THE GLORIOUS BURDEN

THE GLORIOUS BURDEN

The American Presidency

STEFAN LORANT

Harper & Row, Publishers | New York, Evanston and London

Some of the pictures in this work were published by The Macmillan Company in *The Presidency* (copyright 1951 by Stefan Lorant), by Harper & Row in *Lincoln: A Picture Story of His Life* (copyright 1952, 1957), by Doubleday and Company in *The Life and Times of Theodore Roosevelt* (copyright 1958 by Stefan Lorant) and by Simon and Schuster in *FDR: A Pictorial Biography* (copyright 1950 by Stefan Lorant).

Library of Congress Catalog Card Number: 68-15963
Printed by the Murray Printing Company
Bound by The Haddon Craftsmen

For my sons
CHRISTOPHER and MARK

CONTENTS

FOREWORD

The research for this work took me more than twenty years.

Ever since I issued my book *The Presidency,* the first pictorial history of American presidential elections, in 1952, a sizable number of books based on the material of my research have been put on the market and offered to the reading public. The titles of the books varied; one might be called *The History of the Republican Party,* another *The History of the Democratic Party;* still others were labeled with catchwords of the campaigns. The latest of these books not only followed the layout, make-up and appearance of my book of seventeen years ago, but even took its title—which of course is in the public domain.

If imitation is the truest form of flattery, I should really be flattered.

Scores of pictures I had unearthed and whose origin and whereabouts I noted made their reappearance in these books. If I had tracked down an illustration in a century-old issue of the London *Punch,* that same illustration popped up by an amazing coincidence in a number of these other books. One author, using dozens and dozens of my illustrations, seemed to have conscience pangs; he dedicated his book to me—"the pathbreaker." Others were not so squeamish. They took the pictures and made generous use of my text. All these books had one common characteristic: in their bibliographies they omitted any reference to my work, in the apparent hope that the reading public would not notice where the material came from.

Ironically, even my mistakes were slavishly copied. In my earlier study I had identified the cartoon "Mad Tom in a Rage," which appears on page 68, as representing Thomas Jefferson, who with the help of the Devil is tearing down the Federal Government; in my subsequent research I found that the figure with the brandy bottle is not Thomas Jefferson but Tom Paine. Yet that illustration appeared in many other books with the faulty caption, suggesting that the research of these bookmakers did not go much further than the perusal of my volume.

Since my first attempt I have deepened my research and have collected more than thirty thousand illustrations relating to the Presidency. I have combed libraries and private collections, I have compared the quality of the cartoons, I have acquired as much material as I was able for my own collection. Out of these I have selected and included some fifteen hundred illustrations in the present volume.

In the conception and execution of the pictorial layout I followed a preconceived pattern. It is my opinion that a book in which illustrations play a dominant role has to be composed something like a symphony, with motives and melodies carrying forward and developing the theme.

As the reader or viewer of the volume will observe, I have tried to start each chapter with a standing figure of the man elected to the Presidency. This, strange to say, turned out to be an innovation. Before I decided on it I had not imagined that it would be so difficult to find authentic "standing" portraits of all the Presidents. (I have never been able to discover a satisfactory one of Zachary Taylor or James K. Polk.) But I persisted and thus the bulk of the Presidential portraits show them standing, in full figure.

After the opening text page in each chapter I show in a panel the leading candidates as they looked around the time of the election. This too, as I mention in the Appendix, was a far harder task than I had imagined, as no public institution, historical society or library has even collected the likenesses of all the presidential or vice presidential candidates. (To my amusement, I found that the Library of Congress had no portrait of Richard Nixon in its collection, none even of his campaign against Kennedy in 1960—of course this was before his election in 1968.) I directed my research to the candidates' home towns; I had to track down their descendants and find their portraits in private collections and private homes. (I thank all those who generously contributed their suggestions, and have acknowledged their contributions in the Appendix.) But even with all the help I received it took more than a year to complete these panels.

Of the many hundreds of letters I sent out to politicians, artists, librarians, newspaper editors, museum directors and heads of historical societies asking for information and pictures, only one remained unanswered: that to President Johnson's press secretary, George Christian, from whom I sought permission to examine the photographs taken by the outstanding photographer Yoicho Okamoto. Mr. Okamoto, of Japanese descent, has a photographic laboratory in the White House and accompanies the President wherever he goes; he shadows him from morning till night snapping pictures, the best of which are sent with Mr. Johnson's approval to the news media. I am sorry that I was not allowed access to this treasure trove of the Johnson Presidency, so that I might show the work of the first official full-time photographer of an American President.

I am grateful to my old friend Cornell Capa, who generously allowed me to use his magnificent pictures of Adlai Stevenson, John F. Kennedy and Mrs. Kennedy. My thanks also go to John Fell Stevenson for the superb snapshot of his father on election night.

The late Henry R. Luce and *Life* editor Edward K. Thompson graciously allowed me to use the exquisite convention photographs from the files of their magazine.

As to the political cartoons, I hope that my selection is a representative one. I have tried to include as many as space would permit. I think the sheer quantity of these cartoons is far larger than has been printed in any other work which has come to my attention.

In the captions explaining the cartoons I have tried—particularly for the early ones—to give all the pertinent information and identifications which I thought would be useful to the contemporary reader. The text in the "balloons" of the early works is explained and the figures in the drawings identified. This was my aim with the later pictures as well. The reader will notice that I have identified all the important personalities in the illustrations, whether they were at the reception of George Washington in 1790 (pages 40-41), attended the meeting of the Electoral Commission in 1877 (pages 336-337) or were present at President Eisenhower's inauguration in 1957 (page 806).

Many of the illustrations, cartoons and photographs have never been published before. I have refrained from marking such illustrations as "never before published," as one never knows. Some of them may have been printed in an obscure book or magazine. It was not my primary intention to sport "new" material, though the reader will find much of it in the volume; I wanted, rather, to give an all-round picture of the Presidency and of our political history.

Since the book was primarily conceived for the general reader rather than the scholar, I omitted footnotes. However, sources of quotations are given in the main body of the text. The narrative is based on the reports in contemporary newspapers (which I examined in the American Antiquarian Society, Worcester, Massachusetts, in the Library of Congress in Washington, and in the New York Public Library) and on the memoirs and reminiscences of the main participants.

I have also read many of the growing number of Ph.D. dissertations in the leading universities. In recent years many young scholars have enriched and enlarged our knowledge of the Presidency. There is hardly an aspect of the forty-five elections which has not been discussed. (As the list of these theses is a fairly long one, I could find no space for it in the Bibliography, but the interested reader can find the titles of the dissertations in the catalogues of the country's larger libraries or in the publications of the American Historical Society.)

The Bibliography at the end of the volume lists the books I have consulted, but as works on the Presidency are legion, with new and important titles added daily, even there I have not referred to the general histories of such outstanding historians as Justin Winsor, James F. Rhodes, John Bach McMaster, Paxson Oberholtzer, Henry Adams, Samuel Eliot Morison, Henry Steele Commager, John D. Hicks, Allan Nevins and Thomas A. Bailey, whose works I read and studied with great profit.

I had many helping hands during the time I worked on this volume.

My gratitude goes to Evan W. Thomas, under whose editorship the book began to take shape; to Peter Mollman, Production Manager of Harper & Row, who not only looked after the myriad details of production with great effectiveness but gave counsel and advice; to Cass Canfield, Jr. and M. S. Wyeth, Jr., who guided the work to its completion; and to Richard E. Passmore, who read the manuscript, and whose gentle criticism was always beneficial. Though many friends offered suggestions and advice, for the mistakes I alone take the responsibility.

With deep appreciation I thank Nancy and Gil Etheredge, who designed the jacket, the binding and the endpapers, and who spent a great deal of their time straightening out the technical problems.

The layout of the book—the design of the pages—is my own.

The photographic work, reproducing the originals, was most efficiently done by Richard Gilson; the enlargements and the necessary artwork by John Rice.

A book with so many illustrations depends on the quality of reproduction. I was blessed that my publisher decided to give the printing to The Murray Printing Company, Forge Village, Massachusetts. Fritz Walker, the head of the firm, and Kenneth Adams, who supervised the production, did, as the reader will see, an outstanding job. To work with them was a constant pleasure; their effort shows on every page of the book.

I was assisted in my task by two of the most able helpers imaginable.

John Furbish helped me with the research, counted the lines of the captions and made them "fit" so they came out even, to the letter. He did the monumental job of cataloguing the pictures, organizing the files and a hundred other chores. Without him it would have taken many more years to complete the book. He was a most imaginative and resourceful assistant, the best one could wish.

Sally S. Bergmans, who typed the manuscript, at times a dozen drafts of the same chapter, often a dozen or more drafts of the same caption, was always willing, never complaining. Her suggestions on the text were always pertinent and always considered. Her unfailing good humor helped to make the work pleasurable.

In the latter stage of the work Carol Edwards offered reliable and effective assistance.

My wife, Laurie, taking time from her work at New York University, read all the manuscript, helped with the typing, offered criticism and suggestions. Her part in the book is more than can be acknowledged in this space.

Alice said, "What is a book without pictures and conversations?" I agree. Here are the pictures, and here are the conversations.

STEFAN LORANT

"Farview"
Lenox, Massachusetts
November 5, 1968

or cause, the court shall nevertheless proceed to pronounce judgment. The judgment shall be final and conclusive. The proceedings shall be transmitted to the President of the Senate, and shall be lodged among the public records for the security of the parties concerned. Every commissioner shall, before he sit in judgment, take an oath, to be administered by one of the judges of the supreme or superior court of the State where the cause shall be tried, " well " and truly to hear and determine the matter in question, according to the " best of his judgment, without favour, affection, or hope of reward."

Struck out

Sect. 3. All controversies concerning lands claimed under different grants of two or more States, whose jurisdictions, as they respect such lands, shall have been decided or adjusted subsequent to such grants, or any of them, shall, on application to the Senate, be finally determined, as near as may be, in the same manner as is before prescribed for deciding controversies between different States.

Struck out.

X.

Sect. 1. The Executive Power of the United States shall be vested in a single person. His stile shall be, " The President of the United States of Ame-" rica;" and his title shall be, " His Excellency." [He shall be elected by ballot by the Legislature.† He shall hold his office during the term of seven years; but shall not be elected a second time.

to which election a majority of the votes of the members present shall be required

join

Sect. 2. He shall, from time to time, give information ~~to the Legislature~~ of the State of the Union: ~~he may~~ recommend to their consideration such measures as he shall judge necessary, and expedient: he may convene them on extraordinary occasions. In case of disagreement between the two Houses, with regard to the time of adjournment, he may adjourn them to such time as he think proper: he shall take care that the laws of the United States be duly and faithfully executed: he shall commission all the officers of the United States; and shall appoint ~~officers~~ in all cases not otherwise provided for by this constitution. He shall receive Ambassadors, ~~and other public ministers~~ He shall have power to grant reprieves and pardons, ~~but his pardon shall not be pleadable in bar of an impeachment.~~ He shall be Commander in Chief of the Army and Navy of the United States, and of the Militia of the several States. He shall, at stated times, receive for his services, a compensation, which shall neither be encreased nor diminished during his continuance in office. Before he shall enter on the duties of his department, he shall take the following Oath or Affirmation, " I ——— so-" lemnly swear (or affirm) that I will faithfully execute the Office of Presi-" dent of the United States of America." He shall be removed from his office on impeachment by the House of Representatives, and conviction in the Supreme Court, of treason, bribery, or corruption. In case of his removal as aforesaid, death, resignation, or disability to discharge the powers and duties of his office, the President of the Senate shall exercise those powers and duties until another President of the United States be chosen, or until the disability of the President be removed.

Agreed

to the Legislature

and

and

shall

U. S.

Postponed aug. 27

XI *when law & equity*

Sect. 1. The Judicial Power of the United States shall be vested in one Supreme Court, and in such Inferior Courts as shall, when necessary, from time to time, be constituted by the Legislature of the United States.

Agreed.

Sect. 2. The Judges of the Supreme Court, and of the Inferior courts, shall hold their offices during good behaviour. They shall, at stated times, receive for their services, a compensation, which shall not be diminished during their

THE CREATION OF
THE OFFICE

In 1777 Congress approved a plan for a confederacy—the Articles of Confederation. Under the plan each state would have an equal vote regardless of its size or population. The small states considered this provision inequitable; New Jersey, Delaware and Maryland also asked that the large states with claims to Western lands renounce them in favor of the Confederation. As they were unable to agree, the American Revolution was fought under a gentleman's agreement. The Articles were not ratified until 1781.

The Confederation was not so much a government as a league in which the individual states retained a large and important part of their sovereignty—a "firm league of friendship" between the states for their "common defense, the security of their liberties, and their mutual and general welfare." There was no general executive; no general judiciary. Congress, in which each state had but a single vote, could not levy taxes or enlist troops; it could not punish those who broke its laws; and worse, it could raise money only by asking the states to contribute toward the Confederation expenses but had no power to collect it. The states, more concerned about their individual problems than about the common goal, quarreled with each other. They pulled apart, their "friendship" turned into dissension.

The depression which followed the Revolutionary War had a sobering effect on the states; their debt was large—some forty million dollars. Commerce after the separation from Britain suffered. The market for farm produce dwindled. Money became scarce; the states could not pay their share into the common treasury. They issued paper currency, bringing about inflation. The propertied classes protested against the issuance of paper money so welcomed by the debtor classes. With the deepening of the depression, people resorted to barter; they asked that grain or cattle be declared legal tender and they demanded a moratorium on their debts.

In Massachusetts the struggle between the propertied people of the coastal towns and the impoverished farmers in the interior grew into a rebellion. Led by Daniel Shays, the farmers protested against the high taxes, against the foreclosures of their mortgages. Two thousand men under Shays marched on Springfield, forcing the adjournment of the court. Shays' Rebellion, as the uprising became known, was put down by the militia. The growing power of the agrarian and nonpropertied classes frightened the propertied men and forced them to advocate the formation of a more effective government, a closer and more powerful union. Stephen Higginson of Massachusetts wrote Nathaniel Dane, the framer of the Northwest Ordinance: "It is clear in my mind that we cannot long exist under our present system, and unless we soon acquire more force to the Union by some means or other, Insurgents will arise and eventually take the reins from us."

Merchants and creditors despaired at the lack of a uniform currency; soldiers who had received land warrants in part payment for their services in the Revolution, seeing the value of their properties diminish, tried to block the trend. Exporters needed protection so they could market their goods abroad. States in New England set up protective tariffs, others in the South created free ports for European goods. The conditions were anarchical; the situation called for a strong government, a more powerful union.

The first step toward calling a convention came from George Washington. Interested in the navigation of the Potomac, he invited a commission from Virginia and Maryland to his home at Mount Vernon to deliberate on the regulation of the river. The delegates suggested that Pennsylvania and Delaware also should be invited to discuss commercial matters in which they and the other states were interested.

On January 21, 1786, the legislature of Virginia enlarged upon this idea and suggested a general convention of commissioners from the states to "consider how far a uniform system in their commercial relations may be necessary to their common interests and their permanent harmony."

Such a convention met at Annapolis in September 1786. Only five states presented delegates: New York, New Jersey, Pennsylvania, Delaware and Virginia. Because of this meager attendance a report was drawn up—drafted by Alexander Hamilton—which recommended the calling of another meeting with greater powers.

Congress acted promptly upon this recommendation. On February 21, 1787, it resolved that a convention should be called "for the sole and express purpose of revising the Articles of Confederation and reporting to Congress and the several Legislatures such alterations and provisions therein as shall, when agreed to in Congress, and confirmed by the States, render the Federal Constitution adequate to the exigencies of Government, and the preservation of the Union."

With the exception of New Hampshire and Rhode Island, all the states appointed delegates. New Hampshire later sent two men, who arrived in time to discuss the convention's most important resolutions, but the government of Rhode Island (called "Rogue Island" by its angry opponents), in the hands of farmers who insisted on paper money, took no part in the convention's deliberations.

All together sixty-five delegates were appointed by the twelve states, of which fifty-five were in attendance at one time or the other. But the main work of the convention was done by some twenty men.

And what men they were! Jefferson in Paris called them "an assembly of demigods."

Washington, revered and admired by everyone, spoke little; for four months he sat silent, only on the last day did he take part in the discussion. But his presence bound the delegates together, and his few words as recalled by Gouverneur Morris still ring throughout the years: "Let us raise a standard to which the wise and honest can repair."

He was in pain, he nursed a rheumatic shoulder, he wore his arm in a sling for days. And he had his personal griefs: his brother had died at the beginning of the year, both his mother and his sister were ill.

Franklin, the senior member of the convention, rallied the delegates at his house in the off hours for wine and food. He was not in the best of health.

Madison, twenty years younger than Washington, was the acknowledged leader of the delegates who favored a strong central government. His influence was so great that he was called "the master builder of the Constitution." A fragile little man, seemingly melancholy because he could not "expect a long or healthy life," a bookworm who read history, the classics and the philosophers, with a mind as sharp as a rapier, indefatigable, he slept only a few short hours at night. He became the chief recorder of the convention. From May 25 to September 17 he was always present, noting down with accuracy what his colleagues said. These notes on the convention, first published in 1840, provide the most complete record of the proceedings.

Edmund Randolph, the spokesman of the Virginians, was young, tall, handsome, an accomplished orator, the owner of 7,000 acres of land and 200 slaves.

Alexander Hamilton, perhaps the most brilliant among the delegates—the "little lion," as his admirers nicknamed him—delivered a long nationalistic speech on June 19, his main contribution to the debates.

Gouverneur Morris, the leading member of the Pennsylvanians, spoke more often than any of the other delegates. Contemptuous of "democracy," he was for a strong, centralized government in the hands of the rich and the well-born. He believed that if votes were given "to the people who have no property, he will sell them to the rich." The wording of the final document has the mark of his lucid style.

The other Morris was no relation of his. Robert, the "financier of the Revolution," was one of the wealthiest men in Philadelphia. His mansion, with an icehouse and a hothouse, was the most elegant in the city. During the debates Washington who was his friend, stayed there as a guest.

James Wilson, the forceful representative of Pennsylvania, was born in Scotland and came to the New World when he was twenty-one. A student of history, constitutional theory and the science of government, he was professor of law at the University of Pennsylvania. Lord Bryce described him as "one of the deepest thinkers and the most exact reasoners" in the convention.

Rufus King, a Harvard man from Massachusetts with a patrician appearance and a melodious voice, had a promising future before him; he ran for the Vice Presidency on the Federalist slate in 1804 and again in 1808; both times the Pinckney-King ticket was defeated.

Elbridge Gerry (who a quarter-century later, in 1812, became Vice President under Madison) was a thin and small man, with a slight stutter, not too attractive—except to the ladies. His sharp rebuttals during the convention were correctives against would-be errors. His speech on May 31 against popular election of the executive launched the debate with a telling argument: "The evils we experience flow from an excess of democracy. The people do not want virtue, but are the dupes of pretended patriots . . . they are daily misled into the most baneful measures and opinions by the false reports circulated by designing men, and which no one on the spot can refute."

Roger Sherman of Connecticut, preceding Gerry in the discussion with the statement that the people should have as little as possible to do with government as they are liable to be misled, had a certain rusticity of manners. Once a cobbler, now a rich man who had amassed a fortune by importing foreign goods, he was an excellent mathematician, astronomer and lawyer about whom Jefferson once said: "He never said a foolish thing in his life." He was an able and devoted public servant, a Revolutionary patriot about whom John Adams wrote that he was "an old Puritan, as honest as an angel and as firm in the cause of American Independence as Mount Atlas." He spoke out strongly for a national government, and when the convention was shaken by dissension, it was he who brought about the great compromise, often referred to as the Sherman compromise.

What men indeed, what "demigods"! Their ages, their backgrounds and their educations varied widely. Franklin, the oldest, was 81; Charles Pinckney, the youngest, 29. Sherman was 66; Mason, 62; Wilson, 44; Madison, 36; Gouverneur Morris, 35; and King, 33.

They represented a population of about 3,800,000 people, of whom 700,000 were slaves.

Eight large states faced five small states (including Rhode Island). Of the large states Virginia, not counting Kentucky, had about 750,000 population; Massachusetts, including Maine, about 475,000; Pennsylvania, 430,000; North Carolina, 400,000; New York, 340,000; Maryland, 320,000; South Carolina, 250,000; Connecticut, 240,000. This amounted to 3,205,000.

Against this the population of the small states totaled only 534,000. New Jersey had 184,000; New Hampshire, 140,000, Georgia, 80,000; Rhode Island, 70,000; Delaware, 60,000.

Some of the great Revolutionary figures were not in attendance. John Adams was in London, Thomas Jefferson in Paris, both on diplomatic missions; Patrick Henry, Samuel Adams and Tom Paine were not among the delegates either.

The date of the meeting was to be the second Monday in May 1787.

"On Monday the 14th of May, A.D. 1787, and in the eleventh year of the independence of the United States of America, at the State-House in the city of Philadelphia —in virtue of appointments from their respective States, sundry Deputies to the federal-Convention appeared." So begins the *Journal* of the federal convention. But on that day, as Madison noted in his *Journal,* there were not enough deputies assembled "for revising the federal system of Government." The meeting was therefore postponed. Friday, May 25, was a stormy day. On that date twenty-nine delegates from seven states were present, forming a quorum. Bad weather was given as the reason for the poor attendance. But it is interesting to note that during the following months the attendance of the convention was hardly any larger than on the first day.

George Washington was elected unanimously to preside over the convention. His seat, a large carved high-backed chair, was put on a platform. He declared, when conducted to the chair, "that as he never had been in such a situation, he felt himself embarrassed; that he hoped his errors, as they would be unintentional, would be excused."

After some days had passed in organizing the convention — electing officers, considering the delegates' credentials and adopting rules of procedure—the convention could come to order. Thirty-four-year-old Edmund Randolph, Governor of Virginia and chairman of the Virginia delegation, "opened the main business," submitting a set of resolutions, drafted by Madison and carefully discussed beforehand by the seven Virginia delegates. He spoke for more than three hours. He outlined the defects of the Confederation and pointed to the grave situation in the country. "Are we not on the eve of war," he asked, "which is only prevented by the hopes from this convention?"

The resolutions he presented—which during the debates became known as the Virginia Plan—advocated a strong national government composed of three independent departments: the executive, the judiciary and the legislative. The legislative was to have two branches; the lower house was to be elected by the people, the upper house by members of the lower house. The seventh resolution of the Plan called for a national executive to be elected by the national legislature, eligible a second time, which, "besides a general authority to execute the national laws, ought to enjoy the executive rights vested in Congress by the Confederation." It was the first time in the convention that the office of the President was mentioned.

Charles Pinckney, twenty-nine-year-old planter from South Carolina, a soldier of the Revolutionary War, handsome, vain and something of a roué, submitted a proposal regarding the Chief of State. He pleaded "that the executive power be vested in a President of the United States of America which shall be his style; and his title shall be 'His Excellency.' He shall be elected for —— years, and shall be reeligible." With this the debate on the presidential office began.

The meetings were held in an upper room of the State House. The building was closely guarded. The sentries posted at the door turned away anyone who had no business being there. On the pavement outside the building loose earth was thrown to reduce the noise of the traffic, and the windows of the hall were tightly closed so that nothing could be heard outside. On the hot and sticky days—and there were many—the poor New England delegates in their heavy woolen suits felt most uncomfortable.

There was a lot of wild talk in Philadelphia and in the states about what the convention was doing. Rumors spread that they were preparing to institute a monarch, and that a commission would go to England and lay the crown at the feet of George's second son. Sackfuls of mail reached them; the letter writers wanted to know whether that was really the intention of the delegates. On August 22, 1787, the *Pennsylvania Gazette* wrote that the delegates were answering such inquiries with the same reply: "While we cannot affirmatively tell you what we are doing; we never once thought of a King."

Madison in his later years recounted that without the self-imposed secrecy the convention would never have brought results; no Constitution would have been adopted if the debates had been made public. There would have been too much objection to the proposals, there would have been too much criticism to the ideas of the delegates.

It was forbidden to make copies of any entry in the *Journal,* and the delegates were sworn to secrecy about the proceedings. However, some of them kept private notes (Yates, King, Pierce, Paterson, Hamilton, Charles Pinckney, Mason, McHenry); the most complete and exact record, of course, was kept by Madison. It was from his account that the world learned, more than half a century later, what happened in the convention.

Four main principles had to be established regarding the executive. First, in how many persons the power should be vested; second, by what method he should be chosen; third, how long he should hold office; fourth, what his duties should be.

The first question was left unanswered by the Virginians, as the opinions of their members differed. On the first day of June, James Wilson of Pennsylvania, who wrote perceptive thumbnail sketches of the appearance and characteristics of his colleagues and who, according to his fellow delegate William Pierce, "draws the attention not by the charm of his eloquence, but by the force of his reasoning," made the motion that the national executive should "consist of a single person." Pinckney seconded the motion.

The delegates were stunned at the proposal. "A single person" reminded them of George III, a symbol of the rule against which Americans had fought. For them the English monarch was evil and the cause of all their past troubles. They did not want as the head of the new gov-

THE CONSTITUTIONAL CONVENTION IN PHILA-

Painting by J. B. Stearns in 1856

DELPHIA WHERE BETWEEN MAY AND SEPTEMBER 1787 THE OFFICE OF THE PRESIDENT WAS CREATED

17

ernment a single man who might make himself a king; they were afraid of "one man power."

A "considerable pause" ensued. The oldest member of the convention, eighty-one-year-old Benjamin Franklin, broke the silence. It was a point of great importance, Franklin said, and he "wished that the gentlemen would deliver their sentiments on it" before "the question was put." One by one the delegates got up. For the next three days no other business was discussed. John Rutledge of South Carolina "animadverted on the shyness of gentlemen on this and other subjects" and declared that in his opinion the power should be vested in a single person, because a "single man would feel the greatest responsibility and administer the public affairs best." Roger Sherman considered that the elected executive should carry out the will of the legislature, the body that had chosen him; therefore it was for the legislature to appoint one or more men "as experience might dictate."

James Wilson "preferred a single magistrate, as giving most energy, dispatch and responsibility to the office." He would not consider the prerogatives of the British monarch as proper guides in defining the powers of the American executive. This was not Edmund Randolph's opinion; he "strenuously opposed a unity in the Executive magistracy" and regarded it as the "foetus of monarchy." The people, he asserted, were "adverse to the very semblance of monarchy." He further argued that "the Executive ought to be independent. It ought therefore (in order to support its independence) to consist of more than one." He preferred an executive department of three persons, "drawn from different portions of the country." Wilson was against this. In his opinion a plural executive would lead to "uncontrolled, continued and violent animosities." He argued "that Unity in the Executive instead of being the foetus of Monarchy would be the best safeguard against tyranny." As the delegates had such opposing views, the motion for a single magistrate was postponed by common consent, the committee "seeming unprepared for any decision on it." Madison suggested that before "a choice should be made between a unity and a plurality in the Executive—one should decide on the powers of the Executive."

Thus the matter was left in abeyance. The delegates agreed on a national executive, but whether it should be one man or more was not yet decided.

They debated about it again and again. When the first vote on it was taken, seven states voted for a single executive and three—Delaware, Maryland and New Jersey—against it.

The next question was how to elect him and for how long a term. There were two practical ways of selection: one, by popular vote; the other, by the national legislature. The majority of the delegates was strongly against a popular election. Their objections were manifold: some said that it would benefit the large states (their greater

population would be decisive in the election); others held the view that the people of the country would not know the comparative merits of the candidates and would therefore always vote for someone from their own state, someone whom they knew; and there were a few delegates who argued that the common people were neither competent nor could be trusted to make the right selection.

Wilson was for a term of three years with the possibility of reelection. Sherman agreed with him.

Mason recommended a seven-year term without reelection, because in that case the legislature would be most cautious about the choice of the candidate and the executive would have no reason "to intrigue with the Legislature for a reappointment."

Bedford of Delaware was not impressed with Mason's argument. He posed the question: What if the electors made a poor choice and the country were saddled with an incompetent executive for seven long years? Therefore he was for a three-year term, with an ineligibility clause after a period of nine years.

When the motion was put, five states voted for a seven-year term (New York, New Jersey, Pennsylvania, Delaware and Virginia), four voted no (Connecticut, North Carolina, South Carolina and Georgia), and Massachusetts was divided. Washington as presiding officer declared that it was an affirmative vote. However, this was not the final resolution of the matter.

The next question was about the "mode of appointing" the executive.

Wilson was for election by the people. Mason thought this impracticable and voiced the hope that his colleague would take the time to prepare fuller arguments for it.

The following day—on June 2—Wilson made a proposal which would have enabled the people to select the executive without the intervention of the states or the national legislature. It was the electoral system proposal, and it was the first time the idea came before the convention. According to it the people in popular election would choose electors in each district and these electors would then elect the Chief Executive (who could not be chosen from their own ranks), regardless of whether this executive was one man or more. It seemed to be a good idea, but the delegates did not warm up to it.

When the electoral idea came to a vote, it was defeated by eight states against and only two in support.

At this juncture—probably to calm the ruffled tempers —Franklin made a long and earnest appeal against compensation of the executive. He was firmly against offering him any payments for his services, because "there are two passions which have a powerful influence on the affairs of men. They are ambition and avarice; the love of power, and the love of money." He feared that men would want to be the executive simply to earn the money. While the speech was politely listened to, it did not make

MADISON'S NOTES, June 1, 1787, when it was "Resolved that a national executive be instituted; to be chosen by the national legislature; for the term of (blank) years." The Committee of Five was for a seven-year term; the Committee of Eleven reduced this to a four-year term and the convention concurred. There was no word about the number of terms.

much impression.

Then the removability of the executive came up. The proposal that a national legislature should have power to remove the executive was rejected, likewise the suggestion that he should be removed on request by a majority of the legislatures of the individual states. But it was agreed that he should be "removable on impeachment and conviction of mal-practice or neglect of duty."

Once again the debate veered back to whether there should be a single or plural executive.

Randolph again made an appeal against the choice of a single executive, arguing: (1) "The permanent temper of the people was adverse to the very semblance of Monarchy." (2) "Unity was unnecessary." (3) "Necessary confidence could never be reposed in a single Magistrate." (4) "The appointments would generally be in favor of some inhabitant near the center of the Community, and consequently the remote parts would not be on an equal footing." Thus he was in favor of a three-member executive.

Butler opposed this, as in his opinion three men would be the source of constant struggle. Thus the matter was shelved.

The next day was Sunday. The delegates repaired to their quarters in the Indian Queen to discuss the issue over cooling drinks and good food.

On Monday, June 4, the debate continued, with Wilson defending a single executive. He pointed out: "All know that a single Magistrate is not a King." After all, each of the thirteen states had a single man at the head of its government. "The idea of three heads has taken place in none," and added, "If there should be three heads in the national executive, there could be neither vigor nor tranquillity."

Gerry, too, spoke against the three-man proposal: "It would be a General with three heads."

When the vote was taken on this important question, seven states (Massachusetts, Connecticut, Pennsylvania, Virginia, North Carolina, South Carolina, Georgia) voted for a single executive, three states (New York, Delaware and Maryland) against it.

But this was not yet the end. Whether the nation should have a single or plural executive was debated again and again.

On the motion that the executive have the right to negate any legislative act "which shall not be afterwards passed unless by two thirds, parts of each branch of the national legislature," only two voted against it.

Now the paramount issue took precedence over everything else. It was a critical one. Until it was settled there was no sense discussing whether the executive office should be vested in one person or more. This was the question of representation.

On June 15 Paterson of New Jersey brought in a new plan, one in sharp contrast to the Virginia Resolutions. It contained all the weak features of the Articles of Confederation. After a short debate the delegates adopted the Virigina Plan by a seven-to-four vote, with one state divided.

Yet the division between the large and small states was not healed. They faced each other with intense animosity. The large ones pleaded for representation in both houses of the legislature according to population, while the small states insisted on an equal vote for themselves in Congress. The fundamental question was: proportional representation or equal votes for the states?

The small states were apprehensive that they would be swallowed up by the larger ones. On this hung the success or failure of the whole convention—whether the Constitution would be drawn up or whether the delegates were to return to their states unable to reach an agreement.

On July 16 the great compromise was adopted. Its significant feature was that in the upper house each state should have an equal number of seats, while in the lower house representation should be apportioned on the basis of population.

With the acceptance of the compromise the temper of the convention changed. Everything else could be discussed in a more relaxed atmosphere.

The next day—July 17—the problem of the executive was once more introduced for further discussion. For three days the delegates talked about nothing else.

Gouverneur Morris, who spoke more often than any of the others (Morris spoke 173 times, Wilson 168 times, Madison 161 times, Sherman 138 times, Mason 136 times and Gerry 116 times), made a strong appeal against the election of the executive by the national legislature. "If the people should elect," he said, "they will never fail to prefer some man of distinguished character, or services; some man, if he might so speak, of continental reputation," and he added that "if the Legislature elect, it will be the work of intrigue, of cabal and of faction; it will be like the election of a pope by a conclave of cardinals; real merit will rarely be the title to the appointment."

Once more Roger Sherman opposed him and the idea that the executive should be chosen by popular election. He urged that the executive be appointed by the legislature and be made dependent on that body. "An independence of the Executive in the Supreme Legislature, was in his opinion the very essence of tyranny if there was any such thing."

George Mason of Virginia was with Sherman. He said: "It would be as unnatural to refer the choice of a proper character for Chief Magistrate to the people, as it would to refer a trial of colors to a blind man. The extent of the country renders it impossible that the people can

New Hampshire	Massachusetts	Rhode Island	Connecticut	New York	New Jersey	Pennsylvania	Delaware	Maryland	Virginia	North Carolina	South Carolina	Georgia	Questions	ayes	noes	divided
	aye		aye	no		aye	no	no	aye	aye	aye	aye	Single Executive.	7	3	-
	no		aye	no	aye	no	no	no	no	no	aye	no	To strike out the word "People" in the first clause of the 4th resolution; and to insert the word "Legislatures"	3	8	-
	no		aye	aye	no	no	no	no	aye	no	no	no	To add a convenient number of the national Judiciary to the Executive in the exercise of the negative	3	8	-
	aye		aye	aye	aye	aye	aye	aye	aye	aye	aye	aye	That the second Branch of the national Legislature be elected by the individual Legislatures	11		-
	aye		no	no	no	aye	d.	no	aye	no	no	no	To vest the national Legislature with a negative on all state laws which shall appear to them improper	3	7	1
	aye		no	aye	aye	aye	aye	aye	aye	no	aye	aye	To reconsider the mode of appointing the Executive	9	2	
	no		no	no	no	no	d.	no	no	no	no	no	To appoint the national Executive by the Executives of the several States	-	10	1
	aye		aye	no	no	aye	no	d.	aye	aye	aye	aye	That the right of suffrage in the first branch of the national Legislature ought not to be according to the rule established in the confederation, but according to an equitable ratio	7	3	1
	aye		aye	aye	no	aye	no	aye	aye	aye	aye	aye	That the right of suffrage in the first branch be according to the whole number of white and three fifths of the other inhabitants	9	2	
	no		aye	aye	aye	no	aye	aye	no	no	no	no	That in the second branch of the national Legislature each State have one vote	5	6	-
	aye		no	no	no	aye	no	no	aye	aye	aye	aye	That the right of suffrage in the second branch ought to be according to the rule established for the first = an equitable ratio of representation	6	5	-

The National Archives

THE VOTING RECORD of the convention was kept by Major William Jackson of South Carolina, the official Secretary, who tabulated the ayes and nays of the states on several proposals relating to the establishment of the presidential office.

MASSACHUSETTS:

RUFUS KING, who with Gerry, Gorham and Strong formed his state's delegation.

ELBRIDGE GERRY, an old-time revolutionary, feared both democracy and tyranny.

CONNECTICUT:

OLIVER ELLSWORTH initiated the first usage of the phrase "the United States."

ROGER SHERMAN headed the delegation, which also included William Johnson.

NEW YORK: NEW HAMPSHIRE:

ALEXANDER HAMILTON represented his state after Lansing and Yates withdrew.

JOHN LANGDON and Nicholas Gilman were the only spokesmen of their state.

THE VIRGINIANS:

GEORGE WASHINGTON was the respected president of the convention. He spoke only once—at the very end—to lend his great prestige to one of the final amendments.

JAMES MADISON missed no "more than a casual fraction of an hour in any day." He kept a meticulous record of the proceedings, which was made public fifty years later.

THE PENNSYLVANIANS:

BENJAMIN FRANKLIN, at the end of his notable career, attended in spite of illness, his prestige aiding the result. He wanted the meeting place named "Unanimity Hall."

ROBERT MORRIS, the English-born financial wizard, advocated a central government with sufficient "checks and balances." He was a good host to the delegates.

JOHN DICKINSON. His colleagues from the state: Broom, Bedford, Read and Bassett.

LUTHER MARTIN came with J. McHenry, D. Jenifer, J. Mercer and Daniel Carroll.

GEORGE MASON, a Virginia planter, was responsible for the adoption of the Bill of Rights. Refusing to sign the Constitution, he predicted the need for the 11th Amendment.

EDMUND RANDOLPH, Virginia's Governor, led his state's delegation, which included John Blair, George Wythe and James McClurg. He refused to sign the Constitution.

SOUTH CAROLINA:

NORTH CAROLINA:

JOHN RUTLEDGE, who with Butler and the two Pinckneys were the state's delegates.

WILLIAM R. DAVIE with Martin, Spaight, Blount and Williamson were the delegates.

GEORGIA:

NEW JERSEY:

ABRAHAM BALDWIN and Few were signers, Pierce and Houstoun were abstainers.

WILLIAM PATERSON, who served with Brearley, Houston, Livingston and Dayton.

GOUVERNEUR MORRIS, who was not related to Robert, the financier, took greater part in the debates than any other delegate, displaying his erudition and common sense.

JAMES WILSON, one of the great legal minds; the remaining four of Pennsylvania's strong delegation were T. Mifflin, G. Clymer, J. Ingersoll and Thomas Fitzsimons.

have the requisite capacity to judge of the respective pretentions of the candidates."

But no words of the supporter of popular election could change the minds of the delegates. When the proposal was put to a vote, the poll showed that nine states were against popular election and only one, Pennsylvania, for it. And when the question of a choice by the national legislature was put, every state voted in the affirmative.

However, this was not the end of the argument. Those delegates who were against the majority opinion had not given up the fight. They stuck to their convictions. And out of their opposition emerged the institution of the Electoral College.

James Wilson had already offered an electoral plan, but his proposal was voted down. So was Elbridge Gerry's that the President should be elected by the governors of the states. Hamilton, in his five-hour speech on June 19, advocated the election of the executive by electors chosen by the people from election districts, but his plan had not received serious consideration. On July 17 after much discussion the motion that the executive should be chosen "by electors appointed by the legislatures of the several states" was rejected. Then two days later, on July 19, the proposal of Oliver Ellsworth found favor: that the Chief Magistrate should "be chosen by electors appointed by the Legislatures of the States in the following ratio; to wit—one for each State not exceeding 200,000 inhabitants. two for each above yt. number & not exceeding 300,000. and, three for each State exceeding 300,000."

The delegates did not seem to be clear in their purpose —they trod on virgin ground. They had no customs, no tradition, no laws to build upon. They had to create customs, they had to create laws, they had to establish a tradition of their own.

The next day the convention agreed upon the number of electors. Massachusetts, Pennsylvania and Virginia were each to have three; Connecticut, New York, New Jersey, Maryland, North Carolina and South Carolina two each; Rhode Island, New Hampshire, Delaware and Georgia one each.

The tenure of the presidential office was hotly debated, and the question was not settled until the very end. The original Virginia Plan had left the term of office blank. Later the blank was filled in "for the term of seven years." Then the delegates voted that the executive should be ineligible after seven years.

On July 19, following the decision that the election should be by independent electors, Oliver Ellsworth moved that the term should be reduced to six years. For "if the elections be too frequent, the Executive will not be firm enough. There must be duties which will make him unpopular for the moment. There will be *outs* as well as *ins*. His administration therefore will be attacked and misrepresented." The motion was carried. The Chief Magistrate was to serve for six years, but he could be re-elected and hold office for twelve consecutive years.

On July 24 Elbridge Gerry argued that "the longer the duration of his [the executive's] appointment the more will his dependence be diminished—it will be better then for him to continue 10, 15, or even 20 years and be ineligible afterwards."

Luther Martin, representing Maryland, was for an eleven-year term, Elbridge Gerry for fifteen years, William Davie for eight years. And Rufus King, who spoke for Massachusetts, suggested with sarcasm that the executive should rule for twenty years, as "this is the medium life of princes."

The next day Gouverneur Morris spoke against the second term because "a change of men is ever followed by a change of measures. . . . The self-sufficiency of a victorious party scorns to tread in the paths of their predecessors."

A month after the convention ended, and while the delegates were still fresh in his mind, James Madison wrote to Thomas Jefferson: "It was much agitated whether a long term, seven years for example, with a subsequent & perpetual ineligibility, or a short term with a capacity to be re-elected, should be fixed. In favor of the first opinion were urged the danger of a gradual degeneracy of re-elections from time to time, into first a life and then a hereditary tenure, and the favorable effect of an incapacity to be reappointed on the independent exercise of the Executive authority. On the other side it was contended that the prospect of necessary degradation would discourage the most dignified characters from aspiring to the office, would take away the principal motive to ye faithful discharge of its duties—the hope of being rewarded with a reappointment would stimulate ambition to violent efforts for holding over the Constitutional term—and instead of producing an independent administration, and a firmer defence of the constitutional rights of the department, would render the officer more indifferent to the importance of a place which he would soon be obliged to quit forever, and more ready to yield to the encroachments of the Legislature of which he might again be a member."

When the Committee of Five submitted its draft on August 6, the passage read: "The Executive Power of the United States shall be vested in a single person. His style shall be, 'The President of the United States of America'; and his title shall be, 'His Excellency.' He shall be elected by ballot by the legislature. He shall hold his office during the term of seven years; but shall not be elected a second time."

But even this was not the final word. "Upon reconsidering that article," explained Charles Cotesworth Pinckney later in a speech on January 18, 1788, in the South Carolina house of representatives where he was fighting for the ratification of the Constitution, "it was thought that to cut off all hopes from a man of serving again in that elevated station, might render him dangerous, or perhaps indifferent to the faithful discharge of his duty. His term of service might expire during the raging of war, when he might, perhaps, be the most capable man in America to conduct it; and would it be wise and prudent to declare in our Constitution that such a man should not again direct our military operations, though our success might be owing to his abilities? The mode of electing the President rendered undue influence almost impossible; and it would have been imprudent in us to have put it out of our power to re-elect a man whose talents, abilities, and integrity, were such as to render him the object of the general choice of his country."

And Washington wrote about this matter some time later to his friend Lafayette in Paris: "There are other points on which opinions would be more likely to vary. As for instance, on the ineligibility of the same person for President, after he should have served a certain course of years. Guarded so effectually as the proposed Constitution is, in respect to the prevention of bribery and undue influence in the choice of President: I confess, I differ widely myself from Mr. Jefferson and you, as to the necessity of expediency of rotation in that appointment. The matter was fairly discussed in the Convention, and to my full convictions; though I cannot have time or room to sum up the arguments in this letter. There cannot, in my judgment, be the least danger that the President will by any practicable intrigue ever be able to continue himself one moment in office, much less perpetuate himself in it—but in the last stage of corrupted morals and political depravity: and even then there is as much danger that any other species of domination would prevail. Though, when a people shall have become incapable of governing themselves and fit for a master, it is of little consequence from what quarter he comes."

So when the Committee of Eleven, which had to act on "such parts of the Constitution as have been postponed, and such parts of reports as have not been acted on," reported on September 4 that "after the words 'Excellency' . . . of the former resolution" should be inserted "He shall hold his office during the term of four years," the delegates concurred.

There it was: not six years or seven years, not fifteen or twenty, but a short term of four. And re-eligibility was not even mentioned.

The committee's change of heart came after it was agreed that the Chief Magistrate should be chosen through independent electors "equal to the whole number of Senators and members of the House of Representatives," and not by the legislature. Independent electors were a guarantee for the future. Once this decision had been reached, there was no longer the fear that the President would become a servile tool of that body, kept in office for twelve years as a reward for his service or turned out—if recalcitrant—after his first term.

The matter of eligibility for a second, third, or fourth term was left to the people. They could elect the President as many times as they wanted (until the Twenty-second Amendment, limiting the presidential terms to two, became effective in 1951).

On September 8 after the convention approved the draft of the Committee of Detail, a new committee was appointed to revise the style and to arrange the articles which had been agreed upon.

Four days later, on September 12, the Committee of Style (William Samuel Johnson, Alexander Hamilton, James Madison, Rufus King and Gouverneur Morris) had completed its work. The document contained some 4,000 words in 89 sentences, and about 140 distinct provisions. It provided for Electors appointed "in such manner as its Legislature may direct, a number of Electors equal to the whole number of Senators, and members of the House of Representatives. . . ."

On the seventeenth of September thirty-nine delegates signed the Constitution. George Mason refused to put his name under it because it contained no "Declaration of Rights" and because "dangerous power and structure of the government . . . will set out a moderate aristocracy; it is at present impossible to foresee whether it will, in its operation, produce a monarchy, or a corrupt, tyrannical aristocracy; it will most probably vibrate some years between the two, and then terminate in the one or the other."

But the Sage of the Convention had better words for the document. "I confess that there are several parts of this constitution which I do not at present approve," said Franklin in a speech which James Wilson read for him, "but I am not sure I shall never approve them. For having lived long, I have experienced many instances of being obliged by better information or fuller consideration, to change opinions even on important subjects, which I once thought right, but found to be otherwise. It is therefore that the older I grow, the more apt I am to doubt my own judgment, and to pay more respect to the judgment of others. Most men indeed as well as most sects in Religion, think themselves in possession of all truth, and that wherever others differ from them it is so far error. . . . But though many private persons think almost as highly of their own infallibility as of that of their sect, few express it so naturally as a certain french lady, who in dispute with her sister, said 'I don't know how it happens, Sister, but I meet with no body but myself, that's always in the right.'

"In these sentiments, Sir, I agree to this Constitution with all its faults, if they are such. . . ."

The debates were now over. The office of the Presidency had been created.

GEORGE WASHINGTON

Washington had no rival for the presidency. That he would be elected no one doubted. His position was unique; he was respected and trusted by all.

Without him there would have been no army in the Revolutionary War; without his support there would have been no Constitution. He was first in war and first in peace; his influence on his countrymen was unequaled.

But Washington had no desire to become President. He had had his fill of public life, he had "no wish beyond that of living and dying an honest man on my own farm." He wrote to his friend Benjamin Lincoln: "Nothing in this world can ever draw me from [retirement] unless it be a *conviction* that the partiality of men had made my services absolutely necessary." He hoped this would not be the case, but even if it was, he would hold office only as long as he was needed and retire "as soon as my services could possibly with propriety be dispensed with." He viewed his future with apprehension. "May Heaven assist me in forming a judgment," he wrote to Jonathan Trumbull, "for at present I see nothing but clouds and darkness before me."

By the summer of 1788 eleven states had ratified the Constitution (North Carolina did not ratify it until November 21, 1789, and Rhode Island not until May 29, 1790). In the second week of September the Congress of the old Confederation issued a schedule for the first presidential election. This schedule proscribed: On the first Wednesday in January 1789 the states had to choose their presidential electors. A month later, on the first Wednesday in February, these electors were to meet in their respective states and vote for two men; the one with the highest vote became President, the other with the next highest vote, Vice-President. And another month later, on the first Wednesday in March, "be the time, and the present seat of Congress the place, for commencing Proceedings under the said Constitution."

The tight schedule left no time for respite. In less than four months—from September 13, 1788, when Congress published its timetable, to January 7, 1789, when the electors were to be chosen—state legislatures had to be summoned, rules about electoral methods enacted, electors nominated and voted for. The question was: How should the electors be chosen? Should they be named by the legislatures or should they be elected by popular vote?

The shortness of time seemed an indication that the framers of the Constitution expected the state legislatures to make the appointments. "If the people, as hath been asserted, are to choose the electors, is it possible that in the large States of Massachusetts, Virginia, etc., the returns can be made for the choice, notice given to the persons chosen, and the persons thus chosen have time to meet together in the short space of one month?" asked a writer in the *Pennsylvania Packet,* the daily paper of Philadelphia. And he answered: "No, it is impossible and can only be remedied by the legislatures, who, in fact, are 'the states' making the choice."

Thus five states—Connecticut, Delaware, Georgia, New Jersey and South Carolina—chose electors that way, but three others—Pennsylvania, Virginia and Maryland—selected them by popular vote.

In the remaining three states the legislatures debated and argued about the election methods. After protracted argument Massachusetts accepted a complicated proce-

GEORGE WASHINGTON
*Painting by Gilbert Stuart
in the New York Public Library*

CANDIDATES IN 1789

GEORGE WASHINGTON
(1733–1799) held a unique position in the hearts of his fellow Americans. That he would be the unanimous choice for the Presidency was never in doubt. All 69 electors cast their votes for him.

JOHN ADAMS
(1735–1826), revolutionary patriot, delegate to the first Continental Congress, co-author of the Declaration of Independence, our envoy in Europe, was Washington's choice for the Vice Presidency.

JOHN JAY
(1745–1829), a King's College graduate, member of the Continental Congress, Chief Justice of New York, minister to Spain, Secretary of Foreign Affairs under the Confederation, got nine votes.

ROBERT H. HARRISON
(1745–1790) was on General Washington's staff during the Revolutionary War. An eminent lawyer, he became the Chief Justice of the General Court of Maryland. He received six electoral votes.

JOHN RUTLEDGE
(1739–1800), member of both Continental Congresses, Governor of South Carolina, a respected delegate to the Constitutional Convention, received the six electoral votes of South Carolina.

JOHN HANCOCK
(1737–1793), a Harvard graduate, a prosperous merchant, a revolutionary patriot, Governor of Massachusetts, got four electoral votes. His signature on the Declaration of Independence became a byword.

Gilbert Stuart in the Museum of Fine Arts, Boston
MARTHA DANDRIDGE CUSTIS (1731–1802) was married to George Washington on January 6, 1759. She was then 27 years old, the widow of Daniel Parke Custis, whose wife she had been for eight years. They had four children, two of whom died in infancy. From Custis she inherited a 1,500-acre plantation, a Williamsburg house and 200 slaves; she was one of the richest women in Virginia.

dure: The people of the districts were to vote in popular elections for two men, both residents in the same district. Their names then were submitted to the General Court, which chose one out of the two. In addition, the Court also was to name two electors-at-large.

New Hampshire was for popular selection but demanded a majority vote for its five electors. Since many candidates entered the contest, the vote became fragmented; as none of the candidates received the majority, the election came before the assembly where the two houses could not agree whether to vote by a joint or by a separate ballot. It was nearly midnight on the last day when the lower house gave in.

In New York, where a similar argument was raging, the Federalist senate and the anti-Federalist house were deadlocked; thus the state could not cast its vote in the first presidential election.

In the states where popular elections were held, the event caused hardly a ripple. There were no important issues at stake, so only a handful of voters went to the polls. In New York the anti-Federalists, not yet a party, attempted to make Governor George Clinton Vice President; but when Washington let it be known that he regarded John Adams "a safe man" whom he could treat "with perfect sincerity and the greatest candor," Clinton no longer had a chance.

Alexander Hamilton, who nursed a dislike for Adams, tried to ease him out of the vice presidency. He asked General Knox to visit Adams and reason with him. Knox went to Braintree and tried to convince Adams that the vice-presidential post was much too insignificant for him, but Adams thought otherwise.

The "defect of the Constitution" worried Hamilton. If some of the anti-Federalist electors were to hold back "a few votes insidiously" from Washington and give them all to Adams, "the Duke of Braintree" would become President and Washington only Vice President. (One must remember that in this election—as in the next three—the electors had to vote for two men; the one with the highest vote was to become President, the other with the second highest, Vice President.) So Hamilton sent letter after letter to the Federalist electors asking them to "waste" their votes for the second choice, and they responded to Hamilton's suggestion. While Washington received the unanimous vote of all sixty-nine electors, Adams got only thirty-four votes.

The humiliated Adams wrote to his friend, Dr. Rush: "Is not my election to this office, in the scurvy manner in which it was done, a curse rather than a blessing?" In his anger he thought to refuse "the most insignificant office that ever the invention of man contrived or his imagination conceived," but when he calmed down, he changed his mind. He would not create "a great mischief" and thus place an obstacle before the formation of the country's new government.

When Washington received the news of his election, he wrote to Lafayette, his French comrade in arms: "My difficulties increase and magnify as I draw towards a period when, according to the common belief, it will be necessary for me to give a definite answer in one way or another." But about the same time he also sent a letter to General Knox, his American comrade in arms, asking him to buy some "superfine American broadcloth"— enough for a suit—as Washington wanted to take the oath of office in a suit of American-spun cloth.

The new government was to begin operation on March 4, but at that date only eight senators and thirteen representatives were present in New York, the temporary capital. Not until the first day of April had the House of Representatives a quorum to organize itself. By then the hesitancy of Washington had all but vanished. The General prepared himself for the journey. He borrowed £500 to pay some of his most urgent debts and to have some cash on hand. He pondered about the future. "In confidence I assure you," he wrote to Gen-

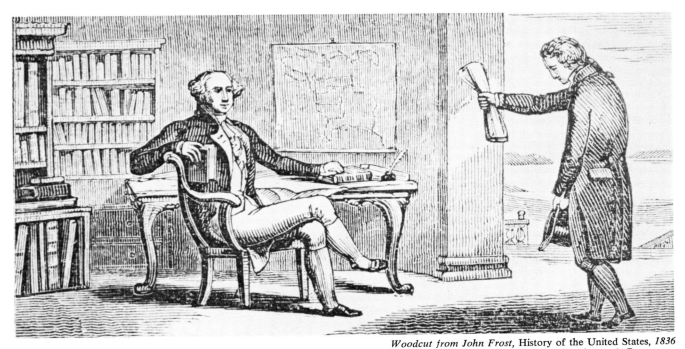

Woodcut from John Frost, History of the United States, *1836*

WASHINGTON IS NOTIFIED OF HIS ELECTION. Charles Thomson, the secretary of the Old Continental Congress, was appointed to bring the news officially to Washington. Thomson mounted his horse in New York on April 7 and, after riding for a full week, he reached Mount Vernon on April 14, 1789, where he told Washington what the General already knew, that he had been elected to the Presidency. Washington said he was ready to begin his journey to New York shortly.

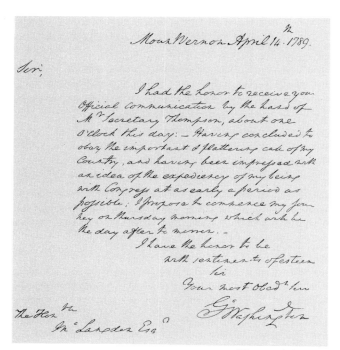

WASHINGTON'S ACCEPTANCE LETTER, addressed to John Langdon, the President pro tempore of the Senate

eral Knox, "with the *world* it would obtain little credit, that my movements to the chair of government will be accompanied by feelings not unlike those of a culprit who is going to the place of his execution; so unwilling am I, in the evening of a life nearly consumed in public cares, to quit a peaceful abode for an ocean of difficulties, without that competency of political skill, abilities, and inclination which are necessary to manage the helm. I am sensible that I am embarking by the voice of the people, and a good name of my own, on this voyage; but what returns will be made for them, Heaven alone can foretell. Integrity and firmness are all I can promise."

On the sixth day of April the Senate had its first quorum and was ready for the official opening and counting of the electoral votes in the presence of members of both houses of Congress. John Langdon, the senator from New Hampshire was elected "president for the sole purpose of opening and counting the votes for President of the United States." After "it appeared that George Washington Esq. was elected President," Charles Thomson, the "perpetual secretary" of the old Continental Congress, was appointed to take the official notification to him. Thomson mounted his horse the next morning—on a Tuesday; two days later he was in Philadelphia; by Sunday he reached Baltimore, and half an hour after noon on Tuesday, the fourteenth of April, exactly a week after he set out from New York, he arrived at Mount Vernon. In a formal little speech he informed Washington what the General already knew— that he was elected to the presidency. Washington made a formal little address in return, promising to be "in readiness to set out the day after tomorrow." He wrote in his journal: "I bade adieu to Mount Vernon, to private life, and to domestic felicity, and with a mind oppressed with more anxious and painful sensations than I have words to express, set out for New York."

The journey from Mount Vernon to New York turned into an ovation from beginning to end. Everywhere along the route Washington was greeted with joyous enthusiasm. A cheering multitude lined the path of his carriage. He had to take part in banquets, listen to speeches, and ride between mounted escorts with shining sabers in city after city. Though he started his day early and traveled late, by the twentieth of the month he was only in Philadelphia, still two and a half days away from New York.

At Elizabeth Town a large barge was waiting for him. Thirteen pilots manned the oars, one for each state, ready to row the craft across the harbor to New York.

At Murray's Wharf at the foot of Wall Street, Governor Clinton and other dignitaries waited for the President-elect. Church bells pealed, cannons boomed, the masses cheered. The *Gazette of the United States,* freshly published in New York, wrote: "May the Rulers of America feel the spirit of their station—feel their hearts beat strong for virtuous fame—feel that they are exalted to be Gods among men, and study to imitate the God of Gods."

Deeply moved by his reception Washington wrote to Edward Rutledge: "I greatly apprehend that my countrymen will expect too much from me. I fear, if the issue of public measures should not correspond with their sanguine expectations, they will turn the extravagant (and I may say undue) praises which they are heaping upon me at this moment, into equally extravagant (though I fondly hope, unmerited) censures."

Inauguration was set for the thirtieth of April. In the morning Washington put on his new brown broadcloth suit with buttons of spread-winged eagles; his stockings were of white silk, his shoe buckles of silver; his dress sword was in a steel scabbard. A joint committee of Congress came to escort him to the Federal Building in Wall Street. He took his seat in a coach drawn by four horses, and other coaches with members of Congress and representatives of foreign nations followed him in a grand procession. Arriving at the Federal Building, Washington walked into the Senate Chamber where he was greeted by Vice President Adams who was so moved by the occasion that he could hardly speak. When he got through his welcome, he led Washington to the portico of the building. Members of Congress followed them.

WASHINGTON ARRIVES AT GRAY'S FERRY. A popular resort patterned after the public gardens of London, the place was lavishly decorated under the direction of Charles Willson Peale, the painter for whom Washington sat during the Constitutional Convention. The President-elect rode over the laurel-arched bridge, cheered by 20,000.

WASHINGTON MOUNTED A HORSE at Trenton, New Jersey, so the people could see him. Thirteen young girls, one for each of the thirteen states, sang: "Welcome, mighty

Woodcuts from the Columbian Magazine, *Philadelphia, May 1789*
Chief! Once more/Welcome to this mighty shore/Now no mercenary foe—/Aims at thee the fatal blow. . . ." At every stop Washington was acclaimed by the multitude.

Chancellor Livingston, the Chief Justice of the New York judiciary, stepped forward to administer the oath. He spoke in measured tones: "I do solemnly swear that I will faithfully execute the office of President of the United States, and will, to the best of my ability, preserve, protect, and defend the Constitution of the United States." Washington repeated the words, adding at the end, "So help me God." Then Livingston called out: "Long live George Washington, President of the United States!"

A thunderous shout rose from the street, from the windows and from the rooftops. Washington bowed and bowed again, then retraced his steps.

"As the company returned into the Senate Chamber," noted Senator Maclay of Pennsylvania, "the President took the chair and the Senators and Representatives their seats. He rose and all rose also and addressed them. This great man was agitated and embarrassed more than ever he was by the levelled cannon or pointed musket. He trembled and several times could scarce make out to read, though it must be supposed he had often read it before. He put the fingers of the left hand into the side of what I think the tailors call the fall of the breeches, changing the papers into his left hand. After some time he then did the same thing with some fingers of his right hand. When he came to the words *all the world,* he made a flourish with his right hand, which left rather an ungainly impression. I sincerely, for my part, wished all set ceremony in the hands of the dancing-masters, and that this first of men had read off his address in the plainest manner, without ever taking his eyes from the paper, for I felt hurt that he was not first in everything." But Maclay was a foe of Federalism, one of the most cantankerous men in Congress, and he disliked ceremonies.

A different description of the event was given by another eyewitness, Fisher Ames, a member of the House from Massachusetts who was a good Federalist and an admirer of Washington. For Ames the scene was touching and solemn. Of Washington, he wrote: "His aspect grave, almost to sadness; his modesty, actually shaking; his voice deep, a little tremulous, and so low as to call for close attention; added to the series of objects presented to the mind, and overwhelming it, produced emotion of the most affecting kind upon the members."

The inaugural address was short; its reading lasted less than ten minutes. And when it was over, Washington, accompanied by the members of Congress, walked across the street to St. Paul's Chapel to hear divine service.

That night the whole city celebrated. Cascades, serpents, fountains of fire lit up the skies. The people sang and danced and cheered. The new country had its president, the first to take office under the Constitution—an event worthy of all the celebration.

WASHINGTON'S ARRIVAL IN NEW YORK. In the afternoon of April 23, 1789, the President-elect reached the temporary capital of the nation. The barge which brought him over the bay from Elizabethtown, New Jersey, had been launched two days before at a cost of some three hundred pounds. It was rowed by thirteen pilots, one for each state in the Union. They were "masters of vessels," not young lads as romanticized in the painting.

As the craft slid across the bay a number of gaily decorated boats swung behind it. On a sloop off Bedloe's Island a choir sang "an elegant ode" to the tune of "God Save the

Painting by A. Rivey in the New-York Historical Society

King" while the Spanish warship *Galveston* gave a salute of thirteen guns in the bay and hoisted the flags of twenty-six nations. There were cheers, huzzahs, singing and shouting.

Murray's Wharf on the East River at the foot of Wall Street was crowded with thousands of "heads standing as thick as ears of corn before the harvest." The steps of the landing were covered with carpets, the rails hung with crimson cloth. Bands played, church bells pealed, guns boomed in salute.

Behind the President-elect in the barge are Colonel David Humphreys, his aide, and Charles Thomson, secretary of the old Congress, who had brought him the notification of his election.

The three men under the baldachin welcoming Washington for the city: New York Governor George Clinton, the Protestant Episcopal Bishop Samuel Provoost, and Chancellor Robert Livingston. Standing behind the women in the left foreground: Alexander Hamilton and his father-in-law, General Philip John Schuyler. After the ceremonious greeting the President-elect led a colorful procession to the Franklin house at Cherry Street, which had been designated as his official residence. His inaugural was still a week away.

33

THE FIRST INAUGURATION. On the morning of April 30, 1789, religious services were performed in all the churches of the city. At noon the procession formed: a military escort, the heads of departments and the committees of Congress in carriages, followed by the President alone in a carriage, his aide-de-camp and secretary behind, and the foreign ministers and citizens bringing up the rear. They proceeded to Federal Hall, where Washington entered the Senate Chamber. Washington went to the open balcony, in full view of the assembled populace. He bowed in response to the enthusiastic applause. On a table was an open Bible on which the President-elect laid his hand when he took the oath from Chancellor Robert Livingston. At the conclusion he said, "I swear—so help me God," and stooped down to kiss the Bible. Livingston stepped to the railing and cried out, "Long live George Washington, President of the United States!" The people cheered.

Engraving by A. S. Sadd after a painting by Tompkins H. Matteson

THE FIRST INAUGURAL ADDRESS. After taking the oath the President returned to the Senate Chamber, where he delivered his inaugural address. Senator Maclay noted that he shook with excitement and had difficulty reading the text: "This great man was agitated and embarrassed more than ever he was by the leveled cannon or pointed musket. He trembled, and several times could scarce make out to read. . . ." Washington started out: "Among the vicissitudes incident to life no event could have filled me with greater anxieties than that of which the notification was transmitted by your order." It was with reluctance that he left Mount Vernon, "summoned by my country, whose voice I can never hear but with veneration and love, from a retreat which I had chosen with the fondest predilection, and, in my flattering hopes, with an immutable decision, as the asylum of my declining years."

He promised to carry out the powers of the Presidency as defined in the Constitution, saying that the government ought not be changed or the Constitution amended before "the future lessons of experience." He stated his intention of refusing any salary over basic expenses.

He ended his address by "resorting once more to the benign Parent of the Human Race in humble supplication that, since He has been pleased to favor the American people with opportunities for deliberating in perfect tranquility, and dispositions for deciding with unparalleled unanimity on a form of government for the security of their union and the advancement of their happiness, so His divine blessing may be equally *conspicuous* in the enlarged views, the temperate consultation, and the wise measures on which the success of this Government must depend."

After the ceremony the President walked to St. Paul's Church, where prayers were offered for the new government.

GEORGE WASHINGTON

The Constitution sketched only the bare outline of the presidential office. The President was to be commander in chief of the army and navy, and was to commission all officers; he was to grant reprieves and pardons for offenses against the United States (except in cases of impeachment); he was to make treaties with the advice and consent of the Senate; he was to appoint ambassadors, ministers and judges of the Supreme Court; he was to inform Congress on the state of the Union and make recommendations to that body; he was on extraordinary occasions to convene both houses, or either of them, and he might also adjourn them; he was to receive ambassadors and other representatives of foreign governments; and he was to take care that the laws of the country were faithfully executed—that was all.

His powers were left vague, they were not spelled out in detail. The reason for this may have been that the founders knew the first President would be George Washington and they had no desire to lay down strict rules for him, and also because they felt that no strict rules could be laid down for leadership.

Congress went into a lengthy and somewhat ridiculous debate on how to address him. Should he be called "His Highness," "His Excellency," "His Elective Highness" or "His Mightiness?" Vice President Adams, ever ready for Old World customs and traditions, suggested "His Highness, the President of the United States and Protector of the Rights of the Same." When Benjamin Franklin heard of this, he remarked that he thought Adams was "always an honest man, often a wise one, but sometimes, and in some things, absolutely out of his

senses." James Madison reminded the House that as the Constitution had referred to the Chief Magistrate as President, that should be his title.

Adams fumed. "What will the common people of foreign countries—what will the sailors and soldiers say when they hear that George Washington is called only 'President of the United States'?" And he answered, "They will despise him." He found "President" undignified since there were "presidents of fire companies and clubs."

Senator William Maclay, the rough-hewn country lawyer from Pennsylvania whose *Journal* left us with vivid insight into the period, had no use for highfalutin titles. He agreed with Madison that since the Constitution called the Chief Executive "The President of the United States," no one had the authority to change that.

Washington told his friends that he would resign if any titles were attached to his office. "President" was good enough for him. So "President" it was, and "President" it remained.

But for the next few weeks Maclay and his Congressional friends mockingly addressed each other "Your Highness of the House" and "Your Highness of the Senate," and they referred to the title-loving Adams as "His Rotundity."

Washington was troubled about his responsibilities. "I walk on untrodden ground," he said. "There is scarcely any part of my conduct that may not hereafter be drawn into precedent." He asked Adams, Hamilton, Jay and Madison about questions of etiquette. Should he reduce the number of his levees? Was it proper to receive as early as eight in the morning?

THE FIRST CABINET had four members.
Henry Knox (War), Thomas Jefferson (State), Edmund Randolph (Attorney General), Alexander Hamilton (Treasury) with the President.
Engraving after a painting by Alonzo Chappel

CANDIDATES IN 1792

GEORGE WASHINGTON

(1733–1799) did not seek a second term, but was urged to remain at the helm of the Government until the new Republic's foundation was secure. After he agreed to serve four more years, all 132 presidential electors cast their votes for him as they felt he was the only person who could rally the loyalties of the competing factions. Washington remains the only President who was elected unanimously.

JOHN ADAMS

(1735–1826), Washington's Vice President, had to bear the brunt of the attacks of the press on the policies of the Federalists as Washington was still sacrosanct, thus unassailable. Adams was called a monarchist and an enemy of democratic institutions; his former writings were cited against him. Hamilton tried to undermine him (he disliked Adams thoroughly) but was unsuccessful in his efforts.

GEORGE CLINTON

(1739–1812), soldier in the Revolutionary War, Governor of New York from 1777 until 1795, filling the office for six consecutive terms, was regarded as the father of the state. He vigorously opposed the adoption of the Constitution. Those who were against the Federalists rallied behind Clinton and gave him 50 votes; not enough to take the Vice Presidency from Adams, who received 77 votes.

THOMAS JEFFERSON

(1743–1826), author of the Declaration of Independence, Governor of Virginia and Washington's Secretary of State, was one of the greatest figures of the early Republic. He opposed Hamilton on the Bank issue, arguing for the strict interpretation of the Constitution. Gradually he built a party against Federalists. Though not a professed candidate in the election, he received four electoral votes.

J. F. Watson, Annals of Philadelphia, 1830

WASHINGTON'S PHILADELPHIA HOME: The Robert Morris mansion on High Street, "the best single house in the city," was rented for him. He repaired, redecorated and refurnished it. In letter after letter he instructed his secretary what he wanted done in the house. In one letter he suggested the use of "bran" to prevent the breakage of ornaments; in another the exchange of "rooming mangles" with Mrs. Morris.

Should he attend large entertainments? Should he accept invitations to the homes of his personal friends? Should he travel through the country to observe conditions or should he stay at home?

Hamilton advised one levee a week, with the President in attendance for no longer than half an hour; he could invite a small number of friends for dinner but not accept return invitations. He also suggested two to four large entertainments a year, but not more. Washington, after considering the recommendations, decided to follow "that line of conduct which combined public advantage with private convenience and which in my judgment, was unexceptionable in itself."

Congress worked on the foundations of the executive structure. It created three departments—State, Treasury and War—and made provisions for an Attorney General. Washington appointed his Cabinet: Thomas Jefferson, who had just returned from France, was to be the Secretary of State; 32-year-old Alexander Hamilton, his aide-de-camp in the war, was to be Secretary of the Treasury; General Henry Knox, his former chief of artillery and the head of the war department under the

CONGRESS MOVES TO PHILADELPHIA. Senator Robert Morris of Pennsylvania leads members of Congress to their new abode. After Jefferson struck his famous bargain with Hamilton (for securing votes for Hamilton's assumption bill, Jefferson was promised the establishment of the permanent capital in the South), Congress moved in November 1789 from New York to the city of Philadelphia, the temporary seat of the government for the next decade—from 1790 to 1800.

Confederation, was to be Secretary of War; Edmund Randolph, the former Governor of Virginia, to be Attorney General. These men were responsible to the President and to him only (not until Theodore Roosevelt's time did the Cabinet receive official status). They were chosen from different geographical areas, and they represented differing political philosophies. Knox and Hamilton were Northerners and centralizers, Randolph and Jefferson, Southerners and states' righters.

The machinery of the government began to turn. Courts and post offices were established, the first ten amendments to the Constitution—the Bill of Rights—were sent to the states for ratification, a census was ordered, salaries fixed. (The President was to receive $25,000 a year, the Vice President, $5,000.)

The administration's most urgent business was to bring order to the country's finances. Hamilton made his report to Congress "for the adequate support of public credit" on January 14, 1790, suggesting that as the debt of the country "was the price of liberty" for which "the faith of America has been repeatedly pledged," therefore all obligations should be paid in full. Thus he proposed to fund all debts at par with full interest and assume the debts of the individual states. He estimated that the foreign debts with arrears of interest amounted to $11.7 million, the domestic debt to $42 million, the state debts to $21.5 million—large sums for a population of less than four million people.

The two proposals—funding and the assumption—were vigorously debated in and out of Congress. Everybody seemed to have personal interest in them; everybody in one way or another was involved in them.

During the war government certificates had been given to farmers, soldiers and shopkeepers for services rendered, for goods supplied or for moneys advanced. However, when they needed cash, they could sell them for only a fraction of their value. Now these same certificates were to be honored in full, giving large profits to those who bought them up. It was understandable that the original holders were enraged, yet the measure passed in Congress with relative ease.

Assumption created even more animosities. The larger states with large debts, like Massachusetts and New York, supported the measure; the smaller states with

39

PRESIDENT WASHINGTON'S REPUBLICAN COURT. The receptions of the President were roundly criticized by all those who feared that the pomp and ceremony of the old world once established in America might lead to monarchy.

As Washington's first residence on Cherry Street was a small one, he sought a more spacious mansion. When he learned that the Macomb House on Broadway would be vacated by the French chargé d'affaires, he promptly rented it for $1,000 a year and redecorated it at considerable expense. On his fifty-eighth birthday in 1790 the Washingtons moved into it. Four days later, they held their first levee.

Mrs. Washington stands on the platform a few steps to the left of the President. Next to her are the wives of Senator Rufus King of New York, Representative Stephen Van Rensselaer, Senator Robert Morris of Pennsylvania, and Nelly Custis, Martha's granddaughter.

Engraving by A. H. Ritchie after a painting by Daniel Huntington
In the left foreground are Chief Justice John Jay, Vice President John Adams and Alexander Hamilton, with Mrs. Adams and Mrs. Hamilton behind them.
The tall figure under the painting to the right of the President is Thomas Jefferson. The man sitting next to the platform is Jonathan Trumbull, then Representative from Connecticut; bending over him is his brother John, the celebrated painter of revolutionary scenes.

small debts, like Virginia and Georgia, opposed it. Sectional differences came to the fore. Southern Representatives threatened to take their states out of the Union if the bill passed.

Hamilton was in despair. He had not enough support for assumption. One day he came upon Jefferson in front of Washington's house, and this is how Jefferson described their encounter:

"He walked me backward and forward before the President's door for half an hour. He painted pathetically the temper into which the legislature had been wrought; the disgust of those who were called the creditor states; the danger of the secession of their members, and the separation of the states.

"I proposed to him," recalled Jefferson, "to dine with me the next day, and I would invite another friend or two, bring them into conference together, and I thought it impossible that reasonable men, consulting together coolly, could fail, by some unusual sacrifices of opinion, to form a compromise which was to save the Union."

At the dinner, with Madison present, the famous bargain was struck: In return for Federalist votes to establish the capital city in the South, Virginia was to help with the passing of the assumption bill. The logrolling pleased North and South, it satisfied Hamilton and Jefferson.

With funding and assumption out of the way Hamilton sent two reports to Congress for the establishment of public credit. In the first—on December 13—he asked for new and higher excise taxes (to cover governmental expenses which he estimated at $2,240,000 a year); in in the second—on December 14—he pleaded for the creation of a central bank.

The latter proposal brought him into sharp conflict with Jefferson, who maintained that the "incorporation of a bank, and the powers assumed by this bill, have not in my opinion, been delegated to the United States by the Constitution." Fearing that a liberal interpretation of the Constitution might lead to unchecked power of the central government, Jefferson demanded a strict observance of the Constitution.

Hamilton replied to Jefferson's objections "that every power vested in a government is in its nature *sovereign* and includes, by *force* of the *term*, a right to employ all the *means* requisite and fairly applicable to the attainment of the *ends* of such power, and which are not precluded by restrictions and exceptions specified in the Constitution, or not immoral, or not contrary to the *essential ends* of political society." Therefore, "there are *implied* as well as *express powers* and . . . the *former* are as effectually delegated as the *latter*."

The positions of the two Cabinet members were worlds apart. Jefferson pleaded for a strict construction of the Constitution, Hamilton for a loose one.

Madison advised the President to return the bill to Congress with the message: "I object to the bill because it is an essential principle of the government that powers not delegated by the Constitution cannot be rightfully exercised; because the power proposed by the bill to be exercised is not delegated; and because I cannot satisfy myself that it results from any expressed power by fair and safe rules of implication." But Washington sided with Hamilton and signed the bill.

The last of Hamilton's financial innovations was embodied in his "Report of Manufactures" in which he asked for protection of the infant industries by import duties and bounties.

All of Hamilton's proposals helped to put a firm financial foundation under the new nation, and they brought those men with property closer to the central government. Because the measures benefited the mercantile and financial North but weakened the agrarian South, Jefferson was forced into opposition.

Jefferson dreamed of a rural America with an agrarian society, Hamilton of a country of cities with a commercial and industrial society. Jefferson hoped to diffuse power, Hamilton to concentrate it; Jefferson was for a weak government, Hamilton for a strong one. Jefferson feared that a strong government with power vested in the hands of a few might lead to corruption and the destruction of liberty, while Hamilton proposed that rather than have a weak government, a strong one should be restrained with controls.

Jefferson trusted the people; he wanted a government for and by them. Hamilton thought the people, whom in an uncontrolled moment he called "a great beast," incapable of wise government; therefore he suggested the rule of the well-educated supported by men of property.

In their hearts Americans were to be for the Jeffersonian ideals, but in their deeds they followed Hamilton.

Gradually the opposing views of Hamilton and Jefferson widened the political division and led to the emergence of political parties, something the founders had not envisaged.

The earliest step in the creation of an opposition party was the fishing and "botanizing excursion" of Jefferson and Madison to New York in the summer of 1791. How many fish the two Virginians caught and how many plants they found is not recorded, but we do know they met with Aaron Burr, the leading New York politician who was in control of the Benevolent Society of the Sons of St. Tammany, and they conferred in Albany with Governor George Clinton. These talks eventually led to a political alliance between the agricultural, rural South and the mercantile, urban North—a coalition which weathered the test of time.

With his term drawing to a close, Washington wanted to return to private life. He passed his sixtieth birthday; he complained of wandering memory, poor hearing and painful dentures—he moaned about the signs of approaching old age. So he asked Madison to compose for him a "valedictory address." Madison argued that without him the Union would break apart.

Jefferson, too, implored Washington to add "one or two more to the many years [he had] already sacrificed to the good of mankind" because within that time "an honest majority" might be established in Congress on the new basis of representation and the President then could return to private life with less danger to the country. "Your being at the helm will be more than an answer to every argument which can be used to alarm and lead the people in any quarter into violence and secession. North and South will hang together if they have you to hang on."

Thus Washington reconsidered. He still had the confidence of the country. Those who were dissatisfied with the Federalists and who opposed Hamilton's fiscal policies aimed their guns at the Vice President. John Adams was an easy target. A man of irascible temper and brusque manners, he made enemies easily. His picturesque phrases—that the country would be better off if it were ruled by "the rich, the well-born and the able," or that the Constitution was "a promising essay toward a well-regulated government"—were well remembered. The opposition assailed him as a supporter of monarchy and as an enemy of democratic institutions. But the attacks had little impact; nobody seemed to care about the election. In the states with popular elections very few voters went to the polls. In the entire state of Pennsylvania less than 4,000 people voted.

Fifteen states participated in the election, five more than in the first one. North Carolina and Rhode Island had ratified the Constitution in the meanwhile, and New York, which had forfeited its vote in the first election, did vote in this one. The two new states which had joined the Union were Vermont and Kentucky.

In most states electors were appointed by the legislatures, but in Virginia, Pennsylvania, Maryland, North Carolina and, in a modified way, in New Hampshire and Massachusetts, the election was by popular vote.

All 132 electors gave their first vote for Washington while they split their second vote. The anti-Federalist alliance of New York and Virginia, bolstered by North Carolina and Georgia, garnered 50 votes for Governor Clinton of New York, not enough to take the second place from Adams, who received 77 votes, but enough to cast a cloud over the political future of the Federalists. If the opposition could show such strength in its first attempt, how much stronger would such an attempt be when Washington was no longer the candidate?

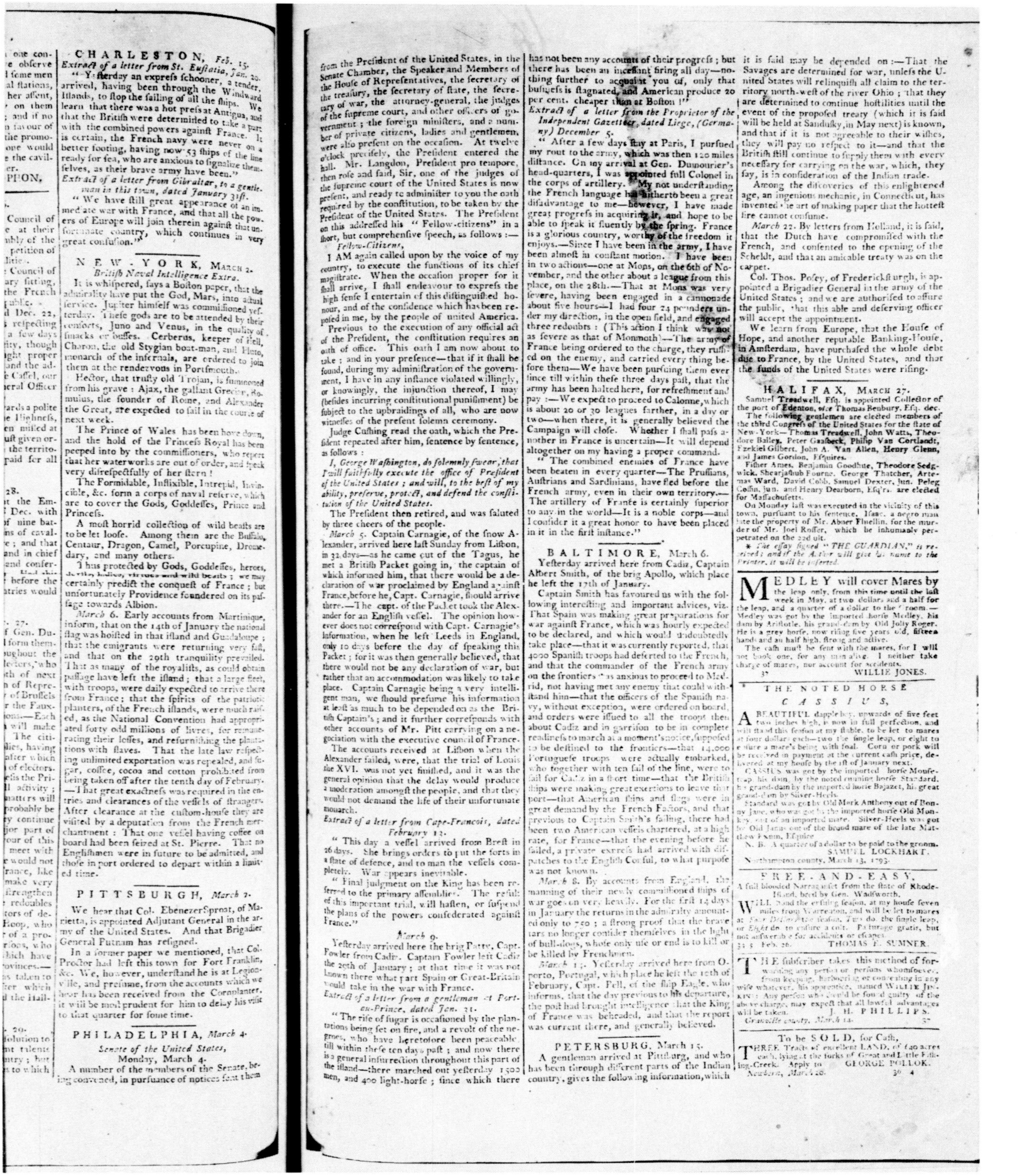

CHARLESTON, *Feb.* 15.

Extract of a letter from St. Eustatia, Jan. 20.

"Yesterday an express schooner, a tender, arrived, having been through the Windward Islands, to stop the sailing of all the ships. We learn that there was a hot press at Antigua, and that the British were determined to take a part with the combined powers against France. It is certain, the French navy were never on a better footing, having now 53 ships of the line ready for sea, who are anxious to signalize themselves, as their brave army have been."

Extract of a letter from Gibraltar, to a gentleman in this town, dated January 31st.

"We have still great appearance of an immediate war with France, and that all the powers of Europe will join therein against that unfortunate country, which continues in very great confusion."

NEW-YORK, March 2.

British Naval Intelligence Extra.

It is whispered, says a Boston paper, that the admiralty have put the God, Mars, into actual service. Jupiter himself was commissioned yesterday. These gods are to be attended by their consorts, Juno and Venus, in the quality of smacks or busses. Cerberus, keeper of Hell, Charon, the old Stygian boat-man, and Pluto, monarch of the infernals, are ordered to join them at the rendezvous in Portsmouth.

Hector, that trusty old Trojan, is summoned from his grave: Ajax, the gallant Grecian, Romulus, the founder of Rome, and Alexander the Great, are expected to sail in the course of next week.

The Prince of Wales has been hove down, and the hold of the Princess Royal has been peeped into by the commissioners, who report that her waterworks are out of order, and speak very disrespectfully of her stern!

The Formidable, Insflexible, Intrepid, Invincible, &c. form a corps of naval reserve, which are to cover the Gods, Goddesses, Prince and Princess.

A most horrid collection of wild beasts are to be let loose. Among them are the Buffalo, Centaur, Dragon, Camel, Porcupine, Dromedary, and many others.

Thus protected by Gods, Goddesses, heroes, ... and wild beasts; we may certainly predict the conquest of France; but unfortunately Providence foundered on its passage towards Albion.

March 6. Early accounts from Martinique, inform, that on the 14th of January the national flag was hoisted in that island and Guadaloupe; that the emigrants were returning very fast, and that on the 20th tranquility prevailed. That as many of the royalists, as could obtain passage have left the island; that a large fleet, with troops, were daily expected to arrive there from France; that the spirits of the patriotic planters, of the French islands, were much raised, as the National Convention had appropriated forty odd millions of livres, for remunerating their losses, and refurnishing the plantations with slaves. That the late law respecting unlimited exportation was repealed, and sugar, coffee, cocoa and cotton prohibited from being taken off after the tenth day of February. —That great exactness was required in the entries and clearances of the vessels of strangers. After clearance at the custom-house they are visited by a deputation from the French merchantment: That one vessel having coffee on board had been seized at St. Pierre. That no Englishmen were in future to be admitted, and those in port ordered to depart within a limited time.

PITTSBURGH, *March* 2.

We hear that Col. Ebenezer Sproat, of Marietta, is appointed Adjutant General in the army of the United States. And that Brigadier General Putnam has resigned.

In a former paper we mentioned, that Col. Proctor had left this town for Fort Franklin, &c. We, however, understand he is at Legionville, and presume, from the accounts which we hear has been received from the Cornplanter, it will be most prudent for him to delay his visit to that quarter for some time.

PHILADELPHIA, *March* 4.

Senate of the United States,
Monday, March 4.

A number of the members of the Senate, being convened, in pursuance of notices sent them from the President of the United States, in the Senate Chamber, the Speaker and Members of the House of Representatives, the secretary of the treasury, the secretary of state, the secretary of war, the attorney-general, the judges of the supreme court, and other officers of government; the foreign ministers, and a number of private citizens, ladies and gentlemen, were also present on the occasion. At twelve o'clock precisely, the President entered the hall. Mr. Langdon, President pro tempore, then rose and said, Sir, one of the judges of the supreme court of the United States is now present, and ready to administer to you the oath required by the constitution, to be taken by the President of the United States. The President on this addressed his "Fellow-citizens" in a short, but comprehensive speech, as follows:—

Fellow-Citizens,

I AM again called upon by the voice of my country, to execute the functions of its chief magistrate. When the occasion proper for it shall arrive, I shall endeavour to express the high sense I entertain of this distinguished honour, and of the confidence which has been reposed in me, by the people of united America.

Previous to the execution of any official act of the President, the constitution requires an oath of office. This oath I am now about to take; and in your presence—that if it shall be found, during my administration of the government, I have in any instance violated willingly, or knowingly, the injunction thereof, I may (besides incurring constitutional punishment) be subject to the upbraidings of all, who are now witnesses of the present solemn ceremony.

Judge Cushing read the oath, which the President repeated after him, sentence by sentence, as follows:

I, George Washington, do solemnly swear, that I will faithfully execute the office of President of the United States; and will, to the best of my ability, preserve, protect, and defend the constitution of the United States.

The President then retired, and was saluted by three cheers of the people.

March 5. Captain Carnagie, of the snow Alexander, arrived here last Sunday from Lisbon, in 32 days—as he came out of the Tagus, he met a British Packet going in, the captain of which informed him, that there would be a declaration of war proclaimed by England against France, before he, Capt. Carnagie, should arrive there.—The capt. of the Packet took the Alexander for an English vessel. The opinion however does not correspond with Capt. Carnagie's information, when he left Leeds in England, only 10 days before the day of speaking this Packet; for it was then generally believed, that there would not be any declaration of war, but rather that an accommodation was likely to take place. Captain Carnagie being a very intelligent man, we should presume his information at least as much to be depended on as the British Captain's; and it further corresponds with other accounts of Mr. Pitt carrying on a negociation with the executive council of France.

The accounts received at Lisbon when the Alexander sailed, were, that the trial of Louis the XVI. was not yet finished, and it was the general opinion that the delay would produce a moderation amongst the people, and that they would not demand the life of their unfortunate monarch.

Extract of a letter from Cape-Francois, dated February 12.

"This day a vessel arrived from Brest in 26 days. She brings orders to put the forts in a state of defence, and to man the vessels completely. War appears inevitable.

"Final judgment on the King has been referred to the primary assemblies. The result of this important trial, will hasten, or suspend the plans of the powers confederated against France."

March 9.

Yesterday arrived here the brig Patty, Capt. Fowler from Cadiz. Captain Fowler left Cadiz the 20th of January; at that time it was not known there what part Spain or Great-Britain would take in the war with France.

Extract of a letter from a gentleman at Port-au-Prince, dated Jan. 31.

"The rise of sugar is occasioned by the plantations being set on fire, and a revolt of the negroes, who have heretofore been peaceable till within these ten days past; and now there is a general insurrection throughout this part of the island—there marched out yesterday 1500 men, and 400 light-horse; since which there has not been any accounts of their progress; but there has been an incessant firing all day—nothing further to acquaint you of, only that business is stagnated, and American produce 20 per cent. cheaper than at Boston!"

Extract of a letter from the Proprietor of the Independent Gazetteer, dated Liege, (Germany) December 5.

"After a few days stay at Paris, I pursued my rout to the army, which was then 120 miles distance. On my arrival at Gen. Dumourier's head-quarters, I was appointed full Colonel in the corps of artillery. My not understanding the French language has hitherto been a great disadvantage to me—however, I have made great progress in acquiring it, and hope to be able to speak it fluently by the spring. France is a glorious country, worthy of the freedom it enjoys.—Since I have been in the army, I have been almost in constant motion. I have been in two actions—one at Mons, on the 6th of November, and the other about a league from this place, on the 28th.—That at Mons was very severe, having been engaged in a cannonade about five hours—I had four 24 pounders under my direction, in the open field, and engaged three redoubts: (This action I think was not as severe as that of Monmouth)—The army of France being ordered to the charge, they rushed on the enemy, and carried every thing before them—We have been pursuing them ever since till within these three days past, that the army has been halted here, for refreshment and pay:—We expect to proceed to Calonne, which is about 20 or 30 leagues farther, in a day or two—when there, it is generally believed the Campaign will close. Whether I shall pass another in France is uncertain—It will depend altogether on my having a proper command.

"The combined enemies of France have been beaten in every quarter—The Prussians, Austrians and Sardinians, have fled before the French army, even in their own territory.— The artillery of France is certainly superior to any in the world—It is a noble corps—and I consider it a great honor to have been placed in it in the first instance."

BALTIMORE, March 6.

Yesterday arrived here from Cadiz, Captain Albert Smith, of the brig Apollo, which place he left the 17th of January.

Captain Smith has favoured us with the following interesting and important advices, viz. That Spain was making great preparations for war against France, which was hourly expected to be declared, and which would undoubtedly take place—that it was currently reported, that 4000 Spanish troops had deserted to the French, and that the commander of the French army on the frontiers was anxious to proceed to Madrid, not having met any enemy that could withstand him—that the officers of the Spanish navy, without exception, were ordered on board, and orders were issued to all the troops then about Cadiz and in garrison to be in complete readiness to march at a moment's notice, supposed to be destined to the frontiers—that 14,000 Portuguese troops were actually embarked, who together with ten sail of the line, were to sail for Cadiz in a short time—that the British ships were making great exertions to leave that port—that American ships and flags were in great demand by the French Factors, and that previous to Captain Smith's sailing, there had been two American vessels chartered, at a high rate, for France—that the evening before he sailed, a private express had arrived with dispatches to the English Consul, to what purpose was not known.

March 8. By accounts from England, the manning of their newly commissioned ships of war goes on very heavily. For the first 14 days in January the returns in the admiralty amounted only to 750; a strong proof that the brave tars no longer consider themselves in the light of bull-dogs, whose only use or end is to kill or be killed by Frenchmen.

March 13. Yesterday arrived here from Oporto, Portugal, which place he left the 12th of February, Capt. Fell, of the ship Eagle, who informs, that the day previous to his departure, the post had brought intelligence that the King of France was beheaded, and that the report was current there, and generally believed.

PETERSBURG, March 15.

A gentleman arrived at Pittsburg, and who has been through different parts of the Indian country, gives the following information, which it is said may be depended on:—That the Savages are determined for war, unless the United States will relinquish all claim to the territory north-west of the river Ohio; that they are determined to continue hostilities until the event of the proposed treaty (which it is said will be held at Sandusky, in May next) is known, and that if it is not agreeable to their wishes, they will pay no respect to it—and that the British still continue to supply them with every necessary for carrying on the war, which, they say, is in consideration of the Indian trade.

Among the discoveries of this enlightened age, an ingenious mechanic, in Connecticut, has invented the art of making paper that the hottest fire cannot consume.

March 22. By letters from Holland, it is said, that the Dutch have compromised with the French, and consented to the opening of the Scheldt, and that an amicable treaty was on the carpet.

Col. Thos. Posey, of Fredericksburgh, is appointed a Brigadier General in the army of the United States; and we are authorised to assure the public, that this able and deserving officer will accept the appointment.

We learn from Europe, that the House of Hope, and another reputable Banking-House, in Amsterdam, have purchased the whole debt due to France, by the United States, and that the funds of the United States were rising.

HALIFAX, March 27.

Samuel Treadwell, Esq. is appointed Collector of the port of Edenton, *vice* Thomas Benbury, Esq. dec.

The following gentlemen are elected members of the third Congress of the United States for the state of New-York—Thomas Treadwell, John Watts, Theodore Bailey, Peter Gansevoort, Philip Van Cortlandt, Ezekiel Gilbert, John A. Van Allen, Henry Glenn, and James Gordon, Esquires.

Fisher Ames, Benjamin Goodhue, Theodore Sedgwick, Shearjashub Bourne, George Thatcher, Artemas Ward, David Cobb, Samuel Dexter, jun. Peleg Coffin, jun. and Henry Dearborn, Esq'rs. are elected for Massachusetts.

On Monday last was executed in the vicinity of this town, pursuant to his sentence, Isaac, a negro man late the property of Mr. Abner Fluellin, for the murder of Mr. Joel Rosser, which he inhumanly perpetrated on the 22d ult.

The essay signed "THE GUARDIAN," is received; and if the Author will give his name to the Printer, it will be inserted.

MEDLEY will cover Mares by the leap only, from this time until the last week in May, at two dollars and a half for the leap, and a quarter of a dollar to the groom. Medley was got by the imported horse Medley, his dam by Aristotle, his grand-dam by Old Jolly Roger. He is a grey horse, now rising five years old, fifteen hands and an half high, strong and active.

The cash must be sent with the mares, for I will not book one, for any man alive. I neither take charge of mares, nor account for accidents.

37 WILLIE JONES.

THE NOTED HORSE
CASSIUS,

A BEAUTIFUL dapple bay, upwards of five feet two inches high, is now in full perfection, and will stand this season at my stable, to be let to mares at four dollars each—two the single leap, or eight to ensure a mare's being with foal. Corn or pork will be received in payment at the current cash price, delivered at my house by the 1st of January next.

CASSIUS was got by the imported horse Mousetrap, his dam, by the noted running horse Standard, his grand-dam by the imported horse Bajazet, his great grand-dam by Silver-Heels.

Standard was got by Old Mark Anthony out of Bonny Jane, who was got by the imported horse Old Monkey, out of an imported mare. Silver-Heels was got by Old Janus out of the blood mare of the late Matthew Exum, Esquire.

N. B. A quarter of a dollar to be paid to the groom.

SAMUEL LOCKHART.

Northampton county, March 13, 1793.

FREE-AND-EASY,

A full blooded Narragansett from the state of Rhode-Island, bred by Gen. Wadsworth,

WILL stand the ensuing season, at my house seven miles from Warrenton, and will be let to mares at *Four Dollars* the season, *Two* do. the single leap, or *Eight* do. to ensure a colt. Pasturage gratis, but not answerable for accidents or escapes.

35 Feb. 26. THOMAS E. SUMNER.

THE subscriber takes this method of forwarning any person or persons whomsoever, from keeping, harbouring or concealing in any wise whatever, his apprentice, named WILLIE JENKINS: Any person who should be found guilty of the above charge, may expect that all lawful advantages will be taken.

J. H. PHILLIPS.

Granville county, March 14. 37

To be SOLD, for Cash,

THREE Tracts of excellent LAND, of 640 acres each, lying at the forks of Great and Little Fishing-Creek. Apply to GEORGE POLLOK.

Newbern, March 26. 36 4

American Antiquarian Society, Worcester, Mass.

NOT ON THE FRONT PAGE. The inauguration of a President was not yet considered an important event. Thus the North Carolina *Journal* began its description of George Washington's second inaugural at the bottom of a left-hand page.

JOHN ADAMS

The waves of the French Revolution swept the American shores. At first when it appeared that France would become a constitutional monarchy through constitutional means, Americans looked upon that revolution as a continuation of their own and approved it. But when in the early months of 1793 news came that Louis XVI had been beheaded, the French Republic established and mass executions were the order of the day, American public opinion became divided. In the main the men of property were against the excesses, denounced mob rule, and attacks on property and religion, while those without means, the farmers of the land and the artisans of the cities, remained in sympathy with the aims of the revolutionaries; they formed democratic societies modeled after the French Jacobin clubs. And when France declared war on Britain, the division in America between French and English sympathizers grew wider. There was a British faction—most of the New England shippers and merchants who needed their trade with England, needed British credit and British pounds—and there was a French faction—predominantly in the South and led by Jefferson—which held that the French were the real friends of America and humanity.

The two countries were bound together by their 1788 treaty of mutual assistance. If France were to be attacked, the United States was to come to her aid.

Washington was in a quandary. To honor the country's obligation to France would lead to war with Britain. To wage such war would be disastrous; the young country was not strong enough, had not enough men, not enough ships, not enough resources. Thus on April 22, 1793, he issued a Neutrality Proclamation which declared that the United States would "pursue a conduct friendly and impartial toward the belligerent powers." It was a repudiation of the French treaty, it was a repudiation of a solemn obligation, but it was in the country's best interest.

The country needed peace, peace, peace. Washington mused: "Nothing short of self-respect, and that justice which is essential to a national character ought to involve us in war, for sure I am, if this country is preserved in tranquility twenty years longer, it may bid defiance in a just cause to any power whatever; such in that time will be its population, wealth and resource." The question was: Would Britain allow America to remain aloof? Would she respect America's neutrality? The answers came soon: She would not.

When the French, anticipating British interference with their West Indian commerce, opened up the islands to neutral shipping, the British began to seize American ships and confiscate their cargoes.

Washington instituted an embargo for two months, during which time no foreign ship was allowed to lay anchor at American ports and no American ship was allowed to carry cargo to foreign lands. It was a gamble and it did not work. The embargo hurt America more than Britain. One-tenth of America's revenue came from customs duties, and three-quarters of all these were on British imports. It was these revenues which paid the expenses of the government.

Britain remained adamant. At war with France and hard pressed, she would not rescind her maritime decrees, she would not change her tough attitude toward

JOHN ADAMS
Painted around 1798 by William Winstanley.
Now at the Adams National Historic Site, Quincy, Mass.

CANDIDATES IN 1796

JOHN ADAMS (1735–1826) was the Federalist choice to follow Washington in the Presidency. But because of Hamilton's meddling he nearly lost the election. He received 71 electoral votes, only 3 more than Jefferson.

THOMAS JEFFERSON (1743–1826) had retired to his beloved Monticello the year before. But as he was the most outstanding figure of the opposition, all those who were against the Federalist administration voted for him.

THOMAS PINCKNEY (1750–1828), soldier of the Revolution and successful negotiator of a Spanish treaty, was the Federalist candidate for the second place. However, the Federalist electors withheld their votes, thus Jefferson won.

AARON BURR (1756–1836), the astute New York lawyer and clever manipulator of the Tammany political machine, was Jefferson's running mate, but because the Southern electors distrusted him, he lost out.

SAMUEL ADAMS (1722–1803), the old revolutionary and now Governor of Massachusetts, was given 15 of Virginia's electoral votes. The defection brought defeat to Aaron Burr, the running mate of Jefferson.

OLIVER ELLSWORTH (1745–1807), brilliant member of the Constitutional Convention, first Senator from Connecticut, who replaced John Jay as Chief Justice of the United States, was backed by three New England states.

Gilbert Stuart, National Gallery of Art, Washington

ABIGAIL SMITH ADAMS (1744–1818), one of the most remarkable women in the early Republic. She had little formal education. "I was never sent to any school. I was always sick," she wrote. But she had a thorough knowledge of the world. She married Adams on October 25, 1764, in a ceremony performed by her father, the Reverend William Smith, a Congregational minister.

As Adams was away from his Quincy home for long periods, Abigail tended the farm and kept close to him through her letters. And what letters they are! Her era lives in them. She was a shrewd observer of the political scene, giving advice to her husband freely. "She would have made a better President than her husband," said President Truman 150 years later.

the United States. And Americans, with their mounting grievances against the mother country, began to say that only a war could settle their differences. Hamilton, who argued that a war would not solve the problems, persuaded Washington to send Chief Justice John Jay to London to seek concessions from the British. For the best part of 1794 Jay negotiated in London, enjoyed social life, kissed the Queen's hand, and by November he had his treaty. It was as good as could be expected. Britain agreed to pay damages for the seizure of American ships; she agreed to "a reciprocal and entirely perfect liberty of navigation, and commerce"; she agreed to evacuate the Northwestern military posts. But on the main grievances—the seizure of American ships, the freedom of American commerce on the high seas and the impressment of seamen—the treaty remained silent. It failed to settle the issue of neutral rights; it failed to

Dear Sir   Monticello Dec. 28. 1796

The public & the public papers have been much occupied lately in placing us in a point of opposition to each other. I trust with confidence that less of it has been felt by ourselves personally. in the retired canton where I am, I learn little of what is passing: pamphlets I see never; papers but a few, and the fewer the happier. our latest intelligence from Philadelphia at present is of the 16th inst. but tho' at that date your election to the first magistracy seems not to have been known as a fact, yet with me it has never been doubted. I knew it impossible you should lose a vote North of the Delaware, & even if that of Pensylvania should be against you in the mass, yet that you would get enough South of that to place your succession out of danger. I have never one single moment expected a different issue; & tho' I know I shall not be believed, yet it is not the less true that I have never wished it. my neighbors, as my compurgators, could aver that fact, because they see my occupations & my attachment to them. indeed it is possible that you may be cheated of your succession by the trick worthy the subtlety of your arch-friend of New York, who has been able to make of your real friends tools to defeat their & your just wishes. most probably he will be disappointed as to you; & my inclinations place me out of his reach. I leave to others the sublime delights of riding in the storm, better pleased with sound sleep & a warm birth below, with the society of neighbors, friends & fellow laborers of the earth, than of spies & sycophants. no one then will congratulate you with purer disinterestedness than myself. the share indeed which I may have had

J. Adams V. President of the U.S.   in

47

THE EVER-CHANGING FACE OF JOHN ADAMS: FROM THE AGE OF FIFTY-

IN 1788 before he left England as the American envoy to the Court of St. James, Adams sat for the young American artist Mather Brown (1761–1832), then a popular portraitist in London.

Jefferson wanted Adams's picture. He had correspondence about it with Adams's son-in-law and with painter John Trumbull, who were to see that Brown fulfilled the commission for which Jefferson eventually paid ten pounds.

LATE IN 1796 OR EARLY 1797 after Adams had been elected to the Presidency, the English painter James Sharples (1751?–1811) made some pastel portraits of him. Two almost identical canvases have come down to us; this one is in the collection of Ima Hogg in Houston, Texas, the other is in the City Art Gallery in Bristol, England.

Sharples generally finished his portraits in a single sitting, charging for a profile picture $15 and for a full face $20.

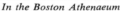

settle the Indian issue in the Northwest; it failed to secure compensation for the slaves which the British had carried away from the South during the Revolutionary War.

Washington realized that the treaty was not the best, but the alternative to it was war. So he signed it.

He was now attacked as never before; he was called "a tyrant," "a dictator," an "impostor." In the *Aurora,* which led the attacks against him, Benjamin Franklin Bache, the grandson of Franklin, wrote that "if ever a

nation was debauched by a man, the American Nation was debauched by Washington."

At the end of his first term when he was ready to lay down his burdens but was persuaded to remain, Madison drafted a valedictory address for him. He had not used the address then; now he sent it to Hamilton for revision. Hamilton composed a new draft, John Jay corrected it, Washington reshaped it. On September 19, 1796, only a few weeks before the election, Washington's Farewell Address was printed in David Claypoole's

THREE TO THE AGE OF EIGHTY-EIGHT, TWO YEARS BEFORE HE DIED

ABOUT 1800, the last year of Adams's Presidency, the French artist Charles B. J. Fevret de Saint-Mémin (1770–1852), who had come to America three years earlier, made this drawing of him with the help of the physiognotrace machine. The instrument, an invention of Gilles Louis Chrétien, enabled the artist to draw the outlines of his sitter in profile exactly. By this method—preceding photography by some forty years—one could obtain a lifelike portrait.

IN 1824 the aging Gilbert Stuart (1755–1828) made this portrait of the 88-year-old Adams in Quincy. Adams enjoyed posing for Stuart "for he lets me do just what I please and keeps me amused by his conversation." Josiah Quincy, later president of Harvard, said that Stuart "caught a glimpse of the living spirit shining through the feeble and decrepit body. He saw [him] at one of those happy moments when the intelligence lights up in its wasted envelope."

American Daily Advertiser. The opposition quickly labeled it a campaign document, "a signal like dropping a hat for the party races to start." In the address Washington warned the country against parties which would lead to division and sectional antagonism; he advised against permanent alliances with foreign countries (no doubt thinking of the 1778 treaty with France which he did not honor), but he favored "temporary alliances" for "extraordinary emergencies."

There was no doubt about the successor—he was to be John Adams, the Vice President. Adams was a man of many faults and many virtues. Temperamental, stubborn, envious, but a sterling patriot who stood above political partisanship, he had the strongest Federalist support; neither Hamilton nor Jay could challenge him. He was elected to the Vice Presidency twice; he was a national figure. Though no one chose officially, it was understood that he would be the Federalist candidate. For his running mate Thomas Pinckney, the negotiator of the successful treaty with Spain, was named.

The opponents of the Federalists, not yet a party, rallied round Thomas Jefferson. They were called in derision "Antis," "Jacobins" and "Republicans," the name which they later adopted. They were to vote for Jefferson for first place and for Aaron Burr for second. Jefferson answered the call reluctantly. He said: "I have no ambition to govern men; no passion which would lead me to delight to ride in a storm."

There was no organized contest; the candidates stayed at home, made no announcements, made no speeches—the battle was fought in pamphlets, in newspapers, in private letters. Character assassination, mudslinging, the later attributes of presidential campaigns, had their origins in this one. The opposition called Adams an "advocate of hereditary power and distinction," and the Federalists the "Monarchist Party"; while Federalist newspapers charged that Jefferson was an atheist, a freethinker, and a man who if elected would reshape the American Government along the lines suggested by the French terrorists.

The Republicans made much of Washington's strong interference in the "Whiskey Rebellion" of two years before, when the President at the urging of Hamilton sent a large military force, 15,000 men, into Pennsylvania to subdue the farmers who refused to pay the excise on whiskey which they distilled from their grain. The unnecessary show of strength antagonized the Scotch-Irish farming communities; it solidified their support of the Republicans and of Jefferson. But Washington proved that the Federal Government was strong and that its laws had to be respected by everyone.

Hamilton, who disliked Adams, took advantage of "the defect of the Constitution" whereby electors were voting for two men and not separately for President and Vice President, and tried to persuade his friends among the Federalist electors to favor General Pinckney, the second on the ticket. He let them know that if Pinckney became President it "would not have been disagreeable to me."

Hamilton suggested to the South Carolina electors that they should vote for Pinckney only and withhold their votes from Adams. If New England, as Hamilton expected, would support the full ticket, the defection of the South Carolina electors would make Pinckney President. But the New England electors were suspicious of Hamilton; they voted as one man for Adams but scattered their second votes on other candidates. Abigail heard of the rumors and warned her husband about Hamilton, and Adams replied that he had never thought much of Hamilton, whom he characterized as "a proud, spirited, conceited, aspiring mortal, always pretending to morality, with as debauched morals as old Franklin."

At times Adams feared the worst—defeat. "The 16 of February will soon come," he wrote his wife, "and then I will take my leave forever. Then for frugality and independence—poverty and patriotism—love and a carrot bed." But he won, if only by a majority of 3 votes. He received 71 votes against Jefferson's 68, Pinckney's 59 and Aaron Burr's 30. Hamilton's meddling secured the Vice Presidency for Jefferson, the only time President and Vice President belonged to opposing factions.

Adams carried the electoral votes of the North, Jefferson those of the South. Before the results became known Jefferson wrote to Madison: "There is nothing I so anxiously hope as that my name may come out either second or third . . . the last would leave me at home the whole year and the other two-third [s] of it." He wanted Adams to be President, and in case of a tie, if the election were to be decided in the House of Representatives, he wanted the Republicans to vote for Adams, who "has always been my senior."

A Baltimore newspaper called the new President "an old fielder," which delighted Adams. He told Abigail that an old fielder was "a tough, hardy, laborious little horse that works very hard and lives upon very little. Very useful to his master at small expense."

Before President Washington left office Bache's *Aurora* fired a parting shot at him: "When a retrospect is taken of the Washingtonian Administration for eight years . . . this day ought to be a JUBILEE in the United States, for the man who is the source of all the misfortunes of our country, is this day reduced to a level with his fellow citizens."

But how fortunate it was for the country to have Washington as its first President. He gave dignity to the office, he kept the opposing factions together, and even though Jefferson and Hamilton resigned from the Cabinet, the unity of the states remained unshaken. The Presidency was molded by him; his achievements became the yardstick for all future Presidents.

He was hurt by the criticism of him and noted sadly: "I now compare myself to the wearied traveller who seeks a resting place, and is bending his body to lean thereon. But to be suffered to do this in peace is too much to be endured by *some*."

He left the Presidency at an appropriate time. Relations with France and Britain were at the breaking point.

Jefferson commented: "The President is fortunate to get off just as the bubble is bursting, leaving others to hold the bag. Yet, as his departure will mark the moment when the difficulties begin to work, you will see that they will be ascribed to the new administration, and that he will have his usual good fortune of reaping credit for the good acts of others and leaving to them that of his errors." This turned out to be an accurate prophecy.

George Washington President of the United States of America

To all and singular, to whom these Presents shall come,— Greeting

Whereas a certain Treaty of amity, Commerce, and Navigation between the United States of America, and his Britannick Majesty, was concluded and signed between their Plenipotentiary the honourable John Jay chief Justice of the United States, and their Envoy Extraordinary to his said Majesty, and the Plenipotentiary of his Britannick Majesty, the Right honourable William Wyndham, Baron Grenville of Wotton, one of his Majesty's privy Council, and his Majesty's Secretary of State for foreign Affairs, at London on the nineteenth day of November, in the Year of our Lord one thousand seven hundred and ninety four; which Treaty is word for word as follows; to wit:

Treaty

"Treaty of Amity Commerce and Navigation, between His Britannick Majesty; and The United States of America, by Their President, with the advice and consent of Their Senate.

"His Britannick Majesty

"and the United States of America, being desirous "by a Treaty of Amity, Commerce and Navigation "to terminate their Differences in such a manner, as "without reference to the Merits of Their respective "Complaints and Pretensions, may be the best calculated "to produce mutual Satisfaction and good understanding: "And also to regulate the Commerce and Navigation "between Their respective Countries, Territories and "People, in such a manner as to render the same "reciprocally beneficial and Satisfactory; They have "respectively named their Plenipotentiaries, and given "them full powers to treat of, and conclude the said "Treaty, that is to say, His Britannick Majesty has "named for His Plenipotentiary The Right Honourable "William Wyndham Baron Grenville of Wotton, One of "His Majesty's Privy Council, and His Majesty's Principal "Secretary of State for Foreign Affairs; and The "President of the said United States, by and with "the advice and Consent of the Senate thereof, hath "appointed

THE MAIN ISSUE of the 1796 election was the Jay treaty—a treaty of amity, commerce and navigation between "His Britannick Majesty" and the United States. In the treaty of 1783 ending the Revolution, Great Britain had promised to give up her forts in the Northwest Territory and make compensation for slaves carried away during the Revolution. These promises were not carried out, and, in addition, there were questions of the boundaries, trade and the impressment of American seamen. Washington sent Chief Justice John Jay to London to negotiate a settlement so war could be prevented. By November 1794 Jay had put his signature to the agreement. It was not the best one, but it was not as bad as its detractors tried to make it. It settled many of the commercial and geographical disputes. Britain agreed to withdraw the military posts south of the Great Lakes; she agreed to arbitration of the disputed boundary between Canada and Maine. Americans were to pay their pre-Revolutionary debts; Britain was to pay for the illegal seizures of American ships and cargoes. But on the principal issue—America's rights as a neutral—the treaty remained silent. There was nothing in it about the search of American ships, about the impressment of seamen into British service. After a protracted debate the Senate passed it, and after soul-searching Washington signed it because it gave the country what it most needed—peace.

For the first time the position of the Chief Executive was changing hands; it had been accomplished smoothly. Chief Justice Oliver Ellsworth administered the oath, and after the ceremony Washington followed Adams deferentially out into the street.

Adams wrote Abigail, who had remained at home in Braintree, that the inauguration was "the most affecting and overpowering scene I ever acted in. I was very unwell, had no sleep the night before, and really did not know but I should have fainted in presence of all the world. I was in great doubt whether to say anything or not besides repeating the oath. And now the world is as silent as the grave. All the Federalists seem to be afraid to approve anybody but Washington. The Jacobin papers damn with faint praise, and undermine with misrepresentation and insinuation. If the Federalists go to playing pranks, I will resign the office, and let Jefferson lead them to peace, wealth, and power if he will."

THOMAS JEFFERSON

ADAMS had a difficult character. He had a bad temper, he was stubborn, he was quarrelsome, he was tactless and he was petty. He was also a poor administrator and he did not get on well with Congress. But he had sterling qualities. He was a true patriot, an honest public servant, a political philosopher of the first order.

He could not be easily swayed; once on the path, he stayed on it. Jefferson characterized him: "He is vain, irritable, and a bad calculator of the force and probable effect of the motives which govern men, but this is all the ill which can possibly be said of him. He is as disinterested as the being who made him; he is profound in his views and accurate in his judgment, except where knowledge of the world is necessary to form a judgment." Jefferson also said that those who really knew Adams would love him. But Hamilton did not, nor did members of the Cabinet, who looked to Hamilton for guidance rather than to President Adams.

The unsolved problems with France caused the most troubles during his administration; peace with that country hung by a thread. After the Jay treaty the feeling in France against America was so strong that the Directory would not deal with Charles Cotesworth Pinckney, the American Minister, and even threatened to arrest him if he did not leave the country. Adams told Congress that as the French Government had "treated us neither as allies, nor as friends, nor as a sovereign state," we should show that "we are not a degraded people, humiliated under a colonial spirit of fear."

The French were hurt about America's disregard of the treaty, which dated from the time France aided America in the Revolution. But did the treaty made with the French King apply to the Republic? The French complained that America bowed to the British view on neutral rights. Under pressure the United States closed its harbors to French shipping, and when on the high seas the British seized neutral vessels taking provisions to France, America remained mute.

France retaliated. She too captured American ships. Provocation after provocation followed until it seemed that war was the only solution. Adams, like Washington before him, knew that the country could not wage a war; it was in no position for it. Its regular army had only 3,500 men. It had hardly any navy, and its fortifications were decrepit. A war would have spelled the ruin of the young republic.

Thus, Adams, keeping a cool head, sent a commission to France consisting of Elbridge Gerry, Charles Cotesworthy Pinckney and John Marshall to negotiate a treaty; but when the envoys reached Paris in October 1797, the French Directory had just made peace with Britain and they were told that the Directory was "exceedingly irritated at some passages of the President's speech" and that "a sum of money was required for the pocket[s] of the Directory and ministers, which would be at the disposal of M. Talleyrand; and that a loan would also be insisted on." It was the old story: "Pay a bribe or else we will not talk to you." The three French intermediaries whom Talleyrand, the Minister of Foreign Affairs, sent to negotiate, and who in the American dispatches were labeled Mr. X, Mr. Y and Mr. Z, asked a $10 million loan for France and another quarter of a million dollars for themselves. Half-deaf

THOMAS JEFFERSON
Painting by Caleb Boyle
Lafayette College, Easton, Pa.

CANDIDATES IN 1800

THOMAS JEFFERSON
(1743–1826), Vice President under Adams, had the support of the Virginia–New York alliance of anti-Federalists for the Presidency. Defeating Adams but tying with his running mate Burr, Jefferson was chosen President by the House of Representatives after 36 ballots and after the Federalists received assurances that some of their demands would be heeded. Ten states voted for Jefferson, four for Burr.

AARON BURR
(1756–1836), son of the president of the College of New Jersey and grandson of the great New England divine Jonathan Edwards, served in the Revolutionary War. A successful lawyer, he became New York's Attorney General in 1789. Two years later he was sent to the U.S. Senate. In 1800 he led his party to a victory in the New York legislature, paving the way for the success of Jefferson.

JOHN ADAMS
(1735–1826) gave the country an able administration, but during his Presidency the opposition rallying around Jefferson made strong inroads. As the nation grew and the power shifted from the Federalist Northeast to the Republican agrarian South and West, the Federalists became divided. One section followed Hamilton, the other supported Adams. Because of this division Adams lost by eight votes.

CHARLES C. PINCKNEY
(1746–1825), lawyer, soldier and diplomat, was the Federalist choice for the Vice Presidency. While a prisoner of the British during the Revolutionary War Pinckney had spurned their offers by saying that if he had any dishonorable blood, he himself "would let it out." A conservative Federalist, an advocate of states' rights, he was respected and admired for his geniality by the members of both parties.

Painting by Thomas Sully
MRS. THOMAS MANN RANDOLPH (1722–1836), the eldest daughter of Thomas Jefferson. Martha and her sister Mary (Mrs. John Wayles Eppes) looked after their father when they were in Washington. Their brother and three of their sisters died in infancy; their mother died in 1782. Martha's seventh child James Madison Randolph was the first baby born in the Executive Mansion.

Pinckney shouted indignantly: "No, no; not a sixpence!"

When the dispatches of the commissioners were published (March 19, 1798), indignation ran high. The country was outraged. Adams advised Congress to be prepared for the worst. "I will never send another minister to France without assurances that he will be received, respected, and honored as the representative of a great, free, powerful, and independent nation."

The Federalists were exultant; the Republicans were dismayed. Their affection for France cooled. They denounced Adams's message to Congress as a "war hawk" cry but they had no other alternative.

The country grew exuberantly patriotic. People cried: "Millions for defense, but not one cent for tribute." An undeclared war followed. The treaties with France were revoked (they had not been kept anyway), appropriations for warships were voted, the Marine Corps revived, the size of the regular army increased.

The Republicans blamed the Federalists for the crisis. They held that had it not been for the Jay treaty, friendly

Contemporary copperplate print published in 1798

THE FIVE-HEADED FRENCH DIRECTORY, standing on a volume labeled "Equality," demands a bribe from the American commissioners, Elbridge Gerry, Charles C. Pinckney and John Marshall, who were in Paris to iron out the difficulties with France so war could be avoided. The cartoon touches on this episode. Scores of American ships had been searched on the high seas by order of the Directory. To eliminate the abuses President Adams sent the three commissioners to Paris to negotiate a treaty. When the American negotiators reached France they were approached by three go-betweens—later called Messrs. X, Y and Z in published dispatches—who asked them for a bribe. Half-deaf Pinckney blurted out: "No, no, not a sixpence!"

In the drawing the French Directory demands "Money, money, money" from the American commissioners and Pinckney tells them that they will not get anything. Underneath the guillotine the devil, a Negro and a Jacobin hold a "civic feast" on a dish of frogs.

When the treatment of the commissioners became public, indignation ran high. The country was ready for war.

relations with France would not have been disturbed and France would not have interfered with American commerce. The Federalists replied that it was not they but the French Revolution which had started the controversy, and they warned that America would be like France if a Republican President were elected.

With patriotic fervor and war hysteria at a peak, the Federalists passed the Alien and Sedition Acts. The object of these laws was to halt the radical French influence and to silence the voices of foreign-born who were critical of the government. The Alien Act gave the President the right to expel or to imprison any alien who was "dangerous" or "suspect" of "any treasonable or secret machinations against the government, while the Sedition Act provided for fining and imprisoning anyone who wrote or distributed "any false, scandalous,

Water color by Nicholas King, City Surveyor, around 1800

THE PRESIDENT'S HOUSE as it looked in 1800. Jefferson moved into it on March 19, 1801, describing it as "a great stone house, big enough for two emperors, one pope and the grand lama in the bargain." The rooms were so large and drafty that thirteen fires had to be kept going constantly to keep off the chill. On the right the large building is the Old Patent Office, where, only a few years previously, Eli Whitney registered his cotton gin.

THE CITY OF WASHINGTON at the time the Federal Government was established there.

In November 1800 the government moved from Philadelphia to the Federal City on the Potomac, which had been planned on a majestic scale by Major L'Enfant, the French engineer.

In the vast empty space in the clearing between the forest and the river stood one wing of the Capitol, the President's "palace," and a few brick houses. The Irish poet Tom Moore, who visited the place at this time, wrote:
This embryo capital, where Fancy sees
Squares in morasses, obelisks in trees;
Which second-sighted seers, ev'n now, adorn
With balconies unbuilt and heroes yet unborn
Though nought but woods and Jefferson they see,
Where streets should run and sages ought *to be.*

An 1801 drawing by G. Beck, engraved by T. Cartwright

and malicious writings" against the Government of the United States, or either house of Congress, or against the President with the intent to "defame said government and to bring them or either of them into comtempt or disrepute." Anybody who was against the President or the government could be prosecuted. Though the Alien law was not enforced, it offended the Irish and the French, who felt that they were singled out for punishment, while the Anglophiles were not molested.

Jefferson wrote: "I consider those laws as merely an experiment on the American mind to see how far it will bear the avowed violation of the Constitution. If this goes down, we shall immediately see attempted another Act of Congress declaring that the President shall continue in office during life, reserving to another occasion the transfer of the succession to his heirs, and the establishment of the Senate for life."

And he penned a set of resolutions against the Acts, which in his opinion had "no force" as they were "not plainly and intentionally authorized by the Constitution." He argued that as the states existed before the Federal Government and as it was they who formed that government, it was only an agent of the states; therefore the states could nullify the Federal laws. (Based on this theory, the Southern states in 1832 nullified the tariff laws, and in 1861 they expanded the theory in the secession doctrine.)

After Jefferson's resolutions were passed by the Kentucky legislature, he sent a copy to Madison, who rewrote them and submitted them to the Virginia legislature. Jefferson hoped other states would adopt the resolutions, but none did.

In the summer of 1798 George Logan, a Philadephia Quaker and a friend of Jefferson, journeyed to Paris and

THE SENATE WING OF THE CAPITOL as it appeared in 1800. From the hill on which it stood one could look over an area nearly as large as that of New York City and see little more than brick kilns and temporary huts for the laborers.

had an interview with Talleyrand as a private citizen. The Foreign Minister told Logan that he would be happy to receive an American Minister if America would send one. Adams, who had already learned of Talleyrand's intention appointed William Vans Murray, the American Minister in Holland, as the new envoy to France. With this the war bubble burst. The military faction in the Federalist party was in retreat. Hamilton and his friends could not defy the President for his attempt to keep the peace. But they suggested that negotiations should be conducted by a mission rather than by a single person. Adams accepted the proposal, naming Chief Justice Oliver Ellsworth and the revolutionary patriot Patrick Henry to assist Murray. When Henry declined, William Davie, governor-elect of North Carolina, served in his stead. By the end of September 1800 the three commissioners came up with a commercial agreement again securing the return to peaceful relations.

By then the presidential candidates had already been chosen. The Federalists in Congress caucused on May 3 and decided on "some hocus-pocus maneuvres," as Jefferson called them, to gain the election. They named Adams and Charles C. Pinckney, and suggested that the North should cast equal votes for both, while South Carolina, Pinckney's home state, should vote for its son alone and not for Adams, thus making Pinckney President.

After Adams heard of the intrigues, he sent a note to the Secretary of War: "The President requests Mr. McHenry's company for a minute." The meeting lasted for more than a minute, much more. Adams berated McHenry, a friend of Hamilton. He told him that Hamilton was "an intriguant, the great intriguant in the world—a man devoid of every moral principle—a bastard and as much a foreigner as Gallatin." McHenry sent in his resignation. Four days later Adams asked Pickering, the Secretary of State and another close friend of Hamilton, to resign too, and when Pickering would not oblige Adams curtly dismissed him.

Adams's dismissal of the two secretaries brought factional bitterness, dividing his party into the Adamites and the Pickeronians. With the election only five months away, the ultra-Federalists attacked the President. They said that he was too old, senile and infirm to perform his duties, that his health was failing, and that he had no teeth, his eyesight was poor and his hands trembled with palsy. Their attacks wrecked their party.

The Republican caucus had chosen Jefferson and Aaron Burr as their candidates. Burr asked for assurance that votes would not be withheld from him, as had been done in the last election. Such assurance was given.

The supporters of Jefferson had to be on the defensive about their candidate's "deism." The Federalists charged Jefferson with infidelity. Jefferson had denied that the shells found on mountain tops were proofs of the great flood. He would rather teach children the Greek and Roman classics than the Bible. And he once wrote that "It does me no injury for my neighbor to say there are twenty Gods, or no God. It neither picks my pocket nor breaks my leg." Thus the Federalists boldly declared that if Jefferson should be elected "religion would be destroyed. Immorality will flourish. The very bonds of society will be loosed."

The Republicans made the usual attacks on Adams's "Toryism" and some of them even alleged that he had sent General Pinckney to England to procure four attractive mistresses—two for the General and two for him. The puritan Adams was amused on hearing the story: "I do declare upon my honor, if this be true General Pinckney has kept them all for himself and cheated me out of my two."

It was a strange campaign in which Hamilton and his Federalist friends assailed their own candidates more than the Republicans. In June Hamilton traveled through the Eastern states talking to Federalist leaders to undermine Adams's chances, but he could not persuade them to rally behind Pinckney for the Presidency.

In August he wrote to Adams asking him for an explanation of why he had called him and his friends "a British faction." Adams did not answer. Nor did he acknowledge Hamilton's second letter, written in October. So the infuriated Hamilton penned a pamphlet about *The Public Conduct and Character of John Adams, Esq., President of the United States.* In it he described Adams's public life from the beginning of the Revolution to the day when he fired the two secretaries from the Cabinet. He wrote that in Adams's character were "great and intrinsic defects" which made him "unfit" for the high office. He had "an imagination sub-

THE FIRST FISTFIGHT IN CONGRESS. In January 1798 the Federalist Roger Griswold of Connecticut, made a disparaging remark about the military record of his fellow Congressman Matthew Lyon of Vermont, whereupon Lyon spat in his face. When it became apparent that the House would not expel Lyon, Griswold attacked his adversary with a cane. Lyon then grabbed a pair of fire tongs and the

An 1801 line engraving called "Congressional Pugilists," printed in the Hartford Echo *in that year*

two legislators wrestled on the floor of the House.

From then on Lyon was violently assailed in the Federalist press. His every move was watched. The Federalists were looking for a reason to punish him. When in a letter to the Vermont *Journal* Lyon charged that under President Adams "every consideration of the public welfare was swallowed up in a continual grasp for power, in an unbounded thirst for ridiculous pomp, foolish adulation and selfish avarice," Lyon was prosecuted under the Sedition Law, sentenced to four months in jail and fined $1,000.

With party spirit running high, Lyon, the Republican, was lampooned in pamphlets. Abigail Adams called him "the beast of Vermont," and he was pilloried as "a wild offensive brute, too wild to tame, too base to shoot."

limated and eccentric, propitious neither to the regular display of sound judgment nor the steady perseverance in a systematic plan of conduct." Noah Webster, who defended Adams against the charges, said that Hamilton's action was "deemed little short of insanity."

On October 22, 1800, Hamilton's harangue was set in type at the press of the New York *Gazette;* copies of it were to be sent in confidence to Federalist politicians and electors. But before Hamilton's friends could receive the pamphlet, a copy of it was in the hands of Aaron Burr, who was in charge of the Republican campaign in New York. (There must have been Republican typesetters in the *Gazette's* plant.) Burr called in two friends and during the night they copied the most telling passages, soon thereafter published in the Philadelphia *Aurora* and the New York *Bee.*

Adams fumed. He loathed Hamilton, whom he called "a creole bastard," and whom he considered a lecher and a schemer. Even years later his temper rose when he thought "of a bastard of a Scotch peddler."

The division among the Federalists brought defeat to Adams. Jefferson and Burr had 73 votes each, Adams 65. But as the Republican candidates had an equal number of votes (elections of President and Vice President were not yet held separately; electors voted for two men; the one with the highest number of votes became President while the next highest became Vice President), the election was thrown into the House of Representatives.

The Federalists still had hopes of turning defeat into victory. They considered prolonging the balloting in the House beyond the fourth of March and thus forcing a new election, and there was strong feeling among them to support Burr, who was not "infected with all the coldblooded vices" and who seemed to them less dangerous than Jefferson. "Mr. Burr has never yet been charged with writing libelous letters against the government of his country to foreigners, and his politics always have been open and undisguised," wrote the *Columbian Centinel.* And Gouverneur Morris noted in his diary: "It seems to be the general opinion that Col. Burr will be chosen President." Men of stature considered that "Burr must be preferred to Jefferson."

But Hamilton, despite all his animosity toward Jefferson, implored his friends to think *first* of their country and only *then* of the party. He thought that Burr was "bankrupt beyond redemption except by the plunder of his country" and he considered him as "the most unfit man in the United States for the office of President." He told Gouverneur Morris: "I trust the Federalists will not finally be so mad as to vote for Burr. I speak with an intimate and accurate knowledge of character. His elevation can only promote the purposes of the desperate and profligate. If there be a man in the world I ought to hate,

it is Jefferson. With Burr I have always been personally well. But the public good must be paramount to every private consideration."

Hamilton's words should not be taken at face value. He was not as friendly with Burr as he pretended. Burr had handed him a stinging defeat in the New York election a few months before, making it sure that the electors of the State would vote for a Republican President.

Wednesday, February 11, 1801, was set for the counting of the votes. Though a heavy snowstorm gripped the city, Washington, the new capital, was crowded. (The government had been moved from Philadelphia the previous June.) Every lodginghouse was full. In one hotel fifty men slept on the floor covered only with their coats.

In the Senate, Jefferson, as the presiding officer, announced that no election had taken place; thus the House would have to decide who should be the next President. Members of the House returned to their own chamber to begin the balloting. All representatives save two were present. One was dead, the other sick—waiting to vote from his bed outside the hall. In the voting each state had a single vote, with the majority of a state's representatives determining that state's position. If the vote was evenly divided, the record was a blank.

Sixteen states took part in the election; thus nine votes were necessary for a choice. On the first trial, eight states voted for Jefferson (New York, New Jersey, Pennsylvania, Virginia, North Carolina, Georgia, Kentucky and Tennessee); six voted for Burr (New Hampshire, Massachusetts, Rhode Island, Connecticut, Delaware and South Carolina); two were divided (Vermont and Maryland). As there was no decision, the voting went on the whole afternoon and evening. Members sent out for pillows and blankets and slept on the floor between ballots. By noon the next day, twenty-eight ballots were taken—with no change yet. After the twenty-third ballot on Saturday, the House adjourned until Monday.

The decision was at razor's edge. Burr could have had the Presidency if he had allied himself with the Federalists and promised to carry on their policies. "The means existed of electing Burr," wrote James A. Bayard, the Delaware delegate. "By deceiving one man (a great blockhead), and tempting two (not incorruptible), he might have secured a majority of the states." And William Cooper, a representative from New York, said: "Had Burr done anything for himself, he would long ere this have been President. If a majority would answer he would have it on every vote."

But even before the election Burr had written to General Samuel Smith, a Baltimore Republican, that in the unlikely event he had an equal number of votes with Jefferson, he would "utterly disdain competition."

THOMAS JEFFERSON
Drawn with the physiognotrace
on November 27, 1804.
By C. B. J. Fevret de Saint-Mémin
Original in the Worcester Art Museum, Mass.

Friends & fellow citizens

Called upon to undertake the duties of the first Executive office of our country I avail myself of the presence of that portion of my fellow citizens which is here assembled to express my grateful thanks for the favor with which they have been pleased to look toward me to declare a sincere consciousness that the task is above my talents, & that I approach it with those anxious & awful presentiments which the greatness of the charge & the weakness of my powers so justly inspire, a rising nation, spread over a wide & fruitful land, traversing all the seas with the rich productions of their industry, engaged in commerce with nations who feel power & forget right advancing rapidly to destinies beyond the reach of mortal eye, when I contemplate these transcendent objects, & see the honour, the happiness, & the hopes of this beloved country committed to the issue & the auspices of this day I shrink from the contemplation, & humble myself before the magnitude of the undertaking. utterly indeed should I despair, did not the presence of many, whom I here see, remind me, that in the other high authorities provided by our constitution. I shall find resources of wisdom, of virtue, & of zeal, on which to rely under all difficulties. to you then, gentlemen, who are charged with the sovereign functions of legislation, & to those associated with you, I look with encouragement for that guidance & support which may enable us to steer with safety the vessel in which we are all embarked, amidst the conflicting elements of a troubled world.

During the contest of opinion —"— through which we have past, the animation of discussions & of exertions has sometimes worn an aspect which might impose on strangers unused to think freely, & to speak & to write what they think. but this being now decided by the voice of the nation enounced according to — the rules of the constitution, all will of course arrange themselves under the will of the law & unite in common efforts for the common good. all too will bear in mind this sacred principle that tho the will of the majority is in all cases to prevail, that will, to be rightful, must be reasonable; that the minority possess their equal rights, which equal laws must protect & to violate would be oppression. let us then fellow citizens unite with one heart & one mind, let us restore to social intercourse that harmony & affection without which liberty, & even life itself, are but dreary things. and let us reflect that having banished from our land that religious intolerance under which mankind so long bled & suffered we have yet gained little if we countenance a political intolerance, as despotic, as wicked, & capable

THE DRAFT OF JEFFERSON'S FIRST INAUGURAL IN HIS OWN HANDWRITING. THE FAMOUS PASas bitter & bloody persecutions. during the throes & convulsions of the antient world, during the agonising spasms of infuriated man, seeking thro' blood & slaughter his long-lost liberty, it was not wonderful that the agitation of the billows should reach even this distant & peaceful shore; that this should be more felt & feared by some & less by others; & should divide opinions as to measures of safety. but every difference of opinion, is not a difference of principle. we have called by different names brethren of the same principle. we are all republicans: we are all federalists. if there be any among us who would wish to dissolve this Union or to change it's republican form, let them stand undisturbed as monuments of the safety with which error of opinion may be tolerated, where reason is left free to combat it. I know indeed that some honest men fear that a republican government cannot be strong that this government is not strong enough but would the honest patriot in the full tide of successful experiment abandon a government which has so far kept us free and firm, on the theoretic & visionary fear, that this government, the world's best hope, may, by possibility, want energy to preserve itself? I trust not. I believe this, on the contrary the strongest government on earth. I believe it the only one, where every man, at the call of the law, would fly to the standard of the law, and would meet invasions of their public order as his own personal concern. some -times it is said that man cannot be trusted with the government of himself. can he then be trusted with the government of others? or have we found angels in the form of kings, to govern him? Let history answer this question.

Let us then, with courage & confidence, pursue our own federal & republican principles; our attachment to Union & representative government. kindly separated by nature & a wide ocean from the exterminat -ing havoc of one quarter of the globe; too high-minded to endure the degradations of the others possessing a chosen country, with room enough for our descendants to the thousandth & thou-sandth generation, enjoying the most favourable temperatures of climate, entertaining a due sense of our equal right to the use of our own faculties, to the acquisitions of our own indus try, to honour & confidence from our fellow citizens, resulting not from birth, but from our action & their sense of them, enlightened by a benign religion, professed indeed & practised in various forms, yet all of them inculcating Honesty, truth, temperance, gratitude & the love of man, acknowleging and adoring an overruling providence, which by all it's dispensations proves that it delights in the happiness of man here, & his greater happiness hereafter; with all these blessings, what more is necessary to make us a happy & a prosperous people? still one thing more fellow citizens. a wise & frugal government which shall restrain men from injuring one another, shall leave them otherwise free to regulate their own pursuits of industry & improvement, & shall not take from the mouth of labor, the bread it has earned. this is the sum of good government, & this is necessary to close the circle of our felicities.

About to enter, fellow citizens, on the exercise of duties which comprehend every thing dear & valuable to you, it is proper you should understand what I deem the essential principles of our government & consequently those which ought to shape it's administration. I will compress them within the narrowest compass they will bear, stating the general principle, but not all it's limitations. _ Equal & exact justice to all men, of whatever state or persuasion religious or political; _ Peace, commerce & honest friendship with all nations, entangling alliances with none: _ the support of the state governments in all their rights, as the most competent administrations for our domestic concerns & the surest bulwarks against anti-republican tendencies: _ the preservation of the General government in it's whole constitutional vigour as the sheet anchor of our peace at home, & safety abroad: _ free & frequent elections by the people in person & the more frequent within the limits of their convenience, & the more a jealous care of the right of election by the people, a mild and safe corrective of abuses which are extensive the right of suffrage, the more perfectly within the definition of a genuine republic lopped by the sword of revolution where peaceable remedies are unprovided: _ _ absolute acquiescence in the decisions of the majority, the vital principle of republics, from which is no appeal but to force the vital principle & immediate parent of despotism: _ a well disciplined militia, our best reliance in peace, & for the first moments of war till regulars may relieve them; _ the supremacy of the civil over the military authority. _ economy in the public expence that labor may be lightly burthened and sacred preservation of the public faith. the honest paiment of our debts. _ encouragement of agriculture; and of commerce as it's handmaid. _ the diffusion of information, & arraignment of all abuses at the bar of the public reason: _ freedom of religion; freedom of the press; & freedom of person, under the ever easing protection of the Habeas corpus: _ and trial by juries, impartially selected. these principles form the bright constellation which has gone before us & guided our steps through an age of revolution & reformation. the wisdom of our sages & blood of our heroes have been devoted to their attainment: they should be the creed of our political faith; the text of civic instruction the touchstone by which to try the services of those we trust and should we wander from them in moments of error or of alarm, let us hasten to retrace our steps, & to regain the road which alone leads to Peace, liberty & safety.

I repair then, fellow citizens, to the post you have assigned me. with experience enough in subordinate offices to have seen the difficulties of this the greatest of all, I have learnt to expect that it will rarely fall to the lot of imperfect man to retire from this station with the reputation, & the favor which bring him into it. without pretensions to that high confidence you reposed in our first and greatest, revolutionary character ~~whose ~~ whose preeminent services had entitled him to the first place in his country's love —. and destined for him the fairest page in the volume of faithful history, I ask so much confidence only as may give firmness & effect to the legal administration of your affairs. I shall often go wrong through defect of judgment. when right, I shall often be thought wrong by those whose positions will not command a view of the whole ground. I ask your indulgence for my own errors, which will never be intentional; and your support against the errors of others who may condemn what they would not, if seen in all it's parts. the approbation implied by your suffrage is a great consolation to me for the past; and my future sollici- tude will be to retain the good opinion of those who have bestowed it in advance, to conciliate that of others by doing them all the good in my power, and to be instrumental to the happiness & freedom of all.

Relying then on the patronage of your good will, I advance with obedience to the work ready to retire from it whenever you become sensible how much better choices it is in your power to make. and may that infinite power which rules the destinies of the universe lead our councils to what is best & give them a favorable issue for your peace and prosperity.

THE CONCLUDING TWO PAGES OF JEFFERSON'S DRAFT TO HIS FIRST INAUGURAL ADDRESS IN 1801

Hamilton pleaded with the electors of his party not to vote for Burr, and when he found them unresponsive he turned to Bayard. The thirty-three-year-old Bayard held an unusual power. He was the sole delegate from Delaware, his single vote counted as much as those of the nineteen delegates of Virginia. He alone could sway the election. Hamilton beseeched him to turn his back on Burr: "Be assured, my dear sir, that this man has no principle, public or private. As a politician, his sole spring of action is an inordinate ambition; as an individual, he is believed by friends as well as foes to be without probity; and a voluptuary by system." But Bay-

ard replied that the Federalists had "a strong inclination" to support Burr and the tide for him was "manifestly increasing."

In a soul-searching analysis Hamilton described the two Republicans. Of Jefferson he said: "I admit that his politics are tinctured with fanaticism; that he is too much in earnest in his democracy; that he has been a mischievous enemy to the principal measures of our past administration; that he is crafty and persevering in his objects; that he is not scrupulous about the means or success, nor very mindful of truth, and that he is a contemptible hypocrite."

Of Burr he wrote: "As to Burr . . . he is a man of *extreme* and *irregular* ambition; that he is *selfish* to a degree which excludes all social affections; and that he is decidedly *profligate*. . . . He is far more *cunning* than *wise*, far more dexterous than able."

But when it became evident that Burr would not cooperate with the Federalists and that either Congress would appoint a President or the country would be without one, Bayard approached John Nicholas, a friend of Jefferson, and told him that three states would stop opposing Jefferson if he would give some assurances as to the future policy of the administration. The four "cardinal points" on which Bayard wanted an assurance were the preservation of the fiscal system, adherence to neutrality toward England and France, preservation of the navy and continuation of the Federalists in office. When General Smith, another friend of Jefferson's, replied that Jefferson had agreed to the conditions, the die was cast.

On the thirty-sixth ballot Lewis Morris of Vermont, one of the two of his state's delegates, stayed away; thus Mathew Lyon, the Jeffersonian elector, swung the state into the Republican column. Half of the Maryland electors who were against Jefferson now voted blank; thus Maryland too moved to the Republicans. (The state would have been for Burr if Joseph Nicholson, sick and racked with fever, had stayed away. But he was brought in, and from his bed in a committee room he held out for Jefferson, keeping Maryland's voted divided until the last.) Jefferson now had ten states, and with them the Presidency. Bayard cast a blank ballot for Delaware, as did the electors of South Carolina.

Later Jefferson wrote to his daughter: "The Federalists were confident at first they could debauch Col. B. from his good faith," but that Burr's "conduct has been honorable & decisive, and greatly embarrasses them."

The inauguration ceremonies were simple. Legend has it that Jefferson rode on horseback to his inaugural and hitched his horse to a fence post. This was not so. The President-elect—six weeks short of his fifty-eighth birthday—walked the two hundred yards from Conrad's boarding house, where he stayed, to the Capitol dressed in his everyday suit, surrounded by his friends and followers and a group of drum-beating and flag-bearing militia. Aaron Burr, who earlier in the morning had taken the oath of office so he could preside over the Senate, received him and led him into the chamber, where John Marshall, the Federalist Chief Justice, administered the oath.

John Adams was not present at the inauguration. He would not attend the swearing in of his successor. Angry at the Republicans he left the muddy village of Washington early in the morning. He was on his way home to his farm in Massachusetts, and to his beloved wife.

With him passed the Federalist regime.

Monumental Inscription.

"That life is long which answers Life's great end."

YESTERDAY EXPIRED,
Deeply regretted by MILLIONS of grateful Americans,
And by all GOOD MEN,
The FEDERAL ADMINISTRATION
Of the
GOVERNMENT of the *United States* :
Animated by
A WASHINGTON, an ADAMS ;—a
HAMILTON, KNOX, PICKERING, WOLCOTT, M'HENRY, MARSHALL,
STODDERT and DEXTER.
Æt. 12 years.

Its death was occasioned by the
Secret Arts, and Open Violence,
Of Foreign and Domestic Demagogues:
Notwithstanding its whole Life
Was devoted to the Performance of every Duty
to promote
The UNION, CREDIT, PEACE, PROSPERITY, HONOR, and
FELICITY of its COUNTRY.

At its birth it found
The Union of the States dissolving like a Rope of snow ;
It hath left it
Stronger than the Threefold cord.

It found the United States
Bankrupts in Estate and Reputation ;
It hath left them
Unbounded in Credit ; and respected throughout
the World.
It found the *Treasuries* of the United States and
Individual States *empty ;*
It hath left them *full and overflowing.*
It found
All the Evidences of Public Debts worthless as rags ;
It hath left them
More valuable than Gold and Silver.

It found
The United States *at war* with the
Indian Nations ;—
It hath concluded *Peace* with them all.
It found
The Aboriginals of the soil *inveterate*
enemies of the whites ,
It hath exercised towards them *justice* and *generosity*,
And *hath left them fast friends.*

ON THE DAY OF JEFFERSON'S INAUGURATION the *Columbian Centinel* of Boston, the mouthpiece of New

It found
Great-Britain in poſſeſſion of all
the *Frontier Poſts* ;
It hath demanded their ſurrender, and
it leaves them in the poſſeſſion
of the United States.
It found
The American ſea-coaſt utterly *defenſeleſs* ;
It hath left it *fortified.*
It found our *Arſenals* empty ; and *Magazines*
decaying ;
It hath left them full of *ammunition*
and *warlike Implements.*
It found our country dependent on Foreign Nations
for *engines of defenſe* ;
It hath left
Manufactories of *Cannon* and *Muſquets*
in full work.
It found
The American Nation at *War* with
Algiers, Tunis, and *Tripoli* ;
It hath
Made *Peace* with them all.
It found
American Freemen in Turkiſh ſlavery, where
they had languiſhed in chains for years ;
It hath
Ranſomed them, and ſet them free.

———

It found the war-worn, invalid *Soldier*
ſtarving from want ;
Or, like BELISARIUS, *begging his refuſe*
meat from door to door ;
It hath left
Ample proviſion for the regular
payment of his *penſion.*

———

It found
The *Commerce* of our country confined
almoſt to *Coaſting Craft* ;
It hath left it
Whitening every ſea with its canvaſs, and
cheering every clime with its *ſtars.*

———

It found our
Mechanics and *Manufacturers* idle in
the ſtreets for want of employ ;
It hath left them
Full of buſineſs, proſperous, contented
and happy.
It found
The Yeomanry of the country oppreſſed with
unequal taxes ;—their farms, houſes and barns
decaying ; their cattle ſelling at the
ſign poſts ; and they driven to
deſperation and *Rebellion* ;
It hath left

Their coffers in caſh ; their houſes in repair ;
their barns full ; their farms overſtocked ; and
their produce commanding ready money,
and a high price.
In ſhort—
It found them *poor, indigent Malcontents* ;
It hath left them
Wealthy Friends to Order and good Government.

It found
The United States *deeply in debt to*
France and *Holland* ;
It hath *paid* ALL *the demands* of the former, and
the principal part of the latter.
It found the Country in a ruinous
Alliance with France ;
It hath honorably diſſolved the connexion,
and ſet us free.

It found
The United States without a ſwivel
on float *for their defenſe* ;
It hath left
A NAVY—compoſed of Thirty-four ſhips of
war ; mounting 918 guns ; and manned
by 7350 gallant tars.

It found
The EXPORTS of our country, a mere ſong, in
value ;
It hath left them worth
Above SEVENTY MILLIONS of Dollars per annum.
In one word,
It found AMERICA *diſunited, poor, inſolvent,*
weak, diſcontented, and *wretched.*
It hath left HER
United, wealthy, reſpectable, ſtrong,
happy and *proſperous.*
Let the faithful Hiſtorian, in after times,
ſay theſe things of its Succeſſor, if it can.
And yet—notwithſtanding all theſe ſervices a d
bleſſings there are found
Many, very many, weak, degenerate Sons,
who loſt to virtue, to gratitude,
and patriotiſm,
Open exult, that this Adminiſtration
is no more.
And that
The " Sun of Federaliſm is ſet for ever."
" *Oh ſhame where is thy bluſh ?*"

As one Tribute of Gratitude in theſe Times,
This MONUMENT
Of the Talents and Services of the deceaſed ;
is raiſed by

March 4th, 1801.   **The Centinel.**

England Federalism, proudly recited the achievements of the Federalist administrations of George Washington and John Adams, now done to death "by the Secret Arts, and Open Violence, of Foreign and Domestic Demagogues."

THOMAS JEFFERSON

The "Revolution of 1800," as Jefferson liked to refer to his election, might more aptly be called "a changing of the guard" than a revolution. The Federalists moved out, the Republicans moved in.

The new administration—supported by a coalition of the agrarian South and West with the mechanics of the cities, by the Clinton-Burr-Livingston machine in New York, and by the aristocrats of South Carolina—brought no overnight changes. Atheism did not become the state religion as the Federalists had warned, there was no blood bath as in the French Revolution, the Constitution was not abandoned, merchants and shipbuilders did not suffer from governmental interference, and, foremost of all, peace was maintained. Though Theodore Dwight could unleash a harangue against the new administration and castigate it, as he did on July 7, 1801, his accusations had little effect. "We have a country governed by blockheads and knaves," orated Dwight; "the ties of marriage with all its felicities are severed and destroyed; our wives and daughters are thrown into the stews; our children are cast into the world from the breast and forgotten; filial piety is extinguished, and our surnames, the only mark of distinction among families, are abolished. Can the imagination paint anything more dreadful on this side of hell?" People listened to such talk but were not convinced that things were really that bad, as the country enjoyed prosperity, enough work and enough food for everyone.

The tone of Jefferson's inaugural address was conciliatory. He offered a friendly hand to the opposition: "We are all Republicans, we are all Federalists." He was now President, President of all the people. He was to adopt some of the Federalist policies. It was said that he outfederalized the Federalists, and this may have been so. But in general he maintained a middle course between the ideas of both parties; he was pragmatic, abandoning theories when they were in the way.

Some of the Federalist laws had to go. When the Alien and Sedition Acts expired, they were not renewed; the naturalization law was changed back to the way it had been before the Federalists tampered with it—no longer did an alien have to prove a fourteen-year residence before naturalization; five years sufficed. The excise tax was repealed, even though its repeal cost a million dollars a year. But otherwise the Hamiltonian finances were left untouched.

Yet life had changed; the new capital on the banks of the Potomac to which the government had moved was a far cry from the elegance of Philadelphia. Washington was a muddy village in the middle of nowhere. It had none of the great homes, none of the elegant social customs. Federalist etiquette, levees and glittering receptions would have been incongruous in such primitive surroundings. Jefferson himself preferred simplicity; he was not ostentatious; he would not let people greet him with stiff and deep bows—he offered his hand instead, a custom kept by all Presidents after him.

He introduced strict governmental economy; with the help of Albert Gallatin, his Swiss-born Secretary of the Treasury, a plan was made to repay the debt, to balance the budget, and to curtail expenditures for the army and the navy. He discontinued the custom initiated by Washington of addressing Congress in per-

TOM PAINE AND THE DEVIL
TEAR DOWN THE GOVERNMENT.
This etching was published in 1801

CANDIDATES IN 1804

THOMAS JEFFERSON (1743–1826) was a most popular President at the end of his first term. The country enjoyed prosperity, taxes were repealed, the Louisiana Territory was acquired. With the nation expanding and developing, the spirits of the people soared and Jefferson rode the crest of the wave. For his second term he scored an overwhelming victory, receiving more than 90% of the votes. He got 162 electoral votes.

GEORGE CLINTON (1739–1812), who replaced Burr as candidate for the Vice Presidency, was the most influential politician in New York. He had been that state's war Governor, serving continuously for six terms. Aaron Burr, whose political career he helped, was his political link with the powerful Livingston family. The 12th Amendment in operation, Clinton received the same number of votes as Jefferson.

CHARLES C. PINCKNEY (1746–1825), who had been the Federalist candidate in the 1804 election, was proposed again by his party for the Presidency. A man of imposing figure and independent judgment, Pinckney was highly regarded by Federalists and Republicans alike. But with the Federalists in decline he was able to get the electoral votes from only three states: Connecticut, Delaware and Maryland, fourteen in all.

RUFUS KING (1755–1827) served as a delegate to both the Continental Congress and the Constitutional Convention, where he proved to be that assembly's most eloquent orator. Later on he became New York's first Senator, a director of the Bank of the United States, and in 1796 he was named envoy to Great Britain. The Federalists selected King for second place on their ticket. He received 14 electoral votes.

son. Not a brilliant speaker, he sent a written message, thus establishing a tradition which remained in force until President Wilson broke it in 1913.

There were problems, big and small, foreign and domestic, right from the outset. Soon after he took office, the precarious situation in the Mediterranean blew up. The Barbary pirates were not satisfied with the amount of ransom they were receiving to leave unmolested American shipping which passed their coast. They made new demands which Jefferson refused to pay, whereupon Tripoli declared war on the United States. Jefferson dispatched the navy, and the war along the Barbary Coast went on with land and naval battles for years; not until the opening of Jefferson's second term was the peace treaty signed. At that time the Pasha of Tripoli received $60,000 for freeing his American prisoners, but he got no more ransom.

At home during the same time, the Jeffersonians had their dramatic battle with the Supreme Court. Adams and the Federalist lame-duck Congress had left an unwelcome legacy, the Judiciary Act of 1801. The law lowered the number of Supreme Court justices from six to five (after a vacancy occurred), raised the number of district courts from thirteen to sixteen and created sixteen new circuit courts. On its merit the law made sense, but Adams appointed only members of his own party. As the law was passed only three weeks before he left the Presidency, he made the appointments in a hurry; some of the commissions were not signed until the night before he moved out of the White House.

The new Republican Congress repealed the Judiciary Act after a prolonged argument. But when Madison, Jefferson's Secretary of State, refused to deliver the signed commissions to the Federalist appointees, one of the "midnight judges"—William Marbury—sued for his. His suit, known as the case *Marbury* vs. *Madison*, led to a far-reaching Supreme Court decision. Though its unanimous decision, written by Chief Justice John Marshall, stated that Marbury was entitled to his commission, the Court would not issue a writ of mandamus to compel Madison to deliver the commission because it was not granted such authority by the Constitution. The power to issue a writ, so the decision read, rested solely on the Judiciary Act of 1789; but since, in the opinion of the Court, Congress had not the power to expand on the Constitution, Section 13 of the 1789 Judiciary Act could not be considered valid. It was the first time that the Supreme Court exercised the "doctrine of judicial review" of Federal legislation, pronouncing a law passed by Congress unconstitutional. The decision was a slap at the Republicans, who readily took up the cudgel to bring the Court into line. They brought impeachment charges against Samuel Chase, one of the associate justices. If Chase was found

LOOK ON THIS PICTURE,

ORDER
LAW
RELIGION

— See what a grace was seated on this brow:—
— An eye like Mars to threaten and command,—
— A combination, and a form, indeed,
Where every God did seem to set his seal,
To give the world assurance of a man:—
THIS WAS—

AND ON THIS.

SOPHISM
NOTES on VIRGINIA
TOM PAINE
CONDORCET
VOLTAIRE

HERE IS—

—— like a mildewd ear,
Blasting his wholesome brother—

Vide Hamlet.

New York, June, 1807.

Engraving from 1807, artist unknown

AN ANTI-JEFFERSON CARTOON comparing Jefferson with Washington. The books under Washington's portrait are labeled "Order," "Law" and "Religion"; the volumes under Jefferson bear the titles "Sophism," "Notes on Virginia," "Tom Paine," "Condorcet" (the French philosopher whose system of state education was adopted by the Assembly) and "Voltaire."

guilty, the next target would be John Marshall. Chase was a staunch Federalist who talked loosely and arrogantly against the Republicans, but who had committed no "high crimes and misdemeanors" for which he could be impeached. In his trial before the Senate, he escaped conviction by a narrow margin when six Republicans sided with the Federalists. In the future, Republicans had to find other means of fighting the Court. Jefferson said that the impeachment attempt was "a farce which will not be tried again."

The high point of Jefferson's first administration was the acquisition of Louisiana. On March 21, 1801, seventeen days after Jefferson took office, Napoleon's envoys signed a treaty in Madrid for its retrocession. That vast territory—one and a half times as big as the entire United States—was the creation of Louis XIV and had been ceded to Spain by France in 1763. France wanted Louisiana back and made repeated offers for its retrocession, but Spain refused. However, when Napoleon proposed the exchange of the Duchy of Parma for it, the Spanish king was willing to make the deal; he desired the duchy for his son-in-law. The bargain was struck and a treaty signed—all in great secrecy.

In the fall of the same year, French envoys signed the preliminary articles of peace with Britain and the war between their nations came to a temporary halt.

Sir

the late President, mr Adams, having not long before his retirement from office, made several appointments to civil offices holden during the will of the President, when so restricted in time as not to admit sufficient enquiry & consideration, the present President deems it proper that those appointments should be a subject of reconsideration & further enquiry. he considers it as of palpable justice that the officers who are to begin their course as agents of his administration should be persons on whom he has personal reliance for a faithful execution of his views. you will therefore be pleased to consider the second appointment you have received as if never made, of which this early notice is given to prevent any derangements which that appointment might produce.

JEFFERSON'S DRAFT canceling Adams's appointments to civil offices. "The present President deems it proper that those appointments should be a subject of reconsideration & further enquiry. He considers it as of palpable justice that the officers . . . of his administration should be persons on whom he has personal reliance for faithful execution of his views."

The peace gave Napoleon opportunity for new adventures, for new conquests—he took Talleyrand's suggestion for a revived French empire in North America.

Thus the ink on the treaty for Louisiana's retrocession was hardly dry before he ordered Leclerc, the husband of his sister, the beautiful Pauline Bonaparte, to embark with an army to Santo Domingo, subdue the rebellion of the Negro slaves and restore order there.

Santo Domingo was the heart of France's overseas power, one of its most valuable possessions. It had 600,000 inhabitants, five-sixths of them Negroes kept in rigid slavery. About two-thirds of France's imports and exports centered on Santo Domingo. Seven hundred oceangoing vessels manned by 80,000 seamen were sailing between the island and France, bringing coffee, sugar, indigo and cotton to the home market. Of the island's 100,000 free citizens, about half were Creoles, and it was they who wielded the political influence, while the other half, the mulattoes with Negro blood in their veins, were without power. The mulattoes were determined to overthrow the Creoles' tyranny, and in this they had the support of the French National Assembly. But the Creoles resisted and the war began. In August 1791, the Negro slaves of the island revolted; from then on Santo Domingo was drenched in blood. In February 1794 the French National Assembly proclaimed the abolition of slavery and the half-million Negroes were given freedom.

Toussaint L'Ouverture, the son of an African chief, took service under the French; by 1797 he had been

Drawing by an unknown artist in 1805, in the New York Public Library

ATTEMPTING TO TAKE WEST FLORIDA FROM SPAIN. President Jefferson, on the right, encourages the Congressional dogs in their fight against the bull, representing Spain. The dogs are labeled with the names of Congressmen: "Peter" Earl, "Caesar" Rodney, Michael "Leib," John B. C. "Lucas," John W. "Eppes," Jefferson's son-in-law, and John "Smilie."

made general in chief of the colony, ruling with absolute power. In 1801 he declared himself a potentate and granted a succession of the power to his children. It was at this stage that Napoleon dispatched the army under Leclerc to subdue Toussaint and restore slavery.

Now Jefferson, who in the past had not given much attention to the events in Santo Domingo, realized how important they were for the future of America.

Reviewing the events some eight decades later, Henry Adams wrote: "If Toussaint and his blacks should succumb, the French Empire would roll on to Louisiana and sweep far up the Mississippi," but if Santo Domingo should resist and succeed, "the recoil would spend its force on Europe, while America would be left to pursue her democratic destiny in peace."

On November 10, 1801, Livingston, the new American envoy, reached Paris and asked Talleyrand about the "rumor" of the retrocession of Louisiana. Talleyrand lied. Though the treaty with Spain had been signed for over a year, he told the envoy that nothing had been concluded. But Livingston was not deceived. A few weeks later he wrote to Rufus King, his colleague in London: "I know that the armament destined in the first instance for Hispaniola [Haiti], is to proceed to Louisiana provided Toussaint makes no opposition."

But Toussaint and the half-million Negroes *did* make opposition. When the 10,000 French soldiers aboard the French fleet reached Santo Domingo, they had to struggle to land. The "war of races" commenced, and proceeded with fury. Leclerc's army withered away. The

73

black generals betrayed Toussaint; putting himself into French hands, he was eventually taken to France, where he died not long afterward. But the black men of Santo Domingo kept on fighting for their freedom. The first French army had been wiped out; the second army had been taken by yellow fever. In mid-September, Leclerc wrote Napoleon that of the 28,000 French soldiers and 500 sailors sent to Santo Domingo, only 4,000 were fit for service, and that "the occupation of Santo Domingo has cost us till now 24,000 men, and we are not yet definitely masters of it." Three weeks later, in another letter Leclerc gave his frank opinion of the country: "We must destroy all the Negroes in the mountains, men and women, keeping only infants less than twelve years old; we must also destroy half of those of the plain, and leave in the colony not a single man of color who has worn an epaulette. Without this the colony will never be quiet." He implored his brother-in-law to send him 12,000 more men "without losing a single day" and be prepared to send another "5,000 more men by the following summer."

Napoleon told Leclerc to arrest all the black generals and send them to France. He believed that once the leaders were out of the way, the rebellion would peter out. And Leclerc replied: "The rebels were exterminated; fifty prisoners were hung. These men die with incredible fanaticism—they laugh at death." In another dispatch he told of 176 deserters whom he caught and out of whom 173 strangled themselves rather than join hands with the French. "There you see the men we have to fight." The Negroes of Santo Domingo resisted the most powerful military nation on earth. They stopped Napoleon; the French suffered tremendous casualties; those who survived the battles died of yellow fever; Leclerc had succumbed.

Jefferson learned of Leclerc's death at about the same time that he heard the news that the Spanish intendant of Louisiana had forbidden Americans to deposit their merchandise at New Orleans. This was a hard blow for the Western farmers who dispatched their goods to the city, where they transshipped them on oceangoing vessels. To the West the "right of deposit" of the goods was a vital necessity. Jefferson had to act. He was informed in the meantime that the French authorities in Santo Domingo had ordered the American consul away, insulted American shipmasters and merchants, put Americans in prison, confiscated American property. Thus in April the President wrote to Livingston: "The day that France takes possession of New Orleans . . . we must marry ourselves to the British fleet and nation." And he sent James Monroe to join Livingston in Paris to buy New Orleans and the Floridas, or New Orleans alone, or some other spot on the east bank of the Mississippi from which Americans

could transship their goods. But such a bargain depended on the black men in Santo Domingo; the future of the United States was in their hands. If they kept on fighting, Napoleon could not occupy Louisiana.

Napoleon had to send another expeditionary force to Santo Domingo, more men, more equipment; and he was to dispatch an army to take over Louisiana—but his resources had been drained: he had not enough ships, not enough soldiers. The expedition to Louisiana, scheduled to sail in September, had to be delayed. In the middle of October the impatient Napoleon made the Spanish king sign another treaty for the deliverance of Louisiana. He wanted to take possession of the land, but the resistance of the Negroes in Santo Domingo blocked his plans. Thus, he had to call a halt to the war, and he had to give up the occupation of Louisiana.

When Monroe reached Paris in early April, Talleyrand told him that Napoleon was ready to sell Louisiana. He was in a hurry; he feared that in the case of war, Britain might take the entire territory. He regarded "the colony as entirely lost." On Easter Monday he told Marbois, one of his ministers: "Irresolution and deliberation are no longer in season. I renounce Louisiana. It is not only New Orleans that I cede; it is the whole colony, without reserve." So Marbois went to see Monroe and began negotiating. By May 2 the treaty was signed. (It was antedated April 30.) The United States acquired 828,000 square miles for 60 million francs and assumed the debts of France to American citizens of 20 million francs. The whole amounted to $15 million, or three cents an acre.

In 1889 Henry Adams reflected on Toussaint and the resistance of the Negroes: "In these days of passion men had little time for thought," wrote Adams; otherwise the "miserable Negro," as Napoleon called Toussaint, would not have been forgotten. He continued: "The prejudice of race alone blinded the American people to the debt they owed to the desperate courage of five hundred thousand Haytian negroes who would not be enslaved." Without their heroic effort to fight for their freedom, there would be no United States today. If Napoleon had won, France would have taken Louisiana, establishing her power in the Middle West, and blocking expansion; Americans could not have passed the barrier and reached the Pacific.

Jefferson, who was always pleading for a strict construction of the Constitution, had no hesitancy in making the purchase, but he hoped for a constitutional amendment to legalize the deal. "Our peculiar security is the possession of a written Constitution," he wrote to Senator Wilson Cary Nicholas. "Let us not make it a blank paper by construction." His political friends, however, persuaded him not to press for such an amendment. The Senate adopted the treaty as it was,

THE LEADER OF THE NEGRO UPRISING Toussaint L'Ouverture, whose heroic stand against French rule thwarted Napoleon's ambition for a North American empire. If the former slaves of Santo Domingo had not fought their oppressors for their freedom, Napoleon would never have sold Louisiana, forever blocking America's path to the Pacific.

THE CHANGING FACE OF THOMAS JEFFERSON—BETWEEN THE YEAR OF 1786, WHEN HE WAS THE

IN 1786 Mather Brown painted the 43-year-old Jefferson in London when he joined John Adams there to negotiate a treaty. The original painting was lost, but a replica of it which John Adams ordered at the time remained with the Adams family. Brown was paid £10 for the portrait.

IN 1800 the young Rembrandt Peale painted the 57-year-old Vice President, soon to be elected to the Presidency. Jefferson sat for him in Philadelphia. The portrait was probably completed in a single sitting, or two at the most; reproductions of it brought Jefferson's image to the people.

considering it in the country's best interest. And Jefferson threw overboard the ideas of strict construction, weak government, and limitation of the powers of the central government by the written Constitution.

He looked with confidence to the next election. Through the purchase the relations of his party with the West—which at that time meant Tennessee, Kentucky and Ohio—were tightened and support was assured.

The stalemate between him and Burr in the last election made a change in the mode of election imperative. Congress passed a resolution for a constitutional amendment whereby electors were to vote separately for President and Vice President rather than for two

men without the designation of office. Before the end of September, the resolution had been ratified by the states and had become the Twelfth Amendment; thus the next contest could be held under its provisions.

The Congressional caucus no longer met in secret. On February 25, 1804, 108 members of Congress convened in an open session and named Thomas Jefferson for the Presidency. They replaced Vice President Burr with George Clinton, the Governor of New York, as Burr had fallen out with his party. In the spring of election year, Burr ran for the governorship of New York but lost, partly because of Hamilton's violent opposition to him; this led to their duel on July 12, 1804,

AMERICAN ENVOY IN PARIS, AND THE YEAR OF 1821, WHEN HE HAD FIVE MORE YEARS TO LIVE.

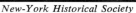

AT THE END OF JANUARY 1805 Rembrandt Peale painted the 61-year-old President in the White House. The portrait was accomplished in three sittings: on January 23, 24 and 31. Actually it was probably already finished by the second sitting; the third was used for making corrections.

IN MARCH 1821 Thomas Sully painted the 78-year-old Jefferson at Monticello. Sully stayed with Jefferson for twelve days "and left the place with the greatest reluctance." He finished the painting after Jefferson's death; it was given to the American Philosophical Society, where it now is.

and to Hamilton's death. Yet even after the duel, Burr presided over the Senate until the end of his term.

The Federalists did not formally nominate their candidates; they just recommended Charles Cotesworth Pinckney and Rufus King.

Pinckney, a brother of Thomas, John Adams's running mate in 1796, was a distinguished soldier in the Revolutionary War, a delegate to the Constitutional Convention, U.S. Senator from New York in the first Congress and again in 1795, Minister to Great Britain in 1796—as good a man as the Federalists could offer, but with no chance of victory.

Jefferson's re-election was a certainty. "Never was

there an administration more brilliant than that of Mr. Jefferson up to this period," wrote John Randolph. "Taxes repealed; the public debt amply provided for . . . sinecures abolished, Louisiana acquired; public confidence unbounded."

Only in Massachusetts, where the Federalists had control over the press and the clergy, was there a contest. There the old charges against Jefferson were re-hashed that he was an infidel, that he was the disciple of the French Revolution, that he was the corrupter of the judiciary and the destroyer of the American military establishment. The Federalist *Columbian Centinel* thundered that under Jefferson "justice has been amended in

Dec. 8. 1801.

Sir.

The circumstances under which we find ourselves at this place rendering inconvenient the mode heretofore practised of making by personal address the first communications between the legislative and Executive branches, I have adopted that by Message, as used on all subsequent occasions through the session. in doing this I have had principal regard to the convenience of the legislature, to the economy of their time, to their relief from the embarrassment of immediate answers, on subjects not yet fully before them, and to the benefits thence resulting to the public affairs. trusting that a procedure, founded in these motives, will meet their approbation, I beg leave through you, sir, to communicate the inclosed message, with the documents accompanying it, to the honorable the Senate, and pray you to accept, for yourself and them, the homage of my high respect and consideration. ——

Th. Jefferson

THE BEGINNING OF A TRADITION. Jefferson, who was not an accomplished orator, sent this letter to the president of the Senate with his first message. In it he explained that he found "inconvenient the mode heretofore practiced" of addressing the assembly in person; therefore, "I beg leave through you, Sir, to communicate the inclosed message . . . to the honorable the Senate." From that time until Woodrow Wilson broke the tradition on the eighth of April 1913, no President appeared before Congress in person.

favor of wicked and abundant violators of the laws of their country; men, destitute of principle and marked only for violence, have consequently obtained the first offices of government." Furthermore, Jefferson had repealed taxes imposed on luxuries, so that "the southern nabobs and whiskey patriots may enjoy their pleasures with the support of government," and to top it all he had purchased "a wilderness [Louisiana] for fifteen millions of dollars which probably might have been acquired more cheaply," over which Mr. Jefferson had been constituted "absolute monarch, clothed with patronage which may ultimately be death to national liberty."

All these charges cut little ice. The voters were for Jefferson. Most of the former Federalists were behind

him because "they saw that not a Federalist had been condemned, that the debt, the bank, and the navy was still preserved; they saw a broad construction of the Constitution, a strong government exercising the inherent powers of sovereignty, paying small regard to the rights of states, and growing more and more national day by day. It is not that Federalists were Republicanized, but the Republicans were Federalized," observed the historian McMaster.

Jefferson scored an overwhelming victory. Of the seventeen states taking part in the election, he carried all but two, Connecticut and Delaware, and he was shy of 2 votes out of 11 in Maryland. His electoral vote stood at 162 against the Federalists' 14.

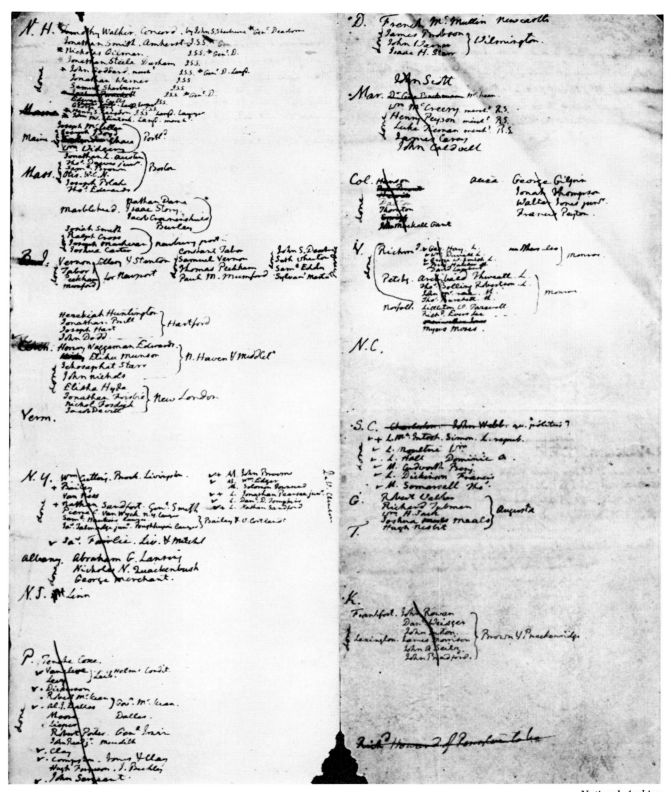

JEFFERSON'S APPOINTMENT LIST, with the names of those who had been helpful in his election. The party men from the various states were given jobs replacing Federalist officeholders. The list proves that in a limited sense the spoils system was established long before Democratic Senator Marcy declared in 1832 that "to the victor belong the spoils."

1808 THE SIXTH ELECTION

JAMES MADISON

Jefferson's second term started off on a high key. The country had peace and prosperity; political strife was at a low ebb; the President was at the peak of popularity. But as his term progressed, troubles began to mount, and toward its end Jefferson was as unpopular as he had been popular before.

The difficulties arose from the war in Europe. Once more Napoleon was fighting Britain and once more American ships were harassed by the two belligerents, neither of them respecting the rights of neutrals. Both the British and the French seized American ships, impounded cargoes, harassed trade and commerce, and impressed seamen.

In response to these indignities Congress, on April 18, 1806, passed a Non-Importation Act forbidding the importation of certain English goods, hoping that the measure might influence the British. It did not. Britain and France kept issuing their Orders in Council and their decrees, blockading each other's ports and interfering with American shipping. It was an untenable situation. Jefferson tried to negotiate the differences with Britain; he sent William Pinkney to London to join James Monroe, the American Minister, with instructions to secure the abandonment of the practice of impressments and America's right on the high seas. The two envoys concluded a pact, but it was so unsatisfactory that Jefferson would not act upon it.

On June 22, 1807, came the attack by a British warship, H.M.S. *Leopard,* on the American frigate *Chesapeake* only ten miles off the coast of Virginia. The British captain asked for the surrender of four sailors on the *Chesapeake* who had supposedly deserted the Union Jack; when the American would not heed the orders, the British let loose their guns. In the encounter three Americans were killed, eighteen wounded, and the four "deserters" were taken off.

Americans were enraged; they cried for retaliation. War fever swept the country.

Jefferson kept a cool head. "If nations go to war for every degree of injury, there would never be peace on earth." He would not be pressured.

To bring Britain to her senses Congress voted the Embargo Act, closing American ports to foreign ships and prohibiting American vessels to carry goods to Europe. Such a policy might have been successful if the British had been so dependent on American produce that they could not do without it. But as it happened, they had had a bumper crop, and furthermore the revolutionary South American republics opened their ports to British trade. Thus the Embargo, instead of bringing Britain to her knees, caused suffering in America. Harbors grew silent—the commerce of the East came to a standstill; in the South and the West farmers were stuck with their cotton, grain and tobacco. The value of exports decreased from $108 million in 1807 to $22 million in 1808.

The Federalist press of New England was fuming with fury. "We are the shipping interest," wrote a correspondent in the Boston paper, "and we will take care that it shall not be destroyed by your attachment. . . ." Another letter writer berated Jefferson: "You Infernal Villain. How much longer are you going to keep this damned Embargo on to starve us poor people?"

JAMES MADISON
By Thomas Sully
Now in the Corcoran Gallery, Washington

CANDIDATES IN 1808

JAMES MADISON
(1751–1836), the guiding spirit and chronicler of the Constitutional Convention, author of the Virginia Resolutions, co-author of *The Federalist* papers, was an outstanding political theoretician. A friend of Jefferson and Secretary of State during his two terms, Madison was handpicked to be his successor and continue the rule of the "Virginia Dynasty." He won easily, receiving 122 electoral votes.

GEORGE CLINTON
(1739-1812), Jefferson's Vice President, was acclaimed by the New York Republicans and their Federalist friends who wanted to see him in the presidential chair. Their support was not strong enough to gain the first place for him but was enough to secure him the Vice Presidency. Clinton disliked Madison and made no secret of his convictions; he opposed the President at every opportunity. He died in office.

C. C. PINCKNEY
(1746–1825), who spent his lifetime serving his country in military and diplomatic posts, became the Federalist candidate for the Presidency for the second time, but had little chance of winning the election. Nevertheless the unsuccessful embargo policy of the Republicans helped increase the Federalist support. Pinckney and King received 47 electoral votes, 33 more than in the previous election.

RUFUS KING
(1755–1827) represented Massachusetts in the Constitutional Convention. After moving to New York he became that state's first Senator, and was named by Washington in 1796 as minister plenipotentiary to Great Britain. Through skillful diplomacy he averted an open break between the two nations. In 1803 he returned home and let his name be put forward for the Federalist vice presidential nomination.

DOROTHY "DOLLEY" PAYNE (1768–1849), the widow of John Todd, by whom she had two sons. She married Madison on September 15, 1794.

Washington Irving described her as "a fine, buxom dame who has a smile and a pleasant word for everybody," and Sarah Seaton, the scintillating wife of the editor of the *National Intelligencer,* wrote of her, "You are aware that she snuffs; but in her hands the snuff-box seems only a gracious implement with which to charm."

Inches taller than "little Madison," she overshadowed her husband at her gay parties. Courageous, tactful, well liked, "Dolley" was the social arbiter of Washington to whom everybody paid homage.

Still others lamented about the embargo's failure:

It promised to make great Bonaparte humble,
It promised John Bull from his woolsack to tumble,
And not to leave either a mouthful to mumble
At our nod to make their caps doff.

But intead of fulfilling all these promises:

The PEOPLE *are left in the dark yet to stumble,*
Their patience worn out, no wonder they grumble
While daily they see their prosperity crumble,
And no hope their condition to mend.

An 1813 wood engraving by Alexander Anderson (1775–1870)

THE EMBARGO ACT, passed by Congress in late 1807, forbade all ships, domestic and foreign, from leaving American ports except for coastal trade. It was hoped that the measure would force Great Britain and France—the two warring nations in need of American raw material and foodstuffs—to reconsider their trade policies.

As England happened to have a bumper crop during those years and as she was able to trade with the South American republics, she did not respond to the embargo. Thus the Act hurt not the enemy but Americans. The harbors on the Atlantic seaboard grew silent; cotton, grain and tobacco were piling up in the South; trade with Europe came to a standstill.

While the embargo was in force, smuggling was rampant; it is the theme of this cartoon. The huge snapping turtle representing the embargo (because of its nickname, "terrapin policy") seizes a smuggler's breeches. The smuggler, carrying goods to an English boat in the harbor, curses the "Ograbme" ("Embargo" spelled backward). The people had fun with the word. They turned the letters about until they read: "Go Bar 'Em" or "Mobrage." And they cursed the "Dambargo."

Smarting under the attacks, Jefferson wrote: "I am tired of an office where I can do no more good than many others, who would be glad to be employed in it. To myself, personally, it brings nothing but increasing drudgery and daily loss of friends." Yet he could have won re-election for another term if he had so wanted; he was still the undisputed leader of his party, he still had the trust of his supporters. But he was firmly against a third term. To Senator Turner of North Carolina, who tried to persuade him, he wrote: "Genl Washington had established a precedent of standing only for two elections . . . that it was a precedent which he thot was obligatory upon himself—and from which he could not depart, and to prove the sincerity of his profession of rotation in office, will be, now that he has the power, to imitate the great Washington and not suffer himself to be a third term candidate." And he suggested that Madison, his old friend and Secretary of State, should be his successor.

Madison, "a withered little apple-John," came from a well-to-do Virginia family. In school he was a studious boy, learning the classics, French and Spanish. He went to the College of New Jersey (Princeton) and after his graduation continued studying theology and

Columbia TEACHING John Bull his new LESSON

An 1813 drawing by William Charles, etched by his partner, S. Kennedy

THE NEW COUNTRY HAD DIFFICULTY KEEPING THE PEACE WITH GREAT BRITAIN AND FRANCE.

Hebrew. In 1776 he was a delegate to the Virginia convention which made a new Constitution. He had been in public life ever since: member of the first Virginia Assembly and of the Governor's Council, a delegate to the Continental Congress, a delegate to the Constitutional Convention. His contributions to *The Federalist* and his efforts in the Virginia convention paved the way for ratification. Elected to the first House of Representatives, he rallied the agrarian opposition against Hamilton's centralizing and capitalistic policies. In 1797 he returned to the 2,500 acres which he was soon to inherit from his father and settled down to live the life of a country gentleman. Jefferson's election brought him back to public life. He became Secretary of State and the President's chief adviser.

Though Madison was the personal choice of the President, some members of his party, particularly from New York, wanted Vice President George Clinton as a candidate, while others, particularly from Virginia, were pleading for the candidacy of James Monroe. This faction, led by John Randolph, distrusted Madison and regarded him, because of his past political tenets, as not a genuine Republican. However, those against Madison's nomination could not agree on a single candidate; thus their efforts came to nothing.

In the latter part of January the Virginia legislature had offered Madison's name, but of the 123 who attended the caucus no less than 57 voted for Monroe. Shortly thereafter, on January 23, Senator Stephen Roe Bradley of Vermont, the previous caucus chairman, called a Congressional caucus in the Senate Chamber, "in pursuance of the powers vested in me," to deliberate

THE CAT *LET OUT OF* THE BAG. { A Scene from a new play under Rehearsal at Boston — Vide the Public Advertiser for Jan'y 21st 1808 —

An 1808 etching by William Charles

A FEDERALIST EDITOR WARNS THE THREE SAILORS AGAINST A WAR WITH THE MOTHER COUNTRY.

on the nominations. Edwin Gray, a Representative from Virginia, resented Bradley's "usurpation of power" as being "an invasion upon the most important and sacred right which belongs only to the people." Still, eighty-nine Representatives and Senators attended the meeting and lined up behind Madison for the Presidency and George Clinton for the Vice Presidency.

"In making the foregoing recommendations," read the announcement, "the members of this meeting have acted only in their individual characters as citizens; that they have been induced to adopt this measure from the necessity of the case; from a deep conviction of the importance of Union to the Republicans throughout all parts of the United States in the present crisis of both our external and internal affairs; and as being the most practicable mode of consulting and respecting the inter-

ests and wishes of all upon a subject so truly interesting to the whole people of the United States."

But with the democratic spirit expanding, the people rebelled against the undemocratic method of caucus selection. John Randolph signed a protest with sixteen others against Madison's candidacy. It assailed the caucus, which without discussion and debate nominated the man most unfit for the place; such action was hostile to the spirit and the plain intent of the Constitution, as that instrument made it the duty of the states to choose electors who in turn were to choose the President. To select one man as the only candidate and have every Republican elector vote for him violated the Constitution and was a gross assumption of power not delegated by the people to any set of men.

The protest went on to say that the country might be

1804: JAMES MADISON AS A YOUNG MAN

on the eve of war with a great maritime power; therefore the Republicans ought to choose a man noted for firmness and energy. Was Madison such a man? "We ask for energy and are told of his moderation. We ask for talents, and the reply is his unassuming merit. We ask what were his services in the cause of public liberty, and we are directed to the pages of the Federalist. . . . "We ask for consistency as a Republican, standing forth to stem the torrent of oppression which once threatened to overwhelm the liberties of the country. We ask for that . . . honorable sense of duty which would at all times turn with loathing and abhorrence from any compromise with fraud and speculation. We ask in vain."

Weathering the attacks, Madison remained the candidate, even though Monroe and Clinton kept on fighting him. Monroe wrote an "anonymous" article (which he did not dare to publish) in which he said that he "will not withhold his services from his country should his fellow citizens be disposed to give him so high a proof of their confidence." Jefferson berated him: "I see with infinite grief a contest arising between yourself and another [meaning Madison]." The dictates of public duty "prescribe neutrality," proceeded Jefferson and told Monroe that though he had no doubt that "the personal conduct of all will be so chaste, as to offer no grounds of dissatisfaction with each other. But your friends will not be as delicate."

Clinton disclaimed foreknowledge of the caucus and would make no comment on his own nomination; yet he struck out at the "intrigue and management of the basest kind" with which Madison secured "success to the caucus nomination." What he really meant to say was that he was willing to take the second place.

The country respected Madison for his work in the framing of the Constitution, for his opposition to Hamiltonian fiscal policies and the Jay treaty, and for his fight against the Alien and Sedition Acts. But one knew little of his actions as Secretary of State. What was his stand on the Embargo?

All this was cleared up and the postcaucus aspirations of Clinton and Monroe were disposed of in one fell swoop during the debates in the Senate over the confirmation of William Pinkney as Minister to Great Britain. As Pinkney was one of the negotiators of the ill-fated British treaty, the Senators wanted to see the correspondence on it before they would take a vote. Jefferson, advised by Madison, sent a message and several letters to the Senate. Vice President Clinton did not notice the "confidential" heading of Jefferson's message and had it read before open galleries—with a British secretary in attendance. Clinton seemed to live up to one of his enemy's characterizations: "He is old, feeble, and altogether incapable of presiding in the Senate. He has no mind—no intellect—no memory."

One of the Federalist Senators from Massachusetts condemned the embargo and the influence of the French in the Cabinet (a jibe at Madison) and asked that all relevant diplomatic correspondence with France and England be made public. Jefferson sent a file of letters to Congress and the clerks read them for six full days. These disclosures helped Madison, as the papers revealed that he had given strong orders on impressment; but they were not carried out. Madison had also outlined a good treaty with England; Monroe and Pinkney had made a poor one. And Madison's policy was not to submit but to stand up to France. The result of the revelations: "Upon the subject of the next President there is literally no division." Madison would have no organized opposition from within his own party.

When the returns of the spring election became known, the Federalists rejoiced. They had won in Massachusetts and had added to their strength in New York.

By the end of June the Republican prospects looked dark. Gallatin wrote his wife that he expected that his party would be turned out in the election. He thought Madison would carry only South Carolina, Virginia and the West and lose all the other states. But by the middle of summer the tide had turned. The Federalists were in disarray. Their leaders tried to persuade De Witt Clinton, the powerful Republican Governor of New York, to join with them in supporting his uncle Vice President George Clinton as the best way to defeat Madison, but De Witt would not enter such a coalition. Thus the Federalists were forced to put up a ticket of their own—it was the same as four years before: Charles Cotesworth Pinkney and Rufus King. They offered no threat to Madison.

The chief campaign issue was the embargo. The policy was under constant attack, particularly in New England. The *Columbian Centinel* of Boston editorialized: "The great foreign object of the Embargo makers was avowedly the destruction of England and her colonies. But after seven months' experience, and bringing thousands of Americanss to beggary, these Virginia Embargoroons find that old England does not essentially feel any misery from the massacre; and that the British Colonies are growing vastly rich on the ruins of American commerce; and some of the late sticklers for the Embargo Laws are calling aloud for their repeal; and for going to *war with England!*"

The New York *Herald,* too, assailed Jefferson, under whom the country had seen "a political intolerance as despotic as wicked, and capable of bitter persecution," and "an adherence to an insidious policy, which has at length brought the nation into the most unexampled state of distress and debasement. . . . We have seen a ruinous embargo, the call of one hundred thousand militia, the equipment of numerous gunboats, and the raising of a standing army, recommended by the President, adopted."

December 22, 1808, was the anniversary of the issuance of the Embargo. The Federalists made it a day of mourning. Flags in New England were lowered; in meeting after meeting the administration's Embargo policy was assailed. "Embargo Day" saw an outpouring of rhymed lament. One was written by William Cullen Bryant, then a thirteen-year-old lad:

> *Go wretch! Resign the Presidential chair,*
> *Disclose thy secret measures, foul or fair;*
> *Go, search with curious eye for horned frogs*
> *'Mid the wild wastes of Louisiana bogs:*
> *Or where Ohio rolls his turbid stream*
> *Dig for huge bones, thy glory and thy theme.*

But all these attacks had little influence on the elec-

By Asher B. Durand, in the New-York Historical Society
1833: JAMES MADISON AS AN OLD MAN

tion. Madison won, receiving 122 electoral votes against his Federalist opponent's 47.

Three days before the inauguration, Jefferson signed a bill repealing the embargo. "Within a few days I retire to my family, my books and farms," he wrote to a friend, "and having gained the harbor myself, shall look on my friends still buffeting the storm, with anxiety indeed, but not with envy. Never did a prisoner, released from his chains, feel such relief as I shall on shaking off the shackles of power."

In the evening of Madison's inauguration, Jefferson attended the inaugural ball of his successor, while the Federalists met at dinners to toast the end of Jefferson's administration and the ruinous embargo.

Soon he was to mount his horse and ride through snow and sleet to his beloved Monticello. Relieved from political responsibilities, he looked forward to a life of peace and serenity.

By the Virtue, Firmness and Patriotism of

JEFFERSON & MADISON,

Our Difficulties with England are settled—our Ships have been preserved, and our Seamen will, hereafter, be respected
while sailing under our National Flag.

NEW-YORK, SATURDAY MORNING, APRIL 22, 1809.

IMPORTANT.

By the President of the United States —A Proclamation.

WHEREAS it is provided by the 11th section of the act of Congrefs, entitled " An
" act to interdict the commercial intercourfe between the United States and Great Bri-
" tain and France, and their dependencies ; and for other purpofes,"—and that " in
" cafe either France or Great Britain fhall fo revoke or modify her edicts as that they
" fhall ceafe to violate the neutral commerce of the United States," the Prefident is au-
thorifed to declare the fame by proclamation, after which the trade fufpended by the faid
act and by an act laying an Embargo, on all fhips and veffels in the ports and harbours of
the United States and the feveral acts fupplementary thereto may be renewed with the
nation fo doing. And whereas the Honourable David Montague Erfkine, his Britannic
Majefty's Envoy Extraordinary and Minifter Plenipotentiary, has by the order and in the
name of his fovereign declared to this Government, that the Britifh Orders in Council
of January and November, 1807, will have been withdrawn, as refpects the United
States on the 10th day of June next. Now therefore I James Madison, Prefident of
the United States, do hereby proclaim that the orders in council aforefaid will have
been withdrawn on the tenth day of June next; after which day the trade of the United
States with Great Britain, as fufpended by the act of Congrefs above mentioned, and
an act laying an embargo on all fhips and veffels in the ports and harbors of the United
States, and the feveral acts fupplementary thereto, may be renewed.

Given under my hand and the seal of the United States, at Washington, the nineteenth day of April, in the year of our Lord, one
(L. S) thousand eight hundred and nine, and of the Independence
of the United States, the thirty-third.

JAMES MADISON.

By the President,
RT. SMITH, *Secretary of State.*

JAMES MADISON

In his inaugural address Madison said that he wanted "to cherish peace and friendly intercourse with all nations having corresponding dispositions; to maintain sincere neutrality towards belligerent nations; to prefer, in all cases, amicable discussion and reasonable accommodation of differences, to a decision of them by an appeal to arms."

He meant what he said. He worked wholeheartedly to keep the peace. He kept on negotiating with the British envoy in Washington, and his minister in Paris was in constant touch with the French government, parlaying for a peaceful solution of the vexing problems. The trouble was that Madison would not stick to a firm policy; he was indecisive and vacillating. The French consul in Philadelphia said of him: "Mr. Madison is an intelligent man, but irresolute, who will always see what ought to be done but will not dare to do it. . . . He will be the slave and not the master of events."

He was timid in dealing with Congress and inept in handling appointments and patronage.

His Cabinet appointments were preposterously weak. He allowed himself to be browbeaten by Senators Smith, Giles and Leib to appoint Smith's brother Robert as Secretary of State—the most incompetent man ever to hold that office. William Eustis of Boston, a surgeon, became his Secretary of War, Paul Hamilton, a former Governor of South Carolina, his Secretary of the Navy. The only outstanding man in the Cabinet was Albert Gallatin, the Secretary of the Treasury.

And yet his administration started out auspiciously. The Non-Intercourse Act, which replaced the Embargo Act, forbade trade with Britain and France and their de-pendencies, but allowed it with other nations. It took no time at all for American shippers to discover that European ports in Holland or Denmark were just as convenient markets to dispose of their produce as were the English and French harbors. Britain, in command of the seas, had plenty of ships to transport American goods from the continental harbors to the homeland. Thus American merchants and American shippers prospered. Before the Embargo the registered foreign tonnage in Massachusetts was 310,000 tons; in 1809 it rose to 324,000 tons, and in 1810 to 352,000 tons. Non-Intercourse also helped the new manufacturers; two years after the Act went into effect the number of spindles in Rhode Island increased tenfold. But while the Act benefited the New England states, it brought disaster to the South, sorely in need of markets for its tobacco and staple products.

Britain and France, fighting each other for supremacy on land and sea, kept on issuing their orders and decrees against neutral shipping. Britain would not allow American merchandise to go to France; France would interfere with American ships taking produce to Britain.

But Britain, constantly short of food, was in need of American goods. A few weeks before Madison took office the London *Times* wrote: "If America will withdraw her Embargo and Non-Importation Acts as far as they relate to England, provided we rescind the Orders in Council we cannot consider this as a disgraceful concession on our part."

Madison, as Secretary of State under Jefferson, was in steady consultation with the British Minister; as President he continued pursuing his way for a peaceful solu-

THE REVOCATION OF THE EMBARGO
A broadside issued on April 22, 1809

CANDIDATES IN 1812

JAMES MADISON

(1751–1836) was chosen by the Republicans to serve a second term. Unassuming and modest, he was a learned and industrious man who, in Herbert Agar's apt phrase, "knew everything about government except how to govern." He was under pressure from the West and South to drive the British from Canada and Spain from the Floridas. In June 1812, the United States declared war on Great Britain.

ELBRIDGE GERRY

(1744–1814), the ardent Republican and former Massachusetts Governor, became the vice presidential candidate after John Langdon declined because of his age. Gerry's name gave "gerrymandering" to the language because under him the districts of Massachusetts were redrawn in such a manner that the Federalists would lose the Senate. Gerry, who died in office two years later, got 113 electoral votes.

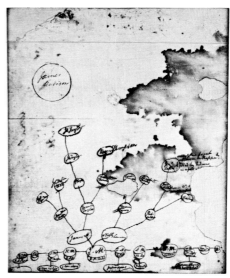

Library of Congress
MADISON'S FAMILY TREE

DEWITT CLINTON

(1769–1828), nephew of George Clinton and long-time mayor of New York City, was the antiwar candidate of the New York and New England Republicans who had had enough of the Southern Presidents and the rule of the Virginia dynasty. In the contest he received sizable support from the Federalists as well. If he could have carried the 25 votes of Pennsylvania, he would have won the election.

JARED INGERSOLL

(1749–1822), a moderate Federalist from Pennsylvania, was the candidate of his party for the second place. He was a Yale graduate, studied law in England and practiced it in Philadelphia, becoming the city's most prominent lawyer. A delegate to the Continental Congress and the Constitutional Convention, Ingersoll was a highly regarded politician, but unfortunately he was not able to carry his own state.

tion of the country's multiplying difficulties.

The signs augured well. The British Minister in Washington, David Montague Erskine, married to an American girl—the eldest daughter of General John Cadwalader of Philadelphia—received new instructions from London in April. Britain was ready to withdraw her Orders in Council against American trade under the following conditions: the United States was to halt its trade embargoes against Britain but enforce them against France; it was to renounce all trade with colonies of Britain's enemies and accept the British "Rule of 1756" under which trade not open to a nation in time of peace could not be opened to that nation in time of war. The last condition was the hardest one for America to swallow; no independent nation could agree to let her ships be seized by the British if found trading with that country's adversaries.

Erskine, though he had exact instructions from George

An etching from 1810 or thereabouts by William Charles, a Scotsman who came to New York around 1806

THE FEDERALISTS OPPOSED WAR, THE DEMOCRATIC-REPUBLICANS DEMANDED IT

Two men are pulling at the pillars "Federalism" and "Democracy" on which the casket "Liberty and Independence" rests. The Democratic-Republican on the left says, "This Pillar Shall not stand—I am determin'd to support a Just and Necessary War," and the Federalist on the right rejoins: "This Pillar must come down. I am a friend of Peace."

The ghost of President Washington, framed in clouds, speaks out: "I left with you a precious Casket of Choicest Blessings Supported by these Pillars—Desist my sons from pulling at them—should you remove one you destroy the whole."

Canning, the British Foreign Secretary, disregarded the letter of his orders and within a short time reached an agreement with the American government. On April 19 he announced that he was "authorized to declare that His Majesty's Orders in Council of January and November, 1807 will have been withdrawn as respects the United States on the 10th of June next," and after that date trade between the two countries "may be renewed." Simultaneously with Erskine's announcement Madison issued a proclamation in regard to British and French trade.

The country was jubilant. Madison was acclaimed by Republicans and Democrats alike. His popularity soared; political harmony with Congress was complete.

But when Canning received Erskine's report, he repudiated the agreement and ordered the envoy home. He would not accept a treaty with America which did not recognize the British "Rule of 1756." To replace Erskine

he sent Francis James Jackson to Washington. Jackson was an unbending English diplomat, with prejudice against everything not English; neither he nor his Prussian wife had respect for Americans.

Tensions mounted. Jefferson felt "war with England inevitable." The British held on to their Orders in Council; America revived Non-Intercourse against Britain. But Canning would not be swayed from his arrogant policy, a policy which made little sense, as it was not in Britain's interest to push America into war.

The Non-Intercourse Act was to expire in the spring of 1810. In December of the previous year Congressman Nathaniel Macon of North Carolina, the chairman of the Committee on Foreign Relations, reported a bill which would allow the importation of British and French goods if carried in American ships. When the Senate defeated the measure, Macon halfheartedly offered a new bill—

An 1809 copperplate print by "Peter Pencil" in the Houghton Library, Cambridge

JEFFERSON IS WAYLAID BY KING GEORGE III AND NAPOLEON, whose countries were in opposition to America's nonintercourse policy. The King says: "Well Tommy! I brought you at last to close Quarters therefore mind what you are about!—If you don't behave gently I'll break your limbs and leave you the rest. . . ." And Napoleon: "Trés bien! Mon Oncle Thomas! Dat is very vell! de more you make Noise, de less dat Jean Boule [John Bull] vill see, dat ve are."

Macon's Bill No. 2—which was to repeal Non-Intercourse but leave the door open for further negotiations with the two warring powers. If France were to withdraw her decrees, America would take up commerce with her, and if Great Britain would rescind her orders, then trade would be resumed with her but not with France.

Congress passed Macon's Bill No. 2 the first day of May, 1810. Three months later in August, the American Minister in Paris was informed by Count Cadore, Napoleon's Foreign Minister, that the French decrees would become ineffective on the first day of November, "it being understood that the English are to revoke the Orders in Council." Though Madison had no guarantee that Napoleon would keep his word, on November 2 he

announced that Non-Intercourse would be reinstated against Britain if she did not repeal her Orders in Council within three months.

This time England felt the squeeze. Napoleon, at the height of his power, successfully undercut British trade with Europe. English goods piled up in the warehouses; they could not be sold. Manufacturing decreased, workers lost their jobs. England needed markets, particularly her American markets. And because of her recent crop failure she was sorely in need of American foodstuffs. Thus, the British Government—with Canning out of office —was forced to change its policy: on June 16 it revoked the Orders in Council. But the move came too late. Before the news reached the United States, America had

JOHN BULL DEMANDS CAPITULATION. "I must have all your Flour," he says, "All your Tobacco—All your Provisions—All your Ships—All your Merchandize." He asks for everything but Porter (David Porter, who successfully harassed English shipping) and Perry (Oliver Hazard Perry, who captured the British fleet at Lake Erie).

The two kneeling Americans beg John Bull not to be hard on them. "You know we were always friendly, even in the time of our Embargo!" The British soldier nudges his civilian buddy, who is carrying barrels of Rum and Tobacco, to push on.

already declared war on Britain.

Why did war come? And why against Britain and not against France? France was no less impervious to America's right on the high seas than Britain. The French seized American ships just as frequently as the British. So why not war with France? Henry Clay put it succinctly: "The one we can strike, the other we cannot reach." Between America and France lay the sea, thousands of miles of it, but Canada, a bastion of British power, was just across the American border.

America's grievances against Britain were varied. The country smarted under the British insults to the American flag; it felt humiliated by George Canning's high-handed attitude toward American sovereignty. Americans held

Britain responsible for the Indian war on the Wabash. The West wanted British monopoly of the fur trade broken, it wanted to prevent the English in Canada from supplying arms to the Indians against the American frontiersmen, and it desired to remove the obstacle of the British military posts.

But the main drive for a confrontation was provided by the War Hawks of the West and South. The election of 1810-1811 changed the balance of power in Congress. Half of the old House members were voted out and replaced by young and vigorous men. It was the coming of a new era. The new Representatives, among them 34-year-old Henry Clay of Kentucky, 29-year-old John C. Calhoun and 30-year-old William Lowndes of South

JUNE 1, 1812: THE FIRST AND LAST PAGES OF THE PRESIDENT'S WAR MESSAGE TO CONGRESS

Carolina, 34-year-old Felix Grundy of Tennessee and others, embodied the spirit of their constituencies; they demanded that Britain be compelled to respect the rights of their country.

These young activists pressed for war to expand the frontier. The West wanted to annex Canada, to move into the territory between the mountains and the Pacific, and the South demanded the whole of Florida to eliminate Spanish influence there. Thus the war which was to be waged for the protection of New England shipping and trading interests turned into a war for the occupation of Canada and Florida.

When war came, Madison had already been renominated by a Congressional caucus, which met on May 18, 1812. Out of the 178 Republicans in Congress only 83

presented themselves, and after endorsing the President they chose for the second place John Langdon of New Hampshire, a signer of the Constitution. When Langdon declined because of his advanced age, the caucus replaced him with Elbridge Gerry, the old revolutionary, Governor of Massachusetts, and a signer of the Declaration of Independence.

The Eastern states, their trade in a shambles, would have liked to see DeWitt Clinton replace Madison. Clinton was endorsed by the Republicans of the New York legislature and he had the blessing of the Federalists, even though they did not endorse him openly. Rufus King and other die-hards would not commit themselves to more than tacit support for a Republican.

The candidacy of Clinton appealed to the voters in the

An 1880 cartoon by Howard Pyle

ONE OF THE MAIN CAUSES FOR THE WAR: THE IMPRESSMENT OF AMERICAN SEAMEN

British warships were always short of seamen, who were recruited by force. They were taken mostly from merchantmen, but as the war with Napoleon went on Britain's merchant marine dwindled and the desertions increased. It was estimated that 20,000 seamen deserted to the United States. Thus the British Navy searched American ships and seized those men who had been born under the English flag, as indeed most Americans were before independence. About 9,000 seamen were taken in this way, even if not all of them had deserted.

The impressments hurt the pride of the new nation. Americans felt humiliated; they were to fight Britain again.

East, who had had enough of the Virginia dynasty and of Southern Presidents. For them Madison represented the war spirit, while Clinton was the peace candidate, though outside New England the Republicans assured the voters that Clinton, once elected, would prosecute the war no less vigorously than Madison.

It was said that Madison sent his war message to Congress because the War Hawks demanded it. It was their price for supporting the President's renomination. It is doubtful that Madison made such a deal; it is more probable that he had changed his policies because he realized the country's position on the war.

The result of the election bared a sectional split. New England (save Vermont) and the middle states (save Pennsylvania and part of Maryland) were for Clinton,

but all the other states backed Madison. He received 128 electoral votes against Clinton's 89. If Clinton could have carried Pennsylvania, the decisive middle industrial state, he would have won the Presidency. But the 25 electoral votes of that state stayed with Madison.

The New England Federalists were dismayed. Their attempt to smash the political power of the South had failed. The South, helped by the slave vote, remained in the saddle. In the seven Southern states that voted for Madison there were about a million slaves, and though they had no voice in the government they had given the President 21 electoral votes (each 45,000 slaves were entitled to one elector).

The policy of the War Hawks, the spirit of expansionism, triumphed. The country wanted war.

95

JAMES MONROE

The war which the country so heartily welcomed turned out to be not an easy one. Wars always look simple before they begin, never after. Canada could not be taken within two months, as the War Hawks had predicted. War also costs money, but Americans felt it "unrepublican" to be taxed for it. In the whole New England area only three million dollars' worth of war bonds were sold.

And though the mood of the country was for war, out of a population of eight million less than 35,000 men volunteered. The brunt of the battle fell on the state militias, a green army commanded by old, feeble and timid officers. Detroit was lost, the attacks at Niagara repulsed. The militiamen were reluctant to fight outside the boundaries of their state; they had no desire to move into Canada.

The defeat at Detroit had proved that without the control of the Great Lakes an attack on Canada was doomed. A small fleet was built on Lake Erie, and when it was ready, it sought out the British squadron. On September 10, 1813, the young Captain Oliver Hazard Perry reported to William Henry Harrison, the commander of the armed forces: "We have met the enemy and they are ours; two ships, two brigs, one schooner and one sloop."

Harrison, too, retrieved the defeats of 1812. In October he attacked Detroit again. The British withdrew after putting a torch to the city. Harrison overtook and defeated them on the banks of the Thames River. His victory secured the Western frontier. The menace of the Indian confederacy had gone. Tecumseh, one of the Indians' best leaders, was killed, presumably by Richard M. Johnson, who later became Vice President under Van Buren.

Two other campaigns—one at Niagara, the other before Montreal—were not so successful. On December 30 the British took Fort Niagara. But earlier that year, General Henry A. S. Dearborn had raided York, the present Toronto, and set fire to the houses of the provincial Parliament.

After the defeat of Napoleon in Europe, the British could send more men and more supplies to America. Their strategy was to attack the mainland on three fronts—at Niagara, Lake Champlain and New Orleans —while their navy would keep on with the siege of the cities and villages along the Atlantic coast.

To relieve the pressure on the Canadian frontier, they landed a force of four thousand soldiers in August 1814 on the west bank of Maryland's Patuxent River, within marching distance of Washington.

Madison prepared a defense of the capital, but the available militia was too small and the commander, General William Henry Winder, was not a great light. Five miles outside of Washington he made a stand against the onrushing British. Madison and other officials came to witness the victory of American arms, so confident were they of the outcome of the battle. But the militiamen broke and ran away; and when the marines and sailors jumped into the breach, trying to stem the tide, they were overpowered. The road to Washington was open. The British took the capital on August 24, 1814, with the President and his Dolley narrowly escaping capture. They left in such a rush that British officers sat down to a dinner which had just

JAMES MONROE
By John Vanderlyn
In the City Hall, New York

CANDIDATES IN 1816

JAMES MONROE (1758–1831), the negotiator of the Louisiana Purchase and Madison's Secretary of State, was in the line of Republican succession. His public career had been varied: member of the Congress of the Confederation, Senator from Virginia in the first U.S. Congress, Minister to France, negotiator with Spain and Britain, Governor of Virginia in 1799 and again in 1811. He received 183 electoral votes.

DANIEL D. TOMPKINS (1774–1825), three times Governor of New York and commander of the New York militia, was the first choice of the New York Republicans for the Presidency, but as he was not known nationally, he had to step aside for William Crawford, the Secretary of the Treasury. However, when Monroe won over Crawford in the caucus, he became the Democratic-Republicans' choice for the second place.

RUFUS KING (1755–1827) was now the Federalists' presidential candidate. He was the leader of those nine men in the Senate who opposed the war, and he made an eloquent speech against the abandonment of Washington after the British had burned the Capitol. But when the war became one of defense, he changed his attitude and approved the administration's measures. He received only 34 electoral votes.

JOHN E. HOWARD (1752–1827), soldier in the Revolution, delegate to the Continental Congress, Governor of Maryland and a U.S. Senator, owned much of the land now covered by the city of Baltimore. He was chosen by the Federalists as their vice presidential candidate; however, he received only the 22 votes of Massachusetts, Connecticut and Delaware. It was the last time the Federalists put up a national ticket.

Painting by Benjamin West
ELIZABETH KORTRIGHT (1768–1830), the daughter of a one-time Tory merchant, married Monroe in New York City on February 16, 1786. They had three children, one of whom died in infancy. Eliza, the eldest daughter, became the wife of George Hay; Maria, the younger daughter, married Samuel Lawrence Gouverneur on March 9, 1820, in the White House's first wedding.

been prepared for Madison at the Executive Mansion.

Next day the British burned the White House (it had been called such long before the British destroyed it and the Americans repainted it, though officially it did not receive the name till Theodore Roosevelt's time) and others in retaliation for the American raid on York the year before. The military significance of taking Washington was small, the blow to the American pride great.

From Washington the British troops moved on to Baltimore, but at Fort McHenry "the flag was still there." Afraid of being too far away from their ships and their supply base, they gave up the attack and embarked for New Orleans.

General Andrew Jackson, in command of American operations in the Southwest, was waiting for them. When they sought the use of Pensacola, Jackson burnt

ELECTION DAY AT THE STATE HOUSE IN PHILADELPHIA IN THE EARLY YEARS OF THE CENTURY

the town. He had already smashed the Indians at Horseshoe Bend, avenging their massacre of Americans at Fort Mims.

In New England the British blockaded the ports; they occupied parts of Maine. The Federalists, smarting under the pinch of war, their business stagnant, their commerce in ruins, were exasperated. They talked of secession and a separate peace with Britain. To discuss a common action, they called a convention at Hartford, Connecticut, on December 15, 1814, to which delegates came from Massachusetts, Rhode Island, Connecticut, Vermont and New Hampshire.

The radicals among the Federalists asked for secession. But with George Cabot presiding, the moderates took charge of the proceedings and, instead of secession, a series of constitutional amendments were discussed.

One recommended that no new state should be admitted to the Union without "the concurrence of two-thirds of the members in both Houses of Congress"; a second that Congress should not have the power "to interdict the commercial intercourse between the United States and any foreign nation" and to "declare war or authorize acts of hostility against any foreign nation"; a third that Congress should not have the power to lay an embargo on ships for more than sixty days; a fourth that naturalized citizens should be ineligible for Congress; a fifth that no President should serve for a second term, nor should the President be elected from the same state for two terms in succession.

Commissioners appointed by the convention took the accepted resolutions to Washington to discuss them with Madison and force their acceptance upon Con-

SHOULD THE UNION BE DISSOLVED? In 1814 delegates from New England states met in a convention at Hartford to discuss secession. The dissolution movement, stirred by the embargo and fomented by the war, had popular support. Its prime mover, Timothy Pickering, Adams's Secretary of State, feared that the new states emerging from the Louisiana Territory might rule the nation in a spirit against New England and that alternative would be promoted at the expense of commerce. Thus Pickering was for the formation of a separate Northern Confederacy. However, when the convention met, the moderates were in control. The convention, under the guidance of Harrison Grey Otis, instead of considering secession, only protested against the unconstitutional acts of Congress and the abuses of poor administrations.

In the cartoon King George III attempts to lure back the

gress. The unlucky men could not have come to the capital at a more unpropitious time. Three days after the adjournment of the Hartford meeting, Andrew Jackson won his spectacular battle at New Orleans. Two thousand British troops lost their lives in the attack, while the Americans lost only a few men. The commissioners found the city celebrating Jackson's victory. And a few days later news reached the country that the peace treaty had been signed in Ghent.

The war was over and the treaty, though it had not settled any serious issues, was welcomed by all factions. Some time later the Federalist politician William Sullivan recalled: "So general and heartfelt was the joy at hearing being at peace again that celebrations were had in all the cities, in which both sexes, all ages, and all parties united, with the strongest enthusiasm. There were splendid processions, bonfires, and illuminations, as though independence of the country had been a second time achieved." In this atmosphere the demands of the Federalists seemed an attack on the Union.

With peace came fresh hope. The war did not make the government collapse, as the Federalists had predicted. Instead of ruining the country, the war led to greater economic self-sufficiency. Factories produced goods in large quantities which formerly were brought from Europe. The country could stand alone; it no longer needed to fear European domination.

A sense of patriotism swept the nation. Gallatin said: "The war has renewed and reinstated the national feelings and character which the Revolution had given, and which were daily lessened. The people have now more general objects of attachment with which their pride and political opinions are connected. They are more Americans; they feel and act more as a nation."

Riding the waves of the nationalistic mood, Madison recommended and Congress passed measures for a sizable increase in the army and navy; it kept the high tariff rates which helped New England with its industrial expansion, and it increased the budget from $10 to $27 million. Madison's program was a Hamiltonian one, yet it was passed by the Jeffersonians.

With election coming up, the Democratic-Republicans had a choice between two men—James Monroe, the Secretary of State, and William H. Crawford, the Secretary of the Treasury.

Crawford was the stronger contender; he seemed to have the support of the majority. Abner Lacock, the Virginia-born Senator from Pennsylvania who tried to get the Presidency for Monroe, went to Crawford and asked him not to challenge Monroe, the last revolutionary hero, and create a disruption in the party. Crawford allowed himself to be persuaded; he was young enough to wait for another occasion. Still, when the Congressional caucus met, he had the support of 54

An 1814 etching by William Charles

three New England states which sent delegates to the convention—Massachusetts, Connecticut and Rhode Island.

The King asks the men to make the leap; there will be "plenty of molasses and Codfish, plenty of goods to Smuggle; Honours, titles and Nobility into the bargain."

Timothy Pickering, the instigator of secession, is praying that the movement should succeed so he may become "Lord of Essex," after his home County in Massachusetts.

members. But as Monroe received eleven more votes, he became the candidate, with Daniel Tompkins, the Governor of New York, as his running mate.

Monroe, another member of the Virginia Dynasty, left William and Mary to serve as the lieutenant in a Virginia regiment during the Revolutionary War. In the battle of Trenton he led a charge against the Hessians, was wounded and through his gallantry became an aide to Lord Stirling, the British-born general who fought with the Americans.

In 1780 he became a student of law with Thomas Jefferson, then the Governor of Virginia, and the two remained friends for life. Monroe turned to politics, was elected to his state's legislature, then to the Congress of the Confederation, where he played a vital role. He was present at the Annapolis Conference of 1786 which prepared the way for the Constitutional Convention the following year. He was not a delegate to the Convention, and as a member of his state convention he opposed ratification. Consequently he ran for Congress but was defeated by Madison.

In 1790 he was named Senator, and though he was inconspicuous in that body, his political career, helped by his friendship with Jefferson, was on the steady rise. Washington appointed him as Minister to France, and it fell to him to explain the Jay Treaty to the French Government—an impossible undertaking. Recalled in 1796, he became Governor of Virginia. When Jefferson became President, he sent Monroe to Paris to negotiate the purchase of Louisiana. His other diplomatic missions with England and Spain were less successful.

His friends wanted him to succeed Jefferson in the Presidency, thus causing a rift between him and Madison. Still, Virginia was with him; in 1810 he was re-elected to the Virginia legislature, and in 1811 he again became Governor of the state. When Madison needed him in his cabinet, he offered him the post of Secretary of State, and Monroe accepted.

As a presidential candidate Monroe was offered as an authentic Revolutionary hero (compared in appearence and deportment with Washington), who had participated in many of the important national questions since independence.

More and more the caucus mode of selection came under attack. An editorial of October 24, 1816, in the Aurora *General Advertiser* signed "Franklin" stated the attitude of the anticaucus men:

"The Constitution of the United States, in order to prevent those corrupt practices, which produced the ruin of other republics, declares that members of Congress shall not be electors, but that a president and vice-president shall be elected by persons chosen for this purpose—all meeting in their several states on the same day. But this sound provision of the Constitution has long been evaded—members of Congress actually exercise the power which elects a president, and the electors contemplated by the Constitution are no more than so many clarks in each state, writing down the decision made in Washington." A week later the same editorial writer summarized the issue: "The real question will be: Caucus usurpation or free election."

The Federalists had not chosen an official slate, but the electors of Massachusetts, Connecticut and Delaware lined up behind Rufus King and John E. Howard. They had no hope; their party was moribund. As political issues did not divert the country, the campaign was listless, causing little stir.

Monroe and Tompkins carried all the states except Massachusetts, Connecticut and Delaware, with 183 electoral votes against King's and Howard's 34.

At the counting of the votes those from Indiana were challenged because that state had been admitted to the Union on December 11, a month after the election. Still, after lengthy discussion the votes were accepted.

In December 1816, after Monroe's election was assured, Congress passed a Calhoun-inspired bill for internal improvements at Federal expense. Madison vetoed the bill—one of the great blunders of his Presidency. Calhoun's bonus bill would have cost only a million and a half dollars for the building of roads and canals, and would have eliminated much of the South's antagonism against the North. But the veto—Madison's last official act sent to Congress the day before his successor's inauguration—was instrumental in keeping the South downtrodden. Without roads to the inland market Southern prosperity was blocked.

Monroe gave his inaugural address on an elevated portico in front of the Capitol. He spoke in the open rather than inside the building because, so the story went, Henry Clay, the Speaker of the House, would not allow the House chamber to be used for the ceremonies. Clay said that the floor of the hall would not be strong enough to hold such a large crowd. Rumor had it that he opposed the use of the chamber because Monroe would not appoint him Secretary of State. As no other appropriate place could be found inside the building, the ceremonies were moved into the open, starting a tradition which has come down to the present.

The new President reviewed the history of America since the Revolution, noting that "During a period fraught with difficulties and marked by very extraordinary events the United States have flourished beyond example. Their citizens individually have been happy and the nation prosperous." And he said that he was pleased to take up the duties of the Presidency in a time of peace, concluding that "gratifying is it to witness the increased harmony of opinion which pervades our Union. Discord does not belong to our system."

An English cartoon published in London on October 4, 1814

THE BURNING WASHINGTON: A CARTOON COMMENT ON MADISON'S FLIGHT FROM THE CITY.

A contemporary engraving in the Smithsonian Institution

THE BURNED-OUT CAPITOL AS IT LOOKED IN 1814

respective Governments, and to the defence of,
our own, which has been atchieved by the
loss of so much blood and treasure, and ma-
tured by the wisdom of their most enlightened
Citizens, and under which we have enjoyed
unexampled felicity, this whole Nation is
devoted. We owe it therefore to Candor, and
to the amicable relations existing between
the United States and those Powers, to declare
that we should Consider any attempt on their
part to extend their System to any portion
of this Hemisphere, as dangerous to our
peace and safety. With the existing Colonies or Dependencies of any European Power
we have not interfered, and shall not interfere. But with the Governments who have
Declared their Independence, and maintained
it, and whose Independence we have, on great
Consideration, and on just principles, acknowledged, we could not view any interposition
for the purpose of oppressing them, or con-
trouling in any other manner their destiny,
by any European Power, in any other light
than as the manifestation of an unfriendly disposition towards the United States.
In the War between those new Governments
and Spain, we declared our neutrality,
at the time of their recognition, and to
this we have adhered, and shall continue
to adhere, provided no change shall

                                    occur

1820 THE NINTH ELECTION

JAMES MONROE

With the war over, foreign issues lost their prominence, and public attention turned to domestic problems: tariff, internal improvements, slavery.

The debates over these issues widened the rift between the sections. Pennsylvania and other manufacturing areas advocated a protective tariff; commercial Massachusetts opposed it. The Middle and Western states wanted internal improvements at government expense; the Northeast was against them. And on the slavery question the views of North and South were so irreconcilable that no solution was in sight.

North and South had grown apart, and the chasm between the manufacturing North and the slaveholding South had steadily widened. The North was apprehensive that the vast land beyond the Mississippi might be turned into slaveholding territory; the South feared Northern domination. When on February 15, 1819, the House committee on territories reported on a bill "enabling" Missouri to draw up a constitution and apply for statehood, the New York Congressman James Tallmadge introduced an amendment prohibiting the extension of slavery into the Louisiana Territory. The South was stung to the quick. It fought the amendment, it would not hear of it. The Northern states were equally adamant. They would not vote for more slaveholding territory. The two sections were in deadlock.

The core of the problem was that in the three decades since the founding of the Republic the country's population had increased threefold. But while at the beginning the population of the South and the North had been roughly equal, now the North had a distinct advantage with its 5,144,000 people to the South's 4,371,000. This meant that in the House of Representatives the North now had 123 Representatives while the South had only 89. In the Senate the political balance remained the same—eleven slave states and eleven free states; however, if the new states of the Louisiana Territory were admitted without slavery, the free states would far outnumber the slave states; the North would be dominant, the South a poor relation. A compromise had to be found to satisfy both North and South. It came when the district of Maine, with Massachusetts' approval, applied for statehood. With Maine as a free state and Missouri as a slave state, the balance in the Senate between North and South could be kept.

The first week of March 1820 President Monroe signed the Missouri Compromise, which declared: "In all territory ceded by France to the United States . . . which lies north of thirty-six degrees and thirty minutes latitude, not included within the limits of the state . . . slavery . . . shall be, and is hereby, forever prohibited." Thus the issue was solved, if only for the time being.

Monroe took no part in the debates over the compromise; he remained silent, and kept neutral. He was the head of the party—the only national party in the land—and he had no wish to antagonize any of the factions. He rode the peak of popularity. Early in his administration the *Columbian Centinel* had coined the phrase, the "Era of Good Feelings," and it had stuck. It was a period of soaring nationalism, of peace, a period in which the country's character took shape.

No one thought of opposing Monroe's candidacy for renomination. He was still the most popular man in the

THE MONROE DOCTRINE
Original in the Library of Congress

CANDIDATES IN 1820

JAMES MONROE
(1758–1831), the President of the "Era of Good Feelings," was the candidate of the whole country. With political animosities dormant no one opposed him. The Federalists were extinct and everyone took cover under the umbrella of the single party. Monroe received all votes but one; the one elector supposedly withheld his vote so that Washington would remain the only President chosen unanimously.

DANIEL D. TOMPKINS
(1774–1825), Monroe's Vice President, ran for the governorship of New York in 1820 and, after he suffered defeat, was once more nominated for the Vice Presidency. In the War of 1812 he recruited 25,000 troops to defend New York City. He borrowed money to pay the troops; large sums passed through his hands and when he could not account for them, his difficulties began.

JOHN QUINCY ADAMS
(1767–1848), son of the second President and Monroe's Secretary of State, was not a candidate in this election but received the single vote of William Plumer of New Hampshire. A man of the world, he attended school in Paris and Amsterdam, studied at Leyden and graduated from Harvard. At fourteen he was private secretary to our Minister in Russia; later, his father's secretary in Britain.

RICHARD STOCKTON
(1764–1828), a lawyer from New Jersey whose father was a signer of the Declaration of Independence, received the 8 votes of the Massachusetts Federalists for the Vice Presidency. The wealthy Stockton, whom his younger colleagues nicknamed "the Old Duke," opposed the war with England as a "political insanity" and fought Monroe's policies. He opposed the "idle doctrine of free trade and sailors' rights."

country. The financial panic of 1819 and the violent political struggle for Missouri's admission left his reputation unscathed. Though a caucus was held in late April, to which were invited not only the pillars of the party but also "other members of Congress as they may think proper to attend," less than fifty showed up. They made no recommendations, but left the selection to the people, so confident were they that it would be Monroe—as, indeed, it was.

The Federalists' influence had gone; no longer could they put up a ticket, no longer did they offer the names of candidates.

Five new states voted in the election: Mississippi (admitted December 10, 1817), Illinois (admitted December 3, 1818), Alabama (admitted December 14, 1819), Maine (admitted March 15, 1820) and Missouri (which adopted a constitution in July 1820 but was not admitted until August 10, 1821)—twenty-four states in all.

Monroe received all the electoral votes but one. The single vote cast for John Quincy Adams came from William Plumer, New Hampshire's former Governor. It was said that Plumer voted for Adams so that George Washington would remain the only President who was elected by a unanimous vote, but those who knew him said that his negative vote was more in disapproval of Monroe's policies than a tribute to Washington.

At the counting of the electoral votes the question arose whether or not a state's votes should be included if that state had not been a part of the Union at the time of the election. It arose because Missouri, not yet formally admitted, had sent in its votes. A joint Congressional committee ruled that if objections were raised against Missouri's votes, they should not be counted; but if no one objected, they could be included in the final figure. There were no objections.

It was a simple inauguration. As the fourth of March fell on a Sunday, the ceremony was held on Monday. It turned out to be a cold day, with sleet and showers, turning Washington into a mudhole. John Quincy Adams described it in his diary: "A quarter before twelve I went to the President's house, and the other members of the Administration immediately afterwards came there. The Marshal and one of his deputies was there, but no assemblage of people. The President, attired in a full suit of black broadcloth of somewhat antiquated fashion with shoe- and knee-buckles, rode in a plain carriage with four horses and a single colored footman. The Secretaries of State, the Treasury, War and the Navy followed, each in a carriage and pair. There was no escort, nor any concourse of people on the way. But on alighting at the Capitol, a great crowd of people were assembled, and the avenues to the hall of the House were so choked up with people pressing for

ON TO THE SECOND INAUGURAL. The Cabinet waits before the White House to accompany Monroe to the ceremony. The painting shows the fresh paint on the White House which was burned by the British in 1814 and not restored until 1817.

admission that it was with the utmost difficulty that the President made his way through them into the House." And the English Minister, who was present, remarked cattily: "In addition to the squeezing and shoving which the poor *Prezzy* experienced at the door, his speech, which was indeed rather long, was occasionally interrrupted by queer sounds from the gallery."

Monroe began the inaugural address on a modest note: "Having no pretensions to the high and commanding claims of my predecessors . . . I consider myself rather as the instrument than the cause of the union which has prevailed in the late election." He dwelt upon the War of 1812 and described new fortifications to prevent future invasions. He added that these military measures "have not been resorted to in a spirit of hostility to other powers. . . . They have been dictated by a love of peace, of economy, and an earnest desire to save the lives of our fellow citizens from that devastation, which is inseparable from war, when it finds us unprepared for it." He went on to extol the achievements of his administration and to describe the growth and vitality of the country. And when he finished, a "cheering shout" went up from the galleries.

After the ceremonies a surging mass flocked to the presidential mansion, restored and painted white since the British had ravaged it in the war. Everybody wanted to shake hands with the President. "All the world was there," wrote Justice Story to his wife. "Hackney coaches, private carriages, foreign ministers and their suites were immediately in motion, and the very ground seemed beaten into powder or paste under the trampling of horses and the rolling of wheels. The scene lasted until 3 o'clock, and then all things resumed their wonted tranquillity."

JOHN QUINCY ADAMS

The "Era of Good Feelings" was a misnomer. To keep political good feelings for any length of time is an unattainable goal. On the surface the political waters during the Monroe administrations were calm, but beneath it the currents were turbulent. Politicians jockeyed for position, struggled for power. There was still one party and no official opposition to it, but halfway through Monroe's second term *Niles' Register* noted sixteen to seventeen candidates ready to succeed the President. By election year the minor contenders had faded away, but six strong ones remained.

The New England states were behind John Quincy Adams, the son of the second President and Monroe's Secretary of State; the South was split between John C. Calhoun of South Carolina, the Secretary of War, and William H. Crawford of Georgia, the Secretary of the Treasury; from the middle states and the West came support for Henry Clay, the former Speaker of the House; large sections of the West clamored for Andrew Jackson, who was the idol of the "common man"; DeWitt Clinton, former Governor of New York, the "father" of the Erie Canal, also had support from the West, but had difficulty in his own state.

Of the six front-runners Crawford was the favorite of the politicians. He had a distinguished public service record; was elected to the Georgia legislature in 1803; four years later he became U.S. Senator; in 1813 he was appointed Minister to France; from 1815 on he served in Madison's Cabinet, first as Secretary of War, then as Secretary of the Treasury. If a caucus selected a candidate, it would be Crawford. Thus all his major opponents—Adams, Clay, Jackson, Calhoun, Clinton

—were ready to "give the caucus a death blow."

Though election time was still far off, the issue of the caucus grew to paramount importance. Should it be held? And if it were held, should its recommendations be followed? These questions were argued in meetings, in newspapers, in the churches and in private talks. Those who were for a caucus mode of selection insisted that it would strengthen the Union, while those who opposed it were certain that it would destroy it.

An increasing number of people demanded a vote in their government. The new Western states added to the rising democratic spirit. The pioneer frontiersmen rejected property qualification as a prerequisite for voting; they rejected the rights of aristocrats to rule the country. And they believed that a good Indian fighter or a good hunter was as qualified for high political office as a university-educated Virginian or a Massachusetts aristocrat. Tennessee elected the half-literate Davy Crockett to the legislature; when he killed 105 bears in one season, his friends were ready to run him for the Presidency.

The new coonskin-capped Americans, no longer in wigs and silver buckled knee breeches, wanted to choose their President; they would not let a Congressional caucus make the decision for them.

The followers of Andrew Jackson asked their legislature to instruct their Senators and Representatives to stay away from the meeting. The Tennessee resolutions called the caucus unconstitutional and inexpedient: unconstitutional because the Constitution did not give Congress the power to recommend a candidate to the electors, inexpedient because such election threatened

JOHN QUINCY ADAMS
Painted by Gilbert Stuart,
completed by Thomas Sully,
in the Harvard Union, Cambridge, Mass.

CANDIDATES IN 1824

JOHN QUINCY ADAMS (1767–1848) followed the precedent of previous Presidents and made the Secretary of State his natural successor. Since the "Era of Good Feelings" under Monroe, the party had split into factions, one behind Adams, the other behind Jackson. In the election Jackson had a larger popular vote than Adams, but in House of Representatives Adams was chosen. Thirteen states voted for him, seven for Jackson.

ANDREW JACKSON (1767–1845) was the son of poor Irish parents who immigrated to America two years before he was born. He was successful at whatever he tried —in business, in politics, in his military career. As a result of his victory at New Orleans, he became the obvious candidate for the Presidency, receiving 99 electoral votes against Adams's 84, Crawford's 41, Clay's 37. But none of them had the majority vote.

LOUISE CATHERINE JOHNSON (1775–1852), daughter of a U.S. Consul, a woman of beauty, intelligence and charm, married Adams in London on July 26, 1797, while he was there on diplomatic business. Their marriage lasted half a century; they had four children, one of whom died in infancy.

WILLIAM H. CRAWFORD (1772–1834), U.S. Senator from Georgia, Minister to France, Secretary of War under Madison and of the Treasury under Monroe, was the foremost aspirant for the Presidency until he was stricken with paralysis in the fall of 1823. For over a year he remained in seclusion, incapacitated and almost blind. Even so he was chosen by the caucus; but 261 Representatives and Senators abstained.

HENRY CLAY (1777–1852), U.S. Senator, member of the House of Representatives, was leader of the "War Hawks" in the Twelfth Congress. An ardent nationalist, he advocated internal improvements, re-charter of the U.S. Bank, protection for industries and a standing army. He pushed the Missouri Compromise through the House. In the election he ran fourth but became President-maker by releasing his votes to Adams.

the liberties of the people by allowing the large states to outvote the small ones.

The resolutions were sent to other states for adoption, but only Maryland and Alabama accepted them.

Though opposition to the caucus was widespread, on February 6, 1824, the *National Intelligencer* carried a call for the Democratic members of Congress to meet on the fourteenth to make recommendations for candidates for the Presidency and the Vice Presidency. Next to the invitation appeared a notice signed by 24 Senators and Representatives which declared that of the 261 members who were entitled to attend the meeting, 181 "deem it inexpedient, under existing circumstances, to meet in a caucus."

The prediction as to the number of opposing Congressmen was not far off the mark. When the caucus met, only 66 members presented themselves, with two

Painting by Samuel F. B. Morse (1791-1872) in the Corcoran Gallery, Washington, D.C.

THE OLD HOUSE OF REPRESENTATIVES WHERE BALLOTING FOR PRESIDENT TOOK PLACE IN 1825.

more sending proxies. The majority of the members—48—represented only four states: New York, Virginia, North Carolina and Georgia. In the balloting Crawford was given 64 votes; John Quincy Adams 2, Andrew Jackson and Nathaniel Macon each 1. For the Vice Presidency Albert Gallatin was chosen.

"In making the foregoing recommendation," said the caucus announcement, "the members of this meeting have acted in their individual characters as citizens, that they have been induced to this measure from a deep and settled conviction of the importance of union among Republicans throughout the United States, and as the best means of collecting and concentrating the feelings and wishes of the people of the Union upon this important subject."

That the caucus should name Crawford was incredible, but politicians are apt to do incredible things.

Full of their own importance, they make decisions, which their "followers" would repudiate. At the time of his nomination Crawford was a seriously ill man. A few months before, he had suffered a stroke; since then he had been paralyzed, unable to attend Cabinet meetings or to sign official papers. Though neither his memory nor his speech was seriously impaired, he walked like a blind man, his feet cold and numb. An observer noted: "But it is the general impression that a slight return of his disorder would prove fatal to him."

His nomination was roundly rejected by the opposition; no one felt obliged to be bound by it. An assembly in Boston's Faneuil Hall proposed John Quincy Adams as the candidate of Massachusetts; he was endorsed by other New England states. Clay was put into nomination by the legislature of Kentucky as "a suitable person to succeed James Monroe as President." Other legislative

John Singleton Copley,
in the Museum of Fine Arts, Boston

1795: 28 YEARS OLD

Charles Willson Peale,
in the Historical Society of Pennsylvania

1825: 58 YEARS OLD

Asher B. Durand,
in the New-York Historical Society

1834: 67 YEARS OLD

Daguerreotype by Mathew B. L
in the National Archives

1847: 80 YEARS OLD

THE CHANGING FACE OF JOHN QUINCY ADAMS

bodies—such as Missouri, Louisiana, Ohio—endorsed him. Jackson was named by the lower house of the Tennessee legislature, Calhoun by the legislature of South Carolina, Clinton by several counties in Ohio.

"King Caucus" was dead—never again were candidates chosen by such an assembly.

To prevent the election from being decided by the House of Representatives, there was feverish activity among the supporters of the other candidates to join forces. The Adams men would have liked to see Jackson in the second place, thus forming a ticket with "John Quincy Adams, who can write, and Andrew Jackson, who can fight," but Jackson would not oblige. Clay, too, was approached; he, too, declined.

The new political issues—tariff, internal improvements, cheap public land—caused dissension among the sections. New England, divided on the tariff, was against internal improvements and against cheap land which diverted its citizens and its business to the West. The middle states, Pennsylvania foremost among them, wanted high tariff protection for their budding industries; they asked for new roads and canals to open the Western market. The South opposed internal improvements as they did not benefit her area, and she was also against high tariff as it interfered with her trade and increased the cost of imported goods.

The major candidates—Adams, Jackson, Crawford, Calhoun, Clay and Clinton—represented the differing political views of the country's sections. Clay advocated Western expansion, internal improvements and a protective tariff; he was also for the U.S. Bank and the recognition of the South American republics. Jackson, while in the Senate, had voted for protective tariff and internal improvement bills. Adams, a nationalist, favored tariff but differed with the Northeast's ideas on internal improvements. Calhoun, also a nationalist, was for tariff and internal improvements, issues which were not favored by his Southern following. But Crawford was a states'-righter and an opponent of the tariff, though he had to keep silent about his political beliefs in order to hold on to his support in the middle states. On internal improvements he followed the conservative course of Madison and Monroe.

Gallatin later removed himself from the vice presidential race; thus Calhoun, the youngest of the four candidates, became the accepted nominee for the second place.

The campaign was spirited; it was fought on platforms, from pulpits and in the press. Clay complained that "the bitterness and violence of the presidential electioneering increase as time advances. It seems as if every liar and calumniator in the country was at work day and night to destroy my character. . . ."

The election began on October 29 and lasted until November 22, since no uniform day had yet been set by the states. Jackson won, receiving 99 electoral votes

1848: IN THE YEAR OF HIS DEATH

Daguerreotype by Southworth and Hawes,
Metropolitan Museum, New York

against John Quincy Adams's 84, William Crawford's 41, and Henry Clay's 37. But Jackson's total was only a plurality—no one had the majority. The Vice Presidency was Calhoun's by a decisive margin.

Since none of the four chief contenders received the majority vote, the House of Representatives was to choose between the three with the highest numbers. Because of this Clay, who ran fourth, wielded unusual power. By releasing his votes to one of the three, he could make the President; so he was ardently courted by the supporters of Jackson, Adams and Crawford.

"I am sometimes touched gently by a friend, for example, of General Jackson," noted Clay, "who will thus address me: 'My dear sir, all my dependence is upon you; don't disappoint us; you know our partiality was for you next to the hero, and how much we want a Western President!' Immediately after, a friend of Mr. Crawford will accost me: 'The hopes of our Republican party are concentrated on you; for God's sake preserve it. If you had been returned instead of Mr. Crawford, every man of us would have supported you to the last hour. We consider him and you as the only genuine Republican candidates.' Next a friend of Mr. Adams comes with tears in his eyes: 'Sir, Mr. Adams has always had the greatest respect for you, and admiration of your talents. There is no station to which you are not equal. Most undoubtedly, you are the second choice of New England and I pray you to consider seriously whether the public good and your own future interests do not point most distinctly to the choice which ought to be made.' How can one withstand all this disinterested homage and kindness?"

Clay had no great difficulty in making his choice between the three of them. Crawford was ruled out because of the state of his health and because he opposed the aspirations of the West. Jackson was ruled out because he was a dictatorial man with no governmental experience, and also because he was a threatening competitor whose rising popularity in the West overshadowed that of Clay. Thus the choice was Adams, whose nationalistic policies were close to his own.

But before coming out for him openly Clay wanted some assurances. At the New Year's Day dinner given by Congress in honor of the Marquis de Lafayette, he happened to sit next to Adams at the head table. Clay suggested a confidential conference "upon public affairs," and Adams accepted. On January 9, Adams relates in his diary that: "Mr. Clay came at six and spent the evening with me in a long conversation explanatory of the past and prospective of the future. He said that time was drawing near when the choice must be made in the House of Representatives of the President from the three candidates presented by the electoral colleges; that he had been much urged and solic-

ited in regard to the part in that transaction that he should take, and had not been five minutes landed at his lodgings before he had been applied to by a friend of Mr. Crawford's, in a manner so gross that it had disgusted him; that some of my friends also, disclaiming, indeed, to have any authority from me, had repeatedly applied to him, directly or indirectly, urging considerations personal to himself as motives to his cause. He had thought it best to reserve for some time his determination to himself. . . . He wished me, as fast as I might think proper, to satisfy him with regard to some principles of great public importance, but without any personal consideration for himself. In the question to come before the House between General Jackson, Mr. Crawford, and myself, he had no hesitation in saying that his preference would be for me."

Some weeks later an anonymous letter writer charged in the Philadelphia *Columbian Observer* that "the friends of Clay have hinted that they, like the Swiss, would fight for those who would pay best. Overtures were said to have been made by the friends of Adams to the friends of Clay, offering him the appointment of Secretary of State for his aid to elect Adams. And the friends of Clay gave this information to the friends of Jackson, and hinted that if the friends of Jackson would offer the same price, they would close with them."

Clay replied angrily in the *National Intelligencer*, calling the letter writer "a base and infamous calumniator, a dastard and a liar," challenged him to a duel, and demanded to know his identity. It turned out that the correspondent was none other than Congressman George Kremer, the dull-witted Representative from Pennsylvania whose main claim to fame was his leopard-skin overcoat. Clay demanded an investigation, but the House committee refused to take Kremer's unfounded accusations seriously.

On February 9 members of the House of Representatives assembled to choose a President. Balloting proceeded by states, with each of the twenty-four states taking part having one vote.

The decision hung on New York. That state's delegation was evenly divided. Adams had 17 men behind him, Crawford 15, and Jackson 2. Van Buren, who managed Crawford's affairs worked hard to keep his delegates in line. The opposition looked for a New York delegate who could be persuaded to switch, and they looked hopefully to Stephen Van Rensselaer. Before the voting the two giants of the Senate, Webster and Clay, descended on him, took him into the Speaker's office and told him that the safety of the country depended on Adam's election on the first ballot. Therefore, they implored him to change his vote to Adams; but Rensselaer, so Van Buren recounts in his autobiography, "took his seat fully resolved to vote for Mr.

Painted from life by Charles Willson Peale in 1819, now in the Masonic Temple, Philadelphia.

THE CANDIDATE WHO HAD MORE ELECTORAL VOTES THAN ADAMS—STILL HE LOST THE ELECTION.
Andrew Jackson, the leader in the west, was ahead in the vote count but as he had not gained the majority the decision was made by the House of Representatives, where Henry Clay released his votes to Adams, making him President.

Crawford, but before the box reached him, he dropped his head upon the edge of his desk and made a brief appeal to his Maker for his guidance in the matter—a practise he frequently observed on great emergencies—and when he removed his hand from his eyes he saw on the floor directly below him a ticket bearing the name of John Quincy Adams. This occurrence, at a moment of great excitement and anxiety, he was led to regard as an answer to his appeal, and taking up the ticket he put it in the box."

His vote put New York in the Adams column, and Adams had the needed majority. He had the support of thirteen states (Maine, New Hampshire, Vermont, Massachusetts, Connecticut, Rhode Island, New York, Maryland, Louisiana, Kentucky, Missouri, Ohio and Illinois) and with it the Presidency. Seven states were for Jackson (New Jersey, Pennsylvania, South Carolina, Alabama, Mississippi, Tennessee and Indiana); the remaining four voted for Crawford (Delaware, Virginia, North Carolina and Georgia).

Jackson felt cheated. He had the largest number of popular votes and also the highest number of electoral votes, and yet he was not given the Presidency. Did Clay's "bargain" with Adams prevent it? Did the House of Representatives betray the people's will? He felt they did.

Whether Jackson was really the people's choice (even though he had the highest popular vote) is arguable. Not all states held popular elections; in six states, including large ones such as New York, electors were named by the legislatures; thus no popular vote was taken. In states like Vermont the popular vote certainly would have favored Adams. Only a few of the states had all four candidates on the ballot. And even in the states with popular elections the voters knew that the decision would be made in the House of Representatives; thus many of them stayed away from the polls. Because of this the voting was light. According to the unofficial count, Jackson received only 152,901 votes, Adams 114,023, Crawford 46,976, and Clay 47,217. Would Jackson have retained his lead if all states had held popular elections? Would he have had the first place if the turnout had been larger? These are questions which will never be answered.

Even before the House of Representatives had made the decision, Jackson wrote to his political associate William B. Lewis that "bargain and sale of the constitutional rights of the people" had been effected. And when Adams appointed Clay as Secretary of State, Jackson burst out in indignation: "So you see the *Judas* of the West has closed the contract and will receive the thirty pieces of silver. His end will be the same. Was there ever witnessed such a barefaced corruption?"

THE FIRST ELECTION CARTOON: The three candidates, John Quincy Adams, William H. Crawford and Andrew Jackson, race for the Presidency; Henry Clay (on the right), the fourth candidate, is pondering.

John Adams (on the left) is waving a cocked hat, encouraging his son "Jack." Next to him a Westerner shouts, "Hurrah for our Jack-son."

Never before had the country taken such interest in the choice of a President. In every state public meetings were held and resolutions passed. The people favored General Jackson; they banded together in Hickory Clubs, they raised hickory poles by the hundreds. One Western newspaper explained: "The popularity of Jackson rests on the gratitude and confidence of the whole people. He is not an

An 1824 engraving by David Claypoole Johnston (1799–1865), the "American Cruikshank," who signed it "Crackfardi"

office seeker, he is not a party man, and if elected will owe it to no congressional caucus nor to any legislative cabal. . . ."

With the Congressional caucus out of fashion, the candidates were proposed by the legislatures of the states. John Quincy Adams was nominated by the legislatures of the New England states; William H. Crawford by the Virginia Legislature; Henry Clay by Kentucky; and Andrew Jackson by Tennessee.

Adams, then Secretary of State, was considered the "safe" candidate. Jackson, the hero of New Orleans, represented the democratic spirit of the frontier. Crawford, the Secretary of the Treasury, had considerable influence since he held the strings of patronage. Of the four candidates, Clay,

the Speaker of the House, had the most clearly defined political program. His "American System" demanded protection of manufactures by high tariff, and asked governmental aid for internal development through the building of roads and canals.

In the 1824 election, as no candidate received the majority of electoral votes, the President had to be chosen by the House of Representatives, where voting proceeded by states with each state having one vote.

Though the electoral college gave Jackson 99 votes, Adams 84, Crawford 41, Clay 37, the House of Representatives chose Adams, making him President. The Jacksonians shouted "fraud and corruption" and began their campaign for the next presidential contest right away.

117

ANDREW JACKSON

"I am a man of reserve, cold, austere, and forbidding manners," wrote John Quincy Adams in his diary. "My political adversaries say a gloomy misanthrope; my personal enemies an unsocial savage. With the knowledge of the actual defects of my character, I have not had the pliability to reform it." He was a scholar and a diplomat, a stern puritan and a cosmopolitan intellectual, austere, brilliant and tactless.

The charge that he had become President by making a deal with Henry Clay haunted him; opposition newspapers reminded the country that he had made a "corrupt bargain" with Clay. Others would have crumbled under such attacks, but not Adams.

"The life that I lead," he wrote, "is more regular than it has perhaps been at any other period. It is established by custom that the President of the United States goes not abroad into any private companies; and to this usage I conform. I am, therefore, compelled to take my exercise, if at all, in the morning before breakfast. I rise usually between five and six; that is, at this time of year, from an hour and a half to two hours before the sun. I walk by the light of moon or stars, or none, about four miles, usually returning here in time to see the sun rise from the eastern chamber of the White House. I then make my fire, and read three chapters of the Bible, with Scott's and Hewlett's Commentaries. Read papers till nine. Breakfast, and from nine till five P.M. receive a succession of visitors, sometimes without intermission—very seldom with an interval of half an hour—never such as to enable me to undertake any business requiring attention. From five to half-past six we dine; after which I pass about four hours in my chamber alone, writing in this diary, or reading papers upon some public business, excepting when occasionally interrupted by a visitor. Between eleven and twelve I retire to bed, to rise again at five or six the next morning."

The campaign for the next election began from the moment of his inauguration and lasted during his entire term. To the "friends of General Jackson"—who would be called Democrats—it was not only a political but a personal contest. Their hero had been cheated out of the Presidency, and they were determined to right the wrong. As a Jacksonian newspaper put it: "It is the sovereign will of the people, the almighty voice of this great nation, that has been set at defiance."

In October 1825, with election time three years away, the Tennessee legislature put forward Andrew Jackson's name for the Presidency. Jackson resigned his seat in the Senate and returned to the Hermitage, where he wrote innumerable letters to friends in preparation for the contest, knitting his followers into a cohesive political organization.

Nominally, the men who were behind him were still Democratic-Republicans, the party of Jefferson, as were the supporters of Adams. But with the deepening cleavage between the two factions, new alignments became a necessity. When the party came into being under Jefferson, it had had definite principles. But since then a quarter of a century had passed and during this time the party had become a political melting pot. Strict constructionists belonged to it, as did loose constructionists; progressive New England financiers and reactionary

ANDREW JACKSON
By Thomas Sully
Now in the Corcoran Gallery, Washington, D.C.

CANDIDATES IN 1828

ANDREW JACKSON (1767–1845) campaigned for four years to undo the "bargain and corruption" of Adams and Clay. No longer did the caucus name the candidates; they were proposed by state legislatures. The two factions of the party drifted apart. The Adams-Clay faction formed the National Republicans, basing their strength in the North; the Jacksonians became the Democrats, with support in the West and South.

JOHN C. CALHOUN (1782–1850), one of the "War Hawks" in the Twelfth Congress, was called "the young Hercules who carried the war on his shoulders" when war finally came. One of the best and most elegant Speakers of the House, he became Monroe's Secretary of War. He was Vice President under Adams, but allied himself with Jackson, hoping to succeed him in the Presidency. The Jackson-Calhoun ticket won easily.

JOHN QUINCY ADAMS (1767–1848), a puritanical personality, was no match for the flamboyant Jackson. In a scurrilous campaign the Adams supporters charged Jackson with bigamy; Jackson never forgave Adams for allowing these attacks which he believed had caused his wife's death. The Jackson men attacked Adams, asserting he had won the Presidency four years before by making a corrupt bargain with Clay.

RICHARD RUSH (1780–1859), son of the celebrated Philadelphia physician, Benjamin Rush, was Secretary of State under Monroe and negotiated a limitation on naval armaments on the Great Lakes. Later a Minister to Britain, he played a part in the negotiations which led to the Monroe Doctrine. When Adams named him to the Treasury, Randolph said it was the worst appointment since Caligula appointed his horse Consul.

Author's collection

RACHEL DONELSON ROBARDS (1767–1828) was married to Captain Lewis Robards in 1785. Five years later Robards was granted the right to sue for divorce and Rachel believed herself to be free. After she married Jackson in 1791 she discovered that the divorce was not valid. In 1794 Robards obtained an official divorce and Rachel once more married Jackson. They had no children.

Southern slaveholders; conservative Federalists, asking protection for the manufacturers, and radical men of the frontier, demanding a wider application of democracy. As it was the only party, it was everybody's party.

And when in the last election four candidates, all belonging to it, had fought for the nomination, the party split. Those who were for Adams and Clay called themselves National Republicans, while the "friends of General Jackson" formed the core of the future Democratic party.

William H. Crawford and Vice President Calhoun now were behind Jackson, as was Senator Martin Van Buren, the New York political "fox" who managed Crawford in 1824 and who now welded the discordant elements into an opposition to Adams and Clay.

The Jacksonians in Congress sharply opposed the President and his policies. In the Senate two of the best orators of the day, Thomas Hart Benton and John Randolph, were speaking for Jackson's cause. Senators

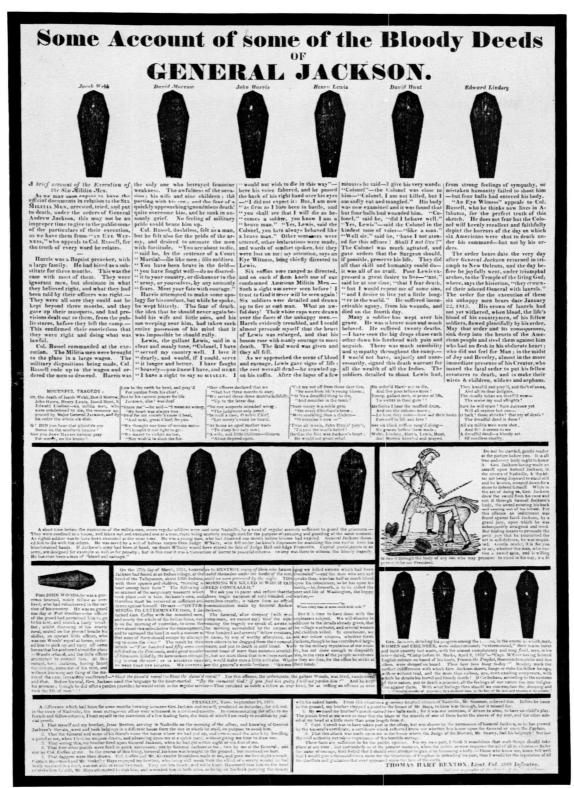

Broadside from 1828

THE COFFIN HANDBILL—a widely circulated anti-Jackson handbill in the campaign. The coffins stand for the death of six militiamen who were tried and executed shortly after the Battle of New Orleans, with Jackson's approval, for crimes of robbery, arson and mutiny during the General's campaign against the Creek Indians of the preceding year. It was printed by publisher John Binns.

John Eaton and Hugh Lawson White were close friends of the General's, and they kept him informed on the events at Capitol Hill.

The Jackson men in Congress pleaded for a limitation of the government's power. They opposed Adams's suggestion to send American envoys to the Congress in Panama. And they refused to help the President build more roads and canals, a national university and a naval academy—all at government expense. When Adams said that the Congress must give the world the impression "that we are palsied by the will of our constituents," his words provided good campaign material for the opposition.

At first the campaign appeared to be a battle between two personalities, but soon it turned into a discussion of political issues. The Jackson men, tired of the succession of Virginia and Massachusetts Presidents, asked for a more equal distribution of wealth and burdens. The newly enfranchised masses demanded a government administered by the people—not by a few holding power in the interests of a few. Thus the campaign narrowed down to the people and the aristocracy.

The sectional differences about tariff, internal improvements and states' rights—the three main political issues of the day—divided the electorate. New England and the middle states, particularly New York and Pennsylvania, were for a tariff because it helped their expanding manufacturers; the West, at first hesitantly, became a supporter of protection as well; the South, with its staple crops, opposed it.

The West wanted internal improvements at Federal expense; since its farmers had to spend a large part of their income transporting their goods to the market, the building of roads and canals was a dire necessity. The East, with plenty of roads, was not so keen to spend money for the benefit of another section.

How did the candidates stand on the issues? Jackson issued a cagey statement: "My real friends want no information from me on the subject of internal improvement and manufactures, but what my public acts has afforded, and I never gratify my enemies. Was I now to come forward and reiterate my public opinions on these subjects, I would be charged with electioneering views for selfish purposes."

Adams supported tariff protection, and, because of his close association with Clay, it was believed he would be for Clay's "American System." New England manufacturers, the conservative remnants of the old Federalists, and the Westerners who asked for internal improvements were behind him.

He also had the backing of a new group, the Antimasons—the first organized third party in America. Their movement began in 1826 because of a grievance. A man named William Morgan, a Freemason who lived

AGAINST THE COFFIN HANDBILLS. John Binns, the publisher of the Philadelphia *Democratic Press* who bore the responsibility for the distribution of the Coffin Handbills, carries the coffins with President Adams and Henry Clay.

Clay cries out: "Hold on Jonny—for I find that the people are too much for us, and I'm sinking with Jack and his Coffins!" Adams says: "I'll hang on to the Chair Harry, in spite of Coffin hand-bills Harris's letter Panama mission or the wishe's of the People." (The Panama mission is a reference to the Panama Congress of South American States held in March 1826.)

An 1828 etching by an unknown artist

Binns complains: "I must have an extra dose of treasury-pap [patronage] or down go the Coffins Harry, for I feel faint already." He became known as "Undertaker Binns" for his printing of the Coffin Handbill.

After the publication of the handbill, Duff Green published an address for the Jackson Central Committee which described Harris as hatching a meeting among 200 militiamen. The Adams press reprinted a circular signed "Truth," which contradicted Green's address, as well as a garbled forgery, "Official Record from The War Department," purported to be an authentic transcript "Ordered to be Printed by the Congress" and sent out as campaign material under the mailing franks of Adams Congressmen.

The Jackson men had the last word. Following the election, citizens of Philadelphia made up their minds to punish "Undertaker Binns" by carrying him through the streets in an open coffin. As they gathered before Binns's house, the editor bolted his doors and fled with his wife to the roof. The people tried to pry the doors, then they settled down, threw stones at the windows and hooted invitations for a moonlight ride at Binns. The scene was repeated for three nights before the demonstrators gave up their fun.

in upper New York State, announced that he would reveal the secrets of Freemasonry, whereupon the master of the village lodge sentenced him to prison for a small debt he owed. Later a group of Masons abducted him and took him to Fort Niagara—and he was never seen again. Eventually a body, believed to be his, was found in the Niagara River. Nobody could say with certainty whether it was his or not, but in the opinion of the New York political boss Thurlow Weed, the body was "a good enough Morgan till after the election." The excitement over Morgan's death spread, swelling the ranks of the Antimasons. The party was a social upheaval rather than a political movement, but politicians organized the bigoted elements into a potent force and swung its support to Adams.

Jackson was the "people's candidate," the man of the Western farmers and of the Eastern laborers, the champion of the "common people," the personification of the new democratic spirit. His campaign managers substituted new election tactics for old ones. They organized mass meetings in which the victories of Jackson were praised. They supplied newspapers with stories on Jackson. A central correspondence committee was formed in Washington, the forerunner of the present national committee; it collected funds, compiled lists of voters and sent them campaign material. Newspapers were established to advance Jackson's cause; broadsides and pamphlets were printed by the thousands. Propaganda and public relations were practiced with telling effect.

Nothing was left to chance. The public was constantly reminded that Adams was a usurper in the presidential chair; that he would never have become President had he not made his corrupt deal with Clay. He was accused of everything they could think of. In the Democratic press Adams's harmless purchase of a billiard table and a set of ivory chessmen for the White House became "gaming table and gambling furniture." He was even charged with making "use of a beautiful girl to seduce the passions of Czar Alexander and sway him to political purposes" when he was minister at St. Petersburg.

The Adams men were not reticent. They and the administration newspapers attacked Jackson in kind. In their parlance Jackson was an adulterer, a gambler, a cockfighter, a bigamist, a Negro trader, a drunkard, a murderer, a thief and a liar. He was supposed to have helped in Burr's conspiracy and usurped the powers of Congress by invading Florida without proper authority. They called him an ignorant and cruel man thirsting for blood and quite insane. A political handbook sets forth the argument: "You know that he is no jurist, no statesman, no politician; that he is destitute of historical, political, or statistical knowledge; that he is unacquainted with the orthography, concord, and government of his language; you know that he is a man of no labor, no patience, no investigation; in short that his whole recommendation is animal fierceness and organic energy. He is wholly unqualified by education, habit and temper for the station of President."

Even Jackson's marriage became an issue. It was alleged that he had married his wife before she had been legally divorced from her first husband. An Adams pamphlet asked: "Ought a convicted adulteress and her paramour husband to be placed in the highest offices of this free and Christian land?"

"Clay is managing Adams's campaign," wrote Isaac Hill, the colorful Jacksonian of the New Hampshire *Patriot,* "not like a statesman of the Cabinet, but like a shyster, pettifogging in a bastard suit before a country squire." Jackson, who was deeply hurt, would not allow his supporters to retaliate. "I never war against females, and it is only the base and cowardly that do," he said when an attack on Adams's wife was suggested to him.

The chief ammunition against Jackson was the so-called Coffin Handbill, a broadside which related the execution of six militiamen who, sentenced by a military court as deserters, had been executed with Jackson's approval at Mobile on January 22, 1815. John Binns, the editor of the Philadelphia *Democratic Press,* conceived the idea to "arrest the public attention and impress the public mind with the injustice and the enormity of the crime of Gen. Jackson in respect to the shooting of these militiamen."

Isaac Hill challenged Binns: "Pshaw! Why don't you tell the whole truth? On the 8th of January, 1815, he murdered in the coldest kind of cold blood 1,500 British soldiers for merely trying to get into New Orleans in search of booty and beauty."

Thus the campaign went on with charges and countercharges, with allegations and counterallegations. Racial, religious and class prejudices cropped up. Adams was charged with being an anti-Catholic because once, in a Fourth of July oration, he had referred to the Church as "that portentous system of despotism and superstition," in which "neither the body nor the soul of the individual was his own." And he was called a monarchist, a ruler above the law, and an old Federalist in disguise. So that he would lose the New England puritan vote, he was denounced for traveling on the Sabbath. The German and Irish communities were heavily canvassed; campaign literature of both candidates was printed in German as well as in English.

Since the last election the method of naming electors by the legislatures had been dying out. Of the twenty-four states, only two—South Carolina and Delaware—had their legislatures still appoint the electors. In the

"Jackson is to be President, and you will be HANGED."

An 1828 wood engraving, artist unknown

AN ANTI-JACKSON WOODCUT, recalling the hanging of two Englishmen during the General's Florida campaign in 1818. The Englishmen—Alexander Arbuthnot and Robert Ambrister—were court martialed and executed because they helped the Seminole Indians who were fighting against Jackson's army of militiamen.

other eighteen states votes were cast on a general ticket. New York and Maine chose one elector from each district, who in turn voted for two additional electors; in Maryland and Tennessee electors were chosen by districts. The actual balloting took place on different days in each state, beginning in September and not ending until November. There was no uniform day set for the voting. Jackson's campaign aroused the country; many who had never voted before went to the polls. The popular vote was three times larger than in the last election. The result was a resounding victory; Jackson received 647,276 votes against Adams's 508,074. The same states which had voted for Thomas Jefferson in 1800 voted for Jackson, and those that went for John Adams voted for his son twenty-eight years later.

Inauguration day was one of great celebration. The Jacksonians from the back country came to the capital to cheer their hero into office. "Where the multitude slumbered last night is unconceivable, unless it were on their Mother Earth, curtained by the unbroken sky," wrote one observer. And Daniel Webster said: "I have never seen such a crowd before. Persons have come five hundred miles to see General Jackson, and they really seem to think that the country has been rescued from some dreadful danger."

Jackson was staying at Gadsby's tavern, cutting a sad figure among the tumultuous mass. Only a few weeks before, his beloved wife had died. "He was in deep mourning," recalled an Englishwoman who was in the hostelry. "He wore his gray hair carelessly but not ungracefuly arranged, and in spite of his harsh, gaunt features looked like a gentleman and a soldier."

Jackson was resentful of Adams, who had allowed Rachel's name to be dragged into the campaign. He believed that the slanders had undermined her health. In one of her last letters Rachel Jackson complained: "The enemys of the Genl have dipt their arrows in wormwood and gall and sped them at me . . . they have Disquieted one that thaey had no rite to do." Rachel left this world with the desire to be "rather a doorkepper in the house of God than to live in that palace at Washington."

At her funeral Jackson swore: "In the presence of this dear saint I can and do forgive all my enemies. But those vile wretches who have slandered her must look to God for mercy." He would not speak to Clay, "the basest, meanest scoundrel that ever disgraced the image of his God"; he would not see Adams, would not make even a courtesy call at the White House.

It was the President who sent a messenger to Gadsby's informing Jackson that the White House would be ready for his occupancy on the fourth of March. "He brought me the answer," recorded Adams in his ever-present diary, "that the General cordially thanked him and hoped that I would put myself to no inconvenience to quit the house, but to remain in it as long as I pleased, even for a month." A few days later, Adams sent another note that his packing might require two or three days beyond the third, to which Jackson replied that he did not wish to inconvenience the President, "but that Mr. Calhoun had suggested that there might be danger of the excessive crowds breaking down the rooms at Gadsby's"; therefore, he wanted to occupy the President's house "after the inauguration on Wednesday next." So Adams "concluded at all events to leave the house on Tuesday."

At half-past eleven on inauguration day Jackson left his hostelry and, accompanied by some of his friends, walked to the Capitol. A shouting mass of his supporters crowded behind him, and more followed in carriages and wagons.

At noon he delivered his inaugural address on the eastern portico and was sworn into office by Chief Justice John Marshall. "The scene," reported the *American Daily Advertiser,* "was a most beautiful and inspiring spectacle. The building, noble in its size, with its richly sculptured capitals and cornices, and the fine group in the pediment; the massy columns (one for each State in the Union); the far-spreading wings and terraces; the grounds and gates, with the crowd of carriages without; the line of soldiers in the park; the towering flight of steps, covered with members of Congress, officers of the army, foreign ministers, ladies dressed in all the varying hues of fashion; the President; the crowd of heads and the innumerable eyes bent on one spot, all taken together presented to the outward eye an assemblage of images never to be forgotten."

After the ceremonies the new President mounted his horse and rode down Pennsylvania Avenue followed by his supporters on horseback. As he rode through the gates of the White House grounds, the mass surged after him. The presidential mansion had never seen such a sight before. Men from the country climbed with their muddy boots on damask chairs; they gobbled the drinks which the waiters brought in. "One hundred and fifty dollar official chairs [were] profaned by the feet of clodhoppers," noted Justice Joseph Story. "I never saw such a mixture. The reign of King Mob seemed triumphant." And Mrs. Bayard Smith related: "The noisy and disorderly rabble . . . brought to my mind descriptions I have read of the mobs in the Tuileries and at Versailles."

Men, women, children, farmers, laborers, ambassadors entangled and filled every corner of the house. "High and low, old and young, black and white poured in one solid column into this spacious mansion. Here was the corpulent epicure grunting and sweating for breath—the dandy wishing he had no toes—the tight-

An 1881 drawing by Howard Pyle
ON THE WAY TO HIS INAUGURATION THE PRESIDENT-ELECT IS ACCLAIMED BY YOUNG AND OLD.

laced miss, fearing her person might receive some permanently deforming impulse. Several thousands of dollars' worth of art glass and china were broken in the attempt to get at the refreshments; punch, lemonade, and other articles were carried out of the house in buckets and pails; women fainted; men were seen with bloody noses; and no police had been placed on duty."

His friends formed a cordon around the President to protect him from well-wishers. Jackson was "sinking into a listless state of exhaustion," and soon escaped through a back door and went to Gadsby's and to bed.

John Quincy Adams did not hear the jubilation. Like his father twenty-eight years before, he left Washington refusing to take part in the inauguration of his successor. Before leaving the White House, he noted: "Three days more, and I shall be restored to private life and left to an old age of retirement, though certainly not of repose. I go into it with a combination of parties and of public men against my character and reputation such as I believe never before was exhibited against any man since this Union existed. Posterity will scarcely believe it, but so it is, that this combination against me has been formed, and is now exulting in triumph over me, for the devotion of my life and of all the faculties of my soul to the Union, and to the improvement, physical, moral, and intellectual, of my country. The North assails me for my fidelity to the Union; the South, for my ardent aspirations of improvement. Yet 'bate I not a jot of heart and hope.' Passion, prejudice, envy, and jealousy will pass. The cause of Union and of improvement will remain, and I have duties to it and to my country yet to discharge."

And so he did. The noblest part of his public career was before him.

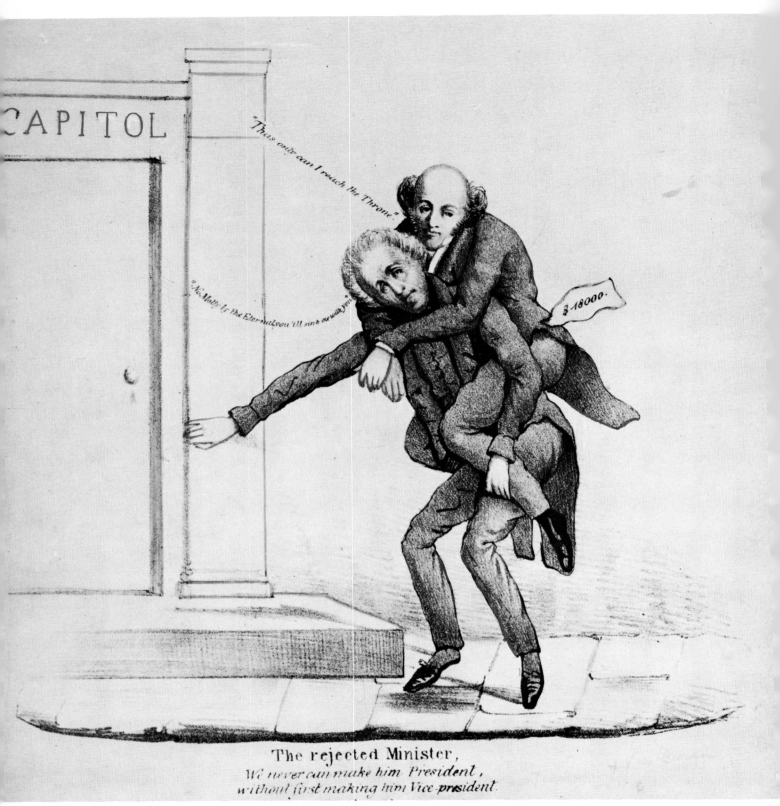

CAPITOL

"Thus only can I reach the Throne"

"No Matty by the Eternal you'll sink me with you"

$18000.

The rejected Minister,
We never can make him President,
without first making him Vice-president.

Lithograph from 1832, published by H. Anstice, New York, in the New-York Historical Society
PRESIDENT JACKSON CARRIES VAN BUREN TO THE CAPITOL, the only way for Martin Van Buren "to reach the throne." When the Senate, after a scurrilous debate, rejected Van Buren's nomination as Minister to London in 1831, Jackson swore by the Eternal to make him first "Vice-President and President afterwards." And he was as good as his word.

ANDREW JACKSON

Andrew Jackson was a new kind of President. He did not come from Virginia like Washington, Jefferson, Madison or Monroe, nor was he raised in Massachusetts like the two Adamses. He was no intellectual, no aristocrat, no political philosopher, no diplomat like his predecessors. His parents were poor; they left Ireland for America two years before his birth. He was only thirteen when he and his brother were captured by the British in the Revolutionary War. Thrown into prison, they contracted small pox. His brother died, leaving him with an undying hatred against everything British.

In his youth he spent more time at the races and cockfights, with girls and at the gaming table than with books. Yet he read law at Salisbury, North Carolina, and was admitted to the bar in 1787. He moved on to the new wilderness frontier, which would soon become the state of Tennessee. There he traded in land, horses and slaves, and owned a general store. A political, judicial and military career followed: Public Prosecutor, Representative to Congress, Senator, Superior Judge of Tennessee, Major General in his state's militia.

In the War of 1812 he was called upon to defend New Orleans. That spectacular battle and his subsequent exploits against the Seminoles in Spanish Florida made him a military hero; his name was revered across the land.

In 1823 he represented Tennessee in the Senate; in the 1824 presidential contest he commanded a larger popular vote than Adams.

He was the first President to begin his life in a modest cabin and reach the splendor of the White House. Roughhewn and quick-tempered, loyal to friends and suspicious of enemies, he shared the virtues and faults of the countrymen of the day. He had a strong character, born to command. He would not equivocate; he would not compromise. He was ever ready to fight a brawl, a duel or a war. In politics he was unbending, impetuous unswerving; in private life charming, chivalrous, courteous.

Once in office he swore to free the Civil Service of corruption and incompetence. Of corruption he found little, of incompetence much. The bulk of civil servants had been holding their jobs so long that they regarded themselves as lifetime appointees. Whether the new civil servants were more capable than the old ones was not examined. "The duties of all public offices are so plain and simple," held Jackson, "that men of intelligence may readily qualify themselves for their performance." And William L. Marcy justified the dismissals in the Senate by saying that he found "nothing wrong in the rule that to the victors belong the spoils of the enemy."

As Jackson began to "cleanse the Augean stables," fear shook the bureaucrats. It was reported that a clerk in the auditor's office cut his throat, while another in the Department of State worried himself into insanity.

Still the spoils system was not as harsh as Jackson's opponents tried to make it appear. During his entire two terms no more than one-fifth of those whom he found in office were replaced. When it came to the removal of old soldiers, Jackson was hesitant to turn them out. "By the Eternal! I will not remove the old man," he said when he was urged to dismiss the postmaster in Albany. "He carries a pound of British lead in his body." Neither would he dismiss the veteran who had lost his leg on the battlefield, even though the man had not supported him.

(turn to page 132)

CANDIDATES IN 1832

ANDREW JACKSON

(1767–1845) was one of the most popular Presidents. He was willing to run for the second time even though in his first message to Congress he had advocated a single term. At Clay's insistence the chief campaign issue became the recharter of the U.S. Bank. In the colorful contest in which the defenders of the Bank fought the President, Jackson won with 687,502 votes against Clay's 530,189.

MARTIN VAN BUREN

(1782–1862), the leader of the "Albany Regency" which controlled the politics of New York State, resigned his Senatorial seat to become Jackson's Secretary of State and his heir apparent. Following the "Eaton Affair" he resigned his post, forcing the Calhoun men out of the Cabinet. When his appointment as Minister to Britain was not confirmed by the Senate, "Old Hickory" made him his Vice President.

HENRY CLAY

(1777–1852), Secretary of State under Adams, was the obvious choice of the National Republicans, later called Whigs. He might have become the candidate of the Antimasons, the first organized third party, if he had approved that party's principles. But he remained silent, and the Antimasons nominated William Wirt. Clay received the support of six states: Conn., Del., Ky., Md., Mass., and R.I.

JOHN SERGEANT

(1779–1852), a Pennsylvania Congressman and intimate friend of Biddle, director of the second U.S. Bank, was the Bank's chief legal and political adviser. Misjudging the mood of the country, he urged Biddle to an all-out attack on Jackson. He became the vice presidential candidate and went down in defeat. The Jackson-Van Buren ticket received 219 electoral votes, the Clay-Sergeant ticket 49.

Photograph by Mathew B. Brady

PEGGY O'NEALE (1796–1879), the daughter of a Washington saloonkeeper, became the center of a storm when she married the wealthy John Henry Eaton, President Jackson's close friend whom he made his first Secretary of War. It was her second marriage; her first husband, a sailor, ran off to sea, later shooting himself.

The fight for Peggy's recognition started harmlessly enough. Mrs. Calhoun and the wives of the Cabinet members refused to receive her, while Jackson was determined to force Peggy, whom he declared as "chaste as a virgin," on Washington's society.

But then the political implications of the struggle became clear. Van Buren, with an eye on the Vice Presidency, sided with Peggy; Calhoun and his Southern friends were against her. Thus Jackson regarded Van Buren as the gallant champion of an innocent female, and Calhoun, the confidant of her traducers. But John Quincy Adams noted: "Calhoun leads the moral party, Van Buren that of the frail sisterhood."

The "Eaton malaria" led to the voluntary resignation of Van Buren and Eaton, and to the involuntary resignation of Calhoun's three friends—Berrien, Branch and Ingham—from the Cabinet. And "Bellona, the goddess of War," as Peggy became known, returned to obscurity. Her husband died, leaving her with a fortune; she married again as an old woman an Italian ballet master who later eloped with her granddaughter.

An 1831 lithograph by Edward Williams Clay

"THE RATS LEAVING A FALLING HOUSE" is the title of this cartoon. As an aftermath of the Peggy Eaton affair Van Buren and Eaton resigned from the Cabinet. Their withdrawals forced the resignation of John Berrien (Attorney General), John Branch (Secretary of Navy) and Samuel Ingham (Secretary of the Treasury).

An 1831 lithograph, attributed to D. Canova, at the Houghton Library

THE CABINET MAKER. President Jackson exclaims: "The four legs are done, now for the bottom. Confound the Rats, if they eat up this piece of old hard Hickory wood I'll have them put under Martial Law."

Published in 1833 (?) by A. Imbert, New York

AGAINST THE BANK. Jackson is pictured as a jackass among chickens representing the Branch Banks. Van Buren is a "sly fox" and Blair of the *Globe* is a "wallowing hog." At left the five dogs labeled with the names of newspapers sing the praises of "the *greatest* and *best* Ass."

An 1832 lithograph in the Library of Cong

THE DEVILS ATTACK JACKSON, cutting his h• from his body before a ship inscribed "Independenc and "Constitution."

Before commercial lithography was established America at the beginning of the 1820s, all illust tions were engraved, etched or cut on steel, copper wood. But after Alois Senefelder, the Bavarian inv• tor, patented his process in 1801, lithography beca a popular means of reproduction, bringing a hu increase in political cartoons drawn on single shee

An 1834 lithograph published by A. Imbert, New Yor•

THE EXPLOSION OF "CONGRESS WATER• blows up Clay, Calhoun, Webster and Biddle, the de fenders of the Bank.

President Jackson tells his supporter: "Aye, Aye Major Downing they thought they'd give us a dose o Congress Water, but they find what we're *Bent or* [a pun on Senator Benton] and we've given 'em a hard Poke into the bargain!" A symbol of Liberty holds a flag proclaiming "Public Confidence in Public funds."

"If he lost a leg fighting for his country, that is vote enough for me," said Jackson.

The President had his troubles right from the outset of his administration and they began with an amusing affair. Major Eaton, his friend and Secretary of War, had married Peggy O'Neale, the not-too-virtuous daughter of a Washington tavern keeper. Jackson, whose own wife had been maligned, was determined to force Peggy, whom he considered as "chaste as a virgin," on Washington society. However, the wives of the Cabinet

132

An 1833 lithograph published by E. Bisbee, New York

OUBLED TREASURES. President Jackson: "evil Take the Treasures and my Secretary too." ary Clay administers Congress water "to a very man sick of the Deposit Fever." The devil takes 0 million United States Treasures with him. Major wning laughs: "Ha! Ha! Ha! I kinder hinted to the eral I ges'd Congress-water and Responsibility uldn't agree on his stomach." He quotes Jackson: ajor that Clay is a bold impudent fellow and will ak out his mind if the Devil stands at the door."

An 1836 lithograph published by H. R. Robinson, New York

CKSON ASKS FRANCE TO PAY UP. For enty years the French government had dodged and layed compensation to American shipping for dam-es during the Napoleonic Wars. Jackson, believing e promise the French made in the 1831 treaty, took strong line to collect the money and was ready to ake redress into our own hands." When war seemed be the only way out, England stepped in to save e face of Louis Philippe with an offer of mediation.

An early 1830s lithograph issued by H. R. Robinson. New York

THE SEVENTH WARD BEGGARS ask for "fiscal patronage." Jackson, on "surplus fund" bales, holds a scepter in one hand and a bag with $100,-000 in the other. The "Courier & Enquirer, Spy in Washington" watches.

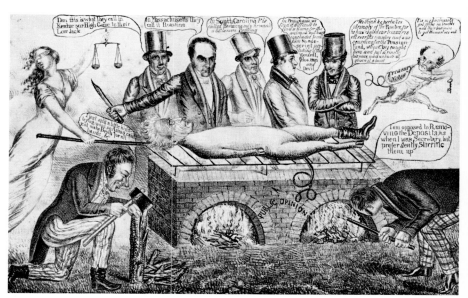

An 1835 lithograph published by H. R. Robinson, New York

POLITICAL BARBECUE. Jackson drawn as a hog lies on the furnace marked "Public Opinion." Behind it Clay, Webster and others hold a discussion. On the right the little hog with Van Buren's head says: " 'Tis my business to get folks in trouble and their business to get themselves out."

members would not bow to his will; when they refused to receive her, a political battle royal ensued.

In the war over Peggy (which was also an attempt to get rid of Eaton) the Cabinet was evenly divided: Van Buren, Eaton and Barry were with the President; Ing-

ham, Branch and Berrien with the Vice President.

That Jackson and Calhoun would clash was inevitable. They were far apart in their political outlook, opposite in character and temperament. The Eaton affair was only the curtain raiser to their estrangement. The

(turn to page 135)

An 1833 lithograph entered by Endicott & Swett, New York

"DESPOTISM—ANARCHY—DISUNION." A cartoon published at the height of the nullification crisis. When the South Carolina convention on November 19, 1832, declared the tariffs of 1828 and 1832 null and void, and forbade Federal officers to collect the revenues in that state, President Jackson announced that the laws of the Federal Government would be strictly enforced. "If a single drop of blood shall be shed there in opposition to the laws of the United States, I will hang the first man I can lay my hands on engaged in such conduct upon the first tree that I can reach." He branded nullification as "incompatible with the existence of the Union, contradicted expressly by the letter of the Constitution, unauthorized by its spirit, inconsistent with every principle on which it was founded, and destructive of the great objects for which it was formed." Jackson asked Congress for authority to use force against South Carolina if necessary, but before any blood was shed Henry Clay introduced a compromise measure for a gradual reduction of duties.

John C. Calhoun walks up the steps "Nullification, South Carolina Ordinance, Treason, Civil War, Deception," toward the crown of "Despotism." James H. Hammond of South Carolina (left), who was active in the military preparations of his state, and Robert Y. Hayne (right), the Governor of South Carolina, give him encouragement. But President Jackson (on the right), trying to pull Hayne back by his coattails, threatens the triumvirate that if they don't stop, "I'll hang you all."

An 1831 lithograph of Pendleton, N.Y., published by H. R. Robinson

THE THREE PRESIDENTIAL CANDIDATES—Henry Clay, William Wirt and John C. Calhoun—play a political game of brag, as poker was called then, with President Jackson. President Jackson's hand is marked "Intrigue, Corruption and Imbecility." William Wirt, candidate of the Antimasons, the first organized third party, exclaims: "I bolt." Vice President Calhoun hides his "Nullification" and "Anti-Tariff" cards under the table. On the left Henry Clay bares his cards, "U.S. Bank, Internal Improvement and Domestic Manufactures."

This is a cartoon in support of Henry Clay's candidacy. At Clay's insistence the recharter of the Bank became the main issue of the campaign. Jackson vetoed the measure because it would have made "the rich richer, and the potent more powerful," and the electorate backed him up. He defeated Clay handsomely and won the Presidency for a second term.

debate between Robert Y. Hayne of South Carolina and Daniel Webster, with Hayne arguing the doctrine of nullification and Webster defending the Union and Federal authority, widened their rift, even though Calhoun kept silent during the debates. Soon thereafter, at the Jefferson Day Dinner the lines were drawn. The President, after listening to a number of nullification toasts, offered one of his own: "Our Union: It must be preserved!"

And Calhoun responded: "The Union, next to our liberty, most dear." A month later, in May, came the final break. Jackson learned that, while he was fighting the Seminoles, Calhoun had proposed in the Cabinet his arrest and trial for insubordination. Jackson now wanted an explanation, and Calhoun's evasive answer gave "full evidence of the duplicity and insincerity of the man." He would no longer speak to Calhoun.

1821: YOUNG HICKORY, painted by Samuel L. Waldo about the time Jackson was military governor of Florida.

1845: OLD HICKORY, a daguerreotype by Mathew B. Brady, taken seven weeks before Jackson's death.

The Cabinet had to be reshaped. Van Buren suggested that he would resign his post as Secretary of State, thus forcing Eaton to follow him; Jackson agreed when Van Buren promised to accept the diplomatic post of Minister to Great Britain. Everything went according to plan: Van Buren resigned, Eaton followed him, and Jackson dismissed from the Cabinet Calhoun's three loyal friends who had opposed him in the Eaton affair.

Calhoun, his hopes of succeeding Jackson in the Presidency gone, resigned from the Vice Presidency and became an opposition Senator. Continuing his fight in the Senate against Van Buren, with the help of Webster and Clay he held up confirmation of his rival's appointment as Ambassador to England. Before the final vote, Churchill C. Cambreleng wrote to Van Buren: "Some of your best friends . . . wish that the Senate would re-

ject you! I know you will be annoyed at such a result—but it's the only thing that can remedy your error in going abroad—it's the only thing that can prevent the election in 1836 from going to the House. . . . If you could but be rejected—you would return in triumph."

Calhoun thought that the rejection would end Van Buren's political career. "It will kill him dead!" he said. "He will never kick, sir, never kick." But Senator Benton knew better. He told Calhoun: "You have broken a Minister and elected a Vice-President."

As election year drew near, speculation was rife about a better mode of selecting candidates. The caucus was discredited. Nomination by the state legislatures would lead to sectional divisions. Nomination by the President was unacceptable. The idea of a convention, with delegates chosen by the people, gained ground.

AN ANTI-JACKSON
BROADSIDE FROM 1832
Author's collection

136

BORN TO COMMAND.

OF VETO MEMORY.

HAD I BEEN CONSULTED.

KING ANDREW THE FIRST.

The first to call such a convention were the Antimasons, who assembled in Baltimore more than a year before election time. In their search for a candidate they approached Clay, who was a Mason and would not compromise his beliefs. They asked Richard Rush, they sounded out Adams, and when both declined they settled on Supreme Court Justice John McLean. However, shortly before the convention McLean bowed out and, after another refusal from John Marshall, the Antimasons turned to William Wirt, the celebrated orator.

In their convention the Antimasons introduced a number of innovations, setting the patterns for the future. One was the formulation of a party platform; others were the naming of a rules committee, the close scrutiny of the delegates' credentials, the conducting of business by means of the committee system and the unanimous acclamation for the candidates after they were chosen.

The National Republicans held their convention in the second week of December 1831. Because of bad weather only 135 came; they chose Henry Clay for the first and John Sergeant for the second place.

The final convention was that of the friends of Jackson, soon to be called the Democratic party. They met in the saloon of the Athenaeum in Baltimore on May 21, 1832, with delegates attending from every state but Missouri. A committee reported the rules, among them one "that two-thirds of the whole number of the votes in the convention shall be necessary to constitute a choice." The two-thirds proposal, which remained the cornerstone of the Democratic conventions for over a hundred years, was offered at Jackson's insistence so Van Buren's nomination could be assured. Another recommendation which became a tradition was the unit rule whereby "the majority of the delegates from each State designate the person for whom the votes for that State shall be cast."

Both Jackson and Van Buren were nominated on the first ballot.

The campaign began without a political issue. For the past year the National Republicans—soon to be called Whigs—had searched for one, and for a while it seemed as though Clay's American System might be it. Webster wrote to Clay: "Parties must now necessarily be started out anew; and the great ground of difference will be the tariff and internal improvements. The question will be put to the country. Let the country decide it."

However, neither the tariff nor the internal-improvement issue caused a stir. Clay hoped that something might turn up to "give a brighter aspect to our affairs."

What did turn up was the recharter of the Bank of the United States. Though the charter did not expire until 1836, the leaders of the anti-Jackson men, Clay, Webster and other National Republicans, pushed through a bill in Congress for its early renewal. Clay was certain

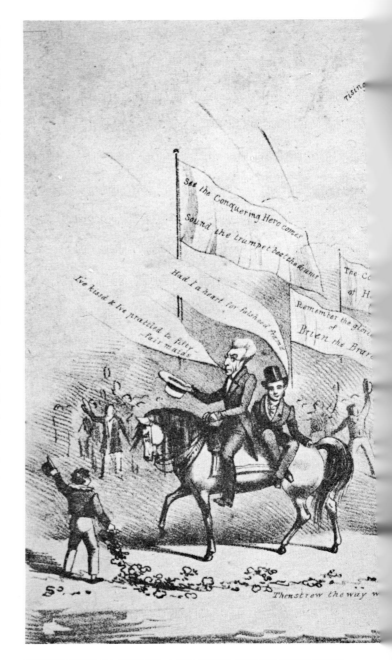

PRESIDENT JACKSON AND VICE PRESIDENT VAN

that Jackson would veto the bill and that the veto would serve him well in the campaign. It turned out otherwise. Jackson's veto (written with the help of Roger B. Taney) turned out to be a superb campaign document. It called the Bank un-American, undemocratic, unconstitutional and injurious to the country, since it would "make the rich richer and the potent more powerful." Jackson summed up the complex and impersonal issue in the sentence: "Shall the rights of the common man

138

An 1833 lithograph drawn by "Hassan Straightshanks," issued by Endicott & Swett, New York

BUREN ON HORSEBACK ARE LEADING THEIR MOTLEY SUPPORTERS IN A CAMPAIGN PROCESSION

be respected or shall the rich rule the country again?" The newly emerged masses in the West, the workingmen in the Eastern cities, the people in the South were with Jackson in the argument.

Clay and his associates misjudged the country's mood. Nicholas Biddle, the imperious president of the Bank, spent vast sums of money for printing and distributing Jackson's veto message, convinced that it would turn the electorate against the President, but Jackson was confident: "The veto works well. Instead of crushing me as was expected & intended, it will crush the bank." And he predicted: "Mr. Clay will not get one electoral vote west of the mountains or south of the Potomac."

The prediction was accurate. Clay received only 49 electoral votes; John Floyd, the 11 votes of South Carolina; William Wirt, the 7 votes of Vermont; the rest —219 electoral votes—went to Jackson. The country wanted him for a second term.

MARTIN VAN BUREN

Jackson regarded his re-election as a mandate against the Bank. He planned to withdraw the government's funds and deposit them in state banks throughout the country. When Louis McLane, his Secretary of the Treasury, refused to sign the order for removal, he dismissed him, as he did the successor William J. Duane. He then named the Bank foe Roger B. Taney, who put his name on the order, even before his appointment came before the Senate to be confirmed.

In the Senate the triumvirate of Clay, Calhoun and Webster combined their attacks on the President. They forced through a resolution that by his removal of the deposits Jackson had "assumed upon himself authority and power not conferred by the Constitution and laws, but in derogation of both."

In a protest to the Senate Jackson denounced the resolution, calling it "subversive of the distribution of powers of government which the Constitution had ordained and established."

For well over three years Senator Benton and other of Jackson's friends fought for the removal of the censure from the Senate *Journal,* but not until 1837 were they successful. Their success was a victory for presidential over parliamentary government. Congress was not to have control over the activities of the President.

At the opening of his administration, Jackson had no clearly defined policy. But by the end of it no one could be in doubt what they were. One could perceive them in his attitude toward the Bank, in his struggle for the reduction of the tariff, in his strong stand against the South Carolina nullifiers, in his firm position on the public land question, in his aggressive foreign policy and his attitude toward the nation's debt.

One of the highlights of Jackson's second term, next to his war on the Bank, was his fight with the South Carolina nullifiers.

Shortly before he was elected for the second time, South Carolina, smarting under the high tariff rates of 1828 ("The Tariff of Abominations") and those of 1832, declared them null and void. In a convention under the chairmanship of the Governor the calling out of the militia was authorized and the state threatened secession if the national government attempted to use force to collect the tariff.

Jackson would not tolerate a state taking upon itself the prerogative of nullifying the laws of the country. In a proclamation issued on December 10, 1832, he declared: "The power to annul a law of the United States, assumed by one State, [is] *incompatible with the existence of the union, contradicted expressly by the Constitution, unauthorized by its spirit, inconsistent with every principle on which it was founded, and destructive of the great object for which it was formed."* He was ready to use force and itched to lead the troops into South Carolina himself to teach that state that the laws of the United States had to be obeyed. Fortunately, it did not come to that. A compromise tariff, proposed by Henry Clay, calmed the ruffled tempers. After a reduction of the rates was promised, gradually reducing the tariff over the next nine years, and after the Force Act—the act which gave the President authority to call out the army and navy to enforce the laws of Congress—was repealed, South Carolina rescinded her ordinance.

MARTIN VAN BUREN
By Henry Inman
in New York's City Hall

CANDIDATES IN 1836

MARTIN VAN BUREN (1782–1862), Jackson's Vice President whom Old Hickory swore to elevate to the Presidency, was chosen by the Democratic convention after the adoption of the 2/3 rule. The Whig press ridiculed him as an aristocratic, corseted dandy. Opposed by a number of Whig regional candidates, he defeated them all. His popular vote was 762,978 against the Whig candidates' combined total vote of 736,250.

RICHARD M. JOHNSON (1780–1850), the hero of the Battle of the Thames in the War of 1812 in which he extricated Harrison from a trap, was the supposed killer of the Indian Chief Tecumseh. Johnson was an intimate friend and loyal supporter of Jackson, who forced on the party his nomination for the Vice Presidency. In the election he could not secure a majority; thus the selection came before the Senate, which chose him.

WILLIAM H. HARRISON (1773–1841), presented as a Whig sectional candidate against Van Buren, was a famed Indian fighter and the first Governor of the Indiana Territory. As a general in the War of 1812 he distinguished himself with his victory in the Battle of the Thames. He served in both houses of Congress. In the election he was the Whigs' biggest vote-getter, receiving 73 electoral votes, not enough for victory.

FRANCIS GRANGER (1792–1868), the son of Jefferson's postmaster general, started in New York politics as a follower of Governor Clinton. Later he joined the Antimasonic movement and allied himself with political boss Thurlow Weed. He ran for the governorship and was defeated. Elected to Congress in 1834, he was nominated for the Vice Presidency as the candidate of the Antimasons and Massachusetts Whigs.

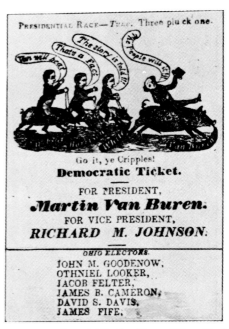

Lorant, The Presidency *(Macmillan)*
AN ELECTORAL TICKET FROM OHIO

As his term went on, the Jackson haters—and there were plenty of them—banded together. Out of their coalition emerged a new party—soon to be called Whigs.

They had no unified political views; they were united only in their hatred of Jackson. National Republicans became Whigs, as did Northern Antimasons. Discontented Democrats joined the fold, as did South Carolina nullifiers. States' righters, Southern conservatives, protectionists, antiprotectionists, pro-Bank and anti-Bank men—they all became Whigs. All those who were determined to end the "tyranny" of Jackson were Whigs.

Jackson wanted Van Buren, his friend and Vice

An 1833 lithograph by Edward W. Clay, published by H. R. Robinson, N.Y.

A PRO-JACKSON CARTOON: THE DOWNFALL OF MOTHER BANK. In 1832 Jackson had vetoed the bill for the renewal of the U.S. Bank's charter and ordered the removal of government funds from that institution. Sharing the West's prejudice against the "moneyed monster," he charged the monopolistic Bank with being unconstitutional.

As Jackson holds up his "Order for the Removal," politicians and editors who received generous loans from the Bank search for refuge in the crumbling columns of the financial temple. Major Jack Downing, the fictitious character, approves Jackson's decision: "Hurrah! Gineral! if this don't beat skunkin I'm a nigger, only see that varmint Nick [Nicholas Biddle, the president of the Bank] how spry he is, he runs along like a Wheatherfield Hog with an onion in his mouth."

President, as his successor. To assure his nomination he proposed as early as February 1835, a year and three-quarters before election time, the calling of a national convention to consider the nomination of candidates for the Presidency and Vice Presidency to which delegates should come "fresh from the people."

Such a convention assembled at the First Presbyterian Church in Baltimore a few weeks later, on May 20, with twenty-two states and two territories—Arkansas and Michigan—represented; only Alabama, Illinois and South Carolina refrained from sending delegates. At the outset of the meeting there was no delegate present from Tennessee, but, as it happened, a

Tennessee gentleman named Rucker was visiting Baltimore, and since he was willing to cast his vote for Van Buren, he was allowed to represent his state, his single vote counting for the entire 15 votes of Tennessee. His action gave us a new word: "ruckerized."

Other states went to the opposite extreme. Maryland with only 10 electoral votes sent 181 delegates, and Virginia's 23 votes were represented by 108 men.

Once more the convention adopted the two-thirds rule, assuring Van Buren's nomination; the Southern opposition could not hope to muster enough strength for anyone else. For the vice-presidential post Jackson himself chose Colonel Richard Mentor Johnson of

143

An 1838 lithograph signed "H.D.," published by H. R. Robinson, N.Y.

DEPRESSION. Van Buren inherited a financial panic from Jackson, his "illustrious predecessor." The bubble of land speculation burst. A panic in England halved the price of cotton. The indiscriminate printing of paper money came to a halt and tradesmen issued "shinplasters"—money of sorts backed by the promise of a haircut or a meal. Because of the crop failure, wheat prices skyrocketed. Everything went up but wages.

The dismayed workman is holding his "New Era" paper in his lap. Two men come in with a "Landlord's Warrant." His wife begs him to find food for their starving children, but he replies: "I have no money and cannot get any work."

Kentucky, his old and faithful supporter and go-between in the Eaton affair. Johnson, a determined opponent of imprisonment for debt, had the working classes of the East behind him, but his private life was a red flag to the Southern delegates. They berated him because of his mulatto mistress, Julia Chinn, with whom he lived and who had borne him two daughters. But the President would not settle on another candidate.

The Whigs ridiculed the "Van Buren convention," calling it a gathering of officeholders and a substitute for the extinct caucus. They would have been happy if they, too, could have held such a convention. But, as they disagreed on political issues, so they could not

agree on a single candidate either. They decided to challenge Van Buren with a number of favorite-son candidates: William Henry Harrison, the aging hero of Tippecanoe, a favorite in the West; Judge John McLean of Ohio; Daniel Webster of Massachusetts, who had the endorsement of Pennsylvania and New York; Jackson's former friend Hugh Lawson White of Tennessee, who was the choice of his state and of Virginia and Illinois; Senator Willie P. Mangum of North Carolina. The Whigs hoped that these men would be favored in their states and regions and prevent Van Buren from obtaining a majority. They hoped that the election then would be thrown into the House of Representatives,

Resolved, That the resolution adopted by the Senate on the 28th day of March, in the year 1834, in the following words, "*Resolved, That the President, in the late Executive proceedings in relation to the public revenue, has assumed upon himself authority and power not conferred by the constitution and laws, but in derogation of both*," be, and the same hereby is ~~ordered~~ to be expunged from the journals of the Senate; because the said resolution is illegal and unjust, of evil example, indefinite and vague, expressing a criminal charge without specification; and was irregularly and unconstitutionally adopted by the Senate, in subversion of the rights of defence which belong to an accused and impeachable officer; and at a time, and under circumstances to ~~the~~ the political rights and pecuniary interests ~~of~~ the people of the United States, ∧ *a serious injury*

∧ *in serious injury and peculiar danger.*]

It was determined in the affirmative — Yeas 33 Nays 13.

On motion by Mr Black,

The yeas & nays being desired by one fifth of the Senators present those who voted in the affirmative are

Messrs Bell, Benton, Brown, Buchanan, Calhoun, Clay, Clayton, Ewing, Frelinghuysen, Goldsborough, Grundy, Hill, Kane, King of Ala, Knight, Leigh, Linn, McKean, Mangum, Moore, Morris, Naudain, Prentiss, Robbins, Robinson, Ruggles, Shepley, Smith, Swift, Tallmadge, ~~Tipton~~, Tomlinson, White, Wright.

Those who voted in the negative are

Messrs Bibb, Black, Cuthbert, Hendricks, Kent, King of Geo. Porter, Preston, Silsbee, Tipton, Tyler, Waggaman, Webster.

On motion by Mr White,

To amend the same by striking out all after the word "is" where it first occurs and inserting in lieu thereof the words — _rescinded_, _reversed_, _repeated_ and _declared to be null and void_

Mr King of Ala moved to amend the original motion of Mr Benton by striking out the words — "ordered to be expunged from the journal of the Senate;" and

Journal of the Senate of the 33rd Congress

THE SENATE CENSURED JACKSON in 1834 because he "has assumed himself authority and power not conferred by the Constitution and laws, but in derogation of both." After his veto of the bill of the renewal of the Bank's charter, the President had removed Secretary of the Treasury Duane for refusing to check out the public funds deposited in the Bank. It was this action which had led to his censure. Not until 1837, three years later and after constant and persistent prodding by Senator Thomas Hart Benton, was the offending censure expunged from the Senate's *Journal*. This was a defeat for those who desired parliamentary government and a victory for those who upheld the idea of presidential government.

An 1837 lithograph signed "Perruquier," published by John Laurence

THE THREE LEADING WHIG CANDIDATES: General William Henry Harrison, Daniel Webster and Henry Clay. Unable to agree on any of them, the Whigs ran a number of favorite-son candidates in opposition to Van Buren, the Democratic nominee. If none of them was to gain a majority, they looked for a decision in the House of Representatives.

where they were strong enough to manipulate a victory.

But all their hopes were shattered when the Democrats remained behind Van Buren and voted for him. The Democrats were not swayed by the Whigs' charge that Van Buren's "mind beats round, like a tame bear tied to a stake, in a little circle, hardly bigger than the circumference of the head in which it is placed, seeking no other object than to convert the government into an instrument to serve himself or his officeholding friends." And they were not impressed by the accusation that "dandy" Van Buren was laced up tightly in corsets, that he was habitually indecisive and effeminate and so behaved like a frail sister that one found it "difficult to tell from his personal appearance whether he was a man or a woman."

As was the fashion of the day, the candidates were asked to give answers about their political beliefs. The questions were: (1) "Will you if elected sign a bill to distribute the surplus revenue?" (2) "Will you if elected distribute the proceeds of sales of public lands?" (3) "Will you sign bills making appropriations to improve navigable streams above ports of entry?" (4) "Will you be willing to sign a bill chartering a national bank?" (5) "Do you believe that Congress has the constitutional right to expunge the records of a previous session?" (By then the Senate was well on the way to

An 1837 lithograph by Napoleon Sarony, published by H. R. Robinson, N.Y.

THE LOCOFOCOS were the radical wing of the Democratic party in New York, denouncing monopoly and vested interests. They asked for equal rights for everyone; thus they were called the Equal Rights party. They got the nickname "locofocos" after an incident at a turbulent Tammany Hall meeting, when the regulars turned off the gaslights, marking the end of the discussion. However, the radicals produced locofocos (matches), lit candles and continued the meeting. In time all Democrats were derisively called "locofocos."

An 1836 lithograph by Edward W. Clay, published by H. R. Robinson, N.Y.
A GAME OF POOL between the Whig candidate Harrison and the Democratic candidate Van Buren.

Webster and Clay, the two prominent Whig leaders (on the left) are betting on Harrison. Webster: "There is a tide in the affairs of men as Shakespeare says." Clay: "I'll go a cool Hundred Harrison wins the game."

On the right Van Buren is flanked by Senator Benton ("I'll bet a cookie he dont make the hazzard") and President Jackson ("By the Eternal! Martin, if Harrison holes you and gets a spot ball on the deep red it is all day with you").

expunging its anti-Jackson resolution.)

Harrison answered all queries in the affirmative except the last. Van Buren was for distribution of the surplus revenue, but was not so sure that he would want to distribute the receipts from the sale of public lands, or improve rivers above ports of entry. He was also opposed to a national bank, and he thought that Congress had the right to expunge any of its resolutions. White was noncommittal, referring his questioners to his Congressional record; but he came out for the improvement of waterways and against the chartering of a national bank.

In the election, a new radical section of the Democratic party made its appearance. This faction fought monopoly and vested interests; opposed paper money and labor-saving machines "by which drones are enabled to grow rich without honest industry." They were against banks, banking and paper money, and they called themselves the Equal Righters because they asked for equal rights for all men. But after an incident at New York's Tammany Hall they became known as Locofocos—a nickname which the opposition later used for all Democrats. It happened that just before the state election in New York the Equal Rights men opposed the Tammany nominations. After a violent argument the Tammany men left the hall, and as they did, they blew out the gaslight; whereupon the Equal Righters lit candles with matches—called locofocos—and "in a moment the platform was lined with fifty sperm lights, and thus the old trick would not take." The meeting proceeded, and the Equal Righters triumphed.

The major issue was the personality of Jackson. Those who admired him voted for Van Buren, those who abhorred him voted for one of the Whig candidates.

An 1836 lithograph published by H. R. Robinson, N.Y.

THE TWO ANTAGONISTS—"The Champion old Tip and the swell Dutchman of Kinderhook" are fighting it out. It is one of the earliest political cartoons in which the candidates are drawn as boxers.

Harrison is seconded by "Western lad," while his bottle-holder is "Old Seventy Six." Van Buren is seconded by Jackson, who exclaims: "By the Eternal! what a severe counter hit." He asks Kendall, the Postmaster General: "Where's the bottle? After this Round put some more into him." But Kendall has found a "Surplus Fund" in it and takes a pull to raise his spirits.

Van Buren won easily, his popular vote about 27,-000 more than the combined votes of the three Whig sectional candidates: Harrison, Webster and White. Of the electoral votes he carried 170 against Harrison's 73, White's 26, Webster's 14 and Mangum's 11.

All twenty-six states which voted in the election (Arkansas had been admitted on June 15, 1836, and Michigan on January 27, 1837), with the exception of South Carolina, now chose electors by popular vote.

As none of the four vice-presidential candidates received a majority, the selection of the Vice President went for the first and only time to the Senate, which chose Richard M. Johnson with 33 votes against Francis Granger's 16.

At the counting of the electoral votes a debate arose over the validity of Michigan's votes, since that state, because of boundary disputes, had not been admitted to the Union at the time of the election. As in a similar instance in the past, the result was announced in two ways: in one, Michigan's votes were not included; in the other, they were. But it made no practical difference.

Inauguration day was a triumph for Jackson. Sick and feeble, he rode to the Capitol with his successor in a phaeton made of wood from the frigate *Constitution*. The masses cheered him along Pennsylvania Avenue. "For once," noted Senator Benton, "the rising was eclipsed by the setting sun."

Next day Jackson visited his old friend Blair to say farewell to him. Making himself comfortable in an easy chair, he lit his pipe and reminisced about his "reign." He spoke of his achievements and he pointed out his failures. And he concluded that he had only two regrets: one, that he had not shot Clay; the other, that he had not hanged Calhoun.

149

WILLIAM HENRY HARRISON and JOHN TYLER

Van Buren had hardly begun his term when the panic of 1837 swept over the country. Bad times would have come even if Jackson had not withdrawn the government's funds from the Bank and deposited them in "pet" banks, but his move speeded up the coming disaster.

The "pet" banks, many of them newly chartered, threw themselves into the banking business with the enthusiasm of newcomers. They issued currency and made liberal loans. In 1829, when Jackson took office, there were 329 banks; in 1837, when the panic broke, there were 788. Their capital grew from $110 million to $290 million, the circulation of their currency from $48 million to $149 milllion, their loans from $137 million to $525 million.

Speculation was widespread. In inflationary times the safest way of maintaining the value of one's money is to get rid of it. One buys; one invests; one speculates. In the West, speculation in land was booming. With adequate roads and easy transportation and with high agricultural prices, good Western land sold at a premium. The trouble was that land speculators already had bought up the choice sites before the settlers got there. Some parcels changed hands a dozen times before they came into the settlers' possession.

In 1834 the government sold four million acres of land; the year after, fifteen million; in 1836, twenty million—five times the acreage of only two years before. This "land-office business" brought the Treasury $4,857,000 in 1834, $24,877,000 in 1836. The yield from it was sufficient to pay for all government expenses and more. And what happened to the money?

The Treasury deposited it in the state banks, which then loaned it out, often to land speculators who bought more land from the government, paying for it with the funds they had just borrowed. Thus the vicious circle continued. The Treasury deposited the money in the banks, speculators borrowed it, bought land with it, transferring "to speculators the most valuable public lands," as Jackson noted, and paying the government "by a credit on the books of the banks."

In July 1836 Jackson stopped "the endless chain." In his *Specie Circular* he announced that the Treasury would not accept paper money for land after August 15. All land purchased after that date had to paid for in "specie"—gold or silver.

The surplus worried Jackson. By 1835 all public debts of the government had been paid off and there were no outstanding obligations. What to do with large sums in the Treasury? Congress voted to lend them to the states. With them the states began to build roads and canals; they made loans to private business. Within two years their debt rose to $170 million, a far larger sum than they could expect to repay from their revenues.

The inflationary trend stimulated business; luxury goods were imported from abroad. The import of silk rose from $6 million in 1831 to almost $23 million in 1836. As money was plentiful and the demand for luxuries great, far more goods were imported than exported; more money flowed out than came in. The situation worsened with the crop failure of 1835, which forced the purchase of wheat from Europe.

Disaster was not far off. American drafts and bills of

WILLIAM HENRY HARRISON
An engraving by John Sartain after a painting by James R. Lambdin

CANDIDATES IN 1840

WILLIAM H. HARRISON (1773–1841), the hero of Tippecanoe, who had proved his strong vote-getting ability in the previous election, again became the choice of the Whigs. In the exuberant and emotional campaign, the wealthy Harrison owning 2,000 acres was transformed into a poor farmer who lived in a log cabin and drank hard cider. He handily won the election with 1,275,016 votes against Van Buren's 1,129,102.

JOHN TYLER (1790–1862), graduate of William and Mary and later its rector and chancellor, also served as Governor of Virginia and U.S. Senator. He was chosen for the Vice Presidency because the Whigs needed a Southerner to balance the Harrison ticket. "Tippecanoe and Tyler too!" won the contest with 234 electoral votes, defeating Van Buren who had only 60. Harrison soon died, and Tyler assumed office.

MARTIN VAN BUREN (1782–1862), who ran for re-election, was destined to lose the race. The Panic of 1837 and the depression which followed it came during his administration so that he was blamed for both. The Whigs assailed him with merciless fury; they pictured him as a haughty aristocrat as opposed to the poor farmer Harrison. In the campaign, issues were little discussed, emotionalism was unrestrained.

RICHARD M. JOHNSON (1780–1850), Van Buren's Vice President, friend of the working man and a military hero was under constant attack from the South because of his mulatto mistresses, one of whom bore him two daughters. The convention did not renominate him, but left the choice to the electorate. He campaigned with the slogan "Rumpsey-dumpsey, rumpsey-dumpsey, Colonel Johnson killed Tecumseh"—and lost.

ANNA TUTHILL SYMMES (1775–1864) married Harrison on November 25, 1795. She bore him ten children—six sons and four daughters. Ill at the time of the inauguration, she remained at North Bend and did not accompany her husband to Washington. Her widowed daughter-in-law looked after Harrison during the four weeks of his tenure.

exchange began to sell at a discount in London and the Bank of England raised its discount rates. English exporters stopped their credit to American customers; they demanded payment in cash and in hard money. American gold supply dwindled to a dangerous low.

The final blow came with the Distribution Act, requiring the "pet" banks to repay the borrowed funds in specie. The banks met the first payment on January 1, 1837, but could not meet the second payment in April. By May—two months after Van Buren's inauguration—all specie payments had been suspended; by summer the country's economic life was paralyzed. In England those firms which could not collect their American debts went into bankruptcy. This brought about a chain reaction. English cotton mills closed, bringing down the price of American cotton. Without the income from

An 1837 lithograph published by H. R. Robinson, N.Y.

THE FIRST APPEARANCE OF THE DEMOCRATIC DONKEY. Jackson rides it, Van Buren follows it. The distribution of the surplus in "pet banks" had far-reaching effects, particularly in the western part of the country. The new banks issued "wildcat" currency, and with the inflated money, speculation in land was booming. To stop it, Jackson issued a Specie Circular, which demanded hard currency—gold or silver—for payments on land from the public reserves.

their cotton, the Southern planters had to curtail their farm purchases from the West; thus the Western farmers, losing a sizable part of their market, cut down their purchases from the Northeast, and Eastern manufacturerers were forced to reduce their production and to dismiss their workers.

Martin Van Buren, like all Presidents before him, subscribed to the laissez-faire philosophy of government. Business was to be left alone; the government was not to interfere with it. The President's duty was to keep the government finances in order, and this Van Buren was determined to do. In a special session Congress repealed the distribution of the surplus, and the government was allowed to issue Treasury notes to meet expenses.

Van Buren advocated the establishment of an inde-

pendent treasury, proposing strong vaults (subtreasuries) in various parts of the country in which the government's funds could be kept. The Whigs opposed the Subtreasury Bill because they felt it was bad for business and because—as Henry Clay said—it would "reduce all property in value by two thirds." But Van Buren held out for the bill, which was passed before his term ended.

By then the Whig National Convention had already met. (James Watson Webb of the *Courier & Enquirer* successfully popularized the term "Whig" as the opposite to Jacksonianism, against King Andrew I and the Tories.) It was a meeting of strangely heterogeneous elements. Cotton planters of South Carolina fuming against protection, manufacturers of Massachusetts asking for protection, bankers of Pennsylvania despis-

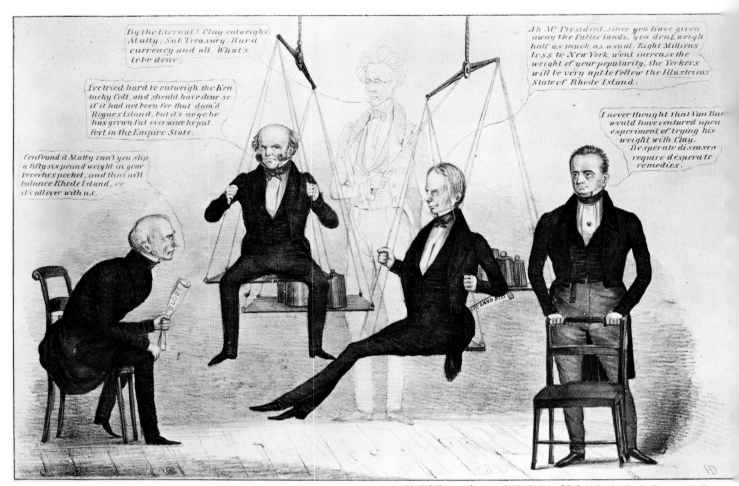

An 1840 lithograph signed "H.D.," published by H. R. Robinson, N.Y.

"WEIGHED AND FOUND WANTING." Blair of the *Globe* (left) and Senator Benton observe the weighing in of Van Buren and Clay. "Confound it, Matty," exclaims Blair, "can't you slip a fifty-six pound weight in your breeches pocket . . ." and Benton says: "I never thought that Van Buren would have ventured upon the experiment of trying his weight with Clay . . ." The ghost of Jackson cries: "By the Eternal! Clay outweighs Matty, Sub-Treasury, Hard Currency and all."

ing Jackson's attitude toward the Bank, Southern conservatives fighting Jackson's "executive tyranny," young Abraham Lincoln, admiring Henry Clay as his "beau ideal of a statesman," financiers afraid of government interference, sugar planters crying for help against Cuba, were now Whigs as were Masons and Antimasons, tariff men and antitariff men, slaveholders and abolitionists, pro-Bank and anti-Bank men. Even Henry Eaton, for whose wife Jackson fought so relentlessly, was now a Whig.

That the various factions were unable to agree on common political ideology was not surprising. A platform was not even proposed; they tried to unite the incongruous elements behind a candidate.

At first the Whigs hoped that Henry Clay might be such a man. He was the favorite of many states, but he had been in public life for three decades and had collected many enemies. He had definite political views—another great handicap for one seeking the nomination. His American System favored a policy of protection; thus he could not count on the votes of the Southern antiprotectionists; and as he was a Mason, he could not hope for the votes of the Antimasons.

When Clay saw he could not get the prize, he let it be known that "If my name creates any obstacle to Union and Harmony, away with it, and concentrate upon some individual more acceptable to all branches of the opposition." Thus the choice remained between two military heroes of the Mexican War—General Winfield Scott and General William Harrison, neither of them experienced in politics, neither of them a colorful personality.

An 1837 lithograph by Edward W. Clay, published by H. R. Robinson, N.Y.

THE EFFECTS OF THE PANIC. Barefoot workers lean against the billboard which advertises "money to loan at 7% per month"; a widow and her child are begging; the factory is "closed for the present"; the Street Hotel is "for sale"; in the sheriff's office, foreclosed property is auctioned off; there is a run on the Mechanics Bank. Only the liquor store and the pawnbroker prosper. In the sky are Jackson's hat and spectacles, symbols of the man thought responsible for the misery.

On the first ballot Clay led with 103 votes against General Harrison's 94 and General Scott's 47. For three full days the balloting went on. Thaddeus Stevens worked for Harrison, as did Thurlow Weed, the influential New Yorker. Stevens got hold of a letter which Scott had written to Francis Granger in an effort to win antislavery support and he saw to it that the letter was read by many delegates, steering them away from Scott. Weed, who at first persuaded the Connecticut delegation to swing from Clay to Scott, now took his state to Harrison, securing him the candidacy. In the final tally, the sixty-eight-year-old warrior received 148 votes against Clay's 90 and Scott's 16. For the second place the Weed-Stevens forces proposed Clay's friend John Tyler of Virginia, a spokesman for the Tidewater aristocracy, to appease the angry Clay suporters.

"There was rhyme," wrote Philip Hone about Tyler's selection later, "but no reason to it." The Whigs cared little about the "reason"; they wanted to win; they wanted the votes of the Federalists in the North and the strict constructionists in the South—thus their ticket became "Tippecanoe and Tyler too."

Clay bemoaned the "diabolic intrigue" which had betrayed him. "I am the most unfortunate man in the history of parties: always run by my friends when sure to be defeated, and now betrayed for a nomination when I, or any one, would be sure of an election."

The Democrats assembled in Baltimore. The night before they met, the Whigs shouted themselves hoarse:

With Tip and Tyler
We'll bust Van's biler.

155

An 1839 lithograph published by H. R. Robinson, N.Y.

CLAY VISITS PRESIDENT VAN BUREN. In the summer of 1839 Henry Clay traveled to Saratoga to meet Thurlow Weed, the New York political boss, to win his favor. After the visit with Weed, Clay paid his respects to the vacationing President, whose successor he desired to be. However, when the Whigs finally made their choice in their Baltimore convention, it was General William Henry Harrison, the hero of Tippecanoe, and not Clay. The hirsute men are supporters of Clay who took an oath not to shave until their hero's election. How long they retained their beards is not recorded.

They had no doubt that Van Buren would be the Democrats' choice to battle Harrison as indeed he was. He was renominated without opposition.

The question was who should be chosen as his running mate. President Jackson, who had virtually hand-picked Johnson four years before, was now against him. The gossip and rumors about Johnson turned Old Hickory against him. An anonymous letter writer wrote—and a Cabinet member saw to it that Jackson read the letter—that Johnson would not have the support of his friends because he "openly and shamefully lives in adultery with a buxom young *negro*."

Jackson wanted his former choice to be replaced. "The people," said he, "have somehow got a prejudice against Col Johnson, that cannot be removed." And he prophesied, "If Col Johnson is the nominee it will loose [*sic*] the democracy thousand[*sic*] of votes."

The embarrassed Democrats were searching for a way out of the difficulty. Before their convention met, Senator Silas Wright even suggested calling it off to avoid the disturbing controversy. But Jackson insisted that the convention "must be held." So the Democratic managers came up with a compromise. Their evasive solution was to leave the vice presidential nomination to "their Republican fellow-citizens in the several states, trusting that before the election should take place, their opinions would become so concentrated as to secure the choice of a vice-president by the Electoral College."

For Jackson this was a spineless proposal and he worked behind the scenes to secure the vice presidential nomination for his protégé James K. Polk. However, as

An 1840 lithograph published by H. R. Robinson, N.Y.

HARRISON, THE RICH OWNER OF 2000 ACRES OF LAND, IS PRESENTED AS A SIMPLE FARMER. An imaginary visit of the Democratic leaders at Harrison's home in North Bend, Ohio. Alighting from the liveried coach are Francis Blair, editor of the *Globe;* Amos Kendall, the Postmaster General; Senator John C. Calhoun and President Van Buren. They are debating how to undermine the Whig candidate. Harrison offers his visitors "a mug of good cider, with ham and eggs, and clean beds." The "dandy" Van Buren pities the poor man who "lives in a log cabin and ploughs his own ground."

the party leaders could not agree on another vice presidential candidate, Johnson's name remained on the ticket.

The Democratic platform came out against internal improvement, for "no more revenue . . . than is required to defray the necessary expenses of Government," against the charter of the U.S. Bank, against the abolitionists who tried "to induce Congress to interfere with questions of slavery," and for "separation of the moneys of the Government from banking institutions," which is "indispensable for the safety of the funds of the Government and the rights of the people."

The campaign which followed was something new; a circus press agent could not have arranged it with more ballyhoo.

The Whigs presented their candidate, the owner of 2,000 acres of land and a sixteen-room house, as a simple backwoodsman. A correspondent of the Baltimore *Republican* wrote that a friend of Clay told him after Harrison's nomination: "Give him a barrel of Hard Cider, and settle a pension of two thousand a year on him, and my word for it, he will sit the remainder of his days in his Log Cabin, by the side of a 'seacoal' fire and study moral philosophy."

The Whig partisans recognized the effectiveness of the phrase. To them goes the credit for introducing modern techniques into the staid presidential campaigns. Thomas Elder, a Pennsylvania banker, and Richard S. Elliott, a Harrisburg editor, thought log cabin and hard cider might be just the right symbols for the party. Elder said that "passion and prejudice, properly aroused and directed, would do about as well as

An 1840 lithograph by Edward W. Clay, published by John Childs, N.Y.

HARRISON KNOCKS OUT THE DEMOCRATS. Kendall and Blair (who holds a globe, the name of his newspaper) tumble over the hard-cider barrel, bringing Van Buren down with them. From the cabin Major Jack Downing calls out: "I swan if the General haint knocked Amos into a cider barrel." Both hard cider and log cabins became Whig symbols in the election; the coon on the cabin wall gradually became a symbol of the Whigs in some of the later political cartoons.

principle and reason in a party contest." So he ordered transparencies showing Old Tippecanoe's log cabin with a coonskin on the wall and a cider barrel next to the entrance. In no time, Elder and Elliott made Harrison into the "log cabin and hard cider candidate," a man who lived in the modest cabin with his door open to all comers, who never drank strong liquor, and who plowed his land with his own hands.

The sentiment caught the imagination of the people. The home of the pioneers was dear to their hearts: many of them were born in log cabins; many of them were still living in them. For them log cabin was the symbol of the country.

The Whigs organized processions, with floats carrying log cabins with the latchstrings hanging out and barrels of hard cider all around the place. Whigs everywhere marched in coonskin caps, offering hard cider to any takers. They wore log cabin badges, distributed log cabin papers and almanacs, sang log cabin songs.

The mass emotionalism stunned the Democrats. Directing their strategy along proven lines, they tried to reason, to discuss and argue the issues. They tried to argue the merits of the Independent Treasury and the assumption of state debts. They attacked Harrison because he was once with the old Federalists whose party had created the National Bank, opposed the War of

An 1841 lithograph by Edward W. Clay, published by John Childs, N.Y.

MATTY'S DREAM. President Van Buren runs out of the White House recounting his horrible dream. He felt himself crushed in a cider press with Harrison's head on it. Senator Calhoun (on the left) and Senator Benton (on the right) try to calm him down, but with little success. Benton does not share Van Buren's dream; he sees only his fallen "mint drops"— gold coins minted in the year of 1834, so dubbed because of the Missouri Senator's continual advocacy of hard currency.

1812, supported high tariffs and internal improvements.

But nobody cared about issues any more. The air was full of cries for log cabins and hard cider. In their parade the Whigs sang:

> *Make way for old Tip, turn out, turn out!*
> *Make way for old Tip, turn out, turn out!*
> *'Tis the people's decree,*
> *Their choice he shall be,*
> *So Martin Van Buren turn out, turn out!*
> *So Martin Van Buren turn out, turn out!*

Farmers called their horses "Tip" and "Ty," and

"The hens in the West never lay an egg nowadays but they cackle: Tip-tip! Tip-tip! Tyler!"

The Whigs' elder leaders, Clay and Webster, campaigned for Harrison. Clay told an audience: "The time for discussion is passed. . . . We are all Whigs—we are all Harrison men. We are *united*. We must triumph." And Webster orated: "The time has come when the cry is change. Every breeze says change. . . . We have fallen, gentlemen, upon *hard* times, and the remedy seems to be HARD CIDER."

A Van Buren man complained that the Whigs had substituted "the exhibition of flags, flagons, and log cabins" for "deliberation and exposition."

THE VIRTUES OF OLD TIPPECANOE WERE EXTOLLED IN NUMEROUS HARRISON ALMANACS.

The huge Whig rallies attracted enormous crowds. "Twenty, thirty, fifty thousand souls" came to hear "the first orators of the nation address the multitudes, not one in ten of whom can hear them," noted John Quincy Adams in his diary. "Here is a revolution in the habits and manners of the people." And Adams added the anxious question: "Where will it end?"

The Whig meetings were described by the acre. "Fifteen acres of men," reported one paper, camped at Tippecanoe battleground to cheer Harrison.

Campaign souvenirs and election merchandise were on display everywhere. The Whigs could buy "Tippecanoe Shaving Soap or Log Cabin Emollient," a handkerchief with the likeness of General Harrison, or a Harrison and Tyler necktie. Pocket brandy and whiskey bottles in the shape of log cabins were popular items. "Old Cabin Whiskey" came from the E.C. Booz Distillery of Philadelphia, introducing to the language another name for liquor.

Thurlow Weed organized the Whig campaign with great skill and professionalism. He designed "a stupendous system." The mailing lists of Whig Congressmen were transferred onto a master list, and everyone on this list received campaign literature, log cabin lithographs, stories of the candidate ready for inclusion in the local papers. The Executive Committee sent orders to the "Central Whig Committees" which sprang up in every county, and the local committees made up lists for every precinct with voters listed as "good, bad or doubtful."

An 1841 lithograph published by T. Sinclair, Philadelphia
THE LOG CABIN grew into a Whig symbol after a Democratic newspaper suggested that if Harrison were given a pension and a barrel of hard cider, he would be happy to sit out the rest of his days in a log cabin. The Whigs took hold of this and from then on the rich Harrison was presented to the electorate as the poor "log-cabin and hard-cider candidate."

A personal committee headed by Charles S. Todd, editor of the Cincinnati *Republican,* was formed to help Harrison. It answered his correspondence, prepared his speeches and wrote pamphlets. Because of this group the Democrats dubbed Harrison "a man in an iron cage."

By 1840, sixteen of the twenty-six states had eliminated all property and taxpaying qualifications on the suffrage. The common man, since Jackson opened the gates, became the main factor in the country's political life. Campaign methods had to be fashioned to the new conditions. Party networks had to be perfected; meetings had to be organized in which speakers brought the issues to the people. Stump oratory became an established feature.

It was still held that the candidates themselves should keep away from personally soliciting votes. Van Buren stayed in the White House writing letters to the newspapers and to politicians advocating his cause. The *National Intelligencer* criticized him for "descending from the Presidential chair into the political arena." In the previous election Nicholas Biddle had advised Harrison to "say not one single word about his principles or his creed—let him say nothing—promise nothing. Let no Committee, no Convention, no town meeting ever extract from him a single word about what he thinks now and will do hereafter. Let the use of pen and ink be wholly forbidden as if he were a mad poet in Bedlam."

At that time Harrison had followed the bank presi-

An 1840 lithograph by Edward W. Clay

"ALL THE WEST GO-
ING FOR MATTY"—
Van Buren, running from
the wild beasts, cries out:
"I wish I was safe at Kinderhook [his home town]!
for I am a used up man!"

THE TWO OPPOSING CAN-
DIDATES and their sup-
porters. Behind Van Buren (on
the left) are Calhoun, Benton
and Kendall; Blair (center) is
snuffing out the candle; behind
Harrison: Webster and Clay.

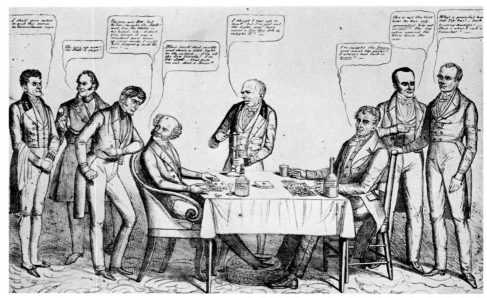

An 1840 lithograph published by John Childs, N.Y.

dent's advice, but he would do so no longer. He broke the long-established tradition and went to the people (though John Adams before the turn of the century was not adverse to making speeches before his election to keep himself in the public eye). He accepted an invitation to appear at Perrysburg, Ohio, for an anniversary celebration of the Battle of Fort Meigs, if only to show that he was in the best of health, vigorous and not a tired old soldier as the Democrats charged. En route to the celebration he stopped at Columbus and spoke from the steps of the National Hotel. As he enjoyed the experience, he continued with his speechmaking, some of his speeches lasting three hours or more. He kept on campaigning up to election day, addressing large audiences, mostly extemporaneously. He was presented by his supporters as a circus animal would be by an animal trainer. At Springfield, Ohio, his friend General Vance cried to the crowd in a loud voice: "This is General Harrison! Look at him!! Look at his bright and beaming eye!!!" The people loved it.

The General was an astute campaigner. He made shrewd appeals to the nationalities. While in Cleveland

"GOING UP SALT RIVER"—the synonym for defeat. Riding the mule with Harrison's head are Clay, Webster and Wise. Van Buren (left) says: "Don't spill your valuable cargo!" They think they have enough "hard cider" to last the trip.

An 1840 lithograph issued by John Childs, N.Y.

An 1840 lithograph by Edward W. Clay

"BUBBLE BURSTING"—Jackson hangs on a branch of a hickory tree holding a bowl of "pap." The *Globe* bubble of Kendall and Blair falls in Salt River, while Van Buren's "Sub Treasury Bubble" lets him down in a cabbage patch at Kinderhook.

he flattered the Native American Society by telling them that he "cared not for the opinions of those who had come over the sea to our shore"; by the time he reached the German communities of Lancaster, he "felt the warmest sympathy for the victims of tyranny and oppression in the Old World, who had fled here for refuge." And in Cincinnati he told a foreign audience that "my republican sympathy for the people of Germany, Ireland, England, or any other land, has been and is warmed into active existence by the remembrance that liberty is equally to all of us."

He was a poor orator and acknowledged it. "I am not a professional speaker, nor a studied orator, but I am an old soldier and a farmer, and as my sole object is to speak what I think, you will excuse me if I do it in my own way," he said in Dayton. His partisans pointed to his modesty, but the Democratic *Globe* counted eighty-one I's in his short Fort Meigs speech: "What a prodigy of garrulous egotism!"

The General's campaign was based on denunciation of the Democrats. Unemployment, closed factories, low cotton prices, diminishing land values—the depression

"THE PEOPLE'S LINE." Van Buren's cab is in collapse, while Harrison's hard-cider locomotive moves merrily along.

"UNCLE SAM'S PET PUPS!" Van Buren and Jackson outside the barrel, Harrison over it, watched by Uncle Sam.

"RAISING THE SPIRIT OF SANTA CLAUS," President Van Buren in the magic circle of log cabins and cider barrels.

with all its hardships—was the Democrats' doing.

To fight the Whigs and Greeley's highly successful *Log Cabin,* the Democrats issued a number of campaign weeklies. In addition to the *Extra Globe* there was a *Magician* in Pennsylvania, the *Old Hickory* in Ohio, the *Rough-Hewer* and the *Kinderhook Dutchman* in New York, and others. Members of Jackson's Kitchen Cabinet, particularly Amos Kendall, the "head devil of the administration," and Francis Blair, the editor of the administration organ *The Globe,* were working hard for Van Buren. Kendall used government employees to present the Democratic case. All postmasters were told to secure subscribers for the *Extra Globe.*

Democratic campaign speakers wooed the foreign voters in the urban areas. They told the immigrants that the Whigs were "Aristocrats, Monarchists, Enemies of the People, especially hostile to Foreigners, and desirous of excluding them from all rights and privileges, if not from the country itself." In Ohio, Democratic officeholders spread the word that all the Germans and Irish were to be sent out of the country if Harrison should be elected. Vituperation and name-calling were in fashion. The *Rough-Hewer* asked the question: "Why do the Whigs call their candidate 'Old Tip'?" and gave the answer: "Because he drinks hard cider," adding, "Old Tip-ler is a pretty name for a candidate for the Presidency."

The Democrats would never call the Whigs by their correct party name, nor did the Whigs the Democrats. Instead of calling them Whigs, the Democrats spoke of Hard Ciderites, Bankites, Black Cockade, Blue Lights, Abolitionists, and Wiggies or Wiggles. And the Whigs talked of the Democrats as Loco-focos, Spoilers, Destructionists, Tories, Levelers. Each side accused the other of allegiance to Federalism. Harrison was forced into repudiating the charge that he had in his youth been a Federalist.

The Whigs distributed a speech of Congressman Charles Ogle, a former law student of Thad Stevens, which he had made in the House on "The Regal Splendor of the President's Palace." It was, in the opinion of the Democrats, a "shameless electioneering trick." For "three mortal days," wrote the Democratic *Globe,* "Mr. Ogle detained the public business with his Omnibus of Lies." Ogle called the White House "as splendid as that of the Caesars, and as richly adorned as the proudest Asiatic mansion"; and he asserted that the garden had rare plants, shrubs and parterres in the style of the Royal Gardens in England and that the men who looked after these were paid with the people's money to spend their time plucking up by the roots burdock and sheep sorrel. Furthermore, the Blue Elliptical Saloon of the presidential mansion was garnished with gilt mirrors as big as a barn door, and in it were chairs that cost $600 a set. The climax of Ogle's speech

THE 1840 CAMPAIGN ADDED NEW EXPRESSIONS TO THE LANGUAGE.

An 1840 woodcut sold by Huestis & Co., New York

THE ORIGIN OF "O.K.," as the illustration suggests, is "Old Kinderhook," Martin Van Buren's nickname, and the name of his home in upstate New York. Led by former President Jackson, Van Buren is walking toward the White House carrying his Subtreasury Bill, which had been adopted by Congress in July 1840 when the presidential campaign was at its height.

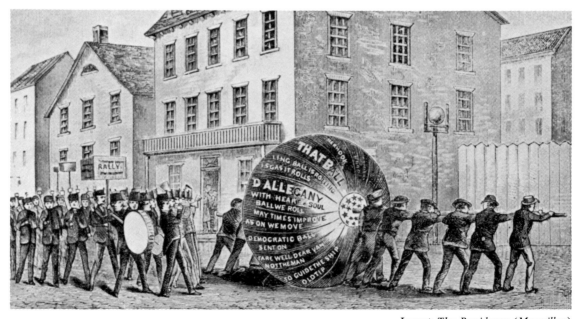

Lorant: The Presidency (Macmillan)

"IT IS THE BALL A-ROLLING on for Tippecanoe and Tyler too," sang the Whigs as they rolled their ball through the streets of Baltimore. Thus "Keep the ball rolling" became part of our language.

An 1840 lithograph by Edward W. Clay, published by John Childs, N.Y.

ON "THE ALMIGHTY LEVER" labeled "Public opinion" march the delegations of the various states. At the "Tip End" (a pun on "Tippecanoe") of the lever stands General Harrison—old Tippecanoe himself. The eagle's banner declares that "Locofocoism will be rolled into oblivion and a gallant soldier raised to the white house. March 4th 1841."

Woodcut in the New York Herald, *March 5, 1841*

HARRISON TAKES THE OATH—the earliest contemporary newspaper illustration of the swearing-in ceremony.

came when he revealed that a bathtub had been installed in the White House. Ogle was "not a little surprised" to find Van Buren the first President to insist upon "the pleasures of the warm or tepid bath" as "proper accompaniments of a palace life."

The Whig press was exuberant in praising the speech and even added some embellishments. One Whig editor complained that a country where the President sleeps on French bedsteads, walks on Royal Wilson carpets and sits on French taborets, eats his *pâté de foie gras* and *dinde désossée* from silver plates with forks of gold, sips his *soup à la Reine* with gold spoons from a silver tureen and rides in a gilded maroon coach—that country could not be called a democracy.

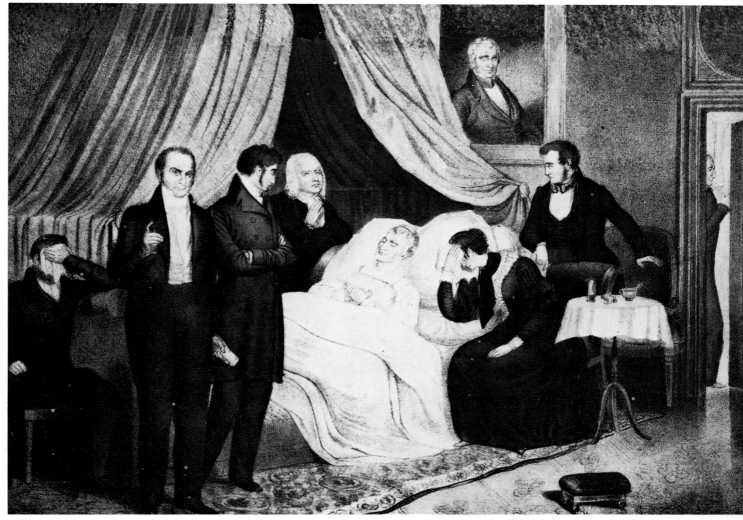

An 1841 lithograph by N. Currier, N.Y

THE DEATH OF HARRISON. On the left, Thomas Ewing, the griefstricken Secretary of the Treasury, sobs into his handkerchief; Secretary of State Daniel Webster and the President's physician are standing next to him. At the head of the bed is the Reverend Hawley with Harrison's niece and nephew. At the door, Postmaster General Francis Granger.

Many Whigs were embarrassed by Ogle's demagogic attack. Young Abraham Lincoln pointed out that less money had been spent for the upkeep of the White House during Van Buren's term than during that of any other President. Never, said Lincoln, had Van Buren requested a single article of furniture. But Greeley denied that Lincoln ever made such a speech—for him the speech was forged by "the Artful Dodgers."

After Ogle's speech the Whigs conducted it as a contest between the simple life of their log cabin candidate and that of the aristocratic Van Buren. The issues were drawn in simple terms: log cabin against palace, hard cider against champagne, Old Tippecanoe against Sweet Sandy Whiskers.

Davy Crockett, the former coonskin Congressman from Tennessee, published a widely distributed *Life of Martin Van Buren* in which he charged (with the help of the man who wrote the book) that the President "struts and swaggers like a crow in a gugar" and that he is "laced up in corsets, such as women in town wear, and, if possible, tighter than the best of them."

The vituperative attacks of Ogle and Crockett gave the country the impression that Van Buren was a royal aristocrat who perfumed his whiskers, ate from gold spoons and looked at himself in nine-foot mirrors.

In the midst of all the excitement the meeting of a small group at Albany was hardly noticed. The men came from six states and laid the foundation for a third

167

National Archives

YOUNG JOHN TYLER as photographed by Mathew B. Brady

Library of Congress

THE FIRST MRS. TYLER—
Letitia Christian (1790–1842)
bore her husband five daughters
and three sons (one daughter
died in infancy). A stroke almost completely paralyzed her
and she lived mostly in a
wheelchair. The only time she
appeared in public at the White
House was for the marriage
of her youngest daughter. She
died during the second year of
her husband's administration.

party, the Abolitionists, which put up candidates for President and Vice President for the first time.

The election began in Ohio and Pennsylvania on October 30 and ended in North Carolina on November 12. The states had not yet a uniform date for the election. The result was close. Harrison received 1,275,016 votes against Van Buren's 1,129,102 and the Abolitionist James G. Birney's 7,069. (Van Buren had about 400,000 more votes in defeat than in his 1836 victory.) In Maine, Harrison won by only 411 votes, and in Pennsylvania by only 349 out of a total of

287,693 votes. But in electoral votes the Whigs had the comfortable margin of 234 to the Democrats' 60.

The Democrats wailed: "The standard-bearer of the Federalist and Abolition party has been elected, if the process by which this has been brought about may be called an election. . . ." The Whigs were jubilant. "The people are free again," cried their newspapers.

The neutral Philadelphia *Public Ledger* summed up the election in a levelheaded way: "For two years past, the most ordinary operations of business have been neglected and President-making has become every citizen's chief concern. The result being uncertain, some have been afraid to engage in new enterprises, others have retired from business, others have not dared to prosecute their business with the old vigor. Millions of dollars will now change hands on election bets; millions of days have been taken from useful labor to listen to stump orators, and millions more to build log cabins, erect hickory poles, and march in ridiculous, degrading,

THE SECOND MRS. TYLER
—Julia Gardiner (1820–1889),
daughter of a New York Senator, married Tyler four months
after her father's death in the
explosion on the warship
Princeton. With a wife thirty
years younger than himself,
"Tyler and his bride are the
laughing stock of this city,"
noted John Quincy Adams. Yet
it was a happy marriage, with
five sons and two daughters.

OLD JOHN TYLER, from a recently discovered daguerreotype

mob-creating processions; millions of dollars have been wasted in soul- and body-destroying intemperance, in paying demagogues for preaching treason and bribing knaves to commit perjury and cast fraudulent votes. However high the hopes inspired by the election of General Harrison, they will prove to be delusive. A national bank cannot be created; the sub-treasury cannot be repealed; the monetary expansion and speculation which the hopes of these measures will create will be quickly followed by contraction, by ruin, and the prostration of the speculators."

On inauguration day Harrison rode to the Capitol on a white charger escorted by his friends. A bitter northeast wind blew and it was cold. Yet Old Tippecanoe would not wear an overcoat and he rode with hat in hand, acknowledging the applause of the masses which lined his route. The crowd before the Capitol was "variously estimated from thirty to sixty thousand."

He wrote his inaugural address at North Bend on sheets of foolscap paper, and when he arrived in Washington he gave it to Webster to read. Webster "respectfully suggested the propriety . . . of striking from it some of the many classical allusions and quotations." After working at the revision Webster arrived late for a dinner engagement. He was asked if anything had happened. "You would think that something had happened if you knew what I have done," said Webster. "I have killed seventeen Roman proconsuls." Still, plenty of them remained in the address, which even for Horace Greeley was "of unusual length."

One month from the day he delivered his inaugural address, Harrison was dead. A cold developed into pneumonia and felled the old warrior. He was succeeded by Vice President John Tyler, the first "accidental" President to become President by succession.

William Cullen Bryant regretted Harrison's death "only because he did not live long enough to prove his incapacity for the office of President."

Brady.   N.Y.

JAMES K. POLK

That a campaign of slogans and manufactured emotionalism could make a President was a novelty for the Democrats. Now that it was over they realized how effective it had been—the log-cabin processions, the hard-cider barrels, the Tippecanoe songs, all that hullabaloo. They berated the Whigs for winning the election through frauds and by deceiving the electorate, and they carefully studied their methods to use them in the future.

The Whigs' joy was short-lived. Their President caught a cold and died of pneumonia a month after his inauguration. The Whigs wondered what kind of executive his successor would be. Would Tyler, a Southern aristocrat, follow the Whigs' nationalistic policies? Before his nomination he declared he was "a firm and decided Whig." But was he? In his past he had opposed a protective tariff, opposed internal improvements, opposed the distribution of receipts from the sale of public lands—all policies of the Whigs. He was an advocate of states' rights, he regarded Jackson's Nullification Proclamation unconstitutional, and he held that the Constitution did not empower the Federal Government to interfere with the institution of slavery.

Tyler soon showed that he had an independent mind and that he would not be dominated by the leaders of his party. He would not allow Clay to tell him what to do. He vetoed the Whigs' bill for a new central bank to replace Van Buren's subtreasury system. When a revised bill was submitted, Clay was confident that Tyler would sign it. "I'll drive him before me," he boasted. But when the bill came to him, Tyler vetoed it as it did not safeguard the rights of the states.

Exasperated at the President's "turns and twists" the Cabinet members, with the exception of Webster who was in the midst of important negotiations with England, resigned, and a caucus of Whig Representatives and Senators declared that in the future "those who brought the President into power can no longer, in any manner or degree, be justly held responsible or blamed for the administration of the executive branch of the government." There was even talk of impeaching him.

Tyler, after losing the support of the Whigs, now appealed to the Democrats. His followers bought Democratic newspapers, replaced the old editors with Tyler's supporters, and the new men set out to convince their readers that Tyler was a regular Democrat. But as Tyler had always opposed Jackson, and as he had signed the repeal of Van Buren's Sub-Treasury Act, the Democrats were not convinced. He could not have been less successful unless he had tried to pass himself off as an abolitionist.

To eliminate Van Buren as a candidate, Tyler sent an intermediary to Van Buren's friend Silas Wright with an offer of a Supreme Court appointment for Van Buren. The envoy told Wright that it was far from certain that Van Buren could be nominated, and if renominated he would surely lose. Wright replied: "Tell Mr. Tyler from me, that if he desires to give to the whole country a broader, deeper, heartier laugh than it ever had and at his expense, he can effect it by making that nomination."

By the spring of election year Tyler's prospects for gaining the nomination were gone. By then it looked like the Whigs would choose Henry Clay, and the

JAMES K. POLK
Photograph by Mathew B. Brady

171

CANDIDATES IN 1844

JAMES K. POLK
(1795–1849), from Tennessee, was Jackson's protégé. After Van Buren spoke against the annexation of Texas, the party sought a candidate who would not alienate the South. It was Polk.

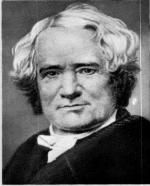

GEORGE M. DALLAS
(1792–1864), a Pennsylvania lawyer and politician, Minister to Russia in Van Buren's administration, became the vice presidential candidate after the chosen nominee, Silas Wright, refused to accept.

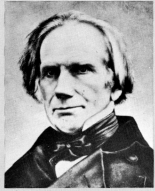

HENRY CLAY
(1777–1852) resigned his Senate seat in 1842 after his break with President Tyler. He was the Whigs' choice for the first place in his third attempt for the Presidency. As in 1824 and in 1832, he lost.

T. FRELINGHUYSEN
(1787–1862), a "Christian gentleman" from New Jersey, was the Whigs' choice for the Vice Presidency. But Polk and Dallas with 1,337,243 votes defeated the Whig ticket, which got 1,209,062 votes.

JAMES G. BIRNEY
(1792–1857), the abolitionist candidate, was the son of one of the richest slaveholders in Kentucky. He moved North to fight slavery. He took enough votes from Clay in New York to give Polk the victory.

JOHN TYLER
(1790–1862), the outgoing President, was backed by a coalition of dissatisfied Whigs and Democrats; but when he realized that he could not gain enough support for the nomination, he withdrew his name.

Library of Congress

SARAH CHILDRESS (1803–1891) married Polk on January 1, 1824. Rumor had it that General Jackson insisted on the marriage to put a halt to Polk's lady-chasing activities.

A beautiful woman with black hair, dark eyes and white complexion, she had a keen interest in politics, working long hours as her husband's secretary. Deeply religious, she ran a spartan household; neither food nor drink was served at her receptions.

Democrats would settle on ex-President Van Buren again. But all of a sudden the political picture changed when Calhoun as Secretary of State concluded a treaty with the Republic of Texas for its annexation, forcing the prospective candidates to take a stand.

A RARE FIND: A RECENTLY DISCOVERED DAGUERREOTYPE taken about 1849, ten years after the invention of photography. President James K. Polk and his wife are in the center. The tall figure on the left with the smudged face is James Buchanan, Polk's Secretary of State. Next to him, his niece Harriet Lane.

The somewhat blurred figure on the right is none other than Dolley Madison, the vivacious widow of the fourth President—she could never hold still. At the time, she was 82 years old, but a man who saw her recounted that her arms and shoulders were as beautiful as those of a young woman. The remaining figures in the group escape positive identification.

Clay declared that "annexation and war with Mexico are identical" and that "Texas ought not to be received into the Union, as an integral part of it, in declared opposition to the wishes of a considerable and respectable portion of the Confederacy."

Van Buren, who in his pronouncement sounded more like a Whig than a Democrat, was also against annexation. He felt that it might lead to war and that the world would regard the United States as the wrongdoer and that this would destroy the country's reputation with

An 1844 lithograph by H. Bucholzer, published by James Baillie, N.Y.

"REQUESTING HIM TO RESIGN." The three New York committeemen ask President Tyler to step down, and while he does, Henry Clay, the Whig candidate, mounts the presidential chair. James K. Polk, the choice of the Democrats, tells his running mate: "I say Dallas—that's nuts for us. . . . I'll stand by to jump in."

Andrew Jackson (left) cries out: "By the Eternal! they are too late! that rascally Clay has got one foot in already!!!"

other nations. As lust for power had never in the past led America to aggression and conquest, said Van Buren, it should not do so now.

Tyler answered the objections of Clay and Van Buren in his message to the Senate. If Texas were not annexed now, it would be lost forever, and he quoted Andrew Jackson's warning that the "golden moment to obtain Texas must not be lost, or Texas must, from necessity, be thrown into the arms of England and be lost to the United States."

As the Whig convention met only four days after Clay's views became known, there was no time to organize an effective opposition to his candidacy. Thus he was renominated by acclamation.

The political principles of the Whigs were muddled.

In their platform they came out for "a well-regulated currency; a tariff for revenue to defray the necessary expenses of the government . . . the protection of the domestic labor . . . the distribution of the proceeds from the sales of public lands; a single term for the Presidency; a reform of executive usurpations; and generally such an administration of the affairs of the country as shall impart to every branch of the public service the greatest practical efficiency, controlled by a well-regulated and wise economy."

As the Democrats were to meet a month later, there was ample time to dislodge the front-running Van Buren, whose stand on Texas was deplored by the Southern wing of the party. Yet as most delegates had been chosen before Van Buren announced his position

An 1844 lithograph published by James Baillie, N.Y.

"POLITICAL COCKFIGHTERS." Clay, the Whig cock, triumphs over Polk, the Democrat cock, while politicians comment on the scene. Webster: "I'll bet one of my best chowders on the Kentucky Rooster." Van Buren: "They rejected me, let them look to their Champion!" Calhoun, Benton, Frelinghuysen (behind Clay) and Dallas (far right) stay silent, but Jackson speaks out: "By the Eternal. I doubt the pluck of that Cock from Tennessee [Polk], if he does go for Texas."

on Texas, they were bound to cast their votes for him.

The mouthpiece of the Democrats, the *Globe,* insisted that Van Buren had not lost a single vote because of his Texas statement. The movement against him was instigated by Calhoun, "the last card of this desperate competitor who has been playing for twenty-five years for the Presidency with the frenzy of a gamester. It cannot win." But it *did* win. The opposition to Van Buren played a clever game. They insisted on the two-thirds rule, which had been so helpful to the "little magician" in the past but now would thwart his ambitions.

One hundred and forty-eight delegates supported the adoption of the two-thirds rule but 116 voted against it. The North was in disarray. United, the delegates could have defeated the motion, but the voting showed that unity could not be accomplished.

Thus the balloting begun. One hundred and seventy-eight votes were needed for victory. On the first trial Van Buren led with 146 votes against 83 for Lewis Cass and 24 for Richard M. Johnson, the Vice-President in the Van Buren administration. Ballot after ballot was taken without a marked change. On the seventh ballot Van Buren's vote sank to a mere 99 votes.

As North and South were in deadlock, unable to agree on either Van Buren or Cass, a compromise candidate had to be found. The historian George Bancroft, a Massachusetts delegate, suggested James K. Polk of Tennessee and made an impassioned plea for him.

Polk was one of the most faithful supporters of

An 1844 lithograph issued by H. R. Robinson, N.Y.

"THE HARRY-CANE" hits Polk as he runs "To Texas" holding the issues: Annexation, Subtreasury and Free Trade. A woolly ram attacks him; the tools of industries which ask for a high protective tariff shower upon his head. Polk exclaims: "It is my opinion, that Wool should be duty-free."

"THE FOX IS BURIED." Ex-President Van Buren, who failed to win the Democratic nomination because of his stand on the Texas issue, is borne to his grave by the decrepit Jackson horse.

The cart is driven by President Tyler, whose son writes "Ahasuerus" on a board (the king in the Bible—Xerxes, the Persian ruler—the conqueror of Greece and the destroyer of Nineveh). The two mourners behind the cart are Senator Benton and Senator Calhoun. Benton holds a sack of his celebrated "Mint Drops" (gold coins). The gravediggers are Webster and Henry Clay.

An 1844 lithograph published by James Baillie, N.Y.

President Jackson, with whom he had been on friendly terms ever since his early days in the Tennessee legislature. As a Congressman he led the fight on Jackson's behalf against the Bank. As Speaker of the House he was accused by the opposition of being a slave of Old Hickory. But most Representatives considered Polk an impartial presiding officer who carried out his duties with composure in spite of taunts from the Whigs.

The Democrats admired Polk, and the Whigs hated him. On one of his last days as Speaker of the House, Henry Clay came over from the Senate to shout with feeling at him from the visitor's gallery: "Go home, God damn you! Go home where you belong!"

Polk had only one term as Governor; in the two subsequent elections he was defeated. By 1844 he was groomed for the Vice Presidency, but after Van Buren issued his Texas statement he was considered as a candidate for the Presidency. Jackson met with his political advisers at the Hermitage and decided on him. And his word carried weight with the party leaders.

"Let Texas be reannexed," the Washington *Daily Globe* reported Polk as saying on May 6, 1844, "and

"THE RACE COURSE." Henry Clay on a shell with a "Tariff and Domestic Manufactures" sail: "We've got the wind and tide in our favor. The people expect me at the White House."

In the water, Polk, Benton and Dallas are clinging to the "Texas Bladder," while the sinking Van Buren cries out: "As I haven't got the bladder, I will try to float on my back."

An 1844 lithograph by H. Bucholzer

An 1844 lithograph issued by H. R. Robinson, N.Y.

POLK'S CONFLICTING STATEMENTS. Riding backward on his donkey, Polk exclaims: "I had steadily, during the period I was a Representative in Congress, been opposed to a Protective Policy"; but his flag reads: "I am in Favor of a Tariff for revenue."

The Negro pulling the tail: "I don't know what Massa Polk tink, me only wish de Jack Donkeys head & ears be on dis end.—and he'll beat himself 10 mile an hour Sartan."

the authority and laws of the United States be established and maintained within her limits, as also in the Oregon Territory, and let the fixed policy of our government be, not to permit Great Britain or any other foreign power to plant a colony or hold dominion over any portion of the people or territory of either."

On the eighth ballot he received 44 votes. On the ninth, Benjamin Butler, who managed Van Buren's candidacy, withdrew Van Buren's name and shifted New York's vote to "Young Hickory." Other states followed, making him, the first genuine "dark horse,"

candidate.

Clay learned of Polk's nomination at his estate in Kentucky. His son came in with a broad smile, asking him to guess who the Democrats nominated. Clay pondered: "Matty? Cass? Buchanan?" but each time his son shook his head no. Then Clay laughed, "Don't tell me they've been such fools as to take Calhoun or Johnson!" His son again said no and the exasperated Clay asked, "Then who the devil is it?" And when he heard "James K. Polk," he poured himself a drink and said, "Beat again, by God!"

An 1844 lithograph by Edward W. Clay, published by A. Donnelly, N.Y.

THE POLKA, the new fashionable dance, was described as "one step forward and two steps back." The dancers are Calhoun, Tyler, Johnson, Cass, Polk and Dallas. The Whig ticket makes comments as Jackson and Van Buren set the tempo.

An 1843 (?) lithograph in the New York Public Library

THE DEVIL SLIPS "Tariff Protection" to Clay: "Beloved Son, these instruments will serve my cause better than anything else I can devise." Frelinghuysen: "They are lovely in their Lives and in their Deaths they will not be divided!"

Silas Wright, Senator from New York, was chosen for the second place. When he learned of his nomination he telegraphed. "I am not and cannot under any circumstances be a candidate before your convention for that office." He felt it inopportune that the presidential and vice presidential candidates should have opposing views on such a vital political issue as annexation: Polk was for it, while Wright opposed it. It was the first and only time in the history of presidential elections that a candidate selected for the office refused to accept the candidacy. The convention then nominated George M. Dallas of Pennsylvania instead.

The Democratic platform was virtually the same as four years before save for three added planks. One of them stated that any law for the distribution of the proceeds from the sale of public lands among the states would be inexpedient and unconstitutional; the other

An 1844 lithograph by H. Bucholzer, issued by James Baillie, N.Y.

SOLD FOR WANT OF USE. The three chained animals—Tyler as an ass, Polk as a goose and Van Buren as a fox—are auctioned off by Clay, who exhorts his running mate, Frelinghuysen: "Stir them up Theodore, and let the gentlemen see."

said that the party was opposed to taking from the President the limited veto which had "thrice saved the American people from the corrupt and tyrannical domination of the Bank of the United States"; the third once declared "that our title to the whole of the Territory of Oregon is clear and unquestionable, that no portion of the same ought to be ceded to England or any other power, and that the reoccupation of Oregon and the reannexation of Texas at the earliest practicable period are great American measures, which the Convention recommends to the cordial support of the Democracy of the Union."

The platform shrewdly linked the "reannexation of Texas" with the "reoccupation of Oregon." (The "re-" meant that Oregon had been part of the United States by settlement and treaty and that Texas had been acquired through the Louisiana Purchase but was later

An 1844 lithograph published by James Baillie, N.Y.

THE STEAMER "BALLOT BOX" pulls Van Buren, Benton, Dallas, Jackson and Polk up the Salt River of defeat. Jackson: "By the eternal! Polk dont give up the ship." Van Buren exclaims: "I never sailed so far up this river before."

An 1844 lithograph published by James Baillie, N.Y.

"CLEANSING THE AUGEAN STABLE"—The Whig candidates Clay and Frelinghuysen throw their rivals Polk and Dallas out the window while Congressman Wise of Virginia refuses to let Lady Texas enter the room. Calhoun is holding Van Buren, "the Kinderhook fox"; Webster is shoveling Senator Benton's popular gold coins—the "mint drops." From the window Jackson calls out: "By the eternal! We shant know the old place, these fellows have gutted it so completely."

surrendered to Spain.) It turned out to be a good campaign slogan—"All of Texas, all of Oregon"—and the Democrats made the most of it. Oregon would add "free" land to the United States and bring in the Northern vote, Texas would enlarge the slave territory and carry Southern approval.

The Democrat voiced the hope that in future campaigns the American democracy would place its trust "not in fictitious symbols, not in displays and appeals insulting to the judgment and subversive of the intellect of the people, but in a clear reliance upon the intelligence, patriotism, and the discriminating justice of the American people." This was their rebuttal of the log-cabin campaign of four years before.

The same day the Democrats met in Baltimore another convention assembled in the same city. It was the meeting of the dissatisfied Whigs and disgruntled Demo-

crats who turned against their parties' policies. Each one of the delegates wore a large button with a star on it to signify the annexation of Texas. Without much enthusiasm they nominated Tyler, but when Tyler saw that he had no hope of winning the election he withdrew his name.

And there was the party of the Abolitionists presenting James G. Birney of New York, with Thomas Morris of Ohio as his running mate. Their platform declared that "human brotherhood is a cardinal principle of true democracy, as well as of pure Christianity, which spurns all inconsistent limitations; and neither the political party which repudiates it, nor the political system which is not based upon it, can be truly democratic or permanent"; therefore "the Liberty Party . . . will demand the absolute and unqualified divorce of the general government from slavery, and also the restoration

JACKSON EXECUTES THE COON, THE SYM
OF THE WHIGS. On the scaffold stand Clay and Fre
huysen; in the foreground, Van Buren and Benton.
An 1844 lithograph published by J. Baillie

Illustrated London News, *November 24, 1844*
THE GREAT WHIG PROCESSION ON BROADWAY

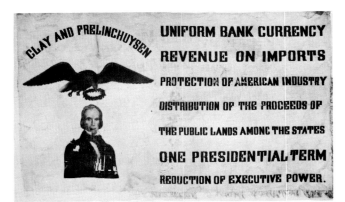

CLAY AND FRELINGHUYSEN

UNIFORM BANK CURRENCY
REVENUE ON IMPORTS
PROTECTION OF AMERICAN INDUSTRY
DISTRIBUTION OF THE PROCEEDS OF
THE PUBLIC LANDS AMONG THE STATES
ONE PRESIDENTIAL TERM
REDUCTION OF EXECUTIVE POWER.

Smithsonian Institution
A CLAY BANNER WITH HIS POLITICAL BELIEFS

Author's collection
ELECTION DAY AT A NEW YORK POLLING BOOTH

of equality of rights among men."

As the campaign got under way, the Democrats proved how much they had learned from the Whigs. Four years ago the Whigs had cried "Tippecanoe and Tyler too"; now the Democrats coined their promising slogans "All Oregon or none" and "Fifty-four forty or fight."

The Whigs circulated the cry of "Who is James K. Polk?"—a question supposedly asked by some Democrats waiting to fire the victory cannon for Van Buren, Calhoun or Cass. In that day of great figures, Polk did not stand out. He could not speak eloquently like Webster, think as well as Calhoun, and he had not the following of Clay. He was short and unimposing. He was known to be incorruptible, a worthy man but not distinguished. Yet General Jackson had given the opinion that in Polk's "extraordinary power of labor, both mental and physical, he united that tact and judgment which are requisite to the successful direction of such an office as that of Chief Magistrate." This was enough for the Democrats; Polk became "Young Hickory." The Whigs might cry "Clay and Frelinghuysen," but the Democrats had the more effective slogan of "Polk, Dallas, Texas, and Democracy."

In spite of their platform reliance on the "discriminating justice of the American people," the Democrats called Clay a heavy gambler and drinker, the inventor of poker, a rake, a derelict, and a Sabbath-breaker. He was accused of saying, "If we cannot have black slaves we must have white ones." The Whigs retaliated by saying that Polk, a Colonel of the Tennessee Militia, had never fired a shot; he was "a petty scoundrel," and a slave driver. And there was always the memory of the "corrupt bargain," with Clay swinging his vote to Adams, and making him President, and being rewarded by becoming his Secretary of State.

A minor issue in the campaign was the one-term limit for the Presidency. The Whigs had a one-term plank in their platform, but Clay kept silent about it. Though the Democrats had no such plank, in his letter of acceptance Polk wrote: "I deem the present to be the proper occasion to declare, that if the nomination made by the convention shall be confirmed by the people, and result in my election, I shall enter . . . the office with the settled purpose of not being a candidate for re-election."

Every trick and fraud was used to further the success of the candidates. The Democratic political bosses rushed through mass naturalization of aliens so the new Americans could cast their votes. In the three weeks before the election alone thousands of aliens in New York State were turned into citizens. A boss at Plaquemines, a parish below New Orleans, sent a boatload of Democrats up the Mississippi. The boat stopped at three different spots so the men could vote at each place.

An 1844 lithograph issued by John Childs, N.Y.

THE RETURNS OF THE ELECTION: The Polk and Dallas ticket defeated Clay and Frelinghuysen. The Whigs' funeral, with the symbol of the party, the coon, moves toward the U.S. Bank, already buried by the Whigs' defeat in the 1832 election. From heaven come the words of Andrew Jackson: "My country is saved! I am now ready for my last resting place."

Though Clay was more popular in the country, the people gave the Presidency to Polk because of his unequivocal stand for annexation. He received 1,337,243 votes against Clay's 1,299,062. It was a close contest. In four states Polk's plurality was no more than ten thousand; in three states less than a thousand. But in the electoral count the Polk-Dallas ticket received 170 votes to 105 for the Whig candidates.

Clay lost New York's 36 electoral votes by 4,000 votes only. If the Abolitionists had not put up a separate candidate polling 62,300 votes, Clay would have won. But Birney took enough votes away from Clay to give victory to Polk. Young Abraham Lincoln in Illinois, then ardently for Clay, said: "If the Whig abolitionists of New York had voted with us . . . Mr. Clay would now be President, Whig principles in the ascendant and Texas not annexed; whereas, by the division, all that either had at stake in the contest was lost."

President Tyler saw in the election returns a mandate for immediate annexation. He asked Congress for a joint resolution (which needed only a simple majority rather than two-thirds in the Senate as for a treaty), and when it was passed early in 1845, he asked Texas to become the twenty-eighth state of the Union. Four days later James K. Polk was inaugurated.

In his inaugural addressed Polk said that "Texas was once a part of our country—was unwisely ceded away to a foreign power—is now independent, and possesses an undoubted right . . . to merge her sovereignty as a separate and indeepndent state in ours." He felt that expansion of the country would "extend the dominions of peace over additional territories and increasing millions." And he spoke of the country's "right" to Oregon.

The road to America's "manifest destiny" was clear.

183

ZACHARY TAYLOR and MILLARD FILLMORE

On the day of his inauguration President Polk confided to George Bancroft, the eminent historian and now his Secretary of the Navy, that he had four objectives: to reduce the tariff, to re-establish the Independent Treasury, to settle the Oregon dispute, and to acquire California. Within a year he had achieved his first three objectives, and before his term ended he had accomplished the fourth as well—California was part of the United States.

Polk was a good administrator; he was a hard-working man. A Washington editor wrote of him: "He works from 10 to 12 hours in every 24. He holds two Cabinet meetings a week. He sees visitors two hours every day when the Cabinet is not employed." And Polk said: "No President who performs his duty faithfully and conscientiously can have any leisure. If he intrusts the details and smaller matters to subordinates constant errors will occur. I prefer to supervise the whole operation of the Government myself rather than intrust the public business to subordinates, and this makes my duties very great."

He fashioned himself after Old Hickory, whom he admired; he wanted to be like Jackson. "He knew how to get things done, which is the first necessity of government, and he knew what he wanted done, which is the second," wrote Bernard De Voto of him.

He exercised firm control over Congress. He not only offered a carefully prepared program, but, as a former Speaker of the House, he knew how to translate this program into law. A Whig Representative remarked that any legislator who dares to differ with the President "must walk the plank. He has but one alternative, either to stand on the platform with the Executive, or be pushed into the sea."

Polk was against Clay and his American System. He was firmly against internal improvements at government expense and the distribution of the surplus between the states. He wanted to "bring the Government back to what it was intended to be, a plain economical Government."

He succeeded in persuading Congress to pass a new tariff bill, reducing the rates somewhat and making it a more equitable one. He also succeeded in reactivating his Independent Treasury Bill, which the Whigs under Tyler had voted down.

On Independence Day, 1845, the Texas legislature voted to join the Union. The Senate ratified the treaty, and Texas became the twenty-eighth state.

America was in an expansive mood. The country's "manifest destiny" pointed to the land between Texas and California, the huge area belonging to Mexico, to the shores of the Pacific. Polk wanted to purchase the territory, but if Mexico could not be persuaded to make the bargain, he was ready to take it by force.

In November, 1845, he sent John Slidell to Mexico, to negotiate the unsettled issues between the countries. Slidell offered to assume Mexico's debt to American citizens if Mexico would recognize the Rio Grande as the southern and western boundary of Texas; he offered for the territory of New Mexico five million dollars and said that "money would be no object for California."

But he was not recognized by the Mexicans. President Herrera would not receive him, nor would General Paredes, who succeeded Herrera.

ZACHARY TAYLOR
Daguerreotype in the Library of Congress

CANDIDATES IN 1848

ZACHARY TAYLOR (1784–1850) had been a regular soldier since 1806. His victories in the Mexican War made him a military hero and the Whig presidential candidate. He won with 1,360,099 votes to 1,220,544 for Cass.

MILLARD FILLMORE (1800–1874), successful lawyer and former Antimason, was the most popular Whig in New York, a state crucial to winning the election. Chosen for the second place, he came to office on Taylor's death.

LEWIS CASS (1782–1866), the prominent Western politician, Governor of the Michigan Territory from 1814 to 1832, Secretary of War, Minister to France and U.S. Senator, became the candidate of the Democrats.

WILLIAM O. BUTLER (1791–1880), former Congressman, served in the War of 1812 and the Mexican War. Nominated for the Vice Presidency by the Democrats, he was chosen mainly because of his military record.

MARTIN VAN BUREN (1782–1862), the former President, was the candidate of the antislavery Free Soilers. He was able to take enough Democratic votes away from Cass to give the election to the Whig ticket.

HENRY A. S. DEARBORN (1783–1851), the son of a military leader in the Revolution, a minor Massachusetts politician, was nominated for the second place by the Native Americans, the party against foreigners and Roman Catholics.

Library of Congress
MARGARET MACKALL SMITH (1788–1852) married Zachary Taylor on June 21, 1810. They had five daughters (two of them died in infancy) and one son.

In delicate health, she did not go with her husband to Washington. Her daughter Betty, the newly married wife of Colonel Bliss, substituted as hostess in the White House.

To strengthen Slidell's bargaining position, Polk sent General Zachary Taylor with a detachment to the Texas border, ready to "protect what, in event of annexation, will be our western frontier." Mexico regarded this as an act of aggression. On May 12, 1846, word reached Washington that Mexican troops had crossed the Rio Grande and that there had been a skirmish between Mexicans and Americans. But by then Polk had already written his message asking Congress for a declaration of war. Bancroft counseled restraint and advised the President to wait until Mexico had committed a definite act of hostility. Now that moment had come, and Polk quickly redrafted his message. "The cup of forbearance has been exhausted," it read. "After reiterated menaces, Mexico has passed over the

An 1848 lithograph published by A. Donnelly, N.Y.

ON TO THE WHITE HOUSE. General Zachary Taylor's locomotive moves toward the White House, from which President Polk calls out: "I wish Trist would hurry up that treaty!" (referring to diplomatic agent Nicholas P. Trist's attempt to negotiate a Texas treaty). From the back of the locomotive, Henry Clay thumbs his nose at Lewis Cass, the Democratic candidate who is racing Zachary Taylor, the Whigs' nominee. In the right background, General Winfield Scott, fatigued with "political, civil, and Military" exertions, wants to get off his high horse for "a hasty plate of soup"—the phrase he once used to explain a brief luncheon absence to the War Secretary. Later on he would be styled "Marshal Tureen."

In the foreground the tombstone is marked, "Hic Jacet Greely," a reference to Horace Greeley's political misfortunes.

boundary of the United States, has invaded our territory and shed American blood upon American soil." The next day, on May 13, Congress declared that "by the act of the Republic of Mexico, a state of war exists between that government and the United States."

Most Whigs, except in the South, were opposed to the war. They questioned whether it was a war of conquest or a war for boundaries, whether it was started by Mexico or by the American troops who invaded Mexico. They charged that Polk had provoked the conflict to enlarge the slaveholding territory of the South. Congressman Abraham Lincoln, "the lonely Whig from Illinois," rose in the House and introduced his "spot resolutions," calling upon the President to name the exact spot on which American blood had been shed.

Was it in Mexico? Or was it on American soil?

But the country was for war. Americans hungered to possess the entire continent; they wanted all the land between the Atlantic and the Pacific.

John C. Frémont, camping with his exploring party near Klamath Lakes, moved into the lower Sacramento Valley. On June 14, 1846, in California, American squatters hoisted a flag with a bear and a star on it and proclaimed the "California Republic." On July 2 Commodore John D. Sloat, in command of the Pacific squadron, took Monterey and proclaimed California part of the United States. On August 1 Colonel Stephen W. Kearny marched into New Mexico, took Santa Fe and led a small detachment to San Diego. Within a few weeks all of the territory of California and New Mexico

An 1848 lithograph published by H. R. Robinson, N.Y.

THE ASSASSINATION OF THE SAGE OF ASHLAND. In choosing their candidate, the Whigs turned to General Zachary Taylor, the hero of the Mexican War, bypassing Henry Clay, the leader of their party.

As the group of political "assassins"—led by Daniel Webster on the left—approaches its victim, they speak lines from Shakespeare's *Julius Caesar* while the unsuspecting Clay continues reading the front page of Greeley's *Tribune*.

was held by the troops of the United States.

In Mexico General Winfield Scott took Vera Cruz the following March, and moved his soldiers into the country's interior. A month earlier, February 22–23, General Zachary Taylor had won the battle of Buena Vista and was pressing the Mexicans from the north. And Scott occupied Mexico City in September.

Polk, as Senator Benton observed, "wanted a small war, just large enough to require a treaty of peace, and not large enough to make military reputations dangerous for the Presidency." It did not work out that way. Both General Scott and General Taylor were Whigs, and both made reputations.

Polk, like other Presidents after him who involved the country in so-called small wars, was like the sorcerer's apprentice—he could not stop once he got started. "What embarrassed Polk," wrote Professor Norman Graebner, "was his need of pursuing the war against an ephemeral enemy that continued to lose all the battles but refused to ask for terms of peace. If the purpose of the war was peace, at what stage in the progression of American victories would a peace be conquered?"

Polk lamented: "I am in the unenviable position of being held responsible for the conduct of the Mexican War, when I have no support either from Congress or

An 1848 lithograph published by James Baillie, N.Y.

WHIG HARMONY. The horses with Taylor's and Clay's heads draw the cart representing the Whig party in opposite directions. Clay, who "would rather be right than to be President," pulls toward "Salt River"—to defeat. The coachmen are Brother Jonathan, symbolizing the American people, and editor Horace Greeley. The wheels of the car roll over a large rock: the Wilmot Proviso, the Congressman's amendment prohibiting slavery in the territory acquired from Mexico.

from the two officers highest in command in the field. How long this state of things will continue I cannot foresee."

Assailed in Congress and in the press, he kept to his path. He dispatched Nicholas P. Trist to join Scott's headquarters and to start negotiations with the Mexican Government. Early in 1848 Trist, who in the meanwhile became a close friend of Scott, was ready with an agreement. The treaty of Guadalupe Hidalgo gave California and New Mexico to the United States. Mexico received $15 million for them; the United States assumed the claim of American citizens against Mexico to the tune of $3 million. "It was not brief, cheap, and bloodless," said Benton about the war. "It had become long, costly and sanguinary."

The other crucial issue during Polk's administration was Oregon. In the platform of the Democratic convention Western delegates had inserted the unattainable demand: "All Oregon or none." They demanded all the territory way up to the Alaskan boundary. "Fifty-four Forty or Fight" was a catchy slogan, but the traditional American offer to Britain had been to divide the territory of Oregon at the forty-ninth parallel. In his message to Congress in December 1845 Polk said that "no compromise which the United States ought to accept can be effected."

Manifest Destiny.

New Mexico, California Chihuahua, Zacatecas. MEXICO. Peru, Yucatan, Cuba.

A WAR PRESIDENT.

GAS

PROGRESSIVE DEMOCRACY.

An 1848 lithograph published by Peter Smith, N.Y.
THE CANDIDATE OF THE DEMOCRATS—LEWIS CASS. Cartoonists used the rhyming of Cass's name with "gass."

But he listened to both sides—to those who were for the 54°40′ and to those who advocated the 49° settlement. Senator Jacob W. Miller of New Jersey noted that the President's position seemed "like the mercury in the barometer, to go up and down according as gentlemen placed their fingers on the bulb. When touched by the warm hands of the Senators from Indiana, from Illinois, and from Ohio, it immediately went up to 54°40′; but when the cool and distinguished Senator from North Carolina put his finger upon it, it fell as quickly to 49°." At last, after much vacillation, Polk accepted the forty-ninth-parallel boundary.

It was before this backdrop that the parties prepared for the election. The Whigs were looking for a winning candidate. Henry Clay was still their leader, but because of his insistence that the party renounce "any wish or desire on our part to acquire any foreign territory whatever, for the purpose of propagating slavery,

or of introducing slaves from the United States," he now faced the opposition of the Southern "Cotton" Whigs, while his former proslavery pronouncements antagonized the New England "Conscience" Whigs, those against slavery.

The fortunes of the party's other giant, Daniel Webster, were no better; he had no support in the South and little strength in the West. Thus the Whigs turned to the war hero, General Zachary Taylor. His victories in Mexico, his Southern birth, his ownership of three hundred slaves, his clean political record (in his entire life he had never cast a vote for anyone) made him the most "available" candidate. What his political beliefs were, Heaven only knew.

On Washington's Birthday in 1848, which coincided with the first anniversary of Buena Vista, the Louisiana state convention formally proposed his nomination.

Taylor made it known that he was "a Whig but not

THE WHIG CANDIDATE—
GENERAL ZACHARY TAYLOR
An 1848 lithograph published by Peter Smith, N.Y.

An 1848 lithograph published by James Baillie, N.Y.

QUESTIONING THE PRESIDENTIAL CANDIDATE. Taylor tells the questioners: "You'll find out what I think, when I'm President, & then it will be my part to command & yours to obey."

In the letter which secured him the nomination, Taylor wrote that on the issues of tariff, currency and internal improvement he would carry out the people's will as expressed through Congress—a noncommittal commitment.

Horace Greeley, who opposed Taylor at first because in his opinion he was not a true Whig, exclaims: "We must take up with Matty [Martin Van Buren]," the other man says: "We must elect Hale [John Hale, the Liberty party candidate]."

an ultra Whig," and "if elected, I would not be the mere President of a party. I would endeavor to act independent of party domination. I should feel bound to administer the government untrammeled by party schemes." This was enough for the Whigs to make him their candidate. As the opposing groups of the party could not agree, no platform was issued.

The Democrats were no less divided; they, too, were split on the slavery issue.

In New York state the "Hunkers" and the "Barnburners" fought for recognition. The Hunkers (named because they "hunkered" for office) were somewhat conservative in their policies; while the Barnburners (a name taken from the story of a Dutch farmer who burned down his barn to get rid of the rats) were mostly old Locofocos, firmly opposed to slavery.

Both groups sent full delegations to the Democratic convention at Baltimore, each claiming to represent the party in New York. Both delegations were admitted, each delegate being given half a vote. As the decision was not acceptable to either faction the Barnburners withdrew and the Hunkers refused to vote.

An 1848 lithograph published by H. R. Robinson, N.Y.

A PHRENOLOGIST reading character from the formation of the skull undertakes to discover the principles of Zachary Taylor, the Whig candidate. Horace Greeley (at left) notes the phrenologist's findings: "Quick fiery temper," "Obstinate & Mulish," "Disregard for things Sacred," "Utterly wanting in all Sympathy." The final judgment is that Taylor is incompetent, "& so say his developments."

And General Taylor says: "When I get to Washington I will turn [Postmaster General] Cave Johnson out, and put a military man in his place." A recent "dead letter" regulation seemingly is the most important thing on his mind.

Polk was not a candidate for re-election, nor was he popular enough to be drafted. To oppose General Taylor the Democrats nominated another general— Lewis Cass of Michigan.

The Democratic platform declared that the powers of government should be construed strictly; that Congress had no authority to carry on internal improvements or to enact a protective tariff. It further held that proceeds from the sale of public lands should not be distributed; that the funds of the government should not be deposited in the banks; that Congress had no power to meddle with the domestic institutions of the states; and finally, that the efforts of the abolitionists to induce Congress to interfere with slavery were dangerous to the stability of the Union.

The Barnburners, who had left the convention, met at Utica again, naming former President Martin Van Buren as their presidential candidate, with Henry Dodge of Wisconsin as his running mate. They adopted a strong antislavery platform.

Another antislavery group from the Whig party met in Buffalo and lined up behind Van Buren, but for the

An 1848 lithograph published by Peter Smith, N.Y.

THE SLAVERY ISSUE was heatedly discussed. Here Horace Greeley pushes Free Soil candidate Martin Van Buren into the arms of the radical abolitionists. John Van Buren, who spurned the Free Soil nomination in his father's favor, looks on. The Free Soil influence was decisive in the election; it split the Democratic vote and gave the Presidency to Taylor.

An 1848 lithograph published by H. R. Robinson, N.Y.

THE THREE CANDIDATES. Both Lewis Cass, the Democratic nominee, and Zachary Taylor, the candidate of the Whigs, are tumbling into Salt River, while Van Buren, the candidate of the Free Soilers, "wins" the buffalo hunt.

second place they chose Charles Francis Adams, son of one President and grandson of another. They adopted an antislavery platform, "in common resolve to maintain the rights of free labor against the aggression of slave power, and to secure free soil for a free people," and were determined "not to extend, nationalize or encourage slavery but to limit, localize and discourage it." Their slogan was "Free Soil, Free Speech, Free Labor, and Free Men."

A host of minor parties named candidates. The Native Americans were for General Henry A. S. Dearborn of Massachusetts for the second place; for the first place they were satisfied with General Taylor. The Liberty or Abolition party named John P. Hale of New Hampshire for President and Leicester King of Ohio for Vice President (later Hale withdrew and threw his support to Van Buren). The Liberty League, a group which had broken away from the Liberty party, offered

An 1848 lithograph published by Peter Smith, N.Y.

TO BRIDGE THE CHASM and avoid falling into "Salt River" (defeat) was Free Soiler Van Buren's aim, here encouraged by the Whig-Abolitionists Garrison, Greeley and "Abby Folsom." Butler, Calhoun, Cass and John Van Buren (on the right) stand on the Democratic platform. Cass notes that Van Buren has been in Salt River once before.

Gerrit Smith for President and the Reverend Charles E. Foote for Vice President. The Industrial Congress, asking for free land for settlers and exemption of the homestead from seizure for debts, endorsed Smith but substituted William Waitt for Vice President.

The slavery issue confused the campaign. The Democrats could not openly advocate the extension of slaveholding territory for fear of losing their support in the North. The Whigs were in a similar predicament with their two opposing factions, the "Conscience" and the "Cotton" Whigs.

Matters came to a head when President Polk asked Congress to appropriate two million dollars for the obvious purpose of making an advance payment to Mexico for the sale of her land. When David Wilmot, a Democratic Congressman from Pennsylvania, introduced his proviso that "neither slavery nor involuntary servitude shall ever exist" in the territory so acquired,

MARTIN
VAN BUREN
Daguerreotype in the Chicago Historical Society

195

THE LAST DAGUERREOTYPE TAKEN OF TAYLOR

THE INAUGURATION OF ZACHARY TAYLOR. The traditional date for the inaugural was the fourth of March. As this fell on a Sunday in 1849, the ceremonies were postponed until Monday. It was a gloomy day, with a raw wind and occasional snow. General Taylor left Willard's Hotel in an open carriage, going to the Irving, where outgoing President Polk joined him. Together they headed the procession down Pennsylvania Avenue.

A special platform had been erected over the steps in front of the east portico of the Capitol building, and an unusually large crowd of thirty thousand persons was on hand. Taylor read his address "very badly as to his pronunciation and manner," thought outgoing President Polk, then took the oath of office from Chief Justice Roger B. Taney.

"THE DEMOCRATIC FUNERAL of 1848"—Martin Van Buren, the "Fox," and Lewis Cass, the "gas bag," are carried to their burial by Democratic Senators Houston, Benton and Calhoun. They are followed by Representatives Allen, Kendall, Woodbury and Worth, who also take the body of President Polk.

ABIGAIL POWERS (1798–1853), the daughter of a clergyman, married Fillmore on February 5, 1826, and bore him two children, Millard and Mary. In the White House she started a library and installed an iron range for cooking. She died in March 1853, the month Fillmore completed his term.

Five years later—on February 10, 1858—Fillmore married again, this time Caroline Carmichael McIntosh.

Photo: Mathew B. Brady
MILLARD FILLMORE (1800–1874), who took the oath of office after Taylor's death on July 9, 1850.

Polk shot back angrily that Wilmot's suggestion was "a mischievous and foolish amendment" which he would veto. In reality there was no need for the proviso; the arid wastes of New Mexico and the cattle ranches of California were not suited to slave labor. But the North upheld it as a matter of principle and strategy.

As the Democratic vote was split between General Cass and Van Buren, the Whigs won the election. Not counting the electoral vote of New York, Taylor and Cass had the same number of votes—127. But as Van Buren received over 120,000 popular votes (which otherwise would have gone to the Democratic ticket), the state's 36 electoral votes went to Taylor, who won.

Taylor's victory had three memorable results: (1) the impressive vote for Martin Van Buren on the Free Soil ticket indicated that the slavery issue could no longer be avoided; (2) the clean sweep which followed in the civil service caused Nathaniel Hawthorne to lose his job in the Salem Custom House, whereupon he began writing *The Scarlet Letter;* (3) a Democratic newspaper dismissed Walt Whitman, giving him time to compose his *Leaves of Grass.*

FRANKLIN PIERCE

Slavery weighed heavily on the national mind, overshadowing and eliminating all other political issues. The dissension among the sections grew to frightening proportions.

Congress argued about the organization of the newly acquired territories; should they be allowed to have slavery or should slavery be prohibited within their borders? Polk ended his term and still no decision had been reached about California, New Mexico or Utah. (Oregon had already been organized as a territory without slavery.)

One of the first acts of the new President was to encourage the inhabitants of California and New Mexico to draw up constitutions and apply for admission to the Union. The Californians, in urgent need of authorized civil government, lost no time in taking President Taylor's advice. The gold rush had brought a mass of "Forty-Niners" to their state, and the temporary military government was inadequate to handle the rough and violent crowd; drunken brawls, robberies, murders, lynchings were the order of the day.

In September 1849 a convention at Monterey drew up a constitution; after it was ratified, the Californians elected a governor and other officers, and they took over the government without waiting for formal admission. The following year New Mexico too adopted a constitution, as did the Mormons of Utah.

The South resented the growth of free territory; if California were to be admitted as a free state, half the territory gained from Mexico would be lost to slavery and the political supremacy of the North would be further enhanced.

The slavery issue split North and South into two hostile camps. The North resisted the establishment of slavery where it had not existed before. The South argued that slaves were property and as such were protected by the Constitution; therefore, slavery should be allowed wherever the flag flew.

To bridge the gap between the two opponents, many compromise proposals were offered. One was to extend the 36°30′ line of the Missouri Compromise to the Pacific, thus dividing the country into two: the Northern part would be free territory, the Southern one would be slaveholding land. Another one advocated popular sovereignty whereby the territories themselves were to decide about the question.

In December 1849, when the new Congress met, President Taylor asked for the admittance of California as a free state while New Mexico and Utah were to join the Union without reference to slavery.

The South was enraged. In a passionate speech the Southern Congressman Robert Toombs threatened: "I do not hesitate to avow before this House and the country, and in the presence of the living God, that if by your legislation you seek to drive us from the territories of California and New Mexico, purchased by the common blood and treasure of the whole people, and to abolish slavery in this District, thereby attempting to fix a national degradation upon half the states of this Confederacy, I am for disunion."

Politicians of both parties searched for a solution. On January 29, 1850, Henry Clay submitted his resolutions to the Senate so "peace, concord and harmony of the Union" could be established.

FRANKLIN PIERCE
Daguerreotype by Mathew B. Brady
Chicago Historical Society

CANDIDATES IN 1852

FRANKLIN PIERCE (1804–1869), the Democratic nominee, was the son of a New Hampshire Governor. A graduate of Bowdoin and a fighter in the Mexican War, he won with 1,601,474 votes to Scott's 1,386,580.

WILLIAM R. D. KING (1786–1853), Senator from Alabama, Minister to France, a moderate states' rights advocate, was the Democratic choice for the second place. He died a month after he took the oath of office in Cuba.

WINFIELD SCOTT (1786–1866), the 66-year-old, six-foot-five general of the Mexican War, became the Whigs' nominee on the fifty-third ballot, defeating Webster and Fillmore. He got only 42 electoral votes to Pierce's 254.

WILLIAM A. GRAHAM (1804–1875), the Governor of North Carolina, Fillmore's Secretary of the Navy and a moving spirit behind the expedition of Admiral Perry to Japan, was the choice of the Whigs for the second place.

JOHN PARKER HALE (1806–1873), U.S. Senator from New Hampshire and an ardent abolitionist, became the presidential candidate of the antislavery Free Soil party. In the election he received over 150,000 popular votes.

GEORGE W. JULIAN (1871–1899), an Indiana politician, was one of the leading antislavery men in Congress who opposed the Compromise. He was selected by the Free Soil party for the vice presidential candidacy.

JANE MEANS APPLETON (1806–1863), the daughter of a former president of Bowdoin College, married Pierce on November 10, 1834. She bore him three sons; all of them died early—the last one was killed before her very eyes in a train accident. Suffering from tuberculosis, she was a chronic invalid. In her depressed state she kept up a correspondence with her dead son.

Clay proposed:

1. Admission of California as a free state;

2. Establishment of territorial governments without any restriction as to slavery in the rest of the territory acquired from Mexico;

3. Determination of the disputed boundary between Texas and New Mexico;

4. Assumption of the bona fide public debt of Texas contracted prior to annexation, upon the condition that Texas relinquish her claim to any part of New Mexico;

5. Agreement that slavery in the District of Columbia might not be abolished without the consent of Maryland, and of the people of the District, and without just compensation to the owners of slaves;

6. Prohibition of slave trade in the District of Columbia;

7. Enactment of a more stringent fugitive slave law;

STUMP SPEAKING FOR A POLITICAL CANDIDATE IN THE COUNTRYSIDE DURING THE FIFTIES

8. Assertion that Congress had no power to interfere with the slave trade between the states.

Clay's compromise proposals gave rise to one of the most distinguished Congressional debates in the nation's history. Clay, Calhoun and Webster held the country spellbound with their oratory. The three had begun public life four decades before; all three were to die within the next two years; but with the last flickers of the fires which had burned so brightly in their souls, they once more spoke out for the country they loved.

With consumption racking his lungs, the 73-year-old Clay held the Senate floor for the better part of two days, pleading concessions from the North, appealing to the South for reasonableness.

Calhoun was so ill that he could not deliver his speech himself; Senator Mason of Virginia read it for him. "I have, Senators," said he, "believed from the first that the agitation of the subject of slavery would, if not prevented by some timely and effective measure, end in disunion." Calhoun admitted that the South was discontented because "the equilibrium between the two sections has been destroyed," and that the only way to save the Union was to allow the South "an equal right in the acquired territory" (meaning the admission of slavery in California and New Mexico). He urged the restoration of the power the South had once possessed and demanded that the North "cease the agitation of the slave question"; otherwise "let the states we represent agree to separate and part in peace. If you are unwilling we should part in peace, tell us so, and we shall know what to do when you reduce the question to submission or resistance."

Webster replied to Calhoun with his momentous Seventh of March speech. He was sixty-eight years old and

201

suffering from a liver ailment, his former magnificent voice was now gone, but the power of his arguments was as strong as ever. He pleaded for the preservation of the Union and for the support of the compromise. "Peaceable secession is an utter impossibility," said Webster. "I see that disruption must produce such a war as I will not describe in its twofold characters."

Webster's speech left a deep impression; it paved the way in the North for a compromise, strengthening the sentiment for the Union. Copies of the speech were in such demand that Webster himself mailed out over a hundred thousand to people who asked for it.

For nine months—from January to September—the Senate debated the compromise. Jefferson Davis was willing to "agree to the drawing of the line of 36°30′ through the territories acquired from Mexico, with the condition that in the same degree as slavery is prohibited north of that line, it shall be permitted to enter south of the line; and that the states which may be admitted into the Union shall come in under such constitutions as they think proper to form."

On July 9, 1850, while the debates were still raging, President Taylor—an opponent of the compromise measures—died. During the Fourth of July ceremonies, he had eaten cherries and wild fruits and had drunk iced water and cold milk to quench his thirst—a combination his constitution was not strong enough to take.

Vice President Millard Fillmore followed him in office, changed the administration's policy. With Webster as Secretary of State, the new President signed five

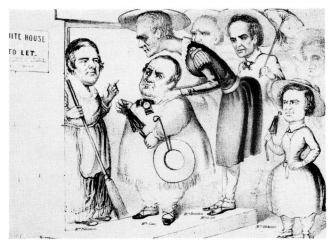

An 1852 lithograph by David C. Johnston in The Old Soldier
HOUSE HUNTING. "Mrs." Fillmore tells the other candidates not to take this one because "its a dreadfull damp nasty place," adding, "We may conclude to keep the house another term—*that is if we can get it.*"

PRESIDENT FILLMORE PEERS FROM A WHITE

WHITE HOUSE.

CASS INTERVENTION

NOMINATION for the PRESIDENCY Salary $24,000 Patronage $60,000,000.

Fillmore. Webster. Scott. Cass Douglass

An 1852 lithograph by David C. Johnston in The Old Soldier

HOUSE WINDOW TO SEE WEBSTER, SCOTT, CASS AND DOUGLAS RUN AFTER THE NOMINATION.

An 1852 lithograph published by N. Currier, New York

THE TWO WHO WERE CHOSEN AND THOSE WHO WERE NOT. Columbia is leading Winfield Scott and Franklin Pierce, the candidates of the two major parties. The others who sought the nomination—Sam Houston, John Crittenden, Thomas H. Benton, Millard Fillmore, John Bell, Lewis Cass, Stephen A. Douglas and Daniel Webster—look on.

bills. The first admitted California as a free state; the second created the Territory of New Mexico without the Wilmot Proviso and provided for the payment of ten million dollars to Texas as an indemnity for the surrender of the New Mexican land; the third created the Territory of Utah; the fourth contained drastic measures against fugitive slaves and against those who helped them to escape; the fifth abolished the slave trade in the District of Columbia.

With the compromise out of the way, the politicians looked to the next presidential contest. Among the Democrats three older men and one younger one were in line for the nomination. Lewis Cass, James Buchanan and William L. Marcy—all of them in public life for more than three decades—were challenged by the candidate of "Young America," 39-year-old Stephen A. Douglas. As none of the four could muster the majority, the balloting of the Democratic convention in Baltimore went on endlessly.

On the twenty-second trial Buchanan's vote rose to 104. Had Marcy come to his support, Buchanan could have been nominated, but Marcy would not make a move. After the thirty-third ballot the Buchanan forces, fearing a Cass victory, asked for adjournment. From their strategy meeting they emerged with an ingenious suggestion. To prove that none of the other candidates had sufficient strength, they proposed to release some of the Buchanan votes (but none from Pennsylvania, Georgia and Alabama) to the other candidates. And if none of those candidates could win with these additional votes, they would then have to give their support to Buchanan. The Buchanan men of course were certain that no other candidate would be able to score a victory. However, the plan did not work. Though none of the principal candidates did gain a majority, neither did Buchanan. The delegates had to look for a compromise candidate. The New Hampshire journalist and politician Edmund Burke wrote to his friend Franklin Pierce of

An 1868 lithograph by J. L. Magee, published by Thomas W. Strong, New York

RACING FOR THE PRESIDENCY. General Scott is riding on a cock; Pierce, on a goose. Scott: "What's the matter, Pierce? feel *Faint?* ha! ha! ha!" (This reference, constantly used in the campaign, is to Pierce's fainting spell on a Mexican Battlefield.) The embarrassed Pierce calls out: "O dear me! I shall *Faint.* I know I shall *Faint,* its *Constitutional.*"

New Hampshire: "The thing is about ripe. We have intimations from Pennsylvania and Virginia that they will soon lead off for you. The South will come in, so will Maine, Connecticut, and I think, all New England. Michigan will also. The prospects are more encouraging than ever."

Burke's prediction was correct. On the forty-seventh and forty-eighth ballots, a few votes were for Franklin Pierce. The Buchanan managers, trying to prove that Pierce could not win either, released a few of their votes to him. But on the forty-ninth ballot, when North Carolina swung to Pierce, the stampede began and in no time the dark-horse candidate from New Hampshire received all but 6 of the 286 votes, and became the Democratic choice. For the Vice Presidency William King of Alabama was chosen.

Pierce was the most acceptable candidate. A smiling, well-mannered politician with a winning personality and a blameless record, he was supported by the North and because of his Southern sympathies he had many friends in the South. "Young America" was delighted—Pierce was only forty-eight.

The son of a Governor of New Hampshire, he entered political life early. He was only twenty-five when he became a member of his state's General Court. In 1833 he was elected to Congress, and after two terms in the House he was sent to the Senate, where he served until 1842. He supported Jackson and followed his lead. Returning to Concord, he practiced law and managed local Democratic campaigns. He enlisted for the Mexican War and led an army from Vera Cruz; then illness put an end to his military career.

The Democratic platform repeated most of the 1848 resolutions and added an explicit plank about slavery, pledging the faithful execution of the compromise, including the Fugitive Slave Law, and promising resistance to "all attempts at renewing, in Congress or out of it, the agitation of the slavery question, under whatever

An 1852 lithograph published by Peter Smith, New York

A CONTESTED SEAT. Scott is holding the presidential chair while Pierce cries from the floor: "Do you want to knock a feller's brains out?" And Scott replies: "Sorry to disappoint you, Pierce; but *the People* wish *me,* to take this chair." Yet when election day came it was not the Whig Winfield Scott but the Democrat Franklin Pierce, whom the people elected.

shape or color the attempt may be made."

When the Whigs met they had as much difficulty in deciding on a candidate as the Democrats. On the first ballot President Fillmore had 133 votes against General Winfield Scott's 131 and Daniel Webster's 29. After fifty ballots there was still no result. At this point the Fillmore supporters promised the Webster managers to release their votes to Webster if he could get 41 votes from the North, but Webster could not round up so many Northern delegates. Thus the convention turned to General Winfield Scott—the hero of the Mexican War—on the fifty-third ballot.

The Whigs' platform acquiesced to the compromise laws "as a settlement in principle and substance of the dangerous and exciting questions which they embrace, and so far as they are concerned, we will maintain them and insist upon their strict enforcement until time and experience shall demonstrate the necessity of further legislation."

Henry J. Raymond, editor of *The New York Times,* revealed that a deal had been made with the Southern delegates, allowing the South to dictate the platform for letting the North nominate the candidate.

Scott's candidacy was not received with universal approval. He was assailed as a puppet of Senator William Seward, whose radical antislavery views were in opposition to those of the Southern Whigs, whereupon Seward issued a statement in which he declined "any public station or preferment whatever at the hands of the President of the United States, whether that President were Winfield Scott or any other man." Scott was also under attack because of his failure to support the compromise, and because he was friendly to the anti-foreign principles of the Native Americans.

A BAD EGG—
A CARICATURE OF PIERCE
Issued in 1852 by Peter Smith, New York

The Whigs' Northern antislavery wing broke away, refusing to support Scott. They joined the party of Free Democracy, which nominated John P. Hale for the Presidency and George W. Julian for the second place. They declared that "slavery is a sin against God, and a crime against man, which no human enactment or usage can make right; and that Christianity, humanity, and patriotism alike demand its abolition." Thus their platform asked for the repeal of the Fugitive Slave Law, for free farms, cheap postage, recognition of Haiti, arbitration of international disputes, internal improvements at Federal expense, and a liberal policy toward the foreign-born, and accepted the slogan "Free soil, free speech, free labor and free men."

There were the usual host of minor candidates. The Liberty Party nominated Gerrit Smith and Charles Durkee, and when both of them declined, a second convention was called in which one section named William Goodell and Charles C. Foot, the other would support John P. Hale and George W. Julian. In the South the Democratic Southern Rights Convention in Montgomery rallied behind George M. Troup of Georgia and General John A. Quitman of Mississippi. In the North some of the discontented New England Whigs and Union Democrats were ready to vote for Webster.

But even with so many contestants before the country, the canvass was sedate. Neither the Democrats nor the Whigs had a definite political program; both of them depended on the personalities of their candidates. Pierce

Webster! this pap is so good, that I really shall be sorry when its gone, I thought it probable I should get another bowlful, but alas! I am doomed to disappointment. —

Oh General! yo[u] neck Oh! how na[...] the seat of my tro[users] so much pepper in [...] nasty it feels, no[...] into my boots. Oh [...] nasty it feels. —

J. L. Magee. del.

"PAP, SOUP AND CHOWDER." Ex-President Fillmore, carried by George Pope Morris, the editor of the New York *Mirror*, eats "Government Pap" (slang for "patronage"); General Scott, the Whig candidate, totters on the shoulders

PIERCE: A BRADY DAGUERREOTYPE

An 1852 lithograph by J. L. Magee, published by Peter Smith, N.Y.

of *Tribune* editor Horace Greeley. A Southern slaveowner pulls him down, spilling his "hasty plate of soup"—a reference to the inept phrase he never could live down. Daniel Webster, spooning his chowder, is carried by James W. Webb, editor of the New York *Courier & Enquirer*.

While the other three contenders laboriously move forward, Democrat Pierce reaches the White House on horseback with the flag: "The Union and the Compromise."

My honest friend, these men are interested parties, I have no further interest in this matter myself, than the inclination to "Serve my "beloved "Country", My Family cannot subsist on less than 25,000 $ a year.

This is the "Ticket" for you, my good friend, I am "Old Sam Houston" if elected I shall not only "lick" all Europe" but all "Creation" to boot.

There, there, go away, go away, dont worry the man, leave him to me, leave him to me.

My good Friend, allow me to present you this Ticket, I am "Old Genl Scott you know me, I licked the British & the Mexicans, if elected I shall probably lick all Europe.

DEMt.

WHIG.

Webster. Houston. Douglas. Scott.

An 1852 lithograph by David C. Johnston in The Old Soldier

SOLICITING A VOTE—Candidates Webster, Houston, Douglas and Scott beg Brother Jonathan for his approval, while Henry Clay watches from the background.

Brother Jonathan was a forerunner of Uncle Sam. During the Revolution, whenever a ticklish problem presented itself, Washington used to say: "We must consult Brother Jonathan"—meaning Jonathan Trumbull, Governor of Connecticut. Thus cartoonists, whenever they wanted to present the people's opinion, used the figure of Brother Jonathan.

was in favor of the compromise measures: what General Scott's beliefs were remained a deeply hidden secret.

The Democrats, confident of victory, went into the election with united ranks. The defeated contestants, Cass, Buchanan, Douglas and Marcy, all stumped for Pierce. The democratic jingle went:

> *We're bound to give the Whigs defeat*
> *With gallant Pierce and King.*

Mudslinging was now an established feature of the campaign. The Whig press called Pierce a drunkard, "a hero of many a well-fought bottle." One voter pleaded

that he "not allow another glass of intoxicating liquor" to pass through his lips. And he was branded as anti-Catholic. He was accused of being a coward because once in the Mexican War he had had a fainting spell and had to be carried from the battlefield. The story failed to mention that Pierce was exhausted by severe pain in his knee, which he had injured the previous day.

The Whigs sang:

> *Two generals are in the field*
> *Frank Pierce and Winfield Scott,*
> *Some think that Frank's a fighting man,*
> *And some think he is not.*

210

An 1852 lithograph by Bela Marsh, Boston

A CRUDE ANTI-SLAVERY CARTOON. Pierce, the Democrat, grovels before a slaveholder with a cat-o'-nine-tails. The figure on the right represents the Austrian General Julius ("The Hyena") Haynau, the executor of the 13 Hungarian generals who led the struggle for their country's independence. The pitcher on his head marked "Barclay's Brewery" refers to Haynau's visit to London in 1850 when at Barclay and Perkins's brewery the draymen beat him up because in Hungary he ordered women stripped and flogged in the streets for speaking to the rebels. Behind Haynau are Cass and Douglas.

'Tis said that when in Mexico,
While leading on his force,
He took a sudden fainting fit,
And tumbled off his horse.

But gallant Scott has made his mark
On many a bloody plain,
And patriots' hearts beat high to greet
The Chief of Lundy's Lane.

And Chippewa is classic ground,
Our British neighbors know,
And if you'd hear of later deeds,
Go ask in Mexico.

The Democratic newspapers hammered on Scott's nickname "Old Fuss and Feathers," which was given to him by his army officers, and made fun of him because of two phrases he had once used. One was "a hasty plate of soup," the other "a fire upon the rear." Scott used the first phrase when during the Mexican War the Secretary of War had called at his office and he was out; on his return he apologized, saying he had left the office only to take "a hasty plate of soup." The second one he had written when he was going to the Rio Grande and, fearing the jealousy of the Democrats, he wanted the support of the administration, "for soldiers had a far greater dread of a fire upon the rear than of the

An 1852 lithograph published by Peter Smith, New York

IN THIS PRECONVENTION CARTOON Webster leads the race for the $100,000 purse—four years of presidential salary—ahead of General Scott and Pierce. But Webster did not win the nomination: within a few months he died.

most formidable enemy in front."

His campaign managers asked Scott to go throughout the country to speak to the Germans and the Irish and to refute the Democratic charge that he was against foreigners. So Scott planned a journey to Blue Lick Springs in Kentucky to inspect the site for a military hospital. On the way he stopped at Pittsburgh, where he reassured his audience that he had not come to the city to campaign but that official duties compelled him to travel West. In Cleveland he said: "Fellow citizens. When I say fellow citizens I mean native and adopted as well as those who intend to become citizens." An Irishman interrupted: "You're welcome here," to which Scott replied: "I hear that rich brogue. I love to hear it. It makes me remember the noble deeds of Irishmen, many of whom I have led to battle and victory." From Cleveland he went to Columbus, and from there to his final destination, Blue Lick Springs, making frequent stops on the way in which he reasserted how much he liked the foreign-born. After inspecting the hospital site

the journey went through Kentucky, Ohio and New York, with Scott reiterating that he was not on a political trip and that he loved that "rich Irish brogue" and that "sweet German accent." The trip was a new departure from tradition—in past campaigns candidates had not solicited votes in person. It was not thought dignified for a President to do it.

Pierce kept silent and left the campaigning to others. He enlisted his close friend from Bowdoin, Nathaniel Hawthorne, to write his campaign biography. Hawthorne emphasized Pierce's exploits in the Mexican War, though not so much as to overshadow the man of peace. Hawthorne was uncertain how to handle the slavery issue, a subject "not to be shirked nor blinked." He tried to put forth Pierce "on the broadest ground possible, as a man for the whole country." Pierce later rewarded his biographer with the comfortable consularship in Liverpool, and the two remained fast friends until the day Hawthorne died quietly in a hotel room with Pierce sitting next to his death-bed.

An 1852 lithograph by Edward W Clay, published by John Childs, New York

ORNITHOLOGY. "Turkey" Scott and "Gamecock" Pierce glare at each other from either side of the Mason-Dixon line. General Scott: "Get out the way fellow! I want the whole road!" and Pierce replies: "But you can't get over this line."

Though Pierce remained at home and made no speeches, he won the election by a comfortable majority. Of the thirty-one states he carried all but four, receiving 1,601,274 votes against Scott's 1,386,580 and John P. Hale's 156,667.

The New York *Herald* declared Pierce had won because the people feared that if Scott had become President, he would have parroted the radical, antislavery views of Seward and this would have led to the breakup of the Union. But the explanation of the *National Intelligencer* sounds more convincing. That paper said the people had voted for Pierce, not only because they looked upon the compromise measures as final settlements on slavery, but because they were tired of the feeble, amicable neutrality of the administration and were ready for something positive, something which would uphold and advance the honor, dignity and power of this great country among the nations of the earth.

Inauguration day was cold with snow flurries and a biting raw wind. For Pierce the cheering multitude did not lighten the gloom of his deep sorrow. A few weeks before he had been in a railroad accident in which his 11-year-old son was killed before his very eyes.

From the ceremonies the Vice President-elect was absent. William R. King of Alabama was in Cuba, ill with tuberculosis; Congress passed a special act allowing him to take the oath of office from the American consul there. He never assumed the office. A month later he was dead.

Pierce delivered his inaugural address freely; he did not read it from a prepared manuscript. His address pleased both North and South, conservatives and "Young America" alike. He endorsed the compromise measures and he committed his administration to America's "Manifest Destiny." All signs pointed to a happy and successful presidential term.

The country was at peace, it enjoyed prosperity; the struggle between the sections had calmed down, the Democratic Congress was ready to support the administration's measures. The future seemed bright indeed.

JAMES BUCHANAN

I fervently hope that the question is at rest," said President Pierce in his inaugural address, "and that no sectional or ambitious or fanatical excitement may again threaten the durability of our institutions or obscure the light of our prosperity." He was of course speaking of the slavery issue, but what he voiced was an idle hope. It was not long before the "fanatical excitement" threatened the durability of the institutions and shook the country to its foundations.

Under the weak and vacillating Franklin Pierce, the Democrats disintegrated. Senator Stephen A. Douglas, fearful of defeat in the next election, tried to stem the tide; he advanced a program of three points: one, about the disposal of the surplus revenue; two, about the improvement of rivers and harbors at Government expense; and three, about the building of a transcontinental railroad to the Pacific.

In the building of the railroad Douglas had a personal stake; he represented Illinois in the Senate and he owned considerable real estate in Chicago and in the Northwest. It was natural that he desired a central and northern railway with its eastern terminal in Chicago. But other cities—St. Paul, Milwaukee, Memphis, Vicksburg, New Orleans—wanted the railroad to begin from their places too.

Congress ordered a survey of the proposed routes. Conducted under the direction of the War Department and Secretary of War Jefferson Davis, it was no surprise that the southern route was recommended. This road had some advantages: it was shorter than the others; it led through the organized territories of Texas and New Mexico, and thus could be built cheaply.

When it became apparent that the southern route had to pass through Mexican territory, Jefferson Davis persuaded Pierce to buy the necessary land. On December 20, 1853, the sandy triangle south of the Gila River was bought from Mexico for $10 million by the Gadsden Purchase—it was the last territorial growth of the United States on the American mainland.

As the central route would have to pass through Indian-populated territory, Douglas anticipated that the red men would fight construction of the railroad and suggested moving them away. With the opening of the Missouri bend to white settlers and with the Indian country organized into a territory, the main obstacles to the building of the railroad would have been cleared.

Before Douglas offered his proposal, the Commissioner of Indian Affairs had already drawn up plans for the removal of the Indians, and the House of Representatives had passed a bill for the organization of the land into the Nebraska Territory. Douglas gave his support to the bill, though he realized that in its present form the Senate would not pass it. Southern Senators would never approve the organization of a new territory in which slavery was forbidden; they would never vote for a bill which would add to Northern power.

So Douglas suggested that since the compromise measures of 1850 had left the territories of New Mexico and Utah free to choose whether to organize themselves with or without slavery, these measures replaced the Missouri Compromise which allowed slavery only south of 36° 30'; thus slavery could *now* be supported even north of that latitude. And it was for the territories to decide whether slavery should be

JAMES BUCHANAN
Photograph by Mathew B. Brady
in the National Archives

CANDIDATES IN 1856

JAMES BUCHANAN (1791–1868), a Jacksonian Democrat from Pennsylvania, diplomat, Secretary of State under Polk, was an unsuccessful presidential aspirant in the last three elections. This time he was chosen and won.

JOHN C. BRECKINRIDGE (1821–1875) of Kentucky, who succeeded Clay in his state's affections, was taken as Buchanan's running mate. The Democratic ticket received 1,838,169 votes against 1,341,264 votes for Frémont.

JOHN C. FRÉMONT (1813–1890) of California, famed Western explorer and husband of Senator Benton's daughter, was the first candidate of the new Republican party. He got 114 electoral votes against Buchanan's 174.

WILLIAM L. DAYTON (1807–1864) of New Jersey lost his Senate seat because he opposed the Compromise. His speech at the Trenton fusion convention resulted in his nomination for Vice President on the Republican ticket.

MILLARD FILLMORE (1800–1874), the former President, was chosen by the Know-Nothings as their presidential candidate. He was also supported by the remnant Whigs, but received only the 8 electoral votes of Maryland.

A. J. DONELSON (1799–1871), nephew and secretary of Andrew Jackson, the editor of the Washington *Union* and a diplomat, was the vice presidential nominee of the Know-Nothings; his ticket received 874,534 votes.

Library of Congress

HARRIET LANE (1830–1903), the youngest of the four children of Buchanan's sister, became a ward of her uncle when her mother died. Buchanan gave the 9-year-old girl a thorough education, and when he moved into the White House, Harriet became his hostess.

She was gay, exuberant and fashion-conscious. She wore low necks and lace berthas, voluminous skirts and elaborate headdresses, and the whole of Washington society copied her.

adopted within their borders. His popular sovereignty idea was in line with the democratic spirit in the West and it held out hope for further slave land to the South.

During the debate in the Senate the bill was amended many times and became far more radical than Douglas intended it to be. One of its provisions outspokenly repealed the Missouri Compromise; another called for the establishment of two territories instead of one: Nebraska to the west of Iowa with a free constitution and Kansas to the west of Missouri with slavery.

The country followed the debates with avid interest. The passage of the Kansas-Nebraska Act pleased the South but enraged the North.

An 1856 lithograph published by Peter Smith, N.Y.

THE THREE PRESIDENTIAL CANDIDATES. John C. Frémont, the new Republican party's first standard-bearer; Millard Fillmore, nominee of the Native Americans and the Whigs; and James Buchanan, the choice of the Democrats.

Abolitionist lecturers incited their audiences with tales about the brutality of slaveholders. Harriet Beecher Stowe's new book *Uncle Tom's Cabin* was read all over the North, fanning the excitement.

Douglas was assailed everywhere. He could have traveled all the way from Boston to Chicago by the light of his own burning effigies. He tried to convince the country of the rightness of his position, but had little success. On one occasion a hostile crowd in Chicago would not allow him to make his speech; it booed and hissed him. Douglas waited for a long while, then took his watch from his pocket, and looking at it carefully, said to the crowd: "It is now Sunday morning; I am going to Church and you can go to hell!"

The fight over the Kansas-Nebraska Act disrupted the parties; it split them into pro- and anti-slavery factions. After its passing suggestions came from all sides for the formation of a new party in which all those who opposed slavery could find a place. Horace Greeley in the New York *Tribune* pressed the proposal; many Whig politicians were for it; Chase, Sumner, Wade endorsed it. Such a new party had a hopeful aspect: it would lure antislavery Democrats and Whigs, Free Soilers and everyone else who opposed the Kansas-Nebraska Act into its ranks. New York Governor Seward spoke out: "We want a bold, outspoken, free-

THE FIRST REPUBLICAN TICKET. Frémont and his running mate Dayton, the "champions of freedom."

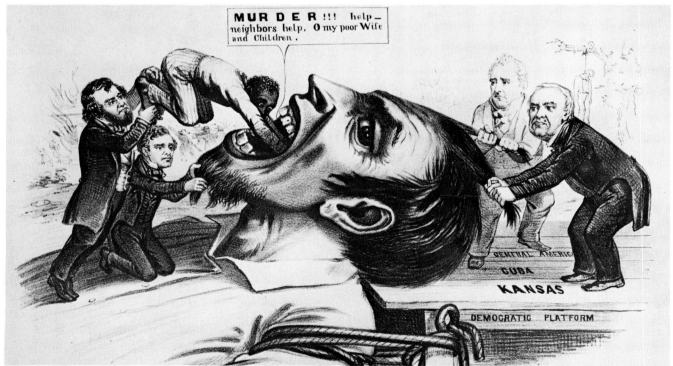

An 1856 lithograph published by J. L. Magee, Philadelphia

THE DEMOCRATS AND THEIR PLATFORM, Douglas, Pierce, Buchanan and Cass try to force slavery on a Free Soiler.

An 1856 lithograph published by Currier & Ives

THE PRESIDENTIAL RACE. The three rival candidates—ex-President Fillmore (in the carriage), Buchanan (on President Pierce's back) and Frémont (in the cart)—on their way to the Executive Mansion.

The cartoon favors Fillmore, the candidate of the Know-Nothings and the Whigs, while Frémont, the Republican standard-bearer, is last in the race, mired in the "Abolition Cess Pool." Horace Greeley nudges the tired animal; Henry Ward Beecher uses a rifle as a lever. "Beecher's Bibles" (as the rifles were called in Kansas) were bought with funds collected in Beecher's Brooklyn church and sent to the Free State settlers so that they could fight "border ruffians."

spoken organization—one that openly proclaims its principles, its purposes, and its objects."

On February 28, 1854, a meeting was held at Ripon, Wisconsin, in which all those present agreed to the formation of a new party which was to take a strong stand against slavery. It was to be called the Republican party.

Not long thereafter, in an oak grove outside the village of Jackson, Michigan, another meeting was held, with resolutions directed against slavery, the "great moral, social and political evil, and the Republican party came into being.

The struggle for the future status of Kansas (that Nebraska would become a free territory was not in doubt) went on. The population of the western part of Missouri was for slavery, and the people thought that Kansas would become a slave state. To make it certain,

many of them crossed over the border, took and occupied the best land. To oppose them, New England abolitionist societies sent groups of men to keep Kansas a free state. The Emigrant Aid Company armed free settlers with Sharpe's rifles—which, because some of the money for them was collected in Reverend Beecher's church, were called "Beecher's Bibles." The poet Whittier gave them the verse:

> *We cross the prairie as of old,*
> *the Pilgrims crossed the sea,*
> *To make the West, as they the East,*
> *the homestead of the free.*

President Pierce appointed a governor and the new governor set a date for the election of a territorial delegate. On the day of the election—with the free settlers showing little interest—Missourians rode into

An 1856 lithograph published by Peter Smith, N.Y.

UNCLE SAM LOOKS AT THE DEMOCRATIC PLATFORM. "Old Bullion" Benton, Franklin "The Last" Pierce and "Prince John" Van Buren (the former President's son) are forming a base for Buchanan ("no longer James Buchanan but the Platform of my party"). A Southerner bears down on the candidate ("I dont care anything about the Supporters of the platform as long as the platform supports me and my Nigger"). From his hole the Kinderhook Fox—Martin Van Buren—comments: "Never mind what we did in '48, Johnny, a change of policy now & then, benefits the political System."

Kansas and voted for a proslavery delegate. At the end of March, 1855, when a territorial legislature was to be elected, the free settlers turned out in force as did the slavery supporters. On election day, scores of Southern "border ruffians" flocked into the territory, "an unkempt, sun-dried, blatant, picturesque mob . . . with guns upon their shoulders, revolvers stuffing their belts, bowie-knives protruding from their boot-tops, and generous rations of whiskey in their wagons." They chased away the election judges and "decided" the result. Of the 5,307 votes cast, hardly more than 1,000 were legal, demonstrating that popular sovereignty did not work. When the elected legislature introduced drastic

slave laws, indignation spread through the free states.

The battle in Kansas went on. On October 23, the antislavery settlers called a convention to Topeka and drew up a constitution prohibiting slavery. After the constitution was adopted by an overwhelming vote, a governor and other state officers were elected and Congress was asked to admit Kansas as a free state.

And while Congress debated whether to accept the pro- or antislavery government, the Federal marshal for the territory served writs upon members of the antislavery government. On May 21, 1856, a mob wrecked the offices of the antislavery newspaper in Lawrence, sacked the town and set fire to the Governor's house.

An 1856 lithograph by Louis Maurer, published by Currier & Ives

THE REPUBLICAN CANDIDATE Frémont receives the homage of his imaginary supporters: A Negro, a Catholic priest, a woman preaching free love, a laborer asking for "an equal division of Property," an advocate of women's rights and a prohibitionist who wants "a law making the use of Tobacco, Animal food and Lager beer a Capital crime."

The new party—based on idealism and moral indignation—attracted the radical elements, all those men and women who were dissatisfied with conditions. The opposition heaped ridicule on them, the party of eccentrics, cranks and do-gooders.

Five men had been killed in the melee. In retaliation John Brown, "a man that had always been from his childhood impressed with the idea that God had raised him up on purpose to break the jaws of the wicked," set out with his sons and neighbors to avenge the deed. They raided a proslavery settlement near Pottawatomie Creek and killed five innocent settlers—the same number killed by the proslavery mob in Lawrence. Brown, the stern puritan, declared: "Without the shedding of blood, there is no remission of sins."

It was a crazy deed, lighting the match under an already explosive situation. The country was in an uproar, Kansas in the throes of civil war.

On May 22, Representative Preston Brooks of South Carolina walked up to the desk of Charles Sumner in the Senate Chamber and beat him with a cane until he fell unconscious to the floor. Sumner, the leading abolitionist from Massachusetts, had made a violent anti-slavery speech on "The Crime Against Kansas" a day before in which he used harsh words against Senator Butler of South Carolina, the uncle of Brooks. This happened only a day after the Lawrence outrage and two days before John Brown's attack.

A week and a half later on June 2, the Democratic convention met at Cincinnati. Its proceedings began with violence. The Missouri "Regulars" knocked down

An 1856 lithograph by Louis Maurer, published by Currier & Ives

"THE MUSTANG TEAM"—Frémont and the editors of four influential New York newspapers (Greeley of the *Tribune*, Bennett of the *Herald*, Raymond of the *Daily Times*, Webb of the *Courier & Enquirer*) are halted by Brother Jonathan. Frémont, often depicted with a cross, was rumored—without foundation—a member of the Roman Catholic Church.

a doorkeeper who attempted to prevent their entrance, but it was of no avail; the committee on credentials would not acknowledge them as the true representatives of their state.

For the presidential nomination the most often-mentioned names were those of President Pierce, James Buchanan, Douglas and Cass. But as both Pierce and Douglas were identified with the Kansas-Nebraska Act —Douglas had introduced it, Pierce had signed it—they were rejected by the antislavery delegates. Thus Buchanan, who had been Minister to Great Britain during the debates and was not involved on either side appeared the most "available" candidate.

He had been a contender in the past three conventions—in 1844, in 1848 and in 1852—but each time another candidate was chosen. Now the time seemed ripe for his selection. He had been in public life all his adult life, first as state legislator, then as Representative

in Congress from 1821 until 1831 when Jackson named him Minister to Russia. After his return in 1834 he became U.S. Senator and won re-election twice. But he had the poor luck of serving in the Senate at the same time as the giants—Clay, Calhoun, Webster— who overshadowed him. In 1844, Buchanan was highly influential in bringing the vote of his state to Polk. When Polk formed his Cabinet, Buchanan became Secretary of State. As such he led the negotiations for the annexation of Texas and for the settlement of the Oregon boundary issue. After the 1848 election, which the Democrats lost, he retured to "Wheatland," his country estate near Lancaster, but in 1852 he was back as a presidential candidate; again he was overlooked. Pierce appointed him Minister to Great Britain; when he returned from London in 1856, he was regarded as the most prominent contender for the Presidency. The Ostend Manifesto, in which he and two of his col-

An 1856 lithograph published by John Fahnestock, Philadelphia

THE SLAVERY MONSTER, with Democratic candidate Buchanan on its back, is pulled over the Mason-Dixon line into Kansas by three "doughfaces" (pro-slavery Democrats from the North)—Cass, Douglas and Pierce. The candidate of the Republicans, Frémont (riding a horse), orders the monster back; Whig nominee Fillmore (on the right) straddles the fence.

leagues recommended the purchase or annexation of Cuba, gave him the approval of the South.

On the first ballot he led with 135½ votes against Pierce's 122½, Douglas's 33 and Cass's 5. His strength increased steadily; on the sixteenth ballot he had 168½ against Douglas's 121 and Cass's 6. Thirty more votes were needed for the necessary two-thirds endorsement. On the next ballot Douglas released his votes "to give effect to the voice of the majority," giving Buchanan the candidacy. For the vice-presidential nomination, John C. Breckinridge of Kentucky was chosen.

The Democratic platform declared that the "party will resist all attempts at renewing, in Congress or out of it, the agitation of the slavery question, under whatever shape or color the attempt be made." It upheld the Kansas-Nebraska Act as "the only sound and safe solution of the slavery question." It also took issue with the "adverse political and religious test which has been

secretly organized by a party claiming to be exclusively American." But "a political crusade in the nineteenth century, and in the United States of America, against Catholics and foreign-born, is neither justified by the past history or future prospects of the country."

This was aimed at the Native Americans, a radical and nationalistic society. They kept their deliberations secret and when asked about their political beliefs they answered, "I know nothing"; thus they became known as "Know-Nothings." For a while, Know-Nothingism was an important political movement directed mainly against foreigners and Roman Catholics. The Know-Nothings opposed the greatly increased immigration of Irish Catholics and German radicals; in the decade between 1845 and 1855 more than 300,000 immigrants arrived, threatening the jobs of American workers. The newcomers voted for those who paid them and who gave them liquor. In general they favored the Democratic party, the Irish because it was "a poor man's party," the Germans because it was a more liberal organization than the Whigs.

The Know-Nothings asked for severe naturalization laws and the exclusion of foreigners and Catholics from all public offices. In the state elections of 1854 they carried Massachusetts and almost won in New York. Their strength came from the cities on the Atlantic seaboard where immigrants competed with American workers, but they also had large support in the South where the European immigration was resented because it increased the antislavery population of the North.

The Republicans held their first national convention at Pittsburgh on Washington's birthday. They adopted a declaration of principles, foremost among them: "We demand, and shall attempt to secure, the repeal of all laws which allow the introduction of slavery into territories once consecrated to freedom, and will resist by every constitutional means the existence of slavery in any of the territories of the United States." They resolved to meet again on June 17, the anniversary of the battle of Bunker Hill, to nominate candidates.

The same day—February 22, 1856—that the Republicans met in Pittsburgh, the Know-Nothings assembled in Philadelphia in their first national nominating convention. They, like the Democrats, were split into Northern and Southern factions. Tempers were boiling. The Southern delegates asked for a platform condemning antislavery and anti-Nebraska agitation, while the Northern delegates opposed any such declaration. And when the Southern view prevailed and the platform remained noncommittal on slavery, seventy-one delegates from the North withdrew, to meet again in another convention later.

The Know-Nothings chose as their candidate former President Fillmore, a man who was neither a Know-Nothing nor in sympathy with their aims. Their platform declared the "Americans must rule America"; it advocated that only native-born citizens should be selected for Federal, state and municipal offices; it asked for "a change in the laws of naturalization, making a continued residence of twenty-one years . . . an indispensable requisite for citizenship"; and urged "opposition to any union between Church and State."

The first national nominating convention of the newly formed Republican party assembled in Philadelphia. "You are here today to give direction to a movement which is to decide whether the people of the United States are to be hereafter and forever chained to the present national policy of the extension of human slavery," orated the chairman of the convention. A crusading fervor pervaded the meeting. The convention was dedicated to resisting slavery. Their short platform was for admitting Kansas to the Union with a free

constitution and for ending civil strife in that territory, and spoke out against "those twin relics of barbarism—polygamy and slavery"—which should be prohibited by Congress in all territories.

As their presidential candidate the delegates chose John C. Frémont, the dashing pathfinder of the West; and for his running mate William L. Dayton, who in the informal ballot triumphed over the Illinois lawyer, Abraham Lincoln, and thirteen other candidates.

Frémont was selected by the Republicans because he was the safest on the slavery issue. Both Seward and Chase had made radical statements, but Frémont had never said anything that would have offended the South, and he "had no political antecedents." Born in Savannah, educated in Charleston, married to Senator Benton's daughter, he had been a Democrat at one time, and he had friendly links not only with the Know-Nothings but with the German groups as well.

It was five days before the Republicans met in their convention that the "North Americans," the Northern seceders of the Know-Nothings, convened in meeting. They wanted Judge McLean as their candidate, hoping that the Republicans would endorse him. But the Republicans were for Frémont, whose nomination was assured long before the convention. If the Know-Nothings did not give up McLean, the Free Soil vote would be split—bringing certain defeat to the antislavery candidates. The Republican managers suggested substituting McLean with Nathaniel P. Banks as the Know-Nothing candidate—and after Frémont officially became the Republican candidate, Banks was to withdraw and release his support to Frémont.

To make the bargain stick, Frémont's managers parleyed with the Know-Nothing delegates and handed out money in a generous manner. If one can believe a report, $30,000 changed hands, after which everything went according to schedule. The Republicans duly nominated Frémont, Banks withdrew and both parties were united behind the Republican standard bearer.

The campaign was already under way when the Whigs—or what was left of them—met, promising their support to the Know-Nothing candidates, but without endorsing their platform. They held that both the Democratic and Republican candidates were fostering sectional strife; thus only Fillmore guaranteed peace and the preservation of the Union. They had "no new principles to announce, no new platform to establish, but are content to broadly rest—where their fathers rested—upon the Constitution of the United States, wishing no safer guide, no higher law."

But the Whigs' days were gone; the majority of their members in the North joined the Republicans; in the South they became either Democrats or Know-Nothings.

With three candidates in the contest, Frémont had to

Frank Leslie's Illustrated Newspaper, *March 1857*
BUCHANAN IS FETCHED BY THE COMMITTEE OF ARRANGEMENT FOR THE INAUGURATION.

carry most of the North to win. The free states had 176 electoral votes against the slave states' 120. But Buchanan was certain of 112 votes from the South. If he could carry his own state and ten more votes, either from Indiana or Illinois, he would be elected.

The main issue was slavery and Kansas. The Republican slogan, "Free soil, free speech, and Frémont," was carried on flags, shouted in torchlight processions and at mass meetings. Republican "Wide-Awake" companies marched through the streets carrying banners and transparencies, Republican fife-and-drum corps played march music; the excitement was like the Tippecanoe campaign of 1840, only this time the emotionalism was based on a burning political issue.

Writers, scientists, professors, clergymen, teachers spoke out for the new party. Ralph Waldo Emerson addressed meetings, as did William Cullen Bryant and Henry Wadsworth Longfellow; intellectuals were crusading with moral fervor against the "peculiar institution." The slavery issue brought not only Whigs to Republican ranks, like Hamilton Fish and Abraham Lincoln, but many Democrats. George Bancroft, the

once ardent Democrat, announced that as the Democratic party had fallen into a hopeless condition under "this bastard race that controls the organization, this unproductive hybrid got by southern arrogance upon northern subserviency," he would not vote for Buchanan.

There were the usual mudslinging and personal invective. Yet the main argument against Frémont remained a political one: that the South would secede and the Union would be dissolved if he were to be elected.

The capitalists of Wall Street, fearing that a Republican victory might upset the money market, made generous contributions to the Democratic campaign chest. August Belmont alone gave $50,000. Against such largesse the new Republican party was powerless; their fresh organization had not yet learned how to tap the coffers of the rich. Horace Greeley wailed: "We Frémonters of this town have not one dollar where the Fillmoreans and Buchaniers have ten each. . . ."

In the state elections in Pennsylvania and in Indiana, Buchanan carried both states. It was an ominous sign

for the Republicans. They tried to effect a last-minute alliance with the Know-Nothings, but their effort came to nothing.

Buchanan won with 1,838,169 popular votes against Frémont's 1,341,264 and Fillmore's 874,534. He had 174 electoral votes against Frémont's 114 and Fillmore's 8. He carried all the Southern and border states, and California, Delaware, Illinois, Indiana, New Jersey and Pennsylvania as well—nineteen states altogether. Frémont took the New England states—New Hampshire, Vermont, Maine, Massachusetts, Connecticut, Rhode Island—the Western States, Iowa, Michigan, Wisconsin, Ohio, and also New York. It was an impressive showing—a "victorious defeat." Thus:

"If months have well-nigh won the field,
What may not four years do?"

National Archives
THE FIRST GROUP PHOTOGRAPH OF A CABINET: On President Buchanan's right: Jacob Thompson (Interior); Lewis Cass (State); John B. Floyd (War). To the President's' left: Howell Cobb (Treasury); Isaac Toucey (Navy); Joseph Holt (Postmaster General); Jeremiah Black (Attorney General). Mathew Brady took the picture.

A NEWLY DISCOVERED PICTURE. This is the first photograph of an inauguration which has come down to us. It was taken at Buchanan's inaugural on March 4, 1857.

Author's collection

227

ABRAHAM LINCOLN

The victory of Buchanan is the victory of Southern bullyism, the acknowledgment of Northern men that 'right or wrong' they yield because the South threatens to secede," remarked a political observer after the 1856 election. But the legalistic mind of Buchanan would not admit that anything was wrong. He said in his inaugural address: "The whole territorial question being thus settled upon the principle of popular sovereignty—a principle as ancient as free government itself—everything of a practical nature has been decided. May we not, then, hope that the long agitation on this subject of slavery is approaching its end, and that the geographical parties to which it has given birth, so much dreaded by the Father of his country, will speedily become extinct?"

Only two days after his inauguration the Supreme Court handed down its decision in the Dred Scott case. Chief Justice Taney, in the name of seven Democratic Justices, five of them from the South, spoke for the majority when he declared that the Negro Dred Scott, who had brought suit for his liberty, was a slave even though he had resided in free territory during part of his life. This meant: Once a slave, always a slave! But Taney went further. He declared the Missouri Compromise unconstitutional as Congress did not have the right to exclude slavery from the Louisiana Territory north of 36°30′. Slaves were property and as such protected under the Constitution whether above or below a geographical line.

The decision was greeted with jubilation in the South, for it made Douglas's proposal of popular sovereignty meaningless. And while the South was happy over the decision, the aroused abolitionists in the North were enraged and demanded strong measures against the spread of slavery.

The flames of antagonism between the sections were fanned by the events in Kansas. Buchanan sent a new proslavery governor to the territory who issued a call for the election of delegates to a constitutional convention. As the Free State party refused to vote, the proslavery men carried the day. Thus in October 1857 a proslavery convention met in Lecompton, framed a constitution and submitted it to the residents of the territory. Although they were asked to vote for a "constitution with no slavery" or a "constitution with slavery," there was a catch to this. If the decision should be for an antislavery constitution, then slavery "should no longer exist in the State of Kansas, except that the right of property in slaves now in this territory shall in no measure be interfered with." Thus whether they voted yes or no, slavery was to remain in Kansas. The Free State men would not participate in such fraud; as they stayed away from the polls, the proslavery constitution was voted upon.

In the Senate Douglas vigorously attacked the Lecompton constitution. "If Kansas wants a slave-state constitution, she has a right to do it. It is none of my business which way the slavery clause is decided, and I care not whether it is voted down or voted up." The "Little Giant" considered the Lecompton document a "trick, a fraud upon the rights of the people," and he broke with the President, who supported it.

The Democratic split was complete. In the mid-term election of 1858 they suffered a resounding defeat.

ABRAHAM LINCOLN
Photograph by Mathew B. Brady
taken on February 9, 1864

CANDIDATES IN 1860

ABRAHAM LINCOLN (1809–1865) of Illinois, the Republican nominee. As the Democrats split on the slavery issue, Lincoln won with 1,866,-452 votes against Douglas's 1,376,957 total, Breckinridge's 849,781, and Bell's 588,879.

HANNIBAL HAMLIN (1809–1891, Senator from the state of Maine, became dissatisfied with the Democrats' stand on slavery and joined the Republicans in 1856. As a Northerner, he was selected as Lincoln's running mate.

STEPHEN A. DOUGLAS (1813–1861), "the Little Giant" from Illinois who served both in the Senate and in the House, became the controversial candidate of the Northern and Western wings of the Democratic party.

JOHN C. BRECKINRIDGE (1821–1875) was chosen Senator by Kentucky a year and a half before his term as Buchanan's Vice President expired. Candidate of the Democratic Southern wing, he supported slaveholding interests.

JOHN BELL (1797–1868), Senator from Tennessee, ran as presidential candidate of the Constitutional Unionists, a party of former Whigs and other conservatives. Their aim was the preservation of the Union.

EDWARD EVERETT (1794–1865), a Massachusetts Governor four times, Harvard's president, Representative, Senator and Secretary of State, the country's greatest orator, was second on the Constitutional Unionists' ticket.

Author's collection

MARY TODD (1818–1882), the well-educated daughter of a Louisville banker, married Lincoln on November 4, 1842. She had a tragic life. Three of her sons died early; her husband was assassinated while she sat beside him.

After Lincoln's death she roamed the world for seventeen years with a clouded mind. She died in Springfield, Illinois, at her sister's home. The ring her husband presented her, bearing the inscription, "Love is Eternal," lay on the night table.

In the senatorial contest of Illinois Douglas was opposed by his old friend Abraham Lincoln. They had known each other from way back when both sat in the Vandalia legislature and when Lincoln served his single term in the House of Representatives. Lincoln's anti-war stand in the Mexican War had made his hopes for re-election futile. Thus he returned to Springfield and to the practice of law; he rode the circuit, made friends, kept his fingers in politics. The debate over the Kansas-Nebraska Act brought him back into the political arena. By 1858 he was considered a worthy opponent to Douglas for the Illinois senatorship. In a series of debates, which were attended by large audiences, and were reported in the nation's press, the two contenders debated the paramount issue of the day: slavery. Lincoln stated his case in a speech in Springfield:

"We are now far into the fifth year since a policy was initiated with the avowed object and confident promise of putting an end to slavery agitation. Under the oper-

An 1861 lithograph by M. A. Woolf, issued by Thomas W. Strong, N.Y.

"OUR NATIONAL BIRD as it appeared when handed to James Buchanan March 4, 1857" and "The identical Bird as it appeared A.D. 1861." The title refers to an old representation used in the past as far back as the Mexican War. The poor bird with a broken chain about her neck has one leg in the shoe "Anarchy," while her wooden stump is labeled "Secession."

ation of that policy, that agitation has not only not ceased but has constantly augmented. In my opinion, it will not cease until crisis shall have been reached and passed. 'A house divided against itself cannot stand.' I believe this government cannot endure permanently half slave and half free. I do not expect the Union to be dissolved—I do not expect the house to fall—but I do expect it will cease to be divided. It will become all one thing, or all the other. Either the opponents of slavery will arrest the further spread of it, and place it where the public mind shall rest in the belief that it is in the course of ultimate extinction; or its advocates will push it forward till it shall become alike lawful in all the States, old as well as new, North as well as South."

During the debates at Freeport Douglas had to contend that popular sovereignty was not incompatible with the Dred Scott decision. The inhabitants of the territory could, so Douglas said, by "unfriendly legislation" jeopardize and make insecure property in slaves and thus destroy the whole institution of slavery itself.

Douglas's Freeport doctrine did not please the Southern hotheads. They asked for a repudiation of his popular sovereignty doctrine and Congressional protection of slavery in all the territories.

The sectional dispute was reaching its climax. Southern members in Congress defeated measures which were to benefit the North (killing the Pacific railroad project and the Homestead Bill); Northern members retaliated by voting "personal liberty laws" (invalidating the Fugitive Slave Law).

Once more the fanatic John Brown entered the scene. With eighteen men he raided the arsenal at Harpers Ferry in a mad attempt to seize firearms and free the slaves in the South. The Southern states viewed the attack as an organized attempt to invoke armed slave insurrection in the South.

It was before this backdrop that the Democratic convention met in Charleston, the center of proslavery

231

THE WIGWAM IN CHICAGO BUILT BY LOCAL POLITICAL CLUBS TO SERVE AS CONVENTION HALL

THE INSIDE OF THE WIGWAM, where on May 18, 1860, the Republican delegates chose Abraham Lincoln.

agitation, on April 23. From the outset the Southern delegates told their colleagues from the other sections: "You must not apologize for slavery; you must declare it right; you must advocate its extension." And they threatened to withdraw if the rights of the South were not upheld in the territories.

The battle raged around Douglas, "the pivot individual." Jefferson Davis told him that if he wanted to get the candidacy he must repudiate the popular-sovereignty idea, agree to a territorial slave code and to the protection of slavery in the new territories. Douglas replied that he would accept the nomination only on the principles of the 1850 Compromise; but if the delegates should vote for "such new issues as the revival of the

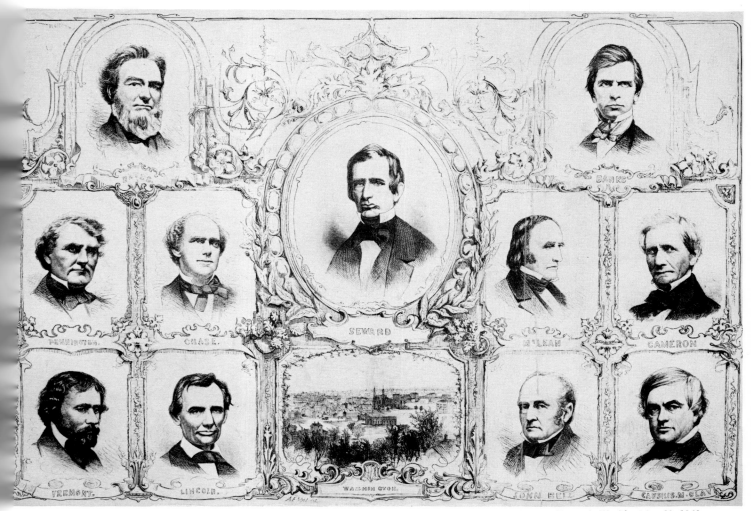

From Harper's Weekly, *May 12, 1860*

THE LEADING REPUBLICAN CANDIDATES as they were pictured in *Harper's Weekly* one day before the opening of the Republican convention. In the center: William H. Seward, the favorite; top left: Edward Bates of Missouri; top right: Nathaniel P. Banks, Governor of Massachusetts. Middle row: William Pennington of New Jersey, the Speaker of the House; Salmon P. Chase, the former Governor of Ohio; John McLean, Supreme Court justice from Ohio; Simon Cameron, Pennsylvania's political boss. Bottom row: John C. Frémont, Abraham Lincoln, John Bell and Cassius M. Clay.

After his election to the Presidency, Lincoln appointed three men from this group for his Cabinet: Chase (Secretary of the Treasury); Cameron (Secretary of War); Bates (Attorney General). Clay was named Minister to Imperial Russia.

African slave trade or a Congressional slave code for the territories," he would not want to be a candidate.

The Douglas supporters made a determined attempt to swamp the convention. Murat Halstead, the young newspaperman, reported to the Concinnati *Commercial,* that "Mills House, where Douglas 'men most do congregate,' is as lively as a molasses barrel with flies. Here is where the outside pressure is brought to bear. It is here that 'public opinion' is represented according to Douglas. Here they tell you Douglas must be the nominee—'All that is to be done is to ratify the voice of the people.' There is nothing but a few ballots, and all is over— Douglas the nominee—South will come down—certain to be elected. The country safe—the party safe."

William Yancey of Alabama, "the prince of fire-eaters," asked for the adoption of the platform before the balloting for the candidates. The Douglas men, realizing that they could not receive the necessary two-thirds vote, were ready to accept the suggestion, hoping for an antislavery platform which then would force some of the Southern delegates to withdraw. They were ready for a "little eruption." They figured that if delegates from three or four Southern states would leave the convention, they would then have the necessary two-thirds support for Douglas from the remaining predominantly Northern delegations.

The debate for the platform went on for days. Reporter Halstead felt that "It is the general impression

-THE "OLD HACK" TURNED OUT TO "GRASS"!

An 1860 drawing by Thomas F. G. Miller
ABANDONING THE FAVORITE. Greeley thumbs his nose at Seward, his erstwhile political friend.

. . . that there will be an explosion of the convention." The excitement over the factional debates was intense: "The hall is very much crowded. Those who have tickets send them out after they get in, and others come in. In this way everybody who understands the trick, and nearly everybody does, gets in. So there is an infernal crowd." When the platform was presented, the majority report of the committee on resolutions supported the Southern position and asked for the protection of slavery in the territories, while the minority report upheld the views of the North and the West. Henry B. Payne of Ohio, who submitted the minority report, said that each one who signed it with him "had felt in his conscience and in his heart that upon the result of our deliberations and the action of this convention, in all human probability, depended the fate of the Democratic party and the destiny of the Union." His words had the ring of truth.

The convention accepted the minority report, with all delegates above the Mason-Dixon line voting for it,

all delegates from below the line voting against it. It was a victory for Douglas and the Northern view, but it was a Pyrrhic victory. The defeated Southern delegations now withdrew. Alabama led the way, followed by Mississippi, Florida, Texas and the majority from Louisiana, South Carolina, Arkansas, Delaware and Georgia—forty-five delegates in all. A Mississippi man cried out emotionally: "We say, go your way and we will go ours. But the South leaves not like Hagar, driven into the wilderness, friendless and alone, for in sixty days you will find a united South standing shoulder to shoulder."

Yet some of the Southern delegates remained. One of them said he would stay "until the last feather be placed upon the back of the camel—I will stay until crushed and broken in spirit, humiliated by feeling and knowing that I have no longer a voice in the counsels of the Democracy of the Union." Then a slave trader from Savannah spoke in support of slavery. He said that if

An 1860 lithograph published by Currier & Ives, N.Y.

THE IRREPRESSIBLE CONFLICT. Seward, who lost the nomination to Lincoln in Chicago, is thrown overboard by Greeley (sitting beside Lincoln); "Over you go Billy! Between you and I there is an 'Irrepressible Conflict.'" Edward Bates and Francis Blair grasp Seward's foot, while other Republicans make their comments. On the riverbank, Brother Jonathan, who now begins to look like Uncle Sam, says: "You wont save your crazy old craft by throwing your pilot overboard."

it were abolished "civilization would go back two hundred years." His outlook on the peculiar institution raised laughter from the delegates, most of them Northerners. In the man's opinion, "the slave trade of Virginia was more inhuman, more unchristian, in every point of view than the African slave trade; for the African slaveholder goes to a heathen land and brings the savage here, and Christianizes and moralizes him, and sends him down to posterity a happy man." He proceeded that he "desired not to be discourteous to Virginia, but with all deference to the state, he believed they were influenced more than they ought to be by the almighty dollar. He had himself purchased some slaves in Virginia and had to pay from one thousand to twelve hundred dollars, while he could buy a better nigger in Africa for fifty dollars." The speech amused the delegates.

The rump convention at last began with the balloting. Douglas needed 202 votes for the nomination. But on the first trial received only 145½. During the next two days fifty-seven ballots were taken, with substantially the same result. As the delegates were not willing to agree on a compromise candidate, the convention adjourned to meet again at Baltimore in June 18.

In the interval two other conventions were held, that of the Constitutional Union party and that of the Republicans. The Constitutional Unionists offered no practical solution to the disruptive forces that were tearing the Union apart. Their conservative platform recognized "no political principle other then the Constitution of the country, the union of the States and the enforcement of the laws." Halstead, that wonderful reporter, satirized the meeting of the "'venerable men' who have come down to us from a former generation of politicians, and whose retirement from the busy scenes of politics have been rather involuntary than otherwise." He wrote that during the sessions "the moment a speaker would say *Constitution; law; Union; American; conservative element; glorious victory; our fathers; our flag; our*

LINCOLN AND HIS SUPPORTERS: A WIDELY CIRCULATED POSTER AGAINST THE REPUBLICAN CANDI-

country; or anything of the sort, he had to pause for some time until the general rapture would discharge itself by stamping, clapping hands, rattling canes, etc. I have likened the enthusiasm to that of an Irish audience at an archbishop's lecture."

And when all the shouting and enthusiasm spent itself, the Constitutional Unionists chose John Bell of Tennessee and the celebrated orator Edward Everett of Massachusetts as their candidates.

Since the last election, when they had put up their

An 1860 lithograph by Louis Maurer, published by Currier & Ives, N.Y.

DATE. GREELEY CARRIES HIM ON A RAIL TO THE LUNATIC ASYLUM, FOLLOWED BY A MOTLEY CROWD.

first presidential candidate, the Republicans had made great strides; they attracted all elements against slavery: former Whigs, Free-Soil Democrats, abolitionists, political reformers, protective tariff devotees alike. Now, as they were to open their convention in Chicago, a multitude of their supporters came to take part in it. The Democratic split made it practically certain that the next President would be a Republican.

William H. Seward, former Governor of New York, was the Republican favorite. He was managed by Thur-

From Harper's Weekly, *April 28, 1860*
THE DEMOCRATIC CONVENTION AT CHARLES-
TON, South Carolina, adjourned after fifty-seven ballots.

From Harper's Weekly, *April 28, 1860*
MIDNIGHT IN CHARLESTON. Two New Yorkers ask,
"Where's them beds of our'n we paid $5 for in advance?"

low Weed, the New York political boss, who brought
with him an efficient political staff and plentiful funds.
As the leader of his party in the Senate, Seward was generally conceded to deserve the nomination. His supporters were so confident of victory that they set up a cannon on the lawn of Seward's home at Auburn to be
fired when the word came.

The managers of the other candidates were no less
active. Edward Bates, a conservative jurist from Missouri, came with the support of Indiana, Maryland and
Delaware as well as his own state; Salmon P. Chase,
Governor of Ohio, had a sizable following even though
he had a rival in his own state, Benjamin Wade. Supreme Court Judge John McLean, a veteran politician,
had Thaddeus Stevens working for him; but perhaps the
most agile were the managers of Abraham Lincoln.

Judge David Davis, with whom lawyer Lincoln had
ridden the circuit in his earlier days, established headquarters at his own expense at the Tremont House.
Assisted by Norman B. Judd, a leading Illinois poli-

FIVE FOOT FOUR
STEPHEN A. DOUGLAS
THE DEMOCRATIC CANDIDATE

From Harper's Weekly, *May 12, 1860*

THE SOUTHERN SECEDERS from the original convention met again in Charleston to choose a candidate.

From Harper's Weekly, *May 12, 1860*

"PLUG-UGLIES," hired to demonstrate support, hear from Charleston that they must pay $50 a day in advance.

tician, and Leonard Swett, another lawyer from the circuit, and also by Joseph Medill and Charles H. Ray from the Chicago *Press & Tribune,* he tried to persuade the anti-Seward delegations that Lincoln, who was neither a radical like Seward nor a conservative like Bates, and who "excited no hates anywhere" and "has made no records to be defended or explained," would be the proper choice of the convention.

The Lincoln managers came to Chicago certain only of the Illinois votes; now they went after the strategic states of Indiana, New Jersey and Pennsylvania, argued with the delegates, bargained and courted them, gave promises freely. When Lincoln wired from Springfield, "I authorize no bargains, and will be bound by none," Dubois, one of the solicitors, cursed, "Damn Lincoln!" and went on with his business. Indiana was won over by promising Caleb B. Smith, the chairman of the delegation, the post of Secretary of the Interior and Willian P. Dole the post of Commissioner of Indian Affairs. It was the strategy of Davis to antagonize no

SIX FOOT FOUR
ABRAHAM LINCOLN
THE REPUBLICAN CANDIDATE

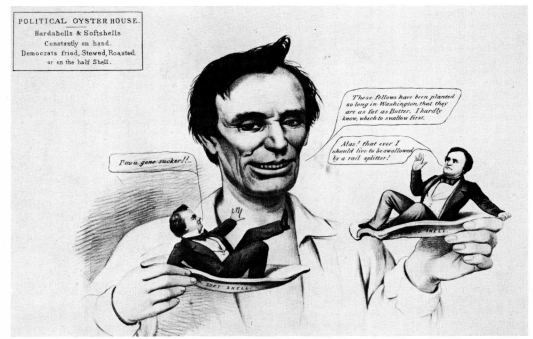

LINCOLN WEIGHING THE TWO OYSTERS, the "Softshell" Democrat Stephen A. Douglas and the "Hardshell" pro-slavery Democrat John C. Breckinridge.

An 1860 lithograph by Currier & Ives

DOUGLAS IS SPANKED by Columbia with a cattail labeled, "News from Maine." Uncle Sam, on the left, approves the spanking, "for he richly deserves it, Give him the Stripes till he sees Stars."

An 1860 lithograph by Currier & Ives

one but secure pledges for Lincoln as the second choice of the states. The Lincoln men told delegates the story of Lincoln's life: his birth in a log cabin, his little schooling, his rail-splitting, the flatboat trip to New Orleans, the lonely rides as a circuit lawyer, and how he bested Douglas in the debates. Davis and Dubois wired Lincoln: "We are quiet but moving heaven & earth. Nothing will beat us but old fogy politicians. The hearts of the delegates are with us."

Seward's strength lay in the East, but this was his weakness, too—these states would vote Republican in any case. And the leaders of three crucial states—Pennsylvania, Indiana and Illinois—were convinced that their local tickets would lose with Seward as the candidate. John A. Andrew, chairman of the Massachusetts delegation, told the men from the doubtful states: "You delegates all say that William H. Seward cannot carry the doubtful states. When we ask you who can,

THE RAIL CANDIDATE.
A Negro and Horace Greeley carry Lincoln on a rail labeled "Republican Platform." Lincoln comments unhappily: "It is true I have split Rails, but I begin to feel as if *this* Rail would split me, it's the hardest stick I ever straddled."

An 1860 lithograph by Louis Maurer, published by Currier & Ives

An 1860 lithograph by Louis Maurer, published by Currier & Ives

THE NATIONAL GAME. The four presidential candidates—Bell, Douglas, Breckinridge and Lincoln —on the baseball field. The rail in Lincoln's hand is marked "Equal Rights and Free Territory"—he rests a foot on "Home Base."

you from New Jersey give us the name of William L. Dayton, a most excellent and worthy man in every way, and entirely satisfactory to us; but when we go to Pennsylvania they name Simon Cameron; and Indiana and Illinois, Abraham Lincoln. Now it is impossible to have all these three candidates, and unless you delegates from the four doubtful states can agree upon some one candidate, who you think can carry these states, we from New England will vote for our choice,

William H. Seward of New York; but if you will unite upon some one candidate and present his name, we will give him enough votes to place him in nomination."

On opening day the "Wigwam," built especially for the occasion, was filled to the rafters; ten thousand people were screaming, shouting, cheering in the hall. Twice that number were on the outside, following the proceedings from the street. Horace Greeley, one of the drafters of the platform, was convinced that "An

An 1860 lithograph by Louis Maurer, issued by Currier & Ives

STORMING THE CASTLE. Lincoln with rail in hand races toward the White House, while the three other candidates—Bell, Douglas and Breckinridge, the last one helped by President Buchanan—try to break into the building by other means. Bell warns Douglas to open the door because the watchman is coming while Breckinridge moans that he is too weak to get up.

Anti-slavery man *per se* cannot be elected; but a tariff, River and Harbor, Pacific Railroad, Free Homestead man may succeed." Therefore he saw to it that the platform comprised all these good things.

The platform out of the way, the convention was ready to begin the balloting. Halstead wrote: "So confident were the Seward men . . . of their ability to nominate their great leader, that they urged an immediate ballot and would have had it if the clerks had not reported that they were unprovided with tally-sheets." So the convention adjourned to meet again the next morning.

During the night Lincoln's managers were working like beavers. It was at midnight that Joseph Medill came upon David Davis in the hotel lobby just as the judge was leaving the room where he had been conferring with the Pennsylvania delegates. "How will they vote?" Medill wanted to know.

"Damned if we haven't got them," responded Davis. "How did you get them?"

"By paying their price." (The price was that the state's favorite son, Simon Cameron, was to become Secretary of the Treasury.)

"Good heavens! Give Cameron the Treasury Department? What will be left?"

"Oh, what's the difference?" replied Davis. "We are after a bigger thing than that; we want the Presidency, and the Treasury is not a great stake to pay for it." (In the end Cameron did not get that plum, but became Secretary of War.)

Early in the morning the confident Seward men began to march through the streets of Chicago, hurrahing their candidate, the "next President of the United States." But they marched a little too far. When they returned to the Wigwam, they could not get into the hall; every seat was occupied. Overnight Lincoln's managers

An 1860 lithograph by Louis Maurer, issued by Currier & Ives

UNCLE SAM MAKES NEW ARRANGEMENTS. He takes down the "help wanted" sign and advises the candidates—Douglas, Breckinridge and Bell—that he has "concluded to take down the Notice and let Old Abe Lincoln have the Place, I find his record all right, and can safely trust him with the management of my affairs." Buchanan is in the White House.

had distributed counterfeit tickets and filled the building with Lincoln supporters. Thus when the balloting began, the large part of the Seward contingent had to stay outside. When Lincoln's name was seconded, every "plank and pillar" in the Wigwam quivered. Halstead noted: "Imagine all the hogs ever slaughtered in Cincinnati giving their death squeals together, a score of big steam whistles going (steam at 160 lbs. per inch), and you conceive something of the same nature."

The first ballot brought no surprises. Maine gave 10 votes to Seward and 6 to Lincoln, Vermont was behind its favorite son, Senator Collamer; Massachusetts cast 21 votes for Seward, 4 for Lincoln; Rhode Island's majority went to Judge McLean; Connecticut's to Bates. New York, Seward's state, was behind its favorite son. New Jersey voted for its favorite son, Dayton; Pennsylvania's majority voted for Cameron; Maryland and Delaware were for Bates. Virginia cast 8 votes for

Seward but 14 for Lincoln. Kentucky was divided among Seward, Lincoln, Chase, McLean and Charles Sumner; Ohio's majority went to Chase. Then came Indiana. A shout broke loose when all 26 of the Hoosier delegates gave their support for Lincoln. Missouri was for Bates, Michigan for Seward, as were Wisconsin and the majority of Texas. Iowa was divided. California and Minnesota were for Seward, and Oregon for Bates. The territories of Kansas and Nebraska and the District of Columbia were behind Seward, giving him 10 votes out of a total of 14.

The result of the first ballot was 173½ for Seward, 102 for Lincoln, 50½ for Cameron, 49 for Chase, 48 for Bates, with the remaining votes divided among a number of lesser candidates.

The convention hall was bursting with excitement. "Call the roll, call the roll," came from thousands of voices.

Lorant: Lincoln: A Picture Story of His Life (*Harper*)
LINCOLN STANDING AT THE DOOR OF HIS SPRINGFIELD HOME WITH FRIENDS AND WELL-WISHERS

The second ballot saw Lincoln in the ascendancy. New Hampshire changed to him, as did Vermont, and 5 more votes were given to him from Rhode Island and Connecticut. Pandemonium broke loose when Pennsylvania switched to Lincoln, increasing his strength by 44 votes. The tally at the end stood: Seward 184½, Lincoln 181. The bandwagon was rolling.

When on the third ballot Lincoln's votes rose to 231½, only 1½ votes short of the nomination, Halstead, watching the excitement, jotted on his pad:

"There are always men anxious to distinguish themselves on such occasions. There is nothing that politicians like better than a crisis. I looked up to see who would be the man to give the decisive vote. . . . In about ten ticks of a watch, Cartter of Ohio was up. I had imagined Ohio would be slippery enough for the crisis. And sure enough! Every eye was on Cartter, and everybody who understood the matter at all knew what he was about to do. . . . He said: 'I rise (eh), Mr. Chairman (eh), to announce the change of four votes of Ohio from Mr. Chase to Mr. Lincoln.' "

The Wigwam was in an uproar. A large photograph of Lincoln was brought into the hall and cheered wildly. Delegation after delegation changed its votes. A secretary with a talley sheet in his hand cried out: "Fire the salute! Abe Lincoln is nominated."

Knapp, a friend of Lincoln, rushed out to wire the news to Springfield: "Abe, we did it. Glory to God!" And Lincoln, who received the message at the *Journal* office, said quietly: "I reckon there's a little short woman down at our house that would like to hear the news." The "little short woman," his wife Mary, who for years suffered a lonely life while her husband was riding the circuit trying law cases and politicking, was now to share the moment of his triumph.

In Chicago the Seward men wept like children, in Springfield the Lincoln supporters got drunk in their joy. Judge Davis telegraphed Lincoln: "Don't come here for God's sake. You will be telegraphed by others to come. It is the united advice of your friends not to come. This is important." The Seward delegates were in such despair that Davis thought it would be disastrous

Drawing in "The Rail Splitter", *Chicago, 1860.*

DOUGLAS ADDRESSING A CHICAGO CROWD—A CARICATURE IN A REPUBLICAN CAMPAIGN PAPER

for Lincoln to confront them in person. In the afternoon the convention completed its work by nominating Hannibal Hamlin, a former Democrat from Maine, for the second place.

Halstead gave his view of the vice presidential nomination. He heard a "thousand voices" call the name of Cassius M. Clay. "If the multitude could have had their way, Mr. Clay would have been put on the ticket by acclamation. But it was stated that Mr. Hamlin was a good friend of Mr. Seward. He was geographically distant from Lincoln, and was once a Democrat. It was deemed judicious to pretend to patronize the Democratic element, and thus consolidate those who were calling the convention an 'old Whig concern.' They need not have been afraid, however, of having it called an old Whig affair, for it was not 'eminently respectable,' nor distinguished for its 'dignity and decorum.' On the other hand, the satanic element was very strongly developed."

The Democrats were still without a candidate. On June 18 they met again, in Baltimore, with many con-

tested Southern delegates asking for admission. For three days the convention discussed nothing else but their status. And when the Douglas factions from Alabama and Louisiana were admitted, all the anti-Douglas delegates from the South withdrew in protest.

The remaining delegates gave Douglas 173 ½ votes, Guthrie 10, and Breckinridge 5, and 3 votes went to others. Sanford Church of New York submitted a resolution that the nomination should be conceded to Douglas as he had received two-thirds of the votes. But when it was pointed out that Douglas had not received the two-thirds vote of *all* the Democratic delegates, but only of those present, Church withdrew his resolution. On the second ballot the Douglas vote increased to 187 ½. Again Church introduced his resolution, and this time it was adopted. Thus Douglas became the candidate of the Northern Democrats. Senator Fitzpatrick was nominated for the Vice Presidency, but he declined. So the national committee replaced him with Herschel V. Johnson of Georgia.

The Southern delegates who had withdrawn from the

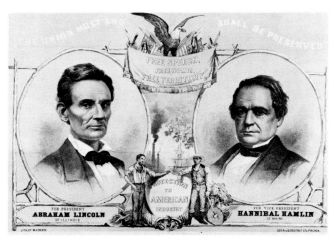

An 1860 lithograph by W. H. Reese, Philadelphia
THE BANNER OF THE REPUBLICAN CANDIDATES

Smithsonian Institution
A LINCOLN BANNER FOR THE GERMAN VOTERS

An 1860 lithograph by Currier and Ives
THE BELL AND EVERETT BANNER

first convention met in the meantime in Richmond; now they met again in another hall in Charleston, joined by the delegates who had left the Baltimore convention. They adopted the rejected majority platform of the first convention calling for the protection of slavery in all territories. And they nominated John C. Breckinridge of Kentucky for the Presidency and Joseph Lane of Oregon for the Vice Presidency.

With this the Democrats had two tickets in the contest, one in the North, the other in the South. Douglas, the Northern candidate, stood on his popular-sovereignty platform; Breckinridge, the candidate of the South, defended slavery.

It was an exciting campaign. Troops of Republi-

can "Wide-Awakes" paraded in New York and other cities wearing black-enameled circular caps, carrying rails with oil lamps and flags. In Boston a rail-splitters' battalion—every one of the men standing at least six feet four inches, as tall as Lincoln in his stocking feet—marched through the streets. The "Bell Ringers" of the Bell and Everett ticket imitated the "Wide-Awakes"; there were also "Union Sentinels" and "Minute Men." In Brooklyn the Douglas men called themselves "The Chloroformers," ready to put the Republican "Wide-Awakes" to sleep.

Lincoln, who made a resolution not to "write or speak anything upon doctrinal points," remained at home in Springfield. He set up his temporary office at the Spring-

Harper's Weekly, *October 13, 1860*

A PARADE OF THE REPUBLICAN WIDE-AWAKES FOR THE LINCOLN-HAMLIN TICKET IN NEW YORK

field State House, receiving officeseekers and visitors by the hundreds. Artists descended on him. Photographers came, painters and sculptors. Friends cried for his picture; people wanted to know what he looked like.

He was asked to say something to reassure the men "honestly alarmed" over the unrest in the South. "There are no such men," he answered. "It is the trick by which the South breaks down every Northern man. If I yielded to their entreaties, I would go to Washington without the support of the men who now support me. I would be as powerless as a block of buckeye wood. The honest men—you are talking of honest men—will find in our platform everything I could say now, or which they would ask me to say."

He would say nothing which might be misconstrued, which might hurt his election. Rallies and political meetings were held almost every night in Springfield, but Lincoln would not attend them. Only when Carl Schurz came in midsummer to give an address did he make an exception. "I will go with and hear what you have to say," he promised.

Schurz has left with us a vivid recollection of the presidential candidate on that day. "The day was blazing hot. Mr. Lincoln expressed his regret that I had to exert myself in such a temperature, and suggested that I make myself comfortable. He indeed 'made himself comfortable' in a way which surprised me not a little, but which was thoroughly characteristic of his rustic

247

BEFORE CONTEST LINCOLN WAS CLEANSHAVEN.

have been farther from his mind than the thought that the world-conspicuous distinction bestowed upon him by his nomination for the presidency should have obliged him to 'put on dignity' among his neighbors. Those neighbors who, from the windows and the sidewalks on that hot afternoon, watched and cheered him as he walked by in the procession behind the brass band, may have regarded him, the future President, with a new feeling of reverential admiration, or awe; but he appeared before and among them entirely unconcerned, as if nothing had happened, and so he nodded to his acquaintances, as he recognized them in the crowd."

While Lincoln stayed at Springfield, Douglas was out campaigning. He warned that a Republican victory would lead to the secession of the South. He repeated to his audiences that "this country is in more danger now than at any moment since I have known anything of public life."

He was aware that he alone could stop Lincoln. Bell had no chance; neither had Breckinridge. But if he could not win, Douglas at least hoped to bring the election to the House of Representatives.

The central issue of the campaign was slavery. Lincoln wanted to exclude it from the territories, to isolate and weaken the existing slave states. Douglas argued that nature already effectively banned slavery in the territories, and that the climate would do what Congress should not. He asked for the toleration of the existing slave states: "If each state will only agree to mind its own business and let its neighbors alone . . . this republic can exist forever divided into free and slave states, as our fathers made it, and the people of each state have decided."

Douglas began his speaking tour in New England; his strength lay in the North. But soon he saw that he would not be able to defeat Lincoln; the Northern states would vote for him and the Republican cause.

He was disturbed that disunionists in Virginia and Maryland might seize the Capital after the election, so he rushed to the South to appeal to their patriotism. When asked in Norfolk whether the South should secede if Lincoln were elected, he answered: "The election of a man to the Presidency by the American people in conformity with the Constitution of the United States *would not justify any attempt at dissolving this glorious confederacy.*" Asked again if the South should be coerced if it did secede, he replied that the President must enforce the laws, "and I, as in duty bound by my oath of fidelity to the Constitution, *would do all in my power to aid the Government of the United States in maintaining the supremacy of the laws against all resistance to them, come from whatever quarter it might.*"

Douglas continued his campaign in New York, where he wished "we had an Old Hickory now alive in order

habits. When he presented himself for the march to the Capitol grounds I observed that he had divested himself of his waistcoat and put on as his sole garment, a linen duster, the back of which had been marked by repeated perspirations and looked somewhat like a rough map of the two hemispheres. On his head he wore a well-battered stovepipe hat which evidently had seen several years of hard service. In this attire he marched with me behind the brass band, after the local campaign committee and the Wide-Awakes. Of course, he was utterly unconscious of his grotesque appearance. Nothing could

Lorant, Lincoln, A Picture Story of His Life (*Harper*)

LINCOLN'S ANSWER to a letter from an 11-year-old girl, Grace Bedell, who suggested that he grow a beard because "all the ladies like whiskers and they would tease their husbands to vote for you and then you would be President."

Photograph by C. S. German, February 9, 1861

AFTER ELECTION HE BEGAN TO GROW A BEARD.

that he might hang Northern and Southern traitors on the same gallows." In October he was in his native Midwest to keep on his warnings to both North and South. While in Iowa he received word that Lincoln had won the electoral votes of Pennsylvania. He told his secretary that "Mr. Lincoln is the next President. We must try to save the Union. I will go South."

And he went. First to St. Louis, then Tennessee and finally to the cotton states, trying to lift the voice of reason. Tired and exhausted, his voice became hoarse. When the party ran short of money he used his own

funds. His life was threatened and numerous attempts were made to wreck his trains, but he went on and on.

It was in Mobile that he heard the election result. His secretary described him as "more hopeless than I had ever before seen him."

When the votes were in, they showed that Lincoln had carried all the Northern states but one. In New Jersey the contest was so close that for days no one knew whether it was for Lincoln or for Douglas. The final tally gave Lincoln 4 and Douglas 3 electoral votes. California was won by Lincoln by a popular majority

Frank Leslie's Illustrated Newspaper, *November 24, 1860*
THE PRESIDENT-ELECT RECEIVES FRIENDS AND OFFICE SEEKERS IN THE SPRINGFIELD STATE HOUSE.

Lorant, Lincoln, A Picture Story of His Life (*Harper*)
LINCOLN SELLS HIS HOUSEHOLD EFFECTS. Following the sale "consisting of Parlor and Chamber Sets, Carpets, Sofas, Chairs, Wardrobes, Bureaus, Bedsteads, Stoves . . . glass, Etc., etc.," which he advertised in the *Illinois State Journal,* Lincoln gave this receipt to the Springfield druggist S. H. Melvin for some of the family belongings.

of only 657 votes out of a total of nearly 80,000.

The South—eleven out of the fifteen slave states—was solidly behind Breckinridge, who had the endorsement of President Buchanan; three states voted for the Bell-Everett ticket, and only one—Missouri—for Douglas. From the Southern States Lincoln did not receive a single electoral vote.

The popular vote stood: Lincoln, 1,866,452; Breckinridge, 849,781; Douglas, 1,376,957; John Bell, 588,879—a clear indication that the overwhelming majority of the country was not for secession and war, but for union and peace. Breckinridge, the only secession candidate, had less than one-fifth of the total.

Lincoln remained in Springfield till early February preparing himself for the ordeal, and growing a beard. Outside his house people were sleeping on the pavement so as to catch him in the morning and petition him

Lorant: Lincoln: A Picture Story of His Life (Harper)
LINCOLN'S FAREWELL SPEECH at Springfield. After
the train left the station, the journalist Henry Villard approached the President-elect for a copy of his speech.
Lincoln took out a pencil and put on paper what he had
said, improving it. As the train rocked, his secretary John
Nicolay took over, completing the page from his dictation.

Lorant: Lincoln: A Picture Story of His Life (Harper)
ON THE MORNING of February 22, 1861, Lincoln
hoisted the flag at Philadelphia's Independence Hall with
a new star honoring Kansas. Lincoln said that if the country
could not be saved without giving up the principle of equality found in the Declaration of Independence, then "I
would rather be assassinated on this spot than surrender it."

for jobs. Dozens of others were waiting in his law office;
everywhere he turned he was surrounded by a demanding crowd. *The New York Times* reporter was greatly
impressed with Lincoln's ability to keep silent on vital
matters without offending the questioners: "Now and
then a blunt old farmer will blurt out something about
the Cabinet, and perhaps suggest the difficulty of meeting the Secessionists. But the truly Republican President
passes it off with a smile, and simply keeps mum. I
never knew a public man who knew so well how to hold
his tongue, and yet not offend his best friends."

The President-elect had two immediate problems before him. One was the formation of a Cabinet, the other
was to write the inaugural speech. Lincoln met with
Hannibal Hamlin, the incoming Vice President, and
with the New York political boss Thurlow Weed. There
was full agreement that Seward should be the Secretary

Illustrated London News, March 1861
IN MUFTI THROUGH BALTIMORE. The 21-year-old
Thomas Nast originally drew Lincoln with a slouched hat,
but the editors of the *Illustrated London News* altered
his drawing to make it agree with the prevalent story.
Thus Lincoln appeared with a plaid and a Scottish cap.

THE INAUGURAL STAND ON THE MORNING OF MARCH 4, 1861, BEFORE THE CEREMONIES BEGIN

Frank Leslie's Illustrated Newspaper, *March 16, 1861*
DOWN PENNSYLVANIA AVENUE. President Buchanan with President-elect Lincoln rides toward the unfinished Capitol.

of State and Salmon P. Chase the Treasury Secretary. To pay the convention debt to Pennsylvania, Simon Cameron had to be given the War office. A similar debt to Indiana made Caleb B. Smith the Secretary of the Interior. The need for two Southerners put Edward Bates, a Unionist from Missouri, in as Attorney General and Montgomery Blair, the Maryland politician, as Postmaster General. The post of the Secretary of the Navy was given to Gideon Welles of Connecticut.

Four members of the Cabinet were former Democrats: Chase, Cameron, Blair and Welles. Thurlow Weed wondered why they should have a majority in the Cabinet. "You seem to forget," said Lincoln, "that I expect to be there; and counting me as one, you see how nicely the Cabinet would be balanced and ballasted."

To compose the inaugural address Lincoln locked himself up in a "dingy, dusty, and neglected back room" over his brother-in-law's store, and in this seclusion began to write. At his elbow he had four references—only four. One was Henry Clay's speech of 1850; another, Andrew Jackson's nullification proclamation; the third, Webster's reply to Hayne; and the fourth, a copy of the Constitution.

When he finished, a compositor of the Springfield *Journal* set it in type; it ran eight galleys. Lincoln revised them and another proof was pulled, this time on seven pages. He was to read the address from these.

Before he left Springfield, Lincoln went to his law office to say good-bye to Billy Herndon, his law partner of sixteen years. Pointing to the shingle, he told Herndon: "Let it hang there undisturbed. Give our clients to understand that the election of a President makes no change in the firm of Lincoln and Herndon. If I live, I'm coming back some time, and then we'll go right on practicing law as if nothing had ever happened."

In the morning of February 11 in the drizzling rain, he bade an affectionate farewell to his friends and neighbors, one of his most touching addresses; then the train took him to Washington over a circuitous route. In Baltimore he changed trains—the detective Pinkerton insisted that he should put on a disguise, a soft hat and an overcoat—to foil an assassination plot. He was

Harper's Weekly, *March 15, 1861*
BUCHANAN AND LINCOLN AS THEY ENTER THE SENATE CHAMBER FOR THE INAUGURAL CEREMONY

whisked through the city in the hours before dawn. He arrived in Washington without fanfare, without reception, a solitary figure in the early morning mist.

The weather on the morning of March 4, 1861, was like the mood of the nation—it wavered between clear and stormy.

Rumors filled the Capital: "There would be a Southern raid upon the Capital," said a man in a public house. Another: "Lincoln will never be inaugurated; he will be shot before sundown."

The military commanders of Washington made careful preparations. Riflemen were placed in squads on the roofs of the houses along Pennsylvania Avenue. General Stone gave orders "to watch the windows on the opposite side, and to fire upon them in case any attempt should be made to fire from those windows on the presidential carriage."

And while the military feared the worst, Lincoln remained calm. As the clock struck noon, President James Buchanan came for him at Willard's Hotel, and together they rode down Pennsylvania Avenue.

To the left and the right of the open carriage rode a squadron of cavalry; vigilant eyes watched the crowds from everywhere. Suddenly there was a commotion; a strange, popping, crackling noise was heard. The police were baffled, but their tension dissipated when they found that the noise came from the boots of the New England section marching behind the carriage. The New Englanders had come in their regular winter footgear, extra soles pegged for heavy snows. The peg timber had shrunk in the warm Maryland sun, causing loud squeaks with every step, "noisy enough, in mass and in unison, to be heard for several blocks." The reporter of the *Evening Star,* paraphrasing Shakespeare, remarked: "Treasons and stratagems cannot be chargeable to men with so much music in their soles."

In his inaugural address Lincoln warned the South: "In your hands, my dissatisfied fellow countrymen, and not in mine, is the momentous issue of civil war. The government will not assail you. You can have no conflict without being yourselves the aggressors. You have no oath registered in heaven to destroy the government, while I shall have the most solemn one to 'preserve, protect, and defend' it." And he pleaded: "We are not

THE CROWD IS WAITING
FOR THE BEGINNING OF
THE INAUGURATION.

Thomas Nast, March 1861

LINCOLN DELIVERS HIS INAUGURAL ADDRESS BEFORE THE UNFINISHED CAPITOL ON MARCH 4, 1861.

Lincoln National Life Foundation

ON AN OPEN BIBLE HE TOOK THE OATH from the trembling and shaking Chief Justice Roger B. Taney, who was described as looking like a "galvanized corpse."

enemies, but friends. We must not be enemies. Though passion may have strained, it must not break, our bonds of affection. The mystic chords of memory, stretching from every battlefield and patriot grave to every living heart and hearthstone all over this broad land, will yet swell the chorus of the Union when again touched, as surely they will be by the better angels of our nature."

A listener wrote his wife: "Old Abe delivered the greatest speech of the age. It is backbone all over."

But no words were strong enough to stop the drift to war. Jefferson Davis had already been inaugurated in the South on February 18. He said, "We have entered upon a career of independence and it must be inflexibly pursued . . . As a necessity, not a choice, we have resorted to the remedy of separation, and henceforth our energies must be directed to the conduct of our own affairs, and the perpetuity of the Confederacy which we have formed."

The attacks on Fort Sumter and the American flag were only weeks away. It was too late to avoid the war between the states.

The Chief Magistrate derives all his authority from the people, and they have conferred none upon him to fix terms for the separation of the States. The people themselves can do this *also* if they choose; but the executive, as such, has nothing to do with it. His duty is to administer the present government, as it came to his hands, and to transmit it, unimpaired by him, to his successor.

Why should there not be a patient confidence in the ultimate justice of the people? Is there any better or equal hope, in the world? In our present differences, is either party without faith *of being* in the right? If the Almighty Ruler of nations, with his eternal truth and justice, be on *on your side of the North, or on yours of the South,* that truth, and that justice, will surely prevail, by the judgment of this great tribunal, the American people.

By the frame of the government under which we live, this same people have wisely given their public servants but little power for mischief; and have, with equal wisdom, provided for the return of that little to their own hands at very short intervals. While the people *retain their virtue, and vigilence, no administration* by any extreme of wickedness or folly, can very seriously injure the government, in the short space of four years.

My countrymen, one and all, *think calmly and* well, upon this whole subject. Nothing valuable can be lost by taking time. If there be an object to *hurry* any of you, in hot haste, to a step which you would never take *deliberately*, that object will be frustrated by taking time; but no good object can be frustrated by it. Such of you as are now dissatisfied, still have the old Constitution unimpaired, and, on the sensitive point, the laws of your own framing under it; while the new administration will have no immediate power, if it would, to change either. If it were admitted that you who are dissatisfied, hold the right side in the dispute, there still is no single good reason for precipitate action. Intelligence, patriotism, Christianity, and a firm reliance on Him, who has never yet forsaken this favored land, are still competent to adjust, in the best way, all our present difficulty.

In *your* hands, my dissatisfied fellow countrymen, and not in *mine*, is the momentous issue of civil war. The government will not assail *you.* You can have no conflict, without being yourselves the aggressors. *You* have no oath registered in Heaven to destroy the government, while *I* shall have the most solemn one to "preserve, protect and defend" it.

I am loth to close. We are not enemies, but friends— We must not be enemies. Though passion may have strained, it must not break our bonds of affection. The mystic chords of memory, stretching from every battle-field, and patriot grave, to every living heart and hearth-stone, all over this broad land, will yet swell the chorus of the Union, when again touched, as surely they will be, by the better angels of our nature.

7744

THE LAST PAGE OF THE INAUGURAL ADDRESS. Set in type back at home in Springfield, it was revised many times. William Seward suggested a different ending; Lincoln approved the suggestion, but revised Seward's pedestrian style.

ABRAHAM LINCOLN and ANDREW JOHNSON

At the time Lincoln took the oath, a Confederate government in the South had already started to operate. Jefferson Davis was the elected head of the Confederacy formed by the states of South Carolina, Mississippi, Florida, Alabama, Louisiana, Georgia and Texas.

A day after his inauguration Lincoln read a report from Major Robert Anderson, the commandant of Fort Sumter in Charleston Harbor. Anderson, whose provisions were running low, reported that after consulting with his officers about possibilities of relief and reinforcement, he came to the conclusion Fort Sumter could be effectively succored only if a combined land and naval force subdued the besieging Confederate batteries on land.

Lincoln knew that if he made an aggressive move, the lower South would retaliate immediately—and once the war began, the upper South might join in the fight too. But he could not allow the garrison to withdraw and abandon the fort.

Secretary of State Seward argued against initiating a war "to regain a useless and unnecessary position," and met with Confederate commissioners in Washington. Lincoln did not oppose a bargain. He was willing to evacuate Fort Sumter if that would prevent the secession of Virginia. "A state for a fort is no bad business." He sent his friend Ward Hill Lamon to South Carolina, where Lamon gave the impression that the fort would not be reinforced.

But as the time passed, Lincoln saw the evacuation would not satisfy the South. He notified the Governor of South Carolina that a peaceful expedition would bring food and other necessities to the garrison of Fort Sumter, but that neither men nor ammunition would be carried.

The Confederate government regarded Lincoln's message as a declaration of war. At 4:30 in the morning of April 12, 1861, General Beauregard's batteries opened fire in Charleston Harbor—the first shots of the Civil War. For a day and a half the barrage continued; on April 13 Anderson and his men surrendered; on April 14 the flag of the Confederacy flew over Fort Sumter.

The outbreak of the war brought political unity to the North. After the fall of Fort Sumter, Douglas went to see Lincoln and the President read to him the draft of the proclamation he would issue the next morning, on April 15, calling for 75,000 volunteers to suppress the rebellion. Douglas, still leader of the Northern wing of the Democratic party, subordinating all personal and political considerations, wholeheartedly endorsed Lincoln's action. He was for sustaining the President, preserving the Union, maintaining the government and defending the capital. He declared: "There can be no neutrals in this war, only patriots or traitors." A few weeks later he died.

But with mounting sacrifices on the battlefields, opposition to Lincoln's policies mounted as well. It was not long before Wendell Phillips spoke of him as "a more unlimited despot than the world knows this side of China," and Charles Sumner said: "Our President is now dictator, *imperator*—whichever you like; but how vain to have the power of a god and not use it godlike."

The reverses on the battlefield, the ineptness of the generals were blamed on Lincoln. He was charged with

ANDREW JOHNSON
*Print from the cracked original
negative of Mathew B. Brady
in the National Archives*

CANDIDATES IN 1864

ABRAHAM LINCOLN (1809–1865) was once again nominated by the Republican party. At first it looked as though he might lose the election to the Democrats, but after General Sherman had taken Atlanta and Admiral Farragut had captured Mobile Bay, his re-election was no longer in doubt. He received 2,330,552 popular votes against McClellan's 1,835,985; the electoral vote total was: Lincoln 212, McClellan 21.

ANDREW JOHNSON (1808–1875), a self-educated former tailor's apprentice in N.C., was a legislator and Senator in Tennessee. He served in Congress ten years, became Governor of his state, U.S. Senator, then military governor of Tennessee. A former Democrat, the Republicans chose him to strengthen the ticket and to win votes in the border states. On April 14, 1865, after the assassination, he was sworn in as President.

GEORGE B. McCLELLAN (1826–1885), West Point graduate, vice president of the Illinois Central Railroad and president of the Ohio and Mississippi Railroad, and erstwhile general of the Union armies during the Civil War, was chosen by the Democrats to oppose Lincoln. Though he repudiated the "stop-the-war" platform, he kept the nomination. Had it not been for major pre-election Union victories, he would have won.

GEORGE H. PENDLETON (1825–1889), a Representative in Congress from Ohio, nicknamed "Gentleman George" because of his bearing and dignity in the free-for-all of Midwestern politics. He was the husband of Francis Scott Key's daughter, the niece of Roger B. Taney. During the Civil War he was the leader of the Democrats' peace wing, the "Copperheads." His party's convention chose him for the Vice Presidential nomination.

ELIZA McCARDLE (1810–1876) married Johnson on May 5, 1827, when she was only 16 years old. She taught him reading and writing. Theirs was a happy marriage, with six children, three sons and three daughters.

Because she was an invalid when Johnson became President, her two daughters —Mrs. Patterson and Mrs. Stover— did the honors at the White House.

inefficiency in the conduct of the war. A joint committee in Congress asked for greater Congressional participation in the decision-making. Lincoln would not hear of it—he would not abdicate his responsibilities. He changed generals who did not work out.

By the summer of 1863, with victories at Gettysburg and Vicksburg, the fortunes of war changed; the initiative now was with the North. Lincoln regained much of his lost popularity. Yet many in his party would have liked to replace him. The man whom they wanted to elevate to the Presidency was Salmon P. Chase, the Secretary of the Treasury, an excellent administrator with a good antislavery record who—so it was assumed —could bring the war to a quick conclusion.

An 1864 cartoon by an unidentified artist

UNCLE SAM REVIEWS THE PRESIDENTIAL CANDIDATES. Behind General McClellan ("Little Mac," with a drum), who was chosen by the Democrats, are Tennessee's Governor Andrew Johnson, who became Lincoln's running mate, and John Frémont, the Republican nominee of eight years before. On Lincoln's left: Secretary of the Treasury Salmon P. Chase; General Benjamin F. Butler, of New Orleans fame; General Nathaniel P. Banks, former Governor of Massachusetts; General Franz Sigel, the leader of the German-Americans; and Secretary of State William H. Seward.

A committee of leading Republicans went to see him early in 1864 to sound him out. And when he expressed his willingness, Samuel Pomeroy, the Kansas Senator, published a circular asserting that, since the re-election of Lincoln was neither possible nor desirable, the new candidate should be Chase. The Secretary sent a note to Lincoln offering his resignation "if there is anything in my action or position which, in your judgment, will prejudice the public interest under my charge." Lincoln answered: "Whether you shall remain at the head of the Treasury Department is a question which I will not allow myself to consider from any other standpoint other than my judgment of the public service, and, in that view, I do not perceive occasion for a change."

Horace Greeley argued in the New York *Tribune* that not only Chase but Frémont, Butler or Grant would make as good a President as Lincoln, and that the selection of any of them would preserve "the salutary one-term principle." Greeley was referring to the custom of the last three decades during which no President had served more than one term. Tyler, Polk, Fillmore, Pierce and Buchanan were not nominated for a second term; Van Buren, though nominated, was defeated in the election.

But Lincoln had a firm base of support. In several states legislative caucuses, political conventions and Union Leagues were for his renomination. He had the backing of the people, of businessmen, of intellectuals.

An 1864 lithograph published by H. H. Lloyd & Co., N.Y.
THE PYGMIES MEASURE LINCOLN'S SHOES. In the group on the left: Salmon P. Chase thumbs his nose; Manton Marble, the anti-Lincoln editor of the New York *World,* and William Cullen Bryant, the editor of the New York *Evening Post,* approach the shoes with rulers. James Gordon Bennett of the New York *Herald* shares a measure with his son (in center). Behind the younger Bennett is Samuel Bowles of the Springfield *Republican,* measuring the right shoe, while Greeley of the New York *Tribune* peers into the left one. The group on the right: Senator Sumner; Hugh Hastings of the Brooklyn *Commercial Advertiser;* Harry J. Raymond of the *New York Times;* and Anna Dickinson, the abolitionist actress.

James Russell Lowell wrote in the *North American Review* that "History will rank Mr. Lincoln among the most prudent of statesmen and the most successful of rulers. If we wish to appreciate him, we have only to conceive the inevitable chaos in which we should now be weltering had a weak man or an unwise one been chosen in his stead." And the botanist Asa Gray told Darwin: "Homely, honest, ungainly Lincoln is the most representative man of the country."

The Radical Republicans, in firm opposition to Lincoln, called a convention in Cleveland "for consultation and concert of action in respect to the approaching presidential election." Their platform declared "that the rebellion must be suppressed by force of arms, and without compromise," and that "the one-term policy for the Presidency adopted by the people is strengthened by the force of the existing crisis, and should be maintained by constitutional amendments." They named John C. Frémont for the Presidency and General John Cochrane for the Vice Presidency.

The decision of the Radicals had no influence on the regular Republicans. On the eve of their convention Seward wrote, "The country is entering on a new and perilous time, a canvass for the Presidency in time of civil war." On June 3 came the battle of Cold Harbor, a defeat for the North, but it had not been fully comprehended and did not lead to any last-minute drive to replace Lincoln. Four days later the Republicans met in Baltimore and renominated the President.

Missouri at first gave her thirty-two votes to Grant,

262

An 1864 pen drawing by an unidentified artist

A DASTARDLY ATTACK ON LINCOLN. The President on the battlefield at Antietam asks his friend Marshal Lamon to "give us that song about Picayune Butler." General McClellan interrupts him: "I would prefer to hear it some other place and time."

A report telling the tale was printed in the New York *World,* whose editor, Manton Marble, was an unrelenting critic of Lincoln. The story was a fabrication, yet it was used. Lincoln wrote a denial of the charge, but never sent it out.

but then changed to Mr. Lincoln. Grant's candidacy had been widely mentioned ever since the Battle of Chattanooga. Lincoln, caring more for the country than for himself, said of his General: "If he takes Richmond let him have the nomination." For his running mate Andrew Johnson, the Democratic Governor of Tennessee who was siding with the North, was chosen. Thaddeus Stevens fumed. Couldn't the Republicans find someone "without going down into one of those d——d rebel provinces to pick one up?" he wanted to know.

When a delegation from the National Union League came to Lincoln to congratulate him, Lincoln made a nice little speech to them: "I do not allow myself to suppose that either the convention or the League have concluded to decide that I am either the greatest or best man in America, but rather they have concluded it is not best to swap horses while crossing the river, and have further concluded that I am not so poor a horse that they might not make a botch of it in trying to swap." Lincoln's phrase, to "swap horses while crossing the river," was often repeated by later Presidents. In time of stress they took refuge in it.

Though Lincoln had the nomination, his election was far from assured. The military picture was poor. The Army of the Potomac was exhausted, the casualties were staggering. The country yearned for peace. "I know," wrote Greeley to Lincoln, "that nine-tenths of the whole American people, North and South, are anxious for peace—peace on almost any terms—and utterly sick of human slaughter and devastation. . . . I firmly

263

Drawn by J. H. Howard in 1864

"I KNEW HIM, HO-RATIO, A FELLOW OF INFINITE JEST," declaims "Hamlet" McClellan, the candidate of the Democrats.

COMPARING THE TWO MEN. Lincoln shakes the hand of a workman, Candidate Mc-Clellan that of Jefferson Davis. The Stars and Stripes of the North fly for Lincoln, the Stars and Bars of the South for Davis.

UNION AND LIBERTY!   AND   UNION AND SLAVERY!

Issued in 1864 by M. W. Siebert, N.Y.

believe that, were the election to take place tomorrow, the Democratic majority in this state and Pennsylvania would amount to 100,000 and that we should lose Connecticut also. Now if the Rebellion can be crushed before November, it will do to go on; if not, we are rushing to certain ruin. . . . I beg you, implore you, to inaugurate or invite proposals for peace forthwith. And in case peace cannot now be made, consent to an *armistice for one year,* each party to retain, unmolested, all it now holds, but the rebel ports to be opened. Meantime, let a national convention be held, and there will

surely be no more war at all events"—a strong advice.

Republicans from New York sent out a call for a fresh Republican convention in Cincinnati to consider the nomination of another candidate in Lincoln's stead.

"Mr. Lincoln is already beaten," wrote Greeley. "He cannot be elected. And we must have another ticket to save us from utter overthrow. If we had such a ticket as could be made by naming Grant, Butler, or Sherman for President, and Farragut for Vice, we could make a fight yet. And such a ticket we ought to have anyhow, with or without a convention."

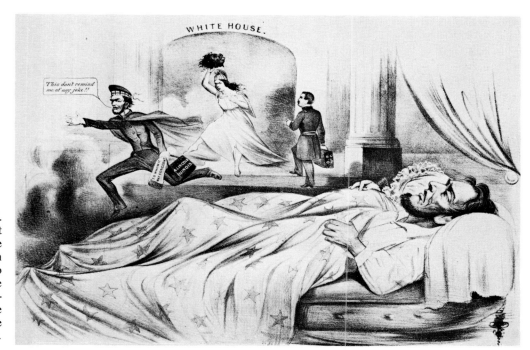

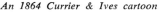

LINCOLN'S DREAM.
Columbia orders him out
of the White House; he
flees with a Scottish cap on
his head (a reference to
the 1861 episode when he
was whisked through Baltimore in disguise), while
General McClellan, on the
other side, moves into it.

An 1864 Currier & Ives cartoon

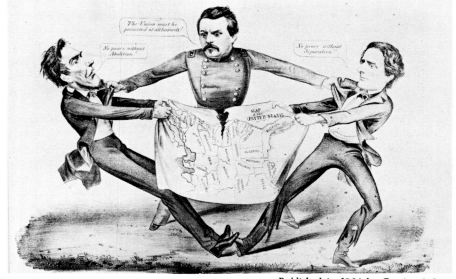

Published in 1864 by Currier & Ives

SUPPORTING THE DEMOCRAT.
George B. McClellan restrains
Abraham Lincoln and Jefferson
Davis from tearing the Union apart.

Politicians and newspapermen suggested that both Frémont and Lincoln, chosen by respective conventions, should withdraw. "The withdrawal of Lincoln and Frémont, and the nomination of a man that would inspire confidence and infuse a life into our ranks would be hailed with general delight," wrote the Cincinnati *Gazette*.

In the latter part of August Thurlow Weed told Seward: "When, ten days since, I told Mr. Lincoln that his re-election was an impossibility, I also told him that the information would soon come to him through other channels. It has doubtless ere this reached him. At any rate, nobody here doubts it, nor do I see anybody from other states who authorizes the slightest hope of success. Mr. Raymond, who has just left me, says that unless some prompt and bold step be now taken all is lost. The people are wild for peace. They are told that the President will only listen to terms of peace on condition that slavery be abandoned."

Gloom descended upon the Republican National Executive Committee; they saw little hope that the President could win re-election. Henry J. Raymond, the

265

> Executive Mansion
> Washington, Aug. 23, 1864.
>
> This morning, as for some days past, it seems exceedingly probable that this Administration will not be re-elected. Then it will be my duty to so co-operate with the President elect, as to save the Union between the election and the inauguration; as he will have secured his election. on on such ground that he cannot possibly save it afterwards,
>
> A. Lincoln

IN THE SUMMER OF 1864, THINKING HE MIGHT BE DEFEATED IN THE ELECTION, LINCOLN HAD

editor of *The New York Times*, wrote Lincoln "the tiding is getting strongly against us," and that the prospects were bad in all parts of the country.

On August 23, the very day he received Raymond's letter, Lincoln wrote a few lines on a double sheet of paper and asked the members of the Cabinet to endorse it on the reverse side—without letting them read it beforehand. What they signed was a promise to cooperate with the new President-elect "to save the Union between the election and the inauguration," as Lincoln regarded his re-election an improbability.

It was about a week later that the Democrats met in Chicago. Under the influence of Clement Vallandigham, the leader of the "Copperheads"—Democrats who opposed the war—the Democratic platform declared that "after four years of failure to restore the Union by the experiment of war . . . during which . . . the Constitution itself has been disregarded in every part, and

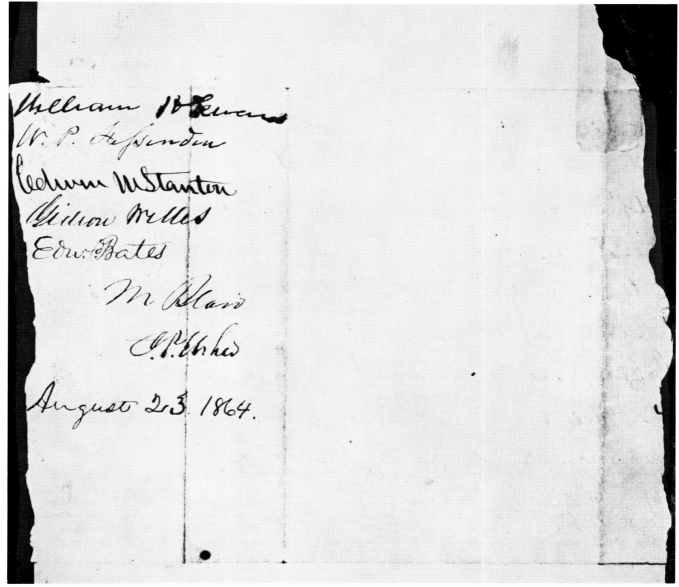

William H Seward
W. P. Fessenden
Edwin M Stanton
Gideon Welles
Edw. Bates
M Blair
J. P. Usher

August 23 1864.

HIS CABINET SIGN THIS NOTE ON THE REVERSE SIDE, NOT TELLING THEM WHAT WAS WRITTEN.

public liberty and private right alike trodden down . . . the public welfare demands that immediate efforts be made for a cessation of hostilities, with a view to an ultimate convention of the States, or other peaceable means, to the end that, at the earliest practicable moment, peace may be restored on the basis of the Federal Union of the States."

The convention turned to General George McClellan, the former commander of the Union forces, and made him their candidate for the Presidency, choosing George Pendleton for the second place. "Little Mac" accepted the nomination but not the platform. "I could not look in the face of my gallant comrades of the army and navy," he wrote, "who have survived so many bloody battles, and tell them that their labors and the sacrifices of so many of our slain and wounded brethren had been in vain; that we had abandoned that Union for which we have so often perilled our lives." And he empha-

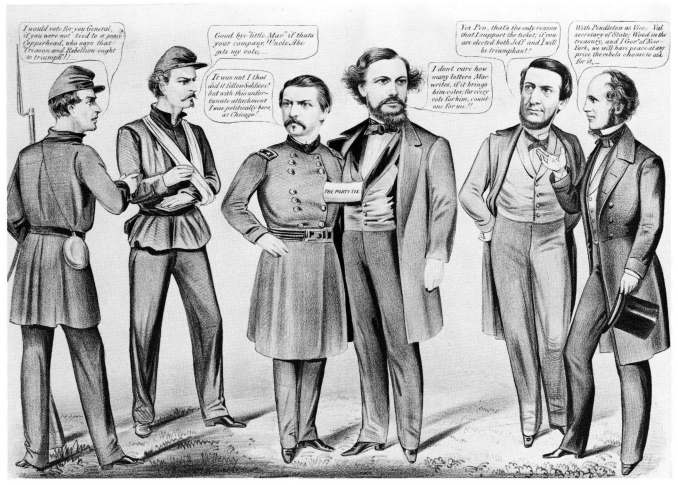

An 1864 lithograph issued by Currier & Ives

AGAINST McCLELLAN. The political Siamese twins—the Democratic candidates McClellan and Pendleton—with Vallandigham and Seymour. Vallandigham was the leader of the Copperheads (Northern Democrats who sympathized with the South, nicknamed for the poisonous snake which strikes without a warning rattle). One of the soldiers says: "I would vote for you General, if you were not tied to a peace Copperhead, who says that Treason and Rebellion ought to triumph!!"

sized: "No peace can be permanent without Union."

Events soon proved that the Democratic platform makers were far from the truth. The war a failure? McClellan had hardly accepted the nomination when the news of Sherman's victory at Atlanta and Farragut's triumph at Mobile Bay flashed through the country. In Seward's opinion: "Sherman and Farragut have knocked the bottom out of the Chicago nominations."

Now that the tide ran in his favor, Lincoln was ready to make a bargain with the radicals in his party who advanced the candidacy of General Frémont. If Frémont would withdraw, Lincoln would drop Montgomery Blair from the Cabinet, which the Radicals demanded. On September 22 Frémont obliged, and a day later Lincoln accepted Blair's resignation. The party was reunited.

On October 2 Salmon P. Chase, who in the mean-while had resigned his Cabinet post, went on stumping for Lincoln, and said: "There is not now, the slightest uncertainty about the re-election of Mr. Lincoln. The only question is by what popular and electoral majority. God grant that both may be so decisive as to turn every hope of rebellion to despair!"

McClellen waged a losing fight. The Democrats used shopworn campaign charges, attacking the "ignorance, incompetency, and corruption of Mr. Lincoln's administration." The New York *World* asked: "Mr. Lincoln, has he or has he not an interest in the profits of public contracts?" and answered that it could be proved that the President had succumbed to opportunities and temptations of his office. " 'Honest old Abe' has few honest men to defend his honesty," said the newspaper.

The President was under steady attack. A campaign

An 1864 drawing by J. E. Bakender

FOR McCLELLAN. The Republicans intimidated voters in the South, forcing them to march between troops to the polls.
The one-legged Union soldier says: "I am an American citizen and did not think I had fought and bled for this, ALAS MY COUNTRY!" But the colored soldier guarding the "free ballot" exclaims: "You can't put in dat you copperhead, traitor, nor any oder 'cept for MASSA LINCOLN." One official protests; the other tells him just to count the votes.

pamphlet, called the *Only Authentic Life of Abraham Lincoln, alias "Old Abe,"* burlesqued his life. It started out by saying that in 1860 "Mr. James Buchanan had been long enough in office, that he was getting soiled, so the nation prepared to put on a clean President." Thus "Abraham, though quite as modest as he was honest, thought this a good chance to make twenty-five thousand a year, so he went to New York and advocated his claims to the position, in a speech at Cooper Institute, charging two shillings admission fee. The Republicans admired his cheek, and nominated him. . . . He accepted, in a letter, in which he said he almost wished they had chosen a statesman instead. The whole country has wished so since." As for the basic fact that he did win the election, "There were two other candidates, and more people voted against Lincoln than voted for

him. He was therefore made President."

The "biography" gave this "description" of Old Abe: "Mr. Lincoln stands six feet twelve in his socks, which he changes once every ten days. His anatomy is composed mostly of bones, and when walking he resembles the offspring of a happy marriage between a derrick and a windmill," and concluded, "Such is Abraham Lincoln. . . . For his friends, who like his administration, he would make a better candidate for re-election than some man they do not like so well. With others, it is different."

The results bore out Chase's prediction: Lincoln won decisively with 2,213,665 popular votes against McClellan's 1,802,237. Even the soldiers—their ballots counted separately—were for Lincoln and not for the soldier candidate, giving the President 116,887 votes against McClellan's 33,748.

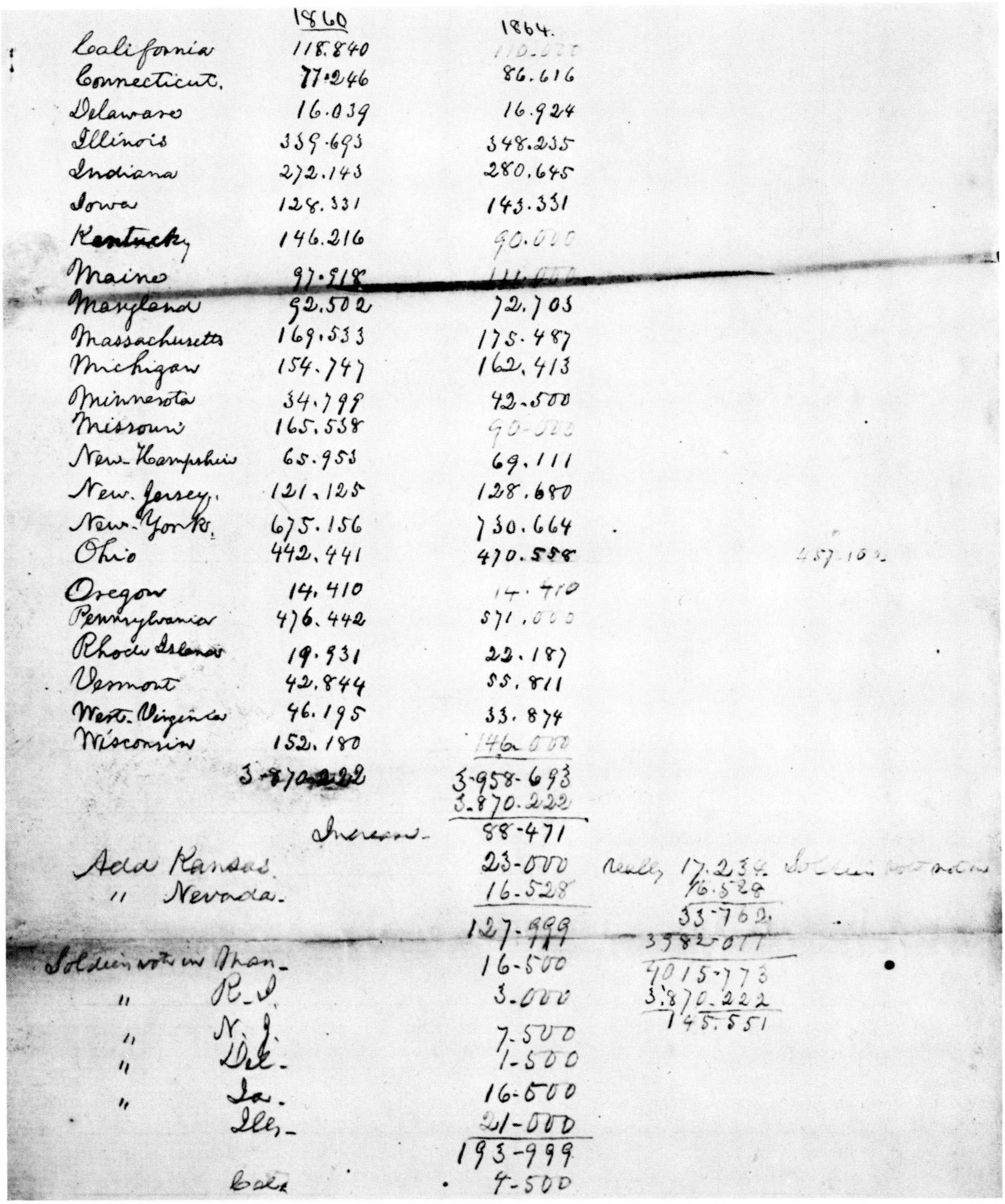

	1860	1864
California	118.840	*110.000*
Connecticut	77.246	86.616
Delaware	16.039	16.924
Illinois	339.693	348.235
Indiana	272.143	280.645
Iowa	128.331	143.331
Kentucky	146.216	*90.000*
Maine	97.918	*114.000*
Maryland	92.502	72.703
Massachusetts	169.533	175.487
Michigan	154.747	162.413
Minnesota	34.799	42.500
Missouri	165.538	*90.000*
New Hampshire	65.953	69.111
New Jersey	121.125	128.680
New York	675.156	730.664
Ohio	442.441	470.558
Oregon	14.410	*14.410*
Pennsylvania	476.442	*571.000*
Rhode Island	19.931	22.187
Vermont	42.844	55.811
West. Virginia	46.195	33.874
Wisconsin	152.180	*146.000*

Ohio 487.16

$$3.870.222 \qquad 3.958.693$$
$$3.870.222$$

Increase 88.471

Add Kansas ...... 23.000   really 17.234 Soldiers vote not in
" Nevada 16.528   16.528
                                            33.762
127.999   3.582.077

Soldiers vote in Penn. 16.500   4.015.773
" R.I. 3.000   3.870.222
" N.J. 7.500   145.551
" Del. 1.500
" La. 16.500
" Ill. 21.000
193.999
Cala 4.500

Lorant: Lincoln: A Picture Story of His Life (*Harper*)

LINCOLN COMPARES HIS VOTE IN 1860 AND 1864: The end result turned out far better than he had anticipated; he won all electoral votes of the free states except Delaware, Kentucky and New Jersey, the three states which went to McClellan by the smallest of margins. The majority of the soldiers' vote favored Lincoln.

Frank Leslie's Illustrated Newspaper, *February 18, 1865*

THE TUMULTUOUS SCENE IN THE HOUSE ON JANUARY 31, 1865: The voting for the Thirteenth Amendment, prohibiting slavery. The next day it was sent to the states for ratification and was ratified before the year was out.

The result was a mandate to the North "to finish the work they had begun." "I give you joy of the election," wrote Emerson to a friend. "Seldom in history was so much staked on a popular vote. I suppose never in history."

Shortly before the votes were counted, Congress passed a resolution that as "the inhabitants and local authorities of the States of Virginia, North Carolina, South Carolina, Georgia, Florida, Alabama, Mississippi, Louisiana, Texas, Arkansas, and Tennessee rebelled against the government of the United States," they were therefore "not entitled to representation in the Electoral College for the choice of President and Vice-President." Lincoln opposed it since the resolution would invalidate the votes of Louisiana and Tennessee, where the governments were recognized by him, with governors friendly and loyal to the Union. He pleaded for a magnanimous reconstruction policy. Instead of accepting his plea, Congress came up with the Twenty-second Joint Rule —giving the two houses the right to decide the issue. Thus the Louisiana and Tennessee governments were rejected.

Senator Charles Sumner had formulated a doctrine of "State suicide." The states which seceded had ceased to exist; Congress had the same power over them that it had over the territories. But Lincoln would not recognize Sumner's thesis in his Proclamation of Amnesty and Reconstruction.

In the original draft of his annual message on December 8, 1863, he argued that "the discussion as to whether a State had been at any time out of the Union is vain and profitless. We know they were, we trust they shall be in the Union. It does not greatly matter whether in the meantime they shall be considered to have been in or out"; but in his revised draft he discarded the statement —he thought it inopportune even to hint that they had been out of the Union.

Lincoln's plan for reconstruction was simple: if one-tenth of the qualified voters (using the 1860 election as the standard) in the Confederate states would take an oath of fealty to the Constitution and swear to abide by the laws of Congress and presidential proclamations dealing with slavery, they could "re-establish a state government" and "such shall be recognized as the true government of the State."

The Radical Republicans objected to this and supported a bill (submitted by Henry Winter Davis in February 1864) requiring a majority of the white male citizens to swear the oath and the states' constitutions to outlaw slavery forever.

At the time of the inauguration the war was almost over. Lincoln offered his hand to the South: "With malice toward none, with charity for all, with firmness in the right as God gives us to see the right, let us strive on to finish the work we are in, to bind up the nation's wounds, to care for him who shall have borne the battle and for his widow and his orphan, to do all which may achieve and cherish a just and lasting peace among ourselves and with all nations."

It was not to be. Five days after General Lee laid down his arms at Appomattox, John Wilkes Booth shot Lincoln while he was enjoying a play in Washington's Ford's Theatre. Early next morning, on April 15, Lincoln died and Vice President Andrew Johnson took the oath to the Presidency.

The Radical Republicans in Congress expected the new President to be a tool in their hands, under whom Lincoln's "tenderhearted" policies toward the South would cease. They had good reasons to hope for this. Johnson was born in the South, he was a poor white who hated "slavocracy" and who once said: "Treason is a crime and crime must be punished. Treason must be made infamous and traitors must be impoverished."

However, after he took office Johnson proclaimed that his policy would be "in all essentials . . . the same as that of the late President." He decided in May that the first steps of reconstruction—the re-establishment of civil government in the Southern states—could be done by executive function. On May 29 he issued two proclamations. One set down the terms for amnesty; the other appointed a provisional governor in North Carolina and had him establish a new state government.

Lorant: Lincoln: A Picture Story of His Life (*Harper*)
MARCH 4, 1865: The crowd had waited patiently since early morning for the beginning of the inaugural ceremonies.

Harper's Weekly, *March 18, 1865*
LINCOLN TAKES THE OATH. Chief Justice Salmon P. Chase, his former Secretary of the Treasury, administers it.

THE SECOND INAUGURAL ADDRESS
As photographed by Alexander Gardner

Fellow Countrymen:

At this second appearing to take the oath of the presidential office, there is less occasion for an extended address than there was at the first. Then a statement, somewhat in detail, of a course to be pursued, seemed fitting and proper. Now, at the expiration of four years, during which public declarations have been constantly called forth on every point and phase of the great contest which still absorbs the attention, and engrosses the energies of the nation, little that is new could be presented. The progress of our arms, upon which all else chiefly depends, is as well known to the public as to myself; and it is, I trust, reasonably satisfactory and encouraging to all. With high hope for the future, no prediction in regard to it is ventured.

On the occasion corresponding to this four years ago, all thoughts were anxiously directed to an impending civil war. All dreaded it—all sought to avert it. While the inaugeral address was being delivered from this place, devoted altogether to saving the Union without war, insurgent agents were in

the city seeking to destroy it without war—seeking to dissolve the Union, and divide effects, by negotiation. Both parties deprecated war; but one of them would make war rather than let the nation survive; and the other would accept war rather than let it perish. And the war came.

One eighth of the whole population were colored slaves, not distributed generally over the Union, but localized in the Southern part of it. These slaves constituted a peculiar and powerful interest. All knew that this interest was, somehow, the cause of the war. To strengthen, perpetuate, and extend this interest was the object for which the insurgents would rend the Union, even by war; while the government claimed no right to do more than to restrict the territorial enlargement of it. Neither party expected for the war, the magnitude, or the duration, which it has already attained. Neither anticipated that

THE SECOND INAUGURAL ADDRESS IN LINCOLN'S WRITING COVERS FOUR FOOLSCAP PAGES. HOW-

Johnson had accepted the "restored loyal governments" of Tennessee, Louisiana, Arkansas and Virginia. With the proclamation for North Carolina he proved that his policy for the seven remaining Southern states would be no less generous than that of Lincoln. Federal agencies were re-established; provisional governors could fill civil offices, both state and local, and also send out calls for constitutional conventions. These conventions were to rewrite the states' laws in accordance with the results of the conflict; they were to invalidate the ordinances of secession, abolish slavery and repudiate the Confederate war debts. But beside these points the states would be free to add others to their constitutions.

Johnson also set terms (similar to those proposed by Lincoln) by which the Southerners could receive amnesty. It was a simple procedure. Anyone who wished to resume relations with the Union was to appear before a Federal officeholder, military or civilian, and take the following oath:

"I———do solemnly swear (or affirm) in the presence of Almighty God that I will henceforth faithfully support, protect and defend the Constitution of the United States and the Union of the states thereunder; and that I will in like manner abide by and faithfully support all laws and proclamations which have been made during the existing rebellion with reference to the emancipation of slaves. So help me God."

During the "Presidential Reconstruction period," as it was called, Congress was in recess. Johnson expected to complete his program before December, when the he cause of the conflict might cease with, or even before, the conflict itself should cease. Each looked for an easier triumph, and a result less fundamental and astounding. Both read the same Bible, and pray to the same God; and each invokes His aid against the other. It may seem strange that any men should dare to ask a just God's assistance in wringing their bread from the sweat of other men's faces; but let us judge not that we be not judged. The prayers of both could not be answered; that of neither has been answered fully. The Almighty has His own purposes. "Woe unto the world because of offences! for it must needs be that offences come; but woe to that man by whom the offence cometh!" If we shall suppose that American Slavery is one of those offences which, in the providence of God, must needs come, but which, having continued through His appointed time, He now wills to remove, and that He gives to both North and South, this terrible war, as the woe due to those by whom the offence came, shall we discern therein any departure from those divine attributes which the believers in a living God always ascribe to Him? Fondly do we hope—fervently do we pray—that this mighty scourge of war may speedily pass away. Yet, if God wills that it continue, until all the wealth piled by the bond-man's two hundred and fifty years of unrequited toil shall be sunk, and until every drop of blood drawn with the lash, shall be paid by another drawn with the sword, as was said three thousand years ago, so still it must be said "the judgments of the Lord, are true and righteous altogether"

With malice toward none; with charity for all; with firmness in the right, as God gives us to see the right, let us strive on to finish the work we are in; to bind up the nation's wounds; to care for him who shall have borne the battle, and for his widow, and his orphan—to do all which may achieve and cherish a just, and a lasting peace, among ourselves, and with all nations.

EVER, HE DID NOT USE THIS MANUSCRIPT BUT READ FROM A PRINTED TWO-COLUMN GALLEY.

new Congress was to assemble. Thaddeus Stevens, the leader of the Radicals, cried out in exasperation: "If something is not done, the President will be crowned King before Congress meets." He reasoned with Johnson to "hold his hand and await the action of Congress," and until then govern the South by "military rulers." Stevens and his political associates were upset about the measures of the new Southern governments.

The worst that the South feared did not come to pass. There were no widespread reprisals upon their sections; there were no wholesale punishments. But they were uneasy about the President's intentions; they were not sure how far Johnson would go in his "forgiving" policy.

The new state conventions procrastinated. Some of them would not nullify secession; they only "repealed" it. Others acknowledged the destruction of slavery by force of arms rather than by proclaiming its abolition. South Carolina and Mississippi refused to repudiate the Confederate debt; Mississippi did not ratify the Thirteenth Amendment.

One of the provisional governors appointed by Johnson said that President Lincoln's death had not been as much of a calamity for the South as imagined. Mississippi's provisional governor organized a local militia, and when the army commander ordered him to desist, Johnson countermanded his order.

But what appalled the North the most was the treatment of the Negroes. The "Black Codes" allowed Negroes to make contracts, acquire property and sue or be sued, but placed harsh restrictions on labor arrange-

275

1861: THE FIRST YEAR OF THE WAR **1862:** AFTER THE REVERSES

THE BURDEN OF THE PRESIDENCY

ments and ownership of the land. The rigorous vagrancy laws assigned Negro youngsters to guardians for whom they were compelled to work without wages. Nowhere in the Black Codes was there a mention of the right to vote. Horace Greeley wanted to know: "If we give the negro a bayonet, why can we not give him a ballot?"

The North wondered whether or not these actions were designed to perpetuate the institution of slavery. The Negroes were uneasy too. They were not sure of their newly acquired status. They wandered "like packs of gypsies" along the roads, "some going to one place and some to another," with no idea of what would hap-

pen when they got there. They were free but they did not know what to do with their freedom.

The South wanted to recoup her old power in Congress. It sent newly elected Senators and Representatives to Washington, many of them former members of the Confederate Congress or officers in the Southern army.

The Northern reaction was violent. When the House met, the Clerk of the House avoided the calling of the Southerners' names. A Joint Committee of Fifteen was formed to judge the qualifications of the Southern Representatives. The committee was under the control of the radicals. Thaddeus Stevens, one of their spokesmen,

1863: AT THE TIME OF THE GETTYSBURG ADDRESS   **1865:** SHORTLY BEFORE HIS DEATH

looked upon the rebel states as "conquered provinces" which should be punished for what they had done. Stevens prepared to delve into the fundamentals of Reconstruction and into the policies of President Johnson. The Representatives of the former Confederate states would have to wait until they were "entitled to be represented in either House of Congress."

The Radicals brought in laws for the South. The Freedmen's Bureau Bill extended the life of the former Bureau which had been set up only for the duration of the war and "for one year thereafter." The Civil Rights Bill voided the unsatisfactory aspects of the Black Codes; it declared all Negroes citizens of the United States, with rights equal to white men in contracts, ownership and in the eyes of the law.

Johnson vetoed the Radical legislation. He refused to sign the Freedmen's Bureau Bill because it would make the Negro the ward of the national government, and because he held that the former slaves had ample protection "without resort to the dangerous expedient of 'military tribunals,'" and he vetoed the Civil Rights Bill, because he thought the Negroes should receive citizenship through the states.

Congress attempted to pass the Freedmen's Bureau

Harper's Weekly, *April 29, 1865*

LINCOLN'S ASSASSINATION. On April 14, 1865, the actor John Wilkes Booth shot the President while Lincoln was seeing the comedy *Our American Cousin,* in Washington's Ford's Theatre. After his deed Booth leaped to the stage shouting: "The South is avenged"—or so people heard him say. As he jumped, he caught the spur of his boot in the flag, fell and broke his leg. Also in the box are Major Henry Rathbone and his fiancée, Clara Harris, daughter of the Senator.

Bill over Johnson's veto, but the Senate would not give it the necessary votes. However, the Civil Rights Bill went through both houses for a second time, and a new Freedmen's Bill was passed over the President's veto. Congress and President were fighting each other furiously.

The Joint Committee of Fifteen proposed a constitutional amendment (the later Fourteenth Amendment) guaranteeing that all persons born in the United States or naturalized should be given full protection in their civil rights. It would penalize states that refused to give voting rights to the Negroes or to allow former rebels to hold Federal offices. Johnson advised the Southern states not to ratify the amendment. With midterm elections coming up, the major issue became whether to accept the harsh proposals of the Radicals or to endorse the magnanimous policies of Johnson.

The Radicals knew that their measures would have to be passed over presidential vetoes, so they concentrated on consolidating their strength in Congress. Johnson had to rely on minority support; he was forced into a defensive position.

His supporters organized a National Union Convention to plan ahead for the Congressional elections, but the convention was noticed less than the riots in Memphis and in New Orleans, where police forces used their guns freely against Negroes.

Johnson was to bring the issue directly to the people. As he was to lay the cornerstone for a monument to Stephen A. Douglas in Chicago, the trip gave a good excuse to make a "swing around the circle," and address audiences along the way. He took with him two popular military heroes—General Grant and Admiral Farragut —and while they were hurrahed wherever they showed

Harper's Weekly, *May 6, 1865*

LINCOLN'S DEATH. At 7:22 in the morning of April 15, 1865, Lincoln breathed his last in a little room opposite the theater. Left: Gideon Welles, Secretary of the Navy; Edwin Stanton, Secretary of War; and Dr. Robert K. Stone, Lincoln's physician. At the head of the bed: Postmaster General Dennison; Senator Sumner; Robert Lincoln, the President's eldest son; and General Halleck. At the door: Quartermaster General Meigs; leaning on the table, Lincoln's secretary, John Hay.

their faces, the President was shouted down and abused; he faced hostile audiences, hecklers goaded him into intemperate remarks. Though Johnson was an experienced stump speaker who spoke with "a living fire," he could not put forward his argument in a convincing way in the face of so much opposition.

At Indianapolis he began: "It is not my intention to make a long speech." Some of the people shouted "Stop" while others cried "Go on." "If you give me your attention for five minutes," the President tried to continue. There were more cries and "No, no, we want nothing to do with traitors." Johnson kept on: "I would like to say to this crowd here tonight." A voice cried out "Shut up! We didn't want to hear from you." Soon, pandemonium followed and the President had to leave without concluding his speech. Such scenes were repeated at other places.

Johnson sought to refute those who called him a Judas to the memory of Lincoln: "I have been maligned; I have been called Judas Iscariot. . . . There was a Judas once, one of the twelve apostles. Oh yes, the twelve apostles had a Christ . . . and he never could have had a Judas unless he had twelve apostles. If I have played the Judas, who has been my Christ that I have played Judas with? Was it Thad Stevens? Was it Wendell Phillips? Was it Charles Sumner?"

And he elaborated: "If the worst come to the worst, if it is blood they want, let them take mine if it be necessary to save the country, for I would freely pour forth my blood as a last libation for its safety and security." He told the crowd that he had no personal ambitions; he had filled most positions "from an alderman up to the Chief Magistracy of the United States," and he attacked those who were against him. "As I go around the circle, having fought traitors at the South, I am prepared to

Lorant: The Life and Times of Theodore Roosevelt (*Doubleday*)
LINCOLN'S FUNERAL IN NEW YORK on April 25, 1865, was observed by a future President. From the second-story window of their grandfather's house, on the corner of Union Square and Broadway, six-year-old Theodore Roosevelt (indicated by the white arrow) and his brother Elliott (the father of Eleanor) are watching the procession on Broadway.

*

Photograph by Jeremiah Gurney, Jr.
THE ONLY PHOTOGRAPH OF PRESIDENT LINCOLN IN HIS COFFIN: It was taken in the City Hall in New York and immediately confiscated by the Secretary of War. The picture came to light some years ago when a young student discovered the faded print among the Stanton papers in the Illinois State Historical Library.

Admiral Davis and Adjutant General Townsend guard the coffin, in front of busts of Daniel Webster and Andrew Jackson.

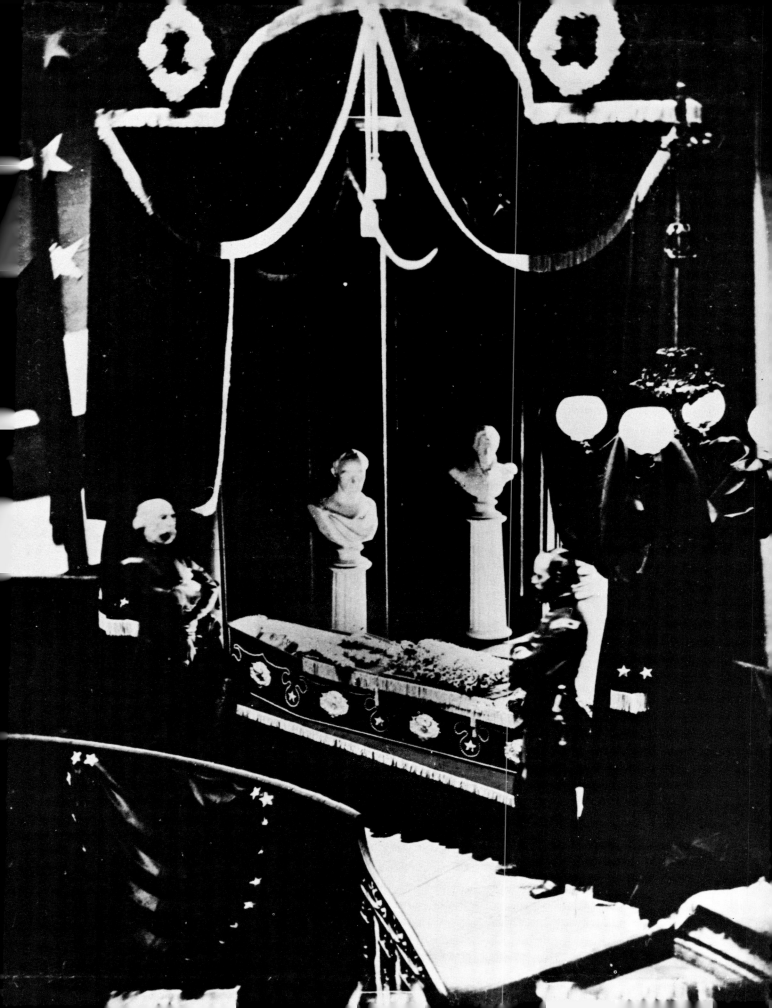

JOHNSON TAKES THE OATH AT HIS RESIDENCE ON APRIL 15, 1865.

BOOTH TOOK HIS LAST REFUGI
in a barn. Soldiers who found his hid
ing place set fire to the barn and one o.
them shot him. "Tell mother I die fo
my country" were Booth's last words

JOHNSON AND HIS CABI-NET: Standing before the new President: Edwin Stanton (War); sitting around the table behind Stanton: James Speed (Attorney General), Gideon Welles (Navy), John Palmer Usher (Interior), William Dennison (Postmaster General) and Hugh McCulloch (Treasury).

fight traitors at the North." At each stop he reminded the people of "the constitution and the flag."

The contemporary humorist Petroleum V. Nasby reported on the tour with memorable pieces, read and laughed at by the country. He concocted his reports as a rebel postmaster from Kentucky who accompanied the President as his chaplain.

Nasby said that in Utica the President spoke "with greater warmth, and jerked more originality than I hed before observed. He introodost here the remark that he

didn't come to make a speech; that he wuz going to shed a tear over the tomb uv Douglas; that, in swingin around the circle, he hed fought traitors on all sides uv it, but that he felt safe. He shood leave the Constooshn in their hands, and ef a martyr wuz wanted, he wuz ready to die with neetness and dispatch."

In Lockport, Michigan, he "wuz sot on savin the country wich hed honored him. Ez for himself, his ambishn wuz more than satisfied. He hed bin Alderman, Member uv the Legislacher, Congressman, Senator,

THE WAR IS OVER. President Johnson, General Grant and Secretary of War Stanton view the parade of the soldiers.

Military Governor, Vice-President, and President. He hed swung around the entire circle uv offises, and all he wanted now wuz to heal the wounds uv the nashen. He felt safe in leavin the Constooshn in their hands."

In Detroit, "This bein a Democratic city, the President wuz hisself agin. His speech here wuz wun uv rare merit. He gathered together in one quiver all the sparklin arrows he had used from Washington to this point, and shot em one by one. He swung around the cirkle; he didn't come to make a speech; he hed bin Alderman uv his native town; he mite hev been Dicktater, but woodent. . . ."

The Radicals won the election. They carried both houses by decisive majorities. Johnson was now a figurehead and remained so for the rest of his term.

In the new Congress the Radicals introduced severe legislation against the South. Their proposal divided the ten Southern states which had not yet ratified the Fourteenth Amendment into five military districts, to be governed by generals of the Union Army. Instead of the

283

Frank Leslie's Illustrated Newspaper, *April 20, 1867*

THE PURCHASE OF ALASKA. President Johnson and Secretary of State Seward, an ardent expansionist, were eager to acquire "Walrussia," as Alaska was nicknamed. Though the price Russia asked for the frigid territory was a modest $7,200,000, Congress hesitated to accept it. Economy-minded Americans had plenty of worries at that time without buying additional territory. Nonetheless, a treaty with Russia transferring Alaska to the United States was signed early in 1867. Legislators voted for it so that the Czar, who had been so friendly to the North during the Civil War, should not be offended. Thus "Seward's Polar Bear Garden" became an American possession.

"reconstructed" governments, new governments were to be elected. Negroes were given the vote. Johnson vetoed the plan, but his veto was overruled. A new era began in the South with carpetbaggers—their earthly belongings in their carpetbags—swarming down from the North and, together with Southern Scalawags and little-educated Negroes, organizing new legislatures. These new carpetbag governments were inept and corrupt; they brought shame and misery to the South.

The Radicals ruled the South with firmness. When a conscience-stricken Republican remonstrated with Thaddeus Stevens that he was bothered about the severe measures, Stevens told him, "Conscience! Tell your conscience to go to the devil, and follow the party line."

The "Crime of Reconstruction"—as the Congressional reconstruction program was called in the South—left lasting bitterness. By giving the vote to the Negro but denying it to the whites, the Republicans could perpetuate their reign. From 1865 till 1884, for two decades, the country had a succession of Republican Presidents.

To check Johnson's power the Radical Republicans

ING ANDY WITH HIS COURTIERS Gideon Welles d William H. Seward as they attend the execution of the olitionists Henry Ward Beecher, Wendell Phillips, harles Sumner, Benjamin F. Butler, Anna Dickinson, orace Greeley and John A. Logan. At the end of the line Thomas Nast, who drew the picture November 1866.

285

ANDREW JOHNSON'S RECONSTRUCTION, AND HOW IT WORKS.

Thomas Nast, September 1866

IN HIS "SWING AROUND THE CIRCLE" from August 28 to September 15, 1866, Johnson attacked the Radicals in Congress, accusing them of planning riots against the Negroes in the South. He was heckled and insulted. "Don't get mad, Andy," they shouted at him, making the President madder than before. During his trip Johnson attempted to drum up support for his lenient reconstruction program, which the Radicals opposed.

left:

The main issue of the midterm election was whether Southern reconstruction was to be carried out with or without the drastic 14th Amendment. Johnson lost his battle: the Radicals rolled up more than a majority in both Houses of Congress.

passed the Tenure of Office Act forbidding the President to issue military orders, to remove civil officeholders of the government or dismiss high military officers without the consent of the Senate. No Cabinet members could be removed by the President.

Johnson held the Act unconstitutional. With Congress between sessions, he asked the resignation of Secretary of War Edwin M. Stanton, who was a friend of the Radicals. When Stanton refused to leave his post "before the next meeting of Congress," Johnson dismissed him swiftly and named General Grant as

ad interim War Secretary. Stanton had "no alternative but to submit under protest to superior force," and there the matter rested for months until Congress convened again. In December, Johnson submitted to the Senate his reasons for removing Stanton, but the Senate refused to concur and demanded that Stanton be reinstated.

The next day the bewildered Grant gave up the key to the War Office, leaving Johnson in the lurch. Johnson once again dismissed Stanton and appointed General Lorenzo Thomas in his stead.

Stanton would not hand over to Thomas "all records,

THE CAUSE OF THE TROUBLE between President and Congress was the Tenure of Office Act, which the Radicals passed over Johnson's veto in 1867. The law required that the President must ask the Senate's consent before removing appointees from office once they had been approved by the Senate. The act's purpose was to perpetuate in office Secretary of War Stanton, a friend of the Radicals. But Johnson, believing the law unconstitutional, dismissed Stanton (on the right) and appointed in his place General Thomas (on the left), whereupon the Radicals voted to impeach the President.

Author's collection

THE IMPEACHMENT COMMITTEE, which was to rule on President Johnson's "high crimes and misdemeanors." Seated: Benjamin F. Butler, Thaddeus Stevens, Thomas Williams and John A. Bingham. Standing behind them are James F. Wilson, George S. Boutwell and John A. Logan.

Photograph by Mathew B. Brady

books, papers and other public property now in [his] custody and charge." Instead he found a Radical judge to swear out a warrent for the arrest of his successor. Thomas posted bail and headed for a confrontation with Stanton, but their debate led nowhere. Stanton offered Thomas a drink and then another one, and locked him out of the War Office.

Then he called in Federal troops to guard the War Department building and stayed in his office day and night. Now Johnson sent to the Senate the name of Thomas Ewing, General Sherman's father-in-law, as a permanent replacement for Thomas. Again the Senate refused to listen to the president.

On February 22, 1868, the House Reconstruction Committee made its report. Thaddeus Stevens recommended that Johnson be impeached—for Stevens the President's crime was so plain that there was no reason even to debate it. A Democratic committee member jumped to his feet and shouted: "Go on, go on, if you choose . . . you may strip him of his office, but you will canonize him among those heroic defenders of constitutional laws and liberty. . . . Suppose you make the President of the Senate the President of the United States, you settle that hereafter a party having a suffi-

THE LAST SPEECH ON IMPEACH-
MENT: Old and infirm Thaddeus
Stevens closing the debate in the House
of Representatives on March 2. Then
the impeachment committee, chosen by
the House, went before the Senate.

Theodore R. Davis, March 1868

THE LADIES' GALLERY in the
Senate during the impeachment
Court, presided over by Chief Justice Salmon P. Chase. The trial was
a tremendous attraction; cards of
admission to it were at a premium.

W. S. Hewett, April 1868

cient majority in the House and the Senate can depose of the President of the United States!"

Other members pointed out that Stanton had been appointed by Lincoln, so it was not strange that Johnson wanted a man of his own choosing.

The Radicals' retort was that Johnson was the "great criminal of our age and country." He had dragged his robes "in the purlieus and filth of treason." He was another Nero and "an ungrateful, despicable, besotted, traitorous man—an incubus and a disgrace."

At five o'clock in the afternoon of February 24, 1868, the House voted—126 to 47—to impeach the President.

The next day Representatives Stevens and John A. Bingham went before the Senate. The old and infirm Stevens, trembling with hate, cried out that "in the name of the House of Representatives and of all the people of the United States, we do impeach Andrew Johnson, President of the United States, of high crimes and misdemeanors. . . ."

Eleven men were appointed to act as a grand jury; on March 4 the articles of impeachment were before the Senate. The first nine dealt with the Tenure of Office Act and the removal of Stanton. Benjamin F. Butler added a tenth charging that Johnson had attacked Con-

left:
IN THE CAPITOL ROTUNDA during the impeachment proceedings: Reporters buttonhole a Senator for news.

below:
EXCITEMENT IN THE CAPITOL

James E. Taylor, May 1868

Harper's Weekly, March 21, 1868
THE   LENGTHY   DEBATES

James E. Taylor, April 1868

gress in his swing around the circle, while Stevens added the last one as a catchall to attract undecided Senators —it was "a mass of indirect allegations of illegal actions by the President."

The Senate was readied as "a court of impeachment for the trial of the President of the United States." Chief Justice Salmon P. Chase was to preside. Henry Stanbery resigned as Attorney General to take charge of the lawyers defending the President. The Radicals' case was presented by Benjamin F. Butler, who said, "I came to the conclusion to try the case as I should try a horse [thievery] case, and I know how to do that."

The Senate consisted of forty-two Republicans against twelve Democrats. The dozen Democrats were four-square behind Johnson. As thirty-six votes were needed for impeachment, the Radicals could not afford to lose seven from the Republican ranks.

On March 30, 1868, Butler began the case: "Now for the first time in the history of the world has a nation brought before the highest tribunal its Chief Executive Magistrate for trial and possible deposition from office. In other times, and in other lands, it has been found that despotisms could only be tempered by assassination, and nations living under constitutional governments even

right:
SERVING OF THE SUMMONS on the President by the sergeant-at-arms.

below:
COUNTING OF THE FINAL VOTE

Frank Leslie's Illustrated Newspaper, *March 28, 1868*

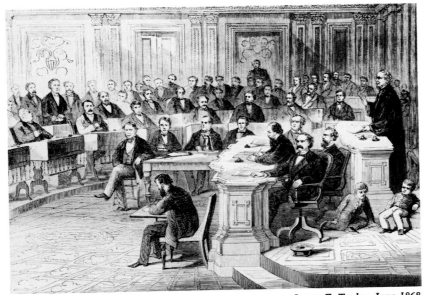

James E. Taylor, June 1868

Harper's Weekly, *March 21, 1868*
TO WIRE THE RESULT: Journalists race to send off their stories.

have found no mode by which to rid themselves of a tyrannical, imbecile, or faithless ruler, save by overturning the very foundation and framework of the government itself. . . . Our fathers, more wisely founding our government, have provided for such and all similar exigencies, a conservative, effectual and practical remedy by the constitutional provision that the 'President . . . shall be removed from office on impeachment for and conviction of treason, bribery or other high crimes and misdemeanors.' "

The lawyer went on to define "an impeachable high crime or misdemeanor to be one in its nature or consequences subversive of some fundamental or essential principle of government, or highly prejudicial to the public interest, and this may consist of a violation of the Constitution, of law, of an official oath, or of duty by an act committed or omitted, or, without violating a positive law, by the abuse of discretionary powers from improper motives or for any improper purpose."

Butler established that the proceeding was not a trial but an inquest of office and that the Senate was a law unto itself "bound only by the natural principles of equity and justice, and that *salus populi suprema est lex.*"

The prosecution paraded a list of witnesses in this

PRESIDENT JOHNSON'S LAST LEVEE OF THE SEASON IN 1868—AT THE TIME OF THE IMPEACHMENT

Theodore R. Davis, March 1868

"solemn, theatrical fiasco"; then, when their proofs seemed shoddy, they began to present witnesses for charges which were not even in the eleven articles. On only one point they showed constraint; they did not present the charge that the President was guilty of complicity in the murder of Abraham Lincoln.

One of Johnson's lawyers, Benjamin R. Curtis, who had served on the Supreme Court, began the appeal for the defense: "Here party spirit, political schemes, foregone conclusions, outrageous biases can have no fit operation. The Constitution requires that here should be a 'trial,' and as in that trial the oath which each one of you has taken is to administer 'impartial justice according to the Constitution and the laws,' the only appeal which I can make in behalf of the President is an appeal to the conscience and the reason of each judge who sits before me. Upon the law and the facts, upon the judicial merits of the case, upon the duties incumbent on that high office by virtue of his office, and his honest endeavor to discharge those duties the President rests his defense."

Curtis pointed out that the whole question of im-

peachment narrowed down to the controversy over the Tenure of Office Act, which "has cut off a power confided to the President by the people through the Constitution . . . and he alone can cause a judicial decision to come between the·two branches of the government to say which of them is right, and after due deliberation, with the advice of those who are his proper advisers, he settles down firmly upon the opinion that such is the character of the law, it remains to be decided by you whether there is any violation of his duty when he takes the needful steps to raise that question and have it peacefully decided."

He attacked the articles of impeachment, taking one after the other. He cited the Constitution and precedents for Johnson's behavior. His arguments were sound and he was on solid ground. The galleries were impressed— but no one could tell how the Senators felt.

The defense brought forth its witnesses. In his cross-examination of them Butler attempted to invalidate their testimony and make them appear ridiculous. He used all the lawyer's tricks. At one point he would call the venerable Stanbery "very young counsel"; at an-

Thomas Nast, in Harper's Weekly, *March 13, 1869*
NAST'S FINAL CARTOON ON THE IMPEACHMENT: "THE POLITICAL DEATH OF THE BOGUS CAESAR"

other, Johnson's lawyers were "five gentlemen of the oldest men in the profession to whom this rule is well known." At another time Butler objected to a witness's testimony of what Johnson had said to him at five in the afternoon, implying that the President would be too much affected by alcohol to speak coherently at that time of the day. Secretary of State Gideon Welles noted in his diary that "Butler gives rules to the Senatorial judges and tells them how to vote, and they obey. Unfortunately they are not legally wise, nor honest, nor candid. They are less safe as triers than an ordinary intelligent jury. The latter would give heed to the clear mind of an intelligent and impartial judge. These Senators are judge and jury in a case of their own, prejudiced, self-consequential, and incompetent. Such a tribunal, it appears to me, is to be treated peculiarly, and not upon trust. They must have it made to appear to them that they are in the wrong. Earnest, vigorous, unwearied efforts are wanted. Scholarly, refined legal ability are not alone sufficient with men who were tested before trial was ordered and who meet in secret caucus daily."

The trial lasted for many months, keeping the country in a high state of excitement. The Radicals' strategy was to keep the Republican Senators from bolting; they put great pressure on the doubtful ones.

On the closing day of the trial, the headline of the New York *Tribune* ran "CONVICTION ALMOST A CERTAINTY."

May 16 was the day of decision. At noon Chief Justice Chase entered the Senate chamber and the court came to order. The Senators decided to vote first on the eleventh article, the catchall article. One pro-Johnson Senator came late; he was so ill that he had to be carried into the hall. The secretary of the Senate called the roll and when it was over Chase announced: "Upon this article 35 Senators vote 'guilty' and 19 Senators vote 'not guilty.' Two-thirds not having pronounced guilty, the President is therefore acquitted on this article." One vote saved him; thirty-six votes would have made the two-thirds. After that the first ten articles were voted upon and went down to defeat. Johnson was not impeached; the presidential office as it had been created by the Constitution was safe.

ULYSSES S. GRANT

Four days after President Johnson was acquitted of the impeachment charges, the Republicans met in Chicago in their nominating convention. Their nominee was a military hero: General Ulysses S. Grant.

The man who "saved the Union" had all the virtues of an ideal candidate. A renowned war leader with a clean record, likable and folksy, his past devoid of scandal; a man of few words, keener on horses, liquor and tobacco than on politics, he was as much a Democrat as he was a Republican.

The only time he had bothered to vote in a presidential election was in 1856, when he had supported the Democrat Buchanan because, as he said, "I knew Frémont." And were it not for the break with President Johnson, Grant might very well have been the Democratic nominee. But after their quarrel over the Tenure of Office Act, he became as shrill for the President's impeachment as were the Radical Republicans.

The New York *World* wrote that Grant was "at first shy; then he wavered; then enveloped himself in a thick mystery—and, at last, he has changed his politics." Yet the Radical Republicans were not sure that he could be trusted. Ben Wade set out for Covington to find out more about the General's politics, and when Dr. Cramer, Grant's brother-in-law, told him that Grant was in full agreement with the Radical Republicans, Wade threw his hat into the air, breaking the globe of a chandelier, so happy was he.

Grant's nomination was a formality. He was decided upon long before the meeting of the convention. All 650 delegates named him by acclamation. There was a sharp contest for the second place. Ben Wade of Ohio was challenged by a number of others, among them Massachusetts Senator Henry Wilson, New York Governor Reuben E. Fenton, the Speaker of the House Schuyler Colfax, Pennsylvania's Governor Andrew G. Curtin. The prize went to Colfax, "a good-tempered, chirping, warbling, real canary bird."

The platform consisted of fourteen planks, and they embraced everything except the two vital issues: Negro suffrage and greenbacks. The first plank congratulated the country "on the assured success of the reconstruction policy of Congress"; the second asked for "equal suffrage to all loyal men at the South," but declared the solution of this question "belongs to the people of those states." The third called for "the payment of the public indebtedness in the uttermost good faith to all creditors at home and abroad"; the fourth for an "equalized and reduced" taxation. The fifth was for a reduction of the national debt "over a fair period"; the sixth advocated diminishing the national debt "so to improve our credit that capitalists will seek to loan us money at lower rates of interest than we now pay"; the seventh proposed that "the government of the United States should be administered with the strictest economy."

The eighth was charged with emotion. "We profoundly deplore the untimely and tragic death of Abraham Lincoln and regret the accession to the presidency of Andrew Johnson, who has acted treacherously to the people who elected him and the cause he was pledged to support; who has usurped high legislative and judicial functions; who has refused to execute the laws; who has used his high office to induce other officers to ignore and violate the laws; who has employed his

CANDIDATES IN 1868

ULYSSES S. GRANT
(1822–1885), a West Pointer, served in the Mexican War. In 1854 he resigned from the army, farmed and sold real estate in St. Louis, worked in his father's Galena hardware and leather store. His Civil War successes led to popular acclaim and thus to his unanimous nomination for the Presidency by the Republicans. He campaigned on "Let us have peace," winning with 3,012,833 votes to Seymour's 2,703,249.

SCHUYLER COLFAX
(1823–1885), the respected Speaker of the House from Indiana, was a former Whig and a supporter of Clay. He joined the Republican party soon after its founding and organized it in his home state. His advanced ideas on Negro suffrage commended him to the Vice Presidency. After a deadlock between the Eastern and Western wings, the Republican convention delegates named him on the fifth ballot.

HORATIO SEYMOUR
(1810–1886) began his political career as secretary to New York's Governor Marcy. Elected to the assembly in 1841, he served a short time as mayor of Utica, was re-elected to the assembly, and in 1852 became Governor. A conservative with Southern sympathies, he was named on the twenty-second ballot by the Democrats for the Presidency after a deadlock between Pendleton and Hendricks.

FRANCIS P. BLAIR, JR.
(1821–1875), son of Jackson's friend and influential editor of the *Globe,* started his political life as a Free-Soiler, organized the Union party in Missouri and led it into the Republican ranks. He was a general in the Civil War. To counteract the Missouri Radicals he rebuilt the Democratic party in the state. He withdrew as candidate for the first place to accept the Democratic delegates' call for the Vice Presidency.

JULIA BOGGS DENT (1826–1902), the daughter of a judge, married Lieutenant Grant on August 22, 1848. They had three sons and a daughter.

A woman of fortitude, she kept the family together while her husband was away for long periods. She was not beautiful; people joked about her crossed eyes. But when, according to a story, she made up her mind to have the condition corrected, Grant told her that he had married her with crossed eyes and he loved her with crossed eyes. She survived him 17 years.

executive powers to render insecure the property, the peace, the liberty and life of the citizen; who has abused the pardoning power; who has denounced the national legislature as unconstitutional; who has persistently and corruptly resisted, by every means in his power, every proper attempt at the reconstruction of the States lately in rebellion; who has perverted the public patronage into an engine of wholesale corruption; and who has been justly impeached for high crimes and misdemeanors, and properly pronounced guilty thereof by the vote of thirty-five senators." This was not even true. Johnson was not "properly pro-

An 1868 photograph by J. Evoli

ULYSSES S. GRANT WITH HIS CHILDREN. Left to right: Ellen ("Nellie," born in 1855), Jesse (born in 1858), a friend of Jesse's, and Ulysses Jr. (born in 1852). The eldest son, Frederick Dent (born in 1850), is not in the picture.

nounced guilty" of the impeachment charges, for even though the thirty-five Senators voted against him, they did not constitute the necessary two-thirds majority.

The ninth plank dealt with "naturalized citizens, who should be protected" in all their rights of citizenship as though they were native-born; the tenth was for "bounties and pensions" for the "brave soldiers and seamen" and for their widows and orphans; the eleventh asked for encouragement and fostering of "foreign immigration, which in the past has added so much to the wealth, development, and resources, and increase of power to this republic." The twelfth—a significantly

short one—read: "This convention declares itself in sympathy with all oppressed peoples struggling for their rights." The thirteenth asked for forbearance and magnanimity toward the people who are "reconstructing the southern state governments upon the basis of impartial justice and equal rights," and suggested that they should be "received back into the communion of the loyal people"; while the fourteenth upheld "the immortal Declaration of Independence."

It was a platform for all seasons and for all occasions. Grant accepted the nomination in a brief note in which he said: "Let us have peace," thus coining the

Drawing by James E. Taylor, May 1868
OPENING THE CONVENTION. Bishop Simpson starts the Chicago Republican National Convention with a prayer.

Drawing by James E. Taylor, May 1868
THE NOMINATION OF GRANT. When General John A. Logan proposed Grant's name, the delegates approved.

Drawing by James E. Taylor, July 1868
THE DEMOCRATIC CONVENTION IN NEW YORK has endorsed the nomination of Seymour and Pendleton.

Frank Leslie's Illustrated Newspaper, *July 25, 1868*
DEMONSTRATION IN NEW YORK'S Union Square on July 9 celebrating the nomination of the Democratic ticket.

slogan of his campaign, and a workable slogan it was.

The Democrats lost no time in tearing into Grant. Their press attacked him without letup; one story accused him of being a thief who went off with a large part of a lady's family silver after he had been entertained in her home during the Civil War; another repeated the old charge that he was a drunkard, "a soaker behind the door and in the dark"; a third one made much of his anti-Semitic "General Order No. 11" of December 1862 in which he forbade Jewish traders to do business with the troops.

For the Democratic nomination no less than forty-seven names were mentioned. The favorites were Chief Justice Salmon P. Chase, "Gentleman George" Pendleton from Ohio, Senator Thomas Hendricks from Indiana, General Winfield Hancock and Francis P. Blair, Jr., of the famous Blair family; but President Johnson had some support as well.

Originally Chief Justice Chase had been a Republican. He had sought the Republican nomination both in 1860 and 1864; both times he lost out to Lincoln. But bitten by the "deadly malady" of presidential fever, he

Sketch by James E. Taylor, May 1868
THE CHEERING GALLERIES. The release of tinted doves when the Republicans nominated their hero Grant.

Published in 1868 by Kellogg & Bukeley, Hartford
THE REPUBLICAN BANNER of General Grant and his running mate, the Speaker of the House Schuyler Colfax.

Frank Leslie's Illustrated Newspaper, *October 24, 1868*
MASS MEETING IN NEW YORK. Democrats marched in a torchlight parade at Union Square on October 5, 1868.

Published in 1868 by Matier & Kent, N.Y.
THE DEMOCRATIC BANNER of former New York Governor Seymour and General F. P. Blair of Missouri.

now wanted to be the candidate of the Democrats. "Nothing would gratify me more than to see the Democracy turn away from past issues and take for its mottoes: 'Suffrage for all, amnesty for all; good money for all; security for all citizens at home and abroad against governmental invasion!'" he declared in April 1868. He had the endorsement of Horatio Seymour, six-time Governor of New York, who felt that Chase might be able to take many votes away from Grant. Yet the Democrats could not become enthusiastic about him even though they admitted that he had "more

qualifications for the Presidency than any other man in the country."

George H. Pendleton of Ohio had a far stronger appeal. He had the backing of the Western states, but because he advocated cheap money—greenbacks to replace national banknotes—he was opposed by the financial and business community of the East. General Blair of Missouri had a good chance until a letter of his to Colonel James O. Brodhead became public; in it Blair said that "the real and only issue in this contest" was the overthrow of the Radicals' reconstruction program,

THE OPPOSING CANDIDATES AND THEIR SUPPORTERS: The Republicans, Grant and Colfax, "The Boys in Blue," are on the left; the Democrats, Seymour and Blair, "The Boys in Gray," are on the right.
Among the Republicans standing behind Grant and Colfax are the Union generals Sheridan, Sherman, Thomas and Burnside. Editor Horace Greeley is reading his paper; Edwin Stanton and Charles Sumner are having a conversation in the

and he proposed that the President should declare the Construction Acts "null and void," compel the army "to undo its usurpations at the South," and "disperse the carpetbag State governments." This was too revolutionary for many a Democrat.

The Democrats met in New York's newly completed Tammany Hall on Independence Day, 1868. The weather was "as hot as weather can well be. Too hot for the warm work on hand here," wrote Kate Chase to her father, the Chief Justice. In the streets outside the

Thomas Nast, in Harper's Weekly, *October 24, 1868*

background. On the hill behind the group, the artillery emplacement has a "Harper's Weekly" flag, while Nast, the cartoonist of the weekly, has drawn himself in the front line, sharpening his pencil for the coming battle.

In the Democratic ranks behind Seymour and Blair are General Robert E. Lee and Jefferson Davis. On the right, barely peering out of a shallow trench, is President Johnson; behind him, General Hancock is surveying the scene with binoculars.

hall the "Pendleton escort" demonstrated with five-dollar-bill badges pinned on their coat lapels, cheering their throats hoarse for their "Young Greenback." They carried banners with the inscription: "The people demand payment of the U.S. bonds in greenbacks and equal taxation. One currency for all. Pendleton the people's nominee. Convention ratify their choice."

The Democratic platform proposed "the immediate restoration of all States to their rights in the Union under the Constitution, and of civil government to the

THE RADICAL PARTY ON A HEAVY GRADE. Grant and Colfax—the Republican candidates—are pulling the carriage labeled "The Chicago Platform" up the hill. The vehicle is crowded with supporters of the ticket, among them George Wilkes, the editor of the "Spirit of the Times"; Edwin Stanton, the former Secretary of War; and Wendell Phillips, Ben Wade, Ben Butler, Charles Sumner and Horace Greeley. Thaddeus Stevens, who has fallen off the vehicle, cries out: "I'd rather fall off than ride with an Old scare crow like you." Greeley says: "We won't stop . . . a pity he hadn't fell off before." Over the White House shines the rising sun—the Democratic candidate, Horatio Seymour.

An 1868 lithograph drawn by Cameron, published by Currier & Ives

American people . . . amnesty for all past political offenses, and the regulation of the elective franchise in the States by their citizens." It declared the Reconstruction Acts "unconstitutional, revolutionary, and void" and it endorsed Pendleton's Ohio Idea—one currency for all the people—the repayment of Civil War bonds in greenbacks. This was a moral issue before the convention. During the war investors, mostly from the East, bought Federal bonds with paper money. These greenbacks had little value, but now the investors wanted to be paid in gold, while Pendleton and the West insisted that they should be paid in greenbacks.

East and West fought over the greenback plank. The West won and the plank read: "One currency for the government and the people, the laborer and the office-

holder, the pensioner and the soldier, the producer and the landholder." It was received with such enthusiasm that it had to be read again.

As the balloting began, Pendleton was in the lead. On the first trial he had 105 votes against President Johnson's 65, General Hancock's 33½ and Sanford E. Church's 34. Chase's name had not yet been submitted. Six more ballots were taken on the first day without considerable change. On the fourth roll call North Carolina cast its vote for Horatio Seymour, who managed Chase's fortunes, but Seymour protested: "I must not be nominated by this convention. I could not accept the nomination if tendered, which I do not expect."

In the succeeding ballots on the next day a seesaw battle developed among Pendleton, Hendricks and

An 1868 lithographic poster

"PATRIOTISM VERSUS BUMMERISM" is the title of this cartoon advocating the Democratic ticket. Seymour and Blair gallop with the Constitution carriage of "White Man's Government" toward the White House, while the rickety cart drawn by Grant and Colfax is pushed by Ben Butler. Death rides with them saying a million slaughtered soldiers block the wheels—"you fooled them, and they now impede your progress." In the foreground are groups of bummers—an army slang used in the Civil War for soldiers who deserted and plundered the countryside. Later the designation was applied to party hangers-on, questionable characters who were given jobs by the government for their services.

Hancock. Until the eighth trial Pendleton led, but thereafter his vote declined. On the eighteenth ballot the Hancock vote rose and the General took the lead with 144½ votes, followed by Hendricks with 87 and Pendleton with only 56½. The convention chairman, sensing a bandwagon move for Hancock, hurriedly adjourned the meeting. By then the General's supporters were so certain of victory that they fired a cannon in front of the convention hall in their candidate's honor.

However, during the night it became evident that Hancock was not acceptable to New York and Ohio, the two most populous states; thus he could not be nominated.

When the balloting resumed, Ohio switched to Hendricks; those delegates from Ohio who were behind Pendleton protested the unit rule, but were overruled. Now the leader of the Ohio delegation, Clement Vallandigham, who was for Chase, went to see Samuel J. Tilden, the chairman of the New York delegation and pleaded for his support. If New York would change to Chase, Ohio would follow suit and make him the nominee. But Tilden had other plans. He wanted an Eastern candidate, a candidate from his own state—Horatio Seymour. To stop Hendricks, who was now leading, Ohio had to move fast. Vallandigham approached Seymour and, leading him to an anteroom, tried to persuade him to become a candidate. Seymour protested, but to no avail; Vallandigham's mind was made up. On the next ballot Ohio swung behind

WHY "THE NIGGER IS NOT FIT TO VOTE"

NEGROES VOTING FOR THE FIRST TIME

Seymour, "a man whom the Presidency has sought and who has not sought the Presidency."

The agitated Seymour rushed to the rostrum. "Gentlemen, I thank you, and may God bless you for your kindness to me, but your candidate I cannot be." Vallandigham spoke up, insisting that Seymour's name must stand. Once more Seymour was walking toward the platform when some of his supporters elbowed him from the hall and drove him to the Manhattan Club. Meeting a friend on the stairs of the club, Seymour, with tears streaming down his cheeks, called out: "Pity me, Harvey! Pity me!"

And while Seymour was in the custody of his friends, in the convention hall the balloting went on. At the end of the twenty-second trial, when Hendricks had 145½ votes, Hancock 103½ and Seymour 22, Wisconsin switched to Seymour, giving the signal for a stampede. Within minutes Kentucky, Massachusetts and North Carolina climbed on the bandwagon and before the ballot was over all states changed their votes, making Seymour the candidate.

All this happened in a flash. Twenty minutes before his nomination Seymour had no inkling that he might be the candidate. He had waited for a propitious time to introduce Chase's name, a moment that didn't come.

But Gideon Welles noted in his diary that the nomination was effected by "duplicity, deceit, cunning management and sharp scheming." Those in the know said that Tilden had planned Seymour's nomination long ahead.

"The Great Decliner"—as Seymour was nicknamed—at first hesitated, then accepted.

> *There's a queer sort of chap they call Seymour,*
> *A strange composition called Seymour,*
> *Who stoutly declines,*
> *Then happiness finds*
> *In accepting, does Horatio Seymour.*

Thus the East got the candidate, the West got the platform. And Blair got the second place on the ticket.

The Republicans were happy. Seymour was no competition to Grant, and they regarded Blair's nomination for the Vice Presidency a mistake. But they would not let themselves indulge in overconfidence. They began their attacks right away. They dug out the story that Seymour had addressed the draft rioters in 1863 as "My friends." They charged that hereditary insanity ran in Seymour's family; therefore the candidate could not be free from it. They attacked Blair because a bill for his two-day stay in a Hartford hotel showed that he spent $10 for board and $65 for whiskey and lemons.

Their organization worked smoothly. It tapped the rich—the Vanderbilts, the Astors—and from their pockets flowed generous contributions to the campaign

Thomas Nast in Harper's Weekly, *September 5, 1868*

"THIS IS A WHITE MAN'S GOVERNMENT." An Irish Catholic, a Confederate soldier and the New York capitalist are trampling on the Negro. A colored orphan asylum and a Southern school are burning in the background. Bodies of men are hanging from the lamppost and from the tree. It is a cartoon assailing the Democrats.

chest. "At no time before in the history of presidential elections," writes the historian Oberholtzer, "was a candidate put under so great a burden of obligation to rich men, which he would be asked to repay."

During the summer the campaign slackened, but grew more spirited with the approach of the state elections in September and October. Day after day the New York *Tribune* headed its political column with Miles O'Reilly's:

> *So, boys! a final bumper*
> *While we all in chorus chant,*
> *For next President we nominate*
> *Our own Ulysses Grant;*
> *And if asked what state he hails from,*
> *This our sole reply shall be,*
> *From near Appomattox Court House,*
> *With its famous apple tree.*

Both the Republicans and Democrats made strong efforts to carry the reorganized Southern states. In Northern towns and villages "hundreds of thousands of meetings are held every evening," wrote Godkin, editor of the *Nation;* "thousands of bands of 'Boys in Blue' with oilskin capes and torches march in procession . . . and there is not a man of any note as a public speaker who has not an 'appointment' to speak somewhere every night until the 1st of November." Republican orators, exaggerating the "outrages" in the South— riots and violence between white and black—inflamed their audiences. Whatever the Democrats said in the South the Republicans used against them in the North. The War Between the States was fought all over again.

Three days before the state elections Gideon Welles wrote: "The elections will, I think, be adverse to the Democrats next Tuesday and also in November. If so, a sad fate I fear awaits our country. Sectional hate will be established."

As Welles predicted, the Republicans won the state elections. Seymour, goaded into action, went on the stump and campaigned vigorously, warning the country against a "man on horseback" who would turn the country into a military dictatorship—but it was far too late.

On October 15, three weeks before election, the New York *World* proposed that Seymour step down and allow either President Johnson or Chief Justice Chase to become the candidate. The suggestion was no help to the Democrats.

Grant won the election, though not so overwhelmingly as was expected. He received 3,012,833 popular votes against Seymour's 2,703,249, carrying twenty-six states with 214 electoral votes against Seymour's eight with 80 electoral votes.

But if he had not had the half-million freedmen vote, controlled by bayonet rule, he would have lost. Of the late Confederate states North Carolina, South Carolina, Florida, Alabama, Arkansas and Tennessee were in the Republican column; Georgia and Louisiana voted for the Democrats. Virginia, Mississippi and Texas had not been accepted as reconstructed states and had not the right to vote.

At the counting of the electoral votes, objections were raised against the Louisiana and the Georgia vote. The objections to the Louisiana vote were overruled,

WAITING FOR THE COUNT.
At his home-town hardware store in Galena, Illinois, Grant marks the time quietly with old friends.

Sketch by Albert Berghaus, November 1868

PRESIDENT ULYSSES S. GRANT DELIVERS HIS FIRST INAUGURAL ADDRESS ON MARCH 4, 1869.

but on the Georgia vote the two houses were unable to agree. The House of Representatives rejected it because Georgia had not fully complied with the Reconstruction Acts; the Senate approved it. To placate both sides the final count was given in two ways: one was with, the other without, the Georgia vote. As to the result it made no difference.

Before the inauguration Grant informed the committee on ceremonies that he would not ride in the same carriage with President Johnson, nor would he speak to him. It was a childish decision, not worthy of him. Thus the committee devised a scheme whereby the outgoing and incoming Presidents were to ride in separate vehicles down Pennsylvania Avenue, the former on the left, the latter on the right side.

But President Johnson showed more dignity. On inauguration day he stayed at his desk at the White House until noon. When the Secretary of State came to escort him to the ceremonies, he said to him: "I am inclined to think that we will finish up our work here by ourselves." And while Grant rode in solitary splendor to the Capitol, Johnson left the Executive Mansion without attention.

Grant's inaugural address was a conglomeration of platitudes. "The responsibilities of the position I feel, but accept them without fear," said the new President, after which a Senator commented: "I am not a religious man, but if I had been elected President, I should not have accepted the responsibilities without fear. I should on my knees have asked God to help me."

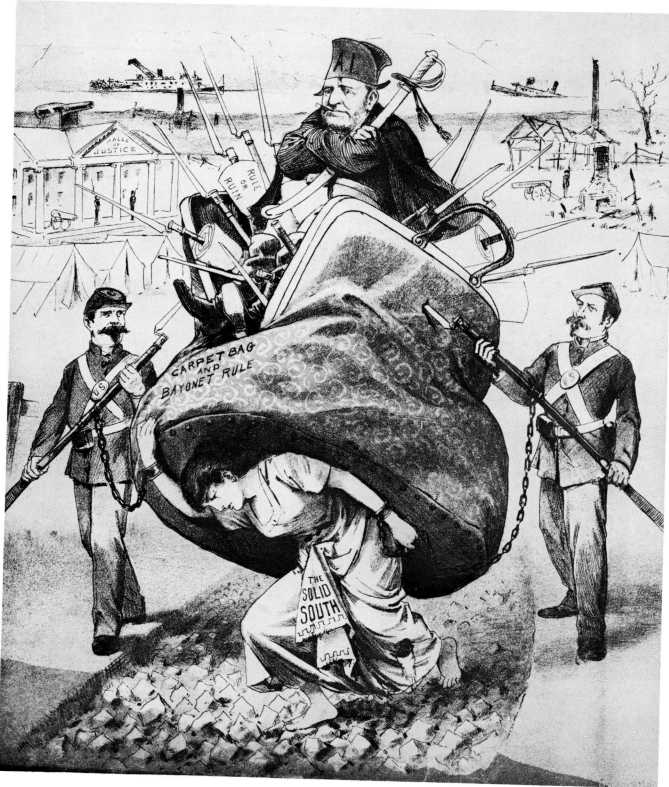

THE REVENGEFUL RECONSTRUCTION PROGRAM of the Radicals, Grant's Bayonet Rule and the corruption of the carpetbag governments embittered the Southern states against the Republican party and brought about "The Solid South."

J. A. Wales, May 1880

ULYSSES S. GRANT

As a rule generals do not make good Presidents. There may be a simple explanation for this. A general commands by giving orders, the President functions by tact, diplomacy and persuasion. Orders have to be obeyed; good soldiers can easily be spotted. But politicians cannot be ordered around, and it is not so easy to find out which one is trustworthy, which one is reliable; thus Grant had a hard time in the Presidency.

He had no critical judgment. He was attracted by the suave, the polished, the rich and the well-mannered; if they were also crooks, he did not notice it. He was a naïve soul. When he received an expensive gift, he was elated over the sender's generosity, not realizing that the gift was nothing but an attempted bribe.

He was friendly with Jay Gould, the sharp financial manipulator who was able to persuade him not to let the Treasury sell gold so that Western farm prices could rise. Grant took the advice, whereupon Gould cornered the gold market and made a fat profit.

Graft and corruption brought the morale of the government to an all-time low. People chased after money; they stole and cheated. The strong exploited the weak; government officials were bribed and bought.

Protesting the malpractices, the Liberal Republicans asked for reforms and a general house-cleaning. Their movement began in Missouri with their opposition to the vindictive anti-Southern provisions of their states' constitutions. When their motion for change was defeated, they offered their own ticket in the mid-term election and won. From then on the movement made rapid strides. In January of election year the Liberal Republicans held a meeting in which they asked for the "uprising of honest citizens," to end the spoils system, and to bring about an honest Civil Service. They wanted to block the renomination of Grant, and to end the regime of the "despot" who endorsed all the "usurpations and corruptions." Later on they got together in their national convention at Cincinnati "to take such action as their convictions and the public exigencies may require." The eight thousand seats of the Exposition Hall were too few to hold all who were there. Henry Watterson described the meeting: "A livelier and more variegated omnium gatherum was never assembled. . . . There were long-haired and spectacled doctrinaires from New England, spiced by stumpy and short-haired emissaries from New York. . . . There were brisk Westerners from Chicago and St. Louis. . . . There were a few rather overdressed persons from New Orleans . . . and a motley array of Southerners of every sort.

The power behind the proceedings was the "Quadrilateral"—the chief editors of four newspapers—Horace White of the Chicago *Tribune,* Samuel Bowles of the Springfield *Republican,* Murat Halstead of the Cincinnati *Commercial,* and Henry Watterson of the Louisville *Courier-Journal.* They wined together, they talked to delegates, argued, cajoled, persuaded them. Their first aim was to block the nomination of David Davis, the gargantuan judge from Illinois who had won the candidacy for his friend Lincoln in 1860. And when they were certain that Davis was out, they limited the candidates to two men: Charles Francis Adams and Lyman Trumbull.

Adams, the son of President John Quincy Adams

CANDIDATES IN 1872

ULYSSES S. GRANT (1822–1885), at the height of his popularity, was renominated unanimously by the Republicans. In the election he got 3,597,132 votes to Greeley's 2,834,079. Of the thirty-seven states he lost only five.

HENRY WILSON (1812–1875), son of a poor day laborer who became a Massachusetts Senator, got the vice presidential nomination as Grant feared Colfax's ambitions. Stricken in the Capitol, he died Nov. 22, 1875.

HORACE GREELEY (1811–1872), the erratic editor of the New York *Tribune,* an influential voice in Whig and Republican politics, was first the Liberal Republicans' choice for the Presidency; Democrats supported him also.

B. GRATZ BROWN (1826–1885), the forward-looking Governor of Missouri, was instrumental in founding the Liberal Republicans in opposition to Grant's policies. He was chosen as their vice presidential candidate.

CHARLES O'CONOR (1804–1884), a successful lawyer who never attained his aspirations for public office, was nominated by those Democrats who wouldn't support Greeley. He was also backed by the Labor Reformers.

THOMAS A. HENDRICKS (1819–1885), Governor of Indiana, a leading contestant for the Presidency in the last election, got most of Greeley's electoral votes as a compliment when Greeley died before the votes were counted.

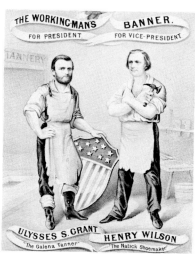

Smithsonian Institution
THE REPUBLICAN BANNER

and the grandson of President John Adams, was the successful negotiator of the *Alabama* claims against Britain; he was a respected politicians who was endorsed by many a Democrat. But he had a cold and aloof character and he would do nothing to win the nomination. Before the convention met he went to Europe for a vacation.

Lyman Trumbull, the grandson of the renowned historian Benjamin Trumbull, was an anti-Nebraska Democrat who served in the Senate for three terms (1855–1873)—first as a Democrat, then as a Republican, and last as a supporter of the Liberal Republicans. He was one of the seven men who saved President Johnson from conviction in his impeachment trial.

The platform, written by Carl Schurz, began with a ringing attack: "The administration now in power has rendered itself guilty of wanton disregard of the laws of the land, and of usurping powers not granted by the Constitution; it has acted as if the laws had binding force only for those who govern. It has thus struck a blow at the fundamental principles of constitutional government and the liberties of the citizen.

"The President of the United States has openly used the powers and opportunities of his high office for the promotion of personal ends.

"He has kept notoriously corrupt and unworthy men in places of power and responsibility, to the detriment of the public interest.

"He has used the public service of the government as a machinery of corruption and personal influence,

Drawing by Matt Morgan, April 6, 1872

THE MODERN BELSHAZZAR. President Grant—the drunken despot—is surrounded by politicians, officeholders, patronage seekers and Cabinet members. Under the canopy of despotism Roscoe Conkling pours from the "2nd Term" bottle.

and has interfered with tyrannical arrogance in the political affairs of States and municipalities.

"He has rewarded with influential and lucrative offices men who had aquired his favor by valuable presents, thus stimulating the demoralization of our political life by his conspicuous example.

"He has known himself deplorably unequal to the task imposed upon him by the necessities of the country, and culpably careless of the responsibilities of his high office."

After this Schurz listed the essential principles for a just government: "Equality of all men before the law . . . equal and exact justice to all, of whatever nativity, race, color, or persuasion, religious or political"; the maintenance of the Union, with "emancipation and enfranchisement," and opposition to "any reopening of the questions settled by the Thirteenth, Fourteenth, and Fifteenth Amendments of the Constitution"; universal amnesty; supremacy of civil over military authority, and "state self-government"; reformed Civil Service, for that service had become "a mere instrument of partisan tyranny and personal ambition, and an object of selfish greed—a scandal and reproach upon free institutions"; a single term for the Presidency; main-

Sketch by James E. Taylor, June 1872

THE REPUBLICAN CONVENTION at Philadelphia's Academy of Music renominated Grant by unanimous vote.

Sketch by James E. Taylor, May 1872

THE LIBERAL REPUBLICAN CONVENTION in Cincinnati named the erratic Horace Greeley for the Presidency.

Sketch by Schaffler, June 1872

THE DEMOCRATIC CONVENTION in Baltimore swung behind Greeley, the choice of the Liberal Republicans.

tenance of the public credit; a "speedy return to specie payment" in the interest of "commercial morality and honest government"; opposition to all further grants of public land to railroad and other private corporations.

On the tariff issue the platform remained vague; to bridge the many opposing views a compromise was adopted, asking for "a system of federal taxation which shall not excessively interfere with the industry of the people, and which shall provide the means necessary to pay the expenses of the government," but, as "there are in our midst honest but irreconcilable differences of opinion with regard to the respective systems of protection and free trade, we remit the discussion of the subject to the people in their congressional districts and the decision of Congress thereon, wholly free from executive interference or dictation."

The evening before the nomination began, B. Gratz Brown, the Liberal Republican Governor of Missouri, and Senator Francis P. Blair, arrived in Cincinnati "fit for stratagems and spoils." They were to advance the candidacy of Horace Greeley, the editor of the New York *Tribune*. Greeley was a brilliant and eccentric man. He was impulsive, unpredictable, vain and vindictive—hardly presidential timber. The Quadrilateral became frightened.

On the first ballot Adams led with 203 votes against 147 for Greeley. Trumbull had 100, Gratz Brown 95, Davis 92½, and Andrew Curtin 62.

To effect Greeley's nomination Gratz Brown withdrew on the third ballot and threw his support to his rival. But even without Gratz Brown in the race Greeley could get only 239 votes; thus the voting had to continue. On the fifth ballot the Adams vote shot up to 279, the Greeley vote to 258. Now, at last, the bandwagon for Greeley was rolling. The sixth ballot saw the end: Greeley received 332 votes against Adams's 324. So Greeley it was.

Thurlow Weed wrote to his friend Hamilton Fish: "Six weeks ago I did not suppose that any considerable number of men, outside of a Lunatic Asylum, would nominate Greeley for President." The liberal newspapers were dumfounded. The *Nation* declared that a greater degree of incredulity and disappointment had not been felt since the news of the battle of Bull Run, while William Cullen Bryant said in the *Evening Post:* "I should at any time beforehand have said that the thing was utterly impossible—that it could not be done by men in their senses, but bodies of men as individuals sometimes lose their wits."

All the New York newspapers attacked Greeley. People just could not think of him as a candidate. Wearing a white linen duster and a porkpie hat, with sideburns on his cheeks and a bald pate at the top of his head, he was more like a character out of a Dickens

THE MOUNTAIN
BRINGS FORTH A MOUSE
A cross between Horace Greeley and B. Gratz Brown
Thomas Nast, May 1872

THIS IS
THE
LIBERAL
MOUNTAIN.

WHAT I KNOW ABOUT GEOLOGY, BY H. G.

CINCINNATI CONVENTION.

CARL SCH... OUR SEC. of S...

Th: Nast

Drawing by Matt Morgan, October 1872

"A USELESS APPEAL"—Emperor Grant, reclining on a pile of money bags, refuses the pleas of begging veterans: "No! No! I make it a rule only to receive. I never give anything." A cartoon by Matt Morgan, who assailed Grant with fury.

Drawing by Matt Morgan, September 1872

GRAND LARCENY. Comparing the profits of Boss Tweed and the President. Grant lectures the New York City Boss: "Now, Tweed, my boy, you see the trouble in your case is, that you did not pocket enough to buy up all your enemies. See what I have done. I have taken so much for myself and them fellows, that they want me to keep on doing it."

novel than a man running for the Presidency.

Those delegates who were dismayed at the convention's selection met at Judge Stallo's house, and while Carl Schurz pounded the piano they gave vent to their pent-up emotions. General Brinkerhoff thought that Greeley and Gratz Brown, who had received the second place, were named by men "as clearly intruders" in the convention hall "as Satan was when he presented himself among the children of light."

Criticism came from all quarters. "With such a head," wrote the New York *Evening Post,* "as is on Greeley's shoulders, the affairs of the nation would not, under his direction, be wisely administered; with such manners as his, they could not be administered with common decorum; with such associates as he has taken to his bosom, they could not be administered with common integrity." *The New York Times* wondered whether "so eminently shrewd a people as this would ever place such a man as Horace Greeley at the head of their government. If any one man could send a great

Thomas Nast, September 1872

"LET US CLASP HANDS OVER THE BLOODY CHASM," said Greeley in his acceptance speech, and cartoonist Thomas Nast of *Harper's Weekly* did not ever let him forget it. In cartoon after cartoon he ridiculed the Republican candidate.

Thomas Nast, July 1872

CINCINNATUS—Farmer Greeley receives the Republican nomination from editor Greeley across "the Bloody chasm."

nation to the dogs, that man is Mr. Greeley."

Greeley heard the news of his nomination in his New York office. Amos Cummings from the *Sun* came to interview him. "I see you are nominated on the sixth ballot, Mr. Greeley." Greeley replied, "Yes, I think it more creditable to be nominated on the sixth than on the first ballot. It is an evidence that our friends had bottom and that their bottom didn't fall out."

Greeley must have felt strange. The party which he had helped to found was now his enemy, and the party which he had fought throughout his entire political career had made him its candidate.

A month later the regular Republicans convened in Philadelphia in their "renomination" convention. They had to nominate Grant if they wanted to remain in power. Though they criticized the President because of his lukewarm attitude toward Civil Service, because

Thomas Nast, August 1872

IT IS ONLY A TRUCE. "Clasp hands over the bloody chasm," Greeley urges the Negro, with an assist from Sumner. The Klansman on the other side says: "Freely accept the hand that is offered, and reach forth thine own in friendly grasp."

of his vacillation on the tariff, because of his fatuous policy against the South, they closed ranks behind him. Every one of the delegates cast his vote for him "whose modest patriotism . . . sound judgment . . . practical wisdom, incorruptible integrity . . . commended him to the heart of the American people." For the second place the convention chose Massachusetts Senator Henry Wilson, the "cobbler of Natick," a man friendly to labor whose nomination was intended to be a slap at Charles Sumner, the other Massachusetts Senator and an enemy of Grant. He replaced Schuyler Colfax, whose presidential ambitions annoyed the President.

The Democrats met in Baltimore under a cloud of gloom. Chastened by their defeat in the last election, they were ready for "a new departure" from old principles. In an act of self-abnegation they accepted not

Thomas Nast, August 1872

LEAVING THE POLLS, Greeley again refers to the chasm, adding, "A great victory has been won in Georgia."

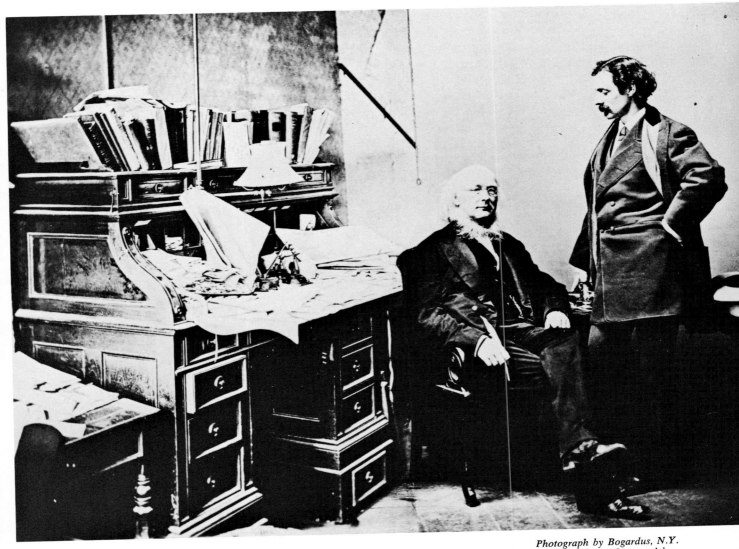

Photograph by Bogardus, N.Y.

HORACE GREELEY IN THE OFFICE OF THE NEW YORK TRIBUNE with Whitelaw Reid, his "first writing editor," who later became his successor. Greeley began his paper in April 1841 with an investment of $2,000. He competed with New York's four Whig newspapers (the *Courier & Enquirer*, the *American*, the *Express* and the *Commercial Advertiser*) and also with the *Sun* and the *Herald*, the "penny press." Before long he was regarded as the most influential publicist in the country, leading crusade after crusade—against slavery, against war, against tobacco and against saloons, brothels, gambling houses and all things sinful.

After the Civil War the young Reid joined Greeley and in time took over the direction of the paper. In 1872, after Greeley's death, with the help of Rhode Island Senator William Sprague and financier Jay Gould, Reid bought the majority of the newspaper's stock. In 1892 Reid, who in 1888 was named Ambassador to France, became Benjamin Harrison's running mate; a decade later, Theodore Roosevelt gave him the coveted diplomatic plum—the ambassadorship in England.

only the platform but also the candidate of the Liberal Republicans—the first and only time that the party did not name its own candidate. Of course, there were dissenters. Representatives Voorhees of Indiana argued that it was a brazen audacity to expect the Democratic party to support Horace Greeley. It would be the same as if "the disciples of the Christian religion would turn away from their faith for one hour and worship Mahomet as the prophet of God." But Voorhees's arguments cut no ice. The Democrats were set to support "anybody to beat Grant." "If the Baltimore Convention puts Greeley in our hymn book," proclaimed the Governor of North Carolina, "we will sing him through if it kills us."

HORACE GREELEY (1811–1872)
A Daguerreotype
in the Chicago Historical Society

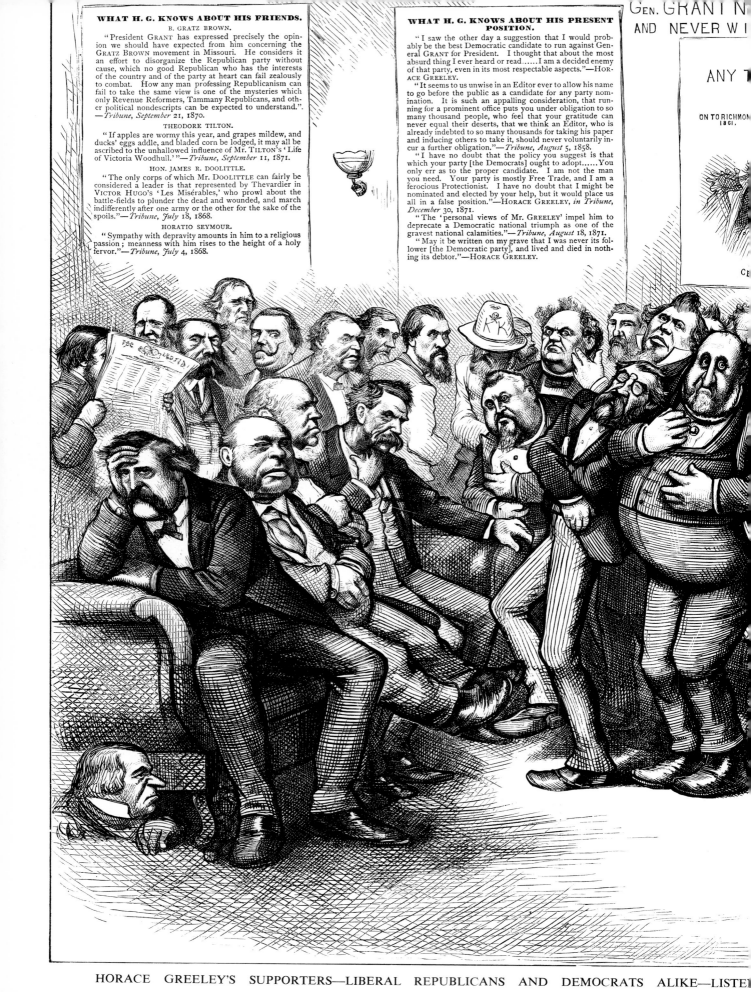

HORACE GREELEY'S SUPPORTERS—LIBERAL REPUBLICANS AND DEMOCRATS ALIKE—LISTE

Thomas Nast, September 1872

MOURNFULLY TO THE CATCHY CAMPAIGN TUNE WHICH CARL SCHURZ PLAYS ON THE PIANO.

An 1872 lithograph of Currier & Ives

THE END OF
LONG BRANCH.
Greeley as he cuts the limb with President Grant: "They make fun of me for what I know about farming, but I guess some folks will soon find out what I know about chopping."

A BANQUET IN THE GROVE. Reception at Greeley's Chappaqua farm for the Democratic National Convention committee.

Sketch by Albert Berghaus, July 1872

Those among the Democrats who could not bring themselves to rally behind Greeley, a "white hat and a white coat," met in a separate convention and named Charles O'Conor as their standard-bearer. The Labor Reform party, dominated by the trade unions, gave its endorsement to O'Conor as well.

In the campaign the personalities of the candidates were more debated than their political philosophies. Greeley was an easy butt of ridicule: his sloppy clothes, his shambling gait, his shapeless trousers and white socks—all provided a fund of material for writers and cartoonists. Thomas Nast caricatured him in *Harper's*

Weekly; the sentence from Greeley's acceptance letter that both North and South were "eager to clasp hands across the bloody chasm" was a recurring theme of his cartoons.

And he was attacked because he was a vegetarian and a brown bread eater, because he was an atheist and a free lover, and he was not allowed to forget that he was a co-signer of Jefferson Davis's bail bond. Poor Greeley wondered whether he was running "for the penitentiary or for the Presidency." He stumped the country, reasoning with audiences, pleading for conciliatory policies toward the South, and denouncing the

THE "LAST DITCH" of the Democratic party. Horace Greeley, holding on to the Cincinnati platform plank: "With this *dead* weight to carry I'm afraid I shall get swamped." The water is marked "Baltimore," the site of the Democratic convention.

Drawn in 1872 by J. Cameron for Currier & Ives

Drawing by Joseph Becker, October 1872

CAMPAIGNING IN THE WEST. Greeley addressed meeting after meeting. Here he speaks from Pittsburgh's St. Charles Hotel.

Republican party for "waving the bloody shirt."

James G. Blaine remembered: "His speeches, while chiefly devoted to his view of the duty and policy of pacification, discussed many questions and many phases of the chief question. They were varied, forcible, and well considered. They presented his case with an ability which could not be exceeded, and they added to the general estimate of his intellectual faculties and resources. He called out a larger proportion of those who intended to vote against him than any candidate had ever before succeeded in doing. His name had been honored for so many years in every Republican household, that the desire to see and hear him was universal, and secured to him the majesty of numbers at every meeting."

He spoke about the tragedy between North and South. "They talk about Rebels and traitors," he said in Pittsburgh. "Are we never to be done with this? We demanded . . . that they surrender their arms and go to their homes. . . . They have done so and now they are asked to repent. Have they not brought forth works meet for repentance? Theirs is a lost cause, but they are not a lost people.'

The Democratic press called Grant a dictator, a

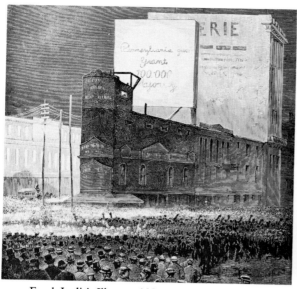

Frank Leslie's Illustrated Newspaper, *November 23, 1872*
ELECTION RETURNS are projected by the stereopticon atop a building at Broadway and 22nd Street.

Frank Leslie's Illustrated Newspaper, *November 23, 1872*
AT PRINTING HOUSE SQUARE IN NEW YORK, "The Sun" and "The Tribune" buildings with the returns on election night.

crook, a drunkard, an ignoramus and stupid; yet he would not answer; he remained silent. The well-oiled Republican organization did the work for him. They had the means and they had the money, both of which Greeley lacked.

"It was one of the strangest campaigns in history," wrote Professor Randall. "Republicans excoriated a Republican President; Liberals labored without enthusiasm for a candidate whose choice was intolerable to them; Democrats supported a violent and abusive opponent; ex-Confederates in the South did battle for a foe who had denounced them as traitors and rebels."

And Professor Roseboom wrote: "Never in American history have two more unfit men been offered to the country for the highest office. The simple soldier, inexperienced in statecraft, impervious to sound advice, and oblivious to his own blundering, was pitted against the vain, erratic, reforming editor whose goodness of heart could not make up for his sad lack of judgment. The man of no ideas was running against the man of too many."

The Republicans appealed to their rich supporters so Greeley, the danger to businessmen and industrialists, could be defeated. The banker Jay Cooke—soon to be bankrupt—alone contributed $50,000. Big business feared that once Greeley was President their juicy pickings would be over. No longer would they be able to enrich themselves without restraint, no longer could they grab for themselves the nation's wealth handed to them with free hands by the Grant administration.

As prosperity stayed on, Grant won easily with 3,597,132 votes against Greeley's 2,834,125 and O'Conor's 29,489. Of the thirty-seven states (for the first time the election was held by popular vote in every state of the Union), thirty-one voted for the President. Greeley carried Missouri, Texas, Georgia, Kentucky, Tennessee and Maryland, but not a single state in the North. Though his defeat was decisive his campaign helped to close "the bloody chasm."

Shortly before the election Greeley's wife died, and he wrote to his friend Margaret Allen: "I am not dead, but wish I were. My house is desolate, my future dark, my heart a stone. I cannot shed tears; they would bring me relief. Shed tears for me, but do not write again till a brighter day, which I fear will never come."

Two weeks later his hallucinations began. Writing in furious haste, as his strength ebbed the words poured out of him. "Utterly ruined beyond hope," he scribbled, "I desire, before the night close its jaws on me forever, to say that, though my running for President has placed me where I am, it is not the cause of my ruin." Soon he was taken to a private home for mental patients in Pleasantville.

Exhausted in mind and body, "the worst beaten man who ever ran for high office," suffering under the blow that the power of his newspaper had passed into other hands, mourning the loss of his wife, he died on November 29, three weeks after his defeat.

The Grant era continued. The worst was yet to come.

WITH GRANT REELECTED
"THE BLOODY CHASM"
CLOSES ON GREELEY.
Drawing by Thomas Nast, November 1872

RUTHERFORD B. HAYES

Fraud and corruption burst into full bloom under Grant. The Navy sold business to contractors, the Interior Department worked hand in hand with land speculators, the "whiskey ring" of revenue officers and distillers railroaded millions away from the government, the Secretary of War received yearly payments from his Indian agents, and so on and on. Public morality was at low ebb. Though the President himself was not tainted with graft, he was so incredibly naïve that he could not see the crookedness of the men around him. Whenever one of the culprits was caught, Grant was the first to shield the scoundrel.

The country grew weary of corruption, weary of the reconstruction policy of the Radical Republicans and of their continuous "waving of the bloody shirt." The financial panic of 1873 led into a full-fledged depression. Five thousand businesses went bankrupt; three years later the number was over nine thousand. Land values went down, business declined, unemployment rose. In the mid-term election of 1874 the Republican preponderance in the House was wiped out.

Grant could not grasp that he might have been responsible for the bad times, and he was ready to run for a third time. Even his supporters were dismayed. The Pennsylvania Republican state convention passed a resolution opposing "the election to the presidency of any person for a third term." In a letter to the convention's chairman, Grant wrote he had no desire to run for a third term any more than he had for the first; and he added that as the Constitution did not restrict the presidential tenure to two terms, the time might come when it would be inadvisable to change a President after eight years in office. Yet he promised to accept the nomination only "under such circumstances as to make it an imperative duty—circumstances not likely to arise." This was not clear enough; the convention expected a straight repudiation of the President's third-term ambitions. New York, Ohio and other states issued resolutions against a third term.

The Democrats were determined that "such circumstances" as Grant mentioned in his letter should not arise and that the country should not be allowed to drift "upon the rock of Caesarism." In December 1875 they introduced a resolution in Congress proclaiming that "the precedent established by Washington and other Presidents of the United States, in retiring from the presidential office after their second term, has become, by universal concurrence, a part of our republican system of government, and that any departure from this time-honored custom would be unwise, unpatriotic and fraught with peril to our free institutions." The resolution was carried by the vast majority of 234 to 18, with a large number of Republicans joining the Democrats, thus shelving Grant's third-term ambitions.

The question was, who should succeed him? James G. Blaine of Maine, the magnetic and money-loving Congressman, was the favorite, closely followed by Roscoe Conkling, who had the support of the administration, and Benjamin H. Bristow, who had prosecuted the Whiskey Ring, the reformers' candidate; and there were the favorite sons: Governor John F. Hartranft of Pennsylvania, Senator Oliver P. Morton of Indiana, Governor Rutherford B. Hayes of Ohio.

At the convention in Cincinnati the silver-tongued

RUTHERFORD B. HAYES
Photograph by Napoleon Sarony

CANDIDATES IN 1876

RUTHERFORD B. HAYES
(1822–1893), Harvard law
graduate, general in the Civil
War, Congressman, three
times Governor of Ohio, was
chosen by the Republicans on
the seventh ballot, defeating
the popular James G. Blaine.

WILLIAM A. WHEELER
(1819–1887), a former Whig
Congressman from New York,
was unknown when the Re-
publicans took him to run
with Hayes. After months of
wrangling, their ticket was
chosen by one electoral vote.

SAMUEL J. TILDEN
(1814–1886), Governor of
New York, famed prosecutor
of the corrupt Tweed ring,
became the choice of the
Democratic convention even
though he had to fight the
opposition of Tammany Hall.

THOMAS A. HENDRICKS
(1819–1885) from Indiana,
who advocated "soft money"
theories, challenged Tilden
for the presidential nomination. But when the convention
decided on Tilden, he reluctantly accepted second place.

PETER COOPER
(1791–1883), New York
manufacturer, inventor and
philanthropist, consented to
run for President on the
Greenback ticket, advocating
"paper money." In the election
Cooper received 81,737 votes.

GREEN CLAY SMITH
(1832–1892) resigned as Governor of the Territory of Montana to become an evangelist.
A keen temperance man, he
became the presidential candidate of the Prohibition party,
receiving 9,522 popular votes.

Rutherford B. Hayes Library, Fremont, Ohio

LUCY WARE WEBB (1831–1889), the daughter of a physician, married Hayes on December
30, 1852. She bore him seven sons and one
daughter; three of the boys died in infancy.

Eleven-year-old Fanny is on one side of her,
eight-year-old Scott Russell on the other. The
girl next to the potted palm is the daughter of
Theodore R. Davis, the *Harper's Weekly* artist.

Lucy Hayes is remembered for her strong
stand against liquor; as she would only serve
soft drinks at the White House, she was nicknamed "Lemonade Lucy—" and the name stuck.

Robert Ingersoll presented Blaine's name in a most
effective nominating address. "Like an armed warrior,
like a plumed knight, James G. Blaine marched down
the halls of the American Congress," he orated, "and
threw his shining lance full and fair against the brazen
forehead of every traitor to his country." The speech
roused the delegates; if the voting had begun then,
Blaine would have won. The opposition quickly asked
for an adjournment, and though the Blaine men resisted
the motion, they had no alternative when someone cut
the gas pipe and the lights went out in the hall.

The next day, when the balloting began, tempers had
cooled down. Though Blaine was leading in the first
few trials, he could not gain the majority. His vote rose
from 285 on the first to 293 on the fifth ballot, 85 short
of victory. On the sixth it jumped to 308, and it looked
as if a stampede was in the making. The next ballot
gave him 351 votes; only 27 more were needed. The
anti-Blaine forces had to act fast. They united behind
Hayes, the most acceptable man to all factions. Ken-

Photograph by Redington & Shaffer, Washington, D.C.

THE SENATE OF THE 43rd CONGRESS: Front row: John Gordon, Ga.; William Windom, Minn.; Lewis Bogy, Mo.; Simon Cameron, Pa.; Reuben Fenton, N.Y.; Matthew Carpenter, Wis.; Daniel Pratt, Md.; Zachariah Chandler, Mich.; John Scott, Pa.; Phineas Hitchcock, Nebr.; Alexander Ramsey, Minn. Second row: George Goldthwaite, Ala.; James Flanagan, Texas; George Dennis, Md.; Bainbridge Wadleigh, N.H.; William Stewart, Nev.; James Alcorn, Miss.; George Wright, Iowa; Thomas Robertson, S.C.; Powell Clayton, Ark.; Thomas Tipton, Nebr.; John Patterson, S.C.; Aaron Cragin, N.H.; Allen Thurman, Ohio. Third row: W. J. McDonald, chief clerk; John Mitchell, Oreg.; James Harvey, Kans.; John Ingalls, Kans.; James Kelly, Oreg.; Henry Davis, W.Va.; John Stevenson, Ky.; Matt Ransom, N.C.; John Sherman, Ohio; William Hamilton, Md.; Arthur Boreman, W.Va.; John Logan, Ill.; Simon Conover, Fla. Last row: J. I. Christy, assistant doorkeeper; William Sprague, R.I.; J. Robert French, sergeant-at-arms; I. Bassett, assistant doorkeeper; John Hager, Calif.; Henry Pease, Miss.

Not in the picture: George Spencer, Ala.; Stephen Dorsey, Ark.; Aaron Sargent, Calif.; Orris Ferry and William Buckingham, Conn.; Eli Saulsbury, Del.; Abijah Gilbert, Fla.; Thomas Norwood, Ga.; Richard Oglesby, Ill.; Oliver Morton, Ind.; William Allison, Iowa; Thomas McCreery, Ky.; Rodman West, La.; Hannibal Hamlin and Lot Morrill, Me.; Charles Sumner and George Boutwell, Mass.; Thomas Ferry, Mich.; Carl Schurz, Mo.; John Jones, Nev.; John Stockton and Frederick Frelinghuysen, N.J.; Roscoe Conkling, N.Y.; Augustus Merrimon, N.C.; William Brownlow and Henry Cooper, Tenn.; Morgan Hamilton, Texas; George Edmunds and Justin Morrill, Vt.; John Johnston and John Lewis, Va.; and Timothy Howe, Wis.

What a pity that not all Senators were present at the picture-taking. It would be interesting to see Thomas Ferry, who counted the votes in the disputed election; Hannibal Hamlin, who had been Lincoln's first Vice President; Carl Schurz, the German-born Republican reformer soon to become Secretary of the Interior under Hayes; Roscoe Conkling, the leader of the Stalwarts; and Charles Sumner, once the powerful chairman of the Foreign Relations Committee.

A member of the lower House has left this description of the 43d Congress' most prominent Senators: "Sumner, Conkling, Sherman, Edwards, Carpenter, Frelinghuysen, Simon Cameron, Anthony, Logan—would have received as a personal affront a private message from the White House expressing a desire that they should adopt any course in the discharge of their legislative duties that they did not approve. If they visited the White House, it was to give, not to receive advice. . . . Each of these stars kept his own orbit and shone in his sphere within which he tolerated no intrusion from the President or from anybody else." And they would not sit "below" a Cabinet member at official dinners.

Thomas Nast, October 1876

THE REPUBLICAN ELEPHANT is trampling on the two-headed Tammany Tiger: Tilden and Hendricks.

A. B. Frost, August 1876

THE TWO-FACED TILDEN, Governor of New York, on the Democratic platform, is pictured as a bogus reformer.

tucky called the signal and switched to Hayes. Other states followed, and before the trial was over Hayes had 384 votes and with them the nomination. For the Vice Presidency the convention chose William A. Wheeler, the New York Congressman.

The platform was a weak document, containing a halfhearted resolution against the spoils system; favoring protection; opposing polygamy; asking public aid to parochial schools; and, though it advocated holding public officials "to a rigid responsibility," it did not offer a remedy for corruption.

A number of resolutions were adopted which radically changed convention procedure in the future. One defined the order of business: first a report of the committee on credentials, then the platform was to be agreed upon, and only after these issues had been disposed of could the nominations and balloting begin. Another resolution asked for a strict adherence to the roll call; after a state had announced its vote, it could not change

it on the same trial, so there could be no stampede. And still another made the unit rule invalid—delegates were to vote as individuals, and not as a unit.

Two weeks later the Democrats met at St. Louis with two serious contenders before them. One was Samuel J. Tilden, the 62-year-old bachelor Governor of New York, prosecutor of the Tweed Ring, a "hard-money man," and the candidate of the reformers; the other was Thomas A. Hendricks of Indiana, a "soft-money man," the candidate of the West.

Long before the opening of the convention a newspaper popularity bureau promoted Tilden's candidacy. Goodsell Brothers, an advertising firm, made surveys of public sentiment, sent releases to local newspapers, mailed Tilden literature to citizens of influence.

But on the convention floor Tilden had to face the political enmity of John Kelly from his own state. Kelly, the leader of Tammany Hall, came with a strong contingent of Tammany men who hung out a banner

330

over their headquarters with the inscription: "New York, the largest Democratic city in the Union, is uncompromisingly opposed to the nomination of Samuel J. Tilden because he cannot carry the State of New York." This was their revenge on Tilden, who had prosecuted corruption in New York politics.

The platform, composed by Manton Marble, editor of the New York *World,* read like an editorial. "Reform is necessary to rebuild . . . the Union, eleven years ago happily rescued from the danger of a secession of States. Reform is necessary to establish a sound currency. Reform is necessary in the scale of public expenses. Reform is necessary even more in the higher grades of the public service." Reform, reform, reform —it was repeated over and over again.

As the balloting began, it became evident that a "reform campaign without Tilden would be like the play of *Hamlet* with Hamlet left out"—thus Tilden was chosen right away. Second place was given to Hendricks, so both hard-money men and soft-money men—both East and West—should be content.

Two new parties made their appearance for the election of 1876. In May the Prohibition Reform party met in Cleveland. Its purpose was to ban the manufacture, sales, importation and exportation of "alcoholic bever-

ages." The female prohibition "Crusaders" and the men who joined with them nominated Green Clay Smith of Kentucky and Gideon T. Stewart, one of the party's founders. About the same time, the Independent National party met in Indianapolis. Its members were all "Greenbackers" determined to give the country paper money. They nominated philanthropist Peter Cooper. Their vice presidential candidate Newton Booth declined the honor and was replaced with Samuel E. Cary.

The issue of the campaign was reform. Both parties cried for reform; but while the Democrats could openly advocate it, the Republicans, carrying the burden of the Grant terms, had to talk about it in subdued tones.

On other issues the views of the two candidates differed little. Hayes was a hard-money man, as was Tilden; Tilden, like Hayes, advocated civil-service reform; Hayes pleaded for the withdrawal of Federal troops from the South, as did Tilden.

Hayes accepted his nomination in a letter in which he denounced unredeemable paper money, deplored conditions in the South, and spoke out for an early return to local self-government free of Federal interference. And asserted his "inflexible purpose" not to be a candidate for re-election. In his diary Hayes wrote: "I have prepared a bold and honest letter of acceptance. It

Thomas Nast, July 1876

THE TWO-HEADED DEMOCRATIC TIGER. Samuel Tilden, the presidential candidate, supports the "Hard Money" theory of the Eastern states; while his running mate, Thomas Hendricks, upholds the "Soft Money" views of the West.

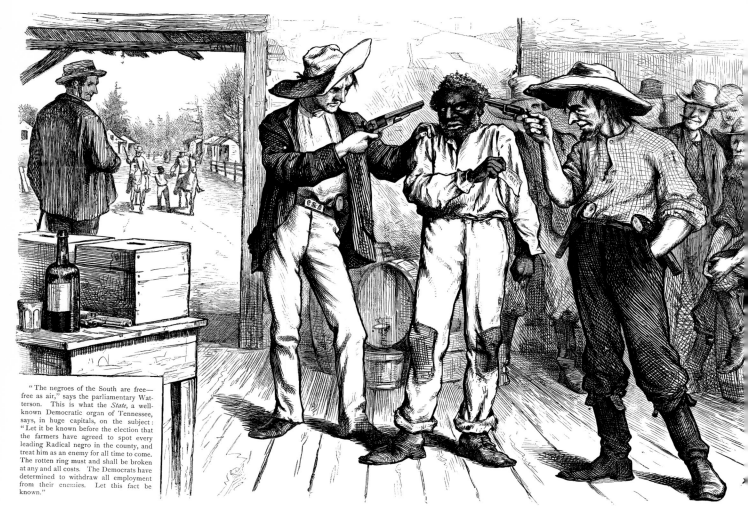

" The negroes of the South are free—free as air," says the parliamentary Watterson. This is what the *State*, a well-known Democratic organ of Tennessee, says, in huge capitals, on the subject: " Let it be known before the election that the farmers have agreed to spot every leading Radical negro in the county, and treat him as an enemy for all time to come. The rotten ring must and shall be broken at any and all costs. The Democrats have determined to withdraw all employment from their enemies. Let this fact be known."

NEGROES MUST VOTE DEMOCRATIC. "Of course he wants to vote the Democratic Ticket!" says the vote solicitor. But in reality both parties reverted to methods of intimidation, bribery and outright violence in order to gain victory.

A. B. Frost, October 1876

will offend some, and cool the ardor of others, but it is sound and I believe will be strong with the people. At any rate it is the true course." His outspoken views gained him many supporters. One of them, Mark Twain, said that Hayes's letter "corralled" his vote at once.

Tilden, too, wrote an acceptance letter—the fashion of the day—which turned out to be three times longer than his party's platform, but comprised nothing new.

As the campaign got under way, the opponents talked more of the past than of the present, the Democrats criticizing the Republicans for their reconstruction policies, the Republicans denouncing the Democrats for their stand in the Civil War. "A bloody-shirt campaign with money and Indiana is safe," wrote a party worker from that state, "a financial campaign and no money, and we are beaten." And while the Republicans waved

the "bloody shirt," the Democrats spoke of the "hard times" and of the scandals under Grant.

Hayes had support from many of the major papers: *Harper's Weekly,* the *Tribune* and the *Evening Post* in New York, the Cincinnati *Commercial* and the Springfield *Republican* among them. He also had endorsement from the reform leader Carl Schurz and most of the independent and liberal Republicans who had nominated Greeley four years earlier. For Schurz, Tilden was "too much of a demagogue—too much of a wire puller and a machine politician," while Hayes was "a man of more than average ability, and decidedly unspoiled as a politician."

The Democratic campaign was in the hands of professional publicity men. Tilden literature was sent to the press; letters by the thousands were mailed to the

THE PENALTY FOR IMPUDENCE
DEATH.
REFORM IS NECESSARY IN NIGGER KILLING.
NO EXCUSE OR PALLIATION COULD POSSIBLY BE FOUND FOR THAT OUTRAGE AND BARBARISM
LAMAR - DEM - MISS.
THE NIGGERS WERE IMPUDENT; WE REFORMED THEM IN COLD BLOOD AFTER THEY HAD SURRENDERED AND WERE UTTERLY DEFENSELESS
IMPUDENT NIGGERS DARING TO CELEBRATE THE 4TH
THE IMPUDENT NIGGER RING BROKEN
NIGGERS REFORMED AT HAMBURG, S.C
ALL QUIET IN TOWN
A REFORM VICTORY IS SURE
"GEN" M.C. BUTLER.
HARD AND SOFT REFORM
Th. Nast

Thomas Nast, August 1876

THE "BLOODY SHIRT" REFORMED. Governor Tilden, the Democratic candidate, with the ribbon "Red Tape" hanging out of his top hat, is pointing to his accomplishments. In the campaign Tilden emphasized that "Reform is necessary."

voters. A literary bureau, a speakers' bureau, a bureau of correspondence answered questions and accusations. Prominent politicians, writers, journalists campaigned for Tilden; Henry George was among them, as were Joseph Pulitzer, John Bigelow, Abram Hewitt, Manton Marble, Henry Watterson and Charles Dana. The Democrats sang lustily:

Sam Tilden is a gentleman,
A true and honest man, sir;
And when we call for honest work
He's just the chap to answer.
He represents the very truths
That we have all been drilled in,
And we couldn't have to lead us on
A better man than Tilden.

Both parties spent freely for the campaign. The Republicans under the direction of the chairman of their national committee, Zachariah Chandler, who was also Secretary of the Interior, squeezed money out of Federal employees. Everybody who worked for a department or bureau of the Government had to contribute. So had the contractors doing Federal business.

Political rallies were held up and down the country with the excitement of cannon, brass bands and partisan orators. But the candidates remained at home. Both Tilden and Hayes were state Governors and wanted to remain inconspicuous in their public duties.

The first state elections beginning in September gave little indication about the outcome of the presidential election. Republican Maine and Vermont remained Republican. Ohio went for the Republicans as expected;

TO CELEBRATE HIS VICTORY, Samuel Tilden's friends gathered at his New York residence at Gramercy Park. However, the Republicans challenged the returns from Florida, Louisiana and South Carolina, the last three Carpetbag states. Tilden received 184 electoral votes—only one more vote from the disputed returns would have given him the victory.

Frank Leslie's Illustrated Newspaper, November 25, 1876

and a Democratic win in Indiana was no surprise. But when the returns from West Virginia favored the Democrats, the Republicans saw that they had little hope for a victory in the Southern states.

The first returns on election night indicated a Tilden victory. By midnight it seemed certain that Tilden had won; Hayes went to bed in the belief that he had lost.

And had it not been for four newspapermen watching the election figures in the office of *The New York Times,* that would have been the end result. But as this group watched the returns, an inquiry came from Democratic State Chairman Magone: "Please give your estimate of electoral votes secured for Tilden. Answer at once." It was an indication that the Democrats were not sure whether they had the Southern vote. John C. Reid, the managing editor of the *Times,* rushed to the Fifth Avenue hotel where Zachariah Chandler, the top manager and director of the Republican campaign, was sleeping in sweet exhaustion. Reid sobered him up

and telegrams were sent to Republican party leaders in Louisiana, South Carolina and Florida: "Hayes is elected if we have carried South Carolina, Florida and Louisiana. Can you hold your state? Answer at once."

The second edition of the *Times*—at six-thirty—gave Tilden 184 and Hayes 181 electoral votes (counting Louisiana and South Carolina for Hayes). To win, Tilden needed 185 votes; he was 1 vote short. But the *Times* said that Florida with its 4 votes was doubtful; therefore, "if the Republicans have carried that state, as they claim, they will have 185 votes—a majority of one." Thus the struggle between Republicans and Democrats for the deciding votes began and kept the country in suspense until inaugural day. Gamblers called "all bets off."

The next day the Republican chairman announced: "Hayes has 185 electoral votes and is elected." But Hayes said in Ohio: "I think we are defeated in spite of recent good news. I am of the opinion that the Demo-

AN ELECTORAL COMMISSION WAS APPOINTED to report to the House of Representatives which set of returns to accept. In the fifteen-man commission the Democrats seemed to have a majority, but when Judge David Davis took the senatorship of Illinois, the balance changed in favor of the Republicans, who voted on party lines, making Hayes President.

crats have carried the country and elected Tilden."

The question was: How would the votes from the three Southern carpetbag states be counted? There were two sets of returns from each of them, one favoring Tilden, the other Hayes. Which returns would be accepted, the Republican ones or the Democratic ones? The candidate who could secure those 19 votes would have the Presidency.

In Florida and South Carolina both sides accused the other of frauds; both the Republican and Democratic electors insisted they were the rightful representatives of their state. In Louisiana the returns were certified by two different governors and two different returning boards, with two different results.

And to add to the confusion, the Governor of Oregon declared a Republican elector ineligible because he was serving as a postmaster, a Federal office, and was thus disqualified under the Constitution. Since the Governor was a Democrat he gave a certificate to the elector

of his party, who had received a thousand fewer votes and was second on the list. As the other two Republican electors would not meet with him, the Democratic elector named two other electors and the three voted—to nobody's surprise—the Democratic ticket.

Both parties sent "visiting statesmen" to the three carpetbag states where they conferred with members of the returning boards and the local officials who juggled the votes, pressing them for acceptance of the rival returns. When talk failed—there was money. The Republicans had the fatter wallets; in addition, they could rely on Federal troop garrisons for "protection." Many prominent leaders of the Republican party went to the South to speak for Hayes; among them were James A. Garfield, John A. Logan, William Evarts, Matt Quay. The Democrats were represented by Lyman Trumbull, George Julian, Henry Watterson, Manton Marble and others for the party.

This was the picture in the three carpetbag states:

THE ELECTORAL COMMISSION OF 1877. William M. Evarts, the chief counsel for Rutherford B. Hayes, presents his opening argument on the Florida vote.

Seated at the bench are the fifteen members of the commission. The first five are the Senators: the Democrats Allen G. Thurman (with beard) and Thomas F. Bayard; the Republicans Frederick T. Frelinghuysen, O. P. Morton and George F. Edmunds. Next to them the five Supreme Court justices: the Republicans William Strong and Samuel F. Miller, the Democrats Nathan Clifford and Stephen J. Field, and the Republican Joseph P. Bradley. Then follow the five members from the House of Representatives: the Democrats Henry B. Payne, Eppa Hunton and Josiah G. Abbott, and the Republicans James A. Garfield and George F. Hoar.

Above the Commission in the gallery are sixty members of the press. The third from the left in the front row is Ben: Perley Poore of the Boston *Journal.* Beside the clock is Mrs. Jane Swisshelm, the free-swinging reform editor. To the left of Poore is the *New York Times* reporter, John Carson. Holding a top hat is T. C. Crawford of the Chicago *Times.* The third woman on his left is Miss Emma Janes of the Toledo *Blade;* the second woman to her left is Mrs. M. P. Lincoln, "Bessie Beech" of the Cleveland *Plain Dealer.* At the left of the gallery is the editor of the Washington *Evening Star,* Crosby Noyes (with full beard). Nearer the center, with his sideburns, is E. B. Wight of the Chicago *Tribune.* Left of him is Miss E. H. Luther of the Boston *Post.* Third to her left is F. A. Richardson of the Baltimore *Sun,* and at his left E. V. Smalley of the New York *Tribune.*

In the foreground, right of center, James G. Blaine, Senator from Maine, is easily recognizable. The second man at his right is editor Henry Watterson of the Louisville *Courier-Journal,* now serving as a Representative. At the right edge is Frederick Douglass, the Negro leader.

Mrs. Abram Garfield, wife of the future President, is by the right shoulder of lawyer Evarts. In front of him is one of Tilden's lawyers, Charles O'Conor, who was an 1872 candidate. Behind Evarts is the white-haired Edwin Stoughton, another counsel for Hayes. The man to Stoughton's left is Zachariah Chandler, Grant's Secretary of the Interior. At his left is the profile of Abram S. Hewitt, the New York Congressman and later Mayor of the city. Second from the front in the group of women behind Evarts is the suffragette Belva M. Lockwood, who in 1884 became the first woman candidate for the Presidency.

To the left of the second bust on the wall is General Ambrose E. Burnside, now a Senator from Rhode Island with his famous "sideburns." The second man to his left, holding a top hat, is Speaker of the House Samuel J. Randall. At the right, in profile, with white hair and mustache, is Representative Fernando Wood, once his state's most powerful boss and three-time Mayor of New York.

In the left foreground, with a drooping handlebar mustache, is Senator John A. Logan of Illinois, famous Civil War general. To his right, with a long white beard, is George Bancroft, the historian, Polk's Secretary of the Navy.

At the near end of the Commission's bench, with small dark sideburns, is William Windom, Senator from Minnesota. By the far end of the bench is Hamilton Fish, Grant's Secretary of State, with his wife on his left.

The painting, now hanging in the Capitol, was done by Mrs. Cornelia Adèle Fassett, the wife of the Chicago photographer who took portraits of Abraham Lincoln in 1859. Mrs. Fassett worked on her large canvas for a number of years, portraying 260 well-known political, social and journalistic personalities, each of them readily recognizable.

Library of Congress

Thomas Nast, February 1877

IT NEARLY CAME TO CIVIL WAR. When Democratic candidate Samuel J. Tilden realized that resistance to the electoral commission's partisan decision could lead to serious consequences and even to a possible disruption of the Union, he bowed to the result. His manager said: "I prefer four years of Hayes' administration to four years of civil war."

In South Carolina the Republicans did have a majority in spite of greater Democratic frauds. Still, the Democrats filed a rival slate.

In Florida the votes were nearly equally divided. But as the returning board had two Republican members to one Democrat, the four votes of the state were audited for Hayes. The Republican Governor certified the choice, even though the Democratic attorney general filed a rival slate. Thus the issue went before the state courts which ruled that the returning board should only have counted the votes as presented. On the recount of the whole state ballot, the Governor became a Democrat; the new board appointed by him was filled with Democrats and they declared the state for Tilden.

In Louisiana the Republican "visiting statesmen" had a problem to solve. In spite of the "bulldozing" of the Negroes, ballot box fraud and "corrected" tally sheets, the Democrats still had a majority of almost nine thousand votes. As it happened, the canvassing board was "for sale to the highest bidder." Thus the returns from the parishes were altered, reducing the Democratic votes by thirteen thousand. The job done, the Republican emissaries journeyed to Columbus and assured Hayes that justice had been done.

But the Democrats were not in the mood to give up. The Senate had a Republican majority, the House a Democratic one. Thus, if the Senate would count the votes, the result would be a Republican victory; and if the House of Representatives was to decide, it would be a Democratic one. For weeks the two houses fought about this. The year went by, 1877 came and they could still not reach an agreement. The only guide in the Constitution is that "The President of the Senate shall, in the presence of the Senate and the House of Representatives, open all the certificates, and the votes shall be counted." Who was to count them and could he

"Any man fit to be President, or even a candidate of a great party for the office, would prefer to be counted out by fraud rather than be counted in by fraud, of which there is a reasonable suspicion. No man in this country has courage enough to accept the office of President, if elected by such a vote; and by courage I mean hardihood, bravado, wickedness, and all the qualities requisite to such an act."—GOV. HAYES, at Athens, O., Nov. 18th, 1876.
"The first successful attempt to gain political power by a fraud upon the ballot would be the end of self-government in our country."—EX-GOV. BIGLER, of Pennsylvania.
"No man worthy the office of President should be willing to hold it if 'counted in' or placed there by any fraud. Either party can afford to be disappointed in the result, but the country cannot afford to have the result tainted by the suspicion of illegal or false returns."
—U. S. GRANT, Nov. 10th, 1876.
HENRY CLAY
FLORIDA
SOUTH CAROLINA FOR HAYES
LOUISIANA
MIGHT IS RIGHT GOV. CHAMBERLAIN

Frank Leslie's Illustrated Newspaper, *January 6, 1877*

IN REALITY IT WAS DIFFERENT. In the drawing Hayes declines the Presidency when the Southern soldier proffers him the election returns from South Carolina, Louisiana and Florida on his bayonet. "I cannot accept a position gained for me by such means as these!" he exclaims. But in reality he accepted the disputed votes and with them the Presidency.

Frank Leslie's Illustrated Newspaper, February 17, 1877
AT THE COUNTING OF THE VOTES in Congress, Republicans objected to the validity of the votes from three Carpetbag states—South Carolina, Louisiana and Florida.

Theodore R. Davis, March 1877
ANNOUNCING THE ELECTION RESULTS. Senator Thomas W. Ferry, the pro tempore president of the Senate, proclaims the final count in the morning of March 2.

Theodore R. Davis, March 1877
THE NIGHT BEFORE THE INAUGURATION. President Grant and his Cabinet stayed at the Capitol to sign bills. Secretary of State Hamilton Fish is behind Grant.

examine the legality of the returns? The House sent Democratic-controlled committees to investigate the disputed returns; the similar committees of the Senate were controlled by the Republicans.

Tilden compiled a book, *The Presidential Counts,* to prove that the result should be determined by Congress, not by the president of the Senate. And for a while it seemed he might have the support of Grant's administration. Grant was angered by Hayes' allusions to his failings during the campaign and by the prominence given to Schurz, who castigated his administration. Grant said, and he repeated it, that in his opinion Tilden had won the election, and he denounced the "fraudulent counting." Conkling, still smarting over his defeat in losing the nomination, would not campaign for Hayes; he too was ready to take Tilden as President. Grant invited Abram S. Hewitt, chairman of the Democratic national committee, to the White House, trying to make a settlement over the Louisiana votes, and keeping them for Tilden. He feared that if the deadlock should continue into March, the nation would be without a President.

Moderates in both parties worked on a compromise. The Electoral Commission Law which Congress passed turned over the dispute to a special commission of fifteen men with power to make a final decision. Five Senators (the Republicans Edmunds, Morton and Frelinghuysen and the Democrats Thurman and Bayard), five Representatives (the Democrats Payne, Hunton and Abbot and the Republicans Garfield and Hoar), and five justices of the Supreme Court. Of the five only four were appointed; the Republicans Miller and Strong and the Democrats Clifford and Field. These four chose the fifth member, Justice David Davis, a liberal Republican who it was understood would favor Tilden. Davis was expected to act as an arbitrator between the two party blocs of seven Republicans and seven Democrats. Tilden accepted the plan, since it seemed to favor him, but five days before the commission was to meet, Justice Davis retired from the Court to become Senator from Illinois and his place was taken by Associate Justice Bradley—a dyed-in-the-wool Republican.

On February 1, 1877, both houses of Congress met jointly to count the electoral votes. The meeting was held in the House of Representatives with over a thousand spectators watching the proceedings. Senator Ferry, the president pro tempore of the Senate, opened the certificates from the states in alphabetical order. When he reached Florida, objection was made and the subject was referred to the commission which waited in the Supreme Court chamber. On February 9 the commission voted on the Florida returns. Its decision was for Hayes by a vote of eight Republicans to seven Democrats. When the decision came before Congress,

STRAYED FROM HIS
HOME!

MY DARLING SOUTH!

WAS LAST SEEN IN THE
COMPANY OF AN ELDERLY

PERSON WHO CLAIMED
TO BE HIS GUARDIAN.

A NATION'S GRATITUDE
SHALL REWARD HIM WHO
RESTORES MY SON TO
HIS DISTRESSED
MOTHER— COLUMBIA.

C. S. Reinhart, October 1877

THE RESULT OF THE DISPUTED ELECTION. One of the new President's first orders was withdrawal of the Federal troops from the last two Carpetbag states. (Florida already had a Democratic governor.) With this the reconstruction era came to an end. In the cartoon the old Irish woman representing the Democratic Party wails that President Hayes has stolen her child—the South—while mother Columbia says, "Oh bless you, sir! You've brought us all together again!" In reality, after the departure of the troops the "Solid South" emerged—the bulwark of the Democratic party ever since.

objection was again raised and the two houses separated to discuss the issue. The Senate sustained the decision; the House rejected it. But under the terms of the Electoral Commission Act, the decision of the commission could not be reversed—thus Florida's four votes went for Hayes. Similarly, the commission approved the Republican returns from Louisiana, South Carolina and Oregon. On every issue the fifteen men voted along partisan lines: eight Republicans against seven Democrats. Thus all Hayes electors were accepted, all Tilden electors rejected.

The Democratic press was outraged. The Democrats in Congress talked of filibustering past the March 4 deadline so that there would be no President. In many states the Democrats organized armed bands to put Tilden in the White House, with "Tilden or blood" as their slogan. Hayes's six-year-old son Scott solemnly told his sister that "R B Hayes is elected, and the Democrats will kill him."

If Tilden had been aggressive, he could have had the Presidency. But he was cautious and indecisive, and he could not make up his mind in a hurry. He was also in poor health. The previous year he had suffered a paralytic stroke, and had been anxious about his symptoms ever since, always carrying a medicine chest with him, watching his diet, and getting regular daily massages. He was so preoccupied with his health that nothing else seemed to matter.

341

Photograph by Mathew B. Brady

THE INAUGURATION OF PRESIDENT HAYES

After a photograph by Mathew B. Brady

HAYES IS SWORN IN BY CHIEF JUSTICE WAITE.

Theodore R. Davis, March 1877

THE INAUGURAL SCENE ON MARCH 4, 1877

But realizing that resistance to the electoral commission's decision would lead to serious disorders, he accepted the verdict. "I prefer four years of Hayes' administration to four years of civil war," he said to his friend Abram Hewitt.

Thus in the early hours of the morning of March 2, Senator Ferry, who presided over the Senate, announced that "Rutherford B. Hayes, having received the majority of the whole number of electoral votes, is duly elected President of the United States for four years, commencing on the 4th of March, 1877." Ferry hoped that the members of Congress and the spectators would refrain from "all demonstrations whatever" and that nothing should "transpire on this occasion to mar the dignity and moderation" which had denoted the proceedings, "in the main so reputable to the American people and worthy of the respect of the world."

It was understood that the Democrats accepted Hayes as President only after they were promised that Federal troops would be withdrawn from Louisiana and South Carolina, the two remaining carpetbag states. (Florida had already inaugurated a Democratic governor on January 2.) Though Hayes denied being a party to the bargain, soon after he took office he withdrew the Federal troops from the South. With this the Radical reconstruction era came to an end.

The news of the final count had not reached Hayes when he left by train for Washington on the first day of March. Heated feelings during the dispute had given rise to threats of assassination; one evening while he was having a family dinner, a bullet was fired through his parlor window. But large friendly crowds greeted him along the way and in spite of the threats he spoke to them. When his train arrived at Harrisburg he learned of Congress's decision.

Grant's term expired at noon on Sunday, the fourth. Previously when the day of inauguration had fallen on a Sunday, the ceremonies were put off until the following day. But for this already complicated election a different procedure was utilized. Grant gave a state dinner for the President-elect at the White House on Saturday evening. Prior to the dinner the President and his son U. S. Grant, Jr. took Hayes and Chief Justice Morrison R. Waite into the "Red Room" where Hayes took the oath of office.

On Monday the official ceremonies took place. Thirty thousand people saw Hayes and Grant dismount and walk arm and arm to the Senate chamber. When Hayes stepped out on the portico loud cheers greeted him. In his speech he repeated the honest pledges of his campaign and pleaded for "not merely a united North or a United South, but a united country." Then he took the oath once more. His speech was received—so newspapers reported—with unprecedented "universal favor."

"ANOTHER SUCH VICTORY AND I AM UNDONE"

Cartoon by Thomas Nast, March 1877

JAMES A. GARFIELD and CHESTER A. ARTHUR

Hayes restored dignity to the presidential office; he weeded out corruption, he supported Civil Service reform and advocated a more decent policy toward the South; he gave the country an honest administration.

The remaining Federal troops from South Carolina and Louisiana were withdrawn, and with this the Reconstruction period came to an end. But the excesses and the irresponsibilities of the carpetbag governments left an undying hatred in Southern hearts against the Republicans. (In the next mid-term election in 1878, the South elected only four Republicans to the House of Representatives, but 102 Democrats.)

For the reformers Hayes was not bold enough; for the regulars in the party he was too independent. The party was split into two factions, the Stalwarts and the Half-Breeds. Hayes and his followers were called the Half-Breeds; in Congress they were led by James G. Blaine, while the Stalwarts were directed by Senator Roscoe Conkling of New York.

In their political beliefs the two factions were not far apart. The *Nation* defined Stalwartism as an "indifference or hostility to civil service-reform, and a willingness to let 'the boys' have a good time with the offices."

The chief difference between them seemed to be that the Stalwarts advocated the return of Grant to the Presidency while the Half-Breeds opposed the ex-President's third term ambitions. Personal animosity between the leaders of the two opposing groups widened the chasm. Ever since Blaine twitted Conkling was "a majestic, supereminent, overpowering, turkey-gobbler strut," Conkling had been his enemy.

In the final year of his term the President reviewed the record of his administration's achievements. He proudly pointed to the fact that the members of his Cabinet were "able gentlemen free from scandals," that there was "no nepotism" and that there were "good morals in the White House." His appointments were free of Congressional dictation, and they were nonpartisan. "I have not done as much to improve the System and Civil Service as I hoped and tried to do," Hayes wrote, "but I have improved the Service in all of its branches until it is equal to any in the world. . . . Look at its purity, efficiency, freedom from Scandals, and decide as to its merits."

He dealt at length on his Southern policy. "My judgment was that the time had come to put an end to bayonet rule. I saw things done in the South which could only be accounted for on the theory that the War was not yet ended. Many Southern people evidently felt that they were justified in acts which could only be justified in time of war towards the common enemy. The Republicans, the North, the colored people if active in politics, were regarded and treated as the public enemy. My task was to wipe out the color line, to abolish sectionalism, to end the war and bring peace. To do this I was ready to resort to unusual measures and to risk my own standing and reputation with my party and the country." He noted that he had appointed many Southern Democrats and had withdrawn the army from the South "because I believe it a constitutional duty and a wise thing to do."

He recalled that General Boynton had suggested that he "be a candidate, or at any rate accept a nomination a second time," but he declared that "I would refuse

JAMES A. GARFIELD
Photograph by Mathew B. Brady
Library of Congress

CANDIDATES IN 1880

JAMES A. GARFIELD (1831–1881), a driver of mules on the Ohio canals, first a graduate, then president of Eclectic Institute (Hiram College), a general in the Civil War, then Congressman, became the Republicans' choice.

CHESTER A. ARTHUR (1830–1886), a member of the Stalwart faction of the Republican party, was chosen for the second place to placate Senator Conkling. After Garfield's death Arthur was sworn in on September 20, 1881.

WINFIELD S. HANCOCK (1824–1886), a West Point graduate, had achieved fame in the Battle of Gettysburg. Called "The Superb," he became presidential candidate of the Democrats, losing by less than ten thousand votes.

WILLIAM H. ENGLISH (1822–1896), a conservative Indiana banker who retired from politics before the Civil War to pursue business and scientific interests, re-emerged on the national political scene as Hancock's running mate.

NEAL DOW (1804–1897), Portland's Quaker mayor and the father of Maine's antiliquor legislation, spent his life crusading for temperance. He was 76 when the Prohibition party nominated him as its candidate.

JAMES B. WEAVER (1833–1912), Iowa politician and Civil War hero, who had been converted to the Free-Soil party by reading *Uncle Tom's Cabin*, was the Greenbackers' choice with B. J. Chambers as running mate.

LUCRETIA RUDOLPH (1832–1918) married Garfield on November 11, 1858. He was then the president of the Eclectic Institute of Hiram College, teaching Latin, Greek, mathematics and other subjects. She bore him seven children—five of them sons.

under all circumstances to depart from my avowed purpose not to be my own successor. In no way could I do the country so great a service as by setting a precedent against a second term. Several presidents have declared themselves when candidates, or when elected, opposed to a second term. I shall be the first who has adhered to the rule." In any case many of the party were against allowing him to seek a second term.

Grant, who the year before had returned from a triumphant two-and-a-half-year world tour, was the hero of Conkling and the Stalwarts. John Russell Young, who had accompanied the General, kept him in the public eye with stories in the *Herald*. The carefully edited "interviews" were collected in two volumes,

Joseph Keppler, October 1880

THE CINDERELLA OF THE REPUBLICAN PARTY AND HER HAUGHTY SISTERS. After ex-President Grant (center) returned from his world tour, Roscoe Conkling (right) and his Stalwart supporters wished to make him President again, ignoring the achievement of President Hayes (by the hearth), who had given the country an honest administration but who could not gain the confidence of either the Stalwarts or the Half-Breeds, the party's two opposing factions.

Around the World with General Grant, which enjoyed a large sale. That he would want the Presidency again after his scandalous two terms was incredible, and it was incredible that such a large number of Republicans should ask for his return to office. But time is a quick healer. Those who were for him had forgotten his poor years in the Presidency and preferred to remember his glory on the battlefields, and they would return him to office with a "whoop and halloo."

John Sherman also sought the nomination hoping that the support of Ohio would be a solid base from which to sweep the convention. But he had incurred the wrath of the Conkling forces by helping Hayes dismiss Chester A. Arthur from the New York Custom House.

On the issues of gold, silver and greenbacks, Sherman compromised by seemingly supporting all three. This was good for the moment, but laid the ground for a crisis later. The unparalleled prosperity he helped bring about as Secretary of the Treasury made a Republican victory a certainty.

The meeting of the Republican convention, which began on June 2 in Chicago's Exposition Building, turned into a momentous battle between Conkling and Blaine. Conkling was confident he could win the nomination for Grant, and Blaine was sure that he could stop it.

Conkling came to the convention with more than three hundred Stalwarts. If the unit rule (requiring each state to vote as a unit) had been enforced, Grant could

Frank Leslie's Illustrated Newspaper, *November 21, 1874*
THE LAST STRAW. Grant's third-term aspirations break
the camel's back—the Republican party. Soaring in the sky
is Stalwart leader Conkling, the leader of the Grant forces.

Thomas Nast, December 1879
BORROWED PLUMES. Roscoe Conkling became Blaine's
enemy when the leader of the Half-Breeds called him a "majestic, supereminent, overpowering, turkey-gobbler strut."

have had the nomination on the first ballot. But the
anti-Grant forces, led by James Garfield of Ohio (who
was managing John Sherman's candidacy), blocked its
acceptance. This freed the votes of more than sixty
delegates in the various states, who could now support
the man of their own choice.

In a short, effective and impassioned speech Roscoe
Conkling presented Grant's name:

> *And when asked what state he hails from,*
> *Our sole reply shall be:*
> *He hails from Appomattox*
> *And its famous apple tree.*

Conkling said that the coming election would determine
whether this country should be "republican or Cossack,"
and he accused all those who opposed Grant and who
cried for reforms of being "charlatans, jayhawkers,
tramps and guerrillas." The aggressive speech did not
sit well with the delegates.

After Conkling finished, Garfield mounted the rostrum to make a friendly and conciliatory address on
Sherman's behalf. He said that Sherman alone could
create party harmony, without which the election could

not be won. "In order to win victory now, we want the
vote of every Republican—of every Grant Republican
and every anti-Grant Republican in America—of every
Blaine man and every anti-Blaine man." His moderate
tone was in sharp contrast to the venomous diatribe of
Conkling.

As the balloting began, Grant was in the lead. At the
end of the first trial he had 304 votes against Blaine's
284, Sherman's 93, George F. Edmunds's 33, Elihu B.
Washburne's 31, and William Windom's 10. Twenty-
eight ballots were taken, with basically the same results.
The vote for Grant fluctuated between 302 and 313, the
vote for Blaine between 282 and 285. Stalwarts and
Half-Breeds held the fort. With Grant and Blaine in a
deadlock and neither of them willing to yield, the search
began for a compromise candidate who would be acceptable to both factions.

On the second ballot a lone Pennsylvania delegate
had cast his vote for Garfield and continued voting for
him until the thirteenth ballot. Other delegates joined
him but then gave up. Between the fourteenth and
eighteenth ballots, Garfield did not receive a single vote.
But on the nineteenth ballot the Pennsylvania delegate
again began to vote for him and was joined on the

thirty-fourth ballot by the majority of the Wisconsin delegation. Garfield protested immediately. "I rise to a point of order," he said. "No man has a right, without the consent of the person voted for, to announce that person's name and vote for him in this convention. Such consent I have not given." But Senator Hoar, the chairman of the convention, would not let him finish his say as he feared Garfield "would say something that would make his nomination impossible." The break came on the next ballot, when 50 of Blaine's votes switched to Garfield. Though Grant was still leading with 313 votes against Blaine's 257 and Sherman's 99, the Garfield bandwagon was now rolling.

It was at about this time that Sherman wired from Washington: "Whenever the vote of Ohio will be likely to assure the nomination of Garfield, I appeal to every delegate to vote for him. Let Ohio be solid. Make the same appeal in my name to North Carolina and every delegate who has voted for me." Thus on the thirty-sixth ballot the convention turned to Garfield, giving him 399 votes; and with the other states changing their votes, he became the candidate. But 306 unyielding Stalwarts clung to Grant until the end. They would not change to accept Garfield's nomination by the usual acclamation.

The Garfield men, paraphrasing the Grant jingle, chanted lustily:

If asked what state he hails from,
Our sole reply shall be:
He comes from old Ohio
And his name is General G.

Sherman wired his lieutenants: "Now give us some first class man for Vice President." But in their elation over the nomination of Garfield, they rushed over to the New York delegation, and to pacify the Stalwarts the Vice Presidency was given to Conkling's friend, Chester A. Arthur, "the gentleman boss" of New York.

Garfield was the last of the log-cabin candidates. In his youth he drove mules on the towpaths of the Ohio Canal. He graduated from Williams College in Massachusetts and taught at Western Reserve Eclectic Institute (later Hiram College), becoming its president. During the Civil War he assembled a regiment, the 42nd Ohio Volunteer Infantry, with many of his Hiram students and gradually rose to the rank of major general. He fought in many engagements, including those at Middle Creek, Shiloh and Chickamauga. In 1862, after

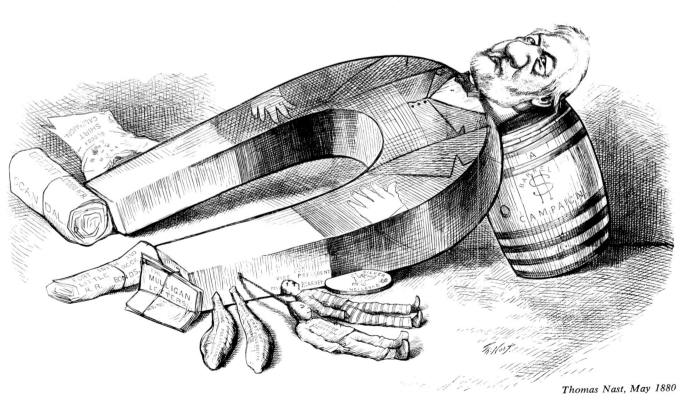

Thomas Nast, May 1880

BLAINE, THE MAGNETIC STATESMAN. At the end of the magnet the scroll reads: "Crédit Mobilier Scandal" and "Fort Smith and Little Rock Railroad Bonds"—two issues which tarnished his reputation. He also attracts a "bloody shirt."

Frank H. Taylor, June 1880

A GROUP OF DELEGATES IN SEARCH OF A ROOM

Frank H. Taylor, June 1880

SOUTH CAROLINA AND FLORIDA DELEGATES

Frank H. Taylor, June 1880

A "SINGLE" IN THE OVERCROWDED HOTELS

THE CONVENTION COMES TO ORDER. ONE OF T

he was elected to Congress as Representative from the 19th Ohio District, he resigned his major-generalcy because Lincoln told him that major generals were easier to procure than administration Republican Representatives. For the next eighteen years—Garfield was re-elected eight times—he served in the House of Representatives, an accomplished parliamentarian, a powerful debater, industrious and hard-working. After Thaddeus Stevens passed from the political stage in 1868, Blaine and Garfield became the leaders in the House, and Blaine's departure for the Senate in 1876 left Garfield without a rival. In 1880 the Ohio legislature elected him to the Senate to succeed Allen G. Thurman, but he never took his seat—on the day his term

RST PHOTOGRAPHS TAKEN AT A CONVENTION.

Sketch by W. Parker Bodfish, June 1880
ARRIVAL OF THE NEW ENGLAND DELEGATES

Sketch by W. Parker Bodfish, June 1880
THE WOMEN'S SUFFRAGE ASSOCIATION MEETS.

Sketch by Frank H. Taylor, June 1880
A DELEGATE TAKES A REST IN A BARBER CHAIR.

was to have begun, he was inaugurated as President.

"The canal boy" was the youngest of the presidential nominees—only forty-eight. Unfortunately, the platform on which he had to conduct his campaign was a meaningless document abounding in such platitudes as: "that the peace regained should be cherished . . . that the liberties secured to this generation should be transmitted undiminished to future generations . . . that the commerce, already so great, should be steadily encouraged," that "the Constitution of the United States is a supreme law, and not a mere contract," and that "the intelligence of the nation is but the aggregate of the intelligence in the several States, and the destiny of the nation must be guided, not by the genius of any one State, but by the

Sketch by Frank H. Taylor, July 1880

THE DEMOCRATIC CONVENTION AT CINCINNATI NOMINATED HANCOCK ON THE SECOND BALLOT.

Frank Leslie's Illustrated Newspaper, *July 31, 1880*

DEPARTMENT OF THE EAST COMMANDER Hancock is notified at his Governor's Island headquarters.

average genius of all." On the whole it was a rehash of the Republicans' platform of four years before. Its other planks came out against polygamy ("slavery having perished in the States, its twin barbarity, polygamy, must die in the Territories"), for the protection of naturalized citizens against Chinese immigration ("as an evil of great magnitude"), and it contained a scathing attack on the Democratic party, which sacrificed "patriotism and justice to a supreme and insatiable lust of office and patronage." At first it contained no declaration for a reform of the Civil Service, but when the delegates demurred, an added plank asked for "a thorough, radical, and complete Civil Service reform."

President Hayes was pleased that Garfield became his party's choice—"the best that was possible"—and was satisfied with Grant's defeat. "There is much per-

Thomas Nast, April 1879

"WE HAVE COME TO STAY"—A PROPHECY WHICH HAS COME TO PASS. The South had its fill of the harsh Republican rule, of the Radical reconstruction program, of corrupt Carpetbag governments. After the Federal troops withdrew, the Southern states swung into the Democratic column and have remained the bulwark of the party until today.

sonal gratification in it. The defeat of those who have been bitter against me. The success of one who has been uniformly friendly. Ohio to the front also and again! The endorsement of me and my Administration. The endorsement of Civil Service reform. The sop thrown to Conkling in the nomination of Arthur, only serves to emphasis [sic] the completeness of his defeat. He was so crushed that it was from sheer sympathy that this bone was thrown to him."

And Hayes went on to note: "Once in about twenty years a campaign on personal characteristics is in order. Gen Jackson in 1820–24 [he meant 1824–28]—Gen Harrison in 1840—Lincoln in 1860—now Garfield in 1880. I know we can't repeat in details but in substance we can. In this instance we stand on the rock of truth. Such struggles with adverse circumstances and such success! The boy on the tow path has become in truth the scholar and the gentleman by his own unaided work. He is the ideal because he is the ideal self made man."

The Democrats were as divided as the Republicans. In the Northern states the regulars were struggling with the former Copperheads, in the South the old Jacksonians were battling with the conservative Bourbons. They, too,

needed a candidate who would be acceptable to all the diverse elements. Tilden, the party's nominee in the disputed election of 1876, saw that he could not be nominated and withdrew. So did Seymour, the candidate of 1868. Many Democrats supported the popular Senate leader Thomas F. Bayard of Delaware, while Indiana still boosted her native son Thomas A. Hendricks. Others seeking the nomination were Representative Henry B. Payne of Ohio; the "Old Roman" Allen G. Thurman; General Winfield S. Hancock; and the House Speaker Samuel J. Randall. But in the end the party turned to General Winfield Hancock, "a good man weighing two hundred and forty pounds," a Civil War general and a military commander in Louisiana under the Reconstruction Acts, whose record was "as stainless as his sword." Though Hancock had no experience in politics and no knowledge of the problems of government, he won the nomination on the second ballot over nineteen other contenders because he had few enemies; his nickname was "Hancock, the Superb." He had been a candidate before the democratic conventions of 1868 and 1876; both times he had lost out.

For the second place the convention chose William H.

W. A. Rogers, October 1880

FRESH BLOOD IS TRANSFUSED into the figure of "Democracy" by Winfield Hancock, the party's candidate. Campaign chairman William Barnum gives a helping hand.

Thomas Nast, November 1880

"WHO IS TARIFF?" Hancock asks in the cartoon, "and why is he for revenue only?" The naïve candidate was ridiculed for his remark that tariff was only a local issue.

354

Joseph Keppler, September 1880

INSPECTING THE DEMOCRATIC CURIOSITY SHOP. General Hancock, the standard-bearer of the Democrats, cries out in dismay at the sight of the patched-up two-ended Democratic donkey: "Great Scott! Am I to be the Head of that?"

English, a millionaire banker from Indiana, who had retired from politics before the war.

The platform was the work of Henry Watterson, the editor of the Louisville *Courier-Journal,* and it read like an editorial. It pledged the party to its constitutional doctrines and traditions; promised opposition to "centralizationism," and the consolidation of the power of all departments in one; it emphasized "the separation of Church and State"; it pleaded for "honest money," but evaded the silver question; it demanded tariff for revenue only; and asked for "a general and thorough reform of the Civil Service." It was for the subordination of the military to civil power and against Chinese immigration, and it denounced the Republicans, particularly for their fraudulent election of 1876. (The Democrats still called the President "Rutherfraud Hayes"; in their press his pictures and cartoons appeared with "fraud" written on his forehead.)

Between Republicans and Democrats there were no clearly defined issues. "Both parties were completely bankrupt," wrote the historian John D. Hicks. "The issues that divided them were historical merely. The Republican Party had come into existence because of the stand it had taken on slavery, and it had lived on because of its determination to free the slaves, to save the Union, and to punish the South. Its program was now finished and its excuse for existence had disappeared. The Democrats, likewise, had so long centered their attention upon the issues of slavery, the Civil War, and reconstruction that they failed to observe that the era in which these issues meant anything had rolled by. . . . Neither Democrats nor Republicans seemed to sense the significance of the vast transformation that was coming over business, nor the critical nature of the relationship between labor and capital, nor even the necessity of doing something definite about civil service reform, the money problem, and the tariff. The Republican Party existed to oppose the Democratic Party."

Joseph Keppler, September 1880

"FORBIDDING THE BANNS." Candidate James Garfield, appears as the bride of Uncle Sam. Behind him are two prim bridesmaids—Carl Schurz and Whitelaw Reid—and also Marshall Jewell, Republican committee chairman. William Barnum, the Democratic chairman, disrupts the ceremony with the "Crédit Mobilier" baby. Garfield, who was supposed to have taken $329—a small sum—from that company's funds, says bashfully: "But it was such a little one."

W. Parker Bodfish, August 1880

CAMPAIGNING. On his way to New York, Garfield gave addresses—as here, in Poughkeepsie—at every train stop.

Thus the campaign substituted for issues a discussion of the behavior and private lives of the candidates. Both Republicans and Democrats boasted of their candidates' war records, heroism, honesty and integrity.

The war was still fresh in the minds of the Republicans—they were determined that no Democrat, even a war hero, should sit in the White House. And some Democrats wanted to repudiate the disputed election results of 1876—this time they would not be robbed of victory. Republican orators attempted to "wave the bloody shirt," but the country was tired of it; sectional hatred was no longer a drawing card. "The war drum throbbed no longer and the battle flags were furled." The Democratic orators tried to revive the fraud charges of the last election, but that did not pull either.

Robert G. Ingersoll, campaigning for the Republicans, simplified the issues: "I believe in a party that

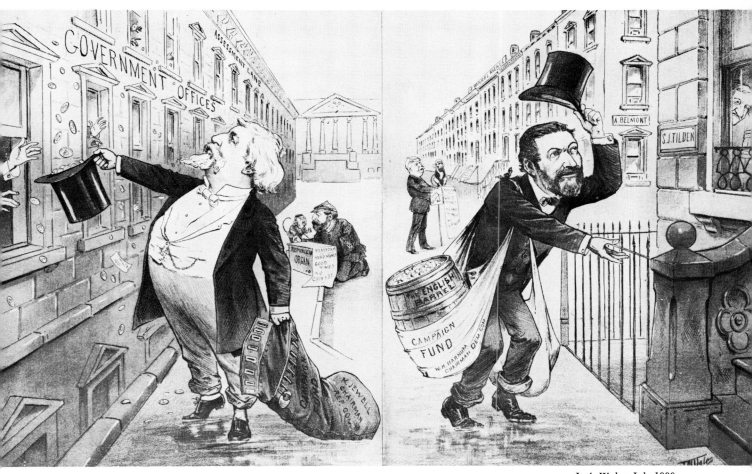

J. A. Wales, July 1880

MONEY FLOWS FREELY IN THE CAMPAIGN. Republican Chairman Jewell and Democratic Chairman Barnum are soliciting funds. The Republican fund raiser urges the government employees to contribute so that they can "keep the places," while the Democratic solicitor encourages the "Barrel Avenue" interests to contribute money "to get the places."

believes in good crops; that is glad when a fellow finds a gold mine; that rejoices when there are forty bushels of wheat to the acre. . . . The Democratic party is a party of famine; it is a good friend of an early frost, it believes in the Colorado beetle and the weevil." So that was that.

There were other candidates from smaller parties. The Greenbackers, who asked for "a government of the people, by the people, and for the people, instead of a government of the bondholders, by the bondholders, and for the bondholders," named James B. Weaver of Iowa and Benjamin J. Chambers of Texas. Two years before, in the mid-term election, they had polled more than a million votes, but with the Panic of 1873 just a memory, with the price of wheat high and the economy expanding, and with Hayes eliminating corruption in government, their influence was on the decline. The Pro-

Thure de Thulstrup, October 1880

EX-PRESIDENT GRANT reviews the "Boys in Blue" torchlight procession near Worth Monument in New York.

Frank Leslie's Illustrated Newspaper, *March 19, 1881*

THE INAUGURAL BALL, with the leading political figures of the day (their heads are drawn larger than those of the others). On the left, behind the uniformed soldier: Roscoe Conkling and Vice President Arthur; in the center: James G. Blaine; behind President Garfield: Carl Schurz and Schuyler Colfax, and farther to the right, ex-President Rutherford Hayes.

hibitionists proposed the indomitable Neal Dow, the father of the "Maine law," and Henry Adams Thompson of Ohio. Like the candidates of the two major parties, the nominees of the Greenbackers and the Prohibitionists were military men. There was an abundance of generals and a conviction that they could—like Jackson, Harrison, Taylor and Grant in the past—stir the popular imagination and carry their party to victory.

Frank Leslie's Illustrated Newspaper, *March 26, 1881*

PRESIDENT GARFIELD'S CABINET. Counterclockwise from the President: James G. Blaine (State), Robert Lincoln (War), Thomas Jones (Postmaster General), Samuel Kirkwood (Interior), Wayne MacVeagh (Attorney General), William Hunt (Navy), William Windom (Treasury).

GARFIELD TAKING THE OATH ON MARCH 4, 1881. He is sworn in by Chief Justice Waite. Mrs. Garfield is on the left; the mustached figure leaning over the balustrade on the right is young Theodore Roosevelt, Representative in the New York legislature. Twenty-four years later he played the principal part in the ceremonies at the same spot.

Arthur Berghaus and Charles Upham, July 1881

THE PRESIDENT IS HURT. On July 2, 1881, at the Washington Railway Station, Garfield was shot by a disappointed office seeker. Next to Garfield is Secretary of State Blaine, while in the background the assassin is taken into custody.

Arthur Berghaus and Charles Upham, July 1881
WAITING FOR THE AMBULANCE. The President, on the floor, is comforted by a Mrs. Smith.

Author's collection
THE ASSASSIN, Charles J. Guiteau, shot Garfield —so he claimed—to elevate Arthur to the Presidency.

It was a dull contest; even the mudslinging was done in an unimaginative way. Garfield was assailed on account of $329 dividend when he had received from Crédit Mobilier, the holding company of the Union Pacific Railroad.

At first Garfield's memory recalled a sum of "about" three hundred dollars, but not a stock dividend. It was, instead, a loan from Oakes Ames to finance a trip to Europe and it had been repaid. When in a moment of panic he sent another payment of $329 to Ames, more explanation was asked. But Garfield's supporters turned the attack to their advantage; they painted the number "329" on transparencies, they shouted "Three twenty-nine," they chalked "329" on walls and scratched it on doors until nobody remembered what the number meant.

And Garfield was attacked because of a supposedly unpaid tailor's bill at Troy, and because is was alleged that during the war he had stolen furniture and bedding from a widow in the South.

Another charge was not so easily dismissed. A man by the name of De Golyer had patents for a wooden pavement which he wanted the Board of Public Works to adopt for Washington. A Congressman had been acting as De Golyer's lawyer, and when he was called out of town, he asked Garfield to present a brief at a Public Works hearing. For this service Garfield was handed the fat sum of $5,000. There could be no doubt that Garfield had been asked to do the chore and was paid the large sum of money because he was the Chairman of the House Appropriations Committee. Even though he did not let the fee influence his actions, he got himself into an embarrassing situation which needed much explaining.

The Stalwarts at first remained aloof and would not take part in the campaign. Garfield was told he must gain the support of the New York "machine" or go down in defeat. In New York and most of the North, "306" Clubs were formed. The "306" stood for the number of Stalwart delegates who stuck with Grant until the end in the convention. Although they were willing to help Garfield, their major aim was to keep Grant's name alive until 1884.

Only after Conkling, Grant and Cameron visited Garfield at his Mentor farm and made the "treaty of Mentor"—which supposedly promised them fair treatment (though what "fair treatment" meant was not spelled out)—they began to campaign for him.

The Republicans had a poor target in Hancock; his past was as clean as a whistle. The General had led an exemplary life; there were no skeletons in his closet.

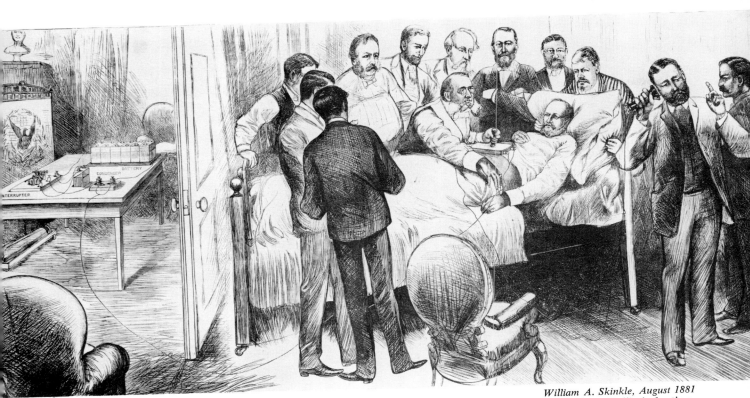

William A. Skinkle, August 1881

IN THE WHITE HOUSE BEDROOM the doctors attempt to locate the bullet with Alexander Graham Bell's induction-balance device. Their persistent probing brought on an infection, which may have caused Garfield's death eleven weeks later.

W. A. Rogers, September 1881

THE CABINET LISTENS to the medical report of Dr. Agnew. From the left, behind Secretary of State Blaine: MacVeagh, Kirkwood, Lincoln, James, Hunt, and Windom.

Drawing by Walter Goater, September 1881

THE PRESIDENT'S WIFE, a faithful nurse for her husband, prepares special food in the White House kitchen.

Grant said of him that "his name was never mentioned as having committed in battle a blunder for which he was responsible." In exasperation the Chicago *Tribune* wrote that Hancock "does nothing but eat, drink and enjoy himself sensually." So those who were against him turned their attacks on his son, who had committed the "crime" of marrying a young lady whose father was a Rebel sympathizer. However, a more effective issue against Hancock offered itself when he told a newspaperman from the Paterson *Daily Guardian* that "the tariff question is a local question." Cartoonists made the most of this remark.

The October state elections gave the Republicans hope. In the crucial states of Ohio and Indiana Democratic gubernatorial candidates were defeated.

The campaign came to life when *Truth*, a New York weekly, printed a forged letter on October 20 supposedly signed by Garfield and addressed to one H. L. Morey of the Employers' Union, Lynn, Massachusetts, in which the importation of cheap Oriental labor for employment in factories was advocated. Though the letter was denounced as a fraud, the Democrats kept on distributing copies of it by the thousands. Because the feelings of the Californians against Chinese labor was strong, Garfield lost that state and almost lost the election. His victory was by the slightest margin: a majority of only 9,464 votes out of a total of nine million; his popular vote stood at 4,454,416 against Hancock's 4,444,952. But he carried all states in the North and West save New Jersey and Nevada. The Republicans regained their majority in the lower House; the Senate was evenly balanced with two Independents maintaining the balance.

The weather was foul on inaugural day; a snowstorm and heavy winds dampened the spirits and kept large crowds away. After Garfield took the oath he kissed his mother, the first mother of a President to witness the inauguration of her son.

When Garfield made up his Cabinet, his appointment of Blaine as Secretary of State was the signal that the fight against the Stalwarts would continue.

On March 20 Conkling was invited to the White House to have a discussion about Federal appointments in New York. The President insisted that even non-Stalwarts from New York must get some of the offices, and Conkling suggested sending them abroad as consuls. Garfield was not in a joking mood. He told Conkling that they did not "deserve exile, but rather a place in the affairs of their own state." To placate his adversary, Garfield sent five of Conkling's suggested choices to the Senate. But when he appointed William Robertson as collector of the Port of New York, a most coveted Federal job, without consulting the Senator, Conkling raged with fury. Patronage in his state was slipping from his grasp; it seemed as if Garfield was building

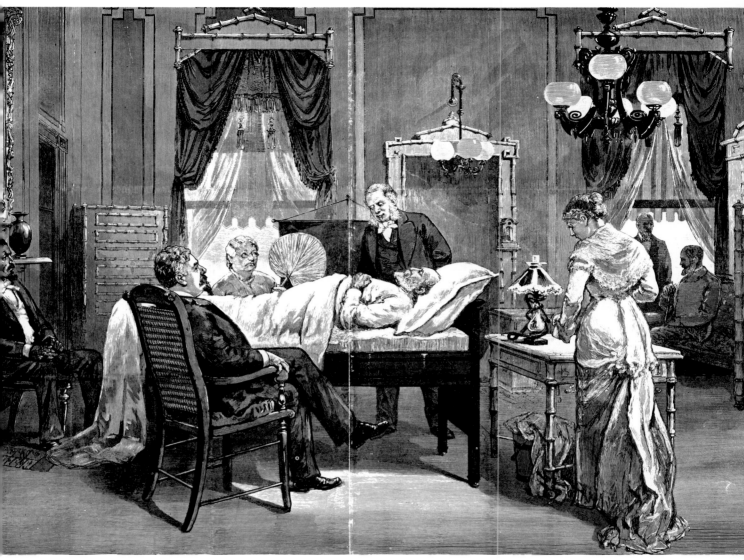

W. A. Rogers, July 1881

THE PRESIDENT'S SICKROOM, AS SKETCHED BY A *HARPER'S WEEKLY* ARTIST FROM THE DOORWAY

up a political machine in New York, to rival his own.

He fought back, asking for the observance of "Senatorial courtesy." Garfield was unyielding; he refused to withdraw Robertson's name. "They may have to take him out of the Senate head first or feet first; I will never withdraw him," he told John Hay. In his opinion the nomination of his appointee "will settle the question whether the President is registering clerk of the Senate or the Executive of the United States. Summed up in a single sentence this is the question: shall the principal port of entry in which more than ninety per cent of all our customs duties are collected be under the control of the administration or under the local control of the fac-

tional Senator?" It was an honest query.

Garfield won, and the Senate confirmed Robertson. Conkling resigned his Senatorial seat. Thomas Platt, the junior Senator from New York, said, "Me, too," expecting that the legislature would rename both of them. But the legislature appointed two moderate men in their stead, thus ending Conkling's political career and sending Platt into temporary oblivion.

The Garfield administration turned out to be the second shortest in American history (only William Henry Harrison's administration was shorter, lasting only one month). On July 2, less than four months after Garfield had taken office, a disappointed office seeker

363

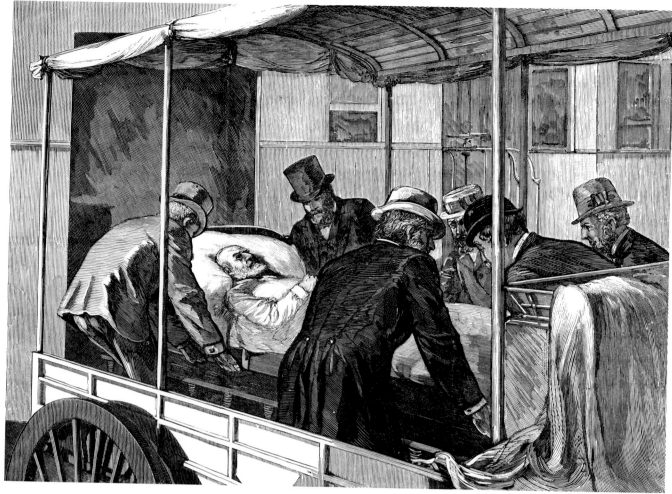

Theodore R. Davis, September 17, 1881

TO ESCAPE THE HEAT IN THE CAPITAL GARFIELD WAS MOVED TO ELBERON, NEW JERSEY.

shot him in the Washington railway station. Charles J. Guiteau, the assassin, who called himself "a Stalwart of the Stalwarts," proclaimed that his reason for shooting the President was to rid the country of a "traitor" and to elevate the "Stalwart" Arthur to the high office.

Guiteau felt that he deserved some kind of job. He had haunted the White House approaches for weeks. And when nothing was given to him and he learned of the President's movements, he went to Union Station where Garfield was to board a train for Williamstown, Massachusetts, to attend his alma mater's commencement.

For weeks the President hovered between life and death. One of those at his side was War Secretary Robert Todd Lincoln, who had been at his father's bedside sixteen years before. And twenty-five years later he would stand near the bedside of another assassinated President—McKinley.

Garfield had been taken to the White House where the doctors probed the wound in repeated attempts to find the bullet. On July 10 Navy engineers rigged up an imaginative plan to keep the sickroom cool; in the next few weeks they would use half a million pounds of ice. But the infection worsened. To escape the stifling heat of the Capital the President was taken to Elberon on the cooler New Jersey shores. There on September 19 he died, and the same night Vice President Arthur swore the oath of office.

The country was shocked. To kill the President so that others could get offices was more than the people could bear. The deed created revulsion against the spoils system; a cry went up for Civil Service reform.

Guiteau's bullet not only killed Garfield but also ended the existence of the Stalwarts. "The stalwarts could no longer hope," wrote Herbert Agar, "as when Hayes was President, to sit through one honest administration and then gaily return to the pigsty."

J. W. Alexander, September 1881

ARTHUR TAKES THE OATH OF OFFICE in the parlor of his Lexington Avenue home in New York at half-past one in the morning of September 20, 1881. New York Supreme Court Justice John Brady swore him in. Two days later, when he returned to Washington, Arthur once more took the oath, this time administered by Chief Justice Morrison R. Waite.

GROVER CLEVELAND

Arthur was named for the Vice Presidency because he was a friend of Roscoe Conkling. After the weary days of balloting, the convention allowed New York to make the selection for the second place on the ticket. The delegates were convinced that "an acceptable man would be presented," and when Arthur's name was given, they were "very much amazed." The candidate's bearing was "most justly and generally condemned," wrote *Harper's Weekly*. Arthur was noted for nothing but grace in presiding at dinners, attendance at meetings and activity in lobbying.

But Arthur had a solid background. Born in Vermont as the son of a Baptist minister, he graduated Phi Beta Kappa from Union College, Schenectady, after which he taught school and studied law. Once admitted to the bar he had helped the antislavery cause. During the Civil War he was quartermaster general of New York, which experience fitted him for a career in politics.

In 1871 Grant appointed him collector of the Port of New York, and he ran the Custom House honestly. But the place was overstaffed with clerks and laborers who regarded their jobs as sinecures. They were party men who felt that their main obligation was to attend party caucuses and conventions and to get out the vote on election day. As a branch of the New York political machine the Custom House was a thorn in the side of President Hayes, who desired a merit system in the Civil Service. Thus in an executive order he directed government employees to refrain from political activity. His Secretary of the Treasury started an investigating committee and reported that the Custom House had far too many employees and that they gave more of their attention to politics than to their jobs. Whereupon Hayes replaced Arthur.

When Arthur assumed the Presidency, he—contrary to expectation—did not fill the Cabinet with Conkling supporters; did not swamp the government with the spoils system; he even allowed a man who replaced him in the Custom House to remain in his post.

In his first message to Congress he asked: "Must this generation die without any return to the traditions of the Fathers without any knowledge of a condition of public affairs where party management for the mere advantage of partisans shall not predominate?" And he declared that "original appointments should be based upon a certain fitness."

To remedy the dismal conditions in the Civil Service, George Pendleton introduced a bill which Congress passed in 1883. The act authorized the President to appoint three Civil Service commissioners who were to provide "open competitive examinations for testing the fitness of applicants for the public service," leaving it to the President to expand the "classified service" as he saw fit. At first only the lowest officers were classified—about 12 percent of the total appointees—but as one Republican President (Arthur) was followed by a Democrat (Cleveland), who was succeeded by a Republican (Harrison), who in turn was replaced by a Democrat (Cleveland), who gave way to a Republican (McKinley), each President in a desire to protect his appointees extended the classified list. Thus the Civil Service grew. By the turn of the century the number of civil servants under the merit system had reached the hundred thousand mark; two decades later it was half a million.

GROVER CLEVELAND
Photograph by C. M. Bell

CANDIDATES IN 1884

GROVER CLEVELAND (1837–1908), Buffalo's reform Mayor and Governor of New York, was the Democrats' choice. The Republican "Mugwumps" deserted Blaine for Cleveland, who won with a skimpy 23,000 vote majority.

THOMAS A. HENDRICKS (1819–1885) of Indiana was Tilden's running mate in 1876. As he held Western views on money matters, he balanced Cleveland's Eastern attitude perfectly. He carried the important vote of his own state.

JAMES G. BLAINE (1830–1893), Speaker of the House and Senator from Maine, won the Republican nomination. Accused of dishonesty, he was abandoned by the reformers of his party, who lined up behind Cleveland.

JOHN A. LOGAN (1822–1886), Illinois Congressman and Senator, Civil War general and a founder of the GAR, was Blaine's running mate. He wore an old fur cap in winter and a straw hat in summer, but never a necktie.

JOHN P. ST. JOHN (1833–1916), whose alcoholic father left him with a hatred for liquor, a former "temperance" Governor of Kansas, was the candidate of the Prohibition party, receiving 150,369 popular votes.

BENJAMIN F. BUTLER (1818–1893), Civil War general and hated military governor of New Orleans, was Massachusetts' Governor when named jointly by the Greenbackers and the Anti-Monopolists. He got 175,365 votes.

Library of Congress

FRANCES FOLSOM (1864–1947) was secretly engaged to the President when she was only twenty. After the inauguration she and her mother visited Europe, while "Uncle Cleve" looked for a house in Washington. Cleveland came to meet them at the dock— but the word was out. Bands played "He's Going to Marry Yum-Yum." When they married in the White House, the whole country wished them well.

She bore her husband, whom she survived by forty years, three daughters and two sons.

Arthur's other major effort was the revision of the tariff. The high protection rates hurt overseas trade; foreign countries erected barriers in retaliation; American raw products met with discrimination abroad. As the country needed the foreign market, tariff revision became imperative.

Both these issues—tariff and Civil Service reform— cut across party lines. In general the Republicans favored high duties, while the Democrats advocated tariff for revenue only, though there were tariff reformers among the Republicans and protectionists among the Democrats. Similarly, Civil Service reformers were found in both parties.

Bernard Gillam in April 1884

THE PRESIDENTIAL RECRUITING OFFICE. Uncle Sam judges the candidates. They are labeled: Evarts, "Too Long-Winded"; Grant, "Retired"; Platt, "Me Too Little"; Conkling, "Too Pigeon-Breasted"; Mahone, "Must be Readjusted"; Dana, "Too Short-sighted"; Logan, "Grammar Feeble"; Blaine, "Too Crooked"; Sherman, "Bloody Shirt Mania"; Croker, "Pigheaded"; Randall, "Protection Madness"; and Bayard, "Unstable." Ben Butler, on the scale, reaches "Notoriety," and the symbol of Puck hands him a rejection slip, "Can't See Straight"; President Arthur has "no backbone"; Payne is identified as "Oil on the Brain," while Samuel Tilden (foreground) is "Rejected—Cipher Catarrh." The only ones "Admitted to competition" (right) are Abram Hewitt, John Carlisle, William Morrison, Robert Lincoln and Senator George Edmunds.

As party lines were not clearly drawn, the outcome of the coming election depended more upon the candidates' personalities than on their political principles.

The Republican convention met first. The chaplain who opened the proceedings in Chicago thanked God for the splendid history of the party and expressed the hope that "the coming political campaign may be conducted with that decency, intelligence, patriotism and dignity of temper which become a free and intelligent people." If Reverend Griswold could have peeped into the future, his words would have been even more fervent.

President Arthur wanted a nomination of his own. And he worked for it in his own way. He had gained some popular support when the price of a postage stamp dropped from three cents to two. Making his appointments, he often paired them—a good one with a bad one. Thus he gained applause from the reformers and at the same time backing from politicians who could help build a personal organization. In the South he had solid strength with the "mercenary brigade" of Federal office-holders. He also had the backing of New York business. But the opposition he faced within his own party far outnumbered his supporters.

General Grant was no longer in the presidential race. The battle in the last convention had left permanent scars. Personal matters added to the reasons for his elimination. The Wall Street firm of Grant and Ward failed in May 1884. The General was not aware of the crookedness of his partner; he was a trusting soul. But to the *Nation* this failure was "the most colossal that ever took place among merely private firms in the United States, and one of the most disgraceful." Grant was left without funds; he lost everything he had. The Senate voted him a pension. He retired from the public eye and was writing his memoirs. Suffering from cancer of the throat, unable to speak, he sat in an old wicker chair at Mount McGregor outside Saratoga, working feverishly in a race against death. Within a year, not long after he wrote the last chapter, he died.

Roscoe Conkling was out of the race as well. After his fight with Garfield over patronage, he resigned from the Senate. When Arthur became President, he hoped that he would be named Secretary of State, but Arthur would not appoint him. As time went by, Conkling was offered a seat on the Supreme Court; "Lord Roscoe" would not take it; he considered it too small a job for his large talents.

Among the others who vied for the nomination were Senator John Sherman of Ohio; General John A. Logan, who tried to solidify the scattered Grant forces; and Senator George Edmunds, who had strong support among the reformers.

But the favorite was James G. Blaine. The Plumed Knight had sought the nomination twice before—in 1876 and in 1880; both times it had eluded him. Garfield appointed him as his Secretary of State, and Blaine started out with bold plans to knit a closer relationship with the South American republics, to expand American trade in Latin America, and to construct across the Isthmus of Panama a canal to be controlled by the United States. However, before he could accomplish his aims, Garfield died and Blaine had to return to private life and to the writing of his memoirs.

From the opening day of the convention Blaine was the center of a violent struggle. The national committee, dominated by his supporters, demanded the temporary chairmanship be given to ex-Governor Powell Clayton of Arkansas, but Henry Cabot Lodge protested and suggested John R. Lynch, a Negro delegate from Mississippi, instead. The delegate-at-large from New York, twenty-five-year-old Theodore Roosevelt, climbed the rostrum, removed his straw hat, and implored the delegates to vote not as units but as individuals for the temporary chairmanship. "Let each man stand accountable to those whom he represents for his vote," said Roosevelt. "Let no man be able to shelter himself behind the shield of his state. . . . One of the cardinal doctrines of American government is the accountability of each man to his people; and let each man stand up here and cast his vote and then go home and abide by

THE THANKSGIVING DINNER of the potential Republican candidates. From left to right: Congressman Richard P. Bland of Missouri; Murat Halstead of the Brooklyn *Standard-Union,* who wrote articles attacking senatorial privilege; Senator William M. Evarts of New

Joseph Keppler, 1884

York; Supreme Court Justice Stephen J. Field; James G. Blaine, Secretary of State; Whitelaw Reid, editor of the New York *Tribune* and Minister to France; John Wanamaker, rich Republican merchant; Senator John A. Logan of Illinois; Joseph Medill of the Chicago *Tribune;* and Senator William B. Allison of Iowa. They have a feast spread—from "Senatorial privilege" soup to a cake of "Tariff" and "Prohibition." The Damocles sword over their heads, "Cleveland's Growing Popularity," keeps them from enjoying their turkey of "Presidential Aspirations."

Frank Leslie's Illustrated Newspaper, *July 19, 1884*

THE DEMOCRATIC NATIONAL CONVENTION AT CHICAGO CHEERS THE NOMINATION OF CLEVELAND.

Frank Leslie's Illustrated Newspaper, *July 19, 1884*

OUTSIDE THE SUN BUILDING in New York City, the bulletin board gives the news of Cleveland's nomination.

what he has done." After Lynch's election the anti-Blaine forces looked forward to further victories.

But the Blaine supporters kept up their attacks. They proposed a resolution whereby delegates who would not pledge themselves in advance to support the nominee of the convention would be denied their seats. "There are already whispers in the air," said George Knight of California, presenting the proposal, "of men high in the Republican party, or that once stood high in the party, openly and avowedly declaring that they will not support one man if he be nominated by this convention. . . . That kind of men we want to know, and the sooner they are out of the Republican party, the better."

As Knight alluded to certain editors in his speech, George William Curtis, the editor of *Harper's Weekly* and one of the targets of Knight's attack, protested in an emotion-laden speech: "A Republican and a free man I came into this convention. Twenty-four years ago I was here in Chicago and took part with the men who

C. Bunnell, in Frank Leslie's Illustrated Newspaper, *June 14, 1884*
THE REPUBLICAN NATIONAL CONVENTION AT CHICAGO CHEERS THE NOMINATION OF BLAINE.

nominated the man who bears the most illustrious name in the Republican party. The gentleman last upon the floor says that he dares any man on this floor to vote against his resolution. I say to him in reply that the presentation of such a resolution in a convention such as this is a stigma, is an insult to every member who sits here." So Knight withdrew his resolution.

After the delegates had adopted a noncommittal platform, the names of the candidates were presented. Judge West offered Blaine with ringing words: "Nominate him and the campfires and beacon lights will illuminate the continent from the Golden Gate to Cleopatra's Needle. Nominate him and the millions who are now waiting will rally to swell the column of victory that is sweeping on." When the Judge finished, pandemonium broke loose. The delegates jumped on the chairs, and their cheers were "fully as deafening as the voice of Niagara." Flags, shields and banners were stripped from the walls, there was dancing in the aisles. "Blaine!

C. Bunnell, June 14, 1884
OUTSIDE CONVENTION HALL the Republicans shout themselves hoarse.

THE TATTOOED MAN—A CARTOON ATTACKING BLAINE BY BERNARD GILLAM, AFTER GERÔME'S

Because of unethical deals with the Little Rock Railroad, Blaine was charged with impropriety. To cartoonist Gillam this suggested the trial of the Greek courtesan of 400 B.C., nicknamed Phryne ("Toad") because of her complexion. During the religious festival at Eleusis she bathed in the nude, thus she was tried for profanity. When the lover

Bernard Gillam in Puck, *June 4, 1884*

PAINTING, "PHRYNE BEFORE THE TRIBUNAL."

who defended her anticipated an unfavorable verdict, he tore open her robe, displaying her loveliness. The judges were so moved that they voted for acquittal.

375

STAR-
ROUTERS'
HEAD-QUARTERS.

FROM THE
MULLIGAN SERIES.

AUGUSTA,
June 29th, 1869.
My Dear Mr. Fisher:
* * * Your offer to admit me to
a participation in the new railroad
enterprise is in every respect as generous as I could expect or desire. I
thank you very sincerely for it, and
in this connection I wish to make a
suggestion of a somewhat selfish
character. It is this: You spoke of
Mr. Caldwell's offer to dispose of a
share of his interest to me. If he
really desires to do so, I wish he
would make the proposition definite,
so that I could know just what to
depend on. Perhaps if he waits till
the full development of the enterprise, he may grow reluctant to part
with the share; and I do not by this
mean any distrust of him. I do not
feel that I shall prove a dead-head in
the enterprise if I once embark in
it. I see various channels in which
I know I can be useful.
Very hastily and sincerely your
friend,

JAMES G. BLAINE.

PUBLIC APPROVAL.

F. Opper

Frank Opper, July 1884

AGAINST BLAINE. His opponents publicized his letters, which indicated he'd been bribed by the Little Rock Railroad.

Blaine! Blaine!" went up the cry, and again "Blaine! Blaine! Blaine!" Men tore off their coats and waved them wildly; it was a scene unrehearsed and fresh, born of enthusiasm. Andrew D. White, president of Cornell University, a delegate-at-large from New York, de-scribed it as "absolutely unworthy of a convention of any party, a disgrace to decency, and a blot upon the reputation of our country."

All together, sixteen nominating speeches were made; the tide of eloquence kept up till dawn.

After a short sleep the balloting began the next morn-ing. On the first trial Blaine was leading with 334½ votes; President Arthur, backed by the South, had 278 votes; Senator Edmunds had 93; General John A. Logan of Illinois, 63½; Senator John Sherman of Ohio, 30; while the remaining votes were scattered among the lesser candidates. General William Tecumseh Sherman, the military hero of the Civil War whose nomination was boosted, declared that "in no event and under no cir-cumstances" would he be a presidential candidate. He

Frank Beard, September 1884

AGAINST CLEVELAND. His opponents attacked him for his affair with Maria Halpin, who bore him a son.

told Blaine that he would account himself "a fool, a madman, an ass" to embark on a political career at sixty-five years of age.

If the Arthur and Edmunds forces had been able to unite behind Arthur, Blaine could have been stopped. But they could not; thus on the fifth ballot Blaine won and became the nominee. The vice presidential candidate became "Black Jack" Logan—one of Blaine's henchmen. He had been named in the Crédit Mobilier scandal and had joined with Blaine in "befriending" the

Little Rock and Fort Smith Railroad. This "neck or nothing partisan" was no more acceptable to the moderates and reformers than Blaine.

The reformers in the party were in an uproar. They were against Blaine; they wanted a candidate who would not be dominated by special groups and party bosses. Blaine's past was tainted by corruption; he had, as Godkin wrote of him, "wallowed in spoils like a rhinoceros in an African pool."

Old-time Republican newspapers turned against the

GLORYING IN THEIR SHAME. Blaine—the thick-skinned animal—enters the ring with Whitelaw Reid, the editor of the *Tribune*, and William Phelps, a New Jersey Congressman, on his back. The cartoon alludes to Godkin's phrase in *The Nation* that when Blaine was Secretary of State he had "wallowed in spoils like a rhinoceros in an African pool."

Thomas Nast, October 1884

Republican nominee. In New York only the *Tribune* supported him. Reform clubs and independent committees within the party "united to rebuke corrupt men and corrupt methods in politics." Reform Republicans told leading Democrats that if the Democratic convention named an honest and progressive candidate, they would give him their support.

This augured well for the Democratic candidate, whoever he might be. And the Democrats had just the right man for the occasion: Grover Cleveland, the reform Governor of New York. Only Tammany Hall stood in the way of his nomination. John Kelly, the leader of the Tammany delegation, pointedly told an interviewer when asked about Cleveland: "Butler is a good man." He was speaking of General Benjamin Butler, the former Radical Republican. And for a while it seemed as if Tammany might be able to put him over. But

Tilden, the presidential candidate in 1876, and now the senior statesman of the party, endorsed Cleveland. After the Brooklyn delegation decided to support him, the vote of New York was safe for him. "Fire and smoke burst from the nostrils of Tammany," reported the *Sun;* "their henchmen paced the lobbies raging like lions."

Still Tammany did not give up the fight; it opposed the unit rule which prevented the delegates from voting individually; it wanted to split New York's vote, and New York was ripe for splitting. But the convention upheld the rule. When Cleveland's name was put before the delegates, one of the leaders of Tammany, State Senator Grady, shouted: "Cleveland cannot carry the state of New York." In the acrimonious debate which followed, Cleveland was alternately praised and abused. Edward S. Bragg of Wisconsin expressed the feelings of the majority when he said that he was sick of Tam-

Frank Beard, October 1884

"CARRYING HIS SIN." The Reverend Henry Ward Beecher, who in his sermons demanded liberal reforms, tells Cleveland, "Your burden is heavy; let me carry it." Beecher's reputation by this time was under a cloud; he was accused of having an illicit relationship.

many; sick of its greed, its jealous spirit, its squabbles and its predictions of defeat. He reminded the convention that Tammany was always kicking and bolting; it had opposed Tilden and stabbed Hancock in the back; it created mischief whenever it could. And he ended by saying that the young men of Wisconsin in whose name he spoke "love Cleveland for his character, but they love him also for the enemies he has made."

Grady jumped to his feet: "On behalf of his enemies I reciprocate the sentiment." But the nomination could no longer be denied to Cleveland, who on the first ballot received 392 votes against Bayard's 170, Thurman's 88 and Randall's 78. It was a majority vote, but not enough for a two-thirds endorsement.

During the night Cleveland's managers bargained with the managers of Samuel J. Randall, Pennsylvania's favorite son; for the release of the Pennsylvania delegates, Randall was promised patronage control in his state. Thus on the second ballot Cleveland became the candidate. To console the old guard, Thomas A. Hendricks of Indiana was chosen for his running mate.

What kind of a man was Cleveland? The Boston *Advertiser* described him: "Cleveland is stout, has a well-fed look, is indeed a good liver, has the air of a man who has made up his mind just how he ought to behave in any position where he may find himself. He is getting bald; he is getting gray—though his white hair does not show conspicuously, as his complexion is sandy. He dresses well, carries himself well, talks well on any subject with which he is familiar, and on any subject with which he is not familiar he does not venture to talk at all."

He was the son of a Presbyterian country clergyman, born in the parsonage at Caldwell, New Jersey. He

THOMAS NAST, THE CELEBRATED CARTOONIST, DREW MANY CARTOONS

Harper's Weekly, *September 20, 1884*
THE PLUMED KNIGHT, as Thomas Nast pictured James G. Blaine, holds the fort behind a barricade of money bags.

Harper's Weekly, *June 28, 1884*
PUTTING ON THE CLEAN SHIRT OF REFORM. Blaine, unfamiliar with the garment, puts it on upside down.

Harper's Weekly, *July 26, 1884*
ASKING FOR THE IRISH VOTE. Blaine promises that when he President he will take steps against Britain.

Harper's Weekly, *October 25, 1884*
FINANCIER GOULD offers a partnership to Blaine, who says he will accept it, if "... I'm let in on the ground floor."

FOR HARPER'S WEEKLY UNDERMINING AND RIDICULING BLAINE.

Harper's Weekly, *October 18, 1884*
LIT PERSONALITY. One part of Blaine wanted to hide
e Mulligan scandal, but the other part wanted to fight it.

Harper's Weekly, *August 30, 1884*
BLAINE'S CARPETBAG refers to his memoirs, *Twenty
Years in Congress*, with which he bid for the nomination.

Harper's Weekly, *October 11, 1884*
KING FOR THE LABOR VOTE, Blaine begs the ques-
: "Does public plunder for private gain protect labor?"

Harper's Weekly, *October 25, 1884*
TWO IRISHMEN TRY TO CARRY JAMES BLAINE into
the White House, but Uncle Sam is blocking the doorway.

started out by working in a general store, taught in the New York Institution for the Blind, then joined the family of his mother's uncle, who lived near Buffalo. There he studied law, was admitted to the bar and soon became assistant district attorney of Erie County. His next job was an unwanted one—sheriff of Erie County —and it was in that post that he had to execute two murderers. In 1881 he was elected Mayor of Buffalo to reform the city's administration, and the following year he was chosen Governor of New York as the "unowned candidate." His administration was honest; he instituted reform; thus when 1884 came and the Democrats needed a new and clean man, he was the obvious choice.

A number of smaller parties entered candidates. The Greenbackers nominated General Benjamin F. Butler for the Presidency, as did the Anti-Monopoly party, which declared in its platform that "labor and capital should be allies" and that "corporations, the creatures of law, should be controlled by law." The Prohibitionists

named John P. St. John, the former Kansas Governor.

The independent Republicans, meeting in New York City, rejected the formation of a third party and agreed to support Cleveland, declaring that "the paramount issue this year is moral rather than political." The *Sun* called them Mugwumps, an Algonquin Indian term meaning "chief" and the name stuck. The Mugwumps— mug on the one side; wump on the other—pleaded for honest and efficient government; they wanted a President of integrity, they called for Civil Service reform.

With the progression of the campaign the strength of the Mugwumps increased. Prominent Republicans became Mugwumps. Carl Schurz, one of the founders of the party, was now a Mugwump, as was the celebrated preacher Henry Ward Beecher. Cabot Lodge was a Mugwump, as was Theodore Roosevelt. Influential Republican newspapers joined in the crusade for honest government. *The New York Times,* the *Herald* and the *Evening Post* turned their backs on Blaine; *Harper's*

AGAINST THE MUGWUMPS

Frank Beard, August 1884
THE INDEPENDENT REPUBLICANS are tempted by George W. Curtis, the reform-demanding editor of *Harper's Weekly,* with a "Cleveland" apple from the Garden of Eden.

Grant Hamilton, November 1884
THE MUGWUMPS WAIT to get into the Capitol. Cleveland stands on the top of the steps. Carl Schurz (in top hat) argues with the Rag Baby—the Independent party.

Grant Hamilton, July 1884

THE INDEPENDENTS. "This is the third time they have marched around. There are just about nine of them, not ninety thousand." L–r: George Curtis, Henry Ward Beecher, Carl Schurz, Theodore Roosevelt and George Jones of the *Times*.

Weekly, the *Nation* and *Puck* went for the Democrats.

Since on the basic issues of national policy there was little difference between the two parties, the campaign turned into a contest of personalities, with many "revelations" about the personal lives of the contestants.

Further compromising letters came to light regarding Blaine's business deals with the Little Rock and Fort Smith Railroad, deepening the suspicion that, although he had professed his innocence after the "Mulligan Letters," he was not as clean as he wanted to appear. No longer a "Plumed Knight," he was now the "tattooed man." He concluded one of his letters to Warren Fisher, a business associate, with "Kind regards to Mrs. Fisher. Burn this letter." When the letter became public, it brought joy to Democrats. They could now chant and sing:

> *Burn this letter! Burn this letter!*
> *Kind regards to Mrs. Fisher.*

and:

> *Blaine! Blaine! James G. Blaine!*
> *The con-ti-nen-tal liar from the*
> *state of Maine.*

Bernard Gillam, October 1883

GENERAL BUTLER, TAMMANY'S CHOICE AND GREENBACKER CANDIDATE, LINES UP HIS SUPPORTERS.
He asks the Solid South to join ranks with his army of Women's Righters, veterans, Irish-Americans, convicts, Greenbackers.

The Republicans retaliated in kind. Cleveland was described as "a small man everywhere except on the hay scales." He had had no experience in national affairs and would be "used by tricksters," a "tool of corrupt rings." Because he had executed two murderers he was called "the hangman of Buffalo." But the worst was yet to come. On July 21 the Buffalo *Evening Telegram* headlined an article, "A *Terrible* Tale: A Dark Chapter in a Public Man's History," and subtitled it: "The Pitiful Story of Maria Halpin and Governor Cleveland's Son." The article revealed that while he was Mayor of Buffalo, Cleveland had had an illicit relationship with a thirty-six-year old widow who had borne him a child.

Cleveland's dismayed friends asked him what to do, and he telegraphed: "Above all, tell the truth!" Yes, it was true that he had had an affair with Mrs. Halpin and that she had borne him a child.

Had the story been known before the convention, Cleveland could not have been nominated. And had

it been made public some time later—nearer to voting day—he would have lost the election. But the accusation came early and the Democrats had enough time to repair the damage. They argued that the real issue of the election was not the private conduct of the candidates but their public integrity. "We are told that Mr. Blaine has been delinquent in office but blameless in private life, while Mr. Cleveland has been a model in official integrity but culpable in his personal relations. We should therefore elect Mr. Cleveland to the public office which he is so qualified to fill and remand Mr. Blaine to the private station which he is admirably fitted to adorn." Godkin, in the *Nation,* was even more to the point. Which was better for the Presidency, he asked, a man like Cleveland, who like Cromwell, Franklin, Hamilton and Webster had been unchaste, or a man like Blaine, who had sold his word in order to destroy documentary evidence of his corruption?

Charles A. Dana of the New York *Sun* retorted:

Grant Hamilton, September 1884

"THE ANGEL OF LIGHT." CLEVELAND AS PAINTED BY THE REVEREND HENRY WARD BEECHER
The result is applauded by Carl Schurz, George W. Curtis and George Jones. The little monkey looks like Thomas Nast.

"We do not believe that the American people will knowingly elect to the Presidency a coarse debauchee who would bring his harlots with him to Washington and hire lodgings for them convenient to the White House."

The Republican marchers now measured their steps to the rhythm of:

Ma! Ma! Where's my pa?

to which the Democrats responded:

Gone to the White House. Ha! Ha! Ha!

At first a number of prominent Republicans refused to stump for Blaine. Roscoe Conkling, Blaine's enemy, said that he was not campaigning for Blaine because "I do not engage in criminal practice." But as the campaign progressed, many of the recalcitrants fell in line—even rebellious Theodore Roosevelt. They went out and

spoke for Blaine—if even reluctantly—for the sake of party unity. Carl Schurz said that their motto was: "Hang moral ideas, we are for the party." Though they conceded that Blaine was not fit for the Presidency, still they worked for him because he was a Republican and because they would rather have a Republican in the Presidency than a Democrat.

Blaine took to the contest like a duck to cold water. In case the "bloody shirt" might not be enough to carry the voters, he said he would "agonize more and more on the tariff." If the epithet "rebel" did not damn the Democrats, "free" trader might. Blaine regarded the Mugwumps who came out against him as just as bad as the Democrats. They, too, were "agents of foreign interests" who wanted to close the mills and factories, throw men out of work and starve their families.

He campaigned hard. He loved to speak, he enjoyed the response of the masses, he was in his element on the platform. His "magnetic" personality made an impact

W. H. McDougall and Gribayedoff, in N.Y. World, *October 30, 1884*
"THE BLOODY BANQUET." James G. Blaine is flanked by the "Money Kings" Gould and Vanderbilt, while the starving laborer and his family are begging for alms. The drawing appeared a few days before the election and caused a sensation. It had a serious effect on Blaine's chances, as he had the poor judgment to accept an invitation to a banquet in his honor at New York's Delmonico's Restaurant when the country was smarting under a severe economic depression.

F. W. Freer, October 1884
POLITICAL DEBATE IN A RURAL POST OFFICE

Grant Hamilton, December 1884
A CARICATURE OF THE REV. BURCHARD, who in a campaign speech referred to the Democratic party as one "whose antecedents have been rum, Romanism and rebellion." Candidate Blaine who was present failed to repudiate Burchard. This cost him the votes of the New York Irish Catholics. Since he lost the state of New York by only 1,149 votes (and with it the election), Blaine's losing the Presidency may have been due to Burchard's phrase.

Frank Leslie's Illustrated Newspaper, *November 8, 1884*

VOTING: WILL THE WINNER BE BLAINE, CLEVELAND OR THE BOTTLED-UP BUTLER?

on the receptive audiences, and he reveled in the people's adulation.

Cleveland, on the other hand, remained in his Governor's office at Albany for most of the time, though he made some brief trips in October. He made no speeches and he would not solicit votes. He told his secretary Lamont: "I had rather be beaten in this race than to buckle to Butler or Kelly. I don't want any pledge made for me that will violate my professions or betray and deceive the good people that believe in me."

It looked as if the election would be close. The Tammany leaders in New York passed the word to their men not to vote for Cleveland, but to support Blaine. If their orders were obeyed, if more than half a million

CLEVELAND AS HAMLET. "Believe in civil service reform," read his belt. Two spoilsmen are restraining him.

*

"STABBED IN THE BACK," a cartoon in the weekly *The Judge*, which supported Blaine, after he had lost the election.

voters under Tammany's control refrained from upholding Cleveland, Blaine would win. Cleveland and his managers were in despair. Then almost at the last moment fate came to Cleveland's rescue. October 29 turned out to be a dark day for Blaine. Two incidents during that day brought disaster and cost him the Presidency.

In the morning the Reverend S. D. Burchard of the Murray Hill Presbyterian Church addressed a meeting at the Fifth Avenue Hotel. Burchard assured Blaine, who was on the platform, that the clergy were with him. Carried away by his peroration, he said that he and his colleagues would not support any candidate put forward by the party of "rum, Romanism and rebellion." This not only evoked Cleveland's old saloon associations and his drinking cronies, but slurred the Catholics and reminded the voters that the Democrats had been on the wrong side in the Civil War. It was a disastrous blunder. The shorthand reporter whom the Democrats had sent to the meeting noted the clergyman's remarks, and though the newspapermen present did not grasp the implication of the phrase, the Democratic campaign managers did.

Overnight they printed thousands of handbills with "Rum, Romanism and Rebellion" in bold letters and distributed them in the poorer districts of New York, the home of the immigrant Irish Catholics. The Irish reacted as expected; they would not heed Tammany's advice and vote for a Catholic-baiter.

On the same evening Blaine attended a fund-raising dinner at fashionable Delmonico's, given for him by New York's wealthiest men. The menu included canvasback duck, terrapin and champagne. Present were a number of millionaires. Next day the New York *World* carried on its front page a cartoon showing "Belshazzar Blaine and the Money Kings." It harmed Blaine even more than Burchard's speech. The country was in the doldrums of depression, the people were starving. It was not the time for the Republican candidate to be wined and dined by men who had made millions under the Republican administration. As the dinner took place just three days before the election, Blaine lost New York by 1,149 votes out of a total of 1,125,159, and with it the election. Without the Burchard speech and the dinner, it

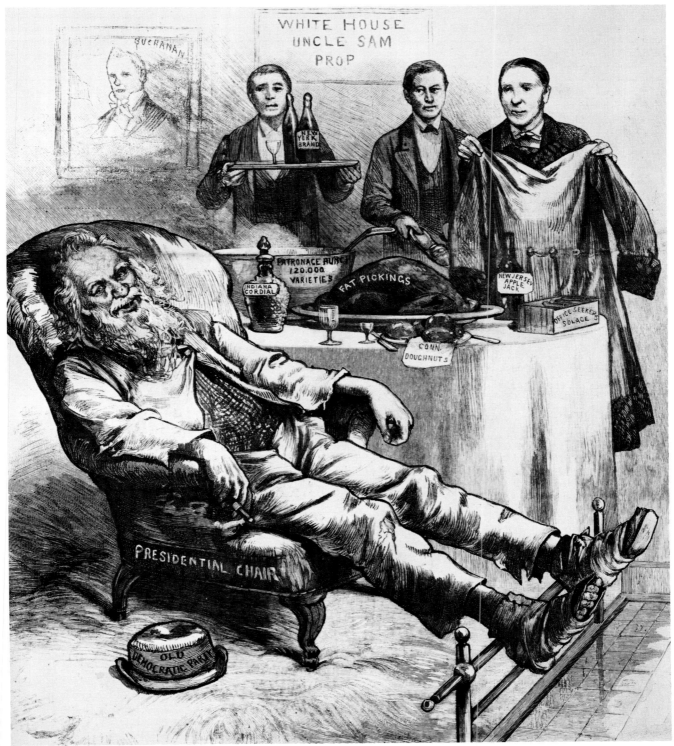

Frank Leslie's Illustrated Newspaper, *November 15, 1884*

AT LAST! AFTER TWENTY-FOUR YEARS THE OLD DEMOCRAT IS BACK IN THE PRESIDENTIAL CHAIR.
The Democratic party, dressed as Rip Van Winkle, warms its feet in the White House for the first time since the days of James Buchanan. Rip smokes an "Office Seekers Solace" cigar. The table is spread with turkey of "Fat Pickings" and 120,000 government jobs available as "Patronage-Punch." Servants bring a robe and slippers. Old Rip was ready to boot the Republicans out of office; "Turn the rascals out!" was his watchword. But Cleveland had been elected with the help of the reformers and was not willing to turn out office holders. But the pressure on him was so great, that he had to yield.

Thure de Thulstrup, March 1885
THE ENTIRE DIPLOMATIC CORPS TOOK PART IN THE DANCING AT THE COLORFUL INAUGURAL BALL.

is fair to assume that he would have won. Cleveland's total majority in the whole country was only 160,000. He received 4,914,986 popular votes to Blaine's 4,854,-981. Butler, the candidate of the Greenbackers and the anti-Monopolists, had 175,365 votes; John St. John, the Prohibitionist contender, received 150,369. Cleveland carried all the Southern and some of the border states in addition to Connecticut, New Jersey, Indiana and New York.

Cleveland took the oath of office from Chief Justice Morrison R. Waite. He spoke without notes, saying, "The people demand reform in the administration of the government, and the application of business principles

to public affairs." He asked for economy in government, a sound financial system, revenue laws which would not only relieve needless taxation but also have "due regard to the interests of capital invested and workingmen employed in American industries," and he wanted no surplus "to tempt extravagance and waste." The speech was a conservative one, and the country liked it.

The partisan *Tribune* noted that Cleveland was "fitly guarded" by a former chief of the "rebel secret service," while other Republicans saw the hated gray uniforms and heard the "Rebel yell."

After twenty-four years of Republican supremacy, the Democrats were back in power again.

CLEVELAND'S INAUGURATION
Chester A. Arthur, his predecessor, on the left

BENJAMIN HARRISON

The Democratic drought was at an end. After twenty-four years in the desert, the Democratic party was back in the promised land, and Democratic job seekers descended on Washington in droves. Cleveland resisted the avalanche manfully; he had no intention of dismissing Federal employees simply because they belonged to the opposition. But of the 126,000 Federal offices only about 12 percent were on the classified list; the rest of the jobs were looked upon as party spoils.

Cleveland had been elected as a "reform" President. But for the Democrats "reform" meant the replacement of Republicans with Democrats: "Turn the rascals out." So Cleveland had to capitulate. Before his term ended, four-fifths of the fourth-class postmasters were replaced; on the other hand, the Civil Service jobs were extended by some 27,000.

Cleveland began well; he had appointed a competent Cabinet; he fought waste and corruption; he vetoed the many pension bills introduced by overgenerous Congressmen for the veterans of the Grand Army of the Republic; he checked appropriations for public buildings, he cut unnecessary expenses. He tried hard to live up to the slogan coined by one of his publicity men: "Public office is a public trust." Realizing that the high tariff was leading to disaster, he dedicated his entire 1887 annual message to that issue, pleading for a general tariff reduction and the removal of duties on raw materials. He pointed out that high rates made life costly for the masses while it piled up fortunes for the few. Because of the high tariff rates the government was amassing a yearly surplus of $100 million when this money should have been in circulation and used for business. "It is a condition which confronts us, not a theory," said Cleveland.

As the Republican Senate would not repudiate the high rates, he pressed the Democrats in the House of Representatives, where they had the majority, to support him in favor of a low-tariff bill. Thus the Mills Bill (introduced by the economy-minded Roger Q. Mills of Texas) proposing lower rates—with wool, flax, hemp, salt, lumber and tin plate on the free list—was passed. However, when it reached the Senate, the Republicans substituted a measure which not only maintained the high rates but increased them.

Congress set aside two nights each week to consider pension matters. These were cases rejected by the lenient Pension Bureau, so these requests generally had little relation to active service. Mostly they were grants to constituents which Congressmen traded among themselves. Congress passed these "pension grabs" by the hundreds and sent them to the President for his signature. Cleveland stayed up until two or three in the morning to write his vetoes. As each "grab" required a separate veto, it was hard work. Cleveland was charged of being a "Vetoing President"—as he had been a "vetoing Governor" and a "vetoing mayor."

Infuriated by Cleveland's intransigence on pension proposals, the Grand Army of the Republic publicized his failure to serve in the war. Like so many others, he had hired a substitute to take his place when he was drafted in 1863. Threats of insulting demonstrations forced him to cancel his plans for attending the annual encampment of the GAR as was the presidential custom. While Cleveland did not care what they thought of him

BENJAMIN HARRISON WITH HIS GRANDSON
Photograph by Parker

CANDIDATES IN 1888

BENJAMIN HARRISON (1833–1901), the grandson of President Harrison, a general in the Civil War and a U.S. Senator from Indiana who was described as "cold as an iceberg," became the Republican candidate when Blaine advised the convention to vote for him. The campaign, run on the tariff issue, was won by Harrison with 233 electoral votes to Cleveland's 168, even though his count was 100,000 less.

LEVI P. MORTON (1824–1920), leading New York banker, Congressman and Minister to France, and later Governor of New York, could have had the vice presidential nomination with Garfield in 1880 and eventually have become President, but declined because of his Senatorial ambitions. Having failed for the third time to win a U.S. Senate seat, he was chosen by the Republicans for the second place.

GROVER CLEVELAND (1837–1908), the first Democratic President since James Buchanan, gave the country a decent and honest administration. But he antagonized the party regulars with his attitude toward the spoils system and made enemies among veterans, farmers and industrialists with his pension, currency and tariff reform policies. He received 5,540,329 votes to Harrison's 5,439,853 but lost in the electoral vote.

ALLEN G. THURMAN (1813–1895), Congressman, Chief Justice of Ohio's Supreme Court, a supporter of Douglas in 1860 and a leader of the "Peace Democrats" in the Civil War, U.S. Senator, was a partisan Jeffersonian Democrat. Called the "Noble Roman" with a red bandanna, he was seventy-five years old when named for the Vice Presidency. It was a strange choice; Thurman's political beliefs were opposite to Cleveland's.

Library of Congress

CAROLINE LAVINIA SCOTT (1832–1892), the first wife of Benjamin Harrison. They were married on October 20, 1853, and she bore him two children, a boy and a girl. She died in 1892, and five years later, when he was out of office, Harrison married again, this time a widow, Mary Scott Lord Dimmick (1858–1948). They had one child, named Elizabeth.

personally, he was appalled at the disrespect shown to the presidential office.

One of Cleveland's dismissals led to a controversy much like the one raised by the Radical Republicans over President Johnson's dismissal of Secretary of War Stanton. When it was found that a postmaster in New York State had failed to submit required reports and had mishandled receipts, the President made a new appointment and asked the Republican-controlled Senate to confirm it. After the Senate adjourned without acting on the appointment, Cleveland dismissed the postmaster, asserting a power denied him in the original Tenure of Office Act.

George Edmunds, the chairman of the Senate Judiciary Committee, regarded this move with aversion. He

Grant Hamilton, 1888

THE REDHEADED GIRLS AND THE WHITE HORSE. The Republican contenders: Evarts of New York, Alger of Michigan, Allison of Iowa, Ingalls of Kansas, Sherman of Ohio, Blaine of Maine, Harrison of Indiana and Depew of N.Y.

had arranged the rules of procedure for the trial of President Johnson and had fought against the partial repeal of the Tenure of Office Act in 1869. Now he was joined by other Republican leaders to oppose Cleveland's appointments—most of them Democrats. The Republicans wanted to know not only why the appointments should be approved, but also why the former officials had been dismissed. Cleveland was ready to comply with the first demand as it was prescribed in the Constitution, but he would not give the reasons for the dismissals. He held that as President he had the power to dismiss civil servants, and he instructed department heads to tell the Senate nothing.

The Senate struck back by refusing to confirm any of the appointments. But the Constitution was with Cleveland: "The President shall have power to fill up all vacancies that may happen during the recess of the Senate by granting commissions which shall expire at the end of their next session." So Cleveland kept making his appointments—and as the Senate was in recess, it could do nothing about them.

In the issue the country backed the President. Even though he was not popular, his integrity was respected, and it was felt that the Senate was hampering him in the fulfillment of his duties. Thus, the Tenure of Office Act, which gave him so much trouble, was discarded.

In the summer of that year Cleveland went to the Midwest and the South—to shake hands, speak to the crowds, to admire the local sights, and also to build up his reputation. In Chicago alone he shook six thousand hands in one evening. His speeches were dull and boring. He returned to Washington exhausted, but feeling that he had done his job.

That Cleveland would be renominated was never in doubt. The Democratic convention at St. Louis chose him by acclamation. No ballots were taken; the shouts of the delegates sufficed. For the Vice Presidency the "noble old Roman" from Ohio, 75-year-old Allen G. Thurman, was selected. As Thurman formerly had backed the West's silver and greenback policies, it was hoped that he would corner the voters from those states. His red bandanna, which he used after taking a pinch of snuff, was his identification mark. The delegates waved a forest of red bandannas in approval after he was named. "I think we have nominated a pocket handkerchief!" said one of them wryly.

The Democratic platform praised the record of the Cleveland administration; it reaffirmed the tariff plank of four years before and endorsed Cleveland's tariff message to Congress. It recommended "the early passage of the bill for the reduction of the revenue now pending in the House of Representatives [the Mills bill]"; it approved statehood for four Western territories; and with an obvious plea for the Irish vote it offered sympathy for Gladstone and Parnell for their valiant efforts to bring home rule to Ireland.

The Republicans met two weeks later in Chicago. A month before their convention convened, many elected delegates came out in favor of:

Blaine, Blaine, James G. Blaine,
We've had him once and we'll have him again.

Blaine had left for Europe the year before, without making it clear whether he wanted the nomination or not. But writing from Italy to the Republican National Committee on January 25, 1888, he requested his name not to be put forward because of "considerations entirely personal to myself." Still his supporters were ready to disregard his wish and went on preparing to draft him. "The Republican Party wants Blaine for the candidate and means to have him," wrote the *Nation.*

A few months later, on May 17, Blaine sent another letter—this time from Paris to Whitelaw Reid, the editor of the New York *Tribune*: "If I should now by speech or by silence, by omission or commission, permit my name in any event to come before the convention, I should incur the reproach of being incandid with those who have always been candid with me."

But even this letter did not cool the ardor of his supporters. "My theory is that Blaine is a candidate, has been from the beginning, and will be until defeated," exclaimed Senator John Sherman, the other favorite contender for the nomination.

There were other politicians to challenge Blaine and Sherman. One was Chauncey Depew, the witty entrepreneur from New York; another was ex-Governor Russell Alger of Michigan; a third one was Senator William B. Allison of Iowa; the fourth one, Senator Benjamin Harrison from Indiana. And Harrison had strong competition in his own state in the person of Walter Q. Gresham.

On the opening ballot Sherman led with 229 votes, followed by Gresham with 111 votes, Depew with 99,

Frank Leslie's Illustrated Newspaper, *June 1886*
THE BACHELOR PRESIDENT MARRIES. Cleveland is the only President who married in the White House. The wedding took place on June 2, 1886. Frances Folsom, the 21-year-old daughter of his deceased law partner, was his bride. Cleveland at that time was forty-nine years old.

Photograph by Prince & Cudlip
CLEVELAND'S FIRST CABINET. Seated: Thomas F. Bayard (State), the President, Daniel Manning (Treasury), Lucius Lamar (Interior). Standing: William Vilas (Postmaster General), William C. Whitney (Navy), William C. Endicott (War), Augustus H. Garland (Att. General).

CLEVELAND'S WALK-OVER
Drawing by Bernard Gillam, 1888

Alger with 84, Harrison with 80, Allison with 72, Blaine with 35; with the other votes scattered among the lesser candidates.

For five ballots the seesaw battle among the major contenders proceeded, none of them being able to secure a majority.

Sherman was implored to withdraw in favor of William McKinley in order to stop the draft for Blaine. Murat Halstead, that keen chronicler of past conventions, wired Sherman, who was in Washington, that "the Ohio delegation is already broken" and that "the Governor goes next ballot for Blaine. He thinks you have no chance left." Halstead was convinced "Blaine will certainly be nominated, unless the movement can be checked by placing McKinley in nomination and concentrating the anti-Blaine forces." Other Sherman men felt the same way. Telegram after telegram rained on Sherman in Washington. George F. Hoar telegraphed him: "Your nomination now seems impossible. If you promptly telegraph Ohio delegation, authorizing them to present McKinley, he will probably be nominated. Otherwise it looks like Blaine." Mark Hanna, who was managing Sherman's campaign, begged him to withdraw in favor of McKinley to "save the party from the Blaine lunatics." D. M. Leggett told him: "Your case looks hopeless, made so by the Blaine tricksters. Blaine must be defeated or we are ruined. Believe a majority would unite on McKinley if he were free. Don't delay final action too long. I believe you have power to defeat Blaine."

But Sherman was adamant; he would not withdraw. He answered Mark Hanna: "Let my name stand. I prefer defeat to retreat. . . . I like McKinley, but such a movement would be unjust to others . . . a breach of implicit faith."

The Blaine men, sensing the end of the Sherman boom, bombarded Blaine with cables, urging him to reverse his stand. Blaine replied from London: "Earnestly requested my friends to respect my Paris letter," and advised them to "refrain from voting for me."

The convention adjourned on Saturday for the weekend. Sunday turned out to be a busy day for the delegates; they kept on bargaining, negotiating deals, forming alliances, and in cables they beseeched Carnegie, Blaine's host in Scotland, to use his influence on his friend. The reply came that Blaine was "immovable." Carnegie's secret code message advised the delegates—in the name of Blaine—to take "Trump and Star," meaning Harrison and Phelps.

On Monday during the next three ballots Harrison's vote increased from 231 on the sixth trial to 544 on the eighth—securing his nomination. For the second place, the convention chose Levi Morton, the wealthy banker from New York and a liberal contributor to past cam-

THE BOSSES OF THE SENATE. "This is the Senate of the monopolists, by the monopolists and for the monopolists," reads the sign on the wall. All the big trusts—oil,

paigns, and not Phelps, as Blaine suggested to them.

Benjamin Harrison was a friend of Blaine's, with a clean and empty political record. A descendant of illustrious forebears—a great-grandson of a signer of

Joseph Keppler, January 1889

copper, lumber interests, insurance and utility companies and railroads—have their spokesmen among the Senators. Because the Senators were still named by the legislatures, it was relatively easy to buy legislators who then voted for those whom the trusts desired. The monopolies were well represented; the People's Entrance is tightly padlocked.

the Declaration of Independence and a grandson of old Tippecanoe—Harrison himself had been a general in the Civil War. In a bid for re-election as a Senator in 1887 he lost by one vote. He then returned to his law practice in Indianapolis, while his friends pushed him toward the Presidency. He was helped by his sound views on the tariff. Once he suggested that a cheaper coat might involve a "cheaper man" under the coat.

U.S. TREASURY

1865 GOING IN

$300,000,000 FOR PENSIONS 188?

Tay—

Drawn by Joseph Keppler, December 1887

THE OPENING OF THE CONGRESSIONAL SESSION. THE ADMINISTRATION'S WORRY WAS THE SURPLUS.

The Blaine supporters consoled themselves:

> *We'll vote this year for Tippecanoe*
> *And for James G. Blaine in '92.*

The platform made clear the Republican position on the tariff. It said, "We are uncompromisingly in favor of the American system of protection. We protest against its destruction, as proposed by the President and his party. They serve the interests of Europe; we will support the interests of America." The lowering of the tariff was denounced, as was the Mills bill. In their other planks the Republicans straddled the currency issue; asked for larger appropriations for the Navy, for public works and for pensions. To appeal to Prohibitionists the platform expressed sympathy "with all wise and well directed efforts for the promotion of temperance and morality." One of the key planks in the platform favored "the entire repeal of internal taxes, rather than the surrender of any part of our protective system." The *Nation* wrote of this: "It is so at variance with all former deliverances of the party, with scores of resolutions of state legislatures under Republican control, with hundreds of speeches and votes of Republican statesmen now living, with the report of the Republican tariff commission only five years ago, and with the recommendation of successive Republican Presidents and Secretaries of the Treasury, that the party can be likened only to the man who made a monster of which he became the unhappy victim. Protection is the Frankenstein of the Republican party."

The Prohibitionists had taken votes away from the

HE AMAZING GROWTH
OF THE PENSION PIG
Drawing by C. J. Taylor, March 1888

Charles Graham and Paul E. Harney, Harper's Weekly, *June 16, 1888*
IN THE DEMOCRATIC CONVENTION at St. Louis, President Cleveland was enthusiastically renominated by acclamation. He had the support of rich and poor alike. The workers trusted him, the bankers and financiers approved his hard-money and anti-silver policies, the merchants and shopkeepers no longer feared that business would go to the dogs under a Democratic administration.

A DEMOCRATIC CAMPAIGN POSTER

Frank Adams in Frank Leslie's Illustrated Newspaper, *June 9, 1888*
THE ARRIVAL OF THE DELEGATES AT ST. LOUIS. A procession down Olive Street passes under the illuminated arch with the slogan: "Public office: a public trust."

Republicans in the previous election. Now they held a convention in Indianapolis to destroy the "saloon power in politics." They jabbed at the Republicans with a plank in favor of reducing the surplus. The "burdens of taxation" were to be removed from the "necessities of life." General Clinton B. Fisk, a New Jersey philanthropist, became their presidential nominee; the Rev. Dr. Brooks, once a chaplain with the Southern troops, was chosen for the second place.

The ensuing campaign was based as expected on the tariff issue. The Republicans asked high protection, the Democrats downward revision. Those who had grown rich on the high duties—the steel men, the industrialists, the manufacturers—contributed freely to the Republican campaign chest. "Put the manufacturers of Pennsylvania under the fire and dry all the fat out of them," advised Matt Quay, the political boss of Pennsylvania and chairman of the Republican National Committee, and his advice was taken by the managers, who collected well over $3 million. Members of the American Iron and Steel Association headed by James Swank were on the top of the list; they could do it without pain since they made tremendous profits be-

HARRISON BREAKS LOOSE! A CARTOON

THE REPUBLICAN CONVENTION at Chicago. A wild demonstration broke out after Governor Foraker's seconding speech for the nomination of Senator John Sherman.

BLAINE COULD HAVE THE NOMINATION but he advised the delegates to "take Harrison." He was visiting millionaire Andrew Carnegie in Scotland when the convention met. The snapshot shows him with his wife and daughters on the left. In the center, Carnegie and the Rev. Charles Eaton (pouring a drink). On the right: Miss Dodge, Blaine, Walter Damrosch (his son-in-law) and Mrs. Phipps.

cause of the protective tariff. Andrew Carnegie could take out no less than $1.5 million out of his mill, and that within a single year. John Wanamaker, the Philadelphia millionaire, played his part well, too. He once called a meeting of ten prominent citizens from his city and within ten minutes raised the first $100,000. He sent a circular to manufacturers: "We want money and we want it quick!" He raised at least a million in all—and it was rumored that there was a secret fund in reserve of two million more dollars.

With the money the Republicans turned out a vast amount of campaign literature, maintained an array of speakers, organized meetings, and foremost of all they bought votes.

Money was used freely to sway dubious states. One such state was Indiana, Harrison's home state. There, twenty thousand votes were for sale. Shortly before the election Wanamaker made a rush appeal for more funds: "We raised the money so quickly that the Democrats never knew anything about it. They had their spies out supposing that we were going to do something, but before they knew what it was we had them beaten."

Blaine returned from Europe early in August on the

THE REPUBLICAN CAMPAIGN BANNER OF '88

BIDDING FOR HIS VOTE. The Democratic and Republican parties both vied for the veteran vote, offering liberal pensions to the Grand Army of the Republic.

THE PARAPHERNALIA OF THE CAMPAIGN. Buttons, ribbons, emblems, and other replicas were the fashion.

A TICKERTAPE PARADE ON WALL STREET

maiden voyage of the *City of New York.* Thousands of Republicans had been brought to New York to cheer his landing. They waited on the expected day of arrival, but the ship was late. Two more days of waiting went by; still no Blaine. As the Republican organizers found it expensive to maintain the paraders in the city, they organized a huge torchlight procession—never mind Blaine. Forty thousand men marched down Fifth Avenue with flags and banners: "Cleveland Runs Well in England," "We Are Not Going to Vote Away Our Wages." The next day, when Blaine's ship arrived, every craft in the harbor opened its steam whistle to welcome him, and there were still two thousand people on hand to greet him. He began to compaign for Harrison, drawing huge audiences, whom he addressed about the tariff. For Blaine tariff protection could never be high enough.

In the industrial plants the workers were told that the reduction of duties would lead to economic collapse and were warned by slips tucked in their pay envelopes that they would be without work if Cleveland was elected. Surprisingly, the most radical of the labor leaders, Terence V. Powderly of the Knights of Labor, campaigned for the Harrison ticket. In the farming areas Republican campaigners blamed the plight of the English farmers on the free-trade principles of that country.

The Democrats begged Cleveland to campaign for his re-election, but he refused; neither would he allow his Cabinet to campaign for him. The people had to take him on his record. Thus the contest was a quiet one with personal invective muted, though the Republicans spread the rumor that Cleveland was a drunkard and that he beat his young wife. They were less conspicuous in this than they had been four years earlier in gloating over Cleveland's illegitimate child. Mrs. Cleveland was forced to issue a statement in which she said

Charles Graham, November 1888
MADISON SQUARE: THE RETURNS COME IN.

Frank Leslie's Illustrated Newspaper, November 10, 1888
THE TARIFF was the chief campaign issue. On New York's Broadway the Harrison men chant: "Trade, trade, no free Trade!" to which the Cleveland men answer: "Don't, don't, don't be afraid; only low tariff so don't be afraid!"

that the charge was "a foolish campaign story without a shadow of foundation," and that she could "wish the women of our country no greater blessing than that their homes and their husbands be as kind, as attentive, considerate and affectionate as mine."

The major Republican plan was "working the free trade racket." They complained long and hard about the end of good wages and profits, the breaking down of business and the end of prosperity. They said that Cleveland was stealing from the people's pockets because the tariff had lowered a barrage of cheap foreign-made goods, thus robbing American workers of their jobs.

To further alarm the voters, the Republicans predicted that most of these foreign goods would be British. Feeling for the mother country had never been great since the Revolution; the War of 1812 and British sympathy for the South during the Civil War had kept it low. To the large numbers of recently arrived Irish, Britain was the enemy. Blaine had long been a John Bull baiter. Each time the English press showed its lack of sympathy for him, and each time an Englishman spoke against him, the party press raised this "proof" before the voting public. It was American to be for the Republican ticket, and not American to favor Cleveland.

Some excitement was generated when the British Minister in Washington, Sir Lionel Sackville-West, answered an inquiry from a "Charles F. Murchison" of California by advising him to vote for Cleveland because a Democratic administration would be more conciliatory and friendly to the mother country than a Republican one. It was a silly kind of advice. Immediately the opposition dubbed Cleveland the "English candidate," with the New York *Tribune* insisting that he would yield to "British interests at the sacrifice of American rights." The Irish in America—most of

Frank Adams, November 1888
THE CAMPAIGN IN INDIANA. The Republican Railroad Club demonstrates through the streets of Indianapolis.

BENJAMIN HARRISON'S INAUGURATION ON MARCH 4, 1889, UNDER A FOREST OF UMBRELLAS. THE

them in the Democratic party—were bitter over the failure of home rule for their homeland, bitter over Gladstone's resignation, and bitter over Balfour's measures against Ireland; they were up in arms against Britain and would not vote for anyone who was friendly to that country. Friends of Cleveland urged the President to hand Sackville-West his passport. The magazine publisher A. K. McClure wrote: "Now kick out Lord Sackville with your biggest boot of best leather, and you've got 'em. *Hesitation is death.*" Cleveland asked the British Government for the Ambassador's recall, but by then the damage had been done.

Outside the South and the border states Cleveland carried only Connecticut and New Jersey; every other state voted Republican. Harrison won the 233 electoral votes against Cleveland's 168, but Cleveland's popular vote was 5,540,329 against Harrison's 5,439,853—about a 100,000 majority.

The candidates of minor parties pulled strongly. Clinton B. Fisk, the Prohibitionist, had 249,506 votes, and Alson J. Streeter, the choice of the Union Labor party, had 146,934.

In New York—the decisive state with thirty-six electoral votes—the Republican majority was barely over

THOUSANDS WHO CAME TO WATCH THE CEREMONIES WERE CHILLED BY THE GUSTY WIND.

Author's Collection

13,000, but enough to bring victory for Harrison. Apparently this was effected through a deal between the Republicans and Tammany Hall, whose candidate David Hill was running for the governorship of the state. In return for Republican votes which gave him a victory, Hill delivered the Democratic Tammany vote to Harrison.

In the other crucial state—Indiana—money was used freely to buy votes. The Republican campaign treasurer, Colonel William W. Dudley, the former head of the pensions bureau, instructed one of his lieutenants to divide the floaters (men whose votes were bought)

into blocks of five, "and put a trusted man in charge of these five with necessary funds, and make him responsible that none get away, and that all vote our ticket." Dudley's letter found its way into the hands of the Democrats and was made public. Righteous indignation followed. However, the letter contained nothing new. Everyone knew that votes could be and were bought. And Harrison won Indiana by the scant majority of 2,348 votes.

Upon learning the result Harrison exclaimed: "Providence has given us the victory," to which Matt Quay retorted: "Think of the man! He ought to know that

The Judge, *March 23, 1889*

THE MOB OF HUNGRY OFFICE SEEKERS. Outgoing President Cleveland is happy to leave it all to his successor. Benjamin Harrison, the incoming President, leans on the door in an effort to keep out the vast hordes of applicants.

Providence hadn't a damn thing to do with it." And the Republican chairman added with an unusual streak of candor that Harrison would never know how many Republicans "were compelled to approach the gates of the penitentiary to make him President."

President-elect Harrison owed many debts to the party leaders, and he began paying them back with the selection of his Cabinet. He said, "I could not name my own Cabinet. They had sold out every place to pay the election expenses." Blaine was the natural choice for Secretary of State. John Wanamaker was to be the Postmaster General as a reward for the millions he had collected for the election. Benjamin F. Tracy, a friend of

New York's boss Tom Platt, was to control the Navy.

In his inaugural address the new President said nothing that had not already been said in the campaign. He indulged in platitudes like "Honorable party service will certainly not be esteemed by me a disqualification for public office," and he promised to do "something more to advance the reform of the civil service." He said that "a treasury surplus is not the greatest evil, it is a serious evil," and he declared that "our pension laws should give more adequate and discriminating relief to the Union soldiers and sailors and to their widows and orphans."

To this, the party newspapers replied, "Go to it."

Frank Opper, October 1888

THE POWER BEHIND THE PRESIDENCY: JAMES G. BLAINE, HARRISON'S SECRETARY OF STATE

READY FOR ANOTHER BOUT
Frank Leslie's Illustrated Newspaper, *August 1892*

GROVER CLEVELAND

Benjamin Harrison was a small man in a big job. A tool of money-grubbing individuals who were more interested in their own welfare than in that of the country, he was the boss of the spoilsmen. (His Postmaster General boasted that within a year he had changed 31,000 out of 55,000 postmasters.) He was the saint of the veterans. (Under his administration the number of pensions for the members of the Grand Army of the Republic was doubled.) He was the pet of the manufacturers and industrialists. (During his term Congress passed the McKinley Tariff Bill, increasing the duties on manufactured articles and helping the industrialists to enormous profits.) These may have helped him politically, but the seeds of disaster were sown.

The surplus which so worried Cleveland soon melted away. "God help the surplus," cried out James Tanner, Harrison's Commissioner of Pensions, and he was as good as his word. Congress spent the taxpayers' money in a lavish fashion. After all, said Speaker Thomas Reed —whose imperial rule over the House brought him the nickname "Czar"—this was a "billion-dollar country." Appropriations for river improvements, for coastal defenses, for Federal buildings increased speedily; within a couple of years the government got rid of the surplus. Then tariff revenues fell off sharply and America became a debtor nation—bills were postponed from day to day, the government was living from hand to mouth.

To such irresponsibilities the country reacted vigorously. In the mid-term election the Republicans suffered defeat; their majority in the lower house was wiped out. The new House had 235 Democrats, with only 88 Republicans.

The Western and Southern states were in an uproar. Farmers, suffering under high mortgages and harsh foreclosures, resentful toward monopolists and bankers whom they regarded as their exploiters, organized themselves in "Alliances," and fought against the abuses of the railroads and the corrupt practices of big business. They were ready to follow the advice of Mary Elizabeth Lease, one of their leaders, who suggested they "raise less corn and more hell." Before long they organized themselves is a third party—the People's party—commonly called the Populists.

In their nominating convention the major parties turned to their past candidates—the Republicans to President Harrison, the Democrats to ex-President Cleveland. Blaine's name was again mentioned, but the Plumed Knight was tired and sick; he would not let his name be put in nomination.

Harrison was not too popular with the leaders of his party The bosses did not regard him as a "good fellow." Platt said that he was "as glacial as a Siberian stripped of his furs," and one wanting to speak with him felt "even in torrid weather like putting on his winter flannels, galoshes, overcoat, mitts and earlaps."

When the Republicans met in their convention in Minneapolis, there were several contenders who were ready to challenge the President. Senator Sherman tried to rally the anti-Harrison men; Mark Hanna was working for Ohio's Governor McKinley; ex-Speaker Reed had many supporters; while Whitelaw Reid saw himself as a compromise choice.

Chauncey Depew, who rose to power in the railroad empire of the Vanderbilts, managed Harrison's precon-

CANDIDATES IN 1892

GROVER CLEVELAND
(1837–1908) was once again the candidate—for the third time—and with the support of the reform elements, he took the Presidency from Harrison with 5,556,543 votes against Harrison's 5,175,582.

ADLAI E. STEVENSON
(1835–1914), from Illinois, was the Democratic choice for the second place. A "soft money" man, his nomination placated the Silverites, whose platform proposals for silver coinage were hooted down.

BENJAMIN HARRISON
(1833–1901), whose moderation had aroused the ill feelings of both the reformers and the party men, was again nominated, but the high tariff and the lavish spending of his administration brought defeat.

WHITELAW REID
(1837–1912), who took over the New York *Tribune* from Horace Greeley and who had been Minister to France, was named for the second place by the Republicans because of his support of Harrison.

JOHN BIDWELL
(1819–1909), California pioneer and one of the first exponents of a transcontinental railroad, became an antimonopolist and was the Prohibitionists' presidential candidate, receiving 255,941 votes.

JAMES B. WEAVER
(1833–1912), Greenbacker candidate in 1880, had taken a leading part in transforming the Farmers' Alliance into the Populists. As the Presidential standard-bearer of the People's party, he got 1,040,886 votes.

Library of Congress
MODELING. The young Mrs. Cleveland, who was married to the President the year before, poses for sculptor Augustus Saint-Gaudens in the summer of 1887 for a bas-relief at his Marion, Massachusetts, studio.

vention campaign. He felt that the best way to thwart the bosses' attempt to replace Harrison required "the greatest publicity," and his hotel room was always open to delegates and the press.

An adroit move lessened the chances of McKinley. The Harrison forces selected him as the permanent chairman. As Quay said, "This makes it impossible for McKinley to Garfield the convention."

In his opening remarks to the convention, McKinley defended the tariff of 1890, which bore his name: "There is not a paragraph that is not patriotic; there is not a page that does not represent true Americanism and the highest possibilities of American citizenship." When he finished his oration, the New York *Herald* reporter noted that all but the blind could see "the shadow of the crown."

The Harrison supporters had another trick up their

Joseph Keppler, September 1889

"A SLAVE OF MANY MASTERS," President Harrison grinds at the "Patronage Mill." Driven by the party chieftains—James Blaine, William Mahone, Thomas Platt, Wade Dudley and Matthew Quay—and also by the various interests such as the District Leader, the Lumber King and others, poor Harrison toils hard to produce offices for deserving Republicans.

sleeves. They brought back the caucus of the first decades of the Republic. The "low-water-mark committee" secretly gathered together almost five hundred delegates. Their leaders were asked, state by state, how many of them were in support of the President. Most of them were, and the result was widely publicized.

Harrison won the nomination on the first ballot with 535⅙ votes to 182½ for Blaine, 182 for McKinley, 4 for Reed and 1 for Robert Lincoln, the son of the martyred President.

Vice President Morton did not want to thrust himself on the party; he waited to hear the call. But the delegates decided to nominate Whitelaw Reid, the publisher of the New York *Tribune* and former associate of Horace Greeley.

The Democrats met in Chicago. Cleveland was once more challenged by Tammany Hall, which preferred David B. Hill, New York's former Governor and now Senator from that state. But Hill's fortunes had been hurt when only South Carolina, under the influence of the Farmer's Alliance leader Benjamin "Pitchfork Ben" Tillman, came out for him, while the local Democrats of all the other Southern states expressed themselves for Cleveland.

But the opposition to Cleveland soon collapsed. There was no doubt that he was the strongest candidate. Even before the balloting, when Senator Vilas was reading the proposed platform, with Cleveland's name mentioned in the first paragraph, "Rank after rank of coatless men, of sometimes hatless men rose by the hundreds, thousands—aye, by the tens of thousands—almost with a wild acclaim that grew from the noisy into the impressive, from the impressive into the awful, as it increased."

Lorant: The Presidency (*Macmillan*)

ON APRIL 30, 1889, ON THE ONE HUNDREDTH ANNIVERSARY of the first inaugural, President Harrison re-enacts Washington's arrival in New York City. His barge is rowed by thirteen oarsmen, one for each of the original states.

The band struck up the national anthem, and the reporter from the New York *Herald* saw a man with a Cleveland banner lead the march "with the set face of a devotee, swinging the censer high above his head while the crazed delegates gazed with eyes of longing and shouted with throats of brass at the swinging picture." The spectators in the galleries "roared themselves black in the face." The commotion was like "the consecration of an army's banners in the sight of the people for whom it went to war."

When the balloting was over, Cleveland had won with 617⅓ votes while Hill received only 144. Carter Harrison of the Chicago *Times* urged the selection of Adlai E. Stevenson as Cleveland's running mate. The delegation from Illinois, Stevenson's home state, took up this suggestion and advanced his name. He won easily on the second ballot.

The platforms of both parties offered little that was new. The Republicans recited the blessings which they had conferred upon the country and reaffirmed their be-

COMMEMORATING THE DAY a hundred years before, President Harrison delivers an address at the very spot where Washington was sworn in. The chair the first President used and the Bible on which he took the oath are on the platform.

lief in "the American doctrine of protection," while the Democrats denounced "the Republican protection as a fraud, a robbery of the great majority of the American people for benefit of the few," demanded a tariff "for the purposes of revenue only," and declared that the McKinley Tarriff Law passed by the Fifty-first Congress was "the culminating atrocity of class legislation."

More notable was the platform of the Populists. "We meet in the midst of a nation brought to the verge of moral, political, and material ruin," it started out. "Cor-

ruption dominates the ballot-box, the legislature, the Congress, and touches even the ermine of the bench. The people are demoralized; most of the states have been compelled to isolate the voters at the polling-places to prevent universal intimidation or bribery. The newspapers are largely subsidized or muzzled; public opinion silenced; business prostrated; our homes covered with mortgages; labor impoverished; and the land concentrating in the hands of the capitalists. The urban workmen are denied the right of organization for self-protection;

TAKING SNAPSHOTS on the White House grounds with the new Kodak. The camera was put on the market in 1888. Using a spool of flexible film on which 100 exposures could be made, it created a boom for amateurs: almost overnight, everybody became a photographer. After the films were exposed, they were taken to a dealer, who either developed them himself or sent them to Kodak in Rochester.

HARRISON'S SECOND CABINET. From left to right: Elkins (War), Noble (Interior), John W. Foster (State), John Wanamaker (Postmaster General), the President, Tracy (Navy), Charles Foster (Treasury), Jeremiah Rusk (Agriculture) and William Miller (Attorney General).

A STATE BEDROOM in the White House. The pillow on the sofa is embroidered "Harrison"; General Sherman's portrait hangs over the door. The furnishings and lighting fixtures are characteristic examples of Victorian taste.

imported pauperized labor beats down their wages; a hireling standing army, unrecognized by our laws, is established to shoot them down, and they are rapidly degenerating into European conditions. The fruits of the toil of millions are boldly stolen to build up colossal fortunes for a few, unprecedented in the history of mankind; and the possessors of these, in turn, despite the republic and endanger liberty. From the same prolific womb of governmental injustice we breed the two great classes of tramps and millionaires." They were the very words which Ignatius Donnelly recited months before when the Populists met in St. Louis to discuss principles.

The platform was divided into three parts: finance, transportation, land. On finance it asked for "a national currency, safe, sound, and flexible"; a "free and unlimited coinage of silver and gold at the present legal ratio of sixteen to one," and that "the amount of circulating medium be speedily increased to not less than fifty dollars per capita." The Populists also pleaded for "a graduated income tax" and for the establishment of postal savings banks.

Their transportation plank read: "Transportation being a means of exchange and a public necessity, the government should own and operate the railroads in the

"HE'S SMALLER THAN ANY OF U
AND YET THEY SAY HE EXPEC
A SECOND TERM!"
Drawing by Frank Opper, May 1890

C. J. Taylor, May 1889

MUZZLING THE PRESS. The President is padlocking with offices the leading newspapermen. The lock on Whitelaw Reid of the New York *Tribune* reads "Minister to France"; on Charles Allen Thorndike Rice of the *North American Review,* "Minister to Russia"; on John C. New of the Indianapolis *Journal,* "Consul General to London"; on John Hicks of the Oshkosh *Northwestern,* "Minister to Peru"; on J. S. Clarkson of the Iowa *State Register,* "Assistant Postmaster General"; on Ellis H. Roberts of the Utica *Herald,* "Assistant U.S. Treasurer." Harrison is removing the lock, "Minister to Germany," from Murat Halstead of the Brooklyn *Standard-Union.* (Halstead's nomination was rejected by the Senate because of his articles denouncing the purchase of senatorial seats.) Next in line are John M. Francis of the Troy *Times,* who sought an office—any office; Elliot Shepard, editor of the *Mail and Express,* who asked for subsidies; Charles E. Fitch of the Rochester *Democrat and Chronicle,* who was appointed U.S. Internal Revenue Collector; Robert P. Porter of the New York *Press,* whose lock reads "Superintendent of the Census"; Elijah W. Halford of the Indianapolis *Journal,* labeled "Private Secretary"; and the President"s son, "Rustle" (Russell), with a chain around his neck. On the end is Charles A. Dana of the *Sun.*

interest of the people." And on their third major issue —land—they declared: "The land, including all the natural sources of wealth, is the heritage of the people, and should not be monopolized for speculative purposes, and alien ownership of land should be prohibited. All land now held by railroads and other corporations in excess of their actual needs, and all lands now owned by aliens, should be reclaimed by the government and held for actual settlers only."

Other principles embodied in the Populist platform were: public ownership of the telegraph and telephone, a secret-ballot system, pensions for ex-Union soldiers and sailors, a rigid enforcement of the eight-hour law, a single presidential term and direct popular voting for Senators. Some of these proposals were adopted by the country in the years ahead; they became the law.

The Populists not only enumerated their political demands but spoke out against monopolies, against greedy financiers, against corrupt railroad corporations. Phrases from their platform were remembered for a long time. "Wealth belongs to him who creates it, and every dollar taken from industry without an equivalent

Joseph Keppler, Puck, *1891*

IN THE CAGE. Secretary of State James G. Blaine, the dominant figure of the Harrison Cabinet, was considered to be in line for the Presidency in 1892. Defeated in 1884, reluctant to run in 1888, he seemed to have an excellent chance in 1892, but before the convention met he announced that he would not be a candidate.

Blaine laid the groundwork for the country's policy toward the South American countries. At a time when foreign issues were given scant attention and when foreign affairs were handled with little diplomatic knowledge, Blaine's imaginative proposals were a novelty. His aim was to unite all the countries in the American hemisphere into a friendly system, with the United States the dominant figure of an "elder sister." He revived the idea of Pan-Americanism, which had been dead since Clay's fiasco with the Congress of Panama in 1826.

With Blaine's full support, a Pan-American Congress met in October 1889 in Washington and laid the foundation of the Bureau of American Republics. Blaine roused the public interest and attracted its attention to international problems. His paternalistic attitude toward the South American nations was taken up by Theodore Roosevelt and subsequent Presidents.

is robbery." "If any will not work neither shall he eat." For their candidates they chose James B. Weaver of Iowa and James G. Field of Virginia; both men had fought in the Civil War, Weaver for the Union, Field on the Confederate side—and Weaver had been the presidential candidate of the Greenbackers in 1880.

The campaign which followed was dull and listless: the streets were no longer jammed by torchlight parades and marching processions; no more "Boys in Blue," no more "Wide-Awakes," tramped through the cities to the tunes of brass bands.

Harrison was obliged to defend the deeds of the Republican Congress—the high tariff, the lavish appropriations for pensioners—and he had to give explanations why the nation's money was spent so extravagantly.

Cleveland had nothing to defend. The public still recalled his first election to the Presidency, when he campaigned on a record of administrative honesty. There were those who remembered his unsuccessful bid four years later when he campaigned against the high tariff. In the present campaign he now had the backing of the conservative bankers and merchants. They were

Joseph Keppler, March 1890

SELLING THE PRESIDENTIAL CHAIR. Republican National Chairman Matt Quay and a party treasurer, Colonel William Wade Dudley, whose special talent was buying the "soldier vote," show that the next election will be very much like the last, in which the Republicans spent a great deal of money to elect Harrison. The "money kings" bid for political influence through party leaders. President Sidney Dillon of the Union Pacific, who had been involved in the Crédit Mobilier scandal, bids mournfully. Russell Sage puts up a frugal bid, while Jay Gould seems to want to keep his money. The others offer cash terms for the entire set—the Presidency, the Vice Presidency and the eight memberships of the Cabinet.

convinced that Cleveland was for sound money policies —for the gold standard—so they made their contributions to the Democratic fund, money which formerly went to the Republicans.

Neither Harrison nor Cleveland stumped the country. Cleveland remained at his summer place at Buzzards Bay on Cape Cod suffering from the gout and "an excess of medicine rather than the lack of it." Harrison stayed at the White House with his ailing wife, who died two weeks before the election.

To make up for their inactivity both candidates presented their political views in letters of acceptance.

Harrison wrote: "There has seldom been a time . . . when a change from the declared policies of the Republican to the declared policies of the Democratic party involved such serious results to the business interests of the country." For him it was Democratic "demolition" versus Republican "development." He said that free coinage of silver by the commercial nations of the world was desirable, but "if the United States should now act independently, it would injure itself." So rather than integrate silver as a backing for the currency, he would hope for "results" from the International Monetary Conference. About half of his

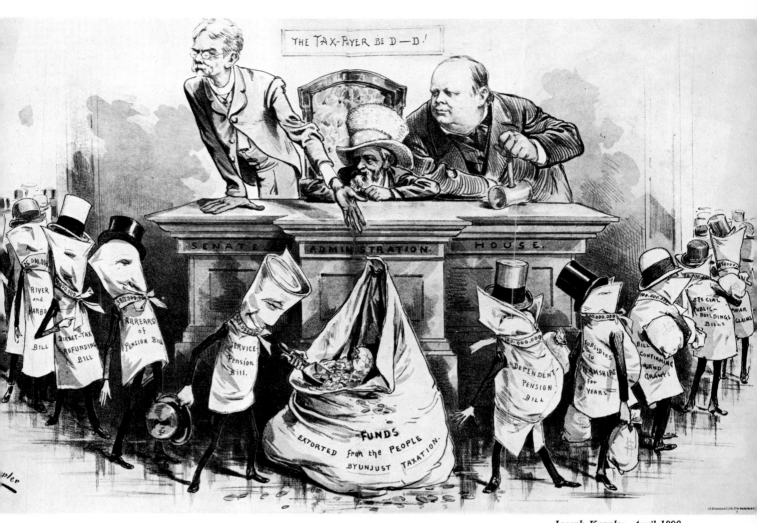

THE TAX-PAYER BE D—D!

SENATE   ADMINISTRATION.   HOUSE.

FUNDS EXTORTED from the PEOPLE BY UNJUST TAXATION.

Joseph Keppler, April 1890

THE TAXPAYER BE DAMNED. Harrison, diminutive under his grandfather's beaver hat, watches as the friends of special interests—Kansas Senator J. J. Ingalls and the bulky speaker of the House, Tom Reed—allow special interests to help themselves from the national grab bag of surplus funds. "God help the surplus!" said a director of the Pension Bureau as he provided for "every old comrade that needs it." Pension expenditures rose from 98 to 157 million dollars. The Sherman Silver Purchase Act and tax refunds to the states were other lavish gifts of Harrison's "billion-dollar Congress." And the exorbitantly high McKinley tariff was one of the means by which funds were "extorted from the people by unjust taxation."

acceptance letter was in defense of the tariff. The Democratic policy was "a new crusade against American shops . . . and American manufacturers," he began. Harrison felt that "There is not a thoughtful businessman in the country who does not know that the enactment into law" of the Democrats' plank on the tariff "would at once plunge the country in a business convulsion such as it has never seen."

Cleveland's letter was only a third as long as Harrison's. A good part of it he used to attack the tariff. He advocated a tariff for revenue only. He believed that the Republican protection of special interests was against

"the spirit of our constitution, and was directly antagonized by every sentiment of justice and fairness of which Americans are pre-eminently proud." And the protective tariff "invites corruption in political affairs by encouraging the expenditure of money to debauch suffrage in support of a policy directly favorable to private and selfish gain." But he pledged there was to be "no exterminating war against any American interest," and he tried to cover the gold-silver controversy with the phrase "sound and honest money."

The vice presidential candidates and other party bigwigs took up the stumping slack. Whitelaw Reid was persuaded to carry the Republican campaign to the West. Governor McKinley made an extended tour from Maine to the Midwest, making a patriotic appeal for a protective tariff as a bulwark of American manufacturers and workingmen.

For the Democrats Adlai E. Stevenson, "the delight of the multitude," campaigned in the Midwest, his native area, and the South. Champ Clark said that Stevenson's information was "wide and varied, his voice musical and far-carrying, his elocution good . . . and he always spoke right out in meeting and did not mince his words." Having been born in Kentucky, he could appeal convincingly to the South. He described the dismal days of Reconstruction and stated that if Harrison were to become President, elections would be controlled again and the evils of Reconstruction revived. He told Cleveland that, though the Populists appealed to the normally Democratic party members in the South, as a result of his own tour, "We are gaining many of them back."

Unlike Harrison and Cleveland, the Populist candidate, General Weaver, crisscrossed the West and South. He was helped on the stump by Mrs. Lease, an "orator of marvelous power and phenomenal psychological

force." The laboring people worshiped her. Wherever the two went, Weaver saw "manifest the peculiar psychological phenomenon which characterized the early Republican meetings throughout the country in 1860." Convictions of justice and right were awakened; people wanted to hear the Populist message. Usually when they stopped, they held two separate meetings; Weaver addressed one, Mrs. Lease the other. "After each had spoken an hour, we alternated so as to reach all the people. We called it exchanging pulpits."

At first they toured the West. In Sacramento a record number of people came to hear them. In Portland they spoke to two assemblies—"one in the afternoon composed of farmers about 3,000 strong; and another at night, which could only be counted by acres." At Seattle, Weaver looked from the train to see "an innumerable crowd of enthusiastic people, which filled the piazza and the streets leading to it to an extent that made it almost dangerous to alight from the cars. It was with great difficulty that we reached our carriages." In Butte "the meeting in the opera house was crowded to suffocation; and the meeting out of doors covered about two acres, solidly packed with people."

Then they moved into the South. In Arkansas they

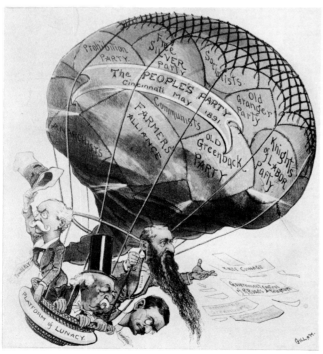

Bernard Gillam, June 1891

THE PEOPLE'S PARTY or, as it was commonly called, the Populists, came into being in Cincinnati in 1891, formed from the remnants of several minor organizations. Its four leaders—Terence V. Powderly, Benjamin F. Butler, Jerry Simpson and William Alfred Peffer—populate the gondola.

C. J. Taylor, February 1888

THE POPULIST MOVEMENT—the first organized struggle of the masses against special privilege—encompassed farmers and laborers, and many workingmen. They held that a high tariff made the monopolists richer, while low farm prices made the mortgaged farmers poorer.

S. Ehrhart, November 1889

A PARALLEL: "THE ROBBER BARONS OF THE MIDDLE AGES AND THE ROBBER BARONS OF TODAY"

spent two hours "arraigning the old parties for their sins of omission and commission, and predicted that the pending movement would never cease till plutocracy was overthrown and the shackles stricken from the limbs of the agricultural class and industries generally."

Everywhere they spoke, large crowds turned out. In Georgia, however, the "spirit of rowdyism" was great. At Macon rotten eggs were thrown at them, and in Atlanta "a similar crowd of rowdies gathered at the point of meeting, bent on tumult and disorder." Weaver speculated that the disrupters of the meeting had the support of those who were afraid that the ranks of the Solid South would be broken because voters were "turning from the old parties almost in armies." In the Carolinas the crowds were five times greater than those that Stevenson had previously drawn. Thus Weaver thought the outlook in the South "magnificent."

Some of the Weaver's campaign funds came from the sale of his book *A Call to Action*. In this he wanted "to call attention to some of the more serious evils which now disturb the repose of American society and threaten the overthrow of free institutions. . . . If the

present strained relations between wealth owners and wealth producers continues much longer they will ripen into frightful disaster." Weaver saw that "the corporation has taken the place of the pirate; and finally a bold and aggressive plutocracy has usurped the government and is using it as a policeman to enforce its insolent decrees."

The national wealth was endangered: "The public domain has been squandered, our coal fields bartered away, our forests denuded, our people impoverished, and we are attempting to build a prosperous commonwealth among people who are being robbed of their homes." He attacked the condition by which "the corporation has been placed above the individual and an armed body of cruel mercenaries permitted in times of public peril, to discharge police duties which clearly belong to the state."

The people knew what Weaver was talking about. The pitched battle between the Pinkerton police and the locked-out steelworkers from the Carnegie plant at Homestead, Pennsylvania was still green in everybody's memory. Only a month before, the company had an-

West Clinedinst, June 1892
THE DEMOCRATIC CONVENTION in Chicago nominated Grover Cleveland once more and Adlai E. Stevenson.

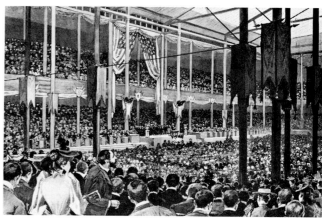

Thure de Thulstrup and Charles Graham, June 1892
THE REPUBLICAN CONVENTION at Minneapolis, which renominated President Harrison and Whitelaw Reid.

Lorant, The Presidency *(Macmillan)*
CARTOONISTS ATTACKED CLEVELAND because he made three consecutive attempts for the Presidency.

W. Bencough, Democratic National Committee
CARTOONISTS ATTACKED HARRISON because he spent the government's surplus with an all too free hand.

nounced a reduction of wages without giving a reason. Business was good, profits were soaring. When the union officials tried to negotiate, the company would not recognize them and closed the works. Carnegie was in Europe, leaving Henry Frick in charge, and Frick gave orders to hire men to replace the locked-out workers and to reopen the plant with them. Expecting resistance, Frick engaged Pinkerton men to protect the

mills. When the Pinkertons approached Homestead in their barges, five thousand workers were on the river banks and gave them battle which lasted for two days. In the end the state militia was called out, and under its protection the mills were opened.

Not only did Weaver assail the inhuman behavior of the management—public opinion as a whole was against it. Republican leaders, apprehensive of the political con-

WHO IS NEXT?

A CRUDE CARTOON OF 1892 LAMPOONING THE REPUBLICAN CANDIDATES WHO SOUGHT THE OFFICE

sequences, appealed to the steel masters to take a milder stand, but their pleas fell on deaf ears. In his acceptance speech Cleveland spoke for the workers' rights. He said that the crushing of the union showed "the tender mercy the workingman receives from those made selfish and sordid by unjust governmental favoritism." Newspapers recalled that the very steel magnates who now arbitrarily reduced the wages had not so long ago pleaded for tariff protection as a means of keeping them high.

The people of the country could not see why wages had to be cut when the industry enjoyed prosperity, why workers should be suffering when the mill owners were making fortunes. As election day was not far off, the riots at Homestead shadowed Republican hopes.

To help their cause the Republicans distributed "poetical patty-pans" made of American tin plate and bear-

ing the labels "Harrison-Reid and Protection." They made two million of these and had children pass them out in the streets, so the Democrats had to come up with something else. Soon they distributed a "neat little bit of so-called American tin plate the shape of the top of a small sardine box" with portraits of Cleveland and Stevenson on one side and on the other the facts about its manufacture. It was noted that the thin black steel sheet was made in Great Britain and imported. The tin coating came from Australia. The machines on which these "poetical patty-pans" of American tin were shaped came from Britain, and they were manned by English workmen who came to the United States in violation of the contract labor laws. Furthermore the men who owned factories for "making American tin plate" were protected by the McKinley tariff. It cost the

Alice Barber Stephens, May 1893
CLEVELAND SWORN IN FOR THE SECOND TIME

W. P. Snyder, March 1893
CLEVELAND REVIEWS THE INAUGURAL PARADE.

American taxpayers fifteen million dollars a year.

Just before the election the Democrats had a major political parade, the biggest ever seen in the city of New York. Forty thousand marching men were reviewed by Cleveland, and watched by half a million spectators. A newspaper report asserted that this was a parade not of mercenaries, as was the usual case, but of men "who have vested interests, who are building the nation, who have contributed to its prosperity. . . ."

The Democrats won decisively. Cleveland had 277 electoral votes to Harrison's 145; he captured not only the doubtful states of New York, New Jersey, Connecticut and Indiana, but Illinois, Wisconsin and California as well. In five Western states—Colorado, Idaho, Kansas, North Dakota and Wyoming—the Democrats voted for the Populist ticket to defeat the Republicans. Farmers who formerly voted Republican now voted for the Populists, and in the South the Republicans allied themselves with the Populists to weaken the Democrats. The result was that the Populists amassed well over a million votes. This was a warning that agrarian resentment could no longer be ignored.

Editor Godkin summed up the election in the *Nation:* "Mr. Cleveland's triumph today has been largely due to the young voters who have come on the stage since the reign of passion and prejudice came to an end, and the era of discussion has opened. If the past canvass has consisted largely of appeals of reason, to facts, to the lessons of human experience, it is to Mr. Cleveland, let us tell them, that they owe it. But they are indebted to him for something far more valuable than this—for an example of Roman constancy under defeat, and of patient reliance on the power of deliberation and persuasion of the American people. Nothing is more important, in these days of boodle, of cheap bellicose patriotism, than that this confidence in the might of common sense and sound doctrine and free speech should be kept alive."

Cleveland accepted his victory with thoughtful words: "While we find in our triumph a result of popular intelligence which we have aroused, and a consequence of popular vigilance which we have stimulated, let us not for a moment forget that our accession to power will find neither this intelligence nor this vigilance dead or slumbering. We are thus brought face to face with the reflection that if we are not to be tormented by the spirits which we have ourselves called up, we must hear, above victorious shouts, the call of our fellow countrymen to public duty, and must put on a garb befitting public servants."

CLEVELAND'S SECOND INAUGURATIC
Ex-President Harrison on the left

WILLIAM McKINLEY

The abundance of crops and the low price for farm produce reduced the farmer's purchasing power; overinvestment in railways halted further expansion; the economic distress of Europe and its dire repercussions at home were telling signs of the coming disaster. Cleveland had hardly begun his Presidency when depression engulfed the nation. Within a year 15,000 businesses failed, 150 banks went into liquidation, 4,000,000 workers became jobless.

While gold was scarce, silver was abundant. Under the Sherman Silver Purchase Act the Treasury was committed to buy a certain amount of silver. But as the silver certificates could also be redeemed in gold, speculators bought them and made quick profits; thus the gold reserve of the Treasury dwindled.

Cleveland called a special session of Congress to repeal the Silver Purchase Act. As many Democrats supported free silver coinage, Cleveland turned to the gold-standard Republicans for help and with their vote the repeal was passed.

Cleveland was for the "sound-money" policies of conservative economists—the Treasury notes must be backed by gold. This would have been effective if gold had been in abundant supply. But the scarcity of gold put a brake on the nation's economy. The farmers of the West were suffering; with farm prices low and mortgages and interests high, they had to produce more for the dollar. They demanded silver coinage and the issuance of unsecured greenbacks, expecting that the resulting inflation would drive prices up and that they could repay their debts in cheaper money. But the Eastern creditors and businessmen held on to the gold standard.

A book published in 1894 advocated the monetary theories of the silverites in a language which could be easily understood. It was *Coin's Financial School* by William H. Harvey. In it Coin, the young financial expert, drew a picture of the times: "Hard times are with us; the country is distracted; very few things are marketable at a price above the cost of production; tens of thousands are out of employment; the jails, penitentiaries, workhouses and insane asylums are full; the gold reserve at Washington is sinking . . . a huge debt hangs like an appalling cloud over the country . . . hungered and half-starved men are banding into armies and marching toward Washington; the cry of distress is heard on every hand . . . riots and strikes prevail throughout the land; schemes to remedy our ills when put into execution are smashed like boxcars in a railroad wreck, and Wall Street looks in vain for an excuse to account for the failure of prosperity to return since the repeal of the Silver Purchase Act."

In Coin's opinion, adherence to the gold standard deepened the depression. Then prosperity or want depended upon money abundance or money scarcity. Since silver money was abolished, there had not been enough currency left for the economy; thus property and commodity values had sunk, while at the same time the price of gold rose. Coin said that the Eastern capitalists were squeezing the West dry, leaving the farmers in misery. To remedy the situation he proposed the coinage of silver so credit could multiply, money circulate and prices rise. The book gave theoretic foundation to the silver crusade.

The campaign for the free coinage of silver at the

WILLIAM McKINLEY
Photograph by C. M. Bell

CANDIDATES IN 1896

WILLIAM McKINLEY
(1843–1901), a captain in the
Civil War, turned into a national figure during his fourteen years as a Congressman.
Following defeat in 1890 he
became Governor of Ohio in
1892. With the loyal support
of his friend Mark Hanna, he
received the Republican nomination on the first ballot.
Conducting a "front porch"
campaign at his Canton, Ohio,
home, he won with 7,111,607
votes to Bryan's 6,509,052.

GARRET A. HOBART
(1844–1899), a leading Republican in New Jersey and
a wealthy businessman who
said he made politics his recreation though his main interests were business and law,
got the vice presidential nomination because of his adherence to the gold standard.
Backed by a lavish campaign
fund, supported by all the industrial states, the Republicans campaigned on the issues
of tariff and currency and won.

WILLIAM J. BRYAN
(1860–1925), former Ne-
braska Congressman, editor
and an advocate of free silver,
was chosen by the Democratic
convention after he roused enthusiasm with his "Cross of
Gold" speech. Endorsed by the
Populists, he campaigned relentlessly, crossing the country
to make hundreds of speeches
for the coinage of silver at 16
to 1. But McKinley's "full dinner pail" campaign beat him.
Still he got 176 electoral votes.

ARTHUR SEWALL
(1835–1900), a wealthy shipbuilder from Maine, was
Bryan's running mate on the
Democratic ticket, but was rejected by the Populists, who,
though accepting Bryan for
the first place, would not take
the plutocratic Sewall for
the second, and nominated
Thomas E. Watson in his
stead. In the electoral vote
Sewall received 149, Watson
27, all together 95 less than
those cast for the Republicans.

IDA SAXTON (1847–1907) married Mc-
Kinley on January 25, 1871. They had two
daughters, both of whom died in infancy.
Their deaths brought her nearer to her husband, in the "fires of mutual grief." She was
an epileptic; McKinley, for whom she nursed
an obsessive love, referred to her seizures as
"her fainting spells" and covered up for them.

old ratio of 16 to 1—the chief Populist issue of 1892
—became intensified; Democrats joined hands with
the Populists; in many Western and Southern states
the silverites took over the party organizations.

The other major issue confronting Cleveland was the
tariff. The Democratic platform had pledged its reduction, and Cleveland was determined to honor the pledge.
However, when the Wilson Bill proposing tariff reduc-
tions reached the Senate, Eastern Democrats allied
themselves with the Republicans to defeat it. They suggested 634 changes, most of them favoring high protection. When the bill was finally passed, the President,
who felt that "a tariff for any other purpose than public
revenue is robbery," denounced it as a product of "party
perfidy and dishonor." He charged that "the livery of

Bernard Gillam, November 1893

"BLAME THE THING—I CAN'T MAKE IT WORK!" COMPLAINS CLEVELAND OVER THE KEYBOARD.

Democratic tariff reform has been stolen and worn in the service of Republican protection." Yet as it offered some relief from the rigid McKinley tariffs, he allowed it to become law without signing it.

"This year, 1894, the year of the Wilson Tariff and the income tax decision, was the darkest that Americans had known for thirty years," wrote Professors Morison and Commager. "Everything seemed to conspire to convince the people that democracy was a failure. Prices and wages hit rock-bottom and there seemed to be no market for anything. Half a million laborers struck against conditions which they thought intolerable, and most of the strikes were dismal failures. Ragged and hungry bands of unemployed swarmed over the countryside, the fires from the hobo camps flickering a message

of warning and despair to affrighted townsfolk."

The Pullman workers in Chicago asked for a restoration of their 20 percent wage cut, and when it was refused, they went on strike. All railway movement around Chicago came to a halt. Over the protest of Illinois Governor Altgeld, Cleveland sent Federal troops against the strikers "to keep the mail flowing," breaking the strike.

Jacob Coxey of Massillon, Ohio, taking with him his wife and small son, Legal Tender, led a march on Washington with an "army" of unemployed. He asked the government to build roads as a means of creating jobs for the unemployed. He was buried in a heap of ridicule, his marchers arrested because they "trespassed" on the Capitol lawn. Coxey was called a lunatic, a

Lorant: **The Presidency** (*Macmillan*)

CLEVELAND'S CABINET—IN 1895 . . . From left to right, starting with President Cleveland: John G. Carlisle (Treasury), Judson L. Harmon (Attorney General), Hillary A. Herbert (Navy), Julius Sterling Morton (Agriculture), Hoke Smith (Interior), William L. Wilson (Postmaster General), Daniel S. Lamont (War), and Richard Olney (State).

C. S. Reinhart, August 1896

AT THE REPUBLICAN HEADQUARTERS, party boss Mark Hanna (in the center), in discussion with Senator Platt. At the left, Senator Quay and Cleveland's Vice President, Hobart; in the background, General Horace Porter.

Lucius Hitchcock, August 1896

THE FRONT-PORCH CAMPAIGN OF McKINLEY. He remained in Canton, Ohio, speaking from his front porch to delegations which came to see him from all over the country. The rest of the campaign was left to the party.

crackpot, but four decades later in the Depression President Roosevelt used his very suggestions to ease the plight of the unemployed.

The mid-term election of 1894 brought defeat to the Democrats. The Republicans, leading in both houses of Congress, boasted that in the forthcoming presidential election any Republican—even a rag doll—could defeat the Democrats. They waited anxiously for the chance.

Mark Hanna, the rich Ohio businessman and a Republican party leader, wanted the Presidency for his friend, William McKinley, the Governor of Ohio. He had a great admiration for McKinley, whom he had once rescued from bankruptcy. "I love McKinley!" Hanna exclaimed. "He is the best man I ever knew."

Photograph by Frances Benjamin Johnson, copyrighted November 11, 1897, Library of Congress

. . . AND THE CABINET MEMBERS' WIVES. With Mrs. Cleveland, in center, are from left to right: Olivia Harmon (wife of the Attorney General), Jane Francis (Interior), Mary Carlisle (Treasury), Agnes Olney (State), Annanine Wilson (Postmaster General), Juliet Lamont (War) and Leila Herbert (Navy). The group was photographed by a woman.

Thure de Thulstrup, October 1896

AT THE DEMOCRATIC HEADQUARTERS, Governor John P. Altgeld of Illinois (on the left), in discussion with candidate William Jennings Bryan (on the right) and James Jones, the chairman of the Democratic national committee.

J. S. Pughe, September 1896

THE WHIRLWIND CAMPAIGN. Bryan traveled 18,000 miles to carry his ideas to the country as no candidate had done since Henry Clay. His recurrent theme was the "coinage of silver and gold at the present legal ratio of 16 to 1."

He hired a railroad car, and in it he sent his friend throughout the country. McKinley made friendly speeches, shook hands by the thousands, made himself known to the people. Billboards welcomed him as "the advance agent of prosperity."

And while McKinley made friends in the open, Hanna worked behind the scenes, talking with local politicians, handing out promises and money. Before the Republican convention met in St. Louis, he had spent more than a hundred thousand dollars, creating a "spontaneous" demand for his friend and assuring McKinley's nomination on an early ballot, preferably the first.

The paramount issue before the delegates was the financial one: should they make a firm declaration about

433

J. S. Pughe, April 1896

WHAT WILL HAPPEN WHEN McKINLEY BECOMES PRESIDENT—A POPULIST CARTOON PREDICTION

The Judge, *October 10, 1896*

AN ANTI-POPULIST CARTOON in which "The Big Humbugs" are attacking the farmer. One insect is marked "Bryan," the other "Watson," the two candidates of the Populists. On the left, William M. Stewart, Senator from Nevada and editor of *The Silver Knight,* is distributing campaign funds. The bug "Tilman" (Senator Benjamin R. Tillman, "Pitchfork Ben," from South Carolina, a Southern agrarian who lost out in the convention because of his violent blast at Cleveland) lies exhausted on the ground; Arthur Sewall—the Democratic vice presidential candidate—is attacking the farmer's horses.

the party's financial policies or should they make a weak one? Hanna was against a firm declaration, but delegates from the East insisted on a firm one.

There is a story that before the opening of the convention a man walked into Hanna's hotel room "and without any preliminary greeting told him: 'Mr. Hanna, I insist on a positive declaration for a gold-standard plank in the platform.' Hanna asked: 'Who in hell are you?' whereupon the stranger introduced himself as 'Senator Henry Cabot Lodge of Massachusetts.' Hanna told him: 'Well, Senator Henry Cabot Lodge of Massachusetts, you can go plumb to hell. You have nothing to say about it.' And Lodge replied: 'All right, sir; I will make my fight on the floor of the convention.' "

But even before Lodge could open his battle the gold-standard men had won their argument. They persuaded the convention that it would be useless to avoid the issue, for it was certain that the Democrats would come out for free silver. So a plank inserted in the platform declared that the party "is unreservedly for sound money . . . unalterably opposed to every measure calculated to debase our currency or impair the credit of our country . . . therefore, opposed to the free coinage of silver."

On the other major issue, the tariff, the platform emphasized the Republicans' allegiance "to the policy of protection as the bulwark of American industrial independence and the foundation of American development and prosperity."

Henry M. Teller of Colorado, who led the silver forces, presented a minority report offering a substitute plank which stated that "the Republican party favors the use of both gold and silver as equal standard money, and pledges its power to secure the free, unrestricted, and independent coinage of gold and silver at our mints at the ratio of sixteen parts of silver to one of gold."

And when his report was rejected, Teller walked out of the hall followed by some thirty delegates. It was a dramatic scene as the men from the Rocky Mountain states took up their banners and marched down the aisle waving their flags while the loyal delegates shouted abuse after them.

After that the nomination of the candidates began. The names of William B. Allison, Thomas B. Reed and Levi P. Morton were offered with colorful oratory; when Joseph B. Foraker proposed McKinley, the delegates cheered enthusiastically; the demonstration was long and noisy. John Thurston, the convention chairman, seconded McKinley's nomination: "On behalf of that dismantled chimney and the deserted factory at its base, that the furnaces may once more flame, the mighty wheels revolve, the whistles scream, the anvils ring, the

spindles hum . . . that the firesides again may glow, the women sing, the children laugh, yes, and on behalf of that American flag and all its stands for and represents, for the honor of every stripe, for the glory of every star, that its power may fill the earth and its splendor fill the sky, I ask for the nomination of that loyal American, that Christian gentleman, soldier, statesman, patriot, William McKinley."

It was not much of a contest. McKinley was chosen on the first ballot with 661½ votes; Reed had only 84½, Quay 61½, Morton 58, and Allison 35½. For the Vice Presidency Garret A. Hobart of New Jersey, another friend of Mark Hanna, was taken.

The Democrats met in Chicago. As thirty states in the West and South had already passed resolutions approving the free coinage of silver, the delegates from these states wrote a "silver" platform. Richard ("Silver Dick") Bland, speaking for the West, orated that "the gold standard meant bankruptcy"; therefore the Democrats should come out for "the free coinage of silver at 16 to 1 and damn the consequences!"

The free-silver men dominated the convention. "The sceptre of political power has passed from the strong,

ATTACKS ON BRYAN

W. A. Rogers, August 1896
"THE DEADLY PARALLEL": THE CANDIDATES

W. A. Rogers, August 1896
LEADER ALTGELD AND HIS "FREE SILVER" MASK

Sculpture caricature by Max Bachmann, 1896

AN ANTI-SEMITIC CARICATURE IN THE CAMPAIGN: "A SURE WINNER IF BRYAN IS ELECTED"

THE REPUBLICAN CONVENTION AT ST. LOUIS. Joseph Foraker presents McKinley's name to the cheering delegates.

THE DELEGATES CHEER during the keynote address by temporary chairman Charles W. Fairbanks of Indiana.

PARTY BOSS MARK HANNA and his candidate, William McKinley, at a private dinner at Hanna's Cleveland home.

certain hands of the East to the feverish, headstrong mob of the West and South," wrote the New York *World.* The silverites defeated the national committee's candidate for the temporary chairmanship; they increased the representation of each territory from two members to six; they unseated the gold-standard delegation from Nebraska and admitted the free-silver delegation headed by William Jennings Bryan; they rejected four gold delegates from Michigan and accepted that state's four silver delegates so Michigan—under the unit rule—could vote with the Silverites.

The platform proclaimed "that the act of 1873 demonetizing silver without the knowledge or approval of the American people has resulted in the appreciation of gold and a corresponding fall in the prices of commodities produced by the people; a heavy increase in the burden of taxation and of all debts, public and private; the enrichment of the money-lending class at home and abroad; the prostration of industry and impoverishment of the people."

And because of this the Democrats were "unalterably opposed to monometallism, which has locked fast the prosperity of an industrial people in the paralysis of hard times. Gold monometalism is a British policy, and its adoption has brought other nations into financial servitude to London. It is not only un-American, but anti-American, and it can be fastened on the United States only by the stifling of that spirit and love of liberty which proclaimed our political independence in 1776 and won in the war of the Revolution. We demand the free and unlimited coinage of both silver and gold at the present legal ratio of sixteen to one."

On the tariff issue the Democrats held that the "duties should be levied for purposes of revenue, such duties to

FREE-SILVERITES SHOW THEIR STRENGTH at the opening of the Democratic convention in Chicago.

THE CANDIDATE AND HIS WIFE posing for the photographers at their home in Upper Red Hook, N.Y.

OUTSIDE THE DEMOCRATIC CONVENTION in Chicago's Coliseum the delegates are patiently waiting for their admission.

be so adjusted as to operate equally throughout the country," and "that taxation should be limited by the needs of the government, honestly and economically administered."

Sixteen delegates of the committee on resolutions submitted a minority report declaring "that the experiment on the part of the United States alone of free silver coinage and a change in the existing standard of value independently of the action of other great nations, would not only imperil our finances, but would retard or entirely prevent the establishment of international bimetallism, to which the efforts of the government should be steadily directed. It would place this country at once upon a silver basis, impair contracts, disturb business, diminish the purchasing power of the wages of labor, and inflict irreparable evils upon our nation's commerce and industry."

Therefore, so the report continued, "until international cooperation among leading nations for the coinage of silver can be secured, we favor the rigid maintenance of the existing gold standard as essential to the preservation of our national credit, the redemption of our public pledges, and the keeping inviolate of our country's honor. We insist that all our paper and silver currency shall be kept absolutely at a parity with gold."

With both the majority and minority reports before the delegates, the debate began. Senator Benjamin "Pitchfork Ben" Tillman of South Carolina argued against the gold standard. He called President Cleveland "a tool of Wall Street" and asked for his impeachment. After other speeches for the minority report, William Jennings Bryan mounted the rostrum. "We do not come as aggressors," he began. "Our war is not a war of conquest; we are fighting in the defense of our homes, our families, and posterity. We have petitioned, and our petitions have been scorned. We have entreated, and our entreaties have been disregarded. We have begged, and they have mocked when our calamity came. We beg no longer, we entreat no more, we petition no more. We defy them." And twenty thousand voices echoed, "We defy them." Bryan asked: "Upon which side will the Democratic party fight, upon the side of the 'idle holders of idle capital' or upon the side of the 'struggling masses'?" There was a hush in the large hall—people felt they were witnessing a great event, as indeed they were. They were listening to one of the greatest speeches ever delivered in a national convention. Bryan's resonant voice carried his message to the furthest corner of the arena. "You come to us and tell us that the great cities are in favor of the gold standard. We reply that the great cities rest upon our broad and fertile prairies. Burn down your cities and leave our farms, and your cities will spring up again as if by magic; but destroy our farms and grass will grow in the streets of every city in the country. . . . Having behind us the producing masses of the nation and the world, supported by the commercial interests, the laboring interests and the toilers everywhere, we will answer their demand for a gold standard by saying to them: You shall not press down upon the brow of labor this crown of thorns, you shall not crucify mankind upon a cross of gold."

Twenty thousand people jumped to their feet. "Bryan, Bryan, Bryan!" went up their shout. The masses had found their leader. The words of "the boy orator of the Platte" (which river, said Senator Foraker, is "only six inches deep but six miles wide at the mouth") stirred the audience.

The "Cross of Gold" speech made Bryan the immediate favorite, a challenger to Richard P. Bland. Though on the first ballot he had fewer votes than Bland (119 to Bland's 235), four trials later he was chosen, with those who were in favor of the gold standard not voting. For the second place the Democrats took Arthur Sewall, a rich shipbuilder from Maine.

The third of the great conventions was that of the People's party. The Populists had made great strides since the last election. In the mid-term election of 1894 they had polled nearly a million and a half votes. Their issue—free silver—was now embedded in the Democratic platform, so that most Populists were ready to accept William Jennings Bryan, the official candidate of the Democrats.

Frank Opper, August 1896

THE SILVER-TONGUED ventriloquist and his dummies. "If the show succeeds, he'll get all the profits"—an inference that Bryan's campaign was conducted to further the interests of the big silver-mine owners of the West.

G. Y. Coffin, August 1896

"PROUD AS A PEACOCK with two tails." William Jennings Bryan ran on the Democratic ticket with Arthur Sewall as his running mate, and also on the Populist ticket with Thomas Watson as the vice presidential candidate.

Lorant: The Presidency (*Macmillan*)

WILLIAM JENNINGS BRYAN IN 1896—AT THE TIME HE RECEIVED THE DEMOCRATIC NOMINATION

PRESIDENT McKINLEY AND THE OUTGOING PRESIDENT CLEVELAND WALK TO THE INAUGURATION.

However, the "middle-of-the-road men" among the Populists asked for separate nominations and no alliance with either the Democrats or the Republicans. They were particularly against Arthur Sewall, the vice presidential candidate. To block Sewall's acceptance, they carried a motion whereby the nomination of the vice presidential candidate was to precede the selection of the presidential candidate. By this maneuver the Populists could name their own man for the Vice Presidency —Thomas E. Watson; for the first place it was Bryan.

The Prohibitionists were also split over the silver issue. The "Narrow Gaugers" opposed free coinage and asked for a narrow platform consisting of only one plank prohibiting the manufacture and sale of intoxicating liquors, while the "Broad Gaugers" wanted a platform of many planks. After the Narrow Gaugers won, the Broad Gaugers withdrew and, meeting again in a separate convention as the National party, they accepted a platform favoring free silver and named Joshua Lever-

ing of Maryland for the Presidency. The Narrow Gaugers nominated Reverend Charles E. Bentley of Nebraska.

The "Gold Democrats" also met in a separate convention; calling themselves the National Democratic party, they opposed silver coinage and named John M. Palmer as their candidate for the Presidency. The "Silver Republicans," who had stalked out of the party's convention gave Bryan his third endorsement.

Though the silver issue was the dominant one of the campaign, the controversy was more than a struggle of the factions over monetary policies. The "battle of the standards" was rather a fight of the agrarian South and West against the industrial East, of debtor and creditor for the control of the government and the economy.

The business leaders contributed vast amounts to the Republican campaign chest to stave off "anarchy." Workers in the factories found slips in their pay envelopes (a device used against Cleveland four years

McKINLEY TAKES THE INAUGURAL OATH FROM CHIEF JUSTICE FULLER AS CLEVELAND LISTENS.

before): "If Bryan is elected, do not come back to work. The plant will be closed."

Bryan campaigned all over the land, making some six hundred speeches, simplifying and dramatizing the causes of economic ills and offering the cure-all: free coinage of silver. He told his audiences that with the abundance of silver money good times would return. He assailed the plutocrats, whom he wanted to be held in check, for if the government was not "greater than the banker of Wall Street," it was "no government at all." He said the financiers knew "not a law, human or divine, which they would respect," because they felt "bigger than the government and greater than the Almighty." It was only the "common people" who had "ever supported a reform that had for its object the benefit of the human race." Bryan exclaimed: "Look at the people who are at the head of the gold-standard propaganda of the United States." Nineteen hundred years ago "the meek and lowly Savior threw the same

kind of people out of His temple because they had made His house a den of thieves." And he exclaimed: "The Creator had made men." He had not used "any superior kind of mud when He made financiers."

He denied the Republican assertion that he was a "revolutionary and an anarchist"—no, he was a crusader for humanity, on the side of the distressed farmers and against those who caused their distress.

And to those who berated his "want of dignity" in the campaign he replied, ". . . I would rather have it said that I lacked dignity than . . . that I lack backbone to meet the enemies of the Government who work against its welfare in Wall Street. What other Presidential candidates did they charge with lack of dignity? (A voice said, "Lincoln.") Yes, my friends, they said it of Lincoln. (Another voice, "Jackson.") Yes, they said it of Jackson. (A voice, "Jefferson.") Yes, and of Jefferson, he was lacking in dignity too."

McKinley listened to the suggestion of the astute

McKINLEY'S INAUGURAL ADDRESS ON MARCH 4, 1897

Thure de Thulstrup, March 1897

COLORFUL SCENE AT THE INAUGURAL BALL IN WASHINGTON'S NEW PENSION OFFICE BUILDING

Mark Hanna—who as "Dollar Mark" was more under attack than the candidate himself—and remained at his home in Canton, where he spoke from the front porch of his home to the delegations which came to see him.

The Republican slogan was: "A full dinner pail"; McKinley's promise was prosperity.

Foreign issues—the annexation of Hawaii and the restoration of the queen to her throne; Britain's controversy with Venezuela which drew such a strong declaration from Cleveland that it was feared it might cause war between England and America; the insurrection in Cuba and the threatening of the American sugar interests—were other topics discussed in the election, but they had little influence on the outcome.

McKinley won handily, receiving over seven million votes against Bryan's 6.5 million. Bryan had the eleven states of the Solid South in addition to the Western states of Colorado, Idaho, Kansas, Montana, Nebraska, Nevada, South Dakota, Utah, Washington and Wyoming;

he was also supported by the border state of Missouri. But the whole industrial North and the Middle West, as well as California and Oregon, were in McKinley's column. Thus the East defeated the West and the South. The Republicans had a comfortable majority in Congress, though in the Senate the Silverites held the balance.

On the night of his election McKinley was kneeling in his bedroom. His mother, her arm around her son, was praying: "Oh, God, keep him humble."

The result brought jubilation to Wall Street. Gold came out from its hiding places; brokers' offices in New York remained open all night, business was so brisk.

Tom Johnson, the liberal Mayor of Cleveland, called the election "the first great protest of the American people against monopoly—the first great struggle of the masses in our country against the privileged classes. It was not free silver that frightened the plutocrat leaders. What they feared then, what they fear now, is free men."

Horace Taylor, January 1, 1900

"WHY HANNA DOES NOT WANT TEDDY RIDING BEHIND McKINLEY." Because Theodore Roosevelt was a colorful personality, Mark Hanna feared that he would overshadow McKinley in the campaign. The Rough Rider dived into the contest like a duck into water. He was here, he was there, he was everywhere. Democratic orators accused President McKinley of abandoning the country's traditional anti-imperial policy. To this Roosevelt replied that McKinley promised in his acceptance letter that "no blow has been struck except for liberty and humanity and none will be" and that the million people who had come under the American flag in Cuba and the Philippines were not subdued but liberated "from the yoke of imperialism."

Roosevelt's flashing smile and his cordiality won votes; his ebullience, his horsemanship and his every action captivated his audiences. "Teddy"—though no one called him that to his face—was a man after the people's hearts, a great personality.

WILLIAM McKINLEY
and THEODORE ROOSEVELT

At the opening of McKinley's term, the worst of the depression was over. Prosperity would have returned even without McKinley, but since it came during his administration, he was given credit for its return. He had a lucky streak. Good harvests and rising prices took the wind out of the Populist revolt and the new discoveries of gold eased the currency problem.

McKinley was not a leader of men. He did what people expected of him. He followed public opinion. When the country grew war-minded, ready to fight over Cuba, he too abandoned his peaceful stance and sent a war message to Congress.

The Republican platform on which he was elected had pledged to revise the tariff and to solve the currency problem. He was determined to honor the campaign pledges. A revised tariff bill bearing the name of Congressman Dingley raised the duties on many products and built a high protective wall around the industries. As to the currency issue, he waited for the midterm election, expecting a reduction in the number of Silver Senators; but the silver issue was solved in a way he had not foreseen. Through the discoveries of new gold mines in Australia, South Africa and the Klondike, and through improved methods of extracting gold from ore, the gold supply of the world doubled; thus the scarcity of the metal ceased to be a problem. The Treasury had enough gold, and as it increased the issue of banknotes the cry for silver abated. A new currency bill made the gold dollar the standard unit of value; all money was redeemable in gold.

The domestic issues diminished in importance. The Cuban problem overshadowed all domestic considerations. The revolution on the island had gained momentum; the insurgents fought against their Spanish overlords, blew up trains, wrecked properties, burned sugar plantations. American investments were in jeopardy; the security of Americans was threatened.

Spain's brutal policy against the Cubans and the concentration-camp methods of General "Butcher" Weyler enraged Americans. Atrocity stories in the "yellow press" kept tempers at a high pitch. Hearst and Pulitzer, the publishers of the *Journal* and the *World* in New York, fought their private war with each other for higher circulation. Jingoism, war hysteria, sensational stories of brutality served their purpose well.

McKinley offered to negotiate a settlement between the contestants, but Spain refused the idea. The President hoped that the conflict could be resolved through peaceful means, but two events put an end to his hopes. One was the letter of the Spanish envoy, Enrique Dupuy de Lôme, which was intercepted by a Cuban revolutionary and printed in Hearst's New York *Journal;* the other was the explosion on the U.S.S. *Maine.* When the country learned that the Spanish Minister had called McKinley a vacillating and shifty politician who was "yielding to the rabble," and when it became known that 268 American lives had been lost in the explosion of the *Maine,* it cried for retaliation.

Hearst sent a bevy of correspondents to Cuba to report on Spanish cruelties. The artist Frederic Remington, seeing no war, asked to be allowed to return home. Hearst wired him: "You furnish the pictures and I'll furnish the war."

Congress appropriated $50 million for national de-

CANDIDATES IN 1900

WILLIAM McKINLEY (1843–1901), under whom the country enjoyed prosperity, was renominated. With the silver controversy settled by new discoveries of gold, the campaign issue became imperialism, brought to the fore by the Spanish-American War and by the projected annexation of the Philippines. The Democrats were against it. McKinley won handily with 7,219,525 votes against Bryan's 6,358,737 vote total.

THEODORE ROOSEVELT (1858–1919), the hero of San Juan Hill who led the Rough Riders' attack against the Spaniards, was elected to the Governorship of New York on his return from the war. An independent executive, he would not bow to the will of political boss Thomas Platt. Thus Platt decided to "elevate" him to the Vice Presidency to get rid of him and to dig his political grave. It turned out to be otherwise.

WILLIAM J. BRYAN (1860–1925), still the leader in the West and the South, wanted to free the Democratic party of Eastern domination. Once more nominated by the Democrats on a platform which endorsed free silver and opposed imperialism and the trusts, Bryan campaigned vigorously—with American policy in the Philippines as the most prominent issue. McKinley received 292 electoral votes, Bryan 155.

ADLAI E. STEVENSON (1835–1914), the former Congressman from Illinois, after serving as Vice President during Cleveland's second term, became a member of the monetary commission to Europe which sought unsuccessfully to pave the way for international bimetalism. Stevenson was for a low tariff and, in opposition to Cleveland, he sympathized with the Silverites; thus he was taken by Bryan for the second place.

Photograph by Clinedinst

THE McKINLEYS POSE FOR A PHOTOGRAPH.

Library of Congress

THEIR BEDROOM IN THE WHITE HOUSE

fense. McKinley still hesitated; he wanted to avoid war. His Undersecretary of the Navy, Theodore Roosevelt, called him a man with "no more backbone than a chocolate eclair."

On April 9, 1898, Spain suspended hostilities against the Cuban rebels, and the American Minister in Spain reported to Washington that all issues could be settled. But it was too late for a peaceful solution. McKinley, yielding to the jingoists, sent his war message to Congress. And the Committee on Foreign Affairs in both the House and the Senate resolved to authorize the President "to intervene at once to stop the war in Cuba, to the end and with the purpose of securing permanent peace and order there."

Louis Dalrymple, April 1900

McKINLEY'S EASTER EGG. The President ponders over the selection of a running mate. Vice President Garret Hobart had died in office, and McKinley was compelled to choose another vice presidential candidate. Which "chicken" should it be? From left to right: Senator Henry Cabot Lodge, former New York governor Frank Black, Interior Secretary Cornelius Bliss and Governor Theodore Roosevelt; getting out of the eggshells are War Secretary Elihu Root, Indiana Senator Albert Beveridge, who later wrote a biography of Abraham Lincoln, and New York's Lieutenant Governor Timothy Woodruff.

After a spirited debate, a significant amendment—the Teller Amendment—was added to the adopted resolutions. In it the United States disclaimed "any disposition or intention to exercise sovereignty, jurisdiction, or control over said island, except for the pacification thereof," and promised that after the restoration of peace, the government and control of the island would be left to its people.

On April 20, 1898, McKinley signed the joint resolution; five days later, America was at war with Spain.

At the outbreak of hostilities the treaty of Hawaiian annexation had not yet been ratified. But after Admiral Dewey's victory at Manila Bay, the Senate was no longer hesitant to act upon it. The Hawaiian government had ceded sovereignty and the Senate "accepted, ratified and confirmed" the cession. On August 12, the American flag was raised at Honolulu.

By then the fighting in Cuba was already over. "It has been a splendid little war," wrote John Hay to his friend Theodore Roosevelt. It was short, it did not cost much money, it did not call for great sacrifice. Young Americans had the opportunity to show their prowess as military heroes—and the girls loved it.

On July 26, Jules Cambon, the French Ambassador, asked for peace terms on behalf of the Spanish Government; McKinley set the terms: Spain was to relinquish Cuba and to cede Puerto Rico and an island in the Ladrones to the United States. In the Philippines,

George B. Luks, in The Verdict, *1899*

HANNA: "THAT MAN CLAY WAS AN ASS. IT'S BETTER TO BE PRESIDENT THAN TO BE RIGHT!" Hanna, the mentor of McKinley, was repeatedly caricatured as a plutocrat with flashing diamond studs and dollar signs on his thumb. Another of Homer Davenport's cartoons showed bankers carting away the statue of George Washington from the front of New York's Subtreasury Building and replacing it with a statue of Hanna, in a suit covered with dollar signs. But ridicule did not impair his effectiveness. He made up his mind to make McKinley President, and he was as good as his word.

Photograph by Barton, Hoffman Photo Co.

MARK HANNA ADDRESSES THE DELEGATES of the Republican convention and presents McKinley's name. In his speech, the autocratic Hanna gave the convention this advice: "I want to make one suggestion, always trust the people."

America was to occupy the city, harbor and bay of Manila pending the final disposition of the islands.

In less than a fortnight, the preliminary peace treaty was agreed upon in Washington; in October, American commissioners were drafting the final terms in Paris. McKinley was in steady cable communication with the commissioners. He directed their talks; nothing was done without his approval.

The unsolved issue of the talks was the fate of the Philippines. The President had no set policy; he asked for advice from politicians and received conflicting suggestions. Thus he turned to the Deity. "I went down on my knees and prayed Almighty God for light and guidance more than one night," McKinley described his search. "And one night late it came to me this way—I don't know how it was, but it came: (1) that we could not give them back to Spain—that would be cowardly and dishonorable; (2) that we could not turn them over to France or Germany—our commercial rivals in the Orient—that would be bad business and discreditable; (3) that we could not leave them to themselves—they were unfit for self-government—and they would soon have anarchy and misrule over there worse than Spain's was; and (4) that there was nothing left for us to do but to take them all, and to educate the Filipinos, and uplift and civilize the Christianize them, and by God's grace do the very best we could by them as our fellow-men for whom Christ also died. And then I went to bed and went to sleep and slept soundly."

The Democrats opposed ratification; they were

Lorant: The Life and Times of Theodore Roosevelt (*Doubleday*)

THE MEETING OF THE REPUBLICAN CONVENTION IN PHILADELPHIA. The arrow points to New York Governor Theodore Roosevelt, who is among his state's delegation. McKinley was renominated quickly. The question was: Who should be his running mate?

Boss Thomas Platt had had enough of his headstrong and unmanageable Governor. The simplest way to get rid of him seemed to be to make him Vice President. Mark Hanna admonished the men who insisted that young Roosevelt should get the second place: "Don't any of you realize that there's only one life between this madman and the White House?" But as Platt persisted, the ticket became "William McKinley, a western man with eastern ideas, and Theodore Roosevelt, an eastern man with western characteristics." The distraught Hanna told McKinley: "Now it is up to you to live."

against the occupation of the Philippines as they had been against the taking of Hawaii. They were against American imperialism. The newly formed Anti-Imperialist League protested against the establishment of a colonial system.

Just when it looked as if the administration would not be able to muster the necessary two-thirds majority for the treaty's ratification, rescue came from an unexpected source. At two-thirty in the afternoon of February 6, 1899—minutes before the final vote—the Republicans were still one vote short, when William Jennings Bryan, the ardent anti-imperialist, persuaded some of his friends in Congress to join with the Republicans and vote for ratification. The reason was—so it

was asserted—that Bryan could use the issue with telling effect.

Long before convention time it was evident that the nominees would be the same as four years before—McKinley would be the candidate of the Republicans and Bryan the standard-bearer of the Democrats.

One other Republican possibility was Admiral George Dewey. He was in the public eye and many Americans thought he would make a good President. The Admiral told a reporter from the New York *World:* "Yes, I realize that the time has arrived when I must definitely define my position." And his position was: "I would be acceptable as a candidate for this great office. . . ." And then Dewey told the interviewer

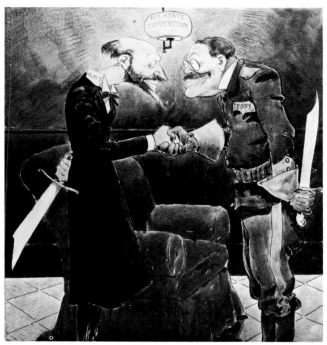

R. L. Bristol, in The Verdict, *1900*
THE "FRIENDLY ENEMIES," Boss Tom Platt and Governor Roosevelt, clashed over legislative and patronage matters. The wily Roosevelt could not be managed by Platt.

E. N. Blue, in Leslie's Weekly, *June 23, 1900*
McKINLEY IS NOMINATED. An enthusiastic delegate gives a hearty cheer for the Republican standard-bearer.

Cartoon in the New York Telegram, *May 1, 1900*
CRIES ROOSEVELT: "I don't want to be Vice President." He firmly believed that it would be the end of his promising political career.

A. Hencke, June 1900
THE REPUBLICAN NATIONAL CONVENTION in Philadelphia, which renominated President McKinley.

THE NATIONAL POPULIST CONVENTION at Sioux Falls, South Dakota, where the Populists named Bryan.

Photograph by A. Hencke and George Stark, July 1900
THE DEMOCRATIC NATIONAL COMMITTEE at the Kansas City Club was led by Chairman Jones (at right).

Photograph by James Burton, July 1900
THE DEMOCRATIC NATIONAL CONVENTION in Kansas City nominated William Jennings Bryan once again.

what he thought of the Presidency. "Since studying this subject," he said, "I am convinced that the office of the President is not such a very difficult one to fill, his duties being mainly to execute the laws of Congress."

That was the end of him as a candidate. The temporary arch for him, erected in New York's Madison Square following his victory at Manila Bay, was never converted into a permanent structure. There was no money for it. The arch was carted to the city dump and Mr. Dooley commented: "When a grateful raypublic, Mr. Hinnessy, builds an ar'rch to its conquering hero, it should be made of brick, so that we can have something convanyient to hurl after him when he has passed by."

The Republican convention in Philadelphia would have been a dull affair without the excitement over the vice presidential candidate. As Vice President Garret A. Hobart had died in office, the delegates had to decide on a new man. McKinley suggested Senator Allison and Mark Hanna proposed Cornelius N. Bliss, but neither of them would accept.

Theodore Roosevelt, the Rough Rider of San Juan Hill and now Governor of New York, had much support among the delegates, but Mark Hanna thought him "unsafe." Ordinarily, if the chairman of the party opposes the nomination of a vice presidential candidate, that is the end of it, but not this time. Thomas Platt, the boss of the New York machine, and Matt Quay, the boss of Pennsylvania, furthered Roosevelt's candidacy not because they believed he would make a good Vice President but because Platt wanted to get rid of the unmanageable Governor.

The Western delegates paraded through the aisles chanting: "We want Teddy! We want Teddy!" The feeling of the convention for Roosevelt's nomination was so marked that Hanna told journalists: "Boys, you can't stop it any more than you could stop Niagara."

In private Hanna's remarks were less amiable. One Washington correspondent noted him talking "in a towering passion" to Henry C. Payne of Wisconsin. Payne asked a simple question and received the answer: "Do whatever you damn please! I'm through! I won't have anything more to do with the convention! I won't take charge of the campaign! I won't be chairman of the national committee again!" Hanna shouted: "Don't any of you realize that there's only one life between that madman and the Presidency?" Payne (a Roosevelt supporter) said that he thought Hanna controlled the convention. "I am not in control! McKinley won't let me use the power of the administration to defeat Roosevelt. He is blind, or afraid, or something!"

Roosevelt had no desire to become Vice President —he felt it would lead to his political oblivion. "What I want is to be Governor of New York," he kept repeating. But as a practical politician he could not

Lorant: The Presidency (*Macmillan*)

BRYAN FORMALLY ACCEPTS THE DEMOCRATIC NOMINATION AT INDIANAPOLIS ON AUGUST 8, 1900.

refuse a genuine call from the delegates. Long before the convention, he wrote Cabot Lodge: "By the way, I did *not* say that I would not under any circumstances accept the vice-presidency. I have been careful to put it exactly as you advised." Roosevelt seemed to have an extremely short memory. On that same day, April 23, he also wrote to Redfield Proctor that he wanted "to make the National leaders understand, what I think the New York State leaders understand, that I will not under any circumstances accept the vice-presidential nomination, and so we might just as well go on with the consideration of somebody else."

McKinley was against selecting his running mate. He telephoned to the convention: "The President's close friends must not undertake to commit the Administration to any candidate. It has no candidate. The convention must make the nomination; the Administration would not if it could. The President's close friends

should be satisfied with his unanimous nomination and not interfere with the vice-presidential nomination. The Administration wants the choice of the convention and the President's friends must not dictate to the convention."

As a delegate at large from New York, Roosevelt made the seconding speech for McKinley's renomination. "We nominate President McKinley," he said, "because he stands indeed for honesty at home and for honor abroad; because he stands for the continuance of the material prosperity which has brought comfort to every home in the Union; and because he stands for that kind of policy which consists in making performance square with promise." After this speech the convention gave the Rough Rider such an ovation that he "stood flushed and almost dazed by the tremendous character of his greeting." Thus, when it came to the vice-presidential nomination, Roosevelt had the vote of every delegate and the ticket became "William McKinley, a Western man with Eastern ideas; and Theodore Roosevelt, an Eastern man with Western characteristics." Roosevelt wrote to Hanna: "I am as strong as a bull moose and you can use me up to the limit, taking heed of but one thing and that is my throat." And Hanna nudged McKinley: "Now it is up to you to live."

Roosevelt confided to Lodge: "It certainly is odd to look back sixteen years when you and I sat in the Blaine convention on the beaten side while the mugwumps foretold our utter ruin, and then in this convention, over which you presided to think how you recognized me to second McKinley's nomination and afterwards declared me myself nominated in the second place on the ticket."

The wily Senator Platt was asked to comment on the nomination. "I am glad that we had our own way," then he quickly corrected himself, "the people, I mean, had their way."

The platform boasted about the administration's achievements. It recalled that four years previously,

"when the people then assembled at the polls, after a term of Democratic legislation and administration, business was dead, industry paralyzed and the national credit disastrously impaired. The country's capital was hidden away, and its labor distressed and unemployed. The Democrats had no other plan with which to improve the ruinous conditions which they had themselves produced than to coin silver at the ratio of 16 to 1." Then the Republicans had restored prosperity "by means of two legislative measures—a protective tariff and a law making gold the standard of value."

On restraining the trusts, the platform used ambiguous words. While recognizing "the necessity and propriety of the honest cooperation of capital to meet new business conditions, and especially our rapidly increasing foreign trade," it condemned "all conspiracies and combinations intended to restrict business, to create monopolies, to limit production or to control prices."

The foreign planks favored "the construction, ownership, control and protection of an isthmian canal," approved "the annexation of the Hawaiian

From Harper's Weekly, *August 11, 1900*

IMPERIALISM WAS THE CHIEF CAMPAIGN ISSUE: On the left, Democratic Chairman Jones holds the two hoops: Free Silver (the issue of the last election) and Imperialism (the issue in the current one). He tells Bryan that the imperialism hoop is safer. On the right, Bryan paints out the old Populist "Free Silver" sign and replaces it with "Imperialism."

ANOTHER EXPLOSION AT HAN
Joseph Keppler, September 1900

SWALLOWED! The Populist boa constrictor with the head of Bryan swallows the Democratic donkey. The Dem-ocrats were fearful that the Populists would take over the party and exclude the conservative ideas of the Eastern

Islands," accepted the Treaty of Paris as the only way "to destroy Spain's sovereignty throughout the West Indies and in the Philippine Islands," and pledged "independence and self-government" for Cuba. All in all, it was a safe platform, and the Republican candidates saw no serious obstacles to victory.

When the Democrats met in Kansas City on July 4, they too did what was expected of them; they nominated William Jennings Bryan by acclamation, and chose Adlai E. Stevenson—Vice President under Cleveland—for the second place.

Their platform was built around the three issues of imperialism, trusts and free silver. "The burning issue of imperialism, growing out of the Spanish War, involves the very existence of the Republic and the destruction of our free institutions. We regard it as the paramount issue of the campaign," read one plank, and it went on: "We hold that the Constitution follows the flag and denounce the doctrine that an Executive or Congress . . . can exercise lawful authority . . . in violation of it. We assert that no nation can long endure half republic and half empire, and we warn the American people that imperialism abroad will lead quickly and inevitably to despotism at home."

J. S. Pughe, July 1900
wing, but it was they who in time assimilated the Populists, appropriated their policies and turned them into laws.

Joseph Keppler, in Puck, *June 6, 1900*
THE "LIVING" ISSUE. Bryan: "They say it's dead! Can't you see it *move?*"—meaning his 1896 free-silver policies.

J. S. Pughe, September 1900

CARL SCHURZ OFFERS UNCLE SAM THE REDUCING TINCTURE assisted by Oswald Ottendorfer, publisher of the New York *Staats-Zeitung,* and by Joseph Pulitzer, of the New York *World.* Measuring Uncle Sam is McKinley.

The platform asked for "a prompt and honest fulfillment of our pledge to the Cuban people and the world that the United States has no disposition nor intention to exercise sovereignty, jurisdiction or control over the island of Cuba, except for its pacification," denounced the Philippine policy of the administration because "the Filipinos cannot be citizens without endangering our civilization," and spoke out against militarism, which "means conquest abroad and intimidation and oppression at home."

The reading of this plank brought on a tumultuous ovation. The delegates marched up the aisles with banners: "Lincoln abolished slavery; McKinley has restored it"; they unfurled a seventy-foot-long flag from the roof of the hall with the words: "The Flag of the Republic forever; of an Empire never!" And they cheered and cheered.

On the trust issue the platform declared that "private monopolies are indefensible and intolerable. They destroy competition, control the price of raw material and of the finished product, thus robbing both producer and consumer"; therefore stringent laws against corporations should be enforced, otherwise "all wealth will be aggregated in a few hands and the Republic destroyed."

And on silver the old 1896 plank for "the free and unlimited coinage of silver and gold at the present legal ratio of 16 to 1" was adopted.

The Democrats condemned the Dingley Tariff Law "as a trust-breeding measure," denounced the currency bill, favored an amendment to the Constitution providing for the election of Senators by popular vote, asked for an "intelligent system of improving the arid lands of the West" and for statehood for the territories of Arizona, New Mexico and Oklahoma. They also advocated home rule and a territorial form of government for Alaska and Puerto Rico, and the "immediate con-

THE PYGMIES ATTACK
Drawing by Joseph Keppler, August 190

From Mrs. Theodore Roosevelt's campaign scrapbook
. . . AND THE GIRLS ADORE HIM.

struction, ownership and control of the Nicaraguan Canal by the United States."

Of the smaller parties holding conventions, the Social Democratic party, appearing for the first time in a national election, named Eugene V. Debs for the Presidency and asked first for "revision of our Federal Constitution, in order to remove the obstacles to complete control of government by the people, irrespective of sex"; second, "the public ownership of all industries controlled by monopolies, trusts and combines"; third, "the public ownership of all railroads, telegraphs and telephones; all means of transportation; all waterworks, gas and electric plants, and other public utilities"; fourth, "the public ownership of all gold, silver, copper, lead, iron, coal and other mines, and all oil and gas wells"; fifth, "the reduction of the hours of labor in proportion to the increasing facilities of production";

sixth, "the inauguration of a system of public works and improvements for the employment of the unemployed, the public credit to be utilized for that purpose"; seventh, "useful inventions to be free, the inventors to be remunerated by the public"; eighth, "labor legislation to be national, instead of local, and international when possible"; ninth, "national insurance of working people against accidents, lack of employment, and want in old age"; tenth, "equal civil and political rights for men and women, and the abolition of all laws discriminating against women"; eleventh, "the adoption of the initiative and referendum, proportional representation, and the right of recall of representatives by the voters"; and finally, "abolition of war and the introduction of international arbitration."

The Populists, having lost a great deal of their influence since the last election, again endorsed Bryan,

From Mrs. Theodore Roosevelt's campaign scrapbook
THE ROUGH RIDER WOOING THEM . . .

Lorant: The Life and Times of Theodore Roosevelt (*Doubleday*)
THEODORE ROOSEVELT ADDRESSES A CROWD AT THE RAMAPO IRON WORKS, HILLBURN, NEW YORK.

Library of Congress
McKINLEY CAMPAIGNS IN THE USUAL MANNER.

From Mrs. Theodore Roosevelt's campaign scrapbook
ROOSEVELT CAMPAIGNS IN THE MODERN WAY.

as did the silver Republicans and the Anti-Imperialist League. But the middle-of-the-road Populists who had disapproved of the fusion with the Democrats in 1896 named their own candidates—Wharton Barker of Pennsylvania for the Presidency and Ignatius Donnelly for the Vice Presidency.

The United Christian party, the Socialist-Labor party, the Union Reform party and the National Prohibition party also offered separate tickets.

In the campaign the Democrats stressed imperialism and legislation against the trusts, while the Republicans stuck to their theme, prosperity and the full dinner pail.

Bryan charged McKinley with the abandonment of America's traditional anti-empire policy and with the subjugation of millions of defenseless people. But in his acceptance letter McKinley had dwelt at length on this issue. He wrote: "The Philippines are ours and American authority must be supreme throughout the archipelago. . . . There must be no scuttle policy. There will be no turning aside, no wavering, no retreat. No blow has been struck except for liberty and humanity and none will be. We will perform without fear, every

Charles Green Bush, in New York World, 1900
HIS RUNNING MATE. To the electorate it seemed that Roosevelt ran for the Presidency, and not McKinley.

Lorant: The Life and Times of Theodore Roosevelt (*Doubleday*)
THE SUCCESSFUL CAMPAIGN SLOGAN IN 1900

T. Dart Walker, October 1900
REPUBLICAN STRATEGISTS: Mark Hanna (at the desk) with Senator Thomas Platt (left), Senator Chauncey Depew and other party leaders in a conference on strategy.

national and international obligation. The Republican Party . . . broke the shackles of 4,000,000 slaves and made them free and to the party of Lincoln has come another supreme opportunity which it has bravely met in the liberation of 10,000,000 of the human family from the yoke of imperialism."

He did not campaign actively, but stayed in the White House with occasional trips to Canton. He explained his stand: "Four years ago I was a private citizen and the candidate of my party for President. It was my privilege to aid in bringing success to my party

by making a campaign. Now I am President of the whole people, and while I am a candidate again, I feel that the proprieties demand that the President should refrain making a political canvass in his own behalf."

Hanna took the stump in the states west of the Mississippi, where Bryan had tremendous strength. Hanna had always been subject to abuse as a friend of the trusts and as the supposed "power behind the throne." In Nebraska he found a huge sign nailed to a telegraph pole: "POPULIST FARMERS BEWARE!!!! Chain Your Children To Yourselves or Put Them Under the

A REPUBLICAN CAMPAIGN POSTER: PROSPERITY

Grant Hamilton, September 1900
LOST! BRYAN IS TRAPPED BY THE DINNER PAILS.

Bed. MARK HANNA IS IN TOWN." However, his earthy manner and straight speech won him more friends than enemies. Herbert Croly, his biographer, wrote: "This trip helped to make Mr. Hanna personally popular throughout the West, just as his first stumping tour in Ohio had made him personally popular in his own State. As soon as he became known, the virulence and malignity with which he had been abused reacted in his favor. When he appeared on the platform, the crowd, instead of seeing a monster, found him to be just the kind of man whom Americans best understand and most heartily like. He was not separated from them by differences of standards and tastes or by any intellectual or professional sophistication. The roughness of much of his public speaking and its lack of form which makes it comparatively poor reading, were an essential part of its actual success. He stamped himself on his speeches just as he had stamped himself upon his business. His audiences had to pass judgment on the man more than on the message and the man could not but look good to them."

Hanna's greatest boost to the campaign was in his management of it. He collected some two and a half million dollars, mostly from big business, and he flooded the country with McKinley emblems and buttons, with posters, pamphlets and leaflets.

Roosevelt was steadily on the campaign trail; he toured the country, speaking morning, noon and night. Audiences loved him; they were amused by his clipped Harvard accent, his flashing teeth, his personality. Everywhere he went, Rough Riders and those who had fought in Cuba turned out en masse. "Buffalo Bill" Cody called him the "American cyclone." He was the delight of the crowds, always outspoken in his views. He told a friend what his campaign was about. "The combination of all the lunatics, all the idiots, all the knaves, all the cowards, and all the honest people who are hopelessly slow-witted is a formidable one to overcome when backed by the Solid South. This is the combination we have to face." He warned the people that a Democratic victory would yield "fearful misery, fearful disaster at home" and he brought up the old issue of free silver, which "would paralyze our whole industrial life." He would do everything in his power to "prevent the throwing over of this Government by Bryan and his followers."

On the main issue of the campaign—imperialism—he declared: "We are not taking a single step which in any way affects our institutions or our traditional policies." For him the question was not "whether we shall expand—for we have already expanded—but whether we shall contract." In another speech he blasted: "We are a nation of men, not a nation of weaklings. The American people were as ready to face their responsibilities in the Orient as they were ready to face them at home."

Roosevelt felt that even more important than imperialism was the issue "of securing good government and moral and material well-being within our own borders. Great though the need is that the nation should do its work well abroad, even this comes second to the thorough performance of duty at home." He attacked Bryan. "What a thorough-faced hypocrite and demagogue he is, and what a small man!" he wrote about him to Cabot Lodge. Before the campaign was over, Roosevelt had made a thousand speeches and had been seen by three million people. " 'Tis Tiddy alone that's runnin'," observed Mr. Dooley, "an' he ain't a-runnin', he's gallopin'!"

Bryan too conducted a relentless campaign even though he did not expect to win. He had said: "I can save more senators, congressmen and governors that way than perhaps may be done by any other candidate and the party machinery will be left in better condition." He worked for the good of the party, giving over six hundred speeches in twenty-four states.

In June he wrote in the *North American Review:* "The issue presented in the campaign of 1900 is the issue between plutocracy and democracy. All the questions under discussion will, in their last analysis, disclose the conflict between the dollar and the man." Getting down to specifics, he said: "To-day three questions contest for primacy—the money question, the trust question and imperialism."

As Cuba and the Philippines were already taken, Bryan could not make much of an issue over them. The problem was now what to do with the territories. The Teller Amendment made provisions for Cuba's future —but what about the Philippines? asked Bryan. He said: "We dare not educate the Filipinos lest they learn to read the Declaration of Independence and the Constitution of the United States." If he were elected, he promised, he would call Congress to a special session and see to it that the Philippines were given a stable, independent government. Then he would apply the Monroe Doctrine to keep other powers from taking the islands after we left them.

Part of Bryan's major speech on imperialism set a lofty tone that the Republicans could not equal. He thundered with all his fervor, "For more than a century this Nation has been a world-power. For ten decades it has been the most potent influence in the world. Not only has it been a world-power, but it has done more to affect the politics of the human race than all the other nations of the world combined. Because our Declaration of Independence was promulgated, others have been promulgated; because the patriots of 1776 fought for liberty, others have fought for it; because our

Photograph by Fred W. Meyer, November 24, 1900
THE PRESIDENT CASTS HIS VOTE IN CANTON.

Photograph by R. L. Dunn, November 1900
ELECTION NIGHT AT THE NEW YORK *TRIBUNE*

F. Cresson Schell, November 1900
OUTSIDE IN NEW YORK'S HERALD SQUARE

467

Photograph by George G. Bain, March 4, 1901

THEODORE ROOSEVELT ON THE WAY TO THE INAUGURATION CEREMONY

J. A. Harper, Library of Congress

THE INAUGURAL BALLROOM IS READY

From Harper's Weekly, March 9, 1901

THE PROCESSION ON THE WAY TO THE CEREMONY

Constitution was adopted, other constitutions have been adopted. The growth of the principle of self-government, planted on American soil, has been the overshadowing political fact of the nineteenth century. It has made this Nation conspicuous among the nations, and given it a place in history such as no other nation has ever enjoyed. Nothing has been able to check the onward march of this idea. I am not willing that this Nation shall cast aside the omnipotent weapon of truth to seize again the weapon of physical warfare. I would not exchange the glory of this Republic for the glory of all the empires that have risen and fallen since time began."

Bryan assailed the Republican full dinner pail—

asking if this covered an average wage of ninety cents a day for the miners. Did it explain why 134,000 of them would go on strike? And he quoted statistics that business failures were increasing. He kept up these attacks day and night on the trail, speaking often as long as four hours at one place.

He attacked the Republican methods: "They will coerce every vote that can be coerced. They will intimidate every laboring man who can be intimidated. They will bribe every election judge who can be bribed. They will corrupt every court that can be corrupted."

His second swing through New York was dubbed "The Second Coming of Bryan." A crowd of 150,000 greeted him. Mr. Hennessy commented: " 'Tis a gr-reat

Lorant: The Life and Times of Theodore Roosevelt (*Doubleday*)

IN DRIZZLING RAIN PRESIDENT McKINLEY IS SWORN IN AGAIN BY CHIEF JUSTICE FULLER.

rayciption they do be givin' Bryan down in New York State." Mr. Dooley came back: "A fine rayciption f'r a State is that he's not dangerously wounded. Anything short iv death is regarded as a friendly an' inthrested rayciption. . . . All ye can say about Willum Jennings Bryan's rayciption is that he got by Wall Sthreet without bein' stoned to death with nuggets fr'm th' goold resarve."

But there were just not enough anti-imperialists around to make Bryan feel confident of winning the crucial Eastern states. He was branded as the Democrats' "old man of the sea," a "fanatical rhetorician' and an anarchist. His message on the dangers of imperialism did not come across. Paxton Hibben wrote: "What

Bryan needed, and needed badly in the campaign of 1900, was a little volume, with pictures if possible, dealing with monopoly in the offhand way *Coin's Financial School* had covered the currency question. From such a work he might have learned to reduce the trust question to words of one syllable for the consumption of the great American public."

Yet the business setback and a rise in unemployment worried the Republicans. John Hay wrote: "There is a vague uneasiness among Republicans, which there is nothing in the elaborate canvasses of the Committee to account for. I do not believe defeat to be possible, though it is evident that this last month of Bryan, roaring out his desperate appeals to hate and envy, is

469

HIS LAST WALK. The President on his way to a reception at the Pan-American Exposition in Buffalo. Shortly after this picture was taken, an assassin shot McKinley.

THE LAST PHOTOGRAPH OF McKINLEY, a souvenir snapshot taken only a few minutes before the assassination.

ANXIOUS MOMENTS. Mark Hanna with prominent Republican friends and reporters waits for news outside the Milburn residence. Inside the doctors are with McKinley.

having its effect on the dangerous classes."

But on election day it was McKinley again. He received 7,219,525 votes against Bryan's 6,358,737; his electoral vote was 292 against Bryan's 155. Roosevelt told his friend Lodge: "Well, I am delighted to have been on the national ticket in this great historic contest, for after McKinley and Hanna, I feel that I did as much as anyone in bringing about the result—though after all it was Bryan himself who did most. . . ."

On inauguration day he stood beside the President in a somber mood. For Platt, who had eased Roosevelt out of the Governorship, it was a happy day. As he walked to the platform to take his seat, he remarked that he was going "to see Roosevelt take the veil!"

Though Roosevelt saw his future in dark colors, his

A LARGE CROWD WAITS TO CHEER McKINLEY.

T. Dart Walker, September 1901

THE ASSASSIN AND THE PRESIDENT. On September 6, as President McKinley attended a public reception in Buffalo's Temple of Music, an anarchist stepped before him and discharged a revolver. For a week the President lay between life and death. On September 14 he died.

LEON F. CZOLGOSZ,
THE ASSASSIN

Roosevelt Memorial Association

THE CROWD WAITS BEFORE THE BULLETIN BOARDS FOR NEWS OF McKINLEY'S CONDITION.

friends did not agree with him. They hoped that he would be the exception to the rule; they were confident that he could break precedent and would be the first Vice President since Van Buren to become President. "I have no doubt that you will be the nominee in 1904," wrote William Howard Taft to him, and Lodge advised him to be careful so that there would be nothing against him when the time came.

Immediately after the inauguration, Roosevelt had taken up the the Vice President's duties as President of the Senate. The Senate session, as it happened, was only a five-day affair devoted primarily to confirming various presidential appointments. The brevity of the session suited Roosevelt admirably, for he had little interest in the role of a parliamentary umpire and had

frequently remarked when his vice presidential candidacy was under discussion that he would find it both boring and exasperating to preside over debates in which he could not actively participate. As Chauncey Depew put it, Roosevelt conspicuously lacked the "equable temper" desirable in such a situation. Nonetheless, his first appearance as Senate president was made into something of a family affair, with his wife Edith, the children and a dozen other members of the Roosevelt clan watching from the gallery. "He was very quiet and dignified," Mrs. Roosevelt recalled. But soon after that, he asked on a motion, "All in favor will say Ay," and bowed to the Republican side as the Senators chuckled. "All those opposed say No," he asked, bowing to the Democrats.

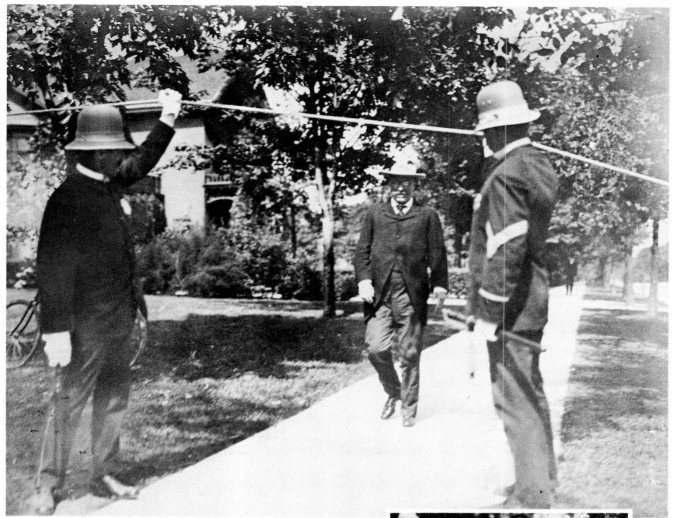

Lorant: The Life and Times of Theodore Roosevelt (*Doubleday*)
THE VICE PRESIDENT ARRIVES after a hurried trip from a vacation on the Isle La Motte in Lake Champlain.

Roosevelt felt that the job of Vice President left him with "unwarranted idleness." He thought it would be well for the Vice President "if, in addition to his vote in the Senate [in case of a tie] . . . he should be given a vote, on ordinary occasions, and perchance on occasion a voice in the debates." He planned to continue his study of law and wanted to teach history.

All of a sudden, his peaceful life was cut short. At four o'clock in the afternoon of September 6, as President McKinley was greeting visitors at a reception in his honor at Buffalo's Pan-American Exposition, the anarchist Leon Czolgosz approached him with a revolver concealed under a handkerchief. As the President reached out to shake hands with him, Czolgosz fired, pumping two bullets into McKinley's body. After

Lorant, The Presidency (*Macmillan*)
THE VICE PRESIDENT IS INTERVIEWED. The doctors' first reports about McKinley's condition were so promising that Roosevelt was ready to continue his vacation and show the country that all was well.

THE FUNERAL OF A PRESIDENT. McKinley's remains are carried to lie in state in the rotunda of the Capitol.

THE CASKET IS REMOVED through the funeral-car window at the railroad station in his home town, Canton.

WHERE ROOSEVELT TOOK THE OATH OF OFFICE: T parlor of the Wilcox residence in Buffalo, where on Septeml 14, 1901, he was sworn in by U.S. District Court Judge John Haz

an emergency operation at the hospital of the Exposition, the President was taken to the home of a friend.

The news of McKinley's assassination reached Roosevelt that afternoon at Isle La Motte on Lake Champlain, where he was attending the annual outing of the Vermont Fish and Game League. He immediately took a special train to Buffalo, and arrived there the following day. To his relief the news was good. He wrote Lodge in Paris: "Long before you receive this letter I believe the last particle of danger will have vanished; nor do I anticipate a long convalescence."

As there seemed to be no emergency, Roosevelt left Buffalo to continue his vacation.

But less than a week later, early on the morning of Friday, September 13, McKinley's condition took a severe turn for the worse and an urgent message was sent to Albany, where a courier was dispatched to notify the Vice President. The day before, Roosevelt, with his wife, his daughter Ethel and three friends, had started an overnight trip into the Mount Marcy area. Roosevelt with his friends had gone to the summit and was on his way down early in the afternoon when a

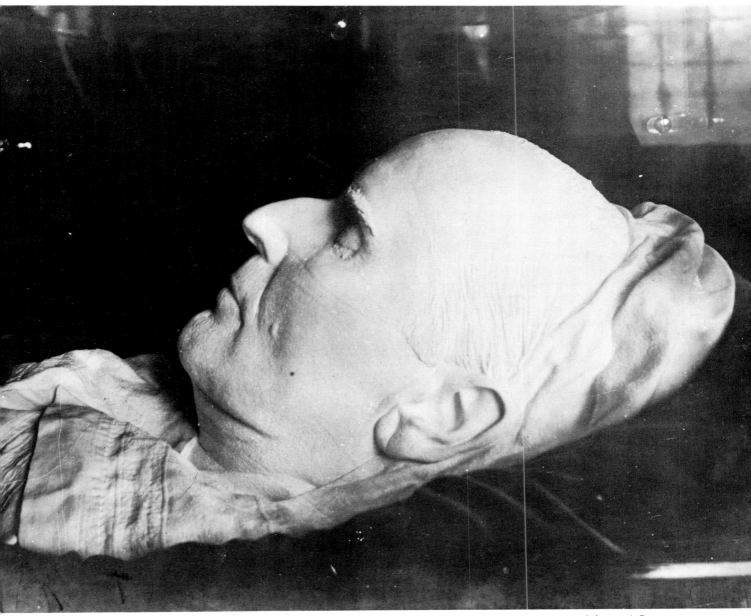

McKINLEY'S DEATH MASK; HIS LAST WORDS WERE "NEARER MY GOD TO THEE, NEARER TO THEE."

guide reached him with the message from Secretary of War Elihu Root: "The President appears to be dying, and members of the Cabinet in Buffalo think that you should lose no time in coming." It was nighttime before he made the thirty-five-mile trip from the clubhouse to the nearest railroad, traveling in a buckboard at break-neck speed through the darkness on rough mountain roads. As he boarded his train in North Creek shortly before dawn, he learned that McKinley had died.

Arriving in Buffalo in the afternoon, Roosevelt joined the Cabinet members in the study of the Ansley Wilcox residence. "I will show the people at once that the administration of the government will not falter in spite of the terrible blow," he declared, his face grim and impassive. "I wish to say that it shall be my aim to continue absolutely unbroken, the policy of President McKinley for the peace, the prosperity, and the honor of our beloved country." He then took the oath of office administered by Judge John R. Hazel of the United States District Court.

Forty-year-old Theodore Roosevelt was now President of the United States.

THEODORE ROOSEVELT

"A smack of Lord Cromer, Jeff Davis a touch of him;
A little of Lincoln, but not very much of him;
Kitchener, Bismarck and Germany's Will,
Jupiter, Chamberlain, Buffalo Bill."

This is how *Punch,* the English weekly, characterized Theodore Roosevelt. Yes, he was all this and more. He came from a well-to-do family; his grandfather was one of the richest men in New York; he graduated from Harvard and studied law at Columbia. He was a writer, a historian, a naturalist. He was also a man of action. He led the Rough Riders up San Juan Hill, he hunted big game, he worked his ranch in the West. A politician with a varied career, he started out as an assemblyman in New York; he became civil service commissioner in Washington under Benjamin Harrison, police commissioner of New York under Grover Cleveland, Assistant Secretary of the Navy under William McKinley. He left his post to volunteer in the Spanish-American War, and when he returned he was a hero acclaimed by young and old. The people elected him Governor of New York in 1898; the party bosses made him Vice President in 1900.

A conservative rather than a radical, he had faith in the existing economic system, but he wanted its abuses to be remedied and to keep a check on the leaders of industry and finance—if possible between dawn and dusk.

As President William McKinley lay close to death, Wall Street was apprehensive. With Roosevelt in the Presidency, the financial world feared an anti-business administration. His brother-in-law warned Roosevelt that "there is a feeling in financial circles here that in case you become President you may change matters so as to upset the confidence . . . of the business world, which would be an awful blow to everybody." But Roosevelt had no such intentions. After McKinley's death he promised to "continue, absolutely unbroken, the policy of President McKinley."

There were rumors of a break between him and Mark Hanna. The Republican chairman, moved by his friend McKinley's death, lamented that now "that damned cowboy is President of the United States." Yet those who were on the funeral train observed a long and friendly talk between the disconsolate Hanna and the new President, after which Hanna reportedly said: "He's a pretty good little cuss after all."

Hanna sent a cordial note advising Roosevelt to "go slow," and Roosevelt listened. His first message to Congress was a moderate one. His criticism of the trusts, in particular, was toned down after a consultation with Hanna, which made Mr. Dooley exclaim of Roosevelt's attitude toward the trusts: 'On wan hand I wud stamp thim under feet; on th' other hand not so fast."

But a man like Roosevelt could not "go slow" for long. Barely a few months had passed when he started to fight the "malefactors of great wealth." Philander Knox, his Attorney General, asked for the dissolution of the Northern Securities Company, a creation of J. P. Morgan for securing a railroad monopoly in the Northwest. The financier raced to Washington. "If we have done anything wrong," he told the President, "send your man [meaning Attorney General Knox] to my man [naming one of his lawyers] and they can fix it

THEODORE ROOSEVELT,
A NEW KIND OF PRESIDENT
Theodore Roosevelt Association

CANDIDATES IN 1904

THEODORE ROOSEVELT
(1858–1919), who succeeded McKinley and became the country's most popular President, desired to gain the office "in his own right" He won hands down with 7,628,785 votes to Parker's 5,084,442.

CHARLES FAIRBANKS
(1852–1918), lawyer and Senator from Indiana, was chosen for the Vice Presidency because, as Roosevelt put it, "Who in the name of heaven else is there?" He campaigned hard, speaking in 33 states.

ALTON B. PARKER
(1852–1926), a "safe and sane" New York judge, was named by the Democrats in the belief he would appeal to Republican businessmen and all those dissatisfied with Roosevelt's advanced policies.

HENRY G. DAVIS
(1823–1916), 81-year-old millionaire, former Senator from West Virginia who started as a railroad brakeman, was chosen as Parker's running mate in the hope he would use his own funds in the campaign.

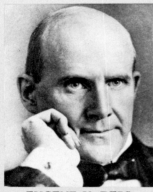

EUGENE V. DEBS
(1855–1926), an early trade unionist, was converted to socialism while in jail following the 1895 Pullman strike. As candidate of the Socialists, he received the impressive total of 402,895 popular votes.

SILAS C. SWALLOW
(1839–1930), a Methodist-Episcopal minister of Pennsylvania called the "Fighting Parson," who opposed dancing, liquor and tobacco, became the Prohibition candidate, receiving 258,950 votes.

Photograph by R. W. Thacher

EDITH KERMIT CAROW (1861–1948), the second wife of Theodore Roosevelt, was his childhood sweetheart. But when at Harvard he fell in love with Alice Lee and married her. She died on February 14, 1884, two days after giving birth to a daughter—the present Alice Longworth. On December 2, 1886, Roosevelt married again, in London—this time it was Edith. They had five children: Theodore (1887–1944), Kermit (1889–1943), Ethel (born 1891), Archibald (born 1894) and Quentin (1897–1917).

The second Mrs. Roosevelt, a frail woman with a strong personality, had a great influence on her husband. To her dying day jealous of his first wife, she presided over the household with an iron hand.

After the funeral for McKinley, with her husband going with the remains to Canton, Mrs. Roosevelt's spirits were low. And a tour of the gloomy upstairs bedrooms of the White House did not raise them. So she wired home: "Send down as many of the children as possible." But she changed her mind and went up for them by train.

The arrival of the young Roosevelts at the White House was "the wildest scramble in history." They brought vans and vans of toys, ponies, books, costumes—enough for a small army. After the forty acres of Sagamore Hill, they found the White House grounds a bit confining, so they would climb the lamp posts along Pennsylvania Avenue to undo the work of the lamplighter.

THE THOUSAND-FACED THEODORE ROOSEVELT: A PHOTO MONTAGE OF THE VERSATILE PRESIDENT

up." The amused Roosevelt replied, "That can't be done," and Knox told Morgan: "We don't want to fix it up; we want to stop it." The disturbed Morgan wanted to know: "Are you going to attack my other interests?" and Roosevelt answered: "Certainly not, unless we find out that in any case they have done something we regard as wrong."

The Northern Securities case was the curtain-raiser in the battle against the trusts. To win it Roosevelt needed popular support. So he left for a speaking tour through New England and the Western states to present his case. He told those who came to hear him that "the biggest corporation, like the humblest citizen, must be held to strict compliance with the will of the people." He lashed out against the well-to-do who "go into wild

speculation and lose their heads," and he berated the rich who get richer while the poor get poorer. His audiences loved it; here was a man after their own hearts—a President who cared for them and who wanted to make life better for them.

The rich saw the handwriting on the wall. James J. Hill, the Western railroad king, complained of the injustice that he and other men like him "should be compelled to fight for our lives against the political adventurers who have never done anything but pose and draw a salary." But among the people Roosevelt's popularity was on the rise. His action in forcing the coal operators and the miners union to settle the paralyzing coal strike was loudly approved and his trust-busting activities heartily endorsed.

479

Photograph by S. L. Stein, June 21, 1904

THE REPUBLICAN CONVENTION at Chicago nominated Theodore Roosevelt by unanimous vote. The large photograph is in memory of the late Mark Hanna.

Collier's Convention Extra, July 12, 1904

THE DEMOCRATIC CONVENTION at St. Louis nominated Judge Alton B. Parker over William Randolph Hearst.

E. M. Ashe, March 1903

THEODORE ROOSEVELT'S CABINET IN 1903. Clockwise from the President: Leslie M. Shaw (Treasury), Philander C. Knox (Attorney General), William H. Moody (Navy), James Wilson (Agriculture), George B. Cortelyou (Secretary of the Department of Commerce and Labor), Ethan A. Hitchcock (Interior), Henry C. Payne (Postmaster General), Elihu Root (War) and John Hay (State).

William A. Rogers, N.Y. Herald, 1904

"THE CONVENTION ARRIVES." It is Roosevelt, Roosevelt, Roosevelt; the face of every delegate arriving on the convention train in Chicago seems to be Roosevelt's.

And he was admired even more for his determined stand in foreign matters. He took as his motto the old African proverb, "Speak softly and carry a big stick," and he boldly interfered when Great Britain, Italy and Germany sent warships to Venezuela to collect the funds owed to them. He prevented the "spanking" of a small country, even if it was ruled by "a villainous little monkey," as he called Cipriano Castro, the Venezuelan President. And when some of the European states, exasperated by Santo Domingo's evasions, threatened to collect pledged customs receipts, he showed equal firmness. He made it clear that the United States adhered to the Monroe Doctrine and added to it a corollary: "Brutal wrongdoing or an impotence which results in a general loosening of the ties of civilized society may finally require intervention by some civilized nation, and in the Western Hemisphere the United States cannot ignore this duty."

America had no stake in Venezuela or in Santo Domingo, but in Colombia it had a vital interest. With its spreading influence in the Pacific, the country needed an isthmian canal. A treaty to build such a canal was submitted to Colombia's legislature; however, that body refused to ratify it. There was a convenient "revolution," which resulted in the establishment of an independent Panama. Roosevelt hurriedly recog-

Maybell in the Brooklyn Daily Eagle, *July 11, 1904*

THE DEMOCRATIC CANDIDATE sent a telegram to the convention, in which Parker declared for the Gold Standard, though the Democratic platform was silent on the issue.

Smithsonian Institution

THE REPUBLICAN BANNER: MORE PROSPERITY

Smithsonian Institution

THE DEMOCRATIC BANNER: JEFFERSONIANISM

Smithsonian Institution

THE SOCIALIST BANNER: "WORKERS UNITE"

nized the new state, and the new Panamanian government acquiesced to the American conditions. The canal was to be built, and Roosevelt could declare years after the event: "I took Panama."

Roosevelt was loved, admired and acclaimed as no President before him, not even Washington, Jefferson or Lincoln. His battle against "the malefactors of great wealth," his wielding of the big stick, his stand in the Philippines and in Panama won him the support of the country. He could do no wrong. But however impressive his achievements, he bemoaned the fact that he was President only by accident, that he had not been voted into office. "I'd rather be elected to that office than have anything tangible of which I know. But I shall never be elected to it. They don't want me," he said with self-pity, and by "they" he meant the party chieftains—Hanna, Platt and the others.

As so often, he had exaggerated. The opposition to him was not so great as he claimed, although it was true that the party bosses would have liked to bring him under their influence. There was some talk of replacing him at the next convention with Mark Hanna, but even before Hanna could make a try, his Ohio opponent, Senator Foraker, threw a bombshell by demanding that the Ohio Republican state convention endorse Roosevelt because he "made a good Presi-

Photograph by Juley, August 1904

JUDGE PARKER IS NOTIFIED OF HIS NOMINATION BY CHAMP CLARK AT ESOPUS, NEW YORK.

dent," and because he was "the most popular man in the United States" and because "I do not know of any reason why Ohio should not declare for him." The implication was clear: If Hanna stopped the endorsement, it was because he wanted the Presidency for himself. Hanna said: "I am not, and will not be, a candidate for the presidential nomination," but he opposed the proposal to commit the Ohio Republicans a year ahead of the national convention. Knowing the sensibilities of Roosevelt, who was then traveling through the West, Hanna wired him: "The issue which has been forced upon me in the matter of our state convention this year endorsing you for the Republican nomination next year has come in a way which makes it necessary for me to oppose such a resolution. When you know all the facts, I am sure you will approve my course."

Roosevelt lost no time with his answer to Hanna, and he handed his reply to the press. "I have not asked any

man for his support," read his telegram. "I have nothing whatever to do with raising this issue. Inasmuch as it has been raised, of course those who favor my administration and my nomination will favor endorsing both, and those who do not will oppose."

Poor Hanna, outmaneuvered on one side by Foraker, on the other by Roosevelt, had to submit. "In view of the sentiment expressed I shall not oppose the endorsement of your administration," he answered. He was ill and tired; he did not want the Presidency; he would not live until the convention.

Roosevelt confided to Cabot Lodge: "Hanna was my only formidable opponent so far as this nomination is concerned. The whole incident has entirely revived me. . . . This last business gave me a new and vivid interest in life."

And he made careful preparations for the forthcoming convention, attending to its every detail. He

E'S GOOD ENOUGH FOR ME—
HE FAMOUS HOMER DAVENPORT CARTOON
the New York Evening Mail, *1904*

Joseph Keppler, in Puck, *November 2, 1904*

PUTTING THE SCREWS ON. George B. Cortelyou, the new Republican finance chairman, is squeezing money out of big corporations. A later investigation showed that 72% of the $2,195,000 which Cortelyou collected came from the trusts.

Photograph by G. V. Buck, Washington, D.C.
THE DEMOCRATIC TICKET. The "safe and sane" candidate Parker and his 81-year-old running mate, Henry G. Davis, who was expected to finance the campaign; but millionaire Davis had no intention of giving up even a penny.

Library of Congress
REPUBLICAN VICE PRESIDENTIAL CANDIDATE, Charles W. Fairbanks, the conservative and stately Indiana Senator, was chosen by Roosevelt as his running mate because, as he put it, "Who in the name of heaven else is there?"

told Elihu Root, who was to make the keynote address, to emphasize the winning of Panama, the Northern Securities suit, Cuban independence, the administration of the Philippines, the Alaska boundary dispute, the formation of the Departments of Commerce and Labor, the Open Door policy to China, the Venezuela affair, the enforcement of the Monroe Doctrine—all signal achievements of his administration.

He sought to prove his appeal in many ways. He courted newspaper reporters by holding press conferences and establishing a special room in the White House for their use. He went before the people on extensive speaking tours, outlining his policies and political philosophy, and by his energy, versatility, informality and outspokenness won their admiration.

Not long before the convention a rich American-born citizen was abducted from his home in Tangier by a Berber highwayman. Rasuli, the bandit, demanded a

large ransom for the American Perdicaris's life. When Roosevelt heard about this, he sent the fleet to Tangier with an ultimatum demanding the immediate release of Perdicaris. Always ready with a succinct expression, he exclaimed: "This government wants Perdicaris alive or Rasuli dead."

When "Uncle Joe" Cannon, the permanent chairman of the convention, read Roosevelt's demand to the Republican delegates, their enthusiasm knew no bounds. For a while the Republican slogan became: "Perdicaris alive or Rasuli dead." Secretary Hay recorded in his diary: "My telegram to Gunmere had an uncalled-for success. It is curious how a concise impropriety hits the public." It is interesting to note that after the election the affair was quietly settled. The Sultan released Perdicaris, and the fleet came home. It turned out that Perdicaris was not even an American citizen, but by then the election was over and won, and

Louis Dalrymple, December 1904

AFTER ROOSEVELT WON he announced: "The wise custom which limits the President to two terms regards the substance and not the form, and under no circumstances will I be a candidate for or accept another nomination." Later, he said: "I would cut my hand off right there," indicating his wrist, "if I could recall that written statement."

J. S. Pughe, March 1905

"ALL HIS OWN." Roosevelt was elated over his victory. On inauguration eve he announced: "Tomorrow I shall come into my office in my own right. Then watch out for me!"

Roosevelt had proven his strength with the people. The President had no opposition; all 994 delegates to the convention voted for him, and they approved his choice of Senator Charles Warren Fairbanks of Indiana, a colorless conservative, for the Vice Presidency.

The platform pledged the Republicans to uphold the protective tariff, preserve the gold standard, maintain a big navy and encourage the development of the merchant marine. It praised Roosevelt's foreign policies and his enforcement of the antitrust laws. It raised no issues—the issue was Roosevelt.

The Democrats were in a difficult position. They had no one who could match Roosevelt's popularity. The Eastern wing of the party was in control; Bryan and the influence of the West was in decline after his two consecutive losses, so they turned to Alton B. Parker, Chief Justice of the New York Court of Appeals, a "safe and sane" man. Cleveland could have had the nomination, but he had no desire for it. The Democrats hoped that Parker's middle-of-the-road stand on issues would be more appealing to conservative businessmen than the radicalism of Roosevelt. His chief opponent was William Randolph Hearst, the publisher, who could not gain enough support to offer a serious threat. To complete the ticket, the Democrats selected 81-year-old Henry G. Davis of West Virginia, one of the weirdest choices on record. The millionaire Davis was chosen so he would contribute to the campaign fund—which he did not.

Bryan, opposing Parker's nomination, asked for a renewal of the party's former free-silver declaration and demanded that an income tax resolution be included in the platform, but he was voted down. Yet he secured a strong antitrust plank.

When Parker was notified of his selection, he wired that he was a firm adherent of the gold standard and if the delegates disagreed with him, he would decline the nomination. The convention answered: "The platform adopted by this convention is silent upon the question of monetary standard, because it is not regarded by us as a possible issue in this campaign, and only campaign issues are mentioned in the platform. Therefore, there is nothing in the views expressed by you in the telegram just received which would preclude a man entertaining them from accepting a nomination on said platform." so Parker, "the enigma from New York," remained the candidate.

Roosevelt relished having the colorless and nationally unknown Parker as an opponent. Accepting the nomination, he attacked the Democrats call for economy as something "they cannot or should not perform." He counseled his friend Taft, who campaigned for him: "Do not in any speech take any position seeming in the least to be on the defensive. Attack Parker. . . . Announce

ROOSEVELT'S INAUGURATION
Next to him are ex-President Clevelan
and Henry Cabot Lodge.
Library of Congress

that we shall not abandon building up the navy and keeping up the army, or abandon rural free delivery, or irrigation of the public land."

The campaign was dull. Republican big business would not line up behind Parker; even though Wall Street and the big corporations were shaken by Roosevelt, they supported him. Morgan, Gould, Frick and other "Robber Barons" contributed freely to the campaign fund. And the one-line editorial of the New York *Sun* read: "Theodore! With all thy faults."

Only when Joseph Pulitzer published an eight-column article in the *World* did the campaign come alive. Pulitzer asked some discomfiting questions of Roosevelt. He wanted to know why the Bureau of Corporations had been so inactive. Was it because big businessmen, "pouring money into your campaign chests, assume they are buying protection?" And why had the head of the bureau become the national chairman? (Roosevelt had chosen George Cortelyou to replace Mark Hanna, who had died early in the year.) And he posed a number of other questions: (1) How much had the beef trust contributed to Mr. Cortelyou? (2) How much had the paper trust contributed to Mr. Cortelyou? (3) How much had the coal trust contributed to Mr. Cortelyou? (4) How much had the sugar trust contributed to Mr. Cortelyou?

At first Roosevelt would not be drawn out. But when Parker said in the campaign that the corporations had paid their blackmail so that the Bureau of Corporations would not reveal damaging facts about them, Roosevelt found his voice: "That contributions have been made is not the question at issue," but "the assertion that there has been any blackmail, direct or indirect, by Mr. Cortelyou or by me is a falsehood."

Roosevelt won the election by the vast majority of 2½ million votes. He received 7,628,785 votes against Parker's 5,084,223. His lead of over two and a half million votes constituted a record. Parker could not carry a single state north of the Mason and Dixon line. Missouri, Maryland and West Virginia were lost to the Democrats. Both houses of Congress were in the Republican fold.

"I am no longer a political accident," cried out Roosevelt happily. In his exuberance he made the rash announcement: "On the 4th of March next I shall have served three and a half years and this . . . constitutes my first term. The wise custom which limits the President to two terms regards the substance and not the form, and under no circumstances will I be a candidate for or accept another nomination."

He was to regret his impulsiveness. "I would cut my hand off right there," he confided to a friend in later years, pointing to his wrist, "if I could recall that written statement."

"AVE THEODORE!" Roosevelt, as a Roman emperor, leads a triumphal procession of his political supporters (Cabot Lodge and Taft in the foreground) and his shackled political captives—Thomas Watson, the Populist candidate; Alton B. Parker, the Democratic candidate; and William Jennings Bryan—toward the White House. In the second chariot, Charles W. Fairbanks, the Vice President, leads his defeated opponent Henry G. Davis.

Joseph Keppler, March 1905

Inauguration day was a happy day for the President. John Hay, who in his youth had been Lincoln's private secretary, gave Roosevelt a ring made of Lincoln's hair, which he wore as he took the oath.

"There'll be a hot time in the old town tonight," played the bands as Roosevelt rode down Pennsylvania Avenue with Rough Riders galloping at the side of his carriage. All his old friends were in Washington lining the parade route:

coal miners of Pennsylvania, grateful to him for settling the anthracite strike; Puerto Ricans and Filipinos; old-style and new-style Indians, with spears and tomahawks and in modern dress; farmers, mechanics and ranchmen who worked with him in the roundups; cowboys and Rough Riders galore. The President wrote his uncle: "How I wish Father could have lived to see it too." It was a new style of inauguration—a Theodore Roosevelt kind of inauguration.

WILLIAM H. TAFT

Tomorrow I shall come into my office in my own right," said Theodore Roosevelt to a friend a day before his inauguration. "Then watch out for me!"

To watch out for him was not a simple task. Roosevelt was all over the place—his fingers were in every pie. He mediated between Russia and Japan; he intervened in the Moroccan crisis; he went to Panama to see how the building of the canal was progressing; he sent the fleet around the world, showing the country's naval strength to Japan; he was here, he was there, he was everywhere.

He had delightful quarrels with General Nelson A. Miles over the findings of a naval court of inquiry on the conduct of Admirals Schley and Sampson at the battle of Santiago; with Maria Longworth Storer, the wife of the American ambassador in Vienna, over making Archbishop Ireland a Cardinal; with Senator Joseph B. Foraker over the Negro troops' dismissals because of the Brownsville, Texas, shootings; with Edward H. Harriman, the railroad king, over a supposed deal for Chauncey Depew's appointment as Ambassador to France. He had controversies with Brander Matthews of Columbia University about simplified spelling; with W. J. Long, whom he called a "nature faker"; he made strong statements against Tolstoy, Gorky, Zola and other literary giants.

He hit the "malefactors of great wealth"; he crusaded against the trusts; he fought the railroads to regulate their rates; he advocated a meat-inspection bill and a pure-food law; and under his guidance a forest reserve for soil conservation was established. "Don't flinch, don't foul, hit the line hard" was his maxim.

With Roosevelt in the White House there was never a dull moment; he gave a good show; he used the Presidency as "a bully pulpit." An Englishman said the two most remarkable things he saw in the United States were "Niagara Falls and the President . . . both wonders of Nature."

If Roosevelt had wished another term in office, it was his for the asking. But his previous statement that "under no circumstances" would he become a candidate for renomination blocked his ambitions.

The question was: Who should become his successor? Who would continue his policies? Whom should he choose?

The names of Secretary of State Elihu Root, Supreme Court Justice Charles Hughes, Vice President Warren Fairbanks, Senator Robert La Follette, Speaker of the House "Uncle Joe" Cannon were mentioned, but in the end Roosevelt settled on that "Dear Old Fellow," his old friend—William Howard Taft.

Their friendship dated back to 1890, when both were at the beginning of their political careers in Washington, Roosevelt a Civil Service commissioner, Taft a Solicitor General.

As President, Roosevelt used Taft as his troubleshooter. When difficulties arose in any part of the earth, he sent Taft to smooth the troubled waters. And Taft, jovial and considerate, was "grabbing a time-table and throwing a change of clothing into a traveling bag," hurrying to the scene of the trouble, soon "making two laughs echo where one groan was heard before." Whether it was in Panama (to iron out construction obstacles) or Tokyo (to calm the excitement which

THE TAFTS WITH
THEIR SON ROBERT

491

CANDIDATES IN 1908

WILLIAM H. TAFT (1857–1930), a jovial 330-pound man with an infectious chuckle, Roosevelt's longtime friend and associate, his Secretary of War and diplomatic troubleshooter, was chosen by him to carry on his policies.

JAMES S. SHERMAN (1855–1912), an archconservative lawyer, businessman, and banker from New York, served in the House of Representatives for two decades. He became Taft's running mate on the ticket.

WILLIAM J. BRYAN (1860–1925), who started his successful weekly, *The Commoner,* after his second presidential defeat in 1900, once more became the Democrats' choice. Taft won with 7,677,788 votes to Bryan's 6,407,982.

JOHN W. KERN (1849–1917), an Indiana lawyer and state senator, was twice Democratic candidate for Governor, losing both times. An intimate friend of William J. Bryan, he was named as his running mate.

EUGENE V. DEBS (1855–1926), Indiana-born spokesman for the labor movement, was the candidate of the Socialist party with the backing of many immigrants. In his third race for the Presidency, Debs got 420,890 votes.

EUGENE W. CHAFIN (1852–1920), an Illinois lawyer with an early interest in temperance and politics, left the Republicans to join the Prohibitionist party and received their nomination as candidate for the Presidency.

Library of Congress

THE TAFT COW, whom the family named Pauline, is grazing on the lawn of the State, War and Navy Building.

followed after California barred Japanese from American public schools and forbade them to own land in America) or Rome (to settle matters with the Vatican regarding the landholdings of Catholic friars in the Philippines) or China (to persuade the government to lift the boycott against American goods), Taft was there and brought back results.

His chuckle was called "one of our great American institutions"; his humanity grew into the country's diplomatic asset. He was fond of people and people liked him. "I think Taft has the most lovable personality I have ever come in contact with," said Roosevelt.

But Taft was not only a kindly soul and an efficient negotiator; he was also a good jurist and a good

Joseph Keppler, April 1907

"WHY DON'T YOU SPEAK FOR YOURSELF, THEODORE?" "John Alden" Roosevelt woos "Priscilla," the Republican party, urging her to choose his friend "Miles Standish" Taft.

In reality Roosevelt did not have to do much wooing. When he made up his mind that Taft would be his successor, nobody had the power to contradict him. At the convention Taft easily won the nomination on the very first ballot.

administrator, proving it as the first governor in the Philippines. And he had the presidential bug.

Ever since late in 1902, when Roosevelt first offered him an appointment on the Supreme Court, Taft had been in a quandary. He would have liked to accept it, as would have his mother, who said: "I do not want my son to be President. A place on the Supreme bench, where my boy would administer justice, is my ambition for him. His is a judicial mind and he loves the law." But Taft's wife and his brother were for larger game.

Thus Taft declined Roosevelt's Supreme Court offer with the lame excuse that he had to remain Governor of the Philippines, as "conditions here would make my withdrawal a violation of duty."

A few months later another seat became vacant on the Court, and Roosevelt again offered it to him: "Dear Will, I am awfully sorry, old man, but . . . I shall have to put you on the Supreme Court."

Once more Taft hesitated. He wrote the President: "I recognize a soldier's duty to obey orders, but I presume on our personal friendship to make one more appeal." So Roosevelt let him "stay where you are. I shall appoint someone else to the Court."

A year later—in the fall of 1903—the President planned to appoint Taft as Secretary of War. Taft, who had made good progress with "the little brown brother" in the Philippines, was tempted to return to Washington. To Mrs. Taft the new offer seemed better because

THE FAMILY OF THEODORE ROOSEVELT. "Home, wife, children," wrote Roosevelt to his eldest son, "they are what really count in life. I have heartily enjoyed many things: the Presidency, my success as a soldier, a writer, a big game hunter and explorer; but all of them put together are not for one moment to be weighed in the balance when compared with the joy I have known with your mother and all of you. . . . "

l. to r.: Quentin, Ethel, Kermit, Theodore, Jr., Archibald. Alice, Roosevelt's daughter by his first wife, was already married.

it was more in line with the kind of work "I wanted my husband to do, the kind of career I wanted for him and expected him to have, so I was glad there were few excuses for refusing to accept it open to him."

So the Tafts came home. Early in 1906, with another vacancy on the Supreme Court, the President asked him for the third time to take a seat on the bench. "It is a hard choice to make," Roosevelt wrote, "and you yourself have to make it. You have two alternatives

before you, each with uncertain possibilities, and you cannot feel sure that whichever you take, you will not afterwards feel that it would have been better if you had taken the other."

For well over three months Taft pondered about the call. His associates urged him to accept it, but again his wife and his brother counseled against it so he could be available when and if the nomination for the Presidency came. He must not set his sights too low.

HIS ELDEST DAUGHTER MARRIES.
Alice Roosevelt's wedding in the White House to Nicholas Longworth, Representative from Ohio, was the social event of the Capital's 1906 season.
Lorant, *The Life and Times of Theodore Roosevelt* (Doubled

THE REPUBLICAN NATIONAL CONVENTION at Chicago nominated William H. Taft on the first roll call.

CELEBRITIES AT THE CONVENTION. Charles P. Taft, the brother of the candidate, with Hiram W. Johnson.

ALONG THE WAY TO THE COLISEUM. The Knox Club, under gay umbrellas, marches to the convention hall.

Taft issued a cagey statement: "I am not seeking the presidential nomination," but added: "I am not foolish enough to say that in the improbable event that the opportunity to run for the great office of President were to come to me, I should decline it, for this would not be true." With this he made himself "available" for the nomination.

One morning in 1908 William Loeb, Jr., Roosevelt's secretary, importuned his boss that "we must have a candidate. If things continue to drift along as now, our friends may lose control."

The President's first choice was Elihu Root. He said that he "would rather see Elihu Root in the White House than any other man now possible. I would walk on my hands and knees from the White House to the Capitol to see Root made President. But I know it cannot be done. He couldn't be elected. There is too much opposition to him on account of his corporation connections." Root too was aware of his limitation; thus when Loeb brought him Roosevelt's offer, he replied: "Please tell the President that I appreciate deeply every word, but I cannot be a candidate. It would mean a fight in the convention and I could not be elected. I've thought it all out. Thank the President, but tell him I am not in the running."

So it had to be Taft. Roosevelt told Loeb: "See Taft and tell of our talk today—tell him all of it so that he will know my mind." Loeb carried the message that "the President has decided to declare for you." Taft was touched: "I must go over and thank Theodore." And when he did, Roosevelt patted his back: "Yes, Will. It's the thing to do."

When the Republican convention met in Chicago, the delegates had nothing more to do but to endorse Roosevelt's choice for his successor. Taft was taken on the first roll call with 702 votes against Philander C. Knox's 68 and Charles E. Hughes's 67.

But even though the delegates voted for Taft, they would rather have had Roosevelt. In an amusing convention letter, Seth Bullock wrote that all the delegates from the Western states were being branded with a circle T [Taft]; "they would only stand for a hair brand, however, and it will be necessary to have them counted quickly at the convention the 16th of June, for if they 'mill around' much the hair will shed off and disclose the Maltese Cross [Roosevelt's ranch in the West] brand burned into their hides by the people and there will be trouble about the ownership. The people want and will insist on the President holding his position for another term so you may expect many bad hours at Chicago."

He was right. When Henry Cabot Lodge, the convention's chairman, reached the passage in his speech that Roosevelt was "the best abused and the most popular

Bernard Partridge, in Punch, *London, June 17, 1908*

"SO THEY SHOULDN'T KNOW THE DIFFERENCE." Roosevelt tells Taft, his chosen successor: "There, there, Sonny, I've fixed you up so they won't know the difference between us." The problem was: Taft was no Roosevelt.

497

Photograph by Mrs. C. R. Miller, July 1908

THE DEMOCRATIC CONVENTION at Denver, where William Jennings Bryan was chosen for the third time.

Photograph by Mrs. C. R. Miller, July 1908

REPUBLICANS VISIT. Nicholas Longworth; H. B. Parker; Mrs. Medill McCormick; Corinne Robinson, Roosevelt's niece; and Alice Longworth, his eldest daughter.

Photograph by Mrs. C. R. Miller, July 1908

THE SPEAKER'S STAND at the Democratic convention: (1) Lewis Nixon of New York; (2) Judge Baker of California; (3) temporary chairman Bell; (4) permanent chairman Clayton; (5) Woodson, National Committee Secretary.

man in the United States today," the applause and cheering for the President kept on for forty-nine minutes. The delegates chanted: "Four—four—four years more," and the enthusiasm was such that Lodge became frightened that the convention was getting out of hand. "Anyone who attempts to use his name as a candidate for the Presidency impugns both his sincerity and his good faith," he cried out.

The anxious Mrs. Taft hoped that the cheers for her husband would last longer, "to get even for the scare that Roosevelt cheer of forty-nine minutes" had given her. Yet when Taft was nominated, the demonstration for him lasted for only twenty-nine minutes.

With the Republican ticket selected, the country turned its attention to the Democratic convention. Whom would they nominate? Their "safe and sane" candidate, Judge Parker, and their "safe and sane" platform of 1904 had brought them a greater defeat than ever before; the party had been "united on the wrong side."

Bryan looked like the logical candidate. He stressed the effort needed to take back his party to the "ethical question" by a "moral awakening." He spoke of "The Brotherhood of Man," and he went on to persuade his supporters to turn away from the materialism of the gilded age and "love one another instead of running riot after money. . . ."

His idea was to change men rather than institutions. For issues meant little in themselves—to work for free silver, for tariff reduction, for government regulation of the trusts was not the most important task; one must instead acknowledge that "The more freely you allow the people to rule, the more quickly will every abuse be remedied."

Bryan was ready to let another man take over the leadership of the party as long as his ideas were not given up. He put forth the names of Woodrow Wilson, George Gray, Governor John A. Johnson of Minnesota and Governor Joseph W. Folk of Missouri. But if they were not acceptable, he was ready to serve.

Governor Johnson, one of the leading candidates, had the backing of ex-President Cleveland; Tammany Hall too was sympathetic to him. Johnson promised that he would not be like Parker and "take nine baths a day in the Hudson and say the party was clean and let it go at that. If I am nominated I'll take Bryan into the campaign with me and he'll have to show his hand in every state."

Woodrow Wilson, another front name for the nomination, was convinced that he had "not a ghost of a chance" to wrest the nomination from Bryan, whom he thought "the most charming and lovable of men personally, but foolish and dangerous in his theoretical beliefs."

Tom Fleming, 1908
ONE OF THE RARE DEMOCRATIC CAMPAIGN POSTERS FOR WILLIAM JENNINGS BRYAN

"SALOME" BRYAN AND THE DEMOCRATIC PARTY, WHICH HAS "LOST ITS HEAD BUT NOT DEAD YET."

By June it was clear that it would be Bryan—two-thirds of the selected delegates were for him even though *The New York Times* said that the selection of Bryan would be a "national calamity" and suggested: "There should be no compromise. Let Bryan nominate himself upon a platform of hostility to the courts, hostility to popular interests, class legislation for labor, the income tax, popular election of senators, the initiative and referendum, confiscation, and all the other doctrines of Bryanite radicalism . . . [when he loses] people will exclaim 'Thank goodness there is an end to that.' "

Joseph Pulitzer, the publisher of the *World,* was for the Republican candidate, but he named sixteen men (a reminder of Bryan's 16-to-1 campaign) whom he

would rather see as the Democratic candidate.

But Bryan it was destined to be. As soon as the name of the "peerless leader" was mentioned in their Denver convention, the delegates screamed, paraded and danced in the aisles. The chant "Bryan! Bryan! Bryan! Bryan!" filled the air. Even Alice Roosevelt Longworth and Ruth Bryan Leavitt, who were in the galleries, waved their scarves as they cheered. For an hour and a half the wild scene went on. And when it came to voting, even this was settled in one ballot. Bryan became the nominee.

For the vice presidential nomination Bryan at first wanted an Easterner; but as a "good" Easterner was not available, the party turned to the Midwest and selected John W. Kern of Indiana, the twice-defeated

Cartoon by J. Campbell Cory

HYPNOTIST BRYAN TRIES TO WORK HIS SPELL ON UNCLE SAM BUT WITHOUT GREAT SUCCESS.

gubernatorial candidate of that state.

The Democratic platform bore the unmistakable mark of Bryan's hand; it was the fourth he had written. The introduction noted "increasing signs of an awakening throughout the country. . . . The conscience of the nation is now aroused to free the Government from the grip of those who have made it a business asset of the favor-seeking corporations. It must become again a people's government, and be administered in all its departments according to the Jeffersonian maxim, 'equal rights to all; special privileges to none.'"

There were not only sentiments of reform but also the feelings of a party which had not gained the Presidency since Cleveland. The rise in Government expenditures and the increase in the number of Federal officeholders were bemoaned. The "absolute domination" of the Republican Speaker of the House was criticized. A passing gibe about Taft was made on the repugnancy of a "forced succession to the Presidency" of a Cabinet officer.

One plank asked that campaign contributions be cleaned up to terminate "the partnership which has existed between corporations of the country and the Republican party under the expressed or implied agreement that in return for the contribution of great sums of money wherewith to purchase elections, they should be allowed to continue substantially unmolested in their efforts to encroach upon the rights of the people."

Others demanded Federal and state controls of interstate commerce and railroads, a lower tariff, legislation

Photograph by George Grantham Bain in 1909
CONTRAST IN PERSONALITIES: WILLIAM HOWARD TAFT, THE EASYGOING REPUBLICAN CANDIDATE.

against the trusts, guarantees for bank funds, an income tax, the eight-hour day in Government work, adding a Department of Labor to the Cabinet, changes in laws relating to labor unions, the direct election of Senators, conservation measures and such progressive proposals.

But the "overshadowing issue" which tied together the Democratic plans was "Shall the people rule?" This was the cardinal point of Bryan's policies.

Next to the Republicans and Democrats, a list of minor parties offered candidates. The Populists nominated Thomas E. Watson; the Socialists named Eugene V. Debs; the Socialist-Laborites at first selected Martin B. Preston, who was serving a term of twenty-five

years' imprisonment in the Nevada State Prison; after he was declared ineligible, he was replaced with August Gilhaus. The Prohibitionists selected Eugene W. Chafin; the Independent party (the outgrowth of Hearst's Independent League) was behind Thomas L. Hisgen.

Neither Taft nor Bryan hoped for a prolonged campaign. Bryan would have liked to stay at home and make "front-porch" speeches; Taft too was against traveling and soliciting votes. But as the contest went into gear, they were forced to change their minds and go to the hustings. Roosevelt advised Taft: "Hit them hard, old man! Let the audience see you smile always,

Photograph July 3, 1908

CONTRAST IN PERSONALITIES: WILLIAM JENNINGS BRYAN, THE FIERY DEMOCRATIC CANDIDATE.

because I feel that your nature shines out so transparently when you do smile—you big, generous, high-minded fellow. Moreover let them realize the truth, which is that for all your gentleness and kindliness and generous good nature there never existed a man who was a better fighter when the need arose."

Taft denounced the Democratic platform and predicted a "devastating panic" if Bryan were elected. Still, there were great similarities in the beliefs of the two candidates. Taft was against the trusts, as was Bryan. Bryan was for a graduated income tax and the direct election of Senators, as was Taft. Thus Bryan spoke on the tariff, on guaranteeing bank deposits, on

the control of campaign contributions, on the labor issue and on the limits of government. A statement that "Justice requires that each individual shall receive from society a reward proportionate to his contribution to society" had subjected Bryan to fire from the Socialists, who believed in the ideal of "From each according to his ability, to each according to his needs."

He began his campaign with an article in _Collier's_ on "My Conception of the Presidency." He set aside the profits from _The Commoner_ for the party and launched a plan to raise money by single subscriptions of a dollar each so that the people could participate with him.

He found no overriding issue like that of free silver

Drawing by William Allan Rogers, May 1908

"FORWARD MARCH!"—Democrat Bryan walks the road of Radicalism; his party takes the path of Conservatism.

William Allan Rogers, February 1908

"THE TWICE-BELTED KNIGHT." Bandaged from previous defeats, Bryan sets out on the Democratic donkey.

in 1896 and anti-imperialism in 1900. There was only the general concern of "Whether the government shall remain a mere business asset of favor-seeking corporations, or be an instrument in the hands of the people for the advancement of the common weal."

Wherever he spoke large audiences turned out to hear him. His wife left a vivid description of such a meeting: "Near the car and at the edge of the crowd stood a thin faced woman with hands clasped convulsively and an expression of the most rapt attention. If she were standing in the presence of Christ she could not have been more worshipful. It made a tear or two drop when I watched her."

Mrs. Bryan observed larger crowds than she had seen before and that "the same types that I have noticed for twelve years are still extant. The long whiskered man who opens his mouth very wide and literally drinks in the speech; the long necked woman, with a small knot of hair and one tooth who waves her apron and shouts; the fond father insisting that his little son shake hands with the candidate; the oldest inhabitant . . . his quavering voice saying he voted first for Andrew Jackson and had never scratched a ticket since—these are here—I welcome them as old friends. . . . In 1896 there was an enthusiasm approaching

frenzy. I have seen men weep and tremble as they grasped [Bryan's] hand. Horny handed men have gripped my hand and breathing hard with suppressed feeling have bade me 'Take good care of him. God has raised him for this work.' In '96, too, there was a large element of good natured curiosity. Now the people are quiet and most attentive. They shout less and apparently think more."

At first it seemed that Bryan might succeed. Roosevelt sent letters to prod Taft. He told him to be less conspicuous in playing golf, and " . . . you ought to be on the stump but only speak *once* or *twice* in each state you visit. Do not answer Bryan; *attack* him. Don't let him make the issues. And never *define* your religious belief! I don't believe you had best say a word about it." Taft wrote back. "I have your letter . . . and if anything can elect me, I believe this letter can."

As Roosevelt's letter hints, Taft was the subject of a minor whispering campaign because he was a Unitarian. Some believed that anyone professing a religion which did not acknowledge the divinity of Christ should not be President. Bryan's religious feeling, which was deep, was sometimes ridiculed—in his Prince of Peace speech he had said that "until you can explain a watermelon do not be too sure that you can set limits to

Bernard Partridge, in Punch, *November 11, 1908*

"ALONE I DIDN'T DO IT." AN ENGLISH CARTOON OF THE AMERICAN PRESIDENTIAL CONTEST

MARCH 4, 1909: ROOSEVELT AND HIS SUCCESSOR

AFTER THE CEREMONIES, which because of inclement weather were held in the Senate Chamber, Taft walks between the throngs of well-wishers to his waiting carriage.

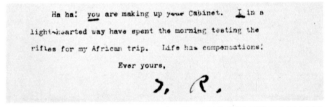

Ha ha! you are making up your Cabinet. I in a light-hearted way have spent the morning testing the rifles for my African trip. Life has compensations!

Ever yours,

T. R.

ROOSEVELT SENT THIS FAREWELL NOTE TO TAFT.

the power of the Almighty."

While Taft had the support of the business community, Bryan courted it. A group of businessmen told him that New York would go for him if he promised to name "safe" justices to any vacancies which might arise on the Supreme Court. Bryan replied that he was not in a mood for deals.

During the last days of the campaign, Bryan stumped New York. In a large rally at Madison Square Garden, he attacked Taft and the Republicans vigorously: "They may be able to defeat me, but they cannot cheat me of the credit that will accord me of giving an impetus to honest politics."

As both multi-millionaires Carnegie and Rockefeller came out for Taft, Bryan hoped this would help his vote in upstate New York. He said: "Mr. Rockefeller's corporation is the most notorious lawbreaker in the United States and he is for Taft because he does not want the law enforced."

At home, waiting for the results, he was in a reminiscent mood and he summed up his eighteen years in politics: "I have helped create a sentiment in favor of

THE WORST INAUGURAL DAY EVER. The capital was beset by snow, sleet and rain. "Even the elements do protest," said Taft as he left the White House. And Theodore Roosevelt replied: "I knew there would be a blizzard when I went out." Taft came back: "You're wrong; it's my storm, I always said it would be a cold day when I got to be President of the United States." But by the afternoon the skies had cleared and President and Mrs. Taft could drive in an open carriage.

politics: "I have helped create a sentiment in favor of reform, and as a candidate I have had but one thing to rely upon, the confidence of the masses in my fidelity to their interests. I've outlived the detraction of my foes."

The Republicans won, 7,677,788 to 6,407,982. Taft polled some 50,000 more votes than Roosevelt four years before; Bryan gained 1,323,000 over Parker.

The Democrats had hoped to carry the entire South and the West, but failed. The two strongest minor candidates, were Chafin with 252,511 votes, and Debs with 420,890. The electoral vote stood at 321 for William

Howard Taft and 162 for William Jennings Bryan.

Inauguration day was beset by heavy snow, sleet and rain. Because the weather was so foul, the ceremonies were held in the Senate chamber. After the oath-taking, Theodore Roosevelt drove to the railroad station and boarded a train for Oyster Bay, leaving the scene to his successor. He was in high spirits and in anticipation of his African trip, "the realization of a golden dream." Taft said to his friend: "Even the elements do protest," and Roosevelt replied: "I knew there would be a blizzard when I went out."

WOODROW WILSON

At the time Roosevelt left for Africa in his search for the "great adventure," there was no shadow over his friendship for Taft. Rumors of a rift between them had no foundation. "People have attempted to represent that you and I were in some way at odds during this last three months," wrote Taft to Roosevelt a few weeks before his inauguration, "whereas you and I know that there has not been the slightest difference between us." But gossipy Washington talked of a letter in which Taft wrote that he owed the Presidency to his brother Charley, and he was accused of ingratitude toward Roosevelt. But what Taft wrote was: "You and my brother Charley made my nomination and election possible."

Roosevelt left the country with full confidence in his successor, and trusting that his policies would be followed. It was not long before he found that Taft was a vacillating President he had no gift for leadership, he was not holding strong to Roosevelt's policies.

The country too felt let down; the air was out of the balloon. Gone were the dramatic quarrels of the Roosevelt days, gone were the exciting news and the amusing phrases—under Taft life had no glamour. Though his administration passed many good laws, his failures were more noticeable than his achievements. Soon he and the Progressive Republicans were feuding.

Their first rift came over the tariff. Taft not only upheld the Payne-Aldrich Bill, a highly protective measure, but defended it as "the best bill the Republican party ever passed." The Progressives were of another opinion. The schism widened when Taft removed Chief Forester Gifford Pinchot, a friend of Roosevelt's, after Pinchot quarreled with the Secretary of the Interior over conservation. And when Taft sided with "Uncle Joe" Cannon, the ultraconservative Speaker of the House, the open break between President and Progressives could no longer be avoided. For the Progressives, Taft had abandoned the Roosevelt line.

With the party factions at sixes and sevens, Republican midterm prospects looked gloomy. Roosevelt was still abroad visiting the capitals of Europe, lecturing, receiving the Nobel Peace Prize and representing the United States at King Edward's funeral. By June 1910 he was on his way home. Before he left England, a letter from Taft reached him, and what a pathetic letter it was. "It is now a year and three months since I assumed office and I have had a hard time," wrote Taft. "I do not know that I have had harder luck than other Presidents, but I do know that thus far I have succeeded far less than have others. I have been conscientiously trying to carry out your policies but my method of doing so has not worked smoothly."

Taft reviewed his achievements, sounding like a schoolboy trying to tell his teacher that he *had* learned his lesson. He assured Roosevelt the tariff bill was "not as radical a change as I favored, but still a change for the better"; he asserted that the tax on corporations would provide "a useful means of discovering and supervising the affairs of our corporations"; he reported that Arizona and New Mexico—the last two of the continental states—would be admitted to the Union; and he boasted that the chief conservation measures would soon become law. But Taft also complained about the insurgent Senators from the Midwest who

CANDIDATES IN 1912

WOODROW WILSON
(1856–1924), Governor of New Jersey whose academic reforms while president of Princeton University brought him public acclaim, became the Democratic candidate after Bryan switched to him.

THOMAS R. MARSHALL
(1854–1925), the successful reform Governor of Indiana, was the Democrats' choice for the Vice Presidency. An apt phrasemaker, his "What this country needs is a really good five-cent cigar" is a byword.

WILLIAM H. TAFT
(1857–1930), the outgoing President, was the candidate of the regular Republicans. In a freewheeling contest with Roosevelt, his former friend and now his enemy, Taft lost, receiving only 3,484,956 votes.

JAMES S. SHERMAN
(1855–1912), lawyer, Mayor of Utica and Congressman from New York, became the first Vice President to be renominated in the history of the Republican party; but he died before the election.

THEODORE ROOSEVELT
(1858–1919) broke away from his party and ran as the candidate of the Progressive —or Bull Moose—party, winning 4,119,507 votes. As he split the Republicans, the election went to Democrat Wilson.

HIRAM JOHNSON
(1866–1945), Governor of California, was Roosevelt's running mate on the Bull Moose ticket to "fight in honorable fashion for the good of mankind" and stand "at Armageddon and battle for the Lord."

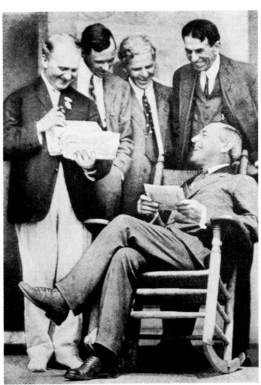

Lorant, The Presidency *(Macmillan)*
WILSON IS CONGRATULATED by reporters after his nomination. The man in white trousers is his secretary, Joseph P. Tumulty, who was instrumental in holding of press conferences.

"have done all in their power to defeat us." For the progressives, he did not begin to fill his predecessor's shoes.

Roosevelt felt "very uncomfortable" hearing about the internal party quarrels. He wrote Cabot Lodge that he was "anything but happy over the prospect of being at home," and added: "As for what you say about the American people looking to me for leadership, it is unfortunately preposterous, and makes me more uncomfortable than ever. That is why I got out of the country, and apparently I ought to have stayed out of the country even longer."

Boardman Robinson, in the New York Tribune, *February 22, 1912*

THE THIRD CUP OF TEA. Roosevelt calls out: "Hey waiter! Bring that over here. When I said I wouldn't take the third cup a little while ago, I only meant I wouldn't take it right on top of the other two." This is an allusion to his statement in 1905, when, heady about his victory at the polls, Roosevelt declared that he would not accept another term.

In other letters from abroad, he excused Taft's actions. "I am sincere when I say that I am not yet sure whether Taft could with wisdom have followed any course save the one he did," said Roosevelt. "The qualities shown by a thoroughly able and trustworthy lieutenant are totally different, or at least may be totally different, from those needed by the leader, the commander. Very possibly if Taft had tried to work in my spirit, and along my lines, he would have failed; that he has conscientiously tried to work for the objects I had in view, so far as he could approve them, I have no doubt."

Roosevelt still had hopes for Taft, saying, "there is at least a good chance that a reaction will come in his favor. Everyone believes him to be honest, and most believe him to be doing the best he knows how. I have noticed very little real personal abuse of him, or indeed attack upon him." But even so he was uneasy about the midterm elections. He smelled defeat. "The trouble is that the Cannon-Aldrich type of leadership down at bottom represents not more than, say, ten per cent of the rank and file of the party's voting strength," said Roosevelt; "but if the great mass—the ninety per cent

THE THIRD-TERM ISSUE

of the party—the men who stand for it as their fathers stood for it in the days of Lincoln, get convinced that the ten per cent are not leading them right, a revolt is sure to ensue." And he added: "Our own party leaders did not realize that I was able to hold the Republican party in power only because I insisted on a steady advance, and dragged them along with me."

Roosevelt hoped "that Taft will retrieve himself yet," but even if he failed to do so, "I most emphatically desire that I shall not be put in the position of having to run for the Presidency, staggering under a load which I cannot carry, and which has been put on my shoulders through no fault of my own. Therefore my present feeling is that Taft should be the next nominee, because, if the people approve of what he has done, it is unfair to me to have to suffer the distrust which others have earned, and for which I am in no way responsible."

However, as soon as he set foot on American soil, his mind seemed to have changed. The insurgent Senators convinced him that only progressive leadership could avert defeat; thus he threw himself headlong into the political whirlpool, forgetting his past promises.

From August until election day he campaigned through the West and South to stem the tide against his party, but to no avail. The House went Democratic (228 Democrats against 161 Republicans); and while the Senate remained Republican, the Republican majority was not overwhelming (51 Republicans against 41 Democrats).

The defeat was proof to the insurgents that if Taft was renominated two years hence he would lose the election; thus they were looking for a better candidate. The newly formed National Progressive Republican League proposed Robert La Follette. Roosevelt, though friendly to the Wisconsin Senator, withheld his endorsement. He decided to wait and see.

He was still friendly to Taft. But when the administration instituted an antitrust suit against U.S. Steel (mainly because of its acquisition of the Tennessee Coal and Iron Corporation in 1907), Roosevelt exploded. It was during his administration that he had approved the acquisition, and he recalled that at that time Taft had been "enthusiastic in praise" of the idea. Roosevelt felt that Taft was "playing small, mean and foolish politics." He became openly hostile.

Taft was bewildered. "If I only knew what the President wanted," he said to his aide, Archie Butt (he still called Roosevelt President), "I would do it, but you know that he has held himself so aloof that I am absolutely in the dark. I am deeply wounded, and he gives me no chance to explain my attitude or learn his." For Taft the motives of his former friend became a puzzle. "I don't know what he is driving at except to make my way more difficult," he said, and added that it was a very painful thing "to see a devoted friendship going to pieces like a rope of sand."

To save his party from defeat Roosevelt made up his mind to become a candidate. The movement for

Charles R. Macauley, in the New York World, *January 18, 1912*

STEALING THE NOMINATION: THE ROUGH RIDER AND THE PRESIDENT. Theodore Roosevelt, disappointed by President Taft's conservatism, was determined to challenge his former friend in the Republican convention. But the party machine behind Taft held firm. The bosses were strong enough to renominate Taft in spite of Roosevelt's ambitions.

"All Hail!" May 4, 1912

"Having a Bully Time," March 30, 1912

IN *HARPER'S WEEKLY* THEODORE ROOSEVELT WAS HARSHLY ASSAILED BY EDWARD W. KEMBLE,

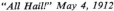

his nomination was already under way when a few progressive Governors issued a petition and called on him to lead the progressive forces.

Roosevelt declared, "My hat is in the ring," and he wrote to the Governors that "I will accept the nomination for President if it is tendered to me, and I will adhere to this decision until the convention has expressed its preference."

Taft went on the offensive. In an ill-conceived speech he lashed out against the men who "are seeking to pull down the pillars of the temple of freedom and representative government," calling them "political emotionalists or neurotics, who have lost that sense of proportion . . . which made our people . . . the greatest self-governing people that the world ever knew."

Now it was open war. The two former friends attacked each other with increasing bitterness. Roosevelt blamed Taft for yielding to "the bosses and to the great privileged interests" and accused him of being "disloyal to every canon of ordinary decency," and Taft replied:

"I deny all of them. I do not want to fight Theodore Roosevelt, but sometimes a man in a corner fights. I am going to fight." In another speech he said: "Condemn me if you will, but condemn me by other witnesses than Theodore Roosevelt. I was a man of straw; but I have been a man of straw long enough. Every man who has blood in his body, and who has been misrepresented as I have . . . is forced to fight."

Roosevelt entered the primaries and challenged Taft to do likewise. The climax of the preconvention battle was in Ohio—Taft's home state—where the two contenders met head on. Within a single week Roosevelt made ninety speeches and covered 1,800 miles throughout the state. Taft too moved around trying to save what he could, but he could not stem Roosevelt's victory.

The result of the primaries was that Roosevelt won nine states against Taft's one and La Follette's two; 278 delegates were with Roosevelt, only 48 with Taft. But from the state party conventions Taft had about five hundred delegates, while Roosevelt could count on

"The Issue," March 23, 1912

"Down With the Bosses," June 1, 1912

WHO CARICATURED THE FORMER PRESIDENT AS A RECKLESS DESTROYER OF THE COUNTRY.

only half that number. Taft had the party with him.

Franklin P. Adams satirized the battle of the two former friends:

> *Or ever the knightly fight was on,*
> *The skirmish of smear and smudge,*
> *I was a king in Washington*
> *And you were a circuit judge.*
>
> *I saw, I took, I made you great,*
> *Friendly, I called you "Will."*
> *And back in Nineteen Hundred and Eight,*
> *Out in Chicago, Ill.,*
> *I made the convention nominate,*
> *And now—the terrible chill.*
>
> *For many a sun has set and shone*
> *On the path we used to trudge,*
> *When I was a king in Washington*
> *And you were a circuit judge.*

> *I passed the lie and you passed it back,*
> *You said I was all untruth;*
> *I said that honesty was your lack,*
> *You said I'd nor reck nor ruth;*
> *You called me a megalomaniac,*
> *I called you a Serpent's Tooth. . . .*

With the struggle growing in bitterness, it was suggested that both of them withdraw in favor of a compromise candidate. But Roosevelt said: "I'll name the compromise candidate. He'll be me. I'll name the compromise platform. It will be our platform."

At the Republican convention in Chicago the Roosevelt men challenged the credentials of more than two hundred Taft delegates, but as the party machine was behind the President, the majority of the contested seats went to Taft. When it became evident that he would not be chosen, Roosevelt issued a statement "The people have spoken, and the politicians will be made to understand that they are the servants and not the masters of

Philadelphia North American, *April 12, 1912*
THE MEN OF EASTON, PA., WANT TO CARRY THEIR HERO ROOSEVELT ON THEIR SHOULDERS.

the rank and file of the plain citizens of the Republican party," he said, charging that "there is no form of rascality which the Taft men have not resorted to."

Each side hired detectives to stop the other from bribing delegates. Police squads were hired to guard against violence and barbed wire put around the rostrum.

This made the indomitable Mr. Dooley say: "I wint to bed last night thinkin' th' counthry was safe, so I put out th' cat, locked th' dure . . . an' pulled into th' siding f'r th' night. Whin I got up I had a feelin' that somethin' was burnin'. . . . But I cudden't find annything wrong till I opened up th' pa-apers an', much to me relief, found that it was not me pants but th' republic that was on fire. Yes, sir; th' republic is doomed to desthruction again."

The night before the balloting began, Roosevelt addressed a large meeting in another hall in Chicago. He told his listeners that Taft had surrendered to the machine and that many delegates were seated in the convention who had no right to be there. "What happens to me is not of the slightest consequence; I am to be used, as in a doubtful battle any man is used, to his hurt or not, so long as he is useful and is then cast aside and left to die. I wish you to feel this. I mean it; and I shall need no sympathy when you are through with me. . . . We fight in honorable fashion for the good of mankind; unheeding of our individual fates; with unflinching hearts and undimmed eyes; we stand at Armageddon, and we battle for the Lord." It was memorable, laying the foundation for a third party.

THE TWO FORMER FRIENDS, OR, WHEN AN IRRESISTIBLE FORCE MEETS AN IMMOVABLE OBJECT

Next day the Republicans named Elihu Root as permanent chairman of their convention, with 558 votes against 501 for McGovern, the candidate of the Roosevelt faction. The Roosevelt men in the galleries demonstrated against the steam-rolling party machine. Every time Root spoke, the shout went up, "Toot, toot! Toot, toot!" and they rubbed sheets of sandpaper together, imitating the noise of a steamroller.

Wild rumors made the rounds. It was said that Roosevelt would come with a faithful group of men and take possession of the convention building at three o'clock in the morning so Taft could not be chosen. Roosevelt had no such plans. At two o'clock in the morning of June 20, after the credentials committee had endorsed the disputed Taft delegates, he said: "So far as I am concerned, I am through. I went before the people and I won. . . ." And he challenged: "Let us find out whether the Republican party is the party of the plain people . . . or the party of the bosses and the professional radicals acting in the interests of special privilege."

Two days later the convention officially nominated Taft with 561 votes to Roosevelt's 107. But Taft's victory was not as large as the figures indicate. The majority of the Roosevelt delegates—344 in all—refrained from voting.

In a separate meeting the Roosevelt supporters cheered: "We will follow Roosevelt, Follow! Follow! Anywhere! Everywhere! We will follow on!" And Roosevelt told them: "If you wish me to make the fight, I will make it, even if only one state should support me."

"His Back to the Wall," New York World, *June 3, 1912*

"The Voice of the People," New York World, *June 7, 1912*

AT THE TIME OF THE REPUBLICAN CONVENTION ROOSEVELT WAS LAMPOONED BY CHARLES R.
In the convention the Roosevelt forces contested 254 seats—about one-third of the total. The National Committee awarded them only 19. Roosevelt's supporters were in a turmoil. Should the credentials committee accept the National Committee's decision, Roosevelt could not be nominated. Mr. Dooley, the creation of the humorist Finley P. Dunne,

The party was irrevocably split; the Roosevelt group had broken away from the regular Republican organization. Whether it meant the formation of a new party was not yet clear. But a few weeks later, when financial support was assured, delegates of the Progressive party met in Chicago in a nominating convention. They sang "Onward, Christian Soldiers" and the "Battle Hymn of the Republic" and infused their meeting with a religious fervor. Roosevelt, who told reporters that he was feeling "as strong as a bull moose," addressed the twenty thousand who had chosen him as their candidate. He called the two parties, the Republicans and the Democrats, "husks, with no real soul within either, divided on artificial lines, boss-ridden and privilege-controlled . . ."

The platform of the new party asked for regulation of the trusts and development of agricultural credit; it endorsed the direct primary, women's suffrage, a downward tariff revision, better working conditions in the factories, minimum-wage standards and an eight-hour day.

With the Republicans divided, the Democrats were

certain of victory even though they had no overwhelming favorite—no potential candidate with the following of a Bryan (who had already lost three times). Champ Clark of Missouri, the Speaker of the House, was backed by newspaper publisher William Randolph Hearst. Alabama's Oscar W. Underwood, chairman of the House Ways and Means committee, had a sizable following, but Alabama was too deep in the South. Governor Judson Harmon of Ohio was the candidate of the conservatives, while Governors Thomas R. Marshall of Indiana and Simeon E. Baldwin of Connecticut ran as favorite sons.

The strongest contender for the nomination was Woodrow Wilson, the Governor of New Jersey—the scholar-politician. He began his career as a professor of American history and political science. In 1902 he was appointed president of Princeton University, and his fight for academic reform earned him national attention. Colonel George Harvey, the publisher of *Harper's Weekly,* helped keep him in the public eye. In 1910 Harvey persuaded the political boss of New Jersey,

"The Machine Gun," New York World, June 14, 1912

"A Perfectly Corking Time," New York World, June 21, 1912

MACAULEY. ALL THESE CARTOONS APPEARED IN THE N.Y. *WORLD* IN THE OPENING DAYS OF JUNE. predicted the convention would be "a combynation iv th' Chicago fire, St. Bartholomew's massacree, the battle iv th' Boyne, the life iv Jessie James, an' th' night iv th' big wind." When his chum Hennessy asked if he was going, Dooley replied: "Iv course I'm goin'!! I haven't missed a riot in this neighborhood in forty years . . ."

James Smith, to let Wilson run for Governor. To the boss's amazement, Wilson won easily and even helped carry the state assembly for the Democrats.

Once in office, Wilson was his own man. The party hacks had to back down; New Jersey was reformed.

In March 1911, he presented himself to the Western states, where he won the hearts of the progressives by attacking "money Power" and "Wall Street," and by calling for direct primaries and the initiative, recall and referendum. The bosses and the conservative Democrats were appalled—Wilson was hardly a "safe and sane" candidate; in fact, he seemed to be "Bryanizing."

In the Democratic convention meeting in Baltimore, Alton B. Parker, the party's standard-bearer of 1904, was chosen as temporary chairman. The incensed Bryan submitted a resolution to oppose "the nomination of any candidate for President who is the representative of or under any obligation to J. Pierpont Morgan, Thomas F. Ryan, August Belmont, or any other member of the privilege-hunting and favor-seeking class." But when he demanded that any *delegate* who represented

those men should withdraw, the delegates demurred. Then Bryan withdrew the last part of his resolution in return for having the first endorsed.

As the voting began, Clark was in the lead. On the first ballot he received 440½ votes against Wilson's 324. The other votes were scattered between Harmon (148), Underwood (117¼), Marshall (31) and the rest. The next few ballots showed little change, but on the tenth Tammany Hall switched its ninety votes from Harmon to Clark, giving him the majority. It seemed that he would be able to get the necessary two-thirds.

Wilson told William McCombs, his manager, to release his delegates, but McCombs would not listen. He persuaded the Underwood delegates to stand firm and not allow a landslide for Clark; thus the balloting continued.

Bryan, angry at Tammany's switch to Clark, bore down on his state's delegation, urging it to change to Wilson. He rose to explain the change. He said that Nebraska would not back anyone "willing to violate the resolution . . . and to accept the high honor of

BRYAN WEIGHS IN
THE DEMOCRATIC CANDIDATES
Drawn by Edward W. Kemble, January 1912

The Newark (N.J.) Advertiser

THE WILSON FAMILY. There were three daughters: Margaret (born 1886, died 1944), Jessie (born 1887, married to Francis Bowes Sayre in 1913, died 1933) and Eleanor (born 1889, married to William G. McAdoo in 1914, died 1967).

the presidential nomination at the hands of Mr. Murphy." After the speech, Wilson's vote rose gradually until on the forty-sixth ballot he had the two-thirds endorsement. As Underwood refused it, the vice presidential nomination went to Thomas R. Marshall.

The campaign was largely a contest of personalities, a three-cornered fight between the placid Taft, the crusading Roosevelt and the rational Wilson. The fourth candidate, Eugene V. Debs, the nominee of the

Socialists, was on his own, attracting large crowds.

Taft told reporters: "I have been told that I ought to do this, ought to do that . . . that I do not keep myself in the headlines. I know it, but I can't do it. I couldn't if I would, and I wouldn't if I could." The shape of the campaign left him discouraged. He wrote his wife: "Sometimes I think I might as well give up so far as being a candidate is concerned. There are so many people in the country who don't like me. Without

Edward W. Kemble, July 1912
THE LATEST ARRIVAL AT THE POLITICAL ZOO

Roosevelt and Johnson

*"For there is neither East nor West,
Border nor Breed nor Birth,
When two strong men stand face to face
Though they come from the ends of the earth."*
—Kipling

Author's Collection
THE POSTER OF THE PROGRESSIVE CANDIDATES

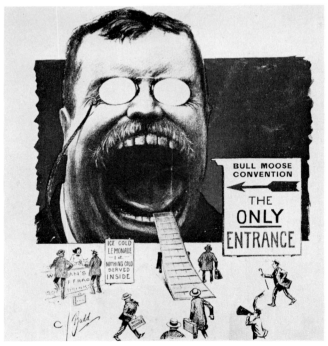

Charles J. Budd, August 1912
ROOSEVELT, THE BULL MOOSE CANDIDATE

knowing much about me, they don't like me—apparently on the Dr. Fell principle . . . they don't exactly know the reason but it is on the principle:

> *'I don't like you Dr. Fell,
> The reason why I cannot tell,*
>
> *'But this I know and know full well,
> I don't like you, Dr. Fell.' "*

Taft's strongest words were reserved for Roosevelt, but at first he did not attack him in public. He could, though, easily write that it was hard to think of Roosevelt "as the fakir, the juggler, the green goods man, the gold brickman that he has come to be. He is to be classed with the leaders of religious cults who promote things over their followers by any sort of physical [psychical] manipulation and deception. He is seeking to make his followers 'Holy Rollers.' "

ROOSEVELT, WHO EXCLAIMED THAT HE WAS AS "FIT AS A BULL MOOSE," ON THE BACK OF HIS ANIMAL.

In his acceptance speech Taft stressed the need for pursuing a constitutional form of government and protecting the exploited classes by "positive law." He explained: "It has been suggested that under our Constitution, such tendency to so-called paternalism was impossible. Nothing is further from the fact. . . . The Republican party stands for the Constitution as it is, with such amendments adapted according to its provisions as new conditions thoroughly understood may require." But what he said was weak compared to Wilson's New Freedom and Roosevelt's New Nationalism.

Roosevelt was a master at catching the headlines. He coined phrases, he attacked his opponents vigorously, he made interesting copy. When Bryan charged that he had stolen his Bull Moose ideas from the Democrats, Roosevelt replied: "So I have. That is quite true. I have taken every one of them except those suited for the inmates of lunatic asylums."

He outlined a program of New Nationalism to create harmony among the workingmen, the farmers and the businessmen. The government would balance the conflicting claims of these groups so that the nation's wealth would be equitably shared. He was scornful of those who tried to enrich themselves at the expense of the country. To him the conservative was as much to be feared as the radical demagogue. But the trusts were not necessarily evil, especially if they could be kept under control. He said: "We are face to face with new conceptions of the relations of property to human welfare"; property is "subject to the general right of the community to regulate its use to whatever degree the public welfare may require it." He would not destroy the trusts; he would regulate them through reforms: fair wages for the workers, including women; child-labor laws; Federal mediation of labor disputes; and a governmental health program.

Wilson realized early in the campaign that his real opponent was Roosevelt and not Taft. "I feel that

P. J. Press Bureau, Philadelphia, July 1912
WILSON promised a New Freedom through tariff reform, regulation of the trusts and a series of new laws for labor.

Lorant, The Life and Times of Theodore Roosevelt (*Doubleday*)
TAFT campaigned little, feeling he should quit: "There are so many people in the country who don't like me."

ROOSEVELT campaigned strenuously to appeal to independents and Democrats. He vied with Wilson to be the

spearhead of the reformers. He felt he could beat Taft, but not Wilson—thus his speeches were, according to the New York *Evening Post*, like those "Custer might have made to his scouts when he saw the Indians coming."

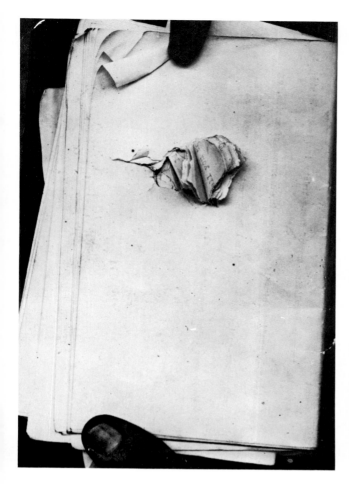

Theodore Roosevelt Association

ROOSEVELT'S MANUSCRIPT and his bloody shirt after an attempt was made on his life at Milwaukee. John Schrank, the assassin, confessed he tried to kill Roosevelt because the late President McKinley appeared in his dreams and ordered him to do so. "Let it be the right and duty of every citizen to forcibly remove a third-termer," he said. Fortunately Roosevelt recovered from the wound; his eyeglasses case and the manuscript in his pocket saved him.

Roosevelt's strength is altogether incalculable. The contest is between him and me, not between Taft and me. I think Taft will run third,—at any rate in the popular, if not in the electoral vote. The country will have none of him. But just what will happen, as between Roosevelt and me, with party lines utterly confused and broken, is all guesswork. It depends upon what the people are thinking and purposing whose opinions do not get into the newspapers,—and I am by no means confident. He appeals to their imagination; I do not. He is a real, vivid person, whom they have seen and shouted themselves hoarse over and voted for, millions strong; I am a vague, conjectural personality, more made up of opinions and academic prepossessions than of human traits and red corpuscles. We shall see what will happen!"

Josephus Daniels managed Wilson's publicity bureau, and the blind Senator Gore took charge of his campaign organization. There was an appeal made for "100,000 earnest citizens to contribute each one honest dollar," and when the response was too moderate, some of the usual sources had to be tapped.

Wilson had stressed the need for tariff reform before the convention, but it was by now a tired issue. He knew the problem of the trusts should be his major issue, but he was not certain how to approach it. He found the inspiration one afternoon in August during a long talk with Louis Brandeis, the young progressive lawyer.

Brandeis was well acquainted with the monopoly question. Though there is no record transcript of their conversation, it seems likely that Brandeis's later memo to Wilson merely elaborated on the same points. He explained that "The Democratic Party insists that competition can be and should be maintained in every branch of private industry; that competition can be and

Lorant: The Life and Times of Theodore Roosevelt (*Doubleday*)
BULL MOOSE CANDIDATE ROOSEVELT CASTS HIS VOTE AT AN OYSTER BAY POLLING PLACE.

AT PROGRESSIVE HEADQUARTERS. Lillian Russell, the darling of the stage, and her publisher husband Alexander Moore at the Chicago office of the Bull Moose party.

should be restored in those branches of industry in which it has been suppressed by the trusts; and that, if at any future time monopoly should appear to be desirable in any branch of industry, the monopoly should be a public one—a monopoly owned by the people and not by the capitalists. The New Party, on the other hand, insists that private monopoly may be desirable in some branches of industry, or at all events, is inevitable; and that existing trusts should not be dismembered or forcibly dislodged from those branches of industry in which they have already acquired a monopoly, but should be made 'good' by regulation. In other words, the New Party declares that private monopoly in industry is not necessarily evil, but may do evil; and that legislation should be limited to such laws and regulations as should attempt merely to prevent the

R. M. Brinkerhoff, in Harper's Weekly, September 28, 1912

AN ANXIOUS MOMENT: EENIE, MEENY, MINY MOE . . . UNCLE SAM MAKES HIS DECISION.

doing of evil. The New Party does not fear commercial power, however great, if only methods for regulation are provided. We believe that no methods of regulation ever have been or can be devised to remove the menace inherent in private monopoly and overweening commercial power." Brandeis went on to summarize: "This difference in the economic policy of the two parties is fundamental and irreconcilable. It is the difference between industrial liberty and industrial absolutism, tempered by governmental (that is, party) supervision."

Wilson assimilated these new ideas with his earlier views and worked them into vibrant speeches. In his first major address, he spoke to 10,00 workers in Buffalo, saying: "And what has created these monopolies? Unregulated competition. It has permitted these men to do anything they choose to do to squeeze their rivals

out and crush their rivals to the earth. We know the processes by which they have done those things. We can prevent these processes through remedial legislation, and so restrict the wrong use of competition that the right use of competition will destroy monopoly. Ours is a programme of liberty; theirs is a programme of regulation. I want you working men to grasp that point because I want to say to you right now that the programme I propose does not look quite so much like acting as a Providence for you as the other programme looks. . . . If you want a great struggle for liberty, that will cost you blood, adopt the Roosevelt regulation programme, put yourself at the disposal of a Providence resident at Washington and then see what will come of it."

Wilson traveled widely and asked the voters to give

529

him a Democratic Congress so that he could enact his progressive legislation. His theme was always the same: "Every form of special privilege and private control must cease. . . . Private control of politics . . . bosses and the machine must go. . . . Private interests, special favors, must not be encouraged by the government." And at another gathering, he said his was a "crusade against powers that have governed us—that have limited our development—that have determined our lives—that have set us in a straitjacket to do as they please. . . . This is a second struggle for emancipation . . . if America is not to have free enterprise, then she can have freedom of no sort whatever."

As a campaigner, Wilson could not match Roosevelt. He was not a glad-hander; he could not bring himself to slap backs or kiss babies; he admitted that his "Presbyterian face" photographed badly; he disliked the glib generalities implicit in whistle-stop oratory. But what his speeches lacked in bombast they more than made up in sense, and his doctrine of the New Freedom held out a hope of an orderly program of reform which would make the government responsible to public

opinion and would guarantee freedom from economic exploitation without recourse to radicalism.

On October 14, as Roosevelt was leaving his Milwaukee hotel to make an address, he was shot by an anti-third-term fanatic. Yet he insisted on going to the auditorium. Two doctors came up from the audience, but the Colonel would not let them examine him: "You just stay where you are! I am going to make this speech and you might as well compose yourself." Again they tried to stop him from speaking. He waved them away. "Get an ambulance or a carriage or anything you like at ten o'clock and I'll go to the hospital, but I won't go until I have finished my speech."

As he went out on the stage a reporter in the audience wrote: "The colonel smiled and waved his hand and the men and women stood up on their seats and cried and shouted their sympathy and affection." Roosevelt pulled out his manuscript from his coat pocket. It was soaked with blood. "Some shouted, some cried, men and women, some silently, some audibly prayed. . . ."

He began in a dramatic manner: "I am going to ask you to be very quiet and please excuse me from making

AND WHEN THE CONTEST WAS OVER, ROOSEVELT'S HOPES WERE SHATTERED.

Edward W. Kemble, November 1912
BOTH ELEPHANT AND MOOSE ARE BATTERED.

Charles R. Macauley, December 1912
THE BULL MOOSE CANDIDATE SEES A MIRAGE.

FOR PRESIDENT

BULL MOOSE
PARTY

Humpty Dumpty sat on the wall.
Humpty Dumpty had a bad fall.
All the ex-bosses
And Bully Moose men,
Can never put Humpty up again.

Kemble

Edward W. Kemble, November 1912

AFTER WILSON WAS ELECTED. The splitting of the vote cost the Republicans the election. Even though Roosevelt received 4,119,507 votes, against Taft's 3,484,956, Wilson amassed 6,293,019 votes, to become the first Democratic President in sixteen years. Roosevelt said: "The fight is over. We are beaten. There is only one thing to do and that is to go back to the Republican party. You can't hold a party like the Progressive party together . . . there are no loaves and fishes."

Lorant: The Presidency (*Macmillan*)
PRESIDENT TAFT AND PRESIDENT-ELECT WILSON LEAVE FOR THE INAUGURAL CEREMONIES.

a long speech. I'll do the best I can, but there is a bullet in my body." It was one of the great moments of his life, and he played his part to the hilt. "I have a message to deliver," he whispered, "and will deliver it as long as there is life in my body."

The audience was under his spell. "I have had an A-1 time in life and I am having it now," Roosevelt kept on, charging that "it was a very natural thing that weak and vicious minds should be inflamed to acts of violence by the kind of awful mendacity and abuse that have been heaped upon me for the last three months . . ." For an hour and a half he held the platform.

Later the X rays showed that his wound was superficial. A surgeon commented with awe: "It is largely due to the fact that he is a physical marvel that he was

not dangerously wounded. He is one of the most powerful men I have ever seen laid on an operating table. The bullet lodged in the massive muscles of the chest instead of penetrating the lung."

In the election Wilson carried forty out of the forty-eight states with 6,283,019 votes to Roosevelt's 4,119,-507 and Taft's 3,484,956. When his students from Princeton came to congratulate him on the night of the election, Wilson told them: "I myself have no feeling of triumph tonight. I have a feeling of solemn responsibility." And Roosevelt said: "The fight is over. We are beaten. There is only one thing to do and that is to go back to the Republican party. You can't hold a party like the Progressive party together. . . . There are no loaves and fishes."

WILSON'S INAUGURATION
On the left, above the flowers, Bryan, Josephus Daniels and Archie Butt (in uniform) on the right, Vice President Marshall.

WOODROW WILSON

In his first inaugural Wilson listed "the things that ought to be altered." He castigated the "tariff which cuts us off from our proper part in the commerce of the world . . . and makes the government a facile instrument in the hands of private interest"; he spoke of the banking and currency system which needed overhauling; he attacked the "industrial system which, take it on all sides, financial as well as administrative, holds capital in leading strings, restricts the liberties and limits the opportunities of labor, and exploits without renewing or conserving the natural resources of the country." He asked for reforms in agriculture and pleaded for effective conservation and irrigation measures. The program he presented was an ambitious one to be accomplished within the framework of the existing social order.

A month after his inauguration the new President went to Congress to deliver his message. Over a century had passed since the Chief Magistrate had appeared in person before the assembled body of both houses. Ever since Jefferson, who sent his messages in writing, it had become a tradition for Presidents to communicate with Congress through the written word. Wilson's departure from this tradition heralded a new era in politics. His message was a short one—newspapers could print it in its entirety on their front page. One of its statements found strong response. "We must abolish everything," said Wilson, "that bears even the semblance of privilege or any kind of artificial advantage."

The President united the Democrats in Congress behind him. He discussed pending legislation in party caucuses, seeking agreements on his policies. On occa-sion he went to the Capitol to confer on strategy or to "persuade" a recalcitrant legislator. Under his leadership the party lost its states' rights tradition and became one of progressive nationalism.

Most of Wilson's reform proposals were written into law. The Underwood-Simmons Tariff reduced the duties of the Payne-Aldrich Tariff. (One of the provisions of the new bill was the income tax—it was made constitutional through the adoption of the Sixteenth Amendment.) The Glass-Owen Federal Reserve Act set up a series of sectional banks, held together by a Federal Reserve Board. The Clayton Antitrust Act and the Federal Trade Commission Act were directed against the formation of monopolies and against the unfair practices of the big corporations.

Several bills were passed to ease the plight of labor. The first Secretary of Labor was appointed; the Keating-Owen Child Labor Bill forbade children under fourteen years from working in factories (a measure which the Supreme Court later found unconstitutional).

Agriculture was not neglected; the Smith-Lever Act provided that the Federal Government should contribute the same amount of money—dollar for dollar—as the states were ready to invest in the extension of agriculture. This "dollar-matching" bill was followed by the Federal Highways Act and many other measures carrying the dollar-matching principle not only into the field of road building but also into education.

All these laws touched on domestic issues. Foreign policy played such little part that in his first message to Congress, Wilson did not even mention it. At his first inauguration, a European war was a distant possibility;

CANDIDATES IN 1916

WOODROW WILSON (1856–1924) was renominated by the Democrats with the campaign slogan: "He kept us out of war." He received 9,129,606 votes against Hughes's 8,538,221, three million more votes than before.

THOMAS R. MARSHALL (1854–1925), a witty man, was a popular Vice President and the first to run for reelection since Calhoun. He was on the threshold of the Presidency from the moment of the President's first stroke.

CHARLES E. HUGHES (1862–1948), a professor of law and former Governor of New York, resigned as Justice of the Supreme Court to accept the Republican nomination. He was also backed by the rest of the Progressives.

CHARLES FAIRBANKS (1852–1918), Roosevelt's Vice President, had retained his control in Indiana politics and was practicing as a railway attorney when once more he became the Republican choice for the second place.

ALLAN L. BENSON (1871–1940), author and writer on politics and economics for *Pearson's Magazine,* was the candidate of the Socialist party with George R. Kilpatrick as his running mate, receiving 585,113 votes.

J. FRANK HANLY (1863–1920), lawyer, editor and lecturer, had been a Congressman and Governor of Indiana. He was nominated by the Prohibitionists as a presidential candidate and received 220,606 votes in the election.

Harper's Weekly, *March 15, 1913*

A PHOTO MONTAGE OF WILSON'S CABINET. Top row: Franklin K. Lane (Interior), William C. Redfield (Commerce), David F. Houston (Agriculture), Albert S. Burleson (Postmaster General). Bottom: Josephus Daniels (Navy), William B. Wilson (Labor), William J. Bryan (State), James C. McReynolds (Attorney General), William McAdoo (Treasury). Front: Lindley Garrison (War).

a year later it was a stark reality. Foreign problems took on a paramount importance.

Before 1914, America's principal foreign troubles were with Mexico. America's billion-dollar investment there had been in jeopardy since the 1910 revolution. President Díaz was followed by Madero in 1911, but two years later Madero—who was friendly to the United States—was murdered and General Huerta took his place. Wilson would not recognize the new Presi-

THEIR LOVE BLOOMED. To the President, the lovely Mrs. Galt was "the only woman I know who can wear an orchid." She accompanied him everywhere—even to the World Series. They married in 1915, a year after the death of his first wife.

dent and declared a policy of "watchful waiting." In April 1914, in order to prevent the landing of German munitions, American marines and bluejackets landed in Mexico and captured Veracruz.

The Mexican controversy had been hardly settled when Europe flamed up. On July 28 Austria declared war on Serbia, on August 1 Germany was at war with Russia, and four days later Germany declared war on France too. On August 4 President Wilson issued his

first neutrality proclamations, stating that the United States would keep out of the European conflict.

The war created a boom for American trade and industry. Factories worked overtime; unemployment dropped; wages and profits rose to new highs. As both belligerents resented the flow of American goods to the enemy, Britain intercepted American ships headed for Germany, and the Germans, suffering from the British blockade, declared a war zone around the British Isles.

The United States was warned that if an American ship should be found in the zone, it would be sunk. Wilson protested. If the "sink-on-sight" rule caused the loss of American lives, Germany would be held to "strict accountability."

On May 7, 1915, the *Lusitania,* the large English passenger liner, was torpedoed by a German submarine. The lives of 1,100 people were lost, including those of 124 Americans. The country cried for retaliation; war fever reached a high pitch. Wilson still struggled to keep the peace. "There is such a thing as a man being too proud to fight," he said. He received a promise from the German ambassador that in the future German submarines would not sink ships without warning, nor disregard the safety of noncombatants.

When on March 24, 1916, in violation of the promise the French steamer *Sussex* was sunk with the loss of three American lives, Wilson sent another protest demanding that Germany "should now immediately declare and effect an abandonment of its present methods of submarine warfare against passenger and freight-carrying vessels," otherwise the United States "can have no choice but to sever diplomatic relations altogether."

The repeated U-boat attacks and other violations convinced Wilson that the war could not be settled through negotiations. During 1916, not unmindful of the impending presidential campaign, he acquiesced to a program of military preparedness which Theodore Roosevelt and his friends had urged for years. With the approval of the business and industrial interests, a series of acts strengthening the military and naval forces of the nation was passed.

That Wilson would be the candidate to succeed himself was never in doubt. He was the leader of his party; he was acclaimed for keeping the country out of war. When the Democratic convention met in St. Louis, the keynoter, Governor Martin Glynn of New York, underlined the President's pacifism. "This policy may not satisfy . . . the fire-eater or the swashbuckler but it does satisfy the mothers of the land at whose hearth and fireside no jingoistic war has placed an empty chair. It does satisfy the daughters of the land from whom bluster and brag have sent no loving brother to the dissolution of the grave."

The enthusiasm which followed the speech made the party leaders uneasy. True, the Democrats were for peace, but not peace at any price, as the Governor seemed to imply. Wilson wanted the issue of Americanism—not pacifism—to be emphasized. He wanted

"Helping the President," by Rollin Kirby, New York World, *July 1915*

"The Castaways," by Rollin Kirby, New York World, *June 1915*

LAMPOONING THE TWO REBELS: ROOSEVELT AND BRYAN

Photograph by A. Marlow, September 2, 1916

THE OFFICIAL NOTIFICATION. Senator Ollie James, the chairman of the Democratic National Convention, hands Wilson the document of his renomination outside the President's home, Shadow Lawn, in Long Branch, New Jersey.

to repeat the ideas which he had stressed in his Flag Day speech—that the English-Americans and the German-Americans were wrong in thinking they could indulge in a double loyalty, and that the first loyalty of every American, even the "hyphenated American," was to America. But when the delegates staged their spontaneous demonstration for pacifism, the Americanism issue was lost. McCombs, one of the party leaders, scrawled on a piece of paper the phrase "But we are willing to fight if necessary" and sent it to Glynn, who added the words to his speech before he finished.

On the second day of the convention, Senator Ollie James of Kentucky, the permanent chairman of the convention, a shrewd orator with "the face of a prize-fighter, the body of an oak and the voice of a pipe organ," made an impressive speech. Sensing the mood, James spoke of Wilson, who "without orphaning a

single American child, without widowing a single American mother, without firing a single gun, without the shedding of a single drop of blood . . . wrung from the most militant spirit that ever brooded above a battlefield an acknowledgment of American rights and an agreement to American demands."

The convention shouted its approval. It wanted to hear more talks like this. The delegates called for their old leader, William Jennings Bryan, and Bryan told the delegates that "I agree with the American people in thanking God we have a President who has kept—*who will keep*—us out of war."

When the balloting began, Senator Hughes moved to suspend the rules and nominate Wilson by acclamation, but a single delegate from Illinois opposed this. So Wilson was nominated "by the vote of 1092 to 1." For his running mate the convention endorsed Vice President

"In Place of the Ermine," New York World, *October 5, 1916*

"Helping Hughes," New York World, *October 2, 1916*

CHARLES EVANS HUGHES, THE REPUBLICAN CANDIDATE, WAS DRAWN BY THE CARTOONIST ROLLIN

Marshall. who was popular enough to run again.

The Democratic platform had two significant planks: one was for "the extension of the franchise to the women of the country by the states upon the same terms as to men"; the other was a denunciation of the hyphenated Americans. "Whoever," this plank said, "is activated by the purpose to promote the interest of a foreign power, in disregard of our own country's welfare . . . and whoever by arousing prejudices of a racial, religious or other nature creates discord and strife among our people so as to obstruct the wholesome process of unification, is faithless to the trust which the privileges of citizenship repose in him and disloyal to his country."

Before the Republican convention met, the party's leaders realized that they needed Roosevelt's support for their candidate. At first the Old Guard wanted to nominate Elihu Root, but Root refused: "You are all bent on killing me. You know that a man seventy-two years old, as I shall be when the next President is inaugurated, cannot bear the burden of the Presi-

dency." So they settled on Charles Evans Hughes, Associate Justice of the Supreme Court.

Hughes had a fine record as Governor of New York, his actions were approved by the Progressives and his decisions on the Supreme Court had won the respect of the conservatives. The conservative Charles W. Fairbanks of Indiana, Roosevelt's Vice President, was nominated for the same post again. The nominations were to heal the wounds of 1912 and to bring unity to the party.

But the Progressives had not yet given up their fight. In a convention of their own, they named Theodore Roosevelt even though he had declared: "It would be a mistake to nominate me unless the country had in its mood something of the heroic." Roosevelt declined the honor. Smarting under his rebuke as a Bull Mooser, he affirmed: "Americans are a two-party people. There is no place for a third party in our politics." (He must have forgotten that the Republican party had come into being as a third party.) Roosevelt declared: "I'll support Hughes, but not unless he declares himself. He must

"Berlin's Candidate," *New York* World, *October 13, 1916*

"Saturday's Parade Epitomized," *New York* World, *November 6, 1916*

KIRBY AS THE FRONT MAN OF THE GERMAN KAISER WILHELM II—A MOST UNFAIR ASSESSMENT.

know where he stands on national honor, national defense and all other great questions before we accept him." Later, as the campaign went into full swing, he gave his full endorsement, although in private he dubbed Hughes as the "whiskered Wilson."

There were the usual number of minor party candidates. The Socialists conducted a primary by mail to nominate Allen L. Benson and George R. Kirkpatrick. The Prohibitionists named J. Frank Hanly and Ira Landrith. The Socialist Labor party put forth the names of Arthur E. Reimer and Caleb Harrison. And the National Woman's party made certain that the suffrage question stayed in the public eye.

The Democrats were confident of victory. Wilson appointed Vance McCormick of Pennsylvania, the "steam engine in boots," to manage his campaign, and he turned out to be an excellent choice. In New York City McCormick built up a strong organization, and he lured many independent voters and Progressive Republicans into supporting the President. Even the Socialists moved to Wilson. The editor of *The Masses* said that Wilson "aggressively believes not only in keeping out of war, but in organizing the nations of the world to prevent war."

Wilson would not take an active part in the campaign. "Don't worry, McCormick," he told him, "this is exactly what the people want. They want the President at a time like this to stay on his job. Let Hughes run about the country if he wishes to." He would not go on the stump. "I am inclined," he wrote to his friend Bernard Baruch, "to follow the course suggested by a friend of mine who says that he has always followed the rule never to murder a man who is committing suicide slowly but surely."

Hughes campaigned energetically. He answered the Democratic campaign slogan, "He kept us out of war," with a demand that America should end its shilly-shally relationship with Mexico. He suggested adopting complete neutrality without a single trace of the Anglophilism which helped Americans to overlook "improper interference with American commerce or with American mails," as done by the British as well as the Germans.

541

THE TWO OPPONENTS APPEAR ON THE CAMPAIGN CIRCUIT IN THE FINAL WEEK OF THE CONTEST.

Collier's, October 7, 1916
". . . THE SITUATION IS IN FLUX."

Boardman Robinson, November 1916
"A VOTE FOR HUGHES IS A VOTE FOR WAR."

But the country, because of its heritage, favored the British.

He was under a steady and violent barrage; newspapers accused him as being pro-German, "crawling on his belly before the Kaiserbund." The *World* wrote that "The followers of the Kaiser in the United States have set out to destroy President Wilson politically for the crime of being an American President instead of a German President. They have adopted Mr. Hughes as their candidate and made his cause their cause."

As the campaign entered the final weeks, Wilson's foreign policy was subjected to heavy criticism. Roosevelt attacked the man who "kept us out of war," distorting the phrase until it sounded like a promise from Wilson that under no circumstances would the country go to war. Roosevelt said that if he had been President when the *Lusitania* was sunk, he would have seized every German vessel interned in American waters. Hughes lamely declared: "I would have made it known . . . that we should not tolerate a continuance of friendly relations . . . if that action were taken, and

the *Lusitania* would never have been sunk."

In his speeches Hughes advocated "a flag that protects the American in his lawful rights wherever his legitimate business may take him," and he attacked the Eight-Hour Law, calling it a "forced law" and "labor's gold brick," stating he was for "America first."

Toward the end of October the Republicans realized that their attack on Wilson's foreign policy had failed, and they turned their attention to the tariff question. Roosevelt kept on his hammering at Wilson. "There should be shadows now at Shadow Lawn" (Wilson's home in New Jersey), said Roosevelt at New York's Cooper Union, "the shadows of the men, women and children who have risen from the ooze of the ocean bottom and from graves in foreign lands; the shadows of the helpless whom Mr. Wilson did not dare protect lest he might have to face danger; the shadows of deeds that were never done; the shadows of lofty words that were followed by no action; the shadows of the tortured dead."

In the last days of the campaign the Democrats distributed printed slogans by the hundreds of thou-

"The New Ringmaster," by Herbert Johnson, August 1916
ISSUES IN THE CAMPAIGN: THE WOMEN VOTE.

"The Eight-Hour Glass," by Herbert Johnson, October 1916
ISSUES IN THE CAMPAIGN: EIGHT-HOUR DAY

sands. "You are working—not fighting!" read one. "Wilson and peace with honor. Hughes with Roosevelt and war," read another. Posters carried the message: "Alive and happy—not cannon fodder!"

When the votes were counted, it was found that New York and every Eastern state north of the Potomac except Maryland and New Hampshire had been carried by Hughes. The Midwest, save Ohio, supported him as well and it seemed that he had won the election. Not counting the thirteen votes of California, he had 254 electoral votes. Thus California was to decide the contest. If the state was for him, he would have 267 electoral votes—one more than the majority.

During the night the New York newspapers conceded that Hughes had won. He went to bed in his suite at the Hotel Astor believing he had been elected President. On the roof of the hotel the large electric sign spelled out the name of the victor: "Hughes."

But when the reports trickled in from California, they indicated that he might be losing that state. A reporter from the *World* called Hughes' room in the Astor for his comments. His valet said, "The President has retired." The reporter shot back: "When he wakes up tell him he is no longer President."

When all the votes were in, Hughes's total in California was some 4,000 less than that of Wilson. Governor Johnson, running for the Senate, amassed a 300,000 majority. Hughes could have won California easily if he had had the support of Governor Hiram W. Johnson, the Bull Moose vice presidential candidate in the last election. But he listened to his advisers, who kept him away from Johnson. He would not talk to him, he would not meet with him, he would not see him.

The New York Congressman John W. Dwight noted that Hughes could have been elected for a single dollar if "a man of sense, with a dollar, would have invited Hughes and Johnson to his room when they were both in the same hotel in California. He would have ordered three Scotch whiskies, which would have been seventy-five cents, and that would have left a tip of twenty-five cents for the waiter. . . . That little Scotch would have brought those men together; there would have been mutual understanding and respect and Hughes would have carried California and been elected." But no one spent that single dollar; thus Wilson remained President.

Wilson, backed by an almost solid South and West, won the election with a majority of well over half a million votes. He had three million more votes than in the previous election. The New York *World* headlined: "A new era in American politics!" and added: "Nothing better has happened in a generation than this shifting of the political balance to a section which still maintains the old ideals of the Republic."

National Archives, March 5, 1917

WILSON'S SECOND INAUGURAL ADDRESS: "We are of the blood of all the nations that are at war. The currents of our trade run quick at all seasons back and forth between us and them. The war inevitably set its mark from the first alike upon our minds, our industries, our commerce, our politics, our social action. To be indifferent to it, or independent of it, was out of the question.

"And yet all the while we have been conscious that we were not part of it. In that consciousness, despite many divisions, we have drawn closer together. We have been deeply wronged upon the seas, but we have not wished to wrong or injure in return, have retained throughout the consciousness of standing in some sort apart, intent upon an interest that transcended the immediate issues of the war itself. . . . We are provincials no longer. The tragic events of the thirty months of vital turmoil through which we have just passed have made us citizens of the world. There can be no turning back. . . . We are being forged into a new unity amidst the fires that now blaze throughout the world. In their ardent heat we shall, in God's Providence, let us hope, be purged of faction and division, purified of the errant humors of party and of private interest, and shall stand forth in the days to come with a new dignity of national pride and spirit. Let each man see to it that the dedication is in his own heart, the high purpose of the nation in his own mind, ruler of his own will and desire."

WARREN G. HARDING and CALVIN COOLIDGE

W ilson wanted to keep the country out of the European war. Though during his campaign he never made a clear pledge to keep neutrality, it was obvious that his election had been brought about by the antiwar sentiment. He was given a mandate because "He kept us out of the war."

However, control of war and peace rested more with Europe's warring nations than with Wilson. After his re-election he sent an appeal to both sides, asking for their terms of peace. The Germans answered that the Central Powers would make their conditions known at the council chamber and that they would be stringent. The Allies' reply, equally unsatisfactory, demanded the return of all territories conquered by the Central Powers and heavy reparations. Thus, it appeared that neither side would accept anything less than a victorious peace.

As his answer to the fighting nations, Wilson addressed the Senate in January 1917, calling for "peace without victory" and outlining terms which he hoped might become the basis for a negotiated settlement. Within a few days Germany, convinced that an economic blockade would bring England to her knees, announced a decision that dashed these hopes. Effective immediately, said the Germans, unrestricted submarine warfare would be resumed against merchant shipping in the war zones, whether Allied or neutral.

The country was forced to break off diplomatic relations with Germany, and Wilson asked for authorization to arm merchantmen. When his measure was blocked by a Senate filibuster, he complained that "a little group of willful men, representing no opinion but their own, have rendered the great government of the United States helpless and contemptible." He then obtained the required power from an unrepealed statute of 1797.

Events soon tipped the scales. On March 1, 1917, it was learned that Germany had proposed an alliance to Mexico for which Mexico would be given, after the Allied-American defeat, the states of Texas, New Mexico and Arizona. When at the end of March the Germans sank three American ships, the cup of forbearance was empty; the President called Congress to a special session and asked for a declaration of war.

In the first months of the war Wilson was at the height of his popularity. His uncompromising idealism made him a natural leader in what Americans felt to be a righteous crusade. He welded the people into a firm national unity which enabled them to accept the sacrifices necessary to effective participation. One of his greatest contributions lay in the formulation of war aims and in his conviction that only a just peace could be a lasting one. He expressed this conviction when he went before Congress with his Fourteen Points in January 1918. Six of these points were general in nature; they called for "open covenants, openly arrived at," freedom of the seas, removal of trade barriers, disarmament, impartial adjustment of colonial claims and establishment of a League of Nations; the remaining eight points cited specific war aims which, though victors' terms, were not unduly harsh on Germany.

Reaction to the Fourteen Points both at home and abroad was enthusiastic. The main significance of Wilson's proposals lay in the fact that Germany, in defeat, seized upon them as a basis for making peace. In October 1918, the Germans appealed to the President

ARREN G. HARDING

CANDIDATES IN 1920

WARREN G. HARDING
(1865–1923), a newspaper
publisher and Senator from
Ohio, was chosen by the Republicans in a "smoke-filled"
room after a deadlock developed between the leading contenders, Wood and Lowden.

CALVIN COOLIDGE
(1872–1933), Governor of
Massachusetts, was the Republican choice for Vice President, his reward for breaking
the Boston police strike the
year before. He succeeded
Harding on August 3, 1923.

JAMES M. COX
(1870–1957), a newspaper
owner, a former Congressman
and Governor of Ohio, be-
came the Democratic nomi-
nee but was badly beaten.
Harding polled 16,153,115
votes against Cox's 9,133,092.

FRANKLIN D. ROOSEVELT
(1882–1945) of New York,
served in the legislature and
as Wilson's Assistant Secretary of the Navy. Named for
the Vice Presidency, he campaigned for the peace treaty
ratification and for the League.

EUGENE V. DEBS
(1855–1926), five-time Socialist candidate, was nominated while in prison for violation of the Espionage Act,
polling 915,490 votes. Debs
was released on Christmas
without regaining citizenship.

PARLEY P. CHRISTENSEN
(1869–1954) of Utah was the
candidate of the Farmer-Labor party with Max S. Hayes
of Ohio as the vice presidential nominee. The Farmer-
Labor ticket polled 265,229
votes for a strong showing.

Library of Congress

FLORENCE KLING (1860–1924) divorced her
husband, Henry De Wolfe, by whom she had one
son, and subsequently married the dashing publisher of the Marion (Ohio) *Star,* Warren Harding,
five years her junior, on July 8, 1891.

The Hardings' marriage was trying. She was over-
bearing, he indulged in extramarital affairs, or, as
William Allen White described it, "a primrose de-
tour from Main Street." One of his amours, Nan
Britton, told about their relations and their illegitimate child in her book, *The President's Daughter.*
Mrs. Harding survived her husband by a year, and
destroyed most of his correspondence; however, a
cache of his love letters to a Marietta merchant's
wife—some of them forty pages long—came to light
recently, causing embarrassment to the heirs.

F. T. Richards, in Life, *June 8, 1920*

THE PRESIDENCY IS UP FOR SALE—A PUNGENT REPRESENTATION OF THE WARREN HARDING ERA

for an armistice; on November 11, the hostilities ended.

In the midterm elections for Congress the Democrats suffered a defeat which was to have a disastrous effect on Wilson's political fortunes. Several factors contributed to this setback: his own mistake in making a public plea for a Democratic Congress, the opposition from "bitter-enders" like Theodore Roosevelt who argued that Wilson's Fourteen Points were not stringent enough, and, at the other extreme, the continuing opposition of the antiwar groups.

The Republicans were now in control of Congress. Though in the Senate their majority amounted to only one vote, it threw control of the Foreign Relations Committee into the hands of the President's personal enemies, chief among them Senator Henry Cabot Lodge.

Wilson was determined to go to Paris as head of the American commission for negotiating the peace. In the commission which accompanied him there was no Republican representation—a fatal mistake.

At Paris Wilson was jubilantly received, but the Allied leaders showed scant respect for the idealism contained in his Fourteen Points. Pitted against the combined strategy of Great Britain, France and Italy, the President had to make compromises. He succeeded on only one major issue: the acceptance of a League of Nations—his cherished dream—as an integral part of the peace treaty.

On his return from Paris Wilson set out to battle

THE CHANGING CABINET

Author's Collection

WILSON'S CABINET IN 1913: From the President's left, clockwise: McAdoo (Treasury), McReynolds (Attorney General), Daniels (Navy), Houston (Agriculture), Wilson (Labor), Redfield (Commerce), Lane (Interior), Burleson (Postmaster General), Garrison (War), Bryan (State).

Author's Collection

WILSON'S CABINET IN 1916: McAdoo (Treasury), Gregory (Attorney General), Daniels (Navy), Houston (Agriculture), Wilson (Labor), Lane (Interior), Burleson (Postmaster General), Baker (War), Lansing (State). Redfield (Commerce) was absent when the picture was taken.

Author's Collection

WILSON'S CABINET IN 1920: From Wilson's left: David Houston (Treasury), Palmer (Attorney General), Josephus Daniels (Navy), Edwin Meredith (Agriculture), William Wilson (Labor), Joshua Alexander (Commerce), John Payne (Interior). Albert Burleson (Postmaster General), Newton Baker (War), Bainbridge Colby (State).

Rollin Kirby, in the New York World, November 1916

WILSON'S FOREIGN-POLICY PROBLEMS. The U-boat menace and the Mexican rebellion were chief concerns.

for the ratification of the treaty. Senate and people were divided: in the Senate there were "ratificationists" who demanded immediate approval for the treaty; there were "mild reservationists" who wanted only minor changes in it and "extreme reservationists" who asked for extensive alterations; and finally there were the "irreconcilables" who wanted no part of the treaty—none at all. But the majority desired to see approval of the treaty and the League if only the President would make some concessions to the reservationists. Wilson would not hear of it.

His unbending attitude played into the hands of Henry Cabot Lodge, the patrician and scholarly Senator from Massachusetts. Although publicly on record as favoring a League of Nations, Lodge saw the situation as an opportunity to bring about a personal defeat for Wilson and to re-establish Republican power. He would kill the League and the treaty in the Senate not by direct attack but by "the indirect method of reservations." He kept the treaty in committee for several months, and then reported it back with fourteen modifying recommendations, a maliciously ironic number. The President's supporters, together with the "irreconcilables," voted it down by a narrow margin.

Wilson by this time was a sick man. In the late summer, when the Foreign Relations Committee was hammering away at the treaty, he took the issue to the people and, against the advice of his physicians, set out

IN APRIL 1917 WILSON ASKED CONGRESS FOR A DECLARATION OF WAR *Underwood & Underwood* AGAINST GERMANY.

WAR!

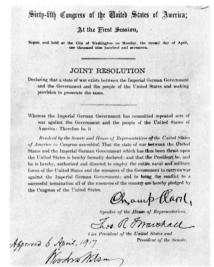

right:
The United States declared war upon Germany on April 6, 1917.

left:
After the war ended, Wilson went to Paris early in 1919 to take part in the treaty deliberations of the Versailles Peace Conference.

551

Keystone

OUTSIDE THE COLISEUM in Chicago, the site of the Republican convention that saw a deadlock between Governor Frank Lowden of Illinois and General Leonard Wood.

Leslie's Weekly, June 26, 1920

THE CHAIRMAN OF THE CONVENTION, Will Hays, introduces Senator Henry Cabot Lodge, chairman of the Senate Foreign Relations Committee, to the delegates.

United Press

THE CANDIDATES DEADLOCK. Governor Lowden and General Wood had about the same number of votes. Ballot after ballot was taken without a change in the results.

United Press

THE COMPROMISE CANDIDATE became Warren G. Harding, the personable Senator from Ohio, chosen in a "smoke-filled room" conference at the Blackstone Hotel.

on a speaking tour. On the evening of September 25, after addressing a crowd at Pueblo, Colorado, he suffered a stroke. He now was confined to his bed, partially paralyzed, mentally exhausted. He saw no visitors, and his dealings with the outside world were channeled through a small coterie headed by his wife.

The nation carried on without a President. When Secretary of State Robert Lansing held informal Cabinet meetings, he was summarily dismissed.

With the war over the country discovered new fears and threats at home. The cost of living soared; workers went on strike for wage increases to keep abreast of the ever-rising costs. In 1919, four million struck. The courts, a great deal of public opinion and, on occasion, Federal troops lined up against the strikers.

The people were in a state of shock over the head-

lines in the news. On one side there were the bombings of anarchists, the "Red scares" and the "un-American" strikes. On the other side were groups of people who took the law into their own hands. The Ku-Klux Klan was revived. Big business tried to destroy the unions with the cooperative police and strikebreakers. The country went mad. Anyone was considered "subversive" who was not "100 per cent American." Anti-intellectualism—the old scourge of American life—came to the surface. Professors, students, writers, editors and actors were victimized and hounded.

The Republicans felt they could win the next election and end the Wilson era. With victory in sight, there were many candidates. The favorite was General Leonard Wood, Theodore Roosevelt's close friend, who made speaking tours repeating that the notion that the

THREE FRIENDS: PRESIDENT WARREN HARDING WITH HENRY FORD AND THOMAS ALVA EDISON

League might prevent war was "idle twaddle and a dream of mollycoddles." He was financed by a "terrific amount" of money from the trusts in the hope "that he would use the military arm of the government to break up strikes and destroy the unions."

The other front runner, Governor Frank O. Lowden of Illinois, was a champion of the agricultural interests. He had been born in a log cabin, worked his way through college and accumulated a fortune before marrying a Pullman heiress.

Another and more liberal contender was Senator Hiram Johnson of California, the former Bull Mooser and Roosevelt's running mate in 1912. A champion of free speech, he condemned the Red hunts, Attorney General Palmer and American intervention in Russia.

And there were the good-looking and easy-going Senator from Ohio, Warren G. Harding, making "America first" speeches; Calvin Coolidge, who had been triumphantly elected Governor of Massachusetts because of his stand on the Boston police strike ("There is no right to strike against the public safety by anybody, anywhere, anytime," he said); and Herbert Hoover, the successful wartime Food Administrator.

In the primaries the main battle was fought between Johnson, Wood, Lowden and Harding. Johnson won more votes than his opponents, but Wood could gather more delegates. Senator Borah, a friend of Johnson, charged that Wood's managers tried to "control the Republican convention by the use of money," and the Senate formed an investigating committee which found that $1,500,000 had been spent on the General's campaign. Lowden too spent freely—even bribing delegates.

THE DEMOCRATIC TICKET: GOVERNOR JAMES M. COX OF OHIO AND FRANKLIN D. ROOSEVELT

Harding had done poorly in the primaries, but, under the guiding hand of Harry Daugherty, his sizable campaign staff started a boom for him. Daugherty told a reporter: "I don't expect Senator Harding to be nominated on the first, second, or third ballots, but I think we can afford to take chances that about eleven minutes after two, Friday morning of the convention, when fifteen or twenty weary men are sitting around a table, someone will say, 'Who will we nominate?' At that decisive time, the friends of Harding will suggest him and can well afford to abide by the result."

The influence of big business pervaded the atmosphere more heavily than it had at any convention since the days of Mark Hanna. From William B. Thompson,

the copper baron, to Harry Sinclair, whose oil empire was to play a sordid part in the destiny of the forthcoming administration, the representatives of special interests made their weight felt.

Senator Lodge, the keynote speaker, declared: "We must be now and ever for Americanism and Nationalism, and against Internationalism!" and he complained about Wilson's Progressive era: "Through long years of bitter conflict, moral restraints were loosened and all the habits, all the conventions, all the customs of life which more even than law hold society together were swept aside." The cheering reached its peak when he said: "Mr. Wilson and his heirs and assigns, or anybody that is his, anybody who with bent knees have

Photo: G. Tolziner

THE REPUBLICAN TICKET: WARREN G. HARDING AND CALVIN COOLIDGE WITH MANAGER HAYS

served his purpose, must be driven from all control of the government and all influence in it."

The party platform, though less dogmatic, confirmed this tone, castigating everything Wilsonian. It charged the Democratic party with lack of preparedness for both war and peace; it favored cutting the public debt and lowering taxes on the wealthy; it denounced the high cost of living but declared for a high protective tariff. On the question of "Wilson's League" the platform was ambivalent—it declared "the Republican Party stands for agreement among nations to preserve the peace," but that this must be done "without compromising national independence." Another plank justified "government initiative" against strikes.

After the balloting got under way it became apparent that no candidate could muster a majority; the support for General Wood and Governor Lowden was equally divided with neither of them making any headway. The scene was now set for a decision "at two o'clock in the morning in a smoke-filled room" which Harry Daugherty had predicted some months before. Over the protests of a majority of the delegates, the party elders called for adjournment and met privately in a suite at the Blackstone Hotel to decide which candidate could be trotted out to break the deadlock.

When the convention met again the next morning, its choice was presented—Warren Gamaliel Harding. For the second place, the party leaders suggested Senator

Harold T. Webster, October 1920
AN ELECTION ISSUE: THE LEAGUE OF NATIONS

F. T. Richards, June 1920
AN ELECTION ISSUE: PROHIBITION

Irvine Lenroot of Wisconsin, but the delegates, in their only burst of rebellion, chose Calvin Coolidge instead.

The nomination of Harding came as a surprise even to the candidate himself. A small-city newspaper publisher with modest political ambitions, his career in the Senate had been unimaginative, unaggressive and unpublicized. A few days before his nomination he had told Nicholas Murray Butler that "the convention will never nominate me" and that he was quitting politics for good. His rescue from obscurity was the work of Daugherty, his shrewd campaign manager, and the accidental factor of the convention deadlock; but even more, it was a result of the peculiar temper of the times. The Republican leaders, sensing America's postwar mood, saw in Harding not only a man who would be amenable to their wishes but also one whose character was almost diametrically opposed to that of Wilson. Where Wilson was cultivated, urbane, aloof, Harding was a jovial small-town personality, friendly to a fault and without intellectual ambitions. Where Wilson was a liberal who distrusted big business, Harding was a conservative who wanted to free businessmen from governmental regulation. Harding's philosophy was neatly summed up in a statement which he made a few weeks before his nomination: "America's present need is not heroics but healing; not nostrums but normalcy; not revolution but restoration." The press pounced upon the word—and "normalcy" became the keyword of his campaign.

The Democratic convention, meeting in San Francisco three weeks later, had little choice but to stand on Wilson's record. The platform urged immediate ratification of the treaty, tax reform, governmental economy and reconstruction measures to combat the high cost of living. It opposed compulsory arbitration of labor disputes ("labor is not a commodity, it is human") and pledged "adherence to the fundamental progressive principles of social, economic, and industrial justice."

Three contenders dominated the field: William Gibbs McAdoo, Wilson's son-in-law and former Secretary of the Treasury; A. Mitchell Palmer, the red-baiting Attorney General; and James M. Cox, the Governor of

556

"Congratulations!" Charles Dana Gibson, in Life, *Oct. 28, 1920*
THE 19TH AMENDMENT HAS BEEN RATIFIED.

A. B. Frost, in Life, *October 4, 1920*
HE AND SHE—AS THEY DRIVE TO THE POLLS

Ohio. Like Harding, Cox was an Ohio newspaper publisher who had gone into politics, but there the resemblance ended. By temperament and conviction he was a progressive in the Wilsonian tradition.

William McAdoo, though he led on the initial ballots, suffered from his vulnerable position as "crown prince." Palmer, who ran second in the early trials, was handicapped by the opposition of the liberals, who despised his atrocious headline-grabbing "Red hunts." As the two-thirds rule was still in force, it took forty-four ballots to nominate Governor Cox.

For his running mate Cox recommended the handsome young New York patrician Assistant Secretary of the Navy during the war years, Franklin Delano Roosevelt. Knowing that young Roosevelt was unpopular with the political bosses in his state, Cox asked the advice of the Tammany boss, Charles F. Murphy, before announcing his preference. "I don't like Roosevelt," Murphy told Cox's emissary. "He is not well known in the country. But this is the first time a Democratic nominee for the Presidency has shown me

courtesy. That's why I would vote for the devil himself if Cox wanted me to. Tell him we will nominate Roosevelt on the first ballot as soon as we assemble."

As the campaign went into gear, neither candidate seemed to generate much excitement. Harding delivered his acceptance speech from an improvised platform in his home town of Marion, and kept up a "front-porch campaign" in the same homely manner. Republican leaders and grass-roots Republican troops came to see him and he made reassuring speeches favoring deflation, the return of the railroads to private ownership, restricted immigration and a high tariff. About the League he was as mealy-mouthed as his party's platform. And he reminisced on "the good old times" of Republican preponderance, to the 1870s and the 1880s of his youth, when the "Republican protective tariff filled the treasury." In one speech he depicted his home town, then asked: "What is the greatest thing in life, my countrymen? Happiness. And there is more happiness in the American village today than in any other place on the face of the earth."

Lorant: The Presidency (*Macmillan*)
ON THE WAY TO THE INAUGURAL. President Wilson, with President-elect Harding; "Uncle Joe" Cannon. one-time all-powerful Speaker of the House; and Senator Philander Knox, Roosevelt's trust-busting Attorney General.

Lorant: The Presidency (*Macmillan*)
TAKING THE INAUGURAL OATH. The swearing in of Warren Harding on March 4, 1921, by Chief Justice Edward D. White. Behind Harding, Philander Knox; Thomas Marshall; and Calvin Coolidge, the new Vice President.

Library of Congress
THE HARDING CABINET: Front row: Weeks (War), Mellon (Treasury), Hughes (State), the President, Vice President Coolidge, Denby (Navy). Back row: Fall (Interior), Hays (Postmaster General), Daugherty (Att. Gen.), Wall (Agriculture), Hoover (Commerce), Davis (Labor).

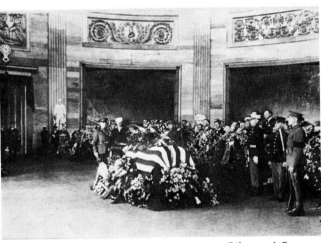

Library of Congress
HARDING'S REMAINS lie in state in the Rotunda of the Capitol. On his return from a journey to Alaska in July 1923, the President was stricken in San Francisco and died shortly thereafter. His sudden death gave vent to rumors that he did not die a natural death, but was poisoned.

In contrast to Harding, Cox stumped with tireless energy. He said his appeal to the people would only be limited by his physical ability. He was arrested for speeding, he was in a railroad accident, and he was plagued by hoarseness, dyspepsia and fatigue. Traveling 22,000 miles, he spoke before 2 million people. On one of his tours he devoted twenty-nine days to a swing through eighteen Western states—from none of which

did he receive a single electoral vote. He stood steadfastly and courageously by Wilson's record and by the League of Nations—neither of them popular stands.

Both the Republican and Democratic candidates ignored prohibition. The Eighteenth Amendment had been ratified in January 1919 and the Volstead Enforcement Act passed over the President's veto in October, so it was deemed best to say nothing at all.

558

Lorant: The Presidency (*Macmillan*)

BY THE LIGHT OF A KEROSENE LAMP, Calvin Coolidge takes the oath of office in the family homestead in Plymouth, Vermont, from his father, Colonel John Coolidge, a justice of the peace, at 2:47 in the morning of August 3, 1923. The news of President Harding's death reached the village shortly before midnight. Coolidge was at a loss how to proceed. The house had no telephone, so he walked to the store nearby to call the Attorney General in Washington.

The composite picture shows only Coolidge and his father, but not the others who were present at the ceremony. Mrs. Coolidge stood at her husband's left. Congressman Dale at his right. The others in the room: Edwin Geiser, Coolidge's secretary, who typed out the oath in triplicate; Joseph McInerny, the government employee who drove the Coolidge car; Leonard Lane, a railway mail clerk; and the editor of the Springfield (Vt.) *Reporter,* 21-year-old Joe Fountain.

In the election—in which only half of the eligible voters cast their ballots—Harding won by a landslide; he got 16,153,115 votes against Cox's 9,133,092. As the Nineteenth Amendment was ratified in the summer of 1920, women could vote in the election. Whether their voice added to the intelligent selection of a President or not, no one was able to tell. Another notable sign of the times: Eugene V. Debs, the candidate of the Socialist party, who during the campaign was in prison serving a term for sedition, received well over 900,000 votes.

From his sickbed, President Wilson had made the prediction that the principles for which he had fought would be vindicated by the American people at the polls. Their overwhelming answer was the final defeat of his career.

CALVIN COOLIDGE

Harding—elected by a record-breaking majority—personified the public's eagerness to substitute a policy of "business as usual" for Wilsonian idealism. One of his first official acts was to throw open the long-shuttered White House gates to sightseers. And Mrs. Harding struck a popular note when she announced that she and the President were "just folks."

A better indication of what was to come was the list of the new Cabinet appointments. The men Harding picked were, in many cases, honest and able—in other cases, just the opposite. Among the former were Charles Evans Hughes, his Secretary of State, and Herbert Hoover, his Secretary of Commerce. Among the latter were Harry F. Daugherty, his campaign manager, whom he made Attorney General, and former Senator Albert B. Fall, whom he appointed Secretary of the Interior. An unprincipled group of Harding's cronies, "the Ohio Gang," followed the new President to Washington, aware that his trusting personality would create lucrative opportunities for them.

With "normalcy" as its goal, the new administration embarked on the job of returning the country to a peacetime footing. Convoking a special session of Congress a month after his inaugural, Harding urged a broad program which included creation of a long-needed federal budget system, establishment of higher tariff barriers, the reduction of wartime taxes, restriction of immigration and extreme governmental economy. At the outset the program met few obstacles. Wartime powers, including governmental ownership of the railroads, were liquidated; federal regulation of the nation's business life was eliminated wherever feasible. Although the

Republicans took their victory as a rebuff for the Treaty of Versailles, they opened negotiations with Germany and on August 25, 1921, a peace treaty was signed.

On the surface, things seemed to be going well, but behind the scenes the President's weakness of character and the carelessness of many of his appointments were bearing ugly fruit. Most of the inside story came out in piecemeal fashion during subsequent years, and it was not until the end of the decade that the whole truth was known; but there was already talk in political circles indicating that corruption in high places was rife. One key figure in the sordid proceedings was Daugherty, the President's principal adviser, whose influence was often for sale. Another was Charles R. Forbes, a political adventurer and former army deserter who, as head of the Veterans Bureau, accepted graft in awarding contracts for hospital buildings and supplies.

Most flagrant of all were the notorious "Teapot Dome" scandals, traced to Secretary of the Interior Fall. Shortly after taking office, Fall had persuaded the Secretary of the Navy to turn over to the Department of the Interior control of naval oil reserves at Teapot Dome, Wyoming, and Elk Hills, California. On the pretext that wells adjacent to these reserves were draining off government oil, Fall proceeded to lease the lands to private oil interests in an arrangement whereby the Navy received a percentage of the oil thus extracted. Outwardly this seemed reasonable, and it was not until considerably later that Fall was found to have accepted substantial bribes from the oilmen for his services.

Harding was not a party to the evildoing of his appointees. That he did know the truth about them by

CANDIDATES IN 1924

CALVIN COOLIDGE (1872–1933) was nominated by the Republicans for a term of his own. As the country was prosperous and calm, he was reelected by the overwhelming majority of 15,719,921 votes against Davis's 8,386,704.

CHARLES G. DAWES (1865–1951), Illinois lawyer and financier, first Director of the Bureau of the Budget, and author of the "Dawes Plan" for a German postwar budget, was chosen by the Republicans as vice presidential candidate.

JOHN W. DAVIS (1873–1955), law professor and West Virginia politician, former Minister to Britain, was nominated on a record 103rd ballot at the Democratic convention breaking the Smith-McAdoo deadlock.

CHARLES W. BRYAN (1867–1945), political secretary and business agent for his brother William J. Bryan, and also editor of *The Commoner* and Governor of Nebraska, became the Democratic party's second-place candidate.

ROBERT LA FOLLETTE (1855–1925), former Governor of Wisconsin, a Senator since 1906, he became the candidate of the newly formed third party, the Progressives. Strongly backed by labor, he polled 4,832,532 votes.

BURTON K. WHEELER (1882——), Massachusetts-born Senator from Montana who helped expose the scandals of the Harding administration, was the vice presidential candidate on La Follette's new Progressive party ticket.

Library of Congress

GRACE ANNA GOODHUE (1879–1957) married Coolidge on October 4, 1905. They had two children: John (born in 1906) and Calvin, Jr. (born in 1908).

Attractive Mrs. Coolidge, with a great sense of humor, loved music and novels, liked people and was liked by them. She played baseball with her sons and rooted for the Washington Senators. A friend remembered that her kindness "cast a sort of glow around her wherever she went."

the summer of 1923, however, seems certain. To add to his difficulties the midterm elections of the previous fall had cut the Republican majorities in Congress substantially and had given the balance of power in the Senate to the radical Republicans of the "farm bloc," who proceeded to obstruct most of his legislative program. Seeking respite from these problems, the President set out on an Alaskan visit in July. On the return trip he received a long coded message from Washington that put him in a state of near collapse, and at San Francisco he was rushed to the Palace Hotel for a rest. On the night of July 28 his physicians described his condition as critical; five days later he was dead.

When a special train carried his body back to Washington to lie in state before being taken to Marion for

AN INFORMAL PRESS CONFERENCE: THE COOLIDGES HOST REPORTERS AT THEIR VERMONT HOME.

burial, the nation's display of grief was described by a *New York Times* reporter as "the most remarkable demonstration in American history of affection, respect and reverence for the dead."

Meanwhile the nation was taking its first close look at the new President, Calvin Coolidge. Although a Vermonter by birth, Coolidge had begun his career as a lawyer in Massachusetts and had worked his way, step by step, to the governorship of the state by the time the Republicans nominated him as Vice President. A man of simple manners and few words (it was said that he could be silent in five different languages), he was conscientious, honest and consistently conservative, both in personal habits and political convictions. His personality, reserved and aloof, contrasted sharply with Hard-

ing's open friendliness. Alice Longworth remarked that he had been "weaned on a pickle."

The manner in which he assumed the highest office was in itself symbolic of the simplicity to which he subscribed. The news of Harding's death had found him vacationing at his family's farmhouse in Vermont. After receiving the message, and after telephoning to Washington about the correct procedure, he took the oath of office in the early hours of the morning from his father, the local justice of the peace.

With Coolidge in the White House the Republican program went ahead with few perceptible deviations, although the dishonest elements were gradually weeded out of the administration. Some of Harding's appointees resigned their offices under fire, a dozen others

THE DELEGATES CHEERED FOR 73 MINUTES WHEN AL SMITH WAS NOMINATED BY ROOSEVELT.

William A. Rogers, 1924

"AW, GIVE A FELLER A CHANCE!" BEGS MCADOO.

—including Fall, Forbes and Colonel T. W. Miller, the Alien Property Custodian—eventually were sent to prison.

It soon became apparent that Coolidge, riding on the crest of a wave of economic prosperity, had grown into a popular President desite his lack of "political glamor." The country wanted a quiet Executive, one who would leave things alone. "Silent Cal" filled the shoe. At the end of 1923 he let it be known that he would seek the presidential nomination in 1924; he had no serious opposition. When Hiram Johnson of California was mentioned as a possible competitor, a Republican committeeman remarked: "I wish my chances of Heaven were as good as the chances of President Coolidge to carry California against Hiram Johnson."

When the Republican convention opened in Cleveland, the senatorial clique which had dominated the 1920 convention was no longer in evidence. Senator

United Press

THE AGING WILLIAM JENNINGS BRYAN at the exhausting sixteen-day Democratic convention. When the favorites Smith and McAdoo stalemated each other, John W. Davis became the compromise choice on the 103rd ballot.

Keystone

THE YOUNG FRANKLIN D. ROOSEVELT puts Al Smith's name in nomination at the Democratic convention. This marked Roosevelt's return into the political arena after three years' absence following his infantile-paralysis attack.

Lodge, whose voice had been the loudest four years before, received no committee appointments and was assigned to such a poor hotel room that he repaired to the quarters of his former secretary.

The party platform was a clear reflection of President Coolidge's views. It stressed governmental economy and debt reduction; it approved the World Court and arms limitation; it promised agricultural reforms, condemned compulsory arbitration of labor disputes, and advocated continued restriction of immigration.

Coolidge received the nomination on the first ballot with only 44 out of 1,209 delegates voting for other candidates. When Governor Lowden of Illinois declined the nomination for the Vice Presidency (he was the second man in presidential history who declined; the other was Silas Wright in 1844), the delegates turned to Charles G. Dawes, a former Chicago banker who had served under Harding as the first Director of the Budget.

Clifford Berryman, Washington Star, *1924*

BRYAN WARNS AGAINST "THAT BIG CITY CHAP."

STUDENT
CALVIN
COOLIDGE

There was a suggestion to ask Senator Borah, but when he was invited by Coolidge to share the ticket, the aging Senator asked: "In what position?" So the ticket was: "Cautious Cal and Charging Charlie."

In contrast to the harmony of the Republican convention, the Democrats assembled in New York's Madison Square Garden amid an atmosphere of wide-open dissension. Senator Pat Harrison of Mississippi, the keynote speaker, capitalized on the Harding scandals; he charged that "in the guarded orchards of this [Republican] administration the golden apples of special privilege have been gathered by the favored few. . . . Show this administration an oil well and it will show you a foreign policy." But no amount of pointing at Republican shortcomings could conceal the fact that the Democratic party was violently split on a fundamental issue: the Ku-Klux Klan.

During the early 1920s the Klan's program of racial and religious bigotry had been gaining eager followers in the South and the West, the Democratic strongholds. Its membership rose from one hundred thousand in 1920 to nearly five million "white male persons, native-

Jay N. "Ding" Darling, September 21, 1923
CARRYING ON WITH THE HARDING PROGRAM

Cartoon by Jay N. "Ding" Darling, June 4, 1924
HOW CAN I BUILD A PLATFORM WITH THAT?

born Gentile citizens of the United States" in 1924.

At the convention the forces were almost evenly divided between the anti-Klan delegates, largely from the East and the large cities, and the delegates who either supported the Klan or felt that it should not be openly disavowed. The first skirmish took place in the platform committee, which, after four days of wrangling, refused to condemn the Klan by name. The fight was carried to the floor, where an amendment proposed by the anti-Klan forces was defeated by a single vote.

On other issues the platform was less explosive. It denounced Republican wickedness and corruption, attacked monopolies, advocated lower railroad rates and lower tariffs, defended the income tax and came out for a government-owned merchant marine. On foreign affairs it promised international cooperation, favoring disarmament and endorsing the League of Nations. As to the repeal of Prohibition, the Democrats would not endorse it.

When it came to the nominations, the party was torn apart once again by the Klan issue. The champion of the anti-Klan forces, New York's popular Governor

GOVERNOR
CALVIN
COOLIDGE

Cartoon by C. H. Sykes, in Life, *April 10, 1924*

Cartoon by C. H. Sykes, in Life, *October 2, 1924*

THE SCANDALS OF THE HARDING ADMINISTRATION WERE PROMINENT ISSUES IN THE CAMPAIGN

Keystone
THE COOLIDGES AT THEIR VERMONT FARM

Keystone
THE COOLIDGES STARTING THE 1924 CAMPAIGN

William A. Rogers
THE TWO BRICKBAT THROWERS IN 1924

Alfred Emanuel Smith, received a seventy-three-minute ovation when Franklin Delano Roosevelt, crippled by infantile paralysis but undaunted in spirit, put his name in nomination. To the pro-Klan delegates Smith's urban liberalism, and above all his Catholicism, were anathema. Their own candidate, though he disavowed much of what they stood for, was William Gibbs McAdoo.

As ballot after ballot was taken the favorite sons dropped out, but neither Smith nor McAdoo could command the two-thirds majority. Endurance records were broken as the fortieth, fiftieth, seventieth, ninetieth ballots were taken. And each time, as the balloting began, more than a million radio listeners heard the booming voice of the Alabama delegate: "Alabama casts twenty-four votes for Oscar Underwood."

Finally, when it became evident that neither major candidate could break the deadlock, the convention turned on the 103rd ballot to John W. Davis, a New

COOLIDGE AUTOGRAPHS A SAP BUCKET WHILE EDISON ASKS MRS. COOLIDGE WHAT'S GOING ON.

York lawyer who had represented West Virginia in Congress before the war and had served under President Wilson as Solicitor General. For the Vice Presidency, Charles W. Bryan, Governor of Nebraska, the brother of William Jennings Bryan was chosen.

Election year was to see the birth of the Progressive party. Its roots went back to the economic unrest of the period just after the war, and its aim was the merging of farmers and laborers into one great party which would "break the power of the private monopoly system over the economic and political life of the American people."

"Craftsmen, railway workers, preachers, priests, housewives, professors, socialists, farmers, alienated Republicans and disgruntled small businessmen mixed in Cleveland in one of the few spontaneous mass movements in American political history," wrote Kenneth MacKay, noting that "These progressives were not convinced, as were many of the worshippers of Mammon in 1924, that telephones, washing machines, and

Rollin Kirby, September 1924
A WHIRLWIND CAMPAIGN BY COOLIDGE

six-cylinder automobiles were not necessarily an index of political morality and economic well-being."

They nominated by acclamation Robert M. La Follette from Wisconsin, who wrote his own platform advocating government ownership of transportation, extensive conservation measures, low tariffs, broad labor legislation, election of federal judges, and a constitutional amendment providing that Congress might, by re-enacting a statute, override a judicial veto. For his running mate, La Follette selected Burton K. Wheeler, the Democratic Senator from Montana. The Progressives did not expect to win, but they hoped to keep Coolidge and Davis from getting a majority and then take their chances in the House.

As the campaigning moved into full swing, it appeared that Coolidge's strongest weapon was the nation's prosperity. Davis charged the Republicans with "corruption in administration and favoritism to privileged classes in legislation," but as the country was not in a mood for reform, he stirred little fervor.

Davis, a corporation counsel to Wall Street interests,

was vulnerable to attacks from farm and labor groups. H. L. Mencken jabbed at him: "Dr. Coolidge is for the Haves and Dr. La Follette is for the Have-Nots. But whom is Dr. Davis for? I'm sure I don't know, and neither does anyone else. I have read all his state papers with dreadful diligence, and yet all I can gather from them is that he is for himself," he said.

During most of the campaign Coolidge remained in Washington. He avoided the limelight. "I don't recall any candidate for President that ever injured himself very much by not talking."

But he stated his political conviction. "I am for economy. After that I am for more economy. At this time and under present conditions, that is my conception of serving the people."

In reply to the Democratic slogan of "A Vote for Coolidge is a Vote of Chaos," the Republicans struck a more popular chord with "Keep Cool and Keep Coolidge." The success of their strategy in identifying Coolidge with prosperity, "standpattism" and spare speaking was well illustrated by the epigram of Oliver

Ellison Hoover, March 6, 1924

BARGAIN DAY IN WASHINGTON. A biting cartoon on the Harding administration's influence on the morality of the capital. All items of an honest government are up for auction; after the vultures have done their part, the junkyard remains.

PRESIDENT COOLIDGE TAKES THE OATH OF OFFICE FROM CHIEF JUSTICE WILLIAM HOWARD TAFT.

Wendell Holmes: "While I don't expect anything very astonishing from him, I don't want anything very astonishing."

The election was a Republican landslide: Coolidge won with 15,725,003 popular votes against Davis's 8,385,586 and La Follette's 4,826,471.

Though La Follette received only the thirteen electoral votes of Wisconsin, he polled four times as many popular votes as Davis in California and twice as many in seventeen states west of the Mississippi.

Shortly after the elections Coolidge's father died in Vermont. The President, who had been unable to leave Washington to be at his bedside, was deep in sorrow. With characteristic understatement, he said later:

"During his last month I had to resort to the poor substitute of a telephone. When I reached home, he was gone. It costs a great deal to be President."

Drawing by Will B. Johnstone, 1925

HERBERT HOOVER

In his inaugural address, the first ever broadcast by radio, President Coolidge repeated his pledge to enforce economy, reduce taxes and avoid governmental interference with business. "We are not without problems," he said. "But our most important problem is not to secure new advantages but to maintain those we already possess." On this note the era of Coolidge prosperity began. It was essentially a negative era from the point of view of governmental activity. For Coolidge and the men around him the best government was the least government. The President made no attempt to work closely with Congress, to take the issues to the people, or to use his executive powers in a forceful manner. It was a period of economic prosperity, and Coolidge felt his task was to encourage private enterprise and keep the government from "rocking the boat."

This did not mean there was complete harmony between President and Congress. Within a few weeks of his inaugural, Coolidge faced a Senate rebellion when he nominated Charles B. Warren, a corporation lawyer and Republican leader from Michigan, for the post of Attorney General. Suspicious of Warren's associations with the "sugar trust," Senate insurgents joined forces with the Democrats and by a one-vote margin refused to confirm the appointment. It was the first time in half a century that a Cabinet appointment had failed to win confirmation, but what hurt Coolidge even more was the fact that Vice President Dawes could have saved Warren if he had voted. It was suggested that Dawes stayed away from the crucial vote because Warren had been against him in the last convention. When Coolidge submitted Warren's nomination for the second time, the vote was forty-six to thirty-nine against confirmation.

On the domestic front the major issue of the Coolidge years was the McNary-Haugen bills for farm aid, a storm center in Congress. Rooted in the depressed agricultural prices which had kept the nation's farmers behind the rest of the country in its march toward economic plenty, the various bills presented by Senator Charles McNary of Oregon and Representative Gilbert N. Haugen of Iowa sought to separate farm produce for export from farm produce for domestic consumption, and thus keep the domestic price structure from being depressed by the world price. After being voted down twice, their bill was submitted again and by the end of 1926 had been passed. Coolidge, whose objections to the bill were primarily based on claims that it represented governmental interference with the nation's economic life, vetoed it, and the veto was sustained. Undaunted, the backers of the bill brought it in again, and again were defeated by a veto. It was not until the following decade that the principles of the McNary-Haugen Bill became law.

The most notable accomplishment of the administration was the initiative provided by the United States in bringing about the Kellogg-Briand Treaty, signed in Paris on August 27, 1928. In it the fifteen signatory powers, including Germany, Italy and Japan, denounced war "as an instrument of national policy"—but neglected to spell out how to do it.

Despite his lack of aggressiveness, Coolidge was a popular President. People liked his dry wit, his frugal habits, his innate conservatism and the "good conscience" which enabled him to sleep eleven hours a day

HERBERT HOOVER WITH HIS WIFE
Photograph by Keystone

CANDIDATES IN 1928

HERBERT C. HOOVER
(1874–1964), engineer, European war relief administrator, Secretary of Commerce under Harding and Coolidge, was the Republicans' standard-bearer. He received 21,437,277 votes to the Democrats' 15,007,698.

CHARLES CURTIS
(1860–1936) of Kansas, Senate majority leader, was nicknamed "Indian" because his mother came from the Kaw tribe. He became the Republican vice presidential candidate with Senator Borah's help.

ALFRED E. SMITH
(1873–1944), Governor of New York, was proposed by Roosevelt in the convention as "the Happy Warrior." The first Catholic candidate, he campaigned for modification of the country's prohibition laws.

JOSEPH T. ROBINSON
(1872–1937), former Representative and Governor of Arkansas, a Protestant and a prohibitionist, had been a Senator since 1913. Chairman of the Democratic convention, he was given the second place.

NORMAN THOMAS
(1884———), a former Presbyterian minister, pacifist, author of several books and editor of *World To-Morrow* and *The Nation,* was the Socialist candidate for the Presidency, polling 265,583 popular votes.

JAMES H. MAURER
(1864–1944), the former machinist president of the Pennsylvania Federation of Labor and a long-time power in Socialist councils, was easily nominated by his party for the vice presidential office.

Library of Congress

LOU HENRY (1875–1944), the daughter of a banker, met Hoover in the geology department of Stanford University, where she was a freshman. They were married on February 10, 1899.

A natural linguist and a collector of antique Chinese porcelain, she also "set the best table that was ever set in the White House." She was a charming companion to her husband. They had two sons, Herbert Jr. (b. in 1903) and Allan Henry (b. in 1907).

on the average. He was just the right man for the times. It was taken for granted he could win the renomination in 1928. One waited eagerly for a word of his intentions, but he offered no clues until August 2, 1927—the fourth anniversary of his succession—when, during an interview at his "Summer White House" in Rapid City, South Dakota, he handed the reporters a slip of paper with the words: "I do not choose to run for President in nineteen twenty-eight."

His statement was like thunder from a clear sky. Did he mean what he said? Did he really "choose" not to run? Some held that the statement was a sincere one; others thought that Coolidge hoped for a deadlock in the national convention between Hoover and his opposition which would force the delegates to draft him. Coolidge explained to Senator Watson of Indiana that "Immediately following the terrible turmoil of that

Author's Collection

THE MEDICINE BALL CABINET OF PRESIDENT HOOVER. Facing the camera on the right is writer Mark Sullivan.

great conflict the people wanted rest, and that is what I was naturally adapted to give them, and did give them. They have prospered under those conditions, because the times demanded them. But a different condition now confronts us. From this time on, there must be something constructive applied to the affairs of government, and it will not be sufficient to say, 'Let business take care of itself. . . .' And so something affirmative must be suggested, and I do not feel I am the man to fill that sort of position or undertake to meet the demand occasioned by that situation." Perhaps the alleged remark of Mrs. Coolidge—"Papa says there's going to be a depression"—had something to do with it.

Though the message seemed ambiguous, the anti-Coolidge faction took it at its face value and began to line up behind other candidates.

The strongest preconvention contender was Herbert

Hoover, the Secretary of Commerce and wartime Food Administrator. His work as a one-man task force during the Mississippi Valley flooding in 1927 was widely acclaimed; Hoover brought order out of chaos, "the one tranquil among the raging floods." Coolidge was not fond of Hoover. On one occasion he said: "That man has offered me unsolicited advice for six years, all of it bad!" On another occasion in 1927, when by a slip of the tongue he referred to him as "President" Hoover, he was so displeased with the resultant speculation that he forbade reporters to quote his remarks in the future.

In December, Coolidge told members of the Republican National Committee: "My decision will be respected." The pro-Hoover men considered this as further encouragement for their activities. Meanwhile, Senator Robert M. La Follette, Jr., gave additional impetus to the anti-Coolidge move by introducing a

Associated Press

HERBERT HOOVER, THE STYLISH ANGLER

Cartoon by Clifford Berryman, 1928

JOINING THE BANDWAGON RUSH FOR HOOVER

Keystone

THE REPUBLICAN CONVENTION IN KANSAS CITY

resolution that no President should serve for more than two terms and complimented Coolidge for conforming to the custom. Senator Fess of Ohio, who still hoped for a Coolidge draft, moved that the clause "complimenting the President" be deleted. In an ironic rejoinder the insurgent Senator Norris of Nebraska replied: "Here is a resolution to be passed by this high legislative body in which we directly commend the President for a patriotic act that he did. . . . Then here come a few earnest, perhaps honest, perhaps ill-advised insurgents and they insist that we shall insult the President of the United States, that at least we shall not commend him for following in the footsteps of Washington."

Though the resolution was passed with the reference to Coolidge deleted, it tended to give a definite inter-pretation to the President's own pronouncements and encouraged the activities of other candidates. Hoover remained the strongest contender, but Governor Lowden of Illinois; Senator Charles Curtis, the majority floor leader from Kansas; Senator Willis of Ohio; and James Watson of Indiana were mentioned as alternatives. However, by the time the delegates assembled in Kansas City, Hoover seemed to have it.

The platform pledged increased economy, tax reduction and high tariffs, urged full enforcement of the Eighteenth Amendment, advocated international cooperation (but without American participation in the League of Nations) and in general took its stand on the accomplishments of the Coolidge administration. The only controversial plank was a renunciation of the McNary-Haugen farm bills which was unsuccessfully

ROOSEVELT AT THE CONVENTION

INP

Library of Congress

THE DEMOCRATIC CONVENTION IN HOUSTON

Associated Press

ALFRED E. SMITH, THE ELEGANT GOLFER

contested in a floor fight.

Hoover won the nomination on the first ballot by an overwhelming majority. As Hoover had been opposed to the McNary-Haugen farm bills, Senator Curtis of Kansas, who had strong farm support and a consistent record of party regularity, became his running mate, the first such candidate with Indian blood.

The Democrats, meeting two weeks later in Houston, Texas, held a convention in marked contrast to their bitter and long-drawn-out session of four years earlier. The conflicts between South and North, wet and dry, urban and rural, and Klan and anti-Klan were still present, but their effects had been nullified in September 1927 by an important pronouncement from William Gibbs McAdoo, the champion of the rural South and West. In a letter to the editor of the Chattanooga

News, McAdoo wrote that, "in the interests of party unity," he would not be a candidate for the nomination. With McAdoo out of the picture, it was expected that New York's Governor Smith would be the choice.

The platform of the Democrats was prepared and adopted with a minimum of discord. It charged that Republican rule had left America with "its industry depressed, its agriculture prostrate," and advocated farm-relief measures, tariff reform and a "constructive" foreign policy (but with no mention of the League or the World Court). The plank dealing with prohibition merely pledged the party to "an honest effort" to enforce the Eighteenth Amendment and castigated the Republicans' failure to do likewise.

For the third time in eight years, Franklin Delano Roosevelt placed the name of Governor Smith in nomi-

The Museum of the City of New York
THE "BROWN DERBY" IN THE CAMPAIGN

INP
THE "STIFF COLLAR" IN THE CAMPAIGN

nation. "We offer one who has the will to win—who not only deserves success but commands it. Victory is his habit—the happy warrior, Alfred Smith." The words rang in the auditorium—Smith had run a hundred thousand votes ahead of Davis in New York to become the first man elected Governor of that state for three terms in nearly a century.

Nine other names were proposed—most notably Senator James A. Reed of Missouri, Representative Cordell Hull of Tennessee, Jesse Jones of Texas and Senator Walter F. George of Georgia—but when Smith received only ten votes less than the necessary two-thirds majority on the first ballot, Ohio switched its vote and "the happy warrior" became the nominee. As a counterbalance for the ticket, the convention nominated Senator Joseph T. Robinson of Arkansas, a Southern Protestant with strong prohibitionist sympathies, for the Vice Presidency. An observer wrote that "the Democratic donkey with a wet head and wagging a dry tail left Houston."

The Republicans' greatest asset in the campaign was

economic prosperity. Hoover emphasized it in his acceptance speech: "We in America today are nearer to the final triumph over poverty than ever before in the history of the land. The poorhouse is vanishing from among us. We have not yet reached the goal, but, given a chance to go forward with the policies of the last eight years, we shall soon, with the help of God, be in sight of the day when poverty will be banished from the nation. There is no guaranty against poverty equal to a job for every man. This is the primary purpose of the policies we advocate." His sentiment was echoed by the popular Republican slogan, "Let's keep what we've got: Prosperity didn't just happen."

Both sides courted the support of business and both sides received large sums of money from it. The campaign expenditures for the Republicans ran to about $10 million; that of the Democrats, over $7 million—three times the amount expended in any previous campaign.

Smith worked hard to convince the business interests they could trust the Democrats. He advocated a protec-

Al Smith at Sedalia, Missouri; A.P.

THE CAVALCADE OF MOTOR CARS GREW INTO A PERMANENT FIXTURE OF CAMPAIGNING.

tive tariff. He chose John J. Raskob, who had risen high within the structure of General Motors and Du Pont, to run his campaign. He gave four more top spots on his staff to wealthy men—Herbert Lehman, Jesse Jones, James W. Gerard and Senator Peter Gerry.

The Bryan-McAdoo wing was unhappy about Smith's campaign. Millionaire John Raskob increased Southern and Western fears of urban Democrats; he was "wet" and also a Catholic. They wondered what Smith was doing to the party.

For the first time since the passage of the Eighteenth Amendment, prohibition was a major issue. Hoover was for full enforcement, describing it as "a great social and economic experiment, noble in motive and far-reaching in purpose" which "must be worked out constructively." Smith, whose personal habits were no secret, came out for modification of the prohibition laws to let the states vote on whether to keep light wines and beer banned. In the damp East, the Republican orators modified Hoover's phrase to read "must be worked *out* of constructively," and the Democrats in the West and South implied Smith's view was just a personal quirk and the party should not fear that he would try to do anything about it.

Another major issue was Smith's Catholicism. Rumors spread that the Pope had his bags packed and that all Protestant marriages would be annulled and Protestant children declared bastards. One preacher told his flock: "If you vote for Al Smith you're voting against Christ and you'll be damned." The Klan was a leader in this fight. Although Hoover repudiated these appeals to bigotry, the feeling was that the election of a Catholic would mean that American policy would be controlled by the Vatican.

Smith was attacked as a "rum-soaked Romanist." Such attacks were not made in the open—they were not printed—but were circulated mouth to mouth. He recalled in his autobiography: "Suddenly, as though by a pre-concerted arrangement a story started to circulate about me, and came from various parts of the country with the same general purport. A woman in Syracuse wrote to a woman in West Virginia that I was intoxi-

Marcus, New York Times, *October 21*

THE SNIPER

Marcus, New York Times, *September 23*

"LISTENING IN"

Jay N. "Ding" Darling, in the New York Tribune

THEY MADE HIM BRING HIS OWN PLANK, TOO!

Jay N. "Ding" Darling, in the New York Tribune

"A BIRD IN THE HAND . . ."

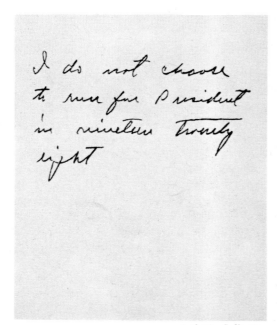

COOLIDGE REFUSES TO RUN AGAIN. On August 2, 1927, in Rapid City, South Dakota, Coolidge handed reporters the above statement. A newspaperman asked him to write it out and the President obliged. Some Republicans thought the words ambiguous and an invitation to a draft, but the Hoover forces took it at face value.

Gluyas Williams, in Life, *February 15, 1929*
CRISIS IN WASHINGTON—the much-publicized cartoon by artist Williams. "Mr. Coolidge refuses point blank to vacate the White House until his other rubber is found."

cated at the New York State Fair on Governor's Day and to such a degree that it required two men to hold me up while I was delivering an address from the grandstand. A Republican state senator who acted as escort to me that day by appointment of the State Department of Agriculture flatly denied that any such thing happened. Photographs and motion pictures had been taken of me from the minute I entered the fair grounds until I stepped aboard the New York Central train to go home. These showed plainly that the story had absolutely no foundation in fact. When the lie was nailed the woman in West Virginia refused to produce the letter and the woman in Syracuse denied that she had written it."

Hoover was also a subject of personal attack, though far less so than Smith. Columnist Heywood Broun called him "The Perfect Hypocrite." He was charged with cheating a Chinese man out of a fortune, and often was called un-American, while many Democrats ridiculed his supposed pro-British sympathies.

Smith had attempted to present himself as the personification of the new dynamics of the cities as he

stumped the country. Wherever he appeared, bands played "The Sidewalks of New York." In the rural areas, his crowds were large, but many came just to hear the man with a city voice and see the famous brown derby and the big cigar.

Kansas editor William Allen White explained the rural opposition; it was "not that Governor Smith is a Catholic and a wet which makes him an offense to the villagers and town dwellers, but because his record shows the kind of a President he would make—a Tammany President" and "Tammany is Tammany, and Smith is its prophet. . . . The whole Puritan civilization which has built a sturdy, orderly nation is threatened by Smith." And as a big-city politician he must be influenced by the city ways. White charged that Smith "had voted ten times against allowing the people to vote on any sort of a restriction on the sale of liquor; four times against stopping gambling and prostitution in connection with saloons; three times against repealing the law keeping saloons open on Sunday; four times in favor of removing zoning restrictions which would keep open saloons from churches and schools and three

Wide World
THREE GENERATIONS OF ROOSEVELTS in the Hyde Park polling place. Franklin Delano Roosevelt, his mother and his daughter, Anna, cast their ballots.

INP, November 1928
WAITING FOR THE ELECTION RESULTS in the New York Armory: Franklin Roosevelt with other Democrats is in the first row; candidate Al Smith is behind him.

times in favor of laws sponsored by organized gambling." Smith challenged his facts. Later White retracted these and similar charges which he felt had "hit below the belt" and were made "without thinking deeply about it."

The Reverend Doctor John Roach Straton, a leader of the Fundamentalists, picked up White's charges and aired them over radio station WQAO. He saw the larger focus of Smith's candidacy—part of the urban ills of "card playing, cocktail drinking, poodle dogs, divorce, novels, stuffy rooms, dancing, evolution, Clarence Darrow, overeating, nude art, prize-fighting, actors, greyhound racing and modernism." One Sunday in August, Straton gave a sermon on "The Moral and Religious Stakes in the Recent Political Situation—A Frank Discussion of the Dangers of Electing as President of the United States Any Man Who Advocates the Nullification of Religious Law, and Whose Election Would Inevitably Give Aid and Comfort to the Forces of Lawlessness, Immorality, Vice and Crime in

America." The sermon was as comprehensive as its title.

Smith asked Straton to allow him to refute the charges of his sermon from the same pulpit, and quoted as the words of Jesus Christ, "Thou shalt not bear false witness against thy neighbor." Straton wrote back that the quotation was not from the New Testament but from the Old and suggested that he and Smith meet in Madison Square Garden. And for the candidate's further edification he reminded him that the Scriptures also declared that "the powers that be [the Constitution of the United States] are ordained of God," including of course the Eighteenth Amendment. Smith replied that it was only fair to have a debate in the church where the charges were made—he did not want to make a circus out of it—and when Straton came up with other ideas, including a series of debates throughout the South patterned on the Lincoln-Douglas meetings, Smith dropped the whole thing.

Smith leveled constant barrages against the Republicans, but Hoover would not debate with him, nor

National Archives

TAKING THE OATH FROM CHIEF JUSTICE TAFT.

INP

THE INCOMING AND OUTGOING PRESIDENTS

would he mention his name in his speeches. Republican speakers reassured their audiences that the poorhouse was vanishing and there was "chicken in every pot and two cars in every garage." Smith cried out again and again, "Let's look at the record"—but people were not in the mood to look at sober facts.

The result was a Republican landslide; Hoover carried forty states, including Smith's own state of New York, all the border states and five in the Solid South. Smith lost even the usual Democratic strongholds Florida, North Carolina, Texas and Virginia, also the border states of Kentucky and Tennessee. Hoover's popular vote was 21,437,227 against Smith's 15,007,-698; his electoral vote stood 444 against Smith's 87. But in his defeat, Smith received twice as many votes as his party's candidate John W. Davis in 1924, who now wrote pessimistically: "In my judgment there is little that can be done at this moment along lines of party regeneration. A beaten army must be permitted to lie in its rest billets and nurse its wounds."

Library of Congress

HOOVER'S CABINET: Sitting: Walter F. Brown (Postmaster General), James W. Good (War), Frank B. Kellogg (State), the President, Andrew W. Mellon (Treasury), William D. Mitchell (Attorney General). Standing: James J. Davis (Labor), Robert P. Lamont (Commerce), Arthur M. Hyde (Agriculture), the Vice President, Ray Lyman Wilbur (Interior), Charles Francis Adams (Navy).

FRANKLIN D. ROOSEVELT

"We have not yet reached the goal," said Herbert Hoover, "but given a chance to go forward with the policies of the last eight years we shall soon, with the help of God, be within sight of the day when poverty will be banished from the nation." When he began his administration, the country was at a high crest of prosperity. The stock market was bullish and the fever of speculation at its peak; from industrialists to cabdrivers, from doctors to dishwashers—everybody speculated, bought and sold shares, chased after easy money. In the single month of January 1929 about a billion dollars of new securities were absorbed by eager investors.

In his inaugural address Hoover said that "in no nation are the fruits of accomplishment more secure," and millionaire John J. Raskob, the chairman of the Democratic National Committee, nodded his assent. "If a man saves $15 a week," said Raskob, "and invests in good common stocks, and allows the dividends and rights to accumulate, at the end of twenty years he will have at least $80,000, and an income from investment of around $400 a month. He will be rich. And because income can do that, I am firm in my belief that anyone not only can be rich, but ought to be rich."

Americans were lulling themselves into the belief that the upward trend of the stock market would continue indefinitely and that their profits would climb to higher and higher levels. But the country's prosperity was not based on solid foundation; the Republican promises of "two cars in every garage" and "two chickens in every pot" were fantasies. While business and industry yielded huge profits, the purchasing power of the farmers declined. While speculators amassed fortunes, the income of wage earners remained static. While industrial production was at a high point, more than a million and a half workers were without jobs.

The stock market speculation, the overexpansion of capital goods, the inadequate purchasing power of the masses, the depression in agriculture, the uncertainty of the foreign markets were leading to an economic collapse. And when it came, it came with a bang.

On October 24, 1929, prices of stocks began to sag. Three days later 12,894,650 shares were dumped on the market. Within the next few weeks securities tumbled $40 billion from their height.

At first people did not believe the seriousness of the crash. Bankers preached confidence. Hoover made encouraging statements. Economists predicted that as soon as the selling hysteria subsided, prosperity would return. But as purchasing power diminished merchandise piled up in the stores; factories curtailed production and dismissed workers. Those who could keep their jobs were forced to take sharp cuts. Salaries of clerks sank to $5 and $10 a week; the wages of domestic servants were reduced to $10 a month.

With wages low the people had not enough money to pay for food and rent; thus they curtailed all nonessential purchases. The cycle of the Depression moved in increasingly wider rings.

When, after months of tumbling prices and diminishing employment, some gains made, Hoover declared that "all evidences indicate that the worst effect of the crash will have been passed within the next sixty days, with the amelioration of seasonal unemployment,

FDR

CANDIDATES IN 1932

FRANKLIN D. ROOSEVELT (1882–1945), the successful Governor of New York, was nominated over Alfred Smith on the fourth ballot. Mencken wrote that he was the "weakest candidate." He promised a new deal for the "little man."

JOHN NANCE GARNER (1868–1967), Speaker of the House from Texas, was given the second place in return for giving the votes of Texas and California to Roosevelt. His ticket had 22,829,501 votes to the Republicans' 15,760,684.

HERBERT HOOVER (1874–1964), was renominated by the Republicans. His inept handling of the Depression brought him the animosity of the jobless masses, assuring his defeat. In the election he carried only six states.

CHARLES CURTIS (1860–1936), the Vice President, was renominated even though he felt no friendship for Hoover. In the past unpretentious but in office pompous, he discarded his Kansas sombrero for a shiny top hat.

NORMAN THOMAS (1884——), presidential nominee of the Socialist party for the second time, was acclaimed by those dissatisfied with the Republicans and the Democrats. He was given a record 884,649 popular votes.

WILLIAM Z. FOSTER (1881–1961) was the presidential candidate of the Communists. He had as running mate James Ford, a Negro labor leader, the first of his race to win one of the nation's top two nominations.

Photograph taken on March 17, 1905

ANNA ELEANOR ROOSEVELT (1884–1962), the daughter of Theodore Roosevelt's brother Elliott, married her distant cousin 23-year-old Franklin on March 17, 1905, in New York. Her uncle, President Theodore Roosevelt, gave her away and stole the limelight from the newlyweds.

The Roosevelts had six children, one girl and five sons: Anna (b. 1906), James (1907), Franklin (1908; died the next year), Elliott (1910), Franklin (1914), John (1916). Mrs. Roosevelt, the outstanding personality of her age, was a remarkable woman. The eyes and ears of her husband, she was a humanitarian forever battling to improve the lot of the poor and underprivileged.

the gaining strength of other forces, and the continued cooperation of the many agencies actively cooperating with the government to restore business and to relieve distress."

To the hard-hit millions the President's advice was a simplistic one: weather the storm. He tried to persuade industry not to make further layoffs, but industrialists would not listen.

As the number of unemployed grew, private charity could no longer cope with the problems of relief, nor could the local and state governments. A cry went up for Federal aid.

Hoover clung tenaciously to the idea of "rugged individualism" and to the *laissez-faire* economic philosophy—it was not the government's task to interfere with business.

Wide World

CONTRAST IN PERSONALITIES. The Roosevelt of 1932 gave the voters the impression of a happy and optimistic extrovert; while the man whom he opposed, President Hoover, gave the image of a dour and pessimistic introvert.

In the mid-term election the Democrats regained their majority in the House of Representatives; the Senate was evenly divided. The Republican future looked bleak. Hoover held on to the beliefs of the past in the midst of a rapidly changing world. He held to the wheel on a rudderless ship.

His administration could be divided into five distinct periods. The first short and happy phase lasted from inauguration day in 1929 until the crash in October. During this time prosperity was on the rise and with it Hoover's popularity. Then came disaster; for a few months Hoover tried to cope by using temporary measures, not realizing the gravity of the events. The third phase, from March 1930 until June 1931, was a time of despair. Hoover said that the Depression was part of the international economic debâcle and advised

CARTOONS OF THE CAMPAIGN

Clifford Berryman, in the Washington Star, *June 22, 1930*

Clifford Berryman, in the Washington Star, *March 9, 1932*

Clifford Berryman, in the Washington Star, *July 21, 1932*

America to free itself "of world influences and make a large measure of independent recovery." During the fourth phase—from June to October 1931—he had to admit the seriousness of the crisis, declared a moratorium on war debts and sought measures to cope with the calamity.

With the nominating conventions around the corner, Hoover was urged not to seek renomination, but he could not be moved. The Republican convention, acceding to his wishes, renominated him on the first ballot. His only avowed rival, Dr. Joseph D. France, the former Senator from Maryland, was bodily carried off the platform when he proposed that the convention should choose ex-President Coolidge instead of Hoover.

The thirty-seven planks of the 8,500-word platform had no constructive proposals for combating the Depression. Amazingly, the Republicans glossed over the nation's economic plight in a few meaningless phrases. On prohibition they proposed that Congress should submit a new amendment on the liquor traffic to state conventions and leave the decision to them.

While the Republicans had little hope of victory, the Democrats were confident. With millions unemployed, with the country's economy on the brink, they were sure to win.

The list of their contenders was a long one. Three former candidates—James M. Cox of 1920; John W. Davis of 1924; Alfred E. Smith of 1928—vied for the candidacy again. The hats of two former vice presidential candidates—Franklin D. Roosevelt of 1920 and Joseph T. Robinson of 1928—were in the ring as well. Among other contenders were Wilson's Secretary of War Newton D. Baker, the Senators J. H. Lewis and James A. Reed, Speaker of the House John N. Garner, the Governors and ex-Governors Albert F. Ritchie, Harry F. Byrd, Harry Moore, George White and William H. Murray.

The forerunners were Al Smith and Franklin D. Roosevelt. Smith had the strong support of the party regulars, though some of them complained that he was no longer the "Happy Warrior" of the brown derby and the cocked cigar, but that he had gone "high-hat, highbrow, and high-life." His handicaps were his religion and his 1928 defeat.

Franklin D. Roosevelt, the Governor of New York, had no such disadvantages. His fame as an energetic, progressive and liberal-minded governor was rising. He was skillfully managed by Louis McHenry Howe, a gnomelike little man with boundless energy. A group of able men under his direction worked assiduously for Roosevelt's nomination. James Farley, who was one of them, recalls that "never in the history of politics was there anything like our letter-writing and long-distance telephone campaign." Democratic county

THE DEMOCRATIC CONVENTION in Chicago gave a lusty cheer to Roosevelt when he promised in his acceptance speech to aid not only the forgotten man but also the forgotten woman, and pledged "a new deal for the American people."

chairmen were asked to report from their districts. Roosevelt signed an avalanche of letters, called politicians on the telephone, sent them autographed photographs. If a county chairman's son were to marry, or his daughter to give birth to a child, he was sure to receive a congratulatory message.

Before the Democrats met in Chicago the Roosevelt men surveyed the delegates, and when these surveys showed that Roosevelt was the favorite, the fact was used with telling effect on delegates who were for other candidates.

In the preconvention skirmishes the Roosevelt forces suffered two setbacks. Their proposals—to abrogate the century-old two-thirds rule and to change the order of proceedings, placing the nominations first and the discussion of the platform afterward—were defeated. (They insisted on the latter because they feared that

Lorant: FDR, A Pictorial Biography (*Simon & Schuster*)
FLYING TO CHICAGO. The Governor, with his wife and sons Elliott and John, flew to the convention city to accept the nomination in person to show the country that disability would not hinder him in his presidential duties.

HOOVER CAMPAIGNING. His slogan, "We want to turn the corner to prosperity," appeared in the streets, but his prophecies—"The worst has passed" and "Prosperity is just around the corner"—were used against him just the same.

THOUSANDS GATHERED at every train stop to hear the President. Here Hoover speaks at Rock Island, Illinois.

the fight over the platform might create such ill feelings among the delegates that Roosevelt would not be able to get the nomination.)

But as soon as the convention settled down to the main business, Roosevelt's strength became manifest. All the pro-Roosevelt delegates from Louisiana and Minnesota were accepted, and Senator Walsh of Montana—a Roosevelt man—was named for the permanent chairmanship.

The Democratic platform was bold and forthright. It promised unemployment relief, unemployment and old-age insurance under state laws, labor legislation, help for the farmer, conservation, development of power resources, regulation of securities exchanges, reciprocal trade agreements; it offered a balanced budget and a sound currency.

At Indianapolis, October 20, 1932

ROOSEVELT CAMPAIGNING. He gave twenty-seven major addresses throughout the country, outlining his program and promising a new deal to the American people. The slogan "Abolish bread lines" greeted him everywhere he went.

The plank proposing the repeal of prohibition was cheered for ten full minutes. But minority reports opposed an out-and-out repeal. Senator Cordell Hull proposed submitting the repeal amendment to the states so that in the election the Democrats should not be branded as either dry or wet. Yet the wets carried the day with 934¾ votes against 213¾.

At three o'clock in the morning on the first day of July the last speaker was through with his nominating speech. The oratory, at long last, came to an end. The weary and sleepy delegates were longing for adjournment, but the Roosevelt managers were anxious to begin with the balloting. The first ballot was taken at 4:25 in the morning. Though Roosevelt led with 666¼ votes against Smith's 301¾, he had 103 votes less than the necessary two thirds. On the second trial the

Lorant: FDR, A Pictorial Biography (*Simon & Schuster*)

THE FARMERS CAME to welcome and listen to the New York Governor, responding to his keen interest in people.

Roosevelt vote increased to 677¾, still not enough for victory. After Roosevelt gained an additional five votes on the third ballot, the convention adjourned until nine o'clock that evening.

During the day frantic efforts were made by Roosevelt's managers to clinch the nomination. Farley offered Sam Rayburn and Silliman Evans of Texas a deal which Roosevelt had endorsed on the telephone. For the Texas and California votes, John Nance Garner, a Texan, would be given the Vice Presidency. But to consummate the deal one had to gain the consent of William Randolph Hearst, the newspaper publisher who controlled the California delegation. At first Hearst would not hear of it, but when Farley threatened to swing the Roosevelt vote to Newton D. Baker, an internationalist and advocate of the League of Nations, Hearst swung behind Roosevelt.

Thus, when the convention reconvened, William McAdoo, the spokesman for the California delegation, mounted the rostrum and amid cheers and catcalls declared: "California came here to nominate a President of the United States. She did not come to deadlock the convention or to engage in another devastating contest like that of 1924. Therefore California casts forty-four votes for Franklin D. Roosevelt." At the end of this trial Roosevelt received 945 votes and with them the nomi-

nation. Mencken noted: "Here was a great convention . . . nominating the weakest candidate before it."

The next day Governor Roosevelt flew from Albany to Chicago. He triumphantly entered to the tune of "Happy Days Are Here Again." He wanted to show that his physical disability (in 1921 he had contracted infantile paralysis) would be no hindrance in the performance of his duties. His speech to the convention was an innovation; it was the first time that a candidate had appeared in person before the delegates to deliver an acceptance speech. Roosevelt said he had "started out on the tasks that lie ahead by breaking the absurd tradition that the candidate should remain in professed ignorance of what has happened for weeks until he is formally notified of that many weeks later. You have nominated me and I know it, and I am here to thank you for the honor. Let it be symbolic that in so doing, I broke traditions. Let it be from now on the task of our party to break foolish traditions."

Roosevelt promised aid to the "forgotten man," to help him realize his hope for a return to the old standard of living in the United States. He upheld the plank about the repeal of prohibition, but he said the dry states would be protected if they decided to keep out intoxicating liquors and prevent the return of the saloon. And he ended his speech: "I pledge you, I pledge myself,

CAMPAIGN CARTOONS BY ROLLIN KIRBY

November 1932

"RUMORS"

September 1932

"THE HAUNTED MAN"

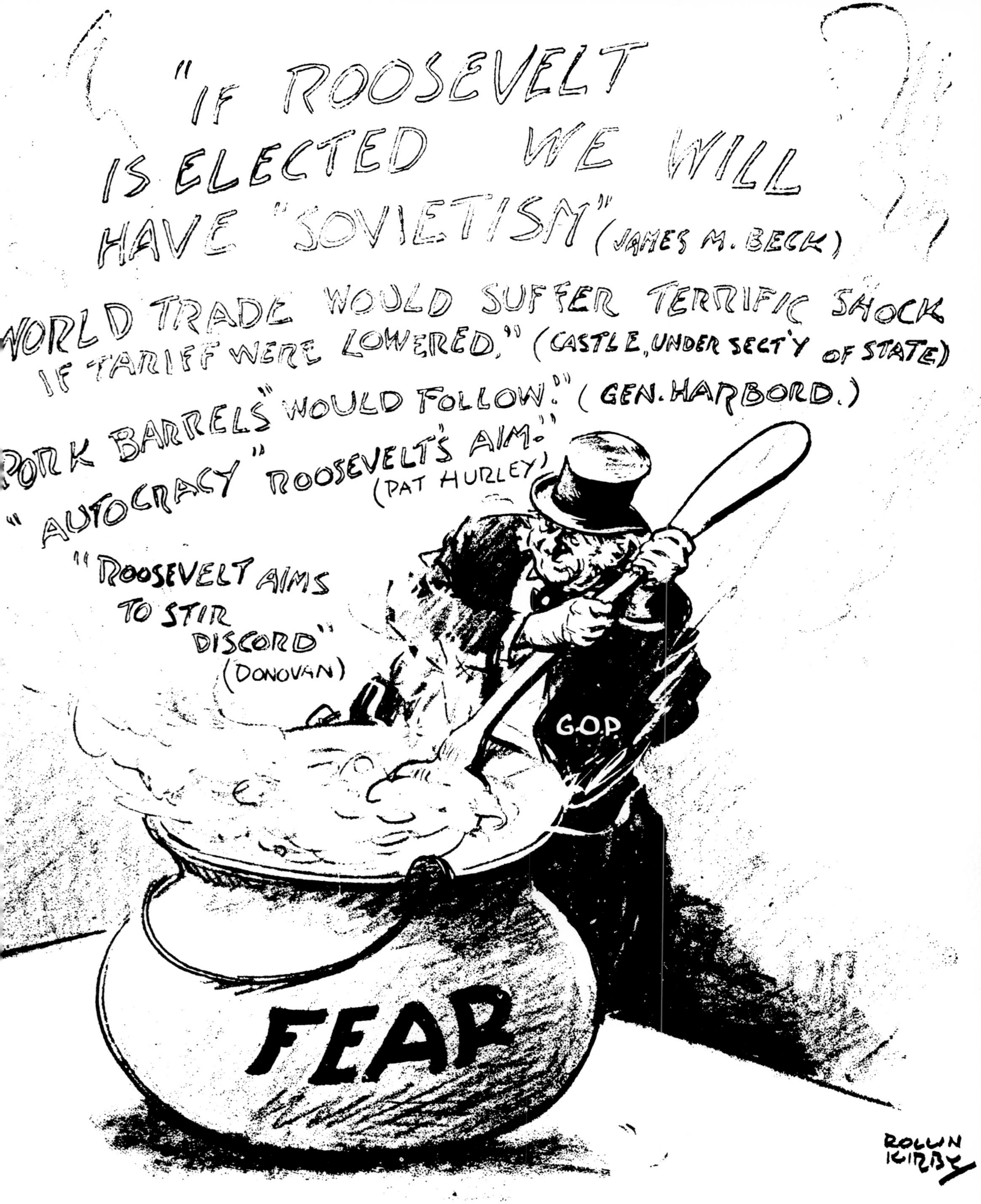

"STIRRING IT UP"
October 1932

Talburt, August 1932

ONE OF THE MAIN ISSUES WAS PROHIBITION. The Republican attitude was halfhearted about the "wet" issue; the Democrats were more outspoken about repeal.

Rollin Kirby, June 1932

TWO CHICKENS IN EVERY GARAGE. The Depression and Hoover's optimistic prophecies were widely criticized.

to a new deal* for the American people. Let us all order of competence and courage. This is more than a political campaign; it is a call to arms! Give me your help, not to win votes alone, but to win in this crusade to restore America to its own people."

With that the campaign was on its way.

The early Republican strategy revolved around three main themes: an attack on the vice presidential candidate Garner as "unsound" and "radical," coupled with the rumor that Roosevelt's health was so poor his election might mean the elevation of Garner to the Presidency; an attack on Roosevelt's "radical" theories; and a whispering campaign in Catholic communities that the preconvention anti-Catholic propaganda against Smith was instigated by Roosevelt.

To refute the Republican allegations about Roosevelt's health, Farley told the country in a radio address: "In various parts of the country hateful stories are cropping up in regard to our candidate's physical and mental health. . . . The Governor recently insured his life for $500,000 with the Warm Springs Foundation as beneficiary. . . . His lameness, which is steadily getting better, has no more effect on his general condition than if he had a glass eye or was prematurely bald. . . . If he were a weakling in any respect, he could not have gone through two grueling campaigns for the governorship of New York. . . . Governor Roosevelt might be handicapped in a footrace, but in no other way need he fear comparison with his adversary."

The strategy of Roosevelt's managers was carefully conceived. Using the newest propaganda methods, Howe, Farley and Charlie Michelson made up elaborate files on all the influential men in the states, and they kept in touch with 140,000 Democratic Committeemen.

Roosevelt traveled around the country giving twenty-seven major addresses and thirty-two shorter ones. *Time* magazine wrote: "If September crowds and applause meant November votes (which one rule says they do), the Pacific Coast was in his bag." At Sacramento Roosevelt praised Hiram Johnson, a progressive Republican; in Nebraska he told Senator George W. Norris, another progressive Republican: "I go along with you because you follow in their footsteps—'radical' like Jefferson, 'demagogue' like Jackson, 'idealist' like Lincoln, 'wild' like Theodore Roosevelt, 'theorist' like Wilson." And Norris said: "What this country needs is another Roosevelt in the White House."

In his speeches he suggested means to end the Depres-

---

*Roosevelt took the phrase "a new deal" from Mark Twain's Connecticut Yankee, who said that "when six men out of a thousand crack the whip over their fellows' backs, then what the other nine hundred ninety-four dupes need is a new deal."

Keystone, July 18, 1932

"JUST A CHAT," Franklin Roosevelt answered reporters when they asked him why he visited Colonel Edward M. House, the political friend and adviser of President Wilson, on the patio of his home in Beverly Farms, Massachusetts.

sion, offering measures for recovery and reform. "At Topeka," as Roosevelt recalled himself, "I outlined a complete national plan for the restoration of agriculture to its proper relationship to the nation. At Salt Lake City I outlined a definite program to give us a definite transportation policy, including the rehabilitation of the railroads of the nation. At Portland I set forth in definite terms a national policy for the conduct of utilities, and especially those engaged in manufacturing and distributing electric power. At Sioux City I proposed a tariff policy aimed to restore international trade and commerce not only with this nation but between all nations. At Boston I championed the principle that the national government has a positive duty to see that no citizen shall starve. At Columbus I proposed the protection of the investing public against the evils and the fraud perpetrated against them during the past ten years. At Pittsburgh I proposed an honest national budget."

Lorant: FDR, A Pictorial Biography (*Simon & Schuster*)

THE TWO FORMER FRIENDS, now "friendly enemies," chat amicably for a brief moment during a garden party.

Photograph by Sammy Schulman, February 15, 1933

THE ATTEMPTED ASSASSINATION OF ROOSEVELT at Miami's Bay Front Park. Joe Zangara, an Italian bricklayer, fired at the President-elect but missed his target; still, one of the bullets hit Anton Cermak, the Mayor of Chicago, who stood nearby. The seriously wounded Cermak was rushed to Jackson Memorial Hospital, where he died three weeks later.

INS, February 15, 1933

THE HAPPY PRESIDENT-ELECT acknowledges the ovation of the large crowd a few minutes before the shooting.

Wherever he went he spoke on repeal of prohibition, a welcome subject for many. There was so much emphasis on repeal that Will Rogers suggested a plank "to show the people where to get some bread with the beer."

Compared to the Roosevelt camp's feverish activity, Hoover's campaign was lifeless. The President gave ten major addresses. He defended his measures in broad terms, asserting that the Depression was not the fault of the administration but was due to foreign causes, and "let no man say it could not have been worse." Often he faced a hostile audience. He was booed in Detroit, Philadelphia, Salt Lake City. Reilly, the White House Secret Service man who accompanied him, recalled that

COUNTING THE VOTE. Vice President Curtis jokingly congratulates Vice President-elect Garner on his election.

people ran out into the streets to thumb their noses at the President.

The Democratic propaganda kept reminding the electorate of Hoover's remarks that "prosperity is just around the corner" and "the worst has passed." A smear campaign on Hoover's character was in high gear; he was accused of not being an American but a Britisher, that he had made a fortune out of Belgian relief funds, that as a German sympathizer during the war he had been responsible for the execution of Edith Cavell, that he practiced crooked finance in Hong Kong, that he employed Chinese coolies in his South African mines.

The Republicans were at a loss to answer the barrage of abuse. Republican orators kept repeating that Hoover was a "great engineer" and a "great humanitarian," and attacked Roosevelt who was "no real farmer, no true Democrat, no real friend of the industrialist, not a genuine Roosevelt and no true disciple of Jefferson in so far as religious tolerance is concerned." They called Roosevelt a radical, a Socialist, a Bolshevist. Roosevelt shot back: "My policy is as radical as American liberty, as radical as the Constitution of the United States." And he said that Hoover's record was like that of the Four Horsemen: "Destruction, Delay, Despair and Deceit."

As the contest came down the stretch, the Republicans reverted to time-worn scare tactics, telling those who still had jobs that they, too, would be unemployed if Roosevelt became President. Hoover said that

Lorant: **FDR, A Pictorial Biography** *(Simon & Schuster)*

HOOVER GREETS ROOSEVELT with a smile as he enters the car at the White House, but his seeming cordiality was only for the public. Beneath that smile lay a strong feeling of animosity. He would not speak; he just sat in silence. The two men rode to the inaugural ceremonies, without saying a word, like children who have been forced to sit together.

"grass would grow in the streets of one hundred cities" and "weeds overrun millions of farms" if the Democratic ticket was elected.

In his address at New York's Madison Square Garden ex-President Coolidge said that "the charge is made that the Republican party does not show any solicitude for the common run of people but is interested only in promoting the interests of a few favored individuals and corporations. . . . All this is a question of method. . . . We have advocated strengthening the position of the employer that he might pay better wages to his em-

ployees." But the country was no longer in a mood to accept trite explanations. The people demanded action, even radical action, so long as the millions of unemployed could regain their jobs.

In his last campaign address Hoover gave a philosophical analysis between the Republican and Democratic positions. "The campaign is more than a contest between two men," he said. "It is a contest between two philosophies of government," and the country had to choose between individualism and regimentation. Then "you cannot extend the mastery of government over the

Lorant: FDR, A Pictorial Biography (*Simon & Schuster*)

DURING THE DRIVE to the Capitol Roosevelt tries to draw Hoover into conversation, but Hoover remains aloof. "I said to myself, 'spinach,'" related Roosevelt later. "The two of us simply couldn't sit there on our hands ignoring each other and everyone else. So I began to wave my own response with my top hat." Still Hoover remained mute. As they passed the unfinished Commerce Building, the exasperated Roosevelt pointed to the skeleton and exclaimed with a smile: "Lovely steel."

daily life of a people without somewhere making it master of people's souls and thought."

On election day, of the forty million men and women who went to the polls, one in every three was without work or regular income. Discontent and gloom hung over the country. The army of bonus marchers, disbanded by government troops with tear gas and bayonets, was still a vivid memory, as were the parades of the hungry. On election eve Herbert Hoover remarked to his secretary: "I'll tell you what our trouble is—we are opposed by six million unemployed, ten thousand

bonus marchers, and ten-cent corn."

A number of smaller parties put up candidates. The Socialists presented Norman Thomas; the Communists, William Z. Foster, and they nominated a Negro, James W. Ford of Alabama, for the second place; the Prohibitionists were behind William D. Upshaw; the Farmer-Labor and Socialist-Labor parties upheld Verne L. Reynolds.

The result was a reversal of 1928: Roosevelt won forty-two states, Hoover only six (Connecticut, Delaware, Maine, New Hampshire, Pennsylvania and

Vermont). Of the popular vote Roosevelt received 22,821,857, Hoover, 15,761,845.

In William Allen White's opinion the overwhelming victory of the Democrats showed "a firm desire on the part of the American people to use government as an agency for human welfare."

On inauguration day Roosevelt attended a church service across Lafayette Park, for "a thought to God is the right way to start off my administration." By then Governor Lehman had declared a four-day bank holiday for New York as did Governor Horner for Illinois. All security and commodity exchanges in New York and Chicago were closed.

Roosevelt took the oath from Chief Justice Charles Evans Hughes on the ancient Dutch Bible which had been in his family for three centuries. He began his address with the ringing phrase: "This is preeminently the time to speak the truth, the whole truth, frankly and boldly." The millions listening on their radios hung on his every word. His voice, as John Dos Passos noted, "after a moment's hoarseness was confident and full, carefully tuned to the microphones; the patroon voice, the headmaster's admonishing voice, the bedside doctor's voice that spoke to each man and to all of us."

Roosevelt went on. "This great Nation will endure as it has endured, will revive and will prosper," he said, thrusting out his pronounced chin in defiance. "So first of all, let me assert my firm belief that the only thing we have to fear is fear itself—nameless, unreasoning, unjustified terror which paralyzes needed efforts to convert retreat into advance." This was a new voice in America. "In such a spirit on my part and on yours we face our common difficulties. They concern, thank God, only material things. Values have shrunken to fantastic levels; taxes have risen; our ability to pay has fallen; government of all kinds is faced by serious curtailment of income; the means of exchange are frozen in the currents of trade; the withered leaves of industrial enterprise lie on every side; farmers find no markets for their produce; the savings of many years in thousands of families are gone. More important, a host of unemployed citizens face the grim problem of existence, and an equally great number toil with little return. Only a foolish optimist can deny the dark realities of the moment."

With bated breath the country listened to the speech: "The money changers have fled from their high seats in the temple of our civilization. We may now restore that temple to the ancient truths. The measure of the restoration lies in the extent to which we apply social values more noble than mere monetary profit."

The solemn crowd blackening forty acres of park and pavement before the speaker nodded their approval, as did the people in their homes. "Happiness lies not in the

Lorant: FDR, A Pictorial Biography (*Simon & Schuster*)

ROOSEVELT TAKES THE OATH from Chief Justice Charles Evans Hughes, resting his hand on the old Dutch Bible which had belonged to the Roosevelt family for generations. Behind him stand his son James and ex-President Hoover.

mere possession of money," continued Roosevelt, "it lies in the joys of achievement, in the thrill of creative effort. The joy and moral stimulation of work no longer must be forgotten in the mad chase of evanescent profits. These dark days will be worth all they cost us if they teach us that our true destiny is not to be ministered unto but to minister to ourselves and to our fellow men."

He promised to accept the responsibility of leading the nation out of the crisis. "Restoration calls, however, not for changes in ethics alone. This Nation asks for action, and action now. Our greatest primary task is to put people to work. I am prepared under my constitu-

tional duty to recommend the measures that a stricken Nation in the midst of a stricken world may require." He was hopeful of the future.

He promised that, if "the normal balance of Executive and legislative authority" proved inadequate to meet the immediate demands of national recovery, "I shall not evade the clear course of duty that will then confront me. I shall ask the Congress for the one remaining instrument to meet the crisis—broad Executive power to wage a war against the emergency, as great as the power that would be given to me if we were in fact invaded by a foreign foe . . . I can do no less."

With this a new era in America's history had begun.

Inaugural Address —

I am certain that my fellow Americans expect that
on my induction into the Presidency I will address them
with a candor and a decision which the present situation
of our nation impels. This is preeminently the time
to speak the truth, the whole truth, frankly and boldly.
Nor need we shrink from ~~being~~ honest *by facing* ~~as to the~~ conditions
~~in~~ of our country today. This great nation will endure
as it has endured, will revive and will prosper. So
first of all let me assert my firm belief that the only
thing we have to fear is fear itself, - nameless, unreasoning,
unjustified terror which paralyzes ~~the needed~~ efforts *needed* *To*
convert retreat into advance.
~~to bring about prosperity once more.~~

In every dark hour of our national life

~~[heavily crossed out lines]~~
a leadership of frankness
and vigor *has* met with that understanding and support of
the people themselves which is essential to victory.

I am convinced that you will again give that support to

leadership in these critical days.

In such a spirit on my part and ~~yours we~~ *on yours* we
our common difficulties. They *concern* thank God,
~~only~~ material things. Values have shrunken to
fantastic levels; taxes have risen ; our ability to
pay has fallen; government of all kinds is faced by
serious curtailment of income; the means of exchange
are ~~being madly hoarded and diverted from~~ *frozen in* the currents
of trade; *the withered leaves of lie on every side;* industrial enterprise ~~is stagnate;~~ farmers
find no markets for their produce; the savings of many
years in thousands of families are gone.

More important, a host of unemployed citizens face
the grim problem of existence, and an equally great
number toil with little return. Only a foolish
optimist can deny the dark realities of the moment.

Yet our ~~[crossed out]~~ distress comes from no failure
of substance. We are stricken by no plague of locusts.
Compared with the perils which our forefathers conquered,

THE FINAL SCRIPT OF FRANKLIN DELANO ROOSEVELT'S FIRST INAUGURAL ADDRESS SHOWS

--5--

minister ~~not only~~ to ourselves *and* ~~but~~ to our fellowmen,
~~[crossed out]~~

Recognition of the falsity of ~~money made~~ *material wealth as the* standard
of ~~(real prosperity)~~ *(of) success* goes hand in hand with the abandonment of the false belief that public office and high
political position are to be valued only by the
standards of pride of place and personal profit; *and there*
must be an end to a conduct in banking and in business
which too often has given to a sacred trust the
likeness of callous and selfish wrongdoing. Small
wonder that confidence languishes, for it thrives
only on honesty, on honor, on the sacredness of
obligations, on faithful protection, on unselfish
performance; ~~without~~ without them it cannot live.

Restoration calls, however, not for changes in
ethics ~~[crossed out]~~ alone *This* ~~the~~ nation asks for action, and
action now.

--6--

Our greatest primary task is to put people to work.
This is no unsolvable problem if we face it wisely and
courageously. It can be accomplished in part by direct
recruiting by the government itself, treating the task
as we would treat the emergency of a war, but at the same
time through this employment accomplishing greatly needed
projects to stimulate and reorganize the use of our natural
resources.

Hand in hand with this
~~[crossed out]~~ we must ~~meet~~ frankly
recognize the ~~[over]~~ overbalance of population in our industrial
centers and, ~~endeavor~~ by engaging on a national scale in
a redistribution, *endeavor* to provide a better use of the land for
those best fitted for the land. *The Task* ~~[crossed out]~~ can be helped by
definite efforts to raise the values of agricultural
products and with this the power to purchase the output of
our cities. It can be helped by ~~[crossed out]~~ *planning* realistically

leave stand

(because they believed and were not afraid) we have

still much to be thankful for. Nature still offers

her bounty and human efforts have multiplied it. ~~There~~

~~is~~ plenty *is at* at our doorstep, but a vast use of it languishes

in the very sight of the supply. Primarily, this is

because the rulers of the exchange of mankind's goods

have failed through their own stubbornness and their own

incompetence, have admitted their failure and abdicated.

Practices   *unscrupulous*

~~The standards~~ of the money changers stand indicted in the

court of public opinion, rejected by the hearts and

minds of men.

True, they have tried, but their efforts have been

cast (~~loos~~) in the pattern of an outworn tradition. Faced

by failure of credit they have proposed only the lending

by which

of more money. Stripped of the lure of profit, to

induce our people to follow their false leadership they

have resorted to exhortations, pleading tearfully for

restored confidence. ~~————————~~

~~————————~~ They know *only* ~~of no other ways~~

of a generation of self-seekers.

~~them~~ the ~~ancient~~ rules. They have no vision, and when

there is no vision the people perish. The money

changers have fled from their high seats in the temple

of our civilization.

We may now restore that temple to the ancient truths.

The measure of the restoration lies in the extent to

social values

which we apply ~~a standard of values~~ more ~~noble~~ noble

~~than~~ mere monetary profit.

Happiness lies not in the mere possession of money;

it lies in the joy of achievement, in the thrill of

joy and   *no longer*

creative effort. The moral stimulation of work must.

forgotten   *by mad chase of*

be ~~no longer merged~~ in ~~the chase of~~ evanescent profits.

~~(—————)~~ These dark days will be worth all they cost

teach us that

us if they ~~—————————————————~~ that our

true destiny is not to be ministered ~~to~~ unto but to

THAT THE PRESIDENT-ELECT KEPT ADDING CORRECTIONS UNTIL THE TIME OF ITS DELIVERY.

the tragedy of the growing loss through foreclosure, of

our small homes and our farms. It can be helped by insistence

that the federal, state and local governments act forthwith

on the demand that their cost be drastically reduced. It

can be helped by the unifying of relief activities which today

and unequal.

are often scattered, ~~inefficient~~ uneconomical.

it can be helped

There are many ways in which ~~————————~~, but

NH   *it*   *never be ed*   *by*

~~————~~ can ~~only be~~ help ~~ed~~ ~~by~~ merely talking about it. We must

act and act quickly.

It can be helped

~~(—— we can accomplish much)~~ by national planning

for and supervision of all forms of transportation and of

communications and other utilities which have a definitely

public character.

Finally, in our progress toward a resumption of work

we require two safeguards against a return of the evils of

the old order: there must be a strict supervision of all

banking and credits and investments; there must be an end

to speculation with other people's money, and there must be

provision for an adequate but sound currency.

These are the lines of attack. I shall presently

urge upon a new Congress in special session detailed measures

for their fulfilment, and I shall seek the immediate

assistance of the several states.

Through this ~~definite~~ program of action we address ourselves

And making income balance outgo

to putting our own national house in order. Our international

trade relations though vastly important, are in point of

time and necessity secondary to the establishment of a sound

national economy. I favor as a practical policy the putting

of first things first. I shall spare no effort to restore

world trade by international economic readjustment, but the

emergency at home cannot wait on that accomplishment.

the

The basic thought that guides t~~hese~~ ~~—————~~ specific

means of national recovery is not narrowly nationalistic.

~~(—————).~~ It is the insistence, as a first consideration, upon the interdependence of the various elements in and parts of the United States -- a recognition of the old and permanently important manifestation of the American spirit of the pioneer.   It is the way to recovery.   It is the immediate way.   It is the strongest assurance that the recovery will endure.

In the field of world policy I would dedicate this nation to the policy of the good neighbor -- the neighbor who resolutely respects himself and because he does so, respects the rights of others -- the neighbor who respects his obligations and respects the sanctity of his agreements in and with a world of neighbors.

If I read the temper of our people correctly we now realise *let it stand* as we have never realised before our interdependence on each other: that we cannot merely take but we must give as well; *more* that we are to go forward we must go forward as a trained and loyal army willing to sacrifice this thing or that thing for

the good of the common discipline, and because without such discipline no progress is made no leadership becomes effective.

We are, I know, ready and willing to submit our lives and property to such discipline because it makes possible a leadership which aims at a larger good. This I propose to offer, pledging that the larger purposes will bind upon us all as a sacred obligation with a unity of duty hitherto evoked only in time of armed strife.

With this pledge taken, I assume unhesitatingly the leadership of this great army of our people dedicated to a disciplined attack upon our common problems.

Action in this image and to this end is feasible under the form of government which we have inherited from our ancestors. Our constitution is so simple and practical that it is possible always to meet extraordinary needs by changes in emphasis and arrangement without loss of essential form.   That is why our constitutional system

has proved itself the most superbly enduring political mechanism the modern world has produced.   It has met every stress of vast expansion of territory, of foreign wars, of bitter internal strife, of world relations.

It is to be hoped that the normal balance of executive and legislative authority may be wholly adequate to meet the unprecedented task before us.   But it may be that an unprecedented demand and need for undelayed action may call for temporary departure from that normal balance of public procedure.

I am prepared under my constitutional duty to recommend the measures that a stricken nation in the midst of a stricken world may require.   These measures, or such other measures as the Congress may build out of their experience and wisdom, I shall, within my constitutional authority, seek to bring to speedy adoption.

12

But in the event that the Congress shall fail to take one of these two courses, and in the event that the national emergency is still critical, I shall not evade the clear course of duty that will then confront me.   I shall ask the Congress for the one remaining instrument to meet the crisis -- broad executive power to wage a war against the emergency, as great as the power that would be given to me if we were in fact invaded by a foreign foe.

For the trust reposed in me I will return the courage and the devotion that befit the time.   I can do no less.

We face the arduous days that lie before us in the warm courage of national unity; with the clear consciousness of seeking old and precious moral values; with the clean satisfaction that comes from the stern performance of duty by old and young alike.   We aim at the assurance of a rounded and permanent national life.

We do not distrust the future of essential democracy. The people of the United States have not failed.   In their

need they have registered a mandate that they want direct vigorous action.   They have asked for discipline and direction under leadership.   They have made me the instrument, the temporary humble instrument of their wishes.   In the spirit of the gift I take it.

In this dedication of a nation we humbly ask the blessing of God.   May he protect each and every one of us.   May he guide me in the days to come.

This was the final draft of the Inaugural at Hyde Park - Wed. March 1st 1933

Franklin D Roosevelt

THE LAST FIVE MANUSCRIPT PAGES OF ROOSEVELT'S INAUGURAL ADDRESS

FRANKLIN D. ROOSEVELT

Franklin D. Roosevelt broke with the philosophy of past governments. No longer would the administration stand aside while millions were without work and suffering privation. Roosevelt felt it was the responsibility of the government to help those who through no fault of their own were in desperate situations. How could there be "business as usual," how could there be "rugged individualism," when the nation's very existence was in peril? The state had to step in, it had to adjust the economic controls.

Roosevelt asked Congress for a far-reaching program of social and economic legislation, and Congress in its memorable hundred-day session complied, enacting a series of relief, recovery and reform measures. A host of Federal agencies came into being to relieve the distress of the vast number of unemployed. The Federal Emergency Relief Administration (FERA) under Harry Hopkins supplied individual states and local communities with Federal funds to the tune of some three billion dollars to help the jobless. The Civil Works Administration (CWA) started projects offering work during the coming winter months. The Works Progress Administration (WPA), which supplanted the FERA, stimulated business by increasing the amount of money in circulation ("priming the pump") and by planning projects of lasting value. Another agency, the Public Works Administration (PWA) under Harold Ickes, mapped out long-range plans of public works, using regular labor (not relief labor) and carrying out heavy construction projects on waterworks, municipal power plants, hospitals and school buildings.

To rehabilitate industry and improve working condi-

tions, the National Recovery Act (NRA) was instituted with the aims of increasing industrial production and employment, of reducing ruthless methods of competition, of securing higher wages (a minimum wage of forty cents an hour), of bettering working conditions, and of reducing working time (a thirty-six-hour week for industrial and a forty-hour-week for clerical workers). The NRA granted labor the right to organize and strike (Section 7A said that "Employees shall have the right to organize and bargain collectively . . . and shall be free from the interference, restraint, or coercion of employers of labor or their agents"); it eliminated child and sweatshop labor, and provided funds for public works and emergency relief.

To uphold labor's right of collective bargaining, the National Labor Board was created, later superseded by the National Labor Relations Board in June 1934. This board, with its associated regional boards, was given power to settle labor disputes and mediate strikes.

Next to labor the Depression brought hardships to the farming communities. To relieve the suffering of farmers, smarting under overproduction, shrinking markets and low prices, the Agriculture Adjustment Act (AAA) introduced a crop-restriction program, paying subsidies for the reduced production of certain staple commodities. Forty million acres were withdrawn from cultivation, cotton crops were reduced by four million bales, wheat reduction brought the farmers a hundred million dollars in benefit payments; tobacco production was cut by one-third, corn by one-fourth; and the government bought six million pigs and hogs for slaughter.

CANDIDATES IN 1936

FRANKLIN D. ROOSEVELT (1882–1945), with the Depression fading away, was unanimously renominated by the Democrats. Acclaimed by the people, hated and denounced by the privileged, he won overwhelmingly.

JOHN NANCE GARNER (1868–1967) was renominated too. He whipped the New Deal measures through Congress though he was not convinced by them. His "Board of Education" sessions where bourbon flowed were famous.

ALFRED M. LANDON (1887——), Governor of Kansas, the new Republican choice, tore into Roosevelt, asking for a prudent fiscal government. Roosevelt's vote was 27,757,333 while Landon received but 16,684,231 votes.

FRANK KNOX (1874–1944), newspaper publisher and Rough Rider with Roosevelt, became Landon's running mate after Senator Vandenberg refused. The *Literary Digest* poll predicted a two-to-one Republican victory.

NORMAN THOMAS (1884——), once again the Socialist party candidate, ran with George A. Nelson. Their platform urged the voters "to defeat the growing forces of fascism and reaction." They were given 187,833 votes.

WILLIAM LEMKE (1878–1950), lawyer from North Dakota, was the choice of the Union party on a platform designed to attract Townsendites, Coughlinites and other reactionary groups. He received 892,267 votes.

Those whom the farm plan condemned to idleness were helped by the Resettlement Administration. Administered by Rexford Tugwell, it gave financial aid to 635,000 farm families, mortgages were adjusted, camps for migratory workers built. The Federal Farm Credit Administration provided funds for new mortgages and loaned money at low interest rates.

To help the middle class and those who were in debt or whose property was mortgaged, the government offered liberal credits. The Commodity Credit Corporation made loans to cotton growers; the Home Owners' Loan Corporation refinanced mortgages on privately owned homes; the Federal Housing Administration insured existing mortgages, gave loans for the repairing of residential and business property and encouraged the building of homes with government financing; and the Reconstruction Finance Corporation—an agency founded under Hoover—gave loans to industrial enterprises.

To protect investors Congress passed measures on banking, finance and revenue. The Glass-Steagall Banking Act restricted the use of bank credit for speculation, separated commercial and investment banking, and made provisions for the insurance of bank deposits. The Securities Exchange Act licensed stock exchanges, required registration of all securities, and fixed strict rules for marginal and speculative loans.

To stop the exploitation and destruction of the nation's natural resources, various measures were undertaken; the most successful was the formation of the Civilian Conservation Corps (CCC), which enrolled young men between the ages of seventeen and twenty-eight. Leaving the slums of the cities, they lived in 26,000 camps around the country planting trees, fighting forest fires, constructing erosion dams, guarding against plant and animal diseases, improving drainage systems. Their work added more than seventeen million acres of new forests to the nation's resources.

The New Deal's reform legislation was wide in scope. To control floods, harness the Tennessee River and supply cheap electric power to backward areas in seven Southern states, the Tennessee Valley Authority (TVA) —one of the signal achievements of the administration— was created. To help young people between sixteen and twenty-five to secure occupational training and employment, the National Youth Administration came into being. The Social Security Act provided unemployment and old-age insurance. The blind, the dependent mothers and their children received benefit payments; money for public health was appropriated.

All these measures were put into effect with such breathless speed that one spoke of the "Roosevelt Revolution." After twelve years of political stagnation the activity of the new administration appeared revolutionary. Actually it was not. The New Deal reforms

(turn to page 610)

Wide World, March 17, 1934
ROOSEVELT GREETS HIS WIFE on their twenty-ninth wedding anniversary outside the Washington Railroad Station.
Eleanor, who loved to travel and see the world, has just returned home from a trip to Puerto Rico and the Virgin Islands.

THE BEGINNING
OF THE
ROOSEVELT ERA

Lorant: FDR, A Pictorial Biography (*Simon & Schuster*)

ROOSEVELT'S FIRST CABINET. In their first meeting, on March 5, 1933, the Attorney General declared that the President had the authority to proclaim a nationwide bank holiday. The others supported him.

Clockwise around the table from Roosevelt: William Woodin (Treasury), Homer Cummings (Attorney General), Claude Swanson (Navy), Henry Wallace (Agriculture), Miss Frances Perkins (Labor), Daniel Roper (Commerce), Harold Ickes (Interior), James Farley (Postmaster General), George Dern (War), Cordell Hull (State).

Lorant: FDR, A Pictorial Biography (*Simon & Schuster*)

THE FIRST FIRESIDE CHAT. A week after the inauguration, the new President explained his banking proposals to the country in terms which everybody could understand. Because some of the banks had already reopened their doors, Roosevelt reassured his listeners that "it is safer to keep your money in the reopened bank than under the mattress."

IN HIS FIRST PRESS CONFERENCE, a smiling FDR told newspaper reporters: "I am told that what I am about to do will become impossible, but I am going to try it. We

are not going to have any more written questions." From then on for 998 press conferences—the number held during his twelve years in office—journalists filed into his study

Lorant: **FDR, A Pictorial Biography** (*Simon & Schuster*)

twice a week. Undismayed by pitfalls, witty in his replies, never at a loss for words, FDR was more than a match for the newsmen, who not only respected but also loved him.

Lorant: The Presidency (*Macmillan*)

THE TWO HAPPY REPUBLICANS—LANDON WITH KNOX, HIS RUNNING MATE, AT TOPEKA, KANSAS

were long overdue. Democratic in spirit and progressive in nature, they were America's solution to the economic crisis which Russia, Germany and Italy met with Communism, Nazism and Fascism. These reforms preserved the capitalist system of individual enterprise by imposing regulations.

Most of the New Deal measures had their roots in the American past. Regulation of business and railroads began in the eighties, agricultural relief under Wilson, conservation under Theodore Roosevelt, supervision of securities exchanges under Harding and Coolidge; and social legislation had been previously enacted in a number of progressive states.

"Taken as a whole, the New Deal legislation contributed greatly to both recovery and reform, improved the status of the farmer and the laborer, prepared the way for a more equitable distribution of wealth, brought business banking, securities, utilities and transportation under more effective regulation, and, most important of all, helped to salvage the natural resources of the nation. At the same time it interfered seriously with the freedom of business enterprise, inaugurated far-reaching controls over labor and farming, encouraged the growth of bureaucracy, created administrative confusion, impaired the integrity of the merit system, encouraged the fear of dictatorship and of class antagonism, greatly increased the national debt, and at some points conflicted with the Constitution." This was the considered judgment of the historians Morison and Commager.

That the new philosophy was under severe attack

Lorant: The Presidency (*Macmillan*)

THE DEMOCRATIC TICKET—ROOSEVELT AND GARNER SMILE AT THE NOTIFICATION CEREMONY.

was not surprising; all new thoughts are. Not only conservatives but progressives turned their guns on Roosevelt. The conservatives insisted that the New Deal measures would lead to Communism; the progressives cried that the reforms were not far-reaching enough. Those who were critical of the relief program charged that it was administered wastefully, that it cost too much, and that it departed from the traditional system of free enterprise. They suggested that the dole was a cheaper way of caring for the unemployed than work relief.

Much of this criticism had validity. To administer a social experiment on such a tremendous scale was not simple. There was a dearth of experienced administrators; the fast-growing and badly paid bureaucrats (241,-000 new positions were added to 583,000 existing ones) were at times ill-suited to their jobs; there was waste and incompetence—a squandering of money. Yet the relief program put millions back to work, fostered their self-respect and maintained their occupational skills. It lifted the country out of the morass.

Under the New Deal the state, as Professor Hacker put it, had become "an enterpriser, buying and selling, lending and borrowing, building and managing; it used its great fiscal and financial powers to redistribute wealth and create income." It had taken over the function of private investors, in much the same manner as it had met the war challenge under Wilson. This was accomplished by added expenditures and a vastly increased public debt. From July 1933 to July 1937 the

THE CAMPAIGN BEGINS: ALFRED LANDON GIVES HIS BEST SMILE TO THE PEOPLE OF NEWARK, N.J.

national debt increased by $14 billion: from roughly $22½ billions in 1933 to $36½ billions in 1937. But those who supported Roosevelt's policies agreed with Professor Arthur M. Schlesinger, Jr. that the President "by extending Federal authority over the nation's economic life . . . hoped to prevent further abuses . . . by financial and industrial interests, to place the business order under firm public control, and to ensure the common folk a fuller, freer and securer existence."

Every one of the New Deal measures was assailed. The subsidy program of the AAA was denounced because it created an "economy of scarcity." The NRA was resented by big business because of its controls, its labor provisions and its "regimentation" (though until the New Deal stopped the worst abuses big business

imposed regimentation through codes, cartels, price-fixing agreements, company-owned towns and company unions); it was also attacked by small business, which feared the increased strength of monopolies, by liberals who were against the suspension of antitrust laws, by labor which pointed to the failing of the codes, by the consumers who resented the higher prices.

Eventually both these major New Deal laws—the NRA and the AAA—were held unconstitutional by the Supreme Court. The decision regarding the NRA proclaimed that "Congress cannot delegate legislative power to the President to exercise unfettered discretion to make whatever laws he thinks may be needed or advisable for the rehabilitation and expansion of trade and industry." And the farm program was overthrown

THE JUBILANT REPUBLICAN CANDIDATE: GOVERNOR LANDON SPEAKS AT CEDAR RAPIDS, IOWA

because of its taxing provisions and because it was "the reserved right of the states," and not of Congress, to "regulate and control agricultural production." (Later the main provisions of both acts were re-enacted.)

With the New Deal battling its way over obstacles, the country was on the way to recovery when the time of the nominating conventions arrived.

In the Republican ranks were four chief contenders: Governor Alfred M. Landon of Kansas led in popularity rating, followed by seventy-one-year-old Senator William E. Borah of Idaho, Senator Arthur H. Vandenberg of Michigan, and the publisher of the Chicago *Daily News,* Frank Knox. Ex-President Hoover was hoping for another nomination but could not gain the support of the party leaders. Before the convention met in Cleveland, there were plans to form a Republican coalition with conservative Democrats to offer the second place on the Republican ticket to an anti-Roosevelt Democrat like Davey of Ohio, Ely of Massachusetts or Al Smith of New York, but nothing came of it.

Before the balloting began, Vandenberg, Knox and other lesser candidates—except Senator Borah—had withdrawn, leaving the nomination to forty-eight-year-old Alfred Mossman Landon, who was chosen on the first trial. The Republicans sang:

> *Landon, oh, Landon*
> *Will lead to victory,*
> *With the dear old Constitution*
> *And it's good enough for me.*

Acme, September 10, 1936

A DOWNPOUR AT CHARLOTTE SOAKED ROOSEVELT TO THE SKIN, BUT HE DID NOT SEEM TO MIND.

Their platform proclaimed: "For three long years the New Deal administration has dishonored American traditions and flagrantly betrayed the pledges upon which the Democratic party sought and received public support." It listed the grievances: the President had usurped the powers of Congress; the integrity and authority of the Supreme Court had been "flaunted"; the "rights and liberties of American citizens" had been violated; a "regulated monopoly [had] displaced free enterprise."

On the more positive side, it promised to "maintain the American system of constitutional and local self-government," to preserve free enterprise, and to provide "encouragement instead of hindrance to legitimate business."

With the New Deal domestic policies—relief, Social Security, the protection of the right of labor "to organize and bargain collectively through representatives of its own choosing without interference from any source," and the provision of ample farm credit "at rates as low as those enjoyed by other industries"—the Republicans had no quarrel. But their platform asked for an efficient Civil Service, a sound currency and a balanced budget, and promised to "stop the folly of uncontrolled spending." As to foreign policy, the platform was firm on the issue: "America shall not become a member of the League of Nations."

When the Democrats met at Philadelphia, their choice was a foregone conclusion. Roosevelt was the only candidate. It was he who drafted the platform outlining a program for the continuation of the New Deal. The opposition to his renomination from a group of conservative Democrats—Al Smith, Bainbridge Colby of New Jersey, James A. Reed of Missouri, Joseph B. Ely of Massachusetts and Daniel F. Cohalan of New York—was too feeble to be effective.

The keynoter was Alben W. Barkley, of Kentucky, who kept the delegates spellbound with his oratory singing the praises of the New Deal. Against the Supreme Court's "tortured interpretation of the Constitution," Barkley placed "the tortured souls and bodies" of working men, women and children. Rhetorically he asked: "Is the Court beyond criticism?" and "May it be regarded as too sacred to be disagreed with?" And the delegates roared back: "No! No!"

A significant achievement of the convention was the decision to abolish the 104-year-old rule which required a two-thirds vote for the selection of the presidential and vice presidential candidates. Adopted at Andrew Jackson's behest in 1832 so Martin Van Buren could secure the nomination for the Vice Presidency, it became a cornerstone of all Democratic conventions and an insurmountable wall to candidates who could not muster Southern support. It had prevented the nomination of "Champ" Clark in 1912, and now his son, Senator Bennett "Champ" Clark, led the fight with all the energy of an avenging fury to overthrow it. Four years before, James Farley had made an attempt to abolished the rule but was unsuccessful. Roosevelt insisted on its abolition. "Now that the party is in power and there is no question about my renomination, we should clear up the situation for all time." Roosevelt might have been thinking of 1940, when the South—with the two-thirds rule in effect—could hinder the naming of a liberal successor.

The Southern delegates fought for the retention of the rule, but they gave up their opposition when a compromise was proposed whereby in the future the states would not be represented according to their population but according to the number of Democratic votes cast in the elections.

The nominating speeches for Roosevelt given by a list of fifty-seven men lasted for a whole day and the better part of a night. When Judge John E. Mack offered Roosevelt's name, the delegates "danced and pranced, whooped and hollered, marched and capered in a mighty effort to display their enthusiasm for their leader. For a full hour the parade milled round and round the hall, giving off all the noise that lungs and instruments could make, carrying placards with which each state tried to outdo the rest in promises of victory." Thus reported the *New York Times*. Senators Connally and McAdoo "went prancing by the speakers' stand like trotting horses, with fixed grins on their faces," while the Massachusetts delegates lifted James Roosevelt, the President's grown son, and carried him around the hall. Under a Mississippi banner, "Three hard years with Hoover," marched an emaciated urchin in rags, followed by a stout woman carrying a banner: "If you can't guess—three good years with Roosevelt." The delegates sang to the tune of "Marching Through Georgia":

Cartoon by Burt Talburt, Washington News

Cartoon by Peter Arno
"Come along, we're going to the Trans-Lux to hiss Roosevelt," which became one of the classic cartoons of the era.

Cartoon by Galbraith
"And if Roosevelt is not reelected, perhaps even a villa in Newport, my sweet," which made everybody chuckle.

TWO CARTOONS OF THE 1936 ELECTION CAMPAIGN WHICH APPEARED IN THE *NEW YORKER*

AP, October 29, 1936
AT HARRISBURG Roosevelt was greeted by Pittsburgh's Mayor David Lawrence and bushy-browed John L. Lewis.

*Herbie Hoover promised us two chickens in
    each pot;
Breadlines and depression were the only
    things we got.
I lost my job, my bank blew up, and I was
    on the spot,
That's why I'm voting for Roosevelt.*

*Hooray, hooray, Herb Hoover's gone away,
Hooray, hooray, I hope he's gone to stay,
For now I'm back to work and get my three
    squares every day,
That's why I'm voting for Roosevelt.*

*They tell us Mr. Landon is a very clever
    gent,*

National Archives

UNION PARTY CANDIDATE: WILLIAM LEMKE ADDRESSES A MASS MEETING OF CONSERVATIVES.

He kids them out in Kansas though he never
    spends a cent.
But Willie Hearst and Standard Oil are
    coughing up his rent,
That's why I'm voting for Roosevelt.

Roosevelt was renominated by acclamation, and John N. Garner was endorsed again for the Vice Presidency.

Roosevelt came to Philadelphia to accept the call. Before he delivered his acceptance address the Philadelphia Symphony Orchestra played Tschaikowsky and Lily Pons sang "Song of the Lark." Raymond Clapper wrote: "Something had happened to that audience. It had been lifted, not to a cheap, political emotional pitch, but to something finer. It was ready for Roosevelt."

National Archives

SOCIALIST NORMAN THOMAS AT CLEVELAND

The President's voice, carried by loudspeakers to every corner of Franklin Field, rang out strongly. "There is a mysterious cycle in human events," he began. "To some generations much is given. Of other generations much is expected. This generation of Americans has a rendezvous with destiny.

"In this world of ours in other lands there are some people who, in times past, have lived and fought for freedom, and seem to have grown too weary to carry on the fight. They have sold their heritage of freedom for the illusion of a living. They have yielded their democracy."

The hundred thousand in the arena listened in silence; many more millions listened to the speech on their radios. "I believe in my heart that only our success can stir their ancient hope. They begin to know that here in America we are waging a great and successful war. It is not alone a war against want and destitution and economic demoralization. It is more than that; it is a war for the survival of democracy. We are fighting to save a great, a precious form of government for ourselves and for the world."

Roosevelt spoke with eloquence of the country, which had shaken off the power of royalists in politics, and said that "new kingdoms were built upon concentration of control over material things." The power to give or refuse jobs, the power to charge high or low prices, the power to permit or block new competing firms—these were the powers of "economic royalists."

Besides Roosevelt and Landon a number of lesser candidates were in the field. The Union party named William Lemke, a Representative from North Dakota who sponsored Federal legislation to shield mortgaged farms from foreclosure. He was supported by all the reactionaries, by the radio speaker Father Charles E. Coughlin, leader of the Native Union for Social Justice, by Dr. Francis E. Townsend, who advocated Federal pensions for the aged, and others. The Socialist party was behind Norman Thomas, the Communists behind Earl Browder, the Socialist-Labor party behind John W. Aiken, and the Prohibitionists behind David L. Colvin.

In both the Republican and the Democratic ranks men crossed party lines. Alfred E. Smith, the Democratic candidate in 1928, "took a walk" and came out for Landon, the Republican nominee. Together with Herbert Hoover, John W. Davis and William Randolph Hearst, he formed the Liberty League, an anti-New Deal organization which came into being in August 1934 under an executive board of millionaires to oppose "the caprice of bureaucracy" and the "tyranny of autocratic power." Bainbridge Colby, Wilson's Secretary of State, said the Roosevelt administration would nullifiy the Constitution, and charged it was linked with men of Communistic leanings. Former Senator Reed of Missouri called a conference of "Jeffersonian Democrats" to Detriot, which issued a declaration against the Roosevelt ticket.

Among Republicans, Senator George W. Norris divorced himself from his party and was renominated as an independent. Senator Robert M. La Follette endorsed Roosevelt, as did Senator James Couzens of Michigan; Senator Borah would not campaign for Landon.

Labor leaders, siding with John L. Lewis, formed the Labor's Non-Partisan League, which worked for Roosevelt's re-election, though the AFL declared it would "adhere to a nonpartisan policy."

The Republicans presented Landon as a plain country boy who was to save the country from the antibusiness and proradical Roosevelt. Under him the New Deal would be abandoned and the nation would return to the *laissez-faire* philosophy of past govenments. The Republican slogan was "Life, Liberty and Landon," their emblem the sunflower—the state flower of Kansas. (At Tiffany's one could buy a nineteen-petal gold sunflower set with yellow diamonds for $815.) To the tune of "Oh Susanna," they sang:

> *The alphabet we'll always have*
> *But one thing sure is true,*
> *With Landon in the New Deal's out*
> *And that means P.D.Q.*
> *Alf Landon learned a thing or two,*
> *He knows the right solution,*
> *And in the White House he will stay*
> *Within the Constitution.*

But Landon was no match for Roosevelt. The "silent Coolidge from Kansas" was no spellbinder, but a colorless man who thought the President a "very fine, charming gentleman." As the campaign progressed, Landon, persuaded by his advisers, reverted to the traditional method of slugging it out, hurling charges of "willful waste" of the taxpayers' money and "strangling of free enterprise" against Roosevelt. Republican speakers derided the relief and reform projects of the New Deal as "boondoggling" and "leaf-raking."

At the Democratic state convention in Syracuse Roosevelt hit back at the Republican charges. "Let me warn you and let me warn the nation against the smooth evasion which says: 'Of course we believe in all these things; we believe in social security; we believe in work for the unemployed; we believe in all these things; but we do not like the way the present administration is doing them. Just turn them over to us. We will do all of them, we will do more of them, we will do them better; and most importantly of all, the doing of them will not cost anybody anything.' . . .

AT HARVARD'S 300TH BIRTH-DAY—FDR told his audience that a hundred years ago Harvard alumni were "sorely troubled" over Andrew Jackson, and fifty years ago over Grover Cleveland. "Now," said FDR with a broad smile, "I am President." As FDR sat in the downpour, Lawrence McKinney, the poet and scholar, whispered to author and editor Frederick Lewis Allen: "This seems Harvard's way of soaking the rich."

Wide World, September 18, 1936

621

TESTING THE VOTE: In Harry's Bar in Paris, the hangout of Hemingway and of others of "the lost generation."

THE RESULT. On election night at New York's Times Square a jubilant crowd cheered Roosevelt's victory.

"You cannot," continued Roosevelt, "be an Old Guard Republican in the East and a New Deal Republican in the West. You cannot promise to repeal taxes before one audience and promise to spend more of the taxpayers' money before another audience. . . . Who is there in America who believes that we can run the risk of turning back our government to the old leadership which brought it to the brink of 1933?"

Roosevelt was at the height of his popularity. James Farley said, "He was more popular than the New Deal itself." And while the people cheered him, newspapers assailed him. He had the support of only 36 percent of the nation's press. William Randolph Hearst attacked him in an editorial saying his "Communist entourage" of Felix Frankfurter, Donald Richberg, Rexford Tugwell, Frances Perkins and Henry Wallace was sufficient proof of the President's radicalism. A Hearst jingle ran:

> The Red New Deal with a Soviel seal
> Endorsed by a Moscow hand;
> The strange result of an alien cult
> In a liberty-loving land.

The Chicago *Tribune* headlined: "Moscow Orders Reds in U.S. to Back Roosevelt," and asked for volunteers to help Landon's cause: "Be a volunteer in the great fight to save the nation!" A Roosevelt victory would mean "Moscow in the White House." This inspired Gail Borden to write in the Chicago *Times*:

> There was a young man from Topeka,
> Whose campaign grew weaker and weaker,
> Till the volunteers came
> And made every old dame
> A bellringer, singer or speaker.

But for the *New York Times* Roosevelt was the "reasoned choice"—since Landon offered little but a secondhand New Deal blighted by his party's traditional isolationism, while Roosevelt would "provide insurance against radicalism of the sort which the United States has most to fear."

The final weeks of the campaign, wrote *Time* magazine, "had demonstrated to what depths of inanity, bad taste, and downright dishonesty American politics can

Lorant: FDR, A Pictorial Biography (*Simon & Schuster*)

ROOSEVELT AND HIS MOTHER ON THEIR WAY TO THE HYDE PARK POLLING PLACE

descend. Normally intelligent men charged Roosevelt and Landon with fascism, communism, nazism—even with belief in bigamy. Leaders like Alfred E. Smith, Hugh Johnson, Harold Ickes, Father Coughlin, Herbert Hoover and Ogden Mills resorted to accusations that even politicians try to avoid."

The Republican National Committee in a last-minute effort launched an offensive against Roosevelt's Social Security Act. Its circulars distributed throughout the industrial areas warned against the bill, which was to call for a one percent deduction from wages and salaries. The leaflets omitted to mention that the money would be used to finance old-page pensions for workers and that employers must also contribute one percent, and they also failed to say that employers alone would bear the cost of a complementary system of employment insurance. The chairman of the Republican National Committee, John Hamilton, made a radio speech in which he declared that the Social Security Act would require every worker to wear a number tag around his neck.

Roosevelt's anger was aroused. He devoted a great

November 3, 1936
ELECTION NIGHT ON THE PORCH AT HYDE PARK

Lorant: FDR, A Pictorial Biography (*Simon & Schuster*)

ROOSEVELT'S SECOND INAUGURAL ADDRESS. The President said:". . . here is the challenge to our democracy: In this nation I see tens of millions of its citizens . . . who at this very moment are denied the greater part of what the very lowest standards of today call the necessities of life. I see millions of families trying to live on incomes so meager that the pall of family disaster hangs over them day by day. I see millions whose daily lives in city and on farm continue under

part of his final campaign address in New York's Madison Square Garden to a defense of Social Security. He pointed out that 77 Republican members of the House voted for the act and only 18 against it, while in the Senate 15 Republican Senators voted for it and only 5 against it. "Never before in all our history have these forces been so united against one candidate as they stand today. They are unanimous in their hate for me— and I welcome their hatred. I should like to have it said of my first administration that in it the forces of selfish-

ness and of lust for power met their match. I should like to have it said of my second administration that in it these forces met their master."

The President's re-election was a certainty, though the *Literary Digest* postcard poll confidently predicted Landon the winner with 370 electoral votes to Roosevelt's 161. The Gallup poll guessed 389 votes for Roosevelt and 141 for Landon.

Both polls were off the mark. Roosevelt won all the states but two—Maine and Vermont. He had 523 elec-

Lorant: FDR, A Pictorial Biography (*Simon & Schuster*)

conditions labeled indecent by a so-called polite society half a century ago. . . . I see millions lacking the means to buy the products of farm and factory and by their poverty denying work and productiveness to many other millions. I see one-third of a nation ill-housed, ill-clad, ill-nourished. It is not in despair that I paint you that picture. I paint it for you in hope—because the Nation, seeing and understanding the injustice in it, proposes to paint it out."

toral votes against Landon's 8. His popular plurality was five million larger than in 1932. The Democratic majority in Congress increased. In the House they had 331 seats against the Republicans' 89; in the Senate 75 seats against the Republicans' 17.

At the time Roosevelt took the oath—the inauguration was now held on January 20, the date having been changed by the Twentieth Amendment—the *New York Times* compared the country's situation with that of four years before. The comparative figures showed that on the stock markets an average of fifty stocks stood at 141.24, while in 1933 they had stood at 50.5. The price of May wheat was now $1.30 and that of hogs $10, while four years earlier May wheat had been quoted at only 4⅞ cents a bushel and hogs at $4. Carloading in 1937 was 96.8 per cent of normal; in 1933 it had been 52 per cent. Steel production in 1937 was 80 per cent, in 1933 only 16.9 per cent, and so forth.

In the four years under Roosevelt the nation had made a miraculous comeback.

FRANKLIN D. ROOSEVELT

President Roosevelt entered his second term determined to continue his fight for social progress. To the new Congress he proposed measures to improve the economic condition of the farmers and better the lot of the workers; he submitted legislation to aid the ill-housed, ill-clad and ill-nourished; he suggested the application of the TVA idea to the nation's six major regions, and asked for a thorough government reorganization.

The Republican minority was powerless to oppose Roosevelt's proposals. They set their hopes on the Supreme Court, where the thoughts of the "Nine Old Men" were anchored in the "good old days" of the "horse and buggy era." The justices resisted the far-reaching social changes brought about under the New Deal and endorsed in elections since 1932.

During the last years of Roosevelt's second term, the Court had invalidated some of the key New Deal legislation. It rejected the NRA and the AAA; it overthrew the Railroad Retirement Plan, the Bituminous Coal Act, the protection of farm mortgages, the Municipal Bankruptcy Act. Occasionally these acts were thrown out on narrow technical grounds, or as one of the justices put it, through a "tortured construction of the Constitution."

Roosevelt felt that "the language and the temper of the decisions indicated little hope for the future." If the Court should continue to cast doubts on "the ability of the elected Congress to protect us against catastrophe by meeting squarely our modern social and economic conditions," and to invalidate his liberal proposals, his administration would be doomed. Particularly, if the

Court should decide against the National Labor Relations Act or the Social Security Act, it would be the end of the New Deal.

In Roosevelt's opinion the Court was out of step with the times, with four conservative justices—McReynolds, Van Devanter, Sutherland and Butler—blocking the reform proposals.

Taking the issue to the people the President pointed out that until he came to office "practically every President of the United States had appointed at least one man to the Supreme Court. President Taft appointed five members and named a Chief Justice; President Wilson three; President Harding four, including a Chief Justice; President Coolidge one; President Hoover three, including a Chief Justice." It was only he—Roosevelt—who during his first administration had not the opportunity of making a single appointment. "Chance and the disinclination of the individuals to leave the Supreme Bench have now given us a Court in which five justices will be over seventy-five years of age before next June and one over seventy." Therefore he offered a plan to infuse the Court with younger blood. If a judge over seventy serving longer than ten years after his seventieth birthday failed to retire, a new judge was to be appointed. However, the number of the new appointees was to be limited to six, so there would never be more than fifteen judges on the Court. Roosevelt pointed out that his plan was not an unusual one; nor was it unconstitutional. The number of justices had been changed in the administrations of John Adams, Thomas Jefferson, Andrew Jackson, Abraham Lincoln and Ulysses Grant.

The outcry following this proposal reverberated

CANDIDATES IN 1940

FRANKLIN D. ROOSEVELT (1882–1945) was nominated for a third term. The war in Europe was raging, Hitler's hordes overran France, Goering's Luftwaffe bombed London—America would not change her commander-in-chief in such crucial times. On foreign policy Willkie agreed with Roosevelt, and he also endorsed most of the New Deal. The Democratic ticket won by 27,313,041 votes to the Republicans' 22,348,480.

HENRY A. WALLACE (1883–1965), son of Harding's Secretary of Agriculture, was Roosevelt's Agriculture Secretary. A thorough student of agriculture, his experiments with hybrid corn brought him a fortune. A progressive, he became the candidate after Roosevelt forced him on the delegates. A dreamy searcher for spiritual truth and a hardheaded administrator too; those "practical" politicians could not understand him.

WENDELL L. WILLKIE (1892–1944), utilities executive, successful corporation lawyer and president of the Commonwealth and Southern, got the nomination of the boisterous convention on the sixth ballot, defeating Taft, Dewey and Vandenberg.

He had the support of influential publishers and bankers, and was helped by the effective organizations of amateurs. Ickes called him the "barefoot boy of Wall Street."

CHARLES L. McNARY (1874–1944), politician from Oregon, state supreme court justice, had been U.S. Senator since 1917. He was the minority leader of the Republicans, thus he was selected for the second place after the party chieftains refused to take Willkie's choice, Governor Baldwin of Connecticut. McNary's conservatism, his advocacy of high tariffs, his opposition to public power, balanced Willkie's liberalism.

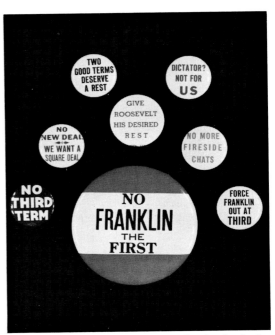

Smithsonian Institution
ANTI-ROOSEVELT CAMPAIGN BUTTONS

across the land. The country was roused. During the next five months—from February 1937, when the President proposed it, until June—Roosevelt's court-packing plan eclipsed all other issues. Roosevelt was accused of taking control of the Court; he was called a dictator who wanted to kill constitutional government by destroying the independence of the judiciary.

Public opinion, fomented by the agitation of the anti-Roosevelt forces, crystallized against the proposal, but a far greater influence in defeating the plan was the change in the Court's attitude, which resulted in the reversal of its opinions in a variety of cases. The Court sustained the Minimum Wage Law of the state of Washington, although a similar measure of the state of New York had been previously held unconstitutional; a revised Farm Mortgage Act, a new Railway Labor Act, the Social Security legislation were sanctioned. "A switch in time saves nine," went the saying.

Lorant: FDR, A Pictorial Biography (*Simon & Schuster*)

AT PRESS CONFERENCES FDR EVADED THE QUESTION: "WILL YOU RUN FOR A THIRD TERM?"

When Roosevelt was forced to shelve his plan, the opposition was jubilant. In their opinion the President had suffered the greatest political defeat of his career. On the surface it looked like defeat. Roosevelt had lost the battle, but in reality he had won his war. During the controversy the Court gradually committed itself to the New Deal policies, and this had been Roosevelt's aim all along.

In August 1937 after government expenditures for relief and recovery were curtailed at the insistence of business and finance, a slump came which lasted more than a year. Roosevelt's critics quickly labeled it the "Roosevelt depression," although conditions were brought about mainly by the fury of the Roosevelt haters, who, in the words of the London *Economist,* were "choking the whole industrial and financial machine."

Unemployment grew and wages fell. The census in 1937 showed that eleven million Americans were jobless and another five and a half million were only partially employed. During that year more than five thousand strikes flared up. The fighting within the ranks of labor added to the difficulties. The newly founded Committee for Industrial Organization (CIO) under the leadership of John L. Lewis, with the aim of unionizing entire industries as units, fought the American Federation of Labor, which was organized according to specific trades. When the CIO started organizing the steel, automobile and textile industries, its efforts were met by determined opposition. The workers retaliated. Sit-down strikes became a new feature of the American scene.

But the political picture was not all dark. Congress passed bills for slum clearance and construction of low-cost housing. A new Farm Security Administration was created, easing the plight of the farmers. But the out-

Lorant, *FDR, A Pictorial Biography* (Simon & Schuster)

THE PURGE. On June 24, 1938, Roosevelt announced that he would enter various Democratic primaries to fight the conservative anti–New Deal Senators who were against his policies. In Georgia he spoke out against Senator Walter George, who "cannot possibly in my judgment be classified as belonging to the liberal school of thought." But after his unfriendly address he shook the Senator's hand warmly and said, "Let's always be friends."

standing New Deal measures of 1938 were the Agriculture Adjustment Act and the Fair Labor Standards Act. The Agricultural Adjustment Act authorized the Secretary of Agriculture to determine the acreage to be planted in crops (if two-thirds of the farmers involved agreed), and to establish marketing controls over the surplus crops. It instituted a "parity payments" system whereby producers of corn, wheat, cotton, tobacco and rice were subsidized; it proposed soil conservation measures; it provided loans for surplus crops and plans for storage. The new measure turned out to be a great success; within a year the cash income of the farm community doubled.

The Fair Labor Standards Act provided for an ultimate maximum work week of forty hours, and a minimum wage of forty cents an hour for all workers producing goods for interstate commerce.

In the Congressional election of 1938 Roosevelt planned to take a stand against those Senators who were fundamentally opposed to the New Deal. He entered the Democratic primary campaign endorsing those candidates who supported his program and opposing those who hampered it. He stumped in Kentucky on behalf of Senator Alben Barkley, in Maryland on behalf of Davey John Lewis who opposed Senator Tydings, in Georgia for Lawrence Camp who opposed Senator Walter F. George, in South Carolina for Governor Olin Johnson who opposed Senator "Cotton Ed" Smith; in New York Roosevelt came out against John O'Connor.

Roosevelt's interference in the Southern primaries

INS

THE NINE OLD MEN who were against the New Deal and were a thorn in the President's side. Not one of them had been appointed by Roosevelt. Some of the justices were in advanced age, most of them were conservatives, and Roosevelt needed a Court to go along with the New Deal legislation. From the left are Attorney General Mitchell; Justices Cardozo, Stone, Sutherland, Van Devanter, Hughes, Brandeis, Butler and Roberts; and Solicitor General Thacher. Justice McReynolds is missing.
Right: Roosevelt with Senator Robinson, who led the fight in Congress for judicial reform. At the height of the battle Robinson died of a heart attack.

met with strong criticism within the party ranks. He was compared to dictators who "purged" their enemies, even though Roosevelt used no force other than the persuasion of open debate. The anti-Roosevelt camp was reinforced when the voters turned against Roosevelt's candidates and re-elected Senator Tydings, Senator George and "Cotton Ed" Smith.

In this presidential election year all the domestic issues faded into insignificance. The questions uppermost in American minds were: Will America enter the war? Will it fight the Nazis? Will it help Britain?

For the anarchical conditions in Europe and the Far East the United States was not without blame. In the years after the First World War the country had retreated into the seemingly secure shell of isolationism,

rendering collective security in the League of Nations unworkable. Without an effective organization to halt them, the aggressors were able to overrun their weaker neighbors.

In 1931 Japan invaded Manchuria and set up a puppet state. In 1935 Mussolini took Ethiopia. In 1936 the Spanish Civil War began—a bloody rehearsal for the world conflagration, with one side supplied by Russian arms and the other strengthened by Nazi equipment. In 1937 Japan plunged the Far East into prolonged hostilities, attacking the Chinese and subjugating their land. In 1939 Hitler overran Czechoslovakia, and in August of that year he signed the nonaggression pact with Russia—the prelude to the Second World War.

Lorant: FDR, A Pictorial Biography (*Simon & Schuster*)

WHO SHALL BE THE SUCCESSOR?—HENRY WALLACE?

. . . JOHN NANCE GARNER?

As early as October 1937 Roosevelt sounded a warning: "It seems to be unfortunately true that the epidemic of world lawlessness is spreading," he said in Chicago. "When an epidemic of physical disease starts to spread, the community approves and joins in a quarantine of the patients in order to protect the health of the community against the spread of the disease."

But the country was not yet ready for action. Isolationists derided him as an alarmist. In July 1939, Senator Borah declared that there would be no war in Europe. Hitler thought otherwise.

On September 21 Roosevelt called Congress into special session and asked for a revised Neutrality Act,*

* The first Neutrality Act to prevent American participation

. . . HARRY HOPKINS?

Lorant: FDR, A Pictorial Biography (*Simon & Schuster*)

which would permit the United States to sell arms and other implements of war to such nations as were able to pay for them in cash and carry them away in ships— a proposal in the interest of Great Britain. Roosevelt also urged Congress to adopt a conscription law

in any foreign war was passed in August 1935 after the Italo-Ethiopian conflict. A year later the Act was strengthened by a clause which prohibited loans to the belligerents. In January 1937 a further resolution forbade the export of munitions to either of the opposing forces in the Spanish Civil War. In May the earlier Neutrality Acts were again changed, giving the President larger discretionary powers. But the great omission of the Act was the failure to distinguish between aggressor and victim nations, thus inadvertently helping the former. Also, the United States would not cooperate closely with the League, so the sanctions against Italy were unsuccessful.

. . . OR JAMES A. FARLEY?

633

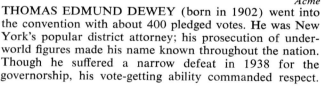

THE CHIEF REPUBLICAN CONTENDERS

THOMAS EDMUND DEWEY (born in 1902) went into the convention with about 400 pledged votes. He was New York's popular district attorney; his prosecution of underworld figures made his name known throughout the nation. Though he suffered a narrow defeat in 1938 for the governorship, his vote-getting ability commanded respect.

ROBERT ALPHONSO TAFT (born in 1889), Ohio Senator, son of President Taft, whose conservative and at times unpopular stands were deplored by the Republican liberals; still he was supported by the party's conservatives, who admired his forthright character. The Taft men hoped to rally at least 300 votes for their candidate on the first ballot.

and not rely on raising an army on a volunteer basis.

The proposals divided the country. The isolationists wanted to keep out of European affairs and not participate in any war. The interventionists, though they too wanted to avoid war, argued that if the dictators Hitler and Mussolini were not checked, America would be their next victim; therefore we should assist the democracies in Europe to defeat totalitarianism.

William Allen White's Committee to Defend America by Aiding the Allies roused the people's conscience to

give help to the mother country; while the America First Committee advocated pacifism and isolationism, its ranks swelled by Anglophobes, anti-Semites, conservatives and reactionaries.

It was against this international backdrop that the nominating conventions met.

Republican gains in the mid-term election of 1938 raised the hopes of the Republican challengers who vied for the nomination. The favorites were: New York's gang-busting District Attorney Thomas Edmund Dewey

William C. Shrout, Life

WENDELL LEWIS WILLKIE (born in 1892), Wall Street lawyer and executive, was a new member of the family. Until recently he had voted for the Democrats. He was backed by astute newspaper publishers and bankers. Keeping himself in the public eye through interviews. magazine articles and radio appearances, his star rose rapidly.

Thomas D. McAvoy, Life

ARTHUR HENDRICK VANDENBERG (born in 1884), Michigan Senator, was thought a compromise choice in case of a Dewey-Taft deadlock, although the names of ex-President Hoover, Willkie, Justice Stone and Governor Bricker were also mentioned as prospective candidates. Later his isolationism gave way to international cooperation.

who was narrowly defeated by Governor Herbert Lehman in the gubernatorial election; Robert Alphonso Taft, Senator from Ohio, the son of the twenty-seventh President, and Michigan's Senator Arthur H. Vandenberg. They were challenged by the forty-eight-year-old Wall Street lawyer and utilities executive, Wendell L. Willkie, who had voted Democratic as late as 1938 but now was a Republican. Other names mentioned were ex-President Hoover, the New York publisher Frank Gannett, the Supreme Court Justices Harlan Stone and

Owen Roberts, and Ohio's Governor John Bricker.

The Republican convention met in Philadelphia only two days after France was forced to sign the armistice with Germany. Dewey was clearly in the lead with some 350 to 400 delegates pledged to him, closely followed by Taft, who had the support of some 300 delegates. But during the months preceding the convention Wendell Willkie had gained support. "Willkie for President" and "Win with Willkie" clubs mushroomed all over the country. Amateur politicians like Russell Davenport and

THE REPUBLICAN CONVENTION at Philadelphia, where amid mounting excitement Willkie was nominated.

WILLKIE WITH WILLIAM A. WHITE of the Emporia *Gazette,* who swung the Kansas delegation for Willkie.

Oren Root, Jr. conducted a well-organized campaign for Willkie, aided by the publicity director for the Committee of Utility Executives and other prominent advertising men. Henry Luce with his magazines was in this group, as were other newspaper publishers, and one heard rumors that the financial House of Morgan had made large investments in the "spontaneous" campaign.

The last Gallup poll taken before the convention gave Dewey 47 percent and Willkie only 29 percent. But headlines of *The New York Times* announced: "Willkie Is Called the Man to Beat" and "Willkie Chief Fear of Dewey Backers."

The platform of the Republicans was, in the words of a historian, "a masterpiece of equivocation, evasion, ambiguity and generalization," with a straddling foreign policy plank which pledged the country to "Americanism, preparedness and peace," and which promised the European victims of aggression "such aid as shall not be inconsistent with the requirements of our own na-

tional defense." It was not a hopeful pronouncement.

A day before the balloting started two notable recruits joined the Willkie group: Representative Frank O. Horton of Wyoming, and keynoter of the convention Harold Stassen, thirty-three-year-old Governor of Minnesota who became Willkie's floor manager. They and the other Willkie men buttonholed delegates asking for support. Willkie himself campaigned actively. In a hotel corridor he approached Jim Watson, the old "standpatter" from Indiana, and this is how Watson recalled their conversation:

"Jim, couldn't you be for me?" asked Willkie.

"No, Wendell, you're just not my kind of Republican."

"I admit I used to be a Democrat."

"Used to be?" snapped Watson.

"You're a good Methodist," replied Willkie. "Don't you believe in conversion?"

"Yes, Wendell. If a fancy woman truly repented and

Lorant: The Presidency (*Macmillan*)
JOSEPH W. MARTIN, the permanent chairman of the convention, presents the beaming candidate to the delegates.

Photograph by John Phillips, in Life
THE GALLERY SHOUTED, danced, stomped and went wild with joy when their candidate won the nomination.

wanted to join my church, I'd welcome her. I would greet her personally and lead her up the aisle to the front pew. But by the Eternal, I wouldn't ask her to lead the choir!"

Whereupon Willkie said with a wave of his hand: "Aw, Jim, you just go to hell!"

On the first ballot Dewey led with 360 votes against 189 for Taft, 105 for Willkie and 76 for Vandenberg. On the second trial Dewey's vote declined to 338, Taft's increased to 203, Willkie's to 171. On the next ballot Willkie had 259, Taft 212. The fourth ballot gave Willkie the lead with 306 votes against Dewey's 250 and Taft's 245.

While the voting went on, the galleries chanted "We want Willkie" and thousands of letters and telegrams urged the delegates to vote for Willkie. On the fifth ballot Willkie's lead increased to 429, Taft's to 377. If Joseph N. Pew, who controlled the majority of the Pennsylvania delegation, had switched to Taft, the

Willkie boom could have been stopped. (Pennsylvania was split: 51 of its delegates voted for Governor Edward Martin as a favorite son, while the other 21 supported Willkie.)

After the fifth ballot Governor Bricker of Ohio tried to propose a recess to stem the Willkie tide, but before he could speak the chairman announced: "There being no majority, the convention will proceed with the sixth ballot." The hall was tense with excitement. All eyes were on the Michigan and Pennsylvania delegates. Before Michigan was called, Willkie gained 29 votes from the other states against 12 for Taft. Then Michigan, released from Vandenberg, threw its full strength to Willkie. The roar from the galleries was deafening. It was to be Willkie. During the roll call the divided Pennsylvania delegates held a final caucus outside the hall. When they returned, Willkie already had 400 votes, only 2 shy of the nomination. Thus shortly after midnight Pennsylvania swung behind Willkie.

THE DEMOCRATIC CONVENTION

John Phillips, Life

THE VOICE FROM THE SEWER. When Mayor Ed Kelly gave a signal, the voice of Thomas McGarry, his superintendent of sewers, boomed over the loudspeakers: "We want Roosevelt. . . . The world needs Roosevelt!"

Lorant: The Presidency (*Macmillan*)

WHEN FDR'S NAME WAS PUT IN NOMINATION for the record-breaking third term, the demonstration lasted an hour. The organ played "Franklin D. Roosevelt Jones," and banner after banner was caught up and carried in parade.

The galleries shouted and went wild with joy. "Nothing exactly like it ever happened before in American politics," reported *Newsweek.* "Willkie had never held public office or even sought it. Virtually a neophyte in politics, he had entered no primaries, made no deals, organized no campaign. . . . His backers were uninitiated volunteers, as strange to the ways of ward bosses and state chairmen as their hero."

But political analyst Thomas L. Stokes wrote that Willkie's nomination was the "culmination of a coup by a strange combination of big-business backers who had financed a short but very effective propaganda campaign on his behalf, beginning only a few months before the convention, and zealous 'amateurs' as they were called, consisting of people all over the country who were weary of the old-type politicians and political hacks and wanted a new face and new blood."

Willkie had chosen as his running mate the Minority

Leader of the Senate Charles L. McNary from Oregon in the hope that he would appeal to the conservatives.

With Willkie as the Republican nominee promising "a crusading, aggressive, fighting campaign," the question was as it had been for the past years: will Roosevelt run for a third term? There was no official word about it, though Washington was buzzing with rumors.

It seems probable that before the beginning of the European war Roosevelt had been against accepting a third term. He told Farley so in the summer of 1939. To reporters who asked him about it he answered: "Put on a dunce cap and stand in the corner." Late in 1939 while discussing a problem with Cordell Hull he said: "That is something the next President will have to worry about, and that will be you, Cordell." The Hopkins papers show that Roosevelt was seriously considering support of Harry Hopkins. And when Farley asked Roosevelt whether he should file his own name in the

FARLEY CONFERS WITH BARKLEY about the nomination of Wallace. Roosevelt wanted his Secretary of Agriculture for his running mate, but many opposed this; the "unsafe" Wallace had been a Republican as late as 1928.

THE PRESIDENT ACCEPTS HIS RENOMINATION: "Today all private plans . . . have been repealed by an overriding public danger. . . . All those who can be of service to the republic have no choice but to offer themselves."

Massachusetts and New Hampshire primaries, Roosevelt told him: "Go ahead, Jim. The water's fine. I haven't an objection in the world."

The President promised Farley to make a statement about the third term announcing his refusal to run, but later he told the Postmaster General: "I could not have issued that statement. It would have destroyed my effectiveness as the leader of the nation in the efforts of this country to cope with the terrible catastrophe raging in Europe. To have issued such a statement would have nullified my position in the world and would have handicapped the efforts of this country to be of constructive service in the war crisis." Besides, the host of candidates and their infighting would have jeopardized the party's chances to remain in power.

It must have been in the middle of May, after Hitler had overrun Holland, Belgium and France, that Roosevelt decided to run again. He was determined to fight

LABOR LEADERS WITH THE VICE PRESIDENTIAL CANDIDATE. Left to right, Tom Kennedy, John L. Lewis and Philip Murray with the satisfied Henry A. Wallace— who had the strong backing of FDR and organized labor.

Acme

FDR CAMPAIGNING IN NEWBURGH, NEW YORK

Photograph by Ralph Morgan, INP

EGGS PELT NORMAN THOMAS IN JERSEY CITY.

the Fascist menace. But even if he had wanted to bow out, it was too late. There was no other candidate on the horizon with whom the Democrats could have won. Neither Secretary of State Cordell Hull, National Chairman James Farley, Vice President John Nance Garner, Federal Security Administrator Paul McNutt, ex-Governor of Michigan Frank Murphy, Secretary of Agriculture Henry Wallace, Attorney General Robert Jackson, nor Justices Stanley Reed and William O. Douglas would have been able to take the election from Willkie.

When the Democratic convention opened in Chicago on July 15, three-fourths of the delegates were pledged to the President. Harry Hopkins, on Roosevelt's behalf, was in firm control of the situation. From his bathroom in the Blackstone Hotel—the only place he could talk

IN A TRIUMPHANT PARADE, WILLKIE RETURNS

TO HIS HOME—ELWOOD, INDIANA—WHERE HE DELIVERED HIS OFFICIAL ACCEPTANCE SPEECH.

Wide World

WILLKIE IS SPEAKING at New York's Times Square, with City Council President Newbold Morris listening closely.

in privacy—he had a private telephone line to the White House. When Senator Barkley in a fighting speech first uttered Roosevelt's name, Mayor Ed Kelley signaled to his superintendent of sewers Thomas McGarry, and McGarry's voice, piped from a room beneath the auditorium, boomed from all the loud-speakers: "We want Roosevelt. . . . The world wants Roosevelt!" The "voice from the sewers," as it was called, continued to repeat the slogans for twenty-two minutes before the demonstration died down. And Barkley concluded his speech: "I and other close friends of the President have long known that he had not wished to be a candidate again. We knew, too, that in no way whatsoever has he exerted any influence in the selection of delegates, or upon the opinions of the delegates to this convention. The President has never had and has not today any desire or purpose to continue in the office of the President, to be a candidate for that office, or to be nominated by the convention for that

office. He wishes in all earnestness and sincerity to make it clear that all delegates to this convention are free to vote for any candidate. This is the message I bear to you from the President of the United States."

The organ now played "Franklin D. Roosevelt Jones"; banner after banner was caught up and carried in the parade. Over the shouting and cheering the thundering voice boomed "The party wants Roosevelt. . . . Illinois wants Roosevelt. . . . The world needs Roosevelt. . . . Everybody wants Roosevelt!"

The next day the platform was read by Senator Robert Wagner, pledging more help to "the land and the farmer," to "industry and worker," to "capital and the businessman." It promised an extension of the party's electric power program, providing cheaper electricity, with "vast economic benefits to thousands of homes and communities," development of Western resources, war on unemployment, the extension of the Social Security system and health service, slum clearance and

CAMPAIGN CARTOONS IN 1940

Rollin Kirby, in the New York Post, *June 29, 1940*
THE REPUBLICANS: "IMPERVIOUS TO HEAT"

Rollin Kirby, in the New York Post, *October 18, 1940*
ITS CANDIDATE: "THE FRUSTRATED SALESMAN"

low-rent housing, consumer's protection against "unjustified price rises," an extension of the Civil Service, fair treatment of war veterans and their dependents, and "equal protection of the laws for every citizen, regardless of race, creed or color."

The platform-makers had a protracted debate over the party's foreign policy plank. The declaration, accepted by both the isolationist and interventionist factions, declared: "We will not participate in foreign wars, and we will not send our army, naval or air forces to fight in foreign lands outside of the Americas, except in case of attack. . . . In self-defense and in good conscience, the world's greatest democracy cannot afford heartlessly or in a spirit of appeasement to ignore the peace-loving and liberty-loving people wantonly attacked by ruthless aggressors. We pledge to extend to these peoples all the material aid at our command consistent with law and not inconsistent with the interests of our own national self-defense." In other words, the Democratic party evaded the question of American responsibility.

Those opposed to a third term proposed James Farley as an alternative to the President. John N. Garner and Millard Tydings were other names on the first ballot. But Roosevelt carried the first ballot with 946 votes against Farley's 72, Garner's 61 and Tydings's 9.

The real fight was reserved for the vice presidential nomination. When Roosevelt let it be known that he had chosen his Secretary of Agriculture Henry A. Wallace, the delegates demurred at his "dictation." The main objection to Wallace was that he had been a Republican as late as 1928. "For God's sake, just because the Republicans nominated an apostate Democrat for President, don't let us put one of those things over," said a delegate from Ohio.

But Roosevelt was firm about Wallace. "He's the kind of fellow I want around. He's honest. He thinks right. He's a digger." When Farley said that Wallace was regarded as a mystic, Roosevelt snapped: "He is not a mystic. He is a philosopher. He's got ideas. He thinks right. He'll help the people think."

Roosevelt's attempt to force Wallace's nomination aroused such ill feelings that Barkley adjourned the afternoon session without allowing the nominating speeches. The recess gave Hopkins and others time to round up the necessary votes for Wallace's nomination.

While the quarreling went on in Chicago, an angry Roosevelt waited at the White House, "determined not to speak or address the convention unless and until the work of the convention has been completed," which

Daniel R. Fitzpatrick, in the St. Louis *Post-Dispatch, July 12, 1940*
THE DEMOCRATS: "AWAITING HIS MASTER"

Daniel R. Fitzpatrick, in the St. Louis *Post-Dispatch, July 12, 1940*
WILLKIE AND MCNARY: "ALL CONNECTED UP"

meant until the Vice President was nominated. He barked at Hopkins on the long-distance phone: "Well, damn it to hell, they will go for Wallace or I won't run, and you can jolly well tell them so." And he prepared a speech refusing the nomination.

The recess over, the delegates gave vent to their feelings about the hand-picked "Republican" vice presidential candidate. "This is no rabbit convention," said a delegate from Missouri. "We want to carry Missouri in November, and we can't do it with a Republican. We want a Democrat for Vice President to run with our Democratic President." Another delegate from Maryland asked for the nomination of Jesse Jones, who was a real Democrat—"and I think I know a Democrat when I see one."

To quell the mood of the convention, Mrs. Roosevelt flew to Chicago and made a gracious speech for Wallace. Farley kept on arguing with Roosevelt over the phone to drop his choice, but when he saw that Roosevelt would not budge, he gave in: "You're the boss. If you say so, I will do all I can to nominate Wallace." Thus it was Wallace on the first ballot.

In the early hours of the morning Roosevelt addressed the convention by radio. "Today all private plans, all private lives have been repealed by an overriding public

danger. In the face of that danger all those who can be of service to the Republic have no choice but to offer themselves." The rebellious delegates were quiet now as they listened to their President. "Only the people themselves can draft a President. If such a draft should be made upon me, I will, with God's help, continue to serve with the best of my ability and with the fullness of my strength."

As to the practical matter of a campaign, Roosevelt said: "I shall not have the time nor the inclination to engage in purely political debate. But I shall never be loath to call the attention of the nation to deliberate or unwitting falsifications of fact."

Some weeks later on August 17 Willkie made his official acceptance speech at Elkwood, Indiana, where he had been born. The place was selected to give Willkie the image of a small-town boy so the voters would forget that he was a wealthy Wall Street lawyer and utilities executive. In his speech Willkie supported Roosevelt's foreign policy (although he criticized the President for seeming to incite us to war) and agreed with most of the New Deal reforms. He endorsed "collective bargaining by representatives of labor's own free choice." He was for wages-and-hours legislation and Federal regulation of interstate utilities, securities mar-

Wide World

IN BOSTON ON OCTOBER 30, 1940, ROOSEVELT DECLARED: "I have said this before, but I shall say it again and again. Your boys are not going to be sent into foreign wars!" Later, when he was accused of misleading the electorate, Roosevelt retorted testily that he never promised Americans not to fight if the country was attacked by a foreign power.

Acme

kets and banking. He favored Federal old-age pensions, unemployment insurance, rural electrification, benefit payments to farmers and agricultural cooperatives.

The Republican candidate challenged Roosevelt to a series of joint debates, hoping for a slugging match with "the champ." But Harold Ickes, speaking for the President, threw cold water on such expectation. "The Battle of Britain could not be adjourned by Roosevelt

IN PHILADELPHIA ON OCTOBER 23 the candidate lashed out: "I consider it a public duty to answer falsifications with facts. I will not pretend that I find this an unpleasant duty. I am an old campaigner and I love a good fight."

Lorant: FDR, A Pictorial Biography (*Simon & Schuster*)

IN NEW YORK ON OCTOBER 28: Answering the Republican candidate's charges of unpreparedness, Roosevelt replied: "Great Britain would have never received help . . . from us if the decision had been left to Martin, Barton, and Fish." Over and over again he repeated the catchy phrase: Martin, Barton and Fish—and the audience joyously joined in the fun.

in order to ride the circuit with Willkie," said the old curmudgeon.

Willkie, called "the simple, barefoot, Wall Street lawyer" running for office as a "rich man's Roosevelt," conducted a traditional campaign, traveling 30,000 miles in thirty-four states, making half a thousand speeches. His principal charges against Roosevelt were that the President thought himself "indispensable," and

IN BROOKLYN ON NOVEMBER 1: The President closed his campaign speech: "I am fighting against the revival of government by special privilege . . . vested in the hands of those who favor . . . foreign dictatorships."

INP

647

that he wanted to perpetuate "one-man rule" by running for a third term. "I deny that Franklin Roosevelt is a defender of democracy. . . . His influence has weakened rather than strengthened democracy throughout the world. . . . If, because of some fine speeches about humanity, you return this administration to office, you will be serving under an American totalitarian government before the long third term is finished."

But while Willkie barnstormed the country, beating Bryan's record of 1896, Roosevelt stayed aloof. He planned to give five major addresses during the last fortnight of the campaign, and he refused to change his mind. Willkie, exasperated by Roosevelt's silence, listened to the advice of his party's tacticians; he now fought hard against the "third-term candidate." With a change in tactics, he told audiences that if they voted for Roosevelt it would mean wooden crosses for their brothers and sons and sweethearts, and that if Roosevelt should become President again, America would soon be involved in a foreign war. He asserted that American boys were already on the transports to foreign shores, that "the floundering management of the New Deal" had "failed to build us a defense system," and that America was "deficient in all the essential items of defense—the airplanes, the guns, the tanks, and even the ability to make them."

Roosevelt began his campaign on October 12 at Philadelphia, and replied to Willkie's charges five days later in New York's Madison Square Garden. He reminded the country that it was not the administration but the Republican opposition in Congress which had tried to keep us unprepared and which had fought against an increased armed force and against aid to Britain. "Great Britain would never have received an ounce of help from us," said Roosevelt, "if the decision had been left to Martin, Barton and Fish." The alliteration caught the audience. They repeated gleefully the cadence: "Martin, Barton and Fish." The President extolled the administration's aims of preparing the country but keeping out of war, and took credit for the Neutrality Act (of which he had in reality disapproved).

It was a strange campaign, with Roosevelt upholding policies in which he did not believe and Willkie making "campaign oratory" which he later had to recant. Basically the political beliefs of the two men were similar. Willkie said: "There is no issue between the third-term candidate and myself on the questions of old-age pensions, unemployment insurance, collective bargaining, laws which guarantee minimum wages and prohibit men working more than so many hours per week, or the elimination of child labor and the retention of Federal relief. I am not alone *for* all these laws, but I advocate their improvement and reinforcement." In effect Willkie was saying: "Let me do the job; I can do it better

THE WINNER
Photograph by Thomas D. McAvoy, in Life,
November 5, 1940

649

INP, October 29, 1940

PICKING A DRAFT NUMBER. The blindfolded Secretary of War, Henry L. Stimson, picks the capsule containing the first number of the peacetime draft lottery—it was 158.

Lorant: FDR, A Pictorial Biography (*Simon & Schuster*)

FDR ADDRESSES CONGRESS. On January 6, 1941, in his Four Freedoms speech Roosevelt advocated the loan of war materials to Britain, to be repaid in kind after the war, as the most effective way of helping that country in her fight.

than Roosevelt." But all were not certain that he could.

Nor was there any disagreement between the two contestants regarding aid to Britain. Willkie said that he was "in favor of aiding Britain at some sacrifice to our own defense program . . . aid to Britain to the limits of prudence for our own safety." The Republican candidate was informed in advance that Roosevelt had decided to give England some fifty overage destroyers in exchange for a ninety-nine-year lease of sea and air bases in islands in the Western Atlantic, and Willkie, who approved the deal, promised not to make a campaign issue of it.

In his third major speech at Boston Roosevelt was urged by influential members of his party to make a strong statement against the entry of America into the war, as Willkie seemed to be gaining ground on the "keeping-out-of-war" theme. So Roosevelt said: "I have said this before, but I shall say it again and again and again: 'Your boys are not going to be sent into foreign wars.' " Robert Sherwood, who claimed responsibility for the statement, recalled that while the speech was being discussed on the train to Boston, Judge Rosenman suggested adding the phrase "except in case of attack," as stated in the Democratic platform. But Roosevelt replied irritably: "Of course we'll fight if we're attacked. If somebody attacks us, then it isn't a foreign war, is it? Or do they want me to guarantee that our troops be sent into battle only in the event of another Civil War?"

When in the same Boston speech Roosevelt referred to Joseph P. Kennedy as "my ambassador," Republicans took up the phrase, saying that the use of the personal pronoun proved Roosevelt's dictatorial ambitions. During his visit to Boston the President was booed by students of the Massachusetts Institute of Technology, who chanted, "Poppa, I wanna be a captain," a reference to the commission given to the President's son Elliott—one of the minor personal issues of the campaign.

In his fourth speech in Brooklyn Roosevelt was in fighting spirit. No longer was he on the defensive. He now attacked the Republicans for joining hands with the Communists, pointing out that "there is something very ominous in this combination that has been forming within the Republican party between the extreme reactionary and the extreme radical elements of this country." He said that "something evil is happening in this country when a full-page advertisement, paid for by Republican supporters, appears—where, of all places? In the *Daily Worker,* the newspaper of the Communist party."

With all the spirit of the old campaigner, Roosevelt pounced on the speech of a Republican judge in Philadelphia who had said: "The President's only supporters

IN HIS THIRD INAUGURAL ADDRESS, ON JANUARY 20, 1941, President Roosevelt sounded a philosophical theme: "Lives of nations are determined not by the count of years, but by the lifetime of the human spirit. The life of a man is three-score and ten: a little more, a little less. The life of a nation is the fullness of the measure of its will to live. . . ."

U.S. Signal Corps

WITH THE WAR AT ITS PEAK, TANKS AND GUNS WERE ON DISPLAY IN THE INAUGURAL PARADE.

are paupers, who earn less than $1,200 a year and aren't worth *that,* and the Roosevelt family." Roosevelt pointed out that half of the nation's population earned less than $1,200. "Paupers," he taunted, "who are not worth their salt—there speaks the true sentiment of the Republican leadership in this year of grace." Such remarks as this, he continued, were a "direct, vicious, unpatriotic appeal to class hatred and class contempt." And moving closer to the microphone he said in a dramatic voice: "That, my friends, is just what I am fighting against with all my heart and soul. I am fighting for a free America—for a country in which all men and women have equal rights to liberty and justice. I am fighting against the revival of government by special privilege—government by lobbyists—government vested in the hands of those who favor and who would have us imitate the foreign dictatorships. And I will not

stop fighting." The cheering for the President echoed through the land.

On election eve Roosevelt appealed to the voters to do their duty, ending his appeal with a prayer remembered from his school days: "Bless our land with honorable industry, sound learning and pure manners. Save us from violence, discord and confusion, from pride and arrogance, and from every evil way. Defend our liberties, and fashion into one united people the multitudes brought hither out of many kindreds and tongues."

There were the usual number of minor party candidates contesting the election. The Socialists put up Norman Thomas for the fourth time on a platform proposing collective ownership of the basic means of production and their operation for use rather than profit as the way to conquer poverty and save democracy. The Socialists were firmly against the "collective

ROOSEVELT IN A FUR-LINED COAT WHICH HE BORROWED FROM AMBASSADOR JOSEPH DAVIES

suicide" of wars, and advocated neutral mediation in behalf of a negotiated peace. The Communists were again behind Earl Browder, who followed the Moscow line (the Nazi-Soviet pact was still in force) and advocated: "Not a cent, not a gun, not a man for war preparations and imperialist war." The Prohibitionists upheld the statistician and market analyst Roger Babson.

On election day everybody was decorated with campaign buttons. Twenty-one million emblems were manufactured boosting the President, thirty-three million were dedicated to Willkie. Besides the usual slogans there were buttons which said: "We don't want Eleanor either" and "Willkie for President—of Commonwealth and Southern." Others said: "No more fireside chats" and "Two good terms deserve another."

Labor leader John L. Lewis made a bombastic radio speech for Willkie, promising that if Roosevelt were re-

elected he would resign as CIO president. But when the votes were counted, it was Roosevelt again. The people of the country had no fear that Roosevelt would become a dictator if they elected him for a third term; they gave little heed to Herbert Hoover's prediction that the defeat of the Republican candidate would mean socialism and totalitarianism in the United States, and they gave no credence to the newspapers which declared that a Roosevelt victory would be the end of free elections. The people knew better.

Roosevelt carried thirty-eight states with 449 electoral votes, receiving 27,243,466 popular votes. Willkie, supported by ten states with 82 electoral votes, won 22,304,755 popular votes.

The Republicans' effort to take the New Deal away from Roosevelt had failed; the country had its first third-term President.

THE WAR MESSAGE: "Yesterday, December 7, 1941—a date which will live in infamy—the United States of America was suddenly and deliberately attacked by naval and air forces of the Empire of Japan," began President Roosevelt in his emergency message to Congress. "I regret to tell you that very many American lives have been lost. . . . Japan . . . has undertaken a surprise offensive extending throughout the Pacific area. The facts of yesterday and today speak for themselves. . . ." The President talked gravely as he asked for a declaration of war against Japan. ". . . No matter how long it may take us to overcome this premeditated invasion, the American people . . . will win through to absolute victory."

1944

FRANKLIN D. ROOSEVELT and HARRY S. TRUMAN

During Roosevelt's third term the overriding issue was the war.

Two days after the Japanese attacked Pearl Harbor, Roosevelt recounted the militant deeds of the Axis. "In 1931 Japan invaded Manchukuo without warning. In 1935 Italy invaded Ethiopia without warning. In 1938 Hitler occupied Austria without warning. In 1939 Hitler invaded Czechoslovakia without warning. Later in 1939 Hitler invaded Poland without warning. In 1940 Hitler invaded Norway, Denmark, the Netherlands, Belgium and Luxembourg without warning. In 1940 Italy attacked France and later Greece without warning. In 1941 the Axis powers attacked Yugoslavia and Greece and they dominated the Balkans without warning. In 1941 Hitler invaded Russia without warning. And now Japan has attacked Malaya and Thailand—and the United States—without warning." Roosevelt concluded: "We are now in this war. We are in it all the way. . . ."

As the country entered the war, Republicans and Democrats shelved their differences and closed ranks. The President called for a vast armament program of 185,000 planes, 120,000 tanks, 55,000 antiaircraft guns, eighteen million tons of shipping. His critics said that such ambitious goals could never be attained.

The early part of 1942 brought defeats. In the Far East Singapore fell, the Burma Road was cut, Bataan was lost, Japanese troops landed in the Aleutians. But as the summer waned, the Marines routed the Japanese at Guadalcanal.

The year of 1943 began auspiciously. In January, British troops took Tripoli; in February, the siege of Stalingrad was lifted; three months later, British and American troops freed Africa from the German invaders.

By 1944 the tide of battle had turned. The defeat of the Axis powers was within reach. Russian troops were pushing the mighty German army out of their land. On June 6, D-Day, the Allies struck at the coast of Normandy and breached the Atlantic Wall; the invasion of Europe was under way.

On June 26 the Republicans met in Chicago, but the country was more interested in the war news than in the proceedings of the convention. Walter Lippmann speculated about the lack of popular interest and came up with the explanation "that the men who organized the convention and are managing it and will write the platform are not the Republicans who could win the election. Even they themselves know it, as one can see from the drab defeatism which the journalists who reflect their views do not conceal."

After Thomas E. Dewey won the Wisconsin primary, defeating Wendell Willkie and forcing his withdrawal, it was evident that the Republican candidate would be the forty-two-year-old Governor of New York. Dewey duly received all but one of the delegates' votes on the first ballot. The lone dissenter, Grant Ritter, a Wisconsin farmer, held out for General Douglas MacArthur because "I'm a man, not a jellyfish." The second place on the ticket went to Ohio's handsome Governor John W. Bricker.

In his acceptance speech Dewey sounded the keynote of his forthcoming campaign. He charged that the Democratic administration had "grown old in office" and had become "tired and quarrelsome," that it was "at

CANDIDATES IN 1944

FRANKLIN D. ROOSEVELT
(1882–1945), was again the Democratic nominee. The war was nearing its end, and Roosevelt was deemed necessary to bring it to a conclusion. Traveling to conferences far away from home, working desperately on the foundation of future peace, he was a sick man, worn by the strain, when he took the call for the fourth term. After a grueling campaign he won; five months later, on April 12, 1945, he died.

HARRY S. TRUMAN
(1884——), farmer, commander of a battery in World War I, partner in a haberdashery store, presiding judge at Jackson County, U.S. Senator from Missouri, chairman of the special Senate committee to investigate the national defense program, was chosen for the Vice Presidency to replace Wallace, who was too radical for the delegates. His ticket got 25,612,610 votes, the Republicans 22,017,617.

AGAINST THE FOURTH TERM

THOMAS E. DEWEY
(1902——), the vigorous Governor of New York, was the Republican choice. He had a reputation as an efficient administrator, moderately liberal in his policies; and he was an effective votegetter. He prophesied that the election would end "one-man government in America." Although he received more votes than any previous Republican, he failed to carry New York or Michigan, his birthplace.

JOHN W. BRICKER
(1893——), Governor of Ohio, had served as a chaplain in the First World War. A conservative politician, called "an honest Harding" by William Allen White, he was chosen as the Republican vice presidential candidate. The platform condemned the Roosevelt administration for waste, inefficiency and the destruction of private enterprise—but had no quarrel with the New Deal domestic issues.

war with Congress and at war with itself"; "wrangling, bungling and confusion" prevailed in the "vital matters of taxation, price control, rationing, labor relations, manpower." He accused the New Deal of failing to eradicate the unemployment problem, which "was left to be solved by the war," and promised that "this election will bring an end to one-man government in America."

His charges found no response in the country. The war was in its final phase—this was not the time to replace an experienced President.

A week before the Democratic convention Roosevelt

"ONWARD, CHRISTIAN SOLDIERS," sang Roosevelt and Churchill at Sunday services aboard the English battleship *Prince of Wales,* and British and American sailors joined in the hymn. Standing behind the main participants are (from left to right) an aide, British Air Chief Marshal Sir Charles Portal, Admiral Ernest King, General George Marshall, and Field Marshal Sir John Dill. Second row: General Henry Arnold, Sumner Welles, Harry Hopkins and Averell Harriman.

handed a letter to Robert E. Hannegan, the chairman of the party's national committee, in which he said that if the convention should renominate him, "I shall accept. If the people elect me, I will serve . . . but I would not run in the usual partisan sense. But if the people command me to continue in this office and in this war, I have as little right to withdraw as the soldier has to leave his post in the line."

Thus on July 20—the very day Tojo resigned as premier of Japan and Hitler escaped death in the attempted assassination by his generals—the Democrats nominated Roosevelt for the fourth time. He received 1,086 votes to 89 for Senator Byrd of Virginia and 1 for James A. Farley on the first ballot.

The rebellion of the Texas delegates, threatening to vote against the President unless white supremacy were upheld and the two-thirds rule reinstituted, was quelled easily. And though the convention did not oppose the renomination of Roosevelt, it was firmly against the renomination of Wallace for the second place. Because of his advocacy of the "century of the common man," his forward stand on social

BUILDING SHIPS. During his inspection tour in the fall of 1942 President Roosevelt (with back to the camera) visited the Kaiser shipyard in Vancouver, Washington, where a complete merchant ship was launched every ten days. The vessels were made battle-ready within four days and turned over to their crews; they were instantly taken out to sea and to duty.

BUILDING PLANES. During September, driving through the assembly line of the Grant-Douglas aircraft plant in Long Beach, California, where Army bombers were built, the President told industrialists to step up war production to 125,000 planes, 75,000 tanks, and 10 million tons of shipping in a year. This, so Roosevelt recalled, "nearly took their breath away."

issues, Wallace was opposed by the city bosses, by the conservatives, by the Southern Bourbons, by all the elements who were against the New Deal. They wanted him off the ticket.

But Roosevelt said about Wallace: "I like him and I respect him and he is my personal friend. For these reasons I personally would vote for his renomination if I were a delegate to the convention."

However, after the unyielding resistance of the delegates, he sent another letter to Hannegan: "You have written me about Harry Truman and Bill Douglas. I should, of course, be very glad to run with either of them and believe that either of them would bring real strength to the ticket." (Grace Tully, Roosevelt's secretary, recalled later that the President placed Douglas's name first and Truman's second, but Hannegan persuaded him to reverse the order; so Truman's name came first.)

Next to Wallace, Douglas and Truman, Roosevelt also encouraged James F. Byrnes, but Philip Murray, president of the CIO, and Sidney Hillman, chairman of its Political Action Committee, said that Byrnes was not acceptable to labor.

When Wallace arrived in Chicago, university students serenaded him:

You can talk about Senator Barkley,
You can talk about Senator Truman,
But the Democratic party has learned that
Wallace fought the battle for the common man,
Common man, common man,
Wallace fought the battle for the common man,
And he'll fight that battle again.

In making the seconding speech for Roosevelt's renomination, Wallace declared his beliefs. "The future

U.S. Signal Corps (Wide World)

AT WASHINGTON, JUNE 11, 1942, with Soviet Foreign Commissar Molotov, who urged Roosevelt to open a second front to give relief to the hard-pressed Russian armies.

U.S. Signal Corps

AT CASABLANCA, JANUARY 24, 1943. Churchill said, "Nothing that may occur in this war will ever come between me and the President." They were now affectionate friends.

U.S. Signal Corps

THE ALLIED LEADERS with the French generals Giraud and De Gaulle. FDR said of De Gaulle: "Yesterday he wanted to be Joan of Arc. Now he wants to be Clemenceau!"

belongs to those," he said, "who go down the line unswervingly for the liberal principles of both political democracy and economic democracy, regardless of race, color or religion. . . . The Democratic party cannot long survive as a conservative party."

The convention gave him a tremendous ovation. The cry went up: "We want Wallace! We want Wallace!" If the balloting had begun then, he would have been chosen. But the chairman asked for adjournment and though delegates and spectators shouted "No!" he adjourned the meeting.

During the night the city bosses lined up delegates for Harry S Truman, Senator from Missouri. Ed Kelly of Chicago, Ed Flynn of New York, Robert Hannegan and Frank Walker worked hard to secure the nomination for him. Arthur Krock wrote in *The New York Times* that it was cleared with Sidney Hillman of the Political Action Committee. Though the "Clear-it-with-Sidney" charge was denied by Roosevelt, Truman later told an interviewer that Hillman assured him that if labor could not have the nomination of Wallace it would be satisfied with Truman.

When it appeared that not enough delegates could be lined up behind Truman on the first ballot, the bosses set up favorite sons to block Wallace's nomination. Even so Wallace led on the first trial with 429½ votes against Truman's 310½, but the votes for the thirteen favorite sons came to 393½. On the second ballot the majority of these votes were railroaded to Truman, giving him the nomination.

Roosevelt made his acceptance speech to the convention over radio, speaking from a private railroad car at San Diego, California: "The people of the United States will decide this fall whether they wish to turn over this 1944 job—this worldwide job—to inexperienced and immature hands, to those who opposed Lend-Lease and international cooperation against the forces of aggression and tyranny, until they could read the polls of popular sentiment; or whether they wish to leave it to those who saw the danger from abroad, who met it head on, and who now have seized the offensive and carried the war to its present stages of success; to those who, by international conferences and united actions, have begun to build that kind of common understanding and cooperative experience which will be so necessary in the world to come."

Roosevelt asked: "What is the job before us in 1944? First, to win the war, to win it fast, to win it overpoweringly. Second, to form worldwide international organizations and to arrange to use the armed forces of the sovereign nations of the world to make another war impossible within the foreseeable future. Third, to build an economy for our returning veterans and for all Americans which will provide employment and a decent

FDR'S SIXTY-FIRST BIRTHDAY. Flying home from Africa, the President cuts his birthday cake. With him are Fleet Admiral William Leahy, the President's Chief of Staff; Harry Hopkins; and Lieutenant Cone, the captain of the plane.

standard of living."

He said he would not campaign in the usual sense. "In these days of tragic sorrow I do not consider it fitting. Besides in these days of global warfare, I shall not be able to find the time. I shall, however, feel free to report to the people the facts about matters of concern to them and especially to correct any misrepresentations."

Thus in the opening months of the contest the Republican candidate did all the talking. In Louisville, Dewey spoke on foreign policy, in Seattle on labor, in San Francisco on government regulation, in Los Angeles on social security. Everywhere he spoke he found apathetic audiences.

He was answered by the members of Roosevelt's Cabinet. The speeches of Harold Ickes, the Secretary of the Interior, "the old curmudgeon," were most effective. At one occasion Ickes said of the Republican candidate:

"Four years ago I observed that Mr. Dewey had thrown his diaper into the ring. At Los Angeles on Friday night, when he upbraided the New Deal for not being New Dealish enough, he threw the sponge after his diaper."

Between the policies of the Republicans and the Democrats, there was little difference. Dewey refrained from attacking the social legislation of the New Deal. Most of it—such as labor's rights, collective bargaining, the SEC, unemployment insurance, the broadening of social security—he endorsed. The administration, Dewey admitted, "did some good things" in its youth. And he did not criticize Roosevelt's conduct of the war, nor offer to change the military leadership if elected. "The military conduct of the war is outside this campaign. It is and must remain completely out of politics," he said.

But Dewey charged that "tired old men" dominated

AT CAIRO, NOVEMBER 22, 1943: Roosevelt, Churchill and Chiang Kai-shek discussed their common Asian strategy against Japan. Their communiqué said that "all the territories Japan has stolen from the Chinese, such as Manchuria, Formosa, and the Pescadores, should be restored to the Republic of China" and "Korea shall become free and independent."

the administration without mentioning that the military leaders were "tired old men" too. Admiral King was sixty-six, General MacArthur and General Marshall were sixty-four, Admiral Halsey was sixty-two, the same age as President Roosevelt.

Republican newspapers attacked the President's Communist and radical support; Republican campaigners denounced Roosevelt as a tool of Sidney Hillman and the PAC. They reminded the country that if he were to remain in office for another term, every member of the Supreme Court would then have been appointed by him. They pointed out that he was in failing health. Vice Admiral Ross McIntire, the President's personal physician, was forced to issue a statement about Roosevelt's health, declaring there was "nothing wrong organically with him at all. He's perfectly O.K. . . . The stories that he is in bad health are understandable enough around

election time, but they are not true."

The Democrats were more troubled about Roosevelt's disinterested attitude toward the campaign than about the Republican attacks on him. "He just doesn't seem to give a damn," said his aide, Pa Watson.

But when Roosevelt made an informal speech at the Teamsters' Union dinner in late September, the campaign caught fire. He began with a mocking smile on his face: "Well, here we are together again—after four years—and what years they have been! I am actually four years older, which seems to annoy some people. In fact, millions of us are more than eleven years older than when we started in to clear up the mess that was dumped in our laps in 1933."

He turned on those Republicans who "suddenly discover" every four years just before election day that they love labor after having attacked labor "for three years

AT TEHERAN, NOVEMBER 28, 1943: Roosevelt met with Premier Stalin for the first time. Together with Churchill they discussed the opening of a second front: the invasion of France across the Channel within the following year, which would bring relief to the Russian army. Stalin promised Russia's entry in the war against Japan after the defeat of Germany.

and six months," and reminded the nation that the Republicans had opposed the National Labor Relations Act, the Wages and Hours Act, and the Social Security Act—statutes which they now upheld in their platform.

Roosevelt demolished the charges which the Republicans hurled against him. But the highlight of the address, the passage which made the country rock with laughter, was the one about his dog Fala. "These Republican leaders," said the President, "have not been content with attacks upon me, or my wife, or my sons— they now include my little dog, Fala. Unlike the members of my family, he resents this. Being a Scottie, as soon as he learned that the Republican fiction writers had concocted a story that I had left him behind on an Aleutian island and had sent a destroyer back to find him at a cost to the taxpayers of two or three or twenty million dollars, his Scotch soul was furious. He has not

"WELL, IKE—YOU'D BETTER START PACKING." In this informal way the General learned from FDR that he would be supreme commander of the invasion armies.

663

INS, June 1944

THE REPUBLICAN CONVENTION AT CHICAGO, WHICH CHOSE THOMAS E. DEWEY AS GOP CANDIDATE

INP, June 28, 1944

ACCEPTING THE NOMINATION, Dewey said that the issue of the war "must remain completely out of politics."

been the same dog since." The audience roared.

"Roosevelt was at his best," wrote *Time* magazine. "He was like a veteran virtuoso playing a piece he has loved for years, who fingers his way through it with a delicate fire, a perfection of tuning and tone, and an assurance that no young player, no matter how gifted, can equal. The President was playing what he loves to play—politics."

Dewey answered Roosevelt's jibes with a hard-hitting counterattack in Oklahoma City. "He asked for it. Here it is!" cried Dewey, and in the manner of a prosecuting attorney he struck out at Roosevelt's so-called Communist sympathies, and cited statements of General Marshall, General Arnold and Senator Truman that in 1940 the Army of the United States was not prepared for war. He charged, "In 1940, the United States could put into the field . . . no more than 75,000 men. The

IN THE DEMOCRATIC CONVENTION AT CHICAGO FDR WAS RENOMINATED FOR THE THIRD TIME.

Army was only '25% ready.' Now Mr. Roosevelt, did those statements come from Goebbels? Was that fraud or falsification? Those are the words of General George C. Marshall."

Dewey quoted General Arnold that "December 7, 1941, found the Army Air Force equipped with plans but not with planes." And he quoted Truman on the floor of the Senate in 1943: "After Pearl Harbor we found ourselves woefully unprepared for war."

The Republican candidate recalled that in 1940 he asked for a two-ocean navy, and the President called the statement "just plain dumb." Dewey's voice rose in anger: "Then as now, we get ridicule instead of action."

Roosevelt decided to make five more major addresses, and despite all the clamor for more, he stuck to his decision. His first address—after "that speech about Fala"—was scheduled for October 21 before the

INP, July 21, 1944
ACCEPTING THE NOMINATION from a railroad car at San Diego. James Roosevelt and his wife listen, at right.

U.S. Signal Corps, July 27, 1944

THE FINAL DRIVE TO CRUSH JAPAN. In Honolulu the President conferred with Admiral Nimitz, commander of the naval forces in the Pacific (pointing to the map), and General MacArthur, commander of Allied forces in the southwest Pacific. Nimitz and MacArthur disagreed. MacArthur wanted to take the Philippines first; Nimitz wanted Formosa.

Foreign Policy Association in New York City. On that day he toured the boroughs of the city in a bitter wind and driving rain. He drove fifty-one miles through the streets of New York, proving to the millions who lined the pavement that he could still take it. Water rolled down his cheeks and dropped from his chin; his thinning hair was pasted flat and the raindrops trickled down the sleeve of his right arm as he raised it again and again to wave to the crowds. Newspapers printed photographs of the tour according to their political sympathies. In the pro-Roosevelt press the President looked smiling and defiant; in the opposition papers he appeared haggard and tired.

Roosevelt's speech on that evening was a forceful attack on Republican shortsightedness on foreign issues. He warned the country of the Republican isolationists who still wielded great power and who would come to the fore if Dewey should be elected. He recalled that the Republicans in Congress had opposed Selective Service in 1940, Lend-Lease in 1941, and the extension of Selective Service in August 1941. "You see," said Roosevelt, "I'm quoting history to you. I'm going by the record, and I am giving you the whole story, and not a phrase here, and half a phrase there. . . ."

Speaking of the future he advocated completion of the United Nations organization before the end of the war. "The Council of the United Nations must have the power to act quickly and decisively to keep the

AP, August 18, 1944

PLANNING THE CAMPAIGN WITH HIS RUNNING MATE. President Roosevelt and Senator Truman are mapping plans for the forthcoming contest at a luncheon meeting beneath the magnolia trees on the White House lawn. Roosevelt suggested that Truman bear the major brunt of the campaign· while he remained at his desk directing the war effort.

peace by force if necessary. A policeman would not be an effective policeman if, when he saw a felon break into a house, he had to go to the Town Hall and call a town meeting to issue a warrant before the felon could be arrested. It is clear that if the world organization is to have any reality at all, our representatives must be endowed in advance by the people themselves, by constitutional means through their representatives in the Congress, with authority to act."

It was about this time Roosevelt learned that Dewey intended to use in his campaign the highly secret information that the United States had broken the Japanese code before the attack on Pearl Harbor. The President said to Harry Hopkins: "My opponent must

be pretty desperate if he is even thinking of using material like this, which would be bound to react against him." However, Dewey—after General Marshall implored him to keep silent about the matter—dropped the plan.

Roosevelt gave his second campaign speech on October 27 in Philadelphia. A few days before, General MacArthur had landed in the Philippines and the Navy had the Japanese on the run. "I wonder whatever became of the suggestion," asked Roosevelt sarcastically, "that I had failed for political reasons to send enough forces or supplies to General MacArthur. Now, of course, I realize that . . . it is considered by some to be very impolite to mention that there's a war on. In that

FDR SPOKE ABOUT HIS DOG FALA at a Teamsters' Union dinner, where he sat between AFL president William Green and Teamster boss Dan Tobin. His audience roared with laughter when he told them that "these Republican leaders have not been content with attacks upon me. . . . They now include my little dog, Fala. . . . I am accustomed to hearing malicious falsehoods about myself. . . . But I think I have a right to object to libelous statements about my dog. . . ."

war I bear a responsibility that I can never shirk. . . . For the Constitution of the United States says—and I hope you'll pardon me if I quote it correctly—the Constitution says the President shall be Commander in Chief of the Army and Navy." He pointed out that all battleships and all but two of the cruisers of Admiral Halsey's victorious Third Fleet had been authorized during his administration, which should be an "answer to a Republican candidate who said that this administration had made 'absolutely no military preparation for

the events that it now claims it foresaw.'"

A day later he spoke again, this time in Chicago, addressing the largest political audience on record—over 100,000 people filled the stadium while another 150,000 listened to his speech outside through loudspeakers. Roosevelt gave his address from his car: "This is the strangest campaign I have even seen," he said. "I have listened to various Republican orators . . . and what do they say? 'Those incompetent blunderers and bunglers in Washington have passed a lot of excellent

Acme, September 11, 1944

THE REPUBLICAN CANDIDATE AT FIRST CONDUCTED A HIGH-LEVEL CAMPAIGN, speaking on specific subjects. But after Roosevelt made his frolicsome Teamsters' Union speech, Dewey's fighting dander was up. Though he declared at Oklahoma City that "I shall not join my opponent in his descent to mudslinging," in his subsequent campaign speeches he charged Roosevelt with leaving the country unprepared for war and accused him of Communist sympathies.

laws about social security and labor and farm relief and soil conservation. . . . Those same quarrelsome, tired old men . . . have built the greatest military machine the world has ever known, which is fighting its way to victory,' and they say, 'If you elect us we promise not to change any of that. . . .' They also say, in effect, 'Those inefficient and worn-out crackpots have really begun to lay the foundation of a lasting world peace. If you elect us we will not change any of that, either.' But they whisper, 'We'll do it in such a way that we

won't lose the support even of Gerald Nye or Gerald Smith [or] the Chicago *Tribune*.' "

The President was in great form. "If anyone feels that my faith in our ability to provide sixty million peacetime jobs is fantastic, let him remember that some people said the same thing about my demand in 1940 for fifty thousand airplanes." And he ended with the promise: "We are not going to turn the clock back. We are going forward, my friends."

The last verbal exchange between the two candidates

THE WEATHER WAS FOUL when Roosevelt, in his navy cape and old hat, which he had worn in his three previous campaigns, drove fifty-one miles through the streets of New York in an open car, proving that he could stand the strain. In Manhattan's garment district (opposite page), confetti and torn telephone books swirled down from the windows. "After the people have seen him," said Robert Hannegan, "they can make up their own minds about his vigor and health."

was in Boston, where Dewey charged that "Mr. Roosevelt, to perpetuate himself in office for sixteen years, has put his party on the auction block—for sale to the highest bidder." He meant the Political Action Committee of Sidney Hillman and the Communist party. Dewey insisted that "the forces of communism" were capturing the Democratic party. It was a poor and tasteless speech not worthy of a presidential candidate.

Roosevelt replied to it three days later: "When any political candidate stands up and says solemnly that there is danger that the government of the United States —your government—could be sold out to the Communists, then I say that candidate reveals shocking lack of trust in democracy—in the spiritual strength of our people."

Speaking of the war Roosevelt explained: "We got

into this war because we were attacked by the Japanese —and because they and their Axis partners, Hitler's Germany and Mussolini's Italy, declared war on us. I am sure that any real American would have chosen, as this government did, to fight when our own soil was made the object of a sneak attack. As for myself, under the same circumstances, I would choose to do the same thing—again, and again, and again." It was the very phrase he had used in his Boston speech four years before and the audience applauded it with enthusiasm.

The keynote of the Republicans was Dewey's crisp American efficiency. At every stop Dewey's campaign procedure was "metronomically precise." If the train was early, it waited in the yards to be able to puff in on schedule. In the larger towns and cities the Republican candidate spoke briefly to the crowd at the station

Wide World

ELECTION NIGHT AT HYDE PARK. The haggard and ill-looking President was wheeled out onto the porch to see the neighbors who came by with torches and a brass band. Noticing a few boys perched in a tree, he recalled that as a child he had climbed the same tree to watch a torchlight parade for President Cleveland.

DEWEY CONCEDES HIS DEFEAT AND CONGRATULATES ROOSEVELT ON HIS FOURTH VICTORY.

before leaving in a twenty-five-car motorcade for his hotel. Then there was a press conference—thirty minutes, no more, no less. When the time was up, Dewey would stride into an adjacent room where local leaders were gathered. He would begin: "Well, I'm here to learn what your problems are."

Emphasizing this image, the Dewey followers glorified their candidate in song:

> *Oh, Tom E. Dewey came to town*
> *A-ridin' on a pony.*
> *He busted gangs and jailed the mobs*
> *And cleared out every phony.*
> *Tom E. Dewey, keep it up,*
> *You're swingin' sharp and handy.*
> *The White House is your home next year*
> *Our Yankee Dewey Dandy.*

Before Dewey was to speak, the height of the lectern was arranged and Dewey would wait in the wings until his name was mentioned, then he walked on stage. He changed suits frequently—gray, pin-striped, brown, blue, all of them single-breasted.

The trouble was that this well-oiled, well-organized, well-planned campaign was not effectual. Dewey always talked to Republican audiences and basked in Republican applause. The people who came to hear him would have voted for him anyway. What Dewey omitted to do was to fight for the decisive independent vote.

He wound up his campaign in New York's Madison Square Garden, once more charging that Roosevelt's "own confused incompetence" had prolonged the war, and that the President had "offered no program, nothing but smears and unspecified complaints, because the New Deal had nothing to offer."

THE FOURTH INAUGURAL—JANUARY 20, 1945. In bitter weather and without an overcoat, Roosevelt takes the oath for the fourth time, this time on the portico of the White House. There was no ceremony. In the second-shortest inaugural address on record—it contained only 573 words—the President said: "And so today in this year of war, 1945, we have learned lessons—at a fearful cost—and we shall profit by them. We have learned that we cannot live alone, at peace. . . . We have learned to be . . . members of the human community. We have learned the simple truth, as Emerson said, that 'the only way to have a friend is to be one.' We can gain no lasting peace if we approach it with suspicion and mistrust or with fear. We can gain it only if we proceed with the understanding and . . . courage which flow from conviction!"

With this the verbal fireworks ended. Roosevelt felt that it was "the meanest campaign of his life. He said he thought they hit him below the belt several times and that it was done quite deliberately and very viciously. He was particularly resentful about the whispering campaign on his failing health which he believed was a highly organized affair." So wrote Robert Sherwood, who had it from Harry Hopkins.

In the campaign the much-derided Political Action Committee of the CIO worked assiduously for the President's re-election. Two million CIO members rang doorbells and distributed literature for him. It was a

INAUGURAL IN WARTIME
Photograph by Merle Hanson, Life

THE CRIMEAN CONFERENCE. At five o'clock in the afternoon, Sunday, February 4, 1945, at the Livadia Palace, the first session of the Yalta Conference began. There was a frank exchange of views on military questions. Clockwise from President Roosevelt: Charles E. Bohlen, Assistant Secretary of State; next to him, but unseen, James F. Byrnes, Director of War Mobilization; Sir Alexander Cadogan, British Permanent Under-secretary of State for Foreign Affairs, is covered by the standing Anthony Eden, Britain Foreign Secretary. Prime Minister Winston Churchill with his oversized cigar is next; the empty chair belongs to his interpreter, Major Birse, who is talking with Eden; Sir Archibald Clark Kerr, British Ambassador to Moscow, makes notes. Then come the Russians: F. T. Gusev, Ambassador to Great Britain; Andrei Y. Vishinsky, Commissar for Foreign Affairs (covered); Marshal Stalin (behind him, Pavlov, his interpreter), Ivan M. Maisky, Deputy Foreign Commissar; Andrei A. Gromyko, Ambassador to the U.S. Then the Americans: Admiral William D. Leahy, FDR's Chief of Staff, Edward R. Stettinius, Jr., Secretary of State. Behind them: Freeman Matthews, Director of European Affairs, and Harry Hopkins, the ever-present friend of the President, his face partly covered by Roosevelt.

A COFFEE CONFERENCE AT YALTA.

new and unique phenomenon proving the importance of labor's political influence. The Republicans met the challenge with posters containing the veiled anti-Semitic appeal: "It's your country. Why let Sidney Hillman run it? Vote for Dewey and Bricker."

The pollsters predicted a close election. Gallup gave the President 51.5 percent of the votes; Elmo Roper predicted a Roosevelt victory by 53.6 percent; *Time* magazine said the election seemed to be so close that the people might not know possibly for weeks after November 7 whether they had elected Tom Dewey or Franklin Roosevelt.

In the Allied powers there was concern whether they might have to deal with a new American leader. The

A HEART-BREAKING PICTURE: ILLNESS MARK
ITS LINES ON ROOSEVELT'S FACE. Behind hir
Fleet Admiral Leahy, Stettinius and General Marsha

REPORT ON YALTA TO CONGRESS. "I come from the Crimean Conference," began Roosevelt, "with a firm belief that we have made a good start on the road to a world of peace. . . . There were two main purposes in this Crimean Conference. The first was to bring defeat to Germany with the greatest possible speed and the smallest possible loss of Allied men. . . . The second purpose was to continue to build the foundation for an international accord which would bring order and security after the chaos of the war, and would give some assurance of lasting peace among the nations of the

New Statesman in London satirized the American concern over the presidential election:

> *If America seems lately*
> *To be burning for a row,*
> *It doesn't matter greatly,*
> *For she's not herself just now.*
> *Her condition is affecting,*
> *For she's just come over queer—*
> *Yes, America's expecting,*
> *And her time is drawing near. . . .*

> *We must not attempt to change her,*
> *Nor her indignation rouse,*
> *Till the Dewey little stranger*
> *Has arrived at the White House,*
> *Or till Roosevelt on election*
> *Celebrates victorious morn—*
> *She'll return our tried affection*
> *Once a President is born.*

But after the election *Time* reported: "It was Franklin Roosevelt in a walkover. His popular percentage was a

Wide World

world." Roosevelt explained the Allied plans to defeat Germany, to end Nazism "and all of its barbaric laws and institutions." And he reported his discussions at Yalta on Poland's future boundaries and government, on the role of France in the postwar world and on other issues of consequence. He advised the members of Congress that the Conference of the United Nations would meet for the first time in San Francisco on April 25. He said with great emphasis: "We shall have to take the responsibility for world collaboration, or we shall have to bear the responsibility for another world conflict."

shade lower than in 1940, his electoral college vote a smashing victory. Once the returns began pouring in there was no doubt." Roosevelt received 25,612,610 against Dewey's 22,017,617. His electoral vote was 432 against Dewey's 99. The pollsters were wrong, off the mark with their predictions.

The result meant that the people were not afraid to elect a President four times in a free election and by a secret ballot. It also meant that they wished to keep the commander in chief, who in the words of *The New York Times* "has a large first-hand knowledge of the problems that will arise in the making of the peace. Moreover, the great prestige and personal following among the plain peoples of the world which he has won with his war leadership might easily prove in itself to be one of the most important cohesive forces binding together a new world organization in its first experimental years." It meant too that the country was turning its back on isolationism and embracing the idea of international cooperation. And finally it meant that it was *not* "time for a change."

The inaugural was one of the simplest. Of the

1932

1936

THE BURDEN OF THE PRESIDENCY

$25,000 appropriated for the event, on Roosevelt's insistence only $2,000 was spent. Roosevelt wanted no celebration while American boys were dying on the battlefield. He took the oath on the portico of the White House (not at the Capitol) before a few thousand invited guests. His address was short, only 573 words. He said: "Today in this year of war 1945, we have learned lessons—at a fearful cost—and we shall profit by them. We have learned that we cannot live alone, at peace; that our own well-being is dependent upon the well-being of other nations far away. We have learned that we must live as men, and not as ostriches nor as dogs in the manger. We have learned to be citizens of the world, members of the human community. We have learned the simple truth, as Emerson said, that 'the

only way to have a friend is to be one.' "

A month later he flew to the Crimea to meet with Stalin and Churchill. The end of the war was in sight and the foundation of the peace had to be laid. On March 1 he appeared before Congress apologizing for reporting on the Yalta conference sitting down. "I know that you will realize it makes it a lot easier for me in not having to carry about ten pounds of steel around the bottom of my legs," he said, for the first time alluding publicly to his infirmity. He looked haggard and ill; his voice lacked the old fire; his precision of speech was gone.

On April 12, 1945, the heart of the nation stood still as the announcement came through the radio that the President had died of a stroke at Warm Springs. "I am

1940

1944

more sorry for the people of the world than I am for us," said Mrs. Roosevelt when she heard of her husband's death.

In the first confused minutes after receiving the news, John Daly spoke on CBS radio without script or notes. "He had gone again to Warm Springs," began Daly in his eulogy, "to try to get new strength to face the San Francisco Conference, to shape there with his own hands, as much as he could, the cause of peace to come, to lead there men of all nations and all faiths, to sit down together around the council table and to give the gift of a peace that would last beyond our time, perhaps beyond our children's time, and to the time of our grandchildren. . . . Probably no man in contemporary history had as deep an understanding and conviction

that the average little man, as we use the term, had definite rights to a decent life."

The people listening to the radio, the people in the streets, the people in their offices, the people everywhere cried. Not only America but the whole world was shocked. Many used the same sentence: "I wonder what will happen to the country now." An old lady in France said, "I shall go into mourning. I felt he was my friend." General De Gaulle talked of Roosevelt as a soldier fallen in the line of duty, leaving "an undying example and an essential message. This message will be heard."

Orson Welles, the actor, wrote a few deeply felt lines: "Desperately we need his courage and his skill and wisdom and his great heart. He moved ahead of us,

Edward Clark, in Life, *April 1945*

FAREWELL. As President Roosevelt's funeral procession leaves Warm Springs, Georgia, where he died on April 12, 1945, Chief Petty Officer Graham Jackson plays "Going Home" on his accordion with an expression mirroring the nation's grief.

showing a way into the future. If we lose that way or fall beside it, we have lost him indeed. Our tears would mock him who never wept except when he could do no more than weep. If we despair because he's gone— he who stood against despair—he had as well never have lived, he who lived so greatly."

Vice President Harry Truman received an urgent call to go to the White House. Mrs. Roosevelt was waiting for him. She placed her arm about his shoulders. "Harry, the President is dead." For a moment Truman was silent, then he asked, "Is there anything I can do for you?" And Mrs. Roosevelt replied calmly, "Is there anything *we* can do for *you?* For you are the one in trouble now."

All top officials flocked to the White House. Truman's daughter Margaret and his wife Bess came to extend their sympathies to Mrs. Roosevelt. At 7:08 P.M. Truman took the oath from Chief Justice Harlan Fiske Stone in the Cabinet Room.

The rest of that evening the new President listened to reports—reports from Europe where the war was drawing to a close, reports on the coming conference in San

Thomas McAvoy, in Life, *April 1945*

THE DESK HE LEFT BEHIND. Roosevelt liked to clutter his White House desk with all kinds of favorite mementos and bric-a-brac sent by friends and admirers. Every item had a cherished memory for him. Fala's toys are scattered on the floor.

Francisco to form a United Nations, reports on "a new explosive of almost unbelievable destructive power."

The next morning after he visited former colleagues at the Capitol to ask for their support he was met by reporters. He shook hands with them. "Boys, if you ever pray, pray for me now. I don't know whether you fellows ever had a load of hay fall on you, but when they told me yesterday what had happened, I felt as though the moon, the stars, and all the planets had fallen upon me."

One reporter said, "Good luck, Mr. President."

And Truman answered sadly, "I wish you didn't have to call me that."

His first decision was to continue with the plans for the San Francisco Conference, which was to meet on April 25. After conferring with the Cabinet he asked Steve Early to tell the press for him that "For the time being I prefer not to hold a press conference. It will be my effort to carry on as I believe the President would have done, and to that end I have asked the Cabinet to stay on with me." The question of continuity seemed uppermost in his mind.

AT EIGHT MINUTES PAST SEVEN O'CLOCK on the evening of April 12, Harry S. Truman took the oath from Chief Justice Harlan F. Stone in the White House. From left to right: Frances Perkins; Harry Stimson; Henry Wallace; Julius A. Krug, War Production Board Chairman; James Forrestal; Claude R. Wickard, Deputy Chairman of

THE PRESIDENT'S FUNERAL

INP, April 15, 1945
THE CORTEGE IN THE SHADOW OF THE CAPITOL

INP, April 15, 1945
ROOSEVELT IS LAID TO REST AT HYDE PARK.

INP, April 15, 1945
FDR'S DAUGHTER AND WIFE AT THE FUNERAL

U.S. Signal Corps
the War Manpower Commission; Secretary of Agriculture Francis L. McNamee (behind Wickard); Francis Biddle; Henry Morgenthau; Mrs. Truman; Harold Ickes; Margaret Truman; Sam Rayburn; Fred Vinson and Joseph Martin.

HARRY S. TRUMAN

Only a superman could have fitted Roosevelt's shoes, and Harry S. Truman was no superman. He was modest and overawed by his job, and the people of the country sympathized with him. Three months after he took office the Gallup Poll gave him an 87 percent rating—87 men out of a 100 backed him up.

Truman's career was the realization of the American Dream. Born on a farm near Lamar, Missouri, he started out as a farmer. During the First World War he served in France as captain with the 120th Field Artillery. After the war he became partner in a haberdashery store—Truman & Jacobson, Men's Outfitters—in Kansas City. When the store went into bankruptcy, Truman turned to politics. He held a number of local offices, among them that of county commissioner, known in Missouri as "county judge."

His real rise in public life began in 1934 when he asked Pendergast, the boss of the Democratic machine in Missouri, for the post of Collector of Internal Revenue. Truman was told—so the story goes—that the job had been promised to someone else, but that he could run for the Senate if he wished. Truman ran and was elected; six years later, when his term expired, he was re-elected for a second term. In the Senate, as chairman of the special committee to investigate first the national defense program, then war production, he won respect for his integrity.

Catapulted into the limelight, supported by conservatives and laborites, he replaced Wallace in the Vice Presidency.

At the time of the inauguration the end of the war was in sight. The Allied armies were in Germany; in the Pacific American forces were ready to invade Japan. On April 28 Mussolini was killed at Lake Como, on April 30 the Russians hoisted their flag over the Reichstag in Berlin, the next day Hitler's suicide was announced. A week later Germany surrendered.

On July 17 Truman crossed the ocean, meeting with Stalin and Churchill (who nine days later was overwhelmingly defeated by Labour in the general election) for a final war conference at Potsdam. On August 6 United States fliers dropped the first atom bomb over Hiroshima; three days later a second bomb was dropped on Nagasaki. Japan asked for terms of surrender. The war was over.

With peace restored, Americans were impatient to throw off wartime restrictions. Truman was accused of bungling the job. His changes in the Cabinet and his appointments to high government posts met with sharp criticism; Harold Ickes said that the new administration was a "government by crony." The President's handling of labor disputes was clumsy; strike followed strike. "To err is Truman," cracked the wits; in the polls the President's popularity declined from 87 percent to 50 percent.

The mid-term election of 1946 sounded a warning: "Had enough? Vote Republican." And the country voted Republican. They recaptured the House by a margin of 28; they captured the Senate by a margin of 2; and they took almost all the governorships outside the South. The Republicans were now ready to end the disastrous four C's: controls, confusion, corruption and Communism.

Truman threw off the mantle of Roosevelt; he was on his own. He battled with Congress. He named General

HARRY S. TRUMAN
Photograph by Mike Ackerman

CANDIDATES IN 1948

HARRY S. TRUMAN
(1884———) was determined to win a term of his own. Though the polls prophesied certain defeat, Truman went to the country, campaigned against the do-nothing 80th Congress and scored a victory.

ALBEN W. BARKLEY
(1877–1956), Senator from Kentucky since 1927 and in politics for almost 45 years, was chosen for the Vice Presidency after his "give 'em hell" keynote speech in the Democratic convention.

THOMAS E. DEWEY
(1902———) was again the Republican choice. Certain of victory, he behaved as if already President. Carefully avoiding specific issues, he indulged in lofty generalities, stressing the theme of unity.

EARL WARREN
(1891———), the popular Governor of California, became Dewey's running mate. He was a liberal, a good administrator, had an attractive family—all of which brought strength to the Republicans.

HENRY A. WALLACE
(1888–1965) left the Democratic ranks and campaigned as the candidate of the Progressives. He started out well, but when the left-wing elements took over his new party, his efforts collapsed.

GLEN H. TAYLOR
(1904———), the guitar-playing Senator from Idaho, was second on Wallace's ticket. His engaging personality was to charm audiences, but people looked on him more as a performer than a candidate.

INP

THE TRUMAN FAMILY. Margaret, the President's only daughter, a concert singer and television personality, was her father's pride. When a music reviewer in Washington wrote critically about her voice, Truman offered to punch his nose.

George Marshall as Secretary of State. He won over conservatives by his firm attitude toward Henry Wallace, who left the Cabinet in September 1946 because of his disagreement with the "get-tough" policy toward Russia. Truman's proposals to aid Greece and Turkey and the Marshall Plan, which proposed United States aid to restore the European economy, gained popular acclaim, and the President was commended for his order to check on the loyalty of government employees.

The conservative middle class approved Truman's policies, but he was criticized by the liberals because of his foreign policy, and assailed by the South because of his stand on civil rights.

By the beginning of 1948 all the old hats of the last election were back in the ring again. It was assumed that Truman would be the Democratic candidate. General Eisenhower, his only serious rival, had removed himself from the race. In a letter released early in 1948 he repeated his former refusal: "I am not available for and could not accept the nomination. . . . The necessary and wise subordination of the military to civil power will be best sustained when life-long professional soldiers abstain from seeking high political office."

Henry A. Wallace led the newly formed Progressive party, which advocated negotiations with Russia and settlement of the issues between the two powers by

Photograph by Charles Cos
A MEMORABLE PHOTOGRAPH. When Truman posed for photographers at a National Press Club party with movie queen Lauren Bacall, he was attacked by the press for his lack of dignity. It was a warning to him to be more careful in the future

ON THE WAY TO BERLIN. President Truman and his Secretary of State, James F. Byrnes, confer during their windy voyage to Germany in July 1945. They were to meet Stalin and Churchill in Potsdam to discuss the problems of peace.

diplomatic means and not through the "cold war."

The Republican favorites were New York's Governor Thomas E. Dewey, liberal in his attitudes, and Senator Robert A. Taft, a conservative, with Harold E. Stassen, running a close third. Others in the race were Senator Arthur Vandenburg (a good compromise if the leading candidates should deadlock each other), Ohio's Senator John Bricker, California's Governor Earl Warren, and General Douglas MacArthur.

The Republican contenders had a battle royal in the primaries. New Hampshire elected 6 delegates to vote for Dewey and 2 to support Stassen. In Wisconsin Harold Stassen defeated General MacArthur, capturing

19 of the state's delegates, leaving only 8 for the General; when MacArthur finished fifth in Nebraska, he was no longer a serious contender. Stassen won that state, but he lost Ohio to Taft, who captured 44 delegates of his home state, leaving Stassen only 9.

Then came the fight for Oregon. In any other election year the primary in that state would have caused little stir, but this time the result in Oregon was of vital importance. Dewey needed the victory to recoup his losses to Stassen in Wisconsin and Nebraska; Stassen needed it to make up for his poor showing in Ohio. They campaigned throughout the state, and they debated before the microphones at Portland: "Should the Commu-

THE THREE MOST POWERFUL MEN IN THE WORLD—Truman, Stalin and Churchill—pose before the opening of the Potsdam conference where, together with Generalissimo Chiang Kai-shek, they discussed terms for Japan's surrender.

U.S. Signal Corps, July 17, 1945

nist party be outlawed in the United States?" Stassen argued for it, Dewey against it.

Dewey won Oregon, carrying it with 111,657 votes to Stassen's 102,419. Arthur Krock wrote in *The New York Times:* "Governor Thomas E. Dewey's substantial victory in Oregon demonstrated that there is no continental demand among Republicans for Harold E. Stassen, just as earlier primaries established the same fact about Senator Robert A. Taft and Mr. Dewey himself."

The Democrats were resigned to the fact that Truman would run and be defeated. But the President was of another opinion. In June he left Washington on a "non-political" tour to put the issues before the people; within twenty-four hours he was openly appealing for his re-election.

It soon became evident that wherever the President spoke his earthy humor and friendly manner evoked a warm response. The people came in droves to listen to him. Truman spoke, as one reporter put it, "the language of Main Street, and Main Street understands it—even to the grammatical errors and slurred words which occasionally made purists on his special train writhe a bit." Here was a friendly man visiting among friendly people, who talked to them simply, in terms which everyone could understand.

THE CLOUD OF A NEW ERA. Three weeks after its successful testing, the first atomic bomb was dropped on Hiroshima, on August 6, 1945, and a second bomb on Nagasaki on August 9, killing 70,000 Japanese. The proclaimed aim of the bombing was to break the fighting spirit of Japan and bring an end to the war.

Truman's main theme was the Republican Congress —"the worst in my memory"—which was more interested "in the welfare of the better classes" than in ordinary men. "We need a Congress that believes in the welfare of the nation as a whole and not in the welfare of special interests," he said in Gary, Indiana, declaring that "when we get a new Congress, maybe we'll get one that will work in the interests of the common people and not in the interests of the men who have all the money."

"Lay it on, Harry!" his audience cried, and Truman responded: "I'm going to, I'm going to. I'm pouring it on and I'm gonna keep pouring it on."

In Spokane Truman said that the Republicans "are going down to Philadelphia in a few days and are going to tell you what a great Congress they have been. Well, if you believe that, you are bigger suckers than I think you are." And he told a labor audience: "I understand that you are not very happy over the labor act of 1948

JAPAN SURRENDERS. On August 14, 1945, Truman announces to the press than Japan has accepted his surrender

Harris & Ewing

terms. Standing behind the President, Secretary of State Byrnes and Attorney General Clark. Sitting on the sofa are Mrs. George S. Schoeneman, Mrs. Truman, Judge Samuel Rosenman, and War Mobilization Director John W. Snyder.

George Silk, in Life

THE PROGRESSIVES BOLT. Wallace endorsed the candidacy of Leo Isaacson, whose success in fighting a by-election in the Bronx raised the hopes of the Progressives.

Thomas D. McAvoy, in Life

THE SOUTH REBELS. In protest over party policies, Southerners stayed away from the annual Jefferson-Jackson Day dinner. The empty table is Senator Johnston's of S.C.

as it is now in effect. But you know the reason for that is that in November 1946 just one-third of the population voted. The people were not interested in what might happen to them. We have that law now, and I am the President and I have to enforce it. Your only remedy is November 1948. And if you continue that law in effect, that is your fault and not mine, because I didn't want it." As his trip wore on, his strategy became clear: it was "the plain people's President against the privileged people's Congress."

In Washington the Republicans grew apprehensive about Truman's impact on the voters. Taft exclaimed: "Our gallivanting President is blackguarding Congress at every whistle-stop in the West." He suggested immediate adjournment because "there is little use in keeping Congress in session while President Truman is delivering an attack on the principles of representative government itself." Taft's "whistle-stop" remark turned out to be a great blunder. Many people in the West

lived at whistle-stop places and they did not like the Senator's patronizing attitude.

On his trip the President scored heavily in his role of a crusader against Congress. On occasion he came out on the platform of his train in his pajamas. In Barstow, California, a woman called up to him that she thought he had a cold. Truman said he didn't. "But you sound like you have a cold," she persisted. "That's because I ride around in the wind with my mouth open," was the retort, and his audience loved it. Truman spiced his speeches with local anecdotes, made compliments about the local scenery, questioned his listeners whether they had been to church, and introduced his wife and daughter to the crowds. "Meet the boss," he would say, pointing to Mrs. Truman. And presenting his daughter he won a laugh when he related how she had worked four years for a diploma from George Washington University, but on the same night that she got hers he got one "for nothing."

Lorant: **The Presidency** (*Macmillan*)

DEWEY ON THE CAMPAIGN TRAIL. The Republican candidate fought a tireless primary campaign, displaying his new personality. Gone was the stiff and ponderous stance of 1944. The new Dewey appeared to be an outgoing and fun-loving man who ate raw beef with Oregon "cavemen" and let himself be kidnaped and hauled off to an initiation ceremony.

THE CLIMAX OF THE OREGON PRIMARY. During this primary Dewey and Stassen debated on Portland's KEX radio station: "Shall the Communist party be outlawed?" Dewey won the primary, the last before the convention. With that the Stassen bandwagon, which had rolled so briskly until then, came to a halt, and Stassen's hopes were shattered.

"His contact with the people," wrote the columnist, Thomas L. Stokes, "recreates again the amiable and friendly fellow who, as a haberdashery store proprietor and a local politician, enjoyed swapping yarns with his friends and exchanging wisecracks of the street-corner variety."

But a reporter of the Washington *Evening Star* was less friendly. "The President, in this critical hour, is making a spectacle of himself in a political junket that would reflect discreditably on a ward heeler," he wrote.

While Truman was trying to turn the tide in his favor in the West, Congress wrestled with an accumulation of unfinished business. The time of adjournment was near, and there was still no decision on civil rights, oleomargarine tax repeal, long-range housing, farm legislation, Federal aid to education, no decision to increase the hourly minimum wages from forty to seventy-five cents; nothing had been done about the Mundt-Nixon Bill, the return of tidelands mineral rights to the states, the broadening of Social Security and many other prob-

lems. In the final weeks of Congress only a few bills were passed: one extended the terms of the Atomic Energy Commissioners for two years; another allowed displaced persons to enter the United States; a third came out for reciprocal trade agreements, a fourth for a stopgap draft.

The inaction of Congress on so many vital issues caused the Republican *Herald Tribune* to write in despair: "For a Congress under Republican leadership to adjourn with such a record in a presidential year would be political suicide." The newspaper suggested Congress should not adjourn but recess and return after the conventions "to finish the job and finish it well. Any other course would mean abdication."

Yet two days before the opening of the Republican convention in Philadelphia, Congress adjourned. The convention's keynote address was given by Governor Dwight H. Green of Illinois and was carried by television into millions of homes. He ripped into the Democratic party, which was "held together by bosses, boodle,

A MISLEADING PHOTOGRAPH "proving" the President could not draw large audiences. The empty hall during Truman's Western tour in June was due to a planning slip-up. The photograph from Omaha lulled the Republicans into overconfidence. They insisted that if the President could draw only small audiences, he would have little chance of victory.

buncombe and blarney," and praised the record of the Eightieth Congress, which had restored faith in representative government, had freed American economy from regimentation, balanced the budget, reduced Federal income taxes, and corrected chaotic conditions in labor relations.

The attractive Clare Boothe Luce spiced her address with wisecracks. She said that President Truman was "a gone goose," whose "time is short and whose situation is hopeless," and whose three years in office were not "the pause that refreshes." She maintained that "Democratic Presidents are always troubadours of trouble, crooners of catastrophe; they cannot win elections except in the climate of crisis. So the party by its composition has a vested interest in depression at home and war abroad."

Each of the Republicans stressed the Democrats' association with Communists. Said Joseph W. Martin, Jr., the Speaker of the House, "The New Deal, over a period of fifteen years of experimenting with statism, had permitted hundreds of enemies of America to infiltrate into

official positions." To this columnist Thomas Stokes retorted: "The Republican cry about Communists in government is, of course, myth. . . . But that does not matter. It's a good issue. It covers up so many omissions by Congress."

The platform emerged after a heated controversy between the "internationalists," led by Senator Henry Cabot Lodge, Jr., chairman of the 104-member resolutions committee, and the "nationalists," under Senator C. Wayland Brooks of Illinois. The chief disagreement was over the foreign policy plank, which, in its accepted version, asked for the continuation of the European Recovery Program "within the prudent limits of our own economic welfare," but omitted any pledge to appropriate money for it. In its other planks the platform supported the United Nations as "the world's best hope," asked recognition of Israel "subject to the letter and spirit of the United Nations Charter," and advocated a foreign policy of "friendly firmness which welcomes cooperation but spurns appeasement."

The platform contained a determined stand on civil rights, promised prompt action to correct "the recent cruelly high cost of living," and urged the maintenance of a strong military establishment. It advocated benefits to veterans, recommended the extension of Social Security, and proposed "equal pay for equal work, regardless of sex." On Federal aid to education the platform was noncommittal: "We favor equality of educational opportunity for all and the promotion of education and educational facilities." On tidelands it declared that the party was in favor of "restoration to the states of their historic rights to the tide- and submerged lands, tributary waters, lakes, and streams." On Communism it pledged "vigorous enforcement of existing laws against Communists and enactment of such new legislation as may be necessary to expose the treasonable activities of Communists and defeat their objective of establishing here a Godless dictatorship controlled from abroad." On labor it promised "continuing study to improve labor-management legislation in the light of experience and changing conditions."

Most of the platform's pledges were in direct contradiction to Republican policies followed in the last Congress. The platform promised support to "the system of reciprocal trade," but in Congress Republicans had fought the reciprocal trade agreements. The platform promised "federal aid to the states for local slum clearance and low-rent housing programs," but in the House the Republicans had supplied a majority to defeat the Taft-Ellender Housing Bill. The platform solemnly upheld the "equality of all individuals in their right to life, liberty and the pursuit of happiness . . . never to be limited in any individual because of race, religion, color, or country of origin," but on Capitol Hill the Republicans had done nothing about abolishing the poll tax, making lynching a Federal crime and removing segregation in the armed forces and discrimination in jobs. In their platform the Republicans favored "progressive development of the nation's water resources," but in Congress they had come out for restriction of the President's public power program.

Seven names were presented for the Republican nomination: Dewey, Taft, Stassen, Warren, Vandenberg, Senator Raymond Baldwin of Connecticut and General MacArthur. "Cheering demonstrations greeted every name," reported the *Herald Tribune*, "but not all the enthusiasm for all the names could conceal the fact that the trading and dealing that has been going on in rooms that were smoke-filled or airy, has left scars that may be bared before the 15,000 spectators when the balloting begins."

Dewey was the acknowledged favorite and his bandwagon received several powerful pushes. After Senator Martin of Pennsylvania withdrew as a favorite son, add-

ing 41 Pennsylvania votes to Dewey's strength, Indiana's favorite son, Charles Halleck, dropped his candidacy and released his state's 29 votes to the New York Governor.

Taft, Stassen, Governor Duff of Pennsylvania and Governor Kim Sigler of Michigan (on behalf of Senator Vandenberg) met in conference to deliberate how to stop Dewey. Duff, raging over Martin's defection, fumed: "We are all agreed that this is the first time in American politics that European blitz tactics have been used to secure a nomination. Yes, and I mean Dewey by that. We have worked out a definite plan to guarantee the delegates the right of free expression."

However, the anti-Dewey men could not agree on any one candidate, for none of them was willing to make a place for the other. "It'll be Tom or me," said Taft, and Stassen would not accept the second place under Taft; thus the meeting ended without any result.

On the first trial Dewey had 434 votes, to 224 for Taft, 157 for Stassen, 62 for Vandenberg, 59 for Warren and 11 for MacArthur. (On this ballot Illinois voted for favorite son Dwight Green, New Jersey for favorite son Governor Driscoll, Connecticut for favorite son Raymond Baldwin.) On the second trial Dewey's vote increased to 515, 33 votes short of victory. On this ballot Taft had 274 votes, Stassen 149, Vandenberg 62 and Warren 57.

After the convention had recessed for a few hours, the opponents of Dewey bowed out and Dewey was made the Republican candidate. For the second place Governor Earl Warren of California was chosen.

Dewey won the nomination, "not because he had principles or even appeal, but because he had a machine," wrote the liberal columnist Max Lerner. "The machine was ruthless and well oiled, run by a group of slick and modern operators. It combined the age-old methods of power politics with the newest strategies of blitz warfare and the precision tools of American industry and administration."

After the Republicans left the City of Brotherly Love, the Democrats moved in. Truman's opponents made a last-minute effort to stop his nomination. The anti-Truman forces embraced three principal groups: the Americans for Democratic Action (ADA), the Southern dissidents and some big-city bosses. They had no common objective except their opposition to Truman's candidacy. The ADA, friendly to labor, supported the President's civil rights program; the conservative Southerners were firmly anti-labor, anti-New Deal, anti-civil rights; the city bosses were against Truman for opportunistic reasons—they wanted to win and not to lose.

But if Truman were not to be the candidate, who would be? The ADA suggested Supreme Court Justice William O. Douglas, but to the Southerners the progres-

BEFORE THE FIGHT ON THE FLOOR. The main contenders for the Republican nomination—Stassen, Dewey and Taft—pose with Speaker of the House Joseph Martin at a welcoming party in Philadelphia before the opening of the convention. Their broad smiles cover the resentment toward one another so obvious in their preconvention maneuvering.

TAFT DEMONSTRATION

DEWEY MEN FROM BUFFALO

THE REPUBLICAN CONVENTION

sive Douglas seemed "just another Wallace in black robes."

There seemed to be one man who could "block Truman" and be a winner—Dwight D. Eisenhower. In the public opinion polls the General was the front runner. The movement to draft him as a Democratic candidate caught momentum; the Georgia and Virginia delegations had pledged themselves in advance to vote for him. On July 3 nineteen party leaders—among them James Roosevelt of California, Colonel Jacob Arvey of Illinois, Governor Strom Thurmond of South Carolina, Senator Lister Hill of Alabama, and the Mayor of New York, William O'Dwyer—wired to the 1592 Democratic delegates and alternates inviting them to a caucus in Philadelphia the Saturday before the opening of the

convention, to "seek for the leader of our party the ablest and strongest man available." The telegram stated that "no man in these critical days can refuse the call to duty and leadership," a hint that Eisenhower was obligated to accept the nomination if it was offered to him.

A day later, on July 4, New Jersey's Frank Hague said on behalf of his State's delegation that "the public will not get world leadership in either Truman or the Republican candidate. General Eisenhower led us to victory through the greatest war in history, and we want him back to complete the job."

But the next day, July 5, the General issued a statement that he "could not accept the nomination for any public office or participate in partisan political contests."

Ralph Morse, in Life
DEWEY DEMONSTRATION

Leonard McCombe, in Life
STASSEN DEMONSTRATION

On that day *The New York Times* survey showed that Truman's nomination was a certainty, for 809 of the convention's delegates were pledged to vote for him— enough to give him victory on the first ballot.

Two days before the opening of the convention the Associated Press reported: "It's all over now but the shouting, and even the shouting will be largely mechanical, organized and half-hearted next week when the Democrats nominate Mr. Truman."

Most columnists composed eloquent obituaries on the Democratic party. Wrote Walter Lippmann: "The country may say to the Democrats as they relinquish the power they have held so long and the heavy responsibility they have borne through dangerous days: 'Hail and farewell. . . . We shall meet again.' " Wrote

Drew Pearson: "Every seasoned Democratic leader is convinced Harry Truman will suffer a historic defeat." Wrote *The New York Times* political correspondent: "Arriving delegates found an atmosphere of gloom and despondency and encountered a spirit of defeatism among the party leaders already here that amounted to confession that President Truman seemed to have little chance of election."

The question was, whom would the Democrats select for the second place. For the past three and a half years the country had been without a Vice President. Truman wanted Justice Douglas, and when Douglas declined, he turned to Senator Alben W. Barkley. "I am willing. . . . But it will have to come quick; I don't want it passed around so long it is like a cold biscuit," said

HERBERT HOOVER warns eloquently: "If you produce nothing but improvised platitudes, you will give no hope."

COLONEL ROBERT McCORMICK, Chicago *Tribune* publisher and head of the Illinois delegation, a Taft man.

DAVID LOW, THE WORLD-FAMOUS CARTOONIST from England, views the antics of the delegates on the floor.

HENRY R. LUCE, the publisher of the nation's most popular magazines, *Time* and *Life,* in the convention hall.

Leonard McCombe, Life

CLARE BOOTHE LUCE, the convention keynoter, leads the cheers for Connecticut's favorite son, Raymond Baldwin.

Leonard McCombe, Life

ALFRED LANDON, the 1936 Republican nominee and Kansas delegation chief, hears the latest convention rumor.

SENATOR LEVERETT SALTONSTALL of Massachusetts (right), listens to the lengthy speeches from the floor.

Ralph Morse, Life

ONE OF THE CHIEF CONTENDERS: Senator Taft, with Dewey, Stassen, and Vandenberg was a favorite candidate.

Leonard McCombe, Life

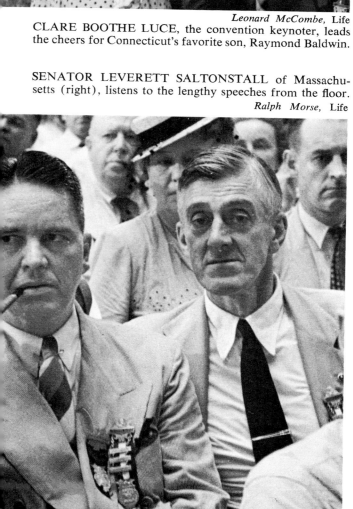

THE MICHIGAN DELEGATES HOLD A CAUCUS AFTER THE SECOND BALLOT INCREASED DEWEY'S LEAD.

Barkley. And it came quick. After Barkley had delivered an old-fashioned sledge-hammer keynote address, no one doubted that the convention would choose him for the Vice Presidency.

But first the platform had to be drawn up. There was a bitter struggle over the civil rights plank. The Southerners, outnumbered three to one on the resolutions committee, were soundly beaten. Their states' rights plank went overboard; none of their other proposals was accepted. The ADA group, led by Minneapolis Mayor Hubert Humphrey, asked for a definite declaration supporting legislation against the poll tax, lynching and segregation in the armed forces, and for fair employment practices. Senator Scott Lucas, on behalf of the administration, opposed an outright declaration because he feared that it might wreck the party, and proposed a plank similar to that of 1944. When the South refused to accept a compromise, the issue was brought

before the convention. In an unprecedented move, the delegates overruled the resolutions committee and by a vote of 651½ to 582½ wrote into the platform a declaration praising President Truman for his courageous civil rights stand and calling on Congress to carry it out, whereupon the Mississippi delegation and half of Alabama's—35 delegates in all—walked out of the hall.

The convention wanted to complete the nomination of President and Vice President by 10:00 P.M. on Wednesday, the third day, when President Truman was to appear before the delegates to deliver his acceptance speech. However, it was well after midnight when the first roll call was completed. Nine hundred forty-seven and a half votes were cast for him against 263 for Senator Richard Russell of Georgia, the hurriedly named candidate of the Southern dissidents. Alben Barkley received the vice presidential nomination by acclamation.

It was two o'clock in the morning when Truman, who

Hank G. Walker, in Life

CALIFORNIA CAUCUS: AFTER FAVORITE SON WARREN BOWED OUT THEY SWITCHED TO DEWEY.

had waited for hours outside the convention hall, made his entrance, opened a black notebook and spoke to the delegates. *Newsweek* reported: "Nothing short of a stroke of magic could infuse the remnants of the party with enthusiasm. But magic he had; in a speech bristling with marching words, Mr. Truman brought the convention to its highest peak of excitement."

"Senator Barkley and I will win this election, and make these Republicans like it, don't you forget that," cried Truman. "We'll do that because they're wrong and we're right." The ten thousand exhausted people in the hall jumped to their feet and cheered. The word *win* electrified them. The President told them that the Democratic party had "been elected four times in succession and I'm convinced it will be elected a fifth time next November. The reason is that the people know the Democratic party is the people's party, and the Republican party is the party of special interests and it always

has been and always will be." The delegates loved it.

He extolled the record of his administration. "Never in the world were the farmers . . . as prosperous . . . and if they don't do their duty by the Democratic party they're the most ungrateful people in the world. . . . And I'll say to labor just what I've said to the farmers. They are the most ungrateful people in the world if they pass the Democratic party by this year."

Truman was in his element. He pointed out that the total national income "has increased from less than forty billion dollars in 1933 to two hundred and three billions in 1947, the greatest in all the history of the world."

He launched into a slashing attack on the Eightieth Congress and the Republican platform. "The Republican party favors the privileged few and not the common, everyday man. Ever since its inception, that party has been under the control of special privilege, and they concretely proved it in the Eightieth Congress. . . .

THE WINNER AND HIS WIFE. Governor and Mrs. Dewey acknowledged the ovation of the cheering delegates.

THE VICE PRESIDENTIAL candidate, Governor Earl Warren of California, and his wife acknowledge the ovation.

THE REPUBLICANS' CHOICE was 46-year-old Dewey, the only candidate in the party's history to receive the nom-

They proved it by the things they failed to do."

Then Truman listed the sins of Congress. It had not extended price controls, therefore prices had "gone all the way off the chart in adjusting themselves at the expense of the consumer and for the benefit of the people who hold the goods." It had not passed the Taft-Ellender-Wagner Housing Bill, which was "to clear the slums in the big cities." Instead of "moderate legislation to promote labor-management relations," it had passed the Taft-Hartley Act, which "disrupted the labor-management relationship and which will cause strife and bitterness to come if it's not repealed." It had done

nothing about an increase in the minimum wage, nothing to improve the Social Security law, nothing about a much needed health plan, nothing about civil rights. But in Truman's estimate two of the greatest failures of the Republican Eightieth Congress were "of major concern to every American family: the failure to do anything about high prices, and the failure to do anything about housing."

Truman pointed out that while the Republican platform asked for the extension and increase of Social Security benefits, when the Republicans actually had the power, "they took 750,000 people off our Social Se-

Hank G. Walker, in Life

ination after having been defeated in a previous election. The "Stop Dewey" movement failed because the opposi-

tion was divided and because neither Taft, Stassen nor Vandenberg had the strength to resist the Dewey machine.

curity rolls. I wonder if they think they can fool the people with such poppycock as that."

The President spoke in anger; he spoke "too rapidly, too jerkily, too emotionally," commented Max Lerner. "But he was caught up in what he was saying. It was a harangue . . . and it was what the polite people call 'demagogic.' But it carried conviction because it was the truth, and had been waiting to be said for a long time. It had no taste: the candidate used un-Dewey-like words like 'lousy,' and called the Republicans the 'enemy.' " But somehow during the speech a rapport was built up between the speaker and an audience "which neither

loved nor admired him. They sensed that this was the most militant presidential acceptance speech in either major party since Bryan. They liked the fact that he came out of his corner fighting."

Truman saved his surprise for the end. "My duty as President requires that I use every means within my power to get the laws the people need on matters of such importance and urgency," he said. Therefore, "On the twenty-sixth day of July, which out in Missouri they call Turnip Day, I'm going to call that Congress back and I'm going to ask them to pass laws halting rising prices and to meet the housing crisis which they say

707

they're for in their platform. At the same time I shall ask them to act on other vitally needed measures such as aid to education, which they say they're for; a national health program, civil rights legislation, which they say they're for; an increase in the minimum wage, which I doubt very much they're for; funds for projects needed in our program to provide public power and cheap electricity . . . an adequate and decent law for displaced persons in place of the anti-Semitic, anti-Catholic law which this Eightieth Congress passed."

Thunderous applause greeted this announcement. "Now my friends," closed Truman, "if there is any reality behind that Republican platform, we ought to get some action out of the short session of the Eightieth Congress. They could do this job in fifteen days if they wanted to do it. . . . What that worst Eightieth Congress does in its special session will be the test. The American people will decide on the record."

Columnist Gerald W. Johnson commented: "Nobody can deny that the Haberdasher has more guts than a fiddle-string factory. Who was the first politician with the nerve to black John L. Lewis' eye? Who punched the nose of Whitney, the railroad trainman . . . ? Battling Harry, the demon necktie salesman." *The New York Times* wrote: "The Democratic party came out of its Philadelphia convention morally stronger, if perhaps numerically weaker, than it went in. It came out with fire in its eye, in place of the glazed look of a week ago."

But the momentary upsurge of confidence could not heal the breach within the party. The progressives left with Wallace, as did the Southern dissidents. The Southerners met in a separate convention at Birmingham, and named Governor J. Strom Thurmond of South Carolina as their presidential candidate and Governor Fielding Wright of Mississippi as his running mate.

Their platform opposed Truman and civil rights for Negroes, proclaimed that the States' Righters "oppose and condemn the action of the Democratic convention in sponsoring a civil rights program calling for the elimination of segregation, social equality by Federal fiat, regulation of private employment practices, voting, and local law enforcement," because "such a program would be utterly destructive of the social, economic and political life of the Southern people, and of other localities in which there may be differences in race, creed, or national origin in appreciable numbers."

Thurmond, the Dixiecrat candidate, exclaimed: "If the South should vote for Truman this year, then we might as well petition the government to give us colonial status. . . . We Southerners are going to cast our vote for candidates who are true believers of states' government."

The hope of the Southern dissidents was that if none of the major presidential candidates could receive a majority vote, the election would be thrown into the House of Representatives, where the South might swing the Presidency to the candidate who opposed legislation on civil rights.

The Progressives, too, had a separate convention; they met in Philadelphia and named Henry A. Wallace for the Presidency and Senator Glen Taylor of Idaho for the second place. Thirty thousand people listened at Shibe Park to Wallace's acceptance speech in which he declared that unlike Truman and Dewey, who boasted that they had accepted their nominations without commitments, he committed himself to place human rights above property rights, to transfer power over big business from private to public hands "wherever necessary," to negotiate peacefully with the Soviet Government and strengthen the United Nations, to develop "progressive capitalism" and protect "truly independent enterprise" from monopoly, to fight restrictive labor legislation, expand health and education facilities, and provide "economic security" for elder citizens.

The Progressive platform repudiated the Marshall Plan, called for the destruction of the atomic stockpile, favored Big Four control of the Ruhr, and asked for cessation of financial and military aid to Chiang Kai-shek.

Besides the already mentioned candidates, a host of others were in the race. The Socialists named Norman Thomas for the sixth time; the Socialist-Labor party selected Edward E. Teichert. Farrell Dobbs was the choice of the Socialist Workers, Gerald K. Smith of the Christian Nationalists, John C. Scott of the Greenbackers, Claude Watson of the Prohibitionists, and John Maxwell of the American Vegetarians.

When Congress reconvened for its special session on Monday, July 25, the mercury hovered near 90 degrees with 88 percent humidity, but the tempers on Capitol Hill registered even higher than that. Republicans branded Truman's recall of Congress "cheap politics and the handiwork of a desperate man."

The President addressed the joint session of Congress in person. He began by asking for Congressional action —"strong, positive action"—to check inflation and the rising cost of living, and he submitted an eight-point program which was "necessary to check rising prices and safeguard our economy against the danger of depression."

He asked for anti-inflationary measures, he asked for "housing at lower prices" and he asked for legislation granting Federal aid to education. He also asked for an increased national minimum wage and expansion of Social Security, for a "more equitable and realistic" pay bill for Federal employees, for civil rights legislation, a better "displaced persons" law, for a $65 million

Cartoon by Herblock, in the Washington Post, *July 18, 1948*
"LOOK, SUPPOSE WE PUT IT TO HIM THIS WAY." A group of disconsolate Democratic politicians deliberates outside the White House on how to persuade Truman to bow out of office and leave the way open for a stronger candidate.

loan for the construction of a permanent UN headquarters in New York City, for Senate ratification of the international wheat agreement, and for a restoration of $56 million for power and reclamation projects, including a TVA steam and generating plant.

But this was not all. He also asked for a comprehensive health insurance plan, a fair and sound labor-management-relations law to replace the Taft-Hartley Act, a long-range farm program, a reciprocal-trade-agreements act, a universal training program, a national science foundation, strengthened antitrust laws, and approval of the St. Lawrence Waterway treaty. Though Truman realized that the limited time of the special session did not "readily permit action" on all the listed measures, "the next Congress should take them up immediately."

Senator Taft said that the President's recommendations were an "omnibus left-wing program." But the Republican New York *Herald Tribune* warned: "Whatever the provocations, the Republican majority will not, we trust, allow itself to be driven into an atitude of intransigence. There are few of its members who can pretend that the record of the Eightieth Congress, hastily concluded as the convention drew near, is perfect or complete. There were measures upon which substantial agreement had already been reached, and for which the pressing need was—and still remains—indisputable. These should be passed as expeditiously as possible."

Yet the Republicans within the Eightieth Congress, confident of victory in November, had no intention of debating legislation in the special session. Republican Senators let their Southern colleagues filibuster the anti-poll-tax bill. Truman's anti-inflation program was given the ax in the banking committees. Thus, after a fruitless fortnight, the special session came to an end.

The stage was set for the campaign. Truman fired the

Francis Miller, *in* Life

THE DELEGATES PRAY AT THE OPENING.

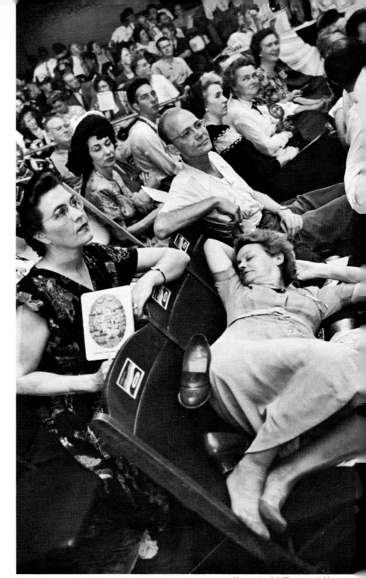

Francis Miller, *in* Life

WHY SHOULD SHE GIVE UP HER NAP?

THE DEMOCRATIC CONVENTION

SENATOR ALBEN BARKLEY, THE KEYNOTER
Lisa Larsen, *in* Life

MRS. TRUMAN WITH BARKLEY'S DAUGHTER
Acme

Francis Miller, in Life

A TRUMAN SUPPORTER VOICES HIS APPROVAL.

Francis Miller, in Life

A DELEGATE IS ONLY MILDLY FOR TRUMAN.

FARLEY GETS A NEW FACE FOR TELEVISION.

Francis Miller, in Life

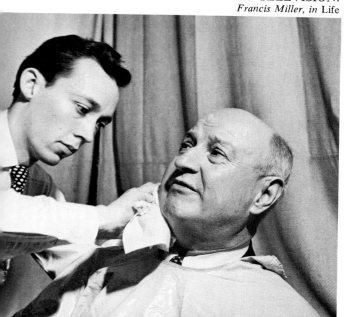

THE ALABAMA DELEGATION PROTESTS LOUDLY.

Francis Miller, in Life

THE DEMOCRATS
NOMINATE TRUMAN.

THE WINNER AFTER A NOMINATION OF HIS OWN.

THE DEMOCRATIC TICKET: Truman and Barkley

AFTER THE CONVENTION GAVE THE NOMINA-

opening gun on Labor Day, addressing large meetings in and around Detroit. Harold Stassen spoke for Dewey in the same city, while Henry Wallace, who had been pelted with eggs and tomatoes in the South, returned to New York to address an audience of fifty thousand.

That very week, on September 9, pollster Elmo Roper stated that Dewey was leading Truman by the unbeatable margin of 44 percent to 31 percent—"an almost morbid resemblance to the Roosevelt-Landon figures as of about this time in 1936"—and therefore he would not issue any more polls for, in his opinion, no amount of electioneering would change a decisive number of votes. "Political campaigns," said Mr. Roper, "are

largely ritualistic. . . . All the evidence we have accumulated since 1936 tends to indicate that the man in the lead at the beginning of the campaign is the man who is the winner at the end of it. . . . The winner, it appears, clinches his victory early in the race and before he has uttered a word of campaign oratory."

On September 17 the President left Washington for an extended campaign tour; Governor Dewey was to follow him two days later. Arthur Krock wrote in *The New York Times:* "If the public opinion pollsters are correct, and they were never more unanimous or certain of their findings, President Truman is launched on a speaking campaign to persuade a majority of the American voters

Thomas D. McAvoy, in Life

TION TO HARRY TRUMAN, HE ROUSED THE DELEGATES WITH A FIGHTING "GIVE 'EM HELL" SPEECH.

to change their minds toward him before November 2. . . . If expert political managers are right in their general belief that a majority opinion of this kind does not shift after early September . . . then Mr. Truman has no chance to achieve the great objective of his gruelling journey."

But despite the pollsters, despite a hostile press, despite the fact that the Democratic party was badly divided and political control in key states was in the hands of Republicans, Truman was convinced that he could turn the tide of public opinion. To Alben Barkley he said: "I'm going to fight hard, I'm going to give them hell." *Them,* of course, meant the Republicans.

He gave his first major address at Dexter, Iowa, where he told an enormous crowd that "there is every reason for the American farmer to expect a long period of good prices—if he continues to get a fair deal. His great danger is that he may be voted out of a fair deal and into a Republican deal."

He tore into "the Wall Street reactionaries," who "are not satisfied with being rich. They want to increase their power and their privileges, regardless of what happens to the other fellow. They are gluttons of privilege." Truman seemingly enjoyed his phrase as he repeated it three times within the next few minutes. He told the farmers that "these gluttons of privilege are now putting up

713

Leonard McComb, in Life

H. L. MENCKEN, the writer, suggests that Wallace's "guru" letters should be explained to the delegates.

Leonard McComb, in Life

NORMAN THOMAS, the perennial Socialist candidate, now a Progressive delegate, asks why Wallace refuses debate.

fabulous sums of money to elect a Republican administration . . . that will listen to the gluttons of privilege first and to the people not at all," and he reminded them that the farmers and workers had been in the past the victims of boom-and-bust cycles, "with the accent on bust."

Then he continued: "You have already had a sample of what a Republican administration would mean to you. Two years ago, in the Congressional elections, many Americans decided that they would not bother to vote. Others thought they would like to have a change, and they brought into power a Republican Congress— the notorious 'do-nothing' Republican Eightieth Congress." This Congress had "stuck a pitchfork in the farmer's back" and done its best to keep price supports

from working. It was the Republican big-business lobbyists, representing the speculative grain trade, who had persuaded Congress not to provide storage bins for the farmers. Concluding, the President told his audience that if the farmers voted for him, they would be voting for themselves.

Two days later—on September 20—Governor Dewey made his first major address at Des Moines. "Tonight," he said, "we will enter upon a campaign to unite America. On January 20 we will enter upon a new era. We propose to install in Washington an administration which has faith in the American people, a warm understanding of their needs, and the confidence to meet them." He ignored Truman's attacks and spoke philosophically and on a lofty plane, avoiding specific issues.

714

Author's Collection
AND THEIR CANDIDATE: HENRY A. WALLACE

Leonard McComb, in Life
DOROTHY THOMPSON, the fiery columnist, rises to challenge Wallace's claim about feudal Yugoslavian estates.

Truman continued his attacks at Salt Lake City, where he charged that the Republicans had helped special interests to "skim the cream from our natural resources," and that the power lobby in Washington, operating through the Congress, had "crudely and wickedly cheated" the people. "The Republican party has shown in the Congress of the last two years that the leopard does not change its spots. It is still the party of Harding-Coolidge boom and Hoover depression."

Again Dewey ignored the President's charges. He spoke at Denver sedately on the theme of conservation.

Though the President faced almost solid opposition in the press, though the polls were dead set against him, wherever he spoke, wherever his train stopped, he attracted large and cheering crowds. *Time* magazine wrote:

Acme
PRO- AND ANTI-WALLACE DEMONSTRATION outside the Negro Mount Olive Baptist Church in Knoxville.

"Newsmen were nonplussed. They had spent most of their time on the train speculating on the extent of Mr. Truman's defeat in November. All across Republican Iowa large crowds turned out to see him. The crowds were friendly, a good deal of the cheering was enthusiastic."

All through Nevada and California Truman repeated his attack on the Eightieth Congress. At Reno he called the Republican chairmen of the Senate and House committees "a bunch of mossbacks." In Los Angeles he suggested that the Progressives should vote for him and not for Wallace, as "a vote for the third party plays into the hands of the Republican forces of reaction whose aims are directly opposed to the aim of American liberalism." At Oakland he blamed the Eightieth Congress for the housing shortage. At El Paso he said that the Republicans would halt the Federal Government's cheap-public-power program and give the benefits and profits from Federally built dams to the private utilities "so they can get rich at your expense." At Deming he declared that Congress had tried to "sabotage the West," and if it had not been for the Democrats, "you would have had your throats cut by this Congress."

By comparison the Dewey speeches were pallid. At Phoenix, Arizona, Dewey orated: "Ours is a magnificent land. Every part of it. Don't let anybody frighten you or try to stampede you into believing that America is finished. America's future—like yours in Arizona—is still ahead of us." But if the people of America had left matters to the government, "there would have been very little progress indeed," and "if it had been up to Washington to develop, let us say, our electrical industry, you can be pretty sure we'd still be using kerosene lamps." In Hollywood he assailed Communism, and at San Francisco he accused the administration of contributing to inflation by "dropping monkey wrenches" into the economic machinery and following "defeatist policies."

While the two chief rivals fought for votes in the West, Henry Wallace toured the Middle West. At St. Louis he blamed both the Democrats and Republicans for failing to make an honest effort to pass Federal laws against racial discrimination and the "Jim Crow" system. In Chicago he said that Russia was "no threat" to the United States despite the fact that "our allies in war" were being "treated as enemies in peace."

The second week of the major campaign found Dewey in Oregon and Washington while the President barnstormed Texas. Again Truman took the offensive. In Dallas he said: "The Republican candidates are 'trying to sing the American voters to sleep with a lullaby about unity in domestic affairs,' but the Republicans 'want the kind of unity that benefits the National Association of Manufacturers, the private power lobbies, the real-estate lobbies, and selfish interests.' " At Fort Worth his theme was that Congress had passed a rich man's tax bill and had taken "freedom away from labor"; in Oklahoma that the Republicans "have not hurt the Communist party one bit—they have helped it"; at Louisville that the NAM had used the Republican party as a tool for killing price control in 1946 in "a conspiracy against the American consumer." The President said that before price control ended, "profits after taxes of all corporations were running at the rate of twelve billion dollars a year," but in the spring of 1948 "they were running at the rate of 20½ billions—an increase of 70 percent in corporation profits." And he posed the question: "Is the government of the United States going to run in the interest of the people as a whole, or in the interest of a small group of privileged big businessmen?"

Dewey repeated his basic contention in all his speeches—that only a Republican President and a Republican Congress could provide the country with the unity it needed to insure peace. On the domestic side he promised a cut in government expenses, thus bringing inflation under control; he spoke for a reduction of the Federal debt, and for a revision of the tax laws to encourage production and savings; he endorsed the farm price subsidies of the government and came out for the strengthening of the soil conservation program and for an acceleration of the reclamation, irrigation and hydroelectric projects. He promised to appoint a Westerner as Secretary of the Interior, and he emphasized his belief that people in the localities affected should have a voice in the planning and operation of the Columbia River and Missouri Valley projects.

Dewey's "soothing-syrup campaign" seemed to fit the mood of the country. "There is a feeling of uncertainty and insecurity abroad in our land," wrote Thomas Stokes. "The people want to be reassured. They want to believe in a fairy tale. They don't want to have to bother their heads about those problems that stare them in the face on the front pages of newspapers every day and about which President Truman talks—troubles in Berlin and Paris; continued high prices here at home and little bits of evidence all around of a boom before a bust; and that 'do-nothing Eightieth Congress' that the President raises up and shakes before them every day.

"Governor Dewey reassures them and flatters them where President Truman scares them and lectures them. Wherever the Republican candidate goes it is 'you good people' and 'your great country out here.' If you'll only have 'faith in yourselves' and 'faith in America' and be of 'stout purpose and a full heart' and 'move forward shoulder to shoulder,' then everything will be fine. For we know 'that every single individual is of priceless importance and that free men against whatever odds have an unbeatable quality,' and so forth and so on.

"Day after day, on every hand, he passes out these

THEY'RE OFF!

165 GROSS OF RARE OLD BOOMERANGS

WALT KELLY

Cartoon by Walt Kelly in the New York Star

CAMPAIGN START: THE THREE CANDIDATES—TRUMAN, DEWEY AND WALLACE—ARE OFF.

Ralph Morse, in Life

THE DEWEY TRAIN RADIATED CONFIDENCE AND EFFICIENCY. The air was full of promise, for the pollsters and experts predicted that the Republicans had the election in the bag. In their minds, Truman was already defeated. Certain of victory, Dewey acted "like a man who has already been elected and is merely marking time, waiting to take office."

pills that are bromides in the real sense of the word, that is, they calm jumpy nerves. The people reach eagerly for them and gulp them down.

"Labor troubles? International tensions and friction? Why, just put competent and honest men in the government and give us 'unity' and 'unity of purpose' and all those things will vanish. There'll be prosperity in the land and peace with all mankind.

"The way he hammers away at the need of competent and honest men in government, you'd think there hadn't been no such in Washington in sixteen years."

And so the first round ended. Truman returned to Washington the second day of October, with public opinion, as reported in the press and on radio, overwhelmingly against him. Fifty of the nation's political writers predicted that Dewey would win. A betting commissioner in St. Louis called Dewey a 15-to-1 favorite. Truman, full of confidence, told a back-platform audience in Lexington, Kentucky, that "I am trying to do in politics what *Citation* has done in the horse races. I propose at the finish-line on November 2 to come out ahead because I think the people understand what the

THE TRUMAN TRAIN WAS FULL OF BANTER AND JOKES. "Did I hear you right?" asks President Truman of a reporter posing a tricky question during the President's whistle-stop tour of Texas. His friendly horseplay and his "give 'em hell, Harry" approach appealed to crowds and newsmen alike as he swung around the country fighting for reelection.

issues are in this campaign." Nobody believed him.

After a few days' respite, Truman was on the road again, keeping on the campaign trail almost without interruption until election day. In Philadelphia he attacked Dewey's "unity" theme. "We don't believe in the unity of slaves, or the unity of sheep being led to the slaughter," he said. "We don't believe in unity under the rule of big business—and we shall fight it to the end."

At Auburn, New York, Representative John Taber's home town, he advised the voters not to re-elect their Representative because Taber had used "a butcher knife, saber, and meat-ax on every forward-looking appropriation in the public's interest that has come before Congress." In Buffalo he said: "The leopard has not changed his spots; he has merely hired some public relations experts. And they have taught him to wear sheep's clothing and to purr sweet nothings about unity in a soothing voice. But it's the same old leopard."

Then Truman returned to Washington to straighten out the confusion which had arisen over his attempt to send Chief Justice Vinson to Moscow to consult with Marshal Stalin on the Berlin crisis. Secretary of State

THOMAS DEWEY conducted a lofty campaign, stressing the theme of unity and confining himself to generalities. He avoided any commitment to spell out specific programs.

HARRY TRUMAN conducted an old-fashioned, slam-bang campaign, vigorously assailing the "do-nothing Republican Congress" and branding the GOP as the party of reaction.

Marshall asked the President not to pursue his plan—not to start bilateral negotiations with the Soviet—but to leave dealings over the Berlin blockade to the Security Council of the United Nations. Truman abandoned the "Vinson Mission," and Dewey capitalized on the President's "tragic blunder."

When Truman resumed his Middle Western tour he repeated his domestic program: "I believe that we should increase the minimum wage from forty cents an hour to at least seventy-five cents an hour. I believe Social Security insurance should be extended to the large groups of people not now protected. I believe that the insurance benefits should be increased by approximately 50 percent. I believe that we should expand our facilities for looking after the nation's health. I believe that the Federal Government should provide aid to the states in meeting the educational needs of our children. I believe the Congress should provide aid for slum clearance and low-rent housing. I believe we should do something, at once, about high prices."

In Pittsburgh Dewey submitted a twelve-point work-

ingman's program. He proposed "firm supports under wages" and a rise of the minimum wage; extension and overhauling of the Social Security system; a more influential labor department; a more effective Federal Conciliation and Mediation Service; encouragement of "unions to grow in responsibility and strengthen the collective bargaining"; enforcing and strengthening of the antitrust laws against business monopolies; provisions of houses "at reasonable cost for our people"; action against soaring prices; removal of the fear of "a boom-and-bust business cycle"; a solution of the problem of "race relations and of discrimination"; the strengthening of civil liberties, and "a world at peace."

Truman called Dewey's speeches "mealy-mouthed" and accused the Republican candidate of having disrupted unity, which he now preached, on questions of foreign relations in his previous campaign during the war. The President denied that the main campaign issues were unity and efficiency. "Maybe the Wall Street Republicans are efficient. We remember that there never was such a gang of efficiency engineers in Washington

THE STATES' RIGHTS SUPPORTERS at their Houston convention showed their contempt not only for the Republicans and Democrats but also for the Progressives.

GOVERNOR J. STROM THURMOND, the standard-bearer of the "Dixiecrats," asked the Southern delegates to vote for one of their own at the Democratic convention.

as there was under Herbert Hoover. We remember Mr. Hoover was himself a great efficiency expert."

He offered a point-by-point rebuttal of Dewey's Pittsburgh speech in the same city. He compared Dewey to a doctor with a magic cure-all. " 'You shouldn't think about issues,' says the doctor. 'What you need is my brand of soothing syrup—I call it *unity.*' " Truman said that Dewey had "opened his mouth and closed his eyes, and swallowed the terrible record of the Republican Eightieth Congress." And he declared that the whole Republican campaign could be summed up with two phrases: "Me, too," and "We're against it."

The Midwestern trip of the President seemed to be a success. Democratic politicians reported a marked improvement in the chances of their own state tickets, and a remarkable upsurge of interest in Truman. Still the consensus of the polls and the press was that Truman would lose in November.

As the campaign reached the final weeks, Truman and Dewey clashed for the first time on major issues—on the bipartisan foreign policy, on labor-management

relations and on social legislation. The foreign policy issue came to the fore through the Vinson incident, which in Dewey's opinion made the United States "appear before the world as a fumbling giant." On labor-management relations Truman said that the Taft-Hartley Law was "an instrument for union-busting by antilabor employers," while Dewey held that "over the plaintive complaints of a helpless administration, the welfare of both labor and the whole of our people has been advanced. As a result, an overwhelming majority of our people approve . . . the law." (Growled John L. Lewis, the miners' chieftain: "That man hasn't even read the act.") On social legislation Dewey held that "the present minimum wage is far too low and it will be raised." Truman retorted that the Republicans "favor a minimum wage—the smaller the minimum, the better."

If one listened to the radio commentators, if one read the pollsters' predictions, if one pondered the columns, one came to the conclusion that Dewey had already won the election. "Thomas E. Dewey's election as President is a foregone conclusion," wrote Leo Egan in the *New*

Walt Kelly, in the New York Star, *October 22, 1948*
SATIRIZING the attitude of all three candidates toward the New Deal, Walt Kelly drew them with identical hats.

Walt Kelly, in the New York Star, *October 27, 1948*
EX-PRESIDENT HERBERT HOOVER guides the mechanical Dewey safely ashore through the political sea.

York Times, while Robert J. Donovan reported in the New York *Herald Tribune* that "Mr. Dewey is confident that the voters long ago made up their minds in favor of a change and that he has the election in the bag." Max Lerner wrote in the New York *Star:* "It is three months to January 20, when Tom Dewey will in all probability move into the White House." And *Time* magazine said that "there was not much left to the presidential campaign except counting the votes. Harry Truman might get a good share of the popular vote, but few people outside of Harry Truman gave him an outside chance." One could read in editorials remarks like this: "The election must be held if for no other reason than to find out which national pollster comes the closest." The press had succumbed to mass hysteria; it took the predictions of the pollsters as the gospel truth. That Truman's audiences in the Middle West had consistently exceeded Dewey's, and that "at every village, town and city the crowds waited in startling numbers," were facts which received little attention.

By this time Wallace's strength had been spent; the Progressive movement was on the verge of collapse. The propaganda in the press and on the air, abusing him as a tool of the Communists, bore fruit: he lost ground. His indecision about supporting liberal Democratic candidates for Congress alienated many of his supporters.

In winding up their campaigns, Truman and Dewey mapped out almost identical itineraries, with Truman speaking one day ahead of Dewey in various cities. In Chicago the President said that "the real danger comes mainly from powerful reactionary forces which are silently undermining our democratic institutions." These forces, working through the Republican party, want to "see inflation continue unchecked," to "concentrate great economic powers in their own hands," and to stir up "racial and religious prejudice against some of our fellow Americans."

Dewey was forced to step down from the lofty level. The President's campaign began to hurt him. He charged that Truman was descending to a new low of "mudslinging" in spreading "fantastic fears" among the people "to promote antagonism and prejudice." He was fighting at last. "We all know the sad record of the present administration. More than three years have passed

Walt Kelly, in the New York Star, November 1, 1948
THE INFLATION GAS of the National Association of Manufacturers is pumped briskly into the Dewey machine.

Walt Kelly, in the New York Star, September 23, 1948
DEWEY'S HIGHLY PUBLICIZED EFFICIENCY is symbolized by showing him as an animated adding machine.

since the end of the war, and it has failed to win the peace. Millions upon millions of people have been delivered into Soviet slavery, while our own administration has tried appeasement on one day and bluster the next. Our country desperately needs new and better leadership in the cause of peace and freedom."

At Cleveland Truman asserted that "we have the Republicans on the run. Of course, the Republicans don't admit that. They've got a poll that says they're going to win." These polls, the President said, were "like sleeping pills to lull the voters into sleeping on election day. You might call them sleeping polls."

Truman expanded on this theme. "These Republican polls are no accident. They are all part of a design to prevent a big vote on November 2 by convincing you that it makes no difference whether you vote or not. They want to do this because they know in their hearts that a big vote spells their defeat. They know that a big vote means a Democratic victory, because the Democratic party stands for the greatest good for the greatest number of the people."

Dewey's answer came the following day in the same

city: "In the opening speech of this campaign at Des Moines, Iowa, I said this will be 'a campaign to unite America.'" He added that the President's campaign was an attempt to split the nation.

The third round of the bout was in Boston, where Truman denounced as a "malicious falsehood" Republican charges that his administration had opened the door to Communists, and ridiculed Dewey's unity theme. "In the old days Al Smith would have said, 'That's baloney.' Today the Happy Warrior would say, 'That's a lot of hooey.' And if that rhymes with anything, it is not my fault."

Yet Dewey kept on repeating that he could "unite our people behind a foreign policy that will strengthen the cause of freedom and bring peace to this world."

The final sparring was in New York's Madison Square Garden, where Truman said that Dewey could follow him in the different cities, but he couldn't follow him in raising the minimum wage to at least seventy-five cents an hour, or in demanding laws for health insurance and medical care, or calling for a repeal of the Taft-Hartley Act, or for a law to control high prices. And he declared

A HAND KISS BY TALLULAH. At the Liberal party rally in New York City, Tallulah Bankhead welcomes the President. The actress, daughter of a former Speaker of the House, campaigned for Truman, convinced that he would be elected.

that whenever Dewey looked at the Democratic program he said, "Me, too," but his party's record said, "Nothing doing." "And his party's record speaks louder than he does."

After Truman's speech, Bartley Crum, publisher of the New York *Star,* came down from the President's suite in the Hotel Biltmore and told the journalists: "The old boy still thinks he's going to win. He's standing there under the shower telling everybody that he'll sweep the country." Everyone laughed—everyone thought it a big joke.

The next day Dewey wound up his campaign, pledging once more an administration devoted to promoting unity among the American people and furthering the cause of world peace. "We agreed that in this grave time we would conduct a campaign worthy of America. I am very happy that we can look back over the weeks of our campaigning and say: 'This has been good for our country!' I am proud that we can look ahead to our

victory and say: 'America won!'" He ridiculed and scorned the type of campaign which Truman had conducted. "But," said Dewey, "our people have not been fooled or frightened. Halloween will be over tomorrow night, but next Tuesday the people of America are really going to bring this nightmare to an end."

By then Truman was on his way home. At St. Louis he said in his final speech that he had "cracked the Republican East" and that "North, South and West are falling in line."

"Now I have an old-fashioned notion that a candidate for public office has a duty to tell the voters where he stands on the issues in a campaign. I have traveled 22,000 miles, made about 270 speeches and taken a positive position on every issue. But the Republican candidate refuses to tell the American people where he stands on any issue. The campaign is ending and you still don't know. All you have got is platitudes and double talk."

Edward Clark, in Life

WELL-WISHERS CONGRATULATE DEWEY AS HE LEAVES AFTER SPEAKING AT ROCK ISLAND, ILLINOIS.

A NEWSPAPERMAN ON THE DEWEY CAMPAIGN TRAIN STRUGGLES WITH THE TURN OF A PHRASE. The frustrated George F. Jenks hits a snag halfway through the copy he must send back home to the Toledo (Ohio) *Blade*.

The President concluded: "The smart boys say we couldn't win. They tried to bluff us with a propaganda blitz, but we called their bluff, we told the people the truth. And the people are with us. The tide is rolling. All over the country I have seen it in the people's faces. The people are going to win this election."

With this the campaign ended. The New York *Herald Tribune* summed it up: "Mr. Dewey's campaign has lacked fireworks because the advocacy of unity and the sober, efficient management of public concerns are not causes which lend themselves to oratorical pyrotechnics. The public reaction to the campaign has been calm, on the whole, because Mr. Dewey represents the viewpoint of the majority. Mr. Truman has won some vociferous support among labor unions by his opposition to the Taft-Hartley Act, but it is minority support."

The pollsters were cocksure of a Dewey victory. On the day before the election the Gallup Poll gave Dewey 49.5 percent of the votes, Truman 44.5 percent, Wallace 4 percent, Thurmond 2 percent. Elmo Roper gave Dewey 52.2 percent, Truman 37.1 percent, Thurmond 5.2 percent, Wallace 4.3 percent, and Thomas 0.6 percent, and declared: "I stand by my prediction. Mr. Dewey is in." Mr. Roper went further. "This is the fourth national election which the polls have shown to be largely settled before the campaigns started," he asserted. "Apparently three years of performance are a more determining factor with voters than three months of campaign oratory."

A day before the election Bert Andrews wrote: "All the signs indicate that Thomas E. Dewey will be elected President on Tuesday over Harry S. Truman. The one big uncertainty is whether the Republicans will retain control of the Senate, which they now dominate by 51 to 45." *Life* magazine had Dewey's picture with the caption: "The next President of the United States." The *Kiplinger News Letter* stated: "Dewey will be in for eight years—until '57." *The New York Times* predicted, after carefully looking into the reports from forty-eight states, that the Dewey-Warren ticket would win with

A QUESTION IS POSED to President Truman after one of his earthy and good-natured back-platform speeches.

MRS. AND MISS TRUMAN were introduced by the President. "Meet the boss," he said, pointing to his wife.

345 electoral votes from twenty-nine states, against the Truman-Barkley ticket with eleven states and only 105 electoral votes. The Thurmond-Wright ticket would carry four Southern states—Alabama, Louisiana, Mississippi and South Carolina—with a total of 38 electoral votes, while four states with 48 electoral votes were doubtful.

In the New York *Sun* George Van Slyke said that "The Republican sweep through the North will give the popular vote of at least thirty-two states to the Dewey-Warren ticket," while Hearst's New York *Journal-American* gave Dewey 337 electoral votes from twenty-seven states. In *Newsweek* Raymond Moley, Franklin D. Roosevelt's former brain truster, opined that "as we view this campaign from a detached position, we all know that the trend is conservative." His colleague on the same magazine, Ernest K. Lindley, declared that "as a national organization the Democratic party is shattered." And the doyen of the pundits, Walter Lippmann, warned that "the course of events cannot be

halted for three months until Mr. Dewey has been inaugurated. There will be need for common sense, good will, cooperation." An editorial in the New York *Herald Tribune* summed up the campaign on the eve of the election: "There can rarely have been a political campaign as strange as the one for the Presidency that ends today. As the polls have made manifest, the contest was over before it got under way. While the conventions were still fulminating, the country had made up its mind that it wanted a change in the White House. The campaign was a ratification meeting, never a debate."

Thus the surprise was great when the first returns were flashed on the screen on election night. They showed no evidence of a Dewey landside. "Wait for the rural regions," repeated the announcers. Tensely the people waited. As the night wore on, Truman's lead became more obvious. In the radio and television studios the pollsters and commentators sweated uncomfortably as they tried to explain why Truman was doing so well.

ABANDONED REPUBLICAN HEADQUARTERS. Early on November 3, Republican headquarters at New York's Hotel Roosevelt were deserted, as the nation awoke to find the election still in doubt and the pollsters trying to save face.

THE DEFEATED CANDIDATE and his family listen to the disappointing returns in the early hours of the morning.

After the first reports Dewey's campaign manager, Herbert Brownell, told newspapermen: "This is definitely a Republican year. The people have made up their minds and have registered their decision in many of the states." The New York *Daily Mirror,* going to press early in the evening, stated: "First returns of the 50,-000,000 all-time voting record throughout the nation yesterday indicated that Governor Thomas E. Dewey and the Republican ticket were headed for a popular vote margin and a possible electoral vote landslide." The Chicago *Tribune* headline was: "Dewey Defeats Truman," reporting a sweeping victory of the Dewey-Warren ticket by "an overwhelming majority of electoral votes."

At this time Truman, who earlier in the evening had left his hotel in Independence, was fast asleep at Excel-

JUBILANT DEMOCRATIC HEADQUARTERS. When late returns indicated a Truman victory, the Democratic campaign workers began to celebrate by forming a "steam roller" at their headquarters in New York's Biltmore Hotel.

Cornell Capa, in Life

sior Springs, a little spa outside the city.

Midnight passed, and still the President was leading. About two o'clock in the morning Fulton Lewis, Jr. told his radio listeners that it looked as if the election would be decided by the House of Representatives and that there anything might happen. The radio newscaster said that the House might even choose Communist sympathizer Marcantonio for President—that is how well versed the commentator was on the Constitution.

At five o'clock in the morning at his New York hotel, Dewey told reporters that he was "still confident." But as the day dawned, the impossible had happened. Truman had won.

The newspapers of November 3, with columns written the day before, made curious reading. "The first post-election question is how the government can get through

THE VICTORIOUS CANDIDATE. President Truman leaves the Muehlebach Hotel in Kansas City for home.

Al Muto, INP

Acme

"THAT'S ONE FOR THE BOOKS," exclaimed the President, pointing to the Chicago *Tribune's* early edition of November 3, which reported a Dewey victory.

DEWEY IS THE NEW PRESIDENT— headlined the *Merkur,* a Munich newspaper.

the next ten weeks. Nowadays, unhappily, time's winged chariot has been equipped with jet propulsion. Events will not wait patiently until Thomas E. Dewey officially replaces Harry S. Truman," wrote the Alsop brothers in the New York *Herald Tribune,* and Drew Pearson wrote that he had "surveyed the close-knit group around Tom Dewey, who will take over the White House eighty-six days from now." Nobody gave Truman a chance.

When the final results were announced proclaiming a Truman victory the wrath of the press turned against the pollsters, blaming them for misleading the country. The poll-takers offered meek alibis. Said Dr. Gallup: "Truman captured many votes from Wallace. Also, a lot of the undecided voters in the poll voted for Truman." Poll-taking, he said, was still "an infant science."

A science? Wilfred J. Funk, the editor of the old *Literary Digest* which made the disastrously inaccurate poll in 1936, was glowing. "I wonder if the word 'science' will continue to be used in connection with this type of public opinion poll."

Elmo Roper confessed: "On September 9 I predicted that Mr. Dewey would win by a wide margin and that it was all over but the shouting. Since then I have had

A. E. Scott, INP

THE WINNERS RETURN TO WASHINGTON. Truman and Barkley were acclaimed on their triumphal return to the capital. In their ride they were accompanied by Mrs. Truman; Margaret; and Mrs. Truitt, the Vice President's daughter.

plenty of chance to hedge on that prediction. I did not do so. I could not have been more wrong. The thing that bothers me most at this moment is that I don't know why I was wrong."

Another pollster, Archibald Crossley, was even more bewildered. "The Crossley Poll showed that the Truman and the Dewey vote would be even if all adult citizens voted. . . . The result clearly showed what happens when one party gets out its vote and the other does not."

Explanations were forthcoming from the columnists. Wrote Marquis Childs: "We were wrong, all of us, completely and entirely, the commentators, the political editors, the politicians—except for Harry S. Truman. And no one believed him. The fatal flaw was reliance on the public opinion polls. No amount of rationalization ever can explain away this mistake by

Harris & Ewing

THE CAMPAIGN IS OVER and the President, accompanied by a Secret Service man, is on the way to work.

Gallup, Roper & Company." Yet the question was: Why?

Arthur Krock's *mea culpa* in the *New York Times* went deeper: "We didn't concern ourselves, as we used to, with the facts. We accepted the polls, unconsciously. I used to go to Chicago and around the country, every election, to see for myself. This time, I was so sure, I made no personal investigation. . . . We have to go back to work on the old and classic lines—to the days when reporters dug in, without any preconception. . . ."

James Reston of the *New York Times* wrote a soul-searching letter to his editor: "Before we in the newspaper business spend all our time and energy analyzing Governor Dewey's failure in the election, maybe we ought to try to analyze our own failure. For that failure is almost as spectacular as the President's victory, and the quicker we admit it the better off we'll be. . . .

"In a way our failure was not unlike Mr. Dewey's: we overestimated the tangibles; we relied too much on techniques of reporting which are no longer foolproof; just as he was too isolated with other politicians, so we were too isolated with other reporters; and we, too, were far too impressed by the tidy statistics of the polls. . . . In short, neither on the train nor in the capitals do we spend much time wandering around talking to the people. We tend to assume that somebody is doing the original reporting in that area, and if the assumptions of the political managers, or the other reporters, or the polls are wrong (as they were in this campaign), then our reports are wrong.

"The great intangible of this election was the political influence of the Roosevelt era on the thinking of the nation. It was less dramatic than the antics of Messrs. Wallace and Thurmond, but in the long run it was more important and we didn't give enough weight to it. Consequently we were wrong, not only on the election, but, what's worse, on the whole political direction of our time."

Time magazine sounded a similar note: "The press was morally guilty of several counts. It was guilty of pride: it had assumed that it knew all the important facts—without sufficiently checking them. It was guilty of laziness and wishful thinking: it had failed to do its own doorbell-ringing and bush-beating, it had delegated its journalist's job to the pollsters."

What were the reasons for Mr. Truman's unexpected victory? Arthur Krock acknowledged that the President was "a master politician and analyst of the people of the United States." Walter Lippmann thought that it could be said "with much justice and without detracting from Mr. Truman's remarkable personal performance, that of all Roosevelt's electoral triumphs, this one in 1948 is the most impressive." I. F. Stone believed that Truman had "waged the kind of campaign Mr. Roosevelt would have waged: for social reforms

and peace." Everybody had an explanation.

Most analysts agreed that Truman won because he got the farmer and labor vote. The strength of the President in the Midwest farm territory was the real surprise. He carried Ohio, Illinois, Wisconsin and Iowa—states which were expected to be in the Republican column. The Republican farmers voted for him because they feared that Dewey would abandon the price-support program.

Labor, which according to the *New Republic* had "finally learned to organize politically as well as economically," and "millions of independent voters who remembered the lessons they learned under Hoover," were firmly behind the President.

Other explanations of Truman's victory were "the bandwagon pressure of the public opinion polls, which encouraged many waverers to vote for the underdog, Truman, just to slow up the expected Dewey landslide, and caused many overconfident Republicans to stay away from the polls entirely"; the President's fighting campaign, which gained him votes and made the voters "revolt against the lofty Dewey platitudes"; the "strength of local Democratic tickets, which gave Harry Truman a boost in almost every key state"; the "pocketbook nerve," which made not only the farmers and workers but the housewives vote for Truman; and the voters' distrust of the Republican party, as mirrored in the Eightieth Congress, a distrust which Tom Dewey's promises of efficient government had never been able to erase."

Dewey, in his first announcement, blamed overconfidence as "one of the outstanding factors." In his opinion "two or three million Republicans stayed at home." (Yet in past elections it was always believed that a large vote favored the Democrats, while a small vote benefited the Republicans.)

In Senator Saltonstall's opinion the principal reason for Dewey's defeat "came from overconfidence, from too great reliance on nationally known polls of public opinion. This led the Republicans to put on a campaign of generalities rather than interesting the people in what a Republican administration could and would do for them if elected."

But the astute analyst Russell Davenport, who helped Willkie eight years before, thought differently: "The theme of the last sixteen years (which must now become twenty years) has been—the Republican party versus the people. And the people have won." Davenport wrote that the Republican party, which had failed to win a presidential election since 1928, "will continue to fail until its members and especially its leaders turn toward the future and away from the past. It will fail until it takes full account of the changes in social and economic thinking which have evolved in the American minds during the last twenty years. It will fail until it realizes

Kick Me!

Cartoon by Talburt, November 6, 1948

BURT TALBURT'S APOLOGY FOR WRONG-GUESSERS APPEARED IN ALL SCRIPPS-HOWARD PAPERS.

that the managerial revolution isn't broad enough to solve the complex problems which confront this nation, until it is convinced that both isolationism and *laissez-faire* are anachronisms."

The unsuccessful Progressive candidates held that Truman had been elected because, as Glen Taylor put

it, "He practically adopted the Progressive platform and began promising to carry it out." Henry Wallace, in a letter to the New York *Herald Tribune,* wrote: "It was the Progressive party alone that made peace an issue in the 1948 campaign. It was our insistence on a return to the Roosevelt one-world policy that forced the bi-partisans to slow down their cold-war program and at least make the gesture of negotiating with Russia. . . . It was the Progressive party which compelled a change in the whole character of the election campaign. It was our party which forced the Democrats to don the mantle of Roosevelt and to promise the American people a return to the New Deal. It was our party which destroyed the plans of reaction, and of the press through which reaction speaks, to deprive the voters of any choice between two programs."

The final figures of the election showed that Truman had polled 24,179,345 votes, carrying twenty-eight states; Dewey had 21,991,291 votes, carrying sixteen states; Thurmond received 1,176,125, Wallace 1,157,-326, and Norman Thomas 139,572 votes. In the Congressional election the Democrats scored a decisive victory. The country elected 263 Democratic Representatives to the House as against 171 Republicans; to the Senate 54 Democrats as against 42 Republicans.

Truman won five states which in 1944 were carried by the Republicans: Colorado, Iowa, Ohio, Wisconsin and Wyoming. He lost nine states to Dewey: Connecticut, Delaware, Maryland, Michigan, New Hampshire, New Jersey, New York, Oregon and Pennsylvania. And because of the civil rights controversy he also lost four states in the South to Governor Thurmond: South Carolina, Mississippi, Alabama and Louisiana. But as he carried all thirteen of the country's largest cities, and the six large agricultural states (California, Iowa, Illinois, Texas, Minnesota and Wisconsin), in addition to the traditionally Republican corn-belt states (Ohio, Wisconsin and Iowa), he came out on the top.

In his annual State of the Union message in January, Truman outlined his Fair Deal program. He asked for legislation in the fields of social welfare, Social Security, education, medical care, economic controls and civil rights. He asked for a balanced budget, partly through a tax increase of four billion a year, and requested broad authority to control inflation. Outstanding among eight anti-inflation points was one to let the government build plants in such industries as steel if private industry "fails to meet our needs." He asked for low-rent public housing and a system of prepaid medical insurance. He called for a repeal of the Taft-Hartley Act, for an increase of the minimum wage to at least seventy-five cents, and for the enactment of his civil rights program.

A fortnight later the capital was ready for the inauguration. The Republican Congress had provided a few hundred thousand dollars to make the ceremonies the "biggest damn inauguration in modern times." Curly Brooks was the head of the committee in charge of the preparations, and money had been spent freely to make the celebrations in honor of a Republican President—the first in sixteen years—memorable. The Democrats now used happily what the Republicans had prepared.

For Truman inauguration day began with a breakfast with his old buddies of World War I—the members of Battery D of the 129th Field Artillery. In a caustic speech he imitated the voice and inflection of radio commentator H. V. Kaltenborn reporting during election night. "While the President is a million votes ahead in the popular vote, when the county vote comes in, Mr. Truman will be defeated by an overwhelming majority," he mimicked. Truman told his friends that after listening to the other radio commentators who said the election would be thrown into the House, he went to bed and to sleep. Awakened at four o'clock, he "turned the darn thing on again." At that time Kaltenborn was saying that while the President had a two-million-vote lead, it was certainly necessary that the House decide the election since Mr. Truman "hasn't an opportunity of being elected by a majority vote."

The streets of Washington were filled with a celebrating crowd. Floats were driven to the assembling places, television technicians and movie operators were at their cameras, bands played, vendors sold badges, the city was ready for its showiest inaugural.

At noon as the President drove to the Capitol he was greeted with affectionate shouts. "Harry" and "Hiya, Harry!"

The inaugural speech was largely devoted to foreign issues. Truman said that the United States would give "unfaltering support" to the United Nations, put its "full weight" behind the European Recovery Program, provide in the North Atlantic Security Pact "unmistakable proof" of the joint determination of the free countries to resist armed attack from any quarter, and embark on "a bold new program for making the benefits of our scientific and industrial progress available for the improvement and growth of underdeveloped areas" of the world. It was not a dramatic address.

After the ceremonies at the Capitol the inaugural parade was watched by millions on television. For the first time organized labor marched in the parade and entered its floats. As Truman reviewed the spectacle, the band played "I'm Just Wild About Harry," and he danced a little jig in time to the music. It was his great day. His face beamed as he stood on the platform.

"Mr. Truman stands there," wrote Gerald W. Johnson in a memorable piece, "not in his own right, but as representing you and me and Joe Dokes down the street, and Martha, his wife, and the kids playing baseball in a vacant lot. He represents a Negro and a Jew and an American-born Japanese. In reality, it is a Minnesota farmer taking the salute, a Georgia cracker, a Pittsburgh steelworker, a New York girl filing clerk, in whose honor the bombers darken the sky over Washington and fill the air with their thunder.

THE INAUGURATION, JANUARY 20, 1949. Chief Justice Fred M. Vinson administers the oath. Others, left to right: Mrs. Max Truitt, daughter of the Vice President; Margaret and Mrs. Truman; Mr. and Mrs. Dean Acheson; Sam Rayburn. At President Truman's side is Vice President Barkley. Holding the Bible is Charles E. Cropley, clerk of the Supreme Court.

"This is more vividly apparent in the case of Mr. Truman than in that of most Presidents; for his election is due to the fact that the common man took matters into his own hands, regardless of the politicians, regardless of the great lords in business and journalism, regardless of the experts and wiseacres. He is conspicuously the common man's choice—and by the same token, the common man's responsibility. . . .

"Mr. Truman's mistakes—and it goes without saying that he will make some—will be our mistakes, his failures will be our defeats. Such strength and wisdom as he has are the strength and wisdom of a common people of this country. . . .

"The ceremonial will be over by midnight and then the long pull will begin. The small man in drab clothes will leave the reviewing stand and take his place behind a desk; you and I will return to our normal occupations. But woe betide us if we forget the parade and what it means. We mean well; but how much of wisdom, how much of patience, how much of steady resolution we must display during the next four years is frightening to contemplate. We can well afford to turn away from the spectacle, murmuring an adaptation of words of the crier of the Supreme Court: 'God save the United States and the nations of the world!' "

To which one can only say: "Amen."

DWIGHT D. EISENHOWER

In his inaugural address President Truman talked of the competition between the Communists and the free world for the minds of the people. "The United States and other like-minded nations find themselves directly opposed by a regime with contrary aims and a totally different concept of life," said Truman. For him the philosophy of Communism was false; therefore it should be fought. He offered a four-point program: support of the United Nations; continuing plans for world economic recovery, such as the Marshall Plan; the strengthening of "freedom loving nations against the dangers of aggression" by means of organizations such as NATO; and "a bold new program for making the benefits of our scientific advances and industrial progress available for the improvement and growth of underdeveloped areas." With these four points Truman hoped to win the cold war against Russia.

The North Atlantic Treaty, pledging the United States and eleven European nations to resist aggression by any outside power, was approved by the Senate by a wide margin (82 to 13). Any outside attack upon any one of the signatories was to be construed as an attack upon all. The critics doubted whether the pact was in the interests of the country, or whether it was an invitation to an increased arms race.

The country's preoccupation with the Russians led to increased spending. Congress voted more than a billion and a half dollars to provide military assistance to "nations which have joined with the United States in collective defense . . . and to other nations whose increased ability to defend themselves against aggression is important to the national interest." Most of the

weapons went to the NATO forces; the rest went to South Korea, the Philippines, Greece, Turkey and Iran.

In Asia Mao Tse-tung assumed the leadership of a new People's Republic of China, and in May 1949 Generalissimo Chiang Kai-shek retreated with his badly mauled forces to the island of Formosa. The mainland of China was now in the hands of the Communists. Their victory had far-reaching consequences. On June 25, 1950, the North Koreans crossed the thirty-eighth parallel in a move to occupy the southern part of the country governed by Dr. Syngman Rhee. Truman made up his mind quickly to help South Korea against the northern invaders. The Security Council of the United Nations voted to send troops to assist the South Koreans. As the Russians had been boycotting the meetings since January, they could not veto the move.

General Douglas MacArthur was named to command the combined American and United Nations forces, and after he cleared South Korea of the invaders, he crossed the thirty-eighth parallel. He urged Truman to allow him to take his troops into China in order to destroy the North Koreans' supply bases. Those who warned of China entering into the war were told that MacArthur's intelligence reports had established the fact that China would not do so. However, when American forces moved toward the border, Chinese "volunteers" in large numbers joined the North Koreans and pushed them back. With the war going poorly and the North Koreans again at the thirty-eighth parallel, Truman was ready for a "diplomatic effort." He ordered MacArthur to maintain the status quo, but MacArthur instead publicly warned China that she

DWIGHT D. EISENHOWER
S. Army photograph

737

CANDIDATES IN 1952

DWIGHT EISENHOWER (1890———), West Point graduate and career officer, had a meteoric military career. As Supreme Commander of the Allied Expeditionary Forces, he led the D-day invasion of Normandy. Retiring from active duty in 1948, he became president of Columbia University. In 1950 Truman named him commander of the NATO forces in Europe. Needing a popular candidate, the Republicans turned to him.

RICHARD M. NIXON (1913———), lawyer and politician from California, had served as a lieutenant commander in the navy during the war. First a Congressman and then a Senator from his state, with a record as a fighter against "the Communist conspiracy," he was chosen by the Republicans as their vice presidential candidate. His ticket won with 33,936,234 votes against the Democrats' 27,314,992 votes.

ADLAI E. STEVENSON (1900–1965), the grandson of Cleveland's Vice President and Governor of Illinois, was Assistant Secretary of the Navy during the war and chief of the delegation to the Preparation Commission of the United Nations. A brilliant intellectual, he was reluctant to offer himself for the presidential nomination and, after a stirring convention address, only accepted when the Democrats drafted him.

JOHN J. SPARKMAN (1899———), son of an Alabama tenant farmer, a delegate to the U.N., served in the House for ten years prior to his election as U.S. Senator. In the upper house Sparkman was a member of the Banking and Foreign Relations committees. Conservative in views, he would, it was thought, balance the ticket and keep the Southern vote. But he could not. Only nine Southern states registered for the Democrats.

UP

MARY GENEVA DOUD (1896———) with her mother, Mrs. John S. Doud, on the way to the inaugural ball. She married Eisenhower on July 1, 1916, a year after he graduated from West Point. Of their two children, the first, David Dwight (b. in 1917), died at the age of three; John Sheldon Doud (b. 1923) is their only surviving child. When "Mamie," as she is called by everybody, set up housekeeping in the White House, it was her thirtieth move in thirty-five years—not one to a house of her own.

would be "doomed to imminent military collapse" should the UN army not "contain the war to the area of Korea." And "Within the area of my authority as the military commander . . . I stand ready at any time to confer in the field with the commander in chief of the enemy forces. . . ."

Truman would neither be pressured into a war with China, a country with a population of eight hundred million, nor would he allow the General to determine national policy. He would not give up his prerogatives as commander in chief. When MacArthur defied the President's orders, Truman removed him. He explained his action to the country: "Full and vigorous debate on matters of national policy is a vital element in the constitutional system of our free democracy. It is fundamental, however, that military commanders must be governed by policies and directives issued to them in

Cartoon by F. B. Modell, March 1952
WHO WILL BE THE REPUBLICAN CANDIDATE? is the theme of this *New Yorker* cartoon. Support was divided between General Eisenhower, Senator Robert H. Taft, General MacArthur, Governor Earl Warren and Harold Stassen.

the manner provided by our laws and Constitution. In time of crisis this consideration is particularly compelling." General Omar Bradley said that MacArthur's strategy would have started a war on the mainland of Asia; the country would have been "in the wrong war, at the wrong place, at the wrong time and with the wrong enemy."

Returning home, MacArthur delivered an emotion-laden address before Congress in which he insisted: "There is no substitute for victory." His closing sentences, "Old soldiers never die. They just fade away," hit the sentimental nerve of the country and for awhile it seemed that he might become the candidate of the Republicans.

Communism was fought not only in Korea but at home as well. Americans began to believe that the Communists were responsible for the unsteady condi-

tions in the world. The hysterical hunt for Communists grew to insane proportions—every Communist was regarded as a superman. People's pasts, their associations, their affiliations were looked into. Guilt by association was decreed. Ultimately there would be thousands of victims in this lapse from national sanity.

Alger Hiss, the head of the Carnegie Corporation and a former State Department official, was accused of supplying secret information to the Russians. In a sensation-laden trial he was jailed for perjury.

In the Senate the publicity-seeking Joseph McCarthy of Wisconsin began to investigate the activities of alleged subversives who, in his opinion, had infiltrated Federal agencies. Truman publicly called the Senator a liar and privately an s.o.b., and declared that the "internal security of the United States is not seriously threatened by the communists in this country."

THE PREY . . . Alger Hiss, president of the Carnegie Foundation for International Peace and former State Department official, is taken to prison. After a sensational confrontation with his former friend, writer Whittaker Chambers, before a House Un-American Activities Committee investigation, Hiss was convicted on a perjury charge and given a five-year sentence, even though the original charges of espionage for the U.S.S.R. were rejected.

. . . AND THE HUNTER. Richard M. Nixon of California, who was first elected to the House in 1946 with anti-Communism as a prominent issue, was one of the most active members of the House Un-American Activities Committee. With the help of Chambers he collected evidence and built his case, linking Hiss with the Communists and causing his spectacular downfall. Nixon later said this was his "first real testing" in the public eye.

McCarthy's shenanigans were helped by a spineless press which printed his every utterance even though reporters knew his "news" was manufactured sometimes on the spur of the moment to get front-page attention, and by cowardly politicians who did not dare to cross him.

Thus the issues of the forthcoming campaign were formed. One was subversion, the other corruption in government. Some high-ranking employees of the Internal Revenue Bureau were found guilty of frauds. A Senate committee found that the Reconstruction Finance Corporation had yielded to Democratic politicians in making loans.

The Republicans made up their formula: "K_1C_2" (Korea, Communism and corruption). Their slogan became "cleaning up the mess." All they needed was a

UP, November 2, 1950

THE ASSASSINATION ATTEMPT ON PRESIDENT TRUMAN. With Clark Clifford and Secret Service men watching him, Truman takes his morning walk—going to work as usual—a day after two Puerto Ricans tried to kill him.

Charles Corte, Acme

ONE WOULD-BE ASSASSIN WAS KILLED . . . Griselio Torresola, a Puerto Rican nationalist, tried to force his way into Blair House, to kill the napping President.

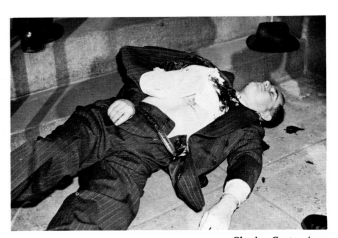

Charles Corte, Acme

. . . THE OTHER WAS WOUNDED. Oscar Collazo lies outside the Blair House. In the exchange of gunfire one of the White House guards was killed, two wounded.

741

Acme, January 6, 1951

THE GENERAL AND THE PRESIDENT. With a friendly handshake and his usual smile President Truman says good-bye to Eisenhower, whom he had appointed to head the NATO forces in Europe, as the General departs for his post.

winning candidate. General Eisenhower's name had been mentioned frequently. When on June 27, 1945, a reporter asked him if he would enter politics, he replied: "Look, I'm in the federal service and I take the orders of my Commander in Chief. All I want is to be a citizen of the United States, and when the War Department turns me out to pasture that's all I want to be. I want nothing else. It is silly to talk about it, but only to settle this matter once for all. I should like to make this as emphatic as possible. There's no use my denying that I'll fly to the moon, because no one has suggested it, and I couldn't if I wanted to. The same goes for politics. I'm a soldier, and I'm positive no one thinks of me as a politician. In the strongest language you can command, you can state that I have no political ambi-

tions at all. Make it even stronger than that if you can. I'd like to go even further than Sherman in expressing myself on the subject."

But by 1948 he spoke differently. Eisenhower could have had the nomination of either party; it was said that Truman not only offered Democratic support to him but was willing to step down and run as Eisenhower's Vice President. The General, meanwhile, assumed the presidency of Columbia University, and late in 1950 he became Supreme Allied Commander, Europe, in charge of NATO. He declared that he had the "highest respect and admiration" for Truman and said that he was "not going to let any sort of talk by others make me a candidate."

Nonetheless, the Eisenhower-for-President move-

UP, April 11, 1951

THE GENERAL AND THE PRESIDENT. With a broad smile Truman bids farewell to MacArthur, whom he had removed from his Pacific command in Korea for the General's insubordination over which way to conduct the war there.

ment gathered momentum. Senator Henry Cabot Lodge of Massachusetts, Governor Thomas Dewey of New York, Senators Frank Carlson of Kansas and James Duff of Pennsylvania, and others organized support for him. For the liberal Republicans, Eisenhower was the answer to a prayer: a military hero and a practicing internationalist, he would dispel the charge that the Republican party was the party of isolationists.

The candidate of the conservatives was Senator Robert Taft of Ohio, the son of a President. On October 15, 1951, a year before election time, he had announced his candidacy, promising to campaign against "creeping control of government encroaching upon the people," as evidenced in regulation of prices, rents and wages, and the Brannan farm plan.

Shortly thereafter the popular Governor of California, Earl Warren, threw his hat in the ring, as did the ever-ready Harold Stassen.

The primary battles turned out to be contests between Eisenhower and Taft. (The write-in attempts for General MacArthur did so poorly that he faded out.)

Early in January 1952, Senator Lodge and Governor Sherman Adams of New Hampshire entered Eisenhower's name in the New Hampshire primary. *The New York Times,* the New York *Herald-Tribune,* the Chicago *Sun-Times* with other leading newspapers across the country endorsed the General's candidacy. "We are confident that he would be able to lead even the laggards among his fellow Republicans away from isolation and towards world responsibility. . . . If Dwight

Letting the Cat Out of a Cellophane Bag.

AM I SURPRISED!

I AM A CANDIDATE

TAFT

Talburt, October 1951

TAFT'S ANNOUNCEMENT WAS NO SURPRISE

You'll Take the High Road, and I'll Take the Low Road I'll Be in the White House Afore You'

IKE

WARREN

TAFT ENDORSEMENT OF McCARTHYISM

Herblock, January 1952

TAFT SINGS TO THE OTHER CANDIDATES.

Eisenhower should be nominated by the Republican party as its candidate for President, we shall support him enthusiastically," wrote the *Times,* and in three editorials argued why "Taft can't win."

Eisenhower won easily in New Hampshire and had a huge write-in vote in Minnesota. However, Taft took Wisconsin and Illinois, and he defeated the General for write-in votes in Nebraska. The result of the primary contest was: in twelve states Taft polled 2,785,790 votes; in nine others Eisenhower received 2,115,430 votes. In the primaries where the two were pitted against each other on equal terms, Eisenhower ran two to one ahead of Taft.

Newsweek commented on the appeal of Eisenhower: "Although recognized by sight and called 'Ike' by almost everybody in the United States, the country knew surprisingly little about him—what he was like, what he thought about the problems facing the nation and the world, what sort of President he might make. Millions already rallied to his support because they knew that, as a soldier, he had led Allied troops to victory in Europe, demonstrating a talent both for diplomacy and leadership, and that he had more recently helped build a dam in Europe against the postwar flood of Commu-

nism. They considered all this qualification enough for the Presidency."

To the joy of his supporters Eisenhower announced in Paris that he would leave NATO on June 1, and that he would quit the army if nominated.

It was assumed by everybody that President Truman would run again. He had served most of Roosevelt's fourth term—three years and nine months of it. The Twenty-second Amendment, which had become effective in 1951, limited a President to two terms, and specified that serving more than two years of a predecessor's term counted as one. However, Truman was exempt from the amendment. But in a surprise announcement at the Jefferson-Jackson Day dinner on March 29, 1952, the President declared: "I shall not be a candidate for re-election. I have served my country long, and I think efficiently and honestly. I shall not accept a renomination. I do not feel that it is my duty to spend another four years in the White House."

His announcement threw the presidential race wide open. Who should follow him? Vice President Alben Barkley; Adlai E. Stevenson, the Governor of Illinois; Estes Kefauver, Senator from Tennessee; Senator Richard Russell of Georgia?

GEORGE III'S DESCENDANT WITH THE HEIR OF THE REBELLIOUS COLONISTS. On the 175th anniversary of the Declaration of Independence, the future Queen Elizabeth II of England meets with the 33rd President of the U.S.

ENTERING EISENHOWER'S NAME in the New Hampshire primary, Senator Henry Cabot Lodge declared: "I am speaking for the General, and I will not be repudiated."

PETITIONS SUPPORTING HIS CANDIDACY are handed by Governor Sherman Adams. Behind him: publisher James Langley and Joseph Geisel, state legislator.

VICTORY. The elated Governor Adams rejoices with the campaign workers after Eisenhower won the primary.

DDE

Supreme Headquarters
Allied Powers Europe
2 April 1952

Dear Mr. Secretary:

I request that you initiate appropriate action to secure my release from assignment as Supreme Commander, Allied Powers Europe, by approximately June 1st, and that I be placed on inactive status upon my return to the United States. A relief date fixed this far in advance should provide ample time for the appointment of a successor and for any preparation and counsel that he may desire from me.

This proposal is in the spirit of the understanding I gained from officials in Washington who outlined the special purposes of my original appointment in December 1950. At that time it was believed by those individuals that, because of past experience, I had relationships with respect to Europe which would facilitate the formation of a common defense structure and the establishment of a pattern for its operation. An assumption on the part of responsible officials of our Government that I could be helpful in the vital task of preserving peace was, of course, a compelling reason for instantaneous return to active service and acceptance of this assignment.

As of now, I consider that the specific purposes for which I was recalled to duty have been largely accomplished; the command has been formed, its procedures established, and basic questions settled. Moreover, a program of growth and development, based on early experience and searching reexamination, has been agreed at governmental levels. There are many difficulties to be overcome but, given the wholehearted support of the NATO community, this program will provide a reassuring degree of security in this region, despite the continued presence of the threat of Soviet Communism. There is every reason to believe that the NATO nations will continue to work together successfully, toward the goal of a secure peace.

Sincerely,

Dwight D. Eisenhower

TURNING INTO A CANDIDATE. Eisenhower's letter to the Defense Secretary asking his release from assignment as Supreme Commander of Allied forces in Europe.

On May 8, Truman jotted a memorandum to himself: ". . . if we can find a man who will take over and continue the Fair Deal, Point IV, Fair Employment, parity for farmers and a consumers' protective policy, the Democratic Party can win from now on. It seems to me now that the Governor of Illinois has the background and what it takes. Think I'll talk to him."

This he did. But Stevenson showed no inclination. He told reporters: "I have repeatedly said that I was a candidate for Governor of Illinois and had no other ambition. To this I must now add that in view of my prior commitment to run for Governor and my desire and the desire of so many who had given their help and confidence in the unfinished work in Illinois, I could not accept the nomination for any other office this summer."

THE HOPE OF THE REPUBLICANS. In April 1952 Lodge flew to France and met with Eisenhower at his SHAPE headquarters. After their conference it was announced that Eisenhower had consented to become a Republican candidate.

UP, April 6, 1952

–AN 'ABE LINCOLN'–   A 'TEDDY ROOSEVELT'   A 'WOODROW WILSON'–   A 'HERBERT HOOVER'–   AN 'F.D.R'–   OR A 'HARRY TRUMAN'?

Cartoon by Vicky in the London News Chronicle

THE GREAT QUESTION: A LONDON CARTOONIST'S SPECULATION ON EISENHOWER AS PRESIDENT

DEMOCRATIC CONTENDER. Estes Kefauver, the crime-fighting Senator, announcing for the nomination.

UP, January 24, 1952

BRAVING NEW HAMPSHIRE WEATHER. Senator Kefauver from Tennessee, in his traditional coonskin cap.

UP, February 21, 1952

THE RESULT OF THE NEW HAMPSHIRE PRIMARY

UP, March 12, 1952

He was asked: "Well, what'll you do if we nominate you anyway?" to which Stevenson answered jokingly, "Guess I'd have to shoot myself."

Truman continued his search for a successor. He thought that Chief Justice Frederick Vinson might be a good choice. Vinson had represented Kentucky in Congress for thirty-five years. He had served as a judge, he was the head of the Economic Stabilization Board during the war, and he had been Truman's Secretary of the Treasury before being named Chief Justice. And when Vinson refused, the President turned to Averell Harriman, who had a long and distinguished government service record. Harriman had been Ambassador to Great Britain and to the Soviet Union, and was now Secretary of Commerce, ably administering the Marshall Plan in Europe. The drawback was that he had never been elected to office.

Others whom Truman considered were Senators Kefauver, Kerr and Russell, but each of them had some political weakness. His crime investigations had made scores of enemies for Kefauver; Kerr was associated with the oil interests; and Russell came from the Deep South. If the popular Barkley had been younger, he would have been the logical candidate, but he was seventy-five years old.

And while the country speculated about the Democratic candidate, the Republicans met in Chicago. In his keynote address, General MacArthur castigated the Truman administration's "headlong retreat from victory" and pinned the "war party" label on the opposition.

There was a dispute over the seating of delegates from Louisiana, Texas and Georgia, as two sets of delegates appeared from each of these states—one for Taft, one for Eisenhower. The Taft-controlled Credentials Committee recommended giving Louisiana to Eisenhower, Georgia's and most of Texas' votes to Taft. The Eisenhower supporters cried "steal." Eisenhower himself saw the move as a betrayal of Republican principles and warned that a party could not clean up corruption in the government "unless that party—from top to bottom is clean itself, and no party can tolerate a rigged convention and hope to win."

When the resolution to approve this decision was before the convention, Donald Eastman rose to ask that the Eisenhower delegates be seated. Senator Dirksen then rose to recall that in 1948 "We followed you before and you took us down the road to defeat." Then he pointed his finger at Dewey, who supported Eisenhower, and said, "and don't do this to us again."

The balloting brought no surprises. On the first trial Eisenhower had 595 votes—nine short of the nomination. Taft had 500, Warren 81, Stassen 20 and MacArthur 10. Then Minnesota switched, and all was over.

TRUMAN WILL NOT BE A CANDIDATE FOR RE-ELECTION. At the Jefferson-Jackson Day dinner, Mrs. Truman and W. B. Williams, chairman of the dinner committee, listen intently as the President makes his declaration, jotted on White House stationery which he inserted in his prepared speech.

In his acceptance speech Eisenhower said: "You have summoned me . . . to lead a great crusade . . . for freedom in America and freedom in the world. I know something of the solemn responsibility of leading a crusade. I have led one. I take up this task, therefore, in the spirit of deep obligation. I accept your summons. I will lead this crusade."

The Republican platform charged the Democrats with the "appeasement of Communism at home and abroad," depriving Americans of precious liberties, disrupting internal tranquillity by fostering class strife, shielding traitors, creating enemies abroad, debauching the dollar, weakening self-government, imposing crushing taxation, turning loose a swarm of bureaucrats "who meddled in the lives of American citizens," and allowing "corruption in high places."

In foreign affairs the platform emphasized air power and massive retaliation; rejected isolationism, supported collective security and mutual aid, attacked the handling of the Korean War, pledged to get rid of Communism and corruption, promised to overhaul the taxation system, to make war on inflation, to revamp the farm program, to balance the budget and to deliver the mail more often.

Eisenhower chose as his running mate the young Senator Richard Nixon of California, a friend of Senator McCarthy, a nationally recognized spokesman

UP, July 14, 1952

THE REPUBLICANS' NEWLY CHOSEN CANDIDATE, with his wife, vice presidential nominee Richard Nixon and his wife, Senators Lodge and John W. Bricker, and convention chairman Joseph Martin, acknowledges the delegates' ovation.

SENATOR TAFT WATCHES THE CONVENTION.
UP, July 7, 1952

against Communism, the prosecutor of Alger Hiss.

Ten days later the Democrats met in the same auditorium. For the first time in two decades no one candidate had the nomination all sewed up; in fact, to the Washington *Post,* "The more avowed candidates arrive in Chicago, the more talk there is about a fugitive from the nomination—Governor Adlai Stevenson of Illinois."

Stevenson made the welcoming speech. "For almost a week pompous phrases marched over this landscape in search of an idea," he began, "and the only idea they found was that the two great decades of progress in

UP, July 11, 1952

THE BATTLE OVER—CONVENTION HALL IS EMPTY AND SILENT. But within a fortnight it would be noisy again, filled with Democrats who would be choosing their candidates in the same hall, in Chicago, and hammering out their platform.

THE REPUBLICAN TICKET IS IN HAPPY SPIRITS.
UP, July 11, 1952

peace, victory in war, and bold leadership in this anxious hour were the misbegotten spawn of socialism, bungling, corruption, mismanagement, waste and worse. . . . After listening to this procession of epithets about our misdeeds, I was even surprised the next morning when the mail was delivered on time." Then he continued in a serious vein: "Where we have erred, let there be no denial; where we have wronged the public trust, let there be no excuses. Self-criticism is the secret weapon of democracy, and candor and confession are good for the political soul."

James Reston wrote in *The New York Times* that

EISENHOWER SUPPORTS SENATOR JOSEPH McCARTHY IN WISCONSIN. Eisenhower said McCarthy had done his work "without recklessly injuring the reputation of innocent people"—one of the strangest statements on record.

Stevenson had "talked himself into the leading candidate's role this afternoon with a fifteen-minute address that impressed the convention from left to right."

Even his divorce was no issue. When the question came up before the predominantly Roman Catholic Massachusetts delegation, one delegate said: "Hell, half of our wives would divorce us if they could."

Barkley now was out of the contest because the C.I.O. denied him support because of his age. But of the other Democrats placed before the convention, Kefauver, Russell and Harriman still had their hopes. Stevenson was still reluctant. "It now looks as though Governor Adlai Stevenson will be dragged protesting to the presidential altar by the Democratic party. His shrieks are growing fainter, his suitor more importunate," wrote columnist Doris Fleeson.

In the Illinois caucus Stevenson asked the delegates not to vote for him, as he had no desire for the office; the delegates said they would vote for him anyway.

Truman flew to Chicago to do his part; and thus Stevenson—the first genuinely drafted candidate since Garfield in 1880—was nominated on the third ballot. In placing Stevenson's name in nomination, Henry Schricker said that "There are times when a man is not permitted to say no. I place before you the man we cannot permit to say no."

Accepting the nomination, Stevenson told the convention: "I have not sought the honor you have done me. I *could* not seek it, because I aspired to another office. . . . I *would* not seek your nomination for the Presidency because the burdens of that office stagger the imagination. Its potential for good and evil, now, and in the years of our lives, smothers exultation and converts sanity into prayer. . . . But from such dread

TAFT	
EISENHOWER	361
OTHERS	129
UNCOMMITTED	91

EISENHOWER VISITS ROBERT TAFT AFTER DEFEATING THE SENATOR FOR THE NOMINATION. *UP* Outwardly everything is serene and everybody seems satisfied—but pictures do not show what goes on beneath the surface.

responsibility one does not shrink with fear. . . . So 'if this cup may not pass from me, except I drink it, Thy will be done.'"

He spoke of the coming campaign: "What does concern me, in common with thinking partisans of both parties, is not just winning the election, but how it is won, how well we can take advantage of this great quadrennial opportunity to debate issues sensibly and soberly. I hope and pray that we Democrats, win or lose, can campaign not as a crusade to exterminate the opposing party, as our opponents seem to prefer, but as a great opportunity to educate and elevate a people whose destiny is leadership, not alone of a rich and prosperous, contented country as in the past, but of a world in ferment. . . .

"Better we lose the election than mislead the people; and better we lose than misgovern the people."

The Democratic platform, like the Republican, compromised on civil rights; it pledged itself to economic and other aid to Western Hemisphere nations and to collective security. It advocated health and tax programs according to one's ability to pay. It called for repeal of the Taft-Hartley Act, for minimum wage and other social legislation, and a basic adherence to the past record of the Democratic party.

The columnists compared and analyzed the candidates. James Reston opined that the contest was basically between a man of action (Eisenhower) and a man of thought (Stevenson). Reston felt that both candidates had more of the "elements of goodness" in them than the "elements of greatness"; both were pragmatic, both appealed to the noblest qualities of the American character; both were middle-of-the-roaders, both were adept at bringing diverse elements together. Neither of them

Cornell Capa, Magnum

TWO DEMOCRATIC CANDIDATES. Adlai Stevenson with his dog King Arthur passes behind the statue of Stephen A. Douglas as he leaves the state capitol at Springfield, Illinois. Douglas opposed Lincoln in the 1860 election.

Cartoon by Marcus, April 1952
A CARTOON ON HIS CANDIDACY

was a professional politician, neither of them aspired to office; both had been forced to run. But while there were great similarities between them, there were also great differences. Stevenson was a more complex man than Eisenhower. He saw many sides to a question while Eisenhower liked to simplify issues. Yet Eisenhower was positive, decisive, optimistic and self-confident while Stevenson was riddled with uncertainties. Stevenson's weapon was the rapier; Eisenhower's was the blunderbuss.

To conduct his campaign, the General was assisted by Senators Lodge of Massachusetts, Seaton of Nebraska and Carlson of Kansas, Governor Adams of New Hampshire, Herbert Brownell and C. D. Jackson, an executive of Time, Inc. Jackson then brought in Emmett John Hughes, a *Life* editor.

An advertising agency was engaged. The firm of Batten, Barton, Durstine and Osborn suggested that as the Republicans were in a minority they should aim for the stay-at-home voters. The strategy should not be the me-tooism of Willkie or Dewey, but rather "Attack! Attack! Attack!" Both Eisenhower and Nixon were seen to have "a high degree of salesmanship in their manner" so that they should not shirk public appearances. Television was the natural means of making "the most of the ticket's human assets." In a phrase the campaign should be: "merchandising Eisenhower's frankness, honesty and integrity, his sincere and wholesome approach."

When Eisenhower appeared to be bothered during the briefing, Sherman Adams asked him why. "All they talked about was how they would win on my popularity. Nobody said I had a brain in my head," replied the General.

Stevenson's campaign manager, Wilson Wyatt, promised that the campaign would be "without exaggeration." A brilliant array of liberals—Arthur Schlesinger, Jr., Willard Wirtz, John Kenneth Galbraith and others—helped the Governor with his speeches. They shared the same habits of thought. Stevenson replaced Democratic National Committee Chairman McKinney with Stephen A. Mitchell, and moved his campaign headquarters from Washington to Springfield. The moves angered Truman. The amateurs in Stevenson's office brought on the enmity of the old Democratic professionals; still Stevenson was determined to run his campaign according to his own rules regardless of the sputtering of the old guard.

He began by attacking the "tidal drift" of power to Washington, asking the states to dike up this drift. He also castigated the Republicans for their "doctrine of change for the sake of change." He had said that he was qualified to clean up the "mess in Washington," a statement which was to haunt him: Republicans re-

TO RUN OR NOT TO RUN
Cornell Capa, Magnum

ON THE EVE OF THE CONVENTION Stevenson tells reporters that he does not want the presidential nomination.

A LITTLE LATER HE RELUCTANTLY ACCEPTS.

garded Stevenson's statement as an admission of corruption. Truman admonished Stevenson to campaign for the New and Fair Deals, not against them.

Opening his campaign in Boise, Idaho, Eisenhower advocated the "Middle Road." He accepted the social gains of the last two decades as "solid floors" upon which private initiative would build a better life. He accepted the achievements of the New Deal and the Fair Deal—social security, workers' unemployment insurance, improved education, protection of workingmen's rights, adequate insurance for farmers—and pledged "to enlist all the resources of private industry and mobilize all resources of our Government to prevent the specter of mass unemployment from once again visiting our land." But he spoke out against the welfare state and against centralized power:

UP, July 26, 1952

PRESIDENT TRUMAN POINTS to the chosen candidate after the convention nominated Stevenson on the third ballot.

"Now we have had for a long time a Government that applies the philosophy of the Left to government. The government will build the power dams, the government will tell you how to distribute your power, the government will do this and that. The government does everything but come in and wash dishes for the housewife. Now their answer to the evils of government is more government. Take agriculture—they offer us the Brannan Plan. Our health—they offer socialized medicine and want our health to be dictated by some bureaucrat."

The cartoonist Herblock drew a cartoon showing Eisenhower reading a long medical report on his health —given to him free—while ranting against medical care for the people.

Both candidates addressed the American Legion

UP, July 27, 1952

THE 1952 TICKET: STEVENSON AND SPARKMAN

Cartoon by Fischetti, September 1952
"THE FORK IN THE ROAD"—LEFT OR RIGHT?

Cartoon by Herblock, October 1952
THE QUESTION IS "WHERE DID EVERYBODY GO?"

convention in New York. Eisenhower proposed that the United States should use its influence to help the Communist-controlled nations of Eastern Europe to throw off the yoke of Russian tyranny. "The American Conscience can never know peace again until these people are restored again to being master of their own fate," he orated, but how this could be accomplished he would not say.

Stevenson denounced the use of patriotism as a club. He called for "free enterprise for the mind" as well as for business. Patriotism, he said, "is a sense of national responsibility which will enable America to remain master of her power—to walk with it in serenity and wisdom, with self-respect and with the respect of all mankind; a patriotism that puts country ahead of self; a patriotism which is not short, frenzied outbursts of emotion, but the tranquil and steady dedication of a lifetime . . . we must take care not to burn down the barn to kill the rats."

Stevenson continued on this theme by advising Eisenhower to get rid of his "gutter counselors." He said: "My opponent's trepidation is understandable. Joe McCarthy may get him if he doesn't watch out."

Eisenhower, against the advice of the professionals,

made up his mind to campaign in the Deep South—every state except Mississippi—the first time in modern times that a Republican presidential candidate had done so. In Atlanta the reception for him was the biggest since the one for Clark Gable and the première of *Gone With the Wind*. In Tampa, Birmingham and Little Rock he spoke out against governmental corruption, and the crowds yelled, "Pour it on." He claimed that corruption was "the inevitable and sure-fire result of an administration by too many men who are too small for their jobs and too big for their breeches and too long in power. . . . The Washington mess is not a one-agency mess, or a one-bureau mess, or a one-department mess. It is a top-to-bottom mess." He urged the South to protect the rights of Negroes, without spelling out how to do it.

Stevenson said in Detroit that he was for repeal of the Taft-Hartley Law, "which has not improved labor relations in a single plant," but was more moderate about it than Truman. Four days later, in Denver, he derided the Republicans for calling "It's time for a change" and at the same time condemning the Democrats as people who wanted to change everything. "I'm beginning to wonder," he said, "if the Republican

THE CAMPAIGN OF 1952

Cartoon by Herblock, September 1952

AS THE CAMPAIGN BEGINS IN EARNEST, IT'S "OFF WE GO!"

UP, September 22, 1952

THREE HAPPY DEMOCRATS. Adlai Stevenson, the presidential candidate; Representative John F. Kennedy, the Massachusetts Senatorial candidate; and Paul Dever, Democratic candidate for a third term as Governor of Massachusetts.

campaign rests on the proposition that Democrats are social revolutionaries who want to keep things exactly as they are."

On September 6 both candidates spoke at the National Plowing Contest in Kasson, Minnesota. Both supported 90 per cent parity and struck out at the other party's farm policies.

In Albuquerque, Stevenson talked of McCarthyism and internal subversion without the hysterical rantings of the Republicans. He said that "the excesses of those who exploit anti-communism do not alter the fact that our nation can never for one moment relax its guard. We must take care not to harm innocent people. We must remember that liberals are not Communists and that socialists are not Communists and that radicals in the American tradition are not Communists."

And while Stevenson barnstormed in the Southwest, Eisenhower met with Senator Taft in New York. Taft had demands to make—for patronage and for the candidate's support of conservative policies. After a two-hour conference at Eisenhower's residence on Morning-side Heights, Taft announced that he and the General were in firm agreement on the fundamental issues and that he would work for Eisenhower's election.

Paul Douglas (who had once hoped to see Eisenhower as the Democratic nominee) said: "The general is a fine and good man. But after he took off his uniform, he got mixed up with the wrong set of folks. He married into the wrong political family. His political mother-in-law, Taft, seems to be running the show, as mothers-in-law so often try to do." And Stevenson remarked about the meeting that Eisenhower's "Great Crusade" had turned into a "Great Surrender" and "Taft lost the nomination but won the nominee."

The campaign of the Republicans was going smoothly until the revelation that Richard Nixon, the vice presidential candidate, had been the beneficiary of a secret "extra expense" fund of $18,235 contributed by seventy-five rich Californians. At first Nixon declared the charge another "smear" from the Alger Hiss

760

UP, July 30, 1952

IT'S A HOT DAY. Governor Adlai Stevenson in a motorcade at his home town, Springfield, on the day he announced he would not be a contestant in the Illinois gubernatorial race. He had already been chosen as presidential candidate.

EISENHOWER AND TAFT MEET at the General's residence and declare they agree on fundamental issues.

AFTER THEIR MORNINGSIDE MEETING Senator Robert Taft leaves the conference with a smile of a winner.

crowd. But the Republicans did not take the accusation lightly. The New York *Herald-Tribune* called for Nixon's immediate withdrawal. Eisenhower withheld his decision until Nixon could appear on television to present his side of the story.

The television appearance of Nixon was a great event. He showed himself to the country as an honest American, his family around him. His homely talk "drenched the soil of the United States with tears." The women of the country were with him. He bared his soul about his financial status—and he talked of his two nice daughters and of his wife who wore not mink but a respectable Republican coat of cloth. The climax of his appeal came when he spoke of another gift— his pet dog Checkers. "The kids, all the kids love the dog . . . and regardless of what they say about it, we are going to keep it." Nixon asked his listeners: "Wire and write the Republican National Committee whether you think I should get off, and whatever their decision is, I will abide by it." The response was mostly in his favor; he had caught the people's sympathy and could remain on the ticket. The next day he met Eisenhower, who told him, "Dick, you're my boy."

Soon thereafter the Republicans charged that Stevenson had given privately contributed funds to certain appointed state employees while he was Governor of Illinois. Following the accusations, both Stevenson and Eisenhower disclosed their personal incomes.

From then on the main issue was Communism. Nixon stressed the evils of Democratic foreign policy and the failure to root out "a dangerous fifth column" at home. He attacked Stevenson as being "soft on Communism" for his deputation on behalf of Alger Hiss before Hiss went on trial. He said that if Stevenson could be duped as easily by Stalin as he was by Hiss, "the Yalta sellout would look like an American diplomatic triumph by comparison."

Early in October, Eisenhower campaigned in Wisconsin, the home state of Senator McCarthy, who was running for re-election. The General's prepared speech on that day to be delivered in Milwaukee included a reference to General Marshall, whom McCarthy had called a traitor. Eisenhower was to say, "Let me be quite specific. I know that charges of disloyalty have, in the past, been leveled against General George C. Marshall. . . . I know him . . . to be dedicated with singular selflessness and the profoundest patriotism . . . this episode is a sobering lesson in the way freedom must *not* defend itself."

But when he delivered his speech, the passage was omitted. Eisenhower allowed himself to be persuaded to give his support to McCarthy's re-election and posed for photographs with the Senator. The General said that he and McCarthy shared the similar purposes "of ridding this Government of the incompetents, the dishonest and above all the subversive and the disloyal" and that they differed only over "methods." The future belonged to the courageous and not to "those who have sneered at the warnings of men trying to drive Communists from high places—but who themselves have never had the sense or the stamina to take after the Communists themselves." Eisenhower insisted that national tolerance of Communism had "poisoned two whole decades of our national life" and had insinuated itself into our schools, public forums, some news channels, some labor unions "and—most terrifyingly—into our Government itself." As his campaign progressed, the General was advocating freeing the government not only of Communists but of "pinks" as well.

The General sounded anti-intellectual. Irked at Stevenson's wit, he said: "Is it amusing that we have stumbled into a war in Korea, that we have already lost in casualties 117,000 of our Americans killed or wounded; is it amusing that that war seems to be no closer to a real solution than ever?" Stevenson replied: "The General has been worrying about my funnybone. I'm worrying about his backbone."

At the University of Wisconsin, Stevenson attacked McCarthy vigorously: "Because we believe in a free mind we are also fighting those who, in the name of anti-communism, would assail the community of freedom itself. . . . The pillorying of the innocent has caused the wise to stammer and the timid to retreat. I should shudder for this country if I thought that we, too, must surrender to the sinister figure of the inquisition, of the great accuser. . . ."

In Detroit he spoke of what the Truman administration had accomplished to combat internal subversion, then noted that Eisenhower had implied that the administration deliberately concealed Communists, but "has offered only thundering silence about a cure. What would he do? Would he fire J. Edgar Hoover . . . General Bedell Smith, head of the Central Intelligence Agency and his own former Chief of Staff . . . Allen Dulles, the brother of his own chief advisor on foreign affairs? . . . I think we are entitled to ask, is the Republican candidate seriously interested in trying to root Communists out of the Government, or is he only interested in scaring the American people to get the Old Guard into the Government?" Stevenson said: "Our country was built on unpopular ideas, on unorthodox opinions. My definition of a free society is a society where it is safe to be unpopular." And he said that "Catching real Communist agents, like killing poisonous snakes or tigers, is not a job for amateurs or children, especially noisy ones."

President Truman too attacked Eisenhower: "He is the man I chose to be a chief lieutenant in some of the

A REPUBLICAN CAMPAIGN BUTTON FROM 1952

Cartoon by Herblock, October 1952
THE MAVERICK REPUBLICAN. Senator Wayne Morse declared the day after the Morningside conference that he would not support Eisenhower because of his capitulation to Taft and because of his endorsement of McCarthy.

UP

A CAMPAIGN SCENE IN WILLIAMSTOWN, MASS.

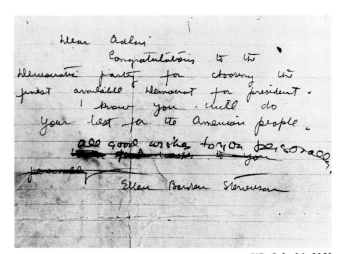

UP, October 25, 1952
THE DEMOCRATIC CANDIDATE MAKES A STOP.

UP, July 26, 1952
HIS FORMER WIFE WISHES STEVENSON WELL.

greatest and gravest undertakings of my Administration" but "the general has betrayed himself . . . by his wild attacks on policies and programs for which he had a great responsibility—and received credit." Truman accused Eisenhower—the "front man" for the power lobby, the railroad lobby, the real estate lobby, the rich man's tax lobby, the oil lobby, the China lobby—of waging a "gutter campaign," and he assailed him of bigotry for his associations with McCarthy and McCarran.

Eisenhower responded to the "vilification" by the opposition: "I have made no deals in this campaign. No one has a claim on me. No one has a promise from me. No one has captured me. I am my own man."

The bombshell of the campaign came in Detroit late in October, when Eisenhower gave his promise to end the war if elected President. "The biggest fact about the Korean war is this—it was never inevitable, it was never inescapable."

And he promised that as President he would take a simple, firm resolution. That resolution will be: To forego the diversion of politics and to concentrate on the job of ending the Korean war—until that job is honorably done.

"That job requires a personal trip to Korea.

"I shall make that trip. Only in that way could I learn how best to serve the American people in the cause of peace.

WHISTLE STOPPING BY THE GOP CANDIDATE *UP*

UP, October 6, 1952
McCARTHY LISTENS TO EISENHOWER SPEAK.

UP
THE REPUBLICAN CANDIDATE IN GOOD SPIRITS

"I shall go to Korea."

The Democrats called Eisenhower's Korea speech irresponsible; they called it a grandstand play. Truman said, "Anyone who poses and talks like a superman is a fraud." Yet the speech impressed the country. Until then the pollsters had been uncertain about the outcome of the contest, giving Eisenhower a slight lead; but after the Korea speech the Eisenhower victory was no longer in doubt.

The Republican tacticians relied on television as much as they did on the traditional whistle-stop campaign. They presented more and more commercials for their candidate. An announcer would declaim: "Eisenhower answers the Nation!" Then followed such scenes as the man-in-the-street asking, "Mr. Eisenhower, what about the high cost of living?" The candidate replied: "My wife, Mamie, worries about the same thing. I tell her it's our job to change that on November fourth." Or another citizen: "It was extra tough paying my income tax when I read about the internal revenue tax collectors being fired for dishonesty." And the General responded: "Well—how many taxpayers were shaken down, I don't know. How many crooks escaped, I don't know. But I'll find out after next January."

Stevenson concluded his campaign in Chicago, offering his version of America: "I see an America where all can work who are able to work—where nobody need be wretched—where the aged dwell in dignity. . . .

UP, September 23, 1952

NIXON TELLS HIS STORY after Democrats exposed the fact that California friends had made contributions to cover his expenses when in the Senate. Nixon defended himself on television. Making the most of the opportunity, he spoke of his wonderful daughters, his dog Checkers, his wife's cloth coat. People loved it—he could stay on the ticket.

"I see an America where slums and tenements have vanished and children are raised in decency and self-respect. . . .

"I see an America where no man is another's master, where no man's mind is dark with fear.

"This is our design for the American cathedral—and we shall build it, brick by brick, stone by stone, patiently, bravely, prayerfully."

The result of the election was a landslide victory for Eisenhower. He received 33,079,308 votes against Stevenson's 26,584,344; the electoral vote stood 442 to 89; Stevenson did not carry a state outside the South.

But the victory of Eisenhower was a personal victory—not one for the Republicans. The Senate was almost evenly divided, with 48 Republicans, 47 Demo-

766

HECKLING NIXON AFTER HIS TELEVISION SPEECH. The Republican vice presidential candidate, about to enter an Oregon hotel two days after his television appeal, is escorted by his bodyguards past a line of good-humored hecklers. They hold sandwich boards with the inscription, "Give Nickels for Nixon." Everybody thought it a funny demonstration.

UP, September 25, 1952

crats and one independent—Wayne Morse—while the House had 221 Republicans and 209 Democrats.

In conceding his defeat in the early hours of the morning in Springfield, Stevenson said in a touching speech: "Someone asked me, as I came in, down on the street, how I felt, and I was reminded of a story that a fellow-townsman of ours used to tell—Abraham Lincoln. He said he felt like a little boy who had stubbed his toe in the dark. He said that he was too old to cry, but it hurt too much to laugh."

Commenting on it, Eisenhower said, "The train, the automobile, and the podium served as in the past, but the plane and television extended the range as never before. 1952 was the last year when whistle-stopping was the major mode of electioneering."

'Sic 'Im, Checkers'

767

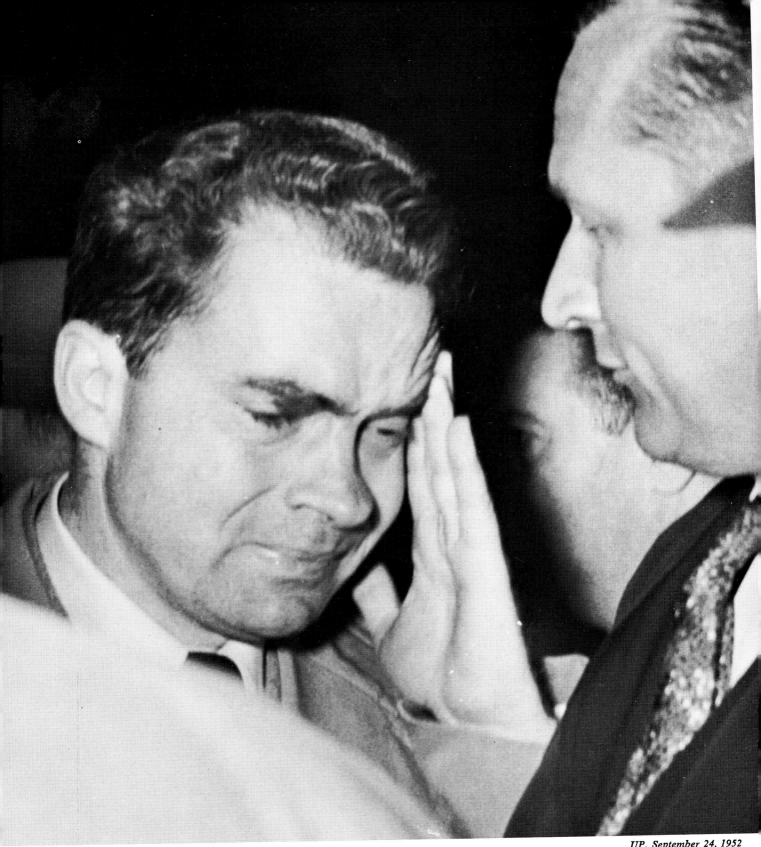

UP, September 24, 1952

OFF CAMERA: Nixon met Eisenhower in Wheeling, West Virginia, a day after his speech. There the General told him, "Dick, you're my boy," and said that he could remain on the ticket. Nixon was overcome with relief and emotion.

UP, September 24, 1952

ON CAMERA: For the benefit of the photographers, their faces are beaming. Eisenhower greets Nixon on his arrival in Wheeling, W. Va., and they shake hands with each other, trying to hide the tension and strain of the past several days.

And Stevenson reflected on the ordeal: "You must emerge, bright and bubbling with wisdom and well-being, every morning at eight o'clock just in time for a charming and profound breakfast talk, shake hands with hundreds, often literally thousands of people, make several inspiring 'newsworthy' speeches during the day, confer with political leaders along the way and with your staff all the time, write at every chance, think if possible, read mail and newspapers, talk on the telephone, talk to everybody, dictate, receive delegations, eat, with decorum—and discretion!—and ride through city after city on the back of an open car, smiling until your mouth is dehydrated by the wind, waving until the blood runs out of your arm, and then bounce easily, confidently, masterfully into great howling halls, shaved and all made up for television with the right color shirt and tie—I always forgot—and a manuscript so defaced with chicken tracks and last minute jottings that you couldn't follow it, even if the spotlights weren't blinding you in the eye every time you looked at them. . . .

"But the real work has just commenced—two or three and sometimes four hours of frenzied writing and editing of the next day's immortal mouthings so you can get something to the stenographers, so they can get something in the mimeograph machine, so they can get something to the reporters, so they can get something to their newspapers by deadline time. . . . Finally sleep, sweet sleep, steals you away, unless you worry—which I do."

Eisenhower had been supported by most of the country's newspapers; 993 daily papers with about 40.1 million readers were for him, while only 201 papers with a tenth of the circulation were for Stevenson.

Errors in handling the campaign had cut into the Stevenson vote. President Truman felt that the firing of the Democratic National Committee chairman was a blunder, as was the moving of Stevenson's headquarters to Springfield, because these decisions alienated the party professionals. The President criticized Stevenson's taking a defensive position on the issue of Com-

UP

STEVENSON BARES HIS TAX DECLARATION. After the Nixon revelations Stevenson published his past ten years' returns, challenging Eisenhower to show his also.

UP, October 2, 1952

CAMPAIGN BALLYHOO. A replica of Stevenson's gubernatorial office was built in a television studio—from where he addressed the nation.

The New York Times.

CITY EDITION
Fair and warm today. Fair and slightly cooler tomorrow.
Temperature Range Today—Max., 68; Min., 50
Temperatures Yesterday—Max., 69; Min., 47
Full U. S. Weather Bureau Report, Page 39

Copyright, 1952, by The New York Times Company.

VOL. CII....No. 34,608.   Entered as Second-Class Matter, Post Office, New York, N. Y.   NEW YORK, SATURDAY, OCTOBER 25, 1952.   Times Square, New York 36, N. Y. Telephone Lackawanna 4-1000   FIVE CENTS

SUBWAYS STALLED BY POWER FAILURE AT HEIGHT OF RUSH

Blast and Fire Short-Circuit Signals of I.R.T. and B.M.T., Force Trains to Crawl

THOUSANDS ARE DELAYED

All of Brooklyn and Most of Manhattan Hit—Bingham Blames Old Equipment

A small explosion and fire in a manhole outside a powerhouse serving the B. M. T. and I. R. T. subway lines caused one of the city's worst delays in transportation last night at the height of the rush hour.

The fire affected the signal light system on the I. R. T. throughout Brooklyn and most of Manhattan, and on the B. M. T. from Times Square to the lower end of Manhattan. Trains crawled through the tubes, halting intermittently between stations to make sure that all precautions were being observed.

Many thousands of homeward-bound riders and others converging into the Times Square area were caught in the slowdown. Others, seeking alternate routes of surface transportation, jammed into buses and waited vainly for empty taxis.

Sidney H. Bingham, chairman of the Board of Transportation, declared the delay would not have occurred had the city heeded his request for new power equipment.

Equipment Held 'Out-moded'

He explained the present "outmoded" circuit-breakers had been installed in 1904 and, with the increase in subway facilities, were unable to "accelerate fast enough to pick up the surge" when trouble developed.

The explosion and fire happened at 6 P. M. in a manhole on Fifty-

Hurricane Injures 70 As It Pounds at Cuba

By The Associated Press.
MIAMI, Fla., Oct. 24—A hurricane packing 165 - mile - per-hour winds slashed a broad path across Cuba today on a course that would take it near South Florida's Gold Coast.

The storm thundered inland over Cuba, with its center near Cienfuegos on the south coast, beating a sixty-mile-wide swath through rich sugar cane and ranch land. Gales lashed outward seventy-five miles from the center of the storm, described as one of the most violent in recent years.

Seventy persons were reported injured when their homes were blown down. These casualty figures covered only two areas in the path of the storm.

Heavy damage to roads, crops and fruit trees was reported in the Cayman Islands, 125 miles below Cuba. The commissioner

Continued on Page 29, Column 2

HARLEM TENEMENT CITED ON 91 COUNTS

First Week of Firetrap Survey Lays 84 Violations to Same Owner in 4 Other Buildings

By CHARLES G. BENNETT
The end of the first week of the city's firetrap survey in Harlem brought a crackdown yesterday by Frederick S. Weaver, Deputy Commissioner of Housing, on the Klahr Realty Corporation, owner of a five-story tenement building at 1 West 118th Street.

Notices that ninety-one violations of the multiple dwelling law had been found at the building, the first one searched by housing inspectors, were sent yesterday by Mr. Weaver to the Klahr Corporation at 1456 Fifth Avenue.

The owner was also notified of eighty-four violations found in four buildings it operates at 1467-66-63

COAL OWNERS ASK PUTNAM TO REVIEW W. S. B. WAGE CURB

Economic Stabilizer Gets Plea for the Approval of 40c Cut From Rise of $1.90 a Day

END OF STRIKE KEY AIM

Moses Says Operators Want to Resume Output—Lewis Role Is Not Indicated

By JOSEPH A. LOFTUS
Special to The New York Times.
WASHINGTON, Oct. 24—Northern soft coal operators asked the Government tonight to reconsider the Wage Stabilization Board's refusal to approve 40 cents of the wage increase of $1.90 a day they contracted to pay the miners. About 350,000 members of the United Mine Workers have been on strike since Monday in protest against the board's decision.

Harry M. Moses, president of the Bituminous Coal Operators Association, representing mainly northern tonnage, filed a petition with Roger L. Putnam, Economic Stabilization Administrator. Whether he also filed a petition with the Wage Stabilization Board could not be learned.

Mr. Moses would not indicate whether his appeal had any basis other than the willingnes of the operators to honor the contract he made and their desire to restore production.

The Wage Board majority of public and industry members held in their decision that an increase of more than $1.50 would give to the miners a larger increase than had been received by workers in any other major industry and might set a pattern for inflation that would break anti-inflation controls.

Putnam Studying Petition

CHINESE RECAPTURE KEY KOREAN CREST

Seize Top of 'Sniper Ridge'— Allied Assaults on Red Strongholds Repelled

By LINDESAY PARROTT
Special to The New York Times.
TOKYO, Saturday, Oct. 25—Chinese Communist infantry in a

EISENHOWER WOULD 'GO TO KOREA'; STEVENSON ASSAILS 'SLICK' PLANS; ACHESON BARS PEACE OF DISHONOR

Support of the U. N. Urged by Nominees

Gen. Dwight D. Eisenhower and Gov. Adlai E. Stevenson declared their support of the United Nations last night and called upon the people of the nation to back the world organization.

[Texts of messages by two candidates appear on Page 2.]

Commending the United Nations for its prompt action in Korea, Gen. Eisenhower asked the American people "to reaffirm their devotion to the peaceful hopes of free men everywhere" and the United States "as a proud member of the United Nations pledge again our strength, our fortune and our sacred honor to the end that no free nation shall ever again be destroyed upon this earth."

In backing United Nation action in Korea, General Eisenhower supported the action taken

Continued on Page 2, Column 6

U.S. EXPLAINS VIEW

Secretary Tells U. N. Unit Washington Is Ready and Eager to End War

ASKS APPROVAL OF EFFORT

Again Rules Out Any Forcible Repatriation and Cites 17 Pacts Signed by Soviet

Excerpts from U. N. address by Mr. Acheson are on Page 4.

By A. M. ROSENTHAL
Special to The New York Times.
UNITED NATIONS, N. Y., Oct. 24—Secretary of State Dean Acheson told United Nations delegates today that the United States was ready and eager to end the Korean war but that peace could not be "purchased at the price of honor."

For almost three hours Mr. Acheson held the floor of the Political and Security Committee of the General Assembly, taking the sixty delegates on a carefully impassioned, calmly spoken and meticulously detailed review of the Korean war, all that led up to it and the long drawn-out attempts to end it. Several times in his speech he carefully underlined the charge that it was the Soviet Union that had trained and equipped the army of North Korea, sent it into a war of aggres-

ACHESON SPEAKS: The Secretary of State addressing the United Nations here yesterday.

The New York Times by Meyer Liebowitz

Stevenson Fears a 'Munich' In Rival's Asian Troop Plan

By W. H. LAWRENCE
Special to The New York Times.
ABOARD STEVENSON TRAIN, in New York, Oct. 24—

GENERAL IN PLEDGE

'First Task' Would Be 'Early and Honorable' End of the War

HE GIVES FOUR PROMISES

Bars Appeasement—Declares 'Record of Failure' Led to Far East Fighting

Text of the Eisenhower speech in Detroit is on Page 8.

By ELIE ABEL
Special to The New York Times.
DETROIT, Oct. 24—Gen. Dwight D. Eisenhower gave the nation his pledge tonight that if elected President he would go to Korea to seek an early and honorable end of the war there.

He promised to "forego the diversions of politics" and to concentrate on the task of closing the war—a conflict that was never inevitable or inescapable, he said, but one that resulted from the Truman Administration's repeated failures to heed the warnings of Republicans. The General made his statements in a speech prepared for a campaign rally at the Masonic Auditorium here.

To pledge an end of the Korean fighting by any "imminent, exact date" would be dishonest, the Republican candidate for President asserted, but it would be equally

New York Times

"I'LL GO TO KOREA"—The headlines of Eisenhower's famous Detroit speech, which secured him the election.

---

munists in government and implying that a mess did exist in Washington.

Nonetheless, Truman thought that on the whole the Democratic candidate had done a good job. "In his campaign for the presidency Stevenson lived up to his reputation as a man of eloquence. His eloquence was real because his words gave a definition and meaning to the major issues of our time. He was particularly effective in expressing this nation's foreign policy. He made no extravagant promises. He was not vague with generalities, but talked to the point. While some felt he may have talked over the heads of some people, he was uncompromising in being himself. His was a great campaign and did credit to the party and the nation. He did not appeal to the weakness but to the strength of the people. He did not trade principles for votes."

Analyzing Stevenson's performance, James Reston said that his greatest strength was his speeches (although many did feel that the candidate spoke over the heads of people), while his greatest weakness was his inability to be free and easy with the voters. He had nothing to match Eisenhower's warm and friendly off-the-cuff manner of delivering his material. The Korea and corruption issues cut into the big-city vote which Stevenson, as a Democrat, ought to have garnered.

Clare Boothe Luce predicted during the campaign that Ike would get the woman's vote because he "exemplifies what the fair sex looks for—a combination of father, husband and son." The General accepted, and thus removed from politics, most New Deal reforms. Once these Democratic achievements were beyond politics, Stevenson could make little political hay with them, and the Democratic slogan, "You never had it so good," which was used to counteract the Republicans' "It's time for a change," came out second best.

Stevenson said: "Even so, if it hadn't been for that going-to-Korea business, I might have beaten him."

But perhaps it was not the issues as much as the personalities. The General's boyish grin and folksy manner made up for his often clumsy speeches. He be-

UP, October 27, 1952

McCARTHY CHARGES that Stevenson associates with subversives and that he "has given aid to the Communist cause."

came a synthetic personality, a trade name advertised all across the country. "I like Ike" buttons were seen everywhere. Americans were eager to believe in a hero who would remove the burdens from them without calling on them for great decisions. "Let Papa do it." Eisenhower was able to appear as many things to many men: as a defender of civil liberties to anti-McCarthyites and as shoulder to shoulder with him in his fight against Communism to the Senator's supporters; as a man not inclined to get involved in foreign entanglements to the isolationist Taft men, and as a firm believer in collective security and international agreements to internationalists. Particularly he could shine as not being a politician. "He was above politics," wrote Marquis Childs. "That was part of his attraction for a people who tend to regard the political process as, at best, a dubious luxury, an expensive kind of fame in which we are forever indulging the players. In so many respects he was uncommitted, a clean slate on which each citizen could write his own hopes and aspirations."

Cartoon by Herblock, October 1952
REBUKING THE MUDSLINGERS

THE EISENHOWER INAUGURATION

UP

THE OLD AND THE NEW. Eisenhower fetches Truman from the White House to drive with him to the ceremony.

UP

NIXON TAKES THE OATH from California's Senator Knowland, with Presidents Truman and Hoover present.

Wingfield, U.S. Army photo

AS CHIEF JUSTICE VINSON GIVES THE OATH.

UP, October 25, 1955

THE FIRST PHOTOGRAPH AFTER THE HEART ATTACK. President Eisenhower faces the cameras on the sun deck of the Fitzsimons Army Hospital in Denver a month after his heart attack. L. to r.: Dr. Howard Snyder, his personal physician, Chief Nurse Lt. Col. Edythe Turner, Col. Byron Pollock, Lt. Lorraine Knox, and Sgts. Walling and Vaughn.

DWIGHT D. EISENHOWER

The administration had a hard beginning. A great many problems—foreign and domestic—faced Eisenhower. The Korean War had to be brought to its conclusion, some kind of accommodation with the Soviets had to be effected.

The new President had to make up his mind on the Bricker Amendment, which proposed to limit the President's powers to enter treaties, thus increasing the authority of Congress over foreign relations; he had to do something about the "enslavement" plank of the Republican platform, repudiating the Yalta agreements and giving "genuine independence of those captive peoples"— meaning the satellites under Soviet rule; he had to cut the budget and had to give a "new look" to the expenditures in the armed forces.

But his most difficult task was how to deal with Congress—which had a bare Republican majority and in which the Republican right-wingers asserted their power. It was such a frustrating struggle that Eisenhower was toying with the idea of forming a new political party into which Republicans and Democrats who shared his moderate views could join.

The Cabinet was a "business administration" dominated by the former heads of large corporations. Charles E. Wilson, the white-haired former president of General Motors, was given the Secretary of Defense post. But before he could be sworn in there was an uproar about his $2½ million worth of stock in General Motors and about his bonuses and other rights in that corporation. As General Motors was the leading Defense Department contractor, Wilson's holdings in that company pointed to a clear conflict-of-interest issue. Wilson was reluctant to sell his securities because he would have to pay heavy taxes on them. In the hearing before the Senate committee, he remarked: "What was good for our country was good for General Motors, and vice versa," which appeared in the press as: "What's good for General Motors is good for the country." Not until he promised to get rid of his holdings, was he confirmed by the Senate. Other appointees also had to dispose of their stocks.

George Humphrey, the head of the National Steel Corporation and Mark Hanna & Co. in Cleveland, who combed his hair the same way as Eisenhower, became Secretary of the Treasury and the strongest influence in the administration. Mrs. Oveta Culp Hobby, the administrator of the Federal Security Agency, was appointed the first Secretary of Health, Education and Welfare. Ezra Taft Benson, the pious Mormon, was named Secretary of Agriculture; John Foster Dulles, Secretary of State. Martin P. Durkin, the former president of the plumbers' union, was to be Secretary of Labor, but, unhappy in the post, he resigned before the year was out.

Eisenhower regarded his Cabinet—"nine millionaires and a plumber"—as a strong one. He was confident he could right the nation's ills with them.

Wage and price controls were ended, military spending reduced, construction work limited; economies were attempted. Still, the forthcoming 1954 budget indicated a whopping ten-million-dollar deficit. Senator Taft berated the President that he had not kept his promise to the American people of a balanced budget and that he was taking the nation "right down the road Truman traveled." Eisenhower, like other Presidents before him, found that it was easier to criticize the "unbalanced

CANDIDATES IN 1956

DWIGHT EISENHOWER
(1890———) possessed the country's confidence. His cheerful smile, his honesty, his father image were reassuring in troubled times; thus he was enthusiastically renominated. In the last weeks of the campaign the Anglo-French-Israeli attack on Egypt and the Hungarian upheaval made Americans rally even more closely behind the President. He won by 35,590,472 votes to Stevenson's 26,022,752.

RICHARD M. NIXON
(1913———), whom President Eisenhower suggested serve in some other capacity during his second term, wanted to continue as Vice President. Stassen of Minnesota, who had organized the "Dump Nixon" move in 1952 after the slush-funds disclosure, tried again to convince the party to choose another candidate. But the majority endorsed Nixon and the Republican ticket won easily.

ADLAI E. STEVENSON
(1900–1965), no longer a reluctant candidate, was renominated by the Democrats. Conducting a strenuous primary campaign, he asked for the voters' support "not in the name of complacency but in the name of anxiety. . . . I do not want to assume that power under any false pretenses." But Eisenhower's popularity was at its peak, and Stevenson's warnings on atomic fallout were too frightening.

ESTES KEFAUVER
(1903–1963), Senator from Tennessee, the well-known head of the committee investigating organized crime, campaigned hard and successfully in the primaries, chalking up victories; but in the convention the party leaders decided again in favor of Stevenson. As a consolation prize he was given second place after a dramatic fight with the young Senator John F. Kennedy whom he defeated narrowly.

UP

THE REPUBLICAN GOLFERS. Eisenhower and Nixon at the Cherry Hills Country Club at Denver. The President, a passionate golfer, often played eighteen holes in the morning and nine in the afternoon. It was after one such day that he suffered his heart attack on Sept. 24, 1955.

budget" than to do something about it. When it came to cuts, the departments screamed, the Senators and Congressmen shouted. They all wanted to cut other figures, not those which affected their departments, which affected their states. And though Eisenhower reduced the new funds for the Air Force by five billion, it was not enough for a balanced budget. (The 1954 budget showed a $3,-116,966,256 deficit, the 1955 budget one of $4,180,-228,922. Of Eisenhower's eight budgets, only 1956, 1957 and 1960 ended with a surplus—about a billion and a half dollars in each of those years; in all other years there was a deficit—in 1959 a record-breaking $12,426,986,751.)

At the time the new President began his term, the Korean War was two and a half years old, and the battle lines had hardened into a stalemate. 33,629 Americans

Abbie Rowe, October 14, 1956

ON HIS SIXTY-SIXTH BIRTHDAY EISENHOWER ACKNOWLEDGES THE GREETINGS OF VISITORS

had been killed in the war, 103,284 wounded, and yet the settlement was far away.

On March 5 Joseph Stalin died. "Well, what do you think we can do about *this?*" Eisenhower asked his associates. He was advised to seek a way to improve relations with Russia. The new Soviet leaders, who took over the government after Stalin's death, had similar ideas—they, too, wanted to reduce the tensions of the cold war; they too searched for peace. Thus in a speech delivered at the annual meeting of the American Society of Newspaper Editors on April 16, Eisenhower said: "We welcome every honest act of peace." He urged disarmament and international control of atomic energy and offered "a substantial percentage of the savings achieved by disarmament to a fund for world aid and reconstruction."

Stalin's death reduced tensions; in Korea the peace negotiations began to make progress. The Communists accepted the UN proposals that sick and injured prisoners be exchanged before an armistice. Eisenhower opposed those who spoke of "stopping the spread of Asian Communism" and was ready to settle for a "limited victory." Accepting the line between North and South Korea—basically the same as before the war—the truce was signed on July 28.

Eisenhower's ending the war was widely acclaimed. He had the love and the trust of Americans, he had the respect of the world. Taft said of him: "He is a man of good will."

Not long after the Korean armistice—in the middle of August—the Russians exploded their first hydrogen

779

Abbie Rowe, May 8, 1953

THE CABINET. Left to right: Henry Cabot Lodge, Ambassador to the United Nations; Douglas McKay (Interior); George Humphrey (Treasury); Vice President Nixon; Herbert Brownell, Jr. (Attorney General); Sinclair Weeks (Commerce); Oveta Culp Hobby (Health, Education, and Welfare); Presidential Assistant Sherman Adams; Philip Young (Civil Service chairman); Joseph Dodge (Budget Director); Robert Cutler (behind Dodge); Arthur Flemming (Defense Mobilization Director); Martin Durkin (Labor); Arthur Summerfield (Postmaster General); John Foster Dulles (State); the President; Charles Wilson (Defense); Ezra Taft Benson (Agriculture); and Harold Stassen (Director of Foreign Operations).

UP

THE "LITTLE" CABINET. William J. Hopkins, executive clerk; Wilton B. Persons, special assistant; Sherman P. Adams, presidential assistant; Emmett J. Hughes, administrative assistant; the President; Gabriel Hauge, administrative assistant; Thomas E. Stephens, appointments secretary; (blocked) Frank K. Saunderson, administrative officer.

bomb. Eisenhower, deeply concerned about the atomic arms race, tried to find a way for peaceful coexistence with the Russians. Consulting with Churchill and with French Premier Laniel in Bermuda, he worked on a speech to be delivered before the United Nations in December. It was the celebrated atoms-for-peace speech. He proposed to the principally involved governments that they "begin now and continue to make joint contributions from their stockpiles of normal uranium and fissionable materials to an International Atomic Energy Agency."

The atoms-for-peace plan fired the imagination of all peace-loving people. It seemed to be a sensible proposal. The Russians listened to it with interest, their diplomats talked about it in Washington and at the Big Four Ministers meeting in the following January, but gradually

THE CABINET WIVES. Left to right, front row: Mrs. Martin Durkin (Labor); Mrs. Douglas McKay (Interior); Mrs. Richard Nixon; Mrs. Eisenhower; Mrs. Charles E. Wilson (Defense); Mrs. Herbert Brownell (Attorney General); Mrs. Harold Stassen (National Security Administrator). Back row: Mrs. Sinclair Weeks (Commerce); Mrs. George Humphrey (Treasury); Oveta Culp Hobby (Federal Security Administrator), who would become first Secretary of Health, Education, and Welfare in the spring of 1953; Mrs. Sherman Adams (Presidential Assistant); Mrs. Arthur Summerfield (Postmaster General); Mrs. Henry Cabot Lodge (Chief U.S. Delegate to the UN); and Mrs. Joseph Dodge (Budget).

their ardor cooled and nothing came of it.

As 1954 opened, internal difficulties increased. In the middle of February, Secretary of Agriculture Benson reduced the support price for dairy products from 90 percent of parity to 75 percent, even though Eisenhower urged a gradual reduction.

At the end of that month came the showdown over the Bricker Amendment. The President, who was hesitant to take a firm stand against the amendment, was now forced to declare that he was "unalterably opposed" to it because "it would so restrict the conduct of foreign affairs that our country could not negotiate the agreements necessary for the handling of our business with the rest of the world." He won—the amendment was defeated by a single vote.

About the same time the storm over Senator McCarthy broke. It arose when McCarthy had the army dentist Major Irving Peress appear before his committee. Peress, accused of Communist activities, invoked the Fifth Amendment and refused to answer the charges. The Senator demanded Peress's court-martial, but the commandant of Camp Kilmer gave the dentist an honorable discharge. McCarthy, raging with fury, called General Zwicker, the commandant of the camp, before his committee and dressed him down. He told him that "he was not fit to wear a uniform" and that he was either dishonest or unintelligent, with "the brains of a five-year-old child."

The cup of forbearance spilled over. McCarthy—who had investigated the Voice of America, who had fought the appointment of Charles Bohlen as Ambassador to

THE END OF AN ERA. On March 5, 1953, Joseph Stalin died. With his death the cold war entered a new phase. Eisenhower said of Stalin: "The extraordinary thirty-year span of his rule saw the Soviet empire expand . . . from the Baltic Sea to the Sea of Japan, finally to dominate 800 million souls. . . ." Under him Russia became a world power.

IN THE QUEST OF PEACE. On Decem 1953, Eisenhower appeared before the G Assembly of the United Nations pleading f limitation of arms, for peaceful uses of the and for friendly relations between East and

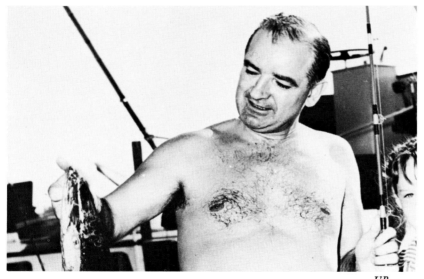

THE SENATOR FROM WISCONSIN, Joseph McCarthy, a reckless demagogue who exploited the country's fear of Communism. He assailed the State Department for harboring Communists and wanted all "subversive" literature taken from public libraries. But President Eisenhower remained silent; he would not "get in the gutter with that guy."

THE McCARTHY INVESTIGATORS, Cohn and G. David Schine, two brash youn, soon to be called "musketeering gumshoes, from one European capital to another, intir ing officials and banning books in USIA lib

Russia, who had attacked the Eisenhower administration on television, who had castigated Britain's "blood trade" with China on the eve of Eisenhower's departure for his conference with Churchill in Bermuda, who had sent his assistants Roy M. Cohn and G. David Schine to Europe where the two "musketeering gumshoes" investigated American information agencies, intimidating officials and ordering books they disliked removed from USIA li-

braries, and whose staff director J. B. Matthews had charged the Protestant clergy with being "the largest single group supporting the Communist apparatus in the United States"—found his nemesis. The army would not let him undermine the military establishment of the nation.

Eisenhower, though aroused, told advisers who urged him to repudiate McCarthy: "I will not get in the gutter

MAKING NEW ALLIANCES. John Foster Dul-
[les] Eisenhower's Secretary of State, was ever on
[the] move to harness together a structure of inter-
[natio]nal alliances and defenses against Commu-
[nism], notably the military "treaty organization."

UP

A NEW CHIEF JUSTICE. On October 5, 1953, Eisenhower appointed
Earl Warren, the former Governor of California, to replace the late
Frederick Vinson. During his two terms Eisenhower appointed four
justices to the Supreme Court. Seated: Frankfurter, Black, Warren, Reed, Douglas. Standing: Clark, Jackson, Burton and Minton.

UP

[TH]E INVESTIGATING FEVER MOUNTS. The
[McC]arthy committee lashed out, recklessly ac-
[cusi]ng people of Communist affiliations. Here
[Rob]ert Kennedy, a committee lawyer, documents
[the] activities of the army dentist Irving Peress.

UP

THE DOWNFALL OF THE DEMAGOGUE. In the famous televised
Army-McCarthy hearings, the country saw what kind of man the
Senator was. And what the President, what the press, what his colleagues in the Senate were too cowardly to do, the homespun Boston
lawyer Joseph N. Welch did—he revealed the Senator's deceptions.

with that guy." But at Dartmouth College he advised the
students, "Don't join the book burners!" and he wired the
religious leaders who appealed to him after Matthews's
attack on the Protestant clergy: "Such attacks betray
contempt for the principles of freedom and decency." Yet
he would not come out openly against the Senator.

The army did. On March 11 each member of the
McCarthy subcommittee received a copy of a report (pre-

pared under the guidance of Sherman Adams, the presidential assistant) charging that Roy Cohn, the chief
counsel for McCarthy, had threatened army officials if
they did not give favored treatment to his chum Private
David Schine.

This led to a televised hearing which kept the country
enthralled for thirty-six days.

What politician and press had failed to do, the television cameras did—they revealed McCarthy's true character. The country could see him in the flesh, how he operated. And when Joseph Welch, the homespun Boston lawyer, cried out in despair, "Don't you have any decency left?" he spoke for most Americans.

And while the army-McCarthy hearing proceeded, in April and May the Communists scored a major military victory in Indochina.

On April 7 Eisenhower exclaimed that Indochina was vital to the free world and if it fell, other states would fall too and be taken over by the Communists. He advanced the domino theory.

"You have a row of dominoes set up, and you knock over the first one," he said, "and what will happen to the last one is the certainty that it will go over very quickly. So you have a beginning of a disintegration that would have the most profound influences." After Indochina would come Burma, Thailand, Malaya and Indonesia—and the falling of these countries would weaken the defenses of Japan, Formosa, the Philippines, and even Australia and New Zealand.

Still he did not compel the United States to get involved in an Asian war. "I cannot conceive of a greater tragedy for America than to get heavily involved now in an all-

out war in any of those regions, particularly with large units."

Exactly a month after his speech — on May 7 — the French garrison of Dienbienphu fell. The Vietminh won a smashing victory. In the peace negotiations at Geneva, France agreed to a partition of Vietnam, giving the northern part of the country to the Communists. Though America was not a participant in the conference, it gave its approval to the treaty.

A few weeks later—in September—the Southeast Asia treaty (SEATO) was signed in Manila, a collective security measure for that part of the world.

Dulles, who had earlier hoped to smash "the organized body of Communist aggression by the end of 1955" and "reduce" the war to a guerrilla war which would be won in 1956 by the Indochinese, was satisfied. The treaty seemed to secure American influence in Indochina. He was convinced that Communism would collapse, but that while it lasted it should be discouraged from aggression. "Local defenses must be reinforced by the further deterrent of massive retaliatory power," Dulles said before the Council on Foreign Relations in New York in January 1954, repeating the President's words from his State of the Union message of a few days earlier. "We shall not be the aggressors, but we and our allies have and will maintain a massive capability to strike back."

With the mid-term election approaching, Eisenhower tried to put through Congress a program which would be helpful to Republican candidates. But Congress was not in a cooperative mood. It passed a comprehensive tax revision bill, giving over a billion dollars in tax relief to individuals and corporations, but it failed to pass amendments to the Taft-Hartley Act, it failed to pass the health insurance bill, it failed to pass the bill allowing eighteen-year-olds to vote, and it failed to pass a number of other bills desired by the President.

The Democrats went into the campaign with high hopes. They had plenty of issues to attack: McCarthyism; a declining economy and recession; the Dixon-Yates contract, which allowed private utility interests to build a plant and provide power for the atomic energy installation in the Tennessee Valley Authority area.

Vice President Nixon campaigned for the Republicans, giving more than two hundred speeches and holding over a hundred press conferences. He antagonized the Democrats by equating them by implication with Communists. He asserted in his speeches that the administration was kicking Communists and fellow travelers out of the government by the thousands. Nixon lumped together all security risks—drunks, deviates, unreliables—and made it appear that they were all Communists. In this he followed the President, who boasted in his State of the Union address that the administration had dismissed 2,200 people under the new security program.

COMMENT ON THE McCARTHY CRAZE

Herblock, October 1954

THE SENATORS RELAX. Henry M. ("Scoop") Jackson of Washington, John F. Kennedy of Massachusetts, Michael J. ("Mike") Mansfield of Montana relax by playing ball on a Sunday afternoon. All three of them had a notable future.

The result of the election was a Republican defeat. Both houses of Congress had a Democratic majority. In the Senate the Democrats had 48 seats against the Republicans' 47 and 1 independent, in the House they had the comfortable majority of 29 (232 seats against the Republicans' 203).

Although the Democrats won, their victory helped Eisenhower. The right wing of his party was clipped of its power; Senator McCarthy lost his chairmanship of his committee and was subsequently censured by the Senate. The Democratic leaders were responsible professionals—they cooperated with the President on important pieces of legislation.

Once more Eisenhower attempted to ease relations with Russia. At the Big Four conference in Geneva he suggested, looking straight at Bulganin and Khrushchev, "that we take a practical step, that we begin an arrangement . . . immediately. These steps would include: To give each other a complete blueprint of our military establishments, from beginning to end, from one end of our countries to the other; lay out the establishments and provide the blueprints to each other.

"Next, to provide within our countries facilities for aerial photography to the other country—we to provide

UP

AFTER EISENHOWER'S HEART ATTACK ON SEPTEMBER 24, 1955, Dr. Paul Dudley White, the famous Boston heart specialist, answers questions from the press at Lowry Air Force Base in Denver. He told them that the President had suffered a coronary thrombosis, caused by a clot in one of the vessels supplying blood to the heart and that, in time, other vessels would replace the damaged one.

IN ANOTHER PRESS CONFERENCE at Chicago on January 21, 1956, Dr. White tells the newspapermen that the President would be physically able to

UP

EVERYTHING IS FINE. Vice President Nixon and press secretary Hagerty vividly reassure the reporters that all is well, after Nixon flew from Washington to Fitzsimmons Army Hospital in Denver to visit with the stricken President.

EVERYTHING IS FINE. A battery of cameramen takes pictures of the President, showing

the facilities within our country, ample facilities for aerial reconnaissance, where you can make all the pictures you choose and take them to your own country to study; you to provide exactly the same facilities for us and we to make these examinations, and by this step to convince the world that we are providing as between ourselves against

the possibility of great surprise attack, thus lessening danger and relaxing tension."

Eisenhower's open skies proposal was acclaimed by a world seeking peace, but like the atoms-for-peace plan it brought no practical results.

The country speculated whether the President would

continue performing his duties as his heart was nearly healed. Next to him (with folded hands) is Dr. Irving Page, president of the Heart Association.

UP

THE DOCTORS TELL THE PRESS in the White House on February 14, 1956, that Eisenhower is physically fit to run for a second term. From left to right: the doctors: Maj. Gen. Leonard Heaton, Commandant of Walter Reed, Col. Byron Pollock, Paul Dudley White, Howard Snyder, the White House Physician, Col. Thomas Mattingly and Walter Thack (Snyder's assistant).

UP

the world that he is well on the way to recovery one month and a day after the heart attack.

UP

EVERYTHING IS FINE. After his return to Washington, Eisenhower tries out his swing on the White House grounds as a photographer captures the event with a telephoto lens. On the right is his son Major John Eisenhower.

run again for re-election. In his memoirs he had written that originally he planned "to limit my political life to the four years ahead." But the party needed him; without him there could be no Republican victory. When a Republican state chairman was asked what he would do if Eisenhower refused, he said: "When I get to that bridge, I will jump off it."

On September 24, 1955, while vacationing in Denver, he was stricken by a heart attack, described at first as "a mild coronary thrombosis." The next day Dr. Paul Dudley White, the prominent cardiologist who was called in from Boston, called it a "moderate attack"—it was

Cartoon by Don Hesse, January 1956

Cartoons by Hungerford, February 1956

"neither mild nor serious."

When Eisenhower recovered, he remained silent about whether he would run again, though he did allow his name to be entered in the New Hampshire primary. Not until the last day of February did Eisenhower come to a "positive, that is, affirmative," decision. "After the most careful and devoutly prayerful consideration . . . I have decided that if the Republican party chooses to renominate me, I shall accept. . . . As of the moment, there is not the slightest doubt that I can perform as well as I ever have all the important duties of the Presidency." On television that evening he told the country that a second term would require "a regime of ordered work activity, interspersed with regular amounts of exercise, recreation and rest."

Even as a part-time President the country wanted him.

On June 9 he had another bout with sickness—this time with ileitis—but after the operation was over, he said he was "in better shape" than before and reassured his supporters that he would run again. His press secretary James Hagerty explained later that the decision came during the President's three-week convalescence at Gettysburg: "It was then that he faced the sheer, god-awful boredom of not being President."

The Democrats once more endorsed Stevenson, and he announced in November 1955: "I shall be a candidate for the Democratic nomination for President next year, which, I suspect, is hardly a surprise."

This time the nomination was not offered to him on a silver platter. He had to fight for it and win. In the primary states of Minnesota, Florida and California he had to lock horns with Estes Kefauver, his main rival. In Minnesota, which was considered safe for him, Stevenson suffered an unexpected defeat, with Kefauver polling about 57 percent of the vote. In Florida, Stevenson won by a narrow margin, but in California he won decisively,

... AND THE WORD CAME ON FEBRUARY 29, 1956

UP

forcing Kefauver to withdraw. The field was now clear.

In these primaries two issues became clear. The first was Stevenson's support for "gradualism" in school integration (he had opposed the use of Federal troops to enforce the 1954 Supreme Court decision and also opposed an amendment to the pending school-aid bill denying Federal aid to any segregated school). However, he angered Southerners by demanding a stronger civil rights plank (including support of the Supreme Court decision) than had been in the previous platform. The other issue was Stevenson's proposal to have the United States cease testing hydrogen bombs and to tell the decision to the world.

Before the opening of the Democratic convention political pundits predicted that Stevenson would take the nomination on the first ballot. But many of the party's influential leaders could not warm up to him. Ex-President Truman made a spirited appeal for Harriman, "who

will make a fighting and successful candidate because he is dedicated to the principles of our party—the New Deal and the Fair Deal." He felt that Stevenson was "too defeatist to win." In his memoirs Truman states that he had made his statement about Stevenson to "make it easier for Stevenson to disassociate himself from me politically."

Despite Truman's opposition, the convention took Stevenson. And after he had been chosen, the candidate told the delegates that it was up to them to select his running mate. "The choice will be yours," he said. "The

Cartoons by Fischetti, October 1955

Cartoon by Herblock, September 1955

profit will be the nation's." The convention decided on Kefauver, who after a spirited battle defeated Senator John F. Kennedy, the young Senator from Massachusetts.

In his acceptance speech Stevenson pledged himself to work for a "New America":

"I mean a new America where poverty is abolished and our abundance is used to enrich the lives of every family.

"I mean a new America where freedom is made real for all without regard to race or belief or economic condition.

"I mean a new America which everlastingly attacks the ancient idea that men can solve their differences by killing each other."

The Democratic platform compromised on civil rights. Omitting a specific pledge to enforce the 1954 Supreme Court decision, it called the decision the "law of the land" and affirmed: "We reject all proposals for the use of force to interfere with orderly determination of these matters by the courts," but the party would "continue its efforts to eliminate illegal discrimination of all kinds."

The platform promised to extend the Civil Service and "secrecy in government" and to improve Congressional procedures; it charged the Eisenhower administration with indecision, drift and contradiction; it pledged arms to Israel; it came out against the admission of Red China

to the United Nations, and supported free access to the Suez Canal; it denounced the Republican farm program and pledged 90 percent and ultimately 100 percent of parity; it promised increased production of atomic power for peace, liberalized Social Security and expanded public housing, the repeal of the Taft-Hartley Act and an increase in the minimum wage, reduced taxes on small businesses and small incomes, more public power and aid to small business.

In contrast to the Democrats, the Republicans' convention was like old home week. Before the meeting, Harold Stassen, special assistant to Eisenhower on disarmament problems, wanted Nixon dumped from the ticket as he would cost it "millions of votes," and promoted the candidacy of Christian Herter, Governor of Massachusetts; but by convention time Stassen had made his peace with Nixon and even seconded his renomination. The ticket was the same as four years before: Eisenhower and Nixon.

The platform praised the Eisenhower record and, citing its achievements, it pledged continued strong defense, a tax reduction "consistent with a balanced budget," a Federal security program to remove the "irresponsible" and unfit from government service, and gave a mild endorsement to the Supreme Court ruling, promising patience and moderation in carrying it out.

Eisenhower based his campaign on the themes of

STEVENSON DRAFTS A RESPONSE
TO THE EISENHOWER ANNOUNCEMENT
Cornell Capa, Magnum

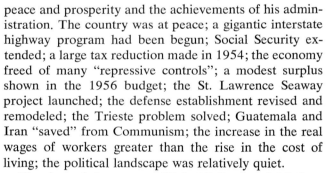

Cartoon by Bill Winstein, July 1956
GETTING READY FOR THE MOMENTOUS SHOW

Cartoon by Herblock, August 1955
"NOVEMBER—AND YOU?"

peace and prosperity and the achievements of his administration. The country was at peace; a gigantic interstate highway program had been begun; Social Security extended; a large tax reduction made in 1954; the economy freed of many "repressive controls"; a modest surplus shown in the 1956 budget; the St. Lawrence Seaway project launched; the defense establishment revised and remodeled; the Trieste problem solved; Guatemala and Iran "saved" from Communism; the increase in the real wages of workers greater than the rise in the cost of living; the political landscape was relatively quiet.

Eisenhower's image was still that "of a cheerful father, a kindly pastor, a modestly confident hero." Leonard Hall, the Republican party chairman, repeated the effective tactic of 1952: he sent out a "Truth Squad," Senators and Congressmen who followed the Democratic candidates, stopped where they stopped, making instant rebuttals of their allegations. Stevenson quipped that the Republican Truth Squad bore the same relationship to truth as a fire department did to a fire. "It will extinguish it if it can."

Stevenson's campaign focused on those states where a slight change of vote would cause a switch. He hoped to induce the Democrats who had supported Eisenhower in 1952 (about 24 percent of the 1948 Democratic vote) to return to the fold. And he hoped to demonstrate by a

public display of energy and stamina the contrast between his and Eisenhower's physical condition.

There was division among his supporters. The intellectuals, led by Willard Wirtz, wanted the same high-level campaign as in 1952; the political in-fighters, like Wilson Wyatt, counseled expediency. "The essential difference between the Stevenson of 1952 and the Stevenson of 1956 is that today he is a willing candidate who fought for and won the nomination on his own terms. It is the difference between being a free agent and a captive of circumstance," wrote Cabell Phillips.

The contest, as usual, began on Labor Day. Stevenson

Cartoon by Hungerford, March 1956
IKE'S RUNNING MATE HOLDS ON TIGHTLY

Cartoon by Fischetti, April 1956
BUTTON, BUTTON, BUTTON, BUTTON, BUTTON

Cartoon by Ivey, St. Petersburg Times

denounced the Republicans for "the smugness, the complacency, the self-satisfaction which are today's great danger in America." He cited the "ugly patches of poverty and insecurity" which still existed. And he asserted that the Republicans "see business as an end in itself, progress as something you measure on a slide rule and prosperity as a statistic."

A day later Eisenhower claimed cold war gains which put the free world in a "stronger" position. "And I don't see how anyone can look at the facts as they exist and deny that."

Stevenson told an American Legion convention in Los Angeles that calling the Democrats the "war party" was "infamy" and part of a "catalogue of deceit." He elaborated on his two provocative proposals: one, to end the draft "at the earliest moment consistent with national safety"; two, to halt the testing of nuclear bombs. He regretted "that the administration chose to casually dismiss my proposal last spring to halt further testing of nuclear devices, conditionally upon adherence by other atomic powers to a similar policy."

While Stevenson and Kefauver were spanning the country and Truman was "giving 'em hell," Eisenhower left it to his Vice President to refute the Democratic charges "on a higher level than in the past," and Nixon promised not to make "personal attacks on the integrity of our opponents." But he added: "You don't win campaigns with a diet of dishwater and milk toast."

Stevenson ripped into Eisenhower for turning over the leadership to Nixon and for not being "master of his own house." He also raised the health issue. "Everyone shares in the sympathy for the circumstances which have created a part-time Presidency. But, we cannot understand—and will not accept—turning the government over to men who work full time for the wrong people or a limited group of people." In a sharply partisan speech, with some of the flavor of Truman's oratory, Stevenson said that Nixon "seems to sail downwind no matter which way the wind

ANOTHER HEALTH CRISIS. Just after midnight on the morning of June 9, 1956, Mrs. Eisenhower called Dr. Howard Snyder, saying that the President had a stomach-ache and could not sleep. Milk of magnesia did nothing, so the doctor went to the White House and stayed at the President's bedside. Before noon it was clear that this was no stomach-ache, and the President was taken by ambulance to Walter Reed Army Hospital. The X rays showed ileitis (causing an inflammation of the small intestine), and the President was operated upon at three o'clock in the morning of the tenth. After the three-hour operation, Eisenhower's press secretary Hagerty told reporters: "The President's condition continues very satisfactory."

blows." Commenting on the similarity of the two party platforms, Stevenson declared: "Well, when someone says to me that the two parties' programs are just about the same, I say that so are two checks signed by different people. The question is which one can be cashed and which one will bounce."

Eisenhower answered him that he was going to stick to the truth and leave "the yelling" to the opposition. "The truth should be our campaign. . . . Although the peace we have is not a secure peace in which we may have confidence, there are still many, many thousands of American mothers that are mighty thankful that their sons are not on the battlefield."

Stevenson issued five major policy papers for a "New America"—a campaign innovation. The first, released in September, concerned the aged—"who have contributed most to making America the land it is today"—going far beyond the party platform in setting forth the goal of

enabling "a person to maintain his accustomed standard of living after the days of his regular employment have ended."

In the second he proposed that national education expenditures be increased by $500 million to a total of one billion dollars a year for the next ten years. "The dream of a New America," he wrote, "begins in the classroom."

Eisenhower answered that the Democrats had killed Federal aid to school construction that year and that Stevenson's program had thus been opposed by his own party; he called this the "strange spectacle of an apparently confused candidate."

Stevenson's third paper dealt with the nation's health, affirming that "Access to good medical care is a basic human right in a civilization founded, as ours is, on the dignity of the individual human being," and proposing that the government promote health care, though not at the expense of the private practitioner.

EVERYTHING IS FINE. The surgeon who operated on the President, General Leonard Heaton, uses a diagram of the intestine to explain about the operation. He said: "We look for a rapid and complete recovery, and feel that he will return to his good health in a short period of time." A reporter asked if the President's life expectancy had been affected. Dr. Snyder (seated) said: "We think it improves it." Then came the question everybody was waiting for—did he think the President should decline to run for re-election? Said Heaton emphatically: "I certainly do not."

But Eisenhower himself had the quote of the day, shortly after his operation when he remarked: "What a bellyache!"

His fourth paper issued in October, gave a "Program for True Economy," in which Stevenson outlined his views on taxation, monetary and budget policy, while his fifth paper, near the end of the campaign, dealt with natural resources: "The most obvious and distressing evidence of the failure of the Eisenhower administration to care for the public good is its giving away parts of the public domain to private interests; letting great natural sites for multi-purpose public projects be exploited for private gain; repudiating public power projects; urging legislation that would transfer private rights in national forests to a privileged few."

In his speeches Stevenson raised many issues. His farm speeches were particularly effective. A poll in *The New York Times* showed that farmers were switching back to him. The reasons for their discontent were low farm prices and resentment of the retention of Agriculture Secretary Ezra Taft Benson. Stevenson quipped that the real reason Eisenhower was running again was that "he can't afford to retire to his farm at Gettysburg while Benson is Secretary of Agriculture." Eisenhower called Stevenson's farm program "mockery and deceit," "a program for politicians, not farmers." Though he offered no definite program, he predicted "better times for every farmer soon." The President's position was that "Rigid supports did not cause high farm income. Wars—with their high demand—did that."

Stevenson kept returning to the issues of war and peace. In Pittsburgh he said: The "Eisenhower administration has not prepared, and evidently is not preparing, to carry out the atoms-for-peace program. . . . I can't accept the apparent administration position that we are powerless to do anything to stop this headlong race for extinction." Eisenhower answered that Stevenson was offering only the delusion of a "cheap and easy" peace that was "unjustified by world realities," and that "the truth

Cornell Capa, Magnum

OUTSIDE HIS HEADQUARTERS Stevenson has a conference in a parked auto with Mrs. Roosevelt and Mrs. Edison Dick.

UP

WATCHING THE KEYNOTE FILM, narrated by Senator Kennedy, are his wife and his sister Eunice Shriver.

before us is clear. Strong—we shall stay free, weak—we shall have only our good intentions to be written as our epitaph."

In Berkeley Stevenson charged that statements on foreign policy by Eisenhower and Dulles were "manifestly untrue," charged "irresponsibility" and "deception" abroad and "Pollyanna politics" at home. He ridiculed statements that our prestige had never been higher. "I sometimes think," he said, "that the most massive retaliation we have to worry about is verbal, and the target is us."

In Chicago he repeated his call for a world pact to end H-bomb testing; he wanted to make this the "first order of business" and was prepared to seek agreement with the Soviet Union, Britain and the other atomic powers "at whatever level, in whatever place" that gave promise of success, in order to avert a "stark, merciless black catastrophe." He called Strontium 90 "the most dreadful

ASKING FOR SUPPORT FROM TEXAS, John Chancellor of N BC broadcasts Senator Lyndon B. Johnson's decision.

Cornell Capa, Magnum

poison in the world." "The search for peace," so Stevenson argued, "won't end. It will begin with the halting of these hydrogen tests. What we will accomplish is a new beginning, and the world needs nothing more than a new beginning."

In Seattle Eisenhower attacked Stevenson's "half-truths" and "hit-and-run statement" and "the big straddle." "This is not a sick America," he declared, "but a healthy America—not a weak nation, but a strong one—not a fearful people, but a confident people."

In Portland he replied to Stevenson's H-Bomb proposals. "We reject," he said, "any thought that we will say: We are going to disarm and we hope that you will do so one day. We will do it in unison." The President called the election a choice in foreign policy between "hard sense and experience versus pie-in-the-sky promises and wishful thinking."

In Youngstown, Ohio, Stevenson returned to his draft

UP

SENATOR HERBERT LEHMAN, who followed Franklin Roosevelt as governor of New York, is for Stevenson.

UP
THE CONVENTION PROGRAM

UP
MRS. EISENHOWER'S CHOICE

UP
JOE MARTIN'S BIG BUTTON

Cartoon by Liederman
NO AD-LIBS, PLEASE!

UP
STASSEN SECONDS NIXON AFTER ALL.

Cartoon by Talburt, August 1956
THE SELF-WAGGING TAIL

proposal. As a substitute for the draft he proposed a professional, specially trained, highly paid volunteer defense corps. He called the present system one of "incredible waste." "There is ample evidence," he said, "that this inexperienced personnel is not meeting today's needs." "I do add, and I think I speak for every person in America, that we will count it a better day when we find that these military needs can best be met by a system which does not mean the disruption of the lives of an entire generation of young men; which lets them plan their education and get started more quickly along life's ordained course."

With the development of the middle East crisis foreign affairs took on more urgency. The State Department, looking with disfavor upon Egypt's recognition of Red China and purchase of arms from Czechoslovakia, had abruptly canceled American support for the Aswan Dam and had persuaded other Western countries to do the same. Nasser then seized the Suez Canal, creating a threat to West European security because most of its oil came through that waterway. Britain and France were

THE CHOSEN REPUBLICAN TICKET ACKNOWLEDGES THE OVATION OF THE DELEGATES. *UP*

preparing for war, but Dulles flew to London and dissuaded the leaders of the two countries from using force. His plan was to apply economic sanctions by rerouting the oil, thus drying up the Suez traffic and undermining Nasser's power. However, Secretary of the Treasury Humphrey threw a wet blanket on the scheme, because it would threaten a balanced budget. By October Britain, France and Israel were convinced that Nasser would close the canal to them and pounce upon Israel while the United States would remain aloof from the

struggle. On October 12 Eisenhower said that the "crisis is behind us." On October 29 Israel, expecting an attack from Egypt, sent her army and paratroopers deep into Egypt's Sinai Peninsula. Though England and France joined in the attack, the United States refused to be drawn into the conflict. Eisenhower asked for a cease-fire in the United Nations and was supported by the Soviet Union.

News came of a revolt in Hungary following upon major unrest in Poland. Budapest students demonstrated in sympathy for the Poles and quoted the lines that had

STEVENSON CAMPAIGNING

Cornell Capa, Magnum

A HAPPY POSE, but Stevenson spoke of serious issues; he advocated the unilateral suspension of our atomic bomb tests and he came out strongly for curtailment of the draft.

A CHARACTERISTIC SN

IN THE PARADE ON
NEW YORK'S 42ND STREET
Cornell Capa, Magnum

SHOT TAKEN BY HIS SON. Wherever he was—in planes, trains, cars—Stevenson wrote and rewrote his speeches.

launched the 1848 revolution against the Hapsburgs: "We vow we can never be slaves." They had been joined by a major part of the populace. But Russian tanks moved into Budapest to put down the rebellion. One observer saw "a column of rioters march with arms outstretched into machine gun fire." Young men took to rifles and submachine guns; they filled wine bottles with gasoline to fight the Russian armor. The Hungarians expected American help, but they received only fiery propaganda from the Voice of America. And the President assured the Soviets of America's peaceful position. Thus the Hungarians, struggling for their freedom, were left

EISENHOWER IN ONE OF HIS CHARACTERISTIC CAMPAIGN STANCES, PARADING ALONG NEW

to their fate.

The Suez and the Hungarian crises helped the chances of Eisenhower. The country would not change Presidents in time of crisis. Americans felt that Eisenhower, the war hero, could better deal with the military situation than the civilian Stevenson.

Stevenson charged that Eisenhower sought to "mislead" the nation and to make "political capital out of a crisis that could engulf the world. . . . A week ago he came before that so-called press conference on television arranged by the advertising agents of the Republican campaign more for adulation than for information. He announced that he had 'good news' about Suez. But there is no good news about Suez. Why didn't the President tell

us the truth? Why hasn't he told us frankly that what has happened in these past few months is that Communist rulers of Soviet Russia have accomplished a Russian ambition that the Czars never could accomplish?"

Eisenhower replied that he would not involve the country in hostilities. The armed action of Britain, France and Israel "can scarcely be reconciled with the principles and purposes of the United Nations Charter," he said, although this statement "in no way minimized our friendship with these nations nor our determination to retain and strengthen the bonds among us."

Soviet Premier Bulganin sent a note on disarmament to the United States in which he said that the U.S.S.R. "fully shares the opinion recently expressed by certain

THE *NEWS* HEADLINES AN IKE SPEECH

UP

UP

'ORK'S EIGHTH AVENUE

THE VICE PRESIDENT'S
CAMPAIGN PLANS
Abbie Rowe

THE WINNING TICKET. On election night in the Sheraton Park Hotel, Washington, President Eisenhower and Vice-President Nixon acknowledge the cheers of their supporters who assembled there in force to learn the result. Behind the happy victors are Eisenhower's son John and Mrs. Eisenhower's mother Mrs. Elivera Carlson Doud.

prominent public figures in the United States concerning the necessity and the possibility of concluding an agreement on the matter of prohibiting atomic weapon tests and concerning the positive influence this would have on the entire international situation."

The President called the note a "propaganda exercise" and said that it "departs from accepted international practice in a number of respects," especially in Bulganin's sending it "in the midst of a national election campaign of which you take cognizance." Stevenson at first criticized Eisenhower for dismissing the note instead of giving it "sober consideration," but the next day he joined him in

RIGHT
DRAFTING THE CONCESSION MESSAGE.
With Willard Wirtz and Arthur Schlesinger, Jr., as photographed by John Fell Stevenson.

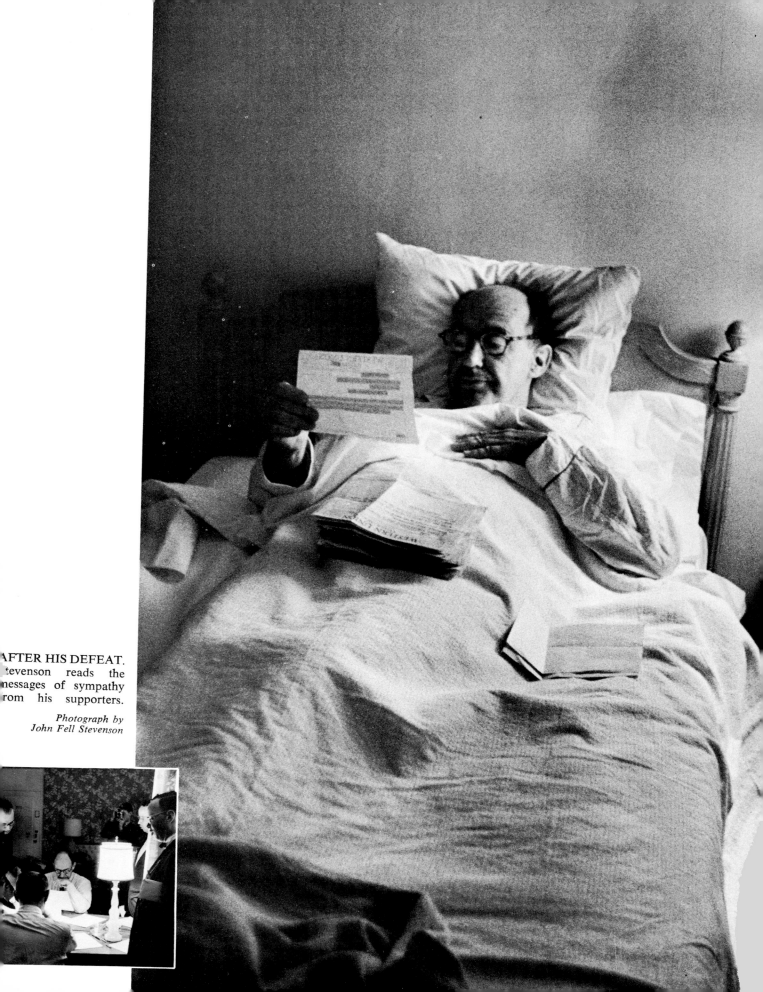

AFTER HIS DEFEAT.
Stevenson reads the
messages of sympathy
from his supporters.

Photograph by
John Fell Stevenson

U.S. Army photograph

TAKING THE OATH OF OFFICE FOR THE SECOND TIME from Chief Justice Earl Warren. John Fey, clerk of the Supreme Court (in the center), holds the Bible. The seats of the temporary stand are filled with prominent figures. Along the left front are former Governor Dewey, Secretary of State Dulles, the President's son Major John Eisenhower, his grandmother Mrs. Doud, and Mrs. Pat Nixon, Mrs. Eisenhower and former President Hoover. Beside Major Eisenhower are Clare Boothe Luce, the wife of the publisher, and the President's personal physician, Major General Snyder.

In the group near Hoover are presidential assistant Sherman Adams (his chin is partly blocked) and Leonard Hall (only his bald head and one eyeglass lens show), who would become the Republican National Chairman. Also with glasses is "Fishbait" Miller, the colorful doorkeeper for the House. Further back are the top military leaders: Admiral Alfred Richmond (Coast Guard), General Randolph Pate (Marine Corps), General Maxwell Taylor (Army), Admiral Arleigh Burke (Navy), General Nathan Twining (Air Force) and Admiral Arthur Radford (Chairman, Joint Chiefs of Staff).

On the right, above Eisenhower, is Arizona's venerable Senator, Carl Hayden. Also on the right are perennial candidate Harold Stassen and John Sparkman, the Democratic Vice Presidential nominee in 1952. To his left are Senator Styles Bridges of New Hampshire and John McCormack of Massachusetts. Then come two of the most powerful men in Congress: the former Democratic Speaker Sam Rayburn and behind him the current Republican Speaker Joseph Martin. Beside Rayburn is Senator Theodore Green of Rhode Island. Back by the column are UN Ambassador Henry Cabot Lodge and Supreme Court Justice Tom Clark. Some of those present were figures of opera and the theater. In the right foreground is Marian Anderson; in the next-to-last row is Pearl Bailey. In the row below her are producer Sol Hurok and Ethel Merman.

806

"resentment at the manner and timing of Premier Bulganin's interference in the political affairs of the United States."

Eisenhower asserted that the present deterrent ability of the United States "could be lost if we failed to hold our superiority" in nuclear weapons. He added that detection of a violation was not always possible "except in the case of the largest weapons" and that a continuance of the "present rate of H-bomb testing—by the most sober responsible scientific judgment—does not imperil the health of humanity." And he offered aid to Poland and other "freedom-loving" satellites. The aid was unspecified, but the President maintained that part of our "mission" was "to help those freedom-loving peoples who need and want and can profitably use our aid that they may advance in their ability for self-support and may add strength to the security and peace of the world."

In his Madison Square Garden speech Stevenson

pressed the issue: "Will the peace and health of the world be advanced if all nations stop exploding hydrogen weapons? The answer is 'yes.'" "Would such an agreement weaken the relative position of the United States? The answer is 'no.' The transcending question before humanity is whether there will be any tomorrow at all."

He emphasized that the Middle East crisis was the product of the "complete" and "catastrophic" failure of Eisenhower's foreign policy. "Our Middle Eastern policy is at an absolute dead end. Had the Eisenhower administration taken a firm stand in the Middle East, had it aided Israel with arms and territorial guarantees, we might, I believe, have been able to prevent the present outbreak of hostilities. And if this government of ours had not alternately appeased and provoked Egypt, I think we would command more influence and respect, not only there, but throughout the Arab world today."

Summing up his ideas on foreign policy, Stevenson

THE INAUGURAL BALL. The Eisenhowers, with Alice Roosevelt Longworth, who married in the White House in one of the major social events of more than half a century ago (see page 479), as they come into the National Guard Armory.

UP

THE INAUGURAL PARADE. The President with two grandchildren, Dwight David and Barbara Anne, and the Vice President with daughters Patricia and Julie. Eleven years later Julie Nixon was engaged to David Eisenhower.

A LITTLE COFFEE BREAK DURING THE PARADE

WELL, WELL . . . FANCY SEEING YOU HERE! The President and his Vice President at opposite ends.

said in Minneapolis: "The last four years have presented America and the free world great opportunities to exploit the weaknesses in the Communist ranks and advance the cause of peace. But this administration has failed to take advantage of them.

"The death of Stalin caught us off guard. The uprisings in East Berlin caught us off guard. The uprisings in Poznan caught us off guard. The most recent revolts in Poland and Hungary obviously caught us off guard. . . . The result is that we have lost our closest and best friends, and what friends have we won? Russia? Egypt? Of course not."

In his final campaign speech in Boston, Stevenson once more raised the issue of Eisenhower's health: "As distasteful as this matter is, I must say bluntly that every piece of scientific evidence we have, every lesson of history and experience indicates that a Republican victory tomorrow would mean that Richard Nixon would probably be President of this country within the next four years."

Mrs. Eisenhower in mink, Mrs. Nixon in her Republican cloth coat. Ex-President Hoover is between the Eisen- howers. Behind him are Clare Boothe Luce and Joseph Martin. Behind the Nixons: the Styles Bridges of N.H.

The result of the election was an overwhelming victory for Eisenhower. The President had a 9½-million popular majority, receiving 35,590,472 votes against Stevenson's 26,022,752. The electoral vote stood 457 for Eisenhower, 73 for Stevenson. Of the Southern states Eisenhower carried not only Virginia, Texas, Tennessee and Florida as in 1952, but Louisiana and Kentucky as well. Stevenson had only six Democratic states in the South: North Carolina, South Carolina, Georgia, Alabama, Arkansas and Missouri. And as in 1952 it was a personal victory, not a Republican one. Democrats retained control over both Houses of Congress, the Senate by 49 to 47, the House by 235 to 200. It was the first time in modern presidential elections that the President failed to carry Congress with him.

For Eisenhower the lesson of the election was: "Modern Republicanism has now proved itself and America has approved of modern Republicanism. Modern Republicanism looks to the future and this means it will gain constantly new recruits."

JOHN F. KENNEDY and LYNDON B. JOHNSON

First terms are the successful ones. During his first term Washington was on the pinnacle of popularity, as were Jefferson, Monroe, Grant, Wilson and Franklin D. Roosevelt. So was Dwight D. Eisenhower. But second terms are the difficult ones. Washington had his troubles with his—at the end of his administration the opposition called him a man who had debauched the country; Jefferson left the office under a cloud; Grant was abused, as was Wilson; Roosevelt brought to his later terms the hatred of his opponents.

Eisenhower was not hated, but the trust in his "infallibility" was shaken. He was still loved. "To most Americans, he seemed before everything else to have the smiling, warmhearted assurance that the comfortable America of the past is still the America of the present," wrote Marquis Childs, but analyzing the President's achievement in his book, *Eisenhower, Captive Hero*, he was more severe. He blamed Eisenhower for the diminishing powers of the Presidency. "Taking a detached view of his own role, the President has been unwilling or unable to exercise many of those powers. Declining in both authority and prestige, the office has resembled much more nearly what it was in the late nineteenth century, when a ceremonial president was content to let the tides of economic destiny have their way."

David Whitney made a similar observation:

"Eisenhower sought to organize the presidency in the style of a commanding general. He tried to have a staff which would keep him informed and provide him with alternate courses of action, although the ultimate responsibility remained his. He did not see himself as the leader of a political party, in the old-fashioned sense, as evi-denced by a note written in his diary a few days before his inauguration in which he commented that he hoped 'that I will be compelled to have little to do, during the next four years, with the distribution of Federal patronage.'"

And even such an admirer of the President as Richard Wilson, one of the editors of *Look* magazine, had to admit that while "Eisenhower understood well his constitutional role, but less well the spiritual and moral leadership of the Presidency, he failed those who expect the President of the United States to be keeper of the nation's conscience."

As President, Eisenhower temporized, he avoided real issues, he passed the problems on to his successor. But he gave the country the breathing spell it desired after the turbulent Roosevelt-Truman years and the Korean War. He was responsible for ending that war, and he genuinely sought peaceful accommodation with the Russians. He was a unique figure in exactly the same sense that General Grant was after the Civil War. Walter Lippmann, who had urged the country to elect him in 1952 rather than Stevenson, made this judgment at the end of the second term: "It was not too difficult to be the national leader on a policy of doing as little as possible in a time when nobody wanted to do very much." And to round up the quotes of the political pundits, here is one by Richard Lee Strout, who dipped his pen in acid when he wrote that Eisenhower, "the beatific general," gave the country "a breathing spell and 'sound' economics, which meant inflation, a rousing deficit, and three recessions in eight years—a combination that really took ingenuity. (Yet, to do him justice, he only slowed the clock down; he didn't

JOHN FITZGERALD KENNEDY
Author's Collection

CANDIDATES IN 1960

JOHN F. KENNEDY
(1917–1963), three times a Congressman and twice elected Senator from Massachusetts, son of Roosevelt's Ambassador to England and grandson of a mayor of Boston, had a winning personality. Harvard graduate, a writer and historian, he won the confidence of youth and the academic community. His handicap was his Catholicism; his asset, his father's millions. He won by a small margin.

LYNDON B. JOHNSON
(1908———) began in Texas as a teacher and entered politics as secretary to a Congressman. Once Texas director of the National Youth Administration, he now was a Senator and the Democrats' powerful floor leader, often giving a helping hand to the Republican administration. When the first place eluded him, he took the Vice Presidency after party leaders insisted on balance for the ticket.

RICHARD M. NIXON
(1913———), Vice President under Eisenhower for two terms, was the Republicans' choice to succeed the President. He campaigned on his maturity and broad experience, but when he accepted Kennedy's challenge to debate with him on television, the country saw that Kennedy was no less mature and no less prepared than Nixon. The Republican ticket lost, with 34,108,157 to 34,226,731.

HENRY CABOT LODGE
(1902———), the former Senator from Massachusetts who lost his seat to John F. Kennedy, was appointed by Eisenhower as the U.S. representative to the United Nations, where he served for seven years. Because of his popular and liberal stand on foreign issues, it was thought that he would bring a good balance to the Republican ticket; thus he received his party's vice presidential nomination.

JACQUELINE LEE BOUVIER
(1929–   ) became a most popular first lady. From a well-to-do family, she was educated at Vassar, the Sorbonne and George Washington University. She first met her husband while interviewing the newly elected Senator for a Washington *Post and Times-Herald* story. They were married on September 12, 1953. Daughter Caroline was born in 1957 and son John Jr., just after his father was elected President. Mrs. Kennedy spoke French, Italian and Spanish, and brought a new note of culture to the Executive Mansion.

UPI, November 9, 1960

THE PRESIDENT WITH HIS FAMILY. Sitting: Eunice Kennedy Shriver; his parents Mr. and Mrs. Joseph P. Kennedy; Jacqueline Bouvier Kennedy; and his youngest brother Edward M. Kennedy. Standing: Ethel Skakel Kennedy, the wife of Robert; Stephen Smith, Jean's husband; Jean Kennedy Smith; the President; Robert F. Kennedy; Pat Kennedy Lawford; Sargent Shriver, the husband of Eunice; Joan Bennett Kennedy, the wife of Edward; and Peter Lawford, the husband of Pat.

set it back.)"

Historians when polled about Eisenhower as President rated him at the bottom of the ladder with Grant and Fillmore. But one is far too close to the Eisenhower era to make a judicious assessment of it, to give a fair picture of Eisenhower's achievements and to bare his failures.

He moved into his second term under a dark cloud, and before the term was over the clouds hung heavier than ever before.

The troubles in the Middle East prompted him to go before Congress with a request for $200 million in economic aid and development funds, and he asked Congressional approval for the use of military forces "to secure and protect the territorial integrity and political independence of such nations requesting such aid against overt armed aggression from any nation controlled by international Communism." The Eisenhower Doctrine, as this became known, did not differ from the adminis-

Abbie Rowe

MAY 9, 1957: President Diem of South Vietnam visits the White House to talk with Eisenhower and Dulles about the aid his government receives.

UPI

JANUARY 10, 1957: The President presents his policy against world Communism.

UPI

SEPTEMBER 26, 1957: Federal troops set a precedent protecting the rights of Negro students to attend school at Little Rock, Arkansas.

Abbie Rowe

JANUARY 3, 1959: Alaska is admitted to the Union, the first new state since 1912.

tration's containment policy. The doctrine had little effect on Egypt, and on the whole it was not successful—though Lebanon and Jordan were saved from the clutches of the Soviets. But Iraq was lost to Arab influence after King Faisal's assassination.

As the summer of 1957 waned and American schools opened their doors, the President was faced with a serious domestic crisis. In Little Rock, Arkansas, nine Negro students attempted to enter Central High School, which

until then had taken only white students. A howling mob opposed their entry into the school. Governor Faubus called out the National Guard and removed it only after the Court ordered him to do so. On September 23, after the troops were gone, the students again attempted to enter the school. Again they were kept away by an unruly mob, turning the demonstration into a riot. The authority of the Federal Government challenged, the laws of the country disobeyed, Eisenhower was forced to send Fed-

OCTOBER 4, 1957: Sputnik I of Russia, the first artificial satellite, starts the space age.

UPI

UPI

JULY 17, 1958: U.S. Marines march in Beirut, Lebanon, to protect the shaky government from toppling, using the Eisenhower Doctrine.

Abbie Rowe

MARCH 18, 1959: Hawaii is admitted to the Union, coming in as the 50th state.

U.S. Army

APRIL 1959: Secretary of State Dulles became seriously ill and was forced to resign his office on April 5. He died of cancer on May 24.

eral troops to Little Rock. The day one thousand paratroopers arrived in the city, the President told the nation on television that events left him no alternative but to enforce the decision of the courts.

October brought more serious troubles. On the fourth of that month Russia launched a satellite to orbit the earth. Sputnik I heralded the beginning of the space age. The country was agog. How could this have happened? How could a primitive, backward country have overcome the most technically advanced civilization in the world? Russia's achievement astounded the nation. Stock jokes about that country's technical inefficiency—"Give a Russian a monkey wrench to tighten a bolt and he will wreck the car"—rang hollow. It was manifest that the Soviets were ahead of the United States in scientific and technical education. "Why can't Johnny read?" was asked. "Why did Ivan do so much better?" people wanted to know.

LISTENING TO THE PRESIDENT'S STATE OF THE UNION MESSAGE IN 1958. The Republican Cabinet (in front) applauding: John Foster Dulles (State), Robert B. Anderson (Treasury), Neil H. McElroy (Defense), William P. Rogers (Attorney General), Arthur Summerfield (Postmaster General); (middle row) Democratic Senators Lyndon B. Johnson (Texas), Mike Mansfield (Montana), Carl Hayden (Arizona), Theodore F. Green (Rhode Island), Harry Byrd (Virginia), (top row) Allen J. Ellender (Louisiana), Albert Gore (Tennessee), A. S. Mike Monroney (Oklahoma), Thomas C. Hennings, Jr. (Missouri), John L. McClellan (Arkansas), Henry Jackson (Washington) and John Kennedy (Massachusetts).

The success of the Sputnik, following so hard on the Little Rock troubles, diminished Eisenhower's stature in the country.

The controversy over school integration, over Russia's technological breakthrough and our inadequate educational system was underscored by the sagging economy. The number of unemployed mounted. "The mood of the country deepened to a dark gray," noted Marquis Childs. "This was the winter of our discontent following on the autumn of our disillusion."

If the opening year of Eisenhower's second term brought poor results, its second year seemed even worse. The slump continued; by July, 5.3 million workers out of

a labor force of 70.4 million were jobless. The President's popularity in the polls dropped by almost twenty points.

Foreign affairs came to the fore. On March 27 Nikita Khrushchev was named Premier of the Soviet Union replacing Bulganin. Once again one man was in full control of the Soviet Union and its people. Khrushchev pledged "peaceful coexistence" with capitalism and better relations with the United States. Four days later Russia suspended its nuclear weapons tests. The United States and Britain followed suit.

Khrushchev came for a look-and-see visit to America and was very warmly welcomed in San Francisco. He moved on to Camp David in Maryland to have "a general

LISTENING TO THE PRESIDENT'S STATE OF THE UNION MESSAGE IN 1959. Front: Supreme Court Justice Hugo L. Black and Chief Justice Earl Warren; Cabinet members Dulles (State), Anderson (Treasury), McElroy (Defense), Rogers (Attorney General), Summerfield (Postmaster General), Seaton (Interior), Benson (Agriculture), Strauss (Commerce), Mitchell (Labor), Flemming (Health, Education, and Welfare); and Lodge (Ambassador to the UN). Second row: Senators Johnson (Texas), Mansfield (Montana), Green (Rhode Island), Hayden (Arizona), Hennings (Missouri), and across the aisle Pastore (Rhode Island), Kennedy (Massachusetts), Gore (Tennessee), Church (Idaho).

discussion of the world situation" with Eisenhower. The cold war grew lukewarm. A thaw was in the offing.

But there were troubles elsewhere. Vice President Nixon went to South America on a goodwill tour and was hooted by anti-American demonstrators. In Lima he was spat upon, shoved and booed; in Caracas the mob attacked his car. The demonstrations marked a low point in American prestige in Latin America.

The Chinese Reds began their massive shelling of the offshore islands Quemoy and Matsu.

The crisis in Little Rock flared up once more in September when the Supreme Court ordered immediate racial integration in the high schools of that city. In re-sponse, schools were closed in Arkansas and Virginia. Eisenhower staved off the storm. In Richard Wilson's opinion, "He could not give his whole heart to the imperatives of justice involving crisis of race and freedom of belief. He could uphold the Presidency by sending para-troopers to enforce school integration in Little Rock, but he could not lead the nation in a relation of the heart and soul to make the white and black man social equals."

His political judgment was questioned, his do-nothing attitude criticized. His administration came under severe attacks when his closest associate was accused of influ-ence-peddling. "Assistant President" Sherman Adams was charged before a Congressional investigating committee of taking presents from his friend, Bernard Gold-fine, a Boston businessman, who had received favors from the government. However valiantly Eisenhower defended Adams, he had to go.

That the forthcoming mid-term election would go against the administration was without question. Little Rock, Sputnik, recession, the influence-peddling of high officials left their mark on the mind of the electorate. The Democratic majority in the Senate increased by 15, and in the House by 48. Eisenhower now was in the hands of the Democratic leadership.

The second half of his term brought more reverses. In January 1959, Castro won control over Cuba. In April 1960, Syngman Rhee of Korea was overthrown. In June of that year the Congo flared up. Eisenhower's three goals, which he had proclaimed so confidently in his first inaugural address—peace, prosperity and progress—were further away than ever. The world was in a turmoil. Chinese Communism was militant in Asia, Russian Communism moved aggressively in Africa and Latin America. Cuba veered toward Communism.

These were the main issues which were to be debated in the forthcoming campaign.

The Democrats were confident of victory; thus many candidates vied for the nomination. The frontrunners were John F. Kennedy, the 43-year-old Senator from Mass-achusetts, and Hubert H. Humphrey, the 49-year-old Senator from Minnesota. Both were liberals, both held advanced political views. Kennedy had the advantage of unlimited funds—his father was a multimillionaire; Hum-phrey's campaign coffers were empty—he was a druggist's son. Kennedy's major handicap, next to his youth, was his religion. No Roman Catholic had ever been elected to the Presidency. The campaign of Al Smith was still fresh in the politicians' minds.

Kennedy's forebears were Irish immigrants, who had risen from poverty to affluence. His father, amassing a fortune in business ventures and on the stock exchange, raised a large family and prepared his four sons for polit-ical life. When the eldest son was killed in the war, the next oldest took over the banner.

Graduated *cum laude* from Harvard in 1940, Kennedy published his senior thesis in book form. *Why England Slept* was an analytical study of Britain's attitude to the

CARTOONIST HERBLOCK COMMENTS ON EISENHOWER'S DILEMMA

Herblock, August 1957
"CONGRESS DIDN'T GIVE US LEADERSHIP."

Herblock, September 1958
"WELL, YOU CAN'T LEAVE US NOW."

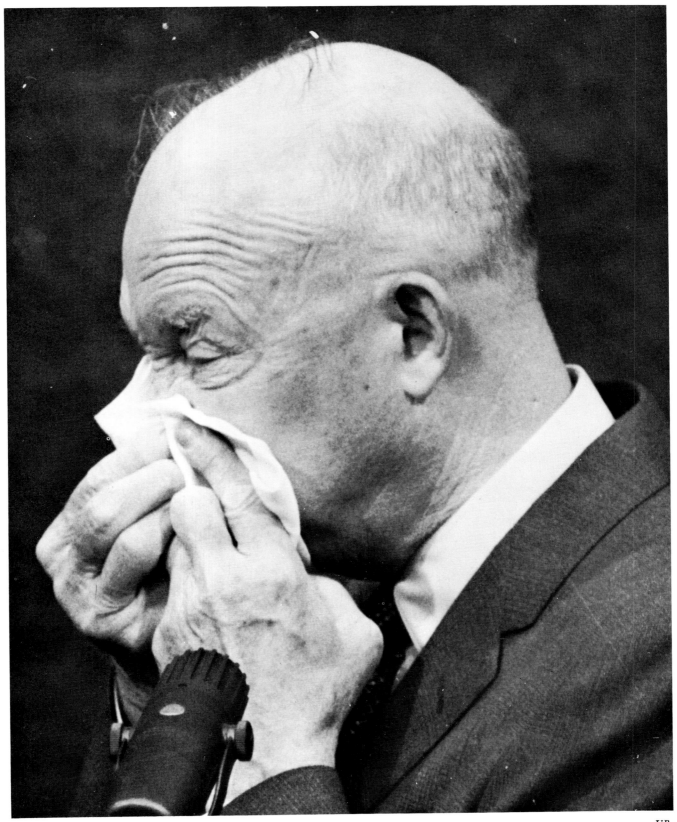

PRESIDENT EISENHOWER SNEEZES AND THE WHOLE COUNTRY TAKES COGNIZANCE OF THE SNEEZE

THE FOUR MAIN CONTENDERS for the Democratic nomination clasp hands in a determination of party solidarity. Senator Stuart Symington of Missouri, Senator Lyndon B. Johnson of Texas, Senator John F. Kennedy of Massachusetts and the two-time Democratic contender Adlai E. Stevenson. On the left, the singer Frank Sinatra who is not a candidate.

Nazi menace. His second book, *Profiles in Courage,* published sixteen years later, in 1956, was written while he was recuperating in the hospital from a near-fatal back operation. It brought him the Pulitzer Prize.

Ambitious, with a winning personality and an attractive wife, he displayed an erudition that captivated his audiences. He was a tremendous vote getter—he was elected three times to the House of Representatives, twice to the Senate, the last time in 1958 with a record-breaking majority of 875,000 votes. He had a fine war record—the well-publicized crash of his PT boat and his rescue of his men won him Marine Corps and Navy medals.

Humphrey was the youngest man to become Mayor of Minneapolis. Before that he taught political science. He was elected to the Senate three times and played an active and impressive part in that body. In the 1948 Dem-

ocratic Convention, he was the standard-bearer for the civil rights plank. In the Senate he was the proponent of legislation for important welfare laws. He worked assiduously for peace. Intelligent, articulate (perhaps too much so—once he started speaking he could never stop), Humphrey too had a winning personality; he too had an attractive wife.

Both men declared their intentions at the opening of election year. Circumstances forced them to enter the primaries. They both had to convince party chieftains of their strong support at the grassroots.

Out of the sixteen primaries, Kennedy entered eight, Humphrey five. Kennedy stayed out of Ohio and California but made arrangements with the two states' favorite sons, Governor Mike DiSalle and Governor Pat Brown, to hold the states for him.

WHAT ARE YOU HIDING? When teen-ager Nicki Hahn came to a Stevenson party with a "Kennedy for President" sign, Stevenson wanted to know what she had; but her friend Nancy McCarthy playfully hid the board out of Stevenson's reach.

The other Democratic hopefuls—Senator Lyndon B. Johnson of Texas and Senator Stuart Symington of Missouri—remained on the sidelines, expecting to succeed through political maneuvering at the convention rather than battling in the primaries. Johnson had the powerful support of the Speaker of the House, Sam Rayburn, while Symington had ex-President Truman in his corner. Adlai Stevenson's candidacy was promoted by Mrs. Roosevelt. The other hopefuls—Averell Harriman, Chester Bowles, G. Mennen Williams—fell by the wayside when Harriman was defeated for the New York governorship by Rockefeller, Bowles could not get the Senate nomination in Connecticut, and Williams had difficulties being re-elected Governor of Michigan.

The first crucial primary between Kennedy and Humphrey shaped up in Wisconsin, in Humphrey's own backyard. It was there the struggle began.

The Kennedy organization was superb, consisting of an array of unusually gifted men. Theodore Sorensen, 31, was his chief aide and speech writer. Kenneth O'Donnell, 35, a Harvard classmate of his brother, and Lawrence O'Brien, 42, were his political tacticians. Pierre Salinger, 34, handled his relations with the press. Louis Harris, 38, conducted the polls. John Bailey, the Democratic State Chairman of Connecticut, was doing the planning under the leadership of Robert Kennedy and Stephen Smith, the husband of Jean Kennedy. The best academic brains offered their services: Kenneth Galbraith, Arthur M. Schlesinger, Jr., Walter Rostow, Paul Samuelson, Harvey Cox.

Kennedy won Wisconsin with 56 percent of the popular vote. It was not a convincing victory; he carried the

Cornell Capa, Magnum
STEVENSON WAITS FOR THE NEWS.

UPI
JACKIE KENNEDY AFTER THE VICTORY

heavily Catholic districts but lost all four of the Protestant ones, and in the nondeclared Seventh District his lead was narrow. When asked by one of his sisters what the results meant, the candidate answered bitterly, "It means that we have to do it all over again. We have to go through every one and win every one of them, West Virginia and Maryland and Indiana and Oregon, all the way to the convention."

The Wisconsin result encouraged Humphrey. He was now ready to fight it out with Kennedy in predominantly Protestant West Virginia.

The religious issue in the state was overriding. To the opposition of an Episcopal bishop, Kennedy answered, "If religion is a valid issue in a Presidential campaign, I shouldn't have served in the House, I shouldn't now be serving in the Senate, and I shouldn't have been accepted in the United States Navy." The oath, so he went on, was the same for all these offices: to defend the constitution.

The last night of the campaign, when interviewed by Franklin D. Roosevelt, Jr., on television, Kennedy speaking with deep emotion poured out his feelings about his faith. He said, "When any man stands in the office of President, he is swearing to support the separation of church and state, he puts a hand on the Bible and raises the other hand to God as he takes the oath. And if he breaks his oath, he is not only committing a crime against the Constitution, for which the Congress can impeach him—and should impeach him—but he is committing a sin against God."

The results in the state gave Kennedy the smashing victory he needed. He carried all but seven of its fifty-five counties. He proved himself in a 95 percent Protestant state. No longer could his nomination be taken lightly. The badly mauled Humphrey was forced to withdraw.

After the West Virginia victory the other primaries went easily. Kennedy won them all. In Oregon he defeated the state's favorite son, Wayne Morse, and won by 73 percent of the votes. Indiana, Nebraska, Maryland were uncontested, but in all these states his vote was impressive. His supporters alleged that he had now enough delegates to win the nomination on the first ballot.

The Republican race for the nomination was simpler. Richard Nixon was the favorite. The President's illnesses had given him the opportunity to become a national figure. His courageous behavior in South America and his verbal exchange with Khrushchev at the opening of the American Exhibit in Moscow won him many admirers. But the image of a hatchet man and the image of "Tricky Dick" still haunted him.

At the outset it looked as though Rockefeller would challenge him. A large personal staff and some advertising agencies laid the groundwork for the Governor's candidacy. They soon discovered that the political and financial powers were behind the Vice President. Thus before

ACCEPT-
SPEECH.
re not here
se the dark-
but to light
candle . . .
and today
edge of a
Frontier—
rontier of
1960's—a
r of un-
opportu-
and perils
frontier of
lled hopes
reats."

UPI

A "FISH-EYE" VIEW OF THE CONVENTION

UPI

THE TICKET: NIXON AND CABOT LODGE

UPI

THE SCENE AFTER THE NIXON NOMINATION

the year was out Rockefeller gave up.

Nixon entered all the primaries to prove his vote-getting power; with no opposition it was a safe exercise.

He received the endorsement of the President with some hesitation. In the middle of January Eisenhower told a news conference that there were about a dozen "virile men in the Republican party" whom he would gladly support. It was mid-March before he endorsed Nixon.

On June 8 Rockefeller, whom Nixon hoped to get for the second place on the ticket, came out with a demand that the leaders of the Republican party should declare promptly "what they believe and what they propose, to meet the great matters before the nation." His request activated the Governor's candidacy, but not enough to pose a danger to Nixon.

Rockefeller, learning of the Republican platform draft, was determined to fight it. Nixon came to him, and the two worked out an agreement covering fourteen points, most of it becoming part of the Republican platform.

As the political moves were completed in the preconvention maneuvers, the conventions offered no surprises. Both Kennedy and Nixon were nominated on the first ballot. Kennedy's vote was 806 against Johnson's 409, Symington's 86 and Stevenson's 79½. Nixon garnered all the votes of the Republican delegates save the 10 from Louisiana, who, angered by the party's civil rights plank, supported Senator Barry Goldwater.

For the second place, the Democratic party leaders prevailed upon Kennedy to offer the Vice Presidency to Johnson to strengthen his Southern support. The liberals were dismayed about the choice. Professor Galbraith quieted the ruffled tempers: "This is the kind of political expedient Franklin Roosevelt would never have used —except in the case of John Nance Garner."

In his acceptance speech the Republican nominee pledged that the fight against Communism would be waged on the social and economic fronts. He asked for a "world-wide strategy, an offensive for peace and freedom" designed to win the battle for freedom without war. For Nixon the major Communist threat was in nonmilitary areas.

The Republican platform called for making a sixth-grade education "conclusive evidence of literacy for voting purposes," for permitting the Attorney General to bring school integration suits, pledged to enact legislation prohibiting labor unions from discriminating on account of race, but it contained no FEPC plank. The platform approved the use of Federal funds to finance segregated facilities. It called for aid to education and additional appropriations to meet defense needs. "There is no price ceiling on America's security"—an apparent departure from Eisenhower's frugal penny-pinching defense policy.

The Democratic platform was a liberal one. It con-

WHEN HE LEARNED
THAT HE WAS CHOSEN
UPI

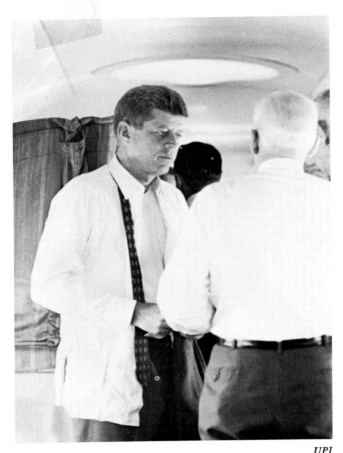

THE CAMPAIGNER TALKS TO A REPORTER . . .

. . . AND PARADES THE STREETS WITH HIS WIFE.

demned the Eisenhower administration for sloth at home and ineptness abroad. In economics it demanded that the Federal Government force the growth of the economy to pay for a welfare program that would go far to erase the last vestiges of inequity in American life.

In defense it charged the Republican administration with allowing the U.S. to slip to a position of second best, of permitting a seven-year lag to develop in military strength in the cold war with the Soviets, and pledged greatly expanded foreign aid to non-Communist nations.

In foreign affairs, it stressed the urgency of peace and disarmament, and blamed Eisenhower for the failure of the summit conference in Paris.

Kennedy was happy with the Democratic platform, which offered the strongest civil rights plank in the party's history (though repudiated by the Southern delegates on the platform committee). The plank proposed means for speeding up school integration, giving the Attorney General power to file suits in Federal courts to prevent any denial of civil rights on account of race, legislation to establish a Federal FEPC, a permanent civil rights commission, opposition to poll taxes and literacy tests.

It pledged new and expanded welfare programs and aid to agriculture and small businesses. It proposed long-term planning for international cooperation in order to replace "tanks with tractors, bombers with bulldozers," without sacrificing American military strength.

In his acceptance speech Kennedy called for more sacrifices on the part of the nation, not more luxuries, as it went its way down the road toward a New Frontier: "Woodrow Wilson's New Freedom promised our nation a new political and economic framework. Franklin Roosevelt's New Deal promised security and succor to those in need. But the New Frontier of which I speak is not a set of promises—it is a set of challenges.

"It sums up not what I intend to offer the American people, but what I intend to ask of them. It appeals to their pride, it appeals to our pride, not our security—it holds out the promises of more sacrifice instead of more security."

The St. Louis Post-Dispatch commented: "The Democratic party nominated not its best man, but its best politician and probably its best vote getter. The question is whether tactical talents will be matched by equal devotion to great purposes. Kennedy's essential self remains to be laid before the country. He faces the same sort of

THE REPUBLICAN CAMPAIGNER: Under large blow-ups, Nixon addresses a college audience at Chicago's Wheaton.

opportunity and in many ways the same sort of crises that Franklin D. Roosevelt faced in the early Thirties."

Prior to the conventions the pollsters predicted a Kennedy victory by a small but comfortable margin. However, after the campaign got under way, the Gallup Poll gave Nixon the edge.

Before Kennedy got his campaign under way, he had to mend some fences. He had been opposed by Truman, Mrs. Roosevelt and other important party figures—and now he had to win them over. He secured Truman's pledge to go "all out" on a coast-to-coast stumping tour, and he got Mrs. Roosevelt's support by promising more social welfare programs and expansion of the Social Security program. And Stevenson, too, fell in line.

Truman commented on what was widely heralded as the "new Nixon," a new image of the Vice President as a soft-spoken, mild-mannered and relaxed campaigner. The ex-President saw no such thing as a "new Nixon." "No, there couldn't be. He's too old to change." Truman could not forgive Nixon's attacks on him in the past, when Nixon had implied that Truman was a traitor. Neither could he forget the angry words in the first Eisenhower election when Nixon, carried away in campaign oratory,

lambasted the President: "To think that Harry Truman, of all people, would try to besmirch Dwight Eisenhower's reputation should make a whole nation rise up in righteous wrath. Why, that piano-playing letter writer!" And Kennedy said: "With all this talk about an old Nixon and a new Nixon, it should be remembered that there was no old Lincoln or a new Lincoln, no old Wilson or new Wilson, no old F.D.R. or new F.D.R. I cannot believe that the American people in these difficult times will choose a man with this fuzzy image of his own political philosophy."

Nixon promised to go to all fifty states, a promise which he was to regret.

A new touch was added to the campaign with the founding of a Republican house advertising agency, Campaign Associates. This may have been what moved the *Nation* to write: "Mr. Nixon creates the impression, in his first post-convention appearances, not so much of being a candidate for the Presidency as a bright young agency executive making a presentation for a client."

In the opening speeches of his campaign Nixon stressed that the contest was not between parties, but between men. "I am not going to begin by saying to those who are

ONE DAY 300,000 TURN OUT FOR HIM—as in this rally in the center of New York's garment district. The beaming face on the extreme left is that of David D. Dubinsky, long-time president of the International Garment Workers Union.

Republicans in this audience, 'Vote for me because I'm a Republican and you're a Republican.' I believe that when we select a President of the United States that our history tells us that the American people look not just to party labels. They look behind them. . . ." In contrast Kennedy stressed ideological differences: "No Democratic candidate," he would say, "for the Presidency has ever run and said, 'Parties don't matter,' because we are proud of our record. We want to be identified with it. We want to follow it."

It was not clear what issues separated the two men.

Both were in favor of Federal aid to schools (though Nixon was not for aid for teachers' salaries, but only for school construction), for loan programs for higher education. Kennedy wanted medical insurance for the aged financed by Social Security. Nixon, in a position paper, endorsed Senator Javits's proposal for care for the aged, a program which gave a choice between private or government-sponsored plans and which went beyond the proposals of the Eisenhower administration. Both candidates wanted a bill to aid depressed areas and more liberal Social Security laws; both were ready to use the

ON ANOTHER DAY ALL THE STREETS ARE EMPTY—as shown in this picture taken early one morning at Portland, Maine, as he makes a swing through New England. With him are Senators Margaret Chase Smith and Edmund Muskie.

power of the Federal Government to fight recession or inflation; both opposed the Benson farm plans—Nixon by dissociating himself from Benson, Kennedy by opposing outright the "Nixon-Benson" farm plan. Thus each candidate tried to identify the other with positions which he, in turn, could criticize. Kennedy had a powerful technique with which he distinguished himself. By constantly using statistics he impressed his audiences with his specific knowledge of their affairs—for example, the wages of female laundry workers in the five largest cities in the country, the amount of the average Social Security check,

the number of workers unprotected by minimum wage, the number of families making under $1,000 a year, the number of Negro judges. He would preface his remarks: "I am not satisfied when . . ." or "Do you realize that . . ." or "Our party will be needed so long as . . ." or "I think we can do better . . ." He would have local information at his fingertips, such as the price of corn in Sanborn, Minnesota, the number of layoffs in International Harvester plants in Illinois.

Television commentator Eric Sevareid remarked—that Nixon "deliberately chose the underdog role. In other

CAMPAIGNING IS HARD WORK. One had to speak and, when the speech is over, prepare the next one. Flying to San Francisco, Nixon works on his next speech. He supports his right leg—the knee was injured earlier in a campaign tour.

words, he initially took the defensive position. He has gone further: Senator Kennedy has used harsh words about Nixon's principles, so Nixon intends to campaign in a more lofty manner, avoiding 'personalities.' Kennedy is tough, so Nixon intends to give the impression of a 'nice guy.' Kennedy was born rich, so Nixon will emphasize his own grocery-store childhood, when he made hamburgers that were cheap but honest. In other words, Mr. Nixon is cutting his cloth to Mr. Kennedy's measure."

Nixon accused Kennedy of taking the "low road," and he promised not to get into personalities. He may have been irked by the glowering photograph of him put out by the Democrats and labeled: "Would you buy a used car from this man?"

Nixon's main argument against Kennedy was his youth and inexperience. The Republican candidate, using a folksy soft sell, stressed his and his running mate's "experience," particularly in the area of foreign affairs. Kennedy reacted sharply: "Mr. Nixon is experienced," he said, "experienced in policies of retreat, defeat, and weakness," which lead to a decline in American prestige all over the world.

On the experience issue Kennedy received an unexpected assist from Eisenhower. When reporters asked the President what major decisions Nixon had participated in, the President answered: "If you give me a week, I might think of one."

It was a grueling campaign, the two candidates racing from one part of the country to the other making speeches, shaking hands, being photographed.

Kennedy attacked the country's political and military weaknesses. He urged America to move ahead. He accused the Republicans of being responsible for the declining national prestige.

Nixon's campaign was based more on his own personality. He told his audiences how his mother baked pies to send him through college, how he tended the family filling station, ground the hamburger in the family store, how his brother's wish for a pony could not be fulfilled. The speech went like this: "I remember that when we were growing up my older brother for one year very desperately wanted a pony. My father could have bought it for about seventy-five dollars. And my brother, who died when I was quite young, kept saying, 'Oh, I want this

830

CAMPAIGNING IS HARD WORK. Kennedy has to accept a dare and ride a mule in the stockyards at Sioux City, Iowa—and what's more he has to look as though he enjoys it. But he felt like Calvin Coolidge under an Indian headdress.

pony more than anything in the world.' Now, being the oldest son, he was kind of a favorite, as you can imagine, with my mother and my father, and they wanted more than anything else to give him what he wanted. It would have been easy for them to say, 'Look, you can have the pony.' But, you know what happened? My mother and father had a little family council and they came in and they said, 'Now, look, if we buy this pony we're not going to have enough money to pay the grocery bill; we're not going to have enough money to pay the clothing bill; we're not going to be able to get the shoes for your younger brother.' It was an awfully hard decision for my mother and father, but it was the right thing."

The newspapermen made their jokes about the speech, but Nixon's audiences ate it up.

Kennedy's religion was a widely discussed issue. Early in September, Eisenhower declared: "I not only don't believe in voicing prejudice—I want to assure you I feel none. And I am sure that Mr. Nixon feels the same." Nonetheless a Protestant group led by Rev. Dr. Norman Vincent Peale charged that a Catholic President would be under "extreme pressure from the hierarchy of his

THE CATHOLIC ISSUE: "I am not the Catholic candidate for President. I am the Democratic party's candidate for President, who happens to be a Catholic."

"I do not speak for my church on public matters—and the church does not speak for me."

"Whatever issue comes before me as President, if I should be elected—on birth control, divorce, censorship, gambling, or any other subject—I will make my decision in accordance with . . . what my conscience tells me to be in the national interest, and without regard to outside religious pressure or dictate. And no power or threat of punishment could cause me to decide otherwise."

THE KENNEDY-NIXON TELEVISION DEBATE INCREASED KENNEDY'S STATURE AND HIS CHANCES.

Long in the Minneapolis *Tribune*

Herblock in the Washington *Post*

Burck in the Chicago *Sun-Times*

CARTOONISTS' COMMENTS ON THE TELEVISION DEBATES

OCTOBER 21, 1960: WITH A CHARACTERISTIC GESTURE KENNEDY CHALLENGES THE SOMBER NIXON.

Church" to align the foreign policy of the United States with that of the Vatican. The group called the National Conference of Citizens for Religious Freedom was more or less representative of the evangelical, conservative Protestants. In rebuttal Kennedy's campaign organization issued a memorandum detailing their candidate's position on the separation of church and state. Discussing his religion Kennedy said that he would resign as President if he could not make every decision in the national interest "without regard to outside religious pressures." Shortly thereafter Peale bowed out, as Reinhold Niebuhr and John Bennett of the Union Theological Seminary accused him and his group of having "loosed the floodgates of religious bigotry."

Nonetheless a *New York Times* survey a few days later found that farmers in the Midwest, despite their hostility to Benson, were not defecting to Kennedy. "There is an undercurrent of anti-Catholic, anti-Kennedy feeling in Midwestern states from Ohio across the Corn-Hog Belt

to Nebraska, and north into the Dakotas," the survey stated. Militant fundamentalist groups received an all-out anti-Kennedy mailing. Their cause was aided when the Catholic bishop in Puerto Rico asked their countrymen not to vote for the liberal Luis Muñoz Marín, thus raising the specter of ecclesiastical interference in politics.

Kennedy kept foreign affairs in the forefront of his campaign. Early in September he said that the United States must regain the lead in the "fight for peace"; that it must rebuild its defenses until it was once again first in military power across the board. He charged the Eisenhower administration with teetering on the brink of war, of lacking solid plans for disarmament negotiations, and of resting on a policy of "swapping threats and insults with the Russians." Nixon stressed in his speeches that "the great issue" was: which candidate could better "keep the peace for America and extend freedom throughout the world."

The United Nations met late in September, with

IN THE HEAT OF THE CAMPAIGN Kennedy shouts: "Hold it, she only wants to shake my hand!" as a Grand Rapids policeman hauls the woman away. He remembered the incident, asking later that she be brought to see him.

Khrushchev and Castro in attendance. The press focused its attention on Khrushchev, who demanded the resignation of Dag Hammarskjöld as secretary general of the United Nations, then launched an attack on Prime Minister Macmillan of Britain. He told the General Assembly that it could only avert war by admitting Red China to membership, and threatened to make a separate peace treaty with East Germany. He boasted that the United States was losing the cold war and that Russian factories were producing rockets like sausages. At one point he became so enraged at the debate that he took off one of his shoes and banged the table with it.

Kennedy warned Khrushchev that Democratic criticism of the Eisenhower administration during the campaign should not be taken as evidence of disunity. "Dem-

ocrats, Republicans and independents alike are united in our opposition to your system and everything it means," he said and pledged that if elected he would move in three ways in his "first ninety days" to strengthen the United States's world position—to build up national defenses, to bring our "more prosperous allies" into a new program of economic aid for underdeveloped areas, and lastly, to "wipe out poverty here in the United States." "This is no time," he went on, "to say we can outtalk or outshout Khrushchev. I want to outdo him—to outproduce him."

Nixon proposed a truce on campaign oratory while Khrushchev was in America. He said that the Democratic nominee had a "special responsibility" to show that all Americans supported Eisenhower in the United Nations: "We have responsibility in avoiding resort to state-

IN THE HEAT OF THE CAMPAIG
Hold it, Lyndon! Kennedy tries to pacify his running mate. But Lady Bird is excited too.
Stern

TELEVISION COMMENTATORS—like the NBC team of Huntley and Brinkley, overseeing a host of reporters—gave the projected results of the election instantly. Still it took until the early morning hours before the results were final.

ments which tend to divide America, which tend to disparage America and which in any way would encourage Chairman Khrushchev and his fellow dictators to believe that this nation, the leader of the free world, is weak of will, is indecisive, is unsure of and hesitant to use her vast power, is poorly defended, is held at bay by imperialistic Communism, is divided in opinion on world affairs, believing that the majority of mankind holds her in disdain."

Kennedy would not take the bait. He attacked Republican leadership for hobbling the nation and permitting the creation of "a Communist satellite ninety miles off the coast of the United States." "I want to make it clear," said he, "that nothing I am saying will give Mr. Khrushchev the slightest encouragement. He is encouraged enough. . . . The most ominous sound that Mr. Khrushchev can hear this week is not of a debate in the United States, but the sound of America on the move, ready to move again."

President Eisenhower, reversing his former statement on his Vice President, now said earnestly: "As a person ready to enter the duties of the presidential office, Dick Nixon has the broadest and deepest preparation and experience of any man I know." Kennedy shot back that this experience meant nothing, and wryly quoted Oscar Wilde that experience is "the name everyone gives to his mistakes." Commenting on Eisenhower's endorsement of Nixon, James Reston wondered whether Eisenhower's popularity was transferable. "And even if it is, would the Democrats in Congress go along with Nixon in 1961 as they did with Eisenhower? The political pros answer 'no' to both questions."

Nixon continued talking about his experience. "After each of my foreign trips, I have made recommendations which were adopted. . . . Through the years I have sat in the National Security Council. I have been in the Cabinet. I have met with the legislative leaders. I have met with

THE EX-PRESIDENT PROUDLY POINTS TO THE VICTORY of the man whose candidacy he vigorously opposed. But Truman is a partisan, the party is the principle—for him any Democratic President is better than a Republican.

the President when he made the great decisions. . . . The President has asked for my advice."

Kennedy answered: "The Vice President and I came to Congress together in 1946. I've been there for fourteen years, the same period of time that he has, so that our experience in government is comparable." And at the Al Smith Memorial Dinner in New York, with Nixon also present, he treated the issue wittily: "I think the worst news for the Republicans this week was that Casey Stengel had been fired. It must show that perhaps experience does not count."

And he went on to say in one of his wittiest speeches: "On this matter of experience, I had announced earlier this year that if successful I would not consider campaign contributions as a substitute for experience in appointing ambassadors. Ever since I made that statement, I have not received one single cent from my father."

Then, taking up Nixon's attacks on Truman's profanity

THE PRESIDENT'S GRANDMOTHER, 96-year-old Mrs. John Fitzgerald, the wife of "Honey Fitz," the erstwhile Boston mayor, rejoiced over her grandson's win.

THE PRESIDENT-ELECT AND HIS WIFE   *UPI*

THE OLD ORDER ALONGSIDE THE NEW   *UPI*

—in a campaign speech Truman said, "If you vote for Nixon, you might go to hell"—Kennedy continued:

"One of the inspiring notes that was struck in the last debate was struck by the Vice President in his very moving warning to the children of the nation and the candidates against the use of profanity by Presidents and ex-Presidents when they are on the stump. And I know after fourteen years in the Congress with the Vice President that he was very sincere in his views about the use of profanity. But I am told that a prominent Republican said to him yesterday in Jacksonville, Florida, that it was 'a damn fine speech' and the Vice President said, 'I appreciate the compliment but not the language.' And the Republican went on, 'Yes, sir, I liked it so much that I contributed a thousand dollars to your campaign.' And Mr. Nixon replied, 'The hell you say.'"

The room rocked with laughter. Cardinal Spellman sitting next to Kennedy chuckled, as did Rockfeller. And even Nixon joined in the merriment.

The highlights of the contest came with the television debates of the two candidates. Four debates were agreed upon. The first was set for September 26 for Chicago, the second for October 7 for Washington, the third for October 13—Nixon was to speak from Los Angeles, Kennedy from New York—and the last one for October 21 from New York.

For Kennedy the outcome of the election hinged on his performance before the television cameras. He had to prove to the country that he was not the inexperienced youngster Nixon made him out.

And Nixon, too, hoped to profit. An experienced debater, he wanted to project the "new Nixon," a dedicated, mature politician, not a mudslinging campaigner of the past, not the "Tricky Dick" of yesterday but the successor of Eisenhower tomorrow.

Kennedy prepared himself thoroughly. The day of the first debate he holed up in his Chicago hotel having cramming sessions with his aides, Sorensen, Goodwin and Feldman. The three tossed him every conceivable question which the panel of interviewers and Nixon might ask in the debates. Kennedy, with the fabulous memory of a seasoned actor, memorized fact cards by the dozen.

Nixon, too, locked himself up in his hotel room and prepared himself for the ordeal. He could not be reached by anyone.

In the studio Kennedy gave off a feeling of confidence. He looked well, he was calm and collected. Nixon looked tired, thin and emaciated. He was not feeling well. The cameras were not kind to his features. His light skin showed every whisker under the surface. Contrary to reports, he was not made up. He used only Lazy Shave, a kind of talcum powder.

Kennedy began with the familiar gambit: "I think the question before the American people is: Are we doing as much as we can do?" He elaborated on the shortcomings of the Eisenhower administration. He charged that under it the country had the lowest rate of economic growth among the industrial nations, that half of America's steel capacity was unused, that natural resources were undeveloped, that there was hunger in some regions, that there were overcrowded schools with underpaid teachers, and that there was racial discrimination.

Nixon replied cautiously: "Our disagreement is not about the goals of America but only about the means to reach these goals." He contradicted Kennedy about his statement about the country's economic strength, but in general he was more in agreement with his opponent's propositions than differing with them.

In the debate Nixon made the fatal error of trying to score points with his rebuttals. He dwelt on the little mistakes and inconsistencies in the Kennedy proposals. Kennedy's tactic was different. He addressed himself over the heads of his opponent and interviewers, disregarding them when it suited him, and spoke to the nation as a whole.

The first debate was a Kennedy victory. Just by standing there next to Nixon, asking questions and answering them in a knowledgeable way, he showed that he was no less experienced than the Vice President. He knew his facts, he knew his figures. He made a great impact on the sixty to seventy million viewers who watched the debate.

The second debate was better for Nixon. He used some makeup, which made Mrs. Roosevelt exclaim, "I had to look at Nixon twice before I recognized him." He had to drop his "inexperience" charge against Kennedy; it was no longer effective after the first debate.

The candidates discussed two main issues: the bombardment of Quemoy and Matsu by the Red Chinese and Cuba under the dictatorship of Castro. Kennedy's position was that the Chinese offshore islands had no strategic value, while Nixon argued that they should not be allowed to fall into the hands of the Communists, because their fall would precipitate a chain reaction—an early statement of the "domino theory." He said that if the islands fell, Formosa and other places would follow. "In my opinion this is the same kind of woolly thinking that led to disaster for America in Korea."

The third debate restated the issues discussed before. Nixon complained again about the forceful language of President Truman, who used swear words against his political opponents.

The fourth debate was dreary. Neither Kennedy nor Nixon had anything new to say. The Cuban issue was discussed once more. Kennedy held that the Eisenhower administration had failed to deal with the Communist menace so near to American shores and suggested the strengthening of the Democratic forces in exile and in Cuba itself so that they could overthrow Castro. Nixon thought this a "most dangerous, irresponsible recommendation," although he must have been aware at that time that the Central Intelligence Agency, with the approval of the President, was already preparing Cuban exiles in Guatemala for a Cuban invasion.

Nixon said about Vietnam that as America had taken a strong stand in Indochina, "the civil war there was ended and today, at least in the south of Indochina, the Communists have moved out and we do have a strong, free position there." The statement proves how dangerous it is to make predictions.

The debates, viewed at one time or another by some 120 million people, established Kennedy's stature and brought disaster for Nixon. They showed that Nixon's "inexperienced" opponent was an intelligent man able to stand up to the Vice President and beat him at his own game. They had a tremendous impact. James Reston wrote about them:

UPI
THE VICE PRESIDENCY CHANGES HANDS, TOO.

"Senator John F. Kennedy is gradually switching roles with Vice President Nixon in these TV debates. He started out, like the Pittsburgh Pirates, as the underdog who wasn't supposed to be able to stay the course with the champ, but is winding up as the character who has more specific information on the tip of his tongue than Mr. Nixon. . . . Mr. Nixon's presentation was general and often emotional; Mr. Kennedy's curt and factual. Mr. Nixon, whose campaign is based on his reputation for knowledge of the facts and experience, was outpointed on facts. Mr. Kennedy, who was supposed to be the matinee idol lacking experience, seldom generalized, plunged into his answers with factual illustrations, and made no appeal to emotion other than the usual Democratic we-take-care-of-the-people argument. . . . In sum, Mr. Kennedy gains as these debates go on even if he does no more than stay level with the Vice President."

Russell Baker, a colleague of Reston's, saw a different picture:

ON TO THE CEREMONIES: The youngest President and Carl Hayden, the oldest Senator, make their way to the portico.

"It is also inescapable that his [Kennedy's] most excited following lies among the young. In some cases the mob scenes seem cast entirely among adolescents too young to vote, and the hysterical edge on the mass shriek is reminiscent of the usual cry that used to fill the Paramount Theatre for the young Frank Sinatra twenty years ago. . . . Should Mr. Kennedy win, the result will have less to do with his daring campaign arguments to the voters than to the impact of a remarkable new political personality which has been dramatized by the happenstance of Mr. Nixon's agreement to appear with him in the four television debates."

All the pollsters and prognosticators predicted a close contest. In mid-October the Gallup Poll refused to predict the outcome because it was too close. It named three issues as major variables: religion, lack of enthusiasm for either candidate, and the closeness in almost every part of the country between the two candidates. "The religious issue could help or hurt either candidate," said Dr. Gallup carefully. And Mort Sahl, the witty commentator of political events, noted with tongue in cheek: "Neither candidate is going to win."

The bulk of the liberals were for Kennedy. In his campaign essay *Kennedy or Nixon: Does It Make Any*

ON TO THE CEREMONIES: The Republican President, his Vice President and members of their party cross the Capitol. *U.S. Army*

Difference? Arthur M. Schlesinger, Jr. wrote: "Kennedy and Nixon stand in sharp contrast—in their personalities, their programs, and their parties. Each asks the American people to repose in him the command of our national policy over the next four years. With Nixon, personality, programs, and party combine to create the expectation of a static government dominated by the forces in our society most opposed to change. With Kennedy, personality, policies, and party combine to create the expectation of an affirmative government dominated by intelligence and vision and dedicated to abolishing the terrifying discrepancy between the American perform-

ance and the American possibility." Schlesinger called Nixon a chameleon with "no political philosophy, no sense of history," a man who is only preoccupied with the popularity of his own public image. And writing in the *New Republic,* Professor James MacGregor Burns felt, "Today on the eve of America's greatest choice, I believe that Kennedy in his campaign has deliberately prepared the way for the most consistently and comprehensively liberal administration in the history of this country."

And even those among the liberals who were not for Kennedy were against Nixon. William Costello wrote

U.S. Army

CHIEF JUSTICE WARREN GIVES THE OATH.

The Gift Outright

The land was ours before we were the land's
She was our land more than a hundred years
Before we were her people. She was ours
In Massachusetts in Virginia
But we were England's still colonials,
Possessing what we still were unpossessed by,
Possessed by what we now no more possessed.
Something we were withholding made us weak
Until we found out that it was ourselves
We were withholding from our land of living
And forthwith found salvation in surrender.
Such as we were we gave ourselves outright
(The deed of gift was many deeds of war)
To the land vaguely realizing westward,
But still unstoried artless unenhanced
Such as she was such as she would become

Robert Frost

For the Inauguration
of John F. Kennedy.

Smithsonian Institution

A POEM FOR THE OCCASION. Robert Frost's "The Gift Outright," which he tried to read at the ceremonies.

THE EYES OF THE WORLD are on the new President. "We observe today not a victory of party but a celebration of freedom—symbolizing an end as well

as a beginning . . . the torch has been passed to a new generation of Americans—born in this century, tempered by war, disciplined by a hard and bitter peace . . . the trumpet summons us—not as a call to bear arms . . . [but to] a struggle against the common enemies of man: tyranny, poverty, disease and war itself . . . And so, my fellow Americans, ask not what your country can do for you: Ask what you can do for your country."

ON THE WAY TO THE INAUGURAL BALL

THE HAPPY SPECTATORS IN THEIR PRIVATE BOX AT THE BALL IN THE NATIONAL GUARD ARMORY

about him: "Working, scheming, talking, fighting, manning the ramparts and battlements of his enclave, he radiates conflict, holds himself poised for attack or defense. His operational code makes him half witch doctor, half soldier of fortune, a mixture of superstition and the latest Madison Avenue gimmickry."

Kennedy was endorsed by *The New York Times,* which had supported Eisenhower in both 1952 and 1956. Two reasons were given for the decision: "One of these is a matter of foreign policy. The other is a question of assuring a unified direction of the nation's affairs at a difficult moment in history. . . . As always, the choice must be made on balance. On balance, our choice is Mr. Kennedy."

As the campaign came to its close, Nixon became the "old Nixon" again, reverting to harsher language, charging his opponent with "barefaced lies." He tried to identify himself with Eisenhower, and asked the President to take an active role in the campaign in its closing week. Eisenhower consented to barnstorm in the crucial states of Ohio and Pennsylvania and also in New York.

In Philadelphia he accused Kennedy of having "cruelly distorted the image of America" abroad and thus showed an "amazing irresponsibility." Kennedy answered the President: "I do not downgrade America, but I do downgrade the kind of leadership America's been getting."

In the final days Nixon made a number of last-minute proposals. He promised a manned flight to the moon by 1966–1969, as well as an East-West summit conference with Khrushchev and a personal tour of Eastern Europe. Later on he added the promise that he would take ex-Presidents Eisenhower, Truman and Hoover along with him.

Kennedy, too, made some proposals. On November 2, he suggested in San Francisco a "Peace Corps" of young men and women who would serve with technical aid missions abroad as an alternative to the draft. These "ambassadors of peace" would supplement other "soldiers for war." He had already endorsed a "Food For Peace" program. "We live in a land of abundance," he said, "a land of such great abundance of food and fiber, in fact, that our 'cup runneth over.' At the same time we live in a world where over 60 percent of the population lives under the shadow of hunger and malnutrition." Thus he suggested a "food-for-peace program that can use America's and the free world's great agricultural productive capability and our large reserve supplies of farm commodities as vital bastions of positive and defensive strength for the entire free world."

Toward the end Nixon sharpened his attacks. He implied that a vote for Kennedy was a vote for war, a vote for higher prices, for inflation, fiscal disaster and government by political and labor bosses. And Kennedy kept repeating that America's national prestige was on the downgrade, that our steel industry was lagging, that the country should be moving forward.

The arrest of Dr. Martin Luther King, Jr., in Atlanta on October 19, roused Kennedy and his friends. Dr. King was arrested, with fifty-two other Negroes, for refusing to leave a table in a restaurant. He was jailed and sentenced to four months' hard labor. It was feared that the beloved Negro leader would not leave the penitentiary alive. When Kennedy learned about the affair, he telephoned Mrs. King promising help. Explaining his call at a news conference, Kennedy said: "She is a friend of mine and I was concerned about the situation."

His brother Robert called the judge who had sentenced Dr. King and obtained his release on bail. The news of the telephone call spread through the Negro neighborhoods. The father of Dr. King said: "Because

SWEARING IN THE CABINET the day after the inauguration. Chief Justice Warren gives the oath to Dean Rusk (State), C. Douglas Dillon (Treasury), Robert

this man was willing to wipe the tears from my daughter's eyes, I've got a suitcase of votes, and I'm going to take them to Mr. Kennedy and dump them in his lap." Booklets by the millions were printed by the Kennedy organization recounting the incident, making certain that every Negro learned about it.

Nixon wound up his campaign with a four-hour telethon from Detroit, asking the voters to "put America first rather than to put party or any other consideration first." Kennedy ended his campaign in Boston, calling the election "a race between the comfortable and the concerned, a race between those who want to be at anchor and those who want to go forward."

THE PRESIDENT
AND HIS SECRETARY
MRS. EVELYN LINCOLN
UPI

McNamara (Defense), Robert Kennedy (Attorney General), Stewart Udall (Interior), Adlai Stevenson (Ambassador to the UN), Orville Freeman (Agriculture), Abraham Ribicoff (Health, Education, and Welfare), behind Warren, Arthur Goldberg (Labor) and Luther Hodges (Commerce). The President and First Lady watch.

Commentators predicted Kennedy's victory. In Samuel Lubell's opinion, "Kennedy will win in an uneven sweep across the country." David Lawrence, writing of a Catholic shift from Eisenhower in 1956 to Kennedy in 1960, wrote: "This is such a sensational shift that, if corroborated by election returns, it could mean not only the landslide for Kennedy but possibly one of the largest popular vote totals ever given to a presidential candidate in American history." *Time, Newsweek* and *U.S. News & World Report* all predicted a Democratic victory.

Kennedy won—but by a hair's-breadth. He had received 118,574 votes more than Nixon (though if one takes into consideration the irregularities in Alabama.

Nixon would have been ahead in the popular vote); Kennedy had 303 electoral votes against Nixon's 219. Yet it had been a personal victory for Kennedy, not a party victory. In Congress Republicans gained two Senate and twenty-two House seats.

Years later Khrushchev reminisced about the election. Calling Nixon a "son of a bitch" who joined with McCarthy when anti-Communism was strong, "and when McCarthy began to fade, Nixon turned his back on him," the Chairman revealed that during the campaign Nixon had asked the Russian government privately for the return of captured U-2 pilot Gary Powers. He told Kennedy when they met in Vienna a few months after the election:

THE CHANGING PORTRAIT ON THE WALL. Kennedy's first Cabinet meeting in January 1961. From left to right: J. Edward Day (Postmaster General); Adlai Stevenson (Ambassador to the U.N.); Vice President Lyndon B. Johnson; Robert McNamara (Defense); Orville Freeman (Agriculture); Arthur Goldberg (Labor); Abraham Ribicoff (Health, Education, and Welfare); Luther Hodges (Commerce); Robert Kennedy (Attorney General); Dean Rusk (State); President Kennedy; Douglas Dillon (Treasury); and Stewart Udall (Interior). They were meeting beneath Jefferson's portrait.

Photograph by Abbie Rowe

FOUR MONTHS LATER, on May 25, the portrait on the wall has been changed to that of George Washington.

"But we guessed his plans. If we had released Powers, Nixon would have won. We decided not to give him any answers and just to give it to you when you moved into the White House. . . . This is the way I voted for you. We made you President."

The election over, Kennedy began to recruit a "ministry of the best available talent." For Secretary of State his choice fell on Dean Rusk, president of the Rockefeller Foundation, a Rhodes scholar and a professor of political science. Robert McNamara, a former professor at the Harvard Graduate School of Business who left teaching to become president of the Ford Motor Company, was to become Secretary of Defense; C. Douglas Dillon, a conservative investment banker with diplomatic service under Eisenhower, the head of the Treasury; Arthur Goldberg, the labor lawyer, Secretary of Labor. Minnesota's former Governor Orville Freeman was chosen for the Agriculture Department, another former Governor,

KENNEDY PUTS UP LINCOLN, helped by his friend William Walton.

Photograph by Cornell Capa, Magnum

Cornell Capa, Magnum

A CABINET MEETING, this time under the gaze of Lincoln. Along the window side are presidential assistants Frederick Dutton, Theodore Sorensen, Walter Heller, Chairman of the Council of Economic Advisers, and McGeorge Bundy.

Abraham Ribicoff of Connecticut, for the Department of Health, Education, and Welfare. North Carolina's Governor Luther Hodges was to become Secretary of Commerce, Stewart Udall of Arizona was named Secretary of the Interior, and J. Edward Day, a California insurance executive, Postmaster General. But the most excitement was created when he let it be known that his brother Robert would become Attorney General. "Don't smile too much or they'll think we are happy about the appointment," Kennedy chided Bobby as they walked to the press conference.

The capital readied itself for the inaugural. Trees along the procession route were sprayed to repel the starlings. The Secret Service organized a guard of five thousand men. The city's mounted police used Spike Jones records to condition their horses for the roar of the crowds. The networks set up connections for their television cameras and microphones for their radios.

By noon of January 19 it seemed that the whole inauguration would be buried in snow. Eight inches of snow fell that night in the city. Washington residents and those who came to the capital abandoned their cars on the streets of the city—tens of thousands of them. Planes could neither take off nor land. But by the morning of inaugural day the snow had stopped and crews had worked through the night to clear the streets.

The ceremonies could not begin on time. The official date of the beginning of the administration was noon—yet

THREE PRESIDENTS AND ONE FUTURE PRESIDENT at the burial of Mrs. Roosevelt. Facing the grave are her children, and Kennedy, Truman and Eisenhower. Vice President Johnson, Stevenson and Ralph Bunche are behind them.

the inaugural program started twenty-one minutes later. Everything seemed to go wrong. Boston's Richard Cardinal Cushing, a friend of the Kennedys', delivered the invocation; while he spoke, smoke caused by a short circuit drifted up from the lectern. Robert Frost stepped up to read a short dedication and poem, the bright sun blinded his eyes, and Vice President Johnson, who had already taken the oath from Sam Rayburn, held up his top hat to shield the paper from the sun. Even so—Frost could not read it, but recited it from memory, faltering as he spoke. After these tense moments, things moved more smoothly.

Kennedy took the oath of office from Chief Justice Earl Warren. Standing without a coat or a hat, he began his inaugural address with words reminiscent of Jefferson: "We observe today not a victory of party, but a celebration of freedom—symbolizing an end, as well as a beginning—signifying renewal, as well as change. For I have sworn before you and Almighty God the same solemn oath our forebears prescribed nearly a century and three-quarters ago."

Then he went on: "We dare not forget today that we are the heirs of that first revolution. Let the word go forth from this time and place, to friend and foe alike, that the torch has been passed to a new generation of Americans—born in this century, tempered by war, disciplined by a hard and bitter peace, proud of our ancient heritage—and unwilling to witness or permit the slow undoing of those

WHILE MOTHER
TENDS THE BABY...

human rights to which this nation has always been committed. . . . Let every nation know, whether it wishes us well or ill, that we shall pay any price, bear any burden, meet any hardship, support any friend, oppose any foe, in order to assure the survival and the success of liberty."

He made a spirited plea for a new quest for peace: "So

...FATHER ATTENDS TO THE AFFAIRS OF STATE

let us begin anew—remembering on both sides that civility is not a sign of weakness, and sincerity is always subject to proof. Let us never negotiate out of fear. But let us never fear to negotiate. . . . And if a beachhead of co-operation may push back the jungle of suspicion, let both sides join in creating a new endeavor, not a new balance

MUSIC AND GAIETY AT THE WHITE HOUSE. The Spanish cellist Pablo Casals plays a classical program for the Kennedys and their guests in the East Room. Casals had last appeared for a President in 1904—for Theodore Roosevelt. He had sworn never to play in any country recognizing Franco—but in his admiration for Kennedy he broke the rule.

THE MONA LISA VISITS THE CAPITAL drawing a multitude of visitors: French cultural minister André Malraux and his wife, the First Family and Johnson.

of power, but a new world of law, where the strong are just and the weak secure and the peace preserved. All this will not be finished in the first hundred days. Nor will it be finished in the first thousand days, nor in the life of this administration, nor even perhaps in our lifetime on this planet. But let us begin. . . . And so, my fellow Americans, ask not what your country can do for you: Ask what you can do for your country."

In the opening days of the new administration "the mood was one of bustle and confidence," recalled Arthur Goldberg, the newly appointed Labor Secretary. "White House reporters found a sharp contrast with the Eisenhower administration. Mr. Eisenhower, with his military background, had been devoted to the staff system and the delegation of authority. President Kennedy gave the impression of being in the thick of things and his eagerness seemed contagious."

In his first news conference Kennedy underlined the

A CONCERT ON THE LAWN. During the warm summer months of the year, orchestras, bands, glee clubs and dancers performed on the White House grounds. The Kennedys' staff was overwhelmed with requests from hundreds of amateur organizations from all over the country that wanted to appear before the President. And in the winter there were sleigh rides.

Abbie Rowe

new sense of spirit. He announced that the Russians would release the two RB-47 fliers who had been shot down over the Arctic in 1960 and said that their release "removes a serious obstacle to improvement of Soviet-American relations."

A few days later in his first State of the Union message, Kennedy said: "I speak today in an hour of national peril and national opportunity." He promised no quick cure for "every national ill," but, he noted, the condition of the economy was disturbing "in the wake of seven months of recession, three and one-half years of slack, seven years of diminished economic growth, and nine years of falling farm income." He continued: "In short, the American economy is in trouble," and promised within the next fortnight to submit measures "aimed at insuring prompt recovery and paving the way for increased long-range growth."

In foreign affairs the task was to convince Russia and

Abbie Rowe

THE PRESIDENTIAL FAMILY WATCHES the colorful parade of a Royal Highland Regiment from a White House balcony. With them is the commander of the Black Watch.

UPI

A WORLD-SHAKING EVENT: MAN ORBITS THE EARTH. Marine Corps Colonel John Glenn, Jr., was the first American astronaut from the Project Mercury team. On February 20, 1962, in the space capsule *Friendship 7* he went around the earth three times and landed in the Atlantic. The trip of 81,000 miles took only four hours and fifty-six minutes.

China "that aggression and subversion will not be profitable routes" to world domination. He urged a greater air-lift capacity, a step-up of the Polaris program and acceleration of the missile program.

And he concluded: "Life in 1961 will not be easy. Wishing it, predicting it, even asking for it, will not make it so. There will be further setbacks before the tide is turned. But turn it we must. The hopes of all mankind rest upon us—not simply upon those of us in this chamber, but upon the peasant in Laos, the fisherman in Nigeria, the exile from Cuba, the spirit that moves every man and nation who shares our hopes for freedom and the future."

In the House of Representatives Speaker Rayburn succeeded in enlarging the Rules Committee, which had been dominated by archconservatives. When the motion for increasing the number in the group was carried, the way for Kennedy's domestic program was open. He

sent a series of messages to Congress: on economic recovery and growth, on the Cuban refugees, on urban renewal, on aid to needy children, on the balance-of-payments deficit, on a minimum wage, on health and hospital care, and on health insurance for the aged.

Fresh in the office, new to his responsibilities, Kennedy let the military carry out the long-planned invasion of Cuba by CIA-trained exile forces. The attack ended in disaster. The Cubans did not rise up against Castro as American intelligence had predicted; his regime did not collapse. The defeat, for which Kennedy accepted full responsibility, had a sobering effect on him. "There is an old saying that victory has a hundred fathers and defeat is an orphan," he commented wryly.

Six weeks after the Cuban invasion the President flew with his wife to Paris to meet President De Gaulle. The visit was a great success. The Parisians went wild over the elegant Jacqueline Kennedy, who had once studied at the

WAR OR PEACE was the underlying issue of this meeting between the President and Soviet Foreign Minister Andrei Gromyko, attended by Dean Rusk, Secretary of State, and Llewellyn Thompson, special adviser on Soviet affairs (on the sofa). Gromyko denied knowledge of Soviet long-range missiles in Cuba, but Kennedy knew better and spoke accordingly.

Sorbonne and wore clothes by French couturiers. When Kennedy rose to address an assemblage in his honor, he said with a smile: "I am the man who accompanied Jacqueline Kennedy to Paris, and I have enjoyed it."

After Paris came Vienna and the meeting with Khrushchev on June 3. "The President was eager to meet Chairman Khrushchev," recalls Pierre Salinger. "He wanted to talk to him about a number of things—to see if progress could be made on a nuclear test ban, to probe the Chairman's intentions on Berlin—but, most of all, he wanted the opportunity to size up the Soviet Chairman face to face."

There were a great number of unsolved problems between the two countries. There was no agreement on control of nuclear testing. There was disagreement on Berlin. Khrushchev threatened to sign a separate treaty with East Germany. Kennedy told the Russian Chairman that America would not allow the access to Berlin to be

AMERICAN INTELLIGENCE PHOTOGRAPHS of the Russian ballistic-missile launch sites at San Cristobal, Cuba.

ONE OF THE GREAT ACHIEVEMENTS OF THE KENNEDY ADMINISTRATION: The signing of the Test Ban Treaty on October 8, 1963. Left to right: Senator Mansfield of Montana; House Speaker Rayburn of Texas; presidential adviser McGeorge Bundy; Senator Pastore of Rhode Island; behind him, Assistant Secretary of State Averell Harriman; Senators Fulbright of Arkansas, Aiken of Vermont, Humphrey of Minnesota, and Dirksen of Illinois; William C. Foster, head of the Arms Control and Disarmament Agency; Senator Howard Cameron of Nevada; Senator Saltonstall of Massachusetts; artist William Walton; and Vice President Johnson. On the wall, the painting is of Lincoln's inaugural ball.

cut. Khrushchev replied that he would meet force with force, and Kennedy reported: "Mr. Chairman, it's going to be a cold winter."

Khrushchev made his threat a reality—he signed a separate peace treaty with East Germany. Calling for an increase in the armed forces, Kennedy said: "I hear it said that West Berlin is militarily untenable. And so was Bastogne. And so, in fact, was Stalingrad. Any dangerous spot is tenable if men—brave men—will make it so. We will not let panic shape our policy, neither will we permit timidity to direct our program." West Berlin

stayed open to the German Federal Republic; and in August the East Germans began to build a wall at the border of their land.

Russia announced that it would break the moratorium and resume nuclear testing in the atmosphere. Kennedy ordered American tests resumed "in the laboratory and underground, with no fallout." The flame for peace flickered sickly.

Asked about the burden of the Presidency, Kennedy said that "the problems are more difficult than I had imagined them to be. The responsibilities placed on the

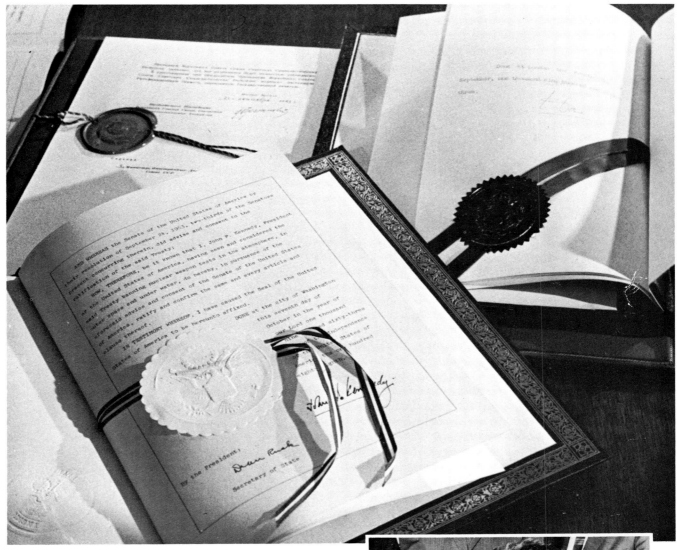

THE FINAL COPY OF THE TEST BAN TREATY which went into effect October 10, 1963. Each of the three signatories received a bound copy. On the top left is the one for the Union of Soviet Socialist Republics; on the right, the copy for Great Britain; and in the foreground the American copy, signed by President Kennedy and Secretary of State Dean Rusk.

United States are greater than I imagined them to be, and there are greater limitations upon our ability to bring about a favorable result than I had imagined them to be. And I think that is probably true of anyone who becomes President, because there is such a difference between those who advise or speak or legislate, and between the man who must select from the various alternatives proposed and say that this shall be the policy of the United States. It is much easier to make the speeches than it is to finally make the judgments, because unfortunately your advisers are frequently divided. If you take

THE PRESIDENT SIGNS THE TREATY.

the wrong course, and on occasion I have, the President bears the burden of the responsibility quite rightly. The advisers may move on to new advice."

The President showed his firmness when the United States Steel Corporation announced a general price increase of 3.5 percent after the Steelworkers Union had been persuaded by the government to cut their wage demands. He felt that he had been betrayed. Enraged, he took to the phone, marshaled his forces and persuaded the other major steel companies not to follow U.S. Steel's lead.

Then came the second Cuban crisis. In October, 1962, the cameras of the U-2 spy planes revealed that missile bases had been built on the island. They were supplied by the Russians, and Russian technicians were making the installation.

Kennedy told the country: "This secret, swift and extraordinary buildup of Communist missiles in an area well known to have a special and historical relationship with the United States and the nations of the Western Hemisphere is a deliberately provocative and unjustified change in the status quo, which cannot be accepted in this country if our courage and our commitments are ever again to be trusted by either friend or foe." It was decided to stop the Russian ships from unloading their cargoes. Defense Secretary McNamara lined up the ships and planes which would enforce the blockade. In the United Nations Stevenson asked the Russian Ambassador to admit there were such bases in Cuba. The Russian replied that he would give his answer in due time. "I am prepared to wait until hell freezes over for your answer," said Stevenson in the tense General Assembly session.

The Organization of American States authorized "the use of armed force" to quarantine Cuba, and the NATO nations pledged their support. At the time the blockade took effect, twenty-four Soviet ships were heading for the island. Half of them turned back; those with non-military cargoes were allowed to proceed. Khrushchev reportedly made an offer to trade his bases in Cuba for American bases in Turkey, but Kennedy would not bargain—the missile bases had to be dismantled. It was said that Khrushchev gave in to the removal of the bases only after a promise that Cuba would not be attacked from the United States.

Kennedy's firm handling of the crisis regained him the prestige he had lost with the Bay of Pigs invasion.

The summer of 1963 took Kennedy to Europe again. He spoke in West Berlin to hundreds of thousands: "Freedom is indivisible and when one man is enslaved, who are free? When all are free, then we can look forward to that day when this city will be joined as one and this great country and this great continent of Europe in a peaceful and hopeful globe." He captured the hearts of all Berliners when he said, "All free men, wherever

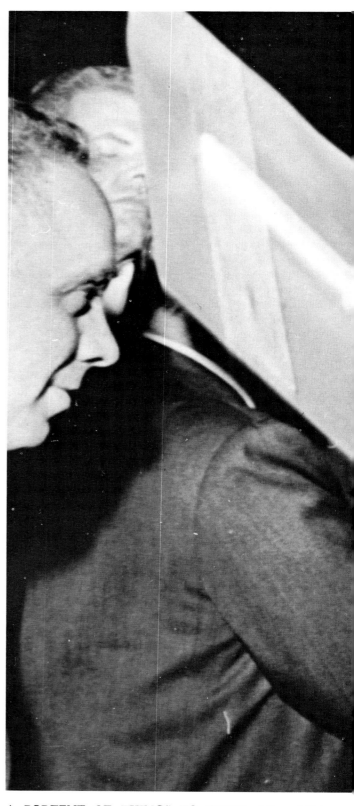

A PORTENT OF THINGS TO COME. After Adlai Stevenson, the American Ambassador to the United Nations, made a speech in Dallas celebrating UN Week, he

was struck with a picket sign and his face was spat upon. Stevenson asked Mrs. Cora Frederickson why she hit him —and received a bawling out. Behind her the sign reads "The House That Hiss Built" (meaning the United Nations). After this, Stevenson wanted to warn the President to postpone his trip to Dallas, then changed his mind.

UPI

ONE OF THE DARKEST MOMENTS IN THE NATION'S HISTORY. On November 22, 1963, John F. Kennedy was shot as he was riding through Dallas. The bullets struck his neck and his head; within the hour he was dead. The stunned country and the sympathetic world were joined in grief by television during his burial.

UPI

THE ASSASSIN

LEE HARVEY OSWALD, who allegedly fired upon the President from the Texas School Book Depository in Dallas, was a confused man who felt himself inadequate. A veteran, he once applied for Russian citizenship, but returned home with his Russian-born wife.

they may live, are citizens of Berlin. And therefore, as a free man, I take pride in the words *Ich bin ein Berliner.*" The cadence of his sentences rang through Europe and the world.

After Berlin he went to the land of his ancestors, Ireland, and from there to Rome to meet with the new Pope, Paul VI.

Kennedy wanted not only men in Berlin to be free, but men everywhere. He was a strong supporter of Negro rights—he urged an end to racial discrimination—its continuation was intolerable. Shortly after taking office he had created a Committee on Equal Employment Oppor-

TAKING THE OATH IN THE CABIN OF AIR FORCE ONE AT 2:38 P.M. (Central Time). Before flying back to Washington, Vice President Johnson is sworn in by U.S. District Court Judge Sarah Hughes (her hand holds the microphone). He is flanked by his wife and Mrs. Kennedy. Behind Mr. Johnson are Dallas Police Chief Jesse Curry, Texas Congressman Homer Thornberry, Texas Congressman Jack Brooks, Dr. George Burkley and Kenneth P. O'Donnell.

tunity to enforce his order on equal rights in hiring by the government and its contractors. He appointed Robert C. Weaver, a Negro, to the Housing and Home Finance Agency and made it a Cabinet post. He ordered the end of all discrimination in housing built or purchased with Federal aid. He called out the National Guard after Governor Ross Barnett and the local authorities would not maintain law and order upon the entrance of student James Meredith to the University of Mississippi. He thwarted Governor George Wallace's attempt to bar a black student from entering the University of Alabama. Kennedy's course was clear: "We are confronted pri-

marily with a moral issue. It is as old as the Scriptures and it is as clear as the American Constitution. The heart of the question is whether all Americans care to be afforded equal rights and equal opportunities; whether we are going to treat our fellow Americans as we want to be treated.

"If an American, because his skin is dark, cannot eat lunch in a restaurant open to the public; if he cannot send his children to the best school available; if he cannot vote for the public officials who represent him; if, in short, he cannot enjoy the full and free life which all of us want, then who among us would be content to have the color of his skin changed and stand in his place?

THE NATION'S HEART STOOD STILL.

A LAST FAREWELL. His wife and daughter pray at the flag-draped coffin, lying in state in the Capitol Rotunda.

UPI

THE PROCESSION ESCORTING THE CASKET

UPI

THE CHIEF MOURNERS: His wife and his brother Robert at the burial in Arlington National Cemetery.

"Who among us would then be content with the counsels of patience and delay? One hundred years have passed since President Lincoln freed the slaves, yet their heirs, their grandsons, are not fully free. They are not yet freed from the bonds of injustice; they are not yet freed from social and economic oppression.

"And this nation, for all its hopes and all its boasts, will not be fully free until all its citizens are free."

The core of his domestic program was to get the economy moving again. During the Eisenhower years the rate of economic growth had been about 2 or 3 percent a year. The philosophy of the "balanced budget" had not been able to prevent recessions—in 1954, in 1958 and in 1960—and a rise in unemployment. In three years under Kennedy the growth rate of the economy rose to 5 percent and unemployment fell. Thus the Keynesian deficit spending became the cornerstone of American economic policies. A barrage of laws was submitted to Congress aimed at the improvement of the economy and the welfare of people. There were proposals for an increase in the minimum wage, a tax cut, measures against air and water pollution, drug labeling, increases in Social Security benefits, fair housing, health facilities, manpower development and training, and others. Congress responded. Of 165 bills introduced by the Kennedy administration, 108 were passed—two out of every three.

Foreign affairs took on a new direction. The essence of the President's philosophy was contained in his statement: "This generation of Americans has already had enough—more than enough—of war and hate and oppression. We shall be prepared if others wish it. We shall be alert to try to stop it. But we shall also do our part to build a world of peace where the weak are safe and the strong are just."

Troubles were brewing in Southeast Asia. The administration supported the pro-Western leaders of Laos. The Laotians were so apathetic about their civil war that it was a relief when the Geneva agreements provided for the country's neutrality. Aid was also given to Thailand and South Vietnam—and when South Vietnam's President Ngo Dinh Diem was ousted, there seemed to be some hope for a government more responsive to the needs of the Vietnamese.

Kennedy kept the armed forces prepared to fight, if the worst should come. But he also worked for a détente in East-West relations—to avoid war. A "limited but practical step forward" was the establishment of the "hot line" between Washington and Moscow. The wheat sales to Russia eased tensions, but the stellar point in American-Russian relations was the signing of a treaty prohibiting nuclear testing in the atmosphere, in space and under water. The diplomats of the three signatory countries—the United States, the Union of Soviet Socialist Republics and Great Britain—stated: "The heads of the three delegations agreed that the test ban treaty constituted an important first step toward the reduction of international tension and the strengthening of peace, and they look forward to further progress in this direction." Kennedy called the treaty "a shaft of light cut into the darkness of cold war discords and tensions."

In the third week of November 1963 Kennedy, ready to campaign for his re-election, journeyed to Texas to repair the rift between the liberal Senator Ralph Yarborough and the conservative Governor John Connally.

At noon on the twenty-second of that month, he rode in an open car through the streets of Dallas toward the place of a luncheon meeting which he was to address. The crowd who lined the route cheered him, and he waved and smiled in response. How often he had ridden in such a cavalcade, sitting in an open car, showing himself to the people. Then, in the flicker of a moment, disaster struck. A gunshot, and another and still another. Kennedy slumped in the seat, his wife holding on to him. In a few minutes America and the world learned that the President had been shot. Churches filled up; the people prayed for their President's recovery. It was not to be. The bulletin from the hospital where Kennedy had been taken announced that the President was dead. A brillant young life was extinguished. A hopeful new era came to an abrupt end. Americans watching the proceedings on television were shocked and stunned.

After Kennedy's death Vice President Johnson drove to the airport and in the cabin of the presidential plane, flanked by his wife and Mrs. Kennedy, took the oath of office. Then, with the coffin bearing the remains of his predecessor, the plane took off for Washington.

Kennedy's coffin was taken to the Capitol, where it lay in state. Men and women, young and old, white and black, filed by in long lines to pay their last respects. Mrs. Kennedy came with her daughter and knelt before the coffin.

On the day of the funeral a caisson pulled by six horses carried the coffin, followed by the riderless "Black Jack" with empty boots facing backward in the stirrups. The widow and the family, the great figures of the Republic and leaders of the world, followed on foot to the funeral services at St. Matthew's Cathedral. After the burial at Arlington National Cemetery, Mrs. Kennedy lit the eternal flame at the grave site.

On that day Alistair Cooke, the brilliant English newspaperman, wrote: "This charming, complicated, subtle and greatly intelligent man, whom the Western world was proud to call its leader, appeared for a split second in the telescopic sight of a maniac's rifle. And he was snuffed out. In that moment, all the decent grief of a nation was taunted and outraged. So that along with the sorrow, there is a desperate and howling note from over the land. We may pray on our knees, but when we get up from them, we cry with the poet:
Do not go gentle into that good night.
Rage, rage against the dying of the light."

AN UNFORGETTABLE PHOTOGRAPH
The grieving widow

LYNDON B. JOHNSON

Every President has wanted to be remembered as a good one, and Johnson's ambitions were bigger than those of any of his predecessors. He wanted to be numbered with the greatest Presidents, to stand on the same pedestal with Washington, Lincoln and Roosevelt.

He started out well, taking firm control after the catastrophe. He knew how to use power—"Power was his business." Under his guidance the dreams of Kennedy became realities: civil rights legislation, aid to education, Medicare. He was on the way to creating the Great Society when, in the words of Tom Wicker, he "found instead an ugly little war that consumed him."

A complex personality, a contradictory character, his tastes and performances shaped by his native Texas, he was restless, ever racing, always on the go. Proud and haughty, he gave the impression of being a supreme egotist. "He was, sadly, mainly interested in Lyndon Johnson and what it all meant for him," wrote his biographer. He would dramatize himself as no other President before him. He had a monumental arrogance. In Vietnam once, when a young army officer pointed with deep respect: "That's your helicopter over there, sir," Johnson replied: "Son, they're all my helicopters."

In the anxious days following the assassination Johnson's first task was to assure the country that he would continue the Kennedy policies. The new President appeared subdued, striking a balance between the humility of his position as Kennedy's successor and the forcefulness required of him as Chief Executive. Political pundits speculated on how Johnson would establish his personal image in the White House, for he was quite different from Kennedy in background, temperament and style. A Texan, a country schoolteacher, a powerful and persuasive Senate infighter, a rancher who knew more about the problems of locating water in a sun-parched land than about international relations, Johnson personified the provincialism and grit of the frontiersman rather than the suave urbanity and cultured wit of his sophisticated predecessor.

At the time of the funeral Johnson met the political leaders of the world who came to Washington to pay their respects to the slain President. Johnson was eager to have a talk with French President De Gaulle to patch up the deteriorating relations between the two countries. He hoped, in the words of the political columnists Evans and Novak, that "his rare combination of persuasion, intimidation and charm . . . could be as effective in the international sphere as it had been in the Senate, reinforced as it now was by presidential power." He hoped to secure De Gaulle's cooperation. After their meeting he boasted: "I think he likes *me*. I am going to try to work *with* him—not force something down his throat. If you force three Bourbons into Luci, it will all come up. I've told everyone who has anything to do with it: stop telling Europeans they have to do *this* or *that*—or *else*."

But the wooing of the French President did not lead to the expected results. Johnson announced that De Gaulle would return for further talks—but De Gaulle denied he had any such intentions. Not long thereafter he granted diplomatic recognition to Red China—a slap in the face of American policy makers.

Johnson's other attempts at personal diplomacy were not too successful, either. Though he obtained a promise from Germany's Ludwig Erhard to stop trading with

THE FATHER OF THE BRIDE
Abbie Rowe

CANDIDATES IN 1964

LYNDON B. JOHNSON (1908———) became President following Kennedy's assassination. An effective Chief Executive, his liberal domestic policies won popular acclaim. At the peak of his popularity Johnson was nominated and campaigned against the warmongering attitude of his Republican opponent. But his involvement in Vietnam led America into a tragic morass, threatening the disruption of the country's moral fiber.

HUBERT H. HUMPHREY (1911———) taught political science and worked for the WPA under the New Deal before he was elected Mayor of Minneapolis. Elected to the U.S. Senate three times, in 1960 he ran in several presidential primaries, but lost to Kennedy. Long thought of as merely a talkative liberal who favored the Negroes and the unions, he was the popular Majority Whip when chosen as Johnson's running mate.

BARRY M. GOLDWATER (1902———), Senator from Arizona and millionaire heir to a department store fortune, was chosen by the conservative wing of the Republican party to offer the voters a "choice, not an echo." He campaigned for a resolute war in Asia, a strong stand against the Russians and against the welfare state at home. He lost disastrously— Johnson had 43,129,489 votes, Goldwater only 27,178,188.

WILLIAM E. MILLER (1914———), a nationally obscure Congressman from New York, was chosen by the Republicans as the vice presidential candidate. Republican national chairman from 1961 to 1964, he headed the party's Congressional campaign committee in 1960, gaining 22 seats for the Republicans. An Easterner and a Roman Catholic known for barbed comments about Democrats, he was not a fortunate choice.

UPI

CLAUDIA ALTA TAYLOR (1912–   ) was raised in a rural corner of northeast Texas. She built up an inheritance of less than $70,000 to an undisclosed figure in the millions, much of it in the LBJ Company. "She's my strength," says Johnson, and columnist Hugh Sidey writes: "She is almost unreal, controlled, determined, subdued, kindly, intelligent, dedicated."

Castro's Cuba, a similar request to Prime Minister Douglas-Home of Great Britain was denied. Relations with the Soviet Union did not improve. Thus his appetite for face-to-face diplomacy waned, particularly after his frigid meeting with the Prime Minister of Canada and after the cancellation of the meetings with the political heads of Pakistan and India. "With all the power of the presidency at his disposal, Johnson was unable to tame the world as he tamed Congress," wrote his biographers.

He focused his attention on domestic issues, which he understood better than the foreign problems. Many pieces of legislation instigated by Kennedy were still not acted upon by Congress—the Civil Rights Bill, the Mass Transit Act, a proposal for hospital construction, medical care for the aged, the tax-cut bill, and others. Johnson

Abbie Rowe, November 28, 1963

FIRST FAMILY. PRESIDENT, 19-YEAR-OLD LYNDA BIRD, FIRST LADY AND 16-YEAR-OLD LUCI BAINES

geared himself to persuade the reluctant law-makers to get the job done; he was a past master at bringing his former colleagues into line. "Let us continue," Johnson intoned in his first address to Congress, to complete the New Frontier legislation and "highly resolve that John Fitzgerald Kennedy did not live—or die—in vain."

The top item on his agenda was the budget. Late in 1962 Kennedy had asked for a $10 billion tax reduction at a time when the country's economy was on the upswing. After Kennedy's death Johnson realized that to get the tax reduction he would have to give up $1½ billion in expenditures. So he whittled the budget down to $97.9 billion, a figure about $3½ billion less than the Kennedy budget and $24 billion less than the original requests from governmental agencies.

Johnson then proceeded to dramatize his role as the nation's responsible economist by one of his characteristic gestures; he ran around switching off the lights in the White House to show off his frugality. That he recommended a $100-billion budget and tried to be frugal on the electric bill tickled the funnybone of Americans. "The White House has gone from Camelot to Johnson City, runs a current wisecrack, and that is about as far as you can go. In turning off the lights at the White House, Mr. Johnson has signaled the end of a brief era in more ways than one," wrote the *New Statesman*.

During the time of transition the country sympathized with Johnson's desire to ensure continuity while at the same time cutting himself loose from the Kennedy mystique and establishing a distinctive style. To win the con-

Cartoon by John Fischetti, Chicago Daily News, *January 1964*

THE PLEA OF THE CARTOONIST: "DON'T SHOOT THE PIANIST—HE DOES THE BEST HE CAN."

fidence of the Kennedy supporters, he had begged the dispirited team of the dead President to work with him ("I need you more than he did"); now he vied for the affection of reporters by inviting them to cookouts, he impressed Washington visitors by asking passers-by to join in brisk impromptu walks around the White House grounds. ("I appreciate your coming here because I feel that I have rapport with you and they won't let me get out of the gate so I am glad they let you in.")

By the time he delivered his first State of the Union address in January 1964, Johnson was ready to strike out on his own: "Let this session of Congress be known as the session which did more for civil rights than the last hundred sessions combined; as the session which enacted the most far-reaching tax cut of our time; as the session which declared all-out war on human poverty and unemployment in these United States; as the session which finally recognized the health needs of all our older citizens; as the session which reformed our tangled transportation and transit policies; as the session which achieved the most effective, efficient foreign-aid program ever; and as the session which helped build more homes, more schools, more libraries, and more hospitals than any single session of Congress in the history of our Republic."

And he declared an "unconditional war on poverty."

The message was well received. "More than any other State of the Union message in a quarter-century of war and cold war, he assigns overwhelming priority to the solution of urgent domestic problems rather than to the strengthening of our military defenses or the undertaking of new ventures in the international field," editorialized *The New York Times,* and Walter Lippmann wrote in his column: "In style and in substance the President's message is an intimate and personal display of the political gifts for which Lyndon Johnson is celebrated. He shows himself to be a passionate seeker with an uncanny gift for finding, beneath the public issues, common ground on which men could stand."

Johnson worked hard to form his image. And this image, as Eric Sevareid put it, "will not be charm, glamour or intellectuality, as with Kennedy. It will not be warmth of personality as with Eisenhower, or the homespun characteristic of Truman. Simply put, it will be strength. If all goes well with him, his public image will be that of 'boss.' "

He plunged into the Presidency of his own, wrote *Time,* "with a headlong velocity. No man in the White House has ever moved faster. . . . Corny as johnnycake,

THE COMING CAMPAIGN IN TWO CARTOONS

Cartoon by Bill Mauldin, January 1964

THE REPUBLICAN ELEPHANT IS BRANDED.

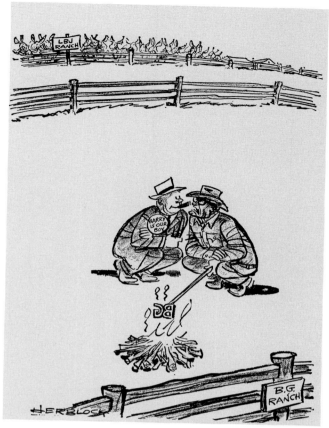

Cartoon by Herblock, January 1964

GOLDWATER SEARCHES FOR HIS OWN HERD.

folksy as a country fiddler, persuasive as a television pitchman, he is also both efficient and effective"—not an accolade to be dismissed lightly coming from that quarter.

The essence of his political philosophy was that politics was a profession and it had to be mastered. He understood that he could only be successful if he could bring the opposite parties together in a compromise. "The people of the world," he said, "prefer reasoned argument to ready attack. That is why we must follow the prophet Isaiah many, many times before we send the Marines, and say, 'Come now, let us reason together.'"

He wanted to do the right thing. One of his close friends observed that "ninety percent of what he wants is right but ninety percent of the way he does it is wrong." And Congressman Wright Patman, who had known him since his childhood, said: "He is not a liberal but a do-gooder," and he added: "He is directed not by a philosophy or a schedule of achievable progress but by glandular gooses, most of them brought on by the approach of November." At heart he was a Jacksonian Democrat and a Populist. He desperately aspired to leave his mark on the Presidency. In the spring of 1964 he said, "Every night when I go to bed I ask myself: 'What did

we do today that we can point to for generations to come, to say that we laid the foundation for a better and more peaceful and more prosperous world?'"

But the moratorium on partisan politics after Kennedy's death soon came to an end. The campaign for the Presidency was off the ground.

Republicans were eager for a crack at the administration. "Big spending, high taxes, a losing war, big giveaways, policing of local affairs by the Federal Government, tolerance of Communism next door in Cuba, relief abuses, lagging weapon development—all these are points along the line of Republican attack," editorialized *U.S. News & World Report.*

One of the foremost Republican contenders was Governor Rockefeller of New York, who had tried for the nomination in 1960, and when he failed he used his influence to update the party platform. In 1962 his wife of thirty years divorced him; that same year he was re-elected Governor by a large margin. But, when he remarried in May 1963, his Gallup Poll rating dropped. His new wife had recently been divorced, leaving four of her small children with her estranged husband. The storm of criticism was more intense than the 13-percentage-point drop in his popularity, indicated by the poll.

THE "DEATH MARCH"—JOHNSON'S PRESS CONFERENCE ON THE WHITE HOUSE GROUNDS

The man who gained from Rockefeller's personal troubles was Barry Goldwater, the conservative Arizona Senator. A winning personality, author of *The Conscience of a Conservative,* he felt that his principles made him "a true Republican and that he alone is qualified to speak for the party." Election year was only three days old when he announced his candidacy. Running against him were the moderate, or middle-of-the-road, men. But all of them were in trouble. Nixon had lost a bid for the governorship of California in 1962—he had to take a "wait and see" attitude. Governor Romney of Michigan had failed to solidify his support. Harold Stassen, once again in the fray, could not be taken seriously. Henry Cabot Lodge had had a benevolent pat on the back from Eisenhower, but he was vulnerable because of his service under the Democrats as Ambassador to South Vietnam. For a while it looked as if Eisenhower would favor Governor Scranton of Pennsylvania, a liberal intellectual from a wealthy family.

And while the Republican contenders were fighting it out, the President, safe in the knowledge of his party's nomination, stayed aloof. He desired to show the country that his main intent was to attend to affairs of state. He would have liked to spend the remainder of his term concentrating on civil rights legislation and his war on poverty, but events around the world forced him to relegate his domestic program to second place.

Not long after his State of the Union message, the administration faced a series of crises. The student demonstrations in Panama against American rule erupted into a full-scale riot. The symbolic issue was whether the flag of Panama should be permitted to fly in the American-leased Canal Zone; the real issue was Panama's demand for re-negotiation of the 1903 treaty between the two countries. When, on January 7, American students defiantly hoisted the Stars and Stripes at Balboa High School, Panamanians took to the streets in protest.

Johnson telephoned Panama's President Chiari, asking for restraint. But Chiari insisted on renegotiation of the treaty. The next day demonstrators stormed the American Embassy in Panama City. Pressured by Senators Dirksen and Russell not to give in to "every little country," Johnson rebuffed an attempt by the Organization of American States to mediate the dispute. Yet the outcry against this action was so strong that he had to agree to "review" the issues with Panama and negotiate a new treaty.

The Panama affair highlighted the "Johnson reaction" to a political crisis—personal attention to every detail by the President to an extent that was alarming to many observers and an omen for the future.

Crisis followed crisis. An American jet trainer was shot down when it violated East German airspace. The government of Zanzibar was overthrown. Malaysia and Indonesia grappled in the South Seas. Greeks and Turks fought on Cyprus. In South Vietnam the second coup in three months removed the American-supported puppet government.

At home civil rights advocates boycotted the New York City school system. The Bobby Baker scandal was revived when the Senate Rules Committee published the testimony of Don B. Reynolds, who had taken Baker into his insurance firm as vice president in the late 1950s in order to exploit his political contacts. Baker, a farm boy from South Carolina, had risen from Senate page to become a Johnson protégé. He was Johnson's eyes and ears in the Senate and rose to wield great authority, eventually controlling campaign funds. Johnson told him: "You're like a son to me, because I don't have a son of my own." While influence peddling was an old story in Washington, the Bobby Baker revelations were a sorry affair, revealing a side of Johnson's character that was not reassuring.

Not having a preferred candidate, the Republicans hoped that the decision would be made in the primaries. Rockefeller and Goldwater were ready to fight it out in three states: New Hampshire, Oregon and California.

In his New Hampshire campaign Goldwater made rash statements. He proposed the use of atomic weapons by NATO area "commanders," he suggested breaking diplomatic relations with the Soviet Union, and he came out for the abolition of the graduated income tax. He often spoke before he had time to think. He was impolitic. He pleaded for voluntary Social Security—and that in a state with a high percentage of elderly citizens. In Tennessee and the depressed areas of Appalachia he advocated that

UPI
"HIM" AND "HER" WALKING THE PRESIDENT

THROUGH SNOW AND SLEET—Senator Goldwater campaigns during a cold February in the New Hampshire primary.

the TVA be sold. Some of his remarks were attempts at friendly banter. On one occasion he said: "Sometimes I think this country would be better off if we could just saw off the Eastern Seaboard and let it float out to sea," and on another: "Let's lob one into the men's room of the Kremlin."

When such remarks appeared in print the Goldwater staff complained that the newspapermen distorted the candidate's statements. But Goldwater's lack of judgment could not be ignored. A flying Major General in the Air Force Reserve, the Senator struck out against reliance on modern missiles instead of SAC bombers: "I don't feel safe at all about our missiles. I wish the Defense Department would tell the American people how undependable the missiles in our silos actually are. I can't tell you—it's classified—and I'll probably catch hell for saying this." He did, from the Defense Secretary and the Pentagon. He returned tit for tat. His opinion of Secretary McNamara was: "If he were my Secretary of Defense, he'd be back making Edsels for Ford the next day."

The more Goldwater talked, the more devil-may-care his attitude seemed. He suggested "defoliating" the jungles of Vietnam with low-yield nuclear weapons; he proposed withdrawing from the United Nations if Red China were admitted.

When in February Fidel Castro cut off the water at the United States naval base in Guantanamo in reprisal for U.S. seizure of four Cuban fishing vessels sailing in Florida waters, Johnson ordered that fresh water be brought in by tankers and insisted on firing some 2,500 Cubans who worked on the base. Goldwater wanted him to go further: "Turn the water on or we are going to march out with a detachment of Marines and turn it on."

And when Goldwater was not attacking the administration for not using American power in international affairs, he was damning Johnson's attempts to mobilize the country's full resources to fight poverty and human misery at home. Leaving his New Hampshire campaign for a day, he gave his ideas before the Economic Club of New York. "We are told that many people lack skills and

THROUGH THE BALMY NIGHTS—Governor Rockefeller campaigns on an evening in May in the California primary.

cannot find jobs because they did not have an education," he said. "That's like saying that people have big feet because they wear big shoes. The fact is that most people who had no skills have no education for the same reason —low intelligence or low ambition."

Coming from a man who had inherited a department store and who lived the luxurious ranch life aspired to by many hard-working people, his statement was particularly offensive.

Despite the endorsement of the ultraconservative Manchester *Union Leader,* the reaction to Goldwater in New Hampshire was negative. His contradictory statements and his half-baked solutions to complex problems antagonized the voters. One of his supporters complained: "If he doesn't mean what he says, then he's just trying to get votes; and if he does mean what he says— then the man is dangerous. So I quit."

Analyzing Goldwater's abilities, Walter Lippmann thought that "his normal political instinct is to dodge these issues in order to allow his less extreme supporters

to say that he never really meant them. But it will be remarkable if the Republicans, whose political lives are mortally challenged, and the Democrats, who are not careless in these matters, allow Senator Goldwater to weasel his way out of the absurdities he has uttered—on the income tax, our relations with Russia, Social Security, the Tennessee Valley, and the racial question. If he tries to retreat to a more moderate position, he will mar his one greatest political asset—the image of himself as a no-nonsense, put-up or shut-up, rough-riding he-man."

To Goldwater's claim that he represented the true conservative tradition, Lippmann rejoined: "Barry Goldwater is not a conservative at all. He appears to be totally without the essential conservative respect and concern for the social order as a living body. He is a radical reactionary who would, if we are to believe what he says, dismantle the modern state. His political philosophy does not have its roots in the conservative tradition but in the crude and primitive capitalism of the Manchester school. It is the philosophy not of the conservators of the social

Cartoon by Burris Jenkins, Jr., April 1964

WHOM SHALL I CHOOSE? The dilemma of the former President. The candidates are lined up, but he cannot decide.

Cartoon by Herblock, July 1964

WILL IT BE B.G.? Some of the Republican liberals band together to prevent the endorsement of Barry Goldwater.

Cartoon by Stannery, July 1964

STILL WAITING FOR THE WORD from party idol ex-President Eisenhower—Governor Scranton worries.

A VIEW OF THE PRESS AND GOLDWATER: "Of course you're prejudiced—you print everything I say," he complains.

Cartoon by Fischetti, August 1964

order but of the newly rich on the make."

Joseph Alsop went even further. "Charmed by the handsome, vital Goldwater exterior and impressed by his enthusiastic following, even the more progressive Republican politicos had supposed that Goldwater was also a clever politician. This was the delusion. For the plain truth is that the hero of the alleged 'conservatives' is much less like a politician than a highly successful Chautauqua lecturer."

As the campaign in New Hampshire progressed, Goldwater's fortunes ebbed—but Rockefeller's did not rise. The choice was "too wide between the two." Even though Rockefeller had presented a balanced budget for his state with no increase in taxes, the thought of the total of nearly $3 billion was too much for a state with no income or sales tax. And there was the question of Happy: "It's not right for a man to throw away his old wife and take up with a younger woman."

Sentiment began shifting toward possible write-in choices—to Nixon as well as Lodge. Nixon did not campaign in the state, and the effort for Lodge was carried out by two men and two women on a shoestring. They made a series of direct-mail appeals, a "madcap adventure, the gayest, the happiest, the most lighthearted enterprise of the entire year."

On voting day it snowed fourteen inches and the result was in keeping with the weather. Lodge, 10,000 miles away in Saigon, won the primary with 33,000 write-in votes. Goldwater trailed with 20,700 votes, Rockefeller with 19,500 and Nixon with 15,600 write-ins.

After his defeat Goldwater concentrated on California and ignored Rockefeller's challenge in Oregon, where Rockefeller campaigned hard to put the party back into the "mainstream" of American life. His motto, "He Cares Enough to Come," gave him a landslide of 93,000 votes. Lodge was second with 78,000, Goldwater a poor third with 50,000, followed closely by Nixon with 48,000.

But behind the scenes, the Goldwater organization had quietly gathered delegates—most of them from state conventions. It was said that Goldwater had 550 delegates "in the bag," and he needed just about a hundred more for victory. With California's 80 delegates he would almost have it; but if he lost the state, his previous support might disappear. It was Rockefeller's last chance to stop his adversary.

Billboards, banners and stickers on cars advertised the final duel. For Goldwater: "We Want a Choice; Not an Echo," "Au H$_2$O = 1964" and "You Know Where He Stands—Vote for the Man You Can Trust." For Rockefeller: "Vote for the Responsible Republican"

UPI, July 13, 1964

OUTSIDE THE CONVENTION James Farmer, the director of CORE, leads demonstrators in an anti-Goldwater parade.

and "Keep America in the Mainstream."

Goldwater had control of the Republican organization. The conservatives reasoned that as the two parties offered the voters essentially the same platform, the large vote untapped in previous elections must represent those alienated conservatives who felt the two parties afforded them no spokesman in government. The Goldwater forces mustered all who felt that peaceful coexistence was appeasement, that the economy was inflationary, that foreign aid was mere mollycoddling of small nations, that states had the right to disobey federal desegregation orders, that the Federal Government was arrogating too much power to itself. There were thousands of ladies—young and old, with and without tennis shoes—and disciplined Young Republicans to go from door to door.

Rockefeller barnstormed the state, making speeches

from early morning to late in the evening. His organization sent a pamphlet, "Who Do You Want in the Room with the H Bomb?," to all of the state's two million registered Republicans. More than a thousand paid telephone workers solicited votes for him. The polls put him ahead of Goldwater. Then on May 30, three days before election day, his new wife Happy gave birth to a son, reminding the electorate of his divorce—a most unfortunate timing.

California went to Goldwater. He won by 68,000 popular votes out of over two million. His victory, in the opinion of *The New York Times,* "will make it difficult —and perhaps impossible—to block his nomination as the Republican Presidential candidate. His designation, however, would be a disaster not only for the Republicans but for all who believe that a vigorous two-party system is

INSIDE THE COW PALACE the delegates wait for former President Eisenhower to address the convention.

necessary to the political health of America. It would put command of the Republican party in the hands of its most backward elements—those who believe that the problems of an era of dynamic change can be met by policies that would have been retrogressive a generation ago."

Those who believed in policies "of an era of dynamic change" had been absent in California. Only some of Lodge's supporters were willing to help Rockefeller. The others—Nixon, Romney and Scranton—stayed on the sidelines waiting for Goldwater to lose. As Rockefeller said bitterly, "All of them are available for the nomination and hoping that lightning will strike."

On June 7 the annual Governors Conference was to meet at Cleveland. Forty-eight hours before the meeting Eisenhower telephoned Scranton, and the Governor went to Gettysburg for a talk. And when Scranton left, he was under the impression that Eisenhower would support him. This brought favorable comment from Walter Lippmann: "The critical question now is not whether Gov. Scranton can at this late date stop the Goldwater machine. The important thing is that the party will not be surrendered without a fight and that there will remain therefore a man around whom the party can rally for the elections of 1966 and 1968."

The next day Scranton arrived in Cleveland, where Romney had already delivered an impassioned appeal to the sixteen Republican governors, a blast with "all the fervor of a missionary statement," to dump Goldwater. Scranton, waiting to appear on the television show *Face the Nation,* learned that Eisenhower had tried to reach him on the phone. When he returned the call the General

BLOCKING THE EXIT OF THE HALL is a sit-in at one of the turnstiles as bi-racial demonstrators protest the platform plank on civil rights.

A DUMMY OF SCRANTON IS CARRIED INSIDE

told him that he would not be part of any "cabal" to stop Goldwater. Thus when the television cameras began to grind, Scranton pocketed the statement announcing his candidacy. Instead he stumbled through a half-hour of questions with awkward answers. He said that he was "available" as a candidate but he would not fight for the nomination. "I don't plan to go out and try to defeat Senator Goldwater. I have no such intention. I do think it is important . . . that the party keep to its sound footing."

Scranton's television appearance and his press conference had disastrous consequences. Newspaper writers called him "the toothless tiger." When Rockefeller was asked if he would support Scranton, he replied: "Governor Scranton said that he was waiting to see where Sen-

ator Goldwater stood. . . . I think I've got to wait to see where he stands." Scranton seemed like a puppet on an Eisenhower string. He knew that if Goldwater was to be stopped, a candidate had to be found instantly. Thus he and Rockefeller and Rhodes of Ohio decided on Romney's candidacy.

For the next two days the Republican governors issued unity-and-harmony statements. The final touch was provided by the appearance of Richard Nixon. In an impromptu press conference Nixon observed that there was a "new force in being to stop extremism"; still, most newsmen speculated that Nixon was using Romney to deadlock the convention and secure the nomination for himself, as the "great healer."

Yet extremism was in the saddle. On June 10 in the Senate, Goldwater voted against cloture on the Civil Rights Act filibuster. And nine days later—a year after the introduction of the Civil Rights Bill—Goldwater was

RUFFLED TEMPERS. Police refused United Press photographer Joel Schrank permission to take a picture of the CORE demonstrators.

UPI

A DEMONSTRATOR IS CARTED OUT OF THE HALL.

UPI

one of the 27 Senators who voted against it. Explaining his vote he said that though he was "unalterably opposed to discrimination," the real answer lay in the good will in the human heart. For Goldwater the Bill succeeded only because "emotion and political pressure, not persuasion, not common sense, not deliberation, had become the rule of the day. . . ." The Senate had ignored the Constitution and "the fundamental concepts of our government system. My basic objection to this measure is, therefore, constitutional." Goldwater argued that the provisions for nondiscrimination in public accommodations and employment would result in a police state, and he concluded, "If my vote is misconstrued, let it be, and let me suffer the consequences. Just let me be judged in this by the real concern I have voiced here and not by words that others may speak or by what others may say about what I think."

But in the Republican party—the party founded on the

slavery issue, the party of Lincoln—the majority sentiment was for the human liberties and civil rights of all citizens, especially as the civil rights movement, with its impressive sit-ins and passive demonstrations, was growing in influence and import.

Since the year of 1954 that movement had come of age; it was no longer a sectional struggle. Negroes all over the country, with increasing support from the white community, resisted openly the humiliations they had endured in the past. They had moral fervor and the idea of a movement with a Christian basis: nonviolence. Their leader, the Reverend Martin Luther King, Jr., told his white colleagues that "we have not made a single gain in civil rights without determined legal and nonviolent pres-

WILLIAM KNOWLAND LEADS THE CHEERS for Goldwater. The other Californians have gold balloons.

THE SCRANTON CHILDREN: Fourteen-year-old Joe and eighteen-year-old Suzan cheer avidly for their father.

SCRANTON DEMONSTRATION shortly after Milton Eisenhower placed the Governor's name in nomination.

GOVERNOR ROCKEFELLER, BOOED and hooted. "This is still a free country, ladies and gentlemen," he said.

sure. . . . We know through painful experience that freedom is never voluntarily given by the oppressor; it must be demanded by the oppressed. . . . For years now I have heard the word 'Wait.' It rings in the ear of every Negro with a piercing familiarity. This 'Wait' has always meant 'Never.'. . . We must come to see with the distinguished jurist of yesterday that 'justice too long delayed is justice denied.' We have waited for more than three hundred and forty years for our constitutional and God-given rights."

The Southern Christian Leadership Conference planned a confrontation through the principles of nonviolence in Birmingham, a city with a black population of 35 per-

cent. Negroes asked to be able to eat at the same lunch counters as whites in the downtown stores, and that a biracial group be set up to plan school desegregation. On April 3, 1963, the first forty of three hundred volunteers were arrested for attempting to be served at lunch counters, forty more the second day; on the third day the shops were closed. Dr. King's movement spread—Birmingham's Negroes joined together in marches—hundreds of them were arrested. On Good Friday Dr. King, too, was arrested and put in prison. By the first week of May the jails of Birmingham were full. When 5,000 Negroes demonstrated, the police dispersed them with dogs and fire

A MOCK FUNERAL is staged after the convention gave the nomination to Barry Goldwater on the first ballot.

SENATOR MORTON orders the aisles cleared after a clash between photographers and the sergeants-at-arms.

THE ROCKEFELLER DEMONSTRATION: But with his recent loss in the California primary it seemed futile.

GOLDWATER ON THE PLATFORM, amidst cascading balloons, accepts the Republican presidential nomination.

hoses—they did not arrest them.

A few days later a truce was worked out. Then a Negro motel and the home of Dr. King's brother were bombed. Riots followed. Alabama state police, the Stars and Bars painted on their helmets, moved in. Once Birmingham quieted, upheavals and demonstrations were reported in Jacksonville, Memphis, Baton Rouge—all over the South —and the cities of the North, too: Chicago, New York, Philadelphia, Detroit. John F. Kennedy's prophetic words "Unless the Congress acts, the Negroes' only remedy is in the street" seemed to be borne out.

President Johnson pressed for the passage of the Civil Rights Bill. Speaking in Gettysburg, he said: "Until justice is blind to color, until education is unaware of race, until opportunity is unconcerned with the color of men's skins, emancipation will be a proclamation but not a fact."

After Goldwater's vote against cloture of the filibuster Eisenhower once more called Scranton and told him how angry he was over Goldwater's vote and expected that Scranton would speak out on the issue. Scranton decided to fight for the nomination, hoping that "even if we lose— we have to create a rallying point in our party for people of our generation." He became officially a candidate, flying from state to state, appearing on television, appealing to Republican delegates. He prodded Goldwater, "I urge you to repudiate your opposition to the civil rights bill. . . . Your views on the subject to date are opposed to the traditional Republican philosophy of equal opportunity for all, and it is of great importance to our party that you now change your views."

He also pointed to the polls in which Johnson led with 62 percent against Goldwater's 29 percent. Yet the Goldwater camp seemed to have the delegates' support. Charles Halleck, the minority leader in the House, told Scranton, "Come back and see me before the second ballot—if there is one."

With his chances dim, Scranton's aim was to "put the nation and the rank and file of the party on the alert to the fact that our leading candidate was impetuous, irresponsible and slightly stupid." The Scranton men tried to override the Goldwater-controlled platform committee. They wanted to have planks against a national right-to-work law, against extremism, for the advocacy of civil rights, for a reaffirmation that only the President—not subordinate military commanders—should be allowed to use nuclear weapons.

And while Scranton was wooing the delegates, his staff composed a letter and sent it to Goldwater. Scranton had not seen it, nor did he sign it. "With open contempt for the dignity, integrity and common sense of the convention, your managers say in effect that the delegates are little more than a flock of chickens whose necks will be wrung at will," read the letter. "You have too often casually prescribed nuclear war as a solution to a troubled world. You have too often allowed the radical extremists to use you. You have too often stood for irresponsibility in the serious business of racial holocaust. You have too often read Taft and Eisenhower and Lincoln out of the Republican Party. . . . In short, Goldwaterism has come to stand for a whole crazy-quilt collection of absurd and dangerous positions that would be soundly repudiated by the American people in November." The Goldwaterites had an easy time turning the blunder to their advantage.

On the second day of the convention in San Francisco, Eisenhower addressed the delegates and dealt the death blow to the hopes of the moderates: "Let us particularly scorn the divisive efforts of those outside our family, including sensation-seeking columnists and commentators, because, my friends, I assure you that these are people who couldn't care less about the good of the party." A delegate shouted, "Down with Walter Lippmann!" and the convention proceeded with an ugly demonstration against the press, the columnists and intellectuals in general. It was a sorry performance, not worthy of a great party. Eisenhower touched on the fears of white America: ". . . let us not be guilty of maudlin sympathy for the

SIGNING THE CIVIL RIGHTS BILL. A study in attitudes. Postmaster General Lawrence O'Brien hands the document to the President. Behind them Speaker John McCormack applauds. In the first row the Republicans Everett Dirksen and Charles Halleck (the main participants in the Ev and Charlie show) approve, together with Senator Humphrey, who always applauds the chief. But Senator Robert Kennedy sits deep in thought.

criminal who, roaming the streets with switchblade knife and illegal firearms seeking a helpless prey, suddenly becomes upon apprehension a poor, underprivileged person who counts upon the compassion of our society and the laxness or weakness of too many courts to forgive his offense." The liberals in the hall were dismayed.

After Eisenhower's speech the platform was read; then late in the evening Rockefeller rose to defend a minority resolution, to denounce those extremists he called "kooks" to their very faces. The galleries responded with yells, klaxons, drums and cries of "We Want Barry." The demonstration against Rockefeller lasted for several minutes. Smiling a weary smile, he weathered the storm and said lamely, "This is still a free country, ladies and gentlemen."

And when the storm abated, he spoke of the attacks of the Goldwater men on him and his supporters. "These things have no place in America. But I can personally testify to their existence. And so can countless others who have also experienced anonymous midnight and early morning telephone calls, unsigned threatening letters, smear and hate literature, strong-arm and goon tactics, bomb threats and bombings"—and the savage noise forced him to stop—"infiltration and take-over of established political organizations by Communist and Nazi methods. Some of you don't like to hear it, ladies and gentlemen, but it's the truth."

The emotion raised in the convention against Rockefeller was more than equaled by the demonstration for Goldwater. Gold foil dropped from the ceiling; gold balloons rose to the rafters. By the end of the first ballot he had 883 votes and the nomination. Scranton was second with 214, Rockefeller had 114, Romney 41, Margaret Chase Smith 27, keynoter Walter Judd 22, and Senator Fong of Hawaii 5.

For his running mate Goldwater chose the upstate New York Congressman William E. Miller, who was thought to provide geographic and ethnic balance to the ticket. A worse choice could hardly have been made; he had no qualification for the high office.

In his acceptance speech, Goldwater said: "The Good Lord raised this mighty Republic to be a home for the brave and to flourish as the land of the free. . . . Our people have followed false prophets. We must, and we shall, return to proven ways—not because they are old, but because they are true." And as patriot he saw the party unalterably pledged to: "Freedom! Freedom—made orderly for this nation by our constitutional government. . . . Freedom—balanced so that order, lacking liberty, will not become the slavery of the prison cell; balanced so that liberty, lacking order, will not become the license of the mob and of the jungle." And he saw "violence in our streets, corruption in our highest offices, aimlessness among our youth, anxiety among our elderly. . . ."

Toward the end of the speech came the sentence: "Extremism in the defense of liberty is no vice! And let me remind you also that moderation in the pursuit of justice is no virtue!" It was there that Goldwater lost the election. He could never live that sentence down, nor could he explain it away. Karl Hess, his speech writer, who wrote it, had probably not imagined what effect those words would have. The Republican moderates were aghast. A reporter cried out: "My God, he's going to run as Barry Goldwater."

The nomination of Goldwater dismayed many of the old-time Republicans. His refusal to disavow the support of the Ku Klux Klan and the militantly anti-Communist John Birch Society was strongly attacked by the Democrats. Johnson denounced "all hate organizations under whatever name they mask and prowl and spread their venom," and said: "Savagery of this kind is completely alien to the entire moral and political tradition of the United States. The efforts to force, bully, and intimidate American citizens—to prevent them from claiming their rights under the Constitution—must be stopped." Even the solidly Republican New York *Herald Tribune* was disquieted about the party's candidate. *The New York Times* saw Goldwater supporters reflecting "the wistful voices of the past . . . a mere minority of a minority." Joseph Alsop asked: "Who, then, among the living and the dead, has been cast from the Republican pantheon?" And he named the most prominent Republicans from Lincoln through Eisenhower. In Europe the columnist John Crosby found that "to the average European, Goldwater is a far more menacing prospect than Mao or Khrushchev. Mao talks as wildly as Goldwater but he has no weapons to speak of."

But James Reston wrote that the coming campaign would be a "useful and even illuminating campaign if Senator Goldwater's philosophy is subjected to fair critical debate. . . . It has been a long time since we have had a really good debate in the United States on the fundamentals of our society, on the reasons for our involvement in the world, on the responsibilities and purposes of our alliances, on the new interdependence of the races, the regions, the free nations, and the state and Federal governments, on the problems of a rapidly growing, increasingly urbanized and secularized society charged with guiding a war in the midst of a political, social and economic revolution. . . ."

Two days later the same columnist observed in a sarcastic vein: "Barry Goldwater has done extremely well in the first few days of the Presidential campaign. He has lost the support of Senators Javits and Keating of New York, but he has picked up the opposition of Wladyslaw Gomulka of Poland and Nikita S. Khrushchev of the Soviet Union. He has won the sympathy of David Lawrence, Clare Boothe Luce, Raymond Moley and Henry

THE HOT SUMMER. Race riots broke out in Harlem after the shooting of a fifteen-year-old Negro boy on the morning of July 16. James Powell was walking with friends to a special summer school in a white neighborhood. A white building superintendent took offense at the youths' boisterousness and drenched them with a garden hose. This led to a mounting series of unplanned responses, ending when an off-duty policeman shot Powell. The news enraged the Negro community.

Taylor, but even more important, he has lost the support of most of the other columnists, most of the big Republican papers, and almost all of the Western European press. . . ."

By the end of July a *Christian Science Monitor* survey showed a Goldwater lead in only thirteen states. If Goldwater had lost the support of the Liberal Republicans, he had the support of Governor Wallace. The Alabama Governor had run in several Northern Democratic primaries, "exploiting all the discontents of a troubled and uncertain time and focusing them on the effort of the Negro to attain equality of status through action by the Federal Government," and receiving the "white backlash" votes: 34 percent in Wisconsin, 30 percent in Indiana, 43 percent in Maryland. He had planned to run as a third-party candidate, expecting at best to throw the election to the House. After the nomination of Goldwater, Wallace withdrew.

Foreign political matters came to the fore. Events in Southeast Asia occupied the public's mind. There had been a series of *coups d'état* and juntos in South Vietnam. There had been public protests and self-immolations by Buddhists. But on August 2, as it was then made public, three North Vietnamese patrol boats attacked the American destroyer *Maddox* in the Gulf of Tonkin. The *C. Turner Joy* joined the *Maddox,* and on August 4 both ships were allegedly attacked by six patrol boats (later investigation cast doubt on the truthfulness of the reports). The American response was to bomb North Vietnamese naval facilities. After a grave national television address by the President pledging to meet force with force, Congress hurriedly passed the "Tonkin Resolution," with only Senators Morse and Gruening dissenting. The resolution supported the President in taking "all necessary measures to repel any armed attack against aggression" and affirmed U.S. intentions to aid any

THE DEMOCRATIC CONVENTION

THE PRESIDENT REVEALS HIS CHOICE for the Vice Presidency: it is Senator Hubert Horatio Humphrey.

THE PRESIDENT'S WIFE, Lady Bird, has reason to be happy; her husband was nominated by acclamation.

HIS BIRTHDAY SPEECH. On August 27, fifty-six-year-old LBJ delivers a hard-hitting address to the convention.

member of the SEATO pact "requesting assistance in defense of its freedom."

It was not long thereafter that the Democratic convention opened in Atlantic City. Johnson was unopposed; the only question was: Whom would he choose as his running mate?

While the convention was in progress and Senator Humphrey, who had led the civil rights walkout in 1948, was working behind the scenes to effect a compromise for the seating of some of the Negro delegates of the Freedom Party of Mississippi, television cameras were showing demonstrators outside the convention and sit-ins within the hall. The note of discord which the President had hoped to avoid was not only marring his consensus convention, it was also being displayed to the nation. Robert Sherrill reported that "a top official of one of the national networks was surprised to receive a personal telephone call from the President himself, telling him, 'Get your goddamn cameras off the niggers out front and back on the speaker's stand inside, goddamn it!'"

Johnson had decided that his running mate would be neither Senator Robert Kennedy nor Senator Eugene McCarthy, Governor Brown nor Secretary McNamara— but Hubert Horatio Humphrey. That same evening the President himself presented Humphrey to the convention. The delegates nominated him by acclamation.

The emotional peak of the convention came when Robert Kennedy rose to eulogize his assassinated brother. The convention applauded for almost half an hour before Kennedy could even start to speak. He ended his memorial with lines from *Romeo and Juliet:*

> *When he shall die, take him and cut*
> *him out in little stars,*
> *And he will make the face of heaven so fine*
> *That all the world will be in love with night,*
> *And pay no worship to the garish sun.*

Then the film *A Thousand Drums* was shown, and there was not a dry eye in the convention hall.

Humphrey accepted his candidacy with a catchy address. He attacked Goldwater:

"The temporary Republican spokesman is not only out of tune with the great majority of his countrymen; he is even out of step with his own party.

"In the last 3½ years most Democrats and Republicans have agreed on the great decisions our nation has made.

"But not Senator Goldwater!

"He has been facing backward—against the mainstream of history.

"Most Democrats and most Republicans in the United States Senate, for example, voted for the nuclear test-ban treaty.

THE ENTIRE DEMOCRATIC CONVENTION IN A PHOTOGRAPH—TAKEN BY THE FISH-EYE CAMERA

BEFORE MAKING A CAMPAIGN ADDRESS at Cleveland, Ohio on October 8, 1964, just a month before the election, President Johnson shakes hands with hundreds of enthusiastic well-wishers, who squeeze his hand until it hurts.

U.P.I.

"But not Senator Goldwater!

"Most Democrats and most Republicans in the United States Senate voted for an 11.5-billion-dollar tax cut for the American people.

"But not Senator Goldwater!

"Most Democrats and most Republicans in the United States Senate—in fact, over *four-fifths* of the members of his own party—voted for the Civil Rights Act of 1964.

"But not Senator Goldwater!"

And so on, through a list of all his senatorial vetoes.

In his acceptance speech Johnson asked for a mandate to continue the Kennedy program and "to supplement that program with the kind of laws that he would have us write." He spoke of his commitment to peace: "To lessen the danger to men without increasing the danger to freedom." He was "offering answers, not retreat; offering unity, not division; offering hope, not fear or smear . . . let us tomorrow turn to our new task! Let us be on our way!"

Early in the campaign Goldwater launched a vicious attack on his opponent: "To Lyndon Johnson, running a country means . . . buying and bludgeoning votes. It means getting a TV monopoly . . . and building a private fortune. It means surrounding himself with companions like Bobby Baker, Billie Sol Estes, Matt McCloskey and other interesting men. . . . It means craving and grasping for power—more and more and more, without end."

The morality issue was milked by the Republicans as the "one slim hope for a monumental political upset."

BEFORE MAKING A SPEECH for the Goldwater ticket on October 15, 1964, Nixon powders his five-o'clock shadow.

THE CAMPAIGN IN FULL SWING. ON HIS PLANE GOLDWATER DICTATES THE DRAFT OF A SPEECH.

Cartoon by De Alba, October 1964
I'm going to send you to Vietnam!

Cartoon by Hayney, September 1964
Why are the other kids afraid to play?

Cartoon by Herblock, October 1964
Do you want to see feelthy pictures?

894

THE PRESIDENT IN BROOKLYN, HELPING ROBERT KENNEDY IN HIS SENATORIAL CAMPAIGN

The Bobby Baker issue, hanging fire in the Senate Rules Committee, had come back into the headlines when Johnson was asked on national television to comment on his relations with Baker. He now disavowed his friendship with the man who had been known as "Lyndon Jr." and "the ninety-seventh Senator." Actually, since becoming President, Johnson had neither seen nor spoken a single word with Baker. Like Henry V repudiating Falstaff, the President had disassociated himself from this political liability. National magazines gleefully carried suggestive reports about the business enterprises of Baker and his cronies; accounts of strings of motels and suggestions that call girls had been provided for ranking Senators cast a lurid glow in the direction of official Washington.

While the Republicans hoped that revelations about Baker's financial dealings would implicate the President, the Rules Committee was being subjected to great pressure to adjourn. After much backstage wheeling and dealing by attorneys Abe Fortas and Clark Clifford the Senate postponed the hearing until after the election.

Johnson ran his campaign in a professional manner. Lawrence O'Brien, the Kennedy strategist, now on the Johnson team, traveled around the country conferring with local politicians and sending his reports to the President. The Quayle organization prepared polls for Johnson. Other groups helped, sending out articles and editorials against Goldwater, creating sentiment against him in the towns which the Republican candidate visited. The backlash—the defection of Democrats to the Republicans on account of the race issue—was more than matched by the frontlash—the defection of Republican voters to Johnson.

Goldwater's attack on Johnson for making a multi-million-dollar fortune while in the Senate (an exposé about this appeared in the *Wall Street Journal* on March 23 and 24, 1964) was repeatedly quoted by the Republicans. The Democrats counterattacked with television films picturing Goldwater as a reckless warmonger who would exercise no restraint in "mashing the button" and

JOHNSON SPEAKING in Pittsburgh's Civic Arena to a crowd of 12,000 which gave him a hearty welcome.

THE CROWD SURROUNDS HIM outside his Miami hotel, breaking through the police lines to shake his hand.

A UNITY CONFERENCE OF THE REPUBLICANS lines up Scranton, Eisenhower, Goldwater and Nixon.

THE ANTAGONISTS ARE FULL OF SMILES: The Rockefellers at the Albany airport with the Goldwaters.

starting an atomic war.

Reports of Johnson's free-wheeling life on the LBJ Ranch in Texas made national headlines. On Easter weekend while entertaining members of the Washington press corps, three of them women, Johnson raced his Lincoln Continental around the ranch with one hand on the wheel and the other on the speaker of his radio-telephone, over which he shouted orders to ranch hands and secretaries while careening at speeds of up to 90 miles an hour. *Time* magazine wrote, "Mr. President, You're Fun," and gave a detailed account of the joyride, de-

scribing LBJ drinking beer from paper cups while he drove with his Texas Stetson hiding the speedometer, all the while relating to his passengers graphic stories of the sex life of his prize Hereford bull.

All this was fuel for the Republican fire. A movie called *Choice* was made for national television, a heavy-handed attempt to link the decline in public morality to the character of the President. But a difference of opinion in the Republican high command, with Senator Goldwater eschewing a smear campaign, kept the film off the screens.

JOHNSON IS HELPED BY BILLY GRAHAM, the
evangelist; they attended services together in Washington.
UPI

THE PRESIDENT IS WELCOMED by a large Louisville
crowd before speaking at the Courthouse (at the right).
UPI

"YES—EXTREME RIGHT," says the little sign under
the billboard put up during the Democratic convention.
UPI

GOLDWATER IS WELCOMED by his enthusiastic
supporters at Mercer County Airport in New Jersey.
UPI

Rowland Evans and Robert Novak wrote: "A vague,
unfavorable image of the President—partly based on
emotion, partly based on his reputation as a Texas
wheeler-dealer not unwilling to cut a corner here and
there—had taken hold throughout the country. . . . The
polls showed that this mood was prevalent even among
some voters who definitely planned to vote for Johnson
anyway." But no matter how sharp criticism of the
President was, Republican attacks lost their sting when
measured against the irresponsible and frightening statements of their candidate.

On the national level Goldwater echoed similar charges
of evils, that "there is a mood of uneasiness. . . . Why do
we see wave after wave of crime in our streets and in
our homes . . . ? A breakdown of the morals of our young
people . . . ? A flood of obscene literature? Corruption
around our highest offices . . . ? The moral fiber of the
American people is beset by rot and decay." This general
sense of crime—the "switchblade issue"—appealed to
those who had "to lock their doors at night."

Goldwater suggested that the President should cut
back some of his programs. He felt "a government that is

Kyuichi Sawada, UPI

THOSE WHO BORE THE SUFFERING . . . A Vietnam family after their bamboo home was destroyed by bombs.

big enough to give everything that you need and want is big enough to take it all away." His goal was to give powers back to "the states, the cities, the people themselves." Many of his ideas were "simply a protest against history," editorialized *The New York Times*. The image most people had of the Republican candidate's domestic program was that of the often-used Democratic advertisement on television—showing a Social Security card, with a man's hands tearing it in two. For the voters, then, this was neither a "choice" nor an "echo."

The civil rights issue had been dropped by both candidates. But even when Goldwater said he would enforce the 1964 Civil Rights Bill if he were elected, even if he could ask how to "build a society of many races with liberty and justice for all"—people remembered his vote against it.

Goldwater's views on a hard line against Communism and liberation in Eastern Europe, though appealing to some, were more than negated by the "finger on the button" issue. Stickers tell the story: "Goldwater for Halloween," "If You Think, You Know He's Wrong," "Vote for Goldwater and Go to War," "Welcome Doctor Strangewater" (an allusion to the film *Dr. Strangelove).*

Television spots, later withdrawn by the Democratic high command, depicted Goldwater as a sinister figure capable of poisoning a little girl's ice-cream cone with strontium 90, or showed petals being plucked from a flower to the accompaniment of a nuclear countdown. The Republican candidate gave the impression of being an irresponsible hothead, ready to lead a holy war against Communism. Johnson reportedly exclaimed, as quoted by Hugh Sidey in his *A Very Personal Presidency* (page 219): "We can't let Goldwater and the Red Chinese both get the bomb at the same time. Then the shit will really hit the fan!"

In Vietnam, which had its third coup in ten months in late September, Goldwater wanted "victory" by "a new winning strategy," while Johnson promised "no wider war." In his hour-long television interview on March 15 he did not even refer to the war, but in campaign speeches he spoke against further American involvement in Vietnam. On August 12 he told the American Bar Association: "They call upon us to supply American boys to do the job that Asian boys should do. They ask us to take a reckless action which might risk the lives of millions and engulf much of Asia and certainly threaten the peace of

898

. . . AND THOSE WHO MADE THE DECISION. The President with his advisers; George Ball, Rusk and McNamara.

UPI

the entire world. Moreover, such action would offer no solution at all to the real problem of Vietnam."

On September 25 he said in Eufaula, Oklahoma: "There are those that say you ought to go north and drop bombs to try to wipe out the supply lines, and they think that would escalate the war. We don't want our American boys to do the fighting for Asian boys. We don't want to get involved in a nation with 700 million people and get tied down in a land war in Asia." On October 8 he repeated at a $100-a-plate dinner in Cleveland: "You don't get peace by rattling your rockets. You don't get peace by threatening to drop your bombs. You must have strength, and you must always keep your guard up, but you must always have your hand out and be willing to talk to anybody, listen to anything they have to say, do anything that is honorable, in order to avoid pulling that trigger, mashing that button that will blow up the world." On October 21 he said again in Akron: "We are not about to send American boys nine or ten thousand miles away from home to do what Asian boys ought to be doing for themselves."

Time magazine lamented that the issues were no longer being discussed by the candidates; they had been clouded

by emotionalism, invective and counterinvective. "There was Vietnam, but it takes two to debate, and Lyndon just hasn't been in a debating mood." South Dakota's Senator George McGovern pointed out later that if all of Johnson's remarks on Vietnam during the campaign were put together, they would hardly fill a single typewritten page. He kept quiet about it, appearing to be for peace.

The New York Times saw that the United States "has gone too far already" in Vietnam by drifting from the original concept of advice and aid. And in comparing the two candidates: ". . . with Barry Goldwater in the White House, a volatile nature, a penchant for military solutions and a philosophy of brinkmanship could combine to create a situation of great danger. Senator Goldwater has never explained precisely what he would do in Vietnam except to send former President Eisenhower there to come back with an answer. . . . The Johnson Administration is making no promises on how and when it will end the war in Viet Nam. But, under Mr. Johnson, all options remain open."

Johnson kept campaigning on the theme of peace and prosperity, now and tomorrow. He was "in favor of a lot of things and . . . against mighty few." Speaking to

HE VOTES LIKE EVERY OTHER AMERICAN. Goldwater waits in line with his family—just like all the others—outside the Cudia Day School in Phoenix, Arizona. His son Barry, Jr., takes a picture of the newsmen who cover the event.

the country from his White House desk, the President said, "We must decide whether we will move ahead by building on the solid structure created by forward-looking men of both parties over the past thirty years. . . . We are now told that we, the people, acting through government, should withdraw from education, from urban renewal and from a host of other vital programs. We are now told that we should end Social Security as we know it, sell TVA, strip labor unions of many of their gains, and terminate all farm subsidies. . . . The choice is yours."

Even the Walter Jenkins episode—Johnson's assistant and close friend was arrested in a public place and charged with homosexuality—breaking less than a month before the election, caused no public outburst of indignation against the morality of the Democrats. It was buried in the news of the resignation of Premier Khrushchev and the first Red Chinese atomic bomb explosion, and Johnson's lead in the polls increased two points.

The Johnson parades and speeches were overwhelming. People responded when he asked them to "come down an' hear the speakin'!" The whole country seemed to be chanting the slogan, "All the way with L.B.J.!"

Mary McGrory of the Washington *Star* described one such parade on the day after the Jenkins scandal: "And the multitudes in Brooklyn would have heartened a cigar-store Indian, which the President is not. For two incredible hours, they poured out of their homes and their bars and their launderettes. The women streamed out of the beauty parlors with curlers in their hair. The men stopped watching the World Series. Hasidic Jews with soft black hats and side whiskers waved wildly. Little boys in their temple skull caps ran after the cavalcade. Lyndon Johnson stood up to full height on the car giving his own special blessing, arms stretched out, shoulders high, fingers rippling. Butchers with their gory aprons greeted him, and bakers with their puffy hats. Women held their children or their dogs high to see him pass. It was wall-to-wall people. . . ."

Johnson made big promises. "We are going to have to rebuild our cities," he said in Los Angeles. "We are going to have to reshape our mass transit facilities. We have to purify our air and to desalt our oceans. We are going to make all the deserts bloom." And the people wanted this dream to become a reality.

900

De Alba, November 1964

MATTER OF HINDSIGHT: "NOW HE TELLS HIM!"

Herblock, November 1963

"HE SAYS THAT HE CAN BRING US PEACE."

On the whole it was a disappointing campaign. It was not a confrontation between two opposing philosophies, but "a wrestling match between volatile personalities." *Time* magazine wrote that the campaign "was going to prove the vital difference between two strong political parties; it was merely shown that one, the G.O.P., is in need of great repair. It was going to pit liberal against conservative; but Lyndon Johnson has stated very few liberal tenets, and many an American conservative now doubts that Barry Goldwater really speaks his language."

Many voters felt that the President was merely the lesser of two evils. Woodrow Wilson's grandson, the Very Reverend Francis B. Sayre, Episcopal Dean of Washington Cathedral, who was born in the White House, described the choice between the two candidates: "one, a man of dangerous ignorance and devastating uncertainty; the other, a man whose public house is splendid in its every appearance, but whose private lack of ethic must inevitably introduce termites at the very foundation." The election, thought Sayre, was a "sterile choice," with "frustration and a federation of hostilities in one party; and in the other, behind a goodly façade, only a cynical manipu-

lation of power."

Johnson won the election by a landslide, receiving 43,128,958 votes against Goldwater's 27,176,873, about a 16-million-vote plurality. (Still, his private ambition was unsatisfied; he did not win by the largest percentage in history. Though he won a smashing 61 percent of the vote, FDR in 1936 won 63 percent, and Warren Harding in 1920 had the record 64 percent.) Goldwater carried only a few Southern states in addition to his native Arizona. Mississippi, Alabama, South Carolina, Louisiana, Georgia voted for him and against Johnson, his Southern-born opponent. But in 32 states outside the South the Republican nominee could not carry a single Congressional District.

In his inaugural address the President charted the future: "If we succeed, it will not be because of what we have, but it will be because of what we are; not because of what we own, but rather because of what we believe. For we are a nation of believers. Underneath the clamor of building and the rush of our day's pursuits, we are believers in justice and liberty and union, and in our own Union. We believe that every man must some day be

INAUGURATION DAY

TAKING THE OATH from Chief Justice Earl Warren as Lady Bird Johnson and Vice President Humphrey watch.

TIMES HAVE CHANGED since the first inaugural in Washington when Jefferson walked to the Capitol accompanied only by a few friends to take the oath as President.

THE INAUGURAL BALL HAS CHANGED, TOO.

THE STATE OF THE UNION MESSAGE on January 4, 1965, in which the newly elected President outlined the details of his "Great Society" in a televised address. He began at 9 P.M., the first nighttime message since Franklin D. Roosevelt, saying, "We're only at the beginning of the road to the Great Society. Ahead now is a summit where freedom from the wants of the body can help fulfill the needs of the spirit." The President outlined his plans for dealing with such problems as the population explosion, urban blight, crime, and peace and freedom. "The Great Society asks not how much, but how good; not only to create wealth but how to use it; not only how fast we are going, but where we are headed."

free. And we believe in ourselves. . . .

"The Great Society," continued Johnson, "is the excitement of becoming—always becoming, trying, probing, falling, resting and trying again—but always trying and always gaining."

He sounded an almost plaintive note when he continued: "This is what America is all about. It is the uncrossed desert and the unclimbed ridge. It is the star that is not reached and the harvest sleeping in the unplowed ground. Is our world gone? We say farewell. Is a new world coming? We welcome it. . . .

"The hour and the day and the time are here to achieve progress without strife, to achieve change without hatred—not without difference of opinion, but without the deep and abiding divisions which scar the Union for generations."

Appendix A

THE ELECTION VOTE FROM 1789 TO 1964

1789

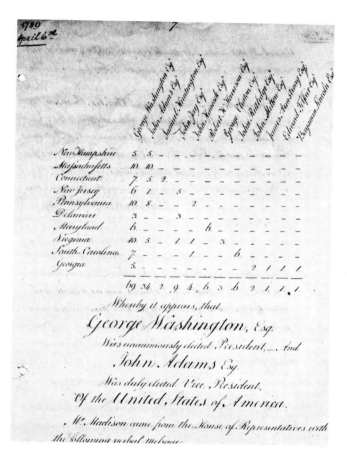

THE FIRST ELECTION RESULT, as recorded in the *Journal* of the United States Senate for April 6, 1789.

Ten states took part in the election. Of the original thirteen states North Carolina and Rhode Island had not yet ratified the Constitution; New York could not agree on the mode of choosing presidential electors.

Electors were appointed entirely by the legislatures of the states of Connecticut, New Jersey, Delaware, South Carolina and Georgia.

In Massachusetts and New Hampshire they were chosen partly by the people and partly by the legislatures.

In Maryland, Pennsylvania and Virginia electors were chosen by popular vote.

1792

Votes.	George Washington	John Adams	George Clinton	Thomas Jefferson	Aaron Burr
New-Hampshire,	6	6			
Massachusetts,	16	16			
Rhode-Island,	4	4			
Connecticut,	9	9			
Vermont,	3	3			
New-York,	12		12		
New-Jersey,	7	7			
Pennsylvania,	15	14	1		
Delaware,	3	3			
Maryland,	8	8			
Virginia,	21		21		
Kentucky,	4			4	
North-Carolina,	12		12		
South-Carolina,	8	7			1
Georgia,	4		4		

THE VOTES IN THE SECOND ELECTION as recorded in the Senate's *Journal* for February 13, 1793.

Fifteen states took part in the election. Rhode Island and North Carolina had ratified the Constitution—the last of the original thirteen states. Vermont had been admitted to the Union on March 4, 1791, Kentucky on June 1, 1792.

In New Hampshire, Maryland, Pennsylvania, Virginia and Kentucky, electors were chosen by popular vote; by the people and the legislature in Massachusetts; in the remaining nine states they were appointed by the legislatures.

In this election the precedent for counting the votes was set. They were tabulated by a Senate teller and the result announced by the Vice President in the presence of Congress.

STATES	John Adams, Mass.	Thomas Jefferson, Va.	Thomas Pinckney, S. C.	Aaron Burr, N. Y.	Samuel Adams, Mass.	Oliver Ellsworth, Conn.	George Clinton, N. Y.	John Jay, N. Y.	James Iredell, N. C.	George Washington, Va.	Samuel Johnston, N. C.	John Henry, Md.	C. C. Pinckney, S. C.
N. H.	6	—	—	—	—	6	—	—	—	—	—	—	—
Vt.	4	—	4	—	—	—	—	—	—	—	—	—	—
Mass.	16	—	13	—	—	1	—	—	—	—	2	—	—
R. I.	4	—	—	—	—	4	—	—	—	—	—	—	—
Conn.	9	—	4	—	—	—	—	5	—	—	—	—	—
N. Y.	12	—	12	—	—	—	—	—	—	—	—	—	—
N. J.	7	—	7	—	—	—	—	—	—	—	—	—	—
Pa.	1	14	2	13	—	—	—	—	—	—	—	—	—
Del.	3	—	3	—	—	—	—	—	—	—	—	—	—
Md.	7	4	4	3	—	—	—	—	—	—	—	2	—
Va.	1	20	1	1	15	—	3	—	—	1	—	—	—
N. C.	1	11	1	6	—	—	—	—	3	1	—	—	1
S. C.	—	8	8	—	—	—	—	—	—	—	—	—	—
Ga.	—	4	—	—	—	—	4	—	—	—	—	—	—
Ky.	—	4	—	4	—	—	—	—	—	—	—	—	—
Tenn.	—	3	—	3	—	—	—	—	—	—	—	—	—
Electoral vote	71	68	59	30	15	11	7	5	3	2	2	2	1

Sixteen states took part in the election. Tennessee had been admitted on June 1, 1796. Electors were chosen by popular vote in N.C., Md., Pa., Va., Ga., and Ky.; by the people and the legislatures in N.H. and Mass.; in the other eight states they were appointed by the legislatures.

STATES	Thomas Jefferson. Va.	Aaron Burr. N. Y.	John Adams. Mass.	C. C. Pinckney. S. C.	John Jay. N. Y.
New Hampshire	—	—	6	6	—
Vermont	—	—	4	4	—
Massachusetts	—	—	16	16	—
Rhode Island	—	—	4	3	1
Connecticut	—	—	9	9	—
New York	12	12	—	—	—
New Jersey	—	—	7	7	—
Pennsylvania	8	8	7	7	—
Delaware	—	—	3	3	—
Maryland°	5	5	5	5	—
Virginia	21	21	—	—	—
North Carolina	8	8	4	4	—
South Carolina	8	8	—	—	—
Georgia	4	4	—	—	—
Kentucky	4	4	—	—	—
Tennessee	3	3	—	—	—
Electoral vote	73	73	65	64	1

° One Maryland elector did not vote.

Sixteen states took part. Popular elections were held in R.I., Md., Va., N.C., Ky.; in the other eleven states electors were appointed by the legislatures. As both Jefferson and Burr had the same number of votes, the election was decided by the House of Representatives.

STATES	PRESIDENT T. Jefferson. Va.	PRESIDENT C. C. Pinckney. S.C.	VICE-PRESIDENT George Clinton. N.Y.	VICE-PRESIDENT Rufus King. N.Y.
New Hampshire	7	—	7	—
Vermont	6	—	6	—
Massachusetts	19	—	19	—
Rhode Island	4	—	4	—
Connecticut	—	9	—	9
New York	19	—	19	—
New Jersey	8	—	8	—
Pennsylvania	20	—	20	—
Delaware	—	3	—	3
Maryland	9	2	9	2
Virginia	24	—	24	—
North Carolina	14	—	14	—
South Carolina	10	—	10	—
Georgia	6	—	6	—
Kentucky	8	—	8	—
Tennessee	5	—	5	—
Ohio	3	—	3	—
Electoral vote	162	14	162	14

Seventeen states took part in the election. Ohio had been admitted on November 29, 1802.

Electors were chosen by the legislatures of Vermont, Connecticut, New York, Delaware, South Carolina and Georgia.

STATES	PRESIDENT James Madison. Va.	PRESIDENT George Clinton. N. Y.	PRESIDENT C. C. Pinckney. S. C.	VICE-PRESIDENT G. Clinton. N. Y.	VICE-PRESIDENT J. Madison. Va.	VICE-PRESIDENT J. Langdon. N. H.	VICE-PRESIDENT J. Monroe. Va.	VICE-PRESIDENT Rufus King. N. Y.
New Hampshire	—	—	7	—	—	—	—	7
Vermont	6	—	—	—	—	6	—	—
Massachusetts	—	—	19	—	—	—	—	19
Rhode Island	—	—	4	—	—	—	—	4
Connecticut	—	—	9	—	—	—	—	9
New York	13	6	—	13	3	—	3	—
New Jersey	8	—	—	8	—	—	—	—
Pennsylvania	20	—	—	20	—	—	—	—
Delaware	—	—	3	—	—	—	—	3
Maryland	9	—	2	9	—	—	—	2
Virginia	24	—	—	24	—	—	—	—
North Carolina	11	—	3	11	—	—	—	3
South Carolina	10	—	—	10	—	—	—	—
Georgia	6	—	—	6	—	—	—	—
Kentucky°	7	—	—	7	—	—	—	—
Tennessee	5	—	—	5	—	—	—	—
Ohio	3	—	—	—	—	3	—	—
Electoral vote	122	6	47	113	3	9	3	47

° One Kentucky elector did not vote.

Seventeen states took part in the election. Electors were appointed by the legislatures in Vermont, Massachusetts, Connecticut, New York, Delaware, South Carolina and Georgia; in the other ten states they were elected by popular vote.

1812

STATES	PRESIDENT		VICE-PRESIDENT	
	James Madison, Va.	De Witt Clinton, N. Y.	Elbridge Gerry, Mass.	Jared Ingersoll, Pa.
New Hampshire	—	8	1	7
Vermont	8	—	8	—
Massachusetts	—	22	2	20
Rhode Island	—	4	—	4
Connecticut	—	9	—	9
New York	—	29	—	29
New Jersey	—	8	—	8
Pennsylvania	25	—	25	—
Delaware	—	4	—	4
Maryland	6	5	6	5
Virginia	25	—	25	—
North Carolina	15	—	15	—
South Carolina	11	—	11	—
Georgia	8	—	8	—
Kentucky	12	—	12	—
Tennessee	8	—	8	—
Louisiana	3	—	3	—
Ohio	7	—	7	—
Electoral vote	128	89	131	86

Eighteen states took part in the election. Louisiana was admitted to the Union on April 8, 1812.

Electors were appointed by the legislatures of Vermont, Connecticut, New York, New Jersey, Delaware, North Carolina, South Carolina, Georgia and Louisiana; in the other states popular elections were held.

1816

STATES	PRESIDENT		VICE-PRESIDENT				
	James Monroe, Va.	Rufus King, N. Y.	D. D. Tompkins, N. Y.	John E. Howard, Md.	James Ross, Pa.	John Marshall, Va.	Robert G. Harper, Md.
New Hampshire	8	—	8	—	—	—	—
Vermont	8	—	8	—	—	—	—
Massachusetts	—	22	—	22	—	—	—
Rhode Island	4	—	4	—	—	—	—
Connecticut	—	9	—	—	5	4	—
New York	29	—	29	—	—	—	—
New Jersey	8	—	8	—	—	—	—
Pennsylvania	25	—	25	—	—	—	—
Delaware	—	3	—	—	—	—	3
Maryland	8	—	8	—	—	—	—
Virginia	25	—	25	—	—	—	—
North Carolina	15	—	15	—	—	—	—
South Carolina	11	—	11	—	—	—	—
Georgia	8	—	8	—	—	—	—
Kentucky	12	—	12	—	—	—	—
Tennessee	8	—	8	—	—	—	—
Louisiana	3	—	3	—	—	—	—
Ohio	8	—	8	—	—	—	—
Indiana	3	—	3	—	—	—	—
Electoral vote	183	34	183	22	5	4	3

Nineteen states took part in the election. Indiana was admitted to the Union on December 11, 1816.

Electors were appointed by the legislatures of Vermont, Massachusetts, Connecticut, New York, Delaware, South Carolina, Georgia, Louisiana and Indiana; in the other states popular elections were held.

While the electoral vote is always exactly reported in the tables, the popular vote shows slight variations according to the source.

The best modern compilation of electoral statistics is Richard M. Scammon's *America Votes* (1965), issued by the Governmental Affairs Institute, Washington, D.C., which contains figures from 1920 to 1964. *Historical Statistics of the United States,* prepared by the Bureau of the Census with the cooperation of the Social Science Research Council (1967), prints the voting figures from 1789 to 1964. Edgar E. Robinson's *The Presidential Vote 1896–1932* (1934) covers the elections from McKinley to Franklin D. Roosevelt, and Robinson's *They Voted for Roosevelt,* the vote from 1932 to 1944; Appleton's *Cyclopaedia,* the votes from 1861 to 1903; McPhearson's *Handbook,* from 1866 to 1894; Walter D. Burnham's *Presidential Ballots, 1836–1892* (1955), from Van Buren to Cleveland; the *National Cyclopaedia of American Biography* (1937), from 1789 to 1933.

The Presidential Counts (1877) is a complete official record of Congressional proceedings at the counting of the electoral votes up to the year 1876.

The *World, Reader's Digest* and *Information Please* almanacs also carry the election tables and figures.

Some of the more interesting contemporary works on the election are Cortez A. Ewing's *Presidential Elections* (1940), L. H. Bean's *Ballot Behavior: A Study of Presidential Elections* (1940) and Svend Petersen's *A Statistical History of the American Presidential Elections* (1963).

In the early elections only the votes of the electors were recorded, but since the age of Jackson the popular vote for presidential electors has been noted as well, with each state supervising the balloting for its own electors.

At the Constitutional Convention the delegates argued at some length about the mode of choosing the Chief Magistrate. As there were no political parties, it was thought that a number of candidates would aspire to the office; thus the founders tried to define some practical means of choosing one man from the many. They wanted to keep the selection free from legislative interference, and they were opposed to popular elections, as they feared the electorate would not be well enough informed to select the right man.

It was James Wilson of Pennsylvania who came up with the idea of having a separate assembly to choose the Pres-

STATES	PRESIDENT		VICE-PRESIDENT				
	James Monroe, Va.	J. Q. Adams, Mass.	D. D. Tompkins, N. Y.	R. Stockton, N. J.	R. G. Harper, Md.	R. Rush, Pa.	D. Rodney, Del.
Maine	9	—	9	—	—	—	—
New Hampshire	7	1	7	—	—	1	—
Vermont	8	—	8	—	—	—	—
Massachusetts	15	—	7	8	—	—	—
Rhode Island	4	—	4	—	—	—	—
Connecticut	9	—	9	—	—	—	—
New York	29	—	29	—	—	—	—
New Jersey	8	—	8	—	—	—	—
Pennsylvania°	24	—	24	—	—	—	—
Delaware	4	—	—	—	—	—	4
Maryland	11	—	10	—	1	—	—
Virginia	25	—	25	—	—	—	—
North Carolina	15	—	15	—	—	—	—
South Carolina	11	—	11	—	—	—	—
Georgia	8	—	8	—	—	—	—
Alabama	3	—	3	—	—	—	—
Mississippi°	2	—	2	—	—	—	—
Louisiana	3	—	3	—	—	—	—
Kentucky	12	—	12	—	—	—	—
Tennessee°	7	—	7	—	—	—	—
Ohio	8	—	8	—	—	—	—
Indiana	3	—	3	—	—	—	—
Illinois	3	—	3	—	—	—	—
Missouri	3	—	3	—	—	—	—
Electoral vote	231	1	218	8	1	1	4

° *In each of these states, one elector died before the electoral meeting.*

Twenty-four states took part in the election. Mississippi was admitted on December 10, 1817, Illinois on December 3, 1818, Alabama on December 14, 1819, Maine on March 15, 1820, and Missouri, after a conditional admission in 1820, on August 10, 1821.

Electors were still appointed by the legislatures in nine states —Vermont, New York, Delaware, South Carolina, Alabama, Georgia, Louisiana, Indiana and Missouri; in all others popular elections were held.

STATES	POPULAR VOTE				ELECTORAL VOTE			
	Andrew Jackson.	John Quincy Adams.	William H. Crawford.	Henry Clay.	A. Jackson, Tenn.	J. Q. Adams, Mass.	W. H. Crawford, Ga.	H. Clay, Ky.
Me.	—	10,289	2,336	—	—	9	—	—
N. H.	—	9,389	643	—	—	8	—	—
Vt.	—	—	—	—	—	7	—	—
Mass.	—	30,687	6,616	—	—	15	—	—
R. I.	—	2,145	200	—	—	4	—	—
Conn.	—	7,587	1,978	—	—	8	—	—
N. Y.	—	—	—	—	1	26	5	4
N. J.	10,985	9,110	1,196	—	8	—	—	—
Pa.	36,100	5,441	4,206	1,690	28	—	—	—
Del.	—	—	—	—	1	2	—	—
Md.	14,523	14,632	3,364	695	7	3	1	—
Va.	2,861	3,189	8,489	416	—	—	24	—
N. C.	20,415	—	15,621	—	15	—	—	—
S. C.	—	—	—	—	11	—	—	—
Ga.	—	—	—	—	—	—	9	—
Ala.	9,443	2,416	1,680	67	5	—	—	—
Miss.	3,234	1,694	119	—	3	—	—	—
La.	—	—	—	—	3	2	—	—
Ky.	6,455	—	—	17,331	—	—	—	14
Tenn.	20,197	216	312	—	11	—	—	—
Mo.	987	311	—	1,401	—	—	—	3
Ohio	18,457	12,280	—	19,255	—	—	—	16
Ind.	7,343	3,095	—	5,315	5	—	—	—
Ill.	1,901	1,542	219	1,047	2	1	—	—
Total	152,901	114,023	46,979	47,217	99	84	41	37

Twenty-four states took part in the election. In six states— Vermont, New York, Delaware, South Carolina, Georgia and Louisiana—electors were appointed by the legislatures.

The election of the President was decided by the House of Representatives, which chose John Quincy Adams. The Vice Presidency was won by John C. Calhoun, who received 182 votes; Nathan Sanford had 30 votes; Nathaniel Macon, 24; Andrew Jackson, 13; Martin Van Buren, 9; and Henry Clay, 2. **Total vote: 361,120.**

ident, with "certain districts in each State which should appoint electors to elect outside of their own body." The delegates felt that the men most qualified to be electors would already be serving in other public office; thus only less able people would be available to be electors. After protracted argument the convention approved Article II, Section 1 of the Constitution:

"The executive power shall be vested in a President of the United States of America. He shall hold his office during the term of four years, and, together with the Vice-President, chosen for the same term, be elected as follows:—

"Each State shall appoint, in such manner as the legislature thereof may direct, a number of electors, equal to the whole number of senators and representatives to which the State may be entitled in the Congress; but no senator or representative, or person holding an office of trust or profit under the United States, shall be appointed an elector.

"The electors shall meet in their respective States, and vote by ballot for two persons, of whom one at least shall not be an inhabitant of the same State with themselves. And they shall make a list of all the persons voted for, and of the number of votes for each; which list they shall sign and certify, and transmit, sealed, to the seat of the government of the United States, directed to the President of the Senate. The President of the Senate shall, in the presence of the Senate and House of Representatives, open all the certifi-

1828

STATES	POPULAR VOTE FOR PRESIDENT		ELECTORAL VOTES FOR PRESIDENT		ELECTORAL VOTES FOR VICE-PRESIDENT		
	Andrew Jackson.	John Q. Adams.	A. Jackson, Tenn.	J. Q. Adams, Mass.	J. C. Calhoun, S. C.	Richard Rush, Pa.	William Smith, S. C.
Me.	13,927	20,733	1	8	1	8	—
N. H.	20,922	24,134	—	8	—	8	—
Vt.	8,350	25,363	—	7	—	7	—
Mass.	6,016	29,876	—	15	—	15	—
R. I.	821	2,754	—	4	—	4	—
Conn.	4,448	13,838	—	8	—	8	—
N. Y.	140,763	135,413	20	16	20	16	—
N. J.	21,951	23,764	—	8	—	8	—
Pa.	101,652	50,848	28	—	28	—	—
Del.	—	—	—	3	—	3	—
Md.	24,565	25,527	5	6	5	6	—
Va.	26,752	12,101	24	—	24	—	—
N. C.	37,857	13,918	15	—	15	—	—
S. C.	—	—	11	—	11	—	—
Ga.	19,363	No. opp.	9	—	2	—	7
Ala.	17,138	1,938	5	—	5	—	—
Miss.	6,772	1,581	3	—	3	—	—
La.	4,603	4,076	5	—	5	—	—
Ky.	39,397	31,460	14	—	14	—	—
Tenn.	44,293	2,240	11	—	11	—	—
Mo.	8,272	3,400	3	—	3	—	—
Ohio	67,597	63,396	16	—	16	—	—
Ind.	22,257	17,052	5	—	5	—	—
Ill.	9,560	4,662	3	—	3	—	—
	647,276	508,074	178	83	171	83	7

Twenty-four states again took part in the election. Democracy was on the march; in only two states—Delaware and South Carolina—were electors appointed by the legislatures.

Total vote: 1,155,350.

1832

STATES	POPULAR VOTES FOR PRESIDENT		ELECTORAL VOTES FOR PRESIDENT				ELECTORAL VOTES FOR VICE-PRESIDENT				
	Andrew Jackson.	Henry Clay.°	A. Jackson, Tenn.	Henry Clay, Ky.	John Floyd, Va.	William Wirt, Md.	M. Van Buren, N. Y.	John Sergeant, Pa.	W. Wilkins, Pa.	Henry Lee, Mass.	A. Ellmaker, Pa.
Me.	33,291	27,204	10	—	—	—	10	—	—	—	—
N. H.	25,486	19,010	7	—	—	—	7	—	—	—	—
Vt.	7,870	11,152	—	—	—	7	—	—	—	—	7
Mass.	14,545	33,003	—	14	—	—	—	14	—	—	—
R. I.	2,126	2,810	—	4	—	—	—	4	—	—	—
Conn.	11,269	17,755	—	8	—	—	—	8	—	—	—
N. Y.	168,497	154,896	42	—	—	—	42	—	—	—	—
N. J.	23,856	23,393	8	—	—	—	8	—	—	—	—
Pa.	90,983	56,716	30	—	—	—	—	—	30	—	—
Del.	4,110	4,276	—	3	—	—	—	3	—	—	—
Md.	19,156	19,160	3	5	—	—	3	5	—	—	—
Va.	33,609	11,451	23	—	—	—	23	—	—	—	—
N. C.	24,862	4,563	15	—	—	—	15	—	—	—	—
S. C.	—	—	—	—	11	—	—	—	—	11	—
Ga.	20,750	—	11	—	—	—	11	—	—	—	—
Ala.	—	—	7	—	—	—	7	—	—	—	—
Miss.	5,919	No can.	4	—	—	—	4	—	—	—	—
La.	4,049	2,528	5	—	—	—	5	—	—	—	—
Ky.	36,247	43,396	—	15	—	—	—	15	—	—	—
Tenn.	28,740	1,436	15	—	—	—	15	—	—	—	—
Ohio	81,246	76,539	21	—	—	—	21	—	—	—	—
Ind.	31,552	15,472	9	—	—	—	9	—	—	—	—
Ill.	14,147	5,429	5	—	—	—	5	—	—	—	—
Mo.	5,192	—	4	—	—	—	4	—	—	—	—
	687,502	530,189	219	49	11	7	189	49	30	11	7

° The figures in the Henry Clay column include the votes for the Anti-masonic candidate William Wirt.

Twenty-four states took part in the election, as in the previous three elections. With the exception of South Carolina all the states chose the electors by popular vote.

Total vote: 1,217,691.

cates, and the votes shall then be counted. The person having the greatest number of votes shall be the President, if such number be a majority of the whole number of electors appointed; and if there be more than one who have such majority, and have an equal number of votes, then the House of Representatives shall immediately choose by ballot one of them for President; and if no person have a majority, then from the five highest on the list the said House shall in like manner choose the President. But in choosing the President, the votes shall be taken by States, the representation from each State having one vote; a quorum for this purpose shall consist of a member or members from two-thirds of the States, and a majority of all the States shall be necessary to

a choice. In every case, after the choice of the President, the person having the greatest number of votes of the electors shall be the Vice-President. But if there should remain two or more who have equal votes, the Senate shall choose from them by ballot the Vice-President.

"The Congress may determine the time of choosing the electors and the day on which they shall give their votes; which day shall be the same throughout the United States."

Before the second election Congress passed a detailed bill to regulate the presidential office. The choice of electors was to be made thirty-four days preceding the first Wednesday in December. They were to meet together and vote on that Wednesday. The electors would make three copies of their

| STATES | POPULAR VOTE | | | ELECTORAL VOTES FOR | | | | | | | | |
| | | | | PRESIDENT | | | | | VICE-PRESIDENT | | | |
	Martin Van Buren.	Whig Candidate.	Name of Whig Candidate.	Martin Van Buren, N. Y.	William H. Harrison, O.	Hugh L. White, Tenn.	Daniel Webster, Mass.	Willie P. Mangum, N. C.	Richard M. Johnson, Ky.	Francis Granger, N. Y.	John Tyler, Va.	William Smith, Ala.
Maine	22,990	15,239	Harrison.	10	—	—	—	—	10	—	—	—
New Hampshire	18,722	6,228	Harrison.	7	—	—	—	—	7	—	—	—
Vermont	14,039	20,996	Harrison.	—	7	—	—	—	—	7	—	—
Massachusetts	33,542	41,287	Webster.	—	—	—	14	—	—	14	—	—
Rhode Island	2,964	2,710	Harrison.	4	—	—	—	—	4	—	—	—
Connecticut	19,291	18,749	Harrison.	8	—	—	—	—	8	—	—	—
New York	166,815	138,543	Harrison.	42	—	—	—	—	42	—	—	—
New Jersey	25,592	26,137	Harrison.	—	8	—	—	—	—	8	—	—
Pennsylvania	91,475	87,111	Harrison.	30	—	—	—	—	30	—	—	—
Delaware	4,153	4,733	Harrison.	—	3	—	—	—	—	3	—	—
Maryland	22,168	25,852	Harrison.	—	10	—	—	—	—	—	10	—
Virginia	30,261	23,468	White.	23	—	—	—	—	—	—	—	23
North Carolina	26,910	23,626	White.	15	—	—	—	—	15	—	—	—
South Carolina°	—			—	—	—	—	11	—	—	11	—
Georgia	22,104	24,876	White.	—	—	11	—	—	—	—	11	—
Alabama	20,506	15,612	White.	7	—	—	—	—	7	—	—	—
Mississippi	9,979	9,688	White.	4	—	—	—	—	4	—	—	—
Louisiana	3,653	3,383	White.	5	—	—	—	—	5	—	—	—
Arkansas	2,400	1,238	White.	3	—	—	—	—	3	—	—	—
Kentucky	33,435	36,955	Harrison.	—	15	—	—	—	—	15	—	—
Tennessee	26,129	36,168	White.	—	—	15	—	—	—	—	15	—
Missouri	10,995	7,337	White.	4	—	—	—	—	4	—	—	—
Ohio	96,948	105,404	Harrison.	—	21	—	—	—	—	21	—	—
Indiana	32,478	41,281	Harrison.	—	9	—	—	—	—	9	—	—
Illinois	18,097	14,983	Harrison.	5	—	—	—	—	5	—	—	—
Michigan	7,332	4,045	Harrison.	3	—	—	—	—	3	—	—	—
	762,978	735,649		170	73	26	14	11	147	77	47	23

° *Electors were appointed by the legislature.*

Twenty-six states took part in the election. Arkansas had been admitted on June 15, 1836; Michigan voted before admission in 1837. As none of the vice presidential candidates received a majority, the Senate had to choose between the two candidates with the highest number of votes, the only time in the history of presidential elections that the Senate performed this function. It selected Richard M. Johnson by a vote of 33 to 16 for Francis Granger.

Total vote: 1,498,627.

votes (two of them to go by separate routes to the Capital; the third to be kept with a district judge as a safeguard), which would be counted on the first Wednesday in January. Congress was to meet for the counting of the votes on the second Wednesday in February, and inauguration date was set for the fourth day of March.

In the 1800 election Thomas Jefferson and Aaron Burr received an equal number of votes; thus the decision had to be made in the House of Representatives with each state having a single vote. To prevent any repetition of this, the Twelfth Amendment was adopted. Ratified on July 27, 1804, it said:

"The Electors shall meet in their respective states and vote by ballot for President and Vice-President, one of whom, at least, shall not be an inhabitant of the same state with themselves; they shall name in their ballots the person voted for as President, and in distinct ballots the person voted for as Vice-President, and they shall make distinct lists of all persons voted for as President, and of all persons voted for as Vice-President, and of the number of votes for each, which lists they shall sign and certify, and transmit sealed to the seat of the government of the United States, directed to the President of the Senate. The President of the Senate shall, in the presence of the Senate and House of Representatives, open all the certificates and the votes shall then be counted—The person having the greatest number of votes for President shall be the President, if such number be a majority of the whole number of electors appointed; and if no person have such majority, then from the persons having the highest numbers, not exceeding three on the list of those voted for as President, the House of Representatives shall choose immediately, by ballot, the President. But in choosing the President the vote shall be taken by States, the represen-

STATES	POPULAR VOTE		ELECTORAL VOTE FOR PRESIDENT		ELECTORAL VOTE FOR VICE-PRESIDENT	
	W. H. Harrison, Ohio. Whig	Martin Van Buren, N. Y. Democrat	W. H. Harrison, Ohio.	Martin Van Buren, N. Y.	John Tyler, Va.	R. M. Johnson, Ky.
Maine	46,612	46,201	10	—	10	—
New Hampshire	26,163	32,761	—	7	—	7
Vermont	32,440	18,018	7	—	7	—
Massachusetts	72,874	51,944	14	—	14	—
Rhode Island	5,278	3,301	4	—	4	—
Connecticut	31,601	25,296	8	—	8	—
New York	225,817	212,527	42	—	42	—
New Jersey	33,351	31,034	8	—	8	—
Pennsylvania	144,021	143,672	30	—	30	—
Delaware	5,967	4,874	3	—	3	—
Maryland	33,528	28,752	10	—	10	—
Virginia	42,501	43,893	—	23	—	22
North Carolina	46,376	33,782	15	—	15	—
South Carolina°	—	—	—	11	—	—
Georgia	40,261	31,921	11	—	11	—
Alabama	28,471	33,991	—	7	—	7
Mississippi	19,518	16,995	4	—	4	—
Louisiana	11,296	7,616	5	—	5	—
Kentucky	58,489	32,616	15	—	15	—
Tennessee	60,391	48,289	15	—	15	—
Missouri	22,972	29,760	—	4	—	4
Arkansas	5,160	6,766	—	3	—	3
Ohio	148,157	124,782	21	—	21	—
Indiana	65,302	51,604	9	—	9	—
Illinois	45,537	47,476	—	5	—	5
Michigan	22,933	21,131	3	—	3	—
	1,275,016	1,129,102	234	60	234	48

° Electors were appointed by the legislature.

Twenty-six states took part in the election.

James G. Birney, Abolitionist candidate, received 7,069 votes.

South Carolina cast its 11 electoral votes for L. W. Tazewell of Virginia for the Vice Presidency; one elector from Virginia voted for James K. Polk, also for the Vice Presidency.

Total vote: 2,411,187.

STATES	POPULAR VOTE			ELECTORAL VOTE	
	James K. Polk, Tenn. Democrat	Henry Clay, Ky. Whig	James G. Birney, N. Y. Abolitionist	Polk and Dallas.	Clay and Frelinghuysen.
Maine	45,719	34,378	4,836	9	—
New Hampshire	27,160	17,866	4,161	6	—
Vermont	18,041	26,770	3,954	—	6
Massachusetts	52,846	67,418	10,860	—	12
Rhode Island	4,867	7,322	107	—	4
Connecticut	29,841	32,832	1,943	—	6
New York	237,588	232,482	15,812	36	—
New Jersey	37,495	38,318	131	—	7
Pennsylvania	167,535	161,203	3,138	26	—
Delaware	5,996	6,278	—	—	3
Maryland	32,676	35,984	—	—	8
Virginia	49,570	43,677	—	17	—
North Carolina	39,287	43,232	—	—	11
South Carolina°	—	—	—	9	—
Georgia	44,177	42,100	—	10	—
Alabama	37,740	26,084	—	9	—
Mississippi	25,126	19,206	—	6	—
Louisiana	13,782	13,083	—	6	—
Kentucky	51,988	61,255	—	—	12
Tennessee	59,917	60,030	—	—	13
Missouri	41,369	31,251	—	7	—
Arkansas	9,546	5,504	—	3	—
Ohio	149,117	155,057	8,050	—	23
Michigan	27,759	24,337	3,632	5	—
Indiana	70,181	67,867	2,106	12	—
Illinois	57,920	45,528	3,570	9	—
	1,337,243	1,299,062	62,300	170	105

° Electors were appointed by the legislature.

Twenty-six states again voted in the election.

Since the last election the number of Representatives in the House had been reapportioned and cut from 242 to 223. Consequently the number of presidential electors was reduced from 294 to 275 (223 plus 52 for each Senator).

Total vote: 2,698,605.

tation from each State having one vote. A quorum for this purpose shall consist of a member or members from two-thirds of the States, and a majority of all the States shall be necessary to a choice. And if the House of Representatives shall not choose a President, whenever the right of choice shall devolve upon them before the fourth day of March next following, then the Vice-President shall act as President, as in the case of the death or other constitutional disability of the President.

"The person having the greatest number of votes as Vice-President shall be Vice-President, if such number be a majority of the whole number of electors appointed; and if no person have a majority, then from the two highest numbers on the list the Senate shall choose the Vice-President; a quorum for the purpose shall consist of two-thirds of the whole number of Senators, and a majority of the whole num-

ber shall be necessary to a choice. But no person constitutionally ineligible to the office of President shall be eligible to that of Vice-President of the United States."

In 1816 a dispute arose about the validity of the vote of a state not yet in the Union. Indiana had approved a state constitution in June, but was not admitted until December 11, 1816. As the time for counting the votes arrived, objections to the state's returns were made; but as the votes would not affect the outcome, the matter was dropped.

A similar argument occurred in 1820. Missouri had approved a state constitution in July 1820, but forbade free Negroes to enter the state. Congress required the Missouri legislature to pledge not to deprive its citizens of their rights under the Constitution. The Missouri legislature was reluctant to act, and not until August 10, 1821, was the state admitted. Congress agreed "that if any objection be made to

1848

| STATES | POPULAR VOTE | | | ELECTORAL VOTE | |
	Zachary Taylor, Louisiana. Whig.	Lewis Cass, Michigan. Democrat.	Martin Van Buren, New York. Free-Soiler.	Taylor and Fillmore.	Cass and Butler.
Alabama	30,482	31,363	—	—	9
Arkansas	7,588	9,300	—	—	3
Connecticut	30,314	27,046	5,005	6	—
Delaware	6,421	5,898	80	3	—
Florida	3,116	1,847	—	3	—
Georgia	47,544	44,802	—	10	—
Illinois	53,047	56,300	15,774	—	9
Indiana	69,907	74,745	8,100	—	12
Iowa	11,084	12,093	1,126	—	4
Kentucky	67,141	49,720	—	12	—
Louisiana	18,217	15,370	—	6	—
Maine	35,125	39,880	12,096	—	9
Maryland	37,702	34,528	125	8	—
Massachusetts	61,070	35,281	38,058	12	—
Michigan	23,940	30,687	10,389	—	5
Mississippi	25,922	26,537	—	—	6
Missouri	32,671	40,077	—	—	7
New Hampshire	14,781	27,763	7,560	—	6
New Jersey	40,015	36,901	829	7	—
New York	218,603	114,318	120,510	36	—
North Carolina	43,550	34,869	—	11	—
Ohio	138,360	154,775	35,354	—	23
Pennsylvania	185,513	171,176	11,263	26	—
Rhode Island	6,779	3,646	730	4	—
South Carolina°	—	—	—	—	9
Tennessee	64,705	58,419	—	13	—
Texas	4,509	10,668	—	—	4
Vermont	23,122	10,948	13,837	6	—
Virginia	45,124	46,586	9	—	17
Wisconsin	13,747	15,001	10,418	—	4
	1,360,099	1,220,544	291,263	163	127

° *Electors were appointed by the legislature.*

Thirty states took part in the election. Florida had been admitted on March 3, 1845, Texas on December 29, 1845, Iowa on December 28, 1846, and Wisconsin on May 29, 1848.

For the first time every state opened its polls on the same day. **Total vote: 2,871,906.**

1852

| STATES | POPULAR VOTE | | | ELECTORAL VOTE | |
	Franklin Pierce, New Hampshire. Democrat.	Winfield Scott, New Jersey. Whig.	John P. Hale, New Hampshire. Free-Soiler.	Pierce and King.	Scott and Graham.
Alabama	26,881	15,038	—	9	—
Arkansas	12,173	7,404	—	4	—
California	40,626	35,407	100	4	—
Connecticut	33,249	30,359	3,160	6	—
Delaware	6,318	6,293	62	3	—
Florida	4,318	2,875	—	3	—
Georgia	34,705	16,660	—	10	—
Illinois	80,597	64,934	9,966	11	—
Indiana	95,340	80,901	6,929	13	—
Iowa	17,763	15,856	1,604	4	—
Kentucky	53,806	57,068	265	—	12
Louisiana	18,647	17,255	—	6	—
Maine	41,609	32,543	8,030	8	—
Maryland	40,020	35,066	281	8	—
Massachusetts	44,569	52,683	28,023	—	13
Michigan	41,842	33,859	7,237	6	—
Mississippi	26,876	17,548	—	7	—
Missouri	38,353	29,984	—	9	—
New Hampshire	29,997	16,147	6,695	5	—
New Jersey	44,305	38,556	350	7	—
New York	262,083	234,882	25,329	35	—
North Carolina	39,744	39,058	59	10	—
Ohio	169,220	152,526	31,682	23	—
Pennsylvania	198,568	179,174	8,525	27	—
Rhode Island	8,735	7,626	644	4	—
South Carolina°	—	—	—	8	—
Tennessee	57,018	58,898	—	—	12
Texas	13,352	4,995	—	4	—
Vermont	13,044	22,173	8,621	—	5
Virginia	73,858	58,572	291	15	—
Wisconsin	33,658	22,240	8,814	5	—
	1,601,274	1,386,580	156,667	254	42

° *Electors were appointed by the legislature.*

Thirty-one states took part in the election. California had been admitted on September 9, 1850.

Daniel Webster got 5,324 votes in Georgia and 1,670 in Massachusetts; an independent Pierce ticket received 5,811 votes. **Total vote: 3,157,326.**

the votes of Missouri, and the counting, or omitting to count, which shall not essentially change the result of the election, in that case they shall be reported by the President of the Senate in the following manner: Were the votes of Missouri to be counted, the result would be, for A. B. for President of the United States, —— votes; if not counted, for A. B. for President of the United States, —— votes. But in either event A. B. is elected President of the United States. And in the same manner for Vice-President."

Opposition to the nominating caucus had grown, and after 1824 it was abandoned. From then on legislatures and state party caucuses suggested the names of the candidates. By

1832 candidates were nominated by national nominating conventions—a custom that has remained with us.

In 1836 the choice of a Vice President fell upon the Senate. There was a question about the validity of the Michigan votes. The question whether or not the votes of the state should be counted was "purposely left undetermined."

In 1848 all presidential electors (with the exception of those from Massachusetts) were appointed on the same day. Subsequent elections were covered by the act stipulating "That the electors of President and Vice-President shall be appointed in each State on the Tuesday next after the first Monday in the month of November of the year in which

1856

| STATES | POPULAR VOTE | | | ELECTORAL VOTE | | |
	James Buchanan, Pennsylvania. Democrat	John C. Frémont, California. Republican	Millard Fillmore, New York. Whig	Buchanan and Breckinridge.	Frémont and Dayton.	Fillmore and Donelson.
Ala.	46,739	—	28,552	9	—	—
Ark.	21,910	—	10,787	4	—	—
Calif.	53,365	20,691	36,165	4	—	—
Conn.	34,995	42,715	2,615	—	6	—
Del.	8,004	308	6,175	3	—	—
Fla.	6,358	—	4,833	3	—	—
Ga.	56,578	—	42,228	10	—	—
Ill.	105,348	96,189	37,444	11	—	—
Ind.	118,670	94,375	22,386	13	—	—
Iowa	36,170	43,954	9,180	—	4	—
Ky.	74,642	314	67,416	12	—	—
La.	22,164	—	20,709	6	—	—
Me.	39,080	67,379	3,325	—	8	—
Md.	39,115	281	47,460	—	—	8
Mass.	39,240	108,190	19,626	—	13	—
Mich.	52,136	71,762	1,660	—	6	—
Miss.	35,446	—	24,195	7	—	—
Mo.	58,164	—	48,524	9	—	—
N. H.	32,789	38,345	422	—	5	—
N. J.	46,943	28,338	24,115	7	—	—
N. Y.	195,878	276,007	124,604	—	35	—
N. C.	48,246	—	36,886	10	—	—
Ohio	170,874	187,497	28,126	—	23	—
Pa.	230,710	147,510	82,175	27	—	—
R. I.	6,680	11,467	1,675	—	4	—
S. C.°	—	—	—	8	—	—
Tenn.	73,638	—	66,178	12	—	—
Tex.	31,169	—	15,639	4	—	—
Vt.	10,569	39,561	545	—	5	—
Va.	89,706	291	60,310	15	—	—
Wis.	52,843	66,090	579	—	5	—
	1,838,169	1,341,264	874,534	174	114	8

° *Electors were appointed by the legislature.*

Thirty-one states again took part in the election.
Total vote: 4,053,967.

they are to be appointed." Thus uniformity was finally introduced in the mode of choosing the electors.

Weather interfered with the 1856 election. A blizzard blanketed Wisconsin on the day of choosing electors and the proceedings had to be delayed for a day. Then when the votes were counted, several Congressmen wanted the Wisconsin vote excluded, but the President *pro tempore* of the Senate refused to entertain any debate. As Wisconsin had voted for the losing side, it made no difference to the result.

The controversy over slavery and the rights of the states led to the withdrawal of eleven states from the Union. By 1864 the pro-Union government in Virginia allowed West Virginia to set herself up as a free state. There were also minority loyalist governments in Tennessee and Louisiana. Congress ignored West Virginia and passed a joint resolution whereby the electoral votes of the eleven Confederate states would not be counted. Lincoln wanted the pro-Union governments in Tennessee and Louisiana recognized; thus he delayed signing the bill. Congress enacted the "twenty-second joint rule," which governed the electoral count until 1877. The rule read:

"The two Houses shall assemble in the hall of the House of Representatives at the hour of one o'clock P.M., on the second Wednesday in February next succeeding the meeting

STATES	POPULAR VOTE				ELECTORAL VOTE			
	Abraham Lincoln, Illinois. Republican	Stephen A. Douglas, Illinois. Democrat	John C. Breckinridge, Kentucky. Democrat	John Bell, Tennessee. Constitutional Union	Lincoln and Hamlin.	Douglas and Johnson.	Breckinridge and Lane.	Bell and Everett.
Alabama	—	13,651	48,831	27,875	—	—	9	—
Arkansas	—	5,227	28,732	20,094	—	—	4	—
California	39,173	38,516	34,334	6,817	4	—	—	—
Connecticut	43,792	15,522	14,641	3,291	6	—	—	—
Delaware	3,815	1,023	7,337	3,864	—	—	3	—
Florida	—	367	8,543	5,437	—	—	3	—
Georgia	—	11,590	51,889	42,886	—	—	10	—
Illinois	172,161	160,215	2,404	4,913	11	—	—	—
Indiana	139,033	115,509	12,295	5,306	13	—	—	—
Iowa	70,409	55,111	1,048	1,763	4	—	—	—
Kentucky	1,364	25,651	53,143	66,058	—	—	—	12
Louisiana	—	7,625	22,861	20,204	—	—	6	—
Maine	62,811	26,693	6,368	2,046	8	—	—	—
Maryland	2,294	5,966	42,482	41,760	—	—	8	—
Massachusetts	106,533	34,372	5,939	22,331	13	—	—	—
Michigan	88,480	65,057	805	405	6	—	—	—
Minnesota	22,069	11,920	748	62	4	—	—	—
Mississippi	—	3,283	40,797	25,040	—	—	7	—
Missouri	17,028	58,801	31,317	58,372	—	9	—	—
New Hampshire	37,519	25,881	2,112	441	5	—	—	—
New Jersey	58,324	62,801	—	—	4	3	—	—
New York	362,646	312,510	—	—	35	—	—	—
North Carolina	—	2,701	48,539	44,990	—	—	10	—
Ohio	231,610	187,232	11,405	12,194	23	—	—	—
Oregon	5,270	3,951	5,006	183	3	—	—	—
Pennsylvania	268,030	16,765	178,871	12,776	27	—	—	—
Rhode Island	12,244	7,707	—	—	4	—	—	—
South Carolina °	—	—	—	—	—	—	8	—
Tennessee	—	11,350	64,709	69,274	—	—	—	12
Texas	—	—	47,548	15,438	—	—	4	—
Vermont	33,808	8,649	1,866	217	5	—	—	—
Virginia	1,929	16,290	74,323	74,681	—	—	—	15
Wisconsin	86,110	65,021	888	161	5	—	—	—
	1,866,452	1,376,957	849,781	588,879	180	12	72	39

° *Electors were appointed by the legislature.*

Thirty-three states took part in the election. Minnesota had been admitted on May 11, 1858, Oregon on February 12, 1859. **Total vote: 4,682,069.**

of the electors of President and Vice-President of the United States, and the President of the Senate shall be their presiding officer. One teller shall be appointed on the part of the Senate, and two on the part of the House of Representatives, to whom shall be handed, as they are opened by the President of the Senate, the certificates of the electoral votes; and said tellers, having read the same in the presence and hearing of the two Houses then assembled, shall make a list of the votes as they shall appear from the said certificates; and the votes having been counted, the result of the same shall be delivered to the President of the Senate, who shall thereupon announce the state of the vote and the names of the persons, if any, elected; which announcement shall be deemed a sufficient declaration of the persons elected President and Vice-President of the United States, and, together with a list of the votes, be entered on the journals of the two Houses.

"If, upon the reading of any such certificate by the tellers, any question shall arise in regard to counting the votes therein certified, the same having been stated by the presiding officer, the Senate shall thereupon withdraw, and said question shall be submitted to that body for its decision; and the Speaker of the House of Representatives shall, in like manner, submit said question to the House of Representatives for its decision; and no question shall be decided affirm-

1864

STATES	POPULAR VOTE		SOLDIERS' VOTE		ELECTORAL VOTE	
	Abraham Lincoln, Illinois.	George B. McClellan, New Jersey.	Abraham Lincoln.	George McClellan.	Lincoln and Johnson.	McClellan and Pendleton.
Calif.	62,134	43,841	2,600	237	5	—
Conn.	44,693	42,288	—	—	6	—
Del.	8,155	8,767	—	—	—	3
Ill.	189,487	158,349	—	—	16	—
Ind.	150,422	130,233	—	—	13	—
Iowa	87,331	49,260	15,178	1,364	8	—
Kan.†	14,228	3,871	—	—	3	—
Ky.	27,786	64,301	1,194	2,823	—	11
Me.	72,278	47,736	4,174	741	7	—
Md.	40,153	32,739	2,800	321	7	—
Mass.	126,742	48,745	—	—	12	—
Mich.	85,352	67,370	9,402	2,959	8	—
Minn.†	25,060	17,375	—	—	4	—
Mo.	72,991	31,026	—	—	11	—
Nev.	9,826	6,594	—	—	2°	—
N. H.	36,595	33,034	2,066	690	5	—
N. J.	60,723	68,014	—	—	—	7
N. Y.	368,726	361,986	—	—	33	—
Ohio	265,154	205,568	41,146	9,757	21	—
Ore.	9,888	8,457	—	—	3	—
Pa.	296,389	276,308	26,712	12,349	26	—
R. I.	14,343	8,718	—	—	4	—
Vt.	42,422	13,325	243	49	5	—
W. Va.	23,223	10,457	—	—	5	—
Wis.	79,564	63,875	11,372	2,458	8	—
	2,213,665	1,802,237	116,887	33,748	212	21

° *One of the three Nevada electors died before the election.*
† *The army vote from Kansas and Minnesota arrived too late for counting.*

Twenty-five states took part in the election. Kansas joined the Union on January 29, 1861, West Virginia on June 20, 1863, Nevada on October 31, 1864.

No valid elections were held in eleven Southern states—Alabama, Arkansas, Florida, Georgia, Louisiana, Mississippi, North Carolina, South Carolina, Tennessee, Texas and Virginia.

Total vote: 4,166,537.

1868

STATES	POPULAR VOTE		ELECTORAL VOTE	
	U. S. Grant, Illinois. Republican	H. Seymour, New York. Democrat	Grant and Colfax.	Seymour and Blair.
Alabama	76,366	72,086	8	—
Arkansas	22,152	19,078	5	—
California	54,592	54,078	5	—
Connecticut	50,641	47,600	6	—
Delaware	7,623	10,980	—	3
Florida°	—	—	3	—
Georgia	57,134	102,822	—	9
Illinois	250,293	199,143	16	—
Indiana	176,552	166,980	13	—
Iowa	120,399	74,040	8	—
Kansas	31,049	14,019	3	—
Kentucky	39,566	115,889	—	11
Louisiana	33,263	80,225	—	7
Maine	70,426	42,396	7	—
Maryland	30,438	62,357	—	7
Massachusetts	136,477	59,408	12	—
Michigan	128,550	97,069	8	—
Minnesota	43,542	28,072	4	—
Mississippi†	—	—	—	—
Missouri	85,671	59,788	11	—
Nebraska	9,729	5,439	3	—
Nevada	6,480	5,218	3	—
New Hampshire	38,191	31,224	5	—
New Jersey	80,121	83,001	—	7
New York	419,883	429,883	—	33
North Carolina	96,226	84,090	9	—
Ohio	280,128	238,700	21	—
Oregon	10,961	11,125	—	3
Pennsylvania	342,280	313,382	26	—
Rhode Island	12,993	6,548	4	—
South Carolina	62,301	45,237	6	—
Tennessee	56,757	26,311	10	—
Texas†	—	—	—	—
Vermont	44,167	12,045	5	—
Virginia†	—	—	—	—
West Virginia	29,025	20,306	5	—
Wisconsin	108,857	84,710	8	—
	3,012,833	2,703,249	214	80

° *Electors were appointed by the legislature.*
† *The "unreconstructed" states of Mississippi, Texas and Virginia were excluded in this election.*

Thirty-seven states took part in the election. Nebraska was admitted on March 1, 1867.

Total vote: 5,716,082.

atively, and no vote objected to shall be counted, except by the concurrent votes of the two Houses, which being obtained, the two Houses shall immediately reassemble, and the presiding officer shall then announce the decision of the question submitted, and upon any such question there shall be no debate in either House; and any other question pertinent to the object for which the two Houses are assembled may be submitted and determined in like manner.

"At such joint meeting of the two Houses, seats shall be provided as follows: for the President of the Senate, the Speaker's chair; for the Speaker, a chair immediately upon his left; for the senators, in the body of the hall, upon the right of the presiding officer; for the representatives, in the body of the hall not occupied by the senators; for the tellers, Secretary of the Senate, and Clerk of the House of Representatives, at the Clerk's desk; for the other officers of the two Houses, in front of the Clerk's desk, and upon either side of the Speaker's platform.

"Such joint meeting shall not be dissolved until the electoral votes are all counted and the result declared; and no recess shall be taken unless a question shall have arisen in regard to counting any of such votes, in which case it shall be competent for either House, acting separately, in the manner hereinbefore provided, to direct a recess, not beyond the

STATES	Ulysses S. Grant, Ill. Republican	Horace Greeley, N.Y. Lib. Republican and Democrat	Charles O'Conor, N.Y. Straight Democrat and Labor Reform	James Black, Pa. Prohibitionist	Ulysses S. Grant, Ill.	Thomas A. Hendricks, Ind.	B. Gratz Brown, Mo.	Horace Greeley, N.Y.	Charles J. Jenkins, Ga.	David Davis, Ill.	Henry Wilson, Mass.	B. Gratz Brown, Mo.	George W. Julian, Ind.	Alfred H. Colquitt, Ga.	John M. Palmer, Ill.	Thomas E. Bramlette, Ky.	Nathaniel P. Banks, Mass.	William S. Groesbeck, O.	Willis B. Machen, Ky.
Alabama	90,272	79,444	—	—	10	—	—	—	—	—	10	—	—	—	—	—	—	—	—
Arkansas	41,373	37,927	—	—	6†	—	—	—	—	—	6†	—	—	—	—	—	—	—	—
California	54,020	40,718	1,068	—	6	—	—	—	—	—	6	—	—	—	—	—	—	—	—
Connecticut	50,638	45,880	204	206	6	—	—	—	—	—	6	—	—	—	—	—	—	—	—
Delaware	11,115	10,206	487	—	3	—	—	—	—	—	3	—	—	—	—	—	—	—	—
Florida	17,763	15,427	—	—	4	—	—	—	—	—	4	—	—	—	—	—	—	—	—
Georgia	62,550	76,356	4,000	—	—	—	6	3	2	—	—	5	—	5	—	—	1	—	—
Illinois	241,944	184,938	3,058	—	21	—	—	—	—	—	21	—	—	—	—	—	—	—	—
Indiana	186,147	163,632	1,417	—	15	—	—	—	—	—	15	—	—	—	—	—	—	—	—
Iowa	131,566	71,196	2,221	—	11	—	—	—	—	—	11	—	—	—	—	—	—	—	—
Kansas	67,048	32,970	596	—	5	—	—	—	—	—	5	—	—	—	—	—	—	—	—
Kentucky	88,766	99,995	2,374	—	—	8	4	—	—	—	—	8	—	—	—	3	—	—	1
Louisiana*	71,663	57,029	—	—	8	—	—	—	—	—	8	—	—	—	—	—	—	—	—
Louisiana†	59,975	66,467	—	—	—	—	—	—	—	—	—	8	—	—	—	—	—	—	—
Maine	61,422	29,087	—	—	7	—	—	—	—	—	7	—	—	—	—	—	—	—	—
Maryland	66,760	67,687	19	—	—	8	—	—	—	—	—	8	—	—	—	—	—	—	—
Massachusetts	133,472	59,260	—	—	13	—	—	—	—	—	13	—	—	—	—	—	—	—	—
Michigan	138,455	78,355	2,861	1,271	11	—	—	—	—	—	11	—	—	—	—	—	—	—	—
Minnesota	55,117	34,423	—	—	5	—	—	—	—	—	5	—	—	—	—	—	—	—	—
Mississippi	82,175	47,288	—	—	8	—	—	—	—	—	8	—	—	—	—	—	—	—	—
Missouri	119,196	151,434	2,439	—	—	6	8	—	—	1	—	6	5	—	3	—	—	1	—
Nebraska	18,329	7,812	—	—	3	—	—	—	—	—	3	—	—	—	—	—	—	—	—
Nevada	8,413	6,236	—	—	3	—	—	—	—	—	3	—	—	—	—	—	—	—	—
New Hampshire	37,168	31,424	100	200	5	—	—	—	—	—	5	—	—	—	—	—	—	—	—
New Jersey	91,656	76,456	630	—	9	—	—	—	—	—	9	—	—	—	—	—	—	—	—
New York	440,736	387,281	1,454	201	35	—	—	—	—	—	35	—	—	—	—	—	—	—	—
North Carolina	94,769	70,094	—	—	10	—	—	—	—	—	10	—	—	—	—	—	—	—	—
Ohio	281,852	244,321	1,163	2,100	22	—	—	—	—	—	22	—	—	—	—	—	—	—	—
Oregon	11,819	7,730	572	—	3	—	—	—	—	—	3	—	—	—	—	—	—	—	—
Pennsylvania	349,589	212,041	—	1,630	29	—	—	—	—	—	29	—	—	—	—	—	—	—	—
Rhode Island	13,665	5,329	—	—	4	—	—	—	—	—	4	—	—	—	—	—	—	—	—
South Carolina	72,290	22,703	187	—	7	—	—	—	—	—	7	—	—	—	—	—	—	—	—
Tennessee	85,655	94,391	—	—	—	12	—	—	—	—	—	12	—	—	—	—	—	—	—
Texas	47,468	66,546	2,580	—	—	8	—	—	—	—	—	8	—	—	—	—	—	—	—
Vermont	41,481	10,927	593	—	5	—	—	—	—	—	5	—	—	—	—	—	—	—	—
Virginia	93,468	91,654	42	—	11	—	—	—	—	—	11	—	—	—	—	—	—	—	—
West Virginia	32,315	29,451	600	—	5	—	—	—	—	—	5	—	—	—	—	—	—	—	—
Wisconsin	104,997	86,477	834	—	10	—	—	—	—	—	10	—	—	—	—	—	—	—	—
	3,597,132	2,834,125	29,489	5,608	286	42	18	—	2	1	286	47	5	5	3	3	1	1	1

Thirty-seven states again took part in the election.

During the counting of the votes many controversies arose. Since objections were raised against the Arkansas and Louisiana votes, the returns of neither state were counted. The popular vote of Louisiana is given in two ways: * marks votes certified by the so-called "Custom-House" board; † marks votes certified by a returning board appointed by the Governor of Louisiana, Henry C. Warmoth, a Republican who joined the Greeley movement (not included in total). The 3 Georgia votes were rejected because Greeley had died before the votes were counted. The remaining 5 Greeley states cast their votes for Hendricks.

Total vote: 6,466,354.

next day at the hour of one o'clock P.M."

Lincoln signed the joint resolution on the day of the count; thus Vice President Hamlin did not present the votes of the disputed states.

In 1869 Congress, controlled by the Radical Republicans, excluded the electoral votes of "States lately in rebellion."

In 1873 there were some problems which were settled under the terms of the twenty-second joint rule. Horace Greeley had died after the election. The question was, should the three votes from Georgia cast for a dead man be counted? The Senate said yes, the House no—thus the votes were not allowed.

In the election of 1876 the returns were disputed in three Southern states. Instead of using the joint rule again, Con-

STATES	S. J. Tilden, N. Y. Democrat	R. B. Hayes, Ohio. Republican	Peter Cooper, N. Y. Greenback	Green Clay Smith, Ky. Prohibitionist
Alabama	102,989	68,708	—	—
Arkansas	58,071	38,669	289	—
California	76,468	78,322	44	—
Colorado°	—	—	—	—
Connecticut	61,934	59,034	774	378
Delaware	13,381	10,752	—	—
Florida†	22,927	23,849	—	—
Florida‡	24,434	24,340	—	—
Georgia	130,088	50,446	—	—
Illinois	258,601	278,232	9,533	—
Indiana	213,526	208,011	17,233	141
Iowa	112,121	171,326	9,901	36
Kansas	37,902	78,322	7,776	110
Kentucky	159,696	97,156	1,944	818
Louisiana†	70,508	75,315	—	—
Louisiana‡	83,723	77,174	—	—
Maine	49,917	66,300	663	—
Maryland	91,780	71,981	33	10
Massachusetts	108,777	150,063	779	84
Michigan	141,095	166,534	9,060	766
Minnesota	48,799	72,962	2,311	72
Mississippi	112,173	52,605	—	—
Missouri	203,077	145,029	3,498	64
Nebraska	17,554	31,916	2,320	1,599
Nevada	9,308	10,383	—	—
New Hampshire	38,509	41,539	76	—
New Jersey	115,962	103,517	712	43
New York	521,949	489,207	1,987	2,359
North Carolina	125,427	108,417	—	—
Ohio	323,182	330,698	3,057	1,636
Oregon	14,149	15,206	510	—
Pennsylvania	366,204	384,184	7,187	1,319
Rhode Island	10,712	15,787	68	60
South Carolina	90,896	91,870	—	—
Tennessee	133,166	89,566	—	—
Texas	104,803	44,803	—	—
Vermont	20,350	44,428	—	—
Virginia	139,670	95,558	—	—
West Virginia	56,495	42,046	1,373	—
Wisconsin	123,926	130,070	1,509	27
Total Republican count	4,286,092	4,032,811	81,737	9,522
Total Democratic count	4,300,814	4,035,161	81,737	9,522

° *Electors were appointed by the legislature to avoid another election.*
† *Republican count.*   ‡ *Democratic count.*

STATES	Hayes and Wheeler.	Tilden and Hendricks.	STATES	Hayes and Wheeler.	Tilden and Hendricks.
Alabama	—	10	Missouri	—	15
Arkansas	—	6	Nebraska	3	—
California	6	—	Nevada	3	—
Colorado	3	—	New Hampshire	5	—
Connecticut	—	6	New Jersey	—	9
Delaware	—	3	New York	—	35
Florida	4	—	North Carolina	—	10
Georgia	—	11	Ohio	22	—
Illinois	21	—	Oregon	3	—
Indiana	—	15	Pennsylvania	29	—
Iowa	11	—	Rhode Island	4	—
Kansas	5	—	South Carolina	7	—
Kentucky	—	12	Tennessee	—	12
Louisiana	8	—	Texas	—	8
Maine	7	—	Vermont	5	—
Maryland	—	8	Virginia	—	11
Massachusetts	13	—	West Virginia	—	5
Michigan	11	—	Wisconsin	10	—
Minnesota	5	—	Total	185	184
Mississippi	—	8			

Thirty-eight states took part in the election. Colorado was admitted on August 1, 1876.

Total vote (Republican count): 8,410,162.
Total vote (Democratic count): 8,427,234.

THE
DISPUTED ELECTION
OF 1876

gress passed the Electoral Commission Law of 1877, setting up a fifteen-man commission to report on the returns. Unless both Houses of Congress rejected a disputed return, that return was to be accepted. With a Democratic House and a Republican Senate, all disputed returns were accepted, and the election went to the Republican Hayes.

After this election many proposals were raised and de-bated about this. On February 3, 1887, the procedure was revised. A new bill set the day for the electors to vote within the states as the second Monday in January, and listed safe-guards for certifying the votes. Also:

"That Congress shall be in session on the second Wednes-day in February succeeding every meeting of the electors. The Senate and the House of Representatives shall meet in

1880

STATES	James A. Garfield, Ohio. Republican	Winfield S. Hancock, Pa. Democrat	James B. Weaver, Iowa. Greenbacker	Neal Dow, Maine. Prohibitionist	Garfield and Arthur.	Hancock and English.
	POPULAR VOTE				ELECTORAL VOTE	
Ala.	56,221	91,185	4,642	—	—	10
Ark.	42,436	60,775	4,079	—	—	6
Calif.	80,348	80,426	3,392	—	1	5
Colo.	27,450	24,647	1,435	—	3	—
Conn.	67,071	64,415	868	409	6	—
Del.	14,133	15,275	120	—	—	3
Fla.	23,654	27,964	—	—	—	4
Ga.	54,086	102,470	969	—	—	11
Ill.	318,037	277,321	26,358	443	21	—
Ind.	232,164	225,522	12,986	—	15	—
Iowa	183,927	105,845	32,701	592	11	—
Kan.	121,549	59,801	19,851	25	5	—
Ky.	106,306	149,068	11,499	258	—	12
La.	38,637	65,067	439	—	—	8
Me.	74,039	65,171	4,408	93	7	—
Md.	78,515	93,706	818	—	—	8
Mass.	165,205	111,960	4,548	682	13	—
Mich.	185,341	131,597	34,895	942	11	—
Minn.	93,903	53,315	3,267	286	5	—
Miss.	34,854	75,750	5,797	—	—	8
Mo.	153,567	208,609	35,135	—	—	15
Neb.	54,979	28,523	3,950	—	3	—
Nev.	8,732	9,613	—	—	—	3
N. H.	44,852	40,794	528	180	5	—
N. J.	120,555	122,565	2,617	191	—	9
N. Y.	555,544	534,511	12,373	1,517	35	—
N. C.	115,874	124,208	1,126	—	—	10
Ohio	375,048	340,821	6,456	2,616	22	—
Ore.	20,619	19,948	249	—	3	—
Pa.	444,704	407,428	20,668	1,939	29	—
R. I.	18,195	10,779	236	20	4	—
S. C.	58,071	112,312	566	—	—	7
Tenn.	107,677	128,191	5,917	43	—	12
Tex.	57,893	156,428	27,405	—	—	8
Vt.	45,567	18,316	1,215	—	5	—
Va.	84,020	128,586	—	—	—	11
W. Va.	46,243	57,391	9,079	—	—	5
Wis.	144,400	114,649	7,986	69	10	—
	4,454,416	4,444,952	308,578	10,305	214	155

Thirty-eight states again took part in the election.

Louisiana voted for two Republican tickets. Maine voted for a fusion Democratic ticket, consisting of three Democrats and four Greenbackers; it also voted for a straight Greenback ticket. Virginia voted for two Democratic tickets.

Total vote: 9,218,251.

1884

STATES	Grover Cleveland, N. Y. Democrat	James G. Blaine, Me. Republican	Benjamin F. Butler, Mass. Greenbacker	John P. St. John, Kan. Prohibitionist	Cleveland and Hendricks.	Blaine and Logan.
	POPULAR VOTE				ELECTORAL VOTE	
Ala.	93,951	59,591	873	612	10	—
Ark.	72,927	50,895	1,847	—	7	—
Calif.	89,288	102,416	2,017	2,920	—	8
Colo.	27,723	36,290	1,953	761	—	3
Conn.	67,199	65,923	1,688	2,305	6	—
Del.	16,964	12,951	6	55	3	—
Fla.	31,766	28,031	—	72	4	—
Ga.	94,667	48,603	145	195	12	—
Ill.	312,355	337,474	10,910	12,074	—	22
Ind.	244,990	238,463	8,293	3,028	15	—
Iowa	177,316	197,089	—	1,472	—	13
Kan.	90,132	154,406	16,341	4,495	—	9
Ky.	152,961	118,122	1,691	3,139	13	—
La.	62,540	46,347	—	—	8	—
Me.	52,140	72,209	3,953	2,160	—	6
Md.	96,932	85,699	531	2,794	8	—
Mass.	122,481	146,724	24,433	10,026	—	14
Mich.	149,835	192,669	42,243	18,403	—	13
Minn.	70,144	111,923	3,583	4,684	—	7
Miss.	76,510	43,509	—	—	9	—
Mo.	235,988	202,929	—	2,153	16	—
Neb.	54,391	79,912	—	2,899	—	5
Nev.	5,578	7,193	26	—	—	3
N. H.	39,183	43,249	552	1,571	—	4
N. J.	127,798	123,440	3,496	6,159	9	—
N. Y.	563,154	562,005	16,994	25,016	36	—
N. C.	142,952	125,068	—	454	11	—
Ohio	368,280	400,082	5,179	11,069	—	23
Ore.	24,604	26,860	726	492	—	3
Pa.	392,785	473,804	16,992	15,283	—	30
R. I.	12,391	19,030	422	928	—	4
S. C.	69,890	21,733	—	—	9	—
Tenn.	133,258	124,078	957	1,131	12	—
Tex.	225,309	93,141	3,321	3,534	13	—
Vt.	17,331	39,514	785	1,752	—	4
Va.	185,497	139,356	—	138	12	—
W. Va.	67,317	63,096	810	939	6	—
Wis.	146,459	161,157	4,598	7,656	—	11
	4,914,986	4,854,981	175,365	150,369	219	182

Thirty-eight states again took part in the election.

No new state had been admitted since 1876, but the census of 1880 changed the apportionment. The number of presidential electors was increased from 369 to 401.

Total vote: 10,095,701.

the hall of the House of Representatives at the hour of one o'clock in the afternoon on that day, and the President of the Senate shall be their presiding officer. Two tellers shall be previously appointed on the part of the Senate, and two on the part of the House of Representatives, to whom shall be handed, as they are opened by the President of the Senate, all the certificates and papers purporting to be the certificates of the electoral vote, which certificates and papers shall be opened, presented, and acted upon in the alphabetical order of the States, beginning with the letter A; and said tellers, having then read the same in the presence and hearing of the two Houses, shall make a list of the votes as they shall appear from the said certificates, and, the votes having been ascertained and counted in the manner and according to the rules

STATES	POPULAR VOTE				ELECTORAL VOTE	
	Benjamin Harrison, Ind. Republican.	Grover Cleveland, N. Y. Democrat.	Clinton B. Fisk, N. J. Prohibitionist.	Alson J. Streeter, Ill. Union Labor.	Harrison and Morton.	Cleveland and Thurman.
Ala.	56,197	117,320	583	—	—	10
Ark.	58,752	85,962	641	10,613	—	7
Calif.	124,816	117,729	5,761	—	8	—
Colo.	50,774	37,567	2,191	1,266	3	—
Conn.	74,584	74,920	4,234	240	—	6
Del.	12,973	16,414	400	—	—	3
Fla.	26,657	39,561	423	—	—	4
Ga.	40,496	100,499	1,808	136	—	12
Ill.	370,473	348,278	21,695	7,090	22	—
Ind.	263,361	261,013	9,881	2,694	15	—
Iowa	211,598	179,887	3,550	9,105	13	—
Kan.	182,934	103,744	6,768	37,726	9	—
Ky.	155,134	183,800	5,225	622	—	13
La.	30,484	85,032	160	39	—	8
Me.	73,734	50,481	2,691	1,344	6	—
Md.	99,986	106,168	4,767	—	—	8
Mass.	183,892	151,856	8,701	—	14	—
Mich.	236,370	213,459	20,942	4,541	13	—
Minn.	142,492	104,385	15,311	1,094	7	—
Miss.	30,096	85,471	218	22	—	9
Mo.	236,257	261,974	4,539	18,632	—	16
Neb.	108,425	80,552	9,429	4,226	5	—
Nev.	7,229	5,362	41	—	3	—
N. H.	45,728	43,458	1,593	13	4	—
N. J.	144,344	151,493	7,904	—	—	9
N. Y.	648,759	635,757	30,231	626	36	—
N. C.	134,784	147,902	2,787	32	—	11
Ohio	416,054	396,455	24,356	3,496	23	—
Ore.	33,291	26,522	1,677	363	3	—
Pa.	526,091	446,633	20,947	3,873	30	—
R. I.	21,968	17,530	1,250	18	4	—
S. C.	13,736	65,825	—	—	—	9
Tenn.	138,988	158,779	5,969	48	—	12
Tex.	88,422	234,883	4,749	29,459	—	13
Vt.	45,192	16,785	1,460	—	4	—
Va.	150,438	151,977	1,678	—	—	12
W. Va.	77,791	79,664	669	1,064	—	6
Wis.	176,553	155,232	14,277	8,552	11	—
	5,439,853	5,540,329	249,506	146,934	233	168

Thirty-eight states again took part in the election.
Total vote: 11,381,031.

in this act provided, the result of the same shall be delivered to the President of the Senate, who shall thereupon announce the state of the vote, which announcement shall be deemed a sufficient declaration of the persons, if any, elected President and Vice-President of the United States, and, together with a list of the votes, be entered on the journals of the two Houses." In the event of objections the Houses were to meet separately and both would have to reject a set of returns.

After the 1876 election many proposals were made in Congress to change the mode of election, none was adopted.

In 1886 the Presidential Succession Act was adopted. It prescribed "that in case of the removal, death, resignation, or inability of both the President and Vice-President of the United States, the Secretary of State, or if there be none, or

STATES	POPULAR VOTE					ELECTORAL VOTE		
	Grover Cleveland, New York. Democrat	Benjamin Harrison, Indiana. Republican	James B. Weaver, Iowa. Populist	John Bidwell, California. Prohibitionist	Simon Wing, Massachusetts. Socialist-Labor	Cleveland and Stevenson.	Harrison and Read.	Weaver and Field.
Alabama	138,138	9,197	85,181	239	—	11	—	—
Arkansas	87,834	46,884	11,831	113	—	8	—	—
California	117,908	117,618	25,226	8,056	—	8	1	—
Colorado	—	38,620	53,584	1,638	—	—	—	4
Connecticut	82,395	77,025	806	4,025	329	6	—	—
Delaware	18,581	18,083	13	565	—	3	—	—
Florida	30,143	—	4,843	475	—	4	—	—
Georgia	129,361	48,305	42,937	988	—	13	—	—
Idaho	—	8,599	10,520	288	—	—	—	3
Illinois	426,281	399,288	22,207	25,870	—	24	—	—
Indiana	262,740	255,615	22,208	13,050	—	15	—	—
Iowa	196,367	219,795	20,595	6,402	—	—	13	—
Kansas	—	157,237	163,111	4,539	—	—	—	10
Kentucky	175,461	135,441	23,500	6,442	—	13	—	—
Louisiana	87,922	13,281	13,282	—	—	8	—	—
Maine	48,044	62,931	2,381	3,062	336	—	6	—
Maryland	113,866	92,736	796	5,877	27	8	—	—
Massachusetts	176,813	202,814	3,210	1,539	649	—	15	—
Michigan	202,296	222,708	19,892	14,069	—	5	9	—
Minnesota	100,920	122,823	29,313	12,182	—	—	9	—
Mississippi	40,237	1,406	10,256	910	—	9	—	—
Missouri	268,398	226,918	41,213	4,331	—	17	—	—
Montana	17,581	18,851	7,334	549	—	—	3	—
Nebraska	24,943	87,227	83,134	4,902	—	—	8	—
Nevada	714	2,811	7,264	89	—	—	—	3
New Hampshire	42,081	45,658	292	1,297	—	—	4	—
New Jersey	171,042	156,068	969	8,131	1,337	10	—	—
New York	654,868	609,350	16,429	38,190	17,956	36	—	—
North Carolina	132,951	100,342	44,736	2,636	—	11	—	—
North Dakota	—	17,519	17,700	899	—	1	1	1
Ohio	404,115	405,187	14,850	26,012	—	1	22	—
Oregon	14,243	35,002	26,965	2,281	—	—	3	1
Pennsylvania	452,264	516,011	8,714	25,123	898	—	32	—
Rhode Island	24,335	26,972	228	1,654	—	—	4	—
South Carolina	54,692	13,345	2,407	—	—	9	—	—
South Dakota	9,081	34,888	26,544	—	—	—	4	—
Tennessee	138,874	100,331	23,447	4,851	—	12	—	—
Texas	239,148	81,444	99,688	2,165	—	15	—	—
Vermont	16,325	37,992	43	1,415	—	—	4	—
Virginia	163,977	113,262	12,275	2,738	—	12	—	—
Washington	29,802	36,460	19,165	2,542	—	—	4	—
West Virginia	84,467	80,293	4,166	2,145	—	6	—	—
Wisconsin	177,335	170,791	9,909	13,132	—	12	—	—
Wyoming	—	8,454	7,722	530	—	—	3	—
	5,556,543	5,175,582	1,040,886	255,941	21,532	277	145	22

Forty-four states took part in the election, six new states having joined the Union.

North Dakota and South Dakota were admitted on November 2, 1889, Montana on November 8, 1889, Washington on November 11, 1889, Idaho on July 3, 1890, and Wyoming on July 10, 1890.

Total vote: 12,050,484.

in case of his removal, death, resignation, or inability, then the Secretary of the Treasury, or if there be none, or in case of his removal, death, resignation, or inability, then the Secretary of War, or if there be none, or in case of his removal, death, resignation, or inability, then the Attorney-General, or if there be none, or in case of his removal, death, resignation, or inability, then the Postmaster-General, or if there be none, or in case of his removal, death, resignation, or inability, then the Secretary of the Navy, or if there be none, or in case of his removal, death, resignation, or inability, then the Secretary of the Interior shall act as President until the disability of the President or Vice-President is removed, or a President shall be elected: *provided,* that whenever the powers and duties of the office of President of the United

1896

| STATES | POPULAR VOTE | | | | | | | ELECTORAL VOTE | | | | |
| | | | | | | | | PRESIDENT | | VICE-PRESIDENT | | |
	William McKinley, Ohio. Republican	William J. Bryan, Nebraska. Democrat	Bryan and Watson. Populist	John M. Palmer, Illinois. Nat. Democrat	Joshua Levering, Maryland. Prohibitionist	C. E. Bentley, Nebraska. National	C. H. Matchett, New York. Socialist Labor	McKinley.	Bryan.	Hobart.	Sewall.	Watson.
Alabama	54,737	131,226	24,089	6,462	2,147	—	—	—	11	—	11	—
Arkansas	37,512	110,103	—	—	839	893	—	—	8	—	5	3
California	146,688	144,766	21,730	2,006	2,573	1,047	1,611	8	1	8	1	—
Colorado	26,271	161,269	2,389	1	1,717	386	160	—	4	—	4	—
Connecticut	110,285	56,740	—	4,336	1,806	—	1,223	6	—	6	—	—
Delaware	20,452	16,615	—	966	602	—	—	3	—	3	—	—
Florida	11,257	31,958	1,977	1,772	644	—	—	—	4	—	4	—
Georgia	60,091	94,672	440	2,708	5,716	—	—	—	13	—	13	—
Idaho	6,324	23,192	—	—	181	—	—	—	3	—	3	—
Illinois	607,130	464,523	1,090	6,390	9,796	793	1,147	24	—	24	—	—
Indiana	323,754	305,573	—	2,145	3,056	2,267	324	15	—	15	—	—
Iowa	289,293	223,741	—	4,516	3,192	352	453	13	—	13	—	—
Kansas	159,541	171,810	46,194	1,209	1,921	630	—	—	10	—	10	—
Kentucky	218,171	217,890	—	5,114	4,781	—	—	12	1	12	1	—
Louisiana	22,037	77,175	—	1,915	—	—	—	—	8	—	4	4
Maine	80,461	34,587	2,387	1,866	1,589	—	—	6	—	6	—	—
Maryland	136,978	104,746	—	2,507	5,922	136	588	8	—	8	—	—
Massachusetts	278,976	105,711	15,181	11,749	2,998	—	2,114	15	—	15	—	—
Michigan	293,582	237,268	—	6,968	5,025	1,995	297	14	—	14	—	—
Minnesota	193,503	139,735	—	3,222	4,363	—	954	9	—	9	—	—
Mississippi	5,123	63,793	7,517	1,071	485	—	—	—	9	—	9	—
Missouri	304,940	363,652	—	2,355	2,169	293	599	—	17	—	13	4
Montana	10,494	42,537	—	—	186	—	—	—	3	—	2	1
Nebraska	103,064	115,999	—	2,797	1,243	797	186	—	8	—	4	4
Nevada	1,938	8,377	575	—	—	—	—	—	3	—	3	—
New Hampshire	57,444	21,650	379	3,520	779	49	228	4	—	4	—	—
New Jersey	221,367	133,675	—	6,373	5,614	—	3,985	10	—	10	—	—
New York	819,838	551,369	—	18,950	16,052	—	17,667	36	—	36	—	—
North Carolina	155,222	174,488	—	578	676	245	—	—	11	—	6	5
North Dakota	26,335	20,686	—	—	358	—	—	3	—	3	—	—
Ohio	525,991	477,497	2,615	1,858	5,068	2,716	1,167	23	—	23	—	—
Oregon	48,779	46,662	—	977	919	—	—	4	—	4	—	—
Pennsylvania	728,300	433,230	11,176	10,921	19,274	870	1,683	32	—	32	—	—
Rhode Island	37,437	14,459	—	1,166	1,160	5	558	4	—	4	—	—
South Carolina	9,313	58,801	—	824	—	—	—	—	9	—	9	—
South Dakota	41,042	41,225	—	683	—	—	—	—	4	—	2	2
Tennessee	148,773	166,268	4,525	1,951	3,098	—	—	—	12	—	12	—
Texas	167,520	370,434	79,572	5,046	1,786	—	—	—	15	—	15	—
Utah	13,491	64,607	—	21	—	—	—	—	3	—	3	—
Vermont	50,991	10,607	461	1,329	728	—	115	4	—	4	—	—
Virginia	135,388	154,985	—	2,127	2,350	—	—	—	12	—	12	—
Washington	39,153	51,646	—	1,668	968	148	—	—	4	—	2	2
West Virginia	104,414	92,927	—	677	1,203	—	—	6	—	6	—	—
Wisconsin	268,135	165,523	—	4,584	7,509	346	1,314	12	—	12	—	—
Wyoming	10,072	10,655	286	—	136	—	—	—	3	—	2	1
	7,111,607	6,509,052	222,583	134,645	131,312	13,968	36,373	271	176	271	149	27

Forty-five states took part in the election. Utah was admitted on January 4, 1896.
Some of the Populist vote for Bryan and Watson is included in the Bryan column.
Total vote: 14,159,540.

States shall devolve upon any of the persons named herein, if Congress be not then in session, or if it would not meet in accordance with law within twenty days thereafter, it shall be the duty of the person upon whom said powers and duties shall devolve to issue a proclamation convening Congress in extraordinary session, giving twenty days' notice of the time of meeting."

A year later, on February 3, 1887, a detailed plan for counting the electoral votes was adopted.

Since then several provisions have been accepted by both parties about the nomination of the President. According to one, if the presidential nominee should die before election day, his party would name another candidate in his place. For the Democrats the selection would be made by the Dem-

1900

STATES	POPULAR VOTE								ELECTORAL VOTE	
	McKinley and Roosevelt, Republican.	Bryan and Stevenson, Democrat.	Wooley and Metcalf, Prohibition.	Debs and Harriman, Social-Democrat.	Malloney and Remmel, Socialist-Labor.	Barker and Donnelly, Mid-Road Populist.	Ellis and Nicholson, Union Reform.	Leonard and Martin, United Christian.	McKinley and Roosevelt.	Bryan and Stevenson.
Alabama	55,512	97,131	2,762	—	—	4,178	—	—	—	11
Arkansas	44,800	81,142	584	27	—	972	341	—	—	8
California	164,755	124,985	5,087	7,572	—	—	—	—	9	—
Colorado	93,072	122,733	3,790	714	684	389	—	—	—	4
Connecticut	102,572	74,014	1,617	1,029	908	—	—	—	6	—
Delaware	22,535	18,863	546	57	—	—	—	—	3	—
Florida	7,420	28,007	2,234	601	—	1,070	—	—	—	4
Georgia	35,056	81,700	1,396	—	—	4,584	—	—	—	13
Idaho	27,198	29,414	857	—	—	232	—	—	—	3
Illinois	597,985	503,061	17,626	9,687	1,373	1,141	572	352	24	—
Indiana	336,063	309,584	13,718	2,374	663	1,438	254	—	15	—
Iowa	307,808	209,265	9,502	2,742	259	613	—	707	13	—
Kansas	185,955	162,601	3,605	1,605	—	—	—	—	10	—
Kentucky	226,801	234,899	2,814	770	299	2,017	—	—	—	13
Louisiana	14,233	53,671	—	—	—	—	—	—	—	8
Maine	65,412	36,822	2,585	878	—	—	—	—	6	—
Maryland	136,185	122,238	4,574	904	388	—	147	—	8	—
Massachusetts	239,147	157,016	6,208	9,716	2,610	—	—	—	15	—
Michigan	316,269	211,685	11,859	2,826	903	837	—	—	14	—
Minnesota	190,461	112,901	8,555	3,065	1,329	—	—	—	9	—
Mississippi	5,753	51,706	—	—	—	1,644	—	—	—	9
Missouri	314,092	351,922	5,965	6,139	1,294	4,244	—	—	—	17
Montana	25,373	37,145	298	708	169	—	—	—	—	3
Nebraska	121,835	114,013	3,655	823	—	1,104	—	—	8	—
Nevada	3,849	6,347	—	—	—	—	—	—	—	3
New Hampshire	54,799	35,489	1,279	790	—	—	—	—	4	—
New Jersey	221,754	164,879	7,190	4,611	2,081	691	—	—	10	—
New York	822,013	678,462	22,077	12,869	12,621	—	—	—	36	—
North Carolina	132,997	157,733	1,006	—	—	830	—	—	—	11
North Dakota	35,898	20,531	731	520	—	111	—	—	3	—
Ohio	543,918	474,882	10,203	4,847	1,588	251	4,284	—	23	—
Oregon	46,526	33,385	2,536	1,494	—	275	—	—	4	—
Pennsylvania	712,665	424,232	27,908	4,831	2,936	638	—	—	32	—
Rhode Island	33,784	19,812	1,529	—	1,423	—	—	—	4	—
South Carolina	3,579	47,233	—	—	—	—	—	—	—	9
South Dakota	54,530	39,544	1,542	169	—	339	—	—	4	—
Tennessee	123,180	145,356	3,860	413	—	1,322	—	—	—	12
Texas	130,641	267,432	2,644	1,846	162	20,981	—	—	—	15
Utah	47,139	45,006	209	720	106	—	—	—	3	—
Vermont	42,569	12,849	383	39	—	367	—	—	4	—
Virginia	115,865	146,080	2,150	145	167	63	—	—	—	12
Washington	57,456	44,833	2,363	2,066	866	—	—	—	4	—
West Virginia	119,829	98,807	1,692	219	—	268	—	—	6	—
Wisconsin	265,760	159,163	10,027	7,048	503	—	—	—	12	—
Wyoming	14,482	10,164	—	—	—	—	—	—	3	—
	7,219,525	6,358,737	209,166	94,864	33,332	50,599	5,598	1,059	292	155

Forty-five states again took part in the election.
Total vote: 13,972,880.

ocratic National Committee; for the Republicans the choice could be effected by either their National Committee or by another national convention.

Another provision is that if the President-elect should die after election day but before the meeting of the Electoral College, the electors would be free to cast their votes for any man of their choice. They would have no obligation to vote for the vice-president-elect.

If both President-elect and Vice President-elect should die, the Electoral College could vote for any two persons even without the consent of the political parties.

The Presidential Succession Act of July 18, 1947, estab-

STATES	POPULAR VOTE						ELECTORAL VOTE	
	Roosevelt and Fairbanks, Republican.	Parker and Davis, Democrat.	Swallow and Carroll, Prohibition.	Debs and Hanford, Socialist.	Corregan and Cox, Socialist-Labor.	Watson and Tibbles, Populist.	Roosevelt and Fairbanks.	Parker and Davis.
Alabama	22,472	79,857	612	853	—	5,051	—	11
Arkansas	46,860	64,434	993	1,816	—	2,318	—	9
California	205,226	89,404	7,380	29,535	—	—	10	—
Colorado	134,687	100,105	3,438	4,304	335	824	5	—
Connecticut	111,089	72,909	1,506	4,543	575	495	7	—
Delaware	23,712	19,359	607	146	—	51	3	—
Florida	8,314	27,040	5	2,337	—	1,605	—	5
Georgia	24,003	83,472	685	197	—	22,635	—	13
Idaho	47,783	18,480	1,013	4,949	—	353	3	—
Illinois	632,645	327,606	34,770	69,225	4,698	6,725	27	—
Indiana	368,289	274,335	23,496	12,013	1,598	2,444	15	—
Iowa	307,907	149,141	11,601	14,847	—	2,207	13	—
Kansas	212,955	86,174	7,306	15,869	—	6,253	10	—
Kentucky	205,277	217,170	6,609	3,602	596	2,511	—	13
Louisiana	5,205	47,708	—	995	—	—	—	9
Maine	64,438	27,649	1,510	2,103	—	—	6	—
Maryland	109,497	109,446	3,034	2,247	—	—	1	7
Massachusetts	257,822	165,772	4,286	13,604	2,365	1,290	16	—
Michigan	364,957	135,392	13,441	9,042	1,036	1,159	14	—
Minnesota	216,651	55,187	6,253	11,692	974	2,103	11	—
Mississippi	3,187	53,374	—	392	—	1,424	—	10
Missouri	321,449	296,312	7,191	13,009	1,674	4,226	18	—
Montana	34,932	21,773	335	5,676	208	1,520	3	—
Nebraska	138,558	52,921	6,323	7,412	—	20,518	8	—
Nevada	6,864	3,982	—	925	—	344	3	—
New Hampshire	54,163	34,074	750	1,090	—	83	4	—
New Jersey	245,164	164,516	6,845	9,587	2,680	3,705	12	—
New York	859,533	683,981	20,787	36,883	9,127	7,459	39	—
North Carolina	82,442	124,121	361	124	—	819	—	12
North Dakota	52,595	14,273	1,140	2,117	—	165	4	—
Ohio	600,095	344,674	19,339	36,260	2,633	1,392	23	—
Oregon	60,455	17,521	3,806	7,619	—	753	4	—
Pennsylvania	840,949	337,998	33,717	21,863	2,211	—	34	—
Rhode Island	41,605	24,839	768	956	488	—	4	—
South Carolina	2,554	52,563	—	22	—	1	—	9
South Dakota	72,083	21,969	2,965	3,138	—	1,240	4	—
Tennessee	105,369	131,653	1,891	1,354	—	2,506	—	12
Texas	51,242	167,200	3,995	2,791	421	8,062	—	18
Utah	62,446	33,413	—	5,767	—	—	3	—
Vermont	40,459	9,777	792	859	—	—	4	—
Virginia	47,880	80,650	1,382	218	56	359	—	12
Washington	101,540	28,098	3,329	10,023	1,592	669	5	—
West Virginia	132,628	100,881	4,600	1,572	—	339	7	—
Wisconsin	280,315	124,205	9,672	28,240	223	530	13	—
Wyoming	20,489	8,930	217	1,077	—	—	3	—
	7,628,785	5,084,338	258,750	402,893	33,490	114,138	336	140

Forty-five states again took part in the election.
Total vote: 13,522,394.

lished new rules, replacing the old ones of January 19, 1886. According to the old act the succession was by "St. Wapniacl" (the first letters of the Departments), meaning the Secretaries of State, Treasury, War, Attorney General, Postmaster General, Navy, Interior, Agriculture, Commerce and Labor. According to the new act if a President were to die, the succession would be: the Vice President, the Speaker of the House of Representatives, the President *pro tempore* of the Senate, then the Secretary of State, the Secretary of Treasury, and so on, as above.

In 1951 the Twenty-second Amendment to the Constitution was ratified, whereby:

STATES	POPULAR VOTE							ELECTORAL VOTE	
	Taft and Sherman, Republican.	Bryan and Kern, Democrat.	Chafin and Watkins, Prohibition.	Debs and Hanford, Socialist.	Gilhaus and Munro, Socialist-Labor.	Watson and Williams, Populist.	Hisgen and Graves, Independence.	Taft and Sherman.	Bryan and Kern.
Alabama	26,283	74,374	665	1,399	—	1,568	495	—	11
Arkansas	56,760	87,015	1,194	5,842	—	1,026	289	—	9
California	214,398	127,492	11,770	28,659	—	—	4,278	10	—
Colorado	123,700	126,644	5,559	7,974	—	—	—	—	5
Connecticut	112,815	68,255	2,380	5,113	608	—	728	7	—
Delaware	25,014	22,071	670	239	—	—	30	3	—
Florida	10,654	31,104	553	3,747	—	1,946	1,356	—	5
Georgia	41,692	72,413	1,059	584	—	16,969	77	—	13
Idaho	52,621	36,162	1,986	6,400	—	—	119	3	—
Illinois	629,932	450,810	29,364	34,711	1,680	633	7,724	27	—
Indiana	348,993	338,262	18,045	13,476	643	1,193	514	15	—
Iowa	275,210	200,771	9,837	8,287	—	261	404	13	—
Kansas	197,216	161,209	5,033	12,420	—	—	68	10	—
Kentucky	235,711	244,092	5,887	4,185	404	333	200	—	13
Louisiana	8,958	63,568	—	2,538	—	—	82	—	9
Maine	66,987	35,403	1,487	1,758	—	—	700	6	—
Maryland	116,513	115,908	3,302	2,323	—	—	485	2	6
Massachusetts	265,966	155,543	4,379	10,781	1,018	—	19,239	16	—
Michigan	333,313	174,619	16,795	11,527	1,086	—	734	14	—
Minnesota	195,843	109,401	11,107	14,527	—	—	426	11	—
Mississippi	4,363	60,287	—	978	—	1,276	—	—	10
Missouri	347,203	346,574	4,284	15,431	868	1,165	402	18	—
Montana	32,333	29,326	827	5,855	—	—	481	3	—
Nebraska	126,997	131,099	5,179	3,524	—	—	—	—	8
Nevada	10,775	11,212	—	2,103	—	—	436	—	3
New Hampshire	53,149	33,655	905	1,299	—	—	584	4	—
New Jersey	265,326	182,567	4,934	10,253	1,196	—	2,922	12	—
New York	870,070	667,468	22,667	38,451	3,877	—	35,817	39	—
North Carolina	114,887	136,928	—	345	—	—	—	—	12
North Dakota	57,680	32,885	1,496	2,421	—	—	43	4	—
Ohio	572,312	502,721	11,402	33,795	721	162	439	23	—
Oklahoma	110,558	122,406	—	21,779	—	434	244	—	7
Oregon	62,530	38,049	2,682	7,339	—	—	289	4	—
Pennsylvania	745,779	448,785	36,694	33,913	1,222	—	1,057	34	—
Rhode Island	43,942	24,706	1,016	1,365	183	—	1,105	4	—
South Carolina	3,965	62,290	—	100	—	—	43	—	9
South Dakota	67,536	40,266	4,039	2,846	—	—	88	4	—
Tennessee	118,324	135,608	300	1,870	—	1,081	332	—	12
Texas	65,666	217,302	1,634	7,870	176	994	115	—	18
Utah	61,165	42,601	—	4,890	—	—	92	3	—
Vermont	39,552	11,496	799	—	—	—	804	4	—
Virginia	52,573	82,946	1,111	255	25	105	51	—	12
Washington	106,062	58,691	4,700	14,177	—	—	249	5	—
West Virginia	137,869	111,418	5,139	3,679	—	—	46	7	—
Wisconsin	247,747	166,662	11,565	28,147	314	—	—	13	—
Wyoming	20,846	14,918	66	1,715	—	—	64	3	—
	7,677,788	6,407,982	252,511	420,890	14,021	29,146	83,651	321	162

Forty-six states took part in the election. Oklahoma was admitted to the Union on November 16, 1907. **Total vote: 14,885,989.**

"No person shall be elected to the office of the President more than twice, and no person who has held the office of President, or acted as President, for more than two years of a term to which some other person was elected President shall be elected to the office of the President more than once."

Ever since the adoption of the Constitution, proposals were made and debated for changing the mode of presidential election. Many suggestions were made to abolish the Electoral College, to vote directly, to let the popular vote decide. Such discussions are still going on.

STATES	POPULAR VOTE						ELECTORAL VOTE		
	Wilson and Marshall, Democrat.	Roosevelt and Johnson, Progressive.	Taft and Sherman, Republican.	Chafin and Watkins, Prohibition.	Debs and Seidel, Socialist.	Reimer and Francis, Socialist-Labor.	Wilson and Marshall.	Roosevelt and Johnson.	Taft and Sherman.
Alabama	82,439	22,689	9,731	—	3,029	—	12	—	—
Arizona	10,324	6,949	3,021	265	3,163	—	3	—	—
Arkansas	68,838	21,673	24,297	898	8,153	—	9	—	—
California	283,436	283,610	3,914	23,366	79,201	—	2	11	—
Colorado	114,223	72,306	58,386	5,063	16,418	—	6	—	—
Connecticut	74,561	34,129	68,324	2,068	70,056	475	7	—	—
Delaware	22,631	8,886	15,998	623	556	1,260	3	—	—
Florida	36,417	4,535	4,279	1,854	4,806	—	6	—	—
Georgia	93,171	22,010	5,190	147	1,014	—	14	—	—
Idaho	33,921	25,527	32,810	1,537	11,960	—	4	—	—
Illinois	405,048	386,478	253,613	15,710	81,278	4,066	29	—	—
Indiana	281,890	162,007	151,267	19,249	36,931	3,130	15	—	—
Iowa	185,325	161,819	119,805	8,440	16,967	—	13	—	—
Kansas	143,670	120,123	74,844	—	26,807	—	10	—	—
Kentucky	219,584	102,766	115,512	3,233	11,647	956	13	—	—
Louisiana	60,966	9,323	3,834	—	5,249	—	10	—	—
Maine	51,113	48,493	26,545	945	2,541	—	6	—	—
Maryland	112,674	57,786	54,956	2,244	3,996	322	8	—	—
Massachusetts	173,408	142,228	155,948	2,754	12,616	1,102	18	—	—
Michigan	150,751	214,584	152,244	8,934	23,211	1,252	—	15	—
Minnesota	106,426	125,856	64,334	7,886	27,505	2,212	—	12	—
Mississippi	57,164	3,627	1,511	—	2,017	—	10	—	—
Missouri	330,746	124,371	207,821	5,380	28,466	1,778	18	—	—
Montana	27,941	22,456	18,512	32	10,885	—	4	—	—
Nebraska	109,008	72,689	54,216	3,383	10,885	—	8	—	—
Nevada	7,986	5,620	3,196	—	3,313	—	3	—	—
New Hampshire	34,724	17,794	32,927	535	1,981	—	4	—	—
New Jersey	178,289	145,410	88,835	2,878	15,801	1,321	14	—	—
New Mexico	20,437	8,347	17,733	—	2,859	—	3	—	—
New York	655,475	390,021	455,428	19,427	63,381	4,251	45	—	—
North Carolina	144,507	69,130	29,139	117	1,025	—	12	—	—
North Dakota	29,555	25,726	23,090	1,243	6,966	—	5	—	—
Ohio	423,152	229,327	277,066	11,459	89,930	2,623	24	—	—
Oklahoma	119,156	—	90,786	2,185	42,262	—	10	—	—
Oregon	47,064	37,600	34,673	4,360	13,343	—	5	—	—
Pennsylvania	395,619	447,426	273,305	19,533	83,164	704	—	38	—
Rhode Island	30,142	16,878	27,703	616	2,049	236	5	—	—
South Carolina	48,355	1,293	536	—	164	—	9	—	—
South Dakota	48,942	58,811	—	3,910	4,662	—	—	5	—
Tennessee	130,335	53,725	59,444	825	3,492	—	12	—	—
Texas	221,589	26,755	28,853	1,738	25,743	442	20	—	—
Utah	36,579	24,174	42,100	—	9,023	509	—	—	4
Vermont	15,350	22,070	23,305	1,154	928	—	—	—	4
Virginia	90,332	21,777	23,288	709	820	50	12	—	—
Washington	86,840	113,698	70,445	9,810	40,134	1,872	—	7	—
West Virginia	113,197	79,112	56,754	4,517	15,248	—	8	—	—
Wisconsin	164,409	58,661	130,878	8,467	34,168	698	13	—	—
Wyoming	15,310	9,232	14,560	434	2,760	—	3	—	—
	6,283,019	4,119,507	3,484,956	207,928	962,573	29,259	435	88	8

Forty-eight states took part in the election. New Mexico was admitted on January 6, 1912, Arizona on February 14, 1912. **Total vote: 15,087,242.**

On February 10, 1967, the Twenty-fifth Amendment to the Constitution was ratified. The Amendment prescribes that if Congress can determine "by two-thirds vote of both Houses that the President is unable to discharge the powers and duties of his office, the Vice President shall continue to discharge the same as Acting President. . . ." Proposed after Eisenhower's heart attack, it also provides for the appointment of a Vice President if there is a vacancy in that office. In the future there can be no President without a Vice President, as under Johnson in 1963-64. ∎

1916

| STATES | POPULAR VOTE | | | | ELECTORAL VOTE | |
	Wilson and Marshall, Democrat.	Hughes and Fairbanks, Republican.	Hanly and Landrith, Prohibition.	Benson and Kirkpatrick, Socialist.	Wilson and Marshall.	Hughes and Fairbanks.
Ala.	99,409	22,809	1,034	1,925	12	—
Ariz.	33,170	20,524	1,153	3,174	3	—
Ark.	112,148	47,148	2,015	6,999	9	—
Calif.	466,200	462,394	27,698	43,259	13	—
Colo.	178,816	102,308	2,793	10,049	6	—
Conn.	99,786	106,514	1,789	5,179	—	7
Del.	24,753	26,011	566	480	—	3
Fla.	55,984	14,611	4,855	5,353	6	—
Ga.	125,845	11,225	—	967	14	—
Idaho	70,054	55,368	1,127	8,066	4	—
Ill.	950,229	1,152,549	26,047	61,394	—	29
Ind.	334,063	341,005	16,368	21,855	—	15
Iowa	221,699	280,449	3,371	10,976	—	13
Kan.	314,588	277,658	12,882	24,685	10	—
Ky.	269,990	241,854	3,036	4,734	13	—
La.	79,875	6,466	—	292	10	—
Me.	64,127	69,506	597	2,177	—	6
Md.	138,359	117,347	2,903	2,674	8	—
Mass.	247,885	268,784	2,993	11,058	—	18
Mich.	285,151	339,097	8,139	16,120	—	15
Minn.	179,152	179,544	7,793	20,117	—	12
Miss.	80,422	4,253	—	1,484	10	—
Mo.	398,025	369,339	3,884	14,612	18	—
Mont.	101,063	66,750	—	9,564	4	—
Neb.	158,827	117,257	2,952	7,141	8	—
Nev.	17,776	12,127	348	3,065	3	—
N. H.	43,779	43,723	303	1,318	4	—
N. J.	211,645	269,352	3,187	10,462	—	14
N. M.	33,693	31,163	112	1,999	3	—
N. Y.	759,426	869,115	19,031	45,944	—	45
N. C.	168,383	120,988	51	490	12	—
N. D.	55,206	53,471	—	—	5	—
Ohio	604,161	514,753	8,080	38,092	24	—
Okla.	148,113	97,233	1,646	45,190	10	—
Ore.	120,087	126,813	4,729	9,711	—	5
Pa.	521,784	703,734	28,525	42,637	—	38
R. I.	40,394	44,858	470	1,914	—	5
S. C.	61,846	1,550	—	135	9	—
S. D.	59,191	64,217	1,774	3,760	—	5
Tenn.	153,282	116,223	147	2,542	12	—
Tex.	286,514	64,999	1,985	18,963	20	—
Utah	84,025	54,137	149	4,460	4	—
Vt.	22,708	40,250	709	798	—	4
Va.	102,824	49,356	783	1,060	12	—
Wash.	183,388	167,244	6,868	22,800	7	—
W. Va.	140,403	143,124	175	6,140	1	7
Wis.	193,042	221,323	7,166	27,846	—	13
Wyo.	28,316	21,698	373	1,453	3	—
	9,129,606	8,532,221	220,606	585,113	277	254

Forty-eight states took part in the election.

J. M. Parker, Progressive for Vice Presidency, received 41,894 votes; Arthur E. Reimer, Socialist-Labor, 13,403.

Total vote: 18,522,843.

1920

| STATES | POPULAR VOTE | | ELECTORAL VOTE | |
	Warren G. Harding, Republican.	James M. Cox, Democrat.	Harding and Coolidge.	Cox and Roosevelt.
Alabama	74,719	156,064	—	12
Arizona	37,016	29,546	3	—
Arkansas	72,316	106,427	—	9
California	624,992	229,191	13	—
Colorado	173,248	104,936	6	—
Connecticut	229,238	120,721	7	—
Delaware	52,858	39,911	3	—
Florida	44,853	90,515	—	6
Georgia	42,981	106,112	—	14
Idaho	91,351	46,930	4	—
Illinois	1,420,480	534,395	29	—
Indiana	696,370	511,364	15	—
Iowa	634,674	227,804	13	—
Kansas	369,268	185,464	10	—
Kentucky	452,480	456,497	—	13
Louisiana	38,539	87,519	—	10
Maine	136,355	58,961	6	—
Maryland	236,117	180,626	8	—
Massachusetts	681,153	276,691	18	—
Michigan	762,865	233,450	15	—
Minnesota	519,421	142,994	12	—
Mississippi	11,576	69,136	—	10
Missouri	727,252	574,699	18	—
Montana	109,430	57,372	4	—
Nebraska	247,498	119,608	8	—
Nevada	15,479	9,851	3	—
New Hampshire	95,196	62,662	4	—
New Jersey	615,333	258,761	14	—
New Mexico	57,634	46,668	3	—
New York	1,871,167	781,238	45	—
North Carolina	232,819	305,367	—	12
North Dakota	160,082	37,422	5	—
Ohio	1,182,022	780,037	24	—
Oklahoma	243,840	216,122	10	—
Oregon	143,592	80,019	5	—
Pennsylvania	1,218,215	503,202	38	—
Rhode Island	107,463	55,062	5	—
South Carolina	2,610	64,170	—	9
South Dakota	110,692	35,938	5	—
Tennessee	219,229	206,558	12	—
Texas	114,658	287,920	—	20
Utah	81,555	56,639	4	—
Vermont	68,212	20,919	4	—
Virginia	87,456	141,670	—	12
Washington	223,137	84,298	7	—
West Virginia	282,007	220,785	8	—
Wisconsin	498,576	113,422	13	—
Wyoming	35,091	17,429	3	—
	16,153,115	9,133,092	404	127

Forty-eight states took part in the election.

Eugene V. Debs and Seymour Stedman, candidates of the Socialist party, received 915,490 votes; Parley P. Christensen and Max S. Hayes of the Farmer-Labor party, 265,229; Aaron S. Watkins and D. Leigh Colvin of the Prohibition party, 189,339; James Ferguson and William J. Hough of the American party, 48,098; William W. Cox and August Gillhaus of the Socialist-Labor party, 30,594. Other votes: 6,347.

In Texas a Black-and-Tan ticket had 27,309 votes.

Total vote: 26,768,613.

1924

STATES	POPULAR VOTE		ELECTORAL VOTE	
	Calvin Coolidge, Republican.	John W. Davis, Democrat.	Coolidge and Dawes.	Davis and Bryan.
Alabama	42,823	113,138	—	12
Arizona	30,516	26,235	3	—
Arkansas	40,583	84,790	—	9
California	733,250	105,514	13	—
Colorado	195,171	75,238	6	—
Connecticut	246,322	110,184	7	—
Delaware	52,441	33,445	3	—
Florida	30,633	62,083	—	6
Georgia	30,300	123,262	—	14
Idaho	69,791	23,951	4	—
Illinois	1,453,321	576,975	29	—
Indiana	703,042	492,245	15	—
Iowa	537,458	160,382	13	—
Kansas	407,671	156,320	10	—
Kentucky	396,758	375,593	13	—
Louisiana	24,670	93,218	—	10
Maine	138,440	41,964	6	—
Maryland	162,414	148,072	8	—
Massachusetts	703,476	280,831	18	—
Michigan	874,631	152,359	15	—
Minnesota	420,759	55,913	12	—
Mississippi	8,494	100,474	—	10
Missouri	648,488	574,962	18	—
Montana	74,138	33,805	4	—
Nebraska	218,985	137,299	8	—
Nevada	11,243	5,909	3	—
New Hampshire	98,575	57,201	4	—
New Jersey	676,277	298,043	14	—
New Mexico	54,745	48,542	3	—
New York	1,820,058	950,796	45	—
North Carolina	190,754	284,190	—	12
North Dakota	94,931	13,858	5	—
Ohio	1,176,130	477,887	24	—
Oklahoma	225,756	255,798	—	10
Oregon	142,579	67,589	5	—
Pennsylvania	1,401,481	409,192	38	—
Rhode Island	125,286	76,606	5	—
South Carolina	1,123	49,008	—	9
South Dakota	101,299	27,214	5	—
Tennessee	130,831	159,339	—	12
Texas	130,794	483,381	—	20
Utah	77,327	47,001	4	—
Vermont	80,498	16,124	4	—
Virginia	73,328	139,717	—	12
Washington	220,224	42,842	7	—
West Virginia	288,635	257,232	8	—
Wisconsin	311,614	68,115	—	—
Wyoming	41,858	12,868	3	—
	15,719,921	8,386,704	382	136

1928

STATES	POPULAR VOTE		ELECTORAL VOTE	
	Herbert Hoover, Republican.	Alfred E. Smith, Democrat.	Hoover and Curtis.	Smith and Robinson.
Alabama	120,725	127,796	—	12
Arizona	52,533	38,537	3	—
Arkansas	77,784	119,196	—	9
California	1,162,323	614,365	13	—
Colorado	253,872	133,131	6	—
Connecticut	296,641	252,085	7	—
Delaware	68,860	35,354	3	—
Florida	145,860	101,764	6	—
Georgia	101,800°	129,604	—	14
Idaho	97,322	52,926	4	—
Illinois	1,769,141	1,313,817	29	—
Indiana	848,290	562,691	15	—
Iowa	623,570	379,011	13	—
Kansas	513,672	193,003	10	—
Kentucky	558,064	381,070	13	—
Louisiana	51,160	164,655	—	10
Maine	179,923	81,179	6	—
Maryland	301,479	223,626	8	—
Massachusetts	775,566	792,758	—	18
Michigan	965,396	396,762	15	—
Minnesota	560,977	396,451	12	—
Mississippi	27,030°	124,538	—	10
Missouri	834,080	662,684	18	—
Montana	113,300	78,578	4	—
Nebraska	345,745	197,950	8	—
Nevada	18,327	14,090	3	—
New Hampshire	115,404	80,715	4	—
New Jersey	926,050	616,517	14	—
New Mexico	69,708	48,211	3	—
New York	2,193,344	2,089,863	45	—
North Carolina	348,923	286,227	12	—
North Dakota	131,419	106,648	5	—
Ohio	1,627,546	864,210	24	—
Oklahoma	394,046	219,174	10	—
Oregon	205,341	109,223	5	—
Pennsylvania	2,055,382	1,067,586	38	—
Rhode Island	117,522	118,973	—	5
South Carolina	5,858°	62,700	—	9
South Dakota	157,603	102,660	5	—
Tennessee	195,388	157,143	12	—
Texas	372,324	344,542	20	—
Utah	94,618	80,985	4	—
Vermont	90,404	44,440	4	—
Virginia	164,609	140,146	12	—
Washington	335,844	156,772	7	—
West Virginia	375,551	263,784	8	—
Wisconsin	544,205	450,259	13	—
Wyoming	52,748	29,299	3	—
	21,437,277	15,007,698	444	87

Forty-eight states voted.

Robert M. La Follette and Burton K. Wheeler, candidates of the Progressive party, received 4,832,532 votes, carrying Wisconsin's 13 electoral votes; Herman P. Faris and Marie Caroline Brehm of the Prohibition party received 56,292 votes; Frank T. Johns and Verne L. Reynolds of the Socialist Labor party, 34,174; William Z. Foster and Benjamin Gitlow of the Communist party, 33,360; Gilbert O. Nations and Leander L. Pickett of the American party, 24,340. Other votes: 7,700.

Total vote: 29,095,023.

Forty-eight states voted.

* In Georgia, Mississippi and South Carolina the Republican totals include votes for two or three elector tickets.

Norman Thomas and James H. Maurer, candidates of the Socialist party, received 265,583 votes; William Z. Foster and Benjamin Gitlow of the Communist party, 46,896; Verne L. Reynolds and Jeremiah D. Crowley of the Socialist Labor party, 21,586; William F. Varney and James A. Edgerton of the Prohibition party, 20,101. Other votes: 6,810.

Total vote: 36,805,951.

1932

	POPULAR VOTE		ELECTORAL VOTE	
STATES	Herbert Hoover, Republican.	Franklin D. Roosevelt, Democrat.	Hoover and Curtis.	Roosevelt and Garner.
Alabama	34,675	207,910	—	11
Arizona	36,104	79,264	—	3
Arkansas	27,465	186,829	—	9
California	847,902	1,324,157	—	22
Colorado	189,617	250,877	—	6
Connecticut	288,420	281,632	8	—
Delaware	57,073	54,319	3	—
Florida	69,170	206,307	—	7
Georgia	19,863	234,118	—	12
Idaho	71,312	109,479	—	4
Illinois	1,432,756	1,882,304	—	29
Indiana	677,184	862,054	—	14
Iowa	414,433	598,019	—	11
Kansas	349,498	424,204	—	9
Kentucky	394,716	580,574	—	11
Louisiana	18,853	249,418	—	10
Maine	166,631	128,907	5	—
Maryland	184,184	314,314	—	8
Massachusetts	736,959	800,148	—	17
Michigan	739,894	871,700	—	19
Minnesota	363,959	600,806	—	11
Mississippi	5,180°	140,168	—	9
Missouri	564,713	1,025,406	—	15
Montana	78,078	127,286	—	4
Nebraska	201,177	359,082	—	7
Nevada	12,674	28,756	—	3
New Hampshire	103,629	100,680	4	—
New Jersey	775,684	806,630	—	16
New Mexico	54,217	95,089	—	3
New York	1,937,963	2,534,959	—	47
North Carolina	208,344	497,566	—	13
North Dakota	71,772	178,350	—	4
Ohio	1,227,319	1,301,695	—	26
Oklahoma	188,165	516,468	—	11
Oregon	136,019	213,871	—	5
Pennsylvania	1,453,540	1,295,948	36	—
Rhode Island	115,266	146,604	—	4
South Carolina	1,978	102,347	—	8
South Dakota	99,212	183,515	—	4
Tennessee	126,752	259,473	—	11
Texas	98,218	771,109	—	23
Utah	84,795	116,750	—	4
Vermont	78,984	56,266	3	—
Virginia	89,637	203,979	—	11
Washington	208,645	353,260	—	8
West Virginia	330,731	405,124	—	8
Wisconsin	347,741	707,410	—	12
Wyoming	39,583	54,370	—	3
	15,760,684	22,829,501	59	472

Forty-eight states voted.

* In Mississippi the Republican total includes votes for two elector tickets.

Norman Thomas and James H. Maurer, candidates of the Socialist party, received 884,649 votes; William Z. Foster and James W. Ford of the Communist party, 103,253; William D. Upshaw and Frank S. Regan of the Prohibition party, 81,872; William H. Harvey and Frank Hemenway of the Liberty party, 53,247; Verne L. Reynolds and John W. Aiken of the Socialist Labor party, 34,043; Jacob S. Coxey and Julius J. Reiter of the Farmer-Labor party, 7,431. Other votes: 4,079.

Total vote: 39,758,759.

1936

	POPULAR VOTE		ELECTORAL VOTE	
STATES	Alfred M. Landon, Republican.	Franklin D. Roosevelt, Democrat.	Landon and Knox.	Roosevelt and Garner.
Alabama	35,358	238,196	—	11
Arizona	33,433	86,722	—	3
Arkansas	32,049	146,765	—	9
California	836,431	1,766,836	—	22
Colorado	181,267	295,021	—	6
Connecticut	278,685	382,129	—	8
Delaware	57,236°	69,702	—	3
Florida	78,248	249,117	—	7
Georgia	36,943	255,363	—	12
Idaho	66,256	125,683	—	4
Illinois	1,570,393	2,282,999	—	29
Indiana	691,570	934,974	—	14
Iowa	487,977	621,756	—	11
Kansas	397,727	464,520	—	9
Kentucky	369,702	541,944	—	11
Louisiana	36,791	292,894	—	10
Maine	168,823	126,333	5	—
Maryland	231,435	389,612	—	8
Massachusetts	768,613	942,716	—	17
Michigan	699,733	1,016,794	—	19
Minnesota	350,461	698,811	—	11
Mississippi	4,467°	157,333	—	9
Missouri	697,891	1,111,043	—	15
Montana	63,598	159,690	—	4
Nebraska	247,731	347,445	—	7
Nevada	11,923	31,925	—	3
New Hampshire	104,642	108,460	—	4
New Jersey	720,322	1,083,850	—	16
New Mexico	61,727	106,037	—	3
New York	2,180,670	3,293,222°	—	47
North Carolina	223,294	616,141	—	13
North Dakota	72,751	163,148	—	4
Ohio	1,127,855	1,747,140	—	26
Oklahoma	245,122	501,069	—	11
Oregon	122,706	266,733	—	5
Pennsylvania	1,690,300	2,353,788	—	36
Rhode Island	125,031	164,338	—	4
South Carolina	1,646°	113,791	—	8
South Dakota	125,977	160,137	—	4
Tennessee	147,055	328,083	—	11
Texas	104,661	739,952	—	23
Utah	64,555	150,248	—	4
Vermont	81,023	62,124	3	—
Virginia	98,336	234,980	—	11
Washington	206,892	459,579	—	8
West Virginia	325,358	502,582	—	8
Wisconsin	380,828	802,984	—	12
Wyoming	38,739	62,624	—	3
	16,684,231	27,757,333	8	523

Forty-eight states voted.

* American Labor party votes are included in the Democratic total for New York. The Republican totals for Delaware, Mississippi and South Carolina include two tickets of electors.

William Lemke and Thomas C. O'Brien of the Union party received 892,267 votes; Norman Thomas and George A. Nelson of the Socialists, 187,833; Earl Browder and James W. Ford of the Communists, 80,171; D. Leigh Colvin and Claude A. Watson of the Prohibitionists, 37,677; John W. Aiken and Emil F. Teichert of the Socialist Labor party, 12,829. Other votes: 2,422.

Total vote: 45,654,763.

1940

STATES	POPULAR VOTE		ELECTORAL VOTE	
	Wendell L. Wilkie, Republican.	Franklin D. Roosevelt, Democrat.	Wilkie and McNary.	Roosevelt and Wallace.
Alabama	42,184	250,726	—	11
Arizona	54,030	95,267	—	3
Arkansas	42,122	157,213	—	9
California	1,351,419	1,877,618	—	22
Colorado	279,576	265,554	6	—
Connecticut	361,819°	417,621	—	8
Delaware	61,440	74,599	—	3
Florida	126,158	359,334	—	7
Georgia	46,495°	265,194	—	12
Idaho	106,553	127,842	—	4
Illinois	2,047,240	2,149,934	—	29
Indiana	899,466	874,063	14	—
Iowa	632,370	578,802	11	—
Kansas	489,169	364,725	9	—
Kentucky	410,384	557,322	—	11
Louisiana	52,446	319,751	—	10
Maine	163,951	156,478	5	—
Maryland	269,534	384,546	—	8
Massachusetts	939,700	1,076,522	—	17
Michigan	1,039,917	1,032,991	19	—
Minnesota	596,274	644,196	—	11
Mississippi	7,364°	168,267	—	9
Missouri	871,009	958,476	—	15
Montana	99,579	145,698	—	4
Nebraska	352,201	263,677	7	—
Nevada	21,229	31,945	—	3
New Hampshire	110,127	125,292	—	4
New Jersey	945,475	1,016,808	—	16
New Mexico	79,315	103,699	—	3
New York	3,027,478	3,251,918°	—	47
North Carolina	213,633	609,015	—	13
North Dakota	154,590	124,036	4	—
Ohio	1,586,773	1,733,139	—	26
Oklahoma	348,872	474,313	—	11
Oregon	219,555	258,415	—	5
Pennsylvania	1,889,848	2,171,035	—	36
Rhode Island	138,654	182,181	—	4
South Carolina	4,360°	95,470	—	8
South Dakota	177,065	131,362	4	—
Tennessee	169,153	351,601	—	11
Texas	212,692	909,974	—	23
Utah	93,151	154,277	—	4
Vermont	78,371	64,269	3	—
Virginia	109,363	235,961	—	11
Washington	322,123	462,145	—	8
West Virginia	372,414	495,662	—	8
Wisconsin	679,206	704,821	—	12
Wyoming	52,633	59,287	—	3
	22,348,480	27,313,041	82	449

Forty-eight states voted.

* The Democratic total for New York includes American Labor party votes. In Connecticut, Georgia, Mississippi and South Carolina the Republican totals include two or three tickets of electors.

Norman Thomas and Maynard C. Krueger of the Socialist party received 116,410 votes; Roger Babson and Edgar V. Moorman of the Prohibition party, 58,708; Earl Browder and James W. Ford of the Communist party, 46,259; John W. Aiken and Aaron M. Orange of the Socialist Labor party, 14,892. Other votes: 2,628.

Total vote: 49,900,418.

1944

STATES	POPULAR VOTE		ELECTORAL VOTE	
	Thomas E. Dewey, Republican.	Franklin D. Roosevelt, Democrat.	Dewey and Bricker.	Roosevelt and Truman.
Alabama	44,540	198,918	—	11
Arizona	56,287	80,926	—	4
Arkansas	63,551	148,965	—	9
California	1,512,965	1,988,564	—	25
Colorado	268,731	234,331	6	—
Connecticut	390,527	435,146	—	8
Delaware	56,747	68,166	—	3
Florida	143,215	339,377	—	8
Georgia	59,900°	268,187	—	12
Idaho	100,137	107,399	—	4
Illinois	1,939,314	2,079,479	—	28
Indiana	875,891	781,403	13	—
Iowa	547,267	499,876	10	—
Kansas	442,096	287,458	8	—
Kentucky	392,448	472,589	—	11
Louisiana	67,750	281,564	—	10
Maine	155,434	140,631	5	—
Maryland	292,949	315,490	—	8
Massachusetts	921,350	1,035,296	—	16
Michigan	1,084,423	1,106,899	—	19
Minnesota	527,416	589,864	—	11
Mississippi	11,613°	168,621	—	9
Missouri	761,175	807,356	—	15
Montana	93,163	112,556	—	4
Nebraska	329,880	233,246	6	—
Nevada	24,611	29,623	—	3
New Hampshire	109,916	119,663	—	4
New Jersey	961,335	987,874	—	16
New Mexico	70,688	81,389	—	4
New York	2,987,647	3,304,238°	—	47
North Carolina	263,155	527,399	—	14
North Dakota	118,535	100,144	4	—
Ohio	1,582,293	1,570,763	25	—
Oklahoma	319,424	401,549	—	10
Oregon	225,365	248,635	—	6
Pennsylvania	1,835,054	1,940,479	—	35
Rhode Island	123,487	175,356	—	4
South Carolina	4,617°	90,601	—	8
South Dakota	135,365	96,711	4	—
Tennessee	200,311	308,707	—	12
Texas	191,423	821,605	—	23
Utah	97,891	150,088	—	4
Vermont	71,527	53,820	3	—
Virginia	145,243	242,276	—	11
Washington	361,689	486,774	—	8
West Virginia	322,819	392,777	—	8
Wisconsin	674,532	650,413	12	—
Wyoming	51,921	49,419	3	—
	22,017,617	25,612,610	99	432

Forty-eight states voted.

* The Democratic total in New York includes votes for the American Labor and the Liberal parties.

Norman Thomas and Darlington Hoopes, candidates of the Socialist party, received 79,003 votes; Claude A. Watson and Andrew Johnson of the Prohibition party, 74,779; Edward A. Teichert and Arla A. Albaugh of the Socialist Labor party, 45,191. Other votes totaled 4,227.

A Texas Regulars elector ticket received 135,444 votes.

Total vote: 47,976,670.

1948

STATES	POPULAR VOTE Thomas E. Dewey, Republican.	POPULAR VOTE Harry S. Truman, Democrat.	ELECTORAL VOTE Dewey and Warren.	ELECTORAL VOTE Truman and Barkley.	ELECTORAL VOTE Thurmond and Wright, States Rights
Alabama	40,930	—	—	—	11
Arizona	77,597	95,251	—	4	—
Arkansas	50,959	149,659	—	9	—
California	1,895,269	1,913,134	—	25	—
Colorado	239,714	267,288	—	6	—
Connecticut	437,754	423,297	8	—	—
Delaware	69,588	67,813	3	—	—
Florida	194,280	281,988	—	8	—
Georgia	76,691	254,646	—	12	—
Idaho	101,514	107,370	—	4	—
Illinois	1,961,103	1,994,715	—	28	—
Indiana	821,079	807,831	13	—	—
Iowa	494,018	522,380	—	10	—
Kansas	423,039	351,902	8	—	—
Kentucky	341,210	466,756	—	11	—
Louisiana	72,657	136,344	—	—	10
Maine	150,234	111,916	5	—	—
Maryland	294,814	286,521	8	—	—
Massachusetts	909,370	1,151,788	—	16	—
Michigan	1,038,595	1,003,448	19	—	—
Minnesota	483,617	692,966	—	11	—
Mississippi	5,043°	19,384	—	—	9
Missouri	655,039	917,315	—	15	—
Montana	96,770	119,071	—	4	—
Nebraska	264,774	224,165	6	—	—
Nevada	29,357	31,291	—	3	—
New Hampshire	121,299	107,995	4	—	—
New Jersey	981,124	895,455	16	—	—
New Mexico	80,303	105,464	—	4	—
New York	2,841,163	2,780,204°	47	—	—
North Carolina	258,572	459,070	—	14	—
North Dakota	115,139	95,812	4	—	—
Ohio	1,445,684	1,452,791	—	25	—
Oklahoma	268,817	452,782	—	10	—
Oregon	260,904	243,147	6	—	—
Pennsylvania	1,902,197	1,752,426	35	—	—
Rhode Island	135,787	188,736	—	4	—
South Carolina	5,386	34,423	—	—	8
South Dakota	129,651	117,653	4	—	—
Tennessee	202,914	270,402	—	11	1
Texas	303,467	824,235	—	23	—
Utah	124,402	149,151	—	4	—
Vermont	75,926	45,557	3	—	—
Virginia	172,070	200,786	—	11	—
Washington	386,314	476,165	—	8	—
West Virginia	316,251	429,188	—	8	—
Wisconsin	590,959	647,310	—	12	—
Wyoming	47,947	52,354	—	3	—
	21,991,291	24,179,345	189	303	39

Forty-eight states voted.

* Liberal party votes are included in the New York Democratic figure. The Mississippi Republican total includes two elector tickets.

J. Strom Thurmond and Fielding L. Wright, candidates of the States' Rights party, received 1,176,125 votes; Henry A. Wallace and Glen H. Taylor of the Progressive party, 1,157,326; Norman Thomas and Tucker P. Smith of the Socialist party, 139,572; Claude A. Watson and Dale H. Learn of the Prohibition party, 103,900; Edward A. Teichert and Stephen Emery of the Socialist Labor party, 29,241; Farrell Dobbs and Grace Carlson of the Socialist Workers party, 13,614. Other votes: 3,412.

Total vote: 48,793,826.

1952

STATES	POPULAR VOTE Dwight D. Eisenhower, Republican.	POPULAR VOTE Adlai E. Stevenson, Democrat.	ELECTORAL VOTE Eisenhower and Nixon.	ELECTORAL VOTE Stevenson and Sparkman.
Alabama	149,231	275,075	—	11
Arizona	152,042	108,528	4	—
Arkansas	177,155	226,300	—	8
California	2,897,310	2,197,548	32	—
Colorado	379,782	245,504	6	—
Connecticut	611,012	481,649	8	—
Delaware	90,059	83,315	3	—
Florida	544,036	444,950	10	—
Georgia	198,961	456,823	—	12
Idaho	180,707	95,081	4	—
Illinois	2,457,327	2,013,920	27	—
Indiana	1,136,259	801,530	13	—
Iowa	808,906	451,513	10	—
Kansas	616,302	273,296	8	—
Kentucky	495,029	495,729	—	10
Louisiana	306,925	345,027	—	10
Maine	232,353	118,806	5	—
Maryland	499,424	395,337	9	—
Massachusetts	1,292,325	1,083,525	16	—
Michigan	1,551,529	1,230,657	20	—
Minnesota	763,211	608,458	11	—
Mississippi	112,966°	172,566	—	8
Missouri	959,429	929,830	13	—
Montana	157,394	106,213	4	—
Nebraska	421,603	188,057	6	—
Nevada	50,502	31,688	3	—
New Hampshire	166,287	106,663	4	—
New Jersey	1,373,613	1,015,902	16	—
New Mexico	132,170	105,661	4	—
New York	3,952,813	3,104,601°	45	—
North Carolina	558,107	652,803	—	14
North Dakota	191,712	76,694	4	—
Ohio	2,100,391	1,600,367	25	—
Oklahoma	518,045	430,939	8	—
Oregon	420,815	270,579	6	—
Pennsylvania	2,415,789	2,146,269	32	—
Rhode Island	210,935	203,293	4	—
South Carolina	168,082°	173,004	—	8
South Dakota	203,857	90,426	4	—
Tennessee	446,147	443,710	11	—
Texas	1,102,878	969,228	24	—
Utah	194,190	135,364	4	—
Vermont	109,717	43,355	3	—
Virginia	349,037	268,677	12	—
Washington	599,107	492,845	9	—
West Virginia	419,970	453,578	—	8
Wisconsin	979,744	622,175	12	—
Wyoming	81,049	47,934	3	—
	33,936,234	27,314,992	442	89

Forty-eight states voted.

* In New York Liberal party votes are included in the Democratic figure. The Republican total in South Carolina includes two elector tickets, and in Mississippi the Republican figure is that of an Independent ticket pledged to Eisenhower and Nixon.

Vincent Hallinan and Charlotta Bass, candidates of the Progressive party, received 140,023 votes; Stuart Hamblen and Enoch A. Holtwick of the Prohibition party, 72,949; Eric Haas and Stephen Emery of the Socialist Labor party, 30,267; Darlington Hoopes and Samuel H. Friedman of the Socialist party, 20,203; Farrell Dobbs and Myra Tanner Weiss of the Socialist Workers party, 10,312. Other votes: 8,733.

Elector tickets supporting General Douglas MacArthur received 17,205 votes.

Total vote: 61,550,918.

1956

STATES	POPULAR VOTE		ELECTORAL VOTE	
	Dwight D. Eisenhower, Republican.	Adlai E. Stevenson, Democrat.	Eisenhower and Nixon.	Stevenson and Kefauver.
Alabama	195,694	280,844	—	10
Arizona	176,990	112,880	4	—
Arkansas	186,287	213,277	—	8
California	3,027,668	2,420,135	32	—
Colorado	394,479	257,997	6	—
Connecticut	711,837	405,079	8	—
Delaware	98,057	79,421	3	—
Florida	643,849	480,371	10	—
Georgia	222,778	444,688	—	12
Idaho	166,979	105,868	4	—
Illinois	2,623,327	1,775,682	27	—
Indiana	1,182,811	783,908	13	—
Iowa	729,187	501,858	10	—
Kansas	566,878	296,317	8	—
Kentucky	572,192	476,453	10	—
Louisiana	329,047	243,977	10	—
Maine	249,238	102,468	5	—
Maryland	559,738	372,613	9	—
Massachusetts	1,393,197	948,190	16	—
Michigan	1,713,647	1,359,898	20	—
Minnesota	719,302	617,525	11	—
Mississippi	60,685°	144,453	—	8
Missouri	914,289	918,273	—	13
Montana	154,933	116,238	4	—
Nebraska	378,108	199,029	6	—
Nevada	56,049	40,640	3	—
New Hampshire	176,519	90,364	4	—
New Jersey	1,606,942	850,337	16	—
New Mexico	146,788	106,098	4	—
New York	4,345,506	2,747,944°	45	—
North Carolina	575,062	590,530	—	14
North Dakota	156,766	96,742	4	—
Ohio	2,262,610	1,439,655	25	—
Oklahoma	473,769	385,581	8	—
Oregon	406,393	329,204	6	—
Pennsylvania	2,585,252	1,981,769	32	—
Rhode Island	225,819	161,790	4	—
South Carolina	75,700	136,372	—	8
South Dakota	171,569	122,288	4	—
Tennessee	462,288	456,507	11	—
Texas	1,080,619	859,958	24	—
Utah	215,631	118,364	4	—
Vermont	110,390	42,549	3	—
Virginia	386,459	267,760	12	—
Washington	620,430	523,002	9	—
West Virginia	449,297	381,534	8	—
Wisconsin	954,844	586,768	12	—
Wyoming	74,573	49,554	3	—
	35,590,472	26,022,752	457	73

1960

STATES	POPULAR VOTE		ELECTORAL VOTE		
	Richard M. Nixon, Republican.	John F. Kennedy, Democrat.	Nixon and Lodge.	Kennedy and Johnson.	Other.
Alabama	237,981	324,050	—	5	6
Alaska	30,953	29,809	3	—	—
Arizona	221,241	176,781	4	—	—
Arkansas	184,508	215,049	—	8	—
California	3,259,722	3,224,099	32	—	—
Colorado	402,242	330,629	6	—	—
Connecticut	565,813	657,055	—	8	—
Delaware	96,373	99,590	—	3	—
Florida	795,476	748,700	10	—	—
Georgia	274,472	458,638	—	12	—
Hawaii	92,295	92,410	—	3	—
Idaho	161,597	138,853	4	—	—
Illinois	2,368,988	2,377,846	—	27	—
Indiana	1,175,120	952,358	13	—	—
Iowa	722,381	550,565	10	—	—
Kansas	561,474	363,213	8	—	—
Kentucky	602,607	521,855	10	—	—
Louisiana	230,980	407,339	—	10	—
Maine	240,608	181,159	5	—	—
Maryland	489,538	565,808	—	9	—
Massachusetts	976,750	1,487,174	—	16	—
Michigan	1,620,428	1,687,269	—	20	—
Minnesota	757,915	779,933	—	11	—
Mississippi	73,561	108,362	—	—	8
Missouri	962,221	972,201	—	13	—
Montana	141,841	134,891	4	—	—
Nebraska	380,553	232,542	6	—	—
Nevada	52,387	54,880	—	3	—
New Hampshire	157,989	137,772	4	—	—
New Jersey	1,363,324	1,385,415	—	16	—
New Mexico	153,733	156,027	—	4	—
New York	3,446,419	3,830,085°	—	45	—
North Carolina	655,420	713,136	—	14	—
North Dakota	154,310	123,963	4	—	—
Ohio	2,217,611	1,944,248	25	—	—
Oklahoma	533,039	370,111	7	—	1
Oregon	408,060	367,402	6	—	—
Pennsylvania	2,439,956	2,556,282	—	32	—
Rhode Island	147,502	258,032	—	4	—
South Carolina	188,558	198,129	—	8	—
South Dakota	178,417	128,070	4	—	—
Tennessee	556,577	481,453	11	—	—
Texas	1,121,310	1,167,567	—	24	—
Utah	205,361	169,248	4	—	—
Vermont	98,131	69,186	3	—	—
Virginia	404,521	362,327	12	—	—
Washington	629,273	599,298	9	—	—
West Virginia	395,995	441,786	—	8	—
Wisconsin	895,175	830,805	12	—	—
Wyoming	77,451	63,331	3	—	—
	34,108,157	34,226,731	219	303	15

Forty-eight states voted.

* The Democratic total for New York includes Liberal party votes; the Republican total for Mississippi includes votes received by two elector tickets.

T. Coleman Andrews and Thomas H. Werdel, candidates of the States' Rights party, received 111,178 votes; Eric Haas and Georgia Cozzini of the Socialist Labor party, 44,450; Enoch A. Holtwick and Edwin M. Cooper of the Prohibition party, 41,937. Other votes: 19,801.

In Alabama, Louisiana, Mississippi and South Carolina, 196,318 votes were cast for unpledged States' Rights tickets.

One Alabama elector voted for Walter B. Jones and Herman Talmadge making the total electoral vote 531.

Total vote: 62,026,908.

Fifty states voted. Alaska became a state on January 3, 1959, Hawaii on August 21, 1959.* Liberal party votes are included in the N.Y. Democratic figure.

Eric Haas and Georgia Cozzini of the Socialist Labor party, received 47,522 votes; Rutherford L. Decker and E. Harold Munn of the Prohibitionists, 46,203; Orval E. Faubus and John G. Crommelin of the National States' Righters, 44,977; Farrell Dobbs and Myra Weiss of the Socialist Workers, 40,165; Charles Sullivan and Merritt Curtis of the Constitution party, 18,162. Other votes: 20,482.

Independent electors received 169,572 votes in Louisiana; an unpledged Democratic ticket in Mississippi polled 116,248 votes.

Senator Harry F. Byrd received 15 electoral votes for President; Senator Barry Goldwater 1.

Total vote: 68,838,219.

1964

STATES	POPULAR VOTE		ELECTORAL VOTE	
	Barry Goldwater, Republican.	Lyndon B. Johnson, Democrat.	Goldwater and Miller.	Johnson and Humphrey.
Alabama	479,085	—	10	—
Alaska	22,930	44,329	—	3
Arizona	242,535	237,753	5	—
Arkansas	243,264	314,197	—	6
California	2,879,108	4,171,877	—	40
Colorado	296,767	476,024	—	6
Connecticut	390,996	826,269	—	8
Delaware	78,078	122,704	—	3
Florida	905,941	948,540	—	14
Georgia	616,584	522,556	12	—
Hawaii	44,022	163,249	—	4
Idaho	143,557	148,920	—	4
Illinois	1,905,946	2,796,833	—	26
Indiana	911,118	1,170,848	—	13
Iowa	449,148	733,030	—	9
Kansas	386,579	464,028	—	7
Kentucky	372,977	669,659	—	9
Louisiana	509,225	387,068	10	—
Maine	118,701	262,264	—	4
Maryland	385,495	730,912	—	10
Massachusetts	549,727	1,786,422	—	14
Michigan	1,060,152	2,136,615	—	21
Minnesota	559,624	991,117	—	10
Mississippi	356,528	52,618	7	—
Missouri	653,535	1,164,344	—	12
Montana	113,032	164,246	—	4
Nebraska	276,847	307,307	—	5
Nevada	56,094	79,339	—	3
New Hampshire	104,029	184,064	—	4
New Jersey	964,174	1,868,231	—	17
New Mexico	132,838	194,015	—	4
New York	2,243,559	4,913,102*	—	43
North Carolina	624,844	800,139	—	13
North Dakota	108,207	149,784	—	4
Ohio	1,470,865	2,498,331	—	26
Oklahoma	412,665	519,834	—	8
Oregon	282,779	501,017	—	6
Pennsylvania	1,673,657	3,130,954	—	29
Rhode Island	74,615	315,463	—	4
South Carolina	309,048	215,723	8	—
South Dakota	130,108	163,010	—	4
Tennessee	508,965	635,047	—	11
Texas	958,566	1,663,185	—	25
Utah	181,785	219,628	—	4
Vermont	54,942	108,127	—	3
Virginia	481,334	558,038	—	12
Washington	470,366	779,699	—	9
West Virginia	253,953	538,087	—	7
Wisconsin	638,495	1,050,424	—	12
Wyoming	61,998	80,718	—	3
District of Columbia	28,801	169,796	—	3
	27,178,188	43,129,484	52	486

* The New York Democratic total includes Liberal party votes.

Eric Haas and Henning A. Blomen, candidates of the Socialist Labor party, received 45,219 votes; Clifton DeBerry and Edward Shaw of the Socialist Workers party, 32,720; E. Harold Munn and Mark R. Shaw of the Prohibition party, 23,267. Other votes: 24,900 .

In Alabama 210,732 votes were cast for an unpledged Democratic ticket.

Total vote: 70,644,510.

Appendix B

PORTRAITS OF THE PRESIDENTS
AND PRESIDENTIAL CANDIDATES

Only a handful of works exist on the iconography of the Presidents.

On George Washington we have *The Life Portraits of Washington and Their Replicas* by John Hill Morgan and Mantle Fielding (printed for the subscribers, Philadelphia, 1931).

On John Adams, the exquisite *Portraits of John and Abigail Adams* by Andrew Oliver (Harvard University Press, 1967).

On Thomas Jefferson, the excellent study of *The Life Portraits of Thomas Jefferson* by Alfred L. Bush (Thomas Jefferson Memorial Foundation, 1962).

On James Madison, the magazine article "The Life Portraits of James Madison" by Theodore Bolton (*The William and Mary Quarterly,* Vol. VIII, No. 1, January 1951).

On Andrew Jackson, the article in *McClure's Magazine,* July 1892, "Life Portraits of Andrew Jackson."

On Abraham Lincoln, Theodore Roosevelt and Franklin D. Roosevelt, the author of this volume has done extensive work. The titles of the books by Stefan Lorant are: *Lincoln: A Picture Story of His Life* (1952), *The Life and Times of Theodore Roosevelt* (1959), and *FDR: A Pictorial Biography* (1950).

General guides on portraits are:

ALA Portrait Index, edited by W. Coolidge and Nina E. Browne (Library of Congress, 1906);

Catalogue of American Portraits in the New-York Historical Society (1941);

Compilation of Works of Art and Other Objects in the United States Capitol (Government Printing Office, 1965);

Dictionary of American Portraits, edited by H. and Blanche Cirker and the staff of Dover Publications, (1967).

The best repository of presidential and other portrait material is in the Frick Art Reference Library, New York. The collection of reproductions and the information about them are all that one can wish; students and researchers owe a deep debt to Miss Helen Frick and the staff of the library for their unique contribution.

It is astonishing that no single American institution, library or museum possesses a collection of portraits depicting the candidates who have run for the presidential office. It took me a full year to collect the illustrations for the panels of the candidates which appear at the opening of each chapter, tracking down the portraits of the presidential and vice presidential candidates one by one. I have tried to show—whenever possible—how the candidates looked in the year they were running for office. Where no picture existed around the time of the campaign, I chose the portraits nearest to the appropriate year.

Hundreds of private persons, historians, librarians, newspaper editors, historical society officials and museum curators helped me in my task. To name every one of them would fill pages—thus I must thank them collectively with deep appreciation for all their kindnesses. But I would like to offer my special thanks to the following persons and institutions:

Bowdoin College Museum of Art, for the Henry A. S. Dearborn painting.

Francis Biddle, the former Attorney General, who helped with the identification of the personalities at Harry S. Truman's oath-taking.

Ellen D. Cattledge of the Corcoran Gallery of Art for several pictures of presidential and vice presidential candidates.

Herbert R. Collins, Assistant Curator, and Philip C. Brooks, Museum Technician, of the Smithsonian Institution, for their kind assistance.

Virginia Daiker and Milton Kaplan of the Library of Congress for their many courtesies.

Mrs. Elizabeth B. Drewry of the Franklin D. Roosevelt Library for a copy of FDR's original inaugural address.

James A. Farley for his reminiscences about the third-term issue.

Harry Fleischman of the National Labor Service for photographs of Norman Thomas.

Margaret Flint of the Illinois State Historical Library for copies of portraits of Stevenson and Douglas.

J. R. Fuchs, Acting Director of the Harry S. Truman Library, for material on President Truman.

Marguerite Gignilliat at Colonial Williamsburg for a copy of the James Madison portrait.

James C. Hagerty, Vice President of the American Broadcasting Corporation, who was President Eisenhower's press secretary, for identification of the personalities at Eisenhower's inauguration.

Elizabeth Harrell, Curatorial Assistant of the Virginia Museum of Fine Arts, for her suggestions about the "Washington Addressing the Constitutional Convention" painting.

Wilhelmina S. Harris, Superintendent of the Adams National Historic Site, for information on the John Adams portraits.

Colonel Grover Heiman, Jr., of the Pentagon for Signal Corps photographs.

Elizabeth S. Henry of the Worcester Art Museum for the copy of the St. Mémin drawing of Jefferson.

Laurence Gouverneur Hoes, President of the James Monroe Memorial Library, for copies of the portrait of President Monroe and the painting of his inauguration.

Donelson F. Hoopes, Curator of the Brooklyn Museum, for help in identifying the figures in the painting of George Washington's reception.

Mrs. Henry W. Howell, Jr., Librarian of the Frick Art Reference Library, for the many courtesies I received from that superb institution, and Mrs. Mildred Steinbach for her research notes.

Joseph Luppino of United Press International, who assisted and guided me through the voluminous material in his firm's collection, and Jack J. Fletcher, Manager of the UPI, for his cooperation.

Watt P. Marchman, Director of the Rutherford B. Hayes Library, for a copy of a picture of the Hayes family.

Elizabeth R. Martin, Librarian of the Ohio Historical Society, for the exquisite McKinley photograph.

Edward E. Martin, brother of the late Joseph Martin, Speaker of the House, for information.

Betty C. Monkman, Curatorial Assistant at the White House, for a copy of a Monroe painting.

James Nelson for information on Norman Thomas.

Beaumont Newhall, Director, and Robert Bretz, Assistant Curator, of the George Eastman House for copies of the Pierce daguerreotypes.

D. Edgar Prina, Secretary of the National Press Club, for his help in identifications.

Paul F. Redding, Curator of Iconography in the Buffalo and Erie County Historical Society, for a Grover Cleveland photograph.

Miss Caroline Rollins of the Yale University Art Gallery for portraits of the early patriots.

Elizabeth E. Roth of the Print Room in the New York Public Library for her assistance in connection with early political cartoons.

Vice President W. G. Rule of the Boatmen's National Bank for his permission to reprint the Bingham painting from the bank's collection.

St. Andrew's Society for permission to reproduce a Charles C. Pinckney painting.

Eugenia M. Southard, Reference Librarian, and Grace Trappan, Librarian, of the Portland Public Library, for information on Neal Dow.

Mrs. Carol J. Smith, Public Information Officer in the United States Department of the Interior, for photographs from the Department's collection.

Maude K. Swingle of the California Historical Society for a Hiram Johnson photograph.

David B. Warren, Curator of the Museum of Fine Arts, the Bayou Bend Collection, for a Jefferson portrait.

Howard W. Wiseman, Curator of the New Jersey Historical Society, for permission to reproduce the Aaron Burr and Richard Stockton portraits in the Society's possession.

Miss Louise Wood, Reference Librarian of the Indiana State Library, for copies of portraits of Fairbanks and Hendricks.

Kay White Zink of the High Museum of Art for the copy of William H. Crawford's portrait.

Credit for the candidate's portraits represented in the panels goes to the following institutions and individuals:

Candidates in 1789—page 28:
GEORGE WASHINGTON, painted by Charles Willson Peale in July 1787, courtesy Pennsylvania Academy of Fine Arts.
JOHN ADAMS, painted by Mather Brown in 1788, courtesy Boston Athenaeum.
JOHN JAY, painted by Joseph Wright, courtesy New-York Historical Society.
ROBERT H. HARRISON, courtesy Library of Congress.
JOHN RUTLEDGE, painted by John Trumbull in 1791, courtesy Yale University Art Gallery.
JOHN HANCOCK, painted by John Singleton Copley, courtesy Museum of Fine Arts, Boston.

Candidates in 1792—page 38:
GEORGE WASHINGTON, painted by Gilbert Stuart (the "Athenaeum" portrait) in 1796 at his Germantown studio, courtesy Museum of Fine Arts, Boston.
JOHN ADAMS, painted by John Trumbull in 1792, courtesy Yale University Art Gallery.
GEORGE CLINTON, painted by John Trumbull, courtesy City Hall, New York.
THOMAS JEFFERSON, painted by Charles Willson Peale in 1791, courtesy Independence Historic National Park.

Candidates in 1796—page 46:
JOHN ADAMS, painted by Charles Willson Peale in 1794, courtesy Independence National Historic Park, Philadelphia.
THOMAS JEFFERSON, painted by James Sharples in 1797, courtesy Independence National Historic Park, Philadelphia.
THOMAS PINCKNEY, painted by John Trumbull in 1791, courtesy Yale University Art Gallery.
AARON BURR, painted by Gilbert Stuart in 1794, courtesy New Jersey Historical Society.
SAMUEL ADAMS, painted by John Singleton Copley, courtesy Museum of Fine Arts, Boston.
OLIVER ELLSWORTH, painted by John Trumbull in 1792, courtesy Yale University Art Gallery.

Candidates in 1800—page 54:
THOMAS JEFFERSON, painted from life by Rembrandt Peale in early 1800's, courtesy Peabody Institute, Baltimore.
AARON BURR, painted by John Vanderlyn between 1802 and 1804, courtesy Oliver Burr Jennings Collection.
JOHN ADAMS, painted by Gilbert Stuart in 1798, completed in 1815, courtesy National Gallery of Art.
CHARLES COTESWORTH PINCKNEY, painted by James Earl before 1796, courtesy Worcester Art Museum.

Candidates in 1804—page 70:
THOMAS JEFFERSON, painted from life by Gilbert Stuart in 1805, courtesy Bowdoin College Museum of Fine Arts.
GEORGE CLINTON, drawn by Charles B. J. Fevret de St. Mémin in 1797-98, courtesy Metropolitan Museum, New York.

CHARLES COTESWORTH PINCKNEY, engraved by E. Wellmore from a miniature by Malbone.
RUFUS KING, painted by John Trumbull in 1792, courtesy Yale University Art Gallery.

Candidates in 1808—page 82:
JAMES MADISON, painted by Gilbert Stuart, courtesy Colonial Williamsburg.
GEORGE CLINTON, painted by Ezra Ames, courtesy New-York Historical Society.
CHARLES COTESWORTH PINCKNEY, painted by Rembrandt Peale, courtesy St. Andrew Society, Charleston, and Frick Art Reference Library.
RUFUS KING, painted by John Trumbull, courtesy Yale University Art Gallery.

Candidates in 1812—page 90:
JAMES MADISON, painted by P. A. Healy, courtesy Corcoran Gallery of Art.
ELBRIDGE GERRY, crayon by John Vanderlyn, courtesy New York Public Library.
DE WITT CLINTON, painted by John Wesley Jarvis, courtesy New-York Historical Society.
JARED INGERSOLL, etching by Albert Rosenthal after a painting by C. W. Peale, courtesy Library of Congress.

Candidates in 1816—page 98:
JAMES MONROE, engraving after a painting, courtesy Library of Congress.
DANIEL D. TOMPKINS, contemporary engraving, courtesy Library of Congress.
RUFUS KING, painted by Gilbert Stuart, courtesy Frick Art Reference Library.
JOHN E. HOWARD, painted by Charles Willson Peale, courtesy Independence National Historic Park, Philadelphia.

Candidates in 1820—page 106:
JAMES MONROE, painted by Rembrandt Peale in the White House between 1817 and 1825, courtesy James Monroe Law Office and Memorial Library.
DANIEL D. TOMPKINS, painted by John Wesley Jarvis about 1820, courtesy New-York Historical Society.
JOHN QUINCY ADAMS, painted by Charles Willson Peale in 1825, courtesy Historical Society of Pennsylvania.
RICHARD STOCKTON, artist unknown, courtesy New Jersey Historical Society and Frick Art Reference Library.

Candidates in 1824—page 110:
JOHN QUINCY ADAMS, painted by Thomas Sully in 1824, courtesy National Gallery of Art.
ANDREW JACKSON, painted by John Vanderlyn sometime between 1819 and 1823, courtesy City Hall, New York.
WILLIAM H. CRAWFORD, painted by Charles Willson Peale, courtesy High Museum of Art.
HENRY CLAY, painted by Samuel S. Osgood, courtesy New-York Historical Society.

Candidates of 1828—page 120:
ANDREW JACKSON, engraving by Longacre, courtesy Widener Library, Cambridge.
JOHN C. CALHOUN, painted by Charles Bird King in 1826, courtesy Corcoran Gallery of Art.

JOHN QUINCY ADAMS, painted by Pieter Van Huffel in 1815, courtesy Smithsonian Institution.
RICHARD RUSH, engraving from a contemporary painting, courtesy New York Public Library.

Candidates in 1832—page 130:
ANDREW JACKSON, painted by Asher B. Durand in 1835, courtesy New-York Historical Society.
MARTIN VAN BUREN, painted by Henry Inman, courtesy City Hall, New York.
HENRY CLAY, painted by Theodore S. Moïse, courtesy Metropolitan Museum of Art.
JOHN SERGEANT, unidentified engraving, courtesy New York Public Library.

Candidates in 1836—page 142:
MARTIN VAN BUREN, painted by George P. A. Healy, courtesy Corcoran Gallery of Art.
RICHARD M. JOHNSON, painted by John Neagle, courtesy Corcoran Gallery of Art.
WILLIAM HENRY HARRISON, engraved by R. W. Dodson after a painting by J. R. Lambdin, Widener Library, Cambridge.
FRANCIS GRANGER, engraving from Vanderhoff, courtesy Library of Congress.

Candidates in 1840—page 152:
WILLIAM HENRY HARRISON, engraving by E. D. Marchan, courtesy Widener Library, Cambridge.
JOHN TYLER, photographed by Mathew B. Brady, courtesy National Archives.
MARTIN VAN BUREN, painted by Henry Inman, courtesy Metropolitan Museum of Art, New York.
RICHARD M. JOHNSON, contemporary engraving, New York Public Library.

Candidates in 1844—page 172:
JAMES K. POLK, photograph by Mathew B. Brady, author's collection.
GEORGE M. DALLAS, contemporary engraving, courtesy New York Public Library.
HENRY CLAY, a photograph in author's collection.
THEODORE FRELINGHUYSEN, engraved by J. A. McDougal, courtesy Library of Congress.
JAMES G. BIRNEY, engraved by Jacques Reich, courtesy New York Public Library.
JOHN TYLER, a daguerreotype, courtesy Chicago Historical Society.

Candidates in 1848—page 186:
ZACHARY TAYLOR, a daguerreotype, author's collection.
MILLARD FILLMORE, a daguerreotype, author's collection.
LEWIS CASS, photograph by Mathew Brady, author's collection.
WILLIAM O. BUTLER, engraved by T. B. Welch, courtesy New York Public Library.
HENRY A. S. DEARBORN, painted by Gilbert Stuart, courtesy Bowdoin College Museum of Fine Arts.

Candidates in 1852—page 200:
FRANKLIN PIERCE, photograph by Mathew Brady, author's collection.

935

WILLIAM R. KING, engraved for the *Democratic Review*.
WINFIELD SCOTT, engraved by J.C. Buttre, courtesy New York Public Library.
WILLIAM A. GRAHAM, engraved by A. H. Ritchie.
JOHN P. HALE, photograph, author's collection.
GEORGE W. JULIAN, photograph, author's collection.

Candidates in 1856 — page 216:
JAMES BUCHANAN, photograph by Mathew Brady, author's collection.
JOHN C. BRECKINRIDGE, photograph by Mathew Brady, author's collection.
JOHN C. FRÉMONT, engraved after a photograph by George E. Peine, courtesy New York Public Library.
WILLIAM L. DAYTON, engraved by A. H. Ritchie from a daguerreotype, courtesy New York Public Library.
MILLARD FILLMORE, daguerreotype by Mathew Brady, author's collection.
A. J. DONELSON, engraved by J. C. Buttre after a photograph by Mathew Brady, courtesy New York Public Library.

Candidates in 1860 — page 230:
ABRAHAM LINCOLN, photograph by C. S. German taken in February 1861, author's collection.
HANNIBAL HAMLIN, photograph by F. B. Johnston, author's collection.
STEPHEN A. DOUGLAS, photograph, courtesy Illinois State Historical Society.
JOHN C. BRECKINRIDGE, an engraving, author's collection.
JOHN BELL, engraved by A.H. Ritchie, author's collection.
EDWARD EVERETT, photograph, author's collection.

Candidates in 1864 — page 260:
ABRAHAM LINCOLN, ANDREW JOHNSON, GEORGE B. McCLELLAN, GEORGE H. PENDLETON, all photographs from the author's collection.

Candidates in 1868 — page 296:
ULYSSES S. GRANT, SCHUYLER COLFAX, HORATIO SEYMOUR, FRANCIS P. BLAIR, JR., all photographs from the author's collection.

Candidates in 1872 — page 310:
ULYSSES S. GRANT, HENRY WILSON, HORACE GREELEY, B. GRATZ BROWN, CHARLES O'CONNOR, all photographs from the author's collection.
THOMAS A. HENDRICKS, photograph, courtesy Indiana State Library.

Candidates in 1876 — page 328:
RUTHERFORD B. HAYES, WILLIAM A. WHEELER, SAMUEL J. TILDEN, THOMAS A. HENDRICKS (after a Brady photograph), PETER COOPER, GREEN CLAY SMITH, all photographs from the author's collection.

Candidates in 1880 — page 346:
JAMES A. GARFIELD, photograph by Brady from the author's collection.
CHESTER A. ARTHUR, photograph from the author's collection.
WINFIELD HANCOCK, engraving by H.B. Hall's Sons, courtesy New York Public Library.
WILLIAM H. ENGLISH, engraving after a photograph by D. Judkins, courtesy New York Public Library.
NEAL DOW, engraving after a photograph, courtesy Maine Historical Society.
JAMES B. WEAVER, engraving after a photograph by C.M. Bell, courtesy New York Public Library.

Candidates in 1884 — page 368:
GROVER CLEVELAND, THOMAS A. HENDRICKS, JAMES G. BLAINE, JOHN A. LOGAN, all photographs from the author's collection.
JOHN P. ST. JOHN, engraved after an 1884 photograph by Bastian, courtesy New York Public Library.
BENJAMIN F. BUTLER, engraved by J. C. Buttre after a photograph by Silsbee & Co., courtesy New York Public Library.

Candidates in 1888 — page 394:
BENJAMIN HARRISON, engraved by H. B. Hall.
LEVI P. MORTON, photograph from the author's collection.
GROVER CLEVELAND, engraved by H.B. Hall, courtesy Buffalo Historical Society.
ALLEN G. THURMAN, photograph from the author's collection.

Candidates in 1892 — page 412:
GROVER CLEVELAND and ADLAI E. STEVENSON, photographs from the author's collection.
BENJAMIN HARRISON, photograph by Bogardus in the author's collection.
WHITELAW REID, photograph, courtesy Library of Congress.
JOHN BIDWELL, engraved by H.B. Hall's Sons, courtesy New York Public Library.
JAMES B. WEAVER, from the author's collection.

Candidates in 1896 — page 430:
WILLIAM McKINLEY, GARRET A. HOBART, WILLIAM J. BRYAN, photographs from the author's collection.
ARTHUR SEWALL, photograph by Gessford, New York.

Candidates in 1900 — page 448:
WILLIAM McKINLEY, photograph, courtesy Ohio State Historical Society.
THEODORE ROOSEVELT, photograph, courtesy Roosevelt Memorial Association.
WILLIAM J. BRYAN, photograph, courtesy Nebraska State Historical Society.
ADLAI E. STEVENSON, photograph, courtesy Illinois State Historical Society.

Candidates in 1904 — page 478:
THEODORE ROOSEVELT, photograph, courtesy Roosevelt Memorial Association.
CHARLES W. FAIRBANKS, photograph, courtesy Indiana State Library.
ALTON B. PARKER, HENRY G. DAVIS, EUGENE V. DEBS, SILAS C. SWALLOW, all photographs from the author's collection.

Candidates in 1908—page 492:
WILLIAM H. TAFT, photograph from the author's collection.
JAMES S. SHERMAN, WILLIAM J. BRYAN, photographs, courtesy Library of Congress.
JOHN W. KERN, EUGENE V. DEBS, photographs from the author's collection.
EUGENE W. CHAFIN, photograph taken in 1908 by Moffett Studio, Chicago, courtesy Chicago Historical Society.

Candidates in 1912—page 510:
WOODROW WILSON, photograph from the author's collection.
THOMAS R. MARSHALL, photograph by Moffett Studio, Chicago, courtesy Library of Congress.
WILLIAM HOWARD TAFT, JAMES S. SHERMAN, photographs from the author's collection.
THEODORE ROOSEVELT, photograph, courtesy Roosevelt Memorial Association.
HIRAM JOHNSON, photograph, courtesy California Historical Society.

Candidates in 1916—page 536:
WOODROW WILSON, THOMAS R. MARSHALL, CHARLES E. HUGHES, CHARLES W. FAIRBANKS, ALLAN L. BENSON, J. FRANK HANLY, all photographs from the author's collection.

Candidates in 1920—page 548:
WARREN G. HARDING, CALVIN COOLIDGE, JAMES M. COX, FRANKLIN D. ROOSEVELT, EUGENE V. DEBS, PARLEY P. CHRISTENSEN, all photographs from the author's collection.

Candidates in 1924—page 562:
CALVIN COOLIDGE, CHARLES G. DAWES, JOHN W. DAVIS, CHARLES W. BRYAN, ROBERT LA FOLLETTE, BURTON K. WHEELER, all photographs from the author's collection.

Candidates in 1928—page 574:
HERBERT C. HOOVER, CHARLES CURTIS, ALFRED E. SMITH, JOSEPH T. ROBINSON, photographs, courtesy Library of Congress.
NORMAN THOMAS, photograph by Cox's Studio, Carbondale, Illinois.
JAMES H. MAURER, photograph from the author's collection.

Candidates in 1932—page 586:
FRANKLIN D. ROOSEVELT, JOHN N. GARNER, HER-
BERT HOOVER, CHARLES CURTIS, photographs from the author's collection.
NORMAN THOMAS, photograph, courtesy Henry Fleischmann.
WILLIAM Z. FOSTER, photograph by Keystone.

Candidates in 1936—page 606:
FRANKLIN D. ROOSEVELT, JOHN N. GARNER, ALFRED M. LANDON, FRANK A. KNOX, NORMAN THOMAS (courtesy Henry Fleischmann), WILLIAM LEMKE, all photographs from author's collection.

Candidates in 1940—page 628:
FRANKLIN D. ROOSEVELT, HENRY A. WALLACE, WENDELL L. WILLKIE, CHARLES L. McNARY, photographs, courtesy Democratic and Republican national committees.

Candidates in 1944—page 656:
FRANKIN D. ROOSEVELT, HARRY S. TRUMAN, THOMAS E. DEWEY, JOHN W. BRICKER, photographs, courtesy Democratic and Republican national committees.

Candidates in 1948—page 688:
HARRY S. TRUMAN, ALBEN W. BARKLEY, THOMAS E. DEWEY, EARL WARREN, HENRY A. WALLACE, GLEN H. TAYLOR, photographs, courtesy Democratic and Republican national committees.

Candidates in 1952—page 738:
DWIGHT D. EISENHOWER, RICHARD M. NIXON, ADLAI STEVENSON, JOHN SPARKMAN, photographs, courtesy Republican and Democratic national committees.

Candidates in 1956—page 778:
DWIGHT D. EISENHOWER, RICHARD M. NIXON, ADLAI STEVENSON, ESTES KEFAUVER, photographs, courtesy Republican and Democratic national committees.

Candidates in 1960—page 812
JOHN F. KENNEDY, LYNDON B. JOHNSON, RICHARD M. NIXON, HENRY CABOT LODGE, official campaign photographs, courtesy Democratic and Republican national committees.

Candidates in 1964—page 870
LYNDON B. JOHNSON, HUBERT H. HUMPHREY, BARRY GOLDWATER, WILLIAM E. MILLER, photographs, courtesy Democratic and Republican national committees.

Appendix C

POLITICAL CARTOONS AND POLITICAL CARTOONISTS

The best work dealing with political cartoons is William Murrell's two-volume *A History of American Graphic Humor* (1933-1938). The slim volume by Allan Nevins and Frank Weitenkampf, *A Century of Political Cartoons: Caricature in the United States from 1800 to 1900* (1944), prints the most famous cartoons of the period. Frank Weitenkampf collated a catalogue of *Political Caricature in the United States in Separately Published Cartoons,* which was first printed in the Bulletin of the New York Public Library (Vol. 56, 1952 ff.). Harry T. Peters' *Currier and Ives, Printmakers to the American People* (1929-1931) contains references to other lithographers and artists as well. His *America on Stone: The Other Printmakers to the American People* (1931) is authoritative. William Dunlap's *History of the Arts of Design* (1917) and Mantle Fielding's *Dictionary of Painters, Sculptors and Engravers* (1926) and *American Engravers Upon Copper and Steel* (1917) are pioneer works.

These are the outstanding American political cartoonists:

ALEXANDER ANDERSON (1775-1870), born in New York, the first noteworthy figure in the country's graphic arts. As a boy he saw some engravings by Hogarth which, as he noted in his diary, "determined my destiny." While studying for a medical degree, which he received around 1795, he became America's first wood engraver. He made hundreds of wood and copperplate engravings for leading magazines and book publishers. A sample of his artistry is his cartoon "OGRABME" (see page 83). His diary is in the library of Columbia College and his biography was written by Frederic M. Burr, *Life and Works of Alexander Anderson* (1893).

WILLIAM CHARLES (1776-1820). Alexander Anderson stated that the birthplace of Charles, the eminent etcher, engraver and caricaturist, was Edinburgh and that he left the British Isles following publication of an engraving reflecting on the Church (probably "A Fallen Piller of the Kirk," 1805). Harry B. Weiss in his pamphlet on Charles (New York Public Library, 1932) asserts that the artist came to New York in 1801, but the date is more likely 1805 or 1806. We know that in 1807 *Charles's Repository of the Arts* was opened in New York. Charles illustrated dozens of toy books for a Philadelphia publisher and he left New York for that city in 1814 to open his own business there.

(Some of Charles' cartoons are printed on pages 84, 85, 91, 93, 100-101.)

DAVID CLAYPOOLE JOHNSTON (1799-1865) was born in Philadelphia, where his father had been a bookkeeper for the printer and publisher, David Claypoole. At the age of fifteen he became an engraver's apprentice. In 1819 he published his first social caricatures, and in 1825 he joined the Boston pioneer lithographic firm of Pendleton, making caricatures of actors and actresses. His paintings were ex-

hibited in the Boston Athenaeum. In addition to political cartoons, of which "A Footrace" (see pages 116-117) is an example, he was active in book illustration and humorous prints. A collection of his comic engravings, *Scraps,* was published in 1850, and his satire of Jefferson Davis, *The House That Jeff Built,* in 1863.

(See pages 202-203, 210 for Johnston's work.)

EDWARD WILLIAMS CLAY (1799-1857) was born in Philadelphia of well-to-do parents. Admitted to the bar in 1825, he became an "artist" three years later, and in 1837 moved to New York. Around 1840, while studying art in Europe, he lost his sight, which put an end to his artistic career. While in Philadelphia he had done etchings and engravings for publishers; two volumes of his satiric caricatures, *Life in Philadelphia* and *Sketches of Character,* were published in 1829. In New York he did lithographic drawings for John Childs and H. R. Robinson. He produced only a few cartoons, all of them of superior quality. His best-known work is "The Times" (see page 131) which he did during the financial panic of 1837.

(For his other cartoons, see pages 143, 148, 155, 158, 159, 162, 166, 178.)

NAPOLEON SARONY (1821-1896) was born in Quebec, the son of a retired Austrian soldier. The Saronys moved to New York around 1830. Young Napoleon sold a lithographic design when he was only ten. While still a boy he was apprenticed to Currier & Ives and H. R. Robinson. The cartoon which he drew in 1837, "An Independent Voter" (see page 147), is a good example of his political caricatures.

In 1846 Sarony started his own commercial lithographic firm, Sarony & Major, later Sarony, Major & Knapp. During the Civil War he was in Europe studying art and photography, and after 1867 he established himself in New York as a leading photographer of celebrities.

CURRIER & IVES. Nathaniel Currier (1813-1888) was the first apprentice of the American commercial lithographic firm, the Pendletons of Boston. In 1835 he founded his own business, N. Currier's, taking James Merritt Ives (1824-1895) as a partner in 1850. The firm became prominent in the field of caricature with the election of 1856. In addition to Maurer and Sarony, Thomas Worth (1834-1917) worked for Currier & Ives as well.

(For Currier & Ives cartoons, see pages 167, 204, 218-219, 235, 240, 265, 268, 322.)

LOUIS MAURER (1832-1932), who lived a full century, was the son of a German cabinetmaker and studied lithography from childhood. Around 1850 his family came to New York, where young Maurer worked for several houses before joining Currier & Ives. He was with this firm from 1852 till 1860, producing horse prints, a fireman series, and a number

938

of caricatures. After leaving Currier & Ives, he established his own business.

(For his work see pages 221, 222, 236-237, 241.)

JOSEPH KEPPLER (1838-1894) was born in Vienna, the son of a confectioner. His father emigrated to Missouri after the 1848 revolution, and around 1868 young Keppler joined him. In St. Louis he studied medicine, then turned to acting. He founded two German-language magazines, both of which failed (one was the first *Puck*). In 1872 he went to New York for *Frank Leslie's Illustrated Newspaper,* doing most of the cover cartoons. In 1876 he founded another German-language *Puck* which was so successful that in March 1877 an English-language edition was added to it.

In the new publication, the main cartoons were printed in color lithography. *Puck* was such a hit that the Republicans started *Judge* to counteract its influence; but *Judge* never reached *Puck's* popularity. Joseph Keppler and Frank Opper did most of the illustrations in *Puck's* early years. H. C. Bunner's *A Selection of Cartoons from Puck by Joseph Keppler* (1893) reproduces some of his work.

(See pages 347, 355, 356, 370-371, 398-399, 401, 404, 413, 419, 420, 421, 456, 459, 461, 484, 488-489, 493, 517.)

MATTHEW SOMERVILLE MORGAN (1839-1890) was born in London; both his parents worked in the theater. He started painting theatrical scenery before becoming artist and correspondent for the *Illustrated London News.* In 1867 he illustrated *Tomahawk,* his own magazine. He did cartoons of the Civil War for *Fun* magazine; some of them are included in his volume *The American War, Cartoons* (1874). He was brought to the United States in 1870 by *Frank Leslie's Illustrated Newspaper* to compete with Thomas Nast, whose cartoons were the chief attraction of *Harper's Weekly.* Morgan was a versatile man; he founded Matthew Morgan's Art Pottery Company in the 1880s, was art editor of *Collier's magazine* (1888-1890), managed Strowbridge Lithographic Company, painted scenery for the theater and, in 1889, for Buffalo Bill's Wild West Show.

(See pages 311, 314, 315.)

THOMAS NAST (1840-1902), the most celebrated cartoonist in America in the latter part of the nineteenth century, was born in Landau, Germany, where his father was a musician in the 9th Bavarian Regiment. He came to New York at the age of six. A gift of crayons from a neighbor led to a passion for drawing. After some training he became at the age of fifteen a sketching reporter on *Frank Leslie's Illustrated Newspaper* at four dollars a week. In 1859 he contributed to two newly established papers: the *New York Illustrated News* and *Harper's Weekly.* After 1862 he worked exclusively for *Harper's Weekly,* moving from reportage to illustrations.

Nast set a new style for political caricature. From the last years of the Civil War till the close of the century, he was the dominant cartoonist in the country. He attacked the Copperheads in the war, he assailed Horace Greeley and his supporters in 1872, he brought defeat to Boss Tweed and his ring, and he ridiculed the aspirations of the "Plumed Knight" James G. Blaine. He was not only a political caricaturist but a great satirist.

Nast ended his association with *Harper's Weekly* in 1886 and began to work for other publications. But his heyday was over. The political scene had changed, and before he was fifty his career had ended. There were no political personalities to attack—only causes—and that was not his strength. In 1892 he began his own *Nast's Weekly,* which lasted for a year and then petered out. He had financial difficulties. In 1902 President Theodore Roosevelt gave him a consular post at Guayaquil, Ecuador, and Nast left to start a new life. Not long after his arrival in Ecuador he died.

The best biography of Nast is Albert Bigelow Paine's reliable and admiring study, *Thomas Nast: His Period and His Pictures* (1904). Recently two books have been published about his work: *Thomas Nast: Political Cartoonist* (1967) by J. Chad Vinton is a poor work; Morton Keller's *The Art and Politics of Thomas Nast* (1968) is a beautiful one, printing many of Nast's cartoons in good reproductions.

(See pages 251, 256, 285, 286, 287, 300-301, 304, 305, 313, 316, 317, 320-321, 325, 330-331, 333, 338, 343, 348, 349, 353, 354, 378, and 380-381.)

BERNHARD GILLAM (1856-1896) was born in England, the seventh of his artist-inventor father's fourteen children. At the age of ten he came with his family to New York. Self-educated, he began to sell drawings in 1876. After his caricatures appeared in *Leslie's Weekly* and the New York *Graphic,* he established himself as a political cartoonist. In 1880 he worked with Thomas Nast during the Garfield campaign. The following year he joined *Puck.* From 1886 on he was part owner and contributor to *Judge, Puck's* rival.

(See pages 369, 374-375, 384, 397, 422, 431.)

CHARLES STANLEY REINHART (1844-1896), a Philadelphian, was more noted as a genre painter and illustrator than as a cartoonist. During the Civil War he was a telegraph operator; afterward he went to Europe to study art. In 1870 he returned to the United States and worked for Harper & Brothers for the next seven years. From 1880 to 1891 he traveled about Europe looking for local color for his illustrations and paintings. He did drawings for G. P. Lathrop's *Spanish Vistas* (1883) and a series on the watering places of America for C. D. Warner's *Their Pilgrimage* (1887). At the time of his death he was beginning a series of Civil War illustrations. Henry James, who admired him, wrote of Reinhart in *Picture and Text* (1893).

(See page 341.)

ARTHUR BURDETT FROST (1851-1928) began to work when he was fifteen, first in a wood engraver's shop in Philadelphia, then in the office of a lithographer. In the evenings he taught himself to draw. In 1875 he joined the staff of *Graphic* magazine as an illustrator. A year later he started to do political cartoons for *Harper's Weekly.* During his career Frost did humorous sketches for *Scribner's Magazine, Harper's Magazine* and *Collier's.* The visual creator of Uncle Remus and Br'er Rabbit, he became one of the most popular book illustrators. His own humorous books, among them *Sports and Games in the Open* (1899) and *Book of Drawings* (1905), were successful. The most recent study on Frost and his art is Henry M. Reed's *A. B. Frost Book* (1968).

(See pages 330, 332, 557.)

JAMES A. WALES (1852-1886), an Ohioan, worked as a wood engraver. During the election of 1872 he sold cartoons to a Cleveland paper. The following year he moved to New York and contributed to *Wild Oats* and *Frank Leslie's Illustrated Newspaper*. In 1875 he went to Paris and London to study. After his return he joined *Puck* and worked extensively for that publication. In 1881 he left *Puck* to work for *Judge,* but returned again to *Puck*.

(See pages 308, 357.)

WILLIAM ALLEN ROGERS (1854-1931), another Ohioan, showed an early aptitude for drawing. His first work was putting fancy scrolls on plows and mowing machines. At the age of fourteen he was selling cartoons to a group of Middle Western papers. After four years on the staff of the original *Daily Graphic,* he began illustrating for *Harper's Weekly* in 1877. During the 1880 campaign one day, when Nast was absent from Harper's office, Rogers started doing political cartoons with the pungent one of Hancock infusing blood in the skeleton "Democracy" (see page 354). During the next forty years his cartoons appeared in *Harper's Weekly, Life, Harper's Monthly Magazine, Puck,* and the New York *Herald.* Some of his works are collected in *Hits at Politics: A Book of Cartoons* (1899) and *America's Black and White Book* (1917). He also illustrated children's books. He wrote an autobiography, *A World Worth While* (1922), and authored *Danny's Partner* (1923) and *A Miracle Mine* (1925).

(See pages 362, 363, 403, 436, 456, 480, 504, 564.)

FREDERICK BURR OPPER (1857-1937) was born in Ohio, where he left school at fourteen to work on a village newspaper. Moving to New York, he sold humorous sketches to *Wild Oats* and other magazines. His graphic debut was an attack on Nast's Catholic phobia. After working for Frank Leslie for three years, in 1876 he joined *Puck,* where he and Keppler were the mainstays of that paper during its first twelve years. He turned to newspaper work (as did other magazine cartoonists such as C. J. Taylor and Edward W. Kemble), staying with the New York *Journal* until he retired in 1932. Opper was one of the best craftsmen among cartoonists; his cartoons against the trusts had great effect. He also illustrated books, among them Mark Twain's, and wrote several of his own: *Willie and His Poppa* (1901), *An Alphabet of Joyous Trusts* (1902), and *John Bull* (1903).

(See pages 376, 409, 416, 440.)

EDWARD W. KEMBLE (1861-1933), a Californian, began his career at *Judge.* In the first issue of that weekly— in October 1881—he had a caricature of Oscar Wilde's farewell to America. The following year he illustrated Mark Twain's *Huckleberry Finn,* which gave him lasting fame. Subsequently he joined *Life* and became known for his drawings interpreting Negroes; he issued these in book form under the title *Comical Coons.* He then worked for *Harper's Weekly* and *Collier's.* By the end of the century he joined the Sunday *World,* and later he became the cartoonist of the New York *Herald,* drawing cartoons against Tammany.

(See pages 514, 515, 520, 522, 533 and 531.)

LOUIS DALRYMPLE (1866-1905) received training at the Pennsylvania Academy of Fine Arts and the Art Students' League in New York. He joined the staff of *Puck* in the late 1880s.

(See pages 449 and 486.)

GRANT E. HAMILTON (1862-1915) was born in Youngstown, Ohio, and worked most of his life in New York City for the *Graphic, Judge* and *Leslie's Weekly.* After Bernard Gillam's death in 1896, Hamilton, "Zim," Flori, and Victor Gillam were the chief cartoonists of *Judge.* W. A. Rogers wrote of Hamilton that he "had more truly the real cartoon idea which, contrary to the notion prevalent among newspaper readers, has nothing to do with comic art." (See pages 382, 383, 385, 386, 388, 395, 466.)

HOMER CALVIN DAVENPORT (1867-1912) also worked as a jockey, a railroad fireman, and a clown in a circus. He was born on an Oregon farm and started doing cartoons early. In 1892 he went to the San Francisco *Examiner.* Three years later William Randolph Hearst brought him to the New York *Evening Journal,* where his work won him an international reputation and one of the highest salaries in the profession. His caricatures were in the great tradition, though never as effective as the cartoons of Nast. His work brought about an attempt in 1897 to pass an anti-cartoon bill in New York. His drawing of Uncle Sam is one of the best; his use of Mark Hanna's dollar-marked suit of clothes and the giant figures of the trusts are permanent contributions to cartoon symbolism. The cartoon "He's Good Enough for Me" (see page 482) was a favorite of Theodore Roosevelt. Davenport's hobby was raising horses on his New Jersey farm, and through a letter from Roosevelt to the Sultan of Turkey, he was able to obtain twenty-seven Arabian horses. In addition to *Davenport's Cartoons* (1898), he had a book of short stories published, as well as *The Dollar or the Man?* (1900).

CLIFFORD BERRYMAN (1869-1949), born in Kentucky, was a self-taught man. At seventeen he was a draftsman in the United States Patent Office. He worked as a general illustrator from 1891 until joining the Washington *Post* in 1896. From 1907 on he did cartoons for the Washington *Evening Star* (as his son does now). He won the Pulitzer Prize in 1943. His *Cartoons of the 58th House* made him the only cartoonist who has cartooned every member of Congress. The *D.A.R.* magazine, Vol. LXVII (1933), includes his "Cartoons of the Presidents."

(See pages 565, 576, 588.)

JOHN S. PUGHE (or PUGH) (1870-1909) was born in Dolgelly, Wales. Of his life not much is known. He was an outstanding craftsman, much admired by his fellow artists. One of his best cartoons is "Swallowed," which he drew for *Puck* in 1900 (see pages 458-459). It shows Bryan as a boa constrictor swallowing the Democratic donkey.

CHARLES RAYMOND MACAULEY (1871-1934) of Ohio began as a cartoonist after winning a fifty-dollar prize from the Cleveland *Press* in 1891. He spent his apprentice years with three other Cleveland papers. In 1894 he moved to New York, where he free-lanced. From 1899 to 1901 he was with the Philadelphia *Inquirer.* His best works date from the decade with the New York *World* (1904-1914). After that he was with the Brooklyn *Daily Eagle* and the *Daily Mirror.* He won the Pulitzer Prize for the best cartoon of 1929. He was the author and illustrator of several books, among them *Fantasmaland* (1904) and *The Red Tavern* (1914). (See pages 513, 518-519, 530.)

"DING" (JAY NORWOOD) DARLING (1871-1962) started as a reporter for the Sioux City *Journal* and began sketching to supplement his stories, doing his first political cartoon, about Theodore Roosevelt, at the turn of the century. In 1906 he joined the Des Moines *Register,* where he stayed for the next eleven years, except for an interlude with the New York *Globe.* He joined the New York *Herald* syndicate in 1917.

Ding was a conservation enthusiast and for a while he headed the U.S. Biological Survey. He was awarded the Pulitzer Prize for cartoons in 1923 and 1942. Some of his work was published in *Aces and Kings* (1918), *Ding Saw Hoover* (1954) and two humorous self-illustrated books, *Ding Goes to Russia* (1932) and *Cruise of the Bouncing Betsey* (1937). A recent book, *Ding's Half Century* (1962), edited by John Henry, provides some biographical data.

(See pages 566, 580.)

BOARDMAN ROBINSON (1874-1952) was born in Nova Scotia and painted for six years in Paris and San Francisco before settling down in New York as an illustrator. From 1907 to 1910 he worked for the *Morning Telegraph;* the following four years for the *Tribune.* In 1915 he traveled with John Reed to the Balkans and Russia for *Metropolitan* magazine. Together they wrote *The War in Eastern Europe* (1916). Robinson's *Cartoons of the War* also was published in that year. He then contributed cartoons and illustrations to *The Masses, Liberator* and *Harper's Weekly.* In 1922 and 1923 he was with *Outlook* in London.

(See pages 511, 543.)

ROLLIN KIRBY (1875-1952) was born in Illinois. His cartoons appeared in *Collier's, McClure's, Life, American* and *Harper's.* In 1912 he joined the staff of the New York *Mail* and the following year the *Sun.* In 1913 he began a series of social cartoons, "Lights of the Town," for the *World,* later joining that newspaper and remaining with it until 1939 (the name of the paper changed to *World-Telegram* in 1931). From 1939 to 1942 he was with the New York *Post.* He then did cartoons for *Look* and for *The New York Times Sunday Magazine.* In addition to sketches, Kirby wrote verse and articles for the old *Life, The New Yorker* and *Vanity Fair.* His *Highlights: A Cartoon History of the Twenties* was published in 1931. He won the Pulitzer Prize three times—in 1921, 1924, and 1928.

(See pages 540-541, 550, 569, 592-593, 594.)

HERBERT JOHNSON (1878-1946), a Nebraskan, started as assistant cartoonist for the Denver *Republican* in 1896. He moved to the Kansas City *Journal* the following year, and remained with that paper until 1903. From 1903 to 1905 he worked as a free-lance cartoonist in New York. Then he joined the Philadelphia *North American,* where he was first manager of the Sunday art department and then became the paper's cartoonist. In 1912 he joined the *Saturday Evening Post.* His *Cartoons* was published in 1936, five years before his retirement. (See page 544.)

HAROLD TUCKER WEBSTER (1885-1955), the creator of Casper Milquetoast, was born in West Virginia and began his career with the Denver *Republican* in 1902. The next three years he worked for the Chicago *Daily News,* and in the same city from 1905 to 1908 for the *Inter-Ocean.* He then spent two years with the Cincinnati *Post* before going to New York to do cartoons for Associated Newspapers. In 1919 he joined the *Tribune;* in 1923 the *World;* and in 1931 the *Herald-Tribune.* In addition to co-authoring several books, he has published *Our Boyhood Thrills and Other Cartoons* (1915) and *Boys and Folks* (1917).

(See page 556.)

DANIEL ROBERT FITZPATRICK (1891-   ) began to work in 1911 with the Chicago *Evening News.* From 1913 to 1958 he was with the St. Louis *Post-Dispatch.* His book, *Cartoons* (1947), includes many of his outstanding works.

(See pages 644, 645.)

HAROLD TALBURT (1895-   ) was born in Toledo, Ohio, where he began his career at *The Toledo News Bee* in 1916. Since 1922 he has been the editorial cartoonist for the Scripps-Howard newspaper *Alliance.* He received the Pulitzer Prize for cartoons in 1933.

(See pages 594, 733.)

HERBERT BLOCK (1909-   ), the best-known living political cartoonist, was born in Chicago and worked for the Chicago *Daily News* from 1929 to 1933. The next decade he drew for the NEA Service. Since 1946 he has been the Washington *Post's* editorial cartoonist. He won the Pulitzer Prize in 1942 and is the only living cartoonist represented in the National Gallery of Art. Several collections of his cartoons have been published: *The Herblock Book* (1952), *Herblock's Here and Now* (1955), *Herblock's Special for Today* (1958), *Straight Herblock* (1958), and *The Herblock Gallery* (1968).

(See page 709 and subsequent pages.)

WALT KELLY (1913-   ), the creator of the comic strip "Pogo," was born in Philadelphia. From 1928 to 1935 he worked for a Connecticut newspaper in Bridgeport. Then he became a Walt Disney Studios animator. In 1941 he did commercial artwork in New York and in 1948 and 1949 was a political cartoonist for the New York *Star.*

(See pages 722, 723.)

WILLIAM H. MAULDIN (1921-   ), born in New Mexico, studied art at the Chicago Academy of Fine Arts. Fame came to him when he drew cartoons for the Mediterranean edition of *Stars and Stripes* in 1943. A year later he received the Pulitzer Prize for his cartoons, and was again awarded the prize in 1958. He was editorial cartoonist for the St. Louis *Post-Dispatch* from 1958 to 1962 and since then for the Chicago *Sun-Times.* His work is reprinted by many other publications. He has several books to his credit, including *Up Front* (1945), *Back Home* (1947); *Bill Mauldin's Army* (1951); *Bill Mauldin in Korea* (1952), and *I've Decided I Want My Seat Back* (1965).

Appendix D

A SHORT SELECTED BIBLIOGRAPHY

In the following list I have attempted to offer some selected titles for the layman and the student who would like to delve more deeply into the lives of Presidents, into Presidential history, and the history of political conventions. It is a short list, with books published up to 1968. I have laid emphasis on the more recent works. The valuable older ones are listed in the bibliographies of the *Dictionary of American Biography* (1928-1944, 22 volumes, including two supplements containing the biographies of those public figures who died before December 31, 1940) and *Harvard Guide to American History* (1954). Most of the books I have listed have comprehensive bibliographies.

I consulted old newspapers of the early years of the Republic in the American Antiquarian Society, Worcester, Massachusetts, in the Library of Congress, Washington, and in the New York Public Library. *The New York Times Index* and microfilms contain material about the second half of our presidential history.

For illustrations I looked at the contemporary weeklies and magazines such as *The Bee* (New York, 1898), *Collier's Weekly* (New York, 1888-1957), *Every Saturday* (Boston, 1866-1874), *Gleason's* and *Ballou's Pictorial* (Boston, 1851-1859), *Harper's Weekly* (New York, 1857-1916), *Judge* (New York, 1881-1939), *Leslie's Weekly* (New York, 1855-1922), *Life,* the humorous weekly (New York, 1883-1936), *Life,* the picture magazine (New York, 1936-   ), *Look* (New York, 1937-   ), *Midweek Pictorial* (New York, 1914-1937), *The New Yorker* (New York, 1925-   ), *Puck* (New York, 1876-1918), and *The Verdict* (1898).

Of general works, I recommend the outstanding works of Herbert Agar, *The Price of Union* (1950) and his subsequent *America Since 1945* (1957) and Eugene H. Roseboom's *A History of Presidential Elections* (1957, revised in 1964); also the entertaining volume by Thomas A. Bailey; *Presidential Greatness* (1966), and Sidney Warren's *The Battle for the Presidency* (1968), with the story of ten presidential elections; in a lighter vein Jack Bell's *The Splendid Misery* (1960) and Robert Bendiner's *White House Fever* (1960).

On presidential quotations: Caroline T. Harnsberger, *A Treasury of Presidential Quotations* (1964), and Arthur B. Tourtellot, *The Presidents on the Presidency* (1964).

Of factual information, Joseph Nathan Kane's *Facts About the Presidents* (1959, 1968) is most excellent.

The inaugural addresses of the Presidents have been published by the U.S. Government Printing Office. *The State of the Union Messages of the Presidents,* edited by F. L. Israel, have been published with a foreword by Arthur M. Schlesinger, Jr. (three volumes, 1966).

The party platforms are compiled by Kirk H. Porter and Donald B. Johnson: *National Party Platforms, 1840-1960* (1956).

Of the vast output on presidential politics, powers, leadership, philosophy, religion, and other related subjects I quote only a few titles: Sidney Hyman (ed.), *Office of the American Presidency* (1956); Wilfred Ellsworth Binkley, *The Man in the White House: His Powers and Duties* (1959); and *The President and Congress* (1937, 3rd ed.); Stuart Gerry Brown, *The American Presidency: Leadership, Partisanship and Popularity* (1966); Louis Brownlow, *The President and the Presidency* (1949); James MacGregor Burns, *Presidential Government: The Crucible of Leadership* (1966); Elmer Eckert Cornwell, *Presidential Leadership of Public Opinion* (1965); Edward S. Corwin and L. W. Koenig, *The Presidency Today* (1956); Corwin, *The President, Office and Powers, 1787-1948: History and Analysis of Practice and Opinion* (1957); Berton Dulce, *Religion and the Presidency, a Recurring American Problem* (1962); Walter Goodman, *All Honorable Men* (1964); Seymour H. Fersh, *The View from the White House: A Study of the Presidential State of the Union Messages* (1961); Herman Finer, *The Presidency: Crisis and Regeneration, an Essay in Possibilities* (1960); Erwin C. Hargrove, *Presidential Leadership: Personality and Political Style* (1966); Sidney Hyman, *The American President* (1954); Francis H. Heller, *The Presidency: A Modern Perspective* (1960); Donald B. Johnson and Jack L. Walker (eds.), *The Dynamics of the American Presidency* (1964); Joseph E. Kallenbach, *The American Chief Executive: The Presidency and the Governorship* (1966); Louis W. Koenig, *The Chief Executive* (1964) and *The Invisible Presidency* (1960); Joseph Kraft, *Profiles in Power: A Washington Insight* (1966); John C. Long, *The Liberal Presidents: A Study of the Liberal Tradition in the American Presidency* (1948); Joan C. MacLean (ed.), *President and Congress: The Conflict of Powers* (1955); Richard E. Neustadt, *Presidential Power, the Politics of Leadership* (1960); Peter H. Odegard, *Religion and Politics* (1960); James E. Pollard, *The Presidents and the Press: Truman to Johnson* (1964); Nelson W. Polsby, *Presidential Elections: Strategies of American Electoral Politics* (1964); Gerald Pomper, *Nominating the President: The Politics of Convention Choice, with a New Postscript on 1964* (1966); Fred Reinfeld, *The Biggest Job in the World: The American Presidency* (1964); Edgar E. Robinson and others, *Powers of the President in Foreign Affairs, 1945-1965* (1966); Clinton L. Rossiter, *The American Presidency* (1956); Edward McC. Sait, *American Parties and Elections* (1952); Theodore C. Sorensen, *Decision-Making in the White House: The Olive Branch or the Arrows* (1963); Rexford G. Tugwell, *The Enlargement of the Presidency* (1960) and *How They Became President: Thirty-Five Ways to the White House* (1965); D. Wallace, *First Tuesday: A Study of Rationality in Voting* (1964); Sidney Warren, *The President as World Leader* (1964); David E. Weingast, *We Elect a President* (1962); Edward A. Weintal and Charles Bartlett, *Facing the Brink,* (1967); and Aaron B. Wildavsky and Nelson W. Polsby, *Presidential Elections* (1964).

On the electoral college: Roger L. MacBride, *The American Electoral College* (1953); Lucius Wilmerding, *The Electoral College* (1958); Neal R. Peirce, *The People's Pres-*

On the first ladies: Bess Truman, *White House Profile* (1951); Marianne Means, *The Woman in the White House* (1963).

On the assassinations: Robert J. Donovan, *The Assassins* (1964); Stewart M. Brooks, *Our Murdered Presidents: The Medical Story* (1966); Charles E. Rosenberg, *The Trial of the Assassin Guiteau* (1968).

There is hardly any aspect of the Presidency which has no documentation. On the Presidents' sports: John Durant, *The Sports of Our Presidents* (1964); on their health: Rudolph Marx, *The Health of the Presidents* (1961); on their horoscopes: Doris C. Doane, *Horoscopes of the U. S. Presidents* (1952); on their wills: John Charles Hogan, *The Wills of the Presidents* (1957). The list is endless.

On the works of the Presidents, their lives and the biographies of their opponents, I suggest the following books:

GEORGE WASHINGTON

Most of Washington's papers, bound in hundreds of volumes and stored in just as many boxes, are in the Library of Congress. The Manuscript Division of the Library published an *Index to George Washington's Papers* (U.S. Government Printing Office, 1964) which serves as a guide.

Douglas Southall Freeman's seven-volume biography on Washington (1948-1957) surpasses all previous works.

Of the single-volume studies, Howard Swiggett's *The Great Man: George Washington as a Human Being* (1953) and Marcus Cunliffe's *George Washington, Man and Monument* (1958) are most readable.

Washington's administration is vividly depicted in George Gibb's *Memoirs of the Administration of Washington and John Adams* (six volumes, 1846); his inauguration in the mammoth illustrated volume, *The History of the Centennial Celebration of the Inauguration of George Washington,* edited by Clarence W. Bowen (1892), *The Journal of William Maclay* (1890), and *The Works of Fisher Ames* (two volumes, 1854).

JOHN ADAMS

The publication of *The Adams Papers* under the able editorship of Lyman H. Butterfield is in progress. Sponsored by the Massachusetts Historical Society, it is published by the Belknap Press of Harvard University Press.

The best biography is Page Smith's *John Adams* (1962).

Catherine Drinker Bowen, *John Adams and the American Revolution* (1950); Zoltán Haraszty, *John Adams, and the Prophets of Progress* (1952); John R. Howe, *The Changing Political Thought of John Adams* (1966); Adrienne Koch, *Adams and Jefferson* (1963); Stephen G. Kurtz, *The Presidency of John Adams* (1957), deal with various aspects of Adams's thoughts and career.

THOMAS JEFFERSON

The publication of the *Thomas Jefferson Papers,* projected in fifty-two volumes, is in progress by the Princeton University Press.

Dumas Malone's four-volume biography, *Jefferson and His Time,* is the latest multi-volume biography; the last volume appeared in 1962.

The administration of Jefferson is best depicted in Henry Adams's *History of the United States of America* (1890) and Frank Van der Linden's *The Turning Point: Jefferson's Battle for the Presidency* (1962). Claude G. Bowers, *Jefferson and Hamilton* (1925); G. Chinard, *Thomas*

Jefferson: The Apostle of Americanism (1929); S. F. Bemis, *Jay's Treaty* (1923), are earlier works.

Margaret Bayard Smith, *First Forty Years of Washington Society* (1906), is a vivid description of the capital's life.

The recent volumes on Aaron Burr are Samuel E. Burr, *Colonel Aaron Burr, the American Phoenix* (1961), and Herbert L. Parmet and Marie B. Hecht, *Aaron Burr, Portrait of an Ambitious Man* (1967).

JAMES MADISON

Writings of James Madison (nine volumes, 1900-1910) was edited by Gaillard Hunt. The Library of Congress issued an *Index to the James Madison Papers* in 1965.

Irving Brant's *James Madison* (six volumes, 1941-1961) is a comprehensive biography.

JAMES MONROE

The Writings of James Monroe (seven volumes, 1898-1903), edited by S. M. Hamilton, is not a complete collection.

The American Secretaries of State and Their Diplomacy (ten volumes, 1927-1929), edited by S. F. Bemis, has many of Monroe's papers.

The standard biography is William P. Cresson's *James Monroe* (1946).

The latest biography of Crawford is Philip Jackson Green, *The Life of William H. Crawford* (1965).

JOHN QUINCY ADAMS

His *Writings* (seven volumes, 1913-1917) were edited by W. C. Ford. His *Memoirs* (twelve volumes, 1874-1877) were edited by Charles Francis Adams; an abridgement of them in two volumes was edited by Allan Nevins (1951).

S. F. Bemis, *John Quincy Adams and the Union* (1956), and Leonard Falkner, *The President Who Wouldn't Retire* (1967), are two of the more recent works.

ANDREW JACKSON

Correspondence of Andrew Jackson (1926-1931), edited by J. S. Bassett.

The best biography is Marquis James's two-volume work *The Border Captain* (1933) and *Portrait of a President* (1937).

On the Jackson era many important studies have been published in the past two decades. Arthur M. Schlesinger, Jr. came out with his excellent *The Age of Jackson* in 1945; Leonard D. White, *The Jacksonians—A Study in Administrative History, 1829-1861,* in 1954; Glyndon G. Van Deusen, *The Jacksonian Era, 1828-1848,* in 1959.

Claude G. Bowers, *The Party Battles of the Jackson Period* (1922), is an early work; Robert V. Remini, *The Election of Andrew Jackson* (1963), is a more recent one.

On life and customs *The Diary of Philip Hone, 1828-1851* (two volumes, 1927) and George Templeton Strong's *Diary, 1835-1875* (four volumes, 1952), both works edited by Allan Nevins, give revealing insights.

Dixon Wecter, *The Hero in America* (1941), is a study of hero worship with Washington, Franklin, Jefferson, Jackson, Lincoln, Lee and Theodore Roosevelt the subjects.

MARTIN VAN BUREN

Calendar of the Papers of Martin Van Buren (1910) was issued by the Library of Congress.

The *Autobiography of Martin Van Buren,* edited by John C. Fitzpatrick, appeared in 1920.

An early work on Van Buren is D. T. Lynch's *An Epoch*

and a Man: Martin Van Buren (1929); a recent one is Robert Vincent Remini's *Martin Van Buren and the Making of the Democratic Party* (1959).

Thomas Hart Benton's *Thirty Years' View* (two volumes, 1854-1856) gives intimate glimpses of the period.

WILLIAM HENRY HARRISON

Messages and Letters of William Henry Harrison (Indiana Historical Collections, two volumes, 1922), edited by Logan Esarey, is the most complete collection of Harrison's writings. The Library of Congress issued an *Index to the William Henry Harrison Papers* in 1960.

Freeman Cleaves, *Old Tippecanoe: William Henry Harrison and His Time* (1939), and James A. Green, *William Henry Harrison, His Life and Times* (1941), are two of the biographies.

Harrison and politics are dealt with by Paul Henry Tobias, *William Henry Harrison—An Interpretation of His Political Ideas and Ideals* (1951), and Robert Gay Gunderson's lively and authoritative *The Log-Cabin Campaign* (1957).

JOHN TYLER

The Letters and Times of the Tylers (three volumes, 1884-1896), edited by Lyon G. Tyler.

Recent biographies and political histories are Robert J. Morgan, *A Whig Embattled: The Presidency Under John Tyler* (1954), and Robert Seager, *And Tyler Too* (1963).

JAMES K. POLK

His papers are in the Library of Congress. *The Diary of James K. Polk During His Presidency, 1845 to 1849,* edited by Milo M. Quaife (four volumes, 1910), was published in an abridged edition by Allan Nevins in 1929.

The latest biographies are Charles Grier Sellers, *James K. Polk, Jacksonian, 1795-1843* (two volumes, 1957), a third in preparation; Charles Allen McCoy, *Polk and the Presidency* (1960); Eugene I. McCormac, *James K. Polk: A Political Biography* (1965).

Recent volumes on Henry Clay: Clement Eaton, *Henry Clay and the Heart of American Politics* (1957); David Lindsey, *Henry Clay and Jackson* (1962).

ZACHARY TAYLOR

The Library of Congress issued an *Index to the Zachary Taylor Papers* in 1960. The largest collection of his papers is in The National Archives.

Biographies: Brainerd Dyer, *Zachary Taylor* (1946); S. B. McKinley, *Old Rough and Ready* (1946); Holman Hamilton, *Zachary Taylor* (two volumes, 1941-1951).

MILLARD FILLMORE

Millard Fillmore Papers were edited by Frank H. Severance (1907) and published by the Buffalo Historical Society.

The latest biography is by Robert J. Rayback, *Millard Fillmore, a Biography of a President* (1959).

FRANKLIN PIERCE

His papers are in the Library of Congress, the New Hampshire Historical Society, and in the hands of his descendants.

Roy Frank Nichols's biography, *Franklin Pierce, Young Hickory of the Granite Hills,* first published in 1931, was completely revised in 1958.

JAMES BUCHANAN

The most recent biography is Philip S. Klein's *President James Buchanan* (1962). An early one is G. Ticknor Curtis's *Life of James Buchanan* (two volumes, 1883).

The political events of the period are brilliantly pictured in Allan Nevins's *The Emergence of Lincoln* (two volumes, 1950). The political conventions of 1856 are described by Murat Halstead in *Trimmers, Truckers and Temporizers,* a slim volume edited by William B. Hesseltine in 1961 containing Halstead's original reports.

On Frémont: Allan Nevins, *Frémont, Pathmaker of the West* (1955), is still the best.

ABRAHAM LINCOLN

Many of Lincoln's letters are in the Library of Congress, most of them having been given to the Library by Robert Todd Lincoln. His *Collected Works* (nine volumes) published by the Abraham Lincoln Association in 1959 supersede earlier volumes, even though the editing is unsatisfactory.

Of biographies of Lincoln there is no end. Well over 5,000 books have been published on him. The most notable ones: William H. Herndon and Jesse W. Weik's *Life of Lincoln* (1888); J. G. Nicolay and John Hay, *Abraham Lincoln: A History* (ten volumes, 1890); Albert J. Beveridge, *Abraham Lincoln, 1809-1858* (1928); Carl Sandburg, *Abraham Lincoln* (six volumes, 1926, 1939); James G. Randall, *Lincoln, The President* (four volumes, 1945-1955).

Special studies of the conventions and elections include: Murat Halstead, *Three Against Lincoln* (edited by William B. Hesseltine, 1960), which prints Halstead's dispatches from the 1860 conventions; Willard Leroy King, *Lincoln's Manager, David Davis* (1960); Melvin L. Hayes, *Mr. L. Runs for President* (1960).

On Douglas: George Fort Milton, *The Eve of Conflict; Stephen A. Douglas and The Needless War* (1934), Gerald M. Capers; *Stephen A. Douglas, The Defender of The Union* (1959). On McClellan: William W. Hassler, *General George B. McClellan, Shield of the Union* (1957).

ANDREW JOHNSON

The Papers of Andrew Johnson, edited by LeRoy P. Graf and Ralph W. Haskins, are projected for ten volumes, of which the first, dealing with the years 1822-1851, appeared in 1968. The Library of Congress issued an *Index to the Andrew Johnson Papers* in 1963.

Biographies and political treatises: R. W. Winston, *Andrew Johnson, Plebeian and Patriot* (1928); Lloyd P. Stryker, *Andrew Johnson* (1929); George Fort Milton, *The Age of Hate: Andrew Johnson and the Radicals* (1930); Eric L. MacKitrick, *Andrew Johnson and the Reconstruction* (1960); Brazilla Carroll Reece, *The Courageous Commoner: A Biography of Andrew Johnson* (1962); Lately Thomas, *The First President Johnson* (1968).

The Johnson era is vividly described in Frank Cowan's *Andrew Johnson: Reminiscences of His Private Life and Character* (1894) and *Memoirs of the White House—The Home Life of our Presidents from Lincoln to Roosevelt, Being Personal Recollections of Col. W. H. Crook* (edited by Henry Rood, 1911).

ULYSSES S. GRANT

Grant's papers are at present being prepared for publication by the Ohio Historical Society for the Ulysses S. Grant Association and the Ohio Civil War Centennial Commission. The Library of Congress issued an *Index to the U. S. Grant Papers* in 1965. The *Personal Memoirs of U. S. Grant* (two volumes, 1885-1886) were republished under the editorship of E. B. Long in 1952.

The projected biography of Grant by the late Lloyd Lewis is being continued by Bruce Catton. Lewis published *Captain*

Sam Grant (1950) before his death; Bruce Catton issued *Grant Moves South* in 1960.

Allan Nevins's *Hamilton Fish: The Inner History of the Grant Administration* (two volumes, 1936, revised edition, 1957) is indispensable for students of the era. Charles Coleman's *The Election of 1868—The Democratic Effort to Regain Control* (1933) is a reliable study.

On Horace Greeley: William Harlan Hale, *Horace Greeley, Voice of the People* (1950), and Glyndon G. Van Deusen, *Horace Greeley, 19th Century Crusader* (1953), are eminently readable.

On Horatio Seymour: Stewart Mitchell, *Horatio Seymour of New York* (1938).

RUTHERFORD B. HAYES

The Hayes papers are in the Rutherford B. Hayes Library at Fremont, Ohio. Hayes's *The Diary of a President 1875-1881* (1964) and *Diary and Letters of Rutherford Birchard Hayes* (five volumes, 1922-1926) contain his writings.

The biography by H. J. Eckenrode, *Rutherford B. Hayes, Statesman of Reunion* (1930), is the standard one. On Tilden: Alexander C. Flick, *Samuel J. Tilden, A Study in Political Sagacity* (1939).

Paul W. Haworth's *The Hayes-Tilden Disputed Election of 1876* (1906) is still valid. Harry Barnard's *Rutherford B. Hayes and His America* (1954) is a valid study.

Of the memoirs, James G. Blaine's *Twenty Years of Congress* (two volumes, 1884) and John Sherman's *Recollections of Twenty Years* (1895) are most enlightening.

JAMES A. GARFIELD

Theodore C. Smith's *The Life and Letters of James Abram Garfield* (two volumes, 1925) is an outstanding biography with much Garfield material.

H. J. Clancy, *The Presidential Election of 1880* (1958), describes that contest.

CHESTER A. ARTHUR

Most of Arthur's papers have been destroyed. The standard biography is George F. Howe's *Chester A. Arthur: A Quarter Century of Machine Politics* (1934).

GROVER CLEVELAND

The Library of Congress issued an *Index to the Grover Cleveland Papers* in 1965. *Letters of Grover Cleveland 1850-1908* (1933) were edited by Allan Nevins.

Biographies: Robert McElroy, *Grover Cleveland, The Man and the Statesman* (two volumes, 1923); Allan Nevins, *Grover Cleveland: A Study in Courage* (1932); and Rexford G. Tugwell, *Grover Cleveland* (1968).

Robert L. O'Brien, *Grover Cleveland as Seen by His Stenographer, July 1892—November 1895* (1951), is what the title indicates.

George H. Knoles's *The Presidential Campaign and Election of 1892* (1942) is about Cleveland's third campaign.

On Blaine: David S. Murray, *James G. Blaine, Political Idol of Other Days* (1934), is the standard work.

BENJAMIN HARRISON

The Library of Congress issued an *Index to the Benjamin Harrison Papers* in 1964.

Harry G. Sievers's *Benjamin Harrison* (two volumes, 1952) is a thoroughly documented life.

Matthew Josephson, *The Politicos, 1865-1896* (1938), describes the political figures of that era.

WILLIAM McKINLEY

The Library of Congress issued an *Index to the Papers of William McKinley* in 1963.

William C. Spielman, *William McKinley: Stalwart Republican* (1954); Margaret Leech, *In the Days of McKinley* (1959); and Howard W. Morgan, *William McKinley and His America* (1963), are the latest works.

On the 1896 campaign we have Douglas D. Woodard, *The Presidential Election of 1896* (1949); George Frisbie Whicher, *William Jennings Bryan and the Campaign of 1896* (1953); P. W. Glad, *McKinley, Bryan and the People* (1964); and of course Bryan's own book, *The First Battle: A Story of the Campaign of 1896* (1896).

On Bryan: Paolo E. Coletta, *William Jennings Bryan: Political Evangelist 1860-1898* (1964). The first volume of a comprehensive life, Lawrence W. Levine, *Defender of the Faith,* appeared in 1965.

On Mark Hanna: Herbert D. Croly, *Mark Hanna, His Life and Work* (1912), and Thomas Beer, *Hanna* (1929).

A chatty memoir is H. H. Kohlsaat's *From McKinley to Harding* (1923).

THEODORE ROOSEVELT

The Letters of Theodore Roosevelt were excellently edited by Elting Morison and others (eight volumes, 1951). Roosevelt's books and literary output were printed in several different editions.

The books on Roosevelt's life: Henry F. Pringle, *Theodore Roosevelt: A Biography* (1931), is a critical one. Carleton Putnam came out with an excellent volume of a projected multi-volume biography (which he unfortunately did not complete), *Theodore Roosevelt: The Formative Years* (1958). George E. Mowry, *The Era of Theodore Roosevelt, 1900-1912* (1958), and John M. Blum's *The Republican Roosevelt* (1954) are excellent studies.

Many in Roosevelt's family left reminiscences. Alice Longworth, *Crowded Hours* (1933); Nicholas Roosevelt, *Theodore Roosevelt: The Man As I Knew Him* (1967), are two of them. On T. R.'s eldest sister: Lilian Rixley's *Bamie* (1963).

WILLIAM HOWARD TAFT

Taft's papers are in the Library of Congress.

Henry F. Pringle, *The Life and Times of William Howard Taft, a Biography* (two volumes, 1939), and Alpheus T. Mason, *William Howard Taft, Chief Justice* (1965), are the outstanding biographies.

Richard Hofstadter, *The Age of Reform: From Bryan to F.D.R.* (1955), and Matthew Josephson, *The President Makers 1896-1919* (1940), are on the politics of the period.

Memoirs: J. B. Foraker, *Notes of a Busy Life* (two volumes, 1916); Chauncey M. Depew, *My Memories of Eighty Years* (1922); and William Allen White, *Mask in a Pageant* (1928).

La Follette's *Autobiography* (1913) is the story of the man who later became the Progressive candidate.

WOODROW WILSON

Public Papers of Woodrow Wilson (six volumes, 1925-1927), edited by Ray Stannard Baker and William E. Dodd. *Woodrow Wilson: Life and Letters* (seven volumes, 1927-1946), *The Papers of Woodrow Wilson* (1966-   ), edited by Arthur S. Link and associates, are now being published by the Princeton University Press.

Of biographies and political studies on Wilson there is no end. Some of the notable works on him: Josephus Daniels, *The Wilson Era* (two volumes, 1944); Arthur S. Link, *Wilson* (two volumes, 1947-1956); John A. Garraty, *Woodrow*

Wilson: A Great Life in Brief (1956); Cary Travers Grayson, *Woodrow Wilson: An Intimate Memoir* (1960); Gene Smith, *When the Cheering Stopped: The Last Years of Woodrow Wilson* (1964).

The 1912 convention is described in William Jennings Bryan, *Tale of Two Conventions* (1912); Victor Rosewater, *Back Stage in 1912* (1932); Frank K. Kelly, *The Fight for the White House: The Story of 1912* (1961).

The Intimate Papers of Colonel House (four volumes, 1928), edited by Charles Seymour, is indispensable for the understanding of the relationship between Wilson and his political friend.

On Hughes: Dexter Perkins, *Charles Evans Hughes* (1956).

WARREN G. HARDING
Most of Harding's correspondence was destroyed by his wife after his death.

Samuel H. Adams, *Incredible Era: The Life and Times of Warren Gamaliel Harding* (1939); Karl Schriftgiesser, *This Was Normalcy* (1948); Burl Noggle, *Teapot Dome—Oil and Politics in the 1920's* (1962); Wesley M. Bagby, *The Road to Normalcy: The Presidential Campaign of 1920* (1962); and Andrew Sinclair, *The Available Man: The Life Behind the Masks of Warren G. Harding* (1965), are the more interesting books on Harding and his time. The latest work is Francis Russell, *The Shadow of Blooming Grove* (1968).

Of memoirs: James M. Cox, *Journey Through My Years* (1946), and William Allen White, *The Autobiography of William Allen White* (1946), are good reading.

CALVIN COOLIDGE
Biographies: William Allen White, *A Puritan in Babylon: The Story of Calvin Coolidge* (1925); Edward Connery Lathem (ed.), *Meet Calvin Coolidge: The Man Behind the Myth* (1960); Howard H. Quint and Robert H. Farrell, *The Talkative President: The Off-the-Record Press Conferences of Calvin Coolidge* (1964); and Donald R. McCoy, *Calvin Coolidge: The Quiet President* (1967).

Memoirs: H. L. Stoddard, *As I Knew Them* (1927); Irwin H. Hoover, *Forty-two Years in the White House* (1934); Nicholas Murray Butler, *Across the Busy Years* (two volumes, 1939-1940).

HERBERT HOOVER
Many of Hoover's papers are in the Hoover Institution on War, Revolution, and Peace at Stanford University.

Of Hoover and his period, there is a voluminous output. The more interesting ones: Herbert Hoover, *Memoirs* (three volumes, 1951-1952); Jay Lovestone, *1928: The Presidential Election and the Workers* (1928); R. V. Peel and T. C. Donnelly, *The 1928 Campaign—An Analysis* (1931); William Starr Myers and Walter H. Newton, *The Hoover Administration: A Documented Narrative* (1936); William Starr Myers and Arthur M. Hyde, *The Hoover Policies* (1937); Broadus Mitchell, *Depression Decade, 1929-1941* (1947); and Eugene Lyons, *Herbert Hoover, a Biography* (1964).

Alfred E. Smith's memoirs, *Up to Now* (1929), is a good personal account. His daughter, Emily Warner, wrote: *The Happy Warrior, a Biography of My Father* (1956); Oscar Handlin, *Alfred Smith and His America* (1958), is a first-rate study; James A. Farley, *Governor Al Smith* (1959), is a personalized account.

E. A. Moore's *A Catholic Runs for President, the Campaign of 1928* (1956) describes the contest.

FRANKLIN DELANO ROOSEVELT
A good-sized library could be filled with books on Roosevelt and his administration.

The Public Papers and Addresses of Franklin D. Roosevelt (fourteen volumes, 1935-1945), compiled by Samuel I. Rosenman, contain his announcements. Letters of his early years, reminiscences of his mother, his wife, his son, his secretary, his associates, of friends and enemies are available in book form.

Biographies: Robert E. Sherwood, *Roosevelt and Hopkins, an Intimate History* (1950); John Gunther, *Roosevelt in Retrospect, a Profile in History* (1950); Frank Freidel, *Franklin D. Roosevelt* (three volumes, 1952); James MacGregor Burns, *Roosevelt—The Lion and the Fox* (1956); Arthur M. Schlesinger, Jr., *The Age of Roosevelt* (three volumes so far, 1957); and Rexford G. Tugwell, *The Democratic Roosevelt; A Biography of FDR* (1957).

Of reminiscences of the family: Eleanor Roosevelt, *This I Remember* (1949); James Roosevelt, *Affectionately, F.D.R., a Son's Story of a Lonely Man* (1959).

Of remembrances of his associates: James Farley, *Behind the Ballots* (1938) and *Jim Farley's Story* (1948); Samuel I. Rosenman, *Working With Roosevelt* (1952); Frances Perkins, *The Roosevelt I Knew* (1946); Ross McIntire, *White House Physician* (1946); Grace Tully, *F.D.R. My Boss* (1949); and many others.

Of the political and social scene: Frederick Lewis Allen, *Only Yesterday* (1931) and *Since Yesterday* (1940); R. V. Peel and T. C. Donnelly, *The 1932 Campaign: An Analysis* (1935); H. L. Mencken, *Making a President* (1932); Raymond Moley, *After Seven Years* (1939); P. H. Odegard, *Prologue to November, 1940* (1940); Basil Rauch, *The History of the New Deal, 1933-1938* (1944); William E. Leuchtenberg, *Franklin D. Roosevelt and the New Deal, 1932-1940* (1963); Warren Moscow, *Roosevelt and Willkie* (1968); Herbert S. Parmet and Marie B. Hecht, *A President runs for a third term* (1968).

On Alf Landon: Donald R. McCoy, *Landon of Kansas* (1966).

On Willkie: Joseph Barnes, *Willkie* (1952); Mary E. Dillon, *Wendell Willkie; 1892-1944* (1952); Muriel Rukeyser, *One Life* (1957); Donald B. Johnson, *The Republican Party and Wendell Willkie* (1960).

HARRY S. TRUMAN
The Public Papers of the Presidents of the United States—Harry S. Truman (1945-1953) (eight volumes, 1945-1953), published by the Government Printing Office.

Memoirs by Harry S. Truman appeared in two volumes (1955-56). His *Mr. Citizen* (1960) offers Truman's announcements, his press conferences, his reminiscences and his thoughts on politics and history.

Jonathan Daniels, *A Man of Independence* (1950), is a biography of the President.

His Presidency and his election in 1948 are handled in John W. Spanier, *The Truman-MacArthur Controversy and the Korean War* (1959); Cabell Phillip's excellent account, *The Truman Presidency: The History of a Triumphant Succession* (1966); Barton J. Bernstein and Allen J. Matusow (eds.), *The Truman Administration: A Documentary History* (1966); the recent excellent study by Irwin Ross, *The Loneliest Campaign: The Truman Victory of 1948* (1968).

DWIGHT D. EISENHOWER
The Public Papers of the Presidents of the United States —Dwight D. Eisenhower (1953-1961) (eight volumes, 1953-

1961) contains his important announcements.

His reminiscences: *Crusade in Europe* (1952) and *The White House Years* (two volumes, 1963). Captain Harry C. Butcher adds to them in *My Three Years with Eisenhower* (1946).

About the Eisenhower years: Robert J. Donovan, *Eisenhower: The Inside Story* (1956); Richard H. Rovere, *The Eisenhower Years: Affairs of State* (1956); Marquis W. Childs, *Eisenhower, Captive Hero: A Critical Study of the General and the President* (1958), Sherman Adams, *First-Hand Report: The Story of the Eisenhower Administration* (1961); Emmet John Hughes, *The Ordeal of Power: A Political Memoir of the Eisenhower Years* (1963).

On Stevenson: Elisabeth S. Ives, *My Brother Adlai* (1956); Kenneth S. Davis, *A Prophet in His Own Country* (1957); Alden Rogers Whitman, *Portrait* (1965); Stuart G. Brown, *Adlai E. Stevenson: A Short Biography* (1965); Edward P. Doyle (ed.), *As We Knew Adlai* (1966); William Severn, *Adlai Stevenson, Citizen of the World* (1966); William Ross, *Adlai Stevenson* (1966). His speeches and addresses are printed in several volumes.

JOHN F. KENNEDY

The number of books on John F. Kennedy and his short administration will probably equal the number of works on Lincoln as time goes by.

His official pronouncements are in *The Public Papers of the Presidents of the United States—John F. Kennedy (1961-1963)* (three volumes, 1961-1963).

He wrote two books, *Why England Slept* (1940) and *Profiles in Courage* (1956).

James MacGregor Burns's political biography in 1960, *John Kennedy: A Political Profile,* annoyed the President and his family; William Manchester's *Portrait of a President: John F. Kennedy in Profile* (1962) pleased the Kennedy clan.

After the assassination some of the Kennedy's associates wrote their remembrances: Arthur M. Schlesinger, Jr., *A Thousand Days: John F. Kennedy in the White House* (1965); Theodore C. Sorensen, *Kennedy* (1965); Pierre Salinger's *With Kennedy* (1966); Evelyn Lincoln, his secretary, *My Twelve Years with John F. Kennedy* (1965).

On the election: Theodore H. White's *The Making of a President: 1960* (1961) is a highly successful effort. Paul T. David (ed.), *The Presidential Election and Transition, 1960-1961* (1961), is a scholarly study. Tom Wicker's *Kennedy Without Tears: The Man Beneath the Myth* (1964) is a tender and touching tribute. Victor Lasky's *JFK: The Man and the Myth* (1963) is a vituperative account.

Richard M. Nixon, who opposed Kennedy in 1960, published his book *Six Crises* in 1962. His biography, *Richard Nixon: A Political and Personal Portrait* (1959), was written by the sympathetic newspaperman Earl Mazo. A revised and expanded version of this book, co-authored by Stephen Hess, is *Nixon: A Political Portrait* (1968).

LYNDON B. JOHNSON

The Public Papers of the Presidents of the United States—Lyndon B. Johnson (1963-1965) (four volumes, 1963-1965) is a Government Printing Office publication.

His election campaign is vividly described by Theodore H. White in *The Making of the President: 1964* (1965); Paul Tillet and others edited *The National Election of 1964* (1966).

Biographies: Favoring Johnson: Hugh Sidey, *A Very Personal Presidency* (1968), a highly readable and amusing book. Against: Robert Sherrill, *The Accidental President* (1967), convincingly written but extremely unfair. Holding a middle ground between the two is *Lyndon Baines Johnson, the Exercise of Power—a Political Biography* (1966) by Rowland Evans and Robert Novak and Jack Bell's *The Johnson Treatment* (1965). Tom Wicker, *JFK and LBJ* (1968), is an excellent study. The chatty volume of Patrick Anderson, *The President's Men* (1968) is good reading about the presidential assistants in the White House from FDR to LBJ.

On Humphrey: Winthrop Griffith, *Humphrey, a Candid Biography* (1965); Robert Sherill and Harry W. Ernst, *The Drugstore Liberal* (1968); Allan H. Ryskind, *Hubert* (1968).

On Goldwater, in addition to his own book, *The Conscience of a Conservative* (1960), are some volumes by his supporters: Stephen C. Shadegg, *How to Win an Election: The Art of Political Victory* (1964); Phyllis Schafly, *A Choice, Not an Echo* (1964); Karl Hess, *In a Cause That Will Triumph* (1967). A brilliant analytical study is Richard H. Rovere, *The Goldwater Caper* (1965).

Appendix E

THE SALARY OF THE PRESIDENT AND VICE PRESIDENT

On September 24, 1789, the first Congress fixed the presidential salary at $25,000 a year, paid in quarterly installments. The salary of the Vice President was to be $5,000.

On March 3, 1873, a day before Grant's second inauguration, Congress increased the salary of the President to $50,000, and that of the Vice President to $10,000.

On June 23, 1906, Congress authorized $25,000 for the traveling expenses of the President.

On March 4, 1909, the day of Taft's inauguration, the presidential salary was raised to $75,000, the vice presidential one to $12,000.

On June 25, 1948, the President's traveling expenses were increased to $40,000 a year.

On January 19, 1949, a day before Truman's inauguration, the presidential salary became $100,000 with an additional $50,000 "to assist in defraying expenses," and the vice presidential salary became $30,000 with an additional $10,000 for expenses.

On March 22, 1955, the vice presidential salary was increased by $5,000 to $35,000. On August 14, 1964, this was increased by another $8,000 to $43,000.

INDEX

Numbers in *italics* indicate pictures